Systematic Theology

Systematic Theology

Roman Catholic Perspectives

Francis Schüssler Fiorenza and John P. Galvin, editors

Fortress Press
MINNEAPOLIS

SYSTEMATIC THEOLOGY
Roman Catholic Perspectives

Cover image: © 2010 Artists Rights Society (ARS), New York / ADAGP, Paris
Cover design: Paul Boehnke
Book design: Zan Ceeley and Ann Delgehausen, Trio Bookworks

Library of Congress Cataloging-in-Publication Data
Systematic theology : Roman Catholic perspectives / Francis Schussler Fiorenza and John P. Galvin, eds. — 2nd ed.
    p. cm.
  Includes bibliographical references and index.
  ISBN 978-0-8006-6291-2 (alk. paper)
  1. Catholic Church—Doctrines. 2. Theology, Doctrinal. I. Fiorenza, Francis Schüssler. II. Galvin, John P., 1944–
  BX1751.3.S97 2011
  230'.2—dc22

2011004851

The paper used in this publication meets the minimum requirements of American National Standard for Information Sciences—Permanence of Paper for Printed Library Materials, ANSI Z329.48-1984.

Manufactured in the U.S.A.

15   14   13   12   11   1   2   3   4   5   6   7   8   9   10

Contents

2.   Faith and Revelation   79

Avery Dulles

God and Trinity

3.1 Approaching the Christian Understanding of God   109

David Tracy

God and Trinity

3.2 The Trinitarian Mystery of God: A "Theological Theology"   131

Anthony J. Godzieba

4. Creation   201

Anne M. Clifford

Contents

Sacraments

9.3 **Eucharist** 515

David N. Power

Sacraments

9.4 Sacrament and Order of Penance and Reconciliation 543

David N. Power

10. Eschatology   621

Jeannine Hill Fletcher

Anne M. Clifford, CSJ, is the Monsignor James Supple Chair of Catholic Studies in the Department of Philosophy and Religious Studies at Iowa State University. She is the author of *Introducing Feminist Theology* (2001) and over forty articles, principally in the areas of Christianity and science, and ecological theology; she is the coeditor of *Christology: Memory, Inquiry, Practice* (2003) and a contributing editor for the *New Catholic Encyclopedia* (2nd edition, 2003).

Avery Cardinal Dulles, SJ (1918–2008), the Laurence J. McGinley Professor of Religion and Society at Fordham University from 1988 until his death in 2008, was an internationally known theologian, lecturer, and author of twenty-five books and over eight hundred articles on theological topics. Past president of both the Catholic Theological Society of America and the American Theological Society, Cardinal Dulles served on the International Theological Commission (1992–1997), as a consultant to the Committee on Doctrine of the United States Conference of Catholic Bishops (1992–2007), and as a member of the United States Lutheran/Roman Catholic Dialogue (1972–1993). Cardinal Dulles was the only United States–born theologian who was not a bishop to be named a Cardinal of the Catholic Church.

 Anne-Marie Kirmse, OP, PhD, who served as Avery Cardinal Dulles's assistant (1998–2008), worked with him to prepare the revised chapter for final publication.

Michael A. Fahey, SJ, is Research Professor of Theology at Boston College. Former editor of the journal *Theological Studies,* he has published widely on ecumenism and on Vatican II, especially contributions to the conciliar documents by particular nations such as Belgium and Canada.

Francis Schüssler Fiorenza is the Charles Chauncey Stillman Professor of Roman Catholic Theological Studies at Harvard University. He is the author of *Foundational Theology: Jesus and the Church* (1984) and coauthored *Religion und Politik* (1982), coedited and translated Friedrich Schleiermacher's *On the Glaubenslehre* (1981), coedited *Habermas, Modernity, and Public Theology* (1984), edited the English version of the *Handbook of Roman Catholic Systematic Theology* (1995), and coauthored with James Livingston the second volume of *Modern Christian Thought: The Twentieth Century* (2000). He has published over one hundred and fifty articles in the areas of political theology, systematic theology, foundational theology, and Roman Catholic theology. A new book, *Rights at Risk,* is forthcoming.

Jeannine Hill Fletcher is Associate Professor of Theology at Fordham University, Bronx, New York. She writes at the intersection of systematic theology, feminist theory, and interreligious concerns. Her publications include *Monopoly on Salvation? A Feminist Response to Religious Pluralism* (2005). Her current work draws on women's voices in interreligious dialogue for a renewed theological anthropology. Jeannine also serves as Faculty Director of Service-Learning at Fordham and works with the Northwest Bronx Community and Clergy Coalition on faith-based justice and advocacy.

John P. Galvin is Professor of Systematic Theology at The Catholic University of America. A priest of the Archdiocese of Boston, he received his licentiate in theology from the Collegium Canisianum (Innsbruck, Austria) and his doctorate in theology from the University of Innsbruck.

Anthony J. Godzieba is Professor of Theology and Religious Studies at Villanova University and editor of *Horizons,* the journal of the College Theology Society. He specializes in fundamental theology, theology of God, Christology, theological anthropology, and philosophical theology. He is the author of *Bernhard Welte's Fundamental Theological Approach to Christology* (1994) and the coeditor of *Christology: Memory, Inquiry, Practice* (2003). His essays have appeared in *Louvain Studies, Theological Studies,* the *Heythrop*

Journal, Philosophy and Theology, New Theology Review, and *Augustinian Studies.* He is completing a book on the theology of God and currently doing research on the intersection of art, music, theology, spirituality, and embodiment in early modern Catholicism.

Roger Haight, SJ, did his doctorate in theology at the Divinity School of the University of Chicago (1973) and has taught at Jesuit graduate schools of theology in Manila, Chicago, Toronto, and Boston. He is currently a scholar in residence at Union Theological Seminary in New York City. He has published works in the areas of theology of grace, liberation theology, fundamental theology, Christology, and ecclesiology. He is a past president of the Catholic Theological Society of America and was named Alumnus of the Year of the Divinity School of the University of Chicago for the year 2005.

Elizabeth A. Johnson is Distinguished Professor of Theology at Fordham University in New York City, where she has received the annual Teaching Award. The author of numerous books, articles, and book chapters, her work has received numerous awards and has been translated into twelve languages. A former president of both the Catholic Theological Society of America and the American Theological Society, her main areas of teaching and writing focus on God, Jesus Christ, Mary and the saints, the problem of suffering, science and religion, ecological ethics, and issues related to justice for women.

David N. Power, OMI, is a native of Dublin, Ireland, and a member of the Congregation of Missionary Oblates of Mary Immaculate. He obtained a doctorate in theology from the Pontifical Liturgical Institute, Rome. He taught theology in Ireland and Rome, and then at the Catholic University of America in Washington, DC, of which he is now Professor Emeritus. Since retirement from CUA he has been a visiting lecturer in Tahiti, South Africa, Canada, and at Oblate School of Theology, San Antonio, Texas. Currently, he is a resident in Lusaka, Zambia, in the formation community of his congregation.

David Tracy is the Andrew Thomas Greeley and Grace McNichols Greeley Distinguished Service Professor Emeritus of Catholic Studies, Professor of Theology and the Philosophy of Religion at the University of Chicago Divinity School, and a member of the Committee on Social Thought. His publications include *The Analogical Imagination: Christian Theology and the Culture of Pluralism* (1981) and *On Naming the Present: Reflections on God, Hermeneutics, and Church* (1994). Dr. Tracy is currently writing a book on God.

AG	*Ad gentes* (Vatican II's Decree on the Mission Activity of the Church)
CCC	*Catechism of the Catholic Church*
DF	*Dei filius* (Vatican I's Constitution on the Catholic Faith)
DH	H. Denzinger and P. Hünermann, eds., *Enchiridion Symbolorum*
DS	H. Denzinger and A. Schönmetzer, eds., *Enchiridion Symbolorum*
DV	*Dei verbum* (Vatican II's Constitution on Divine Revelation)
GS	*Gaudium et spes* (Vatican II's Pastoral Constitution on the Church in the Modern World)
LG	*Lumen gentium* (Vatican II's Constitution on the Church)
NA	*Nostra aetate* (Vatican II's Declaration on Non-Christian Religions)
ND	J. Neuner and J. Dupuis, eds., *The Christian Faith in the Doctrinal Documents of the Catholic Church*
NPNF	*Nicene and Post-Nicene Fathers*
OUI	*Ordo Unctionis Infirmorum Eorumque Pastoralis Cura* (Instruction on Prayer for Healing)
PG	*Patrologia graeca*, ed. J. B. Migne
PL	*Patrologia latina*, ed. J. B. Migne
SC	*Sacrosanctum concilium* (Vatican II's Constitution on the Sacred Liturgy)
ST	*Summa theologiae*, Thomas Aquinas
UR	*Unitatis redintegratio* (Vatican II's Decree on Ecumenism)

Changing Roman Catholic Perspectives

This volume provides an introductory survey of the major theological treatises of systematic theology. At a time of declining theological literacy, an introductory volume should necessarily provide a basic knowledge not only for collegiate religion majors, and not only for beginning theology students in master's programs, both academic and ministerial, but also for interested and informed general readers.

In the twenty years since the appearance of the first edition of these volumes, much has changed in the world, the churches, and theology. The preface to the first edition defined five goals: (1) to explain the diverse theological currents of the Second Vatican Council; (2) to describe the impetus that historical-critical studies of the Scriptures and the Roman Catholic Church's traditions and practices have had on the renewal of theology at the time of Vatican II and on the council's theological, ecclesial, and liturgical reforms; (3) to appropriate and to show the significance that recent hermeneutical theories and philosophical developments had on

contemporary theology; (4) to draw attention to some recent ecumenical and bilateral statements issued by the various Christian churches; and (5) to take into account the current emphasis on practice that exists across diverse liberation theologies.

In approaching the task of revising and updating the essays, the authors have selected various approaches. Some have added to their chapters reflection on developments in the past two decades; others have completely revised their essays. Three original authors—Catherine LaCugna, Monika Hellwig, and Regis Duffy—have died, so new authors were selected: Anthony Godzieba has written a new chapter 3 on the triune God, and Jeannine Hill Fletcher has written a new chapter 10 on eschatology. And since David Power wrote on individual sacraments in the first edition, he was asked to expand his work on chapter 9 to cover all the sacraments except for the section on marriage. Moreover, at the end of every chapter, a new annotated bibliography has been provided.

Avery Cardinal Dulles died soon after he finished his revision of chapter 2 for this volume. We are fortunate that Cardinal Dulles had the same fidelity to deadlines as he has had over the years to his teaching, writing, and service to the church as a theologian. A former colleague at the Catholic University of America, he was extremely encouraging when I first spoke to him about the idea and goals of the original project.

Though the five goals set for the original edition remain the same and are still significant, the context in which they existed has changed. These changes affect the goals, so it is necessary to reflect on how these goals must be expanded, modified, and applied anew. In the four decades since Vatican II, the Roman Catholic Church has seen a continuing discussion of the meaning of the council and the theological currents expressed in it. The theological, cultural, and global situation today is very different from the 1960s, when the council took place or from the 1980s when the first edition was planned and these changing circumstances have widened the scope of the original goals.

The first goal was to present an interpretation of the theological context, background, and consequences of Vatican II. Today the interpretation of the council has moved even more into the center of discussion. Some are questioning the value and significance of the council, and others are even criticizing significant teachings of the council. At the risk of oversimplifying a complex set of issues, these interpretations can be classified into three groups: misinterpretations of the council, basic disagreements with the council documents, and important challenges the council has advanced that still remain as tasks for the Roman Catholic Church.

The misinterpretations of the council often center on *Gaudium et spes* (Pastoral Constitution of the Church in the World of Today),

Dignitatis humanae (Declaration on Religious Freedom), and *Lumen gentium* (Dogmatic Constitution on the Church). It is alleged that *Gaudium et spes* has a too-optimistic attitude toward the modern world and that the declaration on religious freedom operates with the presupposition of the individualism of modern liberalism. Nevertheless, a careful reading of *Gaudium et spes* shows that while it acknowledges the rapid growth in science and technology in the modern world, it criticizes the increased exploitation of the poor as well as the growing distance between the rich and the poor, not only within nations, but also among nations. *Dignitatis humanae* does not ground religious freedom in the private realm and make religious freedom merely an issue of individual preference or choice. Instead, it grounds religious freedom in human dignity (as its Latin title expresses) and in its contribution to the welfare of all.

A somewhat different misinterpretation takes place regarding *Lumen gentium* such that the minority position is now sometimes presented as if it were the decisive meaning. Examples of this include the question of whether the church of Christ is totally and exclusively identical with the Roman Catholic Church or whether the more modest "subsist in" language of the council allows for acknowledgment of the ecclesial reality of other Christian communities. Likewise, the deliberations at the council pointed to the importance of episcopal conferences. *Lumen gentium* clearly underscores the mutual relation between the local churches and the universal church. The local church is not simply the administrative agent of the papacy in a local area. Nor is the universal church simply the aggregate of the local churches.

A more general misinterpretation is the casting of the debate within the categories of a hermeneutics of continuity versus a hermeneutics of discontinuity, as if the choices in interpreting the council were between understanding the council as advocating a discontinuity with the past (one alternative) or a continuity with the past (the other alternative). Such a contrasting alternative simplifies the debate and distorts the interpretations. Many points of reform and change within the council were achieved through a *ressourcement* (return to sources) leading to a recovery of what Karl Rahner would have called the forgotten truths about the church and its sacraments. This approach is evident even where the council broke new ground, such as its efforts to overcome anti-Semitism in the wake of the Holocaust and its grounding of religious freedom in traditions that emphasize God's universal love, human dignity, and the good of human society.

In addition to misinterpretations, there are also the criticisms and disagreements. The schismatic group known as the St. Pius X Fraternity has indeed viewed the decline in religious vocations, the drop in attendance at the Eucharist, and the decreased participation in the sacraments as effects and results of the council itself. The group has also advocated against the ecumenical developments in the council and has contested the council's teaching on religious freedom. These criticisms represent important disagreements between the council and its critics who refused to accept the authority and teaching of the council. As this volume goes to press, the Vatican is engaged in dialogue with the group. The Vatican maintains that anti-Semitism is incompatible with Roman Catholicism, and it affirms the importance of religious freedom while it also objects to religious relativism.

Finally, there are the multiple challenges that the Second Vatican Council lays out with its interpretation of the signs of the time. The council's various diagnoses present unfinished tasks to the Roman Catholic Church that must be taken up. In the wake of the council, we have become even more aware of the multiple challenges entailed in the tension between pluralism and globalization, in the shift from economic and cultural colonialism to the increasing postcolonial resistance to such imperialism, and in the competing imperatives of modernity and postmodernity. Karl Rahner's classical essay about Vatican II best exemplifies this challenge when he explains that the council constitutes a shift in the practice, life, and self-understanding of the church from a European church to a world church. This shift has become increasingly true in the ensuing decades, and its challenge must be met and incorporated into the Catholic Church's theology and practice. Today we are even more aware of the negative impact of European colonialism and imperialism. The awareness of the diverse cultures and practices in which Christianity is embedded contributes to the depth and breadth of the "catholicity" of Christianity.

The first edition achieved its second goal by underscoring the historical diversity and changes that took place in the understanding of theology, God, Christ, the church, the saints and Mary, grace, and the sacraments. The awareness of these historical trajectories has become part and parcel of Catholic theology's self-understanding, one that moved from a more deductive or analytical approach to a more historical and development-oriented perspective. If previously a historical consciousness was viewed as hostile toward Roman Catholic faith, the achievement of Vatican II and of the theology preceding and following it was to retrieve historical studies and to integrate them into the Christian faith. The application of historical-critical studies to the Scriptures and theology had been a point of critical controversy at the turn from the nineteenth to the twentieth xxviii century. However, papal encyclicals and documents of the Pontifical Biblical Commission began to pave the way for the historical criticism that came to fruition in Vatican II.

In the time since Vatican II, two significant developments in historical-critical studies have occurred. One has been the focus on the diverse reception histories of the biblical texts. This has led to an emphasis on the traditional fourfold meaning of Scripture as a way of understanding the meaning and the significance of a text as it was "received" or understood. Consequently, in addition to the historical-critical study of Scripture, there has been a renewed focus on probing the diverse understandings of the multiple meanings of Scripture throughout the ages. How have different groups and different theologians appropriated the Scriptures? In approaching the meaning of the text, the theological task includes not only examining its historical meaning, but also exploring the diverse receptions and interpretations of the Scriptures throughout Christian history, traditions, and practices. Such an approach attends to the rhetoric of the text as well as to an ethics of reading and interpretation. Rather than viewing historical-critical studies as hostile, such an approach takes into account how historical studies have been expanded through social, anthropological, and rhetorical studies.

Another development of historical-critical studies has been the increased attention to popular religiosity and popular religious practices, areas that scholarship had neglected. If previously American religious history focused on religious and theological leadership, today studies seek to uncover the religious practices of immigrant Roman Catholics in the ethnic enclaves of cities or the lived religion embedded in the pious practices and customs of ordinary Catholics. Similar shifts can be seen in the importance

granted the saints and mystics as sources of religious knowledge. In the study of the Reformation and Counter-Reformation, similar shifts in historical research are apparent. One classic study of the influence of the Council of Trent examined the role of five leading bishops as they implemented the council's reforms in their dioceses. More recently, scholars such as Robert W. Scribner examine the religious practices in the post-Reformation period to discover to what extent specific traditions persisted, even within Protestant areas.

An excellent example of this development is Elizabeth Johnson's treatment of the communion of saints and Mary. She not only presents the historical, theological, conciliar, ecumenical, and papal teachings, but also shows the significance of the grassroots diversity, paradigmatic witnesses, and lived religion in Christian communities.

The third goal of the first edition was to incorporate recent hermeneutical theories and philosophical developments. Here change has been substantial, though different fields of theology have a more or less philosophical orientation and consequently are affected differently. In the decades before the Second Vatican Council, several developments took place. There was the blossoming of historical studies of Thomas Aquinas and of Scholasticism that overcame the one-sided interpretation of Neo-Scholasticism. Martin Grabmann, Louis Betrand Geiger, Étienne Gilson, Cornelio Fabro, and Johannes Hirshberger were just a few of the leading historians of Thomism. At the same time, under the influence of *la nouvelle théologie*, the role of Augustine became increasingly emphasized. In addition, the later development of transcendental Thomism sought to bring Thomas into critical confrontation with Kantian philosophy, as in the transcendental Thomism of Joseph

Maréchal, Karl Rahner, Bernard Lonergan, and Emerich Coreth. Further, a unique brand of Thomism represented by Jacques Maritain became influential, especially with his work at the United Nations and on human rights and in political philosophy.

The shift from Kantian philosophy to post-Kantian philosophy has entailed a shift from epistemology to hermeneutics, aesthetics, and social-political philosophy, even though Kant's influence in aesthetic and political philosophy remains strong today in some circles. More recently, in some quarters, there has been a re-emergence of metaphysics, as exemplified by the influence of "Radical Orthodoxy," and its Neo-Platonic metaphysics. At the same time, the influence of Martin Heidegger's critique of Western metaphysics has influenced attempts to understand God beyond the categories of being. The strong emphasis on phenomenology in Europe comes not only from the writings of Pope John Paul II, but also from leading philosophers and theologians such as Jean-Luc Marion and Louise-Marie Chauvet.

Moreover, hermeneutic theories that pointed to the surplus meaning of the text (Paul Ricoeur) or the outstanding and enduring characteristics of classics (Hans-Georg Gadamer) have found a complementary and even alternative emphasis in deconstruction on the aporia of texts (Jacques Derrida) or the postcolonial critique of some of the classics of the West. One can see this shift in David Tracy's writings that moved from an analysis of Bernard Lonergan's method, to an appropriation of hermeneutical theory and then to an appreciation of postmodern theories. His approach to the understanding of God in this volume gives evidence of the latter, especially in its sensitivity to the diversity of resources for theological language about God. David Power's own work on the sacra-

ments displays the shift in recent sacramental theology away from a transcendental approach to one emphasizing the importance of symbol and the category of gift. His chapters on the sacraments illustrate these shifts through his exposition of the work of others and his own systematic construction.

If this volume were complemented by a volume on ethics and social ethics within Roman Catholicism, one would also have to include such diverse strands as the renewed emphasis in Aristotle, the alternative emphasis on John Rawls and Jürgen Habermas, or the emphasis on the communitarian, and the reemphasis of a virtue ethics.

The fourth goal of the previous edition—to include the results of ecumenical advances as recorded in recent bilateral statements—was evident in the statements noted in that edition, and these have been updated. In the chapter on the communion of saints and Mary, Elizabeth Johnson discusses the important dialogues between Lutherans and Roman Catholics on that issue. Roger Haight, in his updated chapter on grace, discusses the important and recent joint statement on justification by Roman Catholics and Lutherans. Michael Fahey has been very engaged in the dialogue between the Roman Catholic Church and Eastern Orthodox churches. His chapter on the church also reflects on the disillusionments and self-doubt that have emerged in recent times within the ecumenical movement itself. To the extent that these dialogues, especially those between Roman Catholic and Lutheran theologians, were a part of the first edition, they have also become a part of this second edition. Although the dialogues in Rome between the Vatican and science do not formally constitute bilateral statements, they do represent an important dialogue taking place in the contemporary Catholic Church.

Anne Clifford's chapter on creation addresses this dialogue, and to the extent that "Intelligent Design" has become a central topic (less within than outside of Roman Catholic theological circles), she deals with this issue in the second edition. Likewise, the influence of some Eastern theologians has led to a more "social" conception of the Trinity in contemporary Western interpretations of the triune God, as Anthony Godzieba indicates.

The fifth goal, which was to include an emphasis on praxis, with specific reference to the diverse liberation theologies, has changed and expanded. Current liberation theologies themselves have undergone changes. They have moved even more clearly and strongly away from any suspicion of a Marxist understanding of praxis. Latin American liberation theology increasingly underscores indigenous American spirituality as well as Christian spirituality as a basis for further understanding the meaning of praxis. At the same time, postcolonial and postmodern theories have decisively influenced the understanding of praxis. This goal is clearly evident in Roger Haight's exposition of grace and in Jeannine Hill Fletcher's presentation of eschatology not only in relation to liberation but also in relation to pluralism. Moreover, with critical theory, there has been an increased critique of the modern West's overemphasis on scientific and technological praxis. Critical theory has also underscored the difficulty in understanding liberation and emphasized a more indeterminate or open-ended conception. The importance of spiritual and liturgical practices also has come increasingly into the center of theological reflection.

As we adopt these five goals and interpret them anew for this edition, the fundamental question that emerges is this: What constitutes Catholicism? In other words, what is the meaning of the book's subtitle, "Roman Catholic Perspectives"? An answer to this question cannot be reduced to a simple or singular formula. Any attempt to contrast Roman Catholic with Lutheran or Reformed approaches to theology is often misleading, because a focus on the areas of disagreement overlooks the more basic Christian beliefs that each shares with the others. Likewise, the contrast between the "Catholic sacramental and substantial" versus the "Protestant prophetic principle" overlooks that much of the substance of Christianity exists in the Reformation churches and much of the prophetic in the Roman Catholic Church. In a similar fashion, the polemic that understands the difference as one between an "either/or" or a "both/and," with the latter representing Roman Catholicism, neglects how the Reformation traditions cannot be limited to the former characterization.

The answer that each of the chapters in this volume seeks to provide is that a Roman Catholic theological approach attempts to articulate the Christian faith and beliefs through an analysis of their biblical roots, the historical developments in their traditions and practices, and their ecclesial fidelity as evident in the explication of the teaching of the various councils and statements of the papacy. Such attempts bring to the fore sacramentality, universality, and union with the bishop of Rome as goals to be reflected in theology. However, these characteristics can best be understood in the categories of "already" and "not yet." One seeks to uncover their presence, but at the same time, one seeks them as a goal yet to be achieved. Such attempts are made in Roman Catholic theology, as Joseph Ratzinger has emphasized, through various forms of correlation between faith and reason, between Christian belief and critical reflection. To the extent that this volume was generated out of the spirit of Vatican II, the authors view the challenges laid down by Vatican II and the Holy Spirit that engendered the council as significant tasks to be taken up and developed in the theological history and reflection of the individual chapters.

—Francis Schüssler Fiorenza,
Harvard Divinity School,
Stillman Professor of
Roman Catholic Theological Studies

Acknowledgments

The first edition of this volume was the idea of John Hollar, then editor at Fortress Press, who discussed it during a luncheon conversation with Francis Schüssler Fiorenza. Unfortunately, Hollar's untimely death occurred before the volume was published; the first edition was dedicated to his memory. Michael West then stepped into the breach, painstakingly and successfully shepherding the volume to its publication. Over the past several years, Michael has encouraged us to bring out a new edition. Without his constant support, encouragement, and advice, this second edition would not have seen the light of day. For that we are grateful. The skilled editorial management of Ann Delgehausen (of Trio Bookworks) and the careful copyediting of Karen Schenkenfelder have been very helpful and deeply appreciated. Jessica Coblentz, a Master of Theological Studies student at Harvard Divinity School, has helpfully prepared the index for the new edition.

The second edition of this volume is dedicated to our colleagues and coauthors of the first edition who are no longer with us but are still fondly remembered as scholars and as friends. Avery Cardinal Dulles, known for his writing in fundamental, systematic, and ecumenical theology, was supportive of the idea from its very beginning. He managed to submit his revised contribution just weeks before his death. Catherine LaCugna's passing took away a scholar in her prime; her contributions to trinitarian theology have provided a decisive marker in subsequent discussions. Monika Hellwig was known for her contribution to liberation theology and practical theology, as was Regis Duffy for his contributions to sacramental theology and pastoral ministry. North American Roman Catholic theology has been enriched by the singular and outstanding contributions of all four theologians, three of whom were presidents of the Catholic Theological Society of America. We are all indebted to them for their contributions to theology. The dedication of this edition to them can only express that gratitude in a small way.

Systematic Theology:
Task and Methods

Francis Schüssler Fiorenza

This chapter seeks to present a historical, descriptive, and systematic introduction to Roman Catholic conceptions of theology and theological method. After some introductory observations on the historical use of the term *theology* and on the Christian Scriptures as theological writings, the first major section will profile three classic conceptions of theology, namely, those of Augustine, Aquinas, and Neo-Scholasticism. The following section will analyze five contemporary approaches to theology, indicating the strengths and weaknesses of each. A third major section will assess the diverse challenges that Roman Catholic theology faces today. It will propose as an adequate method of theology one that seeks to integrate diverse elements and criteria. Since discussions of method are usually more abstract than treatments of particular beliefs, a reader less familiar with or less interested in theological method might prefer to read the other chapters first and to return later to this analysis of theological method.

Fragility of Theology

Theology is a fragile discipline in that it is both academic and related to faith. As an academic discipline, theology shares all the scholarly goals of other academic disciplines: it strives for historical exactitude, conceptual rigor, systematic consistency, and interpretive clarity. In its relation to faith, theology shares the fragility of faith itself. It is much more a hope than a science. It is much more like a raft bobbing on the waves of the sea than a pyramid built on solid ground.

Throughout its history, Christian theology has endured this ambiguity. The relation of theology to faith has always reminded Christian theologians of its fragility, yet they have constantly argued for its disciplinary character and its scientific rigor. For example, Origen and Augustine sought to relate Christian theology to the philosophical knowledge and disciplines of late antiquity. In the medieval university setting, Thomas Aquinas began his *Summa theologiae* by asking whether sacred doctrine as a discipline makes a distinctive contribution to knowledge beyond the philosophical discipline about God. In the nineteenth century, Friedrich Schleiermacher and Johann von Drey argued for theology's rightful status within the modern university against challenges to that status. In the twenty-first century, Christian theologians face the challenge to theology's rightful academic place both by the dominance of the natural sciences and by the emergence of religious studies, which sometimes relegates theology to a confessional discipline not based in the university.

The term *theology* is ambiguous etymologically, historically, and systematically. Etymologically, *theology* means the "word," "discourse," "account," or "language" (*logos*) of God (*theos*). The question, however, remains: Does it mean the word of God as a subjective genitive, namely, God's own discourse? Or is it an objective genitive, meaning discourse about God? The former refers to the divine discourse itself, whereas the second refers to the human effort to understand the divine.[1] Within the early Christian tradition,

---

1. Ferdinand Kattenbusch, "Die Entstehung einer christlichen Theologie: Zur Geschichte der Ausdrücke *theologia, theologein, theologos*," *Zeitschrift für Theologie und Kirche* 11 (1930): 161–205; repr. *Die Entstehung einer christlichen Theologie* (Darmstadt: Wissenschaftliche Buchgesellschaft, 1962). See also Gerhard Ebeling, "Theologie I. Begriffsgeschichtlich," *Religion in Geschichte und Gegenwart*, cols. 754–70; J. Stiglmayr, "Mannigfache Bedeutungen von 'Theologie' und 'Theologen,'" *Theologie und Glaube* 11 (1919): 296–309.

both usages are present. Saint Augustine uses the term *theologia* in the *City of God* in its objective sense to refer to discourse about the divine (*de divinitate ratio sive sermo*).[2] Among the Greek writers, Dionysius the Areopagite (c. sixth century), for example, uses *theologia* to designate not a human science, but the divine discourse itself, particularly the divine discourse of the Holy Scriptures. The Holy Scriptures do not just speak of God but are God's speech. Today this usage no longer prevails, and theology refers primarily to the human study of God.[3]

Historically, the term *theology* emerged as a common and comprehensive term for Christian theology only after the thirteenth century. Among the early Christian writers, the term primarily referred to the pagan philosophical speculation about God rather than to Christian discourse about God, for the latter focused on the divine plan or economy of salvation. Christian discourse, called Christian doctrine, was not simply theology; it was not just another philosophical doctrine about God alone. Instead, Christian discourse explicated God's "economy." It spoke of God's saving plan and action in Jesus Christ and in the Christian community. In the early medieval period, *sacra doctrina, sacra scriptura,* and *sacra* or *divina pagina* were the customary terms for the discipline. They expressed the primacy of the Christian Scriptures in Christian doctrine. As the medieval teaching evolved

from a commentary on the Scriptures or from an exposition of questions appended to scriptural texts to a full-fledged systematic discussion of controversial issues, the term *theology* emerged as the umbrella expression for Christian doctrine. It was in the thirteenth century that the term *theology* came to have the comprehensive meaning that it has for us today.[4]

Considered systematically, the present usage of the term also is ambiguous. *Theology* is often used as an umbrella term to cover all the theological disciplines. Yet the term also denotes a specific discipline known as systematic theology. The division of the theological disciplines is the result of a long process within modern times.[5] *Theology* is also often used in contradistinction from religious studies, the former referring to a confessional approach, the latter prescinding from such commitments.[6] Yet "religious studies" and "theological studies" are sometimes used interchangeably.

The nature and method of theology are issues about which much diversity exists in the history of Christian thought—a diversity of schools, methods, and approaches.[7] Nevertheless, amid all this diversity, there are several constants. In examining the tasks and methods of theology, we must recognize both the diversity and the constancy.

One constant is the Scriptures, a primary element of Christian communities' tradition

---

2. Augustine, *City of God* 8.1.

3. See Joseph Ratzinger, *Principles of Catholic Theology: Building Stones for a Fundamental Theology* (San Francisco: Ignatius, 1987), 320–22.

4. J. Rivière, "Theologia," *Revue des sciences religieuses* 16 (1936): 47–57.

5. Edward Farley, *Theologia: The Fragmentation and Unity of Theological Education* (Philadelphia: Fortress Press, 1983).

6. Francis Schüssler Fiorenza, "Theological and Religious Studies: The Contest of the Faculties," in *Shifting Boundaries: Contextual Approaches to the Structure of Theological Education*, ed. Barbara Wheeler and Edward Farley (Atlanta: Westminster, 1991).

7. Yves Congar, *A History of Theology* (Garden City, NY: Doubleday, 1968).

and identity.[8] Yet the meaning of the Scriptures depends on their interpretation. Augustine's interpretation of the Scriptures relied heavily on his background theory of Neo-Platonic hermeneutics. In the nineteenth century, the historical-critical method came into use as an interpretive tool. Today a multiplicity of hermeneutical theories affect our practices of interpretation. The constant of Scripture remains, yet the means of interpretation vary. The same is true of a community's tradition and creedal statements.

The experience of the community is another constant within theology. Yet that constant has also functioned diversely. Not only do different communities have different experiences, but different theologies have weighted communities' experience differently and have employed quite diverse categories to interpret that experience. The appeal to a community's experience is a constant, but its function differs considerably throughout the history of Christian theology.

Another constant is the reliance on some basic approach, procedure, or method to interpret the Scriptures, tradition, and experience. Such a procedure may be a general, implicit approach or an explicit, specific method. Such procedures constitute what could be called background theories, for they affect how the community interprets its discourse, its tradition, and its experience. Therefore, analyses of the nature of Christian theology, its task and method, should attend to the interplay between the constants of tradition, experience, and background theories that interpret tradition and experience.[9]

Christian Scriptures: Testimony and Theological Reflection

Modern theology has become acutely aware that theological reflection is at the center of the Scriptures. The Scriptures are not simply sources for theological reflection but themselves are examples of theological reflection. The Christian Scriptures do not simply witness to Jesus as the Christ, nor do they merely testify to the faith of the early Christian communities. Their witness takes place in the midst of an attempt to interpret Jesus theologically and is the testimony of a reflective faith. The Christian Scriptures, therefore, are constituted not only by the symbols and testimonies of faith, but also by that theological reflection emerging within those symbols and testimonies.

Such a view of the Christian Scriptures contrasts with previous views. Formerly, the Scriptures were seen primarily as a source providing principles for theology or as the object of theological reflection. In the nineteenth century, some scholars acknowledged only certain writings of the Scriptures as embodiments of theological reflection. They viewed Paul and John as great theologians, for example, but the authors of the Synoptics only as collectors or editors of source materials. Today it is commonly agreed that all the writings are theological. There is no part of the Christian Scriptures that is not at the same time an expression of a reflective witness and a believing theology.

---

8. Francis Schüssler Fiorenza, "The Crisis of Scriptural Authority: Interpretation and Reception," *Interpretation* 44 (1990): 353–68.

9. The systematic nature of the task of attending to tradition, experience, background theory, and community is developed in the final section of this essay.

6

This conviction was strongly affirmed in the Second Vatican Council. The Dogmatic Constitution on Divine Revelation (*Dei verbum*) accented the extent to which theological reflection permeates the New Testament writings. Section 19 in chapter 5 affirms, "The sacred authors wrote the four Gospels, selecting some things from the many which had been handed on by word of mouth or in writing, reducing some of them to a synthesis, explicating [*explanates*] some things in view of the situation of their churches, and preserving the form of proclamation but always in such a fashion that they told us the honest truth about Jesus."[10] This text refers to the selection of materials, the interpretation of traditions, explanations related to specific situations, theological synthesis, and pastoral applications. All of these elements make up the writing of the Gospels. The four Gospels give witness to Jesus in reflecting theologically on his meaning and significance for their particular pastoral situations.

This recognition of the relation between theological reflection and the New Testament writings has entered into the contemporary conceptions of the nature of the Scriptures and their origin.[11] Recent theories of inspiration have related inspiration to the very formation of the Scriptures.[12] The complex elements that led to the formation of the Scriptures—originating events and their interpretation, new situations, and new reflection—are integrated within the theory of inspiration. Inspiration belongs to the whole process of the community's reflection and interpretation of its originating events. This whole process of the formation of the Scriptures provides, some argue, paradigms for our theological reflection.[13]

Today we are aware that the Scriptures are theological. They not only contain the subject matter of theology but also embody specific and differing theological visions. This awareness corresponds to a consensus among Christian theologians and church documents.[14] Moreover, our awareness of the historicity of Christian theology and the Christian Scriptures is one of the specific characteristics of modern theology. Yet before we survey modern and contemporary conceptions of theology, we will examine three classic and influential conceptions of theology.

Three Classic Paradigms of Theology

The Augustinian, Thomistic, and Neo-Scholastic approaches to theology represent the three most influential traditions within Western Roman Catholic theology as an academic discipline. In addition to these approaches, the Roman Catholic tradition contains many other schools of theology. A rich diversity of ascetic,

---

10. Second Vatican Council, Dogmatic Constitution on Divine Revelation (*Dei verbum*), in *The Documents of Vatican II*, ed. Walter M. Abbott (Chicago: Follet, 1966). See also the commentary by Joseph Fitzmyer in *Theological Studies* 25 (1964): 386–408. See the extended commentary on the constitution in vol. 3 of Herbert Vorgrimler, ed., *Commentary on the Documents of Vatican II* (New York: Herder, 1969).

11. Karl Rahner, "Theology of the New Testament" and "Exegesis and Dogmatic Theology," in *Theological Investigations* (New York: Crossroad, 1966), 5:23–41. See also Rahner's *Inspiration in the Bible*, 2nd ed. (New York: Herder, 1964).

12. See Paul Achtemeier, *The Inspiration of Scripture: Problems and Proposals* (Philadelphia: Westminster, 1980).

13. See James P. Sanders, *Canon and Community: A Guide to Canonical Criticism* (Philadelphia: Fortress Press, 1984).

14. See the collection of essays illustrating this point in Roland Murphy, ed., *Theology, Exegesis, and Proclamation* (New York: Herder & Herder, 1971). See also Bruce Vawter, *Biblical Inspiration* (Philadelphia: Westminster, 1971).

spiritual, and liturgical theologies exists in the West. Monastic as well as academic traditions exist. Eastern Christianity contains other rich traditions. My focus on just the Augustinian, Thomistic, and Neo-Scholastic approaches is not meant to slight these other traditions; it is meant to provide a somewhat more detailed examination of the traditions most influential in Western academic theology. Such a focus, moreover, enables one to grasp much more clearly the major changes and transitions that have occurred in the academic study and teaching of Roman Catholic theology.[15]

Augustine: Christian Doctrine as Wisdom

During the early church period, the plurality and diversity of theological conceptions are unmistakable. In the second century, the apostolic fathers (Clement of Rome, Hermas, Ignatius, Polycarp) continually wrestled with the relation between Christianity and Judaism. The Apologists (Justin, Aristides, Athenagoras) sought to relate Christianity to the educated and philosophical culture of the Greco-Roman Empire. Of the anti-Gnostic writers, Irenaeus especially contributed to theological method not only through his understanding of tradition and of the rule of faith, but also through his exposition

"hypothesis" or system of truth.[16] In the third century, the schools of Antioch and Alexandria developed distinctive exegetical approaches, and the beginnings of systematic theology sprouted their roots in the work of Origen.

BEGINNING OF SYSTEMATIC THEOLOGY IN THE GREEK CHURCH

Origen's *On First Principles* (*Peri archon*) makes a threefold contribution to a systematic presentation of the Christian faith. First, Origen attempted to give a foundation for the scientific exegesis of the Scriptures.[17] Second, he developed a systematic theory of religious knowledge. Third, he gave a systematic presentation of theology that indeed has earned him the label of the first systematic theologian.[18] Origen's *On First Principles* (published in 220) has been traditionally seen as a first attempt to bring the truths of the Christian faith into a theological synthesis. The traditional edition of this work, however, distorts its actual genre, which has been brought to light by a recent critical edition.[19] The book is neither a *summa* nor a systematic theology, but rather a systematic exposition of God's relation to the world.

In his preface, Origen explains that the church's tradition contains the canon of faith, and the theologian has the responsibility to

---

15. For a complete survey of the history of Christian theology and doctrine, see the five-volume work by Jaroslav Pelikan, *The Christian Tradition* (Chicago: University of Chicago Press, 1971–88). Earlier and somewhat dated presentations are Reinhold Seeberg, *The History of Doctrines* (Grand Rapids: Baker, 1977; German ed., 1895); Adolf von Harnack, *History of Dogma*, 7 vols. (New York: Dover, 1961; German ed., 1900).

16. See Philip Hefner, "Theological Methodology and St. Irenaeus," *Journal of Religion* 44 (1964): 294–309.

17. See Joseph Wilson Trigg, *Origen: The Bible and Philosophy in the Third-Century Church* (Atlanta: John Knox, 1983).

18. Marguerite Harl, *Origène et la function révélatrice du Verbe Incarné* (Paris: Éditions du Seuil, 1958), 346–59.

19. See Marguerite Harl's essays "Recherches sur le *Peri archon* d'Origène vue d'une nouvelle edition: La division en chapitres," in *Studia Patristica* III, Texte und Untersuchungen zur Geschichte der altchristlichen Literatur 78, ed. F. L. Cross (Berlin: Akademie-Verlag, 1961), 57–67; and "Structure et cohérence du *Peri archon*," in *Origeniana*, ed. Henri Crouzel (Bari, Italy: Istituto di letteratura Cristiana antica, 1975), 11–32. The critical edition is in Henri Crouzel and Manlio Simonetti, eds. and trans., Sources chrétiennes (Paris: Éditions du Cerf, 1978 and 1980).

8 explicate its inner rationale and implications. In seeking to accomplish this task, Origen adopted a specific genre of philosophical literature—one that dealt with questions of physics as the foundation of philosophy. This genre sought a first principle or the first principles of the universe. As a Christian, Origen considered God to be the beginning or first principle of the world. Therefore, he sought to synthesize the issues of physics, philosophy, and theology. The first part of *On First Principles* is a general treatise. It deals with God the Father, Christ, the Holy Spirit, and the Trinity, then with the four types of rational creatures, and finally with the created world and its return to God. The second part, following the same order, deals with special topics under each of these headings. Finally, there is a recapitulation of the topics. The overall effect is to show that all comes from the divine unity and returns to the divine unity. Through such an arrangement, Origen explicated his Christian faith in relation to the philosophical categories and literature of his time.

Augustine's Scientific Conception: Knowledge and Wisdom

Although Origen's originality has led many to consider him the first systematic theologian, it is Saint Augustine who has had the major impact on the development of Christian systematic theology in the West. Augustine's contribution to the development of Western theological method lies in his conception of theology as wisdom, his hermeneutical rules for the interpretation of Scripture, and his influence on the structure of the medieval *summa*.

Significant for Augustine's understanding of theology, or more properly, Christian doctrine, is his distinction between wisdom (*sapientia*) and knowledge (*scientia*). Whereas wisdom has as its object the eternal and unchangeable reality, knowledge is the rational insight into visible, perceptible, changeable, and temporal things.[20] Augustine does not equate knowledge with an empirical rationality, as our modern view does. Instead, Augustine views wisdom and human happiness as the goal of knowledge—a knowledge stemming from three sources: experience, authority, and signs.[21]

Knowledge from *experience* is not, as in modern experimental science, gained from experimentation characterized by confirmation and verification of hypotheses. Instead, this knowledge starts with the world of appearances in order to arrive at the intelligible and the first cause of things. Knowledge proceeds from the visible to the invisible, from appearances to reality. Knowledge from experience is, therefore, knowledge of the intelligible.

Knowledge from *authority* is knowledge based not on what one experiences oneself, but rather on testimony. Although Augustine maintains that knowledge from direct experience is preferable to knowledge based on human authority, he argues that the situation is different in regard to the authority of divine wisdom. The invisible has become visible in Christ. Through his miracles, life, and teaching, Christ is the mediator and revealer of truth; he is the divine authority.[22] Moreover, the Scriptures contain the testimony to his authority as the revealer of the divine truth. This testimony calls for a faith in

---

20. Augustine, *On the Trinity* 12.15.25. See also 12.14.22–23.

21. For an analysis of Augustine's method, see Rudolf Lorenz, "Die Wissenschaftslehre Augustinus," *Zeitschrift für Kirchengeschichte* 67 (1955/56): 29–60 and 213–51.

22. See Augustine, *On the Trinity* 13.19.24, PL 42, col. 1034.

Christ and provides for a knowledge based on his authority.[23]

In addition, there is knowledge from *signs*, which also enables one to go beyond the knowledge of immediate experience.[24] The external form of a perceptible sign refers to something else, hidden from the senses; smoke, for example, refers to a fire. Signs are of two kinds: either natural or "given" (*signa data*). Natural signs make us aware of something without the intention of signifying, as smoke makes us aware of fire. "Given" signs are signs that occur when someone wills they occur.[25] They are given by humans or by God. The most important of them is the Word. As a sign, the Word is a source of knowledge and learning. The words of Scripture are signs that refer to the transcendent. The key task of the interpreter of the Scriptures, therefore, is to interpret their transcendent reference. A genuine interpretation of the Scriptures yields knowledge of the verbal signs of the invisible God. Consequently, a correspondence exists between Augustine's interpretation of the Scriptures and his theory of knowledge.

Augustine's Hermeneutical Rules

In *On Christian Doctrine*, Augustine developed principles and rules for the interpretation of the Scriptures.[26] In so doing, Augustine provided important and influential contributions to rhetoric, education, theology, and hermeneutics. Augustine's hermeneutical theory should be understood in relation to his Neo-Platonic background and his attempt to come to grips with the incarnation of the divine wisdom. The Platonic *chorismos* schema—namely, the distinction between the changeable and unchangeable, the temporal and eternal—provides the background theory to his rules of interpretation.[27] The changeable should be interpreted in relation to the unchangeable, the temporal to the eternal, the world to the transcendent, historical events to the divine plan of salvation, and the human Christ to the divine Word. Augustine's hermeneutical theory bases signification on the ontological priority of the unchangeable eternal to the changeable and material.

This conviction (concerning the ontological priority of the transcendental reality over the material sign) leads Augustine to his basic principle of hermeneutics: what is of primary importance is not so much our knowledge of the material sign that enables us to interpret the eternal reality, but rather it is our knowledge of the eternal reality that enables us to interpret the material sign. This hermeneutical principle

---

23. See Augustine's Letter 120 to Consentius 120.2.9.1–3, *Corpus scriptorum ecclesiasticorum latinorum*, 63, 182, 16–19. See Karl-Heinrich Lütcke, *"Auctoritas" bei Augustinus* (Stuttgart: Kohlhammer, 1968).

24. For Augustine's conception of sign, see R. A. Markus, "St. Augustine on Signs," and B. Darrell Jackson, "The Theory of Signs in St. Augustine's *De doctrina christiana*," in *Augustine: A Collection of Critical Essays*, ed. R. A. Markus (Garden City, NY: Doubleday, 1972), respectively, 61–91 and 92–137.

25. J. Engels, "La doctrine de signe chez saint Augustin," in *Studia Patristica VI*, Texte und Untersuchungen zur Geschichte der altchristlichen Literatur 81, ed. F. L. Cross (Berlin: Akademie-Verlag, 1962), 366–73, argues that *signa data* should not be translated as "conventional signs" because of their intentional character.

26. See Peter Brunner, "Charismatische und methodische Schriftauslegung nach Augustins Prolog zu De doctrina Christiana," *Kerygma und Dogma* 1 (1955): 59–69, 85–103; C. P. Mayer, "'Res per signa': Der Grundgedanke des Prologs in Augustins Schrift De doctrina Christiana und das Problem der Datierung," *Revue des études Augustiniennes* 20 (1974): 100–112; Hermann-Josef Sieben, "Die 'res' der Bibel: Eine Analyse von Augustinus, *De doctr. chris.* I–III," *Revue des études augustiniennes* 21 (1975): 72–90.

27. See Cornelius Petrus Mayer, *Die Zeichen in der gesitigen Entwicklung und in her Theologie des jungen Augustinus* (Würzburg: Augustinus Verlag, 1974), vols. 1–2.

10

applies not only to allegorical and typological but also to literal interpretation. To understand the words of the Bible properly as signs of eternal reality, one must acknowledge that reality.

Knowing the eternal reality requires a spiritual ascent and purification. Such a spiritual purification is, therefore, a presupposition for interpreting Scripture. "A real understanding of Scripture—one that does not stop at the external words—demands a moral purification, and Augustine proposes a scheme of seven stages leading to it."[28] The seven stages are the *fear of God* that leads toward a recognition of God's will; *piety*, so in meekness we attend to the Scriptures; knowledge that grasps that *charity*, the love of God and of neighbor, is the sum of the Scriptures; the gift of *fortitude* in hungering and thirsting for justice; the counsel of *mercy* by which one exercises the love of neighbor and perfects oneself in it; the *purification* of the heart from its attachments to the world; and finally, *wisdom* of divine contemplation.[29]

The interrelation between spiritual purification and the interpretation of the Scriptures points to what in Augustine's view is the major problem of hermeneutics. This problem is not the distance between the horizon of past times and the horizon of present times. Nor is it the problem of grasping the literal meaning in its literalness, as in modern biblical fundamentalism. Though Augustine is aware of historical differences and of linguistic problems in ascertaining the correct literal meaning, for him the central problem of hermeneutics is much more basic. It is the problem of understanding the transcen-

dent referent. The person who interprets the words only in their literal or historical sense and not in their reference to the transcendent has failed to grasp the meaning of the Scriptures.

In cases of doubt, Augustine proposes some basic principles. One principle asks whether the interpretation in question leads to a greater love of God and neighbor. Indeed, he writes that if someone "is deceived in an interpretation which builds up charity, which is the end of the commandments, he is deceived in the same way as a man who leaves a road by mistake but passes through a field to the same place toward which the road itself leads."[30] The knowledge of Scripture entails for Augustine not new information but the discovery of God's will leading to the contemplation of eternal truths, the object of wisdom, and of the blessed life. Another principle underscores the communal context of interpretation, namely, the faith of the church as an interpreting community. This faith is most clearly manifest in the church's rule of faith as expressed in the creed.[31]

Today we face two contrasting tendencies. On the one hand, exegetical practice stresses a scientific objectivity and neutrality that aim to be free from subjective presuppositions. On the other hand, contemporary hermeneutical theory underscores the significance that one's pre-understanding and application have for interpretation. It is contemporary hermeneutical theory that seeks to retrieve and reappropriate (though with a contrasting horizon and different categories) the classic relation between life-practice and interpretation that Augustine

---

28. See Ragnar Holte, *Béatitude et sagesse: Saint Augustin et le problème de la fin de l'homme dans la philosophie ancienne* (Paris: Études augustiniennes, 1962), 342.

29. Augustine *On Christian Doctrine*, 2.7.9–11.

30. Ibid., 1.36.41.

31. See Howard J. Loewen, "The Use of Scripture in Augustine's Theology," *Scottish Journal of Theology* 34 (1981): 201–24.

expressed with his combination of Christian beliefs and Neo-Platonic categories. Hermeneutical theory today affirms that a life-relation to the subject matter to be interpreted is essential to understanding. This hermeneutical affirmation raises the question of the proper life-relation to the subject matter of the Christian Scriptures.

This question (implied in the hermeneutical theories of Martin Heidegger and Hans-Georg Gadamer) has been raised within theological hermeneutics. Yet it has been raised quite diversely by existential hermeneutics and by liberation theology.[32] The existential approach (represented by Rudolf Bultmann's classic essay on hermeneutics) asks: Since the Scriptures are about God's revelation, how then do humans have a pre-understanding of God's revelation?[33] Bultmann's answer refers to Augustine, for it asserts that the issue guiding our approach to the Scriptures is the quest for God that is implied in the question of the meaning of human life. Liberation theology, in contrast, understands this life-relation and pre-understanding as the self-transcendence of solidarity with the poor and oppressed. The existential question of Bultmann's hermeneutics and the solidarity affirmed by liberation theology both stand in a continuity—yet with considerable modifications—with Augustine's stress on self-transcendence and spiritual purification as a condition for the proper understanding of Scriptures. As such, they contrast sharply with the objectivism of much modern historicism.

AUGUSTINE'S INFLUENCE ON THE WEST

Augustine strongly and directly influenced the method, content, and arrangement of medieval theology. His specification of the relation between faith and understanding was decisive for medieval theology and theological method. Augustine quoted an early Latin translation of Isa. 7:9 ("Unless you believe, you will not understand") in order to suggest not only that faith seeks and understanding finds, but also that one seeks understanding on the basis of faith.[34] This verse and idea find their classic formulation in Anselm's prologue to his *Proslogion*: "I do not seek to understand in order to believe, but I believe in order to understand. For I believe even this: that I shall not understand unless I believe."[35] For Anselm, the attempt to gain understanding and rational insight into the truths was an obligatory task and the key to his theological method. Anselm's explication of this Augustinian starting point provided the basis for the Scholastic theological method.

Augustine's view of faith's relation to understanding relates to his understanding of the role of authority in knowledge and the role of the church within theology. Augustine declared

---

32. Martin Heidegger, *Being and Time* (New York: Harper & Row, 1962), secs. 31–32; Hans-Georg Gadamer, *Truth and Method*, 2nd ed. (New York: Crossroad, 1989), 265–307.

33. See Rudolf Bultmann, "The Problem of Hermeneutics" and "Is Exegesis without Presuppositions Possible?" in *New Testament Mythology and Other Basic Writings*, ed. Schubert M. Ogden (Philadelphia: Fortress Press, 1984). Bultmann relates his notion of pre-understanding and question to Augustine: "Unless our existence were moved (consciously or unconsciously) by the question about God in the sense of Augustine's 'Thou hast made us for thyself, and our heart is restless until it rests in thee,' we would not be able to recognize God in any revelation" (p. 87).

34. Augustine, *On the Trinity* 15.2.2. The translation of the Latin Vulgate differed; it had "not abide" instead of "not understand."

35. See chapter 1 of *Proslogion*. For the context and role of Anselm in medieval theology, see Gillian Rosemary Evans, *Anselm and a New Generation* (Oxford: Clarendon, 1980); Richard Campbell, "Anselm's Theological Method," *Scottish Journal of Theology* 32 (1979): 541–62.

12   that the authority of the apostolic sees is what determines which Gospels are canonical; that is, the decisions of the apostolic sees are decisive for determining which texts are acknowledged as Scripture. In addition, the creeds as explications of the rule of faith provide a standard for the interpretation of Scripture. Moreover, Augustine's treatment of the articles of faith in the creed as the reality of faith, and especially the order of his exposition in the *Enchiridion* and *On Christian Doctrine*, influenced the structure and arrangement of topics in the medieval *summas*.[36] *On Christian Doctrine* divides the content of Christian doctrine into reality (*res*) and signs (*signa*). The signs are the words of Scripture, and the reality is the triune God. In *On Christian Doctrine*, Augustine discusses the Apostles' Creed (see book 1, chapters 5–21), and in so doing, he sketches the following outline of Christian doctrine: First is the reality, the triune God, the goal of all human striving. Second is the divine wisdom that has become human and who heals the sick. His teachings and gifts are given to the church, his bride, for the forgiveness of sins. This outline influenced two authors, Gennadius of Marseilles and Fulgentius of Ruspe, who in turn influenced the arrangement of the medieval *Summa sententiarum*.[37] Their treatment of the material is Augustinian and Western, especially insofar as they do not follow the Eastern stress on the economy of salvation, a stress that underscored the soteriological significance of the Christ event and the unity between creation and salvation history. Instead, they follow Augustine's order and discuss first faith and then the objects of faith: God and Christ. They thereby pave the way for Peter Lombard.

After 1215, Peter Lombard's *Four Books of Sentences* was for all practical purposes the medieval textbook. Lombard follows the Augustinian outline, and he distinguishes between reality and signs. Books 1 to 3 treat the *res* (reality): book 1 treats the triune God, book 2 discusses creation, and book 3 discusses Christ (including the virtues). Book 4 is about the signs, the sacraments. Lombard's outline was taken over by many medieval theologians and strongly influenced the order of the presentation of their material.[38]

Besides influencing the systematic arrangement of medieval *summas*, Augustine had an inestimable influence on concrete doctrines. It is impossible for Christian theologians to discuss the doctrine of the Trinity, the nature of sin, the theory of original sin, the role of grace, the efficacy of the sacraments, the nature of ministry, or the relation between church and state without reference to the contributions of Augustine. His influence extends not just to medieval theology, but also to the Reformation and to key theological movements within modern theology. Many of the views of Luther and Calvin were attempts to retrieve Augustine's understanding of grace and human nature. Within the twentieth century, this constructive influence remains: Reinhold Niebuhr's *The Nature and Destiny of*

---

36. See Alois Grillmeier, "Vom Symbolum zur Summa," in *Mit ihm und in ihm: Christologische Forschungen und Perspektiven* (Freiburg: Herder, 1975), 585–636.

37. The outlines of Gennadius of Marseilles's *Liber sive definition ecclesiasticorum dogmatum* and Fulgentius of Ruspe's *Liber de fide ad Petrum* show their indebtedness to Augustine and their contrast with Eastern theological treatises. See Alois Grillmeier, "Patristische Vorbilder frühscholastischer Systematik: Zugleich ein Beitrag zur Geschichte des Augustinismus," in Cross, *Studia Patristica* VI.

38. The outline influenced Thomas in the *Summa theologiae*, with some modifications. Thomas locates the virtues not in his treatment of Christ, but in his anthropology.

Man provided a brilliant reformulation of Augustine's understanding of human nature and sin and then applied that reformulation to political life.[39] Henri de Lubac sought to recover Augustine's understanding of nature and grace over against Neo-Scholasticism.[40] Karl Rahner sought to counter popular misconceptions of the Trinity by retrieving and developing some aspects of Augustine's theology of the Trinity.[41]

Aquinas: Scholastic Method and Thomas's Sacra Doctrina

In 1879 Leo XXIII's encyclical *Aeterni patris* declared Thomas to be the leading Scholastic theologian, the Angelic Doctor, "omnium princeps et magister" ("prince and teacher of all").[42] Thomas's influence upon Roman Catholic systematic theology is indeed unsurpassed. One cannot conceive of Roman Catholic theology without his influence. Yet much of theology that claims to be Thomist represents in reality theological presuppositions, views, and conclusions that are distinct from his. This difference is of such importance that within German theological literature, the terms *Thomanism* and *Thomism* are commonly employed to differentiate Thomas from Thomists.[43] Moreover,

within the course of twentieth century research on Thomas, clear-cut differences have emerged between how the Neo-Thomists understood Thomas that emphasized his Aristotelianism and his philosophical theology, and the current understanding of Thomas that underscores the theological character and purpose of his work and realizes its Augustinian as well as Neo-Platonic background.[44] The Neo-Thomists had interpreted with a specific polemic. They sought to use Thomas's philosophy as both a natural theology and a natural-law ethic to counter what they envisioned to be the influence of Kant on nineteenth-century philosophy and theology. As this polemic waned, so did that specific interpretation of Thomas.

I shall examine Thomas's understanding of theology in three steps. First, I shall consider the development of the Scholastic theological method as the context for his theological method. Second, I shall analyze Thomas's definition of theology and the specific meaning of the title *Sacra doctrina*. Finally, I shall address the criteria of theology. What constitutes for Thomas good theology, or what counts as a considered theological judgment? The answers to these questions display some of the considerable differences between medieval theology and contemporary theology.

---

39. Reinhold Niebuhr, *The Nature and Destiny of Man* (New York: Scribner, 1941).

40. Henri de Lubac, *The Mystery of the Supernatural* (New York: Herder, 1967); idem, *Augustinianism and Modern Theology* (New York: Herder, 1968).

41. Karl Rahner, *The Trinity* (New York: Crossroad, 1970).

42. On the authority of Thomas, see Heinrich Stirnimann, "Non-'tutum'-toto tutius? Zur Lehrautorität des hl. Thomas," *Freiburger Zeitschrift für Philosophie und Theologie* 1 (1954): 420–33.

43. Gottlieb Söhngen, *Der Weg der abendländischen Theologie* (Munich: Pustet, 1959).

44. My brief survey in "The New Theology and Transcendental Thomism," in *Modern Christian Thought*, vol. 2, *The Twentieth Century*, 2nd ed., ed. James Livingston and Francis Schüssler Fiorenza (Minneapolis: Fortress Press, 2006), 197–232 Wayne J. Hankey, "Thomas' Neoplatonic Histories: His Following of Simplicius," *Dionysius* 20 (2002): 153–78; idem, "Reading Augustine through Dionysius: Aquinas' Correction of One Platonism by Another," *Aquinas the Augustinian*, edited by Michael Dauphinais et al. (Washington, DC: Catholic University of America Press, 2007): 243–57.

BACKGROUND TO
SCHOLASTIC METHOD
AND THEOLOGY

The maturation of theology as an academic discipline coincided with the gradual development of the twelfth-century schools into universities. The growth of the universities and the advancement of the liberal arts had a decisive impact on the development of theology, particularly systematic theology.[45] At the beginning of the twelfth century, several kinds of schools existed in Europe: the monastic school, the cathedral school, schools attached to individual scholars, and in Italy, the urban schools that taught liberal arts.

Instruction at the medieval university developed from the reading (*lectio*) to the practice of the disputation (*disputatio*) of questions. This development provided the context for the emergence of the theological *summas* with their diverse "articles."[46] Medieval university lectures first focused on the reading and learning of texts. Since the primary text was sacred Scripture, the discipline was called *sacra doctrina*.[47] The lectures on the text at first amounted to verbal glosses. The lecturer explained the words of the texts, the sense of the passages, and finally the *sentential* or diverse opinions about the more profound meaning and significance of the texts. The questions and opinions that arose in relation to the meaning of the scriptural text increased in number and length. These questions, however, gradually detached themselves from the text in which they had originated. In becoming separated from the text, they were then collected, giving rise to florilegia, compilations, and *summas* in which diverse opinions regarding various questions were collected.[48]

The development from the *lectio* to the *disputatio* entailed an important shift not only in teaching, but also in method. The *lectio* was primarily interpretive, for it consisted of a reading, exposition, and gloss of the text of some recognized authority. The *disputatio* consisted in a lively academic debate. It assumed divergence of opinion and differences among authorities. The method of disputation started out not from an authoritative text, but from a set of questions that pointed to a set of propositions that could be doubted. "From this starting point, the pro and con are brought into play, not with the intention of finding an immediate answer, but in order that under the action of *dubitatio* [doubt], research be pushed to its limit. A satisfactory explanation will be given only on the condition that one continue the search to the discovery of what caused the doubt."[49] The "on the contrary" of the *quaestio* is not the author's thesis, but rather the alternate position. The response of the master follows both posi-

---

45. Gillian Rosemary Evans, *Old Arts and New Theology: The Beginnings of Theology as an Academic Discipline* (Oxford: Clarendon, 1980). For an outstanding survey of recent literature that locates the rhetorical function of his writings, see Mark D. Jordan, *Rewritten Theology: Aquinas after His Readers* (Malden, MA: Blackwell, 2006).

46. M. D. Chenu, *Toward Understanding Saint Thomas* (Chicago: Henry Regnery, 1964). See also his *Théologie comme science* (Paris: J. Vrin, 1943).

47. See Beryl Smalley, *The Study of the Bible in the Middle Ages* (Oxford: Blackwell, 1952); Gillian Rosemary Evans, *The Language and Logic of the Bible* (New York: Cambridge University Press, 1984).

48. For the background to the development of the medieval *summas*, see Johannes Beumer, "Zwischen Patristik und Scholastik: Gedanken zum Wesen der Theologie an Hand des Liber de fide ad Petrum des hl. Fulgentius von Ruspe," *Gregorianum* 23 (1942): 326–47.

49. Chenu, *Toward Understanding*, 94.

tions and resolves the doubts that the question raises.[50]

For this method of instruction, the contribution of Peter Abelard and his student Peter Lombard was decisive. Peter Abelard compiled a set of passages from the patristic writings on issues of Christian doctrine and practice. He called this compilation *Yes and No (Sic et Non)*.[51] As its title suggests, the compilation uncovered the disagreements, contradictions, and differences of opinion in theology. Abelard's approach was innovative insofar as he applied a method common in canon law to issues of doctrine. Medieval canon lawyers, familiar with diverse interpretations of law and practice, sought to educate and to resolve disputes through such collections of conflicting opinions.

Abelard's introduction to *Yes and No* offered several rules for overcoming conflicts of opinion: (1) examine the authenticity of the text or passages; (2) look for later emendations, retractions, or corrections; (3) attend to diversity of intention—for example, the difference between a precept and a counsel; (4) note the distinction of historical times and circumstances; (5) attend to differences in the meaning of terms and their references; and (6) if unable to reconcile the diversity, give greater weight to the stronger witness or greater authority. In this endeavor, the Scriptures retained prime authority. Abelard sought to demonstrate the difference of opinion among Christian authors.[52] It was they,

rather than the Scriptures, that disagreed, and it was their differences of opinion that needed resolution. Abelard's attention to the problem of the disagreements within the tradition came to characterize medieval theological instruction. His student Peter Lombard compiled a collection of diverse opinion that served as a text of medieval education.

Thomas's Understanding of *Sacra Doctrina*

In the twelfth century, the issue was not yet whether theology is a science, but rather whether faith is knowledge. A common answer was that faith is more than opinion but less than knowledge. Faith has more certitude than opinion but less than knowledge. Faith is neither a *scientia opinativa* (operative knowledge) nor a *scientia necessaria* (necessary knowledge), but a *scientia probabilis* (probable knowledge). Faith is, therefore, a form of knowledge that is a grounded opinion with probable certitude.[53] In the twelfth century, *sacra doctrina* was not yet distinct from the interpretation of Scripture. "Yet the idea of a scientific theology, which apodictically derived its conclusions from evident principles, led to a notion of theology as an independent question and consequently led to the question of its relation to the other disciplines."[54]

This question of the relation between *sacra doctrina* and the other disciplines was discussed within the Franciscan schools. Edward

---

50. See F. A. Blanche, "Le vocabulaire de l'argumentation et la structure de l'article dans les ouvrages de Saint Thomas," *Revue des sciences philosophiques et théologiques* 14 (1925): 167–87.

51. D. E. Luscombe, *The Influence of Abelard's Thought in the Early Scholastic Period* (Cambridge: Cambridge University Press, 1969).

52. See the careful analysis of Abelard's intention and the correction of von Harnack's widespread view in Martin Grabmann, *Geschichte der scholastischen Methode* (Freiburg: Herder, 1911), 2:168–229.

53. See Richard Heinzmann, "Die Theologie auf dem Weg zur Wissenschaft: Zur Entwicklung der theologischen Systematik in der Scholastik," *Münchener Theologische Zeitschrift* 25 (1974): 1–17.

54. Charles H. Lohr, "Theologie und/als Wissenschaft im frühen 13. Jahrhundert," *Internationale katholische Zeitschrift* 10 (1981): 327 (my translation). For a comparison of Augustinian and modern conceptions of science, see

16 Kilwardby had asked what the relation is among theology, metaphysics, and other sciences. The *Summa halensis* answers that both theology and metaphysics are wisdom, because they relate to the first causes. When medieval theologians first called theology a "science" (*scientia*), they often used the notion of *scientia* in a general sense.[55] William of Auxerre and Alexander of Hales sought to specify theology as a science by employing Aristotle's notion of science. Thomas, however, went a step further in that he took over Aristotle's division of the sciences and applied the notion of "subalternate science" to describe sacred doctrine as a science.[56]

Thomas's understanding of the nature of *sacra doctrina*, the subject matter of the first article of his *Summa theologiae*, has been and remains an object of considerable controversy. The first commentator on Thomas's *Summa*, Thomas Cardinal de Vio Cajetan (1469–1534), argues that in the first article, *sacra doctrina* refers neither to faith nor to theology, but rather to the knowledge revealed by God. In the second article, it refers to knowledge as an intellectual habit concerning the conclusions drawn from that knowledge.[57] The Louvain theologian Francis Sylvius (1581–1649) argues that *sacra doctrina* is the habit of Scholastic theology derived from the principles of faith.[58] In recent times, Yves Congar interprets *sacra doctrina* as the process of Christian instruction. It is, however, not just the academic theological discipline or simply a collection of theological truths, but rather the whole process of teaching and instruction. Congar interprets the notion of Christian instruction in a broad sense to include both Scripture and theology.[59] Gerald van Ackeran, following Congar, argues that sacred Scripture, sacred doctrine, and theology proper are distinct realities in a causal context. Scripture relates to *sacra doctrina* as an external instrument, as its efficient cause. God, however, is the principal cause.[60] Criticizing these approaches, James Weisheipl, a recent biographer of Thomas, argues that *sacra doctrina* primarily refers to faith,[61] whereas Thomas O'Brien argues that it refers to a distinct academic discipline.[62]

If one locates Thomas within the medieval discussions about academic disciplines, then it becomes clear that by *sacra doctrina*, Thomas meant an academic discipline alongside philosophy. Thomas uses the Aristotelian distinction of sciences to illumine his conception of "sacred doctrine" as distinct from the philosophical understanding of "theology" as the philosophical doctrine of God. Aristotle had distinguished

Charles H. Lohr, "Mittelalterlicher Augustinismus und neuzeitliche Wissenschaftslehre," in *Scientia Augustinianai*, ed. Cornelius Petrus Mayer (Würzburg: Augustinius Verlag, 1975), 157–69.

55. See Peter Lombard *Sententiae* lib. 3, dist. 35, cap. 1.

56. For a survey of the diverse medieval positions, see Ulrich Körpf, *Die Anfänge der theologischen Wissenschaftstheorie im 13. Jahrhundert* (Tübingen: Mohr, 1974).

57. Cajetan, *In I Summa* q. 1, a. 1 and 2.

58. Sylvius, *Opera omnia* I, q. 1, a. 1.

59. Yves Congar, "*Traditio* und *Sacra doctrina* bei Thomas von Aquin," in *Kirche und Überlieferung: Festschrift J. R. Geiselmann* (Freiburg: Herder, 1960), 170–210. French text in *Église et tradition* (Le Puy–Lyon: Mappus, 1963), 157–94.

60. Gerald van Ackeran, *Sacra Doctrina: The Subject of the First Question of the Summa Theologica of St. Thomas Aquinas* (Rome: Catholic Book Agency, 1952).

61. See James Weisheipl, "The Meaning of *Sacra Doctrina* in *Summa theologiae* I, q. 1," *Thomist* 38 (1974): 49–80. See his important biography of Thomas, *Friar Thomas d'Aquino* (New York: Doubleday, 1974); and his essay "The Evolution of Scientific Method," in *The Logic of Science*, ed. V. E. Smith (New York: St. John's University, 1964), 58–86.

62. Thomas O'Brien, "'Sacra Doctrina' Revisited: The Context of Medieval Education," *Thomist* 41 (1977): 475–509.

two kinds of sciences: One proceeds from principles of natural reason, such as arithmetic and geometry. Another proceeds from principles that are from a superior knowledge. For example, optics proceeds from principles of geometry, and music from principles of arithmetic. Thomas suggests that *sacra doctrina* is a science of the second type (a subalternate science) because it proceeds from principles known in a superior science, namely, the knowledge that God possesses. By appealing to Aristotle's doctrine of subalternate science, Thomas not only affirms that *sacra doctrina* is a science, but he also establishes its distinctive source and authority. It is based on the knowledge that God has revealed. The knowledge proper to *sacra doctrina* comes to us only through God's revelation. Its principles are based on the revelation of divine knowledge and divine wisdom.

Thomas's understanding of *sacra doctrina* as a science involves the reduction or resolution (*resolutio*) of theological statements to the articles of faith. Yet such a procedure should not be understood as a purely axiomatic and deductive procedure, as if *sacra doctrina* were just another type of classical geometry. The personal faith in the articles of faith is important to his theological method in the sense that theology is anchored in the prescientific faith, in regard to both its content and its certainty. Through the virtue of faith, the Christian theologian participates in the divine knowledge.[63] Therefore, it could be stated that in addition to its axiomatic character, *sacra doctrina* has a hermeneutical character. Its task is to interpret the prescientific faith.[64]

BASIS AND SUBJECT MATTER OF *SACRA DOCTRINA*

Having argued that *sacra doctrina* is a distinct discipline, Thomas then raises the issue of the mode of argument or authority within the discipline. How does *sacra doctrina* make judgments, and how does it argue? Thomas distinguishes carefully between making judgments according to inclination and making judgments according to knowledge (*per modum cognitionis*). The second way of judging characterizes *sacra doctrina* as an academic discipline. For as Thomas notes, this second way of making judgments is "in keeping with the fact that it [*sacra doctrina*] is acquired through study."[65]

Basis of Sacra Doctrina ◉ The discipline of *sacra doctrina* is based on the Scriptures in two ways. First, since *sacra doctrina* has its origin in divine revelation, its authority is founded on the Scriptures of this revelation. Second, *sacra doctrina* is a distinctive discipline because it has its specific authoritative text, the sacred Scriptures. As a distinctive discipline, *sacra doctrina* has its own authorities. Its arguments proceed from the authority of divine revelation in the Scriptures. In Scholastic theology, the term *authority* has diverse meanings, most associated with a practice of teaching and arguing.[66] Instruction, even in nontheological subjects, was based on the texts of writers who constituted the authority in question. Authority referred to the status of a person who was qualified and whose writings were thereby trustworthy. The text itself, as a quotation from a writer, became a *dictum auctoritatis* (authoritative statement). Author-

---

63. Thomas Aquinas, *Summa theologiae* I–II, q. 110, a. 4: "Homo participat cognitionem divinam per virtutem fidei."

64. See Ludger Oeing-Hanhof, "Thomas von Aquin und die Gegenwärtige Katholische Theologie," in *Thomas von Aquino: Interpretation und Rezeption*, ed. Willehad Paul Eckert (Mainz: Matthias-Grünewald, 1974), 243–306, esp. 260–70.

65. Thomas Aquinas, *Summa theologiae* I, q. 1, a. 6, ad 3.

66. M. D. Chenu, "'Authentica' et 'Magistralia,'" *Divus Thomas (Piacenza)* 28 (1925): 3–31.

ity and quotation thus became interchanged. In the disciplines, this respect for authority meant that academic work was often commentary or interpretation of an authoritative text.[67] Since *sacra doctrina* consisted primarily of a commentary on the Scriptures, it was also called *sacra pagina*, and its authoritative text was the Scriptures. As the disputation of individual questions increased and became independent of the interpretation of the text, the term *theology* came to replace these terms.

The authority that Thomas attributed to Scripture is evident in his division of authorities, where he distinguishes proper or intrinsic authority from necessary and probable argument.[68] *Sacra doctrina* makes use of sacred Scripture *properly*, and its arguments from Scripture carry the weight of necessity. Since Christian faith rests on the revelation given to the apostles and prophets, the canonical Scriptures have, for Thomas, a primal significance and authority. *Sacra doctrina* also uses the authority of the doctors of the church properly, but only with probable effect. *Sacra doctrina* relies on philosophers only as extrinsic and probable. It makes use of them only in those questions in which one can know the truth by natural reason.

This point is significant for understanding the relations between the Roman Catholic and the Lutheran and Reformed traditions of theology. Martin Luther sharply criticized Scholastic theology for excessive reliance on Aristotle's philosophy. Contrasting his theology of the cross with a Scholastic theology of glory, he identified the latter with the natural theology of Scholasticism.[69] In the twentieth century, Karl Barth likewise sharply criticized the defense of natural theology on Thomist philosophy and theology. Such criticisms often overlook the authority and primacy of Scripture within medieval theology and for Thomas Aquinas. A Scandinavian Lutheran theologian, Per Erik Persson, has done a great service in arguing that Thomas attributes an authority to Scripture that is overlooked in the traditional Reformation and Protestant neo-orthodox polemic against Scholasticism.[70]

The primacy that Thomas attributes to Scripture limits the role of philosophy. Philosophy cannot demonstrate the truth of *sacra doctrina*, since the latter's principles are based on revelation. Philosophy can only demonstrate that the truths of revelation do not contradict reason. Furthermore, philosophy can also illumine the meaning of these truths by the use of metaphors and examples. Through logical explication, philosophy elaborates the implications of the articles of faith.[71]

Subject Matter of Sacra Doctrina ☉ *Sacra doctrina* as a discipline has not only distinct principles but also a distinct object: God as the source and goal of all things insofar as they refer to God. Within an Aristotelian conception of science, the subject matter of a discipline is determined by the object or end that provides the unity of that discipline. For Thomas, God is the end that provides the unity of *sacra doctrina*.

---

67. See Edward Schillebeeckx, *Revelation and Theology* (New York: Sheed and Ward, 1967), 1:223–58.

68. Thomas Aquinas, *Summa theologiae* I, q. 1, a. 8.

69. See Martin Luther, "Heidelberg Disputation: Theological Theses," in *Martin Luther's Basic Theological Writings*, ed. Timothy F. Lull (Minneapolis: Fortress Press, 1989), 30–32.

70. Per Erik Persson, *Sacra Doctrina: Reason and Revelation in Aquinas* (Philadelphia: Fortress Press, 1970). Eugene F. Rogers, *Thomas Aquinas and Karl Barth: Sacred Doctrine and the Natural Knowledge of God* (Notre Dame, IN: University of Notre Dame Press, 1995), makes a similar reference to Thomas on Romans.

71. Thomas Aquinas, *Summa theologiae* I, q. 1, a. 5, ad 2.

Only to the extent that created things relate to God as their origin and goal are they the proper subject matter of theology.[72]

This principle determines the theocentric structure of the *Summa theologiae*, which uses the Aristotelian causal schema as well as the Neo-Platonic *exitus-reditus* (procession from and return to) schema to express the relation of all created reality to God. Thomas's arrangement differs from that of other Scholastic authors.[73] Some followed a more systematic or conceptual order. Peter Abelard's arrangement was faith, love, and the sacraments. Peter Lombard referred to *res* and their signs. Others followed the order of salvation history. Hugo of Saint Victor, Alexander of Hales, and Bonaventure referred to the Christ and his redemptive work and benefits. In the decades immediately preceding Thomas, Peter Lombard's arrangement was modified through salvation-historical considerations, not in the sense of a chronological salvation history, but rather as the explication of God's work of creation and re-creation—the invisible re-creation of grace and the visible re-creation in Christ and the sacraments. This outline, evident in Magister Hubertus's *Colligite fragmenta* (1194–1200), is the pattern that Thomas followed.[74] However, Thomas stands in the context of the rediscovery of Aristotle within the West. He uses the Aristotelian conception of science (namely, the appeal to diverse causes:

efficient, final, exemplary, and material) to refer all to God's creative activity. He thereby elaborates God's work of salvation history, namely, creation and re-creation, into the Neo-Platonic *exitus-reditus* schema.

Thomas Aquinas and Magisteria ● The issues of the foundation and authorities underlying theology raise for us the question of the relation between theology and magisterial authority. At the time of Aquinas, an understanding of magisterium prevailed that differs considerably from ours. Today it has become customary to refer to a magisterium in a singular sense. This contemporary use of *magisterium* is the result of a long historical development and has diverse backgrounds.[75] Thomas employed the plural term *magisteria* and distinguished between a pastoral magisterium and a teaching magisterium.

Thomas distinguished between two functions, prelacy and magisterium, and between two kinds of teaching, preaching and doctrinal teaching. The function of prelacy (*praelatio*) belongs to the bishops, and their teaching involves preaching (*doctrina praedicationis*). Theologians have the function of magisterium, and their teaching involves Scholastic doctrine (*doctrina scholastica*). Whereas Thomas ascribes the title of magisterium primarily to the theologian in the forum of teaching magisterium, he attributes to bishops a magisterium of prelacy and

---

72. Wayne J. Hankey, *God in Himself: Aquinas' Doctrine of God as Expounded in the* Summa theologiae (Oxford: Oxford University Press, 1987).

73. For a survey of interpretations, see Otto Hermann Pesch, "Um den Plan der *Summa theologiae* des hl. Thoma von Aquin. Zu Max Seckler's neuem Deutungsversuch," *Münchener theologische Zeitschrift* 16 (1965): 128–37; and his more recent book, *Thomas von Aquin* (Mainz: Matthias-Grünewald, 1988), 381–400.

74. See Richard Heinzmann, "Der Plan der 'Summa theologiae' des Thomas von Aquin in der Tradition der frühscholastischen Systembildung," in Eckert, *Thomas von Aquino*, 455–69.

75. Yves Congar, "Pour une histoire sémantique du terme 'Magisterium'" and "Bref histoire des forms du 'Magistère' et des ses relations avec les docteurs," *Revue des sciences philosophiques et théologiques* 60 (1976): 85–98, 99–112. For the development of the concept of ordinary magisterium, see John P. Boyle, "The 'Ordinary Magisterium': Towards a History of the Concept," *Heythrop Journal* 20 (1979): 380–98; and 21 (1980): 14–29.

20

preaching. To quote Thomas's own terminology, bishops have a "pastoral magisterium" (*magisterium cathedrae pastoralis*), whereas the theologians have a "magisterial magisterium" (*magisterium cathedrae magistralis*).[76]

Concerning what today is called the papal magisterium, Thomas attributes to the pope both judicial and doctrinal competence. Defining matters of faith is a judgment made by the pope, because the more important and difficult questions are referred to him. However, as Yves Congar points out, "It is fact that St. Thomas has not spoken of the infallibility of the papal magisterium. Moreover, he was unaware of the use of magisterium in its modern sense."[77]

Neo-Scholasticism: Its Distinctive Characteristics

In the medieval period of Scholastic theology, diverse schools and traditions flourished. Bonaventure, Duns Scotus, William of Ockham, and many others contributed significantly to theology. Yet in the modern period, Thomism dominates. Thomas's *Summa* replaced Peter Lombard's *Sentences* as the basic textbook of classroom instruction. Although the Neo-Scholasticism that developed in the period following the Renaissance and the Reformation swore its allegiance to Thomas, it manifests decisive differences from Thomas's own thought and categories—differences that twentieth-century historical studies have brought to light.

FROM SCHOLASTICISM TO POST-TRIDENTINE CATHOLICISM

The transformations and shifts from medieval Scholasticism to Neo-Scholasticism were in large part occasioned by the controversies surrounding the Protestant Reformation and by the influence of the Renaissance. Some of the changes in theological method, however, had already begun within late medieval Scholasticism itself. These changes can be traced back to the development of theological censures. It was the issue of theological errors and the awareness of a distinction between theological and philosophical errors that led to a new development in theological method. They led to an increasing emphasis on authority and to a growing number of theological sources.

A comparison between the thirteenth and sixteenth centuries makes this transformation obvious. In the thirteenth century, following Aristotle's notion of science from the *Posterior Analytics*, Thomas considered the articles of faith as the principles of an understanding and presentation of Christian doctrine. Thomas assumed that a basic harmony exists between natural reason and supernatural revelation. Disharmonies resulted from errors in philosophy, and one could correct them through the teaching of Scripture and the doctors of the church.

Certain developments within the fourteenth and fifteenth centuries made it no longer feasible to refer to Scripture and tradition as the basic authorities in the same way that Thomas

---

76. For the distinction between pastoral and teaching magisterium, see Thomas Aquinas, *Questiones de quodlibet.* 3.4.1, ad 3 (Parma ed., 9:490–91). See also *Contra impugnantes dei cultum et religionem*, cap. 2 (Parma ed., 15:3–8). For the theological implications, see Avery Dulles's two essays, "The Magisterium in History: Theological Considerations" and "The Two Magisteria: An Interim Report," in his collection *A Church to Believe In* (New York: Crossroad, 1983), 103–33. See also the special issue of *Chicago Studies* 17, no. 2 (Summer 1978), entitled *The Magisterium, the Theologian, and the Educator.*

77. Yves Congar, "Saint Thomas Aquinas and the Infallibility of the Papal Magisterium (*Summa theol.*, II–II, q. 1, a. 10)," *Thomist* 38 (1974): 102; Ulrich Horst, "Das Wesen der 'potestas clavium' nach Thomas von Aquin," *Münchener theologische Zeitschrift* 11 (1960): 191–201.

did. The controversy about the papacy as well as the conflict among councils, the papacy, and the universities with respect to the authority to watch over doctrine necessitated a more complex theological method. Such a method, initiated by John of Torquemada and used by Johann Eck in his debate with Martin Luther during the Leipzig Disputations in 1519,[78] was further developed by Albert Pigge and Bartolomé Caranza in the polemic of the Counter-Reformation.[79] This theological method sought to determine Catholic truths (*veritates catholicae*) by appealing to Scripture, tradition, the councils, the teaching of the papacy, and so on. Such a method signaled a situation far different from that of Aquinas. In the sixteenth century, the theological method became the search for the evident principles within the diverse sources. This question of the authorities within diverse sources faced Melchior Cano, a Spanish Dominican theologian. His proposals, influencing baroque Scholasticism, initiated the beginning of the development from Baroque Scholasticism to Neo-Scholasticism.[80]

Baroque Scholasticism

Melchior Cano wrote *De locis theologicis* (literally, "concerning theological places"), a book about the sources of theological authority. This book, published posthumously in 1563, represented a new and distinctive theological approach. In the Renaissance, various loci were assembled for different disciplines, and Cano extended this practice to theology. He developed a list of places where theology could look for the sources of its arguments and reasoning.

In adapting the practice of collecting various loci to the discipline of theology, Cano followed not the Aristotelian but rather the humanist concept of locus. This concept, developed by Rudolph Agricola, a humanist, followed Cicero and viewed the loci as *sedes argumentum* (authoritative source of the argument).[81] How Cano differs from Aristotle is important. For Cano, the term *locus* did not refer to either the premises of a syllogism or the principles of theology, as within medieval theology. Instead, the term referred to the place where theology finds its authorities.[82] Cano thereby sought to establish the foundations of Roman Catholic theology with reference to the weight of the authorities that underlie that theology. He listed ten sources of authority from which one could argue theologically: (1) Scripture, (2) oral tradition, (3) the Catholic church, (4) the general councils, (5) the Roman church, (6) the

---

78. See the two works by P. Polman, *Die polemische Methode der ersten Gegner der Reformation* (Münster: Aschendorf, 1931); and *L'élément historique dans la controverse religeuse du XVIe siècle* (Gembloux: J. Duculot, 1932).

79. Albert Pigge, *Hierarchiae ecclesiasticae assertio* (1538), and Bartolomé Caranza, *De necessaria residential personali episcoparorum* (1547). See Charles H. Lohr, "Modelle für die Überlieferung theologischer Doktrin: Von Thomas von Aquin bis Melchior Cano," in *Dogmengeschichte und katholische Theologie*, ed. Werner Löser et al. (Würzburg: Echter, 1985), 148–67, esp. 164–67.

80. For a corrective to many presentations of the significance and contribution of Scholastic schools of theology in Spain, see Melquiades Andres, *La teología española en el siglo xvi* (Madrid: Biblioteca de autores cristianos, 1976), vol. 2. For theological method and Cano, see esp. pp. 386–424.

81. Cano differed not only from Aristotle but also from the Lutheran Scholastic Melanchthon, who used locus as a *locus communis*.

82. Whereas Ambroise Gardeil originally interpreted Cano as understanding loci in the Aristotelian sense, Albert Lang argues that Cano follows Cicero and has a different understanding of loci. See A. Lang, *Die theologische Prinzipienlehre der mittelalterlichen Scholastik* (Freiburg: Herder, 1964). The general interpretation today follows the direction

22 fathers of the church, (7) the Scholastic theologians, (8) human reason, (9) philosophers, and (10) history. The first seven were, according to Cano, properly speaking theological authorities, whereas the last three were extrinsic to theology.[83]

A further development took place from the Baroque Scholasticism of the sixteenth century to the Neo-Scholasticism of the nineteenth and twentieth centuries. For this development, the writings of the Parisian theologian Denis Petau (Dionysius Petavius) were decisive. Today one commonly thinks of Robert Bellarmine and Francis Suarez as the leading theological figures of the sixteenth and seventeenth centuries. At the beginning of the twentieth century, however, Neo-Scholastic theologians considered Denis Petau most significant, so much so that the Neo-Scholastic theologians Carlo Passaglia and Clemens Schrader labeled him "theologorum facile princeps" (prince of theologians).[84] Petau's influence consisted not only in his development of the theological use of historical sources, but also in his understanding of the nature of theology.[85]

Petau developed a conception of theology as a deductive science—a decisive shift from the medieval conception. Petau argued that theology achieves the status of scientific discipline to the degree that it employs a deductive method. Theology advances in knowledge by deducing conclusions from premises of faith by means of premises of reason. Philosophy is the interme-diate link within a syllogistic process of theology. Petau's conception presumed as an implicit background theory that a deductive syllogism constitutes the scientific nature of a discipline. Therefore, theology is a strict science, he argued, only insofar as it uses a deductive process to arrive at theological conclusions. This notion of the deductive, syllogistic theological conclusions became the distinctive Neo-Scholastic conception of theology as a scientific discipline. This understanding of the scientific character formed the structure and procedure of the Neo-Scholastic handbooks of theology.

NEO-SCHOLASTIC THEOLOGY

Characteristic of the Neo-Scholastic approach is the development of the theological manual, which became the major instrument of theological instruction. Whereas Baroque Scholasticism had produced several significant commentaries on Thomas's *Summa theologiae*, Neo-Scholasticism's distinctive contribution was the theological school manual. These manuals followed a set approach. They sought first to clarify the Catholic position on a particular topic, then to demonstrate its veracity with arguments drawn from the Bible and early church writers, and finally to refute the errors of Protestantism. This approach and the methodology of the manuals display the influence of Petau's conception of theological method. Influenced by the Cartesian emphasis on clear and distinct ideas, Neo-Scholasticism sought to incorporate these scientific

established by Albert Lang. See also Elmer Klinger, *Ekklesiologie der Neuzeit* (Freiburg: Herder, 1978); and M. Jacquin, "Melchior Cano et la théologie modern," *Revue des sciences philosophiques et théologiques* 9 (1920): 121–41.

83. Lohr, "Modelle für die Überlieferung theologischer Doktrin," 148–67.

84. See Walter Kasper, *Die Lehre von der Tradition in der Römischen Schule* (Freiburg: Herder, 1962), 379.

85. See Michael Hoffmann, *Theologie, Dogma und Dogmenentwicklung im theologischen Werk Denis Petaus* (Munich: Herbert Lang, 1976); Ignace-Marcel Tshiamalenga Ntumba-Mulemba, "La method théologique chez Denys Petau," *Ephemerides Theologicae Lovanienses* 48 (1972): 427–78; and Leo Karrer, *Die historisch-positive Methode des Theologen Dionysius Petavius* (Munich: M. Hueber, 1970).

ideals into its theological approach.[86] The three elements of Neo-Scholastic theological method display a starting point and approach that differed considerably from medieval Scholastic disputation and from the Baroque Scholastic commentary.

Starting Point: Church Teaching ◉ The Neo-Scholastic manuals began their treatment of theological topics with theses explicating church teaching. The first text that adopted this practice was the 1771 *Theologie Wirceburgensis*— a widely used and distributed manual of theological instruction. The treatment began with a thesis about church teaching because Neo-Scholastic theology considered church teaching to be the immediate rule of faith (*re fidei proxima*). It was this teaching that provided a clear rule and definite standard, enabling believers to ascertain those truths contained in Scriptures and traditions. The Scriptures and traditions themselves were considered to be the remote rule of faith.[87] This distinction between immediate and remote rule of faith expressed the post-Tridentine and apologetical concern of Neo-Scholasticism to elucidate the content of the Roman Catholic faith in the most precise and shortest formulas. The exactitude and brevity facilitated the preaching, teaching, and learning of the formulas of faith.[88]

Such an approach constituted two decisive changes from traditional Scholasticism: one affecting the form of presentation, and the other, the role of Scripture. The manner of presentation changed from the *quaestio* to the thesis. It was the *quaestio* in high Scholasticism and the *disputatio* in late Scholasticism that provided a framework for teaching. Traditional Scholastic teaching began with disputed questions, whereas modern Scholastics began with theses about church teaching. This contrast between modern and medieval Scholasticism has been well described by Chenu, a noted historian: "For an article is a *quaestio*, not a *thesis*, the word that was to be used in the manuals. The change in terms is in itself a denunciation of the heinous reversal to which have been subjected the exalted pedagogical methods set up in the XIIth century universities: 'active methods,' mindful to keep open, even under the dead-weight of school work, the curiosity of both the student and the master."[89]

The second change concerned the role of Scripture. Medieval Scholasticism had given a priority to the Scriptures, and much of the instruction was basically a commentary on Scripture. Disputed questions were resolved by an appeal to authority, the most proper and intrinsic being Scripture, for as Thomas had maintained, an argument based on the authority of the Scriptures bore intrinsic and necessary probity. For Neo-Scholasticism, the situation was radically different. In reaction to the Reformation's appeal to the Scriptures, Neo-Scholastic theologians began to argue that the Scriptures are often misinterpreted. Therefore, they argued that the church's official teaching is the primary and proximate rule of faith.

This specification of official church teaching as the proximate rule of faith led to a distinctive characteristic of the Neo-Scholastic

---

86. Alexander Ganoczy, *Einführung in die Dogmatik* (Darmstadt: Wissenschaftliche Buchgesellschaft, 1983). For an analysis of the three-step method, see B. Durst, "Zur theologischen Methode," *Theologische Revue* 26 (1927): 297–313 and 361–72.

87. See Kasper, *Die Lehre von der Tradition*, 40–47.

88. Ganoczy, *Einführung*, 130–43.

89. Chenu, *Toward Understanding*, 96.

approach, namely, the careful delineation of the binding or obligatory character of church teaching.[90] Theological propositions were classified regarding their centrality to faith, their degree of certitude, and their corresponding censure. Theological propositions could, for example, express truths that were formally revealed. These were classified as "of divine faith" (*de fide divina*), and their denial consisted of heresy. Propositions that were not only formally revealed but also defined as such by the magisterium were considered of "defined divine faith," whereas what the ordinary magisterium taught as revealed truth was labeled simply *de fide*. In the next rank were statements that indirectly flowed from the teaching office of the church. They were defined as belonging to ecclesiastical faith as such, or they were simply and generally acknowledged as belonging to ecclesiastical faith. Other theological positions were classified with corresponding lesser notes, such as proximate to faith, theologically certain, of common opinion, and of probable opinion.[91]

The attempt at clear and distinct classifications of theological propositions corresponded in part to a philosophical attitude prevalent at the time. Neo-Scholasticism had a Cartesian scientific ideal of clear and distinct ideas. Through its distinct classifications, this approach of Neo-Scholasticism set the parameters of theological debates and discussions. Dissent and disagreements were possible but only within the framework of a graded hierarchy of propositions. Although in reaction to the Neo-Scholastic approach many theologians have criticized such distinctions, today a balanced reassessment is taking place. Such classifications are not without value, for they had the advantage of identifying areas for disagreement and dissent. They prevent one from indiscriminately viewing all elements of the tradition as central and essential to the Roman Catholic faith.

Proof from the Sources: Scripture and Tradition ⊚ The second step sought to demonstrate the truth of the thesis in its relation to the sources of faith, namely, Scripture and tradition.[92] The demonstration from the sources followed a definite procedure. The demonstration took place not independent from the magisterial teaching, but precisely from the perspective of that teaching. It was not an attempt to provide a historical-critical analysis of the sources within their own historical context and questions. Instead, the selection and reading of the sources were determined by the proposition that one sought to demonstrate. In practice, the passages from the Scriptures and from early Christian writers were reduced to proof-texts for a particular proposition. They were often cited independently of their context and were interpreted primarily as demonstrations of the truth of a particular doctrinal thesis.

Such a procedure was explicitly justified by the distinction between the proximate and remote rule of faith. The proximate rule of faith provided the interpretive key for understanding the meaning and proof value of the remote source of faith. As one Neo-Scholastic theolo-

---

90. For the distinctiveness of the Neo-Scholastic understanding of magisterium, see T. Howland Sanks, *Authority in the Church: A Study in Changing Paradigms* (Missoula, MT: Scholars, 1974).

91. Francis A. Sullivan, *Creative Fidelity: Weighing and Interpreting Documents of the Magisterium* (New York: Paulist, 1996); and Harold E. Ernst, "The Theological Notes and the Interpretation of Doctrine," *Theological Studies* 63 (2002): 813–25.

92. For an analysis of the Roman School's understanding of tradition, see Kasper, *Die Lehre von der Tradition*.

gian explicitly advocated, "The demonstrative power of the Sacred Scripture, as inspired, as well as that of the documents of the tradition depend upon the church's teaching office because those sources have value for us in the order of knowledge only as a result of the help of the teaching office."[93]

Speculative Exposition ● The third step sought to give a systematic explication of the thesis and thereby lead to a more profound understanding of its truth. The teaching of the church, affirmed in the thesis and demonstrated in the appeals to Scripture and tradition, was then in this final step further illumined through philosophical reflection. This reflection drew upon examples, analogies, and comparisons from natural experience. These examples illustrated the thesis and elaborated its meaning. In this step, the systematic reflection sought to relate the particular thesis to other beliefs and sought thereby to present the coherence of the thesis with the other beliefs.

At the same time, this step sought a certain "actualization" of the thesis. Insofar as it addressed questions of the day, it applied the thesis to concrete issues. In other words, it sought to demonstrate how traditional truths could be correlated with modern questions and contained answers to them. A further element present in this third part was the attempt to resolve the debates among the diverse Scholastic schools (for example, between the Thomists or Scotists or between diverse Thomistic opinions) in order to provide a greater conceptual clarification. Within the framework of Neo-Scholasticism, philosophical reflection served as an instrument or tool or theological reflection rather than as a challenge or critique. The purpose of philosophy was to bring a deeper understanding of theological truths.

CRISIS OF NEO-SCHOLASTIC THEOLOGY

Today Neo-Scholastic theology is often criticized by those seeking to bring theology up-to-date. Such criticisms often overlook the achievements of Neo-Scholastic theology. It sought to deal with problems of its time, just as theologians do today. In the face of rationalist criticisms of revelation and concrete forms of religion, Neo-Scholastic theology sought to develop an apologetic for revelation and for institutional religion. In the face of the rationalist advocacy of clear and distinct ideas, it sought to define as clearly as possible what constituted Christian revelation. Its rationalistic understanding of truth in terms of definite propositions and distinct ideas was in part due to the rationalism against which it fought. In a period of ecumenical controversy, it sought to delineate carefully—though defensively—the distinctiveness of Roman Catholic identity. Neo-Scholastic theology sought to defend its faith against the challenges of its age. What today often appears as its failure can be in part traced to its indebtedness to the currents and categories of its own day.

Nevertheless, two basic problems led to a crisis within Neo-Scholastic theology.[94] These problems occasioned the shift from classical to contemporary approaches to theology. The first was the increased awareness of the historical character of human thought in general, which when applied to theology led to the recognition of the historical character of theological affirmations. The second was the development of a new relationship between theology and philosophy.

---

93. Durst, "Zur theologischen Methode," 310 (my translation).
94. Walter Kasper, *The Methods of Dogmatic Theology* (Shannon, Ireland: Ecclesia, 1969).

26 The development of transcendental, phenomenological, hermeneutical, and existential philosophy affected a shift in the role of philosophy within theological method. Philosophy was no longer limited to an auxiliary or instrumental role within the theological task.

Summary

The three classic theological approaches (Augustinian, Thomist, and Neo-Scholastic) display common elements as well as significant differences. All emphasize the tradition (especially the Scriptures), the scientific character of the discipline of theology, the importance of the community of the church, and the role of experience. Yet how these four elements are interrelated and combined differs considerably. There is a shift from Augustine's emphasis on the relation between personal purification and the correct interpretation of Scripture, to Thomas's emphasis on *sacra doctrina* as an academic discipline with its authorities and rules, to the Neo-Scholastic emphasis on the church's teaching as the proximate rule to interpret Scripture and tradition as the remote rule of faith.

Yet each of these shifts cannot be understood without taking into consideration the background theories informing each approach's conception of what it means to be "scientific" and what it means to interpret the tradition. Augustine is incomprehensible without Neo-Platonism, Thomas without Aristotelianism, and Neo-Scholasticism without its rationalistic and Cartesian reception of Scholasticism. The attempt to think critically and theologically about the objects of the Christian faith is present in these three classic types of Roman Catholic theology, yet all three are intricately linked with specific philosophical and theoretical background theories.

Five Contemporary Approaches to Theology

Within contemporary Roman Catholic theology, many distinctive methods and approaches are employed. To give some idea of this diversity, this section describes several "ideal types": transcendental, hermeneutical, analytical, correlation, and liberation. These approaches represent ideal types to the extent that they are theoretically distinct. However, in practice, these approaches are not mutually exclusive and are indeed often combined. A specific theologian may predominantly follow one approach while at the same time borrowing insights, categories, and methods from other approaches. For example, a liberation theologian may, within a particular argument, employ a transcendental analysis or a recent hermeneutical theory, even though liberation theology as a theological movement is quite distinct from a transcendental or hermeneutical theology.

Transcendental Theology

Much of modern Roman Catholic theology that attends to the challenges of modern philosophy initiated by Descartes and Kant is best characterized by the description "the turn to the subject," that is, the focus on human subjectivity and its role within human knowledge and religious belief. Such a turn was particularly prevalent in the eighteenth and nineteenth centuries, when many theological schools sought to take up the challenges of modern philosophy. These attempts, however, were rebuffed during the pontificates of Pope Pius IX and Pope Leo XIII. The latter sanctioned Thomism as the official philosophy of the Roman Catholic Church. Consequently, in the beginning of the twentieth century, Thomism became the dominant Roman Catholic direction within philosophy and theology. However, in the 1940s and 1950s, a new beginning was made. This time, theology sought to integrate modern philosophy and Thomistic philosophy. This endeavor of engagement with modern philosophy, from its initial attempts to its rebuff and to its renewed attempts, needs to be examined in more detail.

The Turn to the Subject in Modern Theology

The efforts at incorporating modern philosophy came to fruition within the early nineteenth century. Georg Hermes, professor at the Universities of Münster and Bonn, sought to explicate a starting point for theology that incorporated the Cartesian principle of doubt. Anton Günther, though a private scholar and theological author in Vienna, was the most influential German-speaking Roman Catholic theologian of the nineteenth century. He sought to develop theology on the basis of an anthropology and categories that were strongly influenced by Descartes. Theologians of the Tübingen School (von Drey, Möhler, Staudenmeier, Kuhn, and Schell) were in dialogue with German Idealism, especially with such major figures as Hegel, Jacobi, Schleiermacher, and Schelling.[95] They sought to develop Roman Catholic theology by drawing upon these thinkers' insights and categories—though with considerable modifications—in order to relate the content and history of faith to human subjectivity. Although the influence of Schleiermacher's appeal to the human experience is

evident, Roman Catholic theology, especially the Tübingen School, took this influence in a specific direction with its influence upon history and tradition.

The Neo-Scholastic movement reacted against these attempts to reconcile modern philosophy and Roman Catholic theology. Ecclesiastical and political influences were brought to bear on Catholic educational institutions. As a result, several significant theologians lost their teaching positions. The papacy promulgated Thomism as the "official philosophy" of Roman Catholic theology. Yet this Thomism, today called Neo-Thomism, was a special brand of Thomism. It reacted against modern philosophy and the Enlightenment, yet it was as much a child of modernity as it was a foe of modernity. This Neo-Thomism sharply separated nature and grace, expanded the preamble of faith into a full-blown natural theology, and developed a fundamental theology and apologetics in distinction from systematic theology. These developments were deeply indebted to the very modernity that Neo-Thomism opposed.[96]

The dialogue with modern philosophy, however, did not end with the imposition of Neo-Thomism. In time, the antimodernist polemic waned, and Neo-Thomists moved away from their polemic against modern philosophy. Instead, genuine historical studies flourished.[97] Within this context, attempts emerged among the heirs of the Thomist revival to relate Thomas's theology to modern philosophy. Those Roman Catholic theologians most influential at the Second Vatican Council and in postconciliar times were all trained in the Neo-Scholastic

---

95. For a comprehensive survey, see Donald J. Dietrich, *The Goethezeit and the Metamorphosis of Catholic Theology in the Age of Idealism* (Frankfurt: Peter D. Lang, 1979).

96. For the historical development of fundamental theology, see Francis Schüssler Fiorenza, *Foundational Theology: Jesus and the Church* (New York: Crossroad, 1984).

97. The works of Grabmann, Glorieux, and Chenu are just a few examples.

28

tradition and, with the exception of Hans Küng and Joseph Ratzinger, wrote their dissertations or first major works on Thomas. They sought to reinterpret Thomas Aquinas independently from the presuppositions and views of Neo-Scholasticism. They brought to the fore the theological dimensions of Thomas's thought. They recovered the Augustinian elements within Thomas's theology. They demonstrated that the abstract contrast between nature and supernature in Neo-Scholasticism was not authentically Thomist. As a theological movement, this effort was powerful and effective because it neither jettisoned the past out of fascination with the modern nor rejected the modern out of nostalgia for the past. Rather, it opened a way to bring Thomas's theology in contact with modern philosophy.

The results of this movement are indeed impressive. Karl Rahner's study of the epistemology of Aquinas incorporates both Kantian and Heideggerian categories.[98] Bernard Lonergan's two dissertations (on operative grace and on the relation between inner word and ideas) relate Thomas to modern cognitional theory.[99] Edward Schillebeeckx's dissertation on Thomas's understanding of the sacraments relates the sacraments to a phenomenology of encounter.[100] Both Henri Bouillard's study on the relation between grace and nature and Henri de Lubac's historical studies on the development of the notion of the supernatural show the importance of Augustinian elements—which Neo-Thomism had neglected—in Thomas's theology.[101] Even the following generation of theologians (most notably, Johann Baptist Metz, Max Seckler, and Otto Hermann Pesch) continued this dialogue with Thomas Aquinas.[102]

KARL RAHNER'S
TRANSCENDENTAL PHENOMENOLOGY

The development of the transcendental method in Roman Catholic theology is particularly significant.[103] The term *transcendental* is a technical philosophical term with diverse historical meanings. In Scholastic philosophy *transcendental* referred to what was applicable to all being. For example, "goodness" is transcendental because it applies to everything that exists (e.g., God, angels, human persons, objects of nature), whereas quantity applies only to material reality. In modern philosophy, Kant used the term *transcendental* to refer to the a priori conditions of possible experience. A transcendental analy-

98. Karl Rahner, *Spirit and the World* (New York: Herder & Herder, 1968). See the introduction by F. Fiorenza, "Karl Rahner and the Kantian Problematic," xxix–xl.

99. Bernard Lonergan, *Verbum: Word and Idea in Aquinas*, ed. David Burrell (Notre Dame, IN: University of Notre Dame Press, 1967); idem, *Grace and Freedom: Operative Grace in the Thought of St. Thomas Aquinas*, ed. L. P. Burns (New York: Herder & Herder, 1971), 1224–30.

100. Edward Schillebeeckx, *De sacramentele heilseconomie* (Bilthoven: Nelisson, 1952).

101. Henri Bouillard, *Conversion et grâce* (Paris: Éditions du Cerf, 1944); Henri de Lubac, *The Mystery of Salvation* (New York: Herder & Herder, 1967); idem, *Augustinian and Modern Theology* (New York: Herder & Herder, 1969).

102. Johann Baptist Metz, *Christliche Anthropozentrik* (Munich: Kösel Verlag, 1962). See also Max Seckler, *Instinkt und Glaubenswille* (Mainz: Matthias-Grünewald, 1961); idem, *Das Heil in der Geschichte: Geschichtstheologisches Denken bei Thomas von Aquin* (Munich: Kösel, 1964); Otto H. Pesch, *Theologie der Rechtfertigung bei Martin Luther und Thomas von Aquin* (Mainz: Matthias-Grünewald, 1967); and idem, *Thomas von Aquin: Grenze und Grösse mittelalterlicher Theologie* (Mainz: Matthias-Grünewald, 1988).

103. Otto Muck, *The Transcendental Method* (New York: Crossroad, 1968); and Harold Holz, *Transzendentalphilosophie und Metaphysik* (Mainz: Matthias-Grünewald, 1966).

sis, in this sense, investigates the conditions and possibility of knowledge through an analysis of human cognition.

Within contemporary transcendental Roman Catholic Thomism, the term *transcendental* carries a third meaning that combines the previous two. It includes the Kantian meaning to the extent that it refers to the subjective conditions of possible knowledge. In this sense, the term *transcendental* is given a theological twist insofar as it refers to the conditions of our knowledge of revelation. Systematic theology is transcendental when it investigates the "a priori conditions in the believer for the knowledge of important truths of faith."[104] The term *transcendental* also retains an element of its Scholastic sense to the degree that it refers to the infinite horizon of human knowledge. In this sense, transcendental refers to the unlimited dynamism of the human intellect striving to grasp not just specific objects of experience but the meaning of the totality of reality.

The origin of transcendental Thomism lies with Joseph Maréchal, a professor of philosophy at the Belgian Jesuit Scholasticate. He related the metaphysics of Thomas Aquinas to modern philosophy, particularly that of Kant and Fichte. Through his teaching and his five-volume work, *Le point de depart de la métaphysique*,[105] Maréchal had an enormous influence upon continental Roman Catholic philosophers and theologians. Of the theologians influenced by Maréchal who have come to represent the direction of the transcendental approach within theology, Karl Rahner is by far the most influential and renowned. Influenced not only by Maréchal but also by Martin Heidegger (especially his earlier work), Karl Rahner has written about the whole range of Christian theological topics. His editorial work is also extensive and influential. For years, he edited the Denzinger collection of church documents. As editor, he also published several major encyclopedias and dictionaries of theology, *Lexikon für Theologie und Kirche*, *Sacramentum mundi*, *Dictionary of Theology*, and an important series on controversial questions, *Quaestiones disputatae*. He was also influential in establishing the international journal *Concilium*.

Rahner's Starting Point ◉ Central to Rahner's approach is his analysis of human experience of knowledge and freedom as an experience of an "absolute and limitless transcendentality."[106] This experience both constitutes and expresses the historical nature of human persons as radically open toward the transcendent, as oriented to the absolute mystery called God. In Rahner's view, this radical orientation toward the absolute is not only constitutive of human nature, but also results from God's full historical self-communication and presence to humanity—a self-communication that has at the same time a history, namely, the history of God's saving presence to the world.

Rahner's Method ◉ Rahner outlines his method in several points.[107] First, through acts

---

104. Karl Rahner, "Transcendental Theology," in *Sacramentum Mundi* (New York: Herder & Herder, 1970), 6:287.

105. Joseph Maréchal, *Le point de depart de la métaphysique*, 5 vols., 3rd ed. (Brussels: Museum Lessianum, 1944–49).

106. Karl Rahner, "Reflections on Methodology in Theology," in *Theological Investigations* (New York: Crossroad, 1974), 11:94. For the argument that christological interpretation of anthropology avoids the charge of foundationalism that Rahner's critics bring against him, see Francis Schüssler Fiorenza, "Method in Theology," in *The Cambridge Companion to Karl Rahner*, ed. Mary E. Hines and Declan Marmion (New York: Cambridge University Press, 2005), 65–82.

107. Here I follow Rahner's exposition in *Foundations of Christian Faith* (New York: Seabury, 1978), 208–12, which differs slightly from his essay on method.

of knowledge and freedom, human persons transcend themselves. The act of knowing an individual object or the act of willing an individual action has a dimension of unlimited openness. Knowledge and volition are not limited to one object or to one act but are unlimited. The first step is this experience of the limitlessness of our knowing and willing as an experience of the openness of our subjectivity toward the transcending infinite. The unlimitedness of the horizon of our knowing and willing comes to the fore in our questioning and searching for the meaning of the horizon of our existence. We look beyond objects of experience for meaning, and we are confronted with incomprehensible mystery.

Second, in this search for meaning, we experience ourselves as radically finite yet with unlimited questions. We experience reality as an incomprehensible mystery, but at the same time, we hope there is a fulfillment of the highest possibility of human existence. We hope that ultimately reality is meaningful. Though finite and limited, we have the hope for an absolute fullness of meaning. We hope and trust that the absolute mystery of our being is a Thou who is absolutely trustworthy.[108]

Third, Rahner argues for unity between historical existence and subjective human existence. This unity means that God's self-communication (revelation) and the human hope for it are historically mediated. They "appear" together in concrete human history. Consequently, the historical and contingent at the same time announce and awaken hope in the presence of the infinite and absolute. In short, the human hope

for meaning is historical hope that emerges in history as a result of God's presence in human history. In Rahner's interpretation, the historical mediation of the infinite within the finite means that God is first of all present in the historical and contingent as promise and as hope in the face of human finitude and death.[109]

Fourth, since human persons exist in history and time, they search history for God's self-promise as final and irreversible. They search history for an answer to their quest for meaning. They search for what could be considered an absolute fulfillment in itself of the meaning of history. They search for a historical event that brings an irrevocable promise to the world.

Rahner's final point is the development of the notion of "absolute savior," which he explicates with the argument that the historical mediation of God's irreversible presence to the world can be expressed only in a free subject. Only such a free subject can be the "exemplar" of God's presence. For God's presence to be freely offered and accepted, it must be made and accepted in a free human subject. Such an individual accepts human finitude and as such is accepted by God and thus has exemplary significance for the world.

COMPARISON BETWEEN AQUINAS AND RAHNER

A comparison between the *Summa theologiae* of Aquinas and Rahner's *Foundations of Christian Faith* illustrates important shifts in theological presuppositions and method. Thomas wrote the *Summa* as a handbook for students. Rahner wrote his book as a "basic course" (the origi-

---

108. See Francis Schüssler Fiorenza, "The Experience of Trancendence or the Transcendence of Experience: Negiotiating the Difference," in *Religious Experience and Contemporary Theological Epistemology*, ed. Yves de Maeseneer and S. van den Bossche (Louvain: University Press, 2005), 183–218.

109. Rahner, *Foundations of Christian Faith*, 210.

nal German title was *Grundkurs*) that aimed to introduce beginning theological students to Christian theology and faith. Although such a comparison is not entirely appropriate—for the former is a *summa* of theology, whereas the latter is a text of fundamental theology—the comparison is helpful in showing their distinct theological presuppositions.

Rahner begins with an analysis of human persons, their acts of knowing and willing, and their basic existential quest for meaning. The beginning chapters investigate the quest for meaning and experience of absolute mystery coupled with the experience of sin and grace. Rahner's starting point is anthropological not only insofar as he begins with this anthropological analysis, but also insofar as the content of the basic Christian beliefs is related to the anthropological question. God's revelation, salvation history, Christology, the church and sacraments, and eschatology are interpreted in relation to their significance for human nature.

Thomas's starting point and structure are theocentric. After the first question on the nature of *sacra doctrina*, Thomas begins part 1 of the *Summa theologiae* by addressing the issue of the existence and nature of God as one and triune; this is followed by a discussion of what God has created. Part 2 treats human nature and its virtues. Part 3 deals with Christology, the sacraments, and eschatology. This structure has been interpreted as following Aristotelian as well as Neo-Platonic patterns. Neo-Scholastic interpretations of Thomas underscored that the three parts fit Aristotelian categories of causality: part 1, God as the efficient cause; part 2, God as the final cause; and part 3, God as the exemplary

cause of all. Medieval historians pointed to the Neo-Platonic pattern that emphasizes the origin of all things from God and the return of all things to God (*exitus-reditus*).[110] Part 1 is the *exitus*: God and the creation proceeding from God; part 2 is the *reditus*: the return to God; part 3 treats the model as well as the means of the return. These interpretations of the structure of the *Summa* convey its theocentric structure.

The difference between *Foundations* and the *Summa* is most conspicuous in regard to the locus and role of anthropology. Whereas Thomas located anthropology in part 2 of the *Summa*, Rahner locates anthropology in the beginning of *Foundations*. Anthropology constitutes for Rahner the starting point as well as constant reference point of theological reflection. The starting point is the human quest for ultimate meaning that raises the question of God and looks to history—specifically to God's revelation in Christ—for a response. The individual contexts of faith are all related to the structures of human existence and to the human quest for ultimate meaning. In this way, Rahner's theology seeks to relate anthropocentricism and theocentrism. They are not opposed, but proportionately correlated.

Beyond Transcendental Theology

The turn to the subject not only represents an important movement of modern theology, it also underscores the theological task of relating the content and subject matter of theology to human subjectivity. Nevertheless, the turn to the subject is not without its criticisms. Hans Urs von Balthasar especially has argued that the anthropological turn in modern theology,

110. M. D. Chenu, "Le plan de la somme théologique de S. Thomas," *Revue thomiste* 45 (1939): 93–107. For an interpretation that suggests a salvation-historical outline, see Ulrich Horst, "Über die Frage einer heilsökonomischen Theologie bei Thomas von Aquin," *Münchener theologische Zeitschrift* 12 (1961): 97–111.

32

particularly as developed by Karl Rahner, reduces religious truth to the perspective of anthropology and thereby does less justice to other perspectives. Von Balthasar has developed his major systematic work as a triptych: The first part outlines a theological aesthetics that approaches revelation from the standpoint of the beautiful. The second part treats revelation as a dramatic interplay. The third part considers revelation as idea and word. The code words for the three parts are: theo-phany = aesthetics; theo-praxy = dramatic theory; and theo-logy = logic.[111] Von Balthasar has influenced Walter Kasper and Joseph Ratzinger in their respective criticisms of Rahner's transcendental approach. Kasper's own theological approach seeks to complement a transcendental approach with a systematic incorporation of history, the latter being indebted to the nineteenth-century tradition of the Tübingen School.[112]

In addition to such criticism of a transcendental method, other contemporary theological approaches attempt to go beyond a transcendental method insofar as they incorporate into the theological task other dimensions that relocate the role of human subjectivity.[113] Contemporary linguistic philosophy and hermeneutical theory underscore that the human subject exists within a world of language and a tradition of cultural meaning. Political and liberation theologies underscore that the sociopolitical arena is the broader context in which to view the human person. They emphasize the significance of the social and political for the formation and dignity of the human person. The differences from the transcendental approach will become clearer in analysis of these other approaches.

Hermeneutical Theology

Hermeneutics deals with theories of interpretation.[114] All approaches to theology are hermeneutical insofar as they include interpretation, be it the interpretation of the Scriptures, creeds, traditions, or experience. Moreover, some theologians attempt to combine transcendental analysis and hermeneutical theory within their approaches. Nevertheless, recent hermeneutical theory underscores the transcendence of language to human subjectivity in a way that brings to the fore the differences between a transcendental and a hermeneutical approach to theology. At the same time, the emphasis within hermeneutical theory on the transcendence of language and on the universal scope of hermeneutics opens hermeneutical theory to the criticisms raised by liberation and political theologies as well as critical theory.[115]

---

111. For a criticism of Karl Rahner, see Hans Urs von Balthasar, *Cordula oder der Ernstfall*, 3rd ed. (Einsiedeln: Johannes Verlag, 1987). For an introduction to von Balthasar's own position, see Medard Kehl and Werner Löser, eds., *The von Balthasar Reader* (New York: Crossroad, 1982). His own systematic system is developed in three sets of volumes: *The Glory of the Lord*, 7 vols. (San Francisco: Ignatius, 1982–89); *Theo-Drama: Theological Dramatic Theory*: vols. 1–5 (San Francisco: Ignatius, 1988–98); and *Theo-Logic*, vols 1–3 and *Epilogue* (San Francisco: Ignatius, 2004–5).

112. Walter Kasper, *Jesus the Christ* (New York: Paulist, 1976); idem, *The God of Jesus Christ* (New York: Crossroad, 1984); and idem, *Theology and Church* (New York: Crossroad, 1989).

113. Francis Schüssler Fiorenza, "Theology: Transcendental or Hermeneutical," *Horizons* 16 (1989): 329–41.

114. For a history of hermeneutics, see Richard Palmer, *Hermeneutics* (Evanston, IL: Northwestern University Press, 1969); and Kurt Mueller-Vollmer, ed., *The Hermeneutic Reader* (New York: Crossroad, 1985).

115. See Jürgen Habermas's critique of hermeneutical idealism in Justus George Lawler and Francis Fiorenza, eds., *Cultural Hermeneutics* (entire issue of *Continuum* [1970]: 7).

EXPERIENCE AND LANGUAGE

A major distinction between a hermeneutical and a transcendental approach rests on their different interpretation of the relationship between experience and language. Transcendental theology appeals to religious experience that underlies creedal and doctrinal formulations. Such a transcendental approach views language as expressive: doctrinal formulations are propositional statements that express a basic religious experience. At the turn of the twentieth century, modernist theologians viewed religious experience as much more basic than religious doctrine because they considered doctrines as mere linguistic expressions of religious experience. Therefore, they thought doctrinal formulations could be exchanged for different but equivalent formulations.

Hermeneutical theory criticizes this view on the following grounds: Such an expressive view of language and doctrine overlooks the degree to which language does not just express but also constitutes experience. Therefore, religious language is not only expressive, but also constitutive of religious experience. Thus, some hermeneutical theorists argue that one should understand religion not merely as an expressive phenomenon but rather as a cultural linguistic phenomenon.[116] Others argue, on the contrary, that the cultural linguistic view of language is basically a further development that includes transcendental philosophy but goes beyond it.[117] The hermeneutical view of the relation between language and experience has had signifi-cant influence on theological reflection. In this regard, the philosophers Hans-Georg Gadamer and Paul Ricoeur have been especially influential.

CLASSICS:
THE AUTHORITY OF A TRADITION

Gadamer's major point is that "understanding is to be thought of less as a subjective act than as participating in an event of tradition, a process of transmission in which past and present are constantly mediated."[118] Employing several key ideas, Gadamer explicates this notion of understanding as a participation in tradition. The notion of the classic is central to Gadamer's hermeneutics. Classics are significant as outstanding exemplifications of human understanding. Moreover, classics have an "effective-history" to the extent they influence our horizon and specify our self-understanding. Opposing the Enlightenment's prejudice against tradition, Gadamer argues for a "pre-judgment" in favor of the classics. The endurance of the classic through history demonstrates its value and significance. A classic encounters us with a certain authority and claim.

The interpretation of classics is further explicated with the idea of the "fusion of horizons." Understanding takes place not insofar as one abstracts from one's horizon and places oneself in the shoes of the author, but rather insofar as one merges one's own horizon with that of the text and its author. The "fusion of horizons" is achieved when the classic is so interpreted that

---

116. This is the important argument made by George Lindbeck, *The Nature of Doctrine*, 2nd ed. (Philadelphia: Westminster, 2009). His criticisms of Karl Rahner and of David Tracy tend to minimize the role of hermeneutical reflection within their theologies.

117. Charles Taylor, *Human Agency and Language: Philosophical Papers* (New York: Cambridge University Press, 1985), 1:213–92.

118. Hans-Georg Gadamer, *Truth and Method*, rev. ed. (New York: Crossroad, 1989), 290.

its claim upon one's own present is acknowledged.[119]

Gadamer's hermeneutical theory has been further developed and in part modified by Paul Ricoeur's explication of the significance of metaphor and narrative structure, as well as by his stress on the importance of interrelating the modes of explanation and understanding.[120] Commenting on Aristotle's definition of a metaphor in terms of similarity,[121] Ricoeur suggests that a metaphor does not merely further explicate a similarity between images and ideas that is already present. Instead a metaphor produces a resulting similarity. Meanings, previously dissimilar, are brought together. The resulting "semantic shock" creates new meaning. A metaphor, therefore, forges a new meaning by bringing together opposing meanings. Ricoeur extends his analysis from the use of metaphor in sentences to the narrative structure of the whole text. The emplotment of a narrative creates new meaning by bringing together a plot and the characters, occasions, episodes, and events of the story.

Paul Ricoeur modifies Gadamer's hermeneutical approach by introducing "explanation" as complementary to "understanding." The hermeneutical focus on "understanding" takes into account the role of pre-understanding and life-relation vis-à-vis the subject matter of a text. Yet there are also methods of "explanation"— for example, historical-critical, social-critical, and literary-critical analysis, and especially for Ricoeur, the structuralist analysis of sentences and texts. A full interpretation of the subject matter of the text must include not only the attention to our pre-understanding and life-relation, but also structural and analytical analyses.

Using the hermeneutical theories of Gadamer and Ricoeur, David Tracy explores the nature of religious and Christian classics. In addition, he defines systematic theology primarily as hermeneutical and proposes that the task of Christian systematic theology is the interpretive retrieval of the meaning and truth claims of the Christian classic.[122] In explicating his conception of systematic theology as hermeneutical, Tracy accepts Gadamer's notion of understanding as participating in a tradition. However, he accepts Ricoeur's modifications of Gadamer and appropriates some of Ricoeur's categories. Therefore, Tracy underscores the importance of the explanatory modes of historical-critical, literary-critical, and social-critical analysis as complementary to interpretive modes of understanding.

Beyond Hermeneutics

The development of hermeneutical theology coincides with the emergence of several crises. These crises affect not only our understanding of tradition and the sources of theology, but also our understanding of present-day experience.

---

119. Ibid., 369–79. For two good expositions of Gadamer, see Joel C. Weishammer, *Gadamer's Hermeneutics: A Reading of Truth and Method* (New Haven: Yale University Press, 1986); and Georgia Warnke, *Gadamer: Hermeneutics, Tradition and Reason* (Stanford: Stanford University Press, 1987).

120. Paul Ricoeur, *The Rule of Metaphor: Multidisciplinary Studies of the Creation of Meaning in Language* (Toronto: University of Toronto Press, 1977); idem, *Time and Narrative*, 3 vols. (Chicago: University of Chicago Press, 1984–88). See also Josiah Thompson, *Hermeneutics and the Human Sciences* (New York: Cambridge University Press, 1981).

121. Aristotle, *Poetics* 1459a.4–8.

122. David Tracy, *The Analogical Imagination* (New York: Crossroad, 1981), 99–153; idem, *Plurality and Ambiguity: Hermeneutics, Religion, Hope* (New York: Harper & Row, 1987).

The first crisis involves the meaning and significance of tradition. The importance of hermeneutics increases the degree to which the meaning, significance, and validity of the religious tradition become remote and obscure to the present. The more the meaning and the authority of the traditional sources of theology become remote and obscure, the more it becomes necessary to interpret them so as to explicate their meaning and significance.[123] To the extent that the historical, cultural, and social distance between the past and the present increases so as to make the past more obscure, irrelevant, or even oppressive, the need for an interpretation of past traditions increases.

A second crisis affects personal experience. The more personal experience is no longer viewed as transparent, the more the need increases for a hermeneutics of experience. Today one often gives psychological, social, and behavioristic interpretations of human intentions and actions. The meaning of human action is no longer simply identified with the agent's self-interpretation of that action. The result is a conflict of interpretations of human action: one based on conscious intention, explicit motives, and self-interpretation, and another based on unreflective causes, social factors, and hidden reasons. The interpretation of experience and action becomes necessary insofar as the meaning of experience and action is no longer assumed to be manifest and evident.

These two crises lead to a third crisis, the crisis of hermeneutics itself, which emerges when interpretation alone does not suffice to re-solve the other two crises.[124] This crisis occurs when not merely the application of a tradition's meaning and significance is at issue, but rather when the tradition itself is radically challenged or when the conflicts within the tradition are incapable of ready reconciliation. This crisis also occurs when an experience itself is challenged. Then the question is no longer a question how to interpret the experience itself, but rather the adequacy of the experience itself. In Claude Geffré's words, "The crisis of hermeneutics is not simply a crisis of language—it is a crisis of thought."[125] It is then necessary to go beyond interpretation to a reconstruction of either tradition or experience. What is at stake is not just the meaning of a tradition or experience, but its truth. As Joseph Cardinal Ratzinger notes, "Christian theology does not just interpret texts: it asks about truth itself."[126]

Analytical Approaches
to Theology

Some approaches are analytical insofar as they provide analytical tools that help one to carry out the theological task and to clarify theological issues. Two analytical approaches have become especially influential within contemporary Roman Catholic theology. These approaches attempt to underscore either (1) the significance of a metatheory, specifically epistemology for method in general and theological method, (2) or the significant role (often implicit) of models and paradigms in theological reflection.

---

123. See Odo Marquard, *Farewell to Matters of Principle* (New York: Oxford University Press, 1989).

124. Claude Geffré, *The Risk of Interpretation: On Being Faithful to the Christian Tradition in a Non-Christian Age* (New York: Paulist, 1987), 21–45.

125. Ibid., 32.

126. Joseph Ratzinger, *Church, Ecumenism and Politics* (New York: Crossroad, 1988), 154.

METATHEORY:
METHOD IN THEOLOGY

Bernard Lonergan has contributed to contemporary Roman Catholic theology by showing that it is important for theology to address some basic questions of epistemology: What is the nature of human knowledge? What are the basic procedures of human cognition? Lonergan argues that such questions are much more basic than specific theological controversies and that they even underlie particular methodological issues, for epistemological assumptions, often implicit and unexamined, determine the outcome of these theological controversies and methodological issues. Such epistemological assumptions need to be examined, for they are fundamental not just to theology, but to every discipline and to every form of inquiry.

Lonergan has examined such basic questions and assumptions. He has developed an epistemological "metatheory" of human cognition and demonstrated its relevance for theological method. As a metatheory, his analysis of human cognition entails a high degree of abstraction. It analyzes cognitional structures and procedures that are often presupposed but not explicated in concrete theological debates. By examining the issues of epistemological metatheory involved in theological controversies, Lonergan has thereby related concrete theological issues to more general classic and perennial philosophical debates (for example, idealism versus materialism, subjectivism versus objectivism). He often resolves the theological issues with reference to philo-sophical solutions. He shows that his philosophical advocacy of a critical realism over and against idealism and materialism is significant not only for epistemology, but also for concrete theological issues.[127]

Lonergan develops his understanding of critical realism in relation to the transition from the classical Aristotelian understanding of scientific method to a modern empirical method.[128] He affirms that the result of every scientific method is open to further correction and revision. Thereby he emphasizes that genuine objectivity is not a naive realism that equates knowledge with simply taking a look. Objective knowledge is not merely a passive reception; it entails a critical realism in which the subjectivity of the knower also actively orders the world of meaning. This activity of human subjectivity needs to be taken into account in theological method. Lonergan's account of theology does this in two ways: (1) by explicating the structures of human cognition; and (2) by developing the relation between the horizon of subjectivity and the structure of cognition.

Structure of Knowing and Theological Method ◉ Lonergan argues that knowing involves a fourfold structure: the experience of data, the understanding of their meaning, the assessment of their value, and finally an evaluative decision. Since this pattern of knowing takes place in all acts of knowledge, its structure is relevant to all disciplines and sciences, not just philosophy or theology. To illustrate its relevance for theological method, Lonergan

---

127. For example, Lonergan makes the cognitional issues relevant to Christology. See his *The Way to Nicea: The Dialectical Development of Trinitarian Theology* (Philadelphia: Westminster, 1976). The development of trinitarian theology is sketched in relation to epistemology: Tertullian represents the approach of a materialist, Origen an idealist, and Athanasius a critical realist.

128. See Bernard Lonergan, *Insight* (New York: Philosophical Library, 1957); idem, *A Third Collection* (Philadelphia: Westminster, 1985); and the commentary in Vernon Gregson, *The Desires of the Human Heart* (New York: Paulist, 1989).

proposes that the methods and tasks of theology are rooted in the more basic invariant structure of human consciousness with its movement from experience to understanding, to judgment, and finally to decision.

This structure provides a basis for classifying the diverse tasks of theology as diverse functional specialties. Lonergan relates the fourfold structure of knowing to specific intentional objects and to specialties of theology so as to divide the theological task into two phases. The first phase of theology corresponds to the fourfold cognitional structure. It involves research (assembling data), interpretation (understanding its meaning), history (judging the implied assertions and data), and dialectic (clarifying the issues and making a decision or taking a stand). These four procedures are transcendental in that they form the structure of all human knowledge. Everyone (believers, nonbelievers, scientists, philosophers) follows the same basic procedure. If someone wanted to criticize this cognitional scheme, Lonergan argues, that person would in fact prove its validity because he or she would need to assemble data, interpret and evaluate the data, and finally, make a decision.

The second phase of the theological task begins after one has made a decision and taken a stance. This phase, involving the subjective horizon of the theologian, encompasses foundations, doctrinal theology and systematic theology, and communications. It again follows the cognitional structure but in reverse. One moves from the foundation of a decision (foundational theology), to judgments of truth (doctrinal theology), to understanding (systematic theology), and finally, to experience (communications—practical theology).

Conversion and Theological Method ● Crucial to the second phase of the theological task is the foundational role of the decision that is explicated by the category of conversion.[129] The notion of conversion brings out the significance of the intentionality of the knowing and believing subject for the constructive task of theology. Moreover, Lonergan's concrete explication of conversion expands his treatment from the realm of metatheory to a transcendental theology. Lonergan incorporates the intentionality of the knowing and believing subject into theological method through an analysis of conversion. He explicates the intentionality of conversion as intellectual, moral, and religious. Intellectual conversion involves deciding that knowing is not the same as simply taking a good look at the data or forming concepts. Intellectual conversion entails a decision and a movement of self-transcendence, for knowing entails a complex and reflective human operation of continued questioning for evidence, reasons, and comprehensive viewpoints.

Moral conversion changes the criteria for moral decisions from satisfaction to value.[130] Moral conversion entails opting for what one judges to be truly valuable and good, even when value and satisfaction conflict. Such judgments of value comprise knowledge of reality and an intentional response to value. Therefore, moral conversion presupposes intellectual conversion. Moreover, to the degree that value is placed

---

129. For contemporary expositions and further developments of Lonergan's notion of conversion, see Walter Conn, *Conscience: Development and Self-Transcendence* (Birmingham, AL: Religious Education Press, 1981); Stephen Happel and James J. Walter, *Conversion and Discipleship: A Christian Foundation for Ethics and Doctrine* (Philadelphia: Fortress Press, 1986).

130. Lonergan, *Method in Theology* (New York: Crossroad, 1972), 241.

38 above satisfaction, moral conversion is a form of self-transcendence and can be related to cognitive, moral, and affective development.[131]

Religious conversion, like intellectual and moral conversion, entails self-transcendence. Religious conversion, however, goes beyond the self-transcendence of intellectual and moral conversion insofar as it is constituted by that self-transcendence entailed in the shift to ultimate meaning and value. Lonergan characterizes religious conversion with the following set of terms: "being grasped by ultimate concern," "other-worldly falling in love," and "unrestricted love."[132] Religious conversion is not simply a matter of becoming religious, but is rather a total reorientation of one's life.

Lonergan's synthesis is not without its critics. Likening Lonergan to Schleiermacher, Langdon Gilkey has argued that the foundational role given to conversion lessens the public dimension of the theological tasks and opens Lonergan's method to the charge of subjectivism.[133] Although such a charge raises an important issue, it overlooks the hermeneutical dimension of all experience. Understanding presupposes a life-relation to the subject matter to be understood. Therefore, religious knowledge and the interpretation of religious texts presuppose a life-relation to the subject matter of the text. The interpretation of religion involves a double hermeneutic, for that interpretation should be based not only on the model or category that the interpreter uses to understand or to explain a religious event, action, or symbol, but also on the meaning that the religious agents themselves attribute to that religious event, action, or symbol.[134] Lonergan's notion of conversion, coupled with his critical realism, seeks to hold in balance the tension between objectivity and subjectivity in a way that undercuts the criticism.

In addition, the critical question emerges whether major authors and positions in the history of philosophy (Hume, Kant, or Hegel) or in the history of theology (Tertullian, Origen, Athanasius) can be reduced to abstract epistemological categories such as materialistic empiricism, idealism, or critical realism, as Lonergan has often done. Nevertheless, Lonergan has provided an invaluable service. In applying his cognitional metatheory to specific historical theological controversies, he has highlighted the significance of epistemology for concrete theological positions.

MODELS AND CATEGORY ANALYSIS

The use of the term *model* has become widespread in a variety of disciplines. In the natural sciences, a model is a way of representing a phenomenon so as to illustrate some of its basic properties and their interconnections.[135] A model highlights certain features and neglects others. In so doing, it provides an arrangement

---

131. For the relation of Lonergan's understanding of conversion to moral and psychological theories of development, see Walter Conn, *Christian Conversion: A Developmental Interpretation of Autonomy and Surrender* (Mahwah, NJ: Paulist, 1986).

132. Ibid., 241–44.

133. See Langdon Gilkey, "Empirical Science and Theological Knowing," in *Foundations of Theology*, ed. Philip McShane (Notre Dame, IN: University of Notre Dame Press, 1972), 76–101. In the same volume, David Tracy raises a similar criticism; see "Lonergan's Foundational Theology: An Interpretation and a Critique," 197–222.

134. See my *Foundational Theology* (285–301) for arguments for the hermeneutical dimension of experience and the double hermeneutic that seeks to show that appeals to a neutral public or common experience overlook the conditioned nature of all experience.

135. Marx W. Wartofsky, *Models: Representation and the Scientific Understanding* (Boston: Reidel, 1979).

of concepts that delineates a specific vision of a phenomenon from a particular perspective. An analogous use of models has become current within systematic theology to illumine the perspectival nature of theological categories.

Avery Dulles and Models in Theology ⊛ Avery Dulles, one of the leading contemporary Roman Catholic theologians in North America, has consistently made use of models within theology. He has used models to understand the church, revelation, the ecumenical movement, Christology, and Catholicism. His most influential application of models concerns the understanding of the church.[136] In *Models of the Church*, Dulles argues not only that various ecclesiologies differ in their understandings of the church, but also that this difference is in part due to the employment of different models of the church. He identifies institution, mystical communion, sacrament, herald, and servant as different models prevalent in contemporary theology. In later writings, he adds the model of discipleship as another comprehensive model.[137]

The importance of this method (and, in part, a reason for the influence of Dulles's book) is that it enabled Roman Catholics of diverse theological persuasions to understand one another and to engage in a cooperative conversation. Theologians and ministers with an outlook based on the model of the church as institution did not understand the horizon of theologians and ministers influenced by a vision of the church based on the model of communion. The awareness of diverse models implies that each perspective grasps, in a particular way, a significant and indispensable dimension of the church, while at the same time showing that other perspectives are equally valid. In the era following the Second Vatican Council, when diverse ecclesiologies often clashed with one another in theory and practice, such an approach contributed greatly to recognition and acceptance of diverse positions.

In his study of revelation, Avery Dulles proposed the following diverse models for interpreting different theologies of revelation: doctrine, history, inner experience, dialectical presence, and new awareness.[138] He proposes that an understanding of revelation as symbolic can best incorporate the perspectives of each of these models. These diverse models of revelation, moreover, often affect and underlie diverse conceptions of theological method as well as ecumenism.

Category Analysis ⊛ In addition to analyzing implicit epistemologies and models, contemporary theology has become sensitive to the use of diverse categories within theology. There is thus an increasing awareness of the significance and diversity of categories that underlie theological affirmations. The Congregation for the Doctrine of the Faith has taken up this problem in its document *Mysterium ecclesiae*, which deals with the historicity of Christian doctrine.[139] This document affirmed several points: (1) the incompleteness of every doctrinal affirmation; (2) the contextuality of doctrinal affirmations insofar as they are responses to particular questions; (3) the linguisticality of all doctrines; and (4) the distinction between the truth affirmed in a particular doctrinal formulation and the philosophical categories and worldviews used to express that truth.

---

136. Avery Dulles, *Models of the Church* (New York: Doubleday, 1974).

137. Avery Dulles, *A Church to Believe In* (New York: Crossroad, 1982).

138. Avery Dulles, *Models of Revelation* (New York: Doubleday, 1983).

139. The official English translation is "In Defense of Catholic Doctrine," *Origins* 32 (July 19, 1973): 97, 99–100, 110–23. See Ratzinger's commentary in *Principles of Catholic Theology*, 228–30.

Mysterium ecclesiae, written in response to Hans Küng's criticism of papal infallibility,[140] asserts that while doctrinal statements are historically and linguistically conditioned, they still are determinate affirmations of the truth. It maintains that doctrinal statements not only approximate the truth, but express some determinate aspect of truth, albeit in a historical, contextual, linguistic, and categorically specific manner. This affirmation of the historicity of the expressions and categories contained in doctrinal expression poses an important challenge for the understanding and assessment not only of the content of the doctrinal statements, but also of the categories central to theological method.

Traditional doctrines have been formulated with categories borrowed from particular philosophical traditions. Today the adequacy of such categories is often challenged and questioned. Does "transubstantiation" or "transignification" best express the Roman Catholic beliefs about the Eucharist? Is the formula "two natures and one person" adequate to express what traditional christological dogmas affirm? Is the reality expressed by the concept of "hypostatic union" better stated by the concept of "hypostatic identification"? Should the efficacy of the sacraments be expressed with the categories of Aristotelian causality or with categories drawn from a phenomenology of encounter? Hence, within theology, there is debate over whether the new categories or formulations are more or less adequate than the traditional ones. The philosophical debate underlying the theological debate is just as complex. The distinction between content and category or conceptual scheme is as much challenged as it is advocated.[141]

The analysis of basic categories is important for an understanding not only of doctrinal formulations, but also of theological method. Much of contemporary theology cannot be understood unless one takes into account certain shifts in basic categories. One example of such a shift is the result of Martin Heidegger's influence on Roman Catholic theology. In *Being and Time*, Heidegger argued that the ontological categories used from Greek philosophy to Descartes are inadequate to describe the temporality, historicity, and facticity of human existence in the world. Therefore, he sought to replace these categories with categories drawn from an analysis of human existence in its temporality.[142] These categories, which he called "existential," characterize what is specific to human existence: being-toward-death, care, and self-interpretation.[143] Much of Rahner's theology can be adequately understood only when one realizes that beyond traditional Scholastic categories, he has appropriated Heidegger's "existential." In a similar fashion, Lonergan has shifted "from a faculty psychology to intentionality analysis" with the result "that the basic terms and relations of systematic theology will not be metaphysical, as in medieval theology, but psychological."[144] Similar examples could be drawn from other theologians (Edward Schillebeeckx, Piet Schoonenberg, Charles Curran) or from theological movements (e.g., liberation theology). Consequently, contemporary theology needs to engage in metatheoretical reflection

---

140. Hans Küng, *Infallible: An Inquiry* (New York: Doubleday, 1971).

141. See Donald Davidson's classic essay "On the Very Idea of a Conceptual Scheme," now in his collection *Inquiries into Truth and Interpretation* (Oxford: Clarendon, 1984), 183–98.

142. Heidegger, *Being and Time*, 41–49.

143. Ibid., division 2, 277–487.

144. Lonergan, *Method in Theology*, 343.

on the basic categories employed in theological affirmations.

Beyond Metatheory

An important point in considering all metatheories, be they epistemological theories or analyses of models and categories, is that such metatheories are in themselves not theological methods, despite all their utility for theology and theological method. This point has been forcefully raised by Karl Rahner. In his comments on Lonergan's notion of functional specialties in theology, Rahner questions whether Lonergan's method is sufficiently and specifically theological.[145] In his view, Lonergan is not so much developing a theological method as he is describing the cognitional structures involved in every act of human inquiry from searching the skies for clues to the origin of the universe to searching a cookbook for data on how to bake a cake. The very title of Lonergan's book indicates this fact, for the work is not entitled "theological method" but rather *Method in Theology*.[146] A similar criticism can be raised against the use of models in theology. They provide helpful analysis, but theological reflection needs to go beyond merely analyzing the advantages and disadvantages of each model; it needs to take up theology's constructive and systematic task. In this regard, the following approach, employing a method of correlation, provides a more comprehensive view of theological method.

The Method of Correlation

The method of correlation emerged in the nineteenth century as an explicit theological method. In the twentieth century, it became widely accepted, particularly due to the influence of Paul Tillich. Some modified form of the method of correlation has been taken over by many major Roman Catholic theologians. A sketch of Paul Tillich's use of the method of correlation will provide background to its use in contemporary Roman Catholic theology.

Background

The method of correlation has its origins in the "mediation theology" (*Vermittlungs-theologie*) of mid-nineteenth-century German Protestant theology that was a nineteenth-century reaction to Schleiermacher.[147] This theological movement sought to mediate between the traditional theological starting point of Scripture and Schleiermacher's starting point of religious experience. It advocated a method of correlation as a means to mediate science and faith as well as Scripture and reason.

Paul Tillich developed the method of correlation with a specific understanding of correlation.[148] The three possible types of correlation are (1) statistical, as in the correlation of data; (2) logical, as in the interdependence of concepts (for example, whole and part); and (3) real, as in the interdependence of things and events. These three types are also present in theology.

---

145. "Lonergan's theological methodology seems to me to be *so generic that it really fits every science*, and hence is not the methodology of theology as such, but only a very general methodology of science in general, illustrated with examples taken from theology." Karl Rahner, "Some Critical Thoughts on 'Functional Specialties in Theology,'" in McShane, *Foundations of Theology*, 194.

146. Lonergan, *Method in Theology*.

147. Ragnar Holte, *Die Vermittlungstheologie* (Uppsala: University of Uppsala Press, 1965).

148. Paul Tillich, *Systematic Theology* (Chicago: University of Chicago Press, 1951–63), 1:59–66; see also 2:14. See John P. Clayton, *The Concept of Correlation: Paul Tillich and the Possibility of a Mediating Theology* (New York: De Gruyters, 1980).

42 The statistical correlation between religious symbols and what they symbolize constitutes the problem of religious knowledge. The logical correlation between concepts of the divine and those of the human determines the meaning of language about God and the world. And the correlation of the real interdependence of things and events is found in the correlation between one's ultimate concern and that about which one is ultimately concerned. This third correlation is specific to the relationship between the divine and the human within religious experience. This correlation in the divine-human relation expresses a real correlation between the divine and the human on the real and ontological level.

Tillich's definition and application of the method of correlation are diverse. He elaborates the method of correlation in terms of the correlation between question and answer as well as in terms of the correlation between form and content. Concerning the former correlation, he writes, "Theology formulates the questions implied in human existence, and theology formulates the answers implied in divine self-manifestation under the guidance of the questions implied in human existence."[149] His concrete application of the method of correlation is very complex, for he uses correlation not only to express the correlation between question and answer. He also uses the method to express the correlation between the form and content of human experience of finitude and human religious symbolization.[150] Tillich analyzes reason, being, existence, and history to underscore the emergence of a basic question that can then be correlated with the symbols of revelation, God, Christ, Spirit, and the kingdom of God.

CORRELATION IN CONTEMPORARY ROMAN CATHOLIC THEOLOGY

Today many Roman Catholic theologians maintain that a method of correlation best expresses the theological task. As Hans Küng notes, a widespread consensus exists that theology deals with two poles and that these two poles must be correlated. Despite this consensus, important differences exist regarding how each of these poles should be understood and how they should be correlated. A brief description of five particular examples of the method will illustrate significant similarities and differences. These five are Edward Schillebeeckx's critical correlation and structural principles, Hans Küng's use of a critical confrontation between the historical Jesus and the present, Joseph Cardinal Ratzinger's correlation between philosophical and theological inquiry, Rosemary Radford Ruether's correlation with the prophetic principle,[151] and David Tracy's mutually critical correlation.

Critical Correlation and Principles of Identity: Schillebeeckx ⊙ Schillebeeckx formulates the method of correlation as a "critical correlation between the two sources of theology . . . on the one hand the tradition of Christian experiences and on the other present-day experiences."[152] This formulation of correlation differs from Paul Tillich's conception. Tillich distinguishes between the medium and source of revelation in order to affirm that experience is

---

149. Tillich, *Systematic Theology*, 1:61.

150. See Langdon Gilkey, *Gilkey on Tillich* (New York: Crossroad, 1990), 56–78, 171–96.

151. Naturally, Ruether's work can also be categorized in relation to liberation theology and feminist theology—an indication that there is a considerable overlap or crisscrossing in the appropriation of different methods.

152. Edward Schillebeeckx, *Interim Report on the Books "Jesus" and "Christ"* (New York: Crossroad, 1981), 50.

a medium but not a source of revelation. In distinction, Schillebeeckx's correlation is between "two sources" of theology, which he labels the two poles of theology: the experiences of the tradition and present-day experiences. He calls for a "critical correlation and on occasion the critical confrontation of these two 'sources.'"[153] Schillebeeckx further delineates these two poles.

In analyzing the tradition of Christian experience (the first pole), Schillebeeckx maintains that despite their diverse theologies, the New Testament writings have an underlying unity in a basic experience of salvation from God in Jesus. It is "this basic experience that is interpreted in diverse ways but nevertheless the same."[154] That experience is composed of four formative principles: (1) the belief that God wills the salvation of all (theological-anthropological principle); (2) the belief that Jesus is the definitive disclosure of God's starting point (christological mediation); (3) the belief that God's story in Jesus continues in the message and lifestyle of the church (ecclesial mediation); and (4) the belief that the story of salvation cannot be fulfilled on earth (the eschatological dimension).

In analyzing contemporary experience (the other pole), Schillebeeckx proposes that it is characterized by two contrasting elements: its hopeful orientation to the future and its confrontation with an excess of suffering and senseless injustice. The utilitarian individualism of Western modernity is a major reason and cause for this contrast. This utilitarian individualism leads both to the hope for the future and to suffering and injustice. While its central value is freedom, this freedom is permeated with utilitarian individualism, which, linked with science and technology, often becomes a means of maximizing self-interest.

Schillebeeckx argues that a critical correlation should take place between the story of Jesus and modern utilitarian individuals. The story of Jesus evokes and calls us to conversion. The evoking of this metanoia is the goal of a critical correlation. Therefore, for Schillebeeckx, critical correlation primarily means the confrontation with the story of Jesus that elicits conversion. Underlying Schillebeeckx's understanding of the method of correlation is a distinction between ephemeral, conjunctural, and structural history. Ephemeral history is the fact-constituted history of the events of every day that come and go. Conjunctural history is much more expansive and includes the long cultural axes of history. Structural history is invariable, serving as the axis around which the ephemeral and conjunctural revolve.[155] The aim of a critical correlation is to ascertain the structural identity of Christian experience expressed in the diverse categories of conjunctural epochs, for example, Palestinian or Hellenistic. The purpose of ascertaining the structural identity within the conjunctural is to enable the identity of the Christian story to have an impact on the present Christian experience and thereby to allow the story of Christ's salvation to become for us an offer of salvation that confronts modern experience and critically corrects modern attitudes of individualism and possessiveness.

Critical Confrontation and the Living Jesus: Küng ◉ Preferring the term *critical confrontation* over *critical correlation*, Hans Küng has developed the method of correlation as a method of critical confrontation between the living Jesus

---

153. Ibid., 51.
154. Ibid.
155. See Edward Schillebeeckx, *Jesus: An Experiment in Christology* (New York: Crossroad, 1979).

44 and the present situation.[156] Küng changes the term *correlation* to *confrontation*; he prefers to speak of "two poles" rather than "two sources"; and he describes the two poles quite differently than Schillebeeckx does.

The task of theology is to bring about a critical confrontation between the living Jesus and the present situation. The first pole is the living Jesus, rather than the biblical symbol or the Christ of faith. Although, in the course of his writings, Küng has modified his position to include the Christian tradition, his emphasis is on the earthly Jesus. The earthly Jesus—the early Jesus as known through historical-critical research—is the norm and criterion for the Christian faith. In Küng's words, historical-critical research on Jesus can help us see that "the Christ of faith in whom we believe is really the man Jesus of Nazareth and not someone else nor, by some chance, no one at all."[157] Historical-critical research helps us avoid construction or adhering to false images of the Christ of faith. It brings us into contact with the Jesus of history, the norm and criterion of the Christ of faith.

In critically confronting the first pole with the second one, Küng also disagrees with Schillebeeckx's description of the pole of contemporary experience. Küng does not follow Schillebeeckx's view of modernity. It is not so much a utilitarian individualism that characterizes modernity and leads to the excessive suffering of modernity. Instead, modernity is characterized by the proliferation of bureaucracies and a lack of individual freedom. The freedom of Jesus' critique of the law stands in critical confrontation with the law of this bureaucratic modernity.

Correlation between Faith and Reason: Ratzinger ● In underscoring the distinctive and specific nature of Christian theology, Ratzinger argues that the Christian faith views the truth not as a particular truth about some specific thing but rather as the truth of our very being. Though Christian truth becomes accessible in faith, this truth illuminates the meaning of reality and addresses our intellect. Faith does not eliminate the human relation to truth, nor does it bypass analogy of reason. Analogy can be broadened and deepened, but it is not eliminated. Within the limitations of human possibilities, human reason is ordered to the truth. Consequently, Ratzinger maintains that "rationality belongs to the essence of Christianity."[158]

In his defense of analogy, Ratzinger takes sharp exception to Karl Barth's critique of both the *analogia entis* and the role of metaphysics in theology. Ratzinger sets his understanding of correlation in contrast to Barth's opposition to the continuity between the philosophical search for ultimate causes and the theological appropriation of the biblical faith. Ratzinger develops this contrast to Karl Barth by outlining three levels of correlation. The "first level of correlation between philosophical and theological inquiry" emerges when both philosophy and theology confront human mortality and ask about the origin, destination, and meaning of humanity.[159] The "second level of correlation" takes place when "faith advances a philosophical, more precisely, an ontological claim when it professes

---

156. Küng's basic essay on the method of correlation appeared in Leonard Swidler, ed., *Consensus in Theology? A Dialogue with Hans Küng and Edward Schillebeeckx* (Philadelphia: Westminster, 1980), then with modifications in Hans Küng, *Theology for the Third Millennium* (New York: Doubleday, 1988).

157. Küng, *Theology for the Third Millennium*, 111.

158. Joseph Cardinal Ratzinger, *The Nature and Mission of Theology* (San Francisco: Ignatius: 1995), 56.

159. Ibid., 23.

the existence of God, indeed of a God who has power over reality as a whole."[160] The third level of correlation incorporates the element of love.

Ratzinger illustrates this final step of correlation in relation to two answers that Bonaventure presents in justifying the use of philosophical discourse to comprehend the biblical message. The first answer stems from 1 Peter 3:15, the classic scriptural reference within medieval Christianity for the justification of theology. The Greek text clearly underscores what is affirmed, that one should be prepared to give a defense (*apo-logia*) for the reason (*logos*) of our hope. This involves more than the apologetic function—though significant—of explaining to others the reason for what one believes. Such a function shows that faith is not simply a private matter left to individual decision. But on a more profound level, it indicates a missionary function: "Faith has the right to be missionary only if it truly transcends all traditions and constitutes an appeal to reason and an orientation to the truth itself."[161] In addition, Ratzinger notes that there is another justification for theological reflection. Realizing there is a violence of reason that cannot be correlated with faith, Bonaventure posits another motive for inquiry, namely, love.

Correlation and the Prophetic Principle: Ruether ☉ Rosemary Radford Ruether develops the method of correlation from a feminist theological perspective and with an emphasis on the prophetic principle. She does not propose the method of correlation as a method of general consensus, as Hans Küng does. Instead, noting that the method of correlation can be diversely applied, she seeks to develop a liberation theology that takes race, class, and gender into account.[162] She understands the prophetic principle as a dynamic critical principle.[163] It is a principle insofar as it does not refer to a specific tradition or set of texts; rather, it is a principle within diverse traditions and texts. As a dynamic principle, it is not static but changes and is transformed. As a critical principle, it criticizes oppression in the forms of classism, racism, and sexism. In her words, "Feminist theology that draws on Biblical principles is possible only if the prophetic principles, more fully understood, imply a rejection of every elevation of one social group against others as image and agent of God, every use of God to justify social domination and subjugation."[164] As she has developed feminist theology, she has sought to broaden its scope beyond the method of correlation and has sought to incorporate environmental and global concerns.[165]

Mutually Critical Correlation: Tracy ☉ David Tracy suggests that a "widely accepted definition" of the theological task is "to establish mutually critical correlations between an interpretation of the Christian tradition and an interpretation of the contemporary situation"; it is "a revised correlation method" that is "in fact

---

160. Ibid., 24.

161. Ibid., 26.

162. Rosemary Radford Ruether, "Is a New Christian Consensus Possible?" in Swidler, *Consensus in Theology?* 33–39.

163. See Rosemary Radford Ruether, "Feminist Interpretation of the Method of Correlation," in *Feminist Interpretation of the Bible*, ed. Letty M. Russell (Philadelphia: Westminster, 1985), 111–24.

164. Rosemary Radford Ruether, *Sexism and God-Talk: Toward a Feminist Theology* (Boston: Beacon, 1983). See her more recent interpretation in *Feminist Theologies: Legacy and Prospect* (Minneapolis: Fortress, 2007).

165. Rosemary Radford Ruether, *Integrating Ecofeminism, Globalization, and World Religions, Nature's Meaning* (Lanham, MD: Rowman & Littlefield, 2005).

46

nothing other than a hermeneutically self-conscious clarification and correction of traditional theology."[166] It is hermeneutically self-conscious because it does not so much appeal to the Christian fact as it appeals to mutually critical correlations between two sets of interpretations.[167]

In elaborating his conception of the method of correlation, David Tracy takes over and develops the distinction that Schubert Ogden has proposed between criteria of appropriateness to the tradition and criteria of intelligibility to the situation.[168] Taking over the analytical distinction between truth and meaning, Ogden argues that the criteria of appropriateness, drawn from the apostolic witness, determine the meaning or identity of Christianity. The criteria of intelligibility to the situation provide criteria for the truth of the Christian faith.

Tracy carefully distinguishes and defines these criteria in developing his conception of the method of correlation. The criteria of appropriateness, understood as theological criteria, imply that it is "theologically crucial to judge every later theological statement in terms of its appropriateness to the apostolic witness expressed normatively in the Scriptures."[169] Such an interpretation of appropriateness differs considerably from Ruether's emphasis on the prophetic principle or Küng's emphasis on the living Jesus. In distinction to Küng, it is "not the 'historical Jesus' but the confessed witnessed Christ that is theologically relevant."[170]

The criteria of intelligibility address or correlate the message to the present situation. The criteria of intelligibility concern the issue of "relative adequacy" to contemporary experience and situation. It is important that the criteria of relative adequacy to the contemporary be such that they allow the classic event to have a disclosing and transformative impact on the situation. Tracy develops the nature of correlation with the help of the dialectic of event and response, the dialectic of explanatory and interpretive modes, and a model of conversation. The correlation between the two poles is understood as a conversation and a critical correlation. This correlation can differ insofar as the correlation can be one of identity, similarity-in-difference, or even confrontation.[171]

The diversity of approaches advocating that the proper method of theology is a method of correlation indicates how widespread is its acceptance. The method of correlation has much in common with classic conceptions of theology

---

166. Robert M. Grant with David Tracy, *A Short History of the Interpretation of the Bible*, rev. ed. (Philadelphia: Fortress Press, 1984), 170.

167. David Tracy, "What Is Fundamental Theology?" *Journal of Religion* 54 (1974): 13–34. Revised as chapter 2 of *Blessed Rage for Order* (New York: Crossroad, 1975).

168. See Schubert Ogden, *On Theology* (New York: Harper & Row, 1986), 1–22. In addition to *Blessed Rage for Order*, see Tracy, *The Analogical Imagination* and *Plurality and Ambiguity*.

169. Grant and Tracy, *Short History*, 175. Tracy is aware that such a criterion can be taken to imply identity and exclude criticism from later development. Therefore, he nuances his statement: "Criteria of appropriateness insist that all later theologies in *Christian* theology are obliged to show why they are not in radical disharmony with the central Christian witness expressed in the Scriptures. In that restricted sense, Scripture, as the original apostolic witness to Jesus Christ, norms but is not normed (*norma normans sed not normata*) by later witnesses" (p. 176).

170. Tracy, *The Analogical Imagination*, 301–2 n97. See Elizabeth A. Johnson, "The Theological Relevance of the Historical Jesus; A Debate and a Thesis," *The Thomist* 48 (1984): 1–43.

171. David Tracy, "The Uneasy Alliance Reconceived: Catholic Theological Method, Modernity and Postmodernity," *Theological Studies* 56 (1989): 548–70.

yet also differs from these conceptions. On the one hand, it assumes the authority and validity of the pat religious tradition, correctly interpreted, and seeks to apply it to the present. On the other hand, it perceives a greater distance between past message and present situation than did traditional theology. Therefore, correlation is not simply a fact, but rather the result and the goal of the theological task. In working toward this goal, one often combines the theological method of correlation with other methods, such as a transcendental analysis of the religious dimension of human subjectivity or a hermeneutical retrieval of the significance of religious traditions.

BEYOND CORRELATION

Several reservations can be advanced regarding the method of correlation. However, in view of the diverse conceptions of correlation, these reservations are not equally applicable to all. First, the method of correlation often rests on a distinction between language and the reality expressed in language. Such a distinction downplays the historicity of language and culture, for it assumes that different cultural expressions, categories, and language can change while the reality expressed in and through these categories remains the same and, therefore, can be correlated.

Second, the method of correlation emphasizes continuity and identity. It does not sufficiently take into account change and non-identity in the development of faith and theology. Unless one excessively formalized the tradition to an abstract formula, it is necessary to understand the tradition in categories that go beyond correlation and include development, transformation, and change.

Third, the method of correlation does not sufficiently take into account the need for a critique of tradition. The critique I refer to is not simply a matter of criticizing the formulations of tradition in order that the underlying experience or affirmations of the tradition might more readily shine forth. Rather, this critique reexamines the experiences and affirmations themselves.

Liberation Theologies

The term *liberation theology* does not refer to a single theological method but rather to diverse theological movements. In a narrow sense, liberation theology is a contemporary theological movement within Latin America. According to this restricted definition, liberation theology is a movement that focuses on the political, economic, and ideological causes of social inequality within Latin American countries and between Latin America and North America. Strongly influenced by Johann B. Metz's development of a political theology,[172] Latin American theologians offer a distinctive interpretation of modern society, eschatology, and political change. They advocate liberation rather than development as the central theological, economic, and political category. Even within this narrow sense, there is, however, a broad diversity of theological positions and method among Latin American liberation theologians.

In a broad sense, the term *liberation theology* refers to any theological movement that criticizes a specific form of oppression and views liberation as integral to the theological task. Feminist theologies, African-American theologies, and certain Asian theologies are major types of liberation theology. The term has also been appropriated by American Indians, ethnic groups, and

---

172. See Johann Baptist Metz, *Theology of the World* (New York: Crossroad, 1969).

48 other minority groups to express a mode of theological reflection. Despite significant differences among diverse liberation theologians, several common features characterize their methods. These characteristics allow one to speak of a shared method with four distinctive steps in common.

STARTING POINT

Liberation theologies take an analysis of their concrete sociopolitical situation as their starting point. Their analysis seeks to uncover oppression, exploitation, alienation, and discrimination. The interpretation of experience as an experience of oppression is common to all liberation theologies. For example, the stark contrast between the rich and poor within individual countries as well as between the advanced and developing nations leads Latin American liberation theologians to single out the relations of dependency and exploitation between nations as decisive contributing factors to this inequality.[173] African-American liberation theology focuses on the discrimination against Africans and African-Americans in the history of Christianity. Feminist theologians focus on the oppression of women in patriarchally structured societies.

CRITIQUE OF IDEOLOGY

The second common step is to read the tradition from the perspective of the experience of the oppressed. This reading involves a "hermeneutics of suspicion" or a critique of ideology. It looks for ideological distortions in the tradition that led to oppression, and it critiques those elements. The degree and extent of suspicion in this hermeneutic vary from theologian to theologian. Quite often, Latin American liberation theologians seem to indicate that only the tradition subsequent to the New Testament or subsequent to the historical Jesus evidences ideological distortions. Many will, for example, critique this interpretive tradition in order to return to the original intention of the New Testament writings or to the historical Jesus, who was clearly on the side of the poor.[174]

Within feminist liberation theology, the reading of the situation is much more complex.[175] First of all, the New Testament traditions are diverse. Whereas some traditions and texts are permeated with ideas and attitudes discriminatory toward women, other traditions proclaim the equality of male and female in Christ. An example of the former is the household codes of the New Testament that refer to the subordination of women to men and that incorporate an Aristotelian patriarchal order. They originated in an attempt to respond to charges that Christianity was antifamily or against Roman social order. Insofar as Christianity allowed women and slaves to convert to Christianity independently of their "head" or "owner" (the paterfamilias), Romans viewed and criticized Christianity for being antifamily and subversive of the social order. The household codes are in

---

173. See Gustavo Gutiérrez, *A Theology of Liberation*, rev. ed. (Maryknoll, NY: Orbis, 1988). On the relation between political and liberation theology, see Francis Fiorenza, "Political Theology and Liberation Theology: An Inquiry into Their Fundamental Meaning," in *Liberation, Revolution and Freedom: Theological Perspectives*, ed. Thomas McFadden (New York: Seabury, 1975), 3–29.

174. Juan Luis Segundo, *The Historical Jesus of the Synoptics* (Maryknoll, NY: Orbis, 1985); John Sobrino, *Jesus in Latin America* (Maryknoll, NY: Orbis, 1987).

175. For the difference between the approach of Juan Luis Segundo and a feminist critical theory of liberation, see Elisabeth Schüssler Fiorenza, *Bread Not Stone* (Boston: Beacon, 1984), 43–63.

part explainable by this charge.[176] Consequently, the critique of ideology is in some feminist theologies applied not only to the interpretation of the New Testament, but to the New Testament itself.

Standpoints for the critique of ideology differ within liberation theologies. Some liberation theologians relate the current experience of oppression to other standards, such as the historical Jesus or the prophetic principle. The critique of ideology rests then on the correlation between the two standards. For others, such a correlation is often advanced with insufficient historical discernment. For them, the experience of oppression becomes a standard by which the Scriptures are read. Not only is the tradition of interpreting the New Testament "reread" in light of experiences of oppression, but the New Testament itself is also reread in light of those experiences. Therefore, the criterion of the critique becomes the experience of oppression; that experience serves as the basic criterion by which other criteria are evaluated.

Subjugated Knowledge

In addition to criticizing ideological distortions of past and current cultural traditions, liberation theology understands the retrieval of subjugated knowledge as a part of its constructive theological task. The theological task thus includes retrieving forgotten religious symbols, neglected ecclesiastical practices, and ignored experiences. While history often records the memory and interpretation of the victors, it often silences the voices and interpretations of the victims.[177] A task within liberation theology, therefore, is to bring to light the knowledge and experiences of those whose voices have been silenced.[178] Liberation theology uncovers in the past not archetypes, but prototypes of liberation.[179]

Praxis as Criterion

Praxis is, within liberation theologies, not just a goal but also a criterion of theological method.[180] The Greek term *praxis* is deliberately used by liberation theologians to accentuate an important distinction that in fact goes back to Aristotle. In the *Nicomachean Ethics*, Aristotle distinguished practice (*poiesis*) as a technical skill, involved in making something, from practice (*praxis*) as a way of life. Whereas the former is a matter of technical skill (*techne*), the latter expresses a basic way of living.[181] Adopting this Aristotelian notion of praxis, critical theorists and revisionist Marxists have sought to take up Karl Marx's emphasis on social and political praxis while avoiding Marx's technocratic and economic reduction of the notion.[182] Liberation theologians have followed this direction insofar as when they affirm that praxis is both the goal and criterion of their theologies, they are affirming that their goal is not some technocratic

---

176. Elisabeth Schüssler Fiorenza, *In Memory of Her* (New York: Crossroad, 1983): 251–84. See also idem, *Bread Not Stone*, 65–92.

177. See especially Johann Baptist Metz, *Faith in History and Society* (New York: Crossroad, 1980); idem, *The Emergent Church* (New York: Crossroad, 1986); and Matthew Lamb, *Solidarity with Victims* (New York: Crossroad, 1982).

178. Sharon Welch, *Communities of Resistance and Solidarity* (Maryknoll, NY: Orbis, 1985).

179. Rebecca Chopp, *The Power to Speak* (New York: Crossroad, 1989). See her systematic appropriation of Elisabeth Schüssler Fiorenza's notion of prototype in chapter 2.

180. Clodovis Boff, *Theology and Praxis* (Maryknoll, NY: Orbis, 1987); Rebecca Chopp, *The Praxis of Suffering* (Maryknoll, NY: Orbis, 1986).

181. Aristotle, *Nicomachean Ethics* 6.2.1139a.19–20; 6.4.1140a.1–23; 6.7.1141b.16.

182. See especially Jürgen Habermas, *Theory and Practice* (Boston: Beacon, 1973).

50 organization, some social structure, or some economic plan, but rather a way of life. The term *praxis* specifies that the liberation they seek is more than a mere technocratic or economic development—it is a liberation that has religious, social, political, and personal dimensions.

Toward a More Comprehensive Theological Approach

Contemporary theology faces challenges that make the ever-complex task of theology even more complex. Such challenges are cultural, religious, economic, scientific, and political. Moreover, how theologians interpret these challenges often determines how they understand the theological task. If theologians assess the present situation as secularized, as being characterized by the absence of past moral values and the demise of traditional religious meanings, then they view the retrieval of these values and the reactualization of these meanings as the paramount theological task. If they place the political, social, and racial oppressions in the forefront, then overcoming these oppressions is a major goal of theology. If they take human alienation or personal inauthenticity to be the basic problem, then the attainment of authenticity and the overcoming of alienation are their primary goals.

Present life experiences and praxis provide liberation theologians not only sources from which they criticize tradition and the present situation, but also criteria for the assessment of theological affirmations. At the same time, a liberated praxis is also the goal of liberation theology. As such, praxis is the other side of the coin of a hermeneutics of suspicion or the critique of ideology. This emphasis on praxis within liberation theology can be seen as a sort of consequentialism within theology. As a key concept, however, it is in need of clarification. The appeal to praxis is often an appeal to the immediacy of experiences of oppression. Yet at the same time such appeals to praxis as a normative source and an anticipated goal raise the question of the assessment of praxis itself. If judgments are to be made about praxis, then certain legitimate and necessary questions emerge: What is the interpretive framework of such judgments? What background theories are implied or assumed in such judgments? How is praxis itself interpreted and assessed? Such questions move one to a theological method that includes praxis as a central theological and political element, but is a method necessarily broader in scope.

Characteristics of the Modern Situation

This section discusses three characteristics of the modern situation constituting a challenge for the theological task. These characteristics are not external challenges to theology, but are internal to theology and affect the very nature of theological reflection. These challenges are basic ambiguities that characterize our present situation. They are pluralism and unity, rationality and its critique, and, finally, power and its oppressiveness.

AMBIGUITY OF PLURALISM AND UNITY

The impact of cultural pluralism on theology is obvious. Pluralism has philosophical, religious, and political implications for theology. In a widely noted essay, Karl Rahner has argued that previously one could assume a particular philosophy or worldview as a standard to which one could appeal to link theology and culture.[183] This philosophy, whether Thomist, transcendental, phenomenological, existential, or analytical, served as an accepted philosophical standard. Today, however, no single philosophy or philosophical view exists as such a standard or cultural medium for theological reflection. If one expresses Christian belief in particular philosophical categories, then one has not *eo ipso* made that belief more public or more warranted. Philosophical views are often no less particularistic than the religious beliefs themselves.

For theology, the consequences of such pluralism are twofold. First, one can no longer expect a synthesis between theology and culture. Some hold a romantic ideal that such a synthesis occurred in medieval times, and they long for its return, but that is a mere pipe dream. The pluralism of the culture itself hinders such syntheses. Second, this pluralism also implies that theology does not appeal to a particular philosophy as a link between faith and rationality. Instead, theology itself takes up the task of mediation in full awareness of the historicity of philosophy and the pluralism of theology.[184] Theology then seeks to articulate the Christian faith as existing within a pluralistic culture.[185]

In addition to philosophical pluralism, the theological task must confront religious pluralism. The presence of other world religions and the reality of other faiths increasingly make their imprint on Christian theology. The question of Lessing's "Parable of Nathan the Wise" has become paradigmatic for contemporary theology. In this parable, each son (representing Judaism, Islam, and Christianity) maintains that he alone has received the true ring (divine revelation) from his faith. The sons go before a court judge with their contesting claims. The judge observes that the ring is alleged to have a magic power affecting the life-practice of each bearer. Yet not one of them lives such an exemplary life of love that would prove possession of the true ring. The judge concludes that perhaps no one has the ring or maybe only in the future will the ring's power be manifest in one of them. The question remains unresolved and is left to some future and infinitely more capable judge to decide.

Lessing's position is somewhat enigmatic.[186] Is he affirming that no religion possesses the true ring, or is he more likely pointing to the importance of life-practice? Lessing's parable challenges us ever more today. We are more than ever aware that Christianity is one religion among many. Not just Islam and Judaism, but also Buddhism, Confucianism, and many other religions display the vitality and claims of their paradigmatic religious visions. When viewed together, they display the plurality of religious visions. They thereby challenge Christian theology to articulate the significance, meaning, and unconditionality of the Christian vision, not in isolation from other religious visions, but in relation to them.

---

183. Karl Rahner, "Pluralism in Theology and the Unity of the Creed in the Church," *Theological Investigations* (New York: Crossroad, 1974), 11:3–23.

184. For a contemporary account of rationality, see Hilary Putnam, *Reason, Truth and History* (New York: Cambridge University Press, 1981), esp. 103–218.

185. See Claude Geffré, "Pluralité des théologies et unité de la foi," in *Initiation à la pratique de la théologie*, ed. Bernard Lauret and François Refoulé (Paris: Éditions de Cerf, 1982), 117–42; Yves Congar, *Diversity and Communion* (Mystic, CT: Twenty-Third Publications, 1985), 9–43.

186. See Henry E. Allison, *Lessing and the Enlightenment* (Ann Arbor: University of Michigan Press, 1966).

Yet modernity is characterized not only by the growing awareness of philosophical and religious pluralism, but also by the increasing realization of the unity of the world. Economic systems increasingly link nations and groups of nations with each other. Population growth and technological development take place in all nations within a natural ecosystem. Interdependency among all nations is not only economic, but also environmental. All humans depend on the ecosystem. In addition, the increased awareness of human rights (along with their violation) and democratic ideals as extending to all races, nations, and genders points to an increasing awareness of a "common humanity" of all peoples of the earth—an earth increasingly smaller through the growth in communications technology.

The task for theology is both to take pluralism seriously and to explore the particularity and significance of the Christian vision without reducing religious language to an isolated language game that neglects other religious visions and the global situation of humanity.

Ambiguity of Rationality and Its Critique

The task of theology relates to conceptions of rationality. The nature of rationality within the modern world faces a double challenge. It faces the challenge of the modern Enlightenment, and it faces the growing critique of the Enlightenment.[187] Both the Enlightenment and

its critique challenge theology. The Enlightenment and its modern conception of rationality have been significant for Roman Catholic theology, for in the Roman Catholic tradition, theology has always sought a unity between faith and reason. As Joseph Cardinal Ratzinger has recently argued, "Faith is not to be placed in opposition to reason, but neither must it fall under the absolute power of enlightened reason and its methods. . . . It has always been clear from its very structure that Christian faith is not to be divorced from reason."[188]

However, the Enlightenment had a very specific conception of rationality and knowledge. It believed that science had developed correct and cumulative methods of acquiring knowledge. By replacing ancient superstitions, traditional religions, and unexamined authorities, these methods gave promise for eliminating poverty and ignorance, for decreasing disease and hunger, and for providing an increase in material goods and happiness.[189] Today we are aware of the limitations of science and scientific rationality. Though we are aware that scientific rationality has led to great advances in technology and to significant material advantages, we are also aware of its limitations and dangers. The result is that we face a crisis of rationality. This crisis of rationality was articulated forcefully in the critical theory of the 1940s,[190] and the crisis is at the center of the current postmodern critique of technocratic as well as scientific rationality.[191] The modernist belief in the progress of science

---

187. Max Horkheimer and Theodor W. Adorno, *Dialectic of Enlightenment* (New York: Seabury, 1972).

188. Ratzinger, *Principles of Catholic Theology*, 325.

189. See Langdon Gilkey, *Society and the Sacred* (New York: Crossroad, 1988), 3–14, 73–105. See also his earlier work, *Religion and the Scientific Future* (New York: Harper & Row, 1970).

190. Max Horkheimer, *Critique of Instrumental Reason* (New York: Seabury, 1967). See also, from a different perspective, Alvin Gouldner, *The Dialectics of Ideology and Technology* (New York: Basic, 1976).

191. See Jean-François Lyotard, *The Postmodern Condition: A Report on Knowledge* (Minneapolis: University of Minnesota Press, 1984); idem, *The Differend* (Minneapolis: University of Minnesota Press, 1988). For a general survey, see

and reason is intensely criticized for overlooking the negative side of this progress and for a "substitutional universalism," that is, for claiming as universal what is in reality a specifically Eurocentric viewpoint.[192]

This ambiguity of rationality and its critique presents a particularly acute challenge to theology. On the one hand, theological reflection cannot neglect the growth of methodology that has so affected the humanities. The theological analysis of religious classics and even the Scriptures cannot neglect the application of contemporary methods to these texts. In addition, many religious beliefs presuppose particular scientific worldviews, and these worldviews have at least been expressed in the religious beliefs. For theology to overlook the growth in scientific knowledge and rationality would be to withdraw into a ghetto. At the same time, theological reflection needs to avoid scientific positivism that apes the scientism of technocratic rationality. Moreover, since theology articulates the religious belief in transcendence, it has as its task to underscore what transcends scientific rationality. Thereby, theology offers a challenge to positivist and reductionist conceptions of human reason.

AMBIGUITY OF POWER AND ITS OPPRESSIVENESS

The modern world has witnessed an impressive growth of scientific, technological, and political power. The domination of nature and the structural organization of society have led to an increase in material well-being. Yet at the same time, this increase in wealth and health has gone hand in hand with an increase in poverty and hunger. The domination of nature has gone hand in hand with exploitation and devastation of large segments of the globe. Growth in the standard of living has been limited to some people, nations, and continents. Alongside of increased prosperity is increased poverty. These exist not only in separate parts of the world, but side by side in the very same cities and towns. The growth in political power, freedom, and equality for some has been accompanied by racial genocide, gender discrimination, and national oppression. Power is two-edged: it not only enables positive control, but also makes possible exploitative domination.

This ambiguity of power challenges a reflective faith in two ways. First, the ambiguity presents a challenge that affects the mission and structure of faith. It calls for a faith that does justice, for a faith sensitive to the imbalances of power and wealth, for a faith with eyes turned toward the downtrodden and poor. Second, the poor and oppressed bring a view of society and history that is otherwise often neglected.[193] The sociology of knowledge has exposed the degree to which the material conditions of life shape culture and influence thought. The categories with which individuals understand reality or interpret their past develop within structures of power and domination. We stand in a life-relation and a power-relation that influence how we understand ourselves, our world, and others.

Consequently, as liberation theologians emphasize, the task of theology involves not only the critique of nonreligious ideologies that dominate the consciousness of societies, but also the

---

Steven Connor, *Postmodernist Culture: An Introduction to Theories of the Contemporary* (Oxford: Blackwell, 1989). For a critical view, see Jürgen Habermas, *The Philosophical Discourse of Modernity: Twelve Lectures* (Boston: Beacon, 1987).

192. Francis Schüssler Fiorenza, "The Impact of Feminist Theory on My Work," *Journal of Feminist Studies in Religion* (Spring 1991).

193. Gustavo Gutiérrez, *The Power of the Poor in History* (Maryknoll, NY: Orbis, 1983).

54 critique of the very ideologies permeating and fostered by religious traditions. The ambiguity of power challenges theology to be self-critical in its service to God, to humanity, and to nature.

Four Elements
of a Theological Approach

The task of Christian theology is the elaboration of the Christian vision and identity in the face of these challenges. This vision encompasses not only discourse about God and Christ, but also discourse about the Christian community in its relation to other communities. Such a complex task is not arbitrary, but entails diverse criteria.

RECONSTRUCTIVE HERMENEUTICS: THE INTEGRITY OF THE TRADITION

The task of elaborating the Christian vision and identity encompasses many elements, including an interpretation of the Christian community's tradition, Scriptures, creeds, councils, practices, and past reflection. It also encompasses the attempt to bring the Christian community's tradition into relation with philosophical and scientific discourse, with the ongoing experience and practice of faith in the world, and with other communities of discourse with which the Christian community interacts.

Scripture and Tradition ⊛ The interpretation of the Christian community's past involves an interpretation of the authority of its tradition. Within the context of the authority of the tradition, the role of Scripture and its relation to tradition are important issues that have become controverted since the Reformation. They received new significance through the Second

Vatican Council. The major impetus for the renewal of these issues came from intense historical research on the early Christian writers and the early church's liturgy and from the application of historical-critical studies to the Bible. The emergence of the biblical movement within the Roman Catholic Church has shown the importance of the Scriptures for Catholic spirituality, church life, and doctrine. This movement has led to a reexamination of the Council of Trent's teaching in relation to the Reformation's *sola scriptura*.

Two basic views of tradition have emerged, as can be illustrated by the debate between Joseph Geiselmann and Joseph Ratzinger. Geiselmann maintains that tradition is the living presence of Scripture. Tradition does not so much add to Scripture as it has translated Scripture into the living presence of the church. Geiselmann seeks to underscore his argument through a careful interpretation of the Council of Trent's position on the relation between Scripture and tradition and maintains that every age relates to Scripture.[194]

Ratzinger makes a twofold argument that is important for our understanding of tradition. First, Geiselmann's position minimizes the role of the early Christian writers in the post–New Testament times and thereby dehistoricizes tradition. It overlooks that lacunae in the historical foundation do not speak against tradition. The dogmas of 1854 and 1950 affected the Roman Catholic understanding of tradition, for they presupposed that a historical demonstration did not mean that one had to demonstrate that a dogma was explicitly believed in at the beginning of the church, but only that a cross section

---

194. Joseph Rupert Geiselmann, "Das Konzil Trient über das Verhältnis der Heiligen Schrift und der nicht geschriebenen Traditionen," in *Die mündliche Überlieferung*, ed. Michael Schmaus (Munich: Kösel, 1957); idem, *The Meaning of Tradition* (New York: Herder & Herder, 1966).

of the church at times believed in it. Ratzinger in fact maintains that "whatever the whole Church holds to have been revealed *has* been revealed and belongs to the authentic tradition of the Church."[195] The significance of the post–New Testament church has been eliminated by a historical-critical method that reduces faith to the Scriptures.

Second, Ratzinger shows that the understanding of tradition worked out by the Council of Trent was indeed nuanced and complex. Trent combined pneumatological, liturgical, and doctrinal views to emphasize diverse strata within the concept of tradition. Revelation is inscribed not simply in the Bible but also in the hearts of Christians. Consequently, the Spirit speaks through the whole life of the church, including its conciliar and liturgical activity. Trent's teaching on tradition sought to affirm that the revelation of God in Christ "was accomplished in historical facts, but has also its perpetual reality today, because what was once accomplished remains perpetually living and effective in the faith of the Church, and Christian faith never simply refers to what is past but equally to what is present and to what is to come."[196]

Hermeneutics of the Tradition ◉ The importance of tradition and its presence within the Christian church raise the issue of an adequate approach to the interpretation of tradition in regard to both its ongoing development and the continual reconstruction of its integrity. The Congregation for the Doctrine of the Faith's *Mysterium ecclesiae* points out the importance of linguistic categories, historical contextualization, incompleteness, and worldviews in a way

that acknowledges the historicity of tradition. It criticizes a position that in a Neo-Platonic fashion views tradition primarily as approximations to the truth, rather than as historically and linguistically conditioned affirmations of faith. An interpretation of tradition must seek to take into account the historicity of tradition as well as the significance of its affirmations.

It is important to avoid some basic misreading of the nature of tradition. These are views of tradition as static identity, decay, or progressive development. Each of these views captures some aspect of tradition but erroneously extrapolates this aspect into a total view of tradition:

In the view that affirms a *static identity*, neither decay nor development, neither change nor growth takes place. Instead, tradition appears as the affirmation of what always was, is, and will be. This view attempts to crystallize the value of tradition through an affirmation of a lack of change and development.

The second extreme, which views tradition as *decay* away from pristine origins, is more common within a direction of liberal theology influenced by Albrecht Ritschl's critique of metaphysics than within Roman Catholic theological circles, though one does encounter it there also. It views the postbiblical period as a period of decay. The development of doctrine or the institutional growth and development of the church consist of a falling away from the pristine biblical charism. Today some even locate this decay within the New Testament itself. They seek to distinguish sharply between the historical Jesus or the early Christian community's explication of its faith in the Christ

---

195. Ratzinger, *Principles of Catholic Theology*, 139. See also Albert Lang, *Der Auftrag der Kirche* (Munich: Hueber, 1962), 2:290–92; Joseph Ratzinger, "Revelation and Tradition," in Karl Rahner and Joseph Ratzinger, *Revelation and Tradition*, ed. Karl Rahner and Joseph Ratzinger (New York: Herder & Herder, 1966).

196. Joseph Ratzinger, "On the Interpretation of the Tridentine Decree on Tradition," in Rahner and Ratzinger, *Revelation and Tradition*, 65.

56 and the later development of organized structures representing early Catholicism. This view correctly grasps the primal significance of the early New Testament witnesses to Jesus. However, it overlooks the significance of later development, be it the first centuries of Christian community or the medieval and modern development of Christianity. The essence of Christianity should not be reduced to an archaeology of beginnings.[197]

The third view, which considers tradition as a *progressive development* or evolution, often presupposes an organic model of tradition. All development is looked upon as a progressive improvement. Such a view neglects the possibility of distortions. Moreover, it is important to acknowledge that previous ages of Christianity do not relate to the present as childhood or adolescence to maturity, for the non-contemporaneity of a previous stage can be a genuine challenge to the prejudices of modern developments.

Integrity of the Tradition ◉ In the interpretation of tradition, it is important to distinguish between the idea of a principle of Christian faith and the idea of the foundation of Christian faith. This distinction between principles and foundation is often used in moral philosophy and in epistemology.[198] One can illustrate this distinction in regard to the Christian tradition with the example of slavery. Today, as Christians, we affirm that slavery is wrong and that one cannot be a Christian and advocate slavery. Yet we cannot trace to the foundational origins of Christianity a prohibition against slavery. Quite the contrary. Yet today the incompatibility of slavery and Christianity is a principle of Christian faith and morals.

The tradition develops and changes in a way that constantly reconstructs what it considers to be paradigmatic, what it considers to be its vision or "essence." How it does so cannot be adequately addressed in terms of categories of static identity, decay, or development. Instead, there is a constant reconstruction of its understanding of what is paradigmatic to its vision. In this reconstruction, background theories, retroductive warrants, and the community of discourse play important roles. Each of these will be further elucidated in detail in one of the following sections. In brief, background theories are implicit assumptions, philosophical or scientific, about the world and science; the notion of retroductive warrants refers to the way contemporary practices and experiences work backward to affect interpretations or hypotheses and their validation; and finally, the concept of communities of discourse refers to the fact that meaning and assessment take place in the context not of a form of abstract human reason, but in a specific historical tradition and linguistic community.

BACKGROUND THEORIES

The term *background theory* is currently used in the philosophy of science and in ethical theory to designate those implied theories that have an impact on considered hypotheses and judgments. The term has its origin in the philosophy of science. Henri Poincaré coined the term *auxiliary hypotheses* to describe the presupposed hypotheses about physical phenomena that are necessarily assumed in a given practical application of geometry. If the hypothesis does not agree with the observation, then one achieves coherence either by adopting different axioms

---

197. Joseph Ratzinger, *Das Problem der Dogmengeschichte in der Sicht der katholischen Theologie* (Cologne: Opladen, 1966).

198. See Alan Donagan, *The Theory of Morality* (Chicago: University of Chicago Press, 1977).

or by modifying relevant auxiliary hypotheses. Within ethical theory, the application of ethical principles to practice entails relevant background notions about human nature or human society. In general, everyone makes use of some sort of background theories, but specific theories vary from person to person and from age to age.

Historically Considered ☉ Since background theories are implicit, they are often presupposed or assumed without explicit reflection. It is therefore important in reflecting about theological method to attend to the presence of implicit background theories. Judgments about Christian identity or Roman Catholic identity as judgments about the meaning of a religious tradition often rely on implicit background theories not only about the self, society, and the world, but also about the means and methods of interpreting past tradition and present experience. These background theories affect one's judgments about one's Christian or Catholic identity, just as one's judgments about identity affect one's assessment of the nature and appropriateness of various background theories.

The preceding discussion of the history of theological method referred to certain background theories: Augustine's understanding of Christian doctrine presupposed the Neo-Platonic theory of signs, the notion of interior light, and self-transcendence. Aquinas's understanding of *sacra doctrina* presupposed Aristotle's division of sciences, his notion of subalternate science, and the explanatory role of Aristotelian causality. Karl Rahner presupposed in part a transcendental understanding of experience and language as well as Heidegger's analysis of the existential of human *Dasein* (being-there). Con-

temporary hermeneutical theory, with its exposition of the classic, metaphor, and narrative, presupposed an understanding of the relation between language and experience that differs from that of the transcendental approach.

Systematically Considered ☉ The contemporary shift in philosophical background theory has been described by Bernard Lonergan as a shift from logic to method, from essences to systems, from a division of sciences according to formal and material objects to one according to fields and methods, from necessary deduction to probable inferences, and from faculty psychology to intentionality analysis. This shift from logic to method entails for Lonergan a conception of theology as an ongoing process of revision and correction.[199]

My description of theology as encompassing diverse elements—the reconstructive hermeneutic of the tradition, relevant background theories, retroductive warrants, and the community as a community of discourse—concurs with Lonergan's basic description of the shift from logic to method. It suggests that one essential element of the systematic task of theology is the explication of theological reflection in relation to diverse background theories. Such theories are quite diverse. They include philosophical theories about human nature, ethical theories about social justice, psychological theories about personal development, scientific theories about the beginnings of the universe, epistemological theories about human cognition, and literary theories about interpretation—to name a few of the relevant background theories. Each can play a role in the development of a theology.

---

199. Nevertheless, insofar as my proposal suggests a method of broad reflective equilibrium, it places less emphasis than Lonergan does on intentionality analysis and the transcendental analysis of structures of cognition. Instead, it suggests that such analyses of human subjectivity and its structures of cognition provide one of several background theories.

58

The notion of reflective equilibrium suggests that theological reflection advances in part through a critical interaction between one's interpretation of the Christian tradition and one's interpretation of relevant background theories. The correction is mutual. It may very well be that a background theory influences the interpretation of the tradition. Scientific theories of evolution and literary theories about genre have influenced the interpretation of the Genesis accounts of creation. The Christian tradition's understanding of the dignity of the human person has influenced the assessment and adoption of psychological theories of human development. Sometimes the mutual influence is reciprocal: the biblical notion of solidarity with the poor and disadvantaged related to theories of social justice and the notion of a "difference principle" whereby the least advantaged in society are accorded rights.[200]

Any consideration of the relation between background theories and the interpretation of the Christian tradition needs to take into account the historicity of culture and the pluralism of society so that no one background theory is uncritically accepted as an infallible norm, even if it be the latest phenomenological theory about human intentionality, the most recent epistemological theory about the structures of human cognition, or the latest anthropological and psychological account of gender differences. Scientific and philosophical viewpoints of our culture are indeed also historically conditioned and subject to revision. A modernist theology that takes these background theories as infallible standards—be the theory an Aristotelian account of virtue, a Husserlian account of subjectivity, or the latest philosophical theory espousing particularism and relativism—fails to recognize the historicity of culture.

RETRODUCTIVE WARRANTS

The terms *retroductive* and *retroductive warrants* are not commonplace. However, the terms have a specific meaning in current methodological discussion within contemporary philosophy of science, epistemology, and ethics, as well as a specific relevance to theological method. The meaning of the term *retroductive warrant* and its use within theological reflection can be illuminated in various strata: by its use within contemporary philosophy of science, by Newman's illative sense, by liberation theology's appeal to the hermeneutical role of the oppressed, and by Rahner's indirect method of theology.

Theoretical and Practical Fruitfulness ◉ A retroductive warrant within the philosophy of science of epistemology refers to the fertility of a hypothesis, idea, or theory.[201] It refers to the ability of the hypothesis or theory to carry forward the scientific enterprise. Retroductive warrants differ from experimental justifications. A retroductive warrant is not so much an inductive confirmation as it is the theoretical and practical fruitfulness that flows from the imaginative construal of all the available evidence. A warrant is retroductive to the extent that it offers the most feasible and comprehensive explanation of the phenomenon, accounts for unexpected and unanticipated phenomena, and enables the scientific endeavor to move on in practice.

---

200. Francis Schüssler Fiorenza, "Politische Theologie und liberale Gerechtigkeits-Konzeption," in *Mystik und Politik: Johann Baptist Metz zu Ehren*, ed. Edward Schillebeeckx (Mainz: Grünewald, 1988), 105–17.

201. See Ernan McMullin, "The Fertility of Theory and the Unit for Appraisal in Science," *Boston Studies in the Philosophy of Science* 39 (1976): 395–432.

This theoretical and practical fruitfulness is both prospective and retrospective. It is prospective in that a good theory anticipates novel phenomena, that is, phenomena not belonging to the data to be explained. The more novel and unexpected phenomena are predicted and explained, the more adequate the theory. Such fruitfulness prevents a theory from being merely an ad hoc explanation. Such fruitfulness is also retrospective to the extent that it is better able to help organize, integrate, and explain the past data and phenomena.

Recently, Ernan McMullin, a philosopher of science, has compared a scientist's development of a theory to a poet's development of a metaphor.[202] The poet develops the metaphor not by implication but by suggestions. The metaphor explores what is not well understood in advance, and through creative suggestion, it illumines past, present, and future experience. In my opinion, the situation is analogous for theology. Theological theory advances not simply by implication or correlation, but rather through the creative suggestion by which the experience of the community's past, present, and future is illuminated. Theological reflection advances when it offers creative metaphors that enable the community to carry forth and reconstruct its tradition in relation to its ongoing experience.

Illative Sense ◉ The idea of retroductive warrants from experience can also be illustrated by John Henry Newman's notion of an illative sense.[203] This notion of the illative sense in particular influenced twentieth-century Roman Catholic fundamental theology (especially Rahner and Lonergan).[204] With his notion of the illative sense, Newman anticipated much of the contemporary neopragmatic and hermeneutic critique of an abstract conception of reason or of a strictly formal conception of method and rational argumentation. Modern pragmatic philosophers have criticized a Cartesian type of foundationalism that starts from absolute doubt. The illative sense represented Newman's attempt to criticize abstract starting points and steer a middle path between reducing religion to a matter of emotion or sentiment and reducing argumentation to a formal logical or deductive reasoning. He drew on Aristotle's notion of prudent practical judgment (*phronesis*) to illustrate a type of knowledge that he called the illative sense. This illative sense, however, has a theoretical dimension that goes beyond Aristotle's limitation of prudential knowledge to practical knowledge.[205] The detective, the farmer, and the scholar make judgments based on their reflective intuitions. These judgments are related to their experience and character.

Religious judgments are similar to moral judgments. They are not simply the outcome of abstract logic, but result from practical reasoning. Just as practical reason is based on a learned experience, so too does a link exist between moral knowledge and ethical experience. The illative sense is therefore linked to the character and experience of individuals that affect the

---

202. Ernan McMullin, "The Motive for Metaphor," *Proceedings of the American Catholic Philosophical Association* 55 (1982): 27–39; idem, "A Case for Scientific Realism," in *Scientific Realism*, ed. Jarrett Leplin (Berkeley: University of California Press, 1984), 8–40, esp. 26–35.

203. John Henry Newman, *An Essay in Aid of a Grammar of Assent* (Oxford: Clarendon, 1985), esp. chs. 8–10.

204. See Thomas J. Norris, *Newman and His Theological Method* (Leiden: Brill, 1977); Avery Dulles, *Newman* (New York: Continuum, 2002).

205. Gerard Verbeecke, "Aristotelian Roots of Newman's Illative Sense," in *Newman and Gladstone Centennial Essays*, ed. James D. Bastable (Dublin: Veritas, 1978), 177–95.

beginning, process, and conclusion of reasoned and considered judgments. In short, practical experience determines what persons become; it affects not only who they are but also their whole process of reasoning, ranging from the selection of principles to the mode of argumentation, to the construction of conclusions.

Hermeneutical Role of the Oppressed ⊚ The determinations of reasoning by character and experience—determinations illustrative of the illative sense—receive a concrete specification in the various theologies of liberation. Liberation theology attributes a hermeneutical significance to the experience of the oppressed. This experience of oppression affects how the tradition is read, interpreted, and applied. The experience of oppression serves as a retroductive warrant in that it challenges that which is often taken as a matter of course; it provides a view of history from the underside of history; and it suggests new readings and applications of the tradition.[206]

Two examples can illustrate the retroductive and retrospective character of the experience of oppression. The first example has been brought to the fore by feminist theology. Classical theology always emphasized the transcendence of God to all human categories, and it developed theories of analogy that relativized the application of human categories of God, as, for example, when the Fourth Lateran Council affirmed that in every similarity between God and creature, the dissimilarity is even greater.[207] Nevertheless, in popular Christian religious imagery, male language and metaphors have outweighed female metaphors to express God. This popular practice has been philosophically justified by linking male paternity with God's creativity insofar as male paternity has been viewed as the principle of creativity. Today, due to the impact of feminist theology, we are beginning to retrieve nonmale and nonpatriarchal images of God from the Scriptures and from classical attributions.[208] The experience of women is thereby serving as a retroductive warrant for the retrieval, reconstruction, and construction of myriad images of the incomprehensible God. Another significant event for Christianity has been the Holocaust.[209] For centuries, the Christian tradition distinguished its Christian identity from Jewish identity with language, metaphors, and arguments that were often negative and often fed into anti-Judaism or anti-Semitism. The experience of the Holocaust serves as a retroductive warrant propelling Christians to understand their identity in a way that is neither hostile nor degrading to Jews.

Indirect Method ⊚ With reference to Newman's illative sense, Karl Rahner has introduced in fundamental theology the notion of an "indirect method."[210] While acknowledging the importance of historical arguments, Rahner argues that historical arguments need to be

---

206. See Lee Cormie, "The Hermeneutical Privilege of the Oppressed," *Catholic Theological Society of America, Proceedings* 33 (1978): 155–81.

207. Denzinger-Schönmetzer, *Enchiridion symbolorum*, 806: "because it is not possible to affirm a similarity between creator and creature without affirming an even greater dissimilarity" (my translation).

208. Elizabeth Johnson, "The Incomprehensibility of God and the Image of God Male and Female," *Theological Studies* 45 (1984): 441–65; idem, *She Who Is* (New York: Crossroad, 1992); idem, *Quest for the Living God* (New York: Continuum, 2007). For a systematic retrieval of the images of God as mother, lover, and friend in a linguistic, constructive, and pragmatic theological approach, see Sallie McFague, *Models of God: Theology for an Ecological, Nuclear Age* (Philadelphia: Fortress, 1987).

209. See Johann Baptist Metz, *The Emergent Church*, 17–33.

210. Rahner, *Foundations of Christian Faith*, 8–10, 346–68.

supplemented by an indirect method. Such an indirect method appeals in part to formal transcendental considerations and in part to practical experience. A Christian moves from what he or she experiences as a Christian back to a consideration of particular historical beliefs. The indirect method presupposes that the criteria of theological argument are not simply historical or inductive or deductive, but also have a practical experiential dimension. Though more elusive than induction or historical arguments, such an approach moves from Christian experience and practice to an interpretation of one's community and tradition. This indirect method is for Rahner a decision of practical reason directed toward the presence of God in the contingencies of history.[211]

THEOLOGY AND THE COMMUNITY OF THE CHURCH

These diverse dimensions of retroductive warrants show that theology is a theoretical-practical discipline. It entails prudential and considered judgments. These prudential judgments have a basis not only in tradition, but also in an ongoing experience. The plurality of criteria, the practical dimension of experience, and the prudential character of judgments lead to a final consideration: Whose judgments? The question of theological method is not simply a question of academic expertise or individual opinion. Theology relates to a community—a community of discourse and of faith.[212]

Roman Catholicism has a long tradition that points out the relation between the discipline of theology and the community of the church. This venerable tradition affirms that Roman Catholic theology, to be genuinely Roman Catholic, should be "catholic" (that is, universal) and should stand in accord with the bishop of Rome. Roman Catholic identity has been defined in terms of "catholicity" and in terms of unity with the bishop of Rome. This tradition indeed affirms both as intertwined. For an individual, community, theologian, or theological school to separate from communion with the bishop of Rome means detachment from the Roman Catholic Church and thereby loss of the individual's or group's catholicity.

The importance of communion with the bishop of Rome is often translated into the affirmation of obedience to the Roman magisterium. Though such an affirmation expresses a central affirmation of Roman Catholicism, it does not, if taken by itself, totally encompass the relation between the discipline of theology and the community of church or the nature of theology itself. Such a view needs to be complemented by other considerations: the nature of the magisterium within the church; the possibility of dissent and free speech within the church; and the methodological question of how the magisterium itself does theology.[213] Since the first and second issues are treated below in Avery Dulles's chapter on faith and revelation and in Michael Fahey's chapter on the church, the focus here will be on the third issue.

As regards theological method, the issue of the relation to the magisterium involves the complementary and indeed basic methodological

---

211. Rahner seeks to bring Newman's illative sense in relation to Ignatius of Loyola's theology of decision. See "Reflections on a New Task for Fundamental Theology," in *Theological Investigations* (New York: Crossroad, 1979), 16:156–66.

212. See Francis Schüssler Fiorenza, "Foundations of Theology: A Community's Tradition of Discourse and Practice," *Proceedings of the CTSA* 41 (1986): 107–34.

213. For a helpful treatment of the magisterium, see Francis Sullivan, *Magisterium: Teaching Authority in the Catholic Church* (New York: Paulist, 1983).

62 question: How does the magisterium do theology? To the extent that the tradition is challenged by new background theories, by new experiences, and by the emergence of conflicts within the tradition itself, a fundamental methodological question is: How should the magisterium itself meet these challenges, and how does it meet them? For example, in the nineteenth century, the growing acceptance of theories of evolution and the increasing influence of Darwinian views appeared to challenge traditional beliefs about the divine creation of humans. Theories of evolution appeared, at first glance, to discredit the biblical accounts of the creation of the first human couple. They also appeared to invalidate the Aristotelian teleological accounts of human nature and to challenge the specific "dignity" of human nature. Over the past half century, except in certain biblicist or fundamentalist circles, Roman Catholic teaching has shifted away from rejecting theories of evolution. It has acknowledged the diverse literary genres and traditions in the composition of Genesis, and it has sought to integrate Christian belief in divine creation with a theory of evolution and with a historical-critical analysis of the biblical texts.

The shift took place across several fronts: an increasing influence of scientific theories about the evolution of the human race, the increasing acceptance of the applicability of literary forms to an understanding of the Genesis accounts, and the increasing replacement of Aristotelian biology and its notion of teleology by other philosophical and biological conceptions of human nature. Within Roman Catholic theology, the influence of Teilhard de Chardin and Karl Rahner enabled Roman Catholics to understand evolution in a way that was not reductionistic but ennobling. It enabled them to combine a belief in divine creation with a conviction about evolution. At first, some of these attempts were resisted. The Vatican's Pontifical Biblical Commission moved from a cautious, if not negative, stance toward the historical-critical method toward a more positive acceptance. This shift contributed in part to a reinterpretation of the tradition that enabled bringing together new scientific background theories about human origin with the Christian faith in creation. Such an example shows that any account of theology and theological method should include and explain how changes (entailing discontinuity along with continuity) take place within the church, both within official magisterial statements and within the church in general. This broader problem underlies the sensitive and difficult ecclesiological question of the role of a teaching office within the church. It is a distinct, even if not completely separate, issue from that of the nature of authority within the church.

One of the best-known Roman Catholic church historians of the twentieth century, Hubert Jedin, an expert on the Council of Trent, offers a helpful survey and typology of models of how the exercise of theology and the exercise of the teaching office or magisterium de facto existed throughout the history of Roman Catholicism. By describing five historically different models of the exercise of the teaching office within the history of the Roman Catholic Church, Jedin highlights historical facts often neglected, and he suggests that the Roman Catholic community should strive to avoid the one-sidedness and possible weaknesses within each of these historical models.[214]

214. Hubert Jedin, "Theologie und Lehramt," in Remigus Bäumer, ed., *Lehramt und Theologie im 16. Jahrhundert* (Münster: Aschendorff, 1976), 7–21.

1. During the classical period of early Christianity, the leading theologians were bishops, with few major exceptions (Tertullian, Origen, and Clement of Alexandria). In the West, the bishop-theologians were Ambrose and Augustine; in the East, Basil the Great, Gregory of Nazianzus, Gregory of Nyssa, John Chrysostom, and Cyril of Alexandria. The teaching authority was exercised individually and through episcopal synods and ecumenical councils.

2. In the early Middle Ages, the controversy about transubstantiation in the case of Berengar of Tours provided a typical example of the magisterial judgment and decision making in regard to doctrinal issues. First, local synods in Paris (1051) and Tours (1054) evaluated and rejected Berengar's understanding of the Eucharist. Then the case was referred to the bishop of Rome, and the case was discussed by the Roman synod. Finally, the case was referred to the Fourth Lateran Council, as the largest and most universal synod. There were three stages: local synod, Roman synod, and the council as universal synod called and directed by the pope.

3. In the fourteenth and fifteenth centuries, the significant role of university faculties of theology is evident. As Jedin notes, "In the late middle ages, the theological faculties of the universities exercise quite clearly magisterial functions, especially the faculty of the Sorbonne. They condemn theological errors that are known to them or brought before them."[215] Since Pope Innocent III, canons of general councils obtained the power of law only when they were given to the faculties of law and made the subject matter of instruction.[216] Not only did the university theology faculties exercise a teaching office within

the church, but they were corporatively invited to councils along with bishops and abbots. At the Council of Constance, doctors of theology and of canon law were incorporated with voting rights. A concrete illustration of the significance of their right to vote is the Council of Basel. In the vote of December 1436, cardinals and bishops represented less than one-tenth of the voting members.

4. The practice of the Council of Trent provides another model. Theologians were invited to the council by the pope, by the bishops, by superior generals of the religious orders, or by civil rulers (the emperor and the kings of Spain and France). As a general council, Trent had to have representatives of the Christian laity, hence the invitations by the "Christian Princes." In the third session (1561), the earlier medieval practice was followed in that the universities (Louvain, Cologne, and Ingolstadt) were invited as official representatives to Trent. Yet at Trent, many of the bishops, especially the Italian and Spanish bishops, were educated theologians and were influenced by the humanist movement. This was especially true of Italian and Spanish bishops who were members of religious orders.

5. A final model is illustrated by the First and Second Vatican Councils. Here no university faculty of theology was corporatively invited as in the medieval period or as at Trent. The bishops were the voting members, and theologians were present primarily as advisers to the bishops.

Jedin's brief survey shows how the tradition and practice of the Catholic church throughout its history have varied. Today one often encounters one-sided views: Only bishops are teachers

215. Ibid., 12.

216. Knut Wolfgang Nörr, "Päpstliche Dekretalen und römisch-kanonischer Zivilprozess," Walter Wilhelm, ed., *Studien zur europäischen Rechtsgeschichte* (Frankfurt: Klostermann, 1972), 53–65.

64

within the church. Or: Only academic theologians have expertise. The tradition of the Catholic Church has been much broader and more varied. Today, when the task of theology has become so complex, the questions so varied, the problems so pressing, it is important that the voices of diverse faithful within the church be heard and have a rightful impact upon the decision making within the church.

Transitioning to the Twenty-First Century

Whereas Vatican II invoked the image of the church's opening its windows to let in the fresh air of modernity, in the post–Vatican II period, Roman Catholic theology has increasingly faced and sought to engage the criticisms of modernity. Moreover, even though the Second Vatican Council is often reproached for being too open to modernity, it should not be overlooked that it was in fact also critical of modernity. For example, *Gaudium et spes* highlighted the discrepancy between the modern advances in science and technology and the increasing growth of poverty and exploitation.[217] It attacked the growing disparity between the rich and the poor. The post–Vatican II period, however, can be characterized by increased tensions between the calls for further modernization and the criticisms of the very process of modernization.[218] These tensions have become increasingly intensified as the debate has continued among the contrasting directions and opposing views of how theology and the church should go forward. One could say that, on the one hand, there are the diverse liberation theologies, the postcolonial theories, the avant-garde of some postmodern philosophical currents, and the increased awareness of religious and cultural pluralism. On the other hand, there is also the restorationist reaction to modernity and the return to more classical resources and attitudes. But even this contrast is complex. Postcolonial theories bring to the fore the exploitative nature of modernity and therefore seek to accentuate voices and experiences that have been neglected not only in the tradition of the past, but also within the modern West.

The term *postmodern* is often used to interpret these shifts. It remains a popular but ambiguous term that refers to quite distinct attitudes. One direction accentuates the critical aspects of modernity (e.g., Marx's critique of capitalism, Nietzsche's critique of morality, and Freud's analysis of culture). This direction sees postmodernity as an extension of certain critical aspects of modernity and underscores the pluralism of modernities. A contrasting direction highlights the importance of the premodern and the traditional. "Postmodernity" originally emerged as a contrast image to "modernity." The term was used in architecture as a contrast to the formal and functional architecture of modernism. It has become extended to include social and economic theories that have criticized theories of modernization.[219] Where-

---

217. Francis Schüssler Fiorenza, "*Gaudium et spes* and Human Rights," in *The Church and Human Freedom: Forty Years after Gaudium et spes*, ed. Darlene Fozard Weaver (Villanova: Villanova University Press, 2006), 38–65.

218. John W. O'Malley, *What Happened at Vatican II* (Cambridge: Harvard University Press, 2008); Ormond Rush, *Still Interpreting Vatican II: Some Hermeneutical Principles* (Mahwah, NJ: Paulist, 2004).

219. Jean-François Lyotard, *Postmodern Condition: Report on Knowledge* (Minneapolis: University of Minnesota Press, 1984); idem, *The Differend: Phrases in Dispute* (Minneapolis: University of Minnesota Press, 1983); idem, *The Postmodern* (Minneapolis: University of Minnesota Press, 1992).

as developmental theories advocated that Third World countries should "modernize" in order to become more like Western European countries, postmodern theories critically note the degree to which such modernization theories stripped these countries of their cultural traditions and resources. The critique of modernity, therefore often goes hand in hand with a critique of modern European colonialism.

The theological attempts to appropriate postmodern trends for the understanding of theological method have taken diverse and distinctive paths across diverse Christian traditions.[220] In the United States, Hans Frei and George Lindbeck have advocated a "postliberal" direction that has come to be called "the Yale School."[221] Strongly influenced by Karl Barth's criticism of natural theology and the analogy of being, this school criticizes the universalism of transcendental theology, especially as represented in the work of Bernard Lonergan and Karl Rahner. Whereas George Lindbeck advocates a cultural linguistic approach to theology, Hans Frei underscores a thick description of a community's practices and the plain use of scripture.[222] In England, John Milbank has spearheaded a movement called Radical Orthodoxy, which is critical of modernity. He traces the roots of its error back to Duns Scotus. His theology advances a Neo-Platonic theory of participation, retrieves the Eastern fathers, and seeks a radical integration of nature and grace.[223]

Within Roman Catholic theology, the engagement with the postmodern takes a different turn than either the Yale School or Radical Orthodoxy. While this engagement shares in some of the basic criticisms of modernity, it seeks to counter the relativism and particularism of some postmodern theologies. For example, in contrast to Lindbeck, Pope John Paul II strongly advocates universal values in the way he links faith and reason.[224] Ratzinger's advocacy of natural law in the defense of the universality of human rights takes a much more favorable attitude toward natural law than is found in either Karl Barth or in Radical Orthodoxy.[225] His advocacy of a correlation between faith and reason represents a distinctively Roman Catholic approach

---

220. Kevin J. Vanhoozer, ed., *Cambridge Companion to Postmodern Theology* (New York: Cambridge University Press, 2003).

221. George Lindbeck, *The Nature of Doctrine: Religion and Theology in a Postliberal Age*, 25th anniversary ed. (Louisville: Westminster John Knox, 2009); Hans W. Frei, *Types of Christian Theology* (New Haven: Yale University Press, 1992). See Mike Higton, *Christ, Providence, and History: Hans W. Frei's Public Theology* (New York: T&T Clark, 2004).

222. For criticisms of this direction, see Francis Schüssler Fiorenza, "The Cosmopolitanism of Roman Catholic Theology and the Challenge of Cultural Particularity," *Horizons* 35 (Fall 2008): 298–320; idem, "From Interpretation to Rhetoric: The Feminist Challenge to Systematic Theology," in *Walk in the Ways of Wisdom*, ed. Shelly Matthews, Cynthia Briggs Kittredge, and Melanie Johnson Debaufre (Philadelphia: Trinity, 2003), 17–45; idem, "Systematic Theology and Hermeneutics," in *Between the Human and the Divine: Philosophical and Theological Hermeneutics*, ed. Andrzeij Wiercinksi (Toronto: Hermeneutics Press, 2002), 510–30.

223. John Milbank, Catherine Pickstock, and Graham Ward, *Radical Orthodoxy: A New Theology* (New York: Routledge, 1999); and the critical assessment by W. J. Hankey and Douglas Hedley, *Deconstructing Radical Orthodoxy: Postmodern Theology, Rhetoric, and Truth* (Burlington, VT: Ashgate, 2005).

224. John Paul II, *Veritatis splendor* (August 6, 1993), http://www.vatican.va/holy_father/john_paul_ii/encyclicals/documents/hf_jp-ii_enc_06081993_veritatis-splendor_po.html.

225. Pope Benedict XVI, Address to the General Assembly of the United Nations Organization, New York, April 18, 2008, http://www.vatican.va/holy_father/benedict_xvi/speeches/2008/april/documents/hf_ben-xvi_spe_20080418_un-visit_en.html.

66 to theology and ethics, as does his critique of relativism.[226]

The contrasting trends within post–Vatican II Roman Catholic theology involve a decentering of subjectivity through aesthetics and phenomenology; the critique of methodological objectivism; the appeal to memory, tradition, and interruption against a progressive understanding of history; the relevance of lived experience and spirituality in relation to academic approaches; and a move from an individualistic to a dialogical understanding of truth.

Decentering Subjectivity: Aesthetics and Phenomenology

The modern focus on epistemology (theory of knowledge) and on religious experience or religious consciousness as the starting point of theology has been characterized as the anthropocentric turn toward the human subject.[227] The reaction has been to shift the focus to the object of theology through a turn toward aesthetics and phenomenology. Though this appeal had been already present, as the work of Hans Urs von Balthasar documents, in the decades following the council, his influence has increased, just as the influence of phenomenology has grown especially through the writings of Pope John Paul II and Jean-Luc Marion.

The turn toward aesthetics involves two goals. The first implies a specific view of aesthetics in which the beauty and action of the object is emphasized as taking hold of and captivating the human person. This view highlights the degree to which the object of theology should determine and influence human subjectivity. The second goal is directed against a specific interpretation of modernity as a secularization that views nature as having become disenchanted and desocialized.[228] Max Weber identifies this disenchantment of the world with two sources: the scientific revolutions of the sixteenth and seventeenth centuries and the disciplinary practices within Calvinist theology that prefigured the development of capitalism. An aesthetic view of the world seeks to reclaim the world from its disenchantment against theologies of secularization. It notes that ability to wonder at the beauty and sublimity of the world is a central presupposition for a Christian understanding and practice of sacramental life.

Hans Urs von Balthasar's advocacy of aesthetics is paradigmatic for this approach within theology in that his view of aesthetics seeks to undercut a subject-centered theology.[229] For this reason, the influence of his theology has grown in the past two decades. Just as Karl Barth has criticized modern Protestant theology for its anthropocentricism, so too has Hans Urs von Balthasar criticized similar tendencies within Roman Catholic theology. *Love Alone Is Credible* criticizes Karl Rahner's anthropocentric turn and objects that the openness to modern secularity and humanism overlooks the mediation points between immanence and transcendence. It thereby weakens the sensitivity for the transcendence of the divine.[230]

---

226. See also Joseph Ratzinger, *Truth and Tolerance: Christian Belief and World Religions* (San Francisco: Ignatius, 2004).

227. For an attempt to link the notion of freedom in Karl Rahner with postcolonial thought, see Susan Abraham, *Identity, Ethics, and Nonviolence in Postcolonial Theory* (New York: Palgrave Macmillan, 2007).

228. Charles Taylor, *A Secular Age* (Cambridge, MA: Harvard University Press, 2007).

229. See Edward T. Oakes and David Moss, eds., *The Cambridge Companion to Hans Urs von Balthasar* (New York: Cambridge University Press, 2004).

230. Hans Urs von Balthasar, *Love Alone Is Credible* (San Francisco: Ignatius, 2004).

Von Balthasar's theological method itself is complex and incorporates complementary imperatives. (1) He consistently maintains the importance of the analogy of being in relation to the analogy of faith and that at the same time underscores the centrality of the Christian faith as an interpretation of the form of reality. (2) His theological method, therefore, does not echo Barth's critique of the Roman Catholic affirmation of natural theology. Instead, it gives fundamental theology its significant place but underscores the importance of ascetic development of the spiritual senses and an aesthetics experience. (3) Finally, criticizing the neglect of the aesthetics within modern theology, especially modern Protestant theology, von Balthasar develops his distinctive aesthetic theory and shows its importance for the understanding of theology, as well as for Christian and sacramental life.[231]

His major work has a tripartite structure in which aesthetics is complemented by drama and by logic. The theological aesthetics is followed by a theo-drama and by a theo-logic. Each set of volumes is correlated with the transcendentals (i.e., the attributes of all being): Beauty, Goodness, and Truth.[232] As von Balthasar notes, "Our trilogy, presenting a theological aesthetics, dramatics, and logic, is built from within this mutually illuminating light. What one calls the properties of Being that transcend every individual being (the 'transcendentals') seem to give the most fitting access to the mysteries of Christian theology."[233] The theological aesthetics underscores the objective that theology should see the form of God's self-disclosure. The dramatics deals with action, seeing the link between the divine and human action. The mystical and existential knowledge of God and response in freedom are witnesses to God's prior initiative and action. The logic in the theo-logic is not an abstract logic but seeks to display the logic of Christian reality through the Christian living witness to incarnation and through the presence of the Spirit.

A similar decentering of the subject and turn toward the object is evident in the renewed influence of the method of phenomenology within contemporary French Roman Catholic theology. Jean-Luc Marion speaks of the "givenness" of the object with the category of "saturated phenomenon." In talking about God without being, he seeks to think of God after onto-theo-logy.[234] This post-metaphysical thinking of God takes up Heidegger's critique of Western metaphysics and its conception of God. It seeks to avoid the idols of being and of subjectivity in dealing with the God question.[235] Jean-Yves Lacoste takes Heidegger's notion of being in the world and interprets it with the category of liturgy. Michel Henry understands the Gospels as a phenomenology of Christ and refers to the "auto-affection"

231. John D. O'Connor, "Theological Aesthetics and Revelatory Tension," *New Blackfriars* 89 (2008): 399–417.

232. Hans Urs von Balthasar, *The Glory of the Lord*, 7 vols. (San Francisco: Ignatius, 1982–89); idem, *Theo-Drama: Theological Dramatic Theory*, 5 vols. (San Francisco: Ignatius, 1988–98); idem, *Theo-Logic*, 3 vols. and *Epilogue* (San Francisco: Ignatius, 2004–5)

233. Urs von Balthasar, *Epilogue*, 46.

234. Jean-Luc Marion, *Being Given: Toward a Phenomenology of Givenness; Cultural Memory in the Present* (Stanford: Stanford University Press, 2002); idem, *In Excess: Studies of Saturated Phenomena* (New York: Fordham University Press, 2002); *Reduction and Givenness: Investigations of Husserl, Heidegger, and Phenomenology* (Evanston, IL: Northwestern University Press, 1998).

235. Francis Schüssler Fiorenza, "Being, Subjectivity, and Otherness: The Idols of Gods," in *Questioning God*, ed. John D. Caputo, Mark Dooley, and Michael Scanlon (Indianapolis: University of Indiana Press, 2001), 320–50.

of life.[236] Jean-Louis Chrétien uses phenomenology to appeal to a certain religious solicitation or address made to us in experience.[237] This appropriation of phenomenology within theology has not gone without its critics. Dominique Janicaud considers it an illegitimate appropriation of philosophy. In response, it is argued that Janicaud represents a modernist and even Neo-Scholastic understanding of "pure" philosophy.[238] Any full account of human experience should include religious experience in view of the insight of Henri de Lubac and *la nouvelle théologie* (the new theology), which affirmed that there is not de facto pure human nature and underscored the interrelation of grace and nature. In this respect, both Hans Urs von Balthasar and contemporary French theological phenomenologists follow in the footsteps of *la nouvelle théologie*.

Decentering Method and the Interpretation of Meaning

The modern emphasis on scientific objectivity has led to the emphasis on method in general and to development of the historical-critical method within the study of history and the interpretation of historical documents, including the Scriptures. The twentieth century of Roman Catholic theology saw the gradual acceptance of the historical-critical method not only for the study of the history of Christianity, but also for biblical studies.[239] This critique of method has had a significant impact upon systematic theology.[240] In the wake of Vatican II, a shift has taken place, evident in the discussions about the limits of the historical method. Both the influence of hermeneutics (theories of interpretation) and the retrieval of classical motives have shown that important parallels exist between some insights of contemporary hermeneutics and more classical approaches to the interpretation of Scripture.[241] Hans Georg Gadamer's emphasis that a classic has a claim not just its own age, but on subsequent ages, Paul Ricoeur's stress on the surplus of meaning, and Hans Jauss's development of a reception hermeneutic make possible the retrieval of more traditional models of interpretation. Today there is both an increasing appeal to classical interpretations of Scripture, from Henri de Lubac to Joseph Ratzinger, and a defense of the enduring significance of historical criticism.[242] Whereas historical criticism has

---

236. Michel Henry, *Paroles du Christ* (Paris: Éditions du seuil, 2002); idem, *I Am the Truth: Toward a Philosophy of Christianity: Cultural Memory in the Present* (Stanford: Stanford University Press, 2003); idem, *Phénoménologie de la vie* (Paris: Presses universitaires de France, 2003); Michel Henry and Magali Uhl, *Auto-Donation* (Montpellier: Prétentaine, 2002).

237. Jean-Louis Chrétien, *The Call and the Response* (New York: Fordham University Press, 2004); idem, *Hand to Hand : Listening to the Work of Art* (New York: Fordham University Press, 2003.).

238. Dominique Janicaud, *Phenomenology "Wide Open"* (New York: Fordham University Press, 2005); idem, *Phenomenology and the "Theological Turn"* (New York: Fordham University Press, 2000).

239. For a defense of the historical critical method, see Joseph A. Fitzmyer, *The Interpretation of Scripture: In Defense of the Historical-Critical Method* (New York: Paulist, 2008).

240. For Hans Urs von Balthasar's defense of the critique that his theology lacks method, see his *Theo-Logic*, 2:363–65.

241. For a comparison between classical interpretation and contemporary hermeneutics, see Francis Schüssler Fiorenza, "The Conflict of Hermeneutical Tradition and Christian Theology," *Journal of Chinese Philosophy* 27 (2000): 3–31.

242. Compare Matthew Levering, *Participatory Biblical Exegesis: A Theology of Biblical Interpretation; Reading the Scriptures* (Notre Dame, IN: University of Notre Dame Press, 2008), with Joseph A. Fitzmyer, *The Interpretation of Scripture: In Defense of the Historical Critical Method* (Mahwah, NJ: Paulist, 2008).

the goal of discovering the singular meaning of a text based on a grammatical and linguistic interpretation of the text in relation to its historical context, contemporary hermeneutical theory underscores the surplus meaning of a text with its diverse metaphors and narratives. In this sense, the classical multiple meaning of Scriptures that developed during the medieval period is finding a renewed justification in hermeneutical theory. If historical criticism emphasized the objectivity of interpretation to the exclusion of the interpreter's subjectivity, contemporary hermeneutics points to the importance of the interpreter's pre-understanding and social location in the interpretation of texts.[243] Hence, the ancient understanding of pre-understanding (underscored by Augustine's teaching about spiritual purification and ascent) finds its correspondence in the personal orientation toward the question to be posed to the text. If historical criticism emphasized that the text's meaning is located within its conception, hermeneutics underscores that the meaning of the text transcends its context and makes a claim on the present. The distinction between a biblical scholar explaining what a text meant and a systematic theologian asking "What should be the meaning today?" falls by the wayside.[244] The tension between historical criticism and other modes of interpretation presents one of the ongoing challenges of theological method today.

Decentering Progress: Tradition and Memory as Interruption

One of the hallmarks of modernity has been the emphasis on progress, especially through scientific method and technological advance. This understanding of progress has come increasingly under critique. The Frankfurt School's critique of the positivism and scientism of the Enlightenment had argued that its critique of mythology and advocacy of the progress of science had in turn produced a new myth, namely, the myth that science and technology by themselves inevitably lead to progress and happiness.[245] The critique of this myth of progress has been explicitly taken up and developed in various directions.

Johann Baptist Metz makes the memory of suffering central to his theology. The Gospels contain the "dangerous memory" of the death and resurrection of Jesus. Such a memory interrupts history insofar as it brings to the fore the injustice within history and expresses a solidarity with the victims of injustice within history. Metz criticizes the theologians of the preceding generation who lived through the Holocaust yet did not make it a central or even explicit aspect of their theologies.[246] Metz's emphasis on memory of suffering is not only critical of the church's response to the Holocaust within the twentieth century, but is also a critique of viewing history as progressive. The appeal to the memory of

---

243. Francis Schüssler Fiorenza, "The Conflict of Hermeneutical Tradition," specifically 22–24.

244. Elisabeth Schüssler Fiorenza, *Bread Not Stone,* especially the critique of the distinction between what a text meant and means today as employed by Krister Stendhal and Raymond E. Brown. See also her *Rhetoric and Ethic: The Politics of Biblical Studies* (Minneapolis: Fortress Press, 1999).

245. Max Horkheimer, and Theodor W. Adorno, *Dialectic of Enlightenment* (New York: Herder and Herder, 1960).

246. Johannes Baptist Metz, *Memoria Passionis: Ein Provozierendes Gedächtnis in Pluralistischer Gesellschaft* (Freiburg im Breisgau: Herder, 2006). Helmut Peukert, *Science, Action, and Fundamental Theology* (Cambridge: MIT, 1994) has applied Metz's understanding of the memory of victims of injustice to fundamental theological questions. For a development of Metz's notion of interruption in terms of contemporary concerns, see Lieven Boeve, *God Interrupts History: Theology in a Time of Upheaval* (New York: Continuum, 2007).

70

suffering underscores the inadequacy of views of history that take Darwin's evolutionary biology as a pattern for the understanding of history and thereby understand social history as progressive. Such a view does not take into account the injustices of history. The emphasis on memory and interruption is a corrective to any political theology that justifies present political power relations and sees history as unfolding only in a progressive fashion.

Ratzinger decenters the progressive understanding of modernity in several ways. He explicitly takes over the critique or dialectic of the Enlightenment that the early Frankfurt School (Adorno and Horkheimer) had elaborated—namely, that the critique of myth and the positivist scientific method turns in on itself and makes this method into a myth itself.[247] Ratzinger focuses his critique specifically on what he considers a modern approach to truth and understanding. Within modernity, the traditional equation of truth and being has been replaced by an empirical focus on "facts." Facts are what we can know through scientific method and through historical method. Moreover, the turn toward technical thinking sets as paradigmatic a method that combines mathematics and devotion to facts in terms of experiment.[248]

The question of progress and tradition becomes central within Ratzinger's interpretation of Vatican II. On the one hand, he acknowledges that Vatican II has made irreversible progress in going beyond and correcting Pius X's *Syllabus of Errors*. The constitution on religious freedom clearly moves beyond Pius X's collection of errors. On the other hand, he interprets the contribution of Vatican II primarily as a renewal through *ressourcement* (that is, as an appropriation of the best within the tradition), rather than as a progressive innovation. Whereas the former approach interprets Vatican II primarily in continuity with the tradition, the latter emphasizes the innovation and the discontinuity. Ratzinger argues against an interpretation of the Second Vatican Council that divides the texts into two parts—an acceptable progressive part versus an unacceptable old-fashioned part, an acceptable ecclesiology versus a traditional, unacceptable ecclesiology. This becomes clear when one examines how in the Vatican II documents the concept of *communio* is united the understanding of the church and that of the Eucharist.

Decentering Elites: Lived Experience and Spiritual Practices

Historically, theological reflection has taken place and takes place in diverse social and personal contexts: the pastoral activity of the bishop in antiquity, the prayerful life of the monk, the academic discipline of the university, from the medieval to the modern, the contemplative experience of the mystic, and the lived experiences of believers in everyday life. In each context, believing Christians reflect on the meaning of their faith in relation to their lives and activities. Their reflection can be considered a form of theological reflection. However, the more systematic, methodic, and conceptual activity as exercised in the universities has come to be paradigmatic for theological reflection to the detriment of other ways. Too often, the academic conception of theology has neglected other ways of theology.

---

247. See also his debate with Habermas in Jürgen Habermas and Joseph Ratzinger, *The Dialectics of Secularization* (San Francisco: Ignatius, 2005).

248. Joseph Ratzinger, *Introduction to Christianity* (New York: Seabury, 1969), 57–79.

Moreover, such an awareness affects not only theology, but also philosophy. It has become evident through more recent studies that philosophy in antiquity was not understood as abstract method or conceptual discipline, but rather represented a way of life and a discovery of one's self. The philosopher was much more a spiritual adviser than a professor. He exhorted his students to mold themselves through a conversion of attention and through spiritual exercises to follow the paths of wisdom. As Pierre Hadot has noted, the discourse on the transcendent and the spiritual experience of the transcendent, sought in antiquity in philosophy as well as theology to foster a new way of life that required a transformation of the self.[249] In the medieval period, the distinction between the monastic and scholastic approaches has been a constant theme of scholarship that underscored the importance of lived experience, devotion, and spirituality.[250]

Today the emergence of the academic study of religion in the university in the form of religious studies has created a tension that highlights both sides. On the one hand, there has emerged a positivistic understanding of religious studies as an objective discipline that aims for a purely neutral study that precludes any subjective pre-understanding and commitments.[251] It seeks a vision of religious studies that in distinction to other humanistic studies in the universities celebrates its neutrality and objectivity.[252] On the other hand, the emergence of ethnographic studies, participatory sociology, and engaged anthropology has underscored the importance of taking the participants' view of their actions into account in interpreting them. In this view, the academic study of religion entails a study of the lived experiences of the diverse members and groups of a religious community. The study of popular religious practices and rituals, as well as the narratives and lives of the saints, becomes central not only for the study of religions, but these practices and rituals also become sources of theology.[253]

Decentering Individualism: Dialogical Communities of Discourse

The individualism is counterbalanced by dialogical and communal understanding of truth that emphasizes the significance of communities of discourse. The modern approach to philosophy and theology is often associated with Descartes's appeal to consciousness, Kant's appeal to the subject's conditions of knowledge, and Schleiermacher's emphasis on religious experience. This starting with individual consciousness or with religious experience is often interpreted in an individualistic fashion and in a foundational sense, in that an individual's experience provides certitude. Descartes's starting point

---

249. Pierre Hadot, *Philosophy as a Way of Life: Spiritual Exercises from Socrates to Foucault*, ed. Arnold Ira Davidson (New York: Blackwell, 1995).

250. Jean Leclercq, *The Love of Learning and the Desire for God: A Study of Monastic Culture* (London: SPCK, 1978).

251. Francis Schüssler Fiorenza, "Religious and Theological Studies: The Contest of the Faculties," in *Shifting Boundaries: Contextual Approaches to the Structure of Theological Education*, ed. Barbara Wheeler and Edward Farley (Louisville: Westminster John Knox, 1991), 119–49.

252. For a critique, see Francis Schüssler Fiorenza, "Theology in the University," *Bulletin of the Council of Societies for the Study of Religion* 22 (April 1993): 34–39; idem, "Response to Wiebe," *Bulletin of the Council of Societies for the Study of Religion* 23 (April 1994): 6–10.

253. This point has been made by Hans Urs von Balthasar's classic essay, "Theology and Sanctity," now reprinted in *Explorations in Theology*, vol. 1, *The Word Made Flesh* (San Francisco: Ignatius, 1989), 181–210.

for philosophical certitude is often taken as an example, though Schleiermacher's emphasis on the community could serve as a counterexample. Kant thinks that through his analysis of the structures of human cognition, philosophy can achieve a progress similar to that in the natural and mathematical sciences. The Neo-Kantian movement of the early twentieth century sought one-sidedly to reduce Kant's philosophy to a positivistic method of science, to the neglect of what transcended such method in his writing. In reaction, twentieth-century philosophers Martin Buber, Franz Rosenzweig, and Ferdinand Ebner developed a dialogical philosophy and emphasized the I-Thou relationship, and more recently, Emmanuel Levinas placed emphasis on the Other.[254] The Cartesian, "I think, therefore I am" has been replaced with "We exist only in dialogue, and we arrive at truth through dialogue." This dialogical nature of truth has come to expression not only in philosophy but also in theology and ethics—though not without considerable debate. The theological debate concerns the notion of *communio*, the ethical debate concerns a discourse ethics, and the fundamental theological debate concerns the relation between the truth and pluralism.

In theology, the notion of *communio* has become central. The patristic conception is of the church as a *communio* and that we Christians are in communion with each other through our communion with Christ in the Eucharist. The notion of *communio* links local churches not only with other local churches, but also with the past communities. The understanding of *communio*

central to the reflections leading up to Vatican II has in its significance and meaning been at the heart of recent debates.[255] At the twentieth anniversary of the journal *Communio*, Joseph Cardinal Ratzinger reflects on the reception of the Council and suggests that there was a more progressive, in his view, interpretation of the concept of "people of God" as expressing a contrast to hierarchy by emphasizing popular sovereignty and common democratic determination. The notion of *communio* was absorbed into the concept of people of God.[256] The Council brought the notion of *communio* into the forefront not to discard other notions nor to reject the tradition, but instead to integrate *communio* into other understandings of church within the Catholic tradition. This interpretation highlights the importance of relating present understandings of community as *communio* not in opposition to the past, but precisely in communion or in dialogue with the past.

At the same time and in a completely different context, during the last decades the awareness of the importance of community to knowledge and understanding has become central as a result of the linguistic turn and the influence of Wittgenstein's understanding of language on philosophy and theology. This awareness has been sharpened under the influence of Michel Foucault's analysis of the interconnection between power and discourse. His view moves against the binary conception of power of one agent over another agent or group, but shows that power is dispersed through the community. Every community has its set of

---

254. See Samuel Moyn, *Origins of the Other: Emmanuel Levinas between Revelation and Ethics* (Ithaca, NY: Cornell University Press, 2005).

255. See Walter Kasper, *That They May Be One: The Call to Unity Today* (New York: Continuum, 2004). See also Ingolf Dalferth's review of Kasper in *Ecclesiology* 2 (2005): 131–37.

256. Joseph Ratzinger, "*Communio*: A Program," *Communio* 19, no. 3 (1992): 436–49; Hans Urs von Balthasar, "*Communio*—a Program," *Communio* 33 (2006): 153–69.

practices and rules through which meaning and power are mediated.

The understanding of the interconnection among community, knowledge, and power moves in several distinct directions. One direction points to particularity of communities, its experiences, practices, and meanings. This highlights the particular practices and experiences of specific communities and cultures in order to understand their beliefs, values, and claims. Many of the liberation theologies, African American, feminist, Latin American, and Hispanic, take this direction a step further. They point to the experience of a particular community and its culture as illuminating the blind spots of a dominant culture.

Another direction highlights the radical pluralism of knowledge and the significant differences among cultures over against any abstract acknowledgment of universal values, meaning, and truth. In this direction, the experience of particular communities and cultures becomes integral to theological reflection. A third direction points to the role of scientific background knowledge and to the intersection of culture and nature. In this perspective, the unity of nature and the natural environment provides the human race with a basis for unity. Human persons have, despite all cultural differences, some basic similarities. They face sickness, aging, and death. They need food, medicine, and housing. Their housing faces the same laws of gravity and need to offer protections from the hazards of the environment. Peoples of all cultures face dangers from pollution and global warming.

This direction leads many to construct a set of universal rights based on human nature or basic human capabilities.

A position that mediates among these diverse directions is the most helpful and can be expressed by combining the notion of a community of discourse with that of discourse in general. The location of a community within a social-historical context and the interconnection with other communities both become important for fundamental theology, theological method, and ethics. Such a position has to take into account the plurality of cultures and experiences and the necessity of learning from one another. Thus, the particularity of communities exists in relation and in dialogue with other communities. This middle position also underscores the importance of understanding the intersection between the particular discourses and other discourses, and it points to the particularity in a way that one moves beyond particularity insofar as one engages in discourse with other communities.

This pluralism of cultures presents a challenge within Roman Catholic theology and Christian theology, for Christianity exists not across multiple cultures, but within multicultural contexts.[257] In Roman Catholicism, Vatican II is often taken as a watershed. In its wake, as Karl Rahner has argued, Christianity has become a world church.[258] The question of pluralism is often taken as a question of the relation between the individual church and the church as a whole. But the issue of pluralism is much more complex. One aspect of the issue comes to the fore in the debate (for example, between Kasper

257. See Francis Schüssler Fiorenza, "Pluralism: A Western Commodity or Justice for the Other," *Searching Wisdom: Essays in Honor of Wendel Dietrich*, ed. Theodore Vial and Mark Poster (New York: Oxford University Press, 2001), 389–424.

258. Karl Rahner, "The Abiding Significance of the Second Vatican Council," in his *Theological Investigations* (New York: Crossroads, 1981), 20:90–102.

74

and Ratzinger) about the proper role of the unity versus the plurality.[259] A further penetrating debate comes to the fore in the disagreement between von Balthasar and Rahner, wherein von Balthasar seeks to show that the pluralism within the church and theology should be more like the pluralism within a symphony: the various pieces combine to form a unified harmony. Karl Rahner, in contrast, underscores the irreducible nature of pluralism on the cultural level and the positive significance of pluralism within Christianity.[260] Jean-Yves Lacoste contends, "'Theology is a pluralistic discipline by nature. To maintain a plurality of discourses necessarily gives rise to an unstable balance. Were it a merely liturgical discourse, theology would cease to respond to the demands of missionary apologia. Were it merely scientific, it would not respond to the needs of believers' spiritual lives.' What we have here is the recognition that the language of theology consists more of a polyphony."[261]

Conceiving Christian theology and ethics in terms of pluralism invokes an intersubjective theological dialogue with other communities and traditions not only in acknowledging the meaning and truth of other religious traditions, but also in realizing the differences in the relevant background theories and the diverse assessments of the integrity of the tradition in terms of its priorities, paradigms, and relation to lived practice. Theology and ethics practiced

as discourse and dialogue understand not only that we exist in community, but also that our moral obligations stem from our responsibility toward the other and that we stand together a united cosmos and environment. The other as a religious and moral other makes claims on us not only morally, but also intellectually and religiously.

Conclusion

This chapter sought to introduce the nature of theology by presenting a history of the understanding of Christian theology through the centuries, first analyzing three classic paradigms of theology (Augustine, Thomas, and Neo-Scholasticism), then reviewing five contemporary approaches during the last decades of the twentieth century. The elements of these approaches overlap one another. Next, the chapter proposed four elements of a more comprehensive understanding of theology. Finally, the chapter presented new emphases and developments that are apparent as we shift from the twentieth to the twenty-first century.

The task of theology entails a constant challenge to the church as a community of faith and discourse. The challenge is to reconstruct the integrity of the church's tradition in light of relevant background theories and warrants from

---

259. See the debate between Ratzinger and Kasper on the unity of the church versus the pluralism of local communities in Walter Cardinal Kasper, "On the Church," *America* (April 23–30, 2001); and Joseph Cardinal Ratzinger, "The Local Church and the Universal Church: A Response to Walter Kasper," *America* (November 19, 2001).

260. Rahner, *Foundations of Christian Faith*, 367–69. For a comparison between Karl Rahner and George Lindbeck with her own constructive proposal, see Jeannine Hill Fletcher, *Monopoly on Salvation? A Feminist Approach to Religious Pluralism* (New York: Continuum, 2005).

261. Jean-Yves LaCoste, "Theology," in *Encyclopedia of Christian Theology*, ed. idem (New York: Routledge, 2005), 1554–62, quoting from 1561. See also Francis Schüssler Fiorenza, "Changes in Culture and Society and the Interdisciplinarity of Theology," in *Reconsidering the Boundaries between Theological Disciplines*, ed. Michael Welker and Friedrich Schweizer (Münster: LIT, 2005), 201–16.

contemporary experience. Such a task is extremely complex. Bernard Lonergan has noted that it entails a shift from logic to method, and such a shift entails a profound change in consciousness.[262] However, today we are increasingly aware that the shift from logic to method does not suffice. In the decades since Vatican II, it is becoming increasingly clear that the emphasis on method belongs to an academic and scientific approach to theology. It becomes evident that other voices, practices, and discourses need to be attended to. In other words, Lonergan's call for a change in consciousness requires an openness to discourse within the community, heeding not only its past, but also the future. Such a discourse becomes open to the integrity of the past and future when it takes into account the voices of other communities and listens to voices that have not been heard. Theology entails much more than method. It rests on the experiences and discourses of many communities and cultures.

My emphasis on combining retroductive warrants, background theories, the integrity of the tradition, and the catholicity of the church as a community of discourse is not a task that can be simply viewed as a method. It embraces many elements. It seeks to go beyond an understanding of theology as correlation and encourages an understanding of theology that extends beyond the modern focus on method. An adequate theological approach embraces diverse sources, diverse experiences, and a plurality of criteria. It does not simply correlate contemporary questions with traditional answers or symbols. Instead, theological method consists of making

judgments about what constitutes the integrity of the tradition and what is paradigmatic about the tradition. It consists of reflecting on the relevant background theories (both of the tradition and of one's own situation) and taking into account the ongoing practice and experience of the community, as expressed in diverse voices, so that it can be a truly catholic theology.

The shift that is taking place is a move away from method to substantial issues and to issues reflecting the impact that the concrete beliefs and pluralist views are having on theology. The various liberation theologies have called theology to task for failing to reflect on the needs of the poor and disinherited. Postcolonial theology underscores and uncovers the Western and modern biases of much of theology. As Kathryn Tanner has recently noted:

> Such a shift reflected thereby a greater theological respect for the pluralistic world in which we live. Enlightenment challenges to the intellectual credibility of religious ideas could no longer be taken for granted as the starting point for theological work once theologians facing far more pressing worries than academic respectability gained their voices in Europe, the US, and around the globe. Theologians were now called to provide, not so much a theoretical argument for Christianity's plausibility, as an account of how Christianity could be part of the solution, rather than simply part of the problem, on matters of great human moment that make a life-and-death difference to people, especially the poor and the oppressed.[263]

---

262. Lonergan, *A Third Collection*, 3–22.
263. Kathryn Tanner, "Shifts in Theology over the Last Quarter Century," *Modern Theology* 26 (2010): 39–44.

For Further Reading

Histories and Dictionaries of Theology

Beinert, Wolfgang, and Francis Schüssler Fiorenza. *Handbook of Catholic Theology.* English language ed., with new materials. New York: Crossroad, 1995.

> *This one-volume dictionary of systematic theology has been translated from the German and supplemented with some American articles.*

Congar, Yves. *A History of Theology.* Garden City, NY: Doubleday, 1968.

> *A somewhat dated but still valuable introduction to the history of the understanding of theology. It originally appeared as an article in the classic French encyclopedia Dictionnaire de théologie.*

Harnack, Adolf von. *History of Dogma.* 7 vols. New York: Dover, 1961; German ed., 1900.

> *A classic and still informative treatment, though dated. Von Harnack's view of doctrine as a postbiblical, Hellenistic development has been modified by recent work on the Hellenistic period of Judaism.*

Jordan, Mark D. *Ordering Wisdom: The Hierarchy of Philosophical Discourses in Aquinas.* Notre Dame, IN: University of Notre Dame Press, 1986.

> *A collection of the finest studies on Thomas's conception of theology from a leading medievalist. It contains important observations on the rhetorical context of Thomas's work as well as its reception.*

Kerr, Fergus. *Twentieth-Century Catholic Theologians: From Neoscholasticism to Nuptial Mysticism.* Malden, MA: Blackwell, 2007.

> *This survey of some central twentieth-century Catholic theological authors is selective in the choice of theologians. Somewhat Eurocentric in orientation,*

it does consider several important contemporary movements within theology.

Lacoste, Jean-Yves, ed. *Encyclopedia of Christian Theology.* New York: Routledge, 2005.

> *This three-volume English version is the translation of a one-volume French volume of systematic theology. It takes into account contemporary French Catholic theological currents. Jean-Yves Lacoste has also edited Histoire de la théologie (Paris: Éditions du Seuil, 2009), which is an excellent history of Roman Catholic theology. Pierre Gibert has written the biblical section, Patrick Descourtieux the patristic and byzantine section; Marc Ozilou and Gilles Berceville cover the medieval period; and Jean-Yves Lacoste, the editor, covers the sixteenth to twentieth centuries.*

Livingston, James C. *Modern Christian Thought,* vol. 1. James Livingston and Francis Schüssler Fiorenza, *Modern Christian Thought,* vol 2. 2 vols. 2nd ed. Minneapolis: Fortress Press, 2006.

> *This two-volume history of modern Christian theology deals primarily with the nineteenth century (volume 1) and twentieth century (volume 2). The second volume has several chapters on Roman Catholic theology, including Vatican II and its context.*

McBrien, Richard, and Harold W. Attridge. *The HarperCollins Encyclopedia of Catholicism.* New York: HarperCollins, 1995.

> *A comprehensive encyclopedia of Roman Catholicism that is comprehensive in its coverage, brief in its presentation, and written in language easily understood by non-theologians.*

Pelikan, Jaroslav. *The Christian Tradition.* 5 vols. Chicago: University of Chicago Press, 1971–88.

> *A complete and masterful survey. Written as a counterpoint to von Harnack, the volumes take into*

account the role of liturgy and piety as sources of
theology. The annotated bibliography in volume 1, pp.
358–76, provides an important guide.

Rahner, Karl. *Encyclopedia of Theology: The Concise
Sacramentum Mundi*. New York: Crossroad, 1984.
  *Karl Rahner was the editor of the multivolume German
  encyclopedia Lexikon für Theologie und Kirche. This
  volume collects several of Rahner's own essays.*

Nature, Tasks, Divisions, and Method of Theology

Dulles, Avery. *The Craft of Theology: From Symbol to
System*. New York: Crossroad, 1992.
  A collection of essays dealing with the nature of theology.

Ebeling, Gerhard. *The Study of Theology*. Philadelphia:
Fortress Press, 1978.
  *Ebeling, a German Lutheran theologian, proposes a
  conception of theology with attention to the distinct
  disciplines of theology.*

Farley, Edward. *Theologia: The Fragmentation and Unity
of Theological Education*. Philadelphia: Fortress Press,
1983.
  *A historical presentation of the origin of theology's
  division into the fourfold pattern: biblical, historical,
  systematic, and practical.*

Fiorenza, Francis Schüssler. *Foundational Theology: Jesus
and the Church*. New York: Crossroad, 1984.
  *A discussion of the major problems of fundamental
  theology, the resurrection of Jesus, the foundation of
  the church, and the nature of fundamental theology
  with reference to Neo-Scholastic, transcendental,
  hermeneutical, and contemporary approaches to
  theology.*

Jenson, Robert W. *Systematic Theology*. 2 vols. New York:
Oxford University Press, 1997.
  *A two-volume systematic theology from a Lutheran
  perspective.*

Jones, Serene, and Paul Lakeland, eds. *Constructive
Theology: A Contemporary Approach to Classical
Themes*. Minneapolis, Fortress Press, 2005. Print with
CD-ROM.
  *A collaborative attempt of several theologians to present
  systematic theological issues, taking into account both
  historical development and contemporary postmodern
  and postcolonial concerns.*

Kasper, Walter. *The Methods of Dogmatic Theology*.
Shannon, Ireland: Ecclesia, 1969.
  *A booklet that outlines the shift from a Neo-Scholastic
  approach to theology to contemporary and more
  historically oriented approaches.*

Kaufmann, Gordon D. *An Essay on Theological Method*.
AAR Studies in Religion, no. 11. Rev. ed. Missoula,
Mont.: Scholars, 1979.
  *A contemporary reformulation of a liberal Protestant
  understanding of the theological method and the
  constructive task of theology.*

Küng, Hans. *Theology for the Third Millennium*. New
York: Doubleday, 1988.
  *A collection of Küng's essays that deal with the nature of
  theology and theological method.*

Lindbeck, George. *The Nature of Doctrine: Religion and
Theology in a Postliberal Age*. 25th anniversary ed.
Louisville, KY: Westminster John Knox, 2009.
  *This monograph is much more than its title indicates. It
  suggests a cultural linguistic approach to theology over
  against propositional and expressive approaches.*

78 Lonergan, Bernard. *Method in Theology*. New York: Crossroad, 1972.

> *Lonergan explains the significance of human cognitional structures for the use of method within theology and for an eightfold division of disciplines within theology.*

McGrath, Alister E. *Scientific Theology*. 3 vols. Edinburgh: T&T Clark, 2001–3.

> *A three-volume systematic theology subdivided into nature, reality, and theory.*

Metz, Johannes Baptist. *Faith in History and Society: Toward a Practical Fundamental Theology*. New York: Crossroad, 2007.

> *This new translation by Matthew Ashley of Metz's collection of essays illustrates the basic concept of fundamental theology as a practical theology and as a political theology. The introduction and study questions by Ashley are helpful for students.*

Pannenberg, Wolfhart. *Theology and Philosophy of Science*. Philadelphia: Westminster, 1976.

> *Pannenberg, a German Lutheran theologian, presents various conceptions of science and history, a history of conceptions of theology, and his own conception of theology as the history of religion. A sketch of the diverse disciplines of theology is provided.*

Rahner, Karl. *Foundations of Christian Faith*. New York: Seabury, 1978.

> *This book exemplifies Rahner's transcendental fundamental theology as developed in relation to the basic idea of Christianity and the contents of the Christian faith.*

Ratzinger, Joseph. *Principles of Catholic Theology: Building Stones for a Fundamental Theology*. San Francisco: Ignatius, 1987.

> *A collection of Cardinal Ratzinger's essays on Scripture and tradition, church and theology, faith and theology.*

Schleiermacher, Friedrich. *Brief Outline on the Study of Theology*. Atlanta: John Knox, 1966.

> *This classic of Protestantism has had enormous influence on the division of theological disciplines.*

Sobrino, Jon, and Ignacio Ellacuría. *Systematic Theology: Perspectives from Liberation Theology*. Maryknoll, NY: Orbis, 1996.

> *A collection of essays from a large work, Mysterium Liberationis, which was patterned on the first edition of this work.*

Tracy, David. *The Analogical Imagination*. New York: Crossroad, 1981.

> *In this, his first volume, Tracy outlines how the imagination, the use of metaphor, and hermeneutical theory contribute to the theology.*

———. *Plurality and Ambiguity: Hermeneutics, Religion, Hope*. Chicago: University of Chicago Press, 1994.

> *This second volume by Tracy takes into account more recent deconstructive approaches.*

von Balthasar, Hans Urs. *The Glory of the Lord*. 7 vols. San Francisco: Ignatius, 1982–89.
———. *Theo-Drama: Theological Dramatic Theory*. 5 vols. San Francisco: Ignatius, 1988–98.
———. *Theo-Logic*. 3 vols. and *Epilogue*. San Francisco: Ignatius, 2004–5.

> *Von Balthasar's multivolume systematic theology is the culmination of his lifelong work. It exemplifies his basic themes and approaches to theology.*

Faith and Revelation

2

Faith and Revelation

Avery Dulles

It is fundamental to Catholic belief that any salutary relationship to God depends on God's free and gracious manifestation accepted in faith. Described as "the beginning and root of all justification,"[1] faith is seen as an affirmative intellectual response to revelation. Without a prior revelation on God's part, faith would be impossible, for it would have no basis and no object. And without faith, the whole edifice of Christian existence would collapse.

Not only for the Christian life but for theology too, revelation and faith are of constitutive importance. Theology is a disciplined reflection on faith and thus also on revelation. It seeks to serve the church by accurately establishing the contents of revelation, spelling out the theoretical and practical consequences of revelation, critically examining current doctrine and practice in the light of revelation, exhibiting the coherence and credibility of revelation, vindicating the beliefs and practices of the church on the basis of revelation, and refuting views at odds with revelation. Karl Rahner, a representative

contemporary theologian, has declared, "Theology is the science of faith. It is the conscious and methodical explanation and explication of the divine revelation received and grasped in faith."[2] Still more recently, Walter Kasper has described revelation as "the final presupposition, basis, means, and norm of everything that purports to be Christian."[3] The importance of this chapter's theme should therefore be evident.

Revelation

The Concept of Revelation

The word *revelation* (Latin, *revelatio*; Greek, *apocalypsis*) means etymologically the removal of a veil (Latin, *velum*; Greek, *kalymma*), hence, disclosure. The idea that God reveals is pervasive in the Bible and was taken for granted from the dawn of Christianity. Only in the seventeenth century, when rationalists began to deny or minimize revelation, did Christian theologians attempt to define and defend the concept in a

---

1. Council of Trent, Decree on Justification, ch. 8, quoted in H. Denzinger and A. Schönmetzer, eds., *Enchiridion Symbolorum, Definitionum et Declarationum de Rebus Fidei at Morum*, 36th ed. (Freiburg: Herder, 1976), no. 1532. This work will hereafter be cited in the text by the initials DS, followed by the paragraph number.

2. Karl Rahner, "Theology I: Nature," in *Encyclopedia of Theology: The Concise "Sacramentum Mundi*," ed. K. Rahner (New York: Seabury-Crossroad, 1975), 1687.

3. Walter Kasper, "Offenbarung Gottes in der Geschichte. Gotteswort in Menschenwort," in *Handbuch der Verkündigung*, ed. B. Dreher et al. (Freiburg: Herder, 1970), 1:53–96, here 53.

systematic way. Vatican Council I (1869–70) included a chapter on revelation in its Constitution on the Catholic Faith (*Dei filius*; hereafter DF). Here it described revelation as a supernatural manifestation by God "of himself and the eternal decrees of his will"; this manifestation is objectively contained in traditions that come from Christ through the apostles and in Scriptures inspired by the Holy Spirit (DS 3004–6).

Vatican Council II (1962–65), building on the theological probing of several generations since Vatican I, was able to produce a substantial Constitution on Divine Revelation (*Dei verbum*; hereafter DV). Without proposing a strict definition of revelation, the council described it as the action by which God freely makes known the hidden purpose (sacramentum) of the divine will and lovingly speaks to human beings as friends, inviting them "into fellowship with himself" (DV 2). In its chapter on the nature of revelation (chapter 1), *Dei verbum* emphasized the dynamic and interpersonal dimensions. In comparison with Vatican Council I, *Dei verbum* is more personalistic, trinitarian, and christocentric.[4]

The theological concept of revelation, set forth in official church teaching, differs in some respects from current popular usage. In common speech, the word is often applied to a sudden, unexpected disclosure that comes to an individual with exceptional power, depth, and clarity. The Greek word *apocalypsis*, which is the closest equivalent to "revelation" in the Greek Bible, generally refers to an extraordinary psychological experience in which the recipient feels removed from the circumstances of mundane life and transported into a higher world. Theologically, however, revelation does not necessarily involve any such disruption. As we shall see, it can come in a non-ecstatic manner through nature, historical records, current events, and living proclamation. Thus, many biblical terms other than *apocalypsis* may be taken in specific contexts as referring to what modern theology would call revelation. Among them are *logos theou* (Word of God), *phanerosis* (manifestation), *epiphaneia* (appearance), *gnosis* (knowledge), and *aletheia* (truth). We should be on guard against attributing to revelation in the theological sense all the qualities associated with the word in popular usage.

Types of Revelation

To avoid confusion, it is well at the outset to make certain fundamental distinctions. In an *active* or dynamic sense, revelation is the process of God's self-disclosure—a gradual process that extends, as we shall see, over long periods of history. In an *objective* sense, revelation denotes the fund or "deposit" of knowledge, insights, and wisdom resulting from the process just referred to. The fruits of the process, "objectively" contained in Scripture and tradition, are transmitted to believers by education in the church, the living community of faith.

Revelation is said to be *immediate* in the case of persons who receive it directly from God, rather than from other persons who have previously received it. It is *mediate* when passed on from the first recipient to other believers. This distinction should not be made too rigid, since new revelation is normally accorded only to persons who have been prepared for it by the reception of revelation already given, and since the transmission of past revelation may be accompanied by God's present self-manifestation.

---

4. These and other characteristics of Vatican II's theology of revelation are noted by René Latourelle, *Theology of Revelation* (Staten Island, NY: Alba House, 1966), 486–87.

82 A further distinction is between *natural* and *historical* revelation. "Natural" revelation normally means the self-manifestation of God through the regular order of nature as described, for instance, in Paul's sermon at Lystra (Acts 14:15-17). God's self-disclosure through the inner voice of conscience may also be called natural, inasmuch as the law of God is held to be inscribed upon the human heart so that those who have no positive law from God "do by nature what the law requires" (Rom. 2:14; see Vatican II, Pastoral Constitution on the Church in the Modern World [*Gaudium et spes* (hereafter GS)], 16). "Historical" revelation, by contrast, is made to particular individuals and groups through particular events that occur, or have occurred, at special times and places.

The natural revelation described in the preceding paragraph ought to be distinguished, at least conceptually, from the natural knowledge of God obtained by rational inference from created things.[5] Revelation, even when given through nature, is a free and personal self-manifestation of God, calling for the free and personal response of faith. Natural knowledge, in contrast, is an achievement of human reason, which assents necessarily to demonstrative arguments. As we shall see, all revelation, properly so called, is supernatural. Thus, the meaning of natural as opposed to historical should not be confused with the meaning of natural as opposed to supernatural.

It should also be noted that I am concerned in this chapter with *public* revelation, given by God to the whole human race, to an entire people, or to the church as the people of God of the new covenant. I am not concerned with *private* revelation, which may on occasion be given to one or several individuals for some special reason. Public revelation must be communicable to all members of a society and must be certified by signs that make it generally credible. I shall discuss the question of credibility in the second part of this chapter, dealing with faith.

The Modes of Communication

I have already distinguished between natural and historical revelation. Natural revelation is directed in principle to all human beings and may also be called "general." Stating the Catholic position on this point, Vatican Council II asserted, "God, who through the Word creates all things (cf. Jn. 1:3) and keeps them in existence, gives human beings an enduring witness to himself in created realities (see Rom. 1:19-20)" (DV 3). Again, in its Pastoral Constitution on the Church in the Modern World, it declared, "All believers of whatever religion have always heard his [God's] revealing voice [*vocem et manifestationem Eius*] in the discourse of creatures" (GS 36).

Natural revelation is only preliminary. Jews, Christians, and Muslims, among others, hold that God's self-disclosure has occurred more fully and intimately through special events at particular times and places. Historical revelation unfolds in a meaningful sequence of deeds and words, as indicated by Vatican Council II: "This plan of revelation is realized by deeds and words having an inner unity: the deeds wrought by God in the history of salvation manifest and confirm the teaching and realities signi-

---

5. Vatican II in *Dei verbum*, no. 3, refers, as we shall see, to revelation through nature. In *Dei verbum*, no. 6, Vatican II takes up the contrast made by Vatican I in *Die filius* (DS 3004) between revelation and the natural knowledge of God from created things. Thus, Vatican II seems to make a distinction between the natural knowledge of God and revelation through nature.

fied by the words, whereas the words proclaim the deeds and clarify the mystery contained in them" (DV 2).

This sentence needs to be unpacked. On the one hand, the council asserts that revelation is given in historical deeds or facts. The Old and New Testaments are primarily concerned with recounting the great deeds that marked God's self-manifestation to ancient Israel and to the apostles. Central to this history are the events of the exodus (including the Sinai covenant), the conquest of the Holy Land, the exile and return, and in the New Testament, the life, death, and resurrection of Jesus, together with the founding of the Christian church. During the 1940s and 1950s, many Protestant and Catholic scholars, especially biblical theologians, argued for the primacy of deeds or acts over words and concepts as carriers of revelation.

Vatican II, seeking a balanced approach, wisely avoided any dichotomy between deeds and words. Throughout the Bible, the events of salvation history are identified and interpreted by inspired prophets, priests, apostles, and evangelists. Without these highly selective and interpreted accounts, it might not be possible to perceive the revelatory quality of the events themselves. Taken as naked, objective occurrences, the events do not disclose their own divine significance, at least to us, who are unable to reconstruct them in detail. Even to the ancient Israelites, much of their history seemed scarcely reconcilable with the promises made to the patriarchs and kings of old. Only the prophetic interpretation of current events, together with new promises of national restoration, sustained the faith of a pious remnant under conditions of adversity.

We may conclude, then, that "words" in the sense of human language play an essential role in the process of revelation. The words serve to identify the revelatory events, interpret them, preserve their memory, and transmit them together with their saving significance. It may be objected, of course, that the words presuppose that the revelation has already been given and received, for it would not be possible to proclaim what was as yet unknown. The objection rests on a theory according to which thought precedes verbal formulation and expression. In reality, however, thought and formulation develop concurrently, so that our ideas are not mature until we have expressed them, at least to ourselves. Even if, by exception, a revelation were completely imparted before being put into words, it would not at that point be public; it would not have been given to a people as such. I conclude, therefore, that public revelation, even when it first occurs, includes some measure of verbal expression. The original recipients verbalize the revelation to themselves and their community, and this initial verbalization is constitutive of the revelation itself. I shall return to the verbal component in the third part of this chapter, when I consider the transmission of revelation through Scripture and tradition.

External events and spoken or written words, though integral to the process of revelation, are not revelation until their divinely intended meaning is perceived and accepted. For this to happen, they must be apprehended not simply as intramundane phenomena but as self-manifestations of God. They must be seen as communicating God's thoughts and intentions. The primary content of revelation is not some new information about humanity or nature; rather, the primary content is precisely God. To indicate this, Vatican Council I, as quoted above, spoke of revelation as a manifestation by God "of himself and the eternal decrees of his will" (DS 3004), and Vatican Council II stated that by revelation God makes known "himself

84 and the hidden purpose [*sacramentum*] of his will" (DV 2).

Because God "dwells in unapproachable light" (1 Tim. 6:16), revelation is necessarily somewhat mysterious. Vatican Council I stated that the primary contents of revelation, divine mysteries, "so far excel the created intellect that even after they have been given in revelation and accepted in faith, they still remain covered by the veil of faith and wrapped in a kind of darkness as long as, in this mortal life, 'we are away from the Lord, for we walk by faith, not by sight' (2 Cor. 5:6-7)" (DS 3016). Vatican Council II called attention to the interpersonal character of the loving action by which God takes human beings "into fellowship with himself" (DV 2).

Because it is a call to personal union with God, revelation presupposes in the human recipient a certain affinity with the infinite, the divine. Revelation is a grace, an anticipation of the blessed union to be consummated in heaven. God's word, which comes externally through visible and tangible signs, resounds also within, in the depths of the human consciousness.

Involving as it does these two dimensions, revelation normally takes on a symbolic structure.[6] A symbol is a sign pregnant with a plenitude of meaning that must be evoked, because it eludes direct statement. The revelatory events and words of Scripture exemplify this structure. In the Old Testament, the miracles of the exodus, the theophanies of Sinai, and the visions of the prophets and seers are highly symbolic, as are, in the New Testament, events such as the baptism, transfiguration, crucifixion, and resurrection of Jesus. The very events of revelation history are symbols fraught with a meaning deeper than clear concepts or propositional language can convey. Each symbol, taken in its historical and literary context, contains a whole range of interlocking meanings that cannot be spelled out adequately in objective conceptual discourse.

Symbol, as Paul Ricoeur has said, "gives rise to thought"[7] and, indeed, shapes the very thought to which it gives rise. A revelation that begins with symbolic communication gradually generates a whole series of reflections and interpretations that explicate its meaning. Thus the metaphor "Jesus is the Good Shepherd" can be reexpressed to say that Jesus takes care of his followers as a faithful shepherd takes care of his sheep. The propositions clarify the metaphor up to a point, but are abstract and incomplete. By fragmenting the density of the original symbol, they blunt its power. Yet propositional commentary pertains to revelation insofar as it elucidates the meaning of the symbols, preventing certain misinterpretations. The Christian doctrines set limits to the kinds of significance that can be found in the Christian symbols. The doctrines, however, are not independent revelation; they live off the power of the symbols.

The revelatory modes of communication, then, include the order of nature, historical events, symbolic words, interior illuminations, and propositional statements. All of these are integral to the process of revelation. But it is better not to speak of "revealed events," "revealed words," or "revealed propositions," as though these media were the contents of revelation itself. The true content of revelation—revelation in the objective sense—is the divinely intended and humanly perceived significance of the events and words. By participation in the community

---

6. For a fuller discussion of the symbolic structure of revelation, see Avery Dulles, *Models of Revelation* (Garden City, NY: Doubleday, 1983), 131–54.

7. Paul Ricoeur, *The Symbolism of Evil* (Boston: Beacon, 1967), 347–57, esp. 348.

of faith, the individual believer can have reliable access to the revelatory meaning of the signs and symbols through which God's self-disclosure has taken place and through which God's salvific designs have been made known. Through these signs and symbols, believers can grasp God's revelation more fully than they could through the use of unaided reason.

Special Revelation
in Salvation History

As contrasted with the "general" revelation given through the order of nature, the revelation given through particular historical events may be called "special." Christianity rests on a series of such events as presented and interpreted in Holy Scripture. Modern theologians have found meaningful patterns in this history. The Anglican biblical theologian Alan Richardson persuasively presented the opinion that "the distinctive character of Israel's history was that it was built around a series of disclosure situations, which through the activity of prophetic minds became interpretative of Israel's historic destiny and ultimately of the history of all mankind."[8] The events are not self-interpreting, but they lend themselves to the interpretations given to them by the prophets, apostles, and biblical authors. Seen in this light, the events manifest God as personal, free, loving, merciful, just, patient, and powerful. At the same time, salvation history exhibits humanity and the world as objects of God's powerful mercies and as destined by God for redemption and glory. The exceptional events of salvation history, as narrated in the Bible, serve as interpretative keys to illuminate the riddles of life.

According to Christian faith, the history of revelation comes to a climax and focus in the life, teaching, sufferings, death, and resurrection of Jesus Christ, together with the sending forth of the Holy Spirit from the risen Christ. Jesus, as the incarnate Word of God, may in some sense be called revelation itself. Vatican Council II asserts, "The deepest truth about God and the salvation of human beings [the essential content of revelation] is made clear to us in Christ, who is the Mediator and at the same time the fullness of all revelation" (DV 2).

If revelation is understood as symbolic communication, the primacy of Christ is not difficult to grasp. The divine Son, the Word of God, is symbolically present and active in Christ's human nature, which becomes a medium through which the divine manifests itself. For us who do not immediately encounter Christ in his incarnate life, his character and meaning have to be mediated by proclamation, Scriptures, liturgy, and sacraments, and only to the extent that this mediation is successful does Christ become for us the fullness of revelation. But if the mediation is successful, Christ does appear as a uniquely powerful and unsurpassable revelation of God. His life in the flesh, together with his message of forgiveness, supremely manifests what God chooses to be in free grace toward humankind. In Christ's wonderful deeds, especially his miracles, God's kingdom may be seen breaking into the history of the world. The crucifixion, as a symbolic event, expresses the sacrificial character of God's redemptive love. The resurrection symbolizes, by its very reality, the victory of that redemptive love over all that could oppose it, even hatred and death. Without Christ, we could not come to know and respond to God as the one who "so loved the world that he gave his only Son" (John 3:16).

---

8. Alan Richardson, *History Sacred and Profane* (Philadelphia: Westminster, 1964), 224.

Vatican Council II, in its Pastoral Constitution on the Church in the Modern World, concisely stated the revelatory meaning of Christ: "The Church believes that Christ, who died and was raised up for all, can through his Spirit offer human beings the light and the strength to measure up to their lofty vocation. Nor has any other name under heaven been given them by which they can be saved. The Church likewise holds that in its Lord and Master can be found the key, the center, and the goal of all human history" (GS 10; see also GS 44).

Revelation and the Religions

Some authors, notably the Swiss Protestant Karl Barth, have sharply contrasted revelation and religion. Revelation they regard as God's word, coming wholly from above, whereas religion is in their view an effort of sinful human beings to lay hold of the divine. This contrast is overdrawn. Revelation itself demands a human response; it achieves a human and public presence when taken up into religion. Religion, insofar as it is rooted in revelation, is holy and divine.

Judaism and Christianity are the religions directly corresponding to biblical revelation. In them, we can study the dialectical relationship between a specific revelation and the human response. The question then arises whether the nonbiblical religions owe their existence to some kind of revelation, either general or historical, rather than being due simply to human reasoning and initiative. A number of Catholic theologians hold that revelation is reserved to the biblical religions, but official Catholic teaching,

as we have seen, admits that revelation is accessible, in some measure, to people of all cultures and religions.

Vatican Council II, in its Declaration on Non-Christian Religions (*Nostra aetate*; hereafter NA), cautiously hinted that revelation might lie at the root of nonbiblical religions. It spoke of them as being based on "a certain perception of that hidden power which hovers over the course of things and over the events of human life" and, in many cases, on a "recognition" of a supreme divinity and even of God as Father. The teachings of these religions, said the declaration, "often reflect a ray of that Truth which enlightens all human beings." Although "the Catholic Church rejects nothing that is true and holy in these religions," it must never cease to "proclaim Christ as 'the way, and the truth, and the life' (Jn. 14:6)" in whom the fullness of the religious life is to be found (NA 2).

Some theologians, including Karl Rahner,[9] argue to the revelatory character of non-Christian religions from the universal salvific will of God. If God seriously wills that every human person achieve eternal life, it seems altogether probable that grace must be at work in the hearts of the unevangelized. If so, it may be supposed that the myths, rituals, and beliefs of the religions bear traces, at least, of a grace-given awareness of God, and hence of revelation. Although the mutual contradictions among the religions prevent us from holding that all of them are simply revealed, the common themes that underlie many of these religions may well be the effect of God's revealing presence working on the human consciousness.

According to a widespread opinion, God reveals himself in many or all religions, which

---

9. Karl Rahner, *Foundations of Christian Faith* (New York: Crossroad, 1982), 311–21. This theme is recurrent in Rahner's work.

complement each other by manifesting different aspects of the divine mystery. The Congregation for the Doctrine of the Faith in various documents has repudiated this opinion. Christian faith holds that God has fully and definitively revealed himself in Jesus Christ. Any revelation outside of the Christian must therefore be a preparation for, a participation in, or an application of the full revelation in Christ. The doctrines of other religions, insofar as they diverge from Christianity, are not revealed by God and cannot be believed by the virtue of divine faith but only as matters of human conjecture.[10]

Even if one denies revelation in nonbiblical religions, one must acknowledge much good in them. Through dialogue, it may be possible for all the religions, including Christianity, to be enriched and in some ways corrected. In entering such a dialogue, Christians will have no reason to conceal or doubt their own positions regarding Christ as the summit of revelation. Reflections of divine truth are to be sought in all religions.

Revelation:
Past, Present, and Future

Thus far, I have concentrated on the revelation given in the past, especially the special revelation given in biblical times, with its culmination in Jesus Christ. The New Testament writers were convinced that in Christ, God had surpassingly fulfilled the hopes and expectations of Israel and that the mission of the church was to preserve and proclaim God's final self-revelation

in Christ. Increasingly in later books of the New Testament, the term *faith* is used in an objective sense to designate the deposit of revelation committed to the church (Jude 3; 1 Tim. 6:20; 2 Tim. 1:12, 14).

The modern mind, deeply impressed by the limitations imposed by the particularities of time and culture, has difficulty in admitting that there can be any absolute or unsurpassable disclosure within history. Even thinkers who reject the inevitability of progress and deny that "later is better" consider that each age may be able to surpass its predecessors in some respects and that to equate revelation with an ancient deposit would condemn the church to a continual loss of vitality and actuality.

Vatican Council II, conscious of these concerns, avoided repeating the formula sometimes used that revelation "ceased with the death of the last apostle."[11] Instead, after describing Jesus as the perfecter and fulfillment of revelation, it stated, "The Christian dispensation, therefore, as the new and definitive covenant, will never pass away, and we await no further public revelation before the glorious manifestation of our Lord Jesus Christ (see 1 Tim. 6:14 and Tit. 2:13)" (DV 4). In the Constitution on the Church (*Lumen gentium*; hereafter LG), Vatican II depicted the church as capable of showing forth "in the world the mystery of the Lord in a faithful though shadowed way, until at the last it will be revealed in total splendor" (LG 8). These two statements avoid giving the impression that the church already possesses a total grasp of revelation in its fullness, but at the same

---

10. *Dominus Iesus*, secs. 5, 6, 7, 11, 13, 14, 21.

11. On at least two occasions, the Theological Commission or its subcommissions rejected several *modi* requesting that *Dei verbum*, no. 4, be amended to state explicitly that revelation was closed (*clausam*) with the death of the apostles. See the *relations* of July 3, 1964, and November 20, 1964. These are found respectively in the *Acts Synodalia Sacrosancti Concilii Oecumenici Vaticani II*, Periodus 3, vol. 3 (1974), and Periodus 4, vol. 1 (1976), p. 345.

time, they emphasize the church's obligation to adhere faithfully to "the mystery of the Lord," the "Christian dispensation," the "new and definitive covenant."

In the New Testament, the fullness of revelation in Christ is not presented as excluding subsequent revelation. The Gospel of John ascribes this function to the Paraclete, the Spirit of truth, who will declare to the apostles many things that Jesus himself was not able to say in his earthly ministry (John 15:26; 16:12-15). In Acts and the Pauline letters, the apostles are portrayed as receiving revelations to guide them as they shape the doctrine, mission, worship, and structures of the early church. In the Apocalypse (book of Revelation), the seer of Patmos receives visions and locutions that are normative for the churches for which the book is intended (Rev. 22:18-19).

In early patristic times, living prophets continued to play a central role in the direction of the church. Following in the footsteps of Saint Augustine, Saint Bonaventure and many medieval theologians used the term *revelation* to mean the interior illumination and attraction needed for any act of faith.[12] Throughout the Middle Ages, it was held that God's self-disclosure continued through the fathers and doctors of the church and likewise through councils. At the Council of Trent, a prominent theologian declared, "In the general councils the Holy Spirit has revealed to the Church, according to the needs of the time, numerous truths which were not explicitly contained in the canonical books [of Scripture]."[13] Yet it was taken as axiomatic that no postbiblical revelation could essentially change the context of Christian faith.

The theme of ongoing revelation fell into oblivion from the sixteenth through the nineteenth centuries, when revelation was understood almost exclusively as an objective deposit of truth. Some modernist theologians, such as Alfred Loisy, influenced by Hegelian evolutionism, revived the theme at the beginning of the twentieth century, but they gave the impression that God's revelation in Jesus Christ was only a provisional stage on humanity's forward march to an ever deeper unity with the divine. Vatican Council II, while insisting on the permanence of the covenant established in Christ, recognized that God is not silent in our time. Several quotations will illustrate this point.

The Constitution on Divine Revelation asserts that "in the sacred books, the Father who is in heaven meets his children with great love and speaks with them" (DV 21). Not only Scripture but also tradition is seen as a locus of continuing revelation. Through tradition, "God, who spoke of old, uninterruptedly converses with the Bride of his beloved Son; and the Holy Spirit, through whom the living voice of the gospel resounds in the Church, and through it in the world, leads believers to all truth and makes the word of Christ dwell in them abundantly (see Col. 3:16)" (DV 8). The Constitution on the Sacred Liturgy (*Sacrosanctum*

---

12. Latourelle, in his *Theology of Revelation*, briefly summarizes the theme of interior revelation in Augustine (pp. 139–40) and Bonaventure (pp. 155–56). The same theme, he points out, recurs in the sixteenth-century Dominicans Melchior Cano and Domingo Bañex (ibid., 180–83). To the contrary, the Jesuits Francisco Suárez and Juan de Lugo equated revelation with the external proposal of God's word (ibid., 183–87).

13. From a written submission "de traditionibus ecclesiae" (on the traditions of the church) attributed, with some uncertainty, to Claude Le Jay; text in Görres-Gesellschaft, ed., *Concilium Tridentium Diaiorum, Actorum, Epistolarum, Tractatuum Nova Collectio* (Freiburg: Herder, 1930), 12:523. The English translation of Yves Congar's *Tradition and Traditions* (New York: Macmillan, 1966), 122, gives a faulty page reference.

concilium; hereafter SC) emphasizes the multiple presence of Christ in his church, especially in its liturgical celebrations, when the minister performs sacred actions, when the Scriptures are read, and when the congregation prays and sings (SC 7). Finally, the Pastoral Constitution on the Church in the Modern World speaks of the signs of the times as indications of "God's presence and purpose in the happenings, needs, and desires in which this people [the church] has a part along with other people of our age" (GS 11; see also GS 4).

A comprehensive doctrine of revelation, then, cannot limit itself to God's self-disclosure in biblical times. Rather, it must deal with God's active presence to the church and the world today, without which the good news of the gospel, which is admittedly normative, might easily be dismissed as a piece of inconsequential historical information.

The Constitution on Divine Revelation, as I have noted, speaks of "the glorious manifestation of our Lord Jesus Christ" as the consummation of revelation (DV 4). In so doing, it revives the biblical theme of eschatological revelation. Saint Paul addresses the Corinthians as believers who "wait for the revealing of our Lord Jesus Christ" (1 Cor. 1:7). In 2 Thessalonians, Paul speaks of the day "when the Lord Jesus is revealed from heaven with his mighty angels in flaming fire" (2 Thess. 1:7). Elsewhere in the Pauline corpus, we read of the promised time when "Christ who is our life appears" (Col. 3:4). The Letter to the Hebrews speaks of Christ appearing a "second time . . . to save those who are eagerly waiting for him" (Heb. 9:28). The pastoral letters have numerous references to Christ's future coming in glory (e.g., 1 Tim. 6:14; Titus 2:13).

This eschatological dimension of revelation is important not only for the sake of fidelity to the Scriptures but also because of the attunement of our age to progress and to the future. As Joseph Ratzinger notes in his commentary on *Dei verbum*, article 4, the eschatological reference "now shows from within faith the provisional nature of Christianity and hence its relatedness to the future, which exists together with the connection with the Christ event that has taken place once and for all, so that it is impossible to state the one without the other."[14] Christ and his revelation have finality precisely because he is "the one who is to come," bearing in himself the promise of the ultimate future.

The splendor of the risen Christ mediates to the saints in heaven the immediate vision of God. With transformed minds, they gaze upon the splendor of God reflected in the face of the glorious Christ (see 2 Cor. 4:6). The blessed who live with Christ know and will eternally know God through an interior grace that is called, in theological terminology, the light of glory. The light of faith, in the present life, provides faint anticipation of the face-to-face vision that will then be given. The Constitution on the Church eloquently describes the final manifestation of God: "When Christ shall appear and the glorious resurrection of the dead takes place, the splendor of God will brighten the heavenly city and the Lamb will be the lamp thereof (see Apoc. 21:23). Then in the supreme happiness of charity the whole church of the saints will adore God and 'the Lamb who was slain' (Apoc. 5:12), proclaiming with one voice: 'To him who sits upon the throne, and to the Lamb, blessing and honor and glory and might, forever and ever' (Apoc. 5:13-14)" (LG 51).

---

14. Joseph Ratzinger, Commentary on *Dei verbum*, ch. 1, in *Commentary on the Documents of Vatican II*, ed. Herbert Vorgrimler (New York: Herder & Herder, 1969), 3:177.

Faith

The Concept of Faith

In catholic systematic theology, the term *faith* is generally used to designate the provisional knowledge or awareness of the divine that is given in this life to believers who adhere to revelation. Vatican Council I described faith as "the full homage of intellect and will to God who reveals" (DS 3008). Then, in a sentence that sums up the fruits of a long theological development, the council declared, "The Catholic Church professes that this faith, which is the 'beginning of human salvation' (see Trent, DS 1532), is the supernatural virtue whereby, inspired and assisted by the grace of God, we believe that what he has revealed is true, not because the intrinsic truth of the contents is seen by the natural light of reason but because of the authority of God himself, the revealer, who can neither be deceived nor deceive" (DS 3008).

Building on this authoritative statement, Vatican Council II restated the same doctrine with a slight shift of emphasis: "The 'obedience of faith' (Rom. 16:26; see 1:5; 2 Cor. 10:5-6) must be given to God who reveals, an obedience by which one entrusts [*committit*] one's whole self freely to God, offering 'the full submission of intellect and will to God who reveals' (Vatican I, DS 3008), and freely assenting to the revelation given by him" (DV 5).

Before we proceed to a more detailed analysis of these lapidary statements of the two Vatican councils, it may be helpful to situate this conciliar teaching within the range of meanings conveyed by the Greek word *pistis*, the Latin *fides*, and the English word *faith* in other contexts. Faith in the broader sense is not only assent to what a person says. More fundamentally, it is trust in the person, as appears from statements such as "I have faith in you" and "I put my faith in you." Then again, faith or *pistis* can be used to signify faithfulness—for example, in the statements "I have kept faith with you" and "You broke faith with me." Vatican Council I, while emphasizing assent to God's word as true, did not adopt an exclusively intellectualist perspective. It spoke of the homage of both will and intellect to the authority or majesty of God the revealer. Vatican II made a particular effort to build into its statement the dimensions of trust, commitment, obedience, and submission. But it did not minimize the intellectual element of assent to the content of God's revelation. The intellectualist emphasis, already prominent in the Gospel of John, has been strong in the Catholic tradition, especially in the Scholastic theology of the Middle Ages and the Counter-Reformation.

The Virtue and the Act of Faith

Building on certain texts from Saint Paul, such as 1 Cor. 13:13, medieval theologians distinguished sharply among faith, hope, and charity, which they described as the three theological virtues—virtues because they were stable dispositions of the human spirit oriented toward good acts; theological because they had God as their object. Thomas Aquinas explained how the theological virtues order human beings toward the beatific vision. Through faith, we assent to God as our last end and to the way of salvation prescribed by God; through hope, we tend toward the vision of God as something that we can, through grace, attain; through charity, the highest form of love, we enter into an affective union with God, the source of our eternal blessedness.[15]

---

15. Thomas Aquinas, *Summa theologiae* Ia–IIae, q. 62, art. 3.

Charity, as the virtue that makes one a sharer in the divine nature, is the form or soul of all other virtues, including faith. In a person who lacks charity, faith cannot achieve its true purpose. Such a faith is called "dead" or "formless" faith (see James 2:17). According to the Council of Trent, faith without the addition of hope and charity does not unite one to Christ or make one a living member of Christ's body (DS 1531). The faith that offers eternal life is a living faith that "works through charity" (see Gal. 5:6). But a believer who loses charity by willfully turning away from God may still retain the gift of faith. The faith that remains in such a person is still the theological habit of faith, and is a gift of God. It may serve as a basis for repentance and for a return to God's grace and favor.

Virtues are specified and defined by their acts. The principal act of faith, as distinct from other virtues such as hope and charity, is to believe. Belief, however, is not the only act of faith. As Thomas Aquinas explains, faith has a secondary act, which is external: namely, confession in the sense of testimony or witness.[16] It is normal for belief in the heart to give rise to confession with the lips (Rom. 10:9-10; see also 2 Cor. 4:13). A person who sincerely believes will normally be impelled to profess his or her faith, at least when the occasion requires. A culpable silence about—or denial of—one's beliefs can be a sin against the virtue of faith itself.

The concept of confession need not be limited to verbal statements. In a certain sense, the whole life of the committed Christian is an external profession of faith. Good works are not only proofs and consequences of sincere faith; they may be called acts of faith in the secondary sense explained by Saint Thomas.

Formal and Material Objects of Faith

Just as virtues are known by their acts, so acts are known by their objects, the realities in which they terminate. Superficially, it is correct to say that faith has a number of objects—all the truths revealed by God. But on a deeper level, the object of faith is one, for in every assent of faith, the believer is intending to achieve, and actually achieving, union with the mind of God, who is the first truth and the witness to everything accepted in faith. In believing, we assent primarily to God who reveals and only secondarily to this or that particular truth that we believe on the authority of God. Saint Thomas and other Scholastic theologians distinguished between the formal and material objects of faith. The formal object is the ultimate reason for the assent to any particular truth that we accept on the authority of God. In more technical language, the authority of God the revealer is the "formal" object of faith, whereas that to which God attests is the "material" object. The formal object is the inner reason or ground for assent to the material object.

From this analysis, it should be evident that there can be no faith without both a formal and a material object. To make an act of faith in the theological sense is to believe something on the authority of God. One submits to God's authority precisely in accepting what God vouches for.

The material object, revealed truths, requires further discussion. Faith is not an acceptance of a miscellaneous body of disconnected truths but an acceptance of the order of salvation as seen and disclosed by God. In God's mind, the truth is one and undivided. God

---

16. Ibid., IIa–IIae, q. 3, art. 1.

92

knows everything knowable by a single comprehensive idea. The human mind, however, knows piecemeal. It breaks up the totality of revealed truth into distinct truths, separately enunciated in judgments or statements. The articles of the creed and the dogmas of the church are enunciations of revealed truth.

When we make an act of faith, we do not adhere to propositions or statements as the objects of faith, but rather to the reality designated by those propositions or statements. Primarily and directly, we believe in the God who is triune, and in the Son who became incarnate, rather than in the statements that express these realities. Yet the believer does assent, in a secondary way, to the propositions, for without them, the reality would not be humanly affirmable.[17]

As previously stated, there can be no faith without revealed truth, the self-expression of the mind of God. But because of the human element in the articulation of revelation, it is possible for a person of faith to accept an incorrect formulation as though it were God's word or to reject a correct formulation, not recognizing it as God's word. An authentic act of faith can coexist with opinions that are partly incorrect.

The formal object of faith as a theological virtue is the authority of the revealing God. Under this aspect, faith is called "divine." God's authority, however, is normally grasped in some persons or institutions who speak in God's name. The preeminent bearer of revelation is Jesus Christ, who, as the incarnate Logos, gives human utterance to the word of God. Faith may be called "Christian" as well as divine to the extent that it submits to the authority of Christ

as the truth of God incarnate. For the Christian, the truth of God is found not simply in the recorded words of Christ, but primarily in the very being of Christ, who could say of himself, "I am the truth" (John 14:6).

Christ, then, is not simply one among many material objects of faith. As Christians, we believe God as God speaks to us in Christ. Christ in his humanity is not the formal object of faith but is the locus, so to speak, in which the formal object is preeminently encountered. In accepting the word of God, the Christian accepts concurrently the word or self-expression of Christ.

Besides being divine and Christian, faith is, for many Christians, "Catholic." The Catholic Christian adheres to the church because God's word resounds in it. The church is not only a particular content (material object) of revelation; it is a trusted organ through which God's word comes to the faithful. The formal object of faith, according to Thomas Aquinas, is "the first truth [God] as this is made known in Scripture and in the doctrine of the Church, which proceeds from the first truth."[18] The Bible and approved doctrine are the means whereby the church proposes to the faithful the contents of divine revelation.

In brief, then, faith may be called "divine" insofar as it assents to the word of God, "Christian" insofar as it takes Christ to be "the Mediator and fullness of all revelation" (DV 2), and "Catholic" insofar as it submits to the church as the authoritative organ of revelation since the time of Christ. In the Catholic Christian's act of faith, these three dimensions are simultaneously present. When professing a particular ar-

---

17. In the words of Thomas Aquinas, "The act of the believer does not terminate in the propositions but in the reality, for we do not formulate propositions except in order to know things by means of them, whether in science or in faith" (*Summa theologiae* IIa–IIae, q. 1, art. 2, ad 2).

18. Ibid., IIa–IIae, q. 5, art. 3c.

ticle of the creed, the believer accepts it as part of God's revelation given in Christ and proclaimed by the church. Acceptance of particular doctrines would not be an act of faith unless they were accepted precisely on the word of a witness—either God directly encountered or God as represented by some person or organ through whom God chooses to speak.

Faith and Knowledge

The text on faith quoted above (page 90) from Vatican Council I (DS 3008) distinguishes between assent based on reason's grasp of the intrinsic truth of the contents and assent based on the authority of God the revealer. The distinction may be clarified by an analogy from the classroom. A teacher could either tell his or her students the correct answer to a problem in mathematics or else take the students through a series of steps by which they could see for themselves why this must be the answer. In the first case, the students would have a highly imperfect knowledge of the answer, knowing what the solution is without knowing why. Yet they would not be without knowledge. A great deal of what we consider ourselves to know about secular matters depends on an acceptance of the word of others—often very fallible witnesses, such as schoolteachers, books, newspapers, broadcasters, friends, and neighbors. If we discounted all these sources, our knowledge would shrivel to a very small fraction of itself.

It is proper, therefore, to distinguish between two kinds of knowledge. There is evidential knowledge, in which one understands the grounds of one's assent, and faith-knowledge, in which one assents because of the trustworthiness of a witness. Faith-knowledge is imperfect as regards its mode, but it can be certain if the witness is evidently reliable and evidently vouch-

es for what is believed. In divine faith, we assent to something on the word of God, who can neither be deceived nor deceive.

Strictly speaking, we cannot "believe" what we know evidentially. If I could prove by conclusive argument that there are three divine persons, I could not "believe" it. Faith is by nature an obscure form of knowledge in which the inner grounds for the thing believed are hidden from the believer.

Does this mean that faith is irrational? Some Christians have portrayed faith as an arbitrary decision to believe, in which proof or evidence plays no role at all. In the Catholic understanding, however, faith and reason work together. Even though reason cannot by its own powers establish the contents of faith, it can point to adequate motives for believing. Vatican Council I insisted very strongly on this point. The same God, it stated, is the author of faith and reason. Since God is not self-contradictory, truth cannot contradict truth (DS 3017). Faith, therefore, is not against reason. More than this, faith and reason mutually support one another, for right reason is capable of demonstrating the rational grounds of faith and of achieving some understanding of the revealed mysteries. Conversely, faith helps reason by enabling it to avoid certain errors and by giving it access to truth that would otherwise lie beyond its range (DS 3019).

Although faith cannot be an achievement of reason alone, the right use of reason can prepare for faith and confirm it. Reason can show how the contents of faith offer coherent answers to persistent questions to which merely human philosophies give no satisfactory solution. The answers of faith can be seen as having practical value in enabling people to cope with difficulties and reverses and in motivating them to live up to high standards and ideals. Faith gives steadiness, direction, and purpose to human life.

94

Christian revelation, moreover, is accredited by remarkable signs in history, including the prophecies and miracles of Scripture, the resurrection of Jesus from the dead, and the remarkable qualities of the church itself, which Vatican Council I described as a "great and abiding motive of credibility and an irrefragable witness to its own divine mission" (DS 3013). In this connection, the council referred to the wonderful expansion of the church, its exceptional holiness and fruitfulness in good works, its catholic unity and unshakable stability (ibid.). The extent to which all these qualities are apparent is, of course, variable, depending on the fidelity of Christians to their own divine calling.

To conclude this section, then, we may say that although the contents of the Christian message cannot be proved by strict rational argument, they may reasonably be believed. Thanks to the qualities of the Christian message itself and the many signs given in history, the Christian religion may be described as "evidently credible" (Vatican I, DS 3013). That is to say, there are solid rational motives for deciding that one ought to become or remain a believer. To spell out the evidence of credibility by constructing arguments and refuting objections is the task of a special theological discipline known as apologetics. The extent to which any individual believer finds it necessary or useful to articulate the rational grounds of credibility varies enormously from case to case. As John Henry Newman never tired of asserting, the arguments set forth in manuals of apologetics rarely correspond to the spontaneous movement of the mind and heart that commonly brings conviction in matters of religion.[19]

Properties of Faith: Supernaturality, Certainty, Freedom, Obscurity

The signs of credibility have their importance in disposing a person to make an act of faith, in supplying some human confirmation for faith, and in enabling believers to give an account of their faith to others. At most, however, the study of the external evidence can yield only a theoretical assurance that it would be reasonable to believe. Faith itself, as a loving and reverent submission to the testimony of God the revealer, requires a personal preparation that is more than intellectual.

The Roman Catholic Church, in its official teaching, has always insisted that any salutary act of faith depends on the prevenient gift of divine grace. In 529 CE, the Second Council of Orange insisted on the necessity of "the illumination and inspiration of the Holy Spirit, who gives to all [believers] joy [or ease: *suavitatem*] in consenting to the truth and believing it" (DS 377). The Council of Trent in 1547 spoke of God touching the human heart through the enlightenment of the Holy Spirit, and added that the grace of God leaves the recipient free either to accept or to reject the gift of faith (DS 1525–26). The same doctrine is repeated in other words by Vatican Council I (DS 3010) and by Vatican Council II (DV 5).

Theologians explain that God's grace, working on the human heart, produces an existential affinity or connaturality with the good news of the gospel. A person thus prepared by grace feels an inner inclination to believe and is able to reach the practical conviction: it would be good

---

19. See especially Newman's *Fifteen Sermons Preached before the University of Oxford*, 3rd ed. (London: Longmans, Green, 1871; London: SPCK, 1970). Later, as a Catholic, Newman expressed similar ideas in his *Essay in Aid of a Grammar of Assent* (1870). See the edition with an introduction by Nicholas Lash (Notre Dame, IN: University of Notre Dame Press, 1992).

for me to become a believer here and now; I have an obligation to believe. It is not necessary for this realization to be articulated in a distinct judgment, but some such realization is presupposed by the act of faith itself, for as Saint Augustine said, "No one believes anything without first thinking that it ought to be believed."[20]

The illumination of the Holy Spirit does not make the contents of faith demonstrably true; nor does it negate the freedom of the person to reject, for whatever motives, the evidence of credibility. Its specific effect is to make clear to the recipient that he or she is called to become a believer. In so doing, grace overcomes what would otherwise be a hesitation or disinclination to make the full commitment of faith. Grace thus confers a sense of peace and satisfaction upon the assent of faith.

The question whether faith is certain has been much discussed. If by certainty one means a firm commitment, certainty is an ingredient in the very concept of faith. On the other hand, faith is compatible with an acute realization that the evidence is far from compelling and that there are objections that the believer cannot answer. If the signs were so overwhelming that unbelief were impossible, faith, as free assent, would also be impossible. Assent forced on a person by stringent proofs would not be faith in the theological sense of reverent submission to the authority of the divine witness.

Since faith is by definition firm assent, it excludes doubt in the usual sense of that word. But because faith lacks intrinsic evidence, it coexists with a kind of mental dissatisfaction or restlessness that Thomas Aquinas called cogitation (pondering).[21] Without actually doubting the truth of the revealed content, the believer can continue to question how it is possible for things to be as faith asserts that they are; he or she can seek further signs confirming the truth of what is believed and can wrestle with objections that seem to defy solution. Because of these factors, a believer will often feel tempted to doubt. This temptation, though painful, can have a purifying effect; it can banish the illusion that faith rests on strict rational proof.

Faith, therefore, is a *supernatural* assent. It adheres to the revealed message because of the majesty and authority of God the revealer. The *certitude* of faith is proportioned to the reliability of the divine witness, whose voice is heard not only in the externally proclaimed message but in the inner inclination to believe. Faith is reasonable because it is supported by external motives of credibility. It is *obscure* because its essential content—the mystery of God and salvation—surpasses the power of human reason either to discover without revelation or to fathom even after revelation. Finally, faith is *free* both because the grounds of credibility are not stringent and because the grace of God, inclining the mind and will to assent, can be resisted.

Implicit and Explicit Faith

In the Christian theological tradition, the term *implicit faith* is frequently used to convey some important but elusive ideas. The term *implicit* comes from logic, where it describes how a conclusion is contained in its premises. Applying this to theology, we can say that believers implicitly adhere to the logical consequences of the propositions they accept in faith. Thus, in believing that Jesus Christ has a complete human nature, one implicitly believes that he had

---

20. Augustine, *De praedestinatione sanctorum* 2:5 (PL 44:963).
21. Thomas Aquinas, *Summa theologiae* IIa–IIae, q. 2, art. 1.

96

the powers of reasoning, speaking, and laughing. Once the logical consequences of our beliefs are brought to our attention, faith impels us to accept them.

To confine the concept of implicit faith to the logically implicit would, however, be too restrictive. As mentioned earlier in this section, faith is not a mere assent to propositions. Above all else, it is a mysterious union of the mind with God, the first truth, who is both the formal object and the primary material object of faith.

Formally considered, faith is a submission to God's authority as manifested by certain divinely accredited witness or organs. The individual believer may be ignorant of many things actually taught by Christ or the church, but in professing to be a Christian or a Catholic, one implicitly accepts everything that God teaches through these mouthpieces.

Faith, however, should not be understood as a blank check that we sign without any intimation of what will be written on it. The material object of faith, as previously stated, is one. Every act of faith terminates in the one mystery of salvation. Because God is one and the plan of salvation has an inner unity, every authentic act of faith puts us in a living relationship with aspects of the revealed mystery of which we are not explicitly conscious.

Even among Christians, not all know the contents of faith with the same degree of explicitness.[22] To the extent of their capacities, all Christians should explicitly profess the principal mysteries of faith, which are spelled out in the creed and celebrated in the liturgy. Those set over the community as teachers are required to know explicitly some points of faith that the uneducated believe only implicitly.

Taking the doctrine of implicit faith one stage further, Saint Thomas maintained that the ancient Israelites, though the gospel had not yet been proclaimed, had essentially the same faith as Christians, since the real object of their confession was the same.[23] Quoting Heb. 11:13, he asserted that the Israelites of the early centuries beheld the promises from afar, and that the hopes of Israel became more distinct as the time of Christ drew nearer. Thus, an increase in the articles of faith need not involve a change in the real object of faith.

The primary and irreducible content of explicit faith, for Saint Thomas, is that stated in Heb. 11:6, "Whoever would draw near to God must believe that he exists and that he rewards those who seek him." Anyone who accepts this content through supernatural faith may be said to have an implicit grasp of the entire mystery of salvation, including the existence of the triune God, the incarnation, and the resurrection. The implication here is obviously not a matter of formal logic but one of real objective connection, arising out of the affinity between the virtue of faith and its real object.

Faith and Salvation

So often and so emphatically is the connection between faith and salvation stated in the New Testament that the necessity of faith has never been a matter of doubt in Catholic teaching. Relying on texts such as Mark 16:16, Rom. 3:30, and Heb. 11:6, popes and councils have repeatedly taught that no one can be saved without faith. The Council of Trent (DS 1529) and Vatican I (DS 3010) stated in almost the same words that no one attains justification without faith.

---

22. Ibid., arts. 5–6.
23. Ibid., q. 1, art. 7.

The relationship of faith to justification and salvation is not a mere matter of God's positive decree, as though God had arbitrarily laid down faith as a condition. The purpose of the present life is that we may prepare ourselves for, and freely orient ourselves to, the goal for which we are destined. The goal is to behold God by the light of glory. Faith justifies because, by means of it, the future for which we are destined takes hold of us in an inchoative way. "Faith," says Saint Thomas, "is the habit of mind by which eternal life is begun in us, making the intellect assent to things that do not appear."[24]

The anticipation of the beatific vision in this life is necessarily partial and incomplete. We cannot by faith assent explicitly to everything that will be manifested by the light of glory. Thus, it is legitimate to ask what the explicit content of saving faith must be. Saint Thomas, following Saint Augustine and the medieval Augustinian tradition, held that the necessary content varies according to different eras in salvation history and according to the capacities and status of individual persons.[25] In every age and for all persons, according to this theory, it has been necessary to believe that God exists and rewards those who seek God (see Heb. 11:6). Before the time of Christ, unlearned persons were not required to have explicit belief in the mysteries of the Trinity and the incarnation, but in the present age of grace, even uneducated people are bound to have explicit faith in the principal mysteries of Christ's life, especially those solemnly celebrated in the liturgy. While holding this in a general way, Saint Thomas also recognized the principle that people could not be required to have explicit faith in matters they were not in a position to learn.

With the discovery of new continents and civilizations unknown to the theologians of old, the problem of the salvation of the unevangelized has attracted increasing attention. Pius IX, in the course of a severe condemnation of religious indifferentism, conceded that persons invincibly ignorant of the true religion could by the power of divine grace and enlightenment attain to eternal life, provided that they obeyed the natural law inscribed in their hearts.[26] The pope thus made it clear that God does not demand the impossible.

Several documents of Vatican Council II applied the same line of reasoning more specifically to the question of faith. The Decree on Ecumenism (*Unitatis redintegratio*; hereafter UR) teaches that Christians who are not members of the Roman Catholic Church can possess the gift of faith (UR 3). The Decree on the Mission Activity of the Church (*Ad gentes*; hereafter AG) declares that God "in ways known to himself can lead those inculpably ignorant of the gospel to that faith without which it is impossible to please him (Heb. 11:6)" (AG 7). The Pastoral Constitution on the Church in the Modern World affirms that the grace of God works in an unseen way in all human beings, and that the Holy Spirit offers everyone the possibility of being associated with the paschal mystery (GS 22). The Constitution on the Church goes so far as to declare that people who without blame on their part have not yet arrived at an explicit knowledge of God are given the helps necessary for salvation (LG 16). Apparently, the intended meaning is that an atheist in good conscience can have the faith required for justification and salvation.

---

24. Ibid., q. 4, art. 1c.
25. Ibid., q. 2, arts. 7–8.
26. Pius IX, encyclical *Quanta Conficiamur Moerore*, August 10, 1863 (DS 2865–67).

98

Going back to certain very concise texts in Thomas Aquinas, several modern Catholic thinkers have tried to explain how even the professed atheist might be justified by faith.[27] Jacques Maritain maintained that at the dawn of reason, each individual is offered the possibility, by grace, of orienting himself or herself to eternal beatitude by a movement of love. In tending toward that to which human nature is ordered, one orders oneself in fact toward God, even without knowing God in a conceptual way. Maritain contended that this real, nonconceptual knowledge of God, gained through the élan of the will under the leading of grace, satisfies the requirements of Heb. 11:6 and can be salvific for persons who have not as yet been able to attain speculative certainty about God and God's redemptive action.[28]

To affirm the necessity of faith is not to affirm its sufficiency. In the Catholic tradition, it is taught that faith is sufficient for justification and salvation if, and only if, it is informed by charity (*fides caritate formata*). "Dead faith," which lacks the vivifying element of charity, is insufficient. I have referred earlier to the statement of the Council of Trent that "faith, unless it be joined by hope and charity, does not perfectly unite one to Christ or make one a living member of Christ" (DS 1531).

As biblical warrant for this position, Catholic authorities usually appeal to the teaching of James that faith without works is dead (James 2:17) and to Paul's statement that only "faith working through love" avails for salvation (Gal. 5:6). Sometimes also reference is made to Paul's hymn to charity in 1 Corinthians 13, in which the faith that moves mountains is declared unavailing in the absence of charity. Paul's teaching in Romans that justification is given by faith (Rom. 3:28), which might seem to constitute an objection to the Catholic position, is interpreted as referring to what Catholics call "living faith."

Summary: Faith and Revelation

As may be seen from the preceding exposition, faith, in Catholic theology, is the correlative of revelation as provisionally given in the present life. Revelation as such becomes actual when it is accepted in faith, for until it is believed, it has a merely potential or virtual existence.

The formal and material objects of faith are determined by the nature of revelation as God's self-disclosure and as manifestations of the divinely established order. The obscurity of faith corresponds to the mysterious content of revelation and to the symbolic modes whereby this content is communicated. The certainty of faith comes from its divine origin and attestation, both exterior and interior. The external signs of revelation constitute the outward call to faith; the interior illumination and attraction of grace give the inner vocation to faith. The freedom of faith follows from the noncoercive nature of the signs of revelation and of the interior solicitation to believe. The culmination of revelation in Jesus Christ, and its mediation through the church give rise, respectively, to the Christian and Catholic character of faith. The universality

---

27. Jacques Maritain, *The Range of Reason* (New York: Scribner, 1952), part 1, ch. 6, pp. 66–85. This is essentially a commentary on two texts from the *Summa theologiae*, Ia–IIae, q. 89, art. 6, and q. 109, art. 3. A somewhat similar approach, based on the same texts, may be found in Max Seckler, *Instinkt und Glaubenswille nach Thomas von Aquin* (Mainz: Matthias-Grünewald, 1962).

28. For further discussion of the faith necessary for salvation, see Avery Dulles, *Church and Society: The Laurence J. McGinley Lectures, 1988–2007* (New York: Fordham University Press, 2008), 522–34.

of revelation accounts for the possibility of faith that is not explicitly Catholic or even Christian. The inner unity of revelation is the foundation for implicit faith.

Faith, in its theological meaning, issues into belief as its primary and internal act, but faith flows secondarily into external acts of confession by word and deed. Thus faith, without ceasing to be an assent of the mind, involves a trusting commitment of the whole person to God who reveals, together with fidelity and obedience to the saving message.

The provisionality of revelation in the present life accounts for the orientation of faith toward the eternal vision of which it is a foretaste. The consummation of revelation in the light of glory will do away with the very possibility of faith.

Transmission of Revelation

Revelation, which reaches its term in the interior act whereby it is believed, spontaneously comes to expression in a bodily and social manner through external acts of confession. It achieves a public and historical existence when the testimony of the first witnesses becomes constitutive of an enduring community of faith.

Testimony

For the testimony to evoke the response of faith, it must be both humanly credible and divinely fructified by the assistance of the Holy Spirit, who moves the witnesses to give testimony and at the same time enlightens the minds of the hearers. The mediation of revelation, therefore, is not a purely natural process but one that depends on God's continuing activity. To indicate this, some theologians speak in this connection of "dependent" or "repetitive" revelation.[29]

Among the original witnesses to revelation, the prophets of the Old and New Testaments and the apostles of the New Testament period hold a preeminent place. According to the biblical understanding, accepted by the church, these witnesses were empowered, directed, and accredited by God. They were God's agents or instruments. Their words, without being less human than those of other men and women, were in some sense divine, since they gave verbal expression to revelation itself. According to the Gospels, Jesus was able to assure the Twelve and the Seventy, when he sent them on missions, that to receive and hear them was to receive and hear Jesus himself, who in turn spoke for the Father (Matt. 10:40; Luke 10:16; John 20:21). This apostolic mission did not cease with the ascension. Jesus promised to remain with the apostolic leaders (Matt. 28:20; Acts 1:8). Paul, conscious of God's self-communication through his own preaching, was able to congratulate the Thessalonians for having accepted the word they had heard from him "not as the word of men but as what it really is, the word of God, which is at work in you believers" (1 Thess. 2:13).

The expression "word of God" applies most obviously to the spoken and written words of those who are divinely inspired to put the divine message into human language. In a broader sense, however, it is a virtual synonym for

---

29. The theme of *dependent revelation* was proposed by Paul Tillich in his *Systematic Theology* (Chicago: University of Chicago Press, 1951), 1:126–28, and has been taken up in contemporary Catholic theology by Gerald O'Collins, *Fundamental Theology* (New York: Paulist, 1981), 100–102, among others. The term *repetitive revelation* was used by the Anglican John Macquarrie in his *Principles of Christian Theology* (New York: Scribner, 1968), 80–81, 93.

revelation. The Hebrew term for "word," *dabar* (and sometimes its Greek equivalents, *logos* and *rhema*), when applied to God, includes not only speech and writing but all the external signs by which the mind of God is communicated to human beings. Thus, the symbolic gestures of prophets and the expressive actions of inspired believers are forms of the word of God, insofar as these agents are taken up in the process of God's self-communication.

The word of God abides in the church in two closely connected forms, Scripture and tradition. The Council of Trent in one of its first decrees (in 1546) asserted that the Catholic Church accepts sacred Scripture and apostolic traditions with equal devotion and reverence as embodiments of the gospel truth (DS 1501). The First and Second Vatican Councils have reaffirmed the same doctrine (DS 3006; DV 9).

The Bible

The Bible, as understood in Catholic theology, is a fully human work, produced by human authors in the course of a long and complex history.[30] It is a kind of anthology of the sacred literature of Israel and of the primitive church. The selection was made under divine guidance by successive generations of the community of faith and ultimately confirmed by bishops in council and by popes. The Catholic Church accepts as normative for its faith and practice the books that were received as Holy Scripture by the church of the first five centuries and were officially proclaimed as canonical by the Councils of Florence (DS 1334–35) and Trent (DS 1502–3).

The Bible is frequently called, in official Catholic teaching, the "written word of God" (DF, ch. 3 [DS 3011]; DV 9, 21, and passim). God is said to be the "author" of the Bible, not in the sense of having taken the place of the human authors, but in the sense that God's grace impelled the human authors to write and directed them to give a pure and reliable expression of the faith of the people of God at their particular stage of salvation history. In many cases, the biblical books are attributable to the prophets, apostles, and other inspired leaders who helped to shape the faith of Israel and of the early church. In other cases, the biblical authors owed their inspiration, at least in part, to such charismatic leaders. Although much of the inspired literature of the formative period has no doubt perished, a sufficient body of that literature has survived to enable the church to test its own teaching and piety against that of the period when the revelation was freshly given. The Bible thus serves as a critical reference point for the proclamation of the church. Christian faith is historical in the sense that the church, in transmitting it, continues to depend on reliable records of what was originally received.

Biblical inspiration, as Catholics understand it, is the entire complex of interior graces and external helps that enabled the writers and editors of the biblical books to produce normative texts for the church's guidance.[31] The concept of inspiration is often connected with that of inerrancy, meaning freedom from error. In accepting the Bible as the basis for its own belief and teaching, the church certifies that the Bible, taken as a whole, is a reliable witness to God's

---

30. For recent overviews, see Avery Dulles, "The Authority of Scripture: A Catholic Perspective," in *Scripture in the Jewish and Christian Traditions*, ed. Frederick E. Greenspahn (Nashville: Abingdon, 1982), 13–40; and Bruce Vawter, "The Bible in the Roman Catholic Church," in Greenspahn, *Scripture in the Jewish and Christian Traditions*, 111–32.

31. On biblical inspiration, see Karl Rahner, *Inspiration in the Bible*, rev. trans. (New York: Herder & Herder, 1964); see also Bruce Vawter, *Biblical Inspiration* (Philadelphia: Westminster, 1972).

revelation as communicated in the formative period. The inspiration given to the sacred writers prevented them from falsifying what God has revealed. According to Vatican II, "Since, therefore, all that the inspired authors, or sacred writers, affirm should be regarded as affirmed by the Holy Spirit, we must acknowledge that the books of Scripture, firmly, faithfully, and without error, teach that truth which God, for the sake of our salvation, wished to see confided to the sacred Scriptures" (DV 11, Flannery ed.). This statement is carefully phrased. It affirms the value of the Bible as a whole for transmitting in its purity the truth that leads to salvation, but it leaves open the possibility that individual authors may have erred, especially with regard to scientific and historical matters not connected with salvation. This does not mean that the Bible is a patchwork of errant and inerrant passages. As understood by the council, the whole Bible is authoritative and trustworthy in what it affirms about the revelation of God and the plan of salvation. Individual passages, however, must be interpreted according to the intentions of the authors and in their historical and literary context. Vatican II does not favor a fundamentalist literalism in which each sentence, taken in itself, tends to be absolutized.

Some Christians have raised doubts about whether the Old Testament, written prior to the final revelation, still retains its authority. According to a Christian reading, the Old Testament is the inspired literary expression or sedimentation of the faith of the people of God prior to the advent of Jesus Christ. Not everything contained in the Old Testament is directly normative for Christian faith. Certain ideas and practices that were appropriate or perhaps inevitable in an earlier period, before the revelation was complete, are now outdated. This is notably true of the ceremonial prescriptions of the Mosaic Law, which are not binding on Christians. The Old Testament retains its value, however, both because the history of Israel foreshadows and prepares for Christ and because many of the profound religious insights in the Old Testament are not repeated in, or supplanted by, the New Testament. The New Testament, indeed, would not be intelligible except in the light of the Old Testament, which it presupposes.

Tradition as a Source of Doctrine

Since revelation is an organic unity in which the whole is latently present in all the parts, the totality of revelation may be said to be given in the Bible. In bearing witness to Jesus Christ as the definitive disclosure of God, the New Testament presents him who is the "fullness of all revelation." But revelation is never contained in a book alone. The Bible would not be rightly understood if it were taken apart from the living community of faith in and for which it was written. The church, which collected and identified the books of Scripture with the help of the Holy Spirit, has the task of discerning their true meaning, with the help of the same Spirit, in the light of its own history and experience.

The Council of Trent, as we have seen, insisted that traditions that come down from the apostles have no less authority than the books of Scripture.[32] In the next few centuries, many Catholic theologians spoke of revelation as being partly contained in Scripture, partly in

---

32. The teaching of the Council of Trent on tradition has been much discussed. See, for example, Congar, *Tradition and Traditions*, 156–69; and Joseph Ratzinger, "On the Interpretation of the Tridentine Decree on Tradition," in *Revelation and Tradition*, ed. Karl Rahner and J. Ratzinger (New York: Herder & Herder, 1966), 50–68, 73–78.

102 tradition, as in two independent sources. Yet neither Trent nor any other council speaks of "two sources" or asserts that tradition teaches anything that is not in some way contained in Scripture. Vatican II insisted on the unity and coinherence of Scripture and tradition. The two, it asserted, are intimately connected, "for both of them, flowing from the same divine wellspring, in a certain way merge into a unity and tend toward the same end" (DV 9). As a consequence, "Sacred tradition and sacred Scripture form one sacred deposit of the word of God, which is committed to the Church" (DV 10).

Several other shifts in the Catholic theology of tradition should also be noted here.[33] It had become common, especially since the Counter-Reformation, to think of tradition objectively, as a collection of truths communicated to the apostles and preserved in the church. Without rejecting this notion, contemporary Catholicism shows a deeper awareness that tradition cannot be adequately understood as a body of explicit teaching. Many doctrines are contained in a merely implicit way in tradition considered as an activity or process whereby faith is expressed and transmitted. In the words of the Second Vatican Council, tradition "includes everything that contributes to the holiness of life and the increase of faith of the people of God" (DV 8). The church "in its teaching, life, and worship, perpetuates and hands on to all generations all that the Church itself is, all that it believes" (DV 8). Authentic tradition is to be found not only in formal statements but also in "the practice and life of the believing and praying Church" (DV 8).

Tradition, finally, is not static or simply preservative. It develops dynamically. "This tradition which comes from the apostles progresses in the Church with the help of the Holy Spirit" so that, by means of it, the church "constantly moves forward toward the fullness of divine truth until the words of God reach their complete fulfillment in her" (DV 8). Because revelation has an eschatological dimension, tradition too can be future-oriented. It propels the church forward to the day of the Lord, when the church will fully come into its own.

Loci of Tradition

As may be seen from quotations in the preceding paragraph, the process of "traditioning" the faith includes practically everything that the church does. Before we consider formal teaching, it may be appropriate to mention some of the ways in which the church teaches informally or implicitly. Among the most important of these is the life of worship. The liturgy is the place where many of the faithful most vividly experience the saving mysteries and prayerfully reflect on the contents of their faith. For example, the rite of baptism with its accompanying prayers imparts a sense of the universal need for redemption and the removal of sin by grace. The repetition of the words of institution at each Eucharist, together with the elevation of the consecrated elements and the genuflections, impresses on the faithful a realization of the "real presence." Throughout the centuries, a vital interaction between worship and belief has continually occurred, as indicated by the maxim *lex orandi lex credendi* (the

---

33. See Avery Dulles, "Vatican II and the Recovery of Tradition," in his *The Reshaping of Catholicism* (San Francisco: Harper & Row, 1988), 75–92.

rule of prayer is the rule of faith). Sometimes the approved modes of worship give rise to doctrines, and sometimes worship is deliberately modified to reflect and inculcate the church's teaching.[34]

A second important vehicle of tradition is the writings of the church fathers—writers of Christian antiquity distinguished for sanctity and orthodoxy and approved, at least implicitly, by the church as exceptional witnesses to the tradition.[35] The church fathers played a providential role in establishing the canon of Scripture, the articles of the creed, the basic dogmas of the faith, the basic structures of the church, and the essential forms of the liturgy. Their theology was closely related to Scripture, prayer, worship, and preaching, and was less abstract than the academic theology of later centuries. They spoke with a freshness and unction that appeal to many contemporary readers. Although as individuals, many of the church fathers erred on particular questions, they more often achieved answers of lasting value. To the extent that they agreed among themselves, they enjoy strong authority.

A third locus of tradition, not totally separable from the two just mentioned, is the sense of the faithful.[36] Life within the church as the body of Christ has a profound influence on the ways in which people feel and think. The Holy Spirit, animating the church, produces in faithful members an instinctive sense of what agrees or disagrees with revelation. Vatican Council II, in its Constitution on the Church, stated that the sense of the faithful, when it manifests universal agreement in matters of faith and morals, is unerring. Spelling out the effects of this supernatural sense, the same constitution declared that by means of it, the faithful are able to recognize the word of God, adhere to it unfailingly, penetrate its true meaning, and apply it in practice (LG 12). The sense of the faithful has often contributed to the clarification of Christian doctrine either when it arouses protest against certain errors or when it anticipates the official magisterium in discerning truths not yet officially taught.[37]

The sense of the faithful is not a totally autonomous source of doctrine, since it depends in part on the other bearers of tradition and overlaps with them, but it can often help to identify the true content and meaning of tradition, especially when it confirms what is also attested by the other sources. Thus Pius IX, in defining the immaculate conception of the Blessed Virgin, enumerated as witnesses "Holy Scripture, venerable tradition, the constant mind of the Church, and the remarkable convergence [conspiratio] of the Catholic bishops and faithful" (apostolic constitution Ineffabilis Deus, 1854). Because of the close connection between the two, the sense of the faithful leads naturally to

34. See Aidan Kavanagh, *On Liturgical Theology* (New York: Pueblo, 1984), esp. 88–95; see also Edward J. Kilmartin, *Systematic Theology of Liturgy*, vol. 1, Christian Liturgy: Theology and Practice (Kansas City: Sheed & Ward, 1988), 96–99, with references to other literature. For an ecumenical treatment of the relation between *lex orandi* and *lex credendi*, see Geoffrey Wainwright, *Doxology* (New York: Oxford, 1980), 218–83.

35. On the concept and authority of church fathers, see Walter J. Burghardt, "Fathers of the Church," in *New Catholic Encyclopedia*, 5:853–55; Congar, *Tradition and Traditions*, 435–50.

36. On the "sense of the faithful," see William M. Thompson, "Sensus Fidelium and Infallibility," *American Ecclesiastical Review* 167 (1973): 450–86; Jean M. R. Tillard, "Sensus Fidelium," *One in Christ* 11 (1975): 2–29.

37. Still classic is the essay of John Henry Newman, *On Consulting the Faithful in Matters of Doctrine* (1859; rev. ed., 1871). It has been reprinted with an introduction by John Coulson (Kansas City: Sheed & Ward, 1985).

104 the hierarchical magisterium as a teaching organ in the church.

The Hierarchical Magisterium and Infallibility

Since revelation is public, the church requires a way of publicly proclaiming the doctrine that expresses or safeguards that revelation. Roman Catholics find evidence in the New Testament that Christ commissioned Peter and the apostles with the responsibility of overseeing the life and witness of the church. The pope and the other bishops are regarded as successors, respectively, of Peter and the other apostles.[38] One of their most important tasks is to keep the church in the truth of the gospel by proclaiming sound doctrine and condemning doctrinal deviations. In this function, the hierarchy constitutes the church's official teaching body, or magisterium. To perform its doctrinal task successfully, the hierarchy must take the necessary means. It must study the sources and the tradition, consult the sense of the faithful, and make use, on occasion, of the advice of qualified experts. But it is not left to merely human resources. Christ has promised that the powers of death will not prevail against the church founded on the faith of Peter (Matt. 16:18) and that he will remain with the successors of the apostles to the end of time (Matt. 28:20). He has sent the Spirit of truth to guide the apostolic body in bearing witness to his revelation (John 15:26-27; 16:13). In view of these promises, Catholics believe that the magisterium is generally reliable and will never lead the church into error by definitively teaching what is false or contrary to revelation.

When Catholics speak of the infallibility of the magisterium, they mean that in certain specified acts, the popes and bishops, teaching doctrine concerning faith and morals in a way that binds the whole church, are divinely protected from falling into error.[39] As explained in the dogmatic constitutions on the church issued by Vatican Councils I and II, the pope can teach infallibly when, in his capacity as successor of Peter (ex cathedra), he proclaims by a definitive act some doctrine to be held by all the faithful on the basis of divine revelation (DS 3074; LG 25). The same two councils teach that infallibility resides in the whole body of bishops when they exercise their supreme teaching power in union with the successor of Peter. The college of bishops can define matters of faith when it gathers in ecumenical councils. When the college is dispersed, it can teach infallibly if all the bishops are unanimous in holding some doctrine as a matter of faith or morals to be held by all with irrevocable assent (DS 3011; LG 25).

When a pope or ecumenical council defines a dogma, the resulting definition is a human formulation of revealed truth. Catholics accept such teaching as irreversibly true and in that sense as irreformable. Every dogma of the church expresses an authentic aspect of Christian revelation, but the way in which the individual divine mystery is parceled out in dogmas depends on human modes of thinking and speaking that are to some extent culturally conditioned. It is always possible to plumb the

---

38. These points, which will be developed in the chapter on church (ch. 6) by Vatican II in LG 19–24; see also DV 10.

39. On the infallibility of the magisterium, see Francis A. Sullivan, *Magisterium: Teaching Authority in the Catholic Church* (New York: Paulist, 1983), esp. chs. 5–6; see also Avery Dulles, *Magisterium: Teacher and Guardian of the Faith* (Naples, FL: Ave Maria, 2007), ch. 6, pp. 59–81.

truth of revelation more deeply and to express it more aptly in relation to the needs and possibilities of new times and situations. Thus the "irreformability" of dogma does not prevent its reformulation and further refinement. Since John Henry Newman wrote his great *Essay on the Development of Christian Doctrine* (1845), the idea that dogma "develops" has gained general acceptance in the Catholic Church.

Noninfallible Teaching, Religious Submission, and Dissent

Although a great deal of attention has been devoted to infallibility, it should be kept in mind that the vast majority of the church's official statements are not infallible. They are subject to correction in the light of further evidence. According to most theologians, the popes of the past hundred years have uttered only one sentence of clearly infallible teaching: the definition of the dogma of the assumption of the Blessed Virgin by Pope Pius XII in 1950 (DS 3903). Vatican Council II issued some seven hundred pages of statements, but it chose not to invoke its infallibility for any of its teachings. Roman congregations, individual bishops, episcopal conferences, particular councils, and local or national synods issue many doctrinal utterances but have no power to speak infallibly.

Because popes and bishops are set over the church as official teachers, their pronouncements are always to be received with reverence and re-

spect.[40] For Catholics, the teaching of the magisterium has a clear presumption of truth in its favor. It sometimes happens that popes or bishops, when teaching authoritatively though not infallibly, call upon their subjects to submit to their judgment and to cease defending contrary opinions. In such cases, the faithful will strive to adhere sincerely to the teaching of the magisterium and will normally avoid publicly contesting it. The appropriate response to authoritative but noninfallible teaching is frequently called, in Latin, *obsequium animi religiosum* (religious submission of mind; LG 24; *Codex Iuris Canonici*, 753). By this is meant a sincere acceptance based on the authority of the teacher, but one that falls short of the irrevocable assent of faith, which is given to dogmas as revealed truths taught with the charism of infallibility.

While assent to noninfallible doctrine is in principle required, cases arise in which this response is not forthcoming.[41] Doubt or disagreement on the part of the faithful is possible because, even after making an effort to submit, a person may be unable to attain sincere conviction, since the will cannot always force the mind to assent, especially where the special guarantee of infallibility is lacking. In exceptional cases, dissent can be not only subjectively excusable but objectively justified, for, as the very term noninfallible implies, such teaching can in fact be erroneous. Historians of doctrine point out a number of cases in which noninfallible teaching has clearly been in error.[42]

---

40. On the response due to noninfallible teaching, see Sullivan, *Magisterium*, chs. 7–9; and Dulles, *Magisterium*, ch. 7. Sullivan discusses the meaning of *obsequium animi religiosum* on pages 158–61; cf. Dulles, 92–94.

41. On dissent, see Sullivan, *Magisterium*, 166–71 and 215–16; see also Dulles, *The Reshaping of Catholicism*, 93–109.

42. The most celebrated error is no doubt the condemnation of Galileo by the papal inquisition in 1633. Many of the decrees of the Pontifical Biblical Commission issued between 1905 and 1915, dealing chiefly with historical and textual questions, are no longer defended. Other alleged errors and reversals in official Catholic teaching are discussed, for example, in Charles E. Curran and Robert E. Hunt, *Dissent in and for the Church* (New York: Sheed & Ward, 1969), 66–80.

What is the proper conduct for a Catholic who honestly disagrees with some point of official but noninfallible doctrine? First of all, one should critically review one's own contrary opinion. As stated by the German bishops in their pastoral letter of September 22, 1967, "The Christian who believes that he has a right to his private opinion, that he already knows what the church will only come to grasp later, must ask himself in sober self-criticism before God and his conscience, whether he has the necessary depth and breadth of theological expertise to allow his private theory and practice to depart from the present doctrine of the ecclesiastical authorities. The case is in principle admissible. But conceit and presumption will have to answer for their willfulness before the judgment-seat of God."[43]

Assuming that a serious effort to come to agreement with the authoritative teaching has failed, several options remain. One of these is "submissive silence" (*silentium obsequiosum*), in which one keeps one's doubt or dissent to oneself. A second option is to express one's non-acceptance privately to one person or a small number who can prudently evaluate one's difficulties and possibly initiate some steps to clarify or correct, if necessary, the current teaching. A third possibility is to make one's dissent known in a public way by disseminating one's views through speeches and the press. In some cases, public dissent may be "organized" in the sense that one seeks to mobilize public opinion against the official teaching. Public dissent, especially when organized, inevitably inflicts some harm. It weakens the church as a community of faith and witness; it spreads distrust in the hierarchical magisterium and is often a source

of scandal to Catholics and others. For all these reasons, public (especially organized) dissent requires special warrants—namely, that the dissenter be firmly convinced that the official teaching, if unopposed, would cause grave harm and that other, less destructive forms of dissent be unavailing.

Conclusion: Faith, Revelation, and Theology

The present chapter on faith and revelation is not a self-enclosed unit. It opens up toward all the other themes that are taken up in systematic theology.

Faith, as we have seen, has God as its formal object and as its primary material object. In the chapter on God, therefore, faith itself will be more fully elucidated. The chapter on creation, in turn, will provide an occasion for the reader to probe more deeply into what I have been calling God's revelation through nature. In treating the question of Christology, this volume will fill out what has been suggested already concerning Jesus Christ as the Mediator and fullness of all revelation.

The chapter on church will amplify the observations already made about the church as the witness and home of faith. The church will be described as believer, as teacher, and as symbolic realization of revelation in the world. In taking up the themes of sin and grace (theological anthropology), the reader will gain a fuller understanding of the obstacles to faith and of faith as a gift. What will subsequently be said about

---

43. The letter of the German hierarchy is here quoted from Karl Rahner, "Magisterium," in *Encyclopedia of Theology: The Concise "Sacramentum Mundi,"* 878.

Mary and the saints will show how exemplary members of God's faithful people serve to mirror God's revelation in Christ. The chapter on the sacraments will illustrate how the church becomes most tangibly a symbolic presence of Christ in the world, actualizing its essential being, when its pastors and faithful gather in liturgical worship. Finally, the chapter on eschatology will show how faith passes into vision, overcoming the imperfections that necessarily accompany it under the conditions of this present life.

For Further Reading

Congar, Yves. *The Meaning of Tradition.* Sec. 1, vol. 3 of *Twentieth Century Encyclopedia of Catholicism.* New York: Hawthorn, 1964.

> *A condensation, slightly updated, of material given in greater detail in Congar's masterful work* Tradition and Traditions. *This volume is more concise and better organized than its longer and more informative predecessor.*

Coventry, John. *The Theology of Faith.* Notre Dame, IN: Fides, 1968.

> *A simple but thoughtful systematic presentation that stands firmly in the Catholic tradition.*

Dulles, Avery. *Magisterium: Teacher and Guardian of the Faith.* Naples, FL: Sapienta, 2007.

> *A comprehensive treatment of the teaching office in the church. The text is followed by nine appendices, each of which contains an important ecclesial document pertaining to the magisterium.*

———. *Models of Revelation.* Garden City, NY: Doubleday, 1983.

> *A systematic work that proposes a symbolic approach and tests this by comparison with prevalent twentieth-century theories of revelation, both Protestant and Catholic.*

Latourelle, René. *Theology of Revelation.* Staten Island, NY: Alba House, 1966.

> *A standard historical and systematic treatment, especially valuable for its presentation and analysis of official Catholic teaching and of the Catholic theological tradition.*

Newman, John Henry. *Fifteen Sermons Preached before the University of Oxford.* With introductory essays by D. M. MacKinnon and J. D. Holmes. London: SPCK, 1970.

> *A series of sermons preached between 1826 and 1843, showing the author's movement from an evangelical*

Protestant position on faith and reason to the position he was to maintain as a Catholic.

Rahner, Karl. *Foundations of Christian Faith: An Introduction to the Idea of Christianity.* New York: Crossroad, 1982.

> An introduction to theology as a "first-level reflection" on Christian faith. This work gives a rather full presentation of Rahner's transcendental theology of revelation and a helpful summary of his views on faith, Scripture, and magisterium.

Sullivan, Francis A. *Magisterium: Teaching Authority in the Catholic Church.* New York: Paulist, 1983.

> A balanced, carefully reasoned, and clearly written work that concentrates on the exposition and interpretation of official Catholic teaching concerning the magisterium.

Thomas Aquinas. *Faith: Summa theologiae* 31 (2a2ae, Questions 1–7). English translation, introduction, and notes by T. C. O'Brien. London: Blackfriars, 1974.

> Still the most authoritative and incisive Catholic treatise on faith. The terminology is somewhat technical but richly repays those who take the pains to master it.

Vawter, Bruce. *Biblical Inspiration.* Philadelphia: Westminster, 1972.

> A lucid survey of the history of the theology of inspiration by a prominent biblical scholar. Vawter combines fidelity to the tradition with openness, in the final chapters, to recent developments.

God and Trinity 3.1

Approaching the Christian Understanding of God

David Tracy

God and the Revelation of Jesus Christ

A Christian theological understanding of God merges with the question of the identity of God: Who is God? For the Christian, God is the one who revealed Godself in the ministry and message, the cross and resurrection, of Jesus Christ. A Christian theological understanding of God cannot be divorced from the revelation of God in Jesus Christ.

God and Theology

The theological doctrine of God discloses the divine reality that must inform every symbol and doctrine, just as the doctrine of God is informed by every symbol and doctrine (creation-redemption, Christ, eschatology, church, sacrament, revelation). A theological insistence on the interconnection of the central mysteries of the faith is, of course, true of the understanding of every great symbol of Christian faith, but is especially crucial on the question of God. Christian theology must be radically theocentric so that no single symbol or doctrine in the whole system of doctrines can be adequately understood without explicitly relating that symbol to the reality of God.

The theological understanding of God, therefore, may bear a distinct and explicit study only as long as one always recalls that the full Christian theological understanding of God occurs only in and through an entire systematic theology encompassing all the great symbols of

the tradition.[1] One way to remind ourselves of this systematic theological insight is to initiate the discussion of God first with the question of the identity of God as disclosed in Jesus Christ, rather than with the traditional questions of the existence and nature of God. The traditional separation of the tracts *De Deo uno* (*On the One God*) and *De Deo trino* (*On the Triune God*) now seems problematic.[2] The questions and concerns of the tract *De Deo uno* remain, as we shall see below, vital questions for Christian theology. It also remains possible, as is shown by the division of essays in this volume, to have a distinct study of the trinitarian understanding of God. But even that practical need must prove a distinction, never a theoretical separation for systematic theology. For the Christian understanding of God is none other than a trinitarian understanding. Any theology of God that does not affirm that trinitarian self-understanding may, indeed, possess a concept of theism, even radical monotheism, but it becomes a concrete Christian monotheism only as trinitarian.

This section on approaching the Christian understanding of God is written in the context of that trinitarian conviction. I will affirm *that* such a trinitarian understanding of God is the properly Christian one but will not develop *what* analogies are most fruitful for contemporary trinitarian understanding. (Further theological understanding of the triune God will be addressed in chapter 3.2, by Anthony J. Godzieba.) However, the need for this practical division of labor (following the earlier and even less happy division of whole tracts) for an adequate Christian systematic theology of God is not best re-

---

1. The "placement" of the doctrine of God throughout systematic theology (and not as a single "locus") is one of the signal strengths of Schleiermacher's *Glaubenslehre*.

2. The problem is not merely the "manual" genre of traditional manual theologies but the temptations (not necessity) to separate rather than distinguish theistic, monotheistic, and trinitarian understandings of God.

solved, as too often in the past, by analyzing the existence and nature (including attributes) of God first and only then analyzing the concrete identity of God as that identity is revealed in the event and person of Jesus Christ. In sum, the concerns of the traditional tract *De Deo uno* on the one God (insofar as there should continue to be a separate tract at all on the subject—which I admit I doubt) should begin even its own understanding of the "one God" through an analysis of God's self-revelation in Jesus Christ if it is to prove faithful to the *Christian* understanding of God.

This revelational approach to the question of God need not, however, deny the fruitfulness of traditional metaphysical and theological understandings of the nature of God or the fruitfulness of the insistence of Vatican I on the "knowability" of God in natural theology.[3] Rather, both of these important theological concerns (generically, the nature and attributes of God treated in the tract *De Deo uno*, and the arguments on the existence of God studied in the discipline of "natural theology") should be developed, since they clearly are legitimate.

However, these questions should find a more appropriate locus or place in the fuller system of Christian systematic theology.[4] The proper "place" for these legitimate concerns on the nature and existence of God is after an analysis of the scriptural-revelational understanding of God. More exactly, on a Catholic understanding, we understand God foundationally in and through Scripture-in-tradition.

This revised ecclesial principle of Scripture-in-tradition is neither the older Reformation principle "Scripture alone" nor the earlier Roman Catholic formulation "Scripture *and* tradition."[5] The common confession of the Christian church that clarifies the meaning of the creedal belief "We believe in one God" is the confession "We believe *in* Jesus Christ *with* the apostles" (i.e., with the apostolic tradition).[6] More exactly, the ecclesial confession on God can be rendered as "We believe in the God of Jesus Christ with the apostles." We so believe by believing with the apostles *in* Jesus Christ as the very self-revelation of God. This common ecclesial confession, which informs all the classic creeds, finds its scriptural foundation as well as its clearest

---

3. In its Constitution on the Catholic Faith (*Dei filius*), the First Vatican Council affirmed the church's faith in God's omnipotence, eternity, and incomprehensibility, and taught that God can be known from created things by the natural light of human reason. Denzinger-Schönmetzer, *Enchiridion Symbolorum* (hereafter DS), 3001–4, 3021, 3026. The chief study of *Dei filius* is Hermann J. Pottmeyer, *Der Glaube vor dem Anspruch der Wissenschaft* (Freiburg: Herder, 1968); see also Heinrich Ott, *Die Lehre des I. Vatikanischen Konzils: Ein evangelischer Kommentar* (Basel: Reinhardt, 1963). The teaching of Vatican I is reflected in Karl Rahner's observation that "there is a knowledge of God which is not mediated completely by an encounter with Jesus Christ." *Foundations of Christian Faith* (New York: Seabury, 1978), 13.

4. There are few more crucial issues for any systematic theology than the judgment of the proper "place" or "locus" of a particular theological issue.

5. The earlier Catholic-Protestant disputes are well known. The phrase "Scripture-in-tradition" would demand separate theological defense; for this chapter, it may serve as a purely descriptive phrase in the actual practice of many contemporary Catholic and several Protestant theologians. For a representative discussion, see the essays in Richard John Neuhaus, ed., *Biblical Interpretation in Crisis: The Ratzinger Conference on Bible and Church* (Grand Rapids: Eerdmans, 1989).

6. For a fuller explanation, see Robert M. Grant with David Tracy, *A Short History of the Interpretation of the Bible* (Philadelphia: Fortress Press, 1984), 174–87; and my essay "On Reading the Scriptures Theologically," in *Theology and Dialogue: Essays in Conversation with George Lindbeck*, ed. Bruce D. Marshall (Notre Dame, IN: University of Notre Dame Press, 1990), 35–68.

rendering in the plain sense of the passion narrative of the New Testament.[7] That "plain" sense is the plain ecclesial sense—i.e., the obvious and direct sense these proclamatory narratives of God's actions in the cross and resurrection of Jesus of Nazareth have possessed for the Christian community that over the centuries has read these narratives *as Scripture*.[8]

Christians as Christians understand who God is first and foundationally in and through their experience and understanding of Jesus Christ. Christians discover that experience and understanding mediated to them in Word and sacrament through the primary mediation of the ecclesial tradition.[9] Thus do they believe *in* Jesus Christ *with* the apostles. Christian tradition affirms the Jesus Christ proclaimed in the passion narratives of the original apostolic communities and mediated in Word and sacrament in the present ecclesial community in fidelity to the apostolic tradition as truly God and truly human (Chalcedon). Only by thus understanding Jesus Christ does the Christian hope to reach a properly Christian understanding of God.

God and Christ

Christian theology further understands the person and salvific event of Jesus Christ as the very self-revelation of who God is and who we are commanded and empowered to become. A systematic theological understanding of God, therefore, will be developed in direct relationship not only with the doctrine of Christ but also with the doctrines of revelation and salvation. A systematic theological understanding of both revelation and salvation, in turn, is also grounded in the common ecclesial confession and the plain sense of the passion of the Gospels.[10] That "plain sense" remains the surest foundation and clearest explication of the Christian understanding of God. By understanding the proclamatory passion narrative in its details and its unity,[11] Christians begin to understand who God is. They do so by understanding first the identity of the one (Jesus of Nazareth) whose presence as Jesus Christ they experience in Word and sacrament as the very presence of God.

The passion narratives, justly described as "history-like" and "realistic,"[12] disclose the basic Christian understanding not only of the identity of Jesus Christ, but in and through that identity, the identity of the God who acts as agent in and through the actions and sufferings of Jesus of Nazareth.[13] As in any realistic narrative, so too in the passion narrative, an identity is rendered through the plotted interactions of an unsubsti-

---

7. See Hans Frei, *The Identity of Jesus Christ: The Hermeneutical Basis of Dogmatic Theology* (Philadelphia: Fortress Press, 1975); idem, *The Eclipse of Biblical Narrative: A Study in Eighteenth and Nineteenth Century Hermeneutics* (New Haven: Yale University Press, 1974).

8. See David Kelsey, *The Uses of Scripture in Recent Theology* (Philadelphia: Fortress Press, 1975). There is need for a parallel study of the use of Scripture in Catholic theology; see the study (on both Catholic and Protestant biblical interpretation) of Werner Jeanrond, *Theological Hermeneutics: Development and Significance* (London: Macmillan, 1991).

9. The category "mediation" is central to the Catholic understanding of all reality: the primary mediations of Word and sacrament through the mediations of church and tradition.

10. For further reflections on the relationships of confession and narrative, see Tracy, "On Reading the Scriptures Theologically."

11. The phrase "proclamatory passion narrative" refers to the genre of gospel.

12. Frei, *The Identity of Jesus Christ.*

13. For a sensitive hermeneutical and theological account of identity, see ibid.

tutable character (Jesus) and the unique events (betrayal, cross, resurrection) he undergoes. The fact that the Christian understanding of God is grounded not in a general theory of theism but in the concrete history of God's self-disclosure as loving agent in the cross and resurrection of Jesus of Nazareth is the theological foundation of all properly Christian understandings of God.

The passion narrative, moreover, should not remain isolated from the rest of the Scriptures or from the later creeds.[14] Rather, the passion narrative, as foundation and focus of all properly Christian understanding of God, should open up to the larger Gospel narratives of the message and ministry of Jesus and the incarnation of the Logos, the theologies of Paul and John, the Pastorals, the book of Revelation, and all the rest of the New Testament. Again, as focused and grounded in the understanding of God's agency in the passion narrative, the Christian understanding of God should also open anew to the complex and profound disclosures of God's identity in the history of Israel rendered in the many genres (narrative, law, praise, lamentation, wisdom) of the Old Testament.[15] This is clearly not the place to review and interpret the extraordinary complexity of a fuller scriptural understanding of God. This much, however, does need to be affirmed: For the Christian, God is the one who raised Jesus of Israel from the dead. God, for the Christian, is the one who revealed decisively who God is in and through the message and ministry, the incarnation, cross, and resur-

rection of none other than Jesus the Christ. The most profound New Testament metaphor for who God is remains the metaphor of 1 John: "God is love" (4:16; emphasis added). To understand that metaphor—which occurs, let us note, in the first theological commentary on the most theological and meditative of the four Gospels[16]—is to understand, on inner-Christian terms, what has been revealed by God of God's very identity as agent and as love in the incarnation, cross, and resurrection of Jesus Christ.

Therefore, for the Christian faithful, the answer to the question "Who is God?" asked in relation to the self-disclosure of God in Jesus Christ, is this: God is love, and Christians are those agents commanded and empowered by God to love. However, if this classic Johannine metaphor (i.e., "God is love") is not grounded in and thereby interpreted by means of the stark reality of the message and ministry, the cross and resurrection of this unsubstitutable Jesus, who as Christ is God's self-disclosure as love, then Christians may be tempted to think the metaphor is reversible into "Love is God." But this great reversal, on inner-Christian terms, is hermeneutically impossible. "God is love." This identity of God the Christian experiences and knows in and through the proclaimed and narrated history of God's actions and self-disclosure as the God who is love in Jesus Christ, the parable of God.

To affirm that "God is love" is also to affirm, now in the more abstract terms proper to post-

---

14. The temptation of the retrieval of the "passion narrative" as central can lead to a seeming failure of detailed attention to the rest of the individual Gospel—as, for example, in the study of Matthew in Ronald R. Theimann, *Revelation and Theology: The Gospel as Narrated Promise* (Notre Dame, IN: University of Notre Dame Press, 1985), esp. 112–56.

15. See Paul Ricoeur, "Toward a Hermeneutic of the Idea of Revelation," in *Essays in Biblical Interpretation*, ed. Lewis L. Mudge (Philadelphia: Fortress Press, 1980), 73–119.

16. Although technically in the genre of letters, 1 John reads more like a commentary on the understanding of God present in the Gospel of John.

114 scriptural metaphysical theologies,[17] that God, the origin, sustainer, and end of all reality, is characterized by the radical relationality of that most relational of categories, love. God, the one Christians trust, worship, and have loyalty to, can be construed in more abstract terms as the radically relational (and, therefore, personal) origin, sustainer, and end of all reality. To affirm that the Christian understanding of God includes the affirmation that God is the origin, sustainer, and end of all reality is to "place" the Christian understanding of God on the language map of all developed philosophical theisms. To affirm that the Christian understanding of God refers to the one whom Christians worship, trust, and are loyal to is to "place" this Christian understanding on the language map of radical monotheism (shared by Judaism and Islam). To affirm, with 1 John, that "God is love"—an affirmation made in and through the gospel narrative and the ecclesial confession of the incarnation, cross, and resurrection of Jesus Christ—is to affirm the radical relationality of God's nature as personlike (i.e., characterized by intelligence and love).[18] This latter affirmation, moreover, both grounds a theological understanding of the economic Trinity in the primal Christian confession of Jesus Christ and suggests how the immanent Trinity is to be understood in and through the economic Trinity.[19]

For the trinitarian understanding of God is the fullest Christian theological understanding of the radical, relational, loving, kenotic God who revealed Godself in and through the incarnation, the ministry (healing, preaching, actions), the message (the "reign of God"), the fate of the cross, and the vindication of resurrection of Jesus of Nazareth.[20]

Who God is—God's identity—is revealed decisively in this Jesus the Christ. In that precise theological sense, it is impossible to separate theo-logy and Christology. In that same sense, the Christian understanding of the existence and nature of God is grounded in the identity of the God disclosed as kenotic love in Jesus Christ.

God and the Human Quest for God

The Catholic theological understanding of God is, therefore, grounded in the self-revelation of God in Jesus Christ. Jesus Christ is both the self-disclosure of God and God's quest for human beings. Jesus Christ is, therefore, the divine response to the question human beings are to themselves.[21] The further theological question occurs, in the Catholic tradition, of how this christic understanding of God's iden-

---

17. The appropriateness of such abstract categories is demonstrated best by the classic developments of patristic and medieval theologies, as shown by the magisterial work of Bernard Lonergan on Nicaean and medieval developments (*The Way to Nicaea* [London: Longman & Todd, 1976]).

18. For a representative treatment of the understanding of God as person, see Edward Schillebeeckx and Bas van Iersel, eds., *A Personal God?* (New York: Crossroad, 1977; orig. pub. in *Concilium* 103).

19. Karl Rahner, "Remarks on the Dogmatic Treatise 'De Trinitate,'" in *Theological Investigations* (London: Darton, Longman & Todd, 1966), 4:77–102; idem, *The Trinity* (New York: Crossroad, 1970).

20. It is to be noted that the full scriptural history of Jesus is needed for understanding the identity of God. The retrieval of the centrality of the passion narrative (Hans Frei et al.) and the cross (Eberhard Jüngel, Jürgen Moltmann) should not become the occasion to eliminate additional attention to the message and ministry of Jesus.

21. In contemporary Catholic theology, the work of Karl Rahner is especially persuasive here; see Rahner, *Foundations of Christian Faith*.

tity as love correlates with the human quest for God. The word *correlation* here does not imply that the Christian understanding of God must be made to "fit" some already existing understanding of theism or some already completed anthropology or ontology.[22] Rather, the word *correlation* logically allows for the categories of identity (of meaning), nonidentity, or similarity-in-difference.

Credibility and Intelligibility

The Catholic theological tradition has ordinarily (but not always—see, e.g., Meister Eckhart) argued for a similarity-in-difference or analogy[23] between the properly Christian understanding of God and a coherent philosophical (i.e., inevitably metaphysical) understanding of God based on some aspect of the human quest for ultimate meaning and truth.[24] In the modern period, metaphysical accounts of the question of God have often (e.g., Karl Rahner, Edward Schillebeeckx, Bernard Lonergan) also involved an anthropology—the quest for God in the question the human being is to itself. More philosophically stated, classical ontology, in the modern period, often emphasizes an epistemological starting point.

Even Catholic theologians (e.g., Hans Urs von Balthasar) who remain doubtful of the fruitfulness of anthropological "starting points" for the question of God in Christian theology nevertheless also tend to provide some theological anthropology that is argued to correlate with the Christian understanding of God (e.g., the "glory" of God disclosed in the visible form of Jesus Christ and disclosed in other beautiful and true visible forms).[25] An analogy may prove illuminating here.[26] Just as a great work of art may be said to "disclose" both beauty and truth, so, too, the revelation (disclosure) of God in Jesus Christ is experienced as both beautiful and true. But just as we legitimately want to know how our experience of an "event" of revelatory truth in and through a work of art may "correlate" with the rest of our experience, so too the question of how to correlate what we otherwise know or believe to be true with the strictly revelatory event of God's self-disclosure becomes the quest of the human for God.[27] Besides "criteria of appropriateness" for a properly *Christian* understanding of God's identity, therefore, there

---

22. The debates on the "method of correlation" from Paul Tillich's model to the present are well documented in recent theological literature (George Lindbeck, Francis Schüssler Fiorenza, David Tracy, Hans Küng, et al.).

23. For some further analysis here, see David Tracy, "The Analogical Imagination in Catholic Theology," in *Talking about God: Doing Theology in the Context of Modern Pluralism*, ed. David Tracy and John B. Cobb Jr. (New York: Seabury, 1983), 17–29.

24. The phrase "some aspect" refers to the use of the modern "reformed subjectivist principle" of Alfred North Whitehead on some aspect of the human person (e.g., freedom or intelligence) to find one's initial analogy for developing a metaphysics (as "descriptive generalization" or "transcendental analysis") for understanding God.

25. The "disclosure" in other "visible forms" is, of course, understood for von Balthasar only in and through the definitive visible form of God, Jesus Christ. See the brilliant studies of classic and contemporary visible forms in this christological light in Hans Urs von Balthasar, *The Glory of the Lord: A Theological Aesthetics*, 7 vols. (New York: Crossroad, 1983–1991).

26. The analogy depends on the tradition of hermeneutics for understanding truth as manifestation (Paul Ricoeur) or disclosure-concealment (Martin Heidegger) in the work of art.

27. The "coherence" in question will ordinarily claim only a "rough coherence" (Reinhold Niebuhr) with one or another limit-question or limit-experience of human beings.

116 remain theological criteria of credibility or intelligibility for correlating the question of God and God's self-disclosure in Jesus Christ.[28] In Catholic theology, the decrees of Vatican I on the "knowability" of God and the decrees on the possibility of some "analogous" understanding of the mysteries of faith demonstrate the same conviction: human beings, in their quest for God, do not quest in vain.[29] Christians should be willing to give "reasons for the hope that is in them" (see 1 Peter 3:15).[30] One theological way to give such reasons for hope is to attempt to correlate the human quest for God (in all the limit-experiences and limit-questions of human beings as human)[31] with God's own self-disclosure in Jesus Christ.

God and Natural Theology

The classical tradition of "natural theology" and the concerns of the traditional tract *De Deo uno* may be interpreted, therefore, as Catholic theological responses to these questions of intelligibility and credibility. In natural theologies, the "arguments" for the "existence" of God (ontological, cosmological, teleological, and moral) constitute part of the tradition of developing adequate criteria of credibility or intelligibility for the question of God.[32] In theological analyses of God's nature as "one," moreover, the use of various metaphysics or ontologies (e.g., Aquinas's transformation of both Aristotle and Neo-Platonism into his brilliant metaphysics of "*esse*" [to be] whereby the God of Exod. 3:14 is construed as "*Ipsum Esse Subsistens*" [the one Being whose very being it is to be])[33] is part of that same tradition of intelligibility. In the modern period, the "turn to the subject" of much modern thought (as of Augustine in classical theology) has also occasioned several correlational anthropologies, both transcendental and dialogical, that attempt to develop those same classic traditions of credibility and intelligibility in more explicitly modern anthropological directions.[34] None of the classic attempts of natural theology or apologetic theology (as distinct from some exercises in a decadent Neo-Scholasticism) can be read as deductive proofs *sensu stricto* (in the strict sense). Rather, the arguments for the existence of God should be read as reflective attempts to show to any reasonable person the intelligibility or credibility of the ultimate mystery who is the God of Jesus Christ. As such, the traditional "proofs" remain fruitful exercises: "reflective inventories" (Blondel) clarifying how our most basic beliefs and convictions as thinking, existing human beings are rendered intelligible only by grounding them in a basic belief in God—for example, as

---

28. On criteria of appropriateness and criteria of intelligibility, see Schubert Ogden, *On Theology* (San Francisco: Harper & Row, 1986).

29. The decrees of Vatican I were formulated, of course, in the nineteenth-century context of the debates on "faith" and "reason." Nevertheless, they still serve both to articulate the mainline Catholic tradition (e.g., Thomas Aquinas) on these issues and to encourage contemporary Catholic theologies. See, for example, Hans Küng, *Does God Exist? An Answer for Today* (Garden City, NY: Doubleday, 1980).

30. It is striking how often this scriptural saying is appealed to by Catholic theologians.

31. For further analysis, see David Tracy, *Blessed Rage for Order* (New York: Crossroad, 1975).

32. For a classical Thomist position, see Jacques Maritain, *Approaches to God* (New York: Harper, 1954).

33. For a helpful recent study of Aquinas, see W. J. Hankey, *God in Himself: Aquinas' Doctrine of God as Expounded in the* Summa Theologiae (Oxford: Oxford University Press, 1987).

34. The "linguistic turn" and the "turn to the political" have, of course, rendered earlier "transcendental" approaches more controversial.

the necessary coaffirmed horizon of ultimate intelligibility and being of all our acts of knowing (Karl Rahner) or the necessary ground of our most fundamental trust in existence itself (Schubert Ogden).[35]

United to the traditional and modern arguments on the "existence" of God, there are the various philosophical and theological attempts to find credible or intelligible analogies for understanding the nature and attributes of God. Here the theological criteria remain twofold: first, the coherence of any conceptual-theological understanding of God with the revelation of God's identity in Jesus Christ (criteria of appropriateness); second, the internal coherence of the metaphysical concepts employed for understanding God, as well as the coherence of those metaphysical concepts with our other knowledge and basic beliefs.[36] In no responsible theological position is there any claim to understand completely the divine mystery (rationalism). At the same time, the antifideist character of Catholic theology encourages any reasonable attempt to find proper analogical language for understanding the divine mystery more adequately and more intelligibly.

For example, it is correct to insist, as I did previously, (as above) that, abstractly considered the God of Jesus Christ, who *is* love, may also be conceptually construed as the radically relational origin, sustainer, and end of all real-

ity, whose relationality, as love and intelligence, bears all the marks of agency and thereby makes "person" language (God is "who," not "which") appropriate.[37] In that conceptual context, the category of relationality will become the most necessary abstract category for understanding the divine reality. Indeed, how most adequately to understand the divine relationality is the central theological question of God's nature in our period. On the one hand, the recovery of the centrality of the trinitarian understanding of God is the prime instance of the importance of the concept of relationality. This is especially the case in those theologians who have rethought the intrinsic unity of the "economic" and "immanent" Trinity (Karl Rahner, Walter Kasper, et al.).[38] It is also the case in those trinitarian theologians who have rethought the nature of divine relationship of suffering love in the light of the theology of the cross (Eberhard Jüngel, Jürgen Moltmann).[39] In every case of this contemporary trinitarian recovery, the category of relationality has become central for understanding the Christian God. In terms of criteria and appropriateness, therefore, an emphasis on trinitarian relationality is an entirely fruitful and now widespread theological advance.

In terms of criteria of intelligibility, moreover, the new trinitarian theologies have been joined by other theologies (some trinitarian, some not) where ontologies of relationality have

---

35. On the development of Rahner's position from his early emphasis on "intelligibility" to his later emphasis on "holy mystery," see the essays in Leo O'Donovan, ed., *A World of Grace: An Introduction to the Themes and Foundations of Karl Rahner's Theology* (New York: Crossroad, 1980). For Ogden, see Schubert M. Ogden, *The Reality of God* (New York: Harper & Row, 1977).

36. A proper metaphysics will address both kinds of coherence.

37. To claim "person" language as appropriate is not to deny that, like all analogous language for God, it is also finally inadequate for understanding divine intelligence and love.

38. See Rahner, "Remarks on the Dogmatic Treatise 'De Trinitate'"; idem, *The Trinity*; see also Walter Kasper, *The God of Jesus Christ* (New York: Crossroad, 1984), esp. 233–316.

39. Eberhard Jüngel, *God as the Mystery of the World* (Grand Rapids: Eerdmans, 1983); Jürgen Moltmann, *The Trinity and the Kingdom: The Doctrine of God* (New York: Harper & Row, 1980).

come to the forefront of philosophical and theological attention.[40] Process theology (as well as some revisionary forms of Hegelian theology) has led the way in insisting upon relationality as the primary concept needed to render more intelligible the Christian understanding of God for modern persons for whom process, relationality, and freedom are prominent ideals.[41] The question of God, for the Christian, is not primarily (as some classical theists held), How can the absolute one be intelligibly conceived as also relational? The question is, How can the unsurpassably related one best be conceived as absolute? It is to be noted that on the modern process theological view, God—and God alone—is related to all reality, both affecting all reality and affected by all reality.[42] In that sense, the metaphor "God is love" is rendered in explicitly relational terms. At the same time, this same emphasis on love as relationality helps to clarify how God's kenotic love disclosed in the cross of Jesus can be expressed in theological terms that seem both appropriate (to Scripture) and intelligible (to any modern person who believes in the radically relational character of all reality and the centrality of love for human self-constitution).[43]

Part of this issue of intelligibility is, in fact, as much anthropological as it is ontological.[44] The concept of God, for the Christian as for any radical monotheist, must be conceived in terms of perfection-language. As stated by Anselm, "Id quo maius cogitare non potest" (that than which no greater can be conceived).[45] Otherwise, one is not referring to God as understood by Jews, Christians, and Muslims. The question of God, if the discussion is really on God, must be the question of the perfect one. It must, therefore, always be formulated in terms of perfection-language.

Here the language of relationality, even in terms of the human analogue, is a helpful analogous language for the divine nature.[46] Indeed, in a culture of possessive individualism, the theological defense of the relational concept of the human "person," and not the modern concept of the purely autonomous individual, is crucial for those searching for models of human perfection. In the case of God's perfection, of course, any human analogue of perfection, as the Fourth Lateran Council insists on all analogies for God, must realize that "the greater the similarity, the greater still the difference."[47] At the same time, some human analogies for perfection are more fruitful than others. For example, the relational, affecting, and affected person of modern process, Hegelian, and dialogical philosophies does provide more helpful candidates for possible models of human "perfection" than the an-

---

40. For example, John Cobb's theology is not explicitly trinitarian; Norman Pittenger's process theology is.

41. For an important study here, see John Macquarrie, *In Search of Deity: An Essay in Dialectical Theism* (New York: Crossroad, 1985).

42. See John B. Cobb Jr. and David Ray Griffin, *Process Theology: An Introductory Exposition* (Philadelphia: Westminster, 1976); Norman Pittenger, *Catholic Faith in a Process Perspective* (Maryknoll, NY: Orbis, 1981).

43. It should be emphasized that process theologians characteristically appeal not only to a "modern" worldview but also to a biblical hermeneutic on God's relationality to the world.

44. Note Whitehead's use of the "reformed subjectivist principle" here.

45. See Charles Hartshorne, *The Logic of Perfection* (LaSalle, IL: Open Court, 1962); idem, *Anselm's Discovery* (LaSalle, IL: Open Court, 1965).

46. For further analysis, see David Tracy, "Analogy and Dialectic: God-Language," in Tracy and Cobb, *Talking about God*, 29–34.

47. For no similarity can be asserted . . . unless an even greater dissimilarity is included" (DS 806).

cient Greek models of the unaffected (*a-patheia*) person (e.g., of the Stoics) or the modern liberal model of the purely autonomous individual. A relational model of human perfection is clearly a more adequate one for understanding divine perfection than either an ancient individualist or modern autonomous one.[48]

The full Christian theological appropriateness of modern relational thought (Whiteheadean, Hegelian, and dialogical) remains an open question. But the insistence in all these forms of thought on the centrality of relationality (as freedom and love) in finding appropriate human analogues for the radical relationality of the Christian God who is love seems a genuine advance beyond some earlier emphases on "absoluteness" alone in *De Deo uno* followed (coherently?) by "relationality" in *De Deo trino*.

Conclusion: God-Talk in Different Epochs and Today

It is refreshing even today to read the startling achievements of the great patristic and medieval theologians on understanding the God of Jesus Christ by means of their transformation of the Greco-Latin *logos* (word) and *ratio-intellectus* (reason-intellect) of possibility to understand the God of the Scriptures also—partially, analogously but really—as the Ultimate who creates, encompasses, redeems. God is the Mystery of Love and Intelligence. In some ways, these earlier theonomous reflections on understanding God occur through a transformed understanding of Greek notions of love (Augustine's idea of

eros transformed by the gift of divine *agape* into *caritas*) and intelligence (discursive reason become contemplative theological reason). These theologies of God are not merely permanent but in many ways unsurpassed and perhaps unsurpassable achievements of the early and medieval theologians who had the good fortune to live in theonomous cultures.

The long centuries of Christian thought on God were dominated by the oceanic early Christian (especially Greek and medieval) understandings of God as Love and Intelligence. This is still the enriching mainstream of Christian theological reflection on God in both the Christian East and West. However, two alternative unsettling philosophical and theological undercurrents were always at work in Christian reflections on God. The first undercurrent, often named Dionysian after Dionysius the Areopagite, challenged even the highest achievements of the theologians employing Greek understandings of intelligence for attempting a better understanding of Godself as Pure Intelligence. Again and again, the refrain occurs—above all in the great apophatic tradition from Dionysius through John Scotus Erigena as well as through one side of Thomas Aquinas and through Marguerite Porete, Meister Eckhart, and Nicholas of Cusanus. The incomprehensibility of God disclosed in and through God's very comprehensibility became an ever more radical testimony to a powerful apophaticism and mysticism underlying and partly checking the optimism of the classical cataphatic theologies of *logos*, *intellectus*, and *eros*. The apophatic tradition of God's incomprehensibility always functioned as a strong undercurrent in the mainstream become, finally, a powerful undertow to all theological

---

48. Feminist theologies have been especially prominent in developing relational concepts of the "person" and criticizing the "maleness" of many "autonomy" and "individualist" models of the self.

120 language employing the *logos* of Greek intelligibility and possibility (as when Thomas Aquinas said we can know *that* God is but not *what* God is).

At the same time (not through apophatic but through apocalyptic movements and Pauline theologians of the cross), another and even more unsettling undercurrent drove much Western Christian theological reflection. For these thinkers, the reality of God was revealed not principally in glory or *eros*, nor in *logos*, *intellectus*, or intelligence, even apophatically self-aware intelligence, but in the paradoxical, impossible hiddenness of the cross. They held to the belief that God is most truly revealed in the weakness, conflict, and suffering manifested in the passion and cross of Jesus Christ and in the cross-saturated memory of the sufferings of all the oppressed and marginalized peoples of history (the medieval "spiritual" Franciscans). The genre of apocalypse—central in the New Testament itself—and the Pauline theology of the cross sent further shadows over any theology of God focused solely on love and intelligence. The theologies (often mystical) of the incomprehensible God found that the kenotic incarnation and the Divine Love and Intelligence (*Logos*) it manifested must also be read as an intensified kenosis of the cross—and both kenotic incarnation and cross are reread yet again through resurrection and the eschatological not-yet of promise of apocalyptic second coming.

At times, apocalyptic movements and the intense sufferings experienced in history and nature (e.g., the fourteenth-century Great Plague) acted like a flood that invaded and finally overtook the consciousness of many Christians. That flood of suffering invaded individuals (for example, Gregory the Great in his nightmare visions, Mechtild of Magdeburg, Angela of Foligno, and Martin Luther) and changed whole groups (such as the medieval radical, "spiritual" Franciscans, the Reformation Anabaptists, or the contemporary liberation and political theologians flourishing around the globe). These theologians articulate readings of God by listening to the experiences of oppressed and marginalized people. They keep alive the memories of suffering of the living and the dead.

These theological readings of the Christian God resurfaced in the profound sense of the suffering God of the late medieval Franciscans and even more intensely in the hidden-revealed God of Luther, Calvin, Las Casas, Michelangelo, Teresa of Avila, John of the Cross, and later still in the early modern age of an emerging science in Pascal. Pascal, one of the leading scientists and mathematicians of his age, articulated the grandeur of our human situation as our remarkable intelligence-in-act, so brilliantly displayed in modern mathematics and science united to the *misère* of our ego-saturated, self-deluding sense of our power. Pascal's understandings of God is, first, cataphatic (the greatness of the *imago Dei* in us through both the gift of intelligence and the even greater gift of *caritas*), second, apophatic (perhaps only so great a mathematician could see the profound limits of our intelligence at its best), and third and most important for Pascal, that God is a hidden God (Pascal loved to quote Isaiah: "Our God is a hidden God" [Isa. 45:15]). For Pascal, modern science with its great accomplishments had also rendered the universe—so alive, so participatory, so musical and harmonious for the ancients and medievals—silent and empty: "The silence of infinite space terrifies me."[49]

---

49. Blaise Pascal, *Thoughts*, trans. W. F. Trotter, Harvard Classics 45. (New York: P. F. Collier & Son, 1910), section 8, #242.

At the very dawn of modernity, therefore, Pascal sensed both the grandeur of modern science and mathematics and the even deeper incomprehensibility and hiddenness of God. In Western culture as a whole, however, modernity took over with more and more self-confidence, so that the two fragmenting currents of apophaticism-mysticism and apocalypticism went underground again, even for most Christian theologians, because of the impact of the late seventeenth century's scientific revolution, the eighteenth-century Enlightenment, and the nineteenth and early twentieth centuries' (until World War I) overwhelming self-confidence in modern science and technology and Western culture's thoughtless trust in progress. Led by Kant, many moderns now understand the ultimate mystery of God in modern Kantian terms as a limit-concept that can be thought but not known within the limits of modern rational possibility. Others simply dismissed the very notion of God, in Laplace's terms, as a hypothesis that we, the masters of modern rationality, no longer need. The ever more powerful and successful modern scientific *logos* took over *theo-logia* and recast the understanding of God into properly modern (i.e., secular) terms rationally acceptable to a modern mind.

God within the Modern Logos: From Deism to Panentheism

The hidden God of Luther, so explosive in the Reformation, was transformed in early modernity by Pascal into a profoundly anxious sense of the silence of infinite space. Pascal is surely the quintessential early modern who, almost alone, saw both modernity's splendid strength as well as its destructive and self-deluding sense of self-constitution, which undermines the earlier sense of God's reality in self, in history, and in cosmos. Not only the hidden God, but also the Godhead beyond God of Eckhart as well as the whole Dionysian tradition, became a largely forgotten undertow again after a last brilliant efflorescence in the greatest of the Renaissance thinkers, Nicolas of Cusa. Nicolas was the singular early modern theologian in whom the *logos* of modern mathematical intelligibility, the new sense of infinity in early Renaissance modernity, and the apophatic-mystical Dionysian tradition united into one last great creative outburst of a positive *docta ignorantia* (learned ignorance) on the incomprehensible God. In the wider culture, the relentless progress of modernity took over most thought concerning God. God gradually became the rationally possible limit-concept or ceased to exist, save as a cultural memory (what Nietzsche called the "death of God").

The difficulties for modernity on the question of God can now be seen more clearly and understood as reasonable in their context. So strong, so new, so powerful was the modern *logos* that it swept all before it. The horizon of possible intelligibility capsulized in the modern scientific and technological revolutions, as well as in the modern turn to the subject of Descartes and Kant and their many creative successors, climaxed in the modern democratic revolutions and the emergence of modern historical consciousness. No question, including the question of God, could any longer be allowed to be free of the radical rethinking of so amazing a constellation of cultural strength and political-economic achievement (as surely it was). These amazing modern political, scientific, and technological achievements overwhelmed all. By the early twentieth century, religion was privatized, any claim to truth in art marginalized, and reason itself largely reduced in a once public realm to a merely technical reason. By the twentieth century, Max Weber's bureaucratized, rationalized,

122 technologized, disenchanted world made "the death of God" proclaimed by Nietzsche more and more a cultural fact. As a notion of reason, modern rationality was too narrow and self-assured to produce philosophical and theological reflections on God on the level of the ancients, the medievals, and the Renaissance and Reformation thinkers.

The reality of God was recast as a modern question of purely modern rational possibility, if "God" was to be understood at all by a modern mind. Those who still possessed a strong sense of God's reality in their lives became, as Michel de Certeau has shown, marginal to the modern project, which centralized a notion of what could count as reason, much as power was centralized in the modern state. Indeed, intensely religious persons (formerly thought of in religious cultures as just normally religious persons in religious cultures) became what moderns named either mystics (the lovers of the incomprehensible God) or prophets (the beloved of The Impossible). An adjectival dimension to life and culture—the "mystical" as simply a spiritual dimension of mystery alive in all reality—became a noun, the mystic. This noun was used to name and marginalize the large group of outsiders to the modern project: Quietists, Quakers, Pietists, mystics, prophets. All reality must be disciplined by modern thought on what is rationally possible, including the reality of God. The Impossible became, by definition, the passé, the irrational—that is, the modern purely negative sense of the "impossible" as a purely logical category indicating all we must rationally reject. The mystical-metaphysical incomprehensible God and the prophetic-apocalyptic hidden God so lacked modern rational credentials of the conditions of possibility that they were largely forgotten by the increasingly secular culture and largely repressed even by most modern theologians. To call a modern theologian a mystic (e.g., John of the Cross) was as dismissive a charge of irrelevance as to call a philosopher an artist (e.g., John Henry Newman).

More positively, however, the *logos* of modernity—its powerful notion of possible intelligibility—also found new ways to understand God, or more exactly a new series of ways. On the question of God, the modern mind had choices (its *logos* for its *theo-logos*). But the modern choices were principally (it is unfair to say exclusively) determined not so much by the reality of God but by the *logos* of modernity. Philosophical and theological understandings of God adapted no longer to the long and rich traditions of Christian theological reflections on God nor to the actual communal-liturgical or personal spiritual lives of Christians. Even theology became more and more divorced from all that and sought a place solely within the horizon of modern rationality (Michael Buckley).[50] A modern could, for example, be a deist or a modern theist, an atheist or an agnostic. A modern thinker could become, with Spinoza, a modern pantheist (or was he really a God-intoxicated theopanist?). She could also become with Bruno, Hegel, and Whitehead a modern panentheist.

There can be little doubt that these modern understandings of God yielded genuine insights into the reality of God. This is especially the case on the question of panentheism. For it was in modern theology (including modern trinitarian theologies) that the intrinsically relational character of all reality—including, indeed especially, the divine reality—could be understood with the kind of conceptual clarity lacking in much ancient and medieval God-talk. Modern rela-

---

50. Michael Buckley, *At the Origins of Modern Atheism* (New Haven: Yale University Press, 1990).

tional God-talk—Hegelian, process, trinitarian, and most forms of modern feminist theology—solidified relationality as the one necessary category for God-talk. That relational achievement of modern theologies of God stands as its best achievement.

Yet even this now-classic modern achievement came with a high price: in both Hegel and Whitehead, and in many forms of modern relational thought, a question cannot be ignored: Is God rendered a conceptual prisoner of a new intellectual system of modern rationality or modern emancipation with very little memory of God's incomprehensible, hidden infinite mystery? It occurs to no sensible person to insist in the midst of a hurricane that he is experiencing a charming summer breeze. Moreover, if God is greater than all the powers of nature, the biblical God is greater in infinite personal intelligence and love than the overflowing and generous but neither intelligent nor loving impersonal God of all Platonists from Plotinus to Iris Murdoch. The biblical God is not identical to the Nature of the great Romantics. God as God cannot be considered so malleable a reality as to be conceptually grasped.

Even that quintessential modern thinker, René Descartes, insisted, almost despite himself, that the concept of God's infinity had broken through the categories of his modern philosophy. For Descartes, unlike Kant, the concept "the infinite" breaks down all our human categories. For Descartes, God does not merely become a Kantian limit-concept affirmed but not known to us. Rather, in the Third Meditation, Descartes makes an amazing move: the infinite must be a concept given to us. With finite minds, we could not produce the concept of the infinite on its own. Does God break through

Hegel or Whitehead or other contemporary modern forms of understandings of God? For Hegel, once we have grasped the Absolute Idea at the end of the *Phenomenology of Spirit*, we find ourselves capable of understanding "the very mind of God": hence, the *Logic*.[51] For Whitehead, with all his admirable Wordsworthian intuitions and moving Edwardian longings, all his attractive modesty on what metaphysics can and cannot do, all his finely meditative, even contemplative "Adventures" with ideas, God must not—indeed, cannot—be an exception to the axioms of metaphysics. Charles Hartshorne would soon force any earlier Whiteheadian hesitancies to the side and sort out how all namings of God must be one of the isms described in modern rational terms (deism, classical theism, modern atheism, pantheism), with only panentheism able to survive as a proper rational name for the God in modernity.

Hence, even modern theology's greatest achievement in understanding God—the relationality of God and all reality—was always in danger of becoming one more system, one of that long line of modern isms. Those isms began in early modernity with a cold deism and end in late modernity with a warmer process panentheism. However, where is the overwhelming sheer energy of the incomprehensible and hidden understandings of God in many relational understandings of God? This includes, I believe, many overconfident and non-apophatic modern trinitarian theologies. In my judgment, compared to classical theism and modern pantheism, much less modern atheism, panentheistic understandings of God are indeed a genuine rational gain, which too few philosophers and theologians seem willing to admit or even study. However, the modern panentheistic understanding may

---

51. Wilhelm Friedrich Hegel, *Wissenschaft der Logik*, Band 1 (Nürnberg: Johann Leonhard Schrag, 1812–16), 33, 44.

124 also be the end of the purely modern story in the understanding of God unless one allows God's reality as the impossible, incomprehensible Hidden One to break into and through the modern *logos* again. That breakthrough—indeed, that radical disruption—is the central meaning of many postmodern contemporary thoughts on God. Otherwise, modern relational thinkers on God, for all their contribution to greater clarity on God's intrinsically relational (and, for Christians, trinitarian) reality must—unless they rethink the apophatic character of their own genuine modern, rational achievements—fall prey to Heidegger's now-familiar charge of providing merely one more onto-theo-logical understanding of God and reality.[52]

Postmodernity and the Return of God as the Impossible

By its attack on the self-confidence of the modern *logos*, postmodernity provided a new opportunity for serious contemporary thought on God. To be sure, much contemporary thought will (and in my judgment, should) continue to be modern in character and achievement—for example, in the sensitive and impressive reflections on God in some modern cosmologies, in the ecological movements, and some of the "new physics," or in the renewed question of God for several modern scientists and theologians in their mutually informative conversations on science and theology. Much contemporary thought on God, moreover, will prove to be a rediscovery and a necessary (i.e., demythologized) rethinking of the persistent mythological elements in

premodern forms for understanding God. At the same time, the most characteristically postmodern forms of God-talk have allowed the awesome reality of *theos* as the Impossible to charge back in full force. This happens after postmodernity's calling into question of modernity's powerful *logos* of modern rationality and what it will and will not allow to count as rational, as actual, as possible and impossible.

For some postmodern thinkers, to say "the Impossible" as a positive reality is as far as one should go (Derrida).[53] For myself, to say "the Impossible" is to bespeak a new entry to the question of *naming* God as the Impossible. The postmodern positive concept of the Impossible was begun much earlier by Kierkegaard against Kant.[54] For myself, this new postmodern route of the Impossible—especially if joined to the long, diverse, and intellectually fascinating history of the category of the Infinite in its complex and controversial history among the ancients, the medievals, the early moderns, the moderns (especially Descartes), and contemporary science and mathematics—is an exceptionally promising route to naming God anew as the incomprehensible, hidden, all-loving one whom we worship.

Most postmodern philosophical and theological thought tends to be suspicious of almost all traditional and modern arguments on the existence and nature of God, especially all attempts to fit God's reality into a modern horizon of intelligibility (i.e., all the famous modern isms for God from deism and theism through Panentheism). "Let God be God" becomes an authentic cry again. For this impossible, infinite

---

52. Martin Heidegger, *Mindfulness*, trans. Parvis Emad and Thomas Kalary (New York: Continuum, 2006), 9–35.

53. On Jacques Derrida's use of the Impossible, see the study by John D. Caputo, *The Prayers and Tears of Jacques Derrida: Religion without Religion* (Bloomington: Indiana University Press, 1997).

54. Søren Kierkegaard, *Philosophical Fragments*, ed. and trans. Howard V. Hong and Edna H. Hong (Princeton: Princeton University Press, 1985), 37–55.

God reveals Godself in hiddenness: in cross and negativity, in the innocent suffering of all those others whom the grand narrative of modernity has set aside as non-peoples, non-events, non-memories, non-history. As Emmanuel Levinas rightly insists, after a bloodied twentieth century, the question of useless suffering must be the test of any philosophy or theology.[55]

God comes first as empowering hope to oppressed and marginal peoples and their theologies: a God of impossible promise to help liberate and transform all reality personally, communally, economically, socially, politically within the more encompassing horizon of Christian redemption. Emancipation-liberation and redemption are not synonyms. At the same time, they cannot be separated for anyone claiming fidelity (intellectual and existential) to the hidden God of the prophets and their proclamation of God's privileged people as the poor, the marginal, the forgotten, and the oppressed. The question of the "non-person," insists Gustavo Gutiérrez, is now more important and central a question for any thoughtful theologian than the doubts of the modern non-believer.[56] Even modern philosophy need not be read solely as the history of modern epistemology but, as Su-

san Nieman argues, as a history of responses to radical evil.[57] Ethics must concentrate, insists Emmanuel Levinas, on the other, not on the autonomous modern self, if it is to be first "philosophy" challenging all modern ontologies.[58]

God also comes to many postmodern forms of contemporary theology not only as the hidden-revealed God of hope manifested in the passion and negativity of the cross as well as in the memory of suffering and the struggle by, for, and with "others" for justice and love.[59] God also comes as an ever-deeper Hiddenness—the awesome power, the terror, the hope beyond hope for the sake of the hopeless. Hence, the apocalyptic undertow resurfaces with the force of a whirlpool in postmodern thought, insisting on a radical "not-yet."[60] This can be found in the New Testament's threatening, apocalyptic hope of a "second coming" against the raging oppression, injustice, and evil of our world; indeed, "Come, Lord Jesus, come" (Rev. 22:20) are the final words of the New Testament—Jewish words of a messianic Impossibility to come.[61] The African American theologians have led the way here by turning back to their own people's classic narratives and songs (the spirituals, the gospel songs). Thereby they have sensed anew this reality of the

---

55. Emmanuel Levinas, *Of the God Who Comes to Mind*, trans. Bettina Bergo (Stanford: Stanford University Press, 1998), 122–37.

56. Gustavo Gutiérrez, *We Drink from Our Own Wells: The Spiritual Journey of a People*, trans. Matthew J. O'Connell (Maryknoll, NY: Orbis, 1984).

57. Susan Neiman, *Evil in Modern Thought: An Alternative History of Philosophy* (Princeton: Princeton University Press, 2002). See also Richard Bernstein, *Radical Evil: A Philosophical Interrogation* (Cambridge: Cambridge University Press, 2002).

58. Emanuel Lévinas, *Totality and Infinity: An Essay on Exteriority*, trans. Alphonso Lingis (Pittsburgh: Duquesne University Press, 1969). See also the study by Adriaan Peperzak, *To the Other: An Introduction to the Philosophy of Emmanuel Levinas* (West Lafayette, IN: Purdue University Press, 1993).

59. Walter Benjamin, *Theses on the Philosophy of History*, trans. Dennis Redmond (Frankfurt: Suhrkamp Verlag, 1974). Johann Baptist Metz, *The Emergent Church: The Future of Christianity in a Post-Bourgeois World*, trans. Peter Mann (New York: Crossroad, 1981).

60. On Bloch, see the study *Not Yet: Reconsidering Ernst Bloch*, ed. Jamie Owen Daniel and Tom Moylan (London: Verso, 1997).

61. See Caputo, *The Prayers and Tears of Jacques Derrida*, 117–60.

126 hidden-revealed God—the name of the apocalyptic God as the Impossible transforming, not eliminating tragedy. This apocalyptic God has also been rediscovered in the powerful political theology of Johann Baptist Metz and his theological motif of suffering into God.[62] Therefore, it is important to note that the apocalyptic, cross-saturated hidden God returns principally through the memory of the suffering of all victims of gender, race, and class. This list of victims also includes those of Western modernity, such as victims of violent colonial periods of the West—the too often unacknowledged dark side of modernity. Modernity gave our culture the incomparable ethical-political gains of human rights, representative democracy, and a sense of the need for social justice to curb a now-victorious capitalism. Yet there remain many gender, racial, class, and colonialist vestiges of the dark side of modernity.

The hidden-revealed God is now found not principally through the estranged and alienated self of the existentialist theologians, those admirable and deeply troubled modern intellectuals. Rather, a sense of the hidden-revealed God now surfaces principally through the interruptive experience and memory of the suffering of all those ignored, marginalized, murdered, enslaved, or colonized by the grand narrative of Western modernity. In the light of that new apocalyptic interruption of trying to understand the hidden God anew, the modern isms for God begin to seem rather thin. Into that interruption, the apocalyptic hidden God of power, threat, promise, and awe, the God of Lamentations and Job, the God of Jesus' cry on the cross, "My God, my God, why have you abandoned me?" (Mark 15:34), returns to disrupt the power of the modern *logos* over "God" in contemporary theologies.

At the same time, language has come in ever new and self-interrupting guises to disrupt the overreaching claims of modern thought in its own way. The very language that modern thought needs in order to think its horizon of possible intelligibility—the logocentric reality of modern rationality, rendering God into one more modern ism—is now acknowledged as far less clear, less self-present than it thought itself, less logocentric, less in control than modern understandings of language ordinarily assumed. The great nineteenth-century exceptions here are those honorary postmodern thinkers of language, Kierkegaard and Nietzsche. Through postmodern linguistic reflections on the unthought factors in modern thought, the modern *logos* dissolves its own former certainties and disowns its own claims to full self-presence and self-grounding. In fact, the modern *logos* is not stable enough to control its understanding of itself (now decentered), much less able to control an adequate understanding of God. The impossible God returns to fragment, even shatter, the *theos*, at once grounding and domesticated, in modernity's onto-*theo*-logy. The incomprehensible God returns to demand that modernity disown once and for all its overly ambitious claims to understand the reality of God. The incomprehensible God, allied to the hidden God, returns to demand attention. The underground streams have surfaced anew in postmodern theologies with the force of a whirlpool.

Moreover, the two classic traditional clues for understanding God's reality—love and intelligence in the human *imago* created as such by God—also return in new, postmodern forms and sometimes formlessness. "God is love" now becomes an occasion not only to show the reasonableness and relationality of the Divine Re-

---

62. Metz, *The Emergent Church*, 48–66.

ality. Love now also enters postmodernity not solely as relationality but also as transgression, excess, and finally as the transgressive, excessive gift and judgment to name God's impossible love. To recover the great apophatic tradition of Dionysius the Areopagite again—the tradition of the incomprehensible God beyond being—is a new call for thinking God anew. To retrieve the Dionysian tradition is also to challenge modern theology in its most characteristic forms. For the God who is love beyond being and transcendentality is also the God beyond rationality. God is love—i.e., excess, gift, the incomprehensible, impossible Good. That is a thought which modern theology cannot think without yielding its *logos* of rational possibility to the *theos* of what counts for moderns as the Impossible in ways it does not yet seem to know how to do. Job and Lamentations return to haunt contemporary theologians as they attempt to name God in the new hidden-revealed theologies focused on history as interruption. So too such texts as the Song of Songs and the feminist retrievals of God as *Sophia* return to be heard in ways modern theologies did not envisage as even possible, much less desirable. Both intellectually and existentially, desire, body, love, gift have all returned to try to allow God-as-God to be named anew.

When one turns to the second classical clue for understanding God, intelligence, the new postmodern situation is analogous. The modern *logos* in modern theology can no longer suffice for our understanding of God. Another kind of transgression and excess occurs: not new re-

flection on love as gift, but the kind of radical contemplative detachment attendant to a profoundly apophatic theology like that of Meister Eckhart. These postmodern namings of a Godhead beyond God expose modern theology's inability to envisage God beyond its own *logos*.

No one knows, I believe, where those postmodern suspicions and retrievals will finally lead. But this much is clear: thanks to the new reflections on the Impossible, the Infinite, and Love as both radical relationality and gift, excess, and transgression, the reality of God as the incomprehensible, hidden, excessively loving one has returned to the center of theology. Perhaps this is not the time to rush out new propositions on the reality of God, although all such should be welcomed as partial and analogous clarifications of some aspect of the incomprehensible, hidden, loving, trinitarian God. Eventually, it will be time again to try to gather all the fragments into new orderings. However, now is the time for theologians above all to learn to disallow the *logos* of modernity to control their thoughts on God as we learn anew to be attentive to God as the incomprehensible, hidden, and radically, excessively loving God. We must learn somehow to be still and know that God is God and we are not. Neither is the awesome, boundless, finite universe. Even trinitarian language, so necessary to express the central Christian understanding of God as relational love, is likely to become more and more an apophatic trinitarian love as excess. But that is a further question beyond the limits of this chapter.

128 For Further Reading

See also pages 196–99 for further recommended reading.

Araya, Victorio. *God of the Poor: The Mystery of God in Latin American Liberation Theology.* Maryknoll, NY: Orbis, 1988.

> *A major study from a liberation theology perspective.*

Bouillard, Henri. *The Knowledge of God.* New York: Herder & Herder, 1968.

> *A leading Roman Catholic French representative of la nouvelle théologie underscores the relation between language about God and the public nature of theology.*

Burrell, David. *Knowing the Unknowable God.* Notre Dame, IN: University of Notre Dame Press, 1986.

> *An important exposition of Aquinas that highlights his relation to and difference from Moses Maimonides and Ibn-Sina.*

Cobb, John B., Jr., and David Tracy. *Talking about God: Doing Theology in the Context of Modern Pluralism.* New York: Seabury, 1983.

> *A study of some central issues that emerge from Protestant and Catholic standpoints.*

Cone, James. *God of the Oppressed.* New York: Seabury, 1975.

> *A major study of God from the perspective of African American theology.*

Daly, Mary. *Beyond God the Father.* Boston: Beacon, 1973.

> *A significant work of feminist theology in regard to metaphor and language about God.*

Gilkey, Langdon. *Naming the Whirlwind: The Renewal of God-Language.* Indianapolis: Bobbs-Merrill, 1969.

> *Discussion of the problem of God for modern secular culture.*

Hodgson, Peter C. *God in History: Shapes of Freedom.* Nashville: Abingdon, 1989.

> *An effort to rethink the relationship between God and history through a reconstruction of Hegel's trinitarian understanding of God.*

Jüngel, Eberhard. *God as the Mystery of the World.* Grand Rapids: Eerdmans, 1983.

> *An elaboration of the centrality of the Trinity and of a theology of the cross for the Christian understanding of God.*

Kaufman, Gordon. *God the Problem.* Cambridge: Harvard University Press, 1972.

> *A major study of the problem of God for modern thought.*

Küng, Hans. *Does God Exist? An Answer for Today.* Garden City, NY: Doubleday, 1980.

> *Küng articulates many of the central concerns raised by modern thinkers about God.*

Lonergan, Bernard. *The Philosophy of God and Theology.* Philadelphia: Westminster, 1973.

> *Lonergan rethinks the relation between philosophy and religious experience for the question of God.*

———. *The Way to Nicaea.* London: Longman & Todd, 1976.

> *A dialectical study of the emergence of the early conciliar understanding of God.*

Marion, Jean-Luc. *God without Being.* Chicago: University of Chicago Press, 1991.

> *An example of the recent phenomenonological approaches to God.*

McFague, Sallie. *Models of God: Theology for an Ecological, Nuclear Age.* Philadelphia: Fortress Press, 1987.

> *A study of God in relation to the ecological crisis that suggests mother, friend, and lover as new models of God.*

Macquarrie, John. *In Search of Deity: An Essay in Dialectical Theism.* The Gifford Lectures, 1983. New York: Crossroad, 1985.

> *A major attempt to recover the Neo-Platonic tradition on the question of God.*

Ogden, Schubert. *The Reality of God.* New York: Harper & Row, 1977.

> *A major articulation of the reasons for a process understanding of God.*

Rahner, Karl. *Foundations of Christian Faith.* New York: Crossroad, 1978.

> *Rahner's most systematic treatment of divine incomprehensibility.*

Ruether, Rosemary. *Sexism and God-Talk: Toward a Feminist Theology.* Boston: Beacon, 1983.

> *A major feminist study of the doctrine of God/ess.*

God and Trinity

The Trinitarian Mystery of God: A "Theological Theology"

Anthony J. Godzieba

Prelude:
The Limits and Task of Trinitarian Theology

The drama of the revelation of the Trinity bursts the bounds of any metaphor or rational schema. The Trinity, as the great fifth- or sixth-century mystical theologian Pseudo-Dionysius ecstatically proclaims, is "higher than any being, any divinity, any goodness!"[1] For the theologian, whose task is classically defined as "faith seeking understanding," nothing is more resistant to the categories of understanding than the incomprehensible mystery of the triune God; nothing is more excessive. The revelation of the Father's salvific love in the life, death, and resurrection of his Son and the perdurance of the Son's redemptive power through the ongoing activity of the Spirit—contemplating this dramatic activity of divine life in our history led Gregory of Nazianzus to concede that "to tell of God is not possible . . . but to know him is even less possible."[2] Whatever we can affirm of the triune God (kataphatic theology) is constantly shadowed by the ignorance and limitations that God's incomprehensibility forces upon us (apophatic theology). This is because revelation is the interplay of presence and absence; our experience of the triune God conceals at the same time it reveals.

Perhaps, then, the more adequate means to express this drama of love and its salvific effects should indeed be aesthetic: Andrei Rublev's famous gentle icon of the Trinity, or the spectacular and inspiring *Gnadenstuhl* (Throne of Grace) sculpture that hangs high above the altar of the long, narrow Church of St. John Nepomuk (the *Asam-Kirche*) in Munich, or Giovanni Pierluigi da Palestrina's motet "O beata et benedicta et gloriosa Trinitas," whose vocal lines float down from the heights and then rise ecstatically, all the while intertwining in the most delicious harmonies. Or perhaps just making the sign of the cross.

In other words, the doctrine of the Trinity cannot be reduced to a set of rational categories or any sort of metaphysics of substances and essences. Unfortunately, until recently, Roman Catholic theology was full of attempts like this. In the first edition of this volume, Catherine Mowry LaCugna noted that previous Catholic seminary education "often went no further than requiring students to memorize the 5-4-3-2-1 formula, a mnemonic device for retaining the essential elements of the Thomistic doctrine of the Trinity: 'five notions, four relations, three persons, two processions, and one nature.'" She went on to say, though, that "today trinitarian theology is being recovered as a fruitful and intelligible way to articulate what it means to be 'saved by God through Christ in the power of the Holy Spirit.'"[3] This is certainly the case. A recent commentary summarizes this shift in perspective by noting that "much contemporary Trinitarian theology is taken up with how the apparently remote symbol of the triune God has far-reaching implications for our self-understanding, our relationships with others and for

---

1. *The Mystical Theology*, ch. 1, in Pseudo-Dionysius, *The Complete Works*, trans. Colm Luibheid and Paul Rorem, The Classics of Western Spirituality (New York/Mahwah, NJ: Paulist, 1987), 135.

2. Gregory of Nazianzus, Oration 28 [= Second Theological Oration], sec. 4, in *On God and Christ: The Five Theological Orations and Two Letters to Cledonius*, trans. Frederick Williams and Lionel Wickham, Popular Patristics Series (Crestwood, NY: St. Vladimir's Seminary Press, 2002), 39.

3. Catherine Mowry LaCugna, "The Trinitarian Mystery of God," in *Systematic Theology: Roman Catholic Perspectives*, ed. Francis Schüssler Fiorenza and John P. Galvin, 2 vols. (Minneapolis: Fortress Press, 1991), 1:153.

society." This is a contemporary instance of the perduring tension within Christianity "between wanting to preserve the distinct identity of Father, Son and Spirit on the one hand, and the conviction that the triune God is primarily an event, a verb rather than a subject, a pure giving and receiving in an eternal perichoretic communion into which we are invited, on the other."[4]

Attempts to explicate the fundamental Christian confession that "God is love" (1 John 4:16) in purely abstract categories are doomed to frustration; their static character eventually betrays the overall thrust of the New Testament and of the Christian liturgical and spiritual traditions, all of which communicate the drama of our salvation in a much more performative way. Viewing the Trinity as an "event" (an emphasis shared by Thomas Aquinas's description of the inner-trinitarian life as *actus purus*) and as an invitation to participation parallels my suggestion that the mystery of the Trinity as an ensemble of *operations* might best be communicated in those aesthetic *performances*. They draw us in by their beauty and point beyond themselves to suggest, however fleetingly, the drama of divine love that grounds reality, surpasses all human knowledge, and transcends all human expectations.[5] The *active* aesthetic (with its play of light and shadow,

presence and absence, revealing and concealing) can thus suggest the reality of the Trinity, revealed to us in *acts* of love and grace, and mediated by the particularity and limitations of embodied, historically situated experiences.[6]

This does not deny the importance of the systematic task, though. In advocating a more dynamic and personalist view, Walter Kasper rightly argues for a "theological theology," based on the profession of faith in the Trinity, as the robust replacement for the anemic theism that hangs on in many circles, despite the fact that it had been already undermined by the Enlightenment and atheism, and was powerless to respond to either:

> The direct object of the proclamation, as the church's confession of faith, is the economic Trinity and the God of Jesus Christ who in the Spirit gives us love and freedom, reconciliation and peace. Of course, the proclamation cannot stop there. For according to the Lord's farewell prayer true life consists precisely in knowing and glorifying God. For its own sake therefore soteriology must pass over into doxology. For amid all the vicissitudes and instability of history man's salvation consists in having communion with the God who through all eternity *is* love.[7]

---

4. Declan Marmion and Gesa Thiessen, "The Revival of Trinitarian Theology," in *Trinity and Salvation: Theological, Spiritual and Aesthetic Perspectives*, ed. Declan Marmion and Gesa Thiessen, Studies in Theology, Society, and Culture, vol. 2 (Bern: Peter Lang, 2009), 3.

5. The term *operations* comes from Thomas Aquinas by way of Graham Ward. Thomas: "Now God is not known to us in his own nature, but through his works or effects (*ex operationibus vel effectibus ejus*)." *Summa theologiae* Ia, q. 13, a. 8, resp., in *Summa theologiae*, vol. 3 (Ia. 12–13), *Knowing and Naming God*, trans. Herbert McCabe (London: Eyre & Spottiswoode; New York: McGraw-Hill, 1964), 78–79; hereafter cited as ST, part, question (q.), article (a.), response, reply (ad), followed by volume and page(s) in the Latin-English Blackfriars edition, 60 vols. (London: Eyre & Spottiswoode; New York: McGraw-Hill, 1964–76). Ward applies this to Christology, "an analysis of the operations whereby Christ is made known to us. And in being made known we participate in him." *Christ and Culture*, Challenges in Contemporary Theology (Malden, MA: Blackwell, 2005), 1.

6. Cf. Anthony J. Godzieba, "The Catholic Sacramental Imagination and the Access/Excess of Grace," *New Theology Review* 21, no. 3 (August 2008): 14–26.

7. Walter Kasper, *The God of Jesus Christ*, trans. Matthew J. O'Connell (1985; repr., New York: Crossroad, 2005), 316.

134

Communion with God, offered to us in a relationship of love, is at the heart of any reflection on the mystery of the Trinity. The revelation of this mystery is God's loving offer to us of grace and peace; we are the object of God's initiative and saving intentionality. In response, we offer God glory and praise; God is the object of our faith intentionality. Soteriology passes over into doxology. At the nexus of these two active operations occurs our relatively impoverished theological reflection on the mystery of the Trinity. Theology's task in giving "a reason for our hope" (1 Peter 3:15) includes the clarification afforded by reflection. While words ultimately fail and rational categories are exhausted by the Trinity's incomprehensible mystery, explication of some kind is necessary.

This is especially required in our contemporary context, where two contradictory claims about the Trinity immediately jostle for the believer's attention and demand explanation. One emphasizes the Trinity's centrality for human life, while the other proclaims its irrelevance. The first claim is that the heart of Christian belief and the explicitly Christian way of speaking about God is to confess God as Trinity: one God in three persons, Father, Son, and Holy Spirit. We see this in the Nicene Creed: "We believe in one God, the Father almighty, maker of heaven and earth . . . and in one Lord Jesus Christ, the only-begotten Son of God . . . and in the Holy Spirit, the Lord and Giver of life."[8] Thus, for Christians, not only is "Trinity" how God is revealed as the author of our salvation, but "Trinity" is also *precisely* how the long Christian tradition speaks of God when reflecting on how believers have encountered God in their experience as "God-for-us."[9] The other—and polar opposite—claim is the commonly expressed complaint regarding the "relevance" of this doctrine. This comes in a wide range of attitudes, from a popular dismissal of the triune God as unbelievable, nonsensical, or irrelevant to contemporary life all the way up to and including the more sophisticated state of affairs described in Karl Rahner's oft-cited diagnosis that most Christians "are, in their practical life, mere monotheists" and that "should the doctrine of the Trinity have to be dropped as false, the major part of religious literature could well remain virtually unchanged."[10]

How can the Trinity be the foundation of all Christian life as well as the ground of all reality, yet be dismissed as having no "practical" significance? The ambivalence found in many contemporary believers and in many modern and contemporary theologies can already be found in Friedrich Schleiermacher's famous comment that the doctrine of the Trinity, while important, was independent of "the main pivots of the eccle-

---

8. More precisely, the Nicene-Constantinopolitan Creed, the "symbol" of Nicaea (325) as expanded by the first council of Constantinople (381), trans. in J. Neuner and J. Dupuis, *The Christian Faith in the Doctrinal Documents of the Catholic Church* [= ND], 6th ed. (New York: Alba House, 1996), ND 12 (pp. 9–10); Heinrich Denzinger and Peter Hünermann, *Enchiridion symbolorum definitionum et declarationum de reus fidei et morum/Kompendium der Glaubensbekenntnisse und kirchlichen Lehrentscheidungen* [= DH], 38th ed. (Freiburg: Herder, 1999), DH 150. See also Norman P. Tanner, ed., *Decrees of the Ecumenical Councils*, 2 vols. (London: Sheed & Ward / Washington, DC: Georgetown University Press, 1990), 1:24 (Greek/Latin original and English translation on facing pages).

9. See Catherine Mowry LaCugna, *God for Us: The Trinity and Christian Life* (San Francisco: HarperCollins, 1991), 1; Jürgen Werbick, "Trinitätslehre," in *Handbuch der Dogmatik*, ed. Theodore Schneider, 2 vols. (Düsseldorf: Patmos, 1992), 2:481–576, at 481–82.

10. Karl Rahner, *The Trinity*, trans. Joseph Donceel (1970; repr., New York: Crossroad, 2002), 10–11.

siastical doctrine—the Being of God in Christ and the Christian Church."[11] How, then, do we address this ambiguity and build a bridge to get from "irrelevance" to "centrality"? The answer is the use of a natural theology that looks for clues of the presence of God in our experience, and then the pursuit of a theological theology that reflects on the triune God who is revealed to us at the threshold of that experience.

The Role of Natural Theology

We must be careful, though, not to claim too much for natural theology. Thomas Aquinas's caution, reinforcing our earlier point, is worth noting:

> It is impossible to come to the knowledge of the Trinity of divine persons through natural reason. . . . Through natural reason one can know God only from creatures; and they lead to the knowledge of him as effects do to their cause. Therefore by natural reason we can know of God only what characterizes him necessarily as the source of all beings. . . . Whoever tries to prove the trinity of persons by natural powers of reason detracts from faith in two ways. First . . . the object of faith is those invisible realities which are beyond the reach of human reason. . . . Secondly . . . when someone wants to support faith by unconvincing arguments, that person

becomes a laughing stock for the unbelievers, who think that we rely on such arguments and believe because of them.[12]

The distinction between a "natural" and a "theological" theology would leave us with an intractable problem if we held the common view that natural knowledge of God and supernatural divine revelation are distinct and completely separate. Fortunately, there is no real dilemma or forced either-or choice here. That would arise only if one were to approach the question of God with the Enlightenment's assumption of a complete disjunction between so-called pure nature and the supernatural. But that assumption (which unfortunately still colors much of the discussion of God in Western culture) stems from a minimalist view of rationality, faith, and natural theology.

However, we can describe "natural theology" in a much more positive, inclusive, and authentically Catholic way. Faith and reason, while distinct, are mutually related aspects of human experience. Faith is always both "faith seeking understanding" (*fides quaerens intellectum*) and "faith developed in understanding" (*intellectus fidei*).[13] The believer always approaches the truth of God's gratuitous offer of salvation in an active way, interpreting one's life in relation to God and then affirming this relationship as the most meaningful way to actualize the possibilities of human existence. This implicit interaction leads to the more adequate description of natural

---

11. Friedrich Schleiermacher, *The Christian Faith*, ed. H. R. Mackintosh and J. S. Stewart (Edinburgh: T&T Clark, 1989), 741.

12. ST Ia, q. 32, a. 1, resp. (vol. 6 [Ia. 27–32], trans. Ceslaus Verlecky, 102–5; translation modified).

13. Cf. Bernhard Welte, "Credo ut intelligam als theologisches Programm heute," in *Wissenschaft und Verantwortung*, [Freie Universität Berlin] Universitätstage 1962 (Berlin: de Gruyter, 1962), 16–30 ("Credo ut Intelligam—as a Theological Program for our Times," trans. Fidelis J. Smith, *American Church Quarterly* 2 [1962]: 143–52); idem, *Heilsverständnis: Philosophische Untersuchungen einiger voraussetzungen zum Verständnis des Christentums*, Gesammelte Schriften 4/1: Hermeneutik des Christlichen (Freiburg: Herder, 2006; orig. 1966), 32–64.

theology as the search for "the natural 'access-point' of faith" and to describe its task as demonstrating "the internal reasonableness of a faith which has its substantiation in and from itself."[14] The "natural" and the "supernatural" are distinct but not dichotomous; they intersect in everyday, historically shaped lived experience. Within the natural, one recognizes the presence of the mystery of the supernatural, "not as optional like a gift which is proposed but not imposed . . . not as so ineffable as to lack all foothold in our thought and our life, but . . . as indispensable and at the same time inaccessible" to finite human experience.[15] This intersection marks the clearing where knowledge of God unfolds, where faith's desire for God becomes visible, and where revelation begins to be encountered.

There are, however, limits to this search. We agree with Thomas that the natural knowledge of God permits us only an inadequate glimpse of the character of transcendence, never any full comprehension of its nature.[16] Despite this limitation, natural theology discloses something remarkable: the fundamental *religious* character of the structure of human experience, its intentional openness to infinite mystery that forms its transcendental horizon. True, the precise character of this mystery is revealed only by the mystery itself. But the natural knowledge of God opens a vista onto the revelation of the true nature of divine mystery, without daring to claim to actually reach it—much as Moses, on the heights of Mount Nebo, glimpsed the Promised Land without being allowed to enter it (Deut. 34:1-4).

What about this issue when seen within the history of theology? Our approach might appear to echo a difficulty that has plagued mainstream Christian theology since the thirteenth century, and particularly Catholic theology since the late nineteenth century—namely, a perpetuation of the gulf between a theology of the nature and unity of God (the theological treatise *De Deo uno*) and one that deals specifically with God as triune (the treatise *De Deo trino*). More recently, as Catherine LaCugna noted in the first edition, this division of labor "made the doctrine of the Trinity appear as an afterthought, as something added on to a prior, independent philosophical concept of God."[17]

It is ironic that Thomas Aquinas was the first to develop the study of God in this general manner.[18] He began by taking up the earlier scholastic tradition that had been passed down chiefly through Peter Lombard's *Sentences* (*Sententiarum libri IV*, c. 1155–58), the compendium that dominated the study of theology through the latter half of the medieval period. The *Sentences* had divided the material of theology into four treatises (God and Trinity, creation and sin, the incarnation and the virtues, and the sacraments and the four last things). In writing the *Summa theologiae*, however, Thomas reorganized the material dealing with God, under the influence of late Neo-Platonism (especially as conveyed through the writings of Pseudo-

---

14. Walter Kasper, *An Introduction to Christian Faith*, trans. V. Green (New York: Paulist, 1980), 20 ("natural 'access-point'"); idem, *The God of Jesus Christ*, 71 ("internal reasonableness").

15. Maurice Blondel, *The Letter on Apologetics*, in *The Letter on Apologetics and History and Dogma*, trans. Alexander Dru and Illtyd Trethowan (Grand Rapids: Eerdmans, 1994; Fr. orig., 1896), 161.

16. Cf. ST Ia, q. 2, a. 2 (2:8–11).

17. LaCugna, "The Trinitarian Mystery of God," 1:172.

18. Noted also by Rahner, *The Trinity*, 16. For what follows, see LaCugna, *God for Us*, 146–48; W. J. Hankey, *God in Himself: Aquinas' Doctrine of God as Expounded in the* Summa Theologiae (Oxford: Oxford University Press, 1987), 1–35.

Dionysius) and in particular the Neo-Platonic *exitus-reditus* schema (i.e., creatures' procession from and return to God).[19] While the *Sentences* had treated the nature of God within the opening section devoted to the Trinity (*de mysterio Trinitatis*), Thomas was more influenced by the structure of Pseudo-Dionysius's *The Divine Names*. He divided the treatise on God into two distinct parts, called by later commentators *De Deo uno* and *De Deo trino*.[20] The former (*Summa theologiae* Ia, qq. 2–26) examines the issues surrounding the nature of the one God and our knowledge of that nature, while the latter (*Summa theologiae* Ia, qq. 27–43) examines the distinction of persons in the Trinity and their relations.

Thomas never designated one part as purely philosophical and the other as purely theological. Rather, both are theological because they investigate matters that have been revealed to faith and pursued under the rubric of "sacred teaching" (*sacra doctrina*). He insists at the out-

set that theology (also termed *sacra doctrina*) is a discipline practiced from the perspective of faith, which has its grounding in revelation. It is a science whose principles flow "from founts recognized in the light of a higher science, namely God's very own which he shares with the blessed."[21] One cannot appeal, then, either to the structure or the arguments of the *Summa theologiae* to justify the identification of Thomas's *De Deo uno* with the kind of philosophically extrinsicist natural theology we criticized earlier.[22]

After Thomas's death, his twofold division of the study of God was widely imitated in the medieval West and became the model for subsequent discussions. Only much later, with nineteenth-century Roman Catholic Neo-Scholasticism, was the distinction between the two treatises turned into a rigid disjunction that did away with Thomas's carefully crafted plan. The Neo-Scholastic theological manuals identified *De Deo uno* with the philosophical discussion of the one divine nature and *De Deo trino*

---

19. See Paul Rorem, *Pseudo-Dionysius: A Commentary on the Texts and an Introduction to Their Influence* (New York: Oxford University Press, 1993), 172–74. As major influences, he cites Boethius, Proclus (whose *Liber de causis* was believed by Thomas to have been authored by Aristotle), and the Pseudo-Dionysian corpus, particularly *The Divine Names*.

20. Cf. Hankey, *God in Himself*, 10–12. The author of *The Divine Names* had divided them into "the unified names [that] apply to the entire Godhead" (such as "transcendently good," "transcendently existing," "beautiful," and "life-giving") and those "expressing distinctions, the transcendent name and proper activity of the Father, of the Son, of the Spirit." *The Divine Names*, ch. 2, sec. 2, in Pseudo-Dionysius, *The Complete Works*, trans. Colm Luibheid and Paul Rorem, The Classics of Western Spirituality (Mahwah, NJ: Paulist, 1987), 60. In the prologue to ST Ia, q. 2 (2:3), Thomas clearly mentions a *tripartite* outline: the nature of God, "the distinction of persons in God," and "the coming forth from him of creatures." But only the first two parts deal explicitly with the nature of God.

21. ST Ia, q. 1, a. 2, reply (1:11). See also Ia, q. 1, a. 8, ad 2 (1:31–32): "The premises of this teaching [i.e., *sacra doctrina*, Christian theology] are revealed truths, accepted on the word of the teacher who reveals them. . . . All the same *sacra doctrina* also uses human reasoning, not indeed to prove the faith, for that would take away from the merit of believing, but to make manifest some implications of its message. Since grace does not do away with nature but brings it to perfection, so also natural reason should assist faith as the natural loving bent of the will yields to charity. . . . For our faith rests on the revelation made to the prophets and apostles who wrote the canonical books, not on a revelation, if such there be, made to any other teacher" (translation modified).

22. See William Hill's comment on Thomas's "five ways": "What Aquinas seeks out at the very beginning of the work (q. 2) are 'ways' (*viae*, not 'proofs,' 'arguments,' or 'demonstrations') by which the human spirit, in its powers of transcendence, might ascend to an affirmation of God—and in actual fact, that God who has already addressed his Word to man." William J. Hill, *The Three-Personed God: The Trinity as a Mystery of Salvation* (Washington, DC: Catholic University of America Press, 1982), 63.

138

with the theological consideration of mysteries of the Trinity "in the strict sense" (*mysteria stricte dicta*), whose content lay beyond the grasp of human reason and was made available only by means of supernatural revelation. This arrangement clearly reflected the intent of Neo-Scholastic apologists to defend both the legitimacy of Christianity and the objective certainty of supernatural revelation against the criticisms leveled by modern natural religion.[23] The tract *De Deo uno* contained the proofs for the existence of God, the discussion of the nature and attributes of God (e.g., simplicity, immutability, and eternity), and an analysis of the divine operations (knowledge, will, providence, predestination, and omnipotence). *De Deo trino* discussed the distinction, procession, and mission of the divine persons, as well as the intelligibility of the mystery of the Trinity and its philosophical analogues.[24]

Reacting to the perduring influence of this extreme separation, Karl Rahner objected that "the treatise of the Trinity locks itself in even more splendid isolation, with the ensuing danger that the religious mind finds it devoid of interest. It looks as if everything which matters for us in God has already been said in the treatise *On the One God*."[25] The approach we follow here, though, has nothing to do with the rigorous divisions of Neo-Scholasticism. Rather, it has more in common with the method originally suggested by Thomas's *Summa theologiae*, where the study of the nature of the one God and the study of the Trinity are seen as different yet complementary moments of our encounter with revelation. They can be seen as two interlocking Christian responses to the problem of God in Western culture. We can thus discern a genuine connection between our experience of God and a theological (i.e., revelational) theology of the Trinity.

If our contemporary situation is even roughly as many have described it—a time of the celebration of the consumer image, of the dimming of the religious imagination even amid heightened religious expression, or even as a "dark night" of varying intensities that provokes from many, even those of strong Christian belief, the anguished questions "Where is God?" and "Who is God?"—then we must make the strongest arguments for the plausibility of divine transcendence and for the real possibility of personally encountering the living God. In this way, we can reignite the religious imagination. For if the very notion of "God" or "divine transcendence" seems implausible to many,[26] what chance does the doctrine of the Trinity have of being appreciated and appropriated in a way that is helpful to faith?

---

23. Neo-Scholasticism attempted to defend the truth of Catholicism against what it argued were the heresies of modernity by using what amounted to modern means of assuring objective certainty. See Francis Schüssler Fiorenza, "Systematic Theology: Task and Methods," in this volume; idem, "The New Theology and Transcendental Thomism," in James C. Livingston et al., *Modern Christian Thought*, vol. 2, *The Twentieth Century*, 2nd ed. (Minneapolis: Fortress Press, 2006), 198–200; Anthony J. Godzieba, *Bernhard Welte's Fundamental Theological Approach to Christology*, American University Studies, series 7, vol. 160 (New York/Bern: Peter Lang, 1994), 18–30.

24. E.g., see the once-popular seminary manual by Adolphe Tanquerey, *Synopsis Theologiae Dogmaticae, tomus secundus: de Fide, de Deo uno et Trino, de Deo creante et elevante, de Verbo Incarnato*, 24th ed. (Paris: Desclée, 1933).

25. Rahner, *The Trinity*, 17. Rahner's critique applies more to what Thomas's distinction became in the hands of the Neo-Scholastic manualists than to Thomas himself.

26. See, e.g., Charles Taylor's important discussion in *A Secular Age* (Cambridge, MA: Belknap, 2007) of the anthropology (the "buffered self") and the cosmology (an infinite universe and "the dark abyss of time")—both viewed as being devoid of transcendental reference—that dominate contemporary Western culture.

To first seek and find the "clearing" or the natural access point of faith is to promote the human capacity to think and experience otherwise than the unending cycle of commodified images and the seeming claustrophobia of consumer culture. An authentic natural theology heightens our expectations regarding our encounters with God. It widens the parameters by demonstrating that one of the fundamental conditions of human experience is its orientation in the direction of God and transcendence. It also gives us a glimpse—but only a glimpse—of the character of the transcendence for which we long. If natural theology can identify this "clearing" within our experience as the place where God may be encountered, then Christian claims concerning the triune nature and personality of divinity will find a footing in human life and thus be more readily heard and appreciated.

In this clearing, at the threshold of the natural access point of faith, we encounter not only the transcendent horizon of our life and actions, the all-encompassing infinite mystery which we do not hesitate to call "God."[27] We also discover something of its depth, a hint (*Vorgriff*) of the nonnegotiable benevolence of the mystery that *gives* itself to us on its own initiative, a glimpse of the character of absolute freedom that reveals itself to us in a relationship that can best be described as *personal* and ultimately fulfilling. The key elements here are the "givenness" of this experience and the personal relationship that this revelatory giving engenders. At the limits of our experience, divine transcendence can best be described in personal, relational terms: as a gracious giver who encounters us in a personal fashion, freely granting us the space that makes our life and actions possible. In turn, we give ourselves over to the infinite mystery, trusting it to reveal itself as the loving fulfillment that we believe it to be.

What makes this limited yet meaningful vision possible is a revelatory moment already present to human experience. Here is where "natural theology" begins to shade over into "theological theology." The givenness of the infinite mystery makes possible the natural access-point of faith, a moment of grace already present to our experience in the sheer fact of this gift and our recognition of it.[28] We respond and interpret it by placing it within the context of our previous experiences. The most appropriate way to describe this experience of givenness is to employ a personal metaphor: we perceive the givenness that characterizes infinite mystery as a *personal* appeal that creates a *personal* relationship that begins to fulfill us *as persons*. This experience, though, is only a hint, a series of fragmentary anticipations. At this point, natural theology exhausts itself. The presence-absence structure that governs our encounters with God ensures that our affirmations of transcendence, while true, always fall short. Rational reflection can articulate our fundamental openness to the glimpses we receive of divine presence. But the full nature of the giver and the true quality of the relationship always exceed our categories of experience and reflection. They are revealed only in the depths of supernatural revelation itself. If we are to know who God is, then God must reveal God's own self.

---

27. Cf. Karl Rahner, *Foundations of Christian Faith: An Introduction to the Idea of Christianity*, trans. William V. Dych (New York: Crossroad, 1978), 57–75.

28. Indeed, it is the presupposition for our recognition of revelation as supernatural. Cf. Henri Bouillard, *The Knowledge of God*, trans. Samuel D. Femiano (New York: Herder & Herder, 1968), 24–31.

140

At this point, the transition between an authentic natural knowledge of God and trinitarian theology becomes clear. Natural theology's pre-apprehension of the authentic character of God is filled out and intensified by the revelatory encounter we have with God the Father, who saves us through Jesus Christ and who incorporates us into that salvation by means of the Holy Spirit. While natural theology always arrives late on the scene, so to speak, it grasps in fragmentary form that which preexists and pervades every moment of our experience of God. It emphasizes the disclosure that unfolds in terms of presence-and-absence, an action that can be adequately approached only by a theological theology that takes up where natural theology necessarily leaves off. Here, then, is a bridge to a theological theology of the Trinity—not a *proof* of the reality of the triune God, of course, since "reason cannot prove the necessity of the Trinity either from the concept of absolute spirit or from the concept of love. The Trinity is a mystery in the strict sense of the term."[29] Rather, we acknowledge the openness of human experience to an encounter with God and speak, as best we can, about what occurs within that encounter.

"Faith seeking understanding" attempts to express both the revelation of God's own self as a triune communion of persons and the intrinsic relevance of the Trinity for Christian life. One of its fundamental goals, then, is to show that

Christian belief in the triune God is not a doctrine imposed from "outside," but rather that God, in revealing, wills our happiness. Human life, having discovered its intrinsic orientation to God, will find its desires and its created potential fulfilled when it continues to acknowledge and celebrate its rootedness in the Trinity (doxology) and to confess its intrinsic need for the Trinity's loving and saving action (soteriology). To this theological theology of the Trinity we now turn.

The Revelation of the Triune God

The origins of Christian belief in the triune God are found "solely in the history of God's dealings with human beings and in the historical self-revelation of the Father through Jesus Christ in the Holy Spirit."[30] In other words, we become aware of the "inner" or "immanent" reality of God as triune not through abstract speculation, but rather on God's revelatory initiative alone—by God's salvific self-disclosure in history (*oikonomia*, the divine plan or "economy" of salvation), in events first narrated within a tradition of belief before they are reflected upon systematically.[31] Scripture, the divinely inspired interpretive narration of these events, is thus the pivotal resource. While biblical exegetes and theologians agree that there is no explicitly developed

---

29. Kasper, *The God of Jesus Christ*, 267.

30. Ibid., 237. For the development of trinitarian theology, see Gisbert Greshake, *Der dreieine Gott: Eine trinitarische Theologie* (Freiburg: Herder, 1997); Hill, *The Three-Personed God*; Kasper, *The God of Jesus Christ*, 233–316; Catherine Mowry LaCugna, *God for Us*; Wolfhart Pannenberg, *Systematic Theology*, 3 vols., trans. Geoffrey W. Bromiley (Grand Rapids: Eerdmans, 1991–98), 1:259–336; Rahner, *The Trinity*; Stephen Davis, Daniel Kendall, and Gerald O'Collins, eds., *The Trinity: An Interdisciplinary Symposium on the Trinity* (New York: Oxford University Press, 1999).

31. Greshake, *Der dreieine Gott*, 48. For the background and various meanings of "economy" (Greek *oikonomia*; Latin *dispensatio, dispositio*) in relation to salvation, see G. L. Prestige, *God in Patristic Thought*, 2nd ed. (1952; repr., London: SPCK, 1981), 57–67; LaCugna, *God for Us*, 24–30.

doctrine of the Trinity in either the Old or New Testament, nevertheless the classical doctrine is firmly rooted in Scripture's testimony to God's relationship with humanity as it has occurred in history. Additional evidence can be found in the spiritual life and liturgical experiences of the early church, whose members lived under the intense impact and ongoing effects of Christ's resurrection.

Subsequent theological analysis of these formative elements derives from them "the concepts in which the New Testament revelation of the triune God can be formulated as a profession of faith, presents this revelation in its interconnectedness, and renders its meaning recognizable as the center of Christian belief."[32] This very basic description may make development of the doctrine of the Trinity appear to be a simple process, but in reality, it is the fruit of centuries of spiritual experience, liturgical practice, and continuing theological reflection. At every point in this development, the church's fundamental concern has been soteriological, asking how we are to understand the saving activity of God. The theological task, then, is to explain how our salvation is enacted in the intimate communion among the three persons of the Trinity, while at the same time we profess our firm belief in the one God.

The primary scriptural resource for belief in the Trinity is the New Testament, which provides the basis for the doctrine of the Trinity on three interconnected levels: it narrates the historically and culturally embedded events whereby the triune structure of God's saving activity is revealed; it records the early Christian attempts to express this trinitarian structure in reminiscence and confession; and it reflects on how these events and expressions, taken together, articulate the definitive self-revelation of the triune God as love (1 John 4:8, 16).[33] But trinitarian theology also relies on the Old Testament for crucial data about the experiences that ground the New Testament's claims. None is more central than the confession of the unity of God: "Hear, O Israel! The Lord is our God, the Lord alone! Therefore, you shall love the Lord, your God, with all your heart, and with all your soul, and with all your strength" (Deut. 6:4-5). These verses were later incorporated into the *Shema*, the prayer recited twice daily by every devout Jew. The confession of God's oneness and uniqueness was the central pillar of Judaism immediately before and during Jesus' time, and became the basis for Christianity as well.[34]

The Old Testament evidence, however, also shows that this fully formed monotheism was not the starting point of Israel's relationship

---

32. Wolfgang Beinert and Francis Schüssler Fiorenza, eds., *Handbook of Catholic Theology* (New York: Crossroad, 1995), 723, s.v. "Trinity: Doctrine of the" (Wilhelm Breuning).

33. Compare Kasper's assessment of the New Testament evidence, a three-step analysis of "1. the trinitarian structure of the revelational event; 2. the trinitarian explanation of this event in the New Testament; and 3. the connection between this explanation and the essential definition of God that is given in the New Testament." Only in this way can theology keep the confession of the Trinity from being relegated to "a later, purely speculative addition to the original faith in Christ" and instead demonstrate that it "provides the basic structure and ground plan of the New Testament witness, and that with it the belief in the God of Jesus Christ stands or falls." *The God of Jesus Christ*, 244.

34. James D. G. Dunn deems monotheism the first of the four pillars of Second Temple Judaism; see *The Partings of the Ways between Christianity and Judaism and Their Significance for the Character of Christianity* (Philadelphia: Trinity Press International, 1991), 19–21. See also Larry W. Hurtado, *Lord Jesus Christ: Devotion to Jesus in Earliest Christianity* (Grand Rapids: Eerdmans, 2003), 29–31; E. P. Sanders, *The Historical Figure of Jesus* (London/New York: Penguin, 1995 [1993]), 33–39 (on the "common Judaism" of the first century CE).

142

with Yahweh, but rather its mature arrival point. Israel's belief in the oneness and uniqueness of God took centuries to develop into the form that is considered characteristic of Judaism.[35] A number of texts, for example, reflect the character of early Israelite religion when it tolerated other deities (always few in number) alongside Yahweh (e.g., Gen. 35:2-3; Josh. 24:16; Judg. 5:8). Other texts cast light on the conditions of somewhat later Israelite history, when differences existed between the nationalistic cult of Yahweh promoted by the monarchy and other, more syncretistic cultic practices of popular religion (e.g., Baal worship) that originally were tolerated but later were strongly condemned as incompatible with the true worship of Yahweh (1 Kings 18–19; Amos 5:25-27; Hosea 2; Jeremiah 10).[36] The Old Testament clearly depicts a historical development in Israel's relationship with God: from a polytheistic Yahwism or henotheism to a practical monotheism (where one worships Yahweh alone, without deciding on the existence or nonexistence of other deities), and finally to an ethical monotheism (where Yahweh is regarded as the only God; all others are nonentities). The centrality of monotheism was affirmed only around the time of the exile in Babylon in the sixth century BCE, and only in this post-exilic period did monotheism and monolatry become the fundamental dogmas of Judaism. For example, the author of Second Isaiah (Isaiah 40–55), writing just before or during the exile and continuing the Isaian prophetic tradition,[37] boldly and unambiguously affirms

that Yahweh is the only deity in the cosmos and the God of all peoples: "I am the LORD, and there is no other. . . . There is no other god but me, a righteous God and a Savior; there is no one besides me. Turn to me and be saved, all the ends of the earth! For I am God, and there is no other" (Isa. 45:5, 21-22). This insistence on God's unity and uniqueness became the outstanding characteristic of Judaism in the post-exilic period and made Israel unique among its neighbors. It also provoked within Judaism itself "a fierce antipathy to syncretism and virulent hostility to anything which smacked of idolatry,"[38] as Jewish literature from this later period attests (e.g., Jdt. 8:18; Wis. 13:1—15:6).

In the religious experience mirrored in the Old Testament, monotheism was never merely a theoretical issue verified by intellectual "proofs." It arose rather out of Israel's encounters with Yahweh, revelatory experiences whose decisive meaning had to be worked out over time in the context and categories of ancient Near Eastern religion and politics. At the same time, these categories were stretched up to and even beyond their limits. Biblical monotheism is thus "the fruit of religious experience and an expression of practice based on faith." At its heart is "a radical decision in behalf of the one thing necessary," that is, the unshakable truth that "God alone is God; on him alone can one build unconditionally, in him alone can one trust without reserve." A theological analysis of these experiences of faith and of the practices they engender leads to the conclusion that the *oneness* of God neces-

---

35. Mark S. Smith, *The Early History of God: Yahweh and the Other Deities in Ancient Israel*, 2nd ed. (Grand Rapids: Eerdmans / Dearborn, MI: Dove, 2002), 182–99; John J. Scullion, "God: God in the OT," in *The Anchor Bible Dictionary*, ed. David Noel Freedman et al., 6 vols. (New York: Doubleday, 1992), 2:1041–48; Kasper, *The God of Jesus Christ*, 238–39.

36. Smith, *Early History of God*, 183–84.

37. Cf. Richard J. Clifford, "Isaiah, Book of: Second Isaiah," in *The Anchor Bible Dictionary*, 3:490–91.

38. Dunn, *Partings of the Ways*, 20.

sarily implies the *uniqueness* of God: "Only one God can be infinite and all-inclusive; two Gods would limit one another even if they somehow interpenetrated. . . . The singleness of God is therefore not just one of the attributes of God; rather his singleness is given directly with his very essence."[39]

This strict commitment to monotheism provided the matrix not only for first-century CE Judaism, but also for the Jewish movement that formed around Jesus and for the early Christianity that developed from it.[40] To abandon exclusivist monotheism was to abandon Judaism.[41] This is true even in light of the fact that late Second Temple Judaism (post-exilic Judaism from the second century BCE onward) could entertain beliefs in a variety of heavenly intermediary and redeemer figures and even a healthy angelology.[42] While acknowledging the demonstrable elasticity of monotheism within Second Temple Judaism, however, one must make an important distinction between "entertaining a belief in" and "worshipping," and realize how strictly that distinction was held. There is enough evidence that Jewish monotheism during the Roman period certainly "accommodated beliefs and very honorific rhetoric about various principal-agent figures such as high angels and exalted humans like Moses," but at the same time it "drew a sharp line between any such figure and the one God in the area of cultic practice, reserving cultic worship for the one God."[43]

This context makes all the more surprising the extraordinarily high estimation of Jesus of Nazareth among his followers so soon after Easter, as well as early Christianity's worship of Christ as divine, given the fact that belief in Jesus as the son of God arose among first-century CE Jewish disciples who were steeped in exclusivist monotheism.[44] Their fundamental claim was that the historical manifestation of God and God's view of life had occurred most clearly and definitively in the person of Jesus of Nazareth. This belief was anchored in Jesus' preaching of the kingdom of God, in the presence of God's salvific power, which they perceived in Jesus' own life and actions, and in their experiences of the risen Christ after the catastrophe of his crucifixion. Throughout the course of his life, as well as in his death and resurrection, "Jesus reveals God as his own Father in an utterly unique and non-transferable way, while it is only through Jesus that we in turn become the sons and daughters of this Father."[45]

Through his life, words, and practices, Jesus proclaimed the kingdom of God, God's kingly rule and attitude of care toward human life and the world. For Jesus, God's rule transforms

---

39. Kasper, *The God of Jesus Christ*, 239.

40. Hurtado, *Lord Jesus Christ*, 29: "What became 'Christianity' began as a movement within the Jewish religious tradition of the Roman period, and the chief characteristic of Jewish religion in this period was its defiantly monotheistic stance."

41. Ibid., 31.

42. See James D. G. Dunn, *Christology in the Making: An Inquiry into the Origins of the Doctrine of the Incarnation*, 2nd ed. (London: SCM, 1990), 149–59.

43. Hurtado, *Lord Jesus Christ*, 48.

44. For the relatively rapid development of such exalted beliefs in Jesus, see the classic arguments by Martin Hengel in *The Son of God: The Origin of Christology and the History of Jewish-Hellenistic Religion*, trans. John Bowden (Philadelphia: Fortress Press, 1976); and "Christology and New Testament Chronology" in *Between Jesus and Paul: Studies in the Earliest History of Christianity*, trans. John Bowden (Philadelphia: Fortress Press, 1983), 30–47.

45. Kasper, *The God of Jesus Christ*, 244.

144 situations of negativity, suffering, and dehumanization into situations of positivity, joy, and surprising human flourishing beyond any human accomplishment. Such astounding reversals can be accomplished only by God, whom Jesus portrayed in his parables and in his miracles as a surprising and capricious lover who surpasses human expectations and standards and goes to any lengths to make the offer of love and reversal open to all without qualification.[46] Jesus claimed that this long-awaited arrival of the kingdom of God and its ongoing fulfillment was tied in a unique way to his own preaching and prophetic actions. Indeed, the salvific presence of God was present in the very paradox of his person; as John Meier puts it, "Jesus had a direct *theo*-logy (God as object of his preaching), which involved an indirect or implicit *christo*-logy (Jesus as final agent of God). Thus Jesus' identity was absorbed into and defined by his mission."[47] In response to Jesus' aims and the effect his person and ministry had on them, his followers struggled to find appropriate categories and titles to express the extraordinary revelatory character and "otherness" of his presence, while at the same time doing justice to their own commitment to Jewish exclusivist monotheism and to the authentic Jewish character and substance of Jesus' life and preaching. This struggle is rooted in what Meier terms the "basic paradox Jesus presented" to friends and foes alike: "Though he rarely spoke about his status, he implicitly made himself *the* pivotal figure in the eschatological drama he announced and inaugurated. . . . [Jesus] spoke and acted on the presumption that he would be the criterion used for the final judgment. That alone involved a monumental claim to a unique status and role at the climax of Israel's history."[48]

God's action of reversal was revealed not only in Jesus' *announcement* of the kingdom of God, but equally in Jesus' *performance* of its values, especially his overwhelming concern for and action on behalf of the marginalized within first-century Palestinian Jewish society. This activity led to the series of events culminating in his crucifixion and resurrection.[49] That the reversal of negativity and the restoration of human well-being is truly God's salvific will was confirmed for Jesus' followers at Easter; his resurrection is the ultimate reversal, that of death into life. The New Testament clearly shows that the eschatological event of Jesus' resurrection and the disciples' Easter experiences of the risen Lord became the key elements of their interpretation of Jesus' relationship to his Father (*Abba*). Jesus had been revealed as the human face of God, the full self-expression of God's being. Furthermore, as Kasper explains, "The eschatological character of this revelation indirectly makes it clear as well that from eternity God is the God and Father of Jesus Christ and therefore that as Son of God Jesus belongs to the eternal being of God."[50]

The fundamental importance of these revelatory experiences cannot be underestimated,

---

46. For a detailed discussion, see Anthony J. Godzieba, "Method and Interpretation: The New Testament's Heretical Hermeneutic (Prelude and Fugue)," *Heythrop Journal* 36 (1995): 286–306.

47. John P. Meier, "Jesus," in *The New Jerome Biblical Commentary*, ed. R. E. Brown, J. A. Fitzmyer, and R. E. Murphy (Englewood Cliffs, NJ: Prentice Hall, 1990), 1316–28, at 1323 (sec. 29).

48. Ibid.

49. Regarding the advantage of a performance hermeneutic for understanding both Jesus' view of the kingdom of God and our contemporary appropriation of the truth of Jesus' message, see Godzieba, "Method and Interpretation."

50. Kasper, *The God of Jesus Christ*, 244.

given the matrix of Jewish exclusivist monotheism within which they occurred. They provoked the unprecedented development of cultic worship and prayer that included Jesus Christ alongside God the Father, public devotion that is reflected in the New Testament epistolary literature (especially letters by and attributed to Paul) and the book of Revelation.[51] For example, the untranslated Aramaic prayer *marana tha* ("O Lord, come!") preserved in Paul's First Letter to the Corinthians (16:22), which finds a Greek parallel in Revelation 22:20 (*Amên, erchou kyrie Iêsou*; "Amen, come Lord Jesus!"), is a invocation for Jesus to be present, whether at the moment of worship or eschatologically. This prayer has no parallel in Judaism and provides evidence for what Larry Hurtado calls "an incorporation of Jesus into the corporate, public devotional life of early Christians in a way that is otherwise reserved for God."[52] Another example is the Christian hymn quoted by Paul in the Letter to the Philippians (2:6-11); it links the universal confession that "Jesus Christ is Lord" (2:11) with God's exaltation of Jesus (2:9), an exaltation that mirrors God the Father's glory as well (2:11). Colossians 3:17 urges Christians to "do everything in the name of the Lord Jesus, giving thanks to God the Father through him." A number of doxologies (e.g., 1 Thess. 3:11-13; Rom. 1:8; 16:27; 2 Cor. 1:19-20) directly link God the Father and Jesus in prayer,

offering praise to God and invoking Jesus as the mediator between God and humanity.[53] These are thought to quote directly or echo liturgical formulas already in common use in Christian worship in the 50s. These and similar New Testament indicators, taken together, reflect the consistent incorporation of Jesus "into an exclusivistic pattern of devotion in which there is room for only *one God and one Lord* (e.g., 1 Cor. 8:5-6)," a cultic reverencing of Jesus that early Christians believed they were impelled to offer in light of their experience of God.[54]

For the early Christian communities whose beliefs and practices are reflected in these texts, it is clear that Jesus was not considered "another deity of any independent origin or significance; instead, his divine significance is characteristically expressed in terms of his relationship to the one God."[55] The practices of these early communities thus disclose the development of a clearly *binitarian* pattern of belief and devotion. As Hurtado emphasizes, this was "an unparalleled innovation, a 'mutation' or new variant form of exclusivist monotheism in which a second figure (Jesus) was programmatically included with God in the devotional pattern of Christian groups."[56] This devotion paralleled and fostered the development of what have been called "New Testament symbols implying a second in God,"[57] a range of titles for Jesus that attempted to express his unique relationship to God without

---

51. See especially Larry W. Hurtado, *At the Origins of Christian Worship: The Context and Character of Earliest Christian Devotion* (Grand Rapids: Eerdmans, 1999), 63–97; idem, *Lord Jesus Christ*, 134–43; LaCugna, *God for Us*, 112–14.

52. Hurtado, *Lord Jesus Christ*, 141–42.

53. LaCugna, *God for Us*, 112–13.

54. Hurtado, *At the Origins*, 97 (emphasis original). The hymn quoted by Paul in 1 Cor. 8:5-6 confesses that there is "one God, the Father, from whom all things are and for whom we exist, and one Lord, Jesus Christ, through whom all things are and through whom we exist."

55. Hurtado, *Lord Jesus Christ*, 52.

56. Ibid., 64.

57. Hill, *The Three-Personed God*, 6–17.

146   compromising the exclusivist monotheist context from which they arose.

One of these titles is "son of God," originally denoting Yahweh's elect (either corporately or individually) but without overtones of divinity.[58] Early Christian practice, spurred on by the sense of intimate sonship with God that Jesus expressed in his sayings and actions (e.g., Matt. 11:27/Luke 10:22), applied the term to Jesus and eventually narrowed down its focus to signify the distinctive relationship between Jesus and the Father (e.g., Mark 1:1; Rom. 1:3; 8:3; 14–15; Gal. 4:6-7; John 1:14; 1 John 4:9).

Another title is "Lord" (*kyrios*), whose meaning in a Jewish setting was far less ambiguous.[59] In first-century CE Diaspora synagogues where Jews spoke Greek rather than Hebrew, whenever the Scriptures were read aloud in translation, the substitution for the never-to-be-uttered *YHWH* would not have been the Hebrew *Adonai* but rather the Greek *kyrios*. The same translation appears in Christian manuscripts of the Greek translation of the Old Testament, the Septuagint. The word thus had clear connotations of divinity when early Christian communities deliberately chose it as one of their key interpretations of Jesus' relationship to God. In doing so, they expressed their belief that now "Jesus could be hailed as Lord and receive the honour due to God alone, because God had so appointed Christ to this status and these

roles," while at the same time maintaining a distinction between God the Father and Jesus.[60] For example, Peter, in his speech at Pentecost, claims that in Jesus' resurrection and exaltation, "God has made him both Lord (*kyrios*) and Messiah (*christos*)" (Acts 2:36). He cites Psalm 110:1, a popular proof-text in early Christianity: "The Lord said to my Lord, 'Sit at my right hand, until I make your enemies your footstool.'"[61] In Paul's letters, *kyrios* plays a central role. He even claims that preaching "Jesus Christ as Lord" sums up his entire teaching (2 Cor. 4:5) and that this name, precisely because it is "the name that is above every name," deserves to be reverenced by all: "Every tongue [should] confess that Jesus Christ is Lord, to the glory of God the Father" (Phil. 2:9-11).[62] In 1 Corinthians 8, he uses the title in the absolute sense: despite others' claims of "many gods and many lords," for believers there is "one God, the Father . . . and one Lord, Jesus Christ" (1 Cor. 8:5-6). These texts do not spell out the ontological details of the relationship between Jesus and God; such intricate theological discussions developed only later in Christian tradition.

Alongside this binitarian pattern, the New Testament clearly indicates the early development of the *trinitarian* pattern as well, again without compromising the monotheism that governed early Christian experience. Here, too, detailed theological elaboration is bypassed in

---

58. For examples of earlier Jewish usage and of Jesus' own expressions of his sonship, see Dunn, *Partings of the Ways*, 170–71; idem, *Christianity in the Making*, vol. 1, *Jesus Remembered* (Grand Rapids/Cambridge: Eerdmans, 2003), 708–24 (especially his conclusions).

59. For what follows, see Dunn, *Partings of the Ways*, 188–91; see also Hill, *Three-Personed God*, 14–15.

60. Dunn, *Partings of the Ways*, 191: "To call Jesus 'Lord', therefore, was evidently not understood in earliest Christianity as identifying him with God. What Paul and the first Christians seem to have done was to claim that the one God had shared his lordship with the exalted Christ" (italics are in the original).

61. Ibid., 188, 316n16.

62. Dunn notes (ibid., 188) how this passage echoes Isa. 43:22-23: "For I am God; there is no other. By myself I swear. . . . To me every knee shall bend; by me every tongue shall swear."

favor of testimony. The catalyst for this pattern was the immediacy of the presence of God that the earliest Christians continued to experience through the risen Jesus, an intensity of religious experience that led them to recognize their unity with one another and drew them together into the earliest Christian communities.[63] After Easter, believers claimed that the action of the Spirit (*pneuma*) was the source for their continuing participation in God's power (*dynamis*) that Jesus had promised to those who have faith (Mark 9:24; 10:27). The Spirit's action was also the reason for their inclusion within Jesus' relationship to his *Abba* and the resulting community fellowship (*koinônia*).[64] Once again, Jewish tradition provided the model. Various Old Testament texts recount the outpouring of God's "spirit" (in Hebrew, *ruah*; "wind," "breath") as a sign of God's activity in the world, whether as vivifying power (e.g., Job 33:4), creative agency (e.g., Gen. 1:2), or prophetic presence in human beings (e.g., Isa. 61:1), especially in messianic times (e.g., Joel 3:1-5). "Spirit" is understood in these texts more or less impersonally and functionally, as a principle of action.[65] This meaning also governs the use of the term in many New Testament texts. Based on their continuing experience of the risen Christ, however, members of the early church later began to interpret both the process and the implications of God's revelation in Jesus in a way that emphasized how God's "inspiration" of Jesus' disciples is indeed God's *personal* relationship with them, one best

expressed in a *personal* way. They thus expanded the meaning of "spirit" beyond its Old Testament roots in order to acknowledge this distinctive personal divine presence.

This expansion of meaning did not occur all at once, however. The accounts of the baptism of Jesus in the Synoptic Gospels (Mark 1:9-11; Matt. 3:13-17; Luke 3:21-22), for example, appears to follow the earlier Old Testament model. The "voice from heaven" reveals Jesus as the "beloved Son" of the Father; he is portrayed as receiving the "Spirit" (the "Spirit of God" in Matthew; the "Holy Spirit" in Luke) at the inauguration of his ministry. In Paul's letters, too, *pneuma* often reflects this functional Old Testament understanding.[66] Moreover, in several well-known texts, Paul does not clearly differentiate Christ from the Spirit, leaving the relationship ambiguous. In Galatians, for instance, he depicts the role of the Spirit as enabling a believer to replicate in his or her life the intimate relationship with God that Jesus experienced: "As proof that you are children, God sent the spirit of his Son into our hearts, crying out 'Abba, Father!'" (Gal. 4:6).[67] In Rom. 8:9-11, Paul uses "Spirit of God," "Spirit of Christ," and "the Spirit of the one who raised Jesus from the dead" interchangeably to depict the believer's participation in God's life. And in 2 Cor. 3:17-18, he goes so far as to claim that "the Lord is the Spirit." However, there are also striking passages where Paul speaks of the Spirit as distinct from the Father (e.g., Rom. 8:14-17), having

---

63. See James D. G. Dunn, *Unity and Diversity in the New Testament: An Inquiry into the Character of Earliest Christianity*, 2nd ed. (London: SCM / Philadelphia: Trinity Press International, 1990), 174–202, esp. 199–200.

64. Kasper, *The God of Jesus Christ*, 244–45.

65. Joseph A. Fitzmyer, *The Gospel according to Luke (I–IX)*, Anchor Bible 28 (Garden City, NY: Doubleday, 1981), 484; John L. McKenzie, "Aspects of Old Testament Thought," *The New Jerome Biblical Commentary*, 1290–91.

66. For this and what follows, see the discussion in Joseph A. Fitzmyer, "Pauline Theology," *The New Jerome Biblical Commentary*, 1396, secs. 61–65.

67. Cf. Dunn, *Unity and Diversity*, 194.

148 distinguishing characteristics (e.g., 1 Cor. 12:3-11) and even comprehensive knowledge of God: "For the Spirit scrutinizes everything, even the depths of God. . . . No one knows what pertains to God except the Spirit of God" (1 Cor. 2:10-11). At times, Paul emphatically differentiates God, Jesus, and the Spirit, putting them on an equal footing and thereby providing a basis for the language of "distinct persons" found in later dogmatic statements on the Trinity. For instance, 2 Corinthians concludes by saying, "The grace of the Lord Jesus Christ, the love of God, and communion of the Holy Spirit be with all of you" (13:13), a triadic formula that seems to echo liturgical practice.

Two other key New Testament instances significantly expand the meaning of "Spirit." One is Matt. 28:19, Jesus' command to "make disciples of all nations, baptizing them in the name of the Father, and of the Son, and of the Holy Spirit." This parallelism of Father, Son, and Spirit as implicit equals is unprecedented in the Gospel; so, too, is the connection of baptism with Jesus (rather than with John the Baptist). Commentators generally agree that the formula as Matthew presents it most probably originated with the early church, rather than with the historical Jesus, and reflects the church's baptismal practice.[68] But even though the formula may not directly quote Jesus himself, it is warranted by his relationship to his Father and "presents a summary of the early church's development and practice which had been guided by the Spirit of Jesus Christ and to that extent were authorized by Jesus himself."[69] That is, the trinitarian baptismal formula expresses what became the core of early Christianity's developing understanding of its identity, namely, that the life of the church is grounded in God's salvation, which has been incarnated in the person and message of Jesus, and that this life now continues to flourish after Christ's resurrection because of the Father's continuing personal presence to the church through the Spirit. Whoever wishes to join this community of disciples and participate in this offer of personal relationship and salvation must enter through baptism, the origin and ground of Christian life. At baptism, one commits oneself to this trinitarian view of God's saving action. Along with Christ's exalted divine significance, then, Christians early on were called to acknowledge the triune divine life as the necessary precondition for the life of the individual Christian and of the church.

The other key instance is the reference to the Paraclete in John's Gospel, specifically in Jesus' farewell discourse at the Last Supper (John 14–17).[70] There, in intimate conversation with "his own," whom he loved (John 13:1), Jesus promises that, on his return to the Father, he will ask the Father to send "another Advocate (*paraklētos*) to be with you forever. This is the

---

68. E.g., Daniel J. Harrington, *The Gospel of Matthew*, Sacra Pagina (Collegeville, MN: Liturgical, 1991), 1:415–17; W. D. Davies and Dale C. Allison Jr., *A Critical and Exegetical Commentary on The Gospel according to St. Matthew*, 3 vols., International Critical Commentary (Edinburgh: T&T Clark, 1997), 3:676–91, esp. 677–78, 684–87. See also LaCugna, *God for Us*, 113–14.

69. Kasper, *The God of Jesus Christ*, 245.

70. See Raymond E. Brown, *The Gospel according to John XIII–XXI*, Anchor Bible 29A (Garden City, NY: Doubleday, 1970), 1135–44; Rudolf Schnackenburg, *The Gospel according to St. John*, 3 vols., trans. David Smith and G. A. Kon, Herder's Theological Commentary on the New Testament (New York: Crossroad, 1968–82), 3:138–54; John Ashton, "Paraclete," *Anchor Bible Dictionary*, 5:152–54. The discourse contains five sayings regarding the Paraclete: John 14:16-17; 14:26; 15:26-27; 16:7b-11; and 16:13-15. The only other use of *paraklētos* in the New Testament is 1 John 2:1, where it is applied to Christ.

Spirit of truth, whom the world cannot receive" (14:16-17). This Paraclete is "the Holy Spirit, whom the Father will send in my name, [who] will teach you everything, and remind you of all that I have said to you" (14:26). He "comes from the Father" and will testify on Jesus' behalf, as the disciples must do as well (15:26-27). He will come only if Jesus departs, and when he comes, he will convict the world of its false judgments (16:7b-11). As the "Spirit of truth," he will guide the disciples along the way to truth and glorify Jesus, and will take what belongs to Jesus ("All that the Father has is mine") and declare it to the disciples (16:13-15).

No single translation of *paraklêtos* (e.g., "Advocate" or "Comforter") can capture the rich complexity of meaning that the Johannine author intends to express throughout these passages. The term has a range of technical (legal) and nontechnical meanings in Greek: "one called alongside" (*parakalein*) to help—i.e., an advocate, intercessor, or defense counsel; a mediator or spokesperson; a comforter or consoler; and one who encourages and exhorts. Its use in the Gospel has obvious Old Testament antecedents (especially with regard to the prophets as mediators of God's spirit, and personified Wisdom coming to dwell with God's people), as well as precedents in Second Temple Jewish angelology. The Johannine author has creatively combined these traditional meanings and employed them in a unique way to explain how the personal presence of Jesus to the community—its lifeblood, as it were—is sustained after Jesus' return

to the Father. Indeed, the *paraklêtos*, the "Spirit of truth," is "another Paraclete" (14:16), implying that Jesus has already been the first. After Jesus' departure, the Paraclete sent by the Father is portrayed as Jesus' representative, continuing his living presence in the community and personally performing a series of actions: teaching, reminding the disciples of Jesus' words, testifying on Jesus' behalf, defending those disciples suffering persecution, and exposing the guilt of the hostile and unbelieving world, guiding the disciples to the truth about the present and the future.[71] The Paraclete's *personal* actions are instrumental in carrying out his multifaceted relationship to Jesus and to the disciples: "The Paraclete is a *witness* in defense of Jesus and a *spokesman* for him in the context of his trial by his enemies; the Paraclete is a *consoler* and guide of the disciples and thus their *helper*."[72]

The Johannine author has sculpted these diverse meanings into a remarkable theological portrayal of "the Paraclete as the Holy Spirit in a special role, namely, as the personal presence of Jesus in the Christian while Jesus is with the Father."[73] This role is so special and distinctive that the author was compelled to bestow a special title and offer a distinctive interpretation of the Holy Spirit, whose presence the community had already accepted.[74] As Raymond Brown notes, this portrait of the Paraclete is the Fourth Gospel's solution to the "tragedy" of the "death of the apostolic eyewitnesses who were the living chain between the Church and Jesus of Nazareth," and especially the death of the Beloved

---

71. Schnackenburg notes (*The Gospel according to St. John*, 3:142–43) that the Paraclete's "forensic" role as advocate and mediator for disciples who witness to Jesus before hostile persecutors picks up a thread of the early tradition that was known to the synoptics as well (cf. Mark 13:11; Matt. 10:20; Luke 12:11).

72. Brown, *The Gospel according to John*, 1137. See also ibid., 1135, where all the Paraclete's characteristics noted in John 14–16 are tabulated.

73. Ibid., 1139.

74. Ibid., 1140; cf. Schnackenburg, *The Gospel according to St. John*, 3:140, 149–50.

150 Disciple, this community's "eyewitness *par excellence*." How would the community survive without a living connection to Jesus? The Johannine answer is that the connection has been provided by the Spirit, whose presence is due to Jesus and his resurrection (7:39) and who, after the resurrection, enlightened the first disciples so that they would grasp the true meaning of Jesus' earlier words and actions (cf. 2:22; 12:16). In fact, the Gospel insists that the Spirit as Paraclete is the Father's gift to the entire community, guiding not only the Beloved Disciple and other eyewitnesses but every other member as well, now and in the future.[75]

The Gospel of John is not a dogmatic theological treatise. The Johannine author is more interested in the similarities between Jesus and the Spirit than in the distinctions accentuated in later trinitarian theology.[76] But the importance of this Gospel for later Christian reflection on the Trinity is unmistakable, especially for the debates establishing the personal nature of the Holy Spirit.[77] The crucial active and personal role played by the Paraclete in Jesus' farewell discourse clearly implies that the Johannine community had at least an incipient awareness of the trinitarian pattern of God's salvific actions. The unity in love between the Jesus and the Father, expressed in the "priestly prayer" that concludes Jesus' farewell to his disciples (chapter 17), is now made accessible to all believers through the unity of Jesus with his disciples guaranteed by the Spirit as Paraclete.[78] This participation in divine life is the *true* meaning of life—eternal life: "Now this is eternal life, that they should know you, the only true God, and the one whom you sent, Jesus Christ" (17:3). To know the Father means to acknowledge the Father's lordship and to glorify him, thereby discovering that the true meaning of life is communion with God.[79] Jesus makes this communion possible: true life for the disciples means knowing Jesus, the Son who has been sent, and the glory and the love that he has from the Father (17:5, 7, 22-23)—indeed, knowing that "everything that the Father has is mine" (16:15; cf. 17:10). The knowledge of God made available through faith in Jesus "brings communion with him and through him with God. . . . The glorification of the Father by the Son thus has for its goal the participation of the disciples in this glorification and in eternal life."[80] To preserve this communion of the disciples with the Father through Jesus is the role of the Paraclete, the Spirit of truth sent by Jesus (14:16-17), who will reveal not only the union of the Father and the Son, but also how the disciples' own unity among themselves participates in the saving love and unity that is the divine life (17:21, 26). This communion is not for the disciples alone; it must be extended to the world as a sign of God's saving love for the world (17:21, 23).

---

75. Brown, *The Gospel according to John*, 1142: "The later Christian is no further removed from the ministry of Jesus than was the earlier Christian, for the Paraclete dwells within him as he dwelt within the eyewitnesses. And by recalling and giving new meaning to what Jesus said, the Paraclete guides every generation in facing new situations; he declares the things to come."

76. Ibid., 1141.

77. Cf. Schnackenburg, *The Gospel according to St. John*, 3:152–53.

78. For what follows, see Kasper, *The God of Jesus Christ*, 247–48.

79. Schnackenburg comments, "'Knowing God' has the previously established, O[ld] T[estament] meaning of 'having communion with God'. . . . [Johannine theology] is content to present community with God as the fulfillment of man's longing for salvation, achieved in believing and loving union with Jesus Christ." *The Gospel according to St. John*, 3:172–73.

80. Kasper, *The God of Jesus Christ*, 247.

In the light of all these relationships that enfold and give life to the community, the Johannine author thus emphasizes the inherent connection between belief in the Trinity and God's offer of salvation, a connection that is at the heart of Christian belief. The Gospel reveals, in Walter Kasper's words, that "the trinitarian doxology is the soteriology of the world."[81] Salvation consists of our union with God through Christ and consequently with each other; the participative love that is the basis of this union must be revealed and made effective in the world. The Father has given over everything to the Son, the Son gives everything over to the disciples, and the Spirit reveals, preserves, and extends the bond of love that is the catalyst for these acts of giving.

Implicit in this Gospel is the Johannine community's belief that we are offered a glimpse of the triune divine nature through the revelatory events of Christ's own life, lived in intimate relation with his Father, and with the sending of the Spirit—a glimpse that a later writer from the Johannine school will sum up in the simplest terms: God is love. "God abides in those who confess that Jesus is the Son of God, and they abide in God. . . . God is love, and those who abide in love abide in God, and God abides in them" (1 John 4:15-16).[82] Kasper argues that this passage—and the development of trinitarian awareness—is the fundamental summary of the entire message of the New Testament.

In the revelational event which is Jesus Christ God has shown himself to be love. But this revelational event consists precisely in making known the eternal communion of love, life and reciprocal glorification between Father, Son and Spirit, in order that through this revelation the disciples and, with their help, mankind may be drawn into this same communion of love and life. The revelational statement "God is love" is therefore at the same time a statement about the being of God and, as such, a statement about salvation. Only because God is love can he reveal and communicate himself to us as love. The unity of church and world, the peace and reconciliation of mankind have their ultimate ground and ultimate possibility, as seen by Christians, in the acknowledgment of the glory of God in the love of Father, Son and Spirit.[83]

The love of the triune God and the metaphor of personal relationship are, in Kasper's view, the interpretive keys to the Scriptures and to reality as a whole. This interpretation gives us a vantage point from which to summarize and evaluate all the scriptural evidence we have seen. We can discern a pattern, the dialectic of "presence and absence" that is the fundamental logic of God's revelation: the simultaneous knowability-mysteriousness, availability-uncontrollability, immanence-transcendence of God. In the texts we have examined, the traditional categories of divinity have been stretched up to and even beyond their limits to accommodate revelatory experiences of God, who always exceeds human categories, and to respond to God's offer of an always-deeper relationship to humankind. These experiences demand interpretation; their surprising new elements provoke believers to reevaluate their usual expectations and definitions

---

81. Ibid., 248.

82. Regarding the authorship of 1 John, see Raymond E. Brown, *An Introduction to the New Testament*, The Anchor Bible Reference Library (New York: Doubleday, 1997), 389–92.

83. Kasper, *The God of Jesus Christ*, 248.

152

of divinity, a process that takes places under the "pressure" of revelation (the Old Testament theophanies are examples of this). To call this process "development" is too weak a description; any connotations of smooth systematic progress barely hint at the volatility of the call to a deepening personal relationship that occurs when an individual or a community encounters the incomprehensible mystery of God and finds the normal definitions of God shaken or even shattered.

The various categories used by Israel, by Jesus' first disciples, and by early Christianity to understand God and God's activity were constantly expanded and at times surpassed when they were seen as inadequate to the task. As a response to both the devastation of exile and Israel's subsequent miraculous return to its homeland, post-exilic Judaism's rigorous exclusivist monotheism went far beyond earlier polytheistic and henotheistic categories by making the radical claim that Yahweh's salvific presence was absolute and allowed no rivals or subordinates. This revision and expansion continued in the New Testament. Exclusivist monotheism, the essential religious matrix for Jesus, his earliest disciples, and early Christianity, was not an obstacle to the eventual recognition of the triune nature of God, but rather surprisingly acted as a catalyst for new possibilities of understanding and expanding the hard-won faith claim that God is one.

The early growth of the binitarian pattern was one approach. It was an innovative christological expansion of the Jewish understanding of God that developed as a way to do justice to the disciples' original experience of Jesus as the human face of God and God as the *Abba* of Jesus, especially in the light of Jesus' resurrection from the dead. The early communities of believers used this pattern to confess their belief that "from eternity God is the God and Father of Jesus Christ and therefore that as Son of God Jesus belongs to the eternal being of God."[84]

The trinitarian pattern, clearly reflected in the later texts of the New Testament, surpassed binitarianism and in effect critiqued it as ultimately inadequate to deal with the fullness of the early Christian experience of God. Early Christianity's trinitarianism reveals the deeper and (from hindsight) inevitable realization that the manifestation of the relationship of the Father with the Son to us (*oikonomia*; the externalizing "economy" of salvation) and our sharing in that relationship can take place only on God's personal initiative. The confession of the Spirit is the early church's way of recognizing and expressing this initiative by God to enter into a continuing personal relationship with us that saves us. The Christian's experience of revelation and salvation is thus fundamentally trinitarian. This recognition of a "third" in God is not a separate, parallel development, but rather a complementary and even more expansive response to the christological concerns that binitarianism raises.[85]

From a historical point of view, the earlier confession of Jesus as Christ and Lord and the questions that are provoked (who is Jesus? why is he significant? how does his presence live on for us after his departure?) set the stage for the dawning New Testament belief that only by means of the Spirit does the community have a continuing personal share in the reality of Jesus. But once this point was reached, it became clear

---

84. Ibid., 244.

85. Cf. Hill, *Three-Personed God*, 17–28, esp. 26: "An implicit trinitarianism is gradually coming to light in the New Testament itself in function of some of its developing Christologies."

that the believer's ability to recognize Christ as Lord and confess him as such always depended on the already-present power of the Holy Spirit (cf. 1 Cor. 12:3).[86] Thus, Christology and trinitarian theology are inseparably linked in a mutually supportive way. At the same time, though, one must say that Christology finds the completion of its intentional drive or its inherent "logic" in the confession of the Trinity, and that the fundamental structure of revelation and of the New Testament message of salvation is trinitarian.

The Trinitarian Rule of Faith and Its Interpretation

From the New Testament to Nicaea (325 CE)

The simpler confessions and doxologies of the first century CE gave way during the following centuries to both shorter and longer creedal formulas and progressively more detailed theological statements of belief in the Trinity. This is not a story of more and greater abstractions being spun out by theologians in the privacy of their own scholarly disputes and divorced from the church's everyday life. Rather, these developments stemmed directly from the concrete situations of the early church's prayer and liturgical life, its public worship of the triune God (especially the celebrations of baptism and the Eucharist), and the various prayers and formulas

that developed in conjunction with these ritual celebrations. Prayers to God the Father through Christ the mediator, the invocation of the Spirit over the gifts of bread and wine so that they may become the body and blood of the Lord, the threefold confession of Father, Son, and Spirit at baptism—these liturgical actions raised questions in the minds of believers regarding the relations among the Father, Son, and Spirit, and the relation of the trinitarian confession to Christian monotheism. These became the fundamental questions that would occupy the greatest theological minds in the early church over the next few centuries. The development of the trinitarian doctrine provides the earliest documentation of the workings of the ancient principle *lex orandi, lex credendi* ("the rule of prayer is the rule of belief"). One of theology's primary tasks is to interpret with as much clarity as possible the truth of faith that believers already express through personal and liturgical prayer, in order to make that truth more accessible and understandable, and guard it against misinterpretations, distortions, and outright denials.[87]

The *lex orandi*, then, was a vital catalyst to trinitarian reflection. As noted earlier, the New Testament itself contains numerous witnesses to both binitarian and trinitarian patterns of prayer and doxology—a clear sign that Christian communities were already pondering the relations among Father, the risen Christ, and Spirit, with the trinitarian pattern ultimately being judged the most appropriate to the Christian experience of God.[88] The trinitarian confession at baptism was crucial because it

---

86. See ibid., 26–27; Kasper, *The God of Jesus Christ*, 248–49.

87. Cf. Jaroslav Pelikan, *Credo: Historical and Theological Guide to Creeds and Confessions of Faith in the Christian Tradition* (New Haven: Yale University Press, 2003), 166–67; Kasper, *The God of Jesus Christ*, 251. The original form of the principle can be traced back to the Prosper of Aquitaine, writing in the fifth century CE (Pelikan, *Credo*, 166).

88. See LaCugna, *God for Us*, 111–42, for an overview of New Testament and post–New Testament doxologies, Eucharistic prayers, and creeds.

summarized and structured the entire world of belief that the newly baptized Christian was entering. Along with the tripartite baptismal command in Matt. 29:19, other early witnesses to the trinitarian baptismal confession include the *Didache* (late first century), Justin Martyr (first half of second century), and Irenaeus of Lyons (c. 130–c. 200).[89] These early formulas are the roots from which the later creeds developed, a process that began quite early.[90] For example, Irenaeus structures his discussion of the three main "articles" of faith (God the Father and creator of all, Christ as Word and Son, and the Holy Spirit who renews humanity for God) along the lines of the tripartite baptismal confession.[91] The *Apostolic Tradition* (early third century), attributed to Hippolytus of Rome, records a rite of baptism wherein the trinitarian profession has been formulated as a series of three questions (similar to the articles contained in later creeds) posed by the bishop to the one about to be baptized.[92]

The prayers that accompanied the celebration of the Eucharist also developed a trinitarian structure. In the liturgy as described by Justin, the presider takes "bread and a chalice containing wine mixed with water" and "offers praise and glory to the Father of all, through

the name of the Son and of the Holy Spirit."[93] The Eucharistic prayer in the *Apostolic Tradition* gives praise and thanks to God through the mediation of Christ, pronounces an epiclesis that calls on God to "send your Holy Spirit on the presbytery of the holy church," and prays to God in a concluding doxology "that we may praise and glorify you through your child Jesus Christ, through whom be glory and honor to you, with the Holy Spirit in your holy church both now and to the ages of the ages."[94] These examples give a sense of the prevailing understanding in the early church whereby the trinitarian pattern of prayer became the orthodox norm.[95]

What is also evident is that the *lex orandi* contained ambiguities that provoked questions, both liturgical (how to worship God) and theological (how to think about God). These eventually fueled disputes as to precisely what roles Christ and the Spirit play in relation to the Father and to the divine plan of salvation. The prime example is the mediatory pattern that both binitarian and trinitarian prayers consistently took: one prays to the Father "through" or "in the name of" the Son; the Father grants us grace and life "through" Christ and the Spirit.[96] To those influenced by the "hierarchies" of being

---

89. *Didache* 7:1–3, in *The Apostolic Fathers: Greek Texts and English Translations*, rev. ed., trans. J. B. Lightfoot and J. R. Harmer, ed. and rev. Michael W. Holmes (Grand Rapids: Baker, 1999), 258–59; Justin Martyr, *Apology I*, 61, in *Writings of Saint Justin Martyr*, trans. Thomas B. Falls, The Fathers of the Church 6 (New York: Christian Heritage, 1948), 99; Irenaeus of Lyons, *Demonstration of the Apostolic Preaching* 3, 7, in *Proof of the Apostolic Preaching*, trans. Joseph P. Smith, Ancient Christian Writers, no. 16 (New York/Ramsey, NJ: Newman, n.d.), 49, 51.

90. Cf. Pelikan, *Credo*, 377–83.

91. *Demonstration*, 6 (51).

92. *Apostolic Tradition*, 21, in Hippolytus, *On the Apostolic Tradition*, trans. Alistair Stewart-Sykes (Crestwood, NY: St. Vladimir's Seminary Press, 2001), 110–14.

93. *Apology I*, 65 (*Writings*, 105).

94. *Apostolic Tradition*, 4:4, 12–13 (64–65).

95. Pelikan, *Credo*, 380: "The trinitarian force of the baptismal formula—and, apparently on that basis, of the Gloria Patri [Glory be to the Father . . .]—prevailed over any binitarian formulas even though these could claim biblical provenance."

96. Cf. LaCugna, *God for Us*, 22, 114.

or divinity in Hellenistic thinking, these prayers suggested that the Son was subordinate to the Father because of his mediatory role. For others, it raised the question of the subordination of the Holy Spirit, or whether the Spirit was the servant of the Son, the *Logos*. Such contested issues demanded more precision in thought and expression. The theological clarifications that occurred between the end of the first century and the Council of Nicaea (in 325) spoke to this need, contributing to the eventual development of the trinitarian doctrine and to the official ecclesial statements promulgated at the earliest ecumenical councils.[97]

The Apologists of the second century, including such writers as Justin Martyr and Theophilus of Antioch, were committed to the trinitarian pattern and to demonstrating "how the Son and Spirit, who were revealed in the 'Economy' as other than the Father, were yet inseparably one with him in his eternal being."[98] They said much less about the Holy Spirit, however, due to their focus on Christology. They adapted the Hellenistic philosophical concept of *logos* in order to assert Christ's divinity, to explain both his distinction from and his eternal relationship with the Father, and preserve Christianity's commitment to monotheism. *Logos* (meaning both "word" and "reason") had been used in the first century CE by the Stoics and by the Jewish philosopher Philo of Alexandria to name the foundational rational principle that unifies and governs reality and that ultimately is revealed in the rational human mind (also defined as *logos*).[99] Philo further taught that the divine Logos spoke through Israel's prophets and was the means by which the transcendent God of Israel (the "One" or "Monad") was related to the finite materiality of creation.[100]

The Apologists, building on these arguments and on the biblical use of *logos* in John 1:1 ("In the beginning was the Word [*Logos*], and the Word was with God, and the Word was God"), developed a two-stage "*Logos* Christology." The *Logos* is divine and eternally begotten of the one God, preexisting in the mind of the Father as the "immanent Word" (*logos endiathetos*); in the historical coming of Christ, the *Logos* became incarnate as the Son and the Father's "expressed Word" (*logos prophorikos*). In this way, the Apologists attempted to recognize the unity in being as well as the evident plurality in the eternal Godhead (termed "Father," the author of all that exists), and to articulate the distinction between God the Father and Christ in a way that would avoid any overtones of natural, temporal

---

97. For what follows, see Kasper, *The God of Jesus Christ*, 251–63; LaCugna, *God for Us*, 24–30; Pannenberg, *Systematic Theology*, 1:264–80; William G. Rusch, ed. and trans., *The Trinitarian Controversy*, Sources of Early Christian Thought (Philadelphia: Fortress, 1980), 1–27; Edmund J. Fortman, *The Triune God: A Historical Study of the Doctrine of the Trinity* (Philadelphia: Westminster, 1972), 35–170; Wilhelm Breuning, "Gotteslehre," in *Glaubenszugänge: Lehrbuch der katholischen Dogmatik*, ed. Wolfgang Beinert (Paderborn: Schöningh, 1995), 1:274–97.

98. Fortman, *The Triune God*, 108.

99. Cf. Christopher Stead, *Philosophy in Christian Antiquity* (Cambridge: Cambridge University Press, 1994), 46–48, 58–60, 150–58; Henry Chadwick, "Philo and the Beginnings of Christian Thought," in *The Cambridge History of Later Greek and Early Medieval Philosophy*, ed. A. H. Armstrong (1967; repr., Cambridge: Cambridge University Press, 1980), 137–92, at 137–57; Friedo Ricken, *Philosophy of the Ancients*, trans. Eric Watkins (Notre Dame, IN: University of Notre Dame Press, 1991), 190, 194–98, 229; Kasper, *The God of Jesus Christ*, 185–86. The roots of the *logos* concept go back as far as Heraclitus (c. 6th cent. BCE).

100. Chadwick, "Philo," 144: "The Logos is God immanent, the vital power holding together the hierarchy of being, who as God's viceroy mediates revelation to the created order so that he stands midway on the frontier between creator and creature."

156 generation.[101] However, the early development of this Christology with its terminological limitations did not succeed in avoiding a hierarchical subordination of the Logos (seen at times as a second or secondary God) to the Father. This is due to the lack of an adequate correlation between the Hellenistic philosophical conception of the impersonal *logos* (the universal "substance" of reality) and the irreducibly particular, personal, historical reality of Christ, the biblical "Word" who "became flesh" (John 1:14).[102]

Irenaeus of Lyons took a somewhat different approach due to his struggle against the Gnostics. He opposed their view of an utterly inconceivable and ineffable God, their theory of the emanation of the world from the divine (in ever more diluted stages of being), and their dualistic separation of the world from God. Against their overly "Hellenized" view of the Godhead, Irenaeus insisted on the church's rule of faith, "received from the apostles and their disciples . . . in one God the Father Almighty, the Creator of heaven and earth and the seas and all things that are in them; and in the one Jesus Christ, the Son of God, who was enfleshed for our salvation; and in the Holy Spirit, who through the prophets preached the Economies."[103] His incipient reflections on the Trinity and on the roles of Christ and the Spirit in the history of salvation are bound up with his strong theology of creation. He asserts the inherent goodness and dignity of all things, based on their direct creation from nothing by the one God, "the only Lord, Creator, and Father, who alone contains all things and gives them being."[104] On this basis, Irenaeus emphasized most strongly the fundamental unity of creation and redemption in the one economy of salvation: the one and the same God and Father freely creates and saves, and does so by means of his two "hands," Word (Christ the Son) and Wisdom (the Spirit), who are always with God.[105] Irenaeus's position is a type of "economic trinitarianism," arguing that while God's ineffable being is a unity, the Godhead contains from eternity the distinctions of God's Word (the *Logos* or *Verbum*) and God's Wisdom, which are made known to us only when revealed in the economy. Thus, the Son is divine and *always* the Son; he does not become so simply at the incarnation. In discussing the *Logos*, Irenaeus purposely avoids the Apologists' language of "begetting." The Son is *logos ensarkos*, "the enfleshed Word," at once both the "immanent Word" (*logos endiathetos*) and "expressed Word" (*logos prophorikos*) of the Apologists. In the incarnation, Christ as Son and divine *Logos*-made-flesh fully reveals the Father[106]

---

101. See, e.g., Justin, *Apology* 1.21 (*Writings*, 56–57).

102. Cf. Kasper, *The God of Jesus Christ*, 185–86, 252.

103. *Adversus haereses* 1.10, in *Against the Heresies, Volume I, Book I*, trans. and ed. Dominic J. Unger and John J. Dillon, Ancient Christian Writers, no. 55 (New York/Mahwah, NJ: Paulist, 1992), 49. "Economies" here means God's plan of salvation as revealed in the Old and New Testaments (ibid., 185n6).

104. *Adversus haereses* 2.1.1, in *Contre les hérésies, livre II*, ed. and trans. Adelin Rousseau and Louis Doutreleau, Sources chrétiennes 294 (Paris: Éditions du Cerf, 1982), 26–27 (my translation). Irenaeus thereby denies any idea of intermediary stages after an initial creation, and thus rejects the Gnostics' claim of a presently existing "evil" world which differs from the initial intent of the creating demiurge. Cf. G. W. H. Lampe, "Christian Theology in the Patristic Period," in *A History of Christian Doctrine*, ed. Hubert Cunliffe-Jones and Benjamin Drewery (Philadelphia: Fortress Press, 1980), 21–180, at 43–44.

105. *Adversus haereses* 4.pref.4; 20.1, in *Contre les hérésies, livre IV*, ed. and trans. Adelin Rousseau, Sources chrétiennes 100/2 (Paris: Éditions du Cerf, 1965), 390–91, 626–27.

106. *Adversus haereses* 3.6.2, in *Contre les hérésies, livre III*, ed. and trans. Adelin Rousseau and Louis Doutreleau, Sources chrétiennes 211 (Paris: Éditions du Cerf, 2002), 68–71: "Thus, through the Son, who is in the Father and who has

and fully participates in and recapitulates (sums up) all of humanity, thus saving humanity by divinizing it and restoring all creation's communion with God.[107] The role of the Spirit is to reveal the effects of this wondrous exchange as God's plan. The operations of the entire Trinity, then, are the necessary conditions for salvation: "Without the Spirit there is no seeing the Word of God, and without the Son there is no approaching the Father; for the Son is knowledge of the Father, and knowledge of the Son is through the Holy Spirit."[108]

Irenaeus has no fully developed theory of the distinction of persons in the Trinity, and his thought is not without elements that subordinate both *Logos* and Spirit to the Father. He develops, rather, a theology of the economy of salvation that articulates the relationship between God and the world and combats the Gnostics' dualism and their inadmissible separation of God the Creator (Old Testament) from God the Father of Jesus (New Testament). Within this theology, he succeeds in crafting a way of explaining the distinctions within the Godhead while insisting on the unity of God, and rooting this distinction-in-unity firmly in the biblical evidence. By showing how this divine unity is the basis for the unity of creation and salvation, and by emphasizing that in the economy, the distinctive divinizing roles played by the Son's incarnation and the Spirit's revelation could be effective only if they were truly the "two hands" of the Father from eternity, he shows "how the

Son and the Spirit disclosed in the economy as other than the Father were also one with him in his intrinsic being."[109] Incarnation and soteriology are thus inextricably linked in God's plan: "The unity of God thus grounds the unity of the order of salvation, while the order of salvation in turn presupposes the consubstantiality of the Son with the Father. In this brilliant vision of Irenaeus the economic Trinity and the immanent Trinity are one."[110] His insights prove to be influential in later trinitarian debates.

Both Tertullian (c. 160–c. 225) and Origen (c. 185–c. 254) furthered the development of the doctrine by contributing pivotal clarifications and important terminological distinctions. Tertullian attempted to steer a middle course between the extremes of subordinationism and the "modalism" of the Monarchians. Third-century Monarchianism had grown out of a backlash against Apologists' *Logos* Christology, for fear that it undermined the unity of God and led to ditheism. The Monarchians, to safeguard monotheism, argued that the Godhead is an absolute monad—one sole power or substance, a "monarchy" (in Greek *monarchia*, from *monê archê*, "sole origin") devoid of all distinctions. Modalistic Monarchianism, the more philosophically sophisticated of the two versions of modalism extant in the early church, argued that the distinctions that Christians confess— Father, Son, and Spirit—are not real distinctions at all, but merely the different operations, projections, or modalities (*modi*) by which the

---

the Father in himself, the God 'who is' manifests himself—the Father giving witness to the Son, and the Son announcing the Father."

107. *Adversus haereses* 3.16.6; 19.1 (Sources chrétiennes 211, 312–15, 374–75). Cf. Eric Osborne, *Irenaeus of Lyons* (Cambridge: Cambridge University Press, 2001), 22: "God has become man. The purpose of the divine exchange is that man might become what God is. . . . The end of all things is the participation of God in man and of man in God."

108. *Demonstration*, 7 (51–52).

109. Rusch, *The Trinitarian Controversy*, 7.

110. Kasper, *The God of Jesus Christ*, 254.

158 one absolute Godhead manifests God's self in the economy of salvation at different times. This version was argued by such early third-century figures as Sabellius (who came to be seen as the exemplar of modalism—thus "Sabellianism"—and gained an important foothold in Rome), Noetus of Smyrna, and the shadowy Praxeas (which may or may not be a nickname).[111]

Tertullian strove to refute this type of modalism. Its fundamental error, he argued, lay in claiming "that the Father himself came down into the virgin, himself born of her, himself suffered, in short himself is Jesus Christ . . . he [Praxeas] put to flight the Paraclete and crucified the Father."[112] Against this unitarian "patripassianism" (God the Father suffered and died as the Son), he cites the apostolic rule of faith and its trinitarian confession as the authoritative foundation of his argument that the Father is the one from whom the Son proceeds, the Son is born "both man (*hominem*) and God" of the virgin and is named Jesus Christ, who suffered, died, and was raised. The Father and the Son send the Holy Spirit, the Paraclete, who sanctifies those who believe.[113] The ancient rule of faith thus emphasizes that "the threefoldness of God's intrinsic being is disclosed in creation and redemption."[114] Tertullian's interpretation of this confession was the first to introduce the terms "trinity" (*trinitas*) and "person" (*persona*) into the discussion—a theological breakthrough:

> They [Father, Son, and Holy Spirit] are of the one, namely by unity of substance (*per substantiae scilicet unitatem*) while none the less is guarded the mystery of that economy which disposes the unity into trinity (*quae unitatem in trinitatem disponit*), setting forth Father and Son and Spirit as three, three however not in quality but in sequence (*gradu*), not in substance (*substantia*) but in aspect (*forma*), not in power but in [its] manifestation (*specie*), yet of one substance and one quality and one power, seeing it is one God from whom those degrees and aspects and manifestations are reckoned out in the name of the Father and the Son and the Holy Spirit.[115]

In interpreting these relationships, Tertullian retained the concept of *monarchia* but understood it in a more active sense than did his Monarchian opponents. He combined with it his revision of the theory of emanation and with the Apologists' *Logos* Christology, along with a deep concern for the economy of salvation, similar to that of Irenaeus. What resulted was a theology of the immanent Trinity that preserves both unity and distinction in God. A key element is that the *monarchia* of the Father, from which everything proceeds, is not divided by

---

111. Another version, called "dynamic monarchianism" or "adoptionism," held that the man Jesus was never more than human, but was adopted by the Godhead and endowed with divine power (*dynamis*) or inhabited by the *Logos*, one of the Father's attributes, thus becoming "Son of God." Proponents of this version included Paul of Samosata (bishop of Antioch) and Theodotus of Rome.

112. *Adversus Praxean* 1, in *Adversus Praxean liber/Treatise against Praxeas*, ed. and trans. Ernest Evans (London: SPCK, 1948), 89–90 (Latin); 130–31 (English). Hereafter, page numbers for the Latin original (L) and the English translation (ET) are separated by a slash (/).

113. Ibid., 2 (90–91 [L]/131–32 [ET]). The rule of faith is the authoritative touchstone because it "has come down from the beginning of the Gospel" and existed before heresy, and because "whatever is earliest is true and whatever is later is counterfeit." Ibid., 90 (L)/132 (ET).

114. Rusch, *Trinitarian Controversy*, 10.

115. *Adversus Praxean* 2 (90–91[L]/132 [ET]).

the emanation of the Son and the Spirit. Tertullian argued against the Gnostics that emanation does not necessarily imply separation.[116] And contrary to the modalists' explanation, in God there is a distinction of persons, not substances.[117] Tertullian uses *substantia* to refer to the unity of the essential being of Father, Son, and Spirit. Each of the three persons is God, without the Godhead being partitioned: the Father is "the whole substance" (*tota substantia*), the Son second in the sequence (*gradus*) of procession from the whole, and the Spirit third. The Son proceeds from the substance of the Father "not . . . by diversity, but by distribution, not by division but by distinction," and the Holy Spirit proceeds from the Father through the Son.[118] On the basis of these understandings of *monarchia* and emanation/procession, Tertullian proposes a formula "unrivalled in its accuracy"[119] that exerted tremendous influence in later trinitarian discussions: "So the close series of the Father in the Son and the Son in the Paraclete makes three who cohere, the one attached to the other. *And these three are one substance, not one person* (*qui tres unum sunt, non unus*) in the sense in which it was said 'I and the Father are one' [John 10:30], in respect of unity of substance, not of singularity of number."[120]

The other key element of Tertullian's thought, already hinted at with the terms *distribution* and *distinction*, is that relationality is an essential characteristic of what it is to be God. "The rules God has made, he himself observes. A father must have a son so as to be a father, and a son must have a father so as to be a son."[121] The terms *Father, Son,* and *Spirit* (Tertullian often uses the Johannine "Paraclete") designate those relations without which the specific actions of each divine person in the economy could not be understood. The relation of the distinct persons—and therefore plurality—lies at the very center of both the one inner being of God and the revelation of God in the economy of salvation, a "unity in trinity," which is the essential attribute of the immanent as well as the economic Trinity. This insight underlies Tertullian's insistence that Father, Son, and Spirit be called "persons," individual centers of action with specific roles in the history of salvation.[122]

Despite Tertullian's brilliance in perceiving the issues at stake and fending off modalism, his thought does not completely avoid subordinationist tendencies. His portrayal of the Father as "the whole substance" and the Son as "an outflow and portion of the whole (*derivatio totius et portio*),"[123] his depiction of the "perfect birth

---

116. Ibid., 8 (97 [L]/139–40 [ET]).

117. Ibid., 7 (96 [L]/138 [ET]): "Whatever therefore the substance of the Word was, that I call a Person, and for it I claim the name of Son: and while I acknowledge him as Son I maintain he is another beside the Father."

118. Ibid., 7 (94–96 [L]/137–38 [ET], describing the processions); 9 (97–98 [L]/140 [ET], "whole substance" and "distribution . . . distinction"); 13 (103 [L]/147 [ET], each is God [*pater deus et filius deus et spiritus sanctus deus*]).

119. Kasper, *The God of Jesus Christ*, 254.

120. *Adversus Praxean* 25 (121 [L]/169 [ET], emphasis added, translation modified).

121. Ibid., 10 (98 [L]/141 [ET]).

122. See, e.g., ibid., 12 (101 [L]/145 [ET]), where Tertullian explains that at the creation, God says, "Let us make humankind in our image, according to our likeness" (Gen. 1:26) because "there already was attached to him the Son, a second Person, his Word, and a third Person, the Spirit in the Word. . . . He was speaking with the Son who was to assume manhood, and the Spirit who was to sanctify man, as with ministers and mediators in consequence of the unity of the Trinity."

123. Ibid., 9 (97 [L]/140 [ET], translation modified).

of the Word (*sermonis*), when it proceeds from God" at creation,[124] and other such metaphors of emanation, procession, utterance, and extrapolation are signs that his thought remains under the shadow of the Apologists' distinction between *logos endiathetos* and *logos porphorikos*, and that he understands the divine generation of the Son or *Logos* from the Father to have occurred in a gradual fashion.[125] Nevertheless, the precision and clarity of his formulations, as well as his terminological innovations, played a major role in the discussions of the Trinity up to the Council of Nicaea.

Origen's contribution flows from his grand enterprise of constructing a comprehensive Christian view of reality that rests on two pillars: the revelation of the incomprehensible God as found in Scripture (properly interpreted to discover its deeper spiritual meaning) and celebrated in the liturgy, and his interpretation of this revelation within a philosophical framework influenced mainly by the Middle Platonism he had learned from its premier exponent, Ammonius Saccas (c. 175–242).[126] Origen's starting point is the belief handed on by the "apostolic teaching," that God is one, the creator who created all things from nothing, and who sent the Lord Jesus Christ to call both Jews and Gentiles to salvation: "This just and good God, the Father of our Lord Jesus Christ, himself gave the law, the prophets and the gospels, and he is God both of the apostles and also of the Old and New Testaments." Origen emphasizes God's unity and goodness in order to show how the rule of faith decisively refutes the various Gnostic arguments. Christ was "begotten of the Father before every created thing" and was the means by which the Father created the universe. Christ became fully human at the incarnation, truly died, was raised, and ascended into heaven. The Holy Spirit "is united in dignity with the Father and the Son" and inspired the prophets and saints, but the Spirit's origins ("whether he is to be thought of as begotten or unbegotten") are unclear and remain an open question in the church.[127]

In clarifying the meaning of this rule of faith for his contemporaries, Origen employed a Platonic philosophical framework, albeit one tempered by revelation.[128] God as Father is absolutely transcendent, incomprehensible, ungenerated, incorporeal, indivisibly one. He is purely spiritual, "a simple intellectual existence [that] is Unity (*Monas*) [or] Oneness (*Henas*) throughout, and the mind and fount from which originates all intellectual existence or mind."[129]

---

124. Ibid., 7 (94 [L]/136 [ET], translation modified).

125. Johannes Quasten, *Patrology*, vol. 2, *The Ante-Nicene Literature after Irenaeus* (1950; repr., Westminster, MD: Christian Classics, 1984), 326.

126. Ammonius Saccas would also later teach Plotinus. Cf. Chadwick, "Philo and the Beginnings of Christian Thought," 182–83; John Anthony McGuckin, "The Life of Origen," in *The Westminster Handbook to Origen*, ed. John Anthony McGuckin (Louisville: Westminster John Knox, 2004), 1–23, at 5. McGuckin notes also the influence of Aristotle and Pythagoras, and calls the "heart" of Origen's work "the weaving together of the philosophic and mystical imperatives."

127. Origen, *Peri archon* (*De principiis*), pref. 4, in *On First Principles*, trans. G. W. Butterworth (1936; repr., Gloucester, MA: Peter Smith, 1973), 2–4.

128. For what follows, in addition to the sources noted in nn. 125 and 126, see *The Westminster Handbook to Origen*, q.v. "Christology" (C. Kannengieser), 73–78; "God" (R. E. Heine), 108–13; "Trinitarianism" (C. Markschies), 207–9.

129. *Peri archon* 1.1.6 (10). The ancient Latin translation by Rufinus (*De principiis*, the only complete version of *Peri archon* extant) retains the original Greek terms.

The Father, in freedom, has created all reality through his only-begotten Son, who is Wisdom and Logos, the "image of the invisible God" (Heb. 1:3), and who reflects the Father's being to rational creatures and is their way of return to the Father. The relationship of Father and Son is eternal, their union one of love and action.[130] Natural analogies utterly fail to explain "how the unbegotten God becomes Father of the only-begotten Son. This is an eternal and everlasting begetting. . . . For he does not become Son in an external way through the adoption of the Spirit, but is Son by nature."[131]

The better comparison for this ceaseless incorporeal generation, according to Origen, is the operation of the intellect, specifically how "an act of will proceeds from the mind without either cutting off any part of the mind or being separated or divided from it, [thus] in similar fashion has the Father begotten the Son."[132] This description of the generation of the Son as a continuous act of the Father's will, an "immanent intellectual procession" that excludes all materiality, is one of the earliest uses of this intellectual metaphor that will eventually come to dominate Western trinitarian thinking.[133] In comparison, Origen has less to say about the Holy Spirit. The Spirit is divine, "united in honor and dignity with the Father and the Son," proceeds from the Father, and "is ever with the Father and the Son; like the Father and the Son he always is, and was, and will be."[134] However, as previously noted, he was undecided about the Spirit's origins and unsure about the Spirit's precise relation to the Son.

While asserting the union of the Father, Son, and Spirit, Origen emphasizes their distinction as well. He refers to the Father and the Son as "two distinct existences (hypostases), but one in mental unity, in agreement, and in identity of will."[135] Of the Trinity, he is "persuaded that there are three hypostases, the Father, the Son, and the Holy Spirit."[136] Origen here uses hypostasis in its more generic Middle Platonic sense of "substance," "real existence," or "essence," thus nearly equivalent to ousia (the usual word for "substance"), rather than the more precise meaning of "individuality," which developed later, after the Council of Nicaea.[137] He criticized those who would reduce the Father and the Son to one hypostasis, and rejected the use of the term homoousios ("of the same substance," "consubstantial") to describe their relationship.[138] However, the three hypostases could be considered "consubstantial" in the following sense: "Because their respective and specific nature

---

130. Ibid., 1.2.2–6 (16–20); 2.9.2 (130); 4.4.1 (313–16).

131. Ibid., 1.2.4 (18). Origen thus rejects the Apologists' two-stage *Logos* Christology.

132. Ibid., 1.2.6 (19).

133. Fortmann, *The Triune God*, 56.

134. *Peri archon* pref. 4 (3); 1.2.13 (28); *Commentary on Romans* 6.7, quoted in Fortman, *The Triune God*, 57.

135. *Contra Celsum* 8.12, in *Contra Celsum*, trans. Henry Chadwick (Cambridge: Cambridge University Press, 1965), 460–61.

136. *Commentary on John* 2.10.75, in *Commentaire sur Saint Jean, tome I (Livres I–V)*, ed. and trans. Cécile Blanc, Sources chrétiennes 120 (Paris: Éditions du Cerf, 1966), 254–55 (my translation).

137. Markschies, "Trinitarianism," in *Handbook*, 208. Cf. Rusch, *Trinitarian Controversy*, 14; Stead, *Philosophy in Christian Antiquity*, 174–80.

138. Markschies, "Trinitarianism," in *Handbook*, 208, citing the *Commentary on Matthew* 17.14. This rejection may be based on the fear that, during this period, *homoousios* implied the "improper idea of a generic being shared by members of a class" (209).

162

is that of substantial goodness, they can be said to be 'cosubstantive' . . . and to this extent, as cosubstantively good, they are devoid of internal subordinate distinctions."[139]

At the same time, however, Origen's position admits a subordinationist interpretation. Only the Father is God in the absolute sense (*autotheos ho theos*; "God in himself, the God"). Since the Son/*Logos* participates in the Father's divinity, "it would be more just not to call him 'the God' (*ho theos*) but rather 'God' (*theos* [without the article])."[140] The Son/*Logos* is eternally generated from the Father; nonetheless, the Father "caused it to exist."[141] He goes so far as to call the Son "a creature" (*ktisma*)[142] and even "a second God" (*ton deuteron theon*).[143] In emphasizing an immanent hierarchy and the Son's eternal dependence on the Father, Origen is most probably arguing against Gnostic theories of naturalistic emanation. The Spirit is "united in dignity with the Father and the Son" and proceeds from "the original goodness" of God the Father.[144] However, in other texts clearly implying a hierarchy, he claims that the Spirit "needs the mediation [of the Son] in order to be subsistent (*tê hypostasei*)" and is thus at the lowest rank. Despite this, he insists that the Spirit "has more dignity than all the rest and a rank superior to all which has come from the Father through Christ."[145] The three hypostases have different specific actions: the Father has the widest sphere of activity, the Son smaller, and the Spirit smaller still.[146]

However, despite such traces of subordinationism throughout his overall schema, Origen's understanding of salvation is fully trinitarian; that is, salvation is unobtainable apart from the whole Trinity. As the revealed image of God, Christ who is Savior, Son, and Logos is the only means by which human beings, created "in the image and likeness of God" (Gen. 1:26), can gain knowledge of the Father and of "the truth of the noble qualities that are within us."[147] Our understanding of the Son's revelation, in turn, is made possible only by the Holy Spirit,[148] the source of that grace whereby we become holy and thus "capable of receiving Christ afresh in his character of the righteousness of God."[149] Origen's vision of reality follows the circular Neo-Platonic schema of *exitus-reditus* (outflow and return), while always guided by the apostolic rule of faith: the Father, the absolutely transcendent and incorporeal *autotheos*, freely created the universe through the mediation of

---

139. Ibid., 209. Markschies cites *Peri archon* 1.6.2, 1.8.3, and the *Homilies on Numbers* 12.1.

140. *Commentary on John* 2.2.17 (Sources chrétiennes 120, 216–19).

141. *Peri archon* 1.2.9 (23). Earlier in this section, he says that the Son "comes into existence . . . subsisting in its own proper nature, a kind of breath . . . of the first and unbegotten power of God."

142. Ibid., 4.4.1 (314). Rufinus, in his Latin translation of *Peri archon*, omits the mention of the Son as creature (cf. p. 314 nn. 3 and 6), probably in order to distance Origen from accusations of heresy.

143. *Contra Celsum* 5.39 (296), in *Contre Celse, tome III (Livres V et VI)*, ed. and trans. Marcel Borret, Sources chrétiennes 147 (Paris: Éditions du Cerf, 1969), 118–19.

144. *Peri archon* pref. 4, 1.2.13 (28).

145. *Commentary on John* 2.10.76 (mediation), 2.10.75 (rank) (Sources chrétiennes 120, 254–57).

146. *Peri archon* 1.3.5 (33–34). Rufinus omits this potentially troublesome passage from his translation.

147. Ibid., 1.2.6 (20).

148. Ibid., 1.3.4 (32–33). Origen bases his interpretation on one of the Paraclete passages in John's Gospel: "But when he comes, the Spirit of truth, he will guide you to all truth" (John 16:13).

149. Ibid., 1.3.8 (38).

the Son and the Spirit, who are with him eternally, and then calls all back to himself through the grace of the Holy Spirit, which allows us to recognize the revelation of his image in the Son. Without the entire Trinity, we would have no access to the "gifts of God" and thus would be unable to receive salvation.[150] Rather than the determinism that grounds the Gnostic view of reality, Origen finds at the heart of reality the freedom, love, and providence of God.[151]

Because of its desire to "think everything," Origen's theology is full of complexities that at times shade over into obscurities and contradictions. Indeed, Christoph Markschies notes that its "unfinished and experimental character" set off "a struggle at [an] international level over the authoritative interpretation of Origen's Trinitarian schema."[152] Origen's many-faceted synthesis can confound us as well, making his theology of the Trinity difficult to unravel.[153] For example, alongside clearly subordinationist passages such as *Peri archon* 1.3.5 (referred to earlier), Origen can also say that "nothing in the Trinity can be called greater or less, for there is but one fount of deity, who upholds the universe by his word and reason, and sanctifies 'by the spirit of his mouth' all that is worthy of sanctification."[154] In the midst of a difficult discussion of the eternal

relationship of the Spirit with the Father, Origen diagnoses the problem he faces as one having to do with the limits of language: "Of course, these terms that we use, such as 'always' or 'has been,' or any similar ones that bear a temporal significance, must be interpreted with reservations and not pressed; for they relate to time, but the matters of which we are now speaking, though described in temporal language for the purposes of discussion, in their essential nature transcend all idea of time."[155]

Despite the difficulties, we, too, need to wrestle with Origen's theology because of its immense influence on the discussions that led to great doctrinal definitions of Nicaea, Constantinople (381), and Chalcedon (451).[156] His detailed argumentation and introduction of the terms *hypostasis* and *ousia*, played out against a background of mystical spirituality, had a clarifying effect on the trinitarian discussion. He forced it to move to a deeper ontological level in order to handle the still-lingering questions about the relations among Father, Son, and Spirit and the effects on the economy of salvation, questions that became more complex as Christianity grew and had to face rival Hellenistic accounts of reality and divinity. In this way, Origen extended the insights of Irenaeus and Tertullian, and along

---

150. *Commentary on John* 2.10.77 (Sources chrétiennes 120, 256–57).

151. Kasper, *The God of Jesus Christ*, 256: "Origen's entire system has a voluntaristic or, as we would say today, historical character which is profoundly opposed to the naturalism inherent in the gnostic idea of emanation."

152. Markschies, "Trinitarianism," *Handbook*, 207.

153. Markschies notes how Origen's approach admits both subordinationist and "consubstantial" interpretations, depending on one's emphasis. See his "Theologische Diskussionen zur Zeit Konstantins: Arius, der 'arianische Streit' und die Konzil von Nicaea, die nachnizänischen Auseinandersetzungen bis 337" and "'. . . et tamen non tres Dii, sed unus Deus . . .': Zum Stand der Erforschung der altkirchlichen Trinitätstheologie," in *Alta Trinità Beata: Gesammelte Studien zur altkirchlichen Trinitätstheologie* (Tübingen: Mohr Siebeck, 2000), 99–195, at 108–10; 286–309, at 298–99.

154. *Peri archon* 1.3.7 (37). Some commentators hold that Rufinus altered this passage in his translation.

155. Ibid., 1.3.4 (33).

156. As Markschies puts it, "the so-called 'Neo-Nicene' formula (*mia ousia, treis hypostaseis*; 'one substance, three persons') . . . dogmatized through the creed of the Council of Constantinople 381 . . . is a structure of thinking about the Trinity which is fundamentally based on Origen's thinking." "Trinitarianism," *Handbook*, 207.

164 with them helped the church "develop a trinitarian doctrine of its own in which the economic Trinity and the immanent Trinity are inseparably conjoined."[157] Even more specifically, in view of developments in the period immediately following Origen, his approach determined the fundamental "architecture" of orthodox trinitarian doctrine and remains definitive today, as described by Markschies: "After the fourth century the whole body of Trinitarian doctrine was left alone, and to this day its architecture (as witnessed in the Neo-Nicene statements) shows the marks of the compromise (that sought-after balance of disparate emphases) we first find in Origen: a well-balanced mixture of Nicene Antisubordinationism (as in the coequality of the Persons) with legitimate subordinationism (e.g., the taxonomy observed in the Trinitarian aspects of prayer and liturgy and soteriological function)."[158]

At the close of the third century, then, many of the basic elements of a trinitarian "solution" were in place. The next phase of development dealt not only with the clarification of these elements, but also with the noticeably increasing dissonance between biblical revelation and the Hellenistic philosophical framing of the God-issue, which had governed much of the discussion so far. Middle Platonism, the revival and extension of Plato's thought in late antiquity, had provided most of this framework.[159] Its adherents understood God to be the changeless divine monad or sole principle (*archê*) that absolutely transcends time, history, and matter, and created the physical world through a secondary divine figure or demiurge (a concept borrowed from Plato's *Timaeus*; from the Greek *dêmiourgos*, "craftsman"). This doctrine, taught by philosophers such as Numenius (fl. c. mid-second century), appeared under different guises and with many variations in various Christian treatises. However, it clashed with the person- and event-centered understanding of God and God's economy of salvation that had been narrated in the Old and New Testaments. Signs of this growing dissonance surfaced especially during the late third and early fourth centuries, not only in the disputes over the reception of Origen's theology, but in the growing resistance to the subordinationism that, as we have seen, had been a consistent aspect of Christian reflection on God from the Apologists all to way up to Origen.

The controversy sparked by Arius and Arianism put the problem at center stage.[160] Rather than affirm the ambiguous subordinationism that pervaded Origenist descriptions of trinitarian relations, Arius (d. 336) rejected it by absolutizing and radicalizing it. His strict adherence to the Middle Platonic doctrine of God's absolute transcendence determined his interpretation of scripture, his theology of creation, and his Christology. Arius excluded all plurality in

---

157. Kasper, *The God of Jesus Christ*, 257.

158. Markschies, "Trinitarianism," *Handbook*, 209.

159. Cf. Stead, *Philosophy in Christian Antiquity*, 54–75; John M. Dillon, *The Middle Platonists, 80 B.C. to A.D. 220*, rev. ed. (Ithaca, NY: Cornell University Press, 1996).

160. See the summary by Aloys Grillmeier, *Christ in Christian Tradition*, vol. 1, *From the Apostolic Age to Chalcedon (451)*, 2nd ed., trans. John Bowden (Atlanta: John Knox, 1975), 219–48, and the literature cited there, especially G. C. Stead, "The Platonism of Arius," *Journal of Theological Studies* n.s. 15 (1964): 16–31; and Friedo Ricken, "Das Homousios von Nikaia als Krisis des altchristlichen Platonismus," in *Zur Frühgeschichte der Christologie. Ihre biblischen Anfänge und die Lehrformal von Nikaia*, ed. Bernhard Welte, Quaestiones Disputatae 51 (Freiburg: Herder, 1970), 74–99. See also J. N. D. Kelly, *Early Christian Doctrines*, 5th ed. (1977; repr., London/New York: Continuum, 2000), 223–51.

the divine monad, any gradations within divinity, and any inherent connection between God and the material world.[161] In response to complaints raised against his preaching, he defended his position in a letter to his bishop, Alexander of Alexandria, that laid out all the basic elements of his position:

> We know one God—alone unbegotten (*agennêton*), alone eternal, alone without beginning, alone true, alone possessing immortality, alone wise, alone good, alone master, judge of all, manager, director, immutable and unchangeable . . . who begot an only-begotten Son before eternal times, through whom he made the ages and everything. . . . Thus there are three *hypostases*. God being the cause of all is without beginning, most alone; but the Son, begotten by the Father, created and founded before the ages, was not before he was begotten. Rather, the Son begotten timelessly before everything, alone was caused to subsist by the Father. For he is not eternal or as eternal or as uncreated as the Father. Nor does he have identical being with the Father. . . . But God is thus before all things, as Monad (*monas*) and Beginning of all (*archê*). Therefore he is also before the Son, as we have learned from you when you preached throughout the midst of the church.[162]

For Arius, God the Father is uncreated, eternal, utterly transcendent; he is the unique Monad, the *hypostasis* from whom all duality is excluded. Due to the Godhead's absolute transcendence, there can be no direct relationship between divinity and the finite material world. The essence of Godhead is indivisible; it cannot be shared, participated in, or communicated, since this would imply divisibility (and thus change) or even, in the case of participation, a duality of gods.

The Son of God, in contrast, is understood by Arius to be a true creature, inferior to the Father yet superior to all other creatures, created by the Father before time yet not eternal—according to the oft-repeated Arian slogan, "There was when he was not."[163] Thus, the Son is not coeternal with the Father, as Origen held, but had a beginning: he was created before the time of the material world began, and he was the mediating instrument (demiurge) by which the utterly transcendent Father created. Since the Son is of a different order of existence than the Father, he has no direct knowledge of the Father, no communication with him. Whatever divine titles he has (Word, Wisdom, Son of God, etc.) are by courtesy alone: "Even if he is called God, he is not God truly, but by participation in

---

161. Cf. Ricken, "Das Homousios von Nikaia," 99: "Im Arianismus verabsolutiert sich ein mittleplatonisches Denkschema. . . . Der Arianismus stellt insofern eine erste Krisis des mittleplatonischen Denkens dar, der er herausstellt, daß es für den christlichen Glauben keine Stufung des Göttlichen und damit kein Drittes zwischen Transcendenz und geschaffener Welt gibt." ("In Arianism, a middle-Platonist schema of thought becomes absolutized. Arianism thus constitutes a first crisis of middle-Platonist thought. It emphasizes that, for Christian faith, there is no gradation of divinity and therefore no 'third' between transcendence and the created world.")

162. *Letter to Alexander of Alexandria*, 2, 4, in Rusch, *The Trinitarian Controversy*, 31–32 (translation modified, following Stead, "The Platonism of Arius," 18; and Grillmeier, *Christ in Christian Tradition*, 226).

163. Quoted at Nicaea (in the anathema accompanying the creed; see the block quotation on page 166) and by Athanasius, *Contra Arianos*, oratio 1.5, in PG, ed. J.-P. Migne (Paris: 1857–66), 26:21A–B. In his *Letter to Eusebius of Nicomedia*, 5, Arius says that "before [the Son] was begotten or created or defined or established, he was not. For he was not unbegotten. But we are persecuted because we say, 'The Son has a beginning, but God is without beginning.'" In Rusch, *The Trinitarian Controversy*, 30.

grace. . . . He too is called God in name only."[164] The Arians' main concern, then, was to portray God the Father as the monad who by his very nature cannot enter time and history but relates to the world only by means of intermediaries, and to portray as occupying this intermediate sphere the Son, "produced by decree of the will of the Father and not by the communication of his nature or essence," who is on the side of creatures rather than divinity, yet who is the supreme creature and demiurge through whom the transcendent Father creates.[165]

Early in 325, a local council in Antioch condemned the Arian position. Only with Emperor Constantine's explicit intervention was a general council called later that year in Nicaea, with the goal of definitively settling the conflict and thereby securing ecclesial unity. The solution—less definitive than anticipated—was contained in the creed or "symbol" agreed to by the bishops at Nicaea—namely, the definition that the Son is "consubstantial [one in being] with the Father" (homoousios tô patri):

> We believe in one God the Father all powerful, maker of all things both seen and unseen. And in one Lord Jesus Christ, the son of God, the only-begotten (monogenê) begotten from the Father (gennêthenta ek tou patros), that is from the substance (ousia) of the Father, God from God, light from light, true God from true God, begotten not made, consubstantial (homoousion) with the Father, through whom all things came to be, both in heaven and those in earth; for us humans and for our salvation he came down and became incarnate, became human, suffered and rose up on the third day, went up into the heavens, is coming to judge the living and the dead. And in the holy Spirit.
>
> [Anathema:] And those who say, "there once was when he was not", and "before he was begotten he was not", and that he came to be from things that were not, or from another hypostasis or substance, affirming that the son of God is subject to change or alteration—these the catholic and apostolic church anathematizes.[166]

The bishops at Nicaea most probably took up a familiar baptismal creed and inserted various elements and anathemas that specifically ruled out Arianism as a legitimate Christian interpretation of God and God's salvation. In this way, they intended to avoid any divergence between the church's liturgical and pastoral practice and its theological reflection.[167] The creed presents "the saving economy of the Trinity which shows that the Father communicates himself to us in the true Son (and in the Holy

---

164. In Athanasius, *Contra Arianos*, oratio 1.6 (PG 26:24A; translation from Kelly, *Early Christian Doctrines*, 229).

165. I. Ortiz de Urbina, *Nicée et Constantinople*, Histoire des conciles œcuméniques I (Paris: Éditions de l'Orante, 1963), 76. See also Grillmeier, *Christ in Christian Tradition*, 231–32. As LaCugna notes, the Arians could cite scriptural support for their position (e.g., Prov. 8:22; John 14:28), as well as for the widespread subordinationist interpretation of the church's common intercessory prayers to the Father through the Son. *God for Us*, 32. For a somewhat different approach, see Frances M. Young, *From Nicaea to Chalcedon: A Guide to the Literature and Its Background* (Philadelphia: Fortress Press, 1983), 58–64, who views Arius's teaching as driven more by intra-ecclesial exegetical debates than by philosophical argumentation. She describes his major concern as "not so much of demoting the Son as exalting the Father" in order "to avoid attributing physical processes like emanation or generation to God," and Arius himself as being "a reactionary, a rather literal-minded conservative who appealed to scripture and tradition as the basis of his faith" (63–64).

166. Tanner, *Decrees of the Ecumenical Councils*, 1:5.

167. Grillmeier, *Christ in Christian Tradition*, 266.

Spirit), while at the same time showing the truly divine status of the Son and also his soteriological relevance. . . . Jesus Christ is the one true Son of the Father, not a creature."[168] Since the immediate theological discussion focused on Christology, specifically the nature and role of the Son, the baptismal model's brief mention of the Holy Spirit was left undeveloped.

The concept of *homoousios* ("of the same being/substance," "consubstantial") was the most crucial of the additional elements, and the most contested. The term's presence in the creed was initially objectionable to many in the fourth-century church, both at Nicaea and afterward, because of its nonbiblical character, its various shades of meaning,[169] its origins in Valentinian Gnosticism (where it meant a "similarity of being" between different beings), and the fact that the Arian party had been the first to employ it at this stage of the discussion (in order to ridicule and reject it).[170] Nevertheless, the council employed it, at the behest of Constantine and his theological adviser, Ossius of Cordoba, in order to refute the Arian doctrine and to craft a statement to which no Arian could subscribe. In doing so, Grillmeier concludes, "The Fathers of Nicaea had the courage to maintain the tradition of the 'Son of God' to be found in Bible and church in all its strictness, in part with unbiblical words."[171] In a terse, kerygmatic fashion, the concept of *homoousios* summarizes how Sonship relates to the one being of God. It expresses the church's belief that the Son is eternally begotten (*gennêthenta*), not created (*poiêthenta*), thereby uncoupling the concept of "begetting" from any naturalistic concept of "being created in time."[172] Thus, the Son is fully God ("true God from true God"): he belongs on the side of God rather than that of creatures, and possesses the unique and indivisible divine nature that is proper to the Father, without being the Father. Despite its inherent ambiguities, then, *homoousios* can be interpreted in the context of the creed as a whole to mean "unity of being," rather than "same being" (which could connote tritheism) or "identity of being" (which could lead to Sabellian modalism).[173]

The context of the creed as a whole has a very specific character: it is trinitarian from the start and follows the pattern of the economy of salvation, rather than beginning with any sort of philosophical notion of the one being of God. In other words, it does not confess belief in a formal and abstract notion of "divinity" or Godhead. Rather, says Kasper, "the creed starts . . . with the Father and understands him as the 'summit of unity' in which the Son and the Spirit are comprehended. We thus have a genetic conception of the divinity, in which the divinity originates in the Father and streams forth in the Son and

---

168. Ibid., 267.

169. Cf. Kelly, *Early Christian Doctrines*, 234.

170. For the Gnostic prehistory of *homoousios*, see Ricken, "Das Homousios von Nikaia," 92–95. For Arius's first use, see Grillmeier, *Christ in Christian Tradition*, 269–70; and Lampe, "Christian Theology in the Patristic Period," 98.

171. Grillmeier, *Christ in Christian Tradition*, 270.

172. The discussion at Nicaea thus begins the resolution of the persistent ambiguities that had plagued early church discussions of the relationship of the Father with the Son that centered around the linguistic pairs "begotten-unbegotten" (*gennêtos-agennêtos*) and "created-uncreated" (*genêtos-agenêtos*). Note the slight but important variation in spelling. See LaCugna, *God for Us*, 32–34; Grillmeier, *Christ in Christian Tradition*, 267; Kelly, *Early Christian Doctrines*, 227–28.

173. Kasper, *The God of Jesus Christ*, 257–58; Kelly, *Early Christian Doctrines*, 235–36.

168 the Holy Spirit."[174] We also have a clear denial of the Arian argument that the essence of divinity is "self-enclosed" being, and a clear affirmation that it includes relationality and relationship.[175] It turns out, then, that the general trinitarian "architecture" that had been sketched earlier by Origen (and by Tertullian with his reformulation of *monarchia*) remains valid: a dynamic understanding of divine being that balances the coequality of the divine persons (the antisubordinationist affirmation, against the Arians) with a legitimate recognition of the Son's difference from and dependence on the Father (clearly affirmed in the Gospels and numerous other biblical texts),[176] while ruling out any naturalistic understanding of "begetting" or any separation of being between Father and Son.

This was as far as Nicaea's affirmations could go. Despite the emperor's intentions, the problem of reconciling unity and trinity in God remained, and it became even sharper. The council's basic purpose, after all, had been negative: to rule out Arianism as a legitimate Christian interpretation. It gave no further guidance on how *homoousios* should be more precisely and positively defined, since it lacked "the conceptual tools for expressing in an adequate way the unity of being and distinction of persons. . . . The clear distinctions which Tertullian had already made could win adherence only after a long and difficult process of clarification."[177]

From Nicaea to Constantinople I (381 CE)

This process began immediately after Nicaea, with the meaning of *homoousios* as a focus.[178]

Some, like Eusebius of Caesarea (c. 260–c. 340), objected to its materialistic connotations. Others, like the important group of mid-fourth-century theologians known as Homoiousians (misleadingly labeled "Semi-Arians" by one of their contemporaries), tried to develop an orthodox position between the Nicene symbol and the interpretations of the still-active Arian parties. These theologians held just as high a Christology as Nicaea and rejected Arian doctrines, but objected to the unbiblical *homoousios* as well as to the political tactics used by the various parties at the council. They especially feared that confessing the Son as "one in being" with the Father would lead to the Sabellian identification of Father and Son without distinction—i.e., the fear that *homoousios* ("consubstantial") truly meant *tautoousios* ("identical in substance"). They preferred the term *homoiousios* ("like in substance"), and the declaration of the Council of Ancyra (358) codified their view that "the Son, who is an *ousia* (here denoting 'individual entity' or 'person') and not an impersonal divine activity . . . is like the Father in respect of substance."[179] Later statements reflected the Homoiousians' revulsion at the growing radicality

---

174. Kasper, *The God of Jesus Christ*, 258, citing Ortiz de Urbina, *Nicée et Constantinople*, 75–76. Ortiz de Urbina emphasizes that, according to Nicaea, the unity of the persons is "directly revealed and affirmed in its source, who is the Father. It is not deduced by reflection which compares the three persons among themselves" (76).

175. Cf. Greshake, *Der dreieine Gott*, 91–92.

176. Cf. Bernhard Welte, "Zur Christologie von Chalkedon," in *Auf der Spur des Ewigen: Philosophische Abhandlungen über verschiedene Gegenstände der Religion und der Theologie* (Freiburg: Herder, 1965), 429–58, at 454–55.

177. Kasper, *The God of Jesus Christ*, 258. In fact, Constantine considered this lack of precision advantageous; it allowed the various feuding parties to agree to Nicaea's symbol, according to the different shadings of meaning that they accepted.

178. See Kelly, *Early Christian Doctrines*, 237–51; Lampe, "Christian Theology in the Patristic Period," 99–111.

179. Lampe, "Christian Theology in the Patristic Period," 110; see also Kelly, *Early Christian Doctrines*, 250.

of the Arians' claims, as well as the narrowing gap between their own thinking and that of the Nicene party.

Their initial "moderate" compromise solution, unfortunately, could not do justice to the soteriological insight that Nicaea attempted to safeguard with the *homoousios*. Nor did they sort out in any clear fashion the confusing meanings of *ousia* and *hypostasis* that continued to plague the ongoing discussion. (Did *ousia* mean "individual" or something more generic? To what precisely did *hypostasis* refer? Did *ousia* and *hypostasis* mean roughly the same thing?) Some progress began to be made with Athanasius of Alexandria's interventions, both in his post-Nicaea writings and during his leadership of the Synod of Alexandria (362).

Athanasius (c. 296–373) staunchly defended the Nicene doctrine because he grasped the soteriological issue that lay at its core: Only if the Son is truly divine and eternal can he bestow eternal life and save humankind. And the Son can be this and do this only if he is the eternal Son of the eternal Father: "For he [i.e., the *Logos*, the Word of God] himself was made human, so that we might become God; he rendered himself visible by his body, so that we might have an idea of the invisible Father; he took on the insults of men, so that we might have a share in immortality."[180] On seeing how closely the ongoing Homoiousian discussion approximated the Nicene dogma, and despite the inconsistent and even contradictory trinitarian formulas used by the various parties ("three *hypostaseis*" by some, "one *hypostasis*" by others), Athanasius was able to win over the Homoiousians and other moderates. He demonstrated that their concern to avoid the dreaded Sabellianism by maintaining the distinction of persons in the divine Triad, without ever denying the unity of divine being, was yet another legitimate way of expressing Nicaea's concern to affirm the unity of being of Father and Son (i.e., one *ousia*) without denying the distinctions. The church could tolerate both positions and both *hypostasis* formulas; what had separated the parties was fundamentally a difference in emphasis.[181]

Athanasius is also responsible for focusing attention again on the nature and role of the Holy Spirit.[182] Against those who interpreted Scripture as teaching that the Spirit is a creature, his most compelling argument was again soteriological. Citing Paul's challenge "Do you not know that you are the temple of God, and that the Spirit of God dwells in you?" (1 Cor. 3:16), Athanasius argued that "if the Holy Spirit were a creature, we should have no participation in God through him; we would be united to a creature and alien from the divine nature. . . . If he makes men divine, his nature must undoubtedly be that of God."[183] The Spirit is consubstantial (*homoousios*) with the Father and the Son,

---

180. Athanasius, *De incarnatione* 54, 3, in *Sur l'incarnation du Verbe*, ed. and trans. Charles Kannengiesser, Sources chrétiennes 199, 2nd rev. ed. (Paris: Éditions du Cerf, 2000), 458–59. Kannengiesser notes that "these three propositions are rightly considered as summarizing the essentials of the treatise's teaching" (459n1). They echo a theme seen earlier in Irenaeus of Lyons.

181. See Athanasius, *Tomos ad Antiochenos* 5–6 (PG 26:800–4). See also Kelly, *Early Christian Doctrines*, 252–55; Lampe, "Christian Theology in the Patristic Period," 110–11; Joseph T. Lienhard, "*Ousia* and *Hypostasis*: The Cappadocian Settlement and the Theology of 'One *Hypostasis*,'" in Davis et al., *The Trinity: An Interdisciplinary Symposium* (see n. 30), 99–121, at 104–5.

182. See Kelly, *Early Christian Doctrines*, 255–58.

183. *Ad Serapionem* 1, 24 (PG 26:585–88; translation from Kelly, *Early Christian Doctrines*, 258).

170 and hence, due to this indivisible essence, their activity (*energeia*) is one and the same. Whatever the Father accomplishes is effected through the Son in the Holy Spirit.[184]

Athanasius's theology is part of the complex history of Nicaea and its immediate aftermath. The series of animated and at times volatile fourth-century theological discussions helped resolve some (but never all) of the dissonance between the biblically grounded person- and event-centered understanding of the triune God and the Middle Platonic philosophical framework employed to interpret it. Revelation's "excessive" character makes this a necessary dissonance. The biblical view of the loving God who encounters Israel in the Old Testament and all creation through Jesus Christ and the Spirit in the New Testament—in other words, the revelation that God is both immanently and economically *relational*—clashes with, indeed exceeds, Greek ontological categories. The partial resolution in this case was clear: the encounter with the God of the biblical narratives and the incarnational impulse of revelation were given priority over Middle Platonic concepts of absolute transcendence and nonrelational divinity. The categories of being, substance, and divinity had to be rethought and reshaped under the "pressure" of revelation in order to communicate more adequately the realities of the *oikonomia*, the salvific relationship of the triune God with creation that is initiated by the Father and brought to fulfillment in the incarnation of the Son and the persistent power of the Spirit.

If the conflict with Arianism indeed provoked, in Friedo Ricken's phrase, "the crisis of the ancient church's Platonism," then the discussions both at and after Nicaea demonstrate that a parallel crisis of scriptural interpretation had to be faced as well. In an ironic turn of events, the reformulated understandings of the unbiblical notions of *ousia* and *hypostasis* helped guard the biblical Christian experience of the triune God from being swamped by philosophical rigorism. The confession that the loving Father is the source of all things, the recognition of Jesus' intimate sonship with his *Abba* (an intimacy he offers to share with us), the acknowledgment of the Spirit's necessary role in the recognition of Jesus as Lord and as the human face of God—these biblical affirmations are rooted in experiences with God that had provided the basis for early Christianity's fundamental trinitarian structure and its biblical expression. During the early fourth century, however, the meaning of these biblical affirmations came into question. Arius's radically subordinationist interpretation of the Son's relation to the Father had seemed as compelling as the interpretations of those who had emphasized the coequality of the Father and the Son. To solve this dilemma, the soteriological heart of Christianity, the belief that Christ saves us by the power of the Father and gives us a share in the eternal life of God, was brought most strongly to the fore, despite the long tradition of subtly subordinationist liturgical prayer and biblical exegesis.[185]

The result of the Nicene and post-Nicene discussions was the differentiation of two types of subordinationism—one permitted, one banned—similar to what we had seen earlier in the evaluation of Origen's trinitarian "architecture." When speaking of the nature of God and the relations among the divine hypostases, a *logical* subordination of God the Son to God the Father, without any hint of inferiority or superi-

---

184. Ibid., 1, 27–28 (PG 26:593–96).
185. Cf. LaCugna, *God for Us*, 22, 32, 114.

ority of being, is legitimate and permitted, since fathers are logically prior to sons; as the Nicene symbol puts it, "the son of God [is] the only-begotten begotten from the Father." But any *ontological* subordination, implying the superiority of one type of being over another or implying temporal priority, is ruled out.[186] Thus, the soteriological insight that "the Logos himself was made human so that we might become God"— a belief grounded in Christian experience, conveyed by the living tradition of the church, and summed up in the time-honored phrase echoed by Athanasius—became the ultimate standard by which the church interpreted those places in Scripture and in liturgical prayer where the mediating role of Christ could possibly be misrepresented as an "inequality" between the Father and the Son.

What aided theologians in articulating this insight, as well as marking the first steps toward understanding the role of the Holy Spirit, were the unbiblical concepts of *ousia* and *hypostasis*, along with reformulated notions of divinity and being. These categories clarified the soteriology in Scripture in a way that biblical exegesis alone could not. The Nicene symbol itself is a mixture of these two types of language, one a more scriptural presentation of the economy of salvation, the other more abstract, conceptual, argumentative. The life, death, and resurrection of Jesus are narrated in biblical terms, whereas the preceding section on the identity of Christ argues with the technical, abstract terms of Greek philosophy. As Herwi Rikhof explains, "The answer to the question about what Christ did and suffered required not only a focus on the one who acted and suffered, but also a language that could interpret and determine this narrative as clearly as possible. Thus, problems raised with regard to the history of salvation, the *oikonomia*, required a reflection on the level of God-self, the *theologia*."[187]

A final point in connection with this "crisis" is that both the final form of the creed and the subsequent debates over *homoousios* demonstrate the necessity of theological reflection. Rowan Williams is correct in emphasizing the significance of Nicaea's theological hermeneutics (the process of interpretation that clarifies the meanings of Scripture and the lived Christian tradition) for the early church as well as for today:

> There is a sense in which Nicaea and its aftermath represent a recognition by the Church at large that *theology* is not only legitimate but necessary. The loyal and uncritical repetition of formulae is seen to be inadequate as a means of securing continuity at anything more than a formal level; Scripture and tradition require to be read in a way that brings out their strangeness, their non-obvious and non-contemporary qualities, in order that they may be read both freshly and truthfully from one generation to another. They need to be made more *difficult* before we can accurately grasp their simplicities. Otherwise, we read with eyes not our own and think them through with minds not our own; the "deposit of faith" does not really come into contact with *ourselves*. And this "making difficult", this confession that what the gospel says in Scripture and tradition does not instantly and effortlessly make

---

186. See Markschies, "Trinitarianism," *Handbook*, 209.

187. Herwi Rikhof, "Trinity," in *The Theology of Thomas Aquinas*, ed. Rik Van Nieuwenhove and Joseph Wawrykow (Notre Dame, IN: University of Notre Dame Press, 2005), 36–57, at 38.

sense, is perhaps one of the most fundamental tasks for theology.[188]

The conflict of christological interpretations in the early fourth century had exposed the problem of relying on Scripture itself to provide the means necessary for clarifying its meaning. This method failed because of the plurality of plausible interpretations. The danger within Arianism was not only its claim that God was disconnected from the world, but that Scripture could be interpreted to support this claim. It led to the fear that salvation mediated by the ontologically subordinate, nondivine Son might not really be salvific at all. The reality of salvation and the means by which God accomplishes it would thereby be obscured, the Old Testament creation narrative and image-of-God theology would be contradicted, and the role of the Son would be diminished. Without the reflections on being and divinity that used nonbiblical, more philosophical categories (that is, from "outside" the biblical narrative but always in light of biblical revelation), the meaning of Scripture would have remained ambiguous and contested, and its life-giving force in the church undermined. The use of reason to clarify faith claims had been part of Christian tradition from its earliest days. But the official approbation that Nicaea gave to theological reflection, to the point of including its results in the confession of faith that previously had been purely liturgical and doxological, was a momentous step. It provided a model for all subsequent creedal statements. The church insisted that Scripture demands interpretation; the mere recitation of scriptural proof-texts is no guarantee that one has successfully grasped the truth of revelation.

The balanced application of both faith and reason was especially necessary during the polemics of the late fourth century. Despite agreements reached in 362 at the Synod of Alexandria, as well as Athanasius's later interventions, it remained unclear how the distinctions among the divine persons were to be characterized and how *ousia* and *hypostasis* could articulate them. Their overlapping meanings contributed to the confusion; for many writers of the fourth century, *ousia* and *hypostasis* functioned as synonyms meaning "something that subsists."[189] Some, like Marcellus of Ancyra (d. c. 374), argued that Christian monotheism could be defended only by a miahypostatic (one-*hypostasis*) theology. In this tradition, according to Joseph Lienhard, "there is one God, who subsists; He is one *hypostasis*, one *ousia*. . . . This one God utters a Word, or begets a Son, and sends forth his Holy Spirit." This tradition "hesitates to assign any plurality to the Godhead. In general in speaking of God, saying 'one' is always safe, whereas saying 'two' is always dangerous."[190] Many later fourth-century theologians tenaciously held this, arguing that any notion of three *hypostaseis* was tantamount to tritheism.

Through the concerted efforts of the Cappadocian theologians Basil of Caesarea, his friend Gregory of Nazianzus, and Basil's brother Gregory of Nyssa, a way was found to express both the unity and distinction in God as authentically as possible, and this way led eventually to the classic orthodox trinitarian formula of "one *ousia*, three *hypostaseis*." The solution

---

188. Rowan Williams, *Arius: Heresy and Tradition*, rev. ed. (Grand Rapids: Eerdmans, 2001), 236.
189. Lienhard, "*Ousia* and *Hypostasis*," 103–4.
190. Ibid., 108–9.

stemmed from their attempts to work out the explicit distinction between the two terms and then explain how they are related.[191]

Basil (c. 330–379) developed a twofold argument that addresses both the *ousia-hypostasis* question and the begotten-created distinction. He followed Stoic philosophy in claiming that *ousia* and *hypostasis* have different meanings: *ousia* refers to what is common and shared (*ta koinon*), and *hypostasis* to what is proper (*to idion*), the particular way in which *ousia* is received. Each *hypostasis* of the Trinity is thus distinguished from the others by its proper characteristic: paternity (Father), sonship (Son), sanctification (Holy Spirit).[192] Against those who identified unbegottenness (*agennêsia*) with God's essence (*ousia*) and thus concluded that the Son, as begotten, had to be of a different essence and could not be God, Basil contended that unbegottenness is not part of the *ousia* of God, but rather is a proper characteristic of the *hypostasis* of the Father, just as begottenness is a proper characteristic of the Son.[193] As Kasper puts it, "Peculiar to the Father is the fact that he owes his being to no other cause; peculiar to the

Son is his generation from the Father; peculiar to the Holy Spirit is that he is known after and with the Son and that he has his substance from the Father."[194]

Gregory of Nazianzus (329/30–389/90) brought clarity of expression as well as further theological depth to this discussion. He coined various concise formulas to describe the Trinity and was perhaps the first to employ the phrase "one nature and three hypostases."[195] For example, in his Fifth Theological Oration (preached at Constantinople in 380), after presenting a series of arguments against those who denied the divinity of the Holy Spirit (known as the Pneumatomachians or "Spirit-fighters"), he summarized the formal doctrine of the Trinity with great precision:

> The very fact of not being begotten, of being begotten and of proceeding give[s] them whatever names are applied to them—Father, Son, and Holy Spirit respectively. The aim is to safeguard the distinctness of the three hypostases within the single nature (*mia physis*) and quality (*axia*) of the Godhead. The Son is not Father; there is

---

191. For what follows, see esp. Basil Studer, *Trinity and Incarnation: The Faith of the Early Church*, trans. Matthias Westendorff, ed. Andrew Louth (Collegeville, MN: Liturgical, 1993), 139–53; Lienhard, "*Ousia and Hypostasis*," 105–07.

192. *Epistula* [= *Ep.*] (Letter) 214, 4 in *Saint Basile: Lettres*, ed. and trans. Yves Courtonne, 3 vols. (Paris: Belles Lettres, 1957–66), 2:205–6; *Saint Basel: The Letters*, ed. and trans. Roy J. Deferrari, 4 vols., Loeb Classical Library 190, 215, 240, 270 (Cambridge, MA: Harvard University Press, 1962–86), 2:234–35. See also *Ep.* 236, 6 (3:53–54 [Courtonne]; 3:400–3 [Deferrari]).

193. Lienhard, 105, citing Basil, *Contra Eunomium* 2, 26 (PG 29:637). For Eunomius's teaching, including his claim that God's essence can be completely comprehended by human reason, see LaCugna, *God for Us*, 55–56. As Lampe notes, Basil's typology of peculiar properties remains unsatisfactory, since "paternity" and "sonship" are modes of subsistence, while "sanctification" is an activity that logically cannot be restricted to the Spirit. "Christian Theology in the Patristic Period," 114.

194. Kasper, *The God of Jesus Christ*, 259.

195. Cf. Anthony Meredith, *The Cappadocians* (Crestwood, NY: St. Vladimir's Seminary Press, 1995), 44. See, e.g., the passage from the Fifth Theological Oration in the block quotation that begins on this page. In Oration 26, 19, Gregory uses *mia physis, treis idiotêtes* ("one nature, three personalities"). *Discours 24–26*, ed. and trans. Justin Mossay and Guy Lafontaine, Sources chrétiennes 284 (Paris: Éditions du Cerf, 1978), 270–71.

one Father, yet he is whatever the Father is. The Spirit is not Son because he is from God; there is one Only-begotten. Yet whatever the Son is, he is. *The three are one in their Godhead and the one is three in personalities (idiotêsin).*[196]

To refer to the unity in God, Gregory used *ousia* sparingly, preferring *physis* ("nature") or *theotês* ("deity," "Godhead"). To indicate what is three in God, he used *idiotêtes* ("peculiar qualities," "properties") and *prosôpa* ("persons") along with *hypostaseis* and applied the Nicene *homoousios* to all three.[197] He defined what is proper to each hypostases as unbegottenness (Father), generation (Son), and procession (Spirit).[198]

Gregory of Nyssa (c. 330–c. 395) clarified these distinctions even further. He equated *ousia* with the generic, as did Basil. But his analysis of *hypostasis* is more detailed: it refers to "that which is said proper to the individual (*to idiôs*)" and "the conception which, by means of specific notes that it indicates, restricts and circumscribes in a particular thing what is general and uncircumscribed."[199] However, the analogy he used to illustrate how *ousia-hypostasis* is equated with generic-particular (namely, "man" as the genus, and "Peter," "James," and "John" as particular instances of that genus), along with the pronounced individuation it seemed to advocate, led some to accuse him of tritheism (three Gods who share a common divine being). He defended himself by arguing first that language and analogies are only approximations that never succeed in completely comprehending the mysteries of the divine nature, and second that, unlike the three men in the analogy, who are distinguished by the differences in their activities, in the Trinity there is but a single operation or activity (*energeia*) that reveals a unity of being:

> Therefore, then, the holy Trinity works every activity (*energeia*) according to the manner stated, not divided according to the number of the *hypostases*, but one certain motion and disposition of goodwill occurs, proceeding from the Father through the Son to the Spirit.
>
> For . . . the principle of the power of oversight and beholding in Father, Son, and Holy Spirit is one. It starts off from the Father as from a spring; it is effected by the Son, and by the power of the Spirit it completes its grace. No activity (*energeia*) is divided to the *hypostases*, completed individually by each and set apart without being viewed together.[200]

This demonstrates one of the consistent aspects of the Cappadocians' trinitarian thought: it not only affirms the oneness of nature shared by Father, Son, and Spirit, but also emphasizes the distinction of persons within a biblical un-

---

196. Oration 31 [= Fifth Theological Oration], 9 in *Discours 27–31 (Discours théologiques)*, ed. and trans. Paul Gallay and Maurice Jourjon, Sources chrétiennes 250 (Paris: Éditions du Cerf, 1978), 292–93; *On God and Christ: The Five Theological Orations and Two Letters to Cledonius*, trans. Frederick Williams and Lionel Wickham, Popular Patristics Series (Crestwood, NY: St. Vladimir's Seminary Press, 2002), 123 (my emphasis; translation modified).

197. E.g., Oration 31, 10 (Sources chrétiennes 250, 292–93; *On God and Christ*, 123): "What then? Is the Spirit God? Certainly. Is he consubstantial (*homoousios*)? Yes, if he is God."

198. E.g., Oration 25, 16 (Sources chrétiennes 284, 198–99): *agennêsia* (Father), *gennêsis* (Son), *ekpempsis* (Spirit).

199. *On the Distinction between "Ousia" and "Hypostasis"* (once attributed to Basil as his *Ep.* 38), 2–3 (*Basile: Lettres*, 1:82–83 [Courtonne]; *Basil: Letters*, 1:200–201 [Deferrari]).

200. *To Ablabius: That There Are Not Three Gods* (PG 45: 125D–127A, 127C–D; *Gregorii Nysseni Opera*, ed. Werner Jaeger et al., vol. 3/1 [Leiden: Brill, 1958], 48–49, 50; translation in Rusch, *The Trinitarian Controversy*, 155, 156). Cf. Hill, *Three-Personed God*, 48.

derstanding of God focused on salvation and a dynamic and monarchical understanding of divinity, but without subordinationist or Sabellian overtones.[201]

By uniting the Origenist teaching of three hypostases with the Athanasian concern for the unity-in-equality of the Godhead, the Cappadocians' "one nature, three hypostases" formula represents an advance over both positions. By reinterpreting the more abstract Nicene *homoousios* in terms of the saving action of the Trinity confessed at baptism, they bring together the theological concern for the divine unity with the liturgical affirmation of the Trinity's operation in the *oikonomia*.[202]

These crucial terminological clarifications serve as a prelude to the Cappadocians' major contribution, the development of the concept of relationality in support of their arguments. This was a key move in solving much of the unity-distinction dilemma, as well as resolving (as far as possible) the dissonance between the biblical narrative of the economy and Greek philosophical categories.

Gregory of Nazianzus states the point succinctly: "'Father' designates neither substance (*ousia*) nor activity (*energeia*), but is the name of a relation (*scheseôs*) which holds good between the Father and the Son."[203] Basil had first proposed such an understanding of the hypostases in order to defeat Eunomius's claim that by identifying God's *ousia* with unbegottenness and seeing "Father" and "God" as equivalent, one might grasp the essence of God and render God rationally comprehensible. According to Basil, neither "unbegotten" nor "Father" is equivalent to the divine *ousia*. Neither term allows unmediated access to "what" God is; God remains incomprehensible. Rather, they are terms of relation expressing the specific manner of God-being-Father. "Unbegottenness" signifies one proper characteristic, namely, that divine Fatherhood is absolutely independent of any origin. The term *Father* functions similarly as a term of relation, being defined "by relation to the Son, and not just by the absence of all relation to an antecedent term [of origin]. The notion of Father necessarily includes the notion of Son."[204] The terms thus signify *how* God is rather than *what* God is. The mystery of the divine essence is thereby preserved.

Gregory of Nyssa extended this understanding by arguing that the Son and the Spirit are everything the Father is (thus, there is one nature), except that the Son is neither Father nor Spirit, and the Spirit is neither Father nor Son (thus, there are three *hypostaseis*). In agreement with Basil, he held that the Father, Son, and Spirit are distinguished from each other not by essence (*ousia*) or nature (*physis*), but only in terms of the eternal relation (*schesis*) they bear toward one another. The Father is eternally the Father, so the Son must be eternally Son and with the Father as well; no interval separates them. One cannot think of the Father without the Son, nor the Son without the Father.[205]

---

201. In light of this belief, Gregory of Nyssa feels comfortable describing the distinctions in terms of causality; see *That There Are Not Three Gods*, PG 45:133B; *Opera*, 3/1:55–56; Rusch, *The Trinitarian Controversy*, 160.

202. Cf. Studer, *Trinity and Incarnation*, 144–45.

203. Oration 29 (= Third Theological Oration), 16 (Sources chrétiennes 250, 210–11; *On God and Christ*, 84 [translation modified]).

204. LaCugna, *God for Us*, 61, citing Basil's *Contra Eunomium*.

205. *On the Distinction* (= Basil's *Ep.* 38), 7 (1:90–91 [Courtonne]; 1:220–21 [Deferrari]); cf. Studer, *Trinity and Incarnation*, 147.

Indeed, Gregory pushes this line of thinking even further to speak of how Father and Son inhere in each other: "Everything that the Father is is seen in the Son, and everything that the Son is belongs to the Father. The Son in his entirety abides in the Father, and in return possesses the Father in entirety in himself. Thus the hypostasis of the Son is, so to speak, the form and presentation by which the Father is known, and the Father's hypostasis is recognized in the form of the Son."[206] This marks the beginning of the development of the doctrine later known as *perichôrêsis* (Greek) or *circumincessio* (Latin), the mutual permeation or inherence of the persons without any loss of difference in relation.

Finally, the Cappadocians were instrumental in advancing the understanding of the Holy Spirit. All three affirmed the Spirit's divinity, while not quite certain how to differentiate between the Spirit's relation to the Father and the Son's unbegottenness. Basil argued that the Spirit is not to be ranked with creatures but is inseparable from the Father and Son and "completes the all-praised and blessed Trinity." The Spirit shares in "the common [divine] nature (*kata tên physin koinônias*) and "is described to be *of God* . . . because he proceeds from the mouth of the Father, and is not begotten like the Son."[207] Basil never explicitly calls the Spirit "God" or refers to the Spirit as consubstantial, partly out of deference to the terms used for God in Scripture. However, he indirectly affirms the *homoousios* of the Spirit by affirming that the Spirit partakes of the same ineffable nature as the Father and the Son and thus deserves the same honor and adoration that they receive.[208] In light of this, he began to use the liturgical doxology "Glory to the Father *with* the Son, *together with* the Holy Spirit" alongside the more traditional form which gave glory to the Father *through* the Son *in* the Spirit.[209] For Basil, the ultimate convincing argument was the liturgy, since it reflected the long tradition of belief in the Spirit that "was unassailably inherent in the souls of the faithful." The touchstone is especially the long-revered trinitarian baptismal formula, which imposes certain obligations: "The proof of orthodox opinion is not to separate him from the Father and the Son (for we must be baptized as we have received the words of baptism, and we must believe as we are baptized, and we must give glory as we have believed to the Father, the Son, and the Holy Spirit)."[210] Gregory of Nazianzus, as we have seen, had no

---

206. *On the Distinction* 8 (1:92 [Courtonne]; 1:226–27 [Deferrari]; translation from Kelly, *Early Christian Doctrines*, 264).

207. *Peri tou hagiou pneumatos* 18, 45–46 (*Sur le Saint-Esprit*, ed. and trans. Benoît Pruche, 2nd ed., Sources chrétiennes 17bis [Paris: Éditions du Cerf, 2002], 408–90; *On the Holy Spirit*, trans. David Anderson [Crestwood, NY: St. Vladimir's Seminary Press, 1980], 72–73 [translation modified]). This treatise was directed against increased opposition from the Pneumatomachians. See also *Ep.* 125, 3 (2:33–34 [Courtonne]; 2:266–69 [Deferrari]). Basil was originally reluctant to mention the Spirit's divinity in his public homilies, not wishing to create dissension among the members of his congregation.

208. *Peri tou hagiou pneumatos*, 19; 22 (Sources chrétiennes 17bis, 416–25, 440–43; *On the Holy Spirit*, 75–79, 83–85). Cf. Kelly, *Early Christian Doctrines*, 260–61; Yves Congar, *I Believe in the Holy Spirit*, trans. David Smith, Milestones in Catholic Theology (New York: Crossroad, 1997), 1:74.

209. *Peri tou hagiou pneumatos* 1, 3 (Sources chrétiennes 17bis, 256–59; *On the Holy Spirit*, 17). Basil reports that some in his congregation felt this to be contradictory. Kasper describes Basil's formulation as "a doxology based on the one nature or substance of God tak[ing] its place alongside the doxology that reflects the history of salvation." *The God of Jesus Christ*, 261.

210. *Ep.* 125, 3 (2:33 [Courtonne]; 2:266–69 [Deferrari]).

reservations in declaring the Spirit both divine and consubstantial with the Father and the Son in the face of the varied contemporary opinions that denied the Spirit's full divinity, including those who identified "consubstantial" with "begotten" and thus argued that the Spirit could not be another Son. Against the Pneumatomachians, Gregory asserted that the Spirit is truly divine, and differentiated the only-begotten Son's relation to the Father (generation or "filiation") from that of the Spirit, which Gregory called "procession"—without, however, being able to explain it further.[211] Gregory of Nyssa also applied *homoousios* to the Spirit. Taking the other Gregory's insights a step further, he proposed an understanding of the Son as the mediator of the Spirit's procession from the Father, thus assuming a twofold procession of the Spirit (from the Father through the Son).[212]

The treatises and letters of the Cappadocians represent the concluding moves in series of contentious debates that lasted for more than a half century after Nicaea. What were the results? The Cappadocians' insights and success at clarifying the language and concepts used in discussing the Trinity were confirmed at the First Council of Constantinople (381) and in the report of the council sent by the Synod of Constantinople (382) to Pope Damasus and the other bishops in Rome.[213] In the wake of the

recent controversies with Arians, Sabellians, Pneumatomachians, and others, those at the council took up a version of the earlier Nicene creed, made its teaching on the Son's divinity more precise in light of recent theological developments (e.g., omitting the phrase "from the substance [*ousia*] of the Father," adding references to the history of salvation), and greatly expanded the teaching on the Holy Spirit. The result was the following statement:

> We believe in one God the Father all-powerful, maker of heaven and of earth, and of all things both seen and unseen. And in one Lord Jesus Christ, the only-begotten Son of God, begotten from the Father before all ages, light from light, true God from true God, begotten not made, consubstantial (*homoousios*) with the Father, through whom all things came to be; for us humans and for our salvation he came down from the heavens and became incarnate from the holy Spirit and the virgin Mary, became human and was crucified on our behalf under Pontius Pilate; he suffered and was buried and rose up on the third day in accordance with the scriptures; and he went up into the heavens and is seated at the Father's right hand; he is coming again with glory to judge the living and the dead; his kingdom will have no end. And in the Spirit, the holy, the lordly and life-giving one, proceeding forth

---

211. Oration 39, 12, in *Discours 38–41*, ed. Claudio Moreschini, trans. Paul Gallay, Sources chrétiennes 358 (Paris: Éditions du Cerf, 1990), 174–75: "The Holy Spirit is truly the Spirit coming forth (*proïon*) from the Father, not by filiation (for it is not by generation) but by procession (*ekporeutôs*), if I may coin a phrase for the sake of clarity" (my translation).

212. See, e.g., the passage mentioned earlier (n. 201) from *That There Are Not Three Gods* (PG 45:133B; *Opera*, 3/1: 55–56; Rusch, *The Trinitarian Controversy*, 160]): the Spirit's relation to the Father is "through that which depends on the first [i.e., through the Son]." Studer (146n50, 152n101) also cites *Contra Eunomium* 1, 280, 378 (PG 45:336D, 369A) and *Adversus Macedonianos* 6 (PG 45:1308B; *Opera* 3/1: 92–93). Cf. also Kelly, *Early Christian Doctrines*, 262–63.

213. The council's acts have not survived; the only contemporary record is found in the synod's letter summarizing the council's decisions. The council's creed appears in the acts of the Council of Chalcedon (451), where it is quoted alongside the Nicene Creed. Chalcedon declared both creeds to be authoritative doctrinal teaching. See Tanner, *Decrees of the Ecumenical Councils*, 1:21–23 (introduction); 24 (Constantinople I's creed); 25–30 (synodal letter); 84–85 (affirmation by Chalcedon).

from the Father, co-worshipped and co-glorified with Father and Son, the one who spoke through the prophets; in one, holy, catholic and apostolic church. We confess one baptism for the forgiving of sins. We look forward to a resurrection of the dead and life in the age to come. Amen.[214]

The synodal report of 382 makes it clear that the creed's confession of faith in the Trinity is to be understood along the general conceptual lines introduced by the Cappadocians, namely, "that the Father, the Son and the holy Spirit have a single Godhead (*theotêtos*) and power (*dynameôs*) and substance (*ousias*), a dignity deserving the same honour and a co-eternal sovereignty, in three most perfect hypostases, or three perfect persons (*prosôpois*)."[215]

The creed and the synodal letter together signal the resolution of the major trinitarian controversies and constitute the church's definitive statement of what we referred to earlier as the fundamental "architecture" of the Trinity. They also reflect the terminological consensus that had been reached within Eastern (Greek) Christianity by the end of the fourth century. The Western (Latin, Roman) church, diverging from this consensus to some degree, tended to translate *hypostasis* with the Latin *substantia*. Western Christians thus had trouble with the Eastern confession of three *hypostases*; it seemed like a belief in three divine substances, that is,

three Gods. Official Roman statements, such as the "Tome" of Pope Damasus (382), which confirmed Constantinople's decree, spoke instead of one *substantia* and three *personae*, following on Tertullian's insights.[216] Eastern Christians, for their part, had trouble with the Western use of *persona*, since the Greek equivalent *prosôpon* did not connote substantial individuality but rather a mask or mere appearance. The West's use of *personae* sounded like modalism to Eastern ears.

Contemporary commentators have often posited a more profound theological difference behind these terminological distinctions, arguing that the East's trinitarian reflections tended to begin with the distinction of the divine persons and their actions in the economy of salvation, and that the West took more abstract approach, starting from the unity of the divine nature.[217] For example, Walter Kasper claims that "while the creeds of Nicaea and Constantinople start with the Father and then confess the Son and the Spirit to be one in being or substance with the Father, the West replaces this dynamic conception with a more static approach that starts with the one substance and then says that it subsists in three persons."[218] In light of recent research, it is clear that a strict application of any "East = dynamic vs. West = static" schema is an oversimplification; an "Eastern" approach would be just as concerned with the unity of God as a "Western" one. But that

---

214. Ibid., 1:24 (= ND 12, DH 150).

215. Ibid., 1:28. The creed, however, avoids mention of *homoousios* in connection with the Spirit.

216. DH 168 (*de divina substantia*), 173 (*tres personas . . . veras*), 177 (*veram solam unam divinitatem et potentiam, maiestatem et substantiam*) = ND 306/16 ("of the divine substance"), 21 ("three true persons"), 24 ("the one and only true Godhead and might, majesty and substance").

217. The roots of this typology go back to Théodore de Régnon, *Études de théologie positive sur la Sainte Trinité*, 3 vols. (Paris: Retaux, 1892–98). Regarding the inadequacies of de Régnon's schema, despite its pervasive influence, see LaCugna, *God for Us*, 11–12; Michel René Barnes, "Augustine in Contemporary Trinitarian Theology," *Theological Studies* 56 (1995): 237–51; idem, "Rereading Augustine's Theology of the Trinity," in Davis et al., *The Trinity: An Interdisciplinary Symposium* [see n. 30], 145–76.

218. Kasper, *The God of Jesus Christ*, 259.

schema, more broadly conceived, at least points up the differing conceptual starting points behind the obvious terminological distinctions, without turning them into mutually exclusive positions. Eastern trinitarian reflection did seem to be more comfortable with understanding the relations among the divine hypostases in terms of the monarchial metaphor, where God the Father is "the unoriginate origin, source and principle" of the eternal being of God and where "every act of God in creation originates with the Father, proceeds through the Son, and is perfected by the Holy Spirit."[219] On the other hand, the West, in order to rule out all traces of Arianism and subordinationism, seemed more comfortable starting its reflections with the notion of the one divine *substantia* before moving on to treat the distinction of persons.

These differences did not divide the church, however, but rather revealed "the possible plurality and wealth of theologies that are based on a single common faith."[220] These legitimate approaches were brought together at the Second Council of Constantinople (553). Its trinitarian formula is a synthesis of speculative, technical language and more biblical language that reflects the history of salvation:

> If anyone will not confess that the Father, Son and holy Spirit have one nature (*mian physin, unam naturam*) or substance (*ousian, substantiam*), that they have one power and authority, that there is a consubstantial Trinity (*triada homoousion, trinitatem consubstantialem*), one Deity to be adored in three subsistences (*hypostasesin, subsistentiis*) or persons (*prosôpois, personis*): let him

be anathema. There is only one God and Father, from whom all things come, and one Lord, Jesus Christ, through whom all things are, and one holy Spirit, in whom all things are.[221]

This statement brings the historical development of the doctrine of the Trinity to a close. Constantinople II confirms as the church's pivotal belief what we have been calling the fundamental architecture of the doctrine of the Trinity—the expression of the divine trinitarian reality in the language of "nature," "substance," and "person." All subsequent theological reflection on the Trinity in the history of Christian theology is commentary on this doctrinal claim—not "mere" commentary or trivial additions to a basic core, but rather developments that are as legitimate and necessary as what occurred at Nicaea. This is precisely because Christianity has a mandate to proclaim the good news of salvation in every situation, in every epoch. There is the continual need to discern and draw out the doctrine's implications and possibilities and then apply them in contexts far beyond the imaginations of any thinkers in the early church.

The Doctrine of the Trinity in a Contemporary Context

From the moment of baptism ("in the name of the Father, the Son, and the Holy Spirit"), the Trinity is at the core of Christian life. To borrow Kasper's eloquent language, the trinitarian confession expresses "the eschatologically

---

219. LaCugna, "Trinitarian Mystery," 168–69.

220. Kasper, *The God of Jesus Christ*, 259.

221. Tanner, *Decrees of the Ecumenical Councils*, 1:114 (First Anathema against the "Three Chapters," in both Latin and Greek = DH 421 [Greek version only]).

definitive and universal truth about God from which all other talk about God can derive its full truthfulness"—namely, that "God has given of himself through Jesus Christ through the working of the Holy Spirit"—and thereby "holds the entire edifice together like the keystone of a Gothic arch."[222]

The crucial issue we face in rendering the trinitarian doctrine accessible today is explaining what Kasper calls the doctrine's "practical relevance to Christian life."[223] Here, "relevance" does not mean cutting down the mystery of the Trinity to fit ever-shifting cultural standards. Rather, we need to underscore the central truth that the Trinity has been revealed "for us and for our salvation"—for us as we are in the twenty-first century. The connection with the ordinary lives of Christians must be disclosed if the doctrine is to be teachable, preachable, and existentially meaningful for those for whose salvation it has been revealed.[224] Once we say this, though, we begin to recognize the temporal and conceptual distance that exists between the confession of the Trinity as developed in ancient Christianity and our attempts to understand it and live it in the aestheticized postmodern (or even post-postmodern) consumer world of the West. After all, the doctrine's "architecture" and the comprehensive view of reality it engenders have long been expressed in the metaphysical language of "nature" and "substance" and with a quite different view of "person"—ways of thought foreign to a postmodern Western culture seemingly allergic to metaphysics. How do we bridge this hermeneutical gap and disclose

how central the belief in the Trinity is for our times, for a context that in countless ways outruns the imagination of the ancient church?

The keys to bridging the gap are an adequate theological method and an insightful metaphor. First, the method itself must be hermeneutical, based on the recognition that temporal distance and tradition are not disabling factors but rather enabling ones. They allow both the historical rootedness and the necessary newness of our contemporary Christian beliefs and practices to appear in bold relief. Temporal distance and tradition do not prevent understanding; rather, they make a fuller understanding of the trinitarian confession possible through the application of its truth to our present context and its possibilities. That context always exhibits the dual truth of difference *and* continuity: it necessarily differs and stands apart from the originating context of the tradition, yet because of the historically rooted beliefs, practices, and questions that have formed it, it is nonetheless always a part of the tradition. This is the blunt reality of Christian thought and practice.

Graham Ward's comments regarding Christology as a "cultural operation" are pertinent here. Starting with Thomas Aquinas's view that "God is not known to us in his own nature, but through his works (*ex operationibus*) or effects (*effectibus*),"[225] Ward says the fundamental christological question is thus not "who" or "what" Christ is, but "Where is the Christ?" Ward explains, "The Christological enquiry therefore does not begin with the identity of the Christ, what in dogmatics is the nature as

---

222. Kasper, *The God of Jesus Christ*, 233.

223. Ibid.

224. Because of this particular kind of "practical relevance," Kasper argues strongly that a theology of the Trinity must recover the "soteriological motives" that led to the development of the doctrine to begin with and "develop a comprehensive and specifically Christian vision of reality on the basis of the trinitarian confession." Ibid., 263.

225. ST Ia, q. 13, a.8, reply (3:78–79; translation modified).

distinct from the work of Christ; it begins with an analysis of the operations whereby Christ is made known to us. And in being made known we participate in him."[226] This echoes the burning contemporary question "Where is God?" Ward's emphasis on "participation in Christ" is another (very Johannine) way of saying "salvation," and *our* participation, most obviously, begins and develops in the epoch and culture in which we dwell. The Christ-event, while eschatologically oriented, is always culturally situated and inflected as well. As Ward puts it: "Not that the past is irrelevant, for the horizons of today's questions are always configured by what has been handed down to us—including the historical Jesus himself recorded in the Scriptures. But because Jesus Christ is a confession of faith, and faith is a present operation with respect to salvation, then God is made known to us today in ways that differ from [the past]."[227]

The same holds true of the trinitarian confession. The continuous, centuries-long reception of the doctrine—through the practices of liturgy, devotion, and the theological reflections of such thinkers as Augustine and Thomas Aquinas—creates a stream of interpretive and interpreting effects that flow into our own epoch, shape our current framework of beliefs, and connect the ancient confessional statements with our own confession. The trinitarian confession is present to us and for us precisely because of the culturally inflected Christian traditions that stream toward us and touch us with their force. It is clear, then, that bridging the gap means that one takes seriously the whole of the economy of salvation as a "revelatory event" and asks the basic question: How is the Trinity revealed to us, in our own situation? Any answer

must take into account the context-inflected ways in which belief in the Trinity has been interpretively handed down to us throughout the Christian tradition and articulated "for us and for our salvation." A productive method, then, must look both ways: a backward glance at the tradition, and a forward glance at our context and our future.

The second key to bridging the gap is the employment of an insightful metaphor that fuses this historical rootedness with our own context and speaks to our contemporary life of faith. And a successful metaphor opens the way to realizing new possibilities of belief and understanding. The aspect of the ancient confessions of the Trinity that most prominently threads its way into our own faith is the Cappadocian insight into relationality and the use of the metaphor of "person" to explicate the insight and its way of conceiving distinctions in the Trinity. Relationality, the heart of the trinitarian confession of divine unity-and-plurality, is what the theological traditions have labored to articulate—with greater or lesser success—in the centuries after the ancient doctrinal settlements, and our reception of these reflections forms the foundation of our own endeavors of *fides quaerens intellectum* (faith seeking understanding).

The Catholic understanding of the trinitarian confession has been shaped—and to some extent determined—by Augustine and Thomas Aquinas and the ways each chose to format the issue. Augustine (354–430) reflected on the Trinity throughout his career as a Christian theologian, and most especially in the major work *De trinitate*, which Rowan Williams declares "stands alone as a meditation on the trinitarian mystery as a mystery at once of theology

---

226. Ward, *Christ and Culture*, 1 (see n. 5).
227. Ibid., 6.

and anthropology."[228] Augustine's early studies of Neo-Platonism strongly influenced him and led him to see not only the structure of the world as manifesting the being of God (in accordance with Paul in Rom. 1:20: "his invisible attributes of eternal power and divinity have been able to be understood and perceived in what he has made"),[229] but most especially the soul as a reflection of its Creator and thus containing a vestige or image of the Trinity. The way inward through introspection and contemplation thus becomes an ascent toward God. *De trinitate* clearly reveals Augustine's overriding concern for the oneness of God, in order to rule out any trace of Arian subordinationism: "Let us believe that the Father and Son and Holy Spirit are one God, maker and ruler of all creation; and that the Father is not the Son, and the Holy Spirit is neither the Father nor the Son, but that they are a trinity of persons related to each other, and a unity of equal being."[230]

Starting from this emphasis on unity, his argument is driven by the desire to think how oneness and threeness belong together in God, who is made manifest to us in the love of Christ.[231] In books 5–7 of *De trinitate*, he confronts the Arians on the issue of the one divine substance and makes the important point that distinctions in the Trinity do not belong to the substance of divinity but rather to the mutual relations of the inner-trinitarian life.[232] "Father" and "Son" describe the relation between the first and second persons, while the Holy Spirit is "supreme charity conjoining Father and Son to each other and subjoining us to them."[233] However, the central question remains, for if "the Father is God and the Son is God and the Holy Spirit is God," how are believers to understand "that this threesome is not three gods but one God"?[234] Augustine developed various approaches in response to this question,[235] but the most famous and the one with the most impact on the subsequent tradition was the psychological analogy that compares the operations of a person's inner life with the relations within the Trinity. As the human mind is one substance that exists with the distinct powers or operations of memory, understanding, and will, without that substance being divided (the knower remains the same person while exercising these powers),[236] so the one God exists as Trinity, without division or confusion, in the Father's generation of the Word and the procession of the Holy Spirit. All the divine actions are attributable to the entire Trin-

---

228. Allan D. Fitzgerald et al., eds., *Augustine through the Ages: An Encyclopedia* (Grand Rapids: Eerdmans, 1999), s.v. "*De Trinitate*" (by Rowan Williams), 850.

229. Augustine, *De trinitate* 5.1.1 (*The Trinity*, trans. Edmund Hill, ed. John E. Rotelle, in *The Works of Saint Augustine*, part I, vol. 5 [Brooklyn, NY: New City, 1991], 395).

230. Ibid., 9.1.1. (271).

231. Cf. Wilhelm Breuning, "Gotteslehre," in *Glaubenszugänge: Lehrbuch der katholischen Dogmatik*, ed. Wolfgang Beinert, 3 vols. (Paderborn: Ferdinand Schöningh, 1995), 1:289–93, at 290.

232. Cf. Augustine, *De trinitate* 5.8.9 (195): "Whatever that supreme and divine majesty is called with reference to itself is said substance-wise (*substantialiter*); whatever it is called with reference to another is said not substance- but relationship-wise (*non substantialiter, sed relative*)."

233. Ibid., 7.3.6 (224).

234. Ibid., 1.5.8 (70).

235. Cf. Olivier du Roy, *L'Intelligence de la foi en la Trinité selon saint Augustin* (Paris: Études Augustiniennes, 1966).

236. Cf. Augustine, *De trinitate* 10.11.18 (298): "These three then, memory, understanding, and will, are not three lives but one life, nor three minds but one mind. So it follows of course that they are not three substances but one substance."

ity: "The trinity works inseparably in everything that God works."[237]

Any attempt to give a more precise description, however, is defeated by the transcendent mystery of the Godhead. Whatever term is used to answer Augustine's famous question "Three what?"—whether "substance" (*hypostasis*, the preference of "the Greeks") or "person" (Augustine's reluctant choice)—will be merely an inadequate semantic placeholder.[238] This is because "the total transcendence of the godhead (*divinitatis*) quite surpasses the capacity of ordinary speech. God can be thought about more truly than he can be talked about, and he is more truly than he can be thought about."[239] In the final book (book 15), Augustine admits his frustration at not being able to find adequate ways of expressing the distinctions in the Trinity.

Yet this does not block our experience of God. There is still the possibility of mystical ascent through prayer to a contemplative union with the Trinity when one experiences love as a pure gift from God and becomes aware of the presence of God who is love, as 1 John 4:16 proclaims.[240] William Hill explains, "Augustine means to say in effect that the Christian experiences love as the pure gift of God—as grace, thus as a sharing in that love which is proper to God. But to this he now adds his own expanded understanding (not explicit in any Father before

Augustine) that such love in God is the Holy Spirit."[241]

Subsequent Latin tradition, though, emphasized Augustine's psychological analogy rather than this anagogical method. The medieval scholastic tradition also adopted Augustine's focus on the unity of the Godhead and his principle that the divine persons, sharing the same essence, act as one in the economy of salvation (thus the axiom *opera trinitatis ad extra indivisa sunt*, "the works of the Trinity are indivisible in the economy"). As Catherine LaCugna notes, Augustine's principle "tends to blur any real distinctions among the divine persons and thereby formalizes in Latin theology the breach between *oikonomia* and *theologia*. . . . Once it is assumed that the Trinity is present in every instance where Scripture refers to God, and once the axiom *opera ad extra* is in place, no longer, it seems, is there any need to single out any one person in relation to a particular activity."[242] This determined the subsequent shape of Western trinitarian theology.

Thomas Aquinas (c. 1225–74), inheriting this tradition, took up Augustine's psychological analogy, and ontologized it.[243] That is, in Hill's words, he moved "beyond the psychological processes of the soul to its very beingness. The resultant relationality is an ontological one, grounded in being itself as a dynamism and not

---

237. Ibid., 1.5.8 (70). See also ibid., 5.14.15 (199): "With reference to creation Father, and Son, and Holy Spirit are one origin, just as they are one creator and one lord."

238. Ibid., 5.9.10 (196): "Yet when you ask 'Three what?' human speech labors under a great dearth of words. So we say three persons, not in order to say that precisely, but in order not to be reduced to silence."

239. Ibid., 7.4.7 (224–25).

240. Ibid., 8.7.10–8.12 (251–54).

241. Hill, *Three-Personed God*, 58.

242. LaCugna, *God for Us*, 99.

243. For summaries of Thomas's trinitarian theology, see Hill, *Three-Personed God*, 62–78; Gilles Emery, "The Doctrine of the Trinity in St. Thomas Aquinas," in *Aquinas on Doctrine: A Critical Introduction*, ed. Thomas G. Weinandy, Daniel A. Keating, and John P. Yocum (London: T&T Clark, 2004), 45–65. This section is based largely on Emery's essay. References to the *Summa theologiae* (ST) follow the system given in n. 5.

merely a self-referencing achieved by way of the soul's activity."[244] For Thomas, the persons of the Trinity are defined more specifically as "subsistent relations"[245] that in turn are grounded in the inner-divine processions.

Thomas's starting point is the revelation of the Trinity in Scripture, a revelation grasped by faith. Scripture speaks of the distinction of persons within the one God—a distinction characterized by relations—and it is this truth of faith that Thomas attempts to render intelligible. In the *Summa theologiae*, he begins by examining the "immanent processions" or "notional acts," the inner-divine actions that bring about these real relations. In God there are two types of immanent action, intelligence and will. The first, the procession based on intellect (*per modum intellectus*), is the speaking of the Word, the generation of the Son (which also establishes the fatherhood of the Father); the other, the procession based on love (*per modum amoris*), is the procession of the Spirit. These processions cause real relations, not imposed from without ("accidental") but rather generated from within ("substantial"). They are real distinctions in God, standing "in relative opposition to each other. Therefore since in God there is a real relation . . . relative opposition must also be there [and] such opposition implies distinction."[246] The real relations allow us to distinguish the persons in the Trinity while asserting the unity of the divine essence: "While relation in created things exists as an accident in a subject, in God a really existing relation has the existence of the

divine nature and is completely identical with it. . . . Therefore it is clear that in God relation and nature are existentially not two things but one and the same."[247] There are four real relations: active generation or paternity (the relation of the Father to the Son), passive generation or sonship (the Son's relation to the Father), "active spiration" (the relation of the Father and Son to the Spirit), and "passive spiration" or "procession" (the relation of the Spirit to the Father and the Son).[248] Gilles Emery offers this clarification: "Of these relations, three constitute the persons themselves: fatherhood, sonship and procession. For this reason the three relations of origin are known as 'personal properties,' since they constitute the persons in the unity of the divine essence which is communicated. The relation of 'active spiration' . . . is not a personal property, since it is common to the Father and the Son: the Father and the Son are not constituted by the spiration of the Spirit, but by their fatherhood and sonship."[249]

The relations are the focal point of Thomas's argument against both Arianism (diminishing the divinity of any of the persons) and Sabellianism (modalist diminishing of the distinction of persons). In Emery's explanation, "Everything converges in relation, because the divine relation contains both the element of personal distinction (*ratio*), and the element of the hypostatic divine subsistence (*esse*). These two aspects together constitute the theological notion of a divine person."[250] Borrowing Boethius's definition of "person" ("an individual substance

---

244. Hill, *Three-Personed God*, 70.

245. Thomas Aquinas, ST Ia, q. 40, a. 2 (7:144–49).

246. Ibid., Ia, q. 28, a. 3, resp. (6:34–35).

247. Ibid., Ia., q. 28, a. 2, resp. (6:30–31).

248. Ibid., Ia. q. 28, a. 4 (6:34–39).

249. Emery, "The Doctrine of the Trinity," 53.

250. Ibid., 54.

of a rational nature"),[251] with its implications of distinction, existence, and free action (intellect and will), Thomas finds it to be a fitting term for the subsistent relations in God, since "person" refers to that which "is most perfect in the whole of nature, namely what subsists in rational nature."[252] Thus, he defines the divine persons more specifically as "subsistent relations" and avoids both Arian subordinationism and Sabellian modalism: "The divine persons are their own subsisting relations. . . . The divine persons are not distinct in the being wherein they subsist nor in anything else absolute, but exclusively in their being related to one another. Relation, then, is enough to set them apart from each other."[253] With this definition of "person," Thomas can safeguard a strict trinitarian monotheism.

Between these great medieval syntheses and our own time, the field has shifted, and the presuppositions behind the notion of "person" have changed. In modernity and especially the Enlightenment, the word *person* came to be defined psychologically (characterized by self-consciousness) and in terms of autonomy, thereby rendering the earlier use of *person* as defined ontologically (e.g., the Boethian "individual substance") unintelligible in this new context. In reaction to this legacy, Karl Barth (1886–1968) and Karl Rahner (1904–84) both argued that the use of the word *person* with regard to the Trinity is problematic and suggested alternative formulations. Barth claimed that it is preferable

"to say not 'Person' but 'mode of being,' with the intention of expressing by this concept the same thing as should be expressed by 'Person,' not absolutely but relatively better, more simply and more clearly," because "mode of being" was judged closer to the ancient church's use of the term *hypostasis*.[254] Thus, God is one in three distinct and absolutely essential modes of being. Rahner, beginning with God's free self-communication in history and his analysis of human subjectivity in its openness to the transcending horizon of absolute mystery, preferred to say that "the one God subsists in three distinct manners of subsisting."[255] As Walter Kasper notes, while Barth's and Rahner's approaches differ, neither starts with the traditional formula "one substance, three persons"; rather, "they think of God not as substance but as subject, whether as subject of a self-revelation (K. Barth) or as subject of a self-communication (K. Rahner)."[256]

Their alternative formulations flow from their presuppositions. For Barth, the starting point of our reflection on the Trinity is the reality of God's revelation that occurs as an act of divine sovereignty and that "is a ground which has no sort of higher or deeper ground above or behind it, but is simply a ground in itself."[257] Revelation is summed up in the statement "God reveals Himself as the Lord." This is "the root of the doctrine of the Trinity," which states that "God who has revealed Himself according to the witness of Scripture, is the same in unimpaired

---

251. Thomas Aquinas, ST Ia, q. 29, a. 1 (40–47).

252. Ibid., Ia, q. 29, a. 3, resp. (52–53).

253. Ibid., Ia, q. 40, a. 2, ad 1–2 (7:146–49).

254. Karl Barth, *Church Dogmatics*, vol. 1, part 1, *The Doctrine of the Word of God*, trans. G. T. Thomson (1936; repr., Edinburgh: T&T Clark, 1963), 412–13.

255. Rahner, *The Trinity*, 109. He judges this to be "better, simpler, and more in harmony with the traditional language of theology and the Church" than Barth's phrase. Ibid., 110.

256. Kasper, *The God of Jesus Christ*, 300.

257. *Church Dogmatics*, 1/1, 350.

unity, yet also the same in unimpaired variety thrice in a different way." The doctrine is not revelation itself but rather the church's work of understanding it,[258] since revelation means "the self-unveiling, imparted to men, of the God who according to His nature cannot be unveiled to man."[259] Rejecting the quest for vestiges of the Trinity in the world, Barth insists that only Scripture discloses God's freedom to distinguish himself from himself, and that God does so as Revealer, Revelation, and Revealedness, a formula that corresponds both to the unfolding of biblical revelation and to the church's doctrine of the Trinity. Thus, God is understood as the sovereign subject of his own revelation as well as the self-unveiling that makes the human acceptance of revelation possible.[260] While the church traditionally used "person" to explicate this, "the Church doctrine of the Trinity has nothing directly to do with 'personality,'" which would lead to tritheism. Rather, in the doctrine, "we are speaking not of three divine 'I's,' but thrice of the one divine I. The concept of the equality of essence (*homoousia, consubstantialitas*) in Father, Son, and Spirit is thus at every point pre-eminently to be regarded in the sense of identity of essence. From the identity follows the equality of essence in the 'Persons.'"[261]

Rahner, for his part, understands the Trinity in terms of the mystery of salvation as revealed in history. Faith in this holy mystery is the source of his famous axiom: "The basic thesis which . . . presents the Trinity *as a mystery*

of salvation (in its reality and not merely as a doctrine) might be formulated as follows: *The 'economic' Trinity is the 'immanent' Trinity and the 'immanent' Trinity is the 'economic' Trinity.*"[262] Any theological reflection on the Trinity, then, must start with salvation as historically revealed: the free self-communication of God in the world in Christ and in the Spirit, understood upon reflection "as moments, innerly related to each other, yet distinct from one another, of the *one* self-communication of God."[263] This can only be the authentic self-communication of God if the economic Trinity is indeed the immanent Trinity. Any reflection on this must avoid the idea that in God there are three distinct subjectivities and centers of activity—this is the cul-de-sac to which the modern concept of "person" leads. By always using the history of salvation as the benchmark, Rahner believes that a more adequate formulation can be found. That formulation is "distinct manners of subsisting":

> The one self-communication of the one God occurs in three different manners of given-ness, in which the one God is given concretely for us in himself, and not vicariously by other realities through their transcendental relation to God. God is the concrete God in each one of these manners of given-ness—which, of course, refer to each other relatively, without modalistically coinciding. If we translate this in terms of "immanent" Trinity, we may say: the one God subsists in three distinct manners of subsisting.[264]

---

258. Ibid., 351–52.

259. Ibid., 373.

260. Ibid., 361.

261. Ibid., 403.

262. Rahner, *The Trinity*, 21–22 (his emphasis).

263. Ibid., 84–85.

264. Ibid., 109–10.

There are in the Trinity three really distinct subsistences, each identical with the simple essence of God. Historical revelation testifies to the oneness of God and also to the distinction between the Father and the Son, which reflects an eternal differentiation in the immanent Trinity, and between these two and the Holy Spirit, the expression of the mutual love of Father and Son. The true meaning of this doctrine is ultimately not to be found in an abstract formulation about the immanent Trinity, but in how adequately it describes God's salvific activity: "God himself as the abiding and holy mystery, as the incomprehensible ground of man's transcendent existence is not only the God of infinite distance, but also wants to be the God of absolute closeness in a true self-communication, and he is present in this way in the spiritual depths of our existence as well as in the concreteness of our corporeal history."[265]

These influential contemporary attempts to rethink the doctrine of the Trinity respond to the real problem of detraditionalization that affects the classical formulation of the doctrine: what happens to the meanings of "nature," "substance," and "person" when the original experiential context fades and presuppositions change?[266] With regard to Barth and Rahner, Walter Kasper makes the judicious comment that, even though they are valiant attempts to address current understandings of faith, both leave us with problems:

> It is not enough that the trinitarian confession should be marked by logical clarity; this confession is also to be fit for doxological use. But no one can invoke, adore and glorify a distinct manner of subsisting. . . . If, then, we are not to conjure up new misunderstandings and if we are not to turn the trinitarian confession completely into a book with seven seals for the "ordinary" Christian, we have no choice but to retain the traditional language of the church and interpret it to the faithful.[267]

Rather than rejecting the recent concept of "person" as unusable in the doctrine of the Trinity, Kasper suggests that it can be retrieved and joined to the key Cappadocian insight of relationality that led to the official teaching of "one substance, three persons." Here we join in that constructive retrieval.

While "person" will always be an inadequate term for the divine plurality, it is the most fitting word we have, since God relates to us in love and we relate to God in gratitude for creation and salvation. The genius of the post-Nicene theological tradition, signaled by the language of procession and *perichôrêsis*, was to recognize that belief in the Trinity, even during those periods when there was an emphasis on substance as the starting point of trinitarian reflection, always has at its core a recognition of relationality. Kasper puts the point precisely:

> The two processions in God ground three really distinct relative oppositions. The latter are prototypes and primal ground of the dialogical and relational interaction and co-presence of Father, Son and Spirit in the history of salvation. . . . In

---

265. Karl Rahner, *Foundations of Christian Faith: An Introduction to the Idea of Christianity*, trans. William V. Dych (1978; repr., New York: Crossroad, 1989), 137.

266. On the problem of detraditionalization, see Lieven Boeve, *Interrupting Tradition: An Essay on Christian Faith in a Postmodern Context*, Louvain Theological and Pastoral Monographs 30 (Leuven/Dudley, MA: Peeters, 2003).

267. Kasper, *The God of Jesus Christ*, 288.

God substance and relation are really identical; God is relation and exists only in the intra-divine relations; he is wholly love that surrenders and bestows itself. This relational reality of God, which is identical with his being or substance, presupposes real, mutually distinct relational realities. . . . Thus the distinctions based on the relations once again bring out the ecstatic character of God's love.[268]

The term *person* is best situated to bring out this ecstatic, dynamic character because it is a fundamentally relational category. This is a point that the Orthodox theologian John Zizioulas has emphasized by combining the Cappadocian insight with a contemporary understanding of personal existence in order to understand "person" once again in an ontological framework. To say "I am," to assert one's particular being in the face of possible nonbeing (and thus also acknowledge the threat of death) "is the recognition of the limitations or limits of being. It is a *kataphasis* implying an *apophasis*, the possibility or rather the actuality of a *beyond*, a movement of *transcendence*."[269] To be a person, then, is to be ecstatic intentionality with a claim to uniqueness that in turn implies relationship: "Both in the case of God and of man the identity of a person is recognized and posited clearly and unequivocally, but this is so only in and through a *relationship*, and not though an objective ontology. . . . Personal identity is total-

ly lost if isolated, for its ontological condition is relationship.[270] Zizioulas employs this analysis in order to retrieve the Cappadocian fine-tuning of the principle of *monarchia* without subordinationist or modalist overtones: "The fact that God exists because of the Father shows that His existence, His being is the consequence of a free person; which means, in the last analysis, that not only communion but also *freedom*, the free person, constitutes true being. True being comes only from the free person, from the person who loves freely—that is, who freely affirms his being, his identity, by means of an event of communion with other persons."[271]

Kasper, starting from the modern philosophy of freedom, takes a similar tack. Freedom is more originary than self-contained being or substance: "Freedom that goes out of itself and fulfills itself in action, is now the starting point and horizon of thought."[272] Viewed in terms of freedom, the human person is revealed as a unique intentional being marked by two characteristics. First, the person "finds its fulfillment only in the communion of love" and thus exists "only in mutual giving and receiving."[273] Second, the person is marked by a tension between an "irreplaceable individuality" and "an unlimited openness to the whole of reality," a restlessness that cannot be stilled by anything finite but demands definitive fulfillment. This *personal* desire can only be fulfilled in a *personal* way, that is, "only if it encounters a person who is infinite not only in its

---

268. Ibid., 280.

269. John D. Zizioulas, "On Being a Person: Towards an Ontology of Personhood," *Communion and Otherness: Further Studies in Personhood and the Church*, ed. Paul McPartlan (New York: T&T Clark, 2006), 99–112, at 100.

270. Ibid., 112.

271. John D. Zizioulas, *Being as Communion: Studies in Personhood and the Church* (Crestwood, NY: St. Vladimir's Seminary Press, 1985), 18. Cf. also p. 42: "God 'exists' on account of a person, the Father, and not on account of a substance."

272. Kasper, *The God of Jesus Christ*, 153.

273. Ibid., 306.

intentional claims on reality but in its real being; that is, only if it encounters an absolute person" characterized by perfect freedom. Since "person" implies relationality, perfect relationality means the complete emptying of oneself in love. Thus, Kasper concludes, "Seen in the horizon of person, the meaning of being is love. . . . To call God a person is to say that God is the subsistent being which is freedom in love. Thus the definition of God's essence brings us back to the biblical statement: 'God is love' (1 John 4.8, 16)."[274]

A trinitarian theology can be built upon this insight into the category of person as most fundamentally free, intentional, and relational. One can express the divine unity not as some rigid and monolithic unity, but as selfless giving and bestowing that characterizes biblical monotheism:

> If God is to remain God and not become dependent on the world or man, then he must be co-existent within himself. Within the unity and simplicity of his being he must be a communion in love, and this love cannot be a love marked by need but only a love that gives out of the overflowing fullness of his being. . . . Because God in his perfection and simplicity is everything and does not possess anything, he can give only himself. . . . God's oneness must be thought of as love that exists only in the giving of itself.[275]

One can express the distinction of persons with similar "ec-static" language:

> The Father as pure self-giving cannot exist without the Son who receives. But since the Son does not receive something but everything, he exists only in and through the giving and receiving. . . . On the other hand, he would not have truly received the self-giving of the Father were he to keep it for himself and not give it back. . . . But this reciprocal love also presses beyond itself; it is pure giving only if it empties itself of, and gives away, even this two-in-oneness and, in pure gratuitousness, incorporates a third in whom love exists as pure receiving, a third who therefore exists only insofar as he receives his being from the mutual love between Father and Son. The three persons of the Trinity are thus pure relationality; they are relations in which the one nature of God exists in three distinct and non-interchangeable ways. They are subsistent relations.[276]

One advantage of this language is that it follows the biblical precedent: human relationships with God are spoken of in terms of the metaphor of personal relationship, and the New Testament claim that "God is love" (1 John 4:8, 16) can take its rightful place at the core of Christian life. Another is that the connection between the Trinity and creation is made clear: if creation is grounded in God, and God's being is to be a loving communion-in-unity, then, in Kasper's words, "the trinitarian communion-unity shows itself to be the model for a Christian understanding of reality . . . in which person and relation have priority" and in which "the meaning of being is the selflessness of love."[277] A final advantage is that we can claim the doctrine of the Trinity to be "the summation of the entire Christian mystery of salvation and, at the

---

274. Ibid., 154.
275. Ibid., 306.
276. Ibid., 309.
277. Ibid., 310.

190 same time, its grammar,"[278] that is, the structuring principle that acts as the backbone of every Christian claim to truth and the *telos* of all of those claims together.

Ongoing Points of Discussion

The state of the question in trinitarian theology includes several significant issues.[279] Here we focus on three: (1) the issue of "social trinitarianism"; (2) trinitarian theology in ecumenical discussion; and (3) the links between belief in the Trinity, liturgy, and the experience of Christian life.

Relationality and Social Trinitarianism

"Social trinitarianism" is the theory that the perichoretic relationship of the Trinity should provide the model for relationships in human society. According to this argument, the Trinity can be shown in this way to have direct implications for everyday life. The impetus for this strongly influential view comes from the contemporary retrieval of the Cappadocians' "relationality" as a prime element in trinitarian thinking, coupled with a theological anthropology that emphasizes the human person as *imago Dei*.

A "social doctrine of the Trinity" is most closely associated with the Protestant theologian Jürgen Moltmann and his work *The Trinity and the Kingdom of God.* He argues that if one follows Rahner's axiom that "the economic Trinity is the immanent Trinity, and vice versa," and if "God is a community of Father, Son and Spirit, whose unity is constituted by mutual indwelling and reciprocal interpenetration," then "we find the earthly reflection of this divine sociality, not in the autocracy of a single ruler but in the democratic community of free people, not in the lordship of the man over the woman but in their equal mutuality, not in an ecclesiastical hierarchy but in a fellowship church."[280] He proposes the social doctrine as the authentic Christian antidote to a "monotheism" viewed as having long been used to justify domination and repression through monarchical, hierarchical, and patriarchal systems in government, church, and human relations.[281]

Moltmann's student Miroslav Volf has refined this argument further by characterizing it as a "social vision" rather than a "social program." He grounds this vision in the identity of the Trinity as "mutual indwelling" (*perichôrêsis*)

---

278. Ibid., 311.

279. For an overview of the current discussion, see Gerald O'Collins, "The Holy Trinity: The State of the Questions," in Davis et al., *The Trinity: An Interdisciplinary Symposium* (n. 30), 1–25. He sorts the issues into general categories: the recovery of the centrality of trinitarian belief; trinitarian issues in Scripture and early Christian history; the Trinity, Christian life, and interreligious dialogue; and current theological issues, including the relation of the immanent and economic Trinity, the use of personal language, and theological method. See also the diverse topics (historical, ecclesiological, aesthetic, etc.) discussed in Marmion and Thiessen, eds., *Trinity and Salvation* (n. 4).

280. Jürgen Moltmann, *The Trinity and the Kingdom: The Doctrine of God,* trans. Margaret Kohl (1981; Minneapolis: Fortress Press, 1993), 160 (Rahner's axiom), viii ("mutual indwelling," reflection of divine sociality). Citations are from the reprint edition, with a new preface.

281. See, e.g., Jürgen Moltmann, *History and the Triune God: Contributions to Trinitarian Theology,* trans. John Bowden (New York: Crossroad, 1992), xii: "The unity of the triune God is no longer seen in the homogeneous divine subject nor in the identical divine subject, but in the eternal *perichoresis* of Father, Son and Spirit. . . . The monarchical, hierarchical and patriarchal ideas used to legitimate the concept of God are thus becoming obsolete. 'Communion,' 'fellowship,' is the nature and the purpose of the triune God."

and as self-donation that is "enacted in the cross by the power of the Spirit" and that translates into a "divine welcome in Christ" that the New Testament (especially Paul) encourages all believers to emulate.[282]

In Catholic theology, a major representative has been Leonardo Boff, who expands on Moltmann's basic position in his book *Trinity and Society*: "From the perichoresis-communion of the three divine Persons derive impulses to liberation: of each and every human person, of society, of the church and of the poor, in the double—critical and constructive—sense." Humanity is thus called to forsake egoism and live the vocation of communion, society is called to create structures that are "humane, open, just and egalitarian," the church is called to reduce inequalities and practice "unity as co-existence in diversity," and the poor are called to see the Trinity as "the model for a human society based on mutual collaboration—all on an equal footing—and individual differences."[283]

However, others criticize social trinitarianism as being guilty of overreaching, and perhaps even of hubris. Ted Peters argues that since "the concepts of personhood and community are concepts we import into the process of analysis, synthesis, and construction," social trinitarianism, by using such concepts to claim an insight into the immanent Trinity, is ignoring the obvious disjunction between these concepts and the reality of God who infinitely exceeds them: "God alone is God [and] we as creatures cannot copy God in all respects."[284] An even more trenchant criticism accuses social trinitarianism of projecting modern or post-Enlightenment notions of "person" and "egalitarianism" onto the term *perichôrêsis*, and then claiming to discover in the immanent Trinity these very notions and to present this discovery "as an exciting resource Christian theology has to offer the wider world in its reflections upon relationships and relatedness."[285] Rather than viewing this or any doctrine of the Trinity as a "first order discourse" that provides "a deep understanding of the way God really is" and demonstrates God's relevance, Karen Kilby suggests that it should be seen rather as "grammatical" or as a second order "structuring principle" that "specifies how various aspects of the Christian faith hang together."[286] Finally, social trinitarianism has been criticized for misunderstanding the notion of "person" that emanates from the Cappadocian discussion (especially the work of Gregory of Nyssa) and for trying to assimilate it too closely to contemporary philosophical views of the self.[287]

Each side of this contested issue makes an important point. On the one hand, as we emphasized at the outset, the Trinity is and remains an infinite mystery. As Kasper points out, "We

---

282. Miroslav Volf, "'The Trinity Is Our Social Program': The Doctrine of the Trinity and the Shape of Social Engagement," *Modern Theology* 14 (1998): 403–23, at 415–16. See also his summary claim: "[The] primacy of grace in the establishment of its own proper truth and justice is . . . inscribed in the inner logic of divine justification, which is the inner logic of the cross, which is the inner logic of Trinitarian love translated into the world of sin" (417).

283. Leonardo Boff, *Trinity and Society*, trans. Paul Burns (Maryknoll, NY: Orbis, 1988), 236–37.

284. Ted Peters, *God as Trinity: Relationality and Temporality in Divine Life* (Louisville: Westminster John Knox, 1993), 185–86.

285. Karen Kilby, "Perichoresis and Projection: Problems with Social Doctrines of the Trinity," *New Blackfriars* 81/957 (November 2000): 432–45, at 442.

286. Ibid., 443–44.

287. Sarah Coakley, "'Persons' in the 'Social' Doctrine of the Trinity: A Critique of Current Analytic Discussion," in Davis et al., *The Trinity: An Interdisciplinary Symposium*, 123–44.

192 cannot deduce the immanent Trinity by a kind of extrapolation from the economic Trinity."[288] Without a doubt, there is "a strongly apophatic sensibility [that] attends any talk of the 'essence' of God"[289] that should make theologians think twice about making stronger-than-necessary claims about the immanent Trinity. On the other hand, the creed's assertion that the revelation of God in history happens "for us and for our salvation" gives theology a mandate to discern, as far as it is able, how the salvific presence of the triune God occurs "for us." "Relevance" here (*pace* Kilby and other critics) is not code for any attempt to reduce God to fit our limited categories, but rather signals the Christian conviction that there is a connection between the Trinity and history and that it is possible to express in a meaningful way how God's presence interlaces with everyday lived experience, even if the means of expression is ultimately flawed. This conviction stems not only from the belief that the incarnation changes everything, but also from the recognition that the historical revelation of God in Christ ("Rather, he emptied himself . . . coming in human likeness and found human in appearance"; Phil. 2:7) and in the work of the Spirit discloses at the very least a "rhythm of self-giving" that forms "the inner justification, indeed the necessity, of a new trinitarian ontology" that grounds reality and gives us a glimpse (but, again, only a glimpse) of the character of divine life.[290] Theological reflection on the Trinity does not end with the accomplishments of the fourth century; the creed demands that the mystery and its implications for human

life continue to be explored. Indeed, contemporary philosophical reflection on intersubjectivity, relationality, and "the gift" can help theology illuminate the centrality of the Trinity for human life and supplement the Cappadocians' reflections in surprisingly productive ways.

One way to do justice to both sides—arguing on behalf of the "social" metaphor while preserving the infinite mystery of the Trinity—would be to follow Yves Congar and Walter Kasper in revising Rahner's fundamental axiom. Congar emphasizes that "there is a distance between the economic, revealed Trinity and the eternal Trinity. The Trinity is the same in each case and God is really communicated, but this takes place in a mode that is not connatural with the being of the divine Persons."[291] Kasper's rephrasing of the axiom runs thus: "In the economic self-communication the intra-trinitarian self-communication is present in a new way, namely, under the veil of historical words, signs and actions, and ultimately in the figure of the man Jesus of Nazareth." A trinitarian theology must therefore respect both "the kenotic character of the economic Trinity" and "the apophatic character of the immanent Trinity," while recalling that "the immanent Trinity is and remains a *mysterium stricte dictum* in (not: behind!) the economic Trinity."[292]

The Trinity
in Ecumenical Discussion

Enormous strides have been made in the ecumenical dialogues held in the decades after

---

288. Kasper, *The God of Jesus Christ*, 276.

289. Coakley, "'Persons' in the 'Social' Doctrine," 135.

290. Klaus Hemmerle, *Thesen zu einer trinitarischen Ontologie*, Kriterien 40 (Einsiedeln: Johannes Verlag, 1976), 55 (my translation).

291. Congar, *I Believe in the Holy Spirit*, 3:15.

292. Kasper, *The God of Jesus Christ*, 276.

Vatican II. Regarding belief in the Trinity, official Roman Catholic discussions with Lutheran, Reformed, Methodist, and Anglican churches have led to a remarkable consensus.[293] For all those involved in these dialogues, the Trinity is the foundation and ultimate goal of Christian faith, and belief in it is possible because of the life, death, and resurrection of Christ and the sending of the Spirit. While the mystery of divine life exceeds human language and concepts, nonetheless it can be affirmed that the triune God is "a unity of self-communicating and interdependent relationships" (Anglican-Catholic dialogue [ARCIC]) and "an invisible *koinonia*" (Methodist-Catholic dialogue) who calls the church into being for the redemption of humankind. The Father is the source of the processions of the other persons and the source of salvation history. Christ is the Son and Incarnate Word sent by the Father, truly divine and truly human, the unique Lord and mediator who reconciles God and humanity. The Holy Spirit is the bond of unity between Father and Son and bond of communion who unites all Christians. The Spirit is active throughout the history of salvation, bringing transformation and participation in God.

One area that remains controversial is the dispute over the *filioque* ("and from the Son") that continues to separate Roman Catholicism (the Latin West) and the Eastern Orthodox churches.[294] Eastern Christianity holds that the Holy Spirit proceeds from the Father, while according to the West (since the early medieval period), the Holy Spirit proceeds from the Father and from the Son. The West's position (*qui ex Patre Filioque procedit*; "who proceeds from the Father and the Son") was first interpolated into the Nicene-Constantinopolitan Creed of 381 in Spain in 589. Despite criticisms and attempts to suppress the formula (e.g., by Pope Leo III [d. 816]), it spread through western Europe as a safeguard against resurgent christological heresies and was eventually adopted in Rome by 1014. The *filioque* was resisted by the East from the beginning, was condemned by Patriarch Photius of Constantinople in 867, and figured prominently in the mutual exchange of anathemas in 1054 that accelerated the break between Eastern and Western churches. The Latin-led Council of Florence in 1439 declared the reunion of the churches and approved the addition of the *filioque*, but this decree was never officially accepted in the East and was formally rejected in 1484. Despite increasing dialogue and liturgical sharing over the past half century, this separation remains.

The controversy over the *filioque* is really twofold, involving theological and ecclesiological issues. The theological issue, in the words of a recent ecumenical consultation, is "rooted in subtle but significant differences in the way key terms have been used to refer to the Spirit's divine origin." The Greek terms *ekporeuesthai* ("proceed," "issue forth") and *ekporeusis* ("procession") connote "a 'passage outwards' from

---

293. See Walter Kasper, *Harvesting the Fruits: Basic Aspects of Christian Faith in Ecumenical Dialogue* (London/New York: Continuum, 2009), 16–30, which forms the basis of what follows.

294. For a history of the controversy and recent developments, see A. Edward Siecienski, *The Filioque: History of a Doctrinal Controversy*, Oxford Studies in Historical Theology (Oxford/New York: Oxford University Press, 2010). See also the Pontifical Council for Promoting Christian Unity, "The Greek and Latin Traditions Regarding the Procession of the Holy Spirit," *L'Osservatore Romano*, English ed., September 20, 1995 (also at http://www.ewtn.com/library/curia/pccufilq .htm), as well as the statement of the North American Orthodox-Catholic Theological Consultation (NAOCTC), "The *Filioque*: A Church-Dividing Issue?" (October 25, 2003), http://www.usccb.org/seia/filioque.shtml.

194

within some point of origin. . . . Greek theology almost always restricts the theological use of this term to the coming-forth of the Spirit from the Father," thus preserving the monarchical role of the Father among the divine persons (i.e., the "one origin" or "principle without principle").[295] *Proienai* ("movement forward"), in contrast, is used more to describe the Spirit's mission in history. Early Latin translations, however, used *procedere* ("movement outward") and *processio* to translate both meanings. The West thereby attempted to signify "the communication of the consubstantial divinity from the Father to the Son and from the Father, through and with the Son, to the Holy Spirit."[296] However, the East understood the Western use of *procedere/processio* as compromising the role of the Father as the sole *archê* of divine life. The recent North American Orthodox-Catholic discussion, attempting to avoid the theological polemics of the past, has acknowledged a number of consensus points in trinitarian belief, including agreement that "the Holy Spirit is a distinct hypostasis or person within the divine Mystery, equal in status to the Father and the Son," that "the Father is the primordial source (*archê*) and ultimate cause (*aitia*) of the divine being, and thus of all God's operations," and that "both traditions affirm that the three hypostases or persons in God are constituted in their hypostatic existence and distinguished from one another solely by their relationships of origin, and not by any other characteristics

or activities."[297] Such a consensus, building on earlier dialogue agreements and formulas (e.g., "The Spirit proceeds from the Father of the Son" and "The Spirit proceeds from the Father through the Son") has led to calls in Catholic circles for a return to the creed of 381 without the *filioque* interpolation.[298]

The ecclesiological issue involves the teaching authority in the church, specifically regarding the authority of the bishop of Rome to confirm and even alter conciliar decisions. As the report by the North American Orthodox-Catholic Theological Consultation puts it, "So while Orthodox theology has regarded the ultimate approval by the Popes, in the eleventh century, of the use of *Filioque* in the Latin Creed as a usurpation of the dogmatic authority proper to ecumenical Councils alone, Catholic theology has seen it as a legitimate exercise of his primatial authority to proclaim and clarify the Church's faith."[299] This is a serious issue that, at present, seems less amenable to consensus; indeed, it "remains the root issue behind all the questions of theology and practice that continue to divide our communions."[300]

Trinity, Liturgy, and the Christian Life

We would be remiss if we did not recall an important point raised by Catherine LaCugna in the first edition, namely, a more fundamental version of the "relevance" issue: the ongoing task of advocating the centrality of belief in the Trin-

---

295. NAOCTC, "The *Filioque*," 3.1, par. 1. The Eastern understanding is rooted in its interpretation of John 15:26: "When the Advocate comes, whom I will send you from the Father, the Spirit of truth who comes [or proceeds] from the Father (*para tou patros ekporeuetai*), he will testify on my behalf."

296. Pontifical Council for Promoting Christian Unity, "The Greek and Latin Traditions," par. 14.

297. NAOCTC, "The *Filioque*," 3, par. 3.

298. E.g., by Congar, *I Believe in the Holy Spirit*, 3:214.

299. NAOCTC, "The *Filioque*," 3.2.b, par. 1.

300. Ibid., 3.2.b., par. 2.

ity for Christian life. The long-assumed "irrelevance" of Trinity (mentioned at the outset), the portrayal of trinitarian doctrine as too esoteric for ordinary believers, and an impoverished theology of the Holy Spirit (pneumatology) are problems that much contemporary trinitarian theology has worked hard to overcome. But the results have hardly filtered into the everyday life of Catholics, and more must be done, in LaCugna's words, to "bring together the mystery of God and the mystery of salvation."[301]

We can mention two issues that need further discussion. The fundamental importance of these issues is undeniable, especially when one acknowledges the truth of Timothy Radcliffe's succinct identification of "the point of Christianity": "If Christianity is true, then it does not have a point other than to point to God who is the point of everything."[302] How does one acknowledge this ultimate divine point (an exercise in doxology) and live so as to make one's life conform to this point (the experience of salvation, studied by soteriology)?

First, there is a need to underscore an important insight noted both in the early Christian tradition and throughout the history of Christian spirituality: that salvation is indeed "deification" (*theôsis*), "participating in the very life of God, being made like Christ . . . for through Christ we are made sharers in the divine nature (2 Peter 1:4)," and that "the doctrine of the Trinity is the specifically Christian way to explicate the meaning of participation in the life of the triune God."[303] If humanity is created in the image of God, then there is already a path toward that "point," but because of creaturely finitude

and the effects of sin, this transformative participation cannot be achieved without God's grace. The key to reaching that point is summed up by Paul: "The grace of the Lord Jesus Christ and the love of God and the fellowship of the Holy Spirit be with all of you" (2 Cor. 13:13). We have access to the love of God through the grace of Christ offered to us in discipleship (living a Jesus-like life in light of the paschal mystery) and perduring in us and in the midst of our world through the power of the Spirit, who offers us fellowship, a participation in that divine love. Alongside and in consort with the developed Christology that already exists in the church, a more developed understanding of the Holy Spirit (whom some have called "the forgotten person of the Trinity") is needed, along with the development of a trinitarian spirituality that shows how both together ground a life lived according to the values of the kingdom of God. As LaCugna emphasizes, "Union with God (deification) is therefore union with the life of God in the economy. It is at once mystical and active. In a trinitarian spirituality neither a pneumatological nor a christological focus may overtake the other. Christ and the Spirit are the two foci of Christian life. The economy of the Spirit (deification) and the economy of the Son (incarnation) comprise the one divine economy."[304]

The second important issue is the importance of the liturgy for a living trinitarian faith and the retrieval of liturgical theology as a locus for trinitarian theology. For where else is the doctrine of the Trinity as the "summation of the entire Christian mystery of salvation" (Kasper) most often recalled and threaded through our

301. LaCugna, "Trinitarian Mystery," 186.

302. Timothy Radcliffe, *What Is the Point of Being a Christian?* (London/New York: Burns & Oates, 2005), 1.

303. LaCugna, "Trinitarian Mystery," 189 (definition of deification), 190 (doctrine as explication).

304. Ibid., 189.

196 lives than in liturgical prayer, especially the celebration of the Eucharist? Right here is a link to the genius of the Cappadocians: recall that Basil of Caesarea considered the ultimate convincing argument for the divinity of the Spirit to be liturgical prayer, especially the trinitarian baptismal formula, since it was a reflection of the long tradition of belief "in the souls of the faithful."[305] The same confidence in the liturgy and the "sense of the faithful" is reflected in LaCugna's summary of the liturgy as the celebration of the triune God who is revealed "for us and for our salvation": "Doxology is the praise of God, the appreciation of God as God apart from the benefits of God. In praising God we make no distinction between who God is as God, and who God is for us."[306] Here the awareness of our salvation—our incorporation into God's life on God's initiative—is expressed in prayer that unites us "to God's triune mystery and to all believers throughout time, as we place ourselves into the whole history of redemption, particularly its eschatological movement of return to God."[307] Theology should constantly recall, then, how remarkable it is that the simplest prayer to the Trinity can express, as Kasper puts it, how soteriology passes over into doxology:[308] "Glory be to the Father, and to the Son, and to the Holy Spirit."

For Further Reading

Ayers, Lewis. *Nicaea and Its Legacy: An Approach to Fourth-Century Trinitarian Theology.* Oxford/New York: Oxford University Press, 2004.

> An ambitious revisionary reading of a pivotal period in the development of trinitarian theology; supersedes older histories.

Behr, John. *The Nicene Faith.* 2 vols. Vol. 2 of *Formation of Christian Theology.* Crestwood, NY: St. Vladimir's Seminary Press, 2004.

> Analysis of the early development of the doctrines of God, Christ, and Trinity from an Orthodox perspective.

Buckley, Michael J. *At the Origins of Modern Atheism.* New Haven: Yale University Press, 1987.

> An important and influential analysis of how God became a problem in Western culture.

Burrell, David. *Knowing the Unknowable God: Ibn-Sina, Maimonides, Aquinas.* Notre Dame, IN: University of Notre Dame Press, 1986.

> An important exposition of the medieval "dialogue" about God that highlights Thomas's relation to and difference from medieval Jewish and Arab traditions.

---

305. Basil, *Ep.* 125, 3 (2:33 [Courtonne]; 2:266–69 [Deferrari]).
306. Ibid., 186.
307. Ibid., 187.
308. Kasper, *The God of Jesus Christ,* 316.

Congar, Yves. *I Believe in the Holy Spirit.* Translated by David Smith. New York: Crossroad, 1997.

> *A masterful synthesis of Greek and Latin theology and history, ecumenically oriented, with an obvious emphasis on pneumatology.*

Davis, Stephen, Daniel Kendall, and Gerald O'Collins, eds. *The Trinity.* Oxford/New York: Oxford University Press, 1999.

> *Papers on a variety of topics from an interdisciplinary symposium. Especially noteworthy are the contributions of O'Collins, Segal, Lienhard, Coakley, and Barnes.*

Dünzl, Franz. *A Brief History of the Doctrine of the Trinity in the Early Church.* Translated by John Bowden. London/New York: T&T Clark, 2007.

> *A useful overview of the development of the doctrine in the ancient church.*

Emery, Gilles. *The Trinitarian Theology of St Thomas Aquinas.* Translated by Francesca Aran Murphy. New York: Oxford University Press, 2007.

> *An introduction to Thomas's trinitarian synthesis by a master of his thought.*

Greshake, Gisbert. *Der dreieine Gott: Eine trinitarische Theologie.* 2nd ed. Freiburg: Herder, 1997.

> *A major systematic contribution, emphasizing the Trinity as communio. An English translation would be most welcome.*

Hill. William J. *The Three-Personed God: The Trinity as a Mystery of Salvation.* Washington, DC: Catholic University of America Press, 1982.

> *An astute historical and systematic investigation of the doctrine of the Trinity from a contemporary Thomist perspective.*

Johnson, Elizabeth A. *She Who Is: The Mystery of God in Feminist Theological Discourse.* 1992. Reprint, New York: Crossroad, 2002.

> *Steeped both in the tradition and in the contemporary context, this major contribution of feminist theology promotes a deepening and widening of our experience of and discourse about God.*

Jüngel, Eberhard. *God as the Mystery of the World.* Translated by Darrell L. Guder. Grand Rapids: Eerdmans, 1983.

> *A philosophical and theological trinitarian theology based on the centrality of the cross and the hermeneutics of word-as-event.*

Kasper, Walter. *The God of Jesus Christ.* Translated by Matthew J. O'Connell. 1985. Reprint, New York: Crossroad, 2005.

> *A contemporary classic that offers a detailed analysis of the doctrine of the Trinity, a reliable guide to the doctrine's historical development, and a brilliant theological explication of the role the Trinity plays in Christian life today.*

Kelly, J. N. D. *Early Christian Creeds.* 3rd ed. New York: Longman, 1972.

> *Study of the historical development of Christian creeds by a premier historian of theology.*

———. *Early Christian Doctrines.* 5th ed. 1977. Reprint, New York: Continuum, 2003.

> *Standard and reliable history of the development of doctrines in the ancient church.*

198   Küng, Hans. *Does God Exist? An Answer for Today.* Translated by Edward Quinn. 1980. Reprint, Eugene, OR: Wipf & Stock, 2006.

>   *Articulates many of the central concerns about God (especially by the "hermeneutes of suspicion") and provides an interesting counterargument for belief.*

LaCugna, Catherine Mowry. *God for Us: The Trinity and Christian Life.* San Francisco: HarperCollins, 1991.

>   *An analysis of the historical, liturgical, and theological factors in the development of the doctrine, emphasizing the relationality of the Trinity and its centrality for Christian life.*

Marion, Jean-Luc. *God without Being: Hors-Texte.* Translated by Thomas A. Carlson. Chicago: University of Chicago Press, 1991.

>   *A breakthrough work that proposes a view of God after the critique of metaphysics.*

McFague, Sallie. *Models of God: Theology for an Ecological, Nuclear Age.* Philadelphia: Fortress Press, 1987.

>   *A study of God in relation to the environmental crisis that suggests new models of God such as mother, friend, and lover.*

Moltmann, Jürgen. *The Trinity and the Kingdom: The Doctrine of God.* Translated by Margaret Kohl. New York: Harper & Row, 1981.

>   *A theology of the Trinity centered on the cross as a divine event.*

Murray, John Courtney. *The Problem of God.* New Haven: Yale University Press, 1964.

>   *Still an excellent introduction and a classic in Catholic theology.*

O'Collins, Gerald. *The Tripersonal God: Understanding and Interpreting the Trinity.* New York/Mahwah, NJ: Paulist, 1999.

>   *A compact historical and systematic overview of the basic trends of trinitarian thought.*

O'Donnell, John J. *Trinity and Temporality: The Christian Doctrine of God in the Light of Process Theology and the Theology of Hope.* Oxford/New York: Oxford University Press, 1983.

>   *A perspective on trinitarian theology from the point of view of process theology and the political theology of Jürgen Moltmann.*

Pelikan, Jaroslav. *Credo: Historical and Theological Guide to Creeds and Confession of Faith in the Christian Tradition.* New Haven: Yale University Press, 2003.

>   *A more recent study of the development of creeds by a master of historical theology.*

Prestige, G. L. *God in Patristic Thought.* 2nd ed. 1952. Reprint, London: SPCK, 1981.

>   *A still-valuable study of the early developments of patristic terminology.*

Rahner, Karl. *The Trinity.* Translated by Joseph Donceel. 1970. Reprint, New York: Crossroad, 1997.

>   *A pivotal work that set the agenda for many contemporary trinitarian theologies.*

Rusch, William, ed. *The Trinitarian Controversy.* Sources of Early Christian Thought. Philadelphia: Fortress Press, 1980.

>   *A collection of central texts representing the debate over the doctrine of the Trinity.*

Studer, Basil. *Trinity and Incarnation: The Faith of the Early Church.* Edited and translated by Andrew Louth. Collegeville, MN: Liturgical, 1993.

> *A history of the development of the doctrines by a leading authority in the period.*

Ward, Graham, ed. *The Postmodern God: A Theological Reader.* Malden, MA: Blackwell, 1997.

> *Key texts from major thinkers, along with theological commentaries, on the issue of God in a postmodern context. Ward's introduction is especially valuable.*

Welch, Claude. *In This Name: The Doctrine of the Trinity in Contemporary Theology.* New York: Scribner, 1952.

> *A classic summary of Protestant trinitarian theology.*

Young, Frances M. *From Nicaea to Chalcedon: A Guide to the Literature and Its Background.* Philadelphia: Fortress Press, 1983.

> *A detailed and very useful overview of an important period of doctrinal development.*

Creation

Anne M. Clifford

Creation is a belief shared widely among the religions. Descriptive of the relation between God and the world, Christian doctrine of creation proposes that each and every thing that exists is ultimately dependent on a divine creator, the triune God, who possesses the power to bring the world into existence and to provide it with both a lawlike order and the potential for development. A Christian doctrine with importance for understandings of God and for theological anthropology, creation is also intimately related to Christology, especially the belief that the Son of God became incarnate in creaturely flesh, and to Roman Catholic sacramentality, which holds that all of reality is the bearer of God's presence. Because of these beliefs, creation plays a role in Catholic spirituality and morality, including ecojustice. In a comprehensive theology of creation, all of these topics are intertwined, but some may be given more emphasis.

Theology looks closely at the reality of God's creation in order to speak meaningfully to those who are part of it. The need to know about creation is profoundly connected to the human desire for knowledge about the universe, especially our earthly home. Like all the doctrines of the Catholic Church, creation theology is historical and dynamic. Rooted in biblical texts and church doctrines that express communities' beliefs about God, themselves, and the world, creation theology has been shaped by the historical contexts in which it has developed. Creation theology is also dynamic because the dynamism of handing on creation faith in response to societal questions and concerns ensures that it remains a living tradition. Given the pervasive influence of science on contemporary culture, creation theology today necessarily gives serious attention to the challenges and opportunities posed by the natural sciences.

History shows that the Catholic Church has sometimes been in conflict with the natural sciences and wary of their influence. However, the Catholic Church demonstrated the importance of attending to the natural sciences at the Second Vatican Council, when among the signs of the times addressed in the Pastoral Constitution on the Church in the Modern World (1965) was the "scientific spirit" (*Gaudium et spes*, no. 5).[1] The council pointed out that when methodical investigation is carried out in a genuinely scientific manner, it never truly conflicts with religious faith (no. 36).[2]

Twenty-three years later, Pope John Paul II, who as a bishop had participated in the Second Vatican Council, built on the council's treatment of science in a message he sent to a conference on theology and science hosted by the Vatican Observatory.[3] In his "Message" to George V. Coyne, S.J., then the head of the observatory, John Paul II emphasized that while the integrity and autonomy of science and theology must be respected, it is shortsighted for theologians to

---

1. *Gaudium et spes* (Pastoral Constitution on the Church in the Modern World, December 7, 1965), in *Vatican Council: The Conciliar and Post Conciliar Documents* 1, ed. Austin Flannery, O.P. (Grand Rapids: Eerdmans, 1992), 903–1001.

2. The council fathers also made it clear that the "lawful freedom" and "legitimate autonomy of the sciences" were to be respected (GS no. 59).

3. "Message of His Holiness Pope John Paul II to the Reverend George V. Coyne, S.J., Director of the Vatican Observatory" (June 1, 1988), in *John Paul II on Science and Religion: Reflections on the New View from Rome*, ed. Robert John Russell, William R. Stoeger, S.J., and George V. Coyne, S.J. (Notre Dame: University of Notre Dame Press, 1990). The occasion was a conference in honor of the three hundredth anniversary of the publication of Isaac Newton's *Philosophiae Naturalis Principia Mathematica* (*Mathematical Principles of Natural Philosophy*). M before a number corresponds to the pagination of the original message.

ignore the scientific character of modern society. He therefore advocated for honest and in-depth conversation among theologians and scientists, stressing that "knowledge of each other leads us to be more authentically ourselves" (M14). He also called theologians and scientists to search together for a more thorough understanding of one another's disciplines. Anticipating a positive outcome to this search, John Paul II stressed that "a rational unity between science and religion" can be achieved, which would result not in identity or assimilation but in dynamic interchange, with each "radically open to the discoveries and insights of the other" (M9). Further, "science can purify religion from error and superstition; religion can purify science from idolatry and false absolutisms. Each can draw the other into a wider world, a world in which both can flourish" (M13).

Pope John Paul II's hopeful statement, which signals that Catholicism holds that science and theology neither conflict nor must maintain a distant and wary independence, provides a suitable context for a treatment of creation theology. Since sacred Scripture is the primary source and animating principle of creation theology, we will first examine the biblical roots of the doctrine of creation. This examination will attend to some of the complex influences on the formation of biblical creation texts.[4] Granted that biblical interpretation by Christian scholars today is complex and varied, attention to history and literary analysis remains important, especially where creation texts are concerned. This is because a major contributing factor to the perceived conflict between science and Christianity is the insistence on literal interpretation of biblical creation texts by some Christians who judge some scientific theories to be a threat to Christian faith in a creator and to humans as unique among creatures.

The second major section will present major developments in creation belief that took place in the patristic and medieval periods. Attention will be given to two major creation doctrines, *creatio ex nihilo* and *imago Dei*, which were first articulated in the second and early third centuries and then clarified and developed in subsequent centuries. The third major section will address issues that were perceived to challenge Creation faith that arose during the Enlightenment and Modern periods. Here the focus will be on creation theology and the natural sciences with the goal of dispelling popular myths about the Catholic Church's responses to the scientific breakthroughs of Galileo and Darwin. Significant Christian responses to Darwinian evolution, the more problematic of the two, including those that originated in the second half of the twentieth century and remain controversial: Creation Science and Intelligent Design theory will be assessed. The last topic in this third section will be theistic evolution with emphasis on significant contemporary conceptions of God

---

4. Catholic commitment to attending to the historical context of biblical texts is expressed in Pope Pius XII, *Divino afflante spiritu* (On Promoting Biblical Studies), Apostolic See (1943), http://www.vatican.va/holy_father/pius_xii/encyclicals/documents/hf_p-xii_enc_30091943_divino-afflante-spiritu_en.html. The Second Vatican Council furthered Catholic commitment to historical study of the Bible by affirming that God was the ultimate author of the Bible but chose to communicate to humans in a human fashion (*Dei verbum*, no. 11). Therefore, to interpret biblical texts correctly, it is necessary to keep the "divine authorship in mind," while engaging in exegesis that employs historical and literary interpretation (no. 12). See *Dei verbum* (Dogmatic Constitution on Divine Revelation, 1965), in *Vatican Council: The Conciliar and Post Conciliar Documents*, 750–64 (hereafter DV). For more methods for the interpretation of the Bible, see "The Interpretation of the Bible in the Church," presented by the Pontifical Biblical Commission to Pope John Paul II (April 23, 1993), *Origins* 6 (1994), http://catholicresources.org/ChurchDocs/PBC_Interp1.htm.

204 responsive to contemporary science. The final section of this chapter, titled "A Creation Theology That Earth Can Live With," moves beyond the interaction of Catholic theology with science to propose an ecological theology that gives attention to principles of ecojustice.

The Biblical Roots of Christian Creation Theology

The Bible contains passages that focus on creation and numerous verses that touch on it in the context of other topics. Given the diversity of these texts, it is not possible to speak about a theology of creation in the Bible. Rather, what one finds are rich and varied expressions of creation faith over a long span of history. Because of controversy prompted by science-religion debates, treatment of creation has tended to limit the biblical sources to the first two chapters of Genesis. However, creation is also an important theme in the prophetic literature, especially Deutero-Isaiah (chapters 40–55), the Psalms, and Wisdom literature—texts that add further contours to Christian creation faith. In the New Testament, the creation faith of Judaism is presumed and interpreted in christocentric terms.

The Old Testament

The book of Genesis and thus the Bible itself begins with two accounts of creation that provide differently nuanced perspectives on the relationship of God to reality, a relation of Creator to creation. Both texts are imaginative and symbolic. Determining the historical context for Genesis creation accounts with any degree of precision is difficult, since neither the "days of creation" (Gen. 1:1—2:4a) nor the account that focuses on the earth creatures, known as "Adam" and "Eve" (Gen. 2:4b—3:24), address specific events in the history of ancient Israel. While it is impossible to identify the authors or fully reconstruct the histories of the narratives they present, these canonical texts give evidence of being influenced by the prevailing thought patterns of the ancient Near East. In spite of the differences among the Egyptian, Mesopotamian, and Canaanite cultures, their religious creation narratives contain striking commonalities. This fact leads to the conclusion that not only the Genesis creation accounts, but also other Old Testament creation texts, including especially the Psalms, were influenced by the creation mythologies of their neighbors. To illustrate this important element in the history of biblical creation theology, an examination of some similarities that Genesis 1–3 shares with other ancient texts in the region, such as the epic poem *Enuma elish* and the myth entitled *Atrahasis* may prove helpful.

Since its discovery in the 1840s, *Enuma elish* has been compared and contrasted to the first of the Genesis creation narratives. *Enuma elish*, a version of which is traceable to 2000 BCE, provides high drama and graphic description of the events leading up to the creation of the cosmos.[5] The authors of *Enuma elish* describe how the storm god Marduk became the chief god of Babylon and includes a creation epic that attributes deity to freshwater Apsu and to saltwater Tiamat. The first of the seven *Enuma elish* tablets begins with the temporal clause "when

---

5. Leonard W. King traces a form of this creation myth to c. 2100 BCE. *Enuma Elish: The Seven Tablets of Creation* (San Diego: Book Tree, 1998; orig. pub. 1902), 1:lxxvi. Stephanie Dalley traces the Babylonian version to c. 1700 BCE. *Myths from Mesopotamia: Creation, the Flood, Gilgamesh, and Others* (New York: Oxford University Press, 2009), 3.

above the skies had not been named, nor earth below pronounced by name,"[6] and progresses with accounts of the birthing of many gods and of successive conflicts among them. These conflicts set the stage for an epic battle in which Marduk slays Tiamat, described as a sea dragon. By cutting her body in two, Marduk uses the upper half to form the sky, and the other half the basin of the earth. In the sky, the victorious storm god establishes the constellations as "stands for the great gods."[7] After establishing Babylon, Marduk, according to Tablet VI, then rewards the gods who supported him by killing Kingu, who had been Tiamat's ally, creating from his blood the first humans and imposing on them the service of the gods, so that the gods may rest in leisure.

Genesis 1:1—2:4a, like *Enuma elish*, also begins with a temporal clause, commonly translated in Jewish Bibles as "when God began to create the earth"[8] but translated in Christian Bibles, likely due to the influence of the first chapter of the Gospel of John, as "in the beginning God created." Reflecting on the first verse of Genesis 1, Michael Coogan posits, "Creation was the process by which these already existing realities [unformed earth and unruly sea] were transformed into an orderly cosmos."[9] Put simply, the "days of creation" is really about the formation of the world, as the people of the time experienced it. Coogan also proposes that the second verse of Genesis ("the earth being un-

formed and void, with darkness over the surface of the deep and a wind from God sweeping over the water"[10]) alludes to the battle between the storm god Marduk and the primeval sea Tiamat, which is linguistically related to the Hebrew *tehom*, meaning "deep."[11] Genesis 1, in contrast to *Enuma elish*, has no violent winds blowing across the waters. Rather, God orders the watery chaos by a sweeping wind (*ruah* in Hebrew, which also is translated in English Bibles as "breath" or "spirit"). Further, Genesis 1 does not present the human as made from a rebellious slain deity, but rather humankind—male and female—is made in God's image and likeness.

The created cosmos according to Genesis 1 provides no hint of a deadly conflict, but rather results from the utterance of God's creative word. Creation by word appears again in Ps. 33:6 but is not unique to the Bible. Although it is unlikely that Egyptian cosmogony directly influenced the authors of Genesis 1, an Egyptian creation myth speaks of the deity Ptah creating other gods through "what the heart thought and the tongue commanded" (i.e., by word), and it is from these lesser gods that everything emerged.[12]

Similarities of other ancient Near Eastern mythology are also evident for the second account of creation. Genesis 2:4b—3:24, for example, has a plot similar to the creation of humans in the Akkadian epic *Atrahasis*, traceable to the eighteenth century BCE. The second

---

6. King, *Enuma Elish*, 3.

7. Michael D. Coogan cites these words that appear at the beginning of Tablet V of *Enuma Elish* in *The Old Testament: A Historical and Literary Introduction to the Hebrew Scriptures* (New York/Oxford: Oxford University Press, 2006), 7.

8. Adele Berlin and Marc Zvi Brettler, eds., *The Jewish Study Bible* (New York: Oxford University Press, 2004), 12.

9. Coogan, *The Old Testament*, 7.

10. Ibid.,

11. Ibid., 7, 9.

12. James P. Allen, "The Memphite Theology," in *Genesis in Egypt: The Philosophy of Ancient Egyptian Creation Accounts* (New Haven: Yale Egyptological Studies 2, 1988), 43–44.

Genesis creation account employs imagery that depicts God forming the first human from the dust of the earth ('adamah, literally reddish soil or clay) and breathing into this handiwork the breath of life. However, there are also differences between Gen. 2:4b—3:24 and the *Atrahasis* myth. In the latter, the god Enki creates the first humans, with the collaboration of the birth goddess Nintu, from a mixture of clay and the blood of a slain god, associated with knowledge.[13] In addition, humans were created to be servants of the gods, as was the case in *Enuma elish*. *Atrahasis's* human creature, having been made of clay and from a divinity, has a direct link with the earth and with the animals that inhabit it, yet also shares a commonality with the gods. Aspiring to the lofty status of divinity, in *Atrahasis* the humans rebel against their assigned role as the gods' servants.[14]

From only a cursory examination of the two Genesis creation accounts in relationship to the religious mythology of Israel's neighbors, it is clear that the Bible's first creation accounts employ mythological notions found also in the creation accounts of their neighbors, while at the same time adapting some elements and rejecting others. Therefore, while the sun and moon and the stars and their constellations, and even the sea are regarded to be deities by some of ancient Israel's neighbors, for the Jewish writers of Genesis 1, none of these realities is treated as a god. Israel's God in the first creation account transcends creatures; the creaturely world is related to yet distinct from its sole deity. Further, in neither Genesis 1 nor 2 is humankind made explicitly for service to the gods. In Genesis 1:26-28, humans are created in God's own image and likeness. Humans, therefore, can be said to be entrusted with representing God to the world. In Genesis 3, although the first human pair listens to the promise of the tempting serpent who tells them if they eat of the Tree of Knowledge of Good and Bad/Evil, they will be like God, their eating of the forbidden fruit is not a rebellion that seeks an end to servitude, but rather seeks the wisdom that God possesses.

When the first two chapters of Genesis are compared, it is immediately apparent that while both strongly affirm God's creation of the then known world, neither was intended to give a final, single answer to the question of how God created the earth. The similarities and differences that the Genesis creation texts exhibit when compared with the creation texts of their neighbors lead to a logical conclusion: these texts do not lend themselves to empirical explanations about the physical origins of the natural world. While it can be argued that although many of the natural phenomena that ancient people experienced are the same as the ones we experience today, their epistemologies and interpretive frameworks are radically different.

Richard Clifford and John Collins provide some conclusions from their study of the cosmogonies of Israel's neighbors that cast further light on the interpretive framework for the biblical creation tests. Three are worth noting: First, the cosmogonies are "commonly functional," that is, they are read as part of religious functions like communal prayer or dedicating a

---

13. Richard J. Clifford, S.J., and John J. Collins, eds., "Introduction: The Theology of Creation Traditions," in *Creation in the Biblical Traditions* (Washington, DC: Catholic Biblical Association of America, 1992), 5. *Atrahasis* contains both a creation myth and an early flood account that was later incorporated into the Epic of Gilgamesh and likely influenced the biblical flood story (Genesis 6–9).

14. Bernard F. Batto, "Creation Theology in Genesis," in Clifford and Collins, *Creation in the Biblical Traditions*, 22–23.

temple. Historically, creation myths were not told for their own sake with the goal to explain objectively how creation happened. Their purpose was to celebrate the majesty of the Creator and acknowledge their dependence on this deity. Second, the authors of these religious myths assumed that the originating moment explains the present. Finally, there is no good evidence for holding that there were two distinct traditions of creation, one for the creation of the world and the other for the creation of human beings.[15] Human creation is integral to the creation of the cosmos.

While it is striking that many commonalities are shared with the ancient creation myths of the peoples the ancient Jews encountered when articulating their own creation faith, a treatment of these texts as sources for creation theology is incomplete without a treatment of their literary form and content. Genesis's first creation narrative, with its culmination in divine rest on the seventh day, draws attention to the Sabbath (cf. Exod. 20:8-10) and provides a clue to its function in the life of the Jewish community. Its stylized and repetitious pattern lends itself to the conclusion that its intent was for liturgical use. God acting in the role of "priest" confers blessings on each creation (1:22, 28; 2:3). One can imagine a community gathered on the Sabbath, listening to this passage rhythmically chanted, celebrating the presence of God who orders chaos by speech and enlivens by spirit (cf. wind). As the passage unfolds, those gathered for prayer receive a reminder: God, by creative word, fashions a life-world that

is ordered and good. Evil with its disorder is an anomaly in God's creation.

The care with which the creation events that lead up to God's day of Sabbath rest are arranged is apparent if the six-day pattern is analyzed. (see Table 1). The careful arrangement of the days makes concrete the ordering process of God creating. Creation is an intentional multi-stage process, not only initiated in the past, but also experienced in the present. God calls the light into being, sees that it is good, and separates the light from the darkness, but the divine word is only actualized with the separation of night from day. Birds populate the dome of the sky,[16] and the basin of the sea becomes teeming with life as the waters bring forth sea monsters and all the other forms of aquatic life. The creation of plants and the seeds and fruits they produce makes it possible for animals tame and wild to emerge and, it would seem, humans as well. This is so not only because humans are created on the same day as the animals, but also because both are given "every plant yielding seed that is upon the face of all the earth, and every tree with seed in its fruit" as food (v. 29).

There is another pattern in Genesis 1 worthy of attention: the recurring use of "let." The "jussive 'let,'" according to Terrence E. Fretheim, likely means that God's speaking does not function as an imperative; God leaves room for creaturely response. "Hence, the divine speaking in this chapter is of such a nature that the receptor of the word is important in the shaping of the created order."[17] In a sense, creation is envisioned as taking place by God acting not from

---

15. Clifford and Collins, "Introduction," 7–9. Clifford and Collins dispute the argument of the creation of nature and humans as distinct, argued by Claus Westermann, *Genesis 1–11: A Commentary* (Minneapolis: Augsburg, 1984), 19–25.

16. In addition to Gen. 1:20, references to the word *rqyʿ* (expanse, extended surface, firmament) are also found in Gen. 1:7, 8, 14, 15, 17, 20; Ezek 1:22, 23, 25, 26; 10:1; Pss. 19:2; 150:1.

17. Terence E. Fretheim, *God and the World in the New Testament: A Relational Theology of Creation* (Nashville: Abingdon, 2005), 38.

Table 1: God's Well-Ordered, Life-Generating World

Day 1	"Let there be light." (v. 3)	*Day 4*	"Let there be lights in the dome of the sky to separate the day from the night; and let them be for signs and for seasons and for days and years, and let them be lights in the dome of the sky to give light upon the earth." (v. 14)
Day 2	"Let there be a dome in the middle of the waters, to separate one body of water from the other." (v. 6)	*Day 5*	"Let the waters bring forth swarms of living creatures, and let birds fly above the earth across the dome of the sky." (v. 20)
Day 3	"Let the earth put forth vegetation: plants yielding seed, and fruit trees of every kind on earth that bear fruit with the seed in it." (v. 11)	*Day 6*	"Let the earth bring forth living creatures of every kind: cattle and creeping things and wild animals of the earth of every kind." (v. 24) "Let us make humankind in our image, according to our likeness." (v. 26)

outside of the created order but from within it as creation gradually develops. In this development, both nonhuman and human creatures participate together in the activity that God has begun. This participation is a form of cocreation: plants produce seed-bearing fruit, making animal life possible, and in turn, animals and humans multiply.

Humankind, although made on the same day as a host of animals, including those that "creep on the ground," also are singled out as those creatures, male and female, who are made in God's image and likeness (Gen. 1:26). Given the reference to the Sabbath day of rest in Genesis 2:3 and the important role of Sabbath observance in the Mosaic covenant (Exod. 20:8-

11), it may be possible that there is a connection between the Mosaic covenant and the creation of humans. The covenant God initiated calls for refraining from making any images of God, specifying none that "depict heaven above, the earth beneath, or the water under the earth" (Exod. 20:4). Since no graven images can be used for God, it would seem that humans (or perhaps the Jews) are to image God in the sense of acting as God's "representatives," thereby providing clues into the character of the God whom Jews honor and worship. This possibility is proposed with a cautionary note; in the Old Testament as a whole, the notion "image of God" plays no primary role in its references to humanity.[18] In the New Testament, there are

---

18. Walter Brueggemann, *Theology of the Old Testament: Testimony, Dispute, Advocacy* (Minneapolis: Fortress Press, 1997), 452.

references to "image of God" in the Pauline corpus, but it is Jesus Christ who is said to be "the image of God" (2 Cor. 4:4; Phil. 2:6; Col. 1:15).

Although the second creation account, like the first, begins with a temporal clause, "In the day that the Lord God made the earth and the heavens" (Gen. 2:4b), a significant difference becomes apparent in the words that follow. Instead of a watery chaos, the reader is told of a rainless landscape: "When no plant of the field was yet in the earth and no herb of the field had yet sprung up—for the Lord God had not caused it to rain upon the earth" (Gen. 2:5a).

The most striking difference between the first and second Genesis creation accounts is that in the second, anthropomorphic imagery for God abounds. In contrast to the first creation account, which depicts God as transcending the primeval chaos and calling creatures into existence, in the second account, God is a down-to-earth, immanent "hands-on" Creator. God engages in humanlike activities. Like a potter, God shapes the first human earthling from the clay of the soil and then breathes life into this creature (Gen. 2:7). God also plants the garden (Gen. 2:8), makes its "every animal of the field and every bird of the air" (Gen. 2:19), and daily walks in it "at the time of the evening breeze" (Gen. 3:8), .

Not only is the depiction of God strikingly different, but from a literary standpoint, Genesis 2:4b-25 lacks the repetitious refrains and the poetic liturgical form of Gen. 1:1—2:4a. Because Genesis 2 offers explanations of how or why phenomena of nature came about, the second creation account is recognized to be an "etiology," a word derived from the Greek *aitia*, which means "cause." As an etiology, Gen. 2:4b–3:24 provides a causal explanation of human sexual difference and the closeness of the conjugal bond. Noting that it is not good for the newly formed earthling *'adam* (at this stage an androgynous being[19]) to be alone (Gen. 2:18), and perceiving that the newly created animals are not suitable partners, God makes woman from the earthling's rib; *'ish* (a man known as "Adam") and *'ishahah* (woman, given the name "Eve," meaning mother of the living, in Gen. 3:20) result. Having accounted for sexual difference, the story provides a rationale for marriage: "man leaves his father and his mother and clings to his wife, and they become one flesh" (Gen. 2:24). Thus, the story emphasizes that the distinction between the sexes is willed by God.

The story also explains how the blissful life in the garden becomes an unhappy state. Although in the first creation account, human beings, male and female, image God (Gen 1:26-28), in Genesis 3 the first human pair's ambition to be like God is the root of their decision to eat the forbidden fruit and their expulsion from the garden. Violating God's command to refrain from eating of the Tree of Knowledge of Good and Bad/Evil has consequences. Woman will suffer pain in childbirth, and in spite of man's rule over her, she will be attracted to him. Man will endure the difficulties of the labor necessary to eke out sustenance from the soil, which at the end of his life will reabsorb him.

Although Genesis creation narratives are very different, they also share some common themes. In the first account, God repeatedly draws attention to the goodness of creation. In Genesis 2, God's tactile engagement with the creatures that the divine hands have formed gives witness to their goodness. Creaturely goodness, however, is not to be confused with perfection

---

19. This interpretation by Phyllis Trible is widely accepted by biblical scholars today; see her *God and the Rhetoric of Sexuality* (Philadelphia: Fortress Press, 1978), 98–99.

in the sense of completion. As already noted, in Genesis 1, creatures both nonhuman and human participate in the activity that God has begun. This ongoing cocreation of plants, animals, and humans is integral to the blessing God has conferred on creation. Further, humankind, male and female, represent God by exercising dominion (*radah*) over nonhuman creatures; neither man nor woman has dominion over the other (vv. 26-28). Genesis 2 provides concrete content for God in Genesis 1 directing humankind "to subdue the earth" (v. 28). In Gen. 2:15, the human is placed in the garden to till the earth and keep it. Since the Hebrew word *'abad*, translated as "to till," can also be rendered as "to serve," the latter adds nuance to the role of humans as cocreators with God in their activity of subduing the earth. Tilling is not only about humans preparing and cultivating the earth, it is an act of service to God and to the garden, their earthly home. Further, God entrusts humans with naming the creatures of the garden (v. 20). Naming is a way in which humans relate to nonhuman creatures.

Creation also is featured in other parts of the Old Testament, including in the books of the classical prophets. Amos 4:13; 5:8; and Jeremiah 27:5; 31:35-37 speak of creation, but the most extensive treatment is found in Deutero-Isaiah (chs. 40–55), a prophetic text traceable to the Babylonian exile period. In the introductory chapter of Deutero-Isaiah, the prophet is advised by God to speak tenderly to Jerusalem because its service as an exile is coming to an end. Deutero-Isaiah proclaims that the very earth will be re-created: "Every valley shall be lifted up and every mountain and hill be made low; the uneven ground shall become level and the rough places a plain" (Isa. 40:4). Isaiah later speaks of God creating the heavens and earth and, as in Gen. 2:7, breathing the breath of life into the first human (Isa. 42:5-6).

Isaiah also strongly emphasizes that creation as an act of God is connected to Israel's redemption. The creative word by which God made earth and heaven is also the redemptive word by which Israel as a people is created anew: "But now thus says the Lord, he who created you, O Jacob, he who formed you, O Israel: Do not fear, for I have redeemed you; I have called you by name, you are mine" (Isa. 43:1).

Creation is a recurring theme in the Old Testament hymns. Psalm 104, the longest of the creation psalms, praises God not only for setting limits to the oceans (v. 9) but also for continuing to give all creatures "food in due time" (v. 27), thus expressing gratitude for God's providential care for creation. Additional psalms also praise God for creation, including Psalms 8 (in verses 1-19), 19 (verses 1-7), 29, 33, 93, and 96. The Psalter closes with this declaration of praise: "Praise him [God] for his mighty deeds. . . . Let everything that breathes praise the Lord! Praise the Lord!" (Ps. 150:2, 6).

Biblical wisdom literature[20] also speaks of God as Creator and treats creation extensively. Job declares that God's providence has preserved the divine spirit (Job 10:12) and posits that creatures, both animals and plants, have the potential to teach humans about God's ways (Job 12:7-10). Because wisdom literature often deals directly with life questions, the Bible's wisdom writings do not fit neatly into a "salvation history" paradigm, long emphasized in Western Christianity. History is not merely a recollection of key events of the past, but also is concerned

---

20. The biblical Wisdom books are Proverbs, Job, Ecclesiastes (Qoheleth), and the deuterocanonical books Wisdom of Solomon and Sirach (Ecclesiasticus); some authors also designate some of the Psalms as wisdom writings, e.g., Psalm 37.

with the day-to-day experiences of ordinary people. The latter sense of history contributes to the attention that wisdom literature gives to the mysteries of creation, to moral guidance, and to practical instruction.

All three of these are present in the book of Proverbs. In particular, Proverbs contains a great deal of practical human wisdom, but it also treats creation in a different way than any other biblical book. Proverbs 3:16-20 could suggest that wisdom is a divine attribute, but more likely it assumes that God is wise and is speaking of Wisdom personified (Hebrew *Chokmah*; Greek *Sophia*), who holds power over life and its duration.[21] Following her ways, therefore, leads to beatitude:

> Long life is in her right hand;
> in her left hand are riches and honor.
> Her ways are ways of pleasantness,
> and all her paths are peace.
> She is a tree of life to those who lay hold of her;
> those who hold her fast are called happy.
> The LORD by wisdom founded the earth;
> by understanding he established the heavens;
> by his knowledge the deeps broke open,
> and the clouds drop down the dew. (vv. 16-20)

Like a fertile woman, Wisdom is a "tree of life," a symbol first found in Genesis 2:9. Here, "tree of life" is the major metaphor for those who draw Woman Wisdom to themselves. Following Woman Wisdom's ways is the opposite of following folly, which leads to death. The "tree of life" here is the poetic way of calling human beings to a life lived wisely, which is about more

than biological life, although it includes it. Those who embrace Woman Wisdom are filled with blessing.

Wisdom as a female agent of God and not merely a divine quality is not without its critics. It is difficult, however, to dismiss *Chokmah/ Sophia* as an independent female agent when reading Prov. 8:22-31. Wisdom describes herself as having been given center stage in creation, putting to rest doubt that *Chokmah/Sophia* is merely God's abstract intellectual instrument. Yet there is a lack of consensus about her identity and role in creation, due to controversy about how key words should be translated. The first problem is in verse 22 and the meaning of *qānnāî*, which can imply (1) "possessed" or "acquired" by God or (2) "created" or "begotten" by God.[22] Obviously, how one views the nature of Wisdom will affect the translation. If one chooses "possessed," this allows for the possibility that Woman Wisdom existed with God from eternity, while the choice for "created" makes her a creature among others. The second problem is in verse 30. There is uncertainty about the meaning of *'āmôn*, which can be translated as (1) "artisan" in the sense of a craftsperson, which would mean that Wisdom aided God in creating; (2) "confidant"—"constant(ly)," "faithful(ly)"; or (3) nursling or ward—a child God cares for.[23] If artisan/craftsperson is chosen for *'āmôn*, then Woman Wisdom is directly involved in the creation of the world and may be said to possess divine or nearly divine stature.

If we incorporate the first option for both *qānnāî* and *'āmôn*, Prov. 8:22-31 would read as follows:

---

21. Roland E. Murphy refers to Wisdom as "Lady Wisdom" throughout *The Tree of Life*. In Prov. 8:22-31, he associates this female wisdom figure with Maat, the goddess who set the norms for nature and society in ancient Egypt; see *The Tree of Life: An Exploration of Biblical Wisdom Literature*, Anchor Bible Reference Library (New York: Doubleday, 1990), 137.

22. Berlin and Brettler, *The Jewish Study Bible*, 1461.

23. *The Jewish Study Bible* renders *'āmôn* as "confidant" (1462).

212

God *possessed* [*qānnāî*] me at the beginning of
his work,[24]

the first of his acts of long ago. . . .

Before the mountains had been shaped,

before the hills, I was brought forth—

when he had not yet made earth and fields,

or the world's first bits of soil.

When he established the heavens, I was there,

when he drew a circle on the face of the deep,

when he made firm the skies above,

when he established the fountains of the deep,

when he assigned to the sea its limit,

so that the waters might not transgress his
command,

when he marked out the foundations of the earth,

then I was beside him, like an *artisan* ['āmôn];[25]

and I was daily his delight,

rejoicing before him always,

rejoicing in his inhabited world

and delighting in the human race.

This poetic text is enlivened with spontaneity.
God takes delight in Woman Wisdom as she
rejoices in him and the world he has populated
with creatures. Her activity is free. Her delight
in humans is an ecstatic kind of loving. Woman
Wisdom, related so closely to God in the act of
creating, has a permanent place in the work of
creation. She is the necessary precondition for a
well-structured world. She also has a special intimacy with God in that work. Freitheim proposes
that "*wisdom is likely presented as both divine and
creature. As such, wisdom is uniquely capable of
revealing both divine and creaturely worlds.*"[26]

The deuterocanonical book of the Wisdom
of Solomon, attributes to Woman Wisdom (*So-*

phia) a creative role that may be even stronger
than her role as artisan in Proverbs 8, for she
is spoken of as the mother of all things (Wis.
7:12), responsible for their existence and thus
knowing their secrets. Later, unlimited power
is ascribed to Woman Wisdom. Though she is
but one, she can do all things and is the fash-
ioner of all things (7:22). Her image is given
further contours as she is said to have extraordinary power, with which she reaches from one
end of the earth to the other, ordering all things
well (8:1).

The New Testament

The New Testament is strongly influenced by
Wisdom, including in her creation roles. The
Pauline epistles, the earliest New Testament
texts, connect Jesus with Woman Wisdom. In
1 Corinthians, for example, Christ crucified is
presented as "the power of God and the wisdom
of God" (1 Cor. 1:24). As "the wisdom of God,"
Jesus Christ is the central figure in God's plan
of salvation. Later in the same letter, Paul begins the tradition of attributing to Christ the
role in creation given to Proverbs' Woman Wisdom. In 1 Cor. 8:6, Paul declares that it is not
only the "one God, the Father [cf. Creator God],
from whom are all things and for whom we exist," but also the "one Lord, Jesus Christ [cf.
Woman Wisdom] through whom are all things
and through whom we exist." The Woman Wisdom–Creation connection to Jesus Christ develops more explicitly in the hymn that appears
in the first chapter of Colossians (verses 15-20),
attributed to the followers of Paul:

---

24. This is an alternate translation to the NSRV, which reads "The Lord created me at the beginning of his work."

25. "A master worker" in the NRSV.

26. Freitheim, *God and the World in the Old Testament*, 205; emphasis his.

> He is the image of the invisible God, the firstborn of all creation; for in him all things in heaven and on earth were created, things visible and invisible, whether thrones or dominions or rulers or powers; all things have been created through him and for him. He himself is before all things, and in him all things hold together. (Col 1:15-17)

By applying to Christ the characteristics of Woman Wisdom, present "beside God" creating (as she is described as doing in Prov. 8:30), this hymn describes her agency as his. Jesus Christ is celebrated as the mediator of creation.

Most influential of all for the later Christian tradition, however, is the prologue of the Gospel of John (1:1-18). This hymn, interspersed with details about John the Baptist (1:6-8, 15), parallels Col. 1:15-20. The hymn opens with these words:

> In the beginning was the Word, and the Word was with God, and the Word was God. He was in the beginning with God. All things came into being through him, and without him not one thing came into being. What has come into being in him was life, and the life was the light of all people. The light shines in the darkness, and the darkness did not overcome it. (John 1:1-5)

If we replace "Word" with "Wisdom," the influence of Prov. 8:22-31 to describe the divine Word (*Logos*) incarnate in the person of Jesus becomes evident. Why did the author of John choose *Logos* over *Sophia*? The substitution of *Logos* (a masculine noun in Greek) for *Sophia* may have been inspired by the maleness of Jesus,

by the depiction of creation through the divine power of word in the first chapter of Genesis, or by an effort to communicate with Hellenistic Christians.[27] Whatever the motivation, one thing is eminently clear about the initial verses of John's Gospel: they present Jesus as God's creative Wisdom, but with a significant advance beyond Proverbs 8. Jesus is not only "with God," Jesus "was God." Jesus is the preexisting Word/Wisdom of God who has entered the realm of the flesh to dwell with his people (John 1:14). Through his incarnation, creation and redemption are linked.

John's prologue is a confession of faith that Jesus, in his person, reveals God. John's connection of Jesus with Woman Wisdom, "artisan" of creation, makes it clear that Jesus is not exalted with divine status only after his crucifixion and resurrection. From the beginning, Jesus is God, from whom all things come into being. More than God's human emissary, Jesus is the cosmic Christ. It is he who is the light that shines in darkness (1:18) and whose story is told "in order that you may believe that Jesus is the Christ, the Son of God" (John 20:31). Some newly converted Christians, attracted to the Johannine community because of its stirring message about the Son of God, light to the world, will either deny or diminish the significance of his humanity. In response to this development, the author of the letters of John will insist that Jesus Christ "has come in the flesh" (John 1:14a, cf. 1 John 4:1-6; 2 John 1:7).[28]

Rejection of the humanity of Jesus by Johannine Christians, according to Gail R. O'Day, indicates that Gnosticism is making an

---

27. Philo of Alexandria, a Hellenized Jew (c. 20 BCE–50 CE), used *logos* interchangeably with *sophia*.

28. For more on the complexity of the relationship of the Johannine Jesus and *Sophia*, see Elisabeth Schüssler Fiorenza, *Jesus, Miriam's Child, Sophia's Prophet: Critical Issues in Feminist Christology* (New York: Continuum, 1994), 152–54.

impact on the community.[29] Gnosticism and its belief in "saving knowledge," is founded on a hierarchical dualism between spirit, as inherently good, and body (and by extension all of material creation) as inherently evil. The author of the Johannine letters regards flesh-denying Gnosticism a deception and the work of "the spirit of the antichrist" (1 John 4:3; 2 John 1:7). This is strong language, especially for one who writes so eloquently on love (1 John 4:9-21). "Antichrist" draws attention to what is at stake regarding Christian belief in the saving work of Jesus Christ and in the link between salvation in Jesus and the renewal of creation, including the promised "redemption of our bodies" (Rom. 8:18-23).

Creation in Patristic and Medieval Theology

Attending to historical influences on the Bible—including the popular religious myths of the neighbors of the Jews and early Christians—is important for understanding the creation faith of the biblical era. To understand the developments in Christian creation faith in the patristic and medieval periods, it is important to give attention to the history of Christianity's encounters not only with popular religious beliefs but also with philosophical concepts. These encounters result in theological insights that do not simply repeat biblical creation beliefs but rather build on them. Through dialogue with dominant systems of thought concerning the nature of the world and of humans in the world, two creation doctrines were introduced in the early patristic period and further developed through the Middle Ages. These doctrines are *creatio ex nihilo*, meaning creation produced by God from nothing, and *imago Dei*, meaning humans are created in the image of God. The first affirms the complete dependence of creation as a whole on God. The second acknowledges humanity's creaturely capacity for openness to the divine and for God-likeness.

Creatio ex nihilo

In the process of the spread of Christianity throughout the Roman Empire during the centuries after the canonical Gospels were written, nascent church communities attracted members, even with the risk of persecution. Converts to Christianity brought with them visions of the world that differed greatly from those that influenced the Old Testament. Two visions of the world in particular invited scrutiny of the creation faith that Christians inherited from the Jews. One vision combined philosophical pantheism and emanationism, and the other was religious Gnosticism.

Some Christians familiar with Greek philosophy were influenced by philosophies that maintained that the universe was eternal. Plato and Aristotle, the Stoics and Plotinus, in spite of their diversity on many issues, all maintained the eternity of the universe. Christians were familiar with positions that envisioned the creation of nature as coeternal with or out of the divine substance, or as resulting from a series of necessary emanations from one divine source.

In addition, Gnostics attracted to Christianity brought with them beliefs attributed to spiritual elites within their groups, including beliefs about the origins of the world and their

---

29. Gail R. O'Day, "1, 2, 3 John," in *The Woman's Bible Commentary*, ed. Carol A. Newsom and Sharon H. Ringe (Louisville: Westminster John Knox, 1992), 375.

place in it. Gnostics within the Christian community require the church to develop a theology of creation that will provide a response to the Gnostic belief that an inferior creator (a demiurge) made material reality evil, while a supreme godhead, unknown until Christ revealed him, was the source of all that was truly good. As already noted, as early as the late first century and the Gospel of John, Christianity proclaimed that creation came into being through Christ, who in his very flesh affirmed the fundamental goodness of creation.

Well into the second century, Gnostics posed issues to which the unknown author of the *Shepherd of Hermas* (140–150 CE) responded. Though the *Shepherd* is an apocalyptic work more concerned with moral teaching than with theology per se, its author would succinctly state the teaching on creation that a Christian must embrace. The *Shepherd* writes, "First of all, believe that God is one, who created and completed all things and made all that is *from that which is not* and contains all things."[30] This statement implies creation *ex nihilo*, an abstract notion foreign to the writers of the Old Testament creation texts.[31]

The affirmation in Gen. 1:1 of preexisting matter that was formless has the potential of opening the door to Gnostic notions that the material world was inherently disordered and evil, and Gnostic leaders seized upon it. Irenaeus (c. 135–202), bishop of Lyons, would strengthen the position of the *Shepherd of Hermas* to correct the errors of Gnosticism, which

to Irenaeus were synonymous with "knowledge falsely so called," the subtitle of his magnum opus against the Gnostics. Irenaeus's principal foils were Marcion and Vallentinus, who made a sharp distinction between the creator of the Old Testament and the Father God of the New Testament. The creator of the Old Testament is described by them as jealous and violent, and therefore must be rejected. In contrast, the deity of the New Testament is mercy and peace, who through Christ offers salvation from evil and therefore must be embraced. It is not surprising, therefore, that Irenaeus is intent on identifying God, the Father of Jesus Christ, with the Creator, as this selection from *Against the Heresies* demonstrates: "For he [God] is himself uncreated, both without beginning and without end and lacking in nothing. He is himself sufficient for this very thing, existence, but the things which have been made by him have received a beginning. . . . He indeed who made all things can alone, together with his Word, properly be termed God and Lord."[32] Elsewhere, he succinctly states, "God, in the exercise of his will and pleasure, formed all things . . . out of what did not previously exist."[33]

This statement of belief in *creatio ex nihilo*, with its echoes of the statement of the *Shepherd of Hermas*, is complemented by a christocentric creation theology, in which Irenaeus unequivocally links the enfleshed Jesus Christ with creatures. It is Christ, the Son of God incarnate, who recapitulates humanity and the whole of creation together with its history.[34]

---

30. "The Mandates, no. 1," in *The Shepherd of Hermas*, vol. 6 of *The Apostolic Fathers: A New Translation and Commentary*, ed. Graydon F. Snyder (Camden, NJ: Thomas Nelson & Sons, 1968), 63; emphasis mine.

31. Ian G. Barbour, *Religion in the Age of Science* (San Francisco: Harper & Row, 1991), 144.

32. Irenaeus, *Against Heresies: A Refutation and Subversion of Knowledge Falsely So Called*, Ante-Nicene Christian Library 5, trans. and ed. Alexander Roberts and James Donaldson (Edinburgh: T&T Clark, 1968), 3.20.3.

33. Ibid., 1.10.2.

34. Ibid., book 3.13.1; 18.7; and 5.20.2.

Origen (c. 185–254), an influential theologian who lived shortly after Irenaeus, also was determined not to remain silent where the false knowledge of the Gnostics was concerned. In company with Irenaeus, Origen defends the true humanity of Christ as a condition for redemption. Against the Marcionites, he emphasizes both the goodness of the creator, who is one with the Father of Jesus, and the agreement of the Old and New Testaments. Rejecting the opinion of those "who deny either God's creative power or His providential administration of the world," Origen charges those who claim "that matter is uncreated, and co-eternal with the uncreated God" with "impiety."[35] To clinch his argument, Origen draws on 2 Macc. 7:28, "where the mother of seven martyrs exhorts her son to endure torture, this truth is confirmed; for she says, 'I ask of thee, my son, to look at the heaven and the earth, and at all things which are in them, and beholding these, to know that God made all these things when they did not exist.'"[36] To further support his position, Origen then quotes the belief statement from *The Shepherd of Hermas* and adds that the one God who created and arranged all things did so "out of a state of nothingness."[37]

To the voices championing *creatio ex nihilo*, history adds that of Tertullian (c. 160–225), polemicist and apologist.[38] Tertullian is important because he draws from biblical passages to forge the beginnings of a metaphysics of creation that runs contrary to positions of Greek philosophy and the axiom "Nothing comes from nothing" (Latin, *ex nihilo nihil fit*). The document of interest is Tertullian's *The Treatise against Hermogenes*. In the treatise, Hermogenes is identified as a self-proclaimed "Christian" who posed three options for God's creation: (1) out of himself, (2) out of nothing, or (3) out of something— some type of preexisting, perhaps even eternal matter.[39] Favoring the third choice, Hermogenes's rationale is based on the Septuagint's rendering of Gen. 1:2, "the earth was invisible and without order," which to him proves that from preexisting, eternal matter God fashioned the world. Tertullian recognizes that Hermogenes's preference for God and matter being coeternal has important implications for Christian creation faith. If matter is eternal, then it may be said that matter is equal to God.

Applying a lawyer's logic, Tertullian argues that since there is one God, God is the sole one to possess the quality of eternity.[40] Further, if God had needed matter for the creation of the cosmos, then matter would be superior to God. In support of his position, Tertullian draws on biblical texts. In his interpretation of Prov. 8:22–

---

35. Origen, *The Writings* (*De principiis*), trans. Frederick Crombie (Edinburgh: T&T Clark, 1978), 2.2.4, 75–76.

36. Read in context, 2 Macc. 7:28 is more eschatological than protological. Additional scripture passages that are sometimes cited in support of *creatio ex nihilo* are Rom. 4:17 (where God is said to call into being things that are not) and Heb. 11:3 (where the visible world is not created from anything observable).

37. Origen, *The Writings* (*De principiis*), nos. 5, 77.

38. Tertullian, *Against Marcion*, trans. Peter Holmes, vol. 3 of *Ante-Nicene Fathers*, ed. Alexander Roberts, James Donaldson, and A. Cleveland Coxe (Buffalo, NY: Christian Literature, 1885).

39. Tertullian, *The Treatise against Hermogenes*, trans. J. H. Waszink, vol. 24 of *Ancient Christian Writers* (New York: Newman, 1956), ch. 4 (31–32).

40. Ibid., ch. 4, nos. 3–4 (31–32). Elsewhere, Tertullian writes, "He is the unique God for this reason alone, that he is the sole God, and he is the sole God for this reason alone, that nothing existed along with him. So too he must be the first, because all else is after him. All else is after him because all else is from him and from him because they are created out of nothing." Ibid., ch. 17, no. 1 (47).

31, he pointedly argues that the formless abyss of Gen. 1:2 cannot be identified as preexisting matter, because Prov. 8:24 militates against it. This verse, he stresses, says wisdom, a spiritual reality, was created before the abyss, so one can be sure that the abyss itself was also created by God.[41]

To further make his case against matter coeternal with God, Tertullian also proposes an argument "from silence." Since whenever something was made out of another thing, Genesis mentions that second thing, Tertullian concludes that if heaven and earth had been made out of something, surely that thing would have been mentioned.[42] Failing to find an explicit statement about material being used to create heaven and earth, one must conclude that heaven and earth are made by the eternal God from nothing. Further, if one looks to biblical passages that indicate that eventually all things will be reduced to nothing, one must conclude that "all things produced from nothing will in the end come to nothing."[43]

The Treatise against Hermogenes is repetitious and polemical. Christianity would have to wait until Augustine of Hippo (354–430) for stronger support for *creatio ex nihilo*. Augustine's own history makes him well suited to respond to the challenges to Christian faith from Gnosticism and Greek philosophy, especially Neo-Platonism. In his youth, Augustine was attracted to Manichaeism, a form of Gnostic dualism founded by Mani, a third-century Persian.

Manichean mythology emphasized coeternal competing kingdoms. As a result of their competition, the spiritual kingdom, the realm of light and goodness, had become commingled with the material kingdom, the realm of darkness and evil. The effect on humans is that we feel divided about good and evil but are not responsible for the evil we do. In the "end times," there will be salvation, with the separation of good and evil and the liberation of light from the captivity of darkness. Although the Manichean teachings were a source of consolation to Augustine for over a decade, by age twenty-nine, he found them wanting.[44] This prompted him to abandon this popular form of Gnosticism and to take up Platonism and Neo-Platonism before he converted to Christianity.

In *The Confessions*, Augustine provides a counterargument to Gnostic notions of creation emanating from an evil source, by making a case for the self-evidence of creation by drawing attention to its beauty and goodness: "You, therefore, O Lord, who are beautiful, made these things [heaven and earth and all that is in them], for they are beautiful; you who are good made them, for they are good; you have made them, for they are."[45] Later in The Confessions, Augustine makes a case for creatio ex nihilo. Like Tertullian, he draws attention to God, who created all things through Wisdom, but also adds clarity about this God: "You have made heaven and earth, not out of yourself. For then they would have been equal to your Only-

---

41. In *The Treatise against Hermogenes*, Prov. 8:22-31 is treated in ch. 18, no. 1 (49–50) and alluded to in chs. 22–32. For example, wisdom is said to be the "beginning" of God's ways. Ibid., ch. 20, no. 2 (53).

42. In *The Treatise against Hermogenes*, Genesis 1 is treated in chs. 22–32 (57–70), in which Tertullian argues that "beginning" is not matter, but origin in time and first, in the sense of having the first place in order and power. A recurring theme is that God made "the earth invisible and unfinished."

43. Ibid., ch 34, nos. 1–2 (71–72).

44. *The Confessions of St. Augustine*, trans. John K. Ryan (Garden City, NY: Doubleday, 1960), 5.14.24–25 (131).

45. Ibid., 11.4.6 (280).

begotten, and through this equal to you. There was nothing beyond you from which you might make them, O God, one Trinity and trinal Unity. Therefore, you created heaven and *earth out of nothing*, a great thing and a little thing. For you are almighty and good, to make all things good, the great heaven and the little earth."[46]

To those who object to something coming from nothing, in *Genesis against the Manichees*, Augustine replies that it is fitting for Christians to hold *creatio ex nihilo* and not to creation being co-eternal with God: "For we should not be like those who do not believe that Almighty God could have made something. . . . For if something ['eternal matter'] that he had not made helped him to make those things he wanted to make, he was not almighty, and that is sacrilegious to believe."[47] The world does not have the same duration as God, because it does not have "the same eternity as the eternity that God has." God made the world, according to Augustine, and then and only then did time begin. From the perspective of our earthly existence, time may be called "eternal" because it may seem such to us. "Nonetheless, time is not eternal in the same way that God is eternal, because God who

is the maker of time is before time."[48] Time began along with creation.

Augustine revisits the theme of time again in *On the Literal Meaning of Genesis* and accounts for creation being made simultaneously (Ps. 32:9) and also in six days (Genesis 1). Stressing again that God creates through Wisdom, Augustine now adds a further insight: "The change we now see in creatures, measured by the lapse of time, . . . comes to creatures from those causal reasons implanted in them, which God scattered as seeds at *the moment of creation*."[49] Later, Augustine provides this conclusion: "These reasons were created to exercise their causality in either one way or in the other: providing for the ordinary development of new creatures in appropriate periods of time."[50] God's creative act can be said to have two modes: the seminal *informatio* expressed in Genesis 1, and the successive *conformatio* described in Genesis 2. This rationale provides a way for Augustine to harmonize the two Genesis accounts of creation.[51]

Augustine also gives considerable attention to the role of the Trinity in creation, to which he alluded in *The Confessions*. For example, in his unfinished book on Genesis, he writes:

---

46. Ibid., 12.7.7 (308–9), emphasis mine.

47. Augustine, *On Genesis: Two Books on Genesis against the Manichees*, trans. Roland J. Teske, S.J. (Washington, DC: Catholic University of America Press, 1991), 1.6.10 (57–58). Creation from nothing was not an easy concept for Augustine to explain; it is significant that he emphasizes omnipotence, which Greek philosophy attributed to God.

48. Ibid., 1.2.4 (50–51). Augustine no doubt is influenced by Plato, who treated time as a vestige or image of eternity (*Timeaus*, 37d7). Plato in *Timaeus* argued that there were no days and nights and months and years before heaven was created, but when the uncaused and self-subsistent Author constructed heaven, he created them also. "Time and heaven came into being at the same instant, in order that having been created together, if ever there was to be a dissolution of them, they might be dissolved together." See *Timaeus* 37d–38c, in *The Collective Dialogues of Plato*, trans. B. Jowett (Princeton, NJ: Princeton University Press, 1989), cited by Luca Obertello, "Proclus, Ammonius of Hermias, and Zacharias Scholasticus: The Search after Eternity and the Meaning of Creation," in *Divine Creation in Ancient, Medieval, and Early Modern Thought*, ed. Michael Trechow, Willemien Otten, and Walter Hannam (Boston: Brill, 2007), 177–78.

49. *St. Augustine: The Literal Meaning of Genesis*, vol. 1, Ancient Christian Writers, trans. John Hammond Taylor, S.J. (New York: Newman, 1982), 4.33.51 (141), emphasis mine. See also n. 67, pp. 252–54.

50. Ibid., book 6.14.25 (196).

51. Like the theologians of his era, Augustine envisioned sacred Scripture in a unified way as "God's word," thereby ignoring human authors who wrote at different times and in different literary genres.

God the almighty Father made and established all of creation through the only-begotten Son; that is, through the Wisdom and Power that is consubstantial and coeternal with the Father in the unity of the Holy Spirit, who is also consubstantial and coeternal. Therefore the Catholic faith commands that we believe that this trinity is called one God. . . . God has made and created all things . . . not out of the nature of God, but out of nothing. . . . Therefore, we cannot say or believe that the whole of creation is either consubstantial with or coeternal with God.[52]

This argument for the triune God's direct action in creation counters creation conceived as a series of necessary emanations from the divine.

From this survey of creation theology by early church theologians, we can draw three major conclusions that summarize the importance of *creatio ex nihilo* for patristic theology and for the Christian tradition:

1. *Creatio ex nihilo* provides arguments against philosophical pantheism, which obscures a clear distinction between the Creator and creatures. A pantheistic deity lacks sufficient power to be able to bring into existence an autonomous and yet nongodly and unfinished creation.

2. *Creatio ex nihilo* also counters emanationism, which while maintaining God's transcendence, depicts the cosmos as necessarily "flowing forth" from an impersonal deity, thereby blurring the distinction between God as Creator and creatures. A God who freely chooses to create is far more congenial to Christian belief in a personal God, a Trinity of persons who are unified in their creative activity.

3. Against religious Gnosticism and its dualistic conception of good and evil, *creatio ex nihilo* (rather than creation from evil deities) provides a way of stressing the essential goodness of creatures and of adding support to the belief that the Son of God became incarnate as a fully human-fleshy man.

Although there was a consensus of support for *creatio ex nihilo* among the theologians of the church in the patristic period, an official doctrinal statement affirming Christian belief in *creatio ex nihilo* would wait until the thirteenth century and the Fourth Lateran Council (1215). Once again, the church was caught up in a struggle with Gnostics, this time the Albigensians, the roots for whom were the Cathari, eastern Gnostics who had made inroads in Western Europe in the twelfth century. The Albigensians had their own form of dualistic doctrine that held that God created only the spiritual world. The material world, created by the devil, was inherently evil. Their "Christ," therefore, had no real human body. To make it clear that this Gnostic and docetic teaching was an aberrant form of Christianity, the Fourth Lateran council stated, "Firmly we believe and confess simply that the true God . . . Father Son and Holy Spirit . . . at once *from the beginning of time* created each creature *from nothing.* . . . [W]e confess that the Incarnation of the Divinity took place . . . in the Son only . . . having true flesh from the womb of his mother and a human rational soul."[53] This declaration not only affirms that God created

---

52. Augustine, *On the Literal Interpretation of Genesis: An Unfinished Book*, trans. Roland J. Teske, S.J. (Washington, DC: Catholic University of America Press, 1991), 1.2 (145–46).

53. Henricus Denzinger and Aldolphus Schönmetzer, *Enchiridion Symbolorum: Definitionum ed Declarationum De Rebus Fidei et Morum* (Rome: Herder, 1975), 800 (hereafter DS; emphasis mine. Over two hundred years later, at the Council of Florence (1442), Gnostic dualism would be addressed again in a reaffirmation of the belief that God created a good creation out of nothing. DS 1333, 1336.

everything *extra se* without any material-evil cause, but also that time has a beginning. The doctrine of creation is thus inherently bound up with temporal considerations. God brought the universe into being at some point in the past without any antecedent or contemporaneous material cause. The Son of God incarnate is fully human, affirming in his flesh the fundamental goodness of creation.

In addition to responding to a new form of Gnosticism, Lateran IV's emphasis on temporal beginnings also may be a response to Aristotle's philosophy, the most advanced form of knowledge or "science" that was being discussed and debated in the major universities of western Europe during the thirteenth century, not only by Christians, but also by Jews and Muslims.[54] In his *Physics*, Aristotle examines what "motion" entails and concludes, "There was no time nor will there be, when motion was not or will not be." Put simply, for Aristotle: "the being [of the cosmos] is eternal."[55]

Some decades after the Fourth Lateran Council, Thomas Aquinas in the *Summa theologiae* (1266–73)[56] addressed the topic of creation with attention to the issue of its eternity. From the standpoint of Aristotle's philosophy, Aquinas argues that time is irrelevant to the notion of creation: creation *from* nothing does not mean a temporal creation *after* nothing.

In his response to the question regarding whether God alone is eternal, Aquinas declares, "Only God is truly and properly eternal."[57] To say this, however, does not rule out holding that created material reality could be eternal. An eternal, created universe would have no first moment, yet it would have a first cause of its existence. Further, an eternal universe does not necessarily lead to the conclusion that the universe is equal to God or necessary. From a theological standpoint, if *from* nothing is interpreted to mean *temporally after* nothing, then such a notion of creation cannot be demonstrated. It is held on the basis of faith.[58]

Why does Aquinas hold that an eternal creation is possible? To answer this question, one must keep in mind Aquinas's understanding of God and his conception of causality rooted in the thought of Aristotle. Aquinas argued that it was the essence of God to exist.[59] God is not an essence that possesses an existence, but the very act of existence itself. Put simply, God is pure act. God, therefore, is a perfect efficient cause from which all creatures receive existence.[60] Reception of existence by creatures is necessary, because nothing apart from God can be a cause

---

54. In 1215, the same year in which Lateran IV was held, the papal legate to Innocent III prohibited the teaching of Aristotle's *Metaphysics*, *Physics*, and all his writings on the natural sciences at the University of Paris; see Christopher M. Cullen, who cites *Chartularium Universitatis Parisiensis, I*, ed. H. Deniffile and A. Chatelain (Paris: Delalain, 1889), 70, no. 11 in his *Bonaventure* (New York: Oxford University Press, 2006), 197n8.

55. Aristotle, *Physics, or Natural Hearing*, trans. Glen Coughlin (South Bend, IN: St. Augustine's Press, 2005), 8.1.252b5 (162); 8.6.258b10 (174–75). Late in his life, Thomas Aquinas wrote a *Commentary on Aristotle's Physics*, trans. Richard J. Blackwell, Richard J. Spath, and W. Edmund Thirlkel (Notre Dame, IN: Dumb Ox, [1961] 1995), 519.

56. Thomas Aquinas, *Summa theologiae*, trans. Fathers of English Dominican Province (New York: Benzinger Brothers, 1947), hereafter cited as ST. All citations will be from this edition, unless otherwise indicated. Aquinas addressed "Creation" first (c. 1252–56) in *Scriptum super libros Sententiarium* (also known as his commentary on Peter Lombard's *Sentences*).

57. ST I, q. 10, a. 3.

58. Ibid., I, q. 46, a. 2.

59. Ibid., I, q. 3, a. 4.

60. Ibid., I, q. 4, a. 1.

to itself. Everything other than God requires an efficient cause. That said, a time *before* nonbeing cannot be demonstrated either on the part of the world itself or on the part of efficient causality, which allows for God (as causal agent of creation) to have willed the universe always to exist. For Aquinas, God creating "out of nothing" means no ultimate material cause in creation and no restriction on God's freedom. God's willing of creation is an act of love, an act that is the cause of the goodness of created things.[61]

Aquinas also holds that "God is in all things," not as a part of their essence or as an accident, but as a causal agent is present to that upon which it works.[62] In this regard, Aquinas accepts Aristotle's explanation of causality as something happening metaphysically *in* the effect as the result of the activity of the cause.[63] Following this logic, Aquinas envisions God as conjoined with every being insofar as God is its causal source. Every creature depends immediately upon God for its existence, not only when it comes into being, but also at every subsequent moment that it exists. To be created, therefore, is to have existence by participation in God's sheer act of existence.[64] Thus, divine causality results in an ontological dependence of creatures on God.[65]

Aquinas has a strong sense that God transcends creation, which can be expressed symbolically as "God is above all things." The "God above" providentially governs creation through eternal law, which for Aquinas is the rational plan by which all creation is ordered to its proper end.[66] As "First Cause," God does not govern by intervening in creation's processes. Rather, God is present to the world through secondary causes that have a degree of autonomy and are able to act according to their own natures. God's creative act is fully consistent with there being real causes in the natural order. But in the dynamism of divine causality, God is "in all things" with an ongoing causal immanence to creatures.

Aquinas's contemporary, Bonaventure, also gives attention to creation.[67] Bonaventure, in contrast to Aquinas, argues that *creatio ex nihilo* logically implies a temporal (*after* nothing) beginning for creation. He provides several reasons for holding this position, the most straightforward of which is based on his preferred definition of creation: creation is to have being after nonbeing.[68] An eternal universe, therefore, involves an inherent contradiction for Bonaventure. For Bonaventure, *creatio ex nihilo* implied *post nihil*; divine creation meant a temporal beginning

---

61. Ibid. I, q. 20, a. 1–2.

62. Ibid. I, q. 8, a. 1.

63. For a more thorough explanation of Aquinas's appropriation of Aristotelian causality than is possible here, I recommend *Thomas Aquinas: The Treatise on the Divine Nature, Summa theologiae I, 1–13*, translated with commentary by Brian Shanley, O.P. (Indianapolis: Hackett, 2006), 255–58.

64. ST I, q. 44, a. 1–2.

65. For a fuller explanation of this point, see Jan A. Aersten, "Aquinas's Philosophy in Its Historical Setting," in *The Cambridge Companion to Aquinas*, ed. Norman Kretzmann and Eleonore Stump (New York: Cambridge University Press, 1993), 26.

66. ST II, q. 91, a. 1.

67. Bonaventure's starting point for his major work, *The Soul's Journey to God*, is creation. He speaks of creatures as a ladder by which we can ascend into God. See *The Soul's Journey to God: The Tree of Life, The Life of St. Francis*, trans. Ewart Cousins (New York: Paulist, 1978), ch. 1, no. 2 (60).

68. This argument is in Bonaventure's *Commentary on the Sentences of Peter Lombard*, book 2, q. 2, no.6, http://www.franciscan-archive.org/bonaventura/opera/bon02019.html (p. 22). Bonaventure holds that it makes no sense to affirm that creation is out of nothing, unless a sort of change from nothing to something is meant. If one does not affirm a change,

222

of the world. Bonaventure's arguments proceed from his view that creation must fundamentally be understood as a change from nothing to something. Furthermore, the nothingness of creation functions as an exemplar. Not only are creatures made by God from nothing, but also in their being, creatures are "almost nothing in that they participate in a finite way in being."[69] Radically contingent, creatures come to be and cease to exist.

Bonaventure's understanding of creation *ex nihilo* is complemented by his affirmation of the fundamental goodness of creation, a theme given attention, not only by one of his favorite theologians, Augustine, but also in the writings of Francis of Assisi, the founder of the religious order of which Bonaventure was a member. For Bonaventure, the "why" of creation is God manifesting divine goodness and allowing creatures to participate in the divine life. Bonaventure's writings on creation also present a view of creation that is thoroughly *Logos* centered. For Bonaventure, the whole of the world and its history constitutes a magnificent Christophany.[70]

From this survey of medieval theology, we can draw several conclusions:

1. Medieval creation theology affirms the teachings of the patristic period, especially *creatio ex nihilo*, but there is no uniformity in its interpretation.

2. God is the first transcendent cause of the world, bringing the universe into being (*creatio originans*). The initial bestowal of creaturely being by God, the universal principle of being, continues (*creatio continua*) because God is the ground for the fact that there is created causality at all and at every moment.[71] God's agency is the ground of created causality (secondary causation) and is a free expression of divine goodness.

3. Theologizing about creation during the thirteenth century signaled a new development, a "turn to nature" as Aristotle conceived of it. Aristotle not only attended to questions of causality and motion but also offered a theory of knowing that held that knowledge began with sense experience. This Aristotelian innovation in epistemology, spoken of by Aquinas as *conversio ad phantasmata*,[72] helped to pave the way for modern science. Aquinas, in contrast to many of his contemporaries, did not accept that knowing, including knowledge that God exists, is implanted in people by God. He argued, "We cannot know the things that are of God, as they are in themselves; but they are made known to us in their effects."[73] The theology of Aquinas, with its discernible "empiricist character," enabled him to insist that the created world possesses its own intelligibility, which the human mind can grasp.

4. The foundation for natural theology is laid principally by Thomas Aquinas, who argued that from the light of human reason God, the one source and goal of creation, can be known. In the *Summa theologiae*'s questions on

---

then one must mean that "out of nothing" means that nothing itself is that which is a constituent of a creature, as when one says that a table is made out of wood, one means that wood is actually now in the table as the cause of the table. We cannot, however, mean *that* about creatures, for *nothing* is no real principle of anything.

69. Cullen, *Bonaventure*, 128.

70. Ibid., 129.

71. For more on this point, see Zachary Hayes, O.F.M., *The Gift of Being: A Theology of Creation* (Collegeville, MN: Liturgical, 2001), 56ff.

72. E.g., ST I, q. 84, a. 7.

73. Ibid. I, q. 93, a. 2.

or related to creation, the God-talk is almost entirely monotheistic. In only one of his questions on creation does Aquinas directly address the Trinity, which is known not from nature but from divine revelation.[74] This helps to pave the way for further developments in natural theology and the Enlightenment distinction between the Book of God's Works and the Book of God's Words. Although knowledge of God through revelation is far superior, Aquinas demonstrated that God can be known from the study of nature. This is the case because there is consonance between the structures of the natural world and God known through faith. From the created order, through the analogy of being, humans can arrive at knowledge of the Creator.

Imago Dei

A second major creation doctrine traceable to the patristic period and developed in the Middle Ages is *imago Dei*. This doctrine is rooted in Gen. 1:26-28, which presents humankind, male and female, as made in the image and likeness of God. In biblical language, the human is *nephesh* (Gen. 2:7), meaning a living being, an existential whole *with psychosomatic unity*. However, the theological anthropology of patristic and medieval theologians presumes the Greek metaphysical composition of soul and body for *anthropos*.

Beginning with Clement of Alexandria (c. 150–215), the locus of *imago Dei* is the human soul and its intellectual capacities. Clement linked human reason to Jesus Christ, the divine *Logos* incarnate. In his writings on divine pedagogy, Clement presents Christ as the *Logos Paidagogas* for men and women, meaning that both are capable of attaining wisdom in Christ and of being led by Christ to salvation.[75]

Clement envisioned the divine image as a spiritual quality that all humans share; gendered male and female characteristics applied to the bodily level. Mindful that Gnosticism pushed Plato's concept of the human, with its emphasis on the soul and its depreciation of the body, to an extreme, Clement attributed value to the body. He argued, "Those, then, who attack that which was formed [by God], and vilify the body are wrong. They do not see that the human body was formed erect so as to contemplate heaven, and that the organization of the senses tends to knowledge, and that the members and parts are arranged for good, not pleasure."[76] However, while Clement values the bodiliness of humans, he makes it clear that the soul is the better part of the human, and the body its inferior.

Augustine further specifies the soul's superiority over the body by describing the human as a rational soul that uses a mortal and earthly

---

74. Thomas Aquinas raises the question whether creation is the role of a particular person of the Trinity and argues that creation is caused by the "whole Godhead." "Hence to create is not proper to any one Person, but is common to the whole Trinity" (ST I, q. 45, a. 6). Yet the divine Persons, "according to the nature of their procession," are distinguished. God the Father makes the creature through His Word, which is his Son; and through his love, which is the Holy Spirit (q. 45, a. 6).

75. The rationale for this position is found in Clement's claim that although "males are preferable at everything," women are capable of philosophizing "equally with men." "The Stromata or Miscellanies," *The Ante-Nicene Fathers*, Vol. 2, trans. Alexander Roberts and James Donaldson (Grand Rapids: Eerdmans, 1967), 4.8. For more on this point, see Kari Elizabeth Børresen, "God's Image, Man's Image? Patristic Interpretation of Gen. 1:27 and 1 Cor. 11:7," in *The Image of God: Gender Models in Judeo-Christian Tradition*, ed. Kari Elizabeth Børresen (Minneapolis: Fortress Press, 1991), 194–95.

76. Clement, "The Stromata or Miscellanies," 4.26.

224 body.[77] The soul's possession of ideas and its cognitional faculties and capacity for virtue bear witness to the soul's spiritual nature and its higher status in the hierarchy of being. However, he makes it clear that, although the soul is of a higher order than the body, the soul is made not from the substance of God but from nothing. To distinguish the soul from the "substance of God," Augustine speaks of it as "spiritual matter," an intermediate reality between God and physical matter.[78] This was an original innovation on the part of Augustine. Although Augustine is influenced by Platonic/Neo-Platonic hierarchical thinking, as Mary T. Clark points out, "Augustine does not go along with a Platonic identification of man with the soul."[79] Augustine argues in the *City of God*, "For man is not a body alone or a soul alone but a being composed of both."[80] While this statement may seem to be a simple truism, the issue of gendered embodiment and the cultural baggage of masculine and feminine roles make the creational symbol, *imago Dei*, a complex one for Augustine and his contemporaries.

In contrast to the so-called Ambrosiaster, who attributed creational God-likeness exclusively to males, Augustine does not associate the rational soul and, therefore, *imago Dei* exclusively with men. He makes this clear in *The Literal Meaning of Genesis*, where he writes, "Although on the physical side their sexual characteristics may suggest otherwise, namely, that man

alone is said to be the image and glory of God. By the same token, in the original creation of man, in as much as woman was a human being, she certainly had a mind, and a rational mind, and therefore she also was made to the image of God."[81] Augustine holds, therefore, that at the level of *homo interior*, woman images God in spite of her bodily sex, because by its nature, the mind contemplates the truth. However, at the level of the body, the *homo exterior*, woman is the glory of man (cf. 1 Cor. 7:11). He makes the secondary status of the embodied woman clear in *On the Trinity* when he argues, "Man is by himself alone the image of God" and posits that when engaged in temporal things, "woman together with her husband is the image of God."[82]

Arguably for its time, Augustine's treatment of *imago Dei* in a way that acknowledged its presence in women while also upholding the godlike autonomy of men was an original contribution. However, his most original theological contribution was linking the human as *imago Dei* with God as Trinity. Although Augustine lays the groundwork for a trinitarian interpretation of *imago Dei* in *The Confessions*,[83] it is in *On the Trinity* that he painstakingly explores the multiple ways in which humans image the triune God. His exploration culminates with an analogy of the human soul and its faculties applied to the triune God. The mind's capacity for remembering, knowing, and loving affirms the presence of God as Father, Son and Holy Spirit

---

77. Augustine, *The Catholic and Manichaen Ways of Life*, trans. Donald A. Gallager and Idella J. Galliger (Washington, DC: Catholic University of America Press, 1966), 1.27.52.

78. Augustine, *The Literal Meaning of Genesis*, 7.28.43; 7.7.

79. Mary T. Clark, *Augustine* (Washington, DC: Georgetown University Press, 1994), 32.

80. Ibid. Clark cites the *City of God*, 13.24.

81. Augustine, *The Literal Meaning of Genesis*, 3.22.34.

82. Augustine, *The Trinity*, trans. Edmund Hill, O.P., ed. John E. Rotelle, O.S.A. (Brooklyn: New City, 1991), 12.7.10.

83. Augustine, *The Confessions*, 12.7.7, in which Augustine questions how is it possible for any one to understand the "one Trinity and tribunal Unity."

within the soul.[84] This analogy is an example of *ratio superior*, the highest level of mind contemplating God. Not merely a static metaphysical "given," for Augustine, the divine image in the human soul is a dynamic reality whereby the human is oriented toward relationship with God. For through the help of God's grace, one's *imago Dei* can be renewed daily.

Although his primary interest is the "great question" of the human soul and *imago Dei*,[85] Augustine acknowledges that traces of the Trinity can be experienced not only in the rational soul, but also in the "outer man"—the human body.[86] It is by the *ratio inferior* and its focus on external things that one finds in creatures "traces" of the Trinity, which direct one's gaze "at the creator."

Augustine, according to Clark, never made up his mind regarding the question of the origin of the human soul. However, another Western theologian, Hilary of Poitiers (c. 315–367), did. He argued that though flesh is always born of flesh, "the soul of the body [can] be from nowhere else than from God."[87] Later, Thomas Aquinas would echo Hilary. In the context of interpreting Gen. 1:27, where God created humankind in the divine image, Aquinas writes, "Man is like to God in his soul." For him, this means that the human soul could be made only by [direct] creation, even though other life forms [plant and animal species] could come into existence by generation.[88]

The emphasis on the soul should not be construed as Aquinas adhering to the Platonic dualism that depicted the human soul as the self and the body as its instrument. Aquinas accepts Aristotle's notion of the soul as the form-giving first principle that animates any living thing, whether plant, animal, or human.[89] In the case of the human being, the soul that gives form to the body is rational and, therefore, distinct from the vegetative soul of a plant and the sensate soul of an animal. The body is only truly human through the rational soul that determines the body while also transcending it in its spiritual capacities. At the time of death, although the person is one unified substance, the soul of a human does not die. Qualifying the Aristotelian understanding of soul, Aquinas adapts the Platonic notion of the soul as subsistent (self-existent). The soul as rational is incorruptible spirit, surviving after the body dies.[90]

Aquinas envisioned the human creature as an intelligent being and, as such, prone to raise questions. In Question 93 of the *Summa theologiae* I, entitled "The End or Term of the Production of Man," Aquinas poses a series of related questions about the human person as *imago Dei*. He reminds his reader at the outset that only Christ is the perfect image of the invisible God (a. 1). Humans are created toward or after the divine image, because among creatures, humans with their intellectual capacities can contemplate the divine mysteries (a. 2). Aquinas also

---

84. Augustine, *The Trinity*, 17.23.

85. Ibid., 14.2.6.

86. Ibid., 11.prologue.1.

87. Hilary of Poitiers, *On the Trinity*, trans. Stephen McKenna (New York: Fathers of the Church, 1954), 10.22.

88. ST I, q. 90, a. 2; see also Aquinas's *Summa contra Gentiles*, book 2, q. 87. In ST I, q. 90, a. 1, Aquinas will support Augustine's insistence that the soul is not of the substance of God but is created by divine will from nothing.

89. ST I, q. 75, a. 1.

90. Ibid., I, q. 75, a. 6. Aquinas spoke of the incorruptibility of the human soul on the basis of Scripture and reserved immortality for the risen Christ, the first humans in paradise, and human beings after the resurrection of the dead.

provides three ways in which humans image God: (1) as a natural aptitude for understanding and loving, an aptitude common to all humans; (2) as actually and habitually knowing and loving God imperfectly, in conformity to grace; and (3) as knowing and loving God perfectly, in the likeness of God's glory.[91] In the first objection that follows, Aquinas insists, in company with Augustine, that the image of God, "in its principal signification, namely the intellectual nature, is found both in man and in woman." He holds this to be true, even though he argued earlier, following Aristotle, that by nature woman is a "defective and misbegotten" creature (q. 93, a. 1).

Aquinas argues that the image of the Trinity is proper to the soul, but he provides an explanation that differs from that of Augustine. Taking his analysis of the trinitarian processions as his starting point, Aquinas states that the Trinity is found in "the acts of the soul, that is, inasmuch as from the knowledge which we possess, by actual thought we form an internal word and thence break forth into love."[92]

Although emphasizing the soul in his analysis of *imago Dei*, Aquinas does not neglect the question of whether the human body images God. To this question, Aquinas replies that the image of God in man is not to be found in his bodily shape, but since "it is adapted to look upward to heaven, we may rightly say that it is made to God's image and likeness." However, "this is not to be understood as though the image of God were in man's body; but in the sense that the very shape of the human body represents the image of God in the soul by way of a trace."[93]

Aquinas's affirmation of the "trace" of God in the human body resonates with Augustine's affirmation of the trace of the trinitarian image in the bodiliness of humans. Earlier in the *Summa theologiae*, Aquinas speaks of experiencing "traces" of the Trinity in all of creation and speaks of them as manifestations of divine goodness: "[God] brought things into existence so that his goodness might be communicated to creatures, and re-enacted through them. And because one single creature was not enough, he produced many and diverse [creatures], so that what was wanting to one expression of the divine goodness might be supplied by another, for goodness, which in God is single and uniform, in creatures is multiple and scattered. Hence the whole universe less completely than one [creature] alone shares in and represents the divine goodness."[94] Aquinas's words poignantly draw attention to the sacramental character of creation. Each creature, possessing an integrity of its own and in its own distinctive way, is revelatory of God. Further, in his theological reflections on the days of creation, Aquinas calls God's creative processes on days four, five, and six "works of adornment."[95] He professes that birds and fish are called into being by God to embellish creation with beauty. In the richly diverse creation with its multiple traces of the Trinity, God provides humans with a window to the divine.

Patristic and medieval theological reflections on *imago Dei* result in a development that, while taking Gen. 1:27 as its inspiration, exceeds the meaning invested in it by the biblical

---

91. Ibid., 1, q. 93, a. 4.

92. Ibid., 1, q. 93, a. 7.

93. Ibid., 1, q. 93, a. 6.

94. Ibid., 1, q. 47, a. 1.

95. Ibid., 1, qs. 70–72. The works of adornment are distinguished from the works of the other days, which are works of (initial) creation and of distinction.

authors and redactors. Drawing on the insights of the *scientia* of their times, theologians such as Augustine and Aquinas attempted to interpret what it means to say that humans are created in the image of God. Yes, it means that humans are both like and unlike other creatures. Humans have mammal bodies but are more than animals. *Imago Dei* symbolically affirms this "more" by drawing attention to a spiritual core (the rational soul) that makes humans, male and female, somewhat like God. Therefore, to understand the human person, one must first view her/him in relation to God and only then in relation to creatures.

Creation Theology and the Natural Sciences

No treatment of creation theology would be complete without attention to the challenges posed to it by Galileo Galilei (1564–1642) and Charles Darwin (1809–82). Where the conception of the relationship of creation theology and natural science is concerned, the story of Galileo's defense of the Copernican heliocentric system against Roman Catholic Church opposition to it extends beyond factual history and functions as a major iconic myth of the early Enlightenment. Charles Darwin also has long symbolized a clash of authorities: on one side, science and the empirically based evolution theory, and on the other, Christianity and the biblically rooted beliefs about the origin of creatures. Naturalistic evolution, associated with the progressive philosophy of modernity, has long func-

tioned as a symbol for the decline of Christian influence in Western culture.

The Cosmos

In the popular imagination, since Galileo's seventeenth-century clash was with the authorities of the Catholic Church, Catholicism is often typified as obscurantist where scientific progress is concerned. Galileo is seen as championing Nicholas Copernicus's conception of a heliocentric cosmos based on the support of telescopic sightings and mathematical calculations. The church, ignoring Copernicus and seeking to defeat Galileo, is depicted as mindlessly supporting the Aristotelian-Ptolemaic conception of the cosmos as a well-ordered geocentric system that it had assimilated and harmonized with its creation faith during the late Middle Ages.[96] By protecting a geocentric cosmos, church authorities are seen as also protecting the long-held belief that human creatures and their salvation are God's most central concern.

It is true that seventeenth-century Catholic theology, on the basis of Aristotle's common-sense empiricism, assumed that the earth was at rest at the center of the cosmos and that God (the Unmoved Mover) set the heavens in motion in such a way that they rotate around it in concentric spheres. This conception fit well with belief that God created the cosmos in accordance with the divine wisdom and rationality. Since the human, as *imago Dei*, occupies the highest level of the earthly chain of being, humans are capable of participating in the rationality of the Creator. Therefore, in principle, humans

---

96. Although Aristotle's books were banned from public reading by Pope Gregory IX in 1210 at the University of Paris; it would seem that Gregory's long-term plan was to provide Aristotle's works to students in better traslation. In 1366 the legates of Urban V required knowledge of all works of Aristotle for the license to teach there. See Christopher B. Kaiser, *Creational Theology and the History of Physical Science: The Creationist Tradition from Basil to Bohr* (New York: Brill, 1997), 86–87.

228 can understand creation. This was the accepted natural philosophy when Copernicus wrote his treatise *On the Revolutions of the Celestial Spheres* (1543).

The fact that Copernicus's treatise was published two years before the Council of Trent began is significant for the church's judgment against the heliocentric model of the universe when Galileo proposed it in 1616. At Trent, the church rejected Martin Luther's doctrine of private interpretation of the Bible.[97] Authority to interpret sacred Scripture was reserved for the Roman Catholic Church. What was not addressed at the Council of Trent was how biblical texts should be interpreted.

In the years after Trent, Catholic biblical interpretation, like its Protestant counterpart, would de facto take a "turn to the literal."[98] This is evident in Robert Cardinal Bellarmine's *Controversies*, in which he stressed, "In the Scriptures not only the opinions expressed but each and every word pertains to the faith."[99] Application of this criterion led to the judgment that the Aristotelian geocentric model was true because it was compatible with Scripture, including Josh. 10:12-13: "On this day, when the LORD delivered up the Amorites to the Israelites, Joshua prayed to the LORD, and said in the presence of Israel: 'Stand still, O sun, at Gibeon, O moon, in the valley of Aijalon!' And the sun stood still, and the moon stayed, while the nation took vengeance on its foes. . . . The sun halted in the middle of the sky; and did not hurry to set for about a whole day." In accepting this text as literally true, the church's representatives held that the earth's motion around the sun, and not the sun around the earth, was at the very least erroneous, if not heretical. By taking this position, the church ignored the possibility that the description of the earth and sun in Joshua 10 accommodated the commonsense experience of the people for whom it was originally written.

In 1616, Catholic Church authorities formally condemned the Copernican system. Galileo was not mentioned by name. According to Ernan McMullin, Pope Paul V had personally intervened to instruct Cardinal Bellarmine to direct Galileo privately to abandon the Copernican view. Galileo complied until 1632, at which time he published his *Dialogue on Two Chief World-Systems*. In this work, Galileo presented Copernican heliocentrism as a "hypothesis."[100] Largely because of this strategy, he managed to obtain an imprimatur for the *Dialogue*. It was the judgment of Pope Urban VII and the papal court, however, that Galileo had obtained the imprimatur fraudulently. He neglected to inform the censors of the earlier injunction not to hold, defend, or teach the Copernican view. Galileo admitted his noncompliance with the

---

97. At Session IV of the Council of Trent (1546), it was decreed that in matters of faith and morals no one relying on his own judgment could interpret biblical texts contrary to the sense that the church, to whom it belongs to judge their true meaning, has held. In addition, no one was permitted to interpret the Bible contrary to the sense of the unanimous agreement of the Fathers, even though such interpretations were not published. Those who did otherwise could expect punishment in accordance with the penalties prescribed by the law (DS 1507).

98. For more on Catholic biblical literalism, see Irving A. Kelter, "The Refusal to Accommodate: Jesuit Exegesis and the Copernican System," in *The Church and Galileo*, ed. Ernan McMullin (Notre Dame, IN: University of Notre Dame Press, 2005), 38–45.

99. *De controversiis* 2.2.12, cited by Richard J. Blackwell, *Galileo, Bellarmine, and the Bible* (Notre Dame, IN: University of Notre Dame Press, 1991), 31.

100. Ernan McMullin, "Introduction," in McMullin, *The Church and Galileo*, 3–4.

1616 agreement made with Bellarmine, who had died in 1621, and offered to add a new section to the *Dialogue* to soften his positions. The court was not persuaded, and Galileo received a sentence that required him to live under house arrest until his death in 1642.[101]

The language of Galileo's judgment is significant for understanding what was at stake regarding his case. He was judged to be "vehemently suspect of [the] heresy" of "having held and believed a doctrine which is false and contrary to Holy Scripture."[102] Attention not only to Scripture but also to its interpretation by the fathers of the church was of great importance to Galileo's campaign to win over the papacy in support of Copernicus's heliocentric system. This is made clear early on, when in 1615 he wrote a *Letter to the Grand Duchess Christina*, trusting that his generous benefactor would share it widely. In that letter, Galileo was likely influenced by the exegetical principles that Benito Pereyra, S.J., applied in his multivolume work on the book of Genesis.[103] In his *Letter*, Galileo pointed out that the Bible and science have different goals or ends. While granting that the "Bible can never speak untruth—whenever its true meaning is understood," he drew on Augustine to argue that genuine conflict between the two sources of truth—the truth of Holy Scripture and the truth of the solid reasons and experiences of human knowledge—is impossible.

Galileo specifically argued that whether the earth is located at the center of the created cosmos or off to one side is a trivial matter and not heretical, because it has no relevance for the salvation of souls. Surely, where Scripture is concerned, the intention of the Holy Spirit is "to teach us how one goes to heaven, [and] not how heaven goes."[104] By marshaling such a public argument based on his own interpretation of the Bible, Galileo, the astronomer and natural philosopher, put himself in the position of challenging the Catholic Church's authoritative interpretation of biblical texts.

From the perspective of seventeenth-century history, the interaction between Galileo and Roman Catholic Church authorities was not so much a conflict between natural philosophy and Roman Catholic creation doctrine as it was two worldviews bypassing each other without substantive contact. The nascent scientific worldview, with a yet to be widely accepted theory of the then-known universe, was of a different order than a Catholic worldview, which treated sacred Scripture as *the* source of truth without recognition of the limitations of interpreting it through the lenses of literalism and Aristotelian thought.

At the Second Vatican Council in the course of the preparations of *Gaudium et spes* (the Pastoral Constitution on the Modern World), a proposal to acknowledge the church's error with regard to Galileo was made but finally rejected as "inopportune."[105] In 1979, Pope John Paul II judged that the opportune moment for addressing the Galileo case had arrived. A

101. The *Dialogue* was placed on the Index of Forbidden Books, where it would remain until 1822.

102. McMullin, "Introduction," 5.

103. Kelter, "The Refusal to Accommodate," notes that Galileo was influenced by Pereyra's *Commentariorum et disputationum in genesium* (Rome, 1589–98), even though he had "devotion to such scientific ideas as the earth's centrality and mobility" (46–47).

104. Galileo, "Letter to the Grand Duchess Christina," in *Discoveries and Opinions of Galileo* (New York: Doubleday, 1957), 197.

105. McMullin, "Introduction," 7.

commission to study the Galileo case was created in 1981, with a final report presented to the Pontifical Academy of Science in 1992. Upon his reception of the report, John Paul II spoke of the Galileo affair as a "myth . . . far removed from reality."[106]

The heliocentric cosmology of the seventeenth century paved the way for the current widely accepted cosmological theory known as the "big bang." This theory envisions a universe that began a finite time ago from the point of an initial singularity approximately 13.7 billion years ago. The big bang envisions the universe as having originated from a primeval, unimaginably condensed mass of fundamental particles and energy transformed by exploding and then continually expanding to the present observable universe with its billions of galaxies and stars.

Scientists including James S. Trefil have used the term *creation* with reference to big-bang cosmology.[107] To speak of the big bang theory in this way, however, represents the epitome of religious speech. Long before Trefil, an explicitly religious application of creation *ex nihilo* to the big bang theory was made by a noteworthy Christian churchman, Pope Pius XII, who in 1951, prior to the confirmation of the big bang theory, hailed it as unveiling the secrets of nature and thereby disclosing the creative work of God.[108] For Pius XII, the significance of the big bang theory lay in the testimony it gave to creation in time already available from divine revelation.[109]

In 1951, however, Georges Lemaître, one of the chief architects of the big bang theory, objected to the papal endorsement. The objection by Lemaître, a priest and scientist, is particularly significant, since he was a member of the Pontifical Academy of Science.[110] For one thing, Lemaître recognized that the big bang theory had not yet received the support needed to convince the scientific community of its merit. However, even today there are good reasons for theologians not to look to a cosmological theory as corroborating proof for the doctrine of creation, specifically *creatio ex nihilo*. Caution is needed, because although the big bang theory does support an initial singularity nearly 13.7 billion years ago, the big bang does not refer to the ultimate beginning of time. The big bang theory provides a plausible account of the evolution of the universe from a fraction of a second after the initial singularity that set in process the expanding universe we can observe. It does

---

106. John Paul II, "Lessons of the Galileo Case," *Origins* 22 (1992): sec. 11, no. 1, 372.

107. The title of Trefil monograph is *The Moment of Creation: Big Bang Physics from Before the First Millisecond to the Present Universe* (Mineola, NY: Dover, 2004).

108. Support for the big-bang theory was made firm in 1964 by Arno Penzias and Robert Wilson, radio astronomers working at an AT&T Bell Laboratories, who detected microwaves coming to earth from outside of the earth's atmosphere and beyond the Milky Way. This discovery added support to the argument that the universe had expanded from an initial singularity to proportions so enormous that light waves had red-shifted (due to the Doppler effect) to the point where they could be detected as microwave radiation. See James S. Trefil, *The Moment of Creation*, 26–29.

109. Pope Pius XII's address to the Pontifical Academy of Sciences appeared in *Catholic Mind* 50 (1952): 189–91; interest in the pope's appraisal from the scientific community is evident in its publication in the *Bulletin of the Atomic Scientists* 8 (1952): 143–46, 165.

110. Georges Lemaître first formulated the theory of the primeval atom, which prepared the way for the theory of the big bang. Ernan McMullin, a student of Lemaître at the time, gives a firsthand account of his displeasure at the concordism of Pius XII in "How Should Cosmology Relate to Theology?" in *The Sciences and Theology in the Twentieth Century*, ed. Arthur R. Peacocke (Notre Dame, IN: Notre Dame University Press, 1981), 53, n. 25.

not account for an absolute beginning per se. The initial singularity could very well have been preceded by a contraction as part of an infinitely repeatable cycle of an oscillating universe.

Beyond these scientific reasons, on principle, it is unwise for the church or its theologians to equate any scientific theory of the universe's beginnings with the ancient doctrine of creation *ex nihilo*, which at its origins was founded on metaphysical reasoning and not empirical observation and mathematical models. *Creatio ex nihilo* is a doctrine about God who freely chose to create and of the dependence on God for existence. History has demonstrated that at times God has been called upon to explain a "gap" in scientific reasoning, only to have that gap filled later by a new advancement of science. Currently, there are scientists working on theories that may prove to be more adequate explanations of the cosmos than the big bang theory.

The Evolution of Species

Controversy has swirled around Darwinian evolution since *The Origin of Species* was first published in 1859.[111] For the majority of Americans, Darwin is readily associated with conflict between science and religion, because his theory of the origin of species is perceived to challenge the veracity of the Genesis creation accounts.

From this challenge, it would seem to be a short step to questioning the inerrancy of the Bible, the existence of a Creator God, and the doctrine of *imago Dei*.

Darwin's goal, however, was not to oppose biblical creation or a Creator, but rather to point to the shortcomings of Natural Theology, which was the "science" he studied while a theology student at the University of Cambridge. *Natural Theology* by William Paley (1743–1805), which treated observations of nature as a source for demonstrating the existence and attributes of God, was required reading at Cambridge.[112] The purpose of the Natural Theology of Darwin's era was to explain the workings of nature in order to give suitable honor and praise to God. Limiting its focus to the "Book of God's Works," Natural Theology was separate and distinct from the study of the Bible, the "Book of God's Word." Natural Theologians studied nature with the goal of drawing attention to God's design for and direct involvement in creation. Darwin's detailed observations led him to a different emphasis, guided by a fundamental question: How on the basis of observation could one explain the great variety of existing species and the extinction of numerous others? His answer was that species descended over time due to a process of "natural selection" that ensured the "survival of the fittest."[113]

111. Charles Darwin, *The Origin of Species by Means of Natural Selection, or the Preservation of Favored Races in the Struggle of Life* (1st ed., 1859; 6th ed., 1872; New York: Random House, 1993).

112. One of the earliest exponents of natural theology was Raymond de Sabunde, who published *Theologia Naturalis* in 1438. Natural theology gradually rose to importance in England in the seventeenth century. Robert Boyle (1627–91) and Isaac Newton (1642–1727) were technically "natural theologians" (although today they are known as "scientists"); both interpreted the world's operations by mechanical principles within a theistic framework. William Paley, author of *Natural Theology, or Evidences for the Existence and Attributes of the Deity* (London: R. Faulder, 1802), was the most influential Natural Theologian of the nineteenth century. In *Natural Theology*, he proposed the analogy of a watchmaker to support the existence of a transcendent designer—God—who was the source of the well-ordered natural world. A series of books devoted to Natural Theology (1833–40), known as the *Bridgewater Treatises*, supported by a generous grant by F. H. Egerton, Earl of Bridgewater, furthered Paley's project.

113. Darwin, *The Origin of Species*, ch. 5, p. 108 and passim.

Influential naturalists, many of whom were also Anglican clergy, such as William Wilberforce, bishop of Oxford, could not accept Darwin's thesis in *The Origin of Species* because they judged the evidence for natural selection to be not only too thin but also an affront to God's purposeful design of nature and benevolent agency in the world. Darwin questioned the validity of these positions, arguing that the gradual descent of species was in agreement with the "laws impressed on matter by the Creator."[114]

Because of his rejection of a dominant conception of God—a transcendent divine sovereign who not only designed creation but also directly intervened in it by the "special creation" of each species—Darwin's relationship to Christianity is complex, if not outright ambivalent. Darwin believed that science should be agnostic in its goals and methodology. He stressed that expressions used by Natural Theologians, such as the divine "plan of creation" and "special creation," explain nothing, because one gains no new knowledge from such language.[115]

The depth of Darwin's agnosticism, however, is difficult to discern. Two quotes from his writings clearly illustrate this. The first is found in the conclusions section of the sixth edition of *The Origin of Species*, in which he writes, "There is grandeur in this view of life [meaning the descent of species by natural selection] with its several powers, having been originally breathed by the Creator into new forms or into one; and that while this planet has gone cycling on according to the fixed laws of gravity, from so simple a beginning, endless forms most beautiful and most wonderful have been, and are being evolved."[116] Some have argued that Darwin wrote this statement merely to gain the support of Christians for his controversial theory. The second quote is found in his autobiography. There he reflects that it was impossible for him to conceive "that this grand and wondrous universe with our conscious selves, arose entirely through chance. . . . [This] seems to me to be the chief argument for the existence of God."[117]

Whatever his intention in writing these reflections, the emphases in what would come to be known as the natural science of biological evolution resulted in the "revolution" that Darwin anticipated.[118] From the 1650s to about 1860, most people in Great Britain and beyond assumed that the productive harmony between the study of the Book of God's Words and the Book of God's Work would continue. After Darwin, that would not be the case.

What was the Roman Catholic Church's response to Darwin's *The Origin of Species*? Vatican authorities did not condemn the theory of biological evolution but signaled caution. This is evident in the First Vatican Council's *Dei filius* (Dogmatic Constitution on the Catholic Faith, 1870) and the anathemas attached to it. In para-

---

114. Ibid., ch. 15, pp. 645, 647. Some of Darwin's contemporaries supported his explanations of species transformation, arguing that they were compatible with Christianity because they presupposed an original Creator, the primary cause who artfully used secondary causality. See, for example, Frederick Temple's "Apparent Collision between Religion and the Doctrine of Evolution" (1884), reprinted in Tess Cosslett, *Science and Religion in the Nineteenth Century* (Cambridge: Cambridge University Press, 1984), 192–204.

115. Darwin, *The Origin of Species*, ch. 15.

116. Ibid., ch.15, 649.

117. Charles Darwin, *The Autobiography of Charles Darwin, with Two Appendices*, ed. Francis Darwin (1893; repr., London: Watta & Co., 1929), 130.

118. Darwin, *The Origin of Species*, ch. 15, p. 643.

graph 9 of the main text, it states, "All faithful Christians are forbidden to defend as the legitimate conclusions of science those opinions which are known to be contrary to the doctrine of faith" (DS 1798). To this statement are attached more specific anathemas. The first condemns the denial of the one true God, Creator of all things visible and invisible (DS 1801). The second condemns materialism, which affirms the existence of nothing besides matter (DS 1802).

Dei filius was approved before Darwin's second major monograph, *The Descent of Man* (1871), in which he made clear what was implied regarding the evolution of *Homo sapiens* in *The Origin of Species*. All species are descendants of a common ancestor. Humans are historically and organically connected not only to other primates, but also to all of earth's species.

The evolution of the human species would receive the attention of Pope Pius XII in his 1950 encyclical *Humani generis* (Concerning Certain False Opinions).[119] Signaling that the theory of biological evolution was not irreconcilable with Catholic teaching, Pius XII wrote about evolution in general terms, noting the conjectural nature of scientific theories.[120] Apart from a broad treatment of scientific epistemology, Pius XII does have a focal concern, and that is the conception of the origins of the human species. While the church does not prohibit scientific research on the origin of the human body, the pope stresses that the soul cannot be conceived of as merely evolving from matter. Such a position conflicts with church teaching on the creation of the human person and the doctrine of *imago Dei*.[121]

Forty-six years later, another pope, John Paul II, would return to the topic of evolution. In a 1996 message to the Pontifical Academy of Science, John Paul II notes that Pius XII had already affirmed biological evolution to be "an open question, as long as it confines its speculation to the development, from other living matter already in existence, of the human body."[122] Recognizing that evolution now has a much higher degree of acceptance by scientists due to new discoveries, John Paul II points out that evolution is more than an open question, and he effectively accepts the evolutionary framework of biology as scientific fact. He also argues that, since there is a plurality of theories about the mechanisms of evolution, caution is needed. Some theories are dependent on extra-scientific notions borrowed from natural philosophy, which promote reductionistic materialism (the idea that everything, including thoughts, feelings, and religious faith, can be explained in terms of material, physical phenomena).[123]

Citing Pope Leo XIII's position that "[scientific] truth cannot contradict [revealed] truth,"[124]

---

119. By 1950, the so-called New Synthesis of evolution and population genetics, also known as Neo-Darwinism, had signaled a new development in evolutionary biology.

120. Pius XII, *Humani generis* (Concerning Certain False Opinions), in *Acta Apostolicae Sedis* 42 (1950).

121. The question of monogenism versus polygenism (i.e., the question whether the human race must be conceived as descending from a single couple or can be considered to originate from several couples from different parts of the world) is connected with the doctrine of original sin in which the sin of Adam (and Eve) is inherited by all humans. Since Genesis 3 is recognized by Catholic scholars to be symbolic rather than historical, the debate about monogenism versus polygenism is not given attention here.

122. John Paul II, "Message to Pontifical Academy of Sciences on Evolution," *Origins* 26 (1996): 351; the citation is from the encyclical *Humani generis* (Concerning Certain False Opinions), in *Acta Apostolicae Sedis* 42 (1950): 575–76.

123. Ibid.; cf. *Fides et Ratio*, ch. 7.

124. Ibid., 351. John Paul II here is referring to a position in Leo XIII's 1893 encyclical *Providentissimus Deus* (On the

234   John Paul II contends that those theories, which claim that the human spirit emerged from the forces of matter or is a mere epiphenomenon of this matter, are incompatible with a fundamental truth expressed by Pope Pius XII: "Souls are immediately created by God."[125] At the same time, such materialist theories reject the important divinely revealed truth about humans as the creatures made "in the image and likeness of God" (Gen. 1:26).[126] To be human is to have a spiritual soul, the basis for the recognition of "an ontological difference in humans,"[127] which makes *Homo sapiens* a species distinct from the rest of earth's life forms.

Further, the moment of transition to the spiritual in hominids cannot be the object of scientific observation. The sciences can discover valuable signs indicating what is specific to the human species, but since the sciences are limited to the observable, they cannot fully account for humans' spiritual transcendence. For John Paul II, the ontological difference that makes humans distinct from other primates falls within the competence of philosophical analysis. Theology in turn builds on this analysis by articulating "its ultimate meaning according to the Creator's plans."[128]

Christian Challenges to Darwinian Evolution: Creation Science and Intelligent Design

During the forty-six intervening years between the two papal statements on evolution, Christians in the United States initiated two distinct yet related responses to Darwinian evolution: Creation Science and Intelligent Design. Creation Science, traceable to the late 1960s, is defined as "the scientific evidences for creation and inferences from those scientific evidences."[129] By emphasizing scientific evidence and omitting reference to God, Henry Morris (1919–2006), the major founder of "Creation Science," believed he had a biblically compatible science to rival Darwinian evolution.[130]

Beginning not as a result of scientific discovery but as a political movement, Creation Science's major goal was to gain "balanced treatment" alongside Darwinian evolution in American public schools. In the course of its development, Creation Science set itself apart from Darwinian evolution by emphasizing the following core teachings:

Study of Sacred Scripture) (Washington, DC: National Catholic Welfare Conference; reprinted by the Catholic Biblical Association, 1964), 27.

125. "Message to Pontifical Academy of Sciences on Evolution," 352; Once again John Paul II refers to *Humanae Generis*, 575.

126. John Paul II, "Message to Pontifical Academy of Sciences," 352.

127. Ibid.

128. Ibid. In taking this position, Pope John Paul II continues a long tradition, which as already noted, stems from Hilary of Poitiers, who argued that "the soul of the [human] body [can] be from nowhere else than from God." *On the Trinity*, 10.22.413.

129. Section 4 of Arkansas Act no. 590, *Science, Technology and Human Values* 7 (1982): 11.

130. Henry Morris, the founding director of the Institute for Creation Research, earned his doctorate from the University of Minnesota and was a professor of hydraulic engineering at Virginia Polytechnic Institute, Blacksburg, Virginia. For a more thorough treatment of Creation Science than is possible here, see his *History of Modern Creationism*, 2nd ed. (El Cajon, CA: Institution for Creation Research, 1993).

1. The sudden creation of the universe, energy, and life from nothing (cf. *creatio ex nihilo*);

2. The insufficiency of mutation and natural selection in bringing about development of all living species from a single organism (cf. "special creation" of every kind of species);

3. The occurrence of changes in living species only within fixed limits of originally created plant and animal forms (limited acceptance of adaptive microevolution but not of macroevolution resulting in new species);

4. Separate ancestry for humans and apes (*Homo sapiens*' uniqueness among species as *imago Dei*);

5. Explanation of the earth's geology and fossil history by catastrophism, including the occurrence of a worldwide flood (cf. the flood as punishment for sin and Noah's ark; Genesis 6–9);[131]

6. A young earth, less than ten thousand years old (contra big-bang cosmology).[132]

Given Creation Science texts' intended audience—high school students—separating the ancestry of humans and apes was deemed especially important. Morris argued that by teaching Darwinian evolution, schools may be robbing their students' lives of "meaning and purpose in view of the implanted concept that the student is merely a chance product of a meaningless, random process."[133]

To convince others that Creation Science was worthy of inclusion in school curricula, the major strategy was to present Creation Science as superior to Darwinian evolution because evolutionists themselves envision their science as merely theory. In contrast, Creation Science is fact (its underlying source is the inerrant biblical word). The promotion of the use of Creation Science textbooks in public schools sparked a heated controversy—one waged in American courts. On June 19, 1987, the United States Supreme Court struck down the Louisiana Balanced Treatment Act on the grounds that requiring Creation Science to be taught in public schools along side evolution was unconstitutional. Clearly, this law was intended to advance a particular religion.[134]

In the wake of the banning of Creation Science in public schools, a lawyer and law professor named Philip E. Johnson launched a new initiative, which he called Intelligent Design. In a 1990 *First Things* article, Johnson stressed that Darwinian evolution promotes a naturalistic dogma, ruling out not only the creationism of biblical fundamentalists, but also "*any* [italics his] invocation of a creative intelligence or purpose outside the natural order."[135] Johnson did not delve into the ways that a designing

---

131. John C. Whitcomb Jr. and Henry M. Morris, *The Genesis Flood* (Philadelphia: Presbyterian and Reformed, 1961). Two years after *The Genesis Flood* was published, Morris and other like-minded scientists founded the Creation Research Society, dedicated to established scientific support for the Genesis creation story and to fund Creation Science textbooks.

132. Sec. 4 of Arkansas Act no. 590. The full text of this act can be found in *Science, Technology and Human Values* 7 (1982): 11–13.

133. Henry Morris, *Scientific Creationism* (Green Forest, AR: Master, 1974), 15.

134. The full title of the act is the Balanced Treatment for Creation-Science and Evolution Science; the U.S. Supreme Court case is known as *Edwards v. Aguillard*; available at http://www.talkorigins.org/faqs/edwards-v-aguillard.html.

135. Phillip E. Johnson, "Evolution as Dogma: The Establishment of Naturalism," originally published in *First Things*

236 intelligence can be supported scientifically, but did assert that Darwinian evolution cannot account for the perception of intelligence at work in the law-like properties of nature. In a book published a year later, entitled *Darwin on Trial*, Johnson analyzed the demise of Creation Science's balanced-treatment strategy[136] and proposed "intelligent design"[137] not as an attempt to replace biological evolution, but rather to resolve what is lacking in it with a new and superior scientific paradigm.

Unlike Creation Science, contributors to Intelligent Design theory do not subscribe to the sudden creation of the universe less than ten thousand years ago. Nor do they challenge the fossil evidence that there has been a sequence of life forms, which have appeared and become extinct over many millions of years. Intelligent Design, however, does argue that the complexity and variety of life on earth is far too sophisticated to have evolved by chance mutations, as Neo-Darwinism proposes. Some form of unseen intelligence must directly guide the order perceived in nature. To account for the unseen intelligence, William Dembski has proposed a theory known as Design Inference, which he believes "sweeps the field [of biology] clear of chance hypotheses."[138]

Intelligent Design adherents, such as the biochemist Michael Behe, accept the basic process of evolution at the micro level but make a case for the necessity of something like Design Inference for life to have begun and to have developed the "irreducible complexity" evident in living species.[139] To account for the appearance of significant phenomena, such as self-propelling bacteria, explanations based on material causes, random mutations, and the dynamics of natural selection are deemed inadequate.

This assessment of conventional evolution science is in keeping with a major goal of the Intelligent Design movement: the defeat of the metaphysical naturalism that they associate with Neo-Darwinian macroevolution. While the scientific community does have a commitment to *methodological* naturalism and is, therefore, agnostic where the question of God's role in evolutionary processes is concerned, *metaphysical* naturalism is beyond the scope of the natural sciences. Methodological naturalism is why biologists limit themselves to the study of empirical evidence for cause-effect steps oc-

6 (1990): 15–22, reprinted in *Intelligent Design Creationism and Its Critics: Philosophical, Theological and Scientific Perspectives*, ed. Robert T. Pennock (Cambridge/London: Bradford, MIT Press, 2001), 63.

136. Phillip E. Johnson, *Darwin on Trial* (Washington, DC: Regnery Gateway, 1991), 3–14.

137. Ibid., 17 (Intelligent Design is presented as a replacement for Darwinian "purposeless natural processes"), 119, 146, 205 (in an endnote). The term *intelligent design*, however, did not originate with Johnson. It can be found in an early twentieth-century essay by Ferdinand Canning Scott Schiller in which he accepts biological evolution as a credible explanation but argues, "It will not be possible to rule out the supposition that the process of evolution may be guided by an intelligent design." See F. C. S. Schiller, "Darwinism and Design Argument," in Schiller, *Humanism: Philosophical Essays* (New York: Macmillan, 1903), 141.

138. William A. Dembski, *The Design Inference: Eliminating Chance through Small Probabilities* (Cambridge: Cambridge University Press, 1998), 7. The crux of Dembski's argument is his "Law of Small Probabilities," which states, "Specified events of small probability do not occur by chance"; design is inferred (5). From the standpoint of the accepted epistemology of contemporary science, inference is of the order of "an argument from silence" (cf. Tertullian, *The Treatise against Hermogenes*).

139. Michael J. Behe, *Darwin's Black Box: The Biochemical Challenge to Evolution* (New York: Simon & Schuster, 1996), 39–45. Behe self-identifies as a Catholic and is a senior fellow of the Discovery Institute's Center for Science and Culture, Seattle, Washington.

curring in evolution. By keeping within the methodological boundaries of natural science, biologists rule out the question of the existence of a First Cause or of intervening operations by a transcendent designer on the grounds that there is no empirical evidence that provides testable confirmation of either. For supporters of Intelligent Design, such as Phillip Johnson, the naturalism of evolutionary biology is tantamount to a godless materialism.[140]

Intelligent Design critics, such as Robert T. Pennock, point to confusion about methodological and metaphysical naturalism in the writings of Johnson and his Intelligent Design colleagues, arguing that Intelligent Design does not meet the criteria for a scientific theory but rather is a metaphysical concept.[141] The assessment that Intelligent Design does not qualify as science is further supported by the lack of testable research by Intelligent Design's adherents.[142]

In response to this second criticism, the philosophically astute in the Intelligent Design community, such as William Dembski, point out that the problem is not with the research findings of Intelligent Design but rather with the unquestioned reductive philosophical assumptions that have defined what counts as

science since Darwin proposed *natural* selection as the primary mechanism for evolution. Citing Richard Dawkins's opening statement in *The Blind Watchmaker*, "Biology is the study of complicated things that give the appearance of having been designed for a purpose," Dembski questions why one would devote three hundred pages to arguing that design is merely an "appearance." Why not admit that design is actual and integral to scientific explanation?[143] The standard response to Dembski's argument by Intelligent Design's opponents is that the appearance of design from natural processes does not mean that the "design" is intentional, inferring external agency.[144] To account for complex phenomena by attributing evolutionary design to an intelligent agent is to imply God acting, an argument that has no place in science.

Like Creation Science before it, the promotion of teaching of Intelligent Design in United States public schools has been judged not to be constitutional. In 2005, John E. Jones III, the presiding judge in the case of *Kitzmiller v. Dover Area School District*, found that when the school board of Dover, Pennsylvania, added Intelligent Design to the science curriculum, the initiative violated the Establishment Clause of the

140. Phillip E. Johnson, *Reason in the Balance: The Case against Naturalism in Science, Law and Education* (Downers Grove, IL: InterVarsity Press, 1995), 8–9 and passim. See also Johnson's *The Wedge of Truth: Splitting the Foundations of Naturalism* (Downers Grove, IL: InterVarsity, 2000).

141. Robert T. Pennock, "Reply: Johnson's Reason in the Balance," in *Intelligent Design Creationism and Its Critics, Philosophical, Theological, and Scientific*, 102–7.

142. The chairman of the board of directors of the American Association for the Advancement of Science and one of the world's leading botanists, Peter H. Raven, has drawn attention to the deficiency of Intelligent Design's claim to be science: "Intelligent design theory has so far not been supported by peer-reviewed, published evidence." "AAAS Urges Opposition to 'Intelligent Design Theory' within U.S. Science Classes," American Association for the Advancement of Science policy alert with board resolution, posted June 11, 2002, available at http://www.aaas.org/news/releases/2002/1106id2 .shtml.

143. William A. Dembski, "Who's Got the Magic?" in *Intelligent Design Creationism and Its Critics*, 644. See also his *No Free Lunch: Why Specified Complexity Cannot Be Purchased without Intelligence* (Langam, MD: Rowman & Littlefield, 2002), passim.

144. Robert T. Pennock, "The Wizards of ID: Reply to Dembski," in *Intelligent Design Creationism and Its Critics*, 662–63.

First Amendment of the U.S. Constitution.[145]

Upon learning of this judgment, the advocates for Intelligent Design did not abandon their cause. In response to the Dover decision, John H. Calvert, managing director of the Intelligent Design Network, Inc., argued that Judge Jones's decision had a serious discrepancy. The decision takes note of the theistic-friendly implications of support for an intelligent cause for life but omits any discussion of the antireligious implications of Darwinism.[146]

Opponents of Creation Science and Intelligent Design have typified them as successive forms of Christian creationism in conflict with Darwinian evolution and, by extension, with natural science as a whole. This strategy has been used to bolster support for the dismissal of Creation Science and Intelligent Design. However, in their supporters' claims to be "science," both Creation Science and Intelligent Design are actually examples of conflation, namely, attempts to integrate selected scientific evidence with Christian theism.

Further, whether Creation Science or Intelligent Design contributors directly speak of it or not, they recognize that in their confrontation of Darwinian biology, they are confronting far more than the science of evolution. They are opposing the cluster of attitudes and values associated with the umbrella term *social Darwinism*. The term *conflict* more appropriately applies to

their opposition to social Darwinism, in which the supporters of Creation Science and Intelligent Design are engaged to end the hegemony of "naturalism," which they believe is an atheistic ideology and, therefore, a threat to Christian influence in American society.[147]

Intelligent Design has received far more attention from Catholics than Creation Science. Catholic participation in the Intelligent Design movement's advocacy for inclusion in the biology curricula of American public schools in 2005 took the form of a *New York Times* op-ed piece by Cardinal Christoph Schönborn of Vienna entitled "Finding Design in Nature."[148] The cardinal wrote, "Evolution in the sense of common ancestry might be true, but evolution in the [Neo-Darwinian] sense of an unguided, unplanned process of random variation and natural selection is not." He further argued that there is overwhelming evidence for design in biology. To counter Neo-Darwinism's conception of the natural order as an "unguided, unplanned process," he stated, "The Catholic Church, while leaving to science many details about the history of life on earth, proclaims that by the light of reason the human intellect can readily and clearly discern purpose and design in the natural world, including the world of living things."

Cardinal Schönborn further declared that Pope John Paul II's 1996 address to the Pontifical Academy of Sciences on biological evo-

145. "Dover ID Case Decided," MSNBC, December 20, 2005, http://www.msnbc.msn.com/id/10545387/.

146. John H. Calvert, "Outlawing Discussion of Intelligent Design in Schools Is a Violation," originally published in *Watchman* 3 (2006), reprinted in *Intelligent Design versus Evolution*, ed. Louise Gerdes (Farmington Hills, MI: Greenhaven, 2008), 74.

147. For more on this point regarding Creation Science, see Ted Peters and Martinez Hewlett, *Evolution, from Creation to New Creation* (Nashville: Abingdon, 2003), 86–89. For more on Intelligent Design, see my "Intelligent Design 'in the Public Square': Neo-Conservative Opposition to Darwinian Naturalism," in *Faith in Public Life*, ed. William Collinge (Maryknoll, NY: Orbis, 2008), 218–40.

148. Christoph Schönborn, "Finding Design in Nature," *New York Times*, July 7, 2005, http://www.nytimes .com/2005/07/07/opinion/07schonborn.html?ex=1278388800&en=95804823e49fb832&ei=5088&partner=rssnyt& emc=rss.

lution was "rather vague and unimportant."[149] Such language by a cardinal, who is a member of the Vatican's Congregation for Catholic Education, drew considerable attention.[150] A noteworthy member of the Pontifical Academy of Sciences, George Coyne, S.J., then the director of the Vatican Observatory, challenged Schönborn's dismissive treatment of Pope John Paul II's 1996 address on biological evolution, arguing that the cardinal's treatment of the pope's address as "rather vague and unimportant" was a mistake. Coyne referred to the pope's address as an "epoch-making declaration" in which he affirmed Catholic belief that "evolution is no longer a mere hypothesis and then proceeded, far from any thought of incompatibility, to draw reasonable implications for religious belief from that conclusion."[151] Later Coyne offered an even stronger interpretation of the evolution message of John Paul II, stressing that the pope's position is "fundamental church teaching."[152]

Likely to clarify his position, Cardinal Schönborn gave a series of catechetical lectures on creation in Vienna in late fall and winter of 2005–6. These were later published in a monograph entitled *Chance or Purpose? Creation, Evolution, and a Rational Faith*. Early in the opening chapter, he states, "The question of creation is always concerned with the question of the goal of things. It is thereby a matter of the question about a plan, about a 'design' or 'purpose'" for creation.[153] The question is important because, through the exercise of our human reason, humans are capable of knowing a great deal about the Creator. Pointing out that faith in the Creator has not kept up with advances in scientific knowledge, he stresses that "the notion that a Creator somehow intervenes in the wondrous work of nature is—quite rightly—being rejected."[154] In matters of religious faith and the natural sciences, it is important that one observe the proper boundaries of each.

In chapter 4, Cardinal Schönborn treats design in the context of reflection on *creatio continua*, which he describes as "the same sphere of reality that natural science investigates."[155] He stresses at the outset that continuing creation cannot be measured by the empirical methods

---

149. Cornella Dean and Laurie Goodstein, "Leading Cardinal Redefines Church's View on Evolution," July 9, 2005, at "Cardinal Creates Controversy," National Center for Science Education, *New York Times*, http://www.nytimes.com/2005/07/09/science/09cardinal.html?ex=1278561600&en=0c18381d982e5e77&ei=5090&partner=rssuserland&emc=rss. Mark Ryland, a vice president of the Discovery Institute and an acquaintance of the cardinal through the International Theological Institute in Austria, admitted in an interview that he urged the cardinal to write the op-ed.

150. Dean and Goodstein, "Leading Cardinal Redefines Church's View on Evolution." The *Catechism of the Catholic Church* addresses faith and science (no. 159) but makes no direct reference to biological evolution in either the 1994 or 1997 edition.

151. George V. Coyne, "God's Chance Creation," *The Tablet*, August 6, 2005, http://www.thetablet.co.uk/articles/1027/.

152. Catholic News Service, "Vatican Astronomer Says Evolution Important for Insights into God," August 5, 2005, available at http://www.catholicnews.com/data/stories/cns/0504505.htm. Coyne encouraged Christians to move away from the notion of a distant designer intervening in nature and to focus, instead, on the biblical Creator, a personal and loving God. Five months later, in an interview with Mark Lombard, Coyne stressed that the God of Intelligent Design is not the God of love revealed by Jesus Christ. See Mark Lombard, "Intelligent Design Belittles God, Vatican Director Says," *Catholic Online*, January 30, 2006, available at http://www.catholic.org/national/national_story.php?id=18503.

153. Cardinal Christoph Schönborn, *Chance or Purpose? Creation, Evolution, and a Rational Faith*, trans. Henry Taylor (San Francisco: Ignatius, 2007), 18.

154. Ibid., 29.

155. Ibid., 75.

of the natural sciences. Nor can it be condemned on the basis of a "scientific" atheism. He sets himself at a distance from Intelligent Design arguments for direct agency to explain the complexity of the evolution of species. In keeping with his earlier position, he writes, "God's activity is not that of a *deus ex machina*, a 'stopgap,' who has to be brought in for whatever is 'not yet explicable.' It is not a matter of 'intervening, case by case,' from the outside, but of the transcendental creative activity of God, who alone makes it possible for the world to 'hold together,' and for it to climb higher, step by step, in accordance with his plan, for genuinely new elements to appear in it, right up to man."[156] Although he is sympathetic with the fundamental questions raised by Intelligent Design advocates and their recognition that Neo-Darwinism has functioned as an atheistic ideology in Western cultures,[157] it is obvious from this statement that Cardinal Schönborn supports theistic evolution.

The Intelligent Design movement's founder, Phillip Johnson, would likely judge the quoted position of Schönborn, which dismisses God's intervening in nature, to be flawed. For Johnson, theistic evolution is an oxymoron. On the one hand, it asserts that "God rules everything," yet on the other hand, "it claims nature proceeds on its own without supernatural influence."[158] For Johnson, the two positions cannot be reconciled. Attempts to accommodate theism and Darwinism are inherently futile.

In Cardinal Schönborn's assessment, Intelligent Design's conception of design is a misconception, with God analogous to a "divine engineer." He writes, "In order to talk meaningfully about the Creator having a 'design,' we have to retrieve the concept of 'nature.'"[159] Nature is characterized by growth and becoming. The natures of living things have their own form of activity with which they are endowed by the Creator. They reach their goal not by a transcendent force applied from outside, but by "an inner principle" through which God endows creatures with their self-development.[160] It is important to note that the question of cosmic purpose lies beyond the proper realm of the natural sciences. Even if the universe's evolution may imply that some purposes are at work, there is no way scientifically to explain those purposes.

Integral to the "inner principle" of the self-development of species is the need for survival. Darwinism conceives of evolution as an undirected natural process characterized by chance and randomness, two important factors that require clarification. Chance in biology refers to the disorder caused by major events in nature, such as volcanic eruption and hurricanes that can result in adaptive mutations that contribute to the evolution of new species. Chance is also used in reference to unused features of organisms that become useful in a different environment and thereby emerge in a novel function, such as the middle-ear bones of humans that arose from the jawbones of early fish. In Neo-Darwinian evolution, randomness has to do with genetically advantageous characteristics not possessed by every member of a species that have adaptive advantage in a given environment, resulting in mutations that increase the survival

---

156. Ibid., 84.
157. Ibid., 165.
158. Phillip E. Johnson, "Creator or Blind Watchmaker?" in *Intelligent Design Creationism and Its Critics*, 443.
159. Schönborn, *Chance or Purpose?* 98.
160. Ibid., 99.

rates of the organisms and their progeny.[161] Biologists recognize that evolution of new species is possible only under a narrow range of physical and chemical conditions. Put simply, the terms *chance* and *random*, when referring to evolution, do not signify a haphazard throw of the dice.

Randomness and chance are terms that point to the contingent nature of planetary life, in the sense that the existence of species depends on uncertain ecosystem conditions. Regarding chance versus design, scientist and theologian Ian Barbour points out, "If design is understood as a detailed pre-existing plan in the mind of God, then *chance* is the antithesis of *design*. But if design is identified with a general direction of growth toward complexity, life and consciousness, then both law and chance can be part of design."[162]

Evolution, therefore, can be said to proceed through the complex dynamics of law-like necessity and the potential for novelty. When the two come together in the right conditions, the result is the evolution of new life forms. "Emergence" refers to complex phenomena that arise from and depend on more basic phenomena, including the many ancestral steps that led to our hominid ancestors roughly 2.3 million years ago. Cosmic history is punctuated by examples of emergence that show that the universe is neither totally determined nor totally random.

The term *emergence*, of course, is not particular to science. Within theology responsive to science, emerging trends are contributing to new developments in creation theology. One major type of response seeking to bridge the schism between science and Christianity raises this question, "Who is God, and how is God as Creator to be conceived in an era in which evolution plays a major role in the sciences?" A second group is placing emphasis on the health of the planet and is arguing for creation theology with an ecological consciousness. In the sections that follow, attention will be given to each.

Contemporary Conceptions of the Creator

The question of God has been raised again and again by science, or at least by persons who draw on science to dismiss belief in God as unreasonable. A contributing factor is that Christians, at times, have incorporated "God" into science as a stopgap measure. Many have condemned this, including Karl Rahner who argued, "God is not 'something' beside other things that can be integrated into a common homogeneous [scientific] system. If we say 'God' we mean the whole, not indeed a sum of phenomena to be examined, but the whole in its incomprehensible and ineffable origin and ground which transcends the whole to which we and our experimental knowledge belong."[163] Rahner further stresses that because we cannot capture God in a scientific formula, we need not be silent about God. God is everpresent nearness that can draw us, including scientists, into the center of existence, where infinity calls to us. Transcendence and immanence, although spoken of as distinct, are *one* in the holy mystery called "God."[164]

---

161. Patrick H. Byrne, "*Quaestio Disputata*, Evolution, Randomness, and Divine Purpose: A Reply to Cardinal Schönborn," *Theological Studies* 67 (2006): 658–59.

162. Ian G. Barbour, *Nature, Human Nature, and God* (Minneapolis: Fortress Press, 2002), 26.

163. Karl Rahner, "God Is No Scientific Formula," in *The Content of Faith: The Best of Karl Rahner's Theological Writings*, ed. Karl Lehmann and Albert Raffelt, trans. Harvey D. Egan, S.J. (New York: Crossroad, 1992), 225.

164. Ibid., 228–30.

242

Where conceiving of God is concerned, transcendence and immanence have tended to be treated as oppositional terms. Early on, Christian recognition of the immanence of God in creation yielded to emphasis on divine transcendence associated with *creatio ex nihilo*, the doctrine that drew attention to the incompatibility of Greek pantheism with belief in the triune God that the Christian community worshipped. Emphasis on *creatio ex nihilo* and the dependence of creatures on God was accompanied by neglect of *creatio continua*, the doctrine that affirms God's ongoing presence in creation as "Giver of life."

To retrieve God's immanence in the world while not abandoning God's transcendence, some philosophers and theologians have proposed pan*en*theism. When compared with classical theism and pantheism, panentheism is a *tertium quid* (meaning a third intermediate thing); it affirms God's transcendence *of* the world and holds it in tension with God's immanence *in* the world. Anglican theologian and biologist Arthur Peacocke (1924–2006) has employed panentheism as a way to conceive of God's ongoing creativity within nature. Peacocke is opposed to accounts of God as apart from the world altogether (cf. deism) or as oc-

casionally intervening from beyond nature (cf. Intelligent Design theory). He speaks of God's agency as "being in the processes themselves, as they are revealed by the physical and biological sciences."[165] The evolutionary processes are the God-given possibilities that have become actualized. In a sense, God makes things make themselves.[166] For Peacocke, from what we know through science, divine agency cannot be reduced to direct causation because nature—human and nonhuman—is "*in* God." God actively directs the world as a whole.[167]

Lest one conclude that Peacocke is collapsing God and nature, he stresses that God is ultimately more than nature and its processes. He writes, "God in his being transcends, goes beyond, both humanity and nature, [yet] God is either in everything created from the beginning to the end, at all times and all places, or he is not there at all."[168] Peacocke is not alone in proposing panentheism. Other notable theologians have done so as well, including Ian Barbour,[169] Philip Clayton,[170] Denis Edwards,[171] and Sallie McFague.[172]

Panentheism is not without its critics, so it is important to note that Christian panentheism does not abandon biblical revelation about God, but tries to be true to it. As Archbishop Józef

---

165. Arthur Peacocke, "Chance and Law in Irreversible Thermodynamics, Theoretical Biology and Theology," in *Chaos and Complexity: Scientific Perspectives on Divine Action*, ed. Robert John Russell, Nancey Murphy, and Arthur P. Peacocke (Vatican Observatory, Rome: Center for Theology and the Natural Sciences; Berkeley: Vatican Observatory Foundation, 1995), 139. Although rooted in a very different conceptual framework than that of Thomas Aquinas, Peacocke's position resonates with Aquinas's recognition that God is in all things as the causal agent present in the effects caused.

166. Peacocke draws from Charles Kingsley, *The Water Babies* (London: Hodder & Stoughten, 1930; orig. pub. 1863), 143.

167. Peacocke, "Chance and Law in Irreversible Thermodynamics . . .," and his *God and the New Biology* (San Francisco: Harper and Row, 1986), 96.

168. Peacocke, "Chance and Law in Irreversible Thermodynamics," 140.

169. Barbour's panentheism is an adaptation of the conception of God of the process thinkers, Whitehead and Hartshorne; see his *Religion and Science: Historical and Contemporary Issues* (San Francisco: HarperCollins, 1997).

170. Philip Clayton, *God and Contemporary Science* (Edinburgh: Edinburgh University Press, 1997).

171. Denis Edwards, *Breath of Life: A Theology of the Creator Spirit* (Maryknoll, NY: Orbis, 2004), 139–42.

172. Sallie McFague, *The Body of God: An Ecological Theology* (Minneapolis: Fortress Press, 1993), 149–50.

Życiński points out, the panentheistic Creator is the God, according to Paul, in whom "we live and move and have our being" (Acts 17:28).[173] What panentheism does abandon is a Neo-Scholastic framework for conceiving of God. Specifically, it abandons the simplistic notion of God as the distant and abstract prime ("unmoved") mover of a static cosmos and replaces it with a notion of a God who creatively works in, with, and under nature's processes—the evolutionary processes of emergence that are the instruments of God's purposes.

Christian panentheism also abandons God as a monad and envisions the universe to be evolving within the Trinitarian relations of mutual love. In the words of the Catholic theologian Denis Edwards, "The becoming of the world is grounded in the eternal Trinitarian process. There is no necessity which demands that God have a world, since love is realized and expressed in the *perichoresis* (co-indwelling) of the divine Persons." The three persons share an infinite "space" of divine life and "within this space the divine Persons freely make room for the otherness of finite creatures."[174] This "space" is one in which a Christian can experience the finite world as truly sacramental, as a visible manifestation of the triune God's invisible presence that sustains the unfolding world.

An approach to an understanding of God that is also critical of theology influenced by Aristotelian primary causality is that of John Haught, a Catholic theologian. Haught is critical of Aristotle's concept of God as prime mover, which Haught describes as a being "pushing things from the past."[175] Broadly influenced by the process philosophy of Alfred North Whitehead[176] and taking his inspiration from the Jesuit paleontologist and mystic Teilhard de Chardin (1881–1955), Haught proposes a theology of evolution to show how our new awareness of cosmic and biological evolution can enhance Christian teachings about God.

Haught grounds his theology in a "metaphysics of the future," which he describes as "the 'coming of God' in the mode of renewing the future that ultimately explains the novelty in evolution."[177] A key concept in Haught's metaphysics is Teilhard's "Omega," which in Teilhard's schema names the supreme point that is not only the transcendent terminus of the evolutionary process, but, by drawing the world toward the future, is also the actual cause for the universe's growth in complexity and consciousness.[178] Although

---

173. Józef Życiński, *God and Evolution: Fundamental Questions of Christian Evolutionism*, trans. Kenneth W. Kemp and Zuzanna Maślanka (Washington, DC: Catholic University of America, 2006), 176.

174. Denis Edwards, *The God of Evolution: A Trinitarian Theology* (Mahwah, NJ: Paulist, 1999), 32.

175. John F. Haught, *God after Darwin: A Theology of Evolution* (Boulder, CO: Westview, 2000), 81. Aquinas, as already noted, recognized the richness of Aristotle's contribution on motion and causality and most definitely did not envision God as "pushing things from the past." To be created, for Aquinas, is to have potentiality to be actualized and to have existence by participation in God. ST I, q. 44, a. 1–2.

176. Although Haught does not give explicit attention to panentheism, Alfred North Whitehead (1861–1947) can be said to be a panentheist in his conception of the God-world relation. God in the divine primordial nature is the reservoir of all possibility. God, in the consequent nature, is intimately involved, continuously interacting, with the world. Within God is contained the world's complete history, as well as all its possible futures. See Alfred North Whitehead, *Process and Reality: An Essay in Cosmology* (1929), corrected ed., ed. David Ray Griffin and Donald W. Sherburne (New York: Macmillan, 1978).

177. Haught, *God after Darwin*, 115.

178. Pierre Teilhard de Chardin, *The Phenomenon of Man*, trans. Bernard Wall (New York: Harper, 1975); and *The Human Phenomenon*, trans. Sarah Appleton-Weber (East Sussex, UK: Sussex Academic, 1999).

244 Teilhard is a scientist, his Omega is a personal extrapolation that lies beyond empirical data and scientific analysis. This is obvious in Teilhard's association of the Omega Point with the divine *Logos*, Christ, who draws all things to himself (cf. John 12:32). The integration of Christ into his conception of the cosmic Omega gives directionality to evolution with a final goal of union with God. In Teilhard's thought, elements of the science of evolution are complemented by mystical insights.

Haught stresses that the metaphysics of being of Plato and Aristotle incorporated in the theologies of the Western monotheistic religions was appropriate when the cosmos was regarded to be static, but is inadequate in our era. Drawing on Teilhard's ideas, Haught argues that because evolution is a process of constant becoming, of "perpetual movement to the future" toward deeper coherence, the direction of evolutionary processes is not defined by its point of departure but by its goal, the Omega. In his proposed theology of evolution, Haught speaks of God in this way: "'God' . . . must once again mean for us, as it did for many of our biblical forbears, the transcendent future horizon that draws the entire universe, and not just human history, toward an unfathomable fulfillment yet to be realized. This, I think, is what Teilhard means when he says that God must become for us less Alpha than Omega."[179]

Haught believes that his proposed emphasis on radical futurity avoids the pitfalls of metaphysical naturalism in its determinist form that treats the past as determining the present and in its dysteleological form that emphasizes chance while rejecting any goal for or purpose to nature. Against determinism, Haught argues for an emergent evolutionary interpretation of God as gifting creation with the freedom to be itself. Contra dysteleology, which reacts against outdated understandings of divine providence, Haught posits that God does not have a preconceived *plan* for creation so much as a guiding *vision* for creation, filled with love and promise.[180]

Haught's proposal is highly speculative. He recognizes that his grounding of evolutionary novelty in God, which he describes as "the coming God in the mode of a renewing future"[181] will not sit comfortably with conventional Christian thought. Haught questions whether Christianity will be able to gain the critical distance from the classical Greek metaphysics of the "eternal present" to be truly open to a *new* creation. He describes the problem as a conception of creation in which "the natural world is always a deficient reflection of if not a perverse deviation from, a primordial perfection of 'being' that exists forever in a fixed realm generally pictured as 'above creation,' untouched by time."[182] As long as the traditional view continues, the becoming through evolution is rendered a meaningless straying from timeless completeness, rather than a genuinely emergent creation.

Where the natural sciences are concerned, Haught posits that the problem is not the "eternal present," but rather metaphysics oriented to the past. His metaphysics of the future "cannot be translated without remainder into scientifically specifiable concepts, precisely because science typically attributes efficacy only to what lies in the causal past."[183] This metaphysics de-

---

179. Haught, *God after Darwin*, 84.
180. Ibid., 105–9.
181. Ibid., 115
182. Ibid., 85
183. Ibid., 90.

picts nature, as we know it, as having been led out of a dead causal past to the present state of a living complex nature. Such a metaphysics, Haught argues, "no more allows for the emergence of real novelty than does a religious metaphysics fixed on the present."[184]

If we risk abandoning the metaphysics of the past and of the eternal present, then Haught believes we will recognize that God's coming from the future is not only for humans but a coming toward the entire universe, energizing every part of it from within.[185] This insight resonates with the panentheistic conception of God already addressed. It also destabilizes fixation on design that closes off attention to a novel emerging future and shifts it to hopeful promise.

In his emphasis on creation from the future, Haught is in company with other theologians who have made the future a focal point in their theology of God. For example, Karl Rahner speaks of God as the "Absolute Future,"[186] and Wolfhart Pannenberg, Ted Peters, and Jürgen Moltmann speak of God as "the Power of the Future."[187] Future-oriented theologies envision creation to be open and undetermined. The undetermined horizon beckons us to be open to the ineffable mystery of the Creator-God. Openness to our ultimate future calls us to responsibility for the evolving future, not only our own, but that of all creation. For this reason, contemporary creation theology, if it is to be a theology for life, requires attention to the question "For what kind of life?" and therefore to ecology.

A Creation Theology That Earth Can Live With

In a lecture titled "A Theology We Can Live With," Karl Rahner proposed, "If what is meant is the life of people in the West in their consumer-oriented society," then such a theology is without "liveableness."[188] Put simply, not just any conceivable pattern of life can coexist with theology; economics driven by greed is not something that one can live with, because it mutes the message of Christ. What is called for is "a courageous and open theology"[189] that does not shy away from the problematic elements of Western culture. Although ecology was not addressed by Rahner, his negative criticism of consumerism certainly points to it and to the need for a courageous theology, open to a new conception of ourselves and of our relations to the rest of earth's creatures.

Today climate change due largely to centuries of industrialization often driven by short-sighted greed has damaged and, if unchecked, will continue to damage earth's ecosystems, threaten global water supplies, and lessen biodiversity as desertification, erosion, and waste pollution continue to grow. These things col-

---

184. Ibid., 86.

185. Ibid., 99.

186. Karl Rahner, "Marxist Utopia and the Christian Future of Man," in *Theological Investigations* (New York: Crossroad, 1982), 6:59–68. Since eschatology rather than creation is Rahner's focus, it is not being addressed here.

187. Wolfhart Pannenberg, *Metaphysics and the Idea of God* (Grand Rapids: Eerdmans, 2001); Ted Peters, *God—the World's Future* (Minneapolis: Fortress Press, 1992); idem, *Anticipating Omega: Science, Faith, and Our Ultimate Future* (Göttingen, Germany: Vandenhoeck & Ruprecht, 2006); Jürgen Moltmann, *The Future of Creation* (German ed. 1977; Minneapolis: Augsburg Fortress, 2000).

188. Karl Rahner, "A Theology We Can Live With," in *Theological Investigations*, trans. Hugh M. Riley (New York: Crossroad, 1988), 21:100.

189. Ibid., 112.

246 lectively are contributing to accelerated extinction of plant and animal species and to growth in human malnutrition and disease, especially in India and the sub-Saharan African countries. Therefore, it is necessary to make "nature" a *locus theologicus* (meaning context or place for theological reflection) in a creation theology that earth can live with.

Christianity has been criticized for being complicit in the ecological crisis. Lynn White, early in the ecological movement, faulted Christianity, which he described as "the most anthropocentric religion the world has seen."[190] Critical of medieval theologians' emphasis on "man's transcendence of and rightful mastery over nature,"[191] White argued that Christianity is responsible for implanting the notion in Western culture that it is God's will that humans, the only creatures who are said to image God, to exploit nature for their so-called proper ends.

White's critique of medieval theology is accompanied by sweeping generalities and lacks attention to the creation theologies of Thomas Aquinas and Bonaventure treated earlier in this chapter. It would seem, for example, that he failed to take note of Aquinas on experiencing "traces" of the Trinity in all of creation and of his regard for creatures as manifestations of divine goodness.[192] Bonaventure's attention to the sacredness of creation and his assignment of in-trinsic value to everything in the created world are also overlooked.[193]

Arguably, a pattern of thinking and acting traceable to the dawn of the Age of Science and to Francis Bacon (1561–1626) is far more culpable than medieval theology. A highly influential philosopher of science of the seventeenth century, Bacon interpreted the Genesis creation stories as showing that man's control of nonhuman nature was not only man's responsibility, but was God's will.[194] In his interpretation, Bacon combined the two creation stories in Genesis 1–3. Bacon attributed blame for the first sin to Eve's willful disobedience. Eve, therefore, is responsible for man's loss of dominion over the earth. Before the fall, Adam and Eve, made in God's image, were like God, sharing in God's dominion over earth's creatures, all of which had been given to them by God in the Garden of Paradise. With the first sin and subsequent fall from God's favor, this wonderful godly dominion was lost. Bacon envisioned science and its applications in new technologies as the only ways in which "man" (symbolizing scientists and those with monetary resources to sponsor their research) could recover the original dominion lost to him through Eve's disobedience and willful temptation of Adam. Since woman's curiosity caused man's fall from his God-given privileged place of dominion, man's control of

---

190. Lynn White Jr., "The Historical Roots of Our Ecologic Crisis," orig. pub. *Science* 155 (1967): 1203–7, repr. in *Readings in Ecology and Feminist Theology*, ed. Mary Heather MacKinnon and Moni McIntyre (Kansas City: Sheed & Ward, 1995), 31.

191. Ibid., 33.

192. ST I, q. 47, a. 1.

193. Bonaventure, for example, wrote, "Every creature is by its nature a kind of effigy and likeness of the eternal Wisdom." *The Soul's Journey into God*, ch. 2, no. 12 (77).

194. Francis Bacon, *The Works of Francis Bacon*, vol. 4, ed. J. Spedding, R. L. Ellis, and D. Heath (London: Longman, 1857–74), 274, cited by Peter Harrison, "Having Dominion: Genesis and the Mastery of Nature," in *Environmental Stewardship: Critical Perspectives—Past and Present*, ed. R. J. Berry (London: T&T Clark, 2006), 24. (I purposefully use "man" here rather than the gender-inclusive "human" for reasons that will become clear shortly.)

another female, "unruly nature," should be used to regain it. This model of domination has been inimical to the welfare of women and destructive of nonhuman nature.

Obviously, by today's standards of biblical scholarship, Bacon's interpretation of the Genesis creation texts is fundamentally flawed. Dominion entrusted to humans—who are said to bear the divine image—is modeled after a loving God who protects the defenseless and gives justice to the oppressed. The directive to exercise dominion may simply be a reminder to humans not to destroy the fish, birds, and other animals (Gen. 1:26-28). This implies that humans must seek wisdom and strive for right relations, the core meaning of the term *justice*, not only with one another but with all creatures. A pointer to right relations is offered in God's directive to the first human placed in the primordial garden to till it—to serve its life-giving potential (Gen. 2:15).

An appropriate starting point for a creation theology that earth can live with is to lament the interpretations of *imago Dei* used to justify harmful conquest of earth. Throughout the Hebrew Scriptures, lament rises from the depths of the human spirit in times of great distress, especially over the effects of sinful choices. The prophet Jeremiah voices an ecological lament:

> Over the mountains, break out in cries of
> lamentation,
> over the pasture lands, intone a dirge:
> They are scorched, and no one crosses them,
> unheard is the bleat of the flock;

> birds of the air as well as beasts,
> all have fled, and are gone. (Jer. 9:9, NAB)[195]

What sets Jeremiah's lament apart from many found in the Hebrew Scriptures is that its focus is on the effects of sinful human choices on the land and the suffering of all the creatures dependent on it for existence. The land is ravaged; the people are the cause.

A few verses later, Jeremiah calls for the wailing women to assemble:

> Thus says the LORD of hosts:
> Attention! tell the wailing women to come,
> summon the best of them;
> Let them come quickly and intone a dirge
> for us,
> That our eyes may be wet with weeping,
> our cheeks run with tears.
> The dirge is heard from Zion:
> Ruined we are, and greatly ashamed . . .
> Teach your daughters this dirge,
> and each other this lament.
> Death has come up through our windows.
> (vv. 16-20, NAB)

It is difficult to read these words and avoid pondering images of women weeping over the sickness and death of their malnourished children. For it is always the powerless and poor who most directly bear the burden of ecosystem destruction.

A criterion for a constructive "livable" theology for Rahner is that it be "ecclesial," meaning that it be "pursued in harmony" with the

---

195. These selected verses are from a longer section, Jer. 8:4—10:25, in which the dominant theme is disaster and the need for repentance. Lamentation is also the central theme of Jer. 14:1—15:9. See also Hos. 4:3 ("Therefore the land mourns and all that dwell in it languish"); Isa. 24:4-5 ("The earth mourns and fades, the world languishes and fades; both heaven and earth languish. The earth is polluted because of its inhabitants, who have transgressed laws, violated statutes, broken the ancient covenant").

teachings of the church.[196] Teachings of Popes John Paul II and Benedict XVI can provide assistance with creation theology responsive to earth's ecological crisis. In his 1990 World Day of Peace message entitled "Peace with God, the Creator, Peace with All of Creation,"[197] Pope John Paul II connected the issue of world peace to the related issues of the health of the planet and the flourishing of humans. Drawing attention to a lack of due respect for nature, by the plundering of natural resources and by a progressive decline in the quality of life around the world, he called for carefully coordinated solutions to human and ecological problems (nos. 1–2). He stressed, "No peaceful society can afford to neglect either respect for life or the fact that there is an integrity to creation" (no. 7).

Pope John Paul II devotes a section of his message to the "urgent need for solidarity" and emphasizes respect for all creatures (nos. 10–14). Solidarity among humans in the struggle for justice and peace was one of the major themes of John Paul II's social teaching throughout his pontificate. Solidarity is a principle that flows from the emphasis on the dignity of the human person in Catholic Social Teaching. Emphasis on human dignity need not conflict with ecology. In *Renewing the Earth*, the United States

bishops certainly recognized this when they stressed the need "to explore the links between concern for the person and for the earth, between natural ecology and social ecology."[198]

A livable creation theology calls for solidarity to be extended beyond human relationships to the earth's other species, because all are part of God's creation. Solidarity as an ecojustice principle requires the humble awareness of our creaturely kinship with the earth's other species. This is brought to our attention by the Genesis creation accounts that present humans as sharing the same day of creation with other mammals and depict God forming humans and animals from the same dust of the earth. Biblically rooted creaturely kinship is affirmed by Darwinian evolution with its emphasis on the interconnectedness of and cooperation among species. In the words of the U.S. Catholic Bishops, "The web of life is one."[199]

An important ecclesial resource for a creation theology that earth can live with is Pope Benedict XVI's 2009 encyclical *Caritas in Veritate* (Charity in Truth),[200] which treats the moral dimensions of the environment extensively. Benedict XVI speaks of the environment as "God's gift," and as such, it comes with accompanying responsibilities (no. 48). Giving attention

---

196. Rahner, "A Theology We Can Live With," 107. Rahner points out that in matters that have not been definitively settled by the ecclesial teaching office, it is sometimes necessary to criticize the church out of love for it.

197. John Paul II, "Peace with God, the Creator, Peace with All of Creation," World Day of Peace 1990, http://www .vatican.va/holy_father/john_paul_ii/messages/peace/documents/hf_jp-ii_mes_19891208_xxiii-world-day-for-peace_ en.html.

198. United States Catholic Conference, *Renewing the Earth: An Invitation to Reflection and Action on Environment in the Light of Catholic Social Teaching* (1991), in *"And God Saw That It Was Good": Catholic Theology on the Environment*, ed. Drew Christiansen, S.J., and Walter Grazer (Washington, DC: United States Catholic Conference, 1996), 224.

199. Ibid., 224.

200. Benedict XVI, Encyclical Letter *Caritas in Veritate* (29 June 2009), http://www.vatican.va/holy_father /benedict_xvi/encyclicals/documents/hf_ben-xvi_enc_20090629_caritas-in-veritate_en.html. For an earlier treatment of then-Cardinal Ratzinger's creation in which he addressed the exploitation of nature in the name of progress, see his Second Homily, "The Meaning of the Biblical Creation Accounts," in *In the Beginning . . . : A Catholic Understanding of the Story of Creation and the Fall*, German ed., 1986, trans. Boniface Ramsey, O.P. (Grand Rapids: Eerdmans, 1990), 33–39.

to misconceptions associated with biological science, he writes, "When nature, including the human being, is viewed as the result of mere chance or evolutionary determinism, our sense of responsibility wanes." He continues, however, "When nature is rightly understood, the believer recognizes the wonderful result of God's creative activity, which we may use responsibly to satisfy our legitimate needs, material or otherwise, while respecting the intrinsic balance of creation. If this vision is lost, we end up either considering nature an untouchable taboo or, on the contrary, abusing it. Neither attitude is consonant with the Christian vision of nature as the fruit of God's creation" (no. 48).

Benedict XVI stresses that nature is a God-given gift with an inbuilt order, which it is our duty to honor. Honoring nature requires being committed to decisions aimed at strengthening the *covenant between human beings and the environment* (no. 50; italics original). Obviously, Benedict XVI believes that resolutions for the problems of today require far more than technical solutions; what is needed are women and men who heed the appeal of their consciences to act on behalf of the common good (no. 71).

Again, in the 2010 World Day of Peace message entitled "If You Want to Cultivate Peace, Protect Creation,"[201] Pope Benedict XVI gives attention to earth's ecological problems. This is both a realistic message, drawing attention to the environmental migrants who are forced to leave their unproductive lands, and a hopeful one. He speaks of problems providing an *"opportunity for discernment and new strategic planning"* (no. 5; italics original), with the purpose of enabling cultural renewal and the discovery of values that can serve as a solid basis for building a brighter global future (no. 5). Achieving that future requires a plan of action with greater respect for creation and for human development, inspired by "the values proper to charity in truth" (no. 9). Through our loving actions on behalf of the common good, we can experience intimacy with God, who through creation cares for us.

The common good has been traditionally described in Catholic moral theology as "the sum total of social conditions which allow people, either as groups or as individuals, to reach their fulfillment more fully and more easily."[202] Pope Benedict XVI has given attention to this principle in his writings on ecology and has made overtures to extending it beyond the well-being of persons to what is good for all God's creatures. This extension is in keeping with the fundamental Catholic belief in the sacramentality of all of creation and its invitation to develop an aesthetic appreciation for creatures. It also resonates with a Christian panentheism that recognizes that not only humans but also all creatures live and move and have their being in God.

A theology of creation that earth can live with calls for commitment to solidarity with humans and earth's other-kind and to an all-encompassing global common good. For such a theology to be an expression of a living faith in the Creator requires an asceticism of self-imposed moderation and willingness to sacrifice

---

201. Benedict XVI, "*If You Want to Cultivate Peace, Protect Creation*," World Day of Peace, January 1, 2010, http://www.vatican.va/holy_father/benedict_xvi/messages/peace/documents/hf_ben-xvi_mes_20091208_xliii-world-day-peace_en.html.

202. Pontifical Council for Justice and Peace, *Compendium of the Social Doctrine of the Church*, 2004, no. 164, http://www.vatican.va/roman_curia/pontifical_councils/justpeace/documents/rc_pc_justpeace_doc_20060526_compendio-dott-soc_en.html#SECRETARIAT%20OF%20STATE.

for the good of all, accompanied by moral responsibility for a loving ecojustice. In the words of Albert Einstein, "Our task must be to free ourselves from this prison [of self-interest] by widening our circle of compassion to embrace all living creatures and the whole of nature in its beauty."[203] To become this free requires surrender of an anthropocentric view of the world with openness to the God of the future, who breathes life into the emergence of a life-bearing creation.

Conclusion

Over the centuries, beginning with biblical revelation, creation faith has developed, often in response to the challenges of the time. Christian creation beliefs have been forged in the crucible of a long series of controversies, from dualistic matter-depreciating Gnosticism to contemporary atheism that draws on reductionistic empiricism for its warrants. History has shown that for creation theology to be viable, it must be both deeply rooted in the Christian tradition and daringly responsive to emerging challenges.

To be true to the Christian tradition, creation theology must continue the theocentric emphasis of the Bible, giving attention to God and to the Creator's relationship to and agency in the world. Given its theocentric nature, it logically follows that creation theology does not seek to provide an explanation of the origin and evolutionary processes of the universe. However, to be viable, creation theology cannot ignore the knowledge that science can provide about the universe, especially our own planet. Rejection of Creation Science and Intelligent Design theory and atheism that looks to the sciences for its rationale does not rule out innovations in creation theology, but rather clears the way for them.

Life in a time in which evolution science strongly influences the culture requires bringing creation faith to understanding in evolutionary theology that honors the findings of the scientific community. Further, the complex challenges posed by the global ecological crisis require rethinking the riches of the Christian teachings in service of a theology that earth can live with, one that advocates for a renewed creation. Creation theology, at once evolutionary and ecological, offers us the hope that in surrendering our conformity to the patterns of this present age, we will be transformed by the renewing of our minds, "so that we may discern what is the will of God—what is [truly] good and acceptable" (Rom. 12:2).

---

203. Cited by Michael Dowd, *Earth Spirit: A Handbook for Nurturing an Ecological Christianity* (Mystic, CT: Twenty-Third, 1991), 81. Nobody is able to achieve this completely, but the striving for such achievement is in itself a part of the liberation, and a foundation for inner security.

For Further Reading

Barbour, Ian G. *Religion and Science: Historical and Contemporary Issues.* San Francisco: HarperCollins, 1997.

> Barbour is a major contributor to "science and religion" as a subdiscipline within Christian theology and religious studies. This revised and expanded edition of Barbour's 1989–91 Gifford Lectures, first published as Religion in the Age of Science, provides a lucid and detailed overview of major historical developments and issues. Helpful analytical models for relating science and religion from conflict to integration are presented.

Benedict XVI. *In the Beginning . . . : A Catholic Understanding of the Story of Creation and the Fall.* German ed. 1986. Translated by Boniface Ramsey, O.P. Grand Rapids: Eerdmans, 1990.

> This is a collection of homilies on the Genesis creation texts given in 1985 by then-Cardinal Joseph Ratzinger. In the appendix, he argues that to understand "nature" exclusively as an object of scientific study is to misunderstand it. He urges that the theme of creation be made more central to Catholic theology.

Berry, R. J., ed. *Environmental Stewardship: Critical Perspectives—Past and Present.* London: T&T Clark, 2006.

> Berry, past president of the British Ecology Society and of the European Ecological Society, brings together expositions of the concept of stewardship of creation and some noteworthy criticisms of it by religious scholars, theologians, and practical conservationists.

Caruana, Louis, ed. *Darwinism and Catholicism: The Past and Present Dynamics of a Cultural Encounter.* New York: T&T Clark, 2009.

> A collection of historical, philosophical, and theological essays by Catholic scholars with a focus on the influence of Darwinian ideas on Catholicism as an interaction between two worldviews.

Clayton, Phillip, and Arthur Peacocke, eds. *In Whom We Live and Move and Have Our Being: Panentheistic Reflections on God's Presence in a Scientific World.* Grand Rapids: Eerdmans, 2004.

> Scientists and theologians, Catholic, Orthodox and Protestant, address contemporary science and traditional views of God, exploring whether panentheism provides a credible account of divine action for our age.

Deane-Drummond, Celia. *Creation through Wisdom: Theology and the New Biology.* Edinburgh: T&T Clark, 2000.

> This book draws on the wisdom tradition to create a theology responsive to the new biology, including some of the moral dilemmas it presents.

Dempsey, Carol J., and Russell A. Butkus. *All Creation Is Groaning: An Interdisciplinary Vision for Life in a Sacred Universe.* Collegeville, MN: Liturgical, 1999.

> This collection of articles, written by the faculty of the University of Portland, addresses contemporary environmental issues from the perspective of disciplines such as Christian and Islamic theology, the sciences, business, engineering, nursing, and music. It provides insight into what is required for a "wholesale paradigmatic shift in the way humans live on earth" (282).

252 Edwards, Denis. *Breath of Life: A Theology of the Creator Spirit*. Maryknoll, NY: Orbis, 2004.

> This book raises important questions and mines the Christian tradition regarding the role of the Holy Spirit as Creator. A strength of this book is its helpful explanations of important topics, including perichoresis, koinonia, sophia, and panentheism.

Haught, John F. *God after Darwin: A Theology of Evolution*. Boulder, CO: Westview, 2001, 2007.

> A major contributor to science and religion, Haught argues in this book that evolution, rather than being hostile to Christian theology, summons us to read all of nature in terms of the emerging future horizon. He proposes a coming God of the future who makes all things new.

McMullin, Ernan, ed. *The Church and Galileo*. Notre Dame, IN: University of Notre Dame Press, 2005.

> This collection of essays provides a historically accurate, scholarly, and balanced account of Galileo and his complex relationship with the Roman Catholic Church. The 1992 report of the Vatican Commission that studied the Galileo affair is also assessed.

Miller, Kenneth R. *Finding Darwin's God: A Scientist's Search for Common Ground between God and Evolution*. New York: HarperCollins, 1999.

> Miller, coauthor of high school and college biology textbooks and a self-identified Roman Catholic, critiques young- and old-earth Creationism and Intelligent Design. He argues that there are dangers of finding a place for God in the gaps, or in inferences about shadows in scientific knowledge. One never knows when the gap will be filled or when light will be turned on by new scientific discoveries. He also points to the problems with the arguments of atheists, such as Richard Dawkins, who use evolution science to support atheism, arguing that such arguments extend well beyond reasonable boundaries of scientific conclusions.

Peacocke, Arthur R. *Creation and the World of Science*. Oxford: Clarendon, 1979, 2004.

> All of the works of Peacocke, a biochemist and theologian, could be recommended; this one, based on his 1978 Bampton Lectures, is singled out for its assessment of the relationship between Christian faith and science, with attention to the impact of the social sciences.

Peters, Ted, and Martinez Hewlett. *Evolution from Creation to New Creation: Conflict, Conversation and Convergence*. Nashville: Abingdon, 2003.

> Peters, a Lutheran theologian, and Hewlett, a biologist, provide an interdisciplinary treatment of a wide spectrum of views on evolution and Christian theology. Giving attention to the rationale and goals of Creation Science and Intelligent Design theory, they also offer their own constructive theistic evolution.

Russell, Robert John, William R. Stoeger, S.J., and Francisco J. Ayala, eds. *Evolutionary and Molecular Biology: Scientific Perspectives on Divine Action*. Vatican City: Vatican Observatory Foundation / Center for Theology and the Natural Sciences, 1998.

> All of the books in the Divine Action Series are recommended. However, this collection of twenty-two scholarly conference papers on the interaction of theology, philosophy, and evolutionary and molecular biology is especially helpful, given its attention to the importance of evolution in theology-and-science dialogues. This work includes the text of Pope John Paul II's Pontifical Academy of Sciences address on evolution (1996) with an interpretation by George V. Coyne, director of the Vatican Observatory.

Schmitz-Moorman, Karl, in collaboration with James F. Salmon, S.J. *Theology of Creation in an Evolutionary World*. Cleveland: Pilgrim, 1997.

> *The strengths of this book are that it addresses a wide range of sciences, from physics and cosmology to the human sciences, and gives attention to insights from Teilhard de Chardin.*

Schönborn, Christoph. *Chance or Purpose? Creation, Evolution, and a Rational Faith*. Translated by Henry Taylor. San Francisco: Ignatius, 2007.

> *This is a clearly written and engaging collection of catechetical lectures on creation and evolution. Of particular interest is his treatment of continuing creation and divine providence.*

Życiński, Józef. *God and Evolution: Fundamental Questions of Christian Evolutionism*. Translated by Kenneth W. Kemp and Zuzanna Maślanka. Washington, DC: Catholic University of America, 2006.

> *Życiński, archbishop of Lublin, Poland, and a philosopher of science, evaluates the influence of scientific evolution on Catholic belief. In his theology of evolution, Życiński makes a case for harmony between Darwinian evolution and faith in a Creator whose agency is immanent within the processes of evolution.*

Jesus Christ

Jesus Christ

John P. Galvin

At the center of Christian creeds and Christian faith stands the figure of Jesus Christ. For this reason, the study of Christology needs no prolonged justification. While no theology can confine itself exclusively to Christology, no Christian theology would be complete without serious reflection on Jesus Christ.

Yet, though Christology is a perennial topic for theology, both the extent to which christological issues are debated and the form in which such issues are pursued have varied widely from one period of the church's history to another. Among Protestant theologians, Christology has been the focus of impassioned debate for nearly two centuries.[1] Similarly, after a half century in which first the doctrine of grace and then questions concerning the church had largely occupied the creative energies of Roman Catholic theologians, the past four decades have witnessed an extraordinary proliferation of writing on Christology in Catholic circles.[2] (This focus on Christology has increasingly been accompanied by intensified concern with the theology of the Trinity.) The results have included a reexamination of central and foundational christological issues once thought to have been definitively resolved.

Such changes do not occur accidentally. A brief comparison of past and present approaches to Christology will help clarify the present situation; for practical reasons, I shall limit the discussion at this stage to the modern history of Catholic theology.

In the period between the First (1869–70) and Second (1962–65) Vatican Councils, Catholic theology was dominated by the movement known as Neo-Scholasticism. As its name suggests, this school of thought sought to revive, in modified form, the great speculative syntheses of the Middle Ages, especially the work of Thomas Aquinas (1224/25–74). During the hegemony of Neo-Scholasticism, Catholic Christology was characterized by widespread consensus on central issues, such as the divinity of Christ and the theological significance of the crucifixion and the resurrection. With these questions considered settled, debate flourished only with regard to such comparatively peripheral matters as the nature and scope of Christ's human knowledge and the precise relationship of his divine and human natures. Yet the secure exterior masked a deep-seated malaise.

Neo-Scholastic theology, unlike its medieval forebears, divided doctrinal questions into two spheres of inquiry: fundamental theology and dogmatic theology. Each area had its own topics for investigation and a distinct method of argumentation. Fundamental theology, presupposing the results of Scholastic philosophy (including the existence and attributes of God) and arguing by appeal to reason and history, examined the evidence for divine revelation, the status of Christ as divine legate, the inspiration of the Scriptures, and the foundation of the church. Its inquiry drew on the Gospels as reliable historical sources of information about Jesus' public

---

1. For a survey, see John Macquarrie, *Jesus Christ in Modern Thought* (London: SCM, 1990), 175–303, 320–35.

2. As an indication of this development, see the following works, devoted entirely or in large part to Christology, by major Catholic theologians: Walter Kasper, *Jesus the Christ* (New York: Paulist, 1976); Hans Küng, *On Being a Christian* (Garden City, NY: Doubleday, 1976); Karl Rahner, *Foundations of Christian Faith* (New York: Seabury, 1978); Edward Schillebeeckx, *Jesus: An Experiment in Christology* (New York: Seabury, 1979); idem, *Christ: The Experience of Jesus as Lord* (New York: Seabury, 1980); Hans Urs von Balthasar, *Theo-Drama: Theological Dogmatic Theory*, 5 vols. (San Francisco, Ignatius, 1988–98); Raymund Schwager, *Jesus in the Drama of Salvation: Toward a Biblical Doctrine of Redemption* (New York: Crossroad, 1999); Roger Haight, *Jesus, Symbol of God* (Maryknoll, NY: Orbis, 1999); and Hansjürgen Verweyen, *Gottes letztes Wort: Grundriss der Fundamentaltheologie*, 3rd ed. (Regensburg: Pustet, 2000).

life and his resurrection, and found historically credible both Jesus' claim to represent God and a confirmation of that claim through the fulfillment of prophecy and the performance of miracles. Building on bases established in fundamental theology, dogmatic theology studied other doctrinal issues by appeal to the authority of the Bible and of subsequent church teaching. Its treatment of Christ was in turn subdivided into two parts: Christology (in the narrow sense) examined the person of Christ and consisted largely of a theology of the incarnation; soteriology (from the Greek *soteria*, "salvation") explored Christ's salvific work, in particular his atoning death on the cross.

As a result of this organization, Neo-Scholastic study of Christ was fragmented, and many topics were divorced from their appropriate contexts. Jesus' public life and resurrection were considered solely from an apologetic perspective, as evidence for the validity of his divine mission, while the incarnation and crucifixion were studied in isolation. This procedure impeded development of a unified and comprehensive Christology and inhibited efforts to address contemporary christological problems in a constructive and creative manner.[3]

In sharp contrast to the Neo-Scholastic approach, current Catholic authors typically seek to overcome the artificial divisions of the recent past and to present a unified treatment of christological issues.[4] As a general rule, they devote much attention to questions emerging from biblical exegesis and strive to address specific challenges posed to Christianity by modernity. Both concerns promote increased interest in Christology and require intensified consideration of its foundational questions.

To address these concerns adequately, Christology must maintain a broad scope in its inquiries. One issue that must be faced is the question of truth. Theologians cannot rest content with unfolding the implications of standard christological assertions, for these assertions are themselves subjected to challenge. Rather than taking such statements as an unquestioned point of departure, Christology must explore the very basis of the traditional confessions. Indeed, as the Lutheran theologian Wolfhart Pannenberg has cogently argued, examining the ground of Christian faith must take pride of place on the modern theological agenda.[5]

But questions of truth can be addressed only after questions of meaning have been clarified, at least to a degree. To offer an example, the truth of the assertions that "Jesus is the Christ" and that "Jesus is risen" can be considered only after their content has been specified. It may initially appear that the meaning of the words *Christ* and *risen* in these statements is clear, but this assumption will not withstand careful scrutiny. As the obscurity of the creedal references to Christ's descent into hell and his sitting at the right hand of God shows, even the

---

3. Karl Rahner's seminal essay "Current Problems in Christology," *Theological Investigations* (Baltimore: Helicon, 1961), 1:149–200, originally published in 1954, exposed the shortcomings of the prevailing approach and outlined a program for further investigation. The impact of this essay on Catholic theology can scarcely be overestimated. The treatment of Jesus in fundamental theology is thoroughly analyzed in Franz-Josef Neimann, *Jesus als Glaubensgrund in der Fundamentaltheologie der Neuzeit: Zur Genealogie eines Traktats* (Innsbruck: Tyrolia, 1983).

4. This comment is true of the works mentioned in n. 2. Exceptions to the rule are Jean Galot, *Who Is Christ? A Theology of the Incarnation* (Chicago: Franciscan Herald, 1981); Johann Auer, *Jesus Christus—Gottes und Mariä "Sohn"* (Regensburg: Pustet, 1986); and idem, *Jesus Christus—Heiland der Welt; Maria—Christi Mutter im Heilsplan Gottes* (Regensburg: Pustet, 1988).

5. Wolfhart Pannenberg, *Jesus—God and Man* (Philadelphia: Westminster, 1968), 21–37.

258 presence of christological statements in such basic Christian sources as the creeds is no guarantee that their content is self-evident or easy to determine. Clarifying the meaning of Christian beliefs, while often the most arduous part of the theologian's task, can help remove many apparent obstacles to faith.

Among other effects of these developments, foundational questions such as "What does it mean to confess that Jesus is the Christ?" and "What are the grounds for belief that Jesus is the Christ?" have penetrated into the heart of systematic Christology. Their presence inevitably modifies the nature of christological argumentation, for appeal to church teaching is not by itself an adequate response to them. One result is a widespread tendency among contemporary theologians to approach Christology "from below," starting with the historical figure of Jesus, rather than beginning "from above," with the incarnation of the second person of the Trinity.[6] In addition, since similar concerns motivate recent Protestant authors,[7] addressing foundational issues leads to a certain ecumenical convergence in christological questioning. Nonetheless, as we shall see in more detail, much variety remains, since different theologians adopt widely different strategies for analyzing and addressing them.

The pages that follow present an introductory theological examination of Jesus Christ as foundation and content of Christian faith. Following the present section, a relatively brief section will consider diverse Christologies reflected in the writings of the New Testament. Against this background, the third section will examine the development and content of the classical Christian understandings of Christ's person and work; here the focus will be on patristic and medieval thought. The exigencies of the contemporary state of christological questioning will then lead to the fourth section, an investigation of the historical foundations of Christian faith, with particular attention given to Jesus' public life, crucifixion, and resurrection. The fifth section will look at three major modern christological conceptions, and the chapter will conclude with a summary of some basic principles and guidelines for contemporary Christology and an outlook at an issue of particular contemporary concern.

New Testament Christology

While efforts to pinpoint the origin of Christology depend in part on the precise meaning assigned to the term, a rudimentary form of Christology has existed since the public activity of Jesus of Nazareth caused people to wonder what he was about and who he was. His words and deeds provoked reaction—on the part of his wider audience, among the followers he at-

---

6. See ibid., 33–37; and Nicholas Lash, "Up and Down in Christology," in *New Studies in Theology*, ed. S. Sykes and D. Holmes (London: Duckworth, 1980), 1:31–46. The distinction between Christology from below and Christology from above refers to differing starting points and methods of argumentation; it should not be confused with the distinction between high Christology, which affirms the divinity of Christ, and low Christology, which stops short of that affirmation. A more complex typology is offered by Karl Rahner in "Die deutsche protestantische Christologie der Gegenwart," *Theologie der Zeit* 1 (1936): 189–202, where he distinguishes among "christology below," "christology from below," "christology from above," "christology from below and from above," and "christology above."

7. For representative examples of major different approaches to Christology in recent Protestant thought, see, in addition to Pannenberg, Jürgen Moltmann, *The Crucified God* (New York: Harper & Row, 1974); and Schubert M. Ogden, *The Point of Christology* (London: SCM, 1982).

tracted, and on the part of his foes. What he said and did raised questions, which people answered in different ways. An echo of some diverse responses may be found in Mark 8:27-29, where Jesus' disciples report popular identification of him as John the Baptist, Elijah, or one of the prophets, and Peter confesses him as the Messiah.[8] Not all interpretations of Jesus can be called Christology—some are based on rejection—but all do involve at least a tentative assessment of who Jesus is.

As far as Jesus' followers were concerned, this reflection continued during his lifetime but developed more rapidly after his death, for only then was it possible to weigh the whole of his life.[9] The effort included, but was not limited to, attribution to Jesus of various titles (e.g., Messiah, Lord, Son of God), each of which was itself modified in the course of such application As was inevitable, christological thought first developed in unwritten form. Only at a later stage, beginning with the epistles of Paul, did it acquire fixed literary expression.

Our access to the development of Christology in these first twenty years (before and after the crucifixion) is inevitably limited and fragmentary; scholars must seek to retrace their way from material embedded in later documents, often in edited form, to its antecedents. Yet the thought of this foundational age is too decisive to be ignored; indeed, as Martin Hengel has noted, "one is tempted to say that more happened in this period of less than two decades than in the whole of the next seven centuries."[10] Various exegetes have therefore sought to provide plausible reconstructions of the course of christological development. From all indications, early thought about Jesus, on the part of his followers, was quite varied and complex.

Past efforts to analyze early christological development often chose the major christological titles of the New Testament as their point of reference and principle of organization. In an influential study, Oscar Cullmann distinguished titles that refer to Jesus' earthly work (prophet, servant, high priest), future work (Messiah, Son of man), present work (Lord, Savior), and preexistence (Word, Son of God, God). Cullmann summarized the background of each title in Judaism and Hellenism and traced the history of its application to Jesus.[11] Similarly, Ferdinand Hahn investigated the major titles Son of man,

---

8. The historical reliability of this passage is much disputed, but it can in any case serve as an illustration of diverse assessments of Jesus. For an account of the various exegetical positions and a treatment of the issues, see Rudolf Pesch, "Das Messiasbekenntnis des Petrus (Mk 8, 27-30): Neuverhandlung einer alten Frage," *Biblische Zeitschrift* 17 (1973): 178–95; 18 (1974): 20–31.

9. Some authors wish to reserve the term *Christology* for later Christian thought. Thus, Gerald O'Collins holds that "Christology properly began with what we can call the 'post-existent' Jesus." *Interpreting Jesus* (New York: Paulist, 1983), 14. With somewhat different emphasis, Edward Schillebeeckx identifies Christology as "a declaration, made in faith, about the totality of Jesus' life" and notes that such judgment is possible only after death. *Jesus*, 640. Elsewhere (e.g., *Jesus*, 741), Schillebeeckx's descriptions of Christology lack this insistence on totality. In contrast, Hermann Dembowski maintains, "The task of christology can be formulated simply: christology has to speak properly of Jesus." *Einführung in die Christologie* (Darmstadt: Wissenschaftliche Buchgesellschaft, 1976), 21. Illuminating comments on the origin and meaning of the term *Christology* are provided by Gerhard Ebeling, "The Question of the Historical Jesus and the Problem of Christology," in *Word and Faith* (London: SCM, 1963), 288–89n2; and idem, *Dogmatik des christlichen Glaubens* (Tübingen: Mohr, 1979), 2:10–12.

10. Martin Hengel, *The Son of God* (Philadelphia: Fortress Press, 1976), 2.

11. Oscar Cullmann, *The Christology of the New Testament* (London: SCM, 1963). The first German edition was published in 1957.

Lord, Christ, Son of David, and Son of God, and treated in an appendix the theme of eschatological prophet.[12] Though varying significantly on specific points of interpretation, Cullmann and Hahn shared a common focus in their concentration on titles as the reference point for examining the origin and course of christological development.

While continuing to devote considerable attention to titles, Reginald H. Fuller adopted a significantly different principle of organization for his work.[13] Adapting Wilhelm Bousset's sharp dichotomy between Jewish and Hellenistic Christianity,[14] Fuller proposed a three-stage division among Palestinian Judaism, Hellenistic Judaism, and Hellenistic Gentile worlds. To each environment corresponded, in Fuller's judgment, particular christological patterns. The preaching of the earliest stage, the Palestinian church, had two foci: the past word and work of Jesus and his future coming in glory. The second stratum, in a Hellenistic Jewish context, transformed the primitive kerygma into a proclamation of Jesus' present work as exalted Lord and Christ; still more concerned with Jesus' functions than his being, its Christology distinguished two stages in Jesus' activity—his historical ministry and his current reign. Finally, the Hellenistic Gentile mission replaced this twofold pattern with a three-stage framework of preexistence, incarnation, and exaltation. At this time, affirmations about the being of Jesus, not simply his saving functions, began to develop.

Works such as these have significantly enhanced appreciation of the complexities of early christological thought. Yet the presuppositions on which such studies are based have in part been called into question. The sharp division between Palestinian and Hellenistic spheres, even in the modified form advanced by Fuller, overlooks the penetration of Greek influence into Israel during the centuries before Jesus' birth.[15] Discontented with past analyses of early christological development, contemporary exegetes have continued to propose new reconstructions.

Among the many efforts to outline early christological thought, a proposal advanced by Helmut Koester is worthy of note as an initially helpful way of classifying the data. Koester identifies four basic christological trajectories that arose, independently of each other, in different Christian circles in the years between Jesus' death and the writing of the New Testament:[16]

1. An initial type, possibly the most primitive of all, conceived of Jesus as Son of man and coming Lord. Eschatological in focus, this Parousia Christology continued Jesus' own future-oriented preaching, but also identified him as the divine agent who would soon return in glory

---

12. Ferdinand Hahn, *The Titles of Jesus in Christology: Their History in Early Christianity* (Cleveland: World, 1969). This work, Hahn's dissertation at Heidelberg, was completed in 1961.

13. Reginald H. Fuller, *The Foundations of New Testament Christology* (London: Collins, 1965).

14. Wilhelm Bousset, *Kyrios Christos: A History of the Belief in Christ from the Beginnings of Christianity to Irenaeus* (Nashville: Abingdon, 1970). The original edition was published in 1913.

15. See Larry W. Hurtado, "New Testament Christology: A Critique of Bousset's Influence," *Theological Studies* 40 (1979): 306–17. Hurtado is strongly influenced by Martin Hengel, *Judaism and Hellenism*, 2 vols. (Philadelphia: Fortress Press, 1974).

16. For the following, see Helmut Koester, "The Structure and Criteria of Early Christian Beliefs," in *Trajectories through Early Christianity*, ed. James M. Robinson and Helmut Koester (Philadelphia: Fortress Press, 1971), 205–31.

to judge the world. This christological trajectory is reflected in such biblical passages as the apocalyptic discourse of Mark 13, the judgment scene of Matt. 25:31-46, and the Pauline exhortation of 1 Thess. 4:13—5:3. Ecclesiologically, it tends to foster separation of Jesus' followers from the rest of society.

2. In sharp contrast to the Parousia Christology's orientation toward the future, the second christological trajectory looks back on events in Jesus' public life, especially his miracles and exorcisms. Drawing on popular conceptions of the presence of divine powers in gifted religious figures, it understands Jesus as a "divine man" (*theios aner*). Divine-man Christology, evident in references to "Jesus of Nazareth, a man attested to you by God with mighty works and wonders and signs which God did through him in your midst" (Acts 2:22), promoted the handing on and embellishment of miracle stories (see, e.g., Mark 1:23-45); it may also be detected in the opponents Paul criticizes in 2 Corinthians. While not conducive to the development of stable communal consciousness, this model has exerted strong influence on the piety of individual Christians.

3. A third trajectory, wisdom Christology, parallels the second in its concentration on Jesus' public life, but sees him as teacher rather than miracle worker. In this model, Jesus is identified as envoy of divine wisdom (e.g., Matt. 11:25-30; Luke 11:49-51) or even, in more developed forms, as Wisdom incarnate (John 1:1-18; Phil. 2:5-11). The ecclesiological effect is a concentration on teaching, manifest in the development of the parable tradition, with corresponding focus on the theological school.

4. Lastly, a fourth christological model directed its attention to Jesus as crucified and raised from the dead. Reflected in early creedal formulations (e.g., 1 Cor. 15:3-8) and liturgical tradition (1 Cor. 11:23-26), this paschal Christology was strongly promoted by Paul. It took seriously the reality of human life and suffering, eventually created the literary genre of the canonical Gospels, and facilitated the Christian church's self-understanding as a new society created by God.

While approximately equal in age, these four christological models are not, in Koester's judgment, equal in quality. In the canonical New Testament, paschal Christology predominates and functions as the unifying factor. Far from being fortuitous, its preeminence reflects inherent superiority: greater fidelity to the historical Jesus, greater church-building power, and the ability to provide a framework within which the other types could be incorporated and used to enable formation of the gospel tradition.

Reaction to Koester's reconstruction of early christological development has varied. Edward Schillebeeckx has adopted, with some modifications, much of Koester's analysis but differs from Koester on two salient points. First, Schillebeeckx argues that prior to the emergence of any of the four trajectories, Jesus was identified as the long-awaited eschatological prophet, promised to Israel in words God addressed to Moses: "I will raise up for them a prophet like you from among their brethren; and I will put my words in his mouth, and he shall speak to them all that I command him" (Deut. 18:18, RSV). This initial identification of Jesus as the prophet like Moses undergirds the more differentiated models and accounts for the ability of the New Testament to unify them. Second, Schillebeeckx offers a different theological assessment of the various approaches. In his judgment, the identification of Jesus as eschatological prophet holds theological, as well as historical, pride of place. Paschal Christology is placed on the same level as the other models, and Koster's conviction of its inherent superiority is abandoned.[17]

Exegetes have also questioned certain aspects of Koester's work. In an assessment of Schillebeeckx's adaptation of Koester's reconstruction, George MacRae observed that "it is not entirely clear that these and only these are the earliest conceptions," and wondered if "adoptionist" Christology might be equally primitive.[18] Pointing in another direction, Petr Pokorny has stressed the centrality of the resurrection for all strands of Christology and warned against exaggerating the extent of diversity within the New Testament.[19] Appealing to 1 Cor. 15:11, Martin Hengel has also emphasized the unity of the early apostolic preaching.[20] Thus, Koester's reconstruction should not be taken as a definitive solution to the problem of Christology's early development.

Despite such criticisms, Koester's analysis of early christological trajectories can serve as a useful reference point in considering biblical interpretations of Jesus. At the very least, it draws attention to the depth and complexity of Christian thought in the formative years antedating the writing of the New Testament and serves as a warning against facile attempts to reduce christological reflection to a single title or a single perspective.

In the New Testament itself, interpretations of Jesus achieve canonical expression in more developed forms. While past studies of New Testament theology concentrated almost exclusively on Paul and John,[21] methods developed over the past four decades have led to the recognition of distinctive Christologies in other biblical authors as well. Since its inception in the 1950s with the pioneering work of Willi Marxsen on Mark, Günther Bornkamm on Matthew, and Hans Conzelmann on Luke, redaction criticism has succeeded in detecting the theological positions of the individual Synoptic evangelists by studying the ways in which these writers modified the sources on which they drew.[22] More recently, application of the principles of literary criticism to gospel research has shed light on the evangelists' theologies by examining the techniques employed in structuring their narratives.[23] These approaches make clear that the authors of the Synoptic Gospels, far from being mere collectors of available material about Jesus, were accomplished theologians whose works contain rich presentations of Christology not inferior to the more obviously theological reflections of

---

17. For Schillebeeckx's arguments, see *Jesus*, 401–515.

18. George MacRae, review of Edward Schillebeeckx's *Jesus: An Experiment in Christology*, *Religious Studies Review* 5 (1979): 270–73. The citation is from p. 271.

19. Petr Pokorny, *The Genesis of Christology* (Edinburgh: T&T Clark, 1987).

20. Martin Hengel, *The Atonement* (Philadelphia: Fortress Press, 1981), 34–39.

21. See, for example, Rudolf Bultmann, *Theology of the New Testament*, 2 vols. (New York: Scribner, 1951, 1955).

22. The classic texts are Willi Marxsen, *Mark the Evangelist: Studies on the Redaction History of the Gospel* (Nashville: Abingdon, 1969); Günther Bornkamm, Gerhard Barth, and Heinz Joachim Held, *Tradition and Interpretation in Matthew* (London: SCM, 1963); and Hans Conzelmann, *The Theology of Saint Luke* (London: Faber & Faber, 1961). For a more recent and more comprehensive study, see Rudolf Schnackenburg, *Jesus in the Gospels: A Biblical Christology* (Louisville: Westminster John Knox, 1995).

23. See Jack Dean Kingbury, *Jesus Christ in Matthew, Mark, and Luke* (Philadelphia: Fortress Press, 1981); idem, *Matthew* (Philadelphia: Fortress Press, 1978); Paul J. Achtemeier, *Mark*, 2nd ed. (Philadelphia: Fortress Press, 1986); and Frederick W. Danker, *Luke*, 2nd ed. (Philadelphia: Fortress Press, 1987).

the Pauline letters and Johannine writings. Each New Testament author offers a distinctive and valuable interpretation of Jesus' life and work.[24]

New Testament Christology thus spans a considerable range, as it includes the Pauline focus on Jesus' cross and resurrection, the Synoptic interpretations of his public life and passion, the Johannine account of the revelation of God in the Word become flesh, the Letter to the Hebrews' vision of Jesus in priestly categories, and the diverse reflections on Jesus embodied in the other canonical texts. This variety in perspective and content prevents distillation of a common Christology that could be termed *the* biblical conception of Jesus and used as a unified basis for further thought. Nonetheless, the diversity is not without limit;[25] all New Testament authors share a common conviction that in and through Jesus, something decisive for human salvation has occurred. The combination of diversity and unity suggests several elements of the New Testament's permanent legacy to the church's christological reflection.

First, nowhere in the New Testament is Christology developed in isolation from other theological questions. It is inseparable from a theology of history (including an eschatology), a conception of salvation, and a perspective on the church. These interconnections are not a historical accident; they reflect relationships inherent in the nature of Christology.

Second, the diversity of biblical Christology and its close connection with specific issues confronting the church at the time it was developed imply that systematic theology cannot rest content with merely organizing New Testament thought into a more orderly form. The New Testament itself demands that we move beyond it—a fact that in no way detracts from its permanent importance. It is in this sense that Schillebeeckx has observed that "New Testament Christianity can only be a model indirectly, and not directly,"[26] for later Christians.

Third, the importance of the New Testament's references to history, to certain factual events of the past and certain expectations regarding the future, must not be overlooked. Christology is not an expression of timeless truths; it is an assertion of the universal significance of someone who lived and died in a particular time and place.

Fourth, tendencies to divide the New Testament into works that propose a "high Christology" (affirming Jesus' divinity) and those content with "low Christology" (stopping short of that affirmation) should be viewed with suspicion. Such divisions are likely to confuse biblical expressions with similar terminology from the church's dogmatic tradition (e.g., by taking "Son of man" as a designation for Christ's humanity) and to underestimate the christological content articulated in forms unfamiliar to later usage.

Finally, both the content and the diversity of New Testament Christology inevitably pose the question of the legitimacy of the interpretations of Jesus given by the various biblical authors and by the early church in general. Karl Rahner has noted that if the New Testament evaluations

---

24. For a recent treatment of the Christology of the New Testament, see Frank J. Matera, *New Testament Christology* (Louisville: Westminster John Knox, 1999).

25. Gerhard Ebeling, in *The Word of God and Tradition* (Philadelphia: Fortress Press, 1968), 151, has rightly insisted that "in the last resort there has not been an indiscriminate acceptance of anything into the canon." These issues are pursued further in Alex Stock, *Einheit des Neuen Testaments: Erörterung hermeneutischer Grundpositionen der heutigen Theologie* (Einsiedeln: Benziger, 1969).

26. Schillebeeckx, *Christ*, 561.

264

of Jesus are valid, then the further step to the doctrine of the early councils is not especially problematic.[27] While the church recognizes the Scriptures as divinely inspired,[28] the validity of the New Testament's christological affirmations cannot simply be presumed in theological argumentation; it must be examined critically. One portion of that examination is, inevitably, a look at these affirmations' historical basis in Jesus' life and death.[29] Before considering these matters, however, we must first examine the postbiblical development of Christian thought on Jesus and his salvific work.

Classical Christology and Soteriology

The classical expression of the church's teaching about Jesus Christ was forged in the centuries immediately following completion of the New Testament. Christological reflection continued in the second and third centuries, especially in efforts to express Jesus' relationship to the Father and in conjunction with denials of Jesus' true humanity. Yet it was only in the fourth and fifth centuries that the development of classical christological doctrine reached its climax. The fourth-century controversy centered on Arianism and was addressed by the Council of Nicaea, the first ecumenical council, in 325. One hundred years later, the issues of Nestorianism and monophysitism were weighed by the Councils of Ephesus (431) and Chalcedon (451). In the aftermath of these councils, some related christological matters were considered by the Third Council of Constantinople in 681. The first part of this section will consider the formation of christological doctrine during this decisive period.

Motivated by concern for human salvation but formulated in opposition to doctrines judged to be heretical, the teaching of the early ecumenical councils focused on the person of Christ rather than his salvific work. Interpretations of his salvific activity developed at a different pace and never achieved comparable dogmatic status. For this reason, despite the intrinsic connection between the person and work of Christ, I shall postpone consideration of classical soteriological thought until later in this section.

Christology

In the fourth century, the major christological issues were the divinity of Christ and the integrity, or completeness, of his humanity. The chief biblical point of reference was John 1:14: "The Word [*Logos*] became flesh [*sarx*]." In the terms of Koester's models, the Christology of this period was largely a pursuit of one strand of primitive Christian thought: the incarnational type of wisdom Christology reflected in the prologue to the Fourth Gospel.

About the year 318, Arius, a priest in Alexandria (the center of Egyptian Christianity and a major location for theological learning), advanced the teaching that the *Logos* is not truly God, not equal to the Father. Instead, the *Logos* was created out of nothing by the Father as the first and highest creature, the only created reality made directly by God. The Word can be

---

27. Rahner, *Foundations of Christian Faith*, 285–86.

28. On biblical inspiration, see the Second Vatican Council's Dogmatic Constitution on Divine Revelation (*Dei verbum*), nos. 11–13.

29. As will become clear later in the chapter, this last point is not undisputed; such theologians as Rudolf Bultmann and Schubert Ogden deny it.

called Son and even God ("and the Word was God"; John 1:1), but is not of the same substance as the Father. While the Word existed before all other creatures, his existence had a beginning; there was a time when he was not. In due course, the *Logos* functioned as the instrument of the rest of creation ("all things were made through him"; John 1:3), while God remained in exalted distance from the world. In the incarnation, the Word became flesh through union with a human body. No human soul was present, for its place was taken by the *Logos*. Thus, Jesus Christ, in Arian understanding, is an intermediary being, neither divine nor human.

Though all parties agreed in acknowledging the authority of the Bible, proponents and adversaries of Arianism differed in their appeal to and interpretation of relevant biblical texts. In support of aspects of their teaching, adherents of Arianism could draw on passages such as John 14:28, in which Jesus declares, "The Father is greater than I," and Mark 13:32, which implies that the Father's knowledge exceeds that of the Son; in addition, in Prov. 8:22, personified Wisdom, a figure often interpreted christologically in early Christianity, speaks of itself as the first of God's creation. Arius's opponents, for their part, could take recourse to Jesus' statements that "The Father and I are one" (John 10:30) and that "Before Abraham was, I am" (John 8:58). While the issue of Jesus' relationship to the Father cannot be resolved by reference to individual biblical passages in isolation, it is not surprising that, in view of such diverse

biblical material, the dispute proved intractable.

An appealing figure, Arius quickly won popular support. In 320, he was condemned and excommunicated by a regional synod at Alexandria, but these measures proved ineffective, as his following had grown too large. Finally, in May 325, the emperor Constantine convened a general synod of bishops at Nicaea (in modern Turkey, not far from Istanbul). This first ecumenical council was well attended, with 220 to 300 participants. (Estimates vary; the traditional figure of 318 is symbolic, based on the number of Abraham's warriors in Genesis 14:14.)

After long and bitter debate, during which Arius was supported by several bishops, the anti-Arian party prevailed. An ancient creed of uncertain origin was reworked into the Nicene Creed, still used liturgically, though in expanded form. Subordination of the *Logos* to the Father was unambiguously rejected. The council professed that the Son is "true God from true God, begotten not made, of one substance (*homoousios*) with the Father." Of particular importance was the introduction of the nonbiblical term *homoousios*, which precluded diminution of the divinity of Christ and became the touchstone of fidelity to the conciliar teaching. To the creed itself the council appended an anathema directed against those who maintained characteristic Arian tenets.[30]

Despite condemnation at Nicaea, Arianism persisted for some time in many variants, as several compromise formulations were proposed. The controversy focused on Arianism's denial of

---

30. For the Greek text and an English translation, see J. N. D. Kelly, *Early Christian Creeds*, 3rd ed. (New York: McKay, 1972), 215–16. On Arianism and the Council of Nicaea, see ibid., 205–62; Kelly, *Early Christian Doctrines* (New York: Harper & Row, 1960), 223–51; Leo D. Davis, *The First Seven Ecumenical Councils (325–787): Their History and Theology* (Wilmington, DE: Glazier, 1987), 33–80; Alois Grillmeier, *Christ in Christian Tradition*, 2nd ed. (Atlanta: Knox, 1975), 1:219–73; John Courtney Murray, *The Problem of God* (New Haven: Yale University Press, 1964), 31–60; I. Ortiz de Urbina, *Nicée et Constantinople* (Paris: Éditions de l'Orante, 1963), 13–136; and Klaus Schatz, *Allgemeine Konzilien: Brennpunkte der Kirchengeschichte* (Stuttgart: UTB, 2008), 27–44.

266 Christ's divinity; those involved in the controversy took less account of the fact that Arianism also undercut Christ's humanity. In the ensuing disputes, the chief proponent of Nicaea's teaching was Athanasius, who had been present at the council as an Alexandrian deacon and in 328 became bishop of Alexandria. His chief argument against the Arians was soteriological: "He became man that we might be divinized."[31] Salvation is participation in divine life (see 2 Peter 1:4). Unless the *Logos* is divine, Athanasius argued, salvation through Christ is impossible; an adequate theology of salvation requires rejection of all forms of Arianism.

With much difficulty, Nicaea's rejection of Arianism won general acceptance in East and West over the course of the next half century. Eventually, the climate became emphatically anti-Arian, with heavy stress on the divinity of Christ in theology and general piety.[32]

Before we proceed to the christological councils of the fifth century, a few remarks must be made about earlier thought on the humanity of Christ. At an early date, some denied the reality of Christ's body, often on the basis of a general conviction that matter is evil. Gnostics and Manicheans held that his body was only a costume worn to conceal his true identity (a position called docetism, from the Greek *dokeo*, "seem"). Among other things, these views entail denial of the reality of the crucifixion.

A more specifically christological rejection of the integrity of Christ's humanity is the denial of the presence in him of all or part of a human soul. Arianism held this position, along with its denial of his divinity. While affirming the divinity of the *Logos*, Apollinarianism (named after Apollinarius, bishop of Laodicea from c. 360) held that the active principle of the soul, the *nous*, was replaced in Christ by the *Logos*. In its subordination to the *Logos*, Christ's humanity lacked its own active principle. This teaching was rightly repudiated by most Christians. The First Council of Constantinople (381), though more concerned to defend the divinity of the Holy Spirit against the Pneumatomachians, also rejected Apollinarianism in passing.[33] Operative in theological criticism of Apollinarianism was the soteriological principle already mentioned: if Christ does not have a human soul, then he is not truly human; if he is not truly human, then we are not truly saved.

Arianism and Apollinarianism, and also much orthodox Christology, have a common basis in the use of what has been called a *Logos-sarx* (Word-flesh) christological model. Typical of Alexandria, this approach is represented by Athanasius, among others. The terminology is derived from John 1:14. There, *sarx* does not mean body as distinguished from soul, but rather full human reality.[34] Later *Logos-sarx* Christology, however, typically compared the unity of divinity and humanity in Jesus with the union of soul and body in all human beings, and either denied the presence of a human soul in Christ (Arius, Apollinarius) or affirmed the integrity of his humanity without seeing his human soul (intellect and will) as a major salvific

---

31. Athanasius *De incarnatione* 54 (*Patrologia graeca*, ed. J. B Migne [hereafter PG], 25, 192b).

32. On the effects, see Josef A. Jungmann, *The Place of Christ in Liturgical Prayer* (Staten Island, NY: Alba House, 1965).

33. On this council, see Davis, *The First Seven Ecumenical Councils*, 81–133; and Ortiz de Urbina, *Nicee et Constantinople*, 137–242.

34. On this verse, see Raymond E. Brown, *The Gospel according to John* (Garden City, NY: Doubleday, 1966), 1:13, 30–35.

factor (Athanasius). This Alexandrian Christology continued into the fifth century, with Cyril (patriarch of Alexandria, 412–444) its major proponent. In this approach, the unity of Christ, based on the rule of the *Logos*, is so emphasized that the role of Christ's humanity is obscured, though its reality is not denied.

In the late fourth and early fifth centuries, a new type of Christology arose further to the East. Centered in Antioch, this approach has been called a *Logos-anthropos* (Word-man) Christology. Its chief early figures, Diodor of Tarsus (d. before 394) and Theodore of Mopsuestia (d. 428), were connected with Antioch's school of catechists. In contrast to Alexandria, the Antiochene school emphasized the distinction of two natures in Christ and sought to give full scope to his human nature. It encountered difficulty, however, in articulating clearly the unity of Christ.

Behind the thought of each school lie legitimate christological concerns. Yet, in the fifth century, when each school absolutized its position and ignored or rejected the intention of the other, serious problems arose. Christological debate raged from 428, when controversy erupted in Constantinople, to 451, when a widely (though not universally) accepted resolution was produced at the Council of Chalcedon. To understand Chalcedon's achievement, it is necessary to grasp the history of the dispute. The first stage is marked by the rise and rejection of Nestorianism.

In 428, Nestorius, an Antiochene monk, was appointed patriarch of Constantinople by Emperor Theodosius II. Later that year, he was drawn into a dispute concerning the use of *theotokos* (bearer of God) as a title for Mary.

Though the title was ancient and enjoyed considerable popularity, Nestorius supported its critics and recommended instead honoring Mary as *christotokos*, bearer of Christ. That term was certainly unobjectionable, but the legitimacy of *theotokos* remained a matter of contention.

While the language directly concerns Mary, the underlying issue is christological and was immediately recognized as such: Is the unity of Christ such that his mother can be called Mother of God? Aside from considerations of context, the word *theotokos* can have varying meanings. Its use as a Marian title cannot mean that Mary is divine or that she is the source of Christ's divinity. Nonetheless, since motherhood relates to a person and since the person of Jesus is divine, Mary is rightly called Mother of God. As far as Jesus' natures are concerned, she is the source of his human reality, not his divinity. Thus, the term *theotokos*, ambiguous in itself, has a legitimate Christian sense.[35]

In 428, the christological terminology used in the preceding paragraph, especially *person* and *nature*, was not yet available for common use. The dispute quickly became bitter. Monks in Constantinople, Alexandrian in their theological orientation, opposed Nestorius and immediately sent excerpts from his writings to Alexandria and Rome. The patriarch of Alexandria, Cyril, and Nestorius then exchanged letters. Cyril offered a detailed commentary on the teaching of Nicaea and urged Nestorius to alter his views. Nestorius in turn accused Cyril of misunderstanding Nicaea. Each wrote to Rome seeking support, but only Cyril strengthened his case by providing translations of the disputed texts. In 430, a local Roman synod under Celestine I condemned Nestorius's

---

35. These issues are discussed helpfully by Karl Rahner in remarks cited by Klaus Riesenhuber, *Maria im theologischen Verständnis von Karl Barth und Karl Rahner* (Freiburg: Herder, 1973), 72–73n49.

teaching and authorized Cyril to obtain from Nestorius a repudiation of his previous position. When Nestorius refused to comply, Cyril conducted a synod in Alexandria. The synod produced a christological confession and a list of twelve anathemas,[36] which were sent to Constantinople for Nestorius to sign. In addition to speaking of Mary as *theotokos*, the text refers to a "natural union" in Christ and compares the union of his divinity and humanity to the union of soul and body in all human beings. The Alexandrians were apparently unaware that such language would inevitably awaken suspicions of Apollinarianism.

Hoping to reestablish peace, Emperor Theodosius convened a council to assemble in Ephesus on June 7, 431. On the appointed day, over two hundred bishops, including Cyril and Nestorius, were present, but the Eastern bishops, led by John of Antioch, had not yet arrived. On June 22, despite their continued absence, Cyril forced the opening of the council, over the protests of at least sixty bishops and the imperial representative. Under the circumstances, Nestorius refused to appear. On its first day, the council read the Nicene Creed, Cyril's second letter to Nestorius, and Nestorius's reply. The letter of Cyril was approved, and Nestorius's response was condemned as contrary to Nicaea. The twelve anathemas of the Alexandrian synod were received favorably but not voted on. Finally, Nestorius was deposed.

Four days later, the Eastern bishops arrived in Ephesus. Upon hearing what had happened, they immediately assembled and condemned Cyril, both for his procedure and for favoring Arianism and Apollinarianism. In early July,

the papal legates reached Ephesus and, in accordance with their instructions, confirmed the condemnation of Nestorius. Cyril's party then excommunicated the bishop of Antioch. At this point, the emperor's representative ended the council. Theodosius eventually took Cyril's part and exiled Nestorius from Constantinople, first to Antioch and then to Egypt. Cyril returned to Alexandria a theological and political success.

The Council of Ephesus produced no new creed and no new christological formula. Its accomplishments were limited to condemning Nestorianism, affirming the legitimacy of *theotokos* as a title for Mary, and accepting Cyril's second letter to Nestorius as an authentic interpretation of Nicaea. A complete victory for the Alexandrian school, the council was too one-sided to bring about reconciliation.[37]

From the conclusion of the council until Cyril's death in 444, notable efforts were made to reunite the two factions. Both John of Antioch and Cyril were anxious to bring about reconciliation. In 433, Theodoret of Cyrrhus, the last great Antiochene theologian, composed a creed of union and an explanation of proper christological vocabulary,[38] which were acceptable to Cyril. The creed speaks of two natures in Christ yet also confesses that there is but "one Christ, one Son, one Lord." The title *theotokos* is applied to Mary. Drawing on the terminology of Nicaea but expanding its use, the creed teaches that Christ is *homoousios* with the Father according to his divinity and *homoousios* with us according to his humanity. While the creed of union was not universally accepted (some Alexandrians felt that Cyril conceded too much in

---

36. See Denzinger-Schönmetzer, *Enchiridion Symbolorum* (hereafter DS), 252–63.
37. On Nestorianism and the Council of Ephesus, see Grillmeier, *Christ in Christian Tradition*, 1:443–87.
38. DS 271–73.

accepting reference to two natures), the new formula resulted in a relatively peaceful period that lasted until Cyril's death in 444.[39]

Cyril was succeeded at Alexandria by his archdeacon Dioscorus, a foe of the two-natures terminology and of Cyril's policy of reconciliation. Four years later, Eutyches, the leader of the monks in Constantinople, rejected the formula of union and accused its defenders of Nestorianism; he taught instead the presence of one nature in Christ (monophysitism). Under the leadership of the patriarch Flavian, a synod in Constantinople condemned Eutyches, but he found support from Dioscorus and from Emperor Theodosius. Over the opposition of the bishop of Rome, Leo the Great (440–461), the emperor summoned a new general council to meet again in Ephesus. Dioscorus was designated to preside, and the council was intended to repeat the condemnation of Nestorianism, condemn Flavian, and rehabilitate Eutyches.

The assembly convened on August 8, 449. Roman legates arrived with a dogmatic letter from Leo,[40] which stressed the unity of Christ and confessed the presence of two natures.[41] The legates were not allowed to have the letter read. Instead, Eutyches defended his teaching and was declared orthodox by about 80 percent of the 130 to 140 bishops in attendance. When the minority protested efforts to have Flavian deposed, Dioscorus had the assembly disrupted by imperial soldiers and a crowd of monks. A later meeting, which the papal legates refused to attend, condemned the major Antiochene theologians. Alexandria had once again triumphed, and the reunion of 433 was annulled.

Yet the meeting at Ephesus won no general acceptance. Both Flavian and the papal legates protested to Rome. Leo denounced the assembly as a gathering of robbers and demanded that a new council be convened. In July 450, the death of Theodosius brought with it a shift in imperial policy. Theodosius's influential and antimonophysite sister Pulcheria quickly married Marcian, a former military commander, and aided her husband's ascent to the throne. The new emperor exiled Eutyches from Constantinople and called a council, initially intended for Nicaea in deliberate imitation of Constantine, but finally convened at Chalcedon, very near Constantinople, on October 8, 451.

Chalcedon was the best attended of the early councils, with approximately 350 bishops in attendance, all but seven from the East. Influenced by Roman legates and imperial commissioners, its early sessions reaffirmed the Nicene Creed and Leo's letter to Flavian. Dioscorus was then tried and deposed. In the fifth session, a crisis developed, as the imperial representatives insisted on formulating a new creed in order to achieve complete clarity. After a first draft was found ambiguous, especially by the Roman legates, a commission of bishops succeeded in drawing up an acceptable text, which was then adopted. This creed became the classical formulation of christological doctrine. Its purpose is to profess both the unity of Christ and the completeness of his divinity and humanity:

> Following then the holy Fathers, we all with one voice teach that it should be confessed that our Lord Jesus Christ is one and the same Son, the

---

39. For an English translation of the formula of union, see Davis, *The First Seven Ecumenical Councils*, 161–62.

40. DS 290–95.

41. For a study of Leo's Christology in its historical context, see Susan Wessel, *Leo the Great and the Spiritual Rebuilding of a Universal Rome* (Boston: Brill, 2008).

Same perfect in Godhead, the Same perfect in manhood, truly God and truly man, the Same (consisting) of a rational soul and a body; *homoousios* with the Father as to his Godhead, and the Same *homoousios* with us as to his manhood; in all things like unto us, sin only excepted; begotten of the Father before ages as to his Godhead, and in the last days, the Same, for us and for our salvation, of Mary the Virgin *Theotokos* as to his manhood.

One and the same Christ, Son, Lord, Only begotten, made known in two natures (which exist) without confusion, without change, without division, without separation; the difference of the natures having been in no wise taken away by reason of the union, but rather the properties of each being preserved, and (both) concurring into one Person (*prosopon*) and one *hypostasis*—not parted or divided into two persons (*prosopa*), but one and the same Son and Only-begotten, the divine Logos, the Lord Jesus Christ; even as the prophets from of old (have spoken) concerning him, and as the lord Jesus Christ himself has taught us, and as the Symbol of the Fathers has delivered to us.[42]

The council expresses its doctrine in a variety of ways. The definition first professes belief in the unity of Christ with the simple confession that "our Lord Jesus Christ is one and the same Son." The phrase "one and the same" is used twice, and the word *same* four other times, thus emphasizing the unity. Here the text draws on the creed of union of 433 but uses nontechnical expressions that both schools, Alexandrian and Antiochene, could understand, thus establishing a context for reconciling the conflicting terminologies.

In an equally understandable way, stress is laid on both the divinity and the humanity of Christ. To accomplish this, the most disputed word of the previous century, *homoousios*, is used twice: Christ is *homoousios* with the Father and *homoousios* with us. (The meaning is, of course, not the same in each case: there is only one divine nature, while there are many human beings.)

Yet the fifth-century debate had to be addressed more precisely. Chalcedon therefore spoke of Christ as one "in two natures" (not "from two natures"), a clear rejection of monophysitism. The creed then confesses that the difference of the natures (divine and human) is not removed by their union but rather preserved, as the two natures are united in one person (*prosopon*) and one hypostasis. The term *hypostasis* is used in addition to *prosopon* to stress that in this context, *prosopon* signifies something real and not what its original meaning in profane Greek would suggest: a mask, or appearance. In English, it is customary to speak of the "hypostatic union" of the two natures in the one person of Christ.

Of special importance is the council's use of four adverbs that express in summary form key characteristics of the union: *asygchytos* (without confusion), *atreptos* (without change), *adiairetos* (without division), and *achoristos* (without separation). The first two adverbs contain a rejection of monophysitism, by insisting that neither nature is destroyed in the union; the final pair rejects nestorianism by insisting on Christ's unity. The juxtaposition of the four words reflects Chalcedon's concern to oppose the extreme positions of both Alexandria and Antioch. The balance that results accounts in large part for the council's success.[43]

---

42. The translation is taken from Robert V. Sellers, *The Council of Chalcedon: A Historical and Doctrinal Survey* (London: SPCK, 1953), 210–11. For the original Greek text (with Latin translation), see DS 301–2.

43. For further indication of the issues Chalcedon's definition helps to clarify, see Bernard Lonergan, "Christ as Subject: A Reply," in *Collection* (New York: Herder, 1967), 192–93. "Two natures" answers the question of "what" Jesus Christ

Chalcedon's use of *person* and *nature* is not identical with the way these terms were used in any particular ancient philosophy. Nor does the council seek to provide a precise definition of its technical vocabulary. Rather, the meaning of the terms is specified operatively, that is, by the way they are used. Like other dogmatic definitions, Chalcedon's teaching entails an ecclesial regulation of language: in this case, the church determines authoritatively that certain words (*nature*, *person*) are to be used in a specific way in christological application. This decision contributes to preserving and promoting Christian unity in faith by providing a common language for use in speaking about Christ. Yet it does not preclude use of other terminology in speaking about Christ. Nor does it imply that the words in question have always had the meaning attributed to them by the council.[44]

The standard argument in support of Chalcedon's teaching appeals to the communication of idioms, or the exchange of attributes. Presupposing biblical Christology, this argumentation notes that in the New Testament, both divine and human attributes are predicated of the one subject, Christ. Reference is made to such passages as Acts 3:15 ("You have killed the author of life") and John 17:5 ("Father, glorify me with the glory which I had with you before the world was made"). Such statements are possible only if both natures, divine and human, are present

and united in a single person; a merely moral union would not be sufficient to justify speaking in this way of death and suffering.

Despite its balance, Chalcedon was not universally accepted. Most Egyptian bishops rejected the two-natures terminology as a betrayal of Ephesus and Cyril, while Nestorians remained unwilling to accept *theotokos*. Both monophysite and Nestorian churches still exist; Coptic Christians (chiefly in Egypt and Ethiopia) remain monophysite, and there are Nestorians in Syria and India. As a result of ecumenical dialogue in recent decades, the Catholic Church has signed (separately) joint christological statements with non-Chalcedonian churches representing the Alexandrian and the Antiochene traditions; these texts affirm the churches' common christological faith, notwithstanding their historical variations in christological terminology. Nonetheless, controverted ecclesiological matters remain a stumbling block to full ecclesial communion.[45]

In the years after Chalcedon, various efforts were made to reconcile the monophysites, chiefly by retaining Chalcedon's formula but placing greater stress on the unity of Christ. One such effort had significant doctrinal repercussions. To allay fears about division within Christ, the patriarch Sergius of Constantinople (610–638) taught that although there are two natures in Christ, there is only one operation of the will,

---

is; "one person" answers the question of "who" he is. As Lonergan's series of questions and answers imply, the issues, though pertinent to many christological issues, come to a head in the understanding of Jesus' crucifixion.

44. On the regulation of language inherent in all dogmatic definitions, see Karl Rahner, "What Is a Dogmatic Statement?" in *Theological Investigations* (Baltimore: Helicon, 1966), 5:42–66. On the council's use of words as technical terms, see Frans Jozef van Beeck, *Christ Proclaimed: Christology as Rhetoric* (New York: Paulist, 1979), 131–33.

45. See Alois Wilhelm Grillmeier, *Christ in Christian Tradition*, vol. 2, part 1 (Atlanta: Knox, 1987); de Vries, "The Reasons for the Rejection of the Council of Chalcedon by the Oriental Orthodox Churches," *Wort und Wahrheit*, supplement 1 (Vienna: Herder, 1972), 54–60; Ronald G. Roberson, "The Modern Roman Catholic–Oriental Orthodox Dialogue," *One in Christ* 21 (1985): 238–54. The "Common Christological Declaration between the Catholic Church and the Assyrian Church of the East," signed in Rome on November 11, 1994, by Pope John Paul II and Patriarch Khanania Mar Dinkha IV, is an example of contemporary christological agreement after centuries of discord.

272 which is both divine and human. Many mono-physites found this formulation acceptable. The resulting reconciliation of several provinces with Constantinople won the approval of the emperor Heraclius (610–641), who in 638 signed a decree confessing "one will of our Lord Jesus Christ." This teaching is open to the interpretation that the exercise of Jesus' human freedom was always an act of the one person (in that case, it is faithful to Chalcedon), but it could also be taken as a denial of the existence of a human will in Jesus (in which case, the integrity of his human nature is abbreviated).

While Pope Honorius (625–638) did not object to the teaching,[46] others—for example, Maximus Confessor and Sophronius of Jerusalem—saw the problem more clearly. In 649, a Lateran synod condemned monothelitism (one will in Christ) and taught instead the presence of two harmoniously united wills, one divine, one human.[47] After fierce controversy, during which the aged Maximus was barbarically tortured at the hands of monothelites, the matter was finally addressed at the Third Council of Constantinople (680–681).[48] The christological definition of Constantinople III cites Chalcedon, teaches the presence of two wills and two operations of the wills in Jesus, and notes the submission of his human will to the divine will.

This teaching does not add to the content of Chalcedon, for two natures imply two wills, but it was an important explication and defense of Chalcedonian doctrine. More than an abstract principle is at stake, for without a human will, Christ could exercise no human freedom.[49]

With the Third Council of Constantinople, the development of church doctrine on the person of Jesus is substantially complete. Christological issues, in this sense, were not at stake in the division of the Eastern and Western churches or at the time of the Reformation, and thus did not evoke additional official reaction. More recently, such mid-twentieth-century Neo-Scholastic theologians as Paul Galtier and Pietro Parente have debated the implications of the hypostatic union for Christ's psychological constitution,[50] and many authors have analyzed the differences between the use of the terms *person* and *nature* in the ancient councils and the meaning of these words in contemporary usage.[51] But modern official statements on the person of Christ, such as Pope Pius XII's encyclical *Sempiternus rex* (1951) and the Congregation for the Doctrine of the Faith's declaration *Mysterium Filii Dei* (1972), largely confine themselves to paraphrasing the teachings of the early councils and insisting on their continued validity.[52]

---

46. See DS 487–88.

47. DS 510.

48. DS 553–59.

49. On the history of Constantinople III, see Davis, *The Seven Ecumenical Councils*, 258–89. The theological significance of the issue is discussed by Raymund Schwager, *Der wunderbare Tausch: Zur Geschichte und Deutung der Erlösungslehre* (Munich: Kösel, 1986), 135–60.

50. See Paul Galtier, *L'unité du Christ: Être, personne, conscience* (Paris: Beauchesne, 1939); Pietro Parente, *L'Io di Christo* (Brescia: Morcelliana, 1951). On this debate, see Alois Grillmeier, "The Figure of Christ in Catholic Theology Today," in *Renewal in Dogma*, vol. 1 of *Theology Today* (Milwaukee: Bruce, 1965), 92–97.

51. See, e.g., Karl Rahner, "Current Problems in Christology," 158–63; Piet Schoonenberg, *The Christ* (New York: Herder & Herder, 1971), 50–105. Freedom and self-consciousness are now often associated with "person" rather than "nature."

52. For the original Latin texts, see *Acta Apostolicae Sedis* 43 (1951): 625–44 and 64 (1972): 237–41; for English translations, see *Eastern Churches Quarterly* 9 (1952): 229–44; *Catholic Mind* 70 (1972): 61–64.

In recent centuries, the development of classical christological dogma has been assessed in widely varying ways, which can be grouped into three basic categories. A theologian's assessment of this issue is a reliable indication of that author's overall christological position:

1. Some authors consider the dogmatic development an aberration that replaced New Testament Christology with philosophical reflection on the person and natures of Christ. From this perspective, the Christology of the patristic period has been rejected as a Hellenization of Christianity, in which Greek metaphysical speculation supplanted the Bible's historical mode of thought and fostered an often intolerant preoccupation with doctrine. Criticisms of this sort were registered in the past by liberal Protestant theology; Adolf von Harnack (1851–1930), who opposed gospel to dogma, is an important historical example. More recently, Leslie Dewart has advocated a similar position, and Hans Küng's *On Being a Christian* reflects some similar tendencies.[53]

2. Diametrically opposed to this position is a conception that Avery Dulles has termed the dogmatic approach to Christology.[54] Authors of this persuasion typically conceive the conciliar development as a movement from the New Testament's concern with more functional Christology (Christ in his significance for us) to a more ontological Christology (Christ himself), and evaluate this step as progress from the order in which realities become known to us to the order in which they exist in themselves. The conciliar development can then be taken not only as true, but also as providing the proper framework for further christological questioning. Bernard Lonergan's Latin writings on Christology provide an example of this position, which is also reflected in more recent work influenced by Lonergan's conception of theological method.[55]

3. A third position judges the early councils' doctrine to be a true expression of the reality of Christ, and usually considers itself still bound by their authoritative regulation of christological language. Nonetheless, it finds the development of dogma marked by a gradual narrowing of the question. While issues concerning Christ's divinity and humanity are important, they are not the only significant questions for Christology to address. Adherents of this third approach often note that, although the patristic period was moved by soteriological concerns, its final formulations do not incorporate an explicit soteriology. Thus, the conciliar teaching, while true, neither exhausts the matter nor determines the agenda for all future christological investigation. This assessment is widespread among major contemporary theologians.[56]

In my judgment, only the third position does justice to all dimensions of the actual development. Christology is free to develop new terminology and to address issues that the early councils did not face. This is all the more neces-

---

53. See Harnack's widely read lectures on the essence of Christianity, delivered at the University of Berlin in 1899–1900 and translated as *What Is Christianity?* (Philadelphia: Fortress Press, 1986); and L. Dewart, *The Future of Belief* (New York: Herder, 1966). For a telling critique of Dewart, see Bernard Lonergan, "The Dehellenization of Dogma," in *A Second Collection* (Philadelphia: Westminster, 1974), 11–32.

54. Avery Dulles, "Contemporary Approaches to Christology: Analysis and Reflection," *Living Light* 13 (1976): 119–44.

55. See B. Lonergan, *De Verbo Incarnato*, 3rd ed., 4 vols. (Rome: Pontifica Universitas Gregoriana, 1964); Daniel A. Helminiak, *The Same Jesus: A Contemporary Christology* (Chicago: Loyola University Press, 1986).

56. See especially Karl Rahner, "Current Problems in Christology."

sary in view of the ease with which ancient terminology can be misunderstood in the modern world.[57] Yet contemporary Christology should be measured against the conciliar teaching, especially that of Chalcedon, to ensure that its content does not fall short of expressing what the church has recognized in Jesus. Chalcedon's regulation of the christological use of the terms *person* and *nature* also continues to deserve respect.

Soteriology

To complete this survey of classical Christology and soteriology, we must now turn explicitly to the question of Christ's work. While not completely separable from the person of Christ, soteriology has its own distinctive history and must be considered by itself. In this area, we have no official teaching comparable to the dogmas of Nicaea and Chalcedon regarding Christ's person. Soteriology has been more varied (perhaps necessarily so) than Christology, where a fixed terminology has been more firmly established.

In classifying soteriologists, it is useful to ask what aspect or aspects of Christ's existence are seen as salvific. The four major points of reference are Christ's incarnation, public life, crucifixion, and resurrection, either alone or in some combination.[58] Is salvation attributed to God's presence in Jesus? To Jesus' teaching and example? To his death on the cross? To his exaltation after death? Or must these items be drawn together more closely than this series of questions suggests? Various positions have been

held in the history of Christian thought. Each choice reflects basic theological intentions; each choice has consequences and can be assessed in part with reference to those consequences. A sketch of the historical development will help clarify the issues.

In the patristic period, there was no unified systematic soteriology. The Fathers developed instead a wide variety of themes and images, each of which contributed something to the overall picture. Only a few significant features can be mentioned here, without any attempt to discuss individual authors in detail.

A basic theme is an antidualist principle, stressed especially in anti-Gnostic writing. The question of salvation is often cast in terms of a struggle between good and evil, between God and the devil. Yet this conception, much praised by such modern authors as Gustaf Aulen for its dramatic thrust and for its emphasis on salvation as the work of God,[59] is always accompanied by an insistence that creation is good. While patristic soteriology speaks of conflict and opposition in the history of salvation, and even of God's triumph over hostile powers (see also Col. 2:15), it rejects any metaphysical dualism in which the world is seen as evil by nature. Salvation is salvation of the world, not escape from the world.

A more specific theory, perhaps the most important theme of the period, is the idea of recapitulation. This conception derives from Irenaeus of Lyons, though it has biblical foundation in Paul's epistles. Christ is seen as the

---

57. A particular danger is that reference to "one person" may be misunderstood as denial of Jesus' humanity. Conversely, of course, to speak of Jesus as a "human person" departs from the conciliar regulation of language and may be construed as a denial of his divinity.

58. See Cornelius Mayer, "Von der satisfaction zur liberatio? Zur Problematik eines neuen Ansatzes in der Soteriologie," *Zeitschrift für Katholische Theologie* 96 (1974): 405–14.

59. See Gustaf Aulen, *Christus Victor: An Historical Study of the Three Main Types of the Idea of the Atonement* (New York: Macmillan, 1969). The book is based on lectures delivered at the University of Uppsala in 1930.

new Adam (see Romans 5; 1 Corinthians 15), the new head of creation who summarizes or recapitulates in himself the whole of creation. His coming is the fullness of time (Gal. 4:4), the climax of human history. The central biblical text for this approach is Eph. 1:10, which speaks of God's plan to sum up (*anakephalaiosasthai*) all things in Christ. In patristic thought, the incarnation is the beginning and foundation of such recapitulation, but there is also a resurrectional component; it is as "firstborn of the dead" (Col. 1:18) that Christ restores to the human race the existence in the image and likeness of God that had been lost in Adam.

This theory, which combines several biblical themes, especially from Pauline sources, remained influential throughout the patristic period. Closely connected with the principle that what is not assumed in Christ is not saved, it focuses attention on the incarnation. More ontological than juridical in its terminology, it conceives of salvation primarily as communication of and participation in divine life (2 Peter 1:3-4), not primarily as forgiveness of sin. Salvation is the perfection of creation.

Yet patristic thought is not exhausted in the notion of recapitulation. Many authors, including those who favored the theme of recapitulation, also accented the idea of divine education of the human race in and through Christ. Here emphasis is placed on the teaching and example of Jesus' public life. Irenaeus, for example, writes that Christ wanted to be our teacher so "that through imitation of his works and performance of his words we might have commu-

nion with him" and that "had the truth already been known, the coming of the Redeemer into the world would have been superfluous."[60] This theme, also to be found in later authors, prevents the idea of salvation through recapitulation from becoming an automatic physical process.[61]

Finally, the idea of divine triumph over the devil was often elaborated in detail. On the basis of Jesus' reference to giving his life as a ransom for many (Matt. 20:28; Mark 10:45), Origen and numerous other theologians developed the idea that Christ was a ransom offered to the devil for the fallen human race, which had become the devil's property through sin. Deceived through inability to perceive Christ's divinity, Satan swallowed the bait, exchanging control over the rest of the human race for Christ. When Christ rose from the dead, the devil was completely overcome. While popular at the time, the theory of ransom paid to the devil always met resistance; Gregory of Nazianzus, among others, rejected its notion of God as blasphemous.[62]

While patristic thought drew upon a multiplicity of images to suggest a variety of soteriological insights, medieval theologians, especially in the West, developed a more rigorously reasoned theoretical account of Christ's salvific activity. Salvation was envisioned as forgiveness of sin, attention fixed firmly on the cross, and theology developed in juridical categories. The chief figure in this process was Anselm of Canterbury (1033/34–1109).

A strong critic of any notion of ransom paid or offered to the devil, Anselm sought to show that the Christian idea of the incarnation is

---

60. Irenaeus, *Adversus Haereses* 5.1.1; 2.18.6.

61. This theme is particularly accented by Gisbert Greshake, "Der Wandel der Erlösungsvorstellungen in der Theologiegeschichte," in *Gottes Heil—Glück des Menschen* (Freiburg: Herder, 1983), 50–79; this essay is based on a widely noted lecture delivered in Munich in 1972. For a differing emphasis and critique of Greshake's position, see Hans Urs von Balthasar, *Theo-Drama 4* (San Francisco: Ignatius, 1994), 244–54.

62. The conception is analyzed in more detail by Raymund Schwager, *Der wunderbare Tausch*, 32–53.

276 compatible with God's dignity. Entitling his work *Cur Deus homo?* (*Why God Became Man?*) he divides his argument into two parts. First, he seeks to demonstrate that without the incarnation, salvation of the human race would be impossible (book 1). Then, against this background, he argues that salvation is God's intention for the human race (book 2). The incarnation, far from being inappropriate for God, is in fact a necessary element in fulfilling God's purpose in creation. In the course of these analyses, Anselm develops his theory of satisfaction, which has influenced Western thought to the present day.

Anselm's starting point is an assessment of sin and its effects. Instead of concentrating on the content of specific sinful deeds, Anselm views sin formally, as an offense against God. Drawing on the legal theory of his day, he measures guilt and the resulting debt in qualitative terms, with reference to the dignity of the offended party. In the case of sin, the offended party is God, and the resulting debt is therefore infinite. Either punishment or satisfaction is necessary. As long as the matter remains unresolved, the proper order of the universe is disrupted, for God is not a private figure but Creator of heaven and earth.

Like sin, payment of the appropriate satisfaction is also measured qualitatively, but here the point of reference is the one who offers satisfaction in repayment of the debt. Concretely, this means that the human race, left on its own, is unable to pay the debt it has contracted. Any attempted satisfaction would remain finite and therefore insufficient, and in any case, the human race has nothing that it does not already owe to God. On purely human terms, the disrupted cosmic order cannot be restored.

Yet punishment is no adequate solution. Punishment of humanity would leave God's plans for creation frustrated—an intolerable notion. To forget or ignore the debt is equally impossible, for divine mercy is inseparable from divine justice, and in any case, ignoring the debt would leave the proper order disturbed. At the same time, since human dignity and freedom must be respected, satisfaction must be offered by a member of the human race.

From a combination of these ideas, Anselm concludes to the necessity of the incarnation. The debt must be repaid, and a human being must repay it; yet apart from the incarnation, no human being can do so. Therefore, given both God's initial free choice in creating the human race for a specific end and the fact of human sin, the incarnation of God's Son is needed to achieve the divine purpose. Since death is a consequence of sin and Christ is sinless, he did not have to die. Nonetheless, as a true human being composed of body and soul, he was able to die if he freely chose to do so. Because of the dignity of his person as true God, his death is of infinite value and constitutes the necessary satisfaction for sin. Incarnation is the necessary presupposition of a necessary redemption.[63]

In the centuries that followed, Anselm's theory achieved widespread acceptance in the West, though it has never been defined as a dogma by the church. In the course of its reception, however, various modifications were introduced into Anselm's conception. The most influential change derives from Thomas Aquinas. Aquinas in general supported Anselm, though he also used other models in his soteriology. Yet Thomas opposed Anselm's idea that the incarnation was necessary for redemption. In his

---

63. An English translation of *Cur Deus Homo?* is available in *Saint Anselm: Basic Writings* (LaSalle, IL: Open Court, 1968), 171–288.

judgment, the incarnation was very appropriate ("convenient"), a fitting and reasonable thing for God to do, but not strictly necessary. Thomas held that the incarnation was necessary only on the condition that God demands full satisfaction. Why God requires this and why satisfaction is accomplished precisely in Christ's death remain mysteries of divine freedom. Had God so willed, redemption could have been accomplished differently.

Later developments can be mentioned more briefly. While Martin Luther revived certain aspects of patristic thought on Christ's salvific work in criticism of Scholastic theology, this issue was not a central point of controversy at the time of the Reformation.[64] In classical Protestant theology, atonement was often conceived as a punishment of Christ (instead of others) by God. In Catholic thought, especially in Neo-Scholasticism, different schools developed, as varying emphases were placed on Christ's obedience and his physical suffering. In some circles, a highly abstract evaluation of Christ's acts developed: it was argued that, since Christ is divine, any free act on his part could have infinite value as satisfaction. This approach, of course, sharply reduces the significance of the crucifixion.[65]

Many modern theologians, especially liberal Protestants, have criticized Anselm sharply, both for his reliance on legal categories and for his concentration on the crucifixion. Much of this criticism can itself be criticized: As to

the first matter, liberal theology's dichotomy between legal and personal categories must be questioned, for legal categories are personal. As to liberal theology's charge that Anselm concentrated too much on the crucifixion, it is fair to reply that liberal theology has suffered from an opposing tendency to reduce Christ's significance to the content of his ethical teaching and the example of his life. Anselm does tend, however, to separate Christ's death from his public life. In addition, the choice of the need to overcome sin and its consequences as his point of departure narrows the soteriological question, in comparison with the patristic theme of divinization. Nonetheless, as Gisbert Greshake has observed, there is much value in Anselm's stress on the exercise of Christ's human freedom and in his insistence that salvation is a public act, the removal of the public consequences of sin.[66]

There is more to be criticized in the reception of Anselm than in Anselm himself. The various modifications of his thought separate incarnation and redemption, and make the actual salvific events seem arbitrary. One effect of these modifications is a lack of intrinsic connection between Christology and the doctrine of grace. Excessive efforts to safeguard divine freedom can lead to positions in which God's actions are arbitrary and therefore border on intrinsic meaninglessness; if salvation of the human race can be accomplished in an infinite number of ways, then the actual history of salvation loses importance.

---

64. On Luther's thought, see Aulen, *Christus Victor*, 101–22; Schwager, *Der wunderbare Tausch*, 192–231.

65. On developments after Anselm, see Franz Lakner, "Salvation B: Satisfaction," in *Sacramentum Mundi*, ed. Karl Rahner et al. (New York: Herder & Herder, 1970), 5:433–35.

66. Evaluations of Anselm's work range from Aulen's sharp criticism in *Christus Victor*, 84–92, 143–59, to Greshake's praise in *Gottes Heil*, 80–104, summarized under the title "Redemption and Freedom," *Theology Digest* 25 (1977): 61–65. For further analyses, see Schwager, *Der wunderbare Tausch*, 161–91; Hans-Ulrich Wiese, "Die Lehre Anselms von Canterbury über den Tod Jesu in der Schrift 'Cur Deus homo,'" *Wissenschaft und Weisheit* 41 (1978): 149–79; 42 (1979): 34–55; and Michel Corbin, ed., *L'Oeuvre d'Anselme de Cantorbery* (Paris: Cerf, 1986–90). For a thought-provoking assessment of common soteriological conceptions, see Thomas Marsh, "Soteriology Today," *Irish Theological Quarterly* 46 (1979): 145–57.

278   As the substance of Anselm's theory of satisfaction became widely accepted in the West, Scholastic theologians began to inquire thematically into the motive for the incarnation. The standard way of posing the question was to ask if the Word would have become flesh if Adam had not sinned. While broaching the subject in unreal terms and envisioning a hypothetical answer, this speculation was based on legitimate concerns about the role of Christ in world history. The traditional answers (no unanimity was reached) remain of interest, for the underlying issues are still important.

The answer of the Thomist school is negative: the Word would not have become flesh had Adam not sinned. The motive of the incarnation is the overcoming of sin; without sin to overcome, the incarnation would not have taken place. The biblical basis for this position is found chiefly in Paul's insistence that Christ died for our sins, though it is recognized that the New Testament does not precisely address the later question. An ancient liturgical expression of the idea is enshrined in the Exsultet of the Easter Vigil: "O happy fault! . . . O truly necessary sin of Adam." The Thomist position entails the consequence that both creation and the initial offer of grace are not intrinsically related to the incarnation. The incarnation is the divine response to a factor eternally foreseen but not willed by God.

The Scotists hold the opposite position: the Word would have become flesh even if Adam had not sinned. The motive of the incarnation is the perfection of creation. While not denying that Christ in fact overcame sin, the Scotists see this as a subordinate effect, accomplished in the process of fulfilling God's original design. The biblical basis is sought especially in the hymn of Colossians, which praises Christ as the "first-born of all creation" and confesses that "all things were created through him and for him" (1:15-16). The Scotist position sees creation and all grace in christological terms.[67]

Contemporary theologians rarely discuss this issue in the terms familiar to medieval thought. Yet the interrelationship of Christ, grace, and sin remains an object of questioning. Many recent authors, such as Karl Barth and Karl Rahner, favor the more christocentric Scotist view. Rahner even takes matters a step further by arguing that, while the offer of grace is a free act on God's part, grace itself is inherently directed toward the incarnation of the second person of the Trinity as an indispensable component of the elevation of the human race to participation in the divine life. Edward Schillebeeckx and Raymund Schwager, in contrast, develop in varying ways a more Thomistic perspective; their soteriologies focus more on overcoming evil than on perfecting what is by nature good. But before examining such modern conceptions in more detail, we must first consider the background of all christological assertions: the life, death, and resurrection of Jesus of Nazareth.

Historical Foundations

To this point, we have examined various Christian interpretations of Jesus' person and work. Such theological assertions are statements of faith, but they are not arbitrary; even if not susceptible of proof in a strict sense, they can be assessed by reference to the figure whom they claim to interpret. Against the background of the doctrinal history surveyed in the preced-

---

67. For a penetrating study of the issues, see Felix Malmberg, *Über den Gottmenschen* (Freiburg: Herder, 1960), 9–26.

ing sections, the following portion of this chapter will study the historical reference points of Christology in the public life, death, and resurrection of Jesus.

Reference to these items as historical foundations requires some qualification. First, our historical knowledge of Jesus is mediated chiefly by documents written to promote theological understanding, not by works of history in the modern sense. The extent and the theological significance of our historical access to Jesus are subject to dispute and will have to be weighed in our treatment of Jesus' public life. Consideration of the crucifixion requires attention to issues ranging from Jesus' approach to death to the origin of theological interpretations of the crucifixion. Finally, since the resurrection can hardly be classified as a historical event in the same sense as Jesus' public life and death, a series of different questions will demand attention on that score. Despite these complications, the three topics to be investigated here share common ground as foundational factors influential (or possibly influential) in the development of faith in Jesus.

Public Life

The chief sources of information about Jesus' public life (almost nothing is known about his earlier years) are the four Gospels. For much of the church's history, the Gospels were taken in a straightforward manner as reliable sources of information about Jesus' actual words and deeds, though their theological content was recognized as well. Since its inception in the late eighteenth century, critical biblical scholarship has gradually led to recognition that the Gospels are primarily expressions of Christian preaching. To retrieve from them historical data about Jesus remains possible, but this task requires careful, methodical investigation and entails a willingness to settle for fragmentary results. Yet some historical knowledge of Jesus seems essential for Christology, especially for examination of its foundational dimensions.[68]

The following account of Jesus' public life will begin with a look at the chief stages of modern inquiry into this question, since familiarity with this background is indispensable for grasping current research. It must be borne in mind throughout that the range of possible historical investigation is not restricted to the issues selected for notice here, and that historical study of Jesus' life does not exhaust the task of interpreting the Gospels.

The work of Hermann Samuel Reimarus (1694–1768), a rationalist thinker and teacher of Near Eastern languages in Hamburg, is usually identified as the origin of critical research into Jesus. Between 1774 and 1778, Gotthold Ephraim Lessing published seven lengthy excerpts from Reimarus's defense of rationalist religion, without revealing the author's name. Two of these *Fragments* considered the aims of Jesus and his disciples and the story of the resurrection. Their publication aroused a storm of controversy and shattered untroubled acceptance of the Gospels as historical documents.[69]

Distinguishing sharply between Jesus' aims and the later aims of his disciples, Reimarus identified Jesus as a messianic pretender who

---

68. For further discussion of these theological issues, see John P. Galvin, "From the Humanity of Christ to the Jesus of History: A Paradigm Shift in Catholic Christology," *Theological Studies* 55 (1994): 252–73.

69. For an English translation, see C. H. Talbert, ed., *Reimarus: Fragments* (Philadelphia: Fortress Press, 1970). The full text of Reimarus's *Apologie* was not published until 1972.

preached the nearness of the kingdom of heaven in a political, nationalistic sense. His activity was limited to Israel and involved no break with the law (see Matt. 5:17-18). While the Messiah could be called Son of God, this royal title did not imply divinity. Jesus twice came close to achieving his goals, once during his ministry in Galilee and later at his triumphant entrance into Jerusalem, but the desired popular response ultimately failed to materialize, and he was executed. His last words ("My God, my God, why have you forsaken me?"; Matt. 27:46) are in admission of failure.

Jesus' disciples, who shared their master's hopes during his lifetime, were totally unprepared for his death. (Reimarus rejects the predictions of the passion as unhistorical, with the argument that the disciples' reaction to Jesus' arrest and crucifixion betrays no sign of preparation.) After Jesus' death, they had recourse to a different strand of Jewish messianic expectation. While Jesus had seen himself as Messiah in the royal, Davidic sense, the disciples turned after his failure to an apocalyptic strand of hope for a messiah who would come twice, first in human weakness, then in divine glory: a supernatural Son of Man coming on the clouds of heaven (see Dan. 7:13). To carry out this reinterpretation, the disciples stole Jesus' body (see Matt. 28:11-15, where the evangelist tries to refute this allegation) and after waiting fifty days so that their claims could not be disproved, proclaimed his resurrection from the dead and imminent return in power. Soon his death was proclaimed a redemptive event, and Christianity became sufficiently well established to survive Jesus' failure to return. As a final stage of the subterfuge, the Gospels seek to depict Jesus'

life in conformity with the disciples' later ideas. Fortunately, elements of the true story continue to show through (especially in Matthew, which at the time of Reimarus was considered the oldest Gospel) and make exposure of the fraud possible.

Reimarus erred in many respects, especially in attributing nationalistic ideas to Jesus and deliberate deception to the disciples. His work remains important, however, for having questioned forcefully the relationship of what would later be called the historical Jesus to the Christ of faith. The issues that he addressed have remained matters of serious theological concern.

The period immediately after publication of Reimarus's *Fragments* did not produce important new insights. Instead, two types of literature on Jesus abounded: traditional harmonizings of the Gospels, and rationalist lives that sought to provide natural explanation for unusual events, especially the miracles. The next major contribution was the publication of David Friedrich Strauss's *The Life of Jesus Critically Examined* in 1835–36.[70]

Highly influenced by Hegel's philosophy, Strauss sought to contribute to systematic theology by developing a variant of the Hegelian notion of myth. As an initial step in this ambitious project, he subjected the Gospels to close examination. Proceeding scene by scene and accompanying each account with detailed criticism, he presented the traditional harmonizing of the different texts and the recent naturalist explanation. Against this twofold background, Strauss advanced his "mythical" interpretation as the third stage of the dialectic. In his judgment, the Gospels result from application of Old Testament themes, especially messianic ideas,

---

70. Strauss's work, published when the author was twenty-seven, eventually appeared in four editions. The English translation, *The Life of Jesus Critically Examined* (Philadelphia: Fortress Press, 1972), is by the novelist George Eliot.

to the life of Jesus: apart from a few basic facts about Jesus' life, they contain primitive Christian ideas expressed in historical form. Unlike Reimarus, Strauss did not consider the Gospels a product of deceit. That the gospel tradition is historically unreliable is due not to fraud, but to the inevitable growth of poetic legend around a venerated figure.

In any case, for Strauss, the important point is early Christian thought, not the history of Jesus. Critical historical examination of Jesus' life is but a means to an end, for Jesus is simply the vehicle used to express messianic ideas and is no more important than any other human being. The ideas that the Gospels present in mythical form by applying them to Jesus must now be reexpressed as truths about the human race as a whole, for no idea can be confined to one individual: "Humanity is the union of the two natures—God become man."[71] Within this framework, neither the historical Jesus nor any other individual can be the object of faith; Christology, shorn of its reference to Jesus, is transformed into a theological-philosophical anthropology.

Despite Strauss's speculative goal, his major impact was as an exegete and historian. His *Life* sparked intense debate, especially among Protestant theologians,[72] and caused books on the historical Jesus to proliferate. The most fundamental objection to his recasting of Christology is that Strauss failed to see the personal importance of Jesus for the development of the "christological idea": the Gospels are not the mere expression of existing ideas with reference to Jesus, but a critical adaptation of such ideas on the basis of who Jesus was. Nonetheless, Strauss re-

mains important for urging two basic—perhaps the two basic—christological questions: What is the relationship of the historical Jesus to the Christ of faith? And is the Christian message of salvation separable from its historical origin in Jesus?

As the nineteenth century progressed, liberal Protestant thought came to dominate critical research on the life of Jesus. Liberal Protestantism was opposed to the dogmatic Christ of the early councils and suspicious of the Christologies of Paul and John. Judging these developments a falsification of the true picture of Jesus, it devoted its efforts to reconstructing from the Synoptic Gospels a biography of Jesus as an ethical teacher. Here, inquiry into the historical Jesus is associated with a "low Christology" that denies the divinity of Christ.

The resulting effort to uncover the historical Jesus soon concluded that the only suitable sources were the Synoptic Gospels. Methodical study of the texts gradually led to recognition of the priority of Mark and to identification of a common source, termed Q, behind the texts of Matthew and Luke. As the oldest material, Mark and Q were presumed to be a reliable basis for reconstructing Jesus' public life. These liberal Protestant interpretations of the life of Jesus depict him as an ethical teacher who preached the kingdom of God as an interior, moral reality. Much attention is devoted to psychological description of his personality and inner development, which are seen as a model for our imitation. Biographical presentation is thus essential to the theological enterprise.

The most influential example of this unitarian theology is a series of lectures on the essence

---

71. Ibid., 780.

72. On the Catholic reaction, see William Madges, "D. F. Strauss in Retrospect: His Reception among Roman Catholics," *Heythrop Journal* 30 (1989): 273–92.

282 of Christianity delivered in 1899–1900 at the University of Berlin by the eminent church historian Adolf von Harnack. Harnack identified three basic principles in Jesus' teaching: (1) the coming of the (ethical) kingdom of God, (2) the Fatherhood of God and the infinite value of the human soul, and (3) the better justice (see Matt. 5:20) and the command of love. Jesus' preaching is concerned exclusively with the individual, who is called to repent and believe. Dogmas, especially christological and trinitarian doctrine, are later Hellenizations of the gospel. In a famous, oft-criticized passage, Harnack states, "The Gospel, as Jesus proclaimed it, has to do with the Father only and not with the Son," though he does hasten to add that Jesus "was its personal realization and its strength, and this he is felt to be still."[73] Central to this position are a rejection of classical Christology, an optimistic assurance that exegetes can reach the historical Jesus, and the image of Jesus as preacher and model of an ethical message of the kingdom of God. The apocalyptic, eschatological element in the Gospels is dismissed as an incidental residue of Jewish cultural influences.

Positions of this sort, while now discredited in theological circles, still exert a certain popular influence. It is important to note that they have been rejected not simply out of fidelity to postbiblical tradition, but due to internal deficiencies. Their inadequacy is best seen in conjunction with the development of research around the turn of the century, when the liberal quest was

jolted by the publication of four books. Each in its own way challenged an essential element of the synthesis prevailing in liberal circles.

In 1892, the exegete Johannes Weiss published a brief but important study of Jesus' preaching. Weiss argued that Jesus' understanding of the kingdom of God was eschatological; the ethical interpretation of his message was a false modernization of his actual teaching. This critique called into question the liberal image of Jesus as an ethical teacher.[74]

In the same year, Martin Kähler, a systematic theologian opposed to liberal Christology, rejected the quest for the historical Jesus as historically fruitless and theologically bankrupt. Kähler held that, given the limitations of our sources, finding the Jesus of history is impossible. Furthermore, even if better sources were available, no historian can reach what alone interests believers: the suprahistorical Savior. Fearing that liberal theology makes Christian faith dependent on the shifting sands of historical research, Kähler insists that "the real Christ is the Christ who is preached," not the product of a scholarly reconstruction.[75]

Shortly thereafter, in 1901, Wilhelm Wrede published his study of the messianic secret in the Gospels. Wrede argued that the structure of Mark and the Gospel's messianic material were the product of the evangelist and could not serve as a guide to the actual events of Jesus' life. Details of Jesus' life, including the sequence of events, which is indispensable for

---

73. Harnack, *What Is Christianity?* 144, 145.

74. The first edition was sixty-seven pages long; an expanded second edition appeared in 1900. For an English translation of the original text, see Johannes Weiss, *Jesus' Proclamation of the Kingdom of God* (Philadelphia: Fortress Press, 1971). A comparable emphasis on future eschatology in Jesus' message is reflected in Alfred Loisy, *The Gospel and the Church* (Philadelphia: Fortress Press, 1976; French orig. 1902), a widely read work composed in conscious opposition to Harnack. Significant presence of eschatology in Jesus' teaching does not exclude ethics from his message, but it does rule out conceiving Jesus solely as moral teacher.

75. For an English translation, see Martin Kähler, *The So-Called Historical Jesus and the Historic, Biblical Christ* (Philadelphia: Fortress Press, 1964). The citation is taken from p. 66.

psychological reconstruction, are unavailable to us. As Wrede realized, his insight into the character of the Gospels sounded the death knell for psychological biographies of Jesus.[76]

Finally, Albert Schweitzer summarized a vast amount of research on the Jesus of history and brought it into intelligible order. While sympathetic to liberal Protestantism's goals, he showed that its portrait of Jesus was a modernization unduly influenced by nineteenth-century theological views. Schweitzer did not deny the possibility of reaching the historical Jesus; he rejected Wrede's doubts on this point and held that an accurate picture of Jesus could be obtained. But the Jesus of history was an apocalyptic preacher who mistakenly expected God's kingdom to arrive with cosmic force in the near future. As a high-water mark of Jewish apocalypticism, he is even more foreign to modernity than is the conciliar Christology that liberal theology sought to supplant. Since the historical Jesus provides no support for liberal thought, the search for "the Jesus of history as an ally in the struggle against the tyranny of dogma" must be declared a failure.[77]

The nineteenth-century quest of the historical Jesus never recovered from these assaults. Liberal theology, so accommodated to a particular culture, lost its prominence in the aftermath of World War I. In the period that followed, Paul and John again became the decisive voices of the New Testament, and pursuit of the historical Jesus receded in favor of focus on the preached Christ. Karl Barth, whose impassioned commentary on Romans inaugurated a new theological epoch in 1919, repeated Kähler's charge that the quest was both impossible and illegitimate. Wholeheartedly repudiating all that liberal theology stood for, Barth insisted that we know Christ only by faith. In a famous exchange of letters with Adolf von Harnack, he went so far as to maintain that the meager results of historical inquiry into Jesus could paradoxically serve a good purpose by demolishing a place where faith might be tempted to seek false support.[78] In a similar vein, Rudolf Bultmann opined that "we can now know almost nothing concerning the life and personality of Jesus,"[79] and insisted that theology needs knowledge only of the fact of Jesus' existence, not further information about his life.[80] While Bultmann offered an account of Jesus' message and spoke of a Christology implicit in his words and deeds,[81] he was convinced that theology should focus on the preaching of the cross, rather than on Jesus' public life.

Lack of theological interest in the historical Jesus prevailed in large part—never universally—for a generation.[82] In 1953, an important

---

76. See Wilhelm Wrede, *The Messianic Secret* (Cambridge: Clarke, 1971). Wrede's specific interpretation of Mark's theological activity is itself open to objection.

77. Schweitzer's work was originally published in 1906 under the title *Von Reimarus zu Wrede*. For an English translation, see *The Quest of the Historical Jesus: A Critical Study of Its Progress from Reimarus to Wrede* (London: Black, 1911). The citation is from p. 4. This work is the classic history of the "quest." For a briefer informative account and critique, see Ben F. Meyer, *The Aims of Jesus* (London: SCM, 1979), 25–59.

78. See H. Martin Rumscheidt, *Revelation and Theology: An Analysis of the Barth-Harnack Correspondence of 1923* (Cambridge: Cambridge University Press, 1972), 35, where Barth's text is translated.

79. Rudolf Bultmann, *Jesus and the Word* (New York: Scribner, 1934), 8.

80. Rudolf Bultmann, "The Primitive Christian Kerygma and the Historical Jesus," in *The Historical Jesus and the Kerygmatic Christ*, ed. C. Braaten and R. Harrisville (Nashville: Abingdon, 1964), 20–21, 25.

81. See Bultmann, *Jesus and the Word*; and idem, *Theology of the New Testament*, 1:43.

82. This generalization does not apply to Catholic theology, which in this period rightly rejected bifurcation of the

lecture by Ernst Käsemann, one of Bultmann's students, inaugurated the "new quest" of the historical Jesus.[83] Intense theological interest in the historical Jesus, now on the part of Catholic as well as Protestant scholars, has persisted since that time. Initially, Jesus' preaching was the focus of attention, but other major aspects of his public life now attract equal interest. In view of the purpose of this chapter, the following recapitulation of the major conclusions of modern research emphasizes matters that bear directly on Christology.[84]

The central content of Jesus' public life can be determined with great certitude. Addressing Israel as a whole, Jesus preached and exemplified in his conduct the coming of God's kingdom. The kingdom is expected to arrive in the (near) future yet has already begun to be present among Jesus' hearers. Since preaching the coming of God's rule entails a summons to repent, Jesus' message has both eschatological and ethical dimensions.

Jesus did not make himself the focus of his own teaching. Nonetheless, the coming of the kingdom of God, and the message of the coming of that kingdom, are in Jesus' view inseparably tied to his person. The kingdom begins to arrive in and through his presence and conduct. His actions and words presuppose and reflect a conviction that he is God's definitive representative, not to be surpassed in the future. A prophetic figure, he is (in his own self-understanding) incapable of being replaced by a later prophet. Thus, Jesus' preaching of the kingdom has christological presuppositions and implications.[85] Among other things, the link between his person and message implies that the truth of the message is inseparable from his personal destiny.

The indirect self-reference of Jesus' public preaching and conduct is often termed implicit Christology: Christology because of its personal claims about Jesus, and implicit because the claims are not expressed through explicit use of titles. There is no consensus among contemporary exegetes about the existence of explicit Christology during Jesus' lifetime.[86] In any case, however, the decisive theological issue is the presence of implicit Christology in Jesus' words and deeds, for without this reference point, any verbal claim to messianic status or to other christological titles would be hollow. Explicit Christology cannot stand on its own; implicit Christology can.

Like the rejection of the original quest, renewal of research on the historical Jesus is defended on both historical and theological

---

historical Jesus from the Christ of faith but lacked adequate appreciation of the difficulty inherent in recovering historical data about Jesus from the New Testament. For official Catholic recognition of the theological interests that affect the work of the evangelists, see the Second Vatican Council's Dogmatic Constitution on Divine Revelation (*Dei verbum*), no. 19.

83. Ernst Käsemann, "The Problem of the Historical Jesus," in *Essays on New Testament Themes* (London: SCM, 1964), 15–47.

84. For a succinct and balanced account, see John P. Meier, "Jesus," in *The New Jerome Biblical Commentary*, ed. R. Brown et al. (Englewood Cliffs, NJ: Prentice Hall, 1990), 1316–28. For more detailed discussions, see Meyer, *The Aims of Jesus*; Schillebeeckx, *Jesus*, 41–319; and E. P. Sanders, *Jesus and Judaism* (Philadelphia: Fortress Press, 1985).

85. In this context, Edward Schillebeeckx refers to Jesus' "abba-experience" as the foundation of his preaching and conduct (*Jesus*, 256–71), and Karl Rahner notes Jesus' consciousness of unsurpassable proximity to God (*Foundations of Christian Faith*, 251–54). The intrinsic connection of Jesus' message and person is also expressed in Wolfhart Pannenberg's thesis: "The office of Jesus was to call men into the Kingdom of God, which had appeared with him." *Jesus—God and Man*, 212.

86. On these issues, see Raymond E. Brown, *Biblical Reflections on Crises Facing the Church* (New York: Paulist, 1975), 20–37. On the individual titles, see Meier, "Jesus," 1323–25.

grounds. On the historical side of the question, it is argued that our inability to write a biography of Jesus, as we might write a biography of a modern figure, does not preclude uncovering accurate historical information of more limited scope. While care must be taken neither to retroject later material into Jesus' life nor to divorce Jesus from his historical context, application of such criteria as multiple attestation (the presence of similar material in varying forms and in mutually independent sources) and dissimilarity (identification of material that cannot be ascribed either to early Christian or to Jewish sources other than Jesus) makes it possible to distinguish what stems from Jesus from other material attributed to him in the Gospels.[87] Moreover, the basic picture of Jesus obtained in this way is more certain and more stable than are judgments with regard to the origin of individual texts.

Perhaps even more important than this historical argumentation is the changed theological situation. The new quest's chief difference from Bultmann lies not in its description of the historical Jesus but in the theological importance it attributes to this information. "Kerygmatic theology" feared the original quest as an attempt to replace faith with historical research, and in some respects, its suspicion was well founded. In contrast to both nineteenth-century research and its critics, modern scholars frequently assert that investigation into the historical Jesus, far from being excluded by faith, is a basic imperative arising from faith itself. This argument, common to exegetes and theologians, has two distinct aspects.

The first aspect of the argument, advanced especially in the early years of the new quest, is the need to ask if the Christian kerygma's reference to and interpretation of Jesus is legitimate. Since the biblical message is not self-justifying, the question of continuity between Jesus and the preaching of the church must be addressed. This point has been expressed emphatically by Gerhard Ebeling: "If it were to be shown that Christology had no basis in the historical Jesus, but was a misinterpretation of Jesus, then Christology would be ruined."[88] In a similar vein, Nicholas Lash has observed, "If I were to become convinced that Jesus did not exist, or that the story told in the New Testament of his life, teaching and death was a fictional construction ungrounded in the facts, or a radical *misinter*pretation of his character, history and significance, then I should cease to be a Christian."[89]

The second aspect of the argument, more emphasized now than in the initial phase of the revival of research on Jesus, is the need for historical knowledge of Jesus in order to understand christological assertions. To understand what is meant by confessing that "Jesus is the Christ," it is necessary to know something about his life. Historical knowledge of Jesus is important not only for studying the foundation of christological statements, but also for grasping their content. On both grounds, these scholars argue, Christian faith requires historical knowledge of its object.

As is clear from the history of research, the theological function attributed to the historical Jesus (whether to Jesus himself in history, or to historical knowledge of Jesus in contemporary

---

87. For discussion of criteria, see Meier, "Jesus," 1317–18; Meyer, *The Aims of Jesus*, 76–94; and Schillebeeckx, *Jesus*, 81–102.

88. Gerhard Ebeling, "The Question of the Historical Jesus," 289; translation slightly modified. See also idem, *Theology and Proclamation* (Philadelphia: Fortress Press, 1966), 54–81.

89. Nicholas Lash, *Theology on Dover Beach* (New York: Paulist, 1979), 84.

theology)[90] is an issue distinct from the question of the extent of our historical knowledge about him. While the terminology used in discussing these matters varies from one author to another, three basic positions may be distinguished:

1. Some authors, such as David Friedrich Strauss, have denied any theological significance to the historical Jesus. A position this extreme is not common.

2. Other theologians, such as Bultmann, restrict or seek to restrict theologically relevant historical material about Jesus to the mere fact of his existence. It is easier to articulate this position than to carry it out consistently; even Bultmann would hardly have been able to find significance in the preaching of the cross if Jesus had not been crucified. The major contemporary representative of a position akin to Bultmann's is Schubert Ogden, who argues that the historical point of reference for Christian faith and theology is the earliest apostolic preaching, not the life of Jesus. Distinguishing between the empirical-historical Jesus and the existential-historical Jesus (Jesus as known through the earliest apostolic witness), Ogden holds that contemporary Christology typically suffers from the flaw of "asking about the being of Jesus in himself, as distinct from asking about the meaning of Jesus for us." In fact, Ogden argues, the necessary and sufficient condition for the appropriateness of a christological assertion is its compatibility with the earliest apostolic witness, not its basis in Jesus' self-understanding.[91]

3. Most contemporary authors attribute greater theological significance to Jesus himself and to our historical knowledge of him. For the reasons previously noted, though with variations in detail, these authors consider certain elements of Jesus' life and of our information about him to be indispensable presuppositions of christological assertions.[92] Divergences among theologians on the theological significance of the historical Jesus are closely related to differences on other theological issues. Authors who conceive of Christian faith as closely related to history tend to attribute more theological significance to the historical Jesus than do those who divorce faith from history and perhaps even see factual historical knowledge as inimical to faith conceived as risk. Similarly, theologians who profess the divinity of Christ may require more historical material to support their affirmations than do those who are content with a low Christology depicting Jesus solely as teacher and example. Still, the divisions I have noted do not follow strictly on these lines, for numerous factors influence such theological judgments.

In my opinion, only the third of these positions takes into adequate account the historical nature of Christian faith and the centrality of the basic Christian confession that *Jesus* is the Christ.[93] As described here, however, the third

---

90. On the issues involved here, see John P. Meier, "The Historical Jesus: Rethinking Some Concepts," *Theological Studies* 51 (1990): 3–24.

91. See Ogden, *The Point of Christology*; the citation is from pp. 15–16. For further assessment, see my review in *Heythrop Journal* 26 (1985): 67–69. A position similar to Ogden's is represented by David Tracy, who holds with regard to Christology that "the primary content criterion should be the Jesus-kerygma of the original apostolic witness." *The Analogical Imagination: Christian Theology and the Culture of Pluralism* (New York: Crossroad, 1981), 272. See ibid., 248–338, esp. 300–301n97; and idem, *Blessed Rage for Order: The New Pluralism in Theology* (New York: Seabury, 1975), 204–36.

92. For an example of this position, see Karl Rahner's reflections on the systematic issues and summary of major aspects of our historical knowledge of Jesus, in *Foundations of Christian Faith*, 243–49.

93. See Elizabeth A. Johnson, "The Theological Relevance of the Historical Jesus: A Debate and a Thesis," *Thomist* 48 (1984): 1–43; John P. Galvin, "'I Believe . . . in Jesus Christ, His Only Son, Our Lord': The Earthly Jesus and the Christ of

category is quite broad; it leaves within itself considerable room for pluralism. One disputed issue is of major importance: the sufficiency of the historical Jesus as the historical reference point of Christology.

Most theologians concerned with foundational christological issues (Pannenberg, Kasper, Küng, O'Collins, Schwager, and Rahner in several writings) identify the public life of Jesus and the resurrection as the two major poles upon which Christology is built; in their judgment, knowledge of Jesus' public life is a necessary but not a sufficient basis for Christology.[94] Other authors equally interested in developing a high Christology (Ebeling, Rudolf Pesch, Franz Schupp, Verweyen, some lines of thought in Rahner) consider the historical Jesus the exclusive historical reference point for Christology; the resurrection, while not denied, is classified as a confession of faith, rather than part of the historically establishable foundation of faith.

Differences on this score often reflect varying evaluations of the crucifixion, as well as alternative conceptions of the role of the resurrection in christological argumentation. Authors who consider the resurrection the second pole on which Christology is based frequently assess Jesus' death in negative terms, as an end that calls into question the validity of his entire life. Consequently, their references to the historical Jesus typically encompass his life up to but not including his crucifixion. Conversely, those who envision the historical Jesus as sufficient basis for Christology typically include his death in their point of historical reference, for they find his crucifixion revelatory of God. Thus, the

question of the theological significance of Jesus' public life leads inescapably to consideration of his death.

Crucifixion

As is evident from even a cursory reading of the New Testament, Jesus' death on the cross has long been the focal point of vigorous controversy. That Jesus was crucified is beyond doubt, though the precise date of his death can no longer be determined.[95] At issue in theological discussion is not the fact of the crucifixion but its meaning, for "Christ crucified, a stumbling block to Jews and folly to Gentiles," is "to those who are called, both Jews and Greeks, Christ the power of God and the wisdom of God" (1 Cor. 1:23-24).

Jesus' Approach to Death

As a prelude to considering theological interpretation of the crucifixion, we must first examine a historical issue with far-reaching theological implications: Jesus' personal stance toward death. The importance of this matter, accented in the reference to "a death he freely accepted" in the Second Eucharistic Prayer of the Roman liturgy, has been articulated clearly in a statement on Christology issued in 1979 by the International Theological Commission: "If, for Jesus, the Passion was a failure and a shipwreck, if he felt abandoned by God and lost hope in his own mission, his death could not be construed then, and cannot be construed now, as the definitive act in the economy of salvation. A death undergone in a purely passive manner could not be a

---

Faith," in *Gospel Interpretation: Narrative-Critical and Social-Scientific Approaches*, ed. Jack Dean Kingsbury (Harrisburg, PA: Trinity Press International, 1997), 273–82.

94. For a clear defense of this position, see Pannenberg, *Jesus—God and Man*, 53–114.

95. On crucifixion as a means of punishment in antiquity, see Martin Hengel, *Crucifixion* (Philadelphia: Fortress Press, 1977).

'christological' saving event. It must be the consequence, the willed consequence, of the obedience and love of Jesus making a gift of himself."[96] As this passage suggests, the meaning of Jesus' crucifixion rests in part on its relationship to his earlier life.

The issues entailed in inquiry into this relationship are multidimensional. In a more objective respect, we can ask why Jesus was put to death, and we can inquire into the compatibility of his message of God's kingdom with his own execution. More subjectively, we can ask if Jesus foresaw his death, and seek to determine if and how he interpreted it and incorporated it into his understanding of his mission.[97]

Answers to such questions may seem self-evident, for the Gospels show Jesus predicting his passion (e.g., Mark 8:31; 9:31; 10:33-34, 45; John 10:18) and interpreting his death as salvific (e.g., Mark 10:45; 14:22-24). But while these texts have traditionally been read as historical reports, they are suspect from a critical perspective of being creations of the early church. In addition, there is tension between Jesus' public preaching of the kingdom of God (see, e.g., Mark 1:15) and an attribution, on his part, of salvific efficacy to his death.[98]

The strongest adversary of the traditional understanding is Rudolf Bultmann, who denies that we can establish a positive connection between Jesus' life and his death. Objectively, Bultmann considers Jesus' crucifixion as a political criminal a sign that his religious message (in Bultmann's judgment, nonpolitical) was misinterpreted as a threat to Roman rule. On this view, Jesus' death is linked to his public activity only insofar as his purposes were misunderstood. On the subjective level, Bultmann insists that our sources permit no firm conclusions about Jesus' personal approach to death and even leave open the possibility that he suffered a complete collapse. The Gospel passages that interpret the crucifixion as salvific are expressions of early Christian theology, developed after the crucifixion and retrojected into Jesus' life.[99]

Both aspects of Bultmann's position have rightly been challenged. As Jürgen Moltmann and others have argued, Jesus' death flowed from his public activity. It is not that Jesus wished to be executed or directed his actions toward that end. But his death resulted from rejection, not misunderstanding. To the Jewish religious leaders, Jesus' stance toward the Law was blasphemous and endangered their own

---

96. See "Select Questions on Christology," in *International Theological Commission: Texts and Documents 1969–85*, ed. Michael Sharkey (San Francisco: Ignatius, 1989), 197.

97. Scholastic and Neo-Scholastic theology deduced from the hypostatic union that Jesus' human intellect enjoyed the beatific vision and knowledge of all past, present, and future reality from the moment of his conception; to these authors, it is a priori clear that Jesus foresaw his death and recognized its salvific significance. In contrast, contemporary theologians typically ascribe to Jesus a consciousness of unsurpassable proximity to God that does not imply unlimited knowledge of factual data. See, e.g., Rahner, *Foundations of Christian Faith*, 249, 253–54. From this perspective, questions such as those noted above cannot be answered a priori. The nature and extent of Christ's human knowledge was much discussed in the 1950s and early 1960s. Influential modern analyses include Engelbert Gutwenger, *Bewusstsein und Wissen Christi* (Innsbruck: Felizian Rauch, 1960); and Karl Rahner, "Dogmatic Reflections on the Knowledge and Self-Consciousness of Christ," in *Theological Investigations* (Baltimore: Helicon, 1966), 5:193–215. On the history of thought, see Helmut Riedlinger, *Geschichtlichkeit und Vollendung des Wissens Christi* (Freiburg: Herder, 1966).

98. This point is urged especially by Anton Vögtle, "Todesankündigungen und Todesverständnis Jesu," in *Der Tod Jesu: Deutungen im Neuen Testament* (Freiburg: Herder, 1976), 51–113.

99. See Bultmann, *Jesus and the Word*, 213–14; idem. "The Primitive Christian Kerygma and the Historical Jesus," 23–24.

status. To Roman civil authority, his efforts to gather Israel represented a political threat in a highly volatile situation, though Jesus himself was neither a political activist nor a revolutionary. Death was the inevitable result of fidelity to his own preaching, given the failure of his message to win general acceptance.[100]

Bultmann's views on Jesus' personal stance toward death have also been criticized, most notably in several closely reasoned studies of Heinz Schürmann. Schürmann argues that, given the historical context, Jesus must have realized from the start of his public life the possibility of provoking opposition and meeting death at the hands of his adversaries. As opposition mounted, he must have recognized the increasing danger, so that toward the end of his life, the final outcome became clear. In addition to these general considerations, a text from the Last Supper plays an important role in Schürmann's argumentation. In a passage widely judged authentic, Jesus tells his disciples, "Amen, I say to you, I will not drink again of the fruit of the vine until that day when I drink it new in the reign of God" (Mark 14:25). This saying of Jesus both predicts death and expresses certitude that his death will prevent neither the coming of God's kingdom nor Jesus' own participation in it.[101] Thus, Jesus' faithfulness to his message remained constant to the end.

Positions akin to Schürmann's have been adopted by many theologians. Walter Kasper,

Hans Küng, Raymund Schwager, and Gerald O'Collins offer similar reflections, and Edward Schillebeeckx, though hesitant on some points, follows the same basic line of argumentation. Karl Rahner, enumerating the main points of our historical knowledge about Jesus, asserts that "he faced his death resolutely and accepted it as the inevitable consequence of fidelity to his mission and as imposed on him by God."[102] Thus, it is possible to speak of a widespread consensus about Jesus' free acceptance of death on the part of recent Catholic theologians. While Jesus' death was not an explicit topic of his public preaching, we can be certain that he accepted personally the most radical consequences of the message he had proclaimed and embodied in his deeds.

INTERPRETATIONS OF THE CRUCIFIXION

Against this background, it is possible to weigh various theological interpretations of the crucifixion. As a first step, drawing in large part on Edward Schillebeeckx's summary of exegetical studies, I shall identify three major early Christian assessments of Jesus' death and consider the relationship of these interpretations to Jesus himself. The present look at the crucifixion will then conclude by noting the thought of some modern authors on the immediate theological implications of the crucifixion.

The Death of a Prophet-Martyr ◎ Consistent with Jesus' status as a prophetic figure,

---

100. On these issues, see Jürgen Moltmann, *The Crucified God*, 126–45. The trinitarian aspect of Moltmann's interpretation of the crucifixion is not at issue here. Wolfhart Pannenberg observes more soberly that "Jesus' cross is . . . the not fortuitous consequence of his preaching." "Den Glauben an ihm selbs fassen und verstehen," *Zeitschrift für Theologie und Kirche* 86 (1989): 366.

101. See especially Heinz Schürmann, *Gottes Reich—Jesu Geschick* (Leipzig: St. Benno, 1983), 183–251. For a more detailed summary and for discussion of other authors, see John P. Galvin, "Jesus' Approach to Death: An Examination of Some Recent Studies," *Theological Studies* 41 (1980): 713–44.

102. Rahner, *Foundations of Christian Faith*, 248. The sense is that God imposes death on Jesus inasmuch as it is entailed in fidelity to his mission. For the other authors, see Kasper, *Jesus the Christ*, 114–21; Küng, *On Being a Christian*, 320–25; O'Collins, *Interpreting Jesus*, 79–92; Schillebeeckx, *Jesus*, 294–312; and Schwager, *Jesus in the Drama of Salvation*.

one pattern of thought took recourse to the Old Testament experience that prophets often encounter rejection and even violent death. The sufferings of Jeremiah are a case in point, though Jeremiah's trials stop short of execution. In the New Testament, Jesus' lament over Jerusalem (Luke 13:33-34) and Stephen's speech to the high priest (Acts 7:51-52) express the general theme of persecution of the prophets, and the parable of the vineyard (Mark 12:1-12) places Jesus' death in this traditional context. While development of this line of thought can suggest that a prophet-martyr's woes have salvific value for others, the basic point is that persecution and death do not undermine prophetic standing; on the contrary, genuine prophets must expect opposition. Jesus' crucifixion does not disprove his claim to represent God.

The Death of the Righteous Sufferer ⊛ Prominent in the Psalms of lament (e.g., Psalm 22) and in the wisdom literature (e.g., Wis. 2:12-20; 5:1-23) is the theme of the current travail and eventual triumph of the righteous sufferer. To outward appearances utterly abandoned, the victim is eventually vindicated by God. The theme can involve simply the suffering of the innocent, as in the book of Job, or persecution of the righteous precisely because of their justice. Readily applicable to the death of Jesus, these ideas exercise formative influence on the passion narratives, and are reflected with particular clarity in the Gospels accounts of the crucifixion (Matt. 27:46-48; Mark 15:34-36; Luke 23:46-47; John 19:28-30).

An Atoning, Redemptive Death ⊛ The chief Old Testament background for the understanding of Jesus' death as redemptive is the fourth servant song of Second Isaiah (Isa. 52:13—53:12): "He was wounded for our transgressions, he was bruised for our iniquities; upon him was the chastisement that made us whole, and with his stripes we are healed" (52:5). Here salvific effects are attributed to suffering, which benefits others and atones for sin. New Testament references to Jesus' death as ransom (Mark 10:45) and expiation (Rom. 3:25), as death for our sins (1 Cor. 15:3), and as death "for many" (Matt. 26:28; Mark 14:24) or "for you" (Luke 22:20; 1 Cor. 11:24) reflect this strand of thought, which centuries later gave rise to Anselm's theory of satisfaction. While the first two types may maintain simply that Jesus is salvific despite his death, the third approach explicitly recognizes salvific value in the crucifixion.[103]

Whether all or any of these interpretations of the crucifixion can be retraced to Jesus is disputed. Schillebeeckx speaks of Jesus' death as a prophetic sign left for others to interpret in the light of Jesus' life, and Rahner seems content to leave open the issue of explicit interpretation by Jesus. In contrast, Schürmann judges that Jesus expressed the salvific character of his death, at least unthematically, and Rudolf Pesch traces all three types of interpretation to the period shortly before the crucifixion.[104] There are telling arguments on both sides (in addition to exegeting individual texts, each has to provide a plausible account of Christology's early devel-

---

103. For Schillebeeckx's treatment of these issues, see *Jesus*, 274–94. Marie-Louise Gubler, *Die frühesten Deutungen des Todes Jesu* (Fribourg: Universitätsverlag, 1977); Günter Bader, *Symbolik des Todes Jesu* (Tübingen: Mohr, 1988); and Hengel, *The Atonement* provide further information.

104. See Schillebeeckx, *Jesus*, 318–19; Rahner, *Foundations of Christian Faith*, 248–49; Schürmann, *Gottes Reich*, 198–223; Rudolf Pesch, *Das Abendmahl und Jesu Todesverstandnis* (Freiburg: Herder, 1978). For further consideration, see Galvin, "Jesus' Approach to Death."

opment), and it is not likely that consensus will be reached. In any case, the validity of theological interpretations of the crucifixion depends on their corresponding to the way Jesus lived and died, not on their explicit origin with Jesus.

Attention to these divergent strands of early interpretation of the crucifixion gives rise to the question of the immediate theological implications of Jesus' death. The position most commonly held by contemporary theologians (e.g., Pannenberg, Kasper, O'Collins, Schwager) is that Jesus' disgraceful execution called into question the validity of his preaching and his claim to speak on behalf of God—a state of affairs overcome only by his resurrection and its manifestation. Other authors (Pesch, Rahner in some texts), however, appeal to the traditions of the prophet-martyr and the righteous sufferer to argue that Jesus' death did not imply that his claims were illegitimate, either historically, in the eyes of the disciples, or factually, as far as later theological assessment is concerned.

At stake in this discussion is the relationship among Jesus' public life, death, and resurrection. While it seems inconsistent to recognize that his public life led to his crucifixion yet to assess his life in positive terms and his death negatively, the issue cannot be pursued until we look more closely at the resurrection.

Resurrection

While factual data concerning Jesus' public life and death have important theological ramifications, they often neither presuppose nor entail Christian faith. Nonbelievers may note that Jesus preached the coming of God's kingdom and that he was crucified, yet judge that he was mistaken in his message and that his death lacks the significance that Christians attribute to it. The resurrection falls into a different category. It is hard to imagine anyone agreeing that Jesus is risen, in the sense that Christians affirm, yet not being or becoming Christian.[105] Here event and meaning are so intimately linked that distanced historical description is scarcely possible.

The importance of the resurrection, classically expressed in Paul's dictum that "if Christ has not been raised, then our preaching is in vain and your faith is in vain" (1 Cor. 15:14), is acknowledged by all Christians. Nonetheless, theologians differ significantly in specifying what is meant by the confession that Jesus is risen, and especially in conceiving the relationship of the resurrection to the crucifixion. Indeed, as C. F. Evans has observed, "the principal difficulty here is not to believe, but to know what it is which offers itself for belief."[106] To examine the various aspects of the topic, the following section will consider both biblical material and major modern theologies of the resurrection.

BIBLICAL DATA

"Resurrection narratives" differ in kind from crucifixion narratives. While crucifixion narratives, though always permeated with theological interpretation, are in fact accounts of the crucifixion, no canonical resurrection narrative purports to describe the resurrection directly.[107] Instead, the chief New Testament texts fall

---

105. Pinchas Lapide, an apparent exception, conceives of the resurrection as a resuscitation. *The Resurrection of Jesus: A Jewish Perspective* (Minneapolis: Augsburg, 1983). See John P. Galvin, "A Recent Jewish View of the Resurrection," *Expository Times* 91 (1979–80): 277–79.

106. C. F. Evans, *Resurrection and the New Testament* (London: SCM, 1970), 130.

107. The *Gospel of Peter*, an apocryphal second-century text, portrays the resurrection directly (IX.35–X.42): "In the night whereon the Lord's day dawned, as the soldiers were keeping guard two by two in every watch, there came a great

292 into two categories: stories of the discovery of the empty grave and of appearances of the risen Lord, and brief formulas that proclaim Jesus' resurrection.[108]

Each of the Gospels includes an account of Jesus' burial[109] and of discovery of the empty tomb (Mark 15:42—16:8; Matt. 27:57—28:15; Luke 23:50—24:11; John 19:38—20:18). While unanimous in reporting that women found Jesus' grave empty two days after his crucifixion, the accounts differ in several respects: The number and names of the women, their motivation in visiting the tomb, the events that occur in their presence, the number of heavenly figures whom they encounter, the message they receive, and their reaction to these events all vary considerably from text to text. Matthew alone includes mention of a Roman guard, and John alone (but see Luke 24:12, 24) mentions a story of two disciples racing to the grave. Matthew and John include divergent accounts, not paralleled in Mark and Luke, of an appearance of the risen Jesus at the tomb. These differences, which reflect the evangelists' theological perspectives, cannot be completely harmonized on a historical level.

The narratives of appearances of the risen Lord exhibit even greater variations. The stories vary in location (Jerusalem in Luke 24, John 20, and Acts 1; Galilee in Matthew 28 and John 21),

in the circumstances of the appearances, and in the words ascribed to the risen Lord. Like the accounts of the empty grave, the appearance narratives are of considerable theological import. The texts weigh the nature and divine origin of faith, the identity and the transformation of the risen Jesus, and several sacramental themes (baptism, Eucharist, forgiveness of sins) and ecclesiological themes (mission, apostleship, the role of Peter). But on a historical level, they resist amalgamation into a coherent unified account.

In addition to these narratives, the New Testament also contains numerous brief formulas that profess faith in Jesus' glorification. Such passages, most common in Paul's letters but also found in the Gospels, may embody hymns (Phil. 2:5-11), catechetical instruction (1 Cor. 15:3-8), and liturgical acclamations (Luke 24:34). They vary in vocabulary, sometimes speaking of resurrection (e.g., 1 Thess. 4:14; Rom. 10:9) and sometimes of exaltation (e.g., Phil. 2:9). Older than the writings into which they have been incorporated, these formulas have sometimes been modified or expanded for use in their current context.

In modern discussion, pre-Pauline formulas have assumed a central role in studies of the resurrection. Because of its content and age, 1 Cor. 15:3-8 is particularly significant in this respect:

---

sound in the heaven, and they saw the heavens opened and two men descend thence, shining with a great light, and drawing near unto the sepulcher. And that stone which had been set on the door rolled away of itself and went back to the side, and the sepulcher was opened and both of the young men entered in. When therefore those soldiers saw that, they waked up the centurion and the elders (for they also were there keeping watch); and while they were yet telling them the things which they had seen, they saw again three men come out of the sepulcher, and two of them sustaining the other, and a cross following after them. And of the two they saw that their heads reached unto heaven, but of him that was led by them that it overpassed the heavens. And they heard a voice out of the heavens saying: 'Hast thou preached unto them that sleep?' And an answer was heard from the cross, saying: Yea." Cited, with slight modifications, from M. R. James, *The Apocryphal New Testament* (Oxford: Oxford University Press, 1953), 52–53.

108. Reginald H. Fuller offers a thorough account of the relevant texts in *The Formation of the Resurrection Narratives* (New York: Macmillan, 1971). For a helpful chart illustrating the similarities and differences of the Gospel narratives, see Raymond E. Brown, "The Resurrection of Jesus," in *The New Jerome Biblical Commentary*, 1376.

109. On the burial, see Raymond E. Brown, "The Burial of Jesus (Mark 15:42-47)," *Catholic Biblical Quarterly* 50 (1988): 233–45.

For I delivered to you as of first importance what I also received, that Christ died for our sins according to the scriptures, that he was buried, that he was raised on the third day according to the scriptures, and that he appeared to Cephas, then to the twelve. Then he appeared to more than five hundred brethren at one time, most of whom are still alive, though some have fallen asleep. Then he appeared to James, then to all the apostles. Last of all, as to one untimely born, he appeared also to me.

The core of this passage, fixed in wording before Paul received it, may be retraced to within a few years of the crucifixion. Neither its original language (Aramaic or Greek) nor its geographical origin (Damascus, Antioch, and Jerusalem are the chief possibilities) can be determined with certitude. Nonetheless, the antiquity of the formula is beyond question. Its importance for historical questioning is enhanced by verse 8, where Paul numbers himself among the recipients of "appearances" of the risen Christ. Here he applies to his own experience the same verb (*ophthe*) used three times in the preceding verses to designate appearances to prior witnesses to the resurrection. The text contains no reference to the empty grave and no narrative of a resurrection appearance. Unlike the Gospel stories, however, it is the direct expression of one who claims to have been an eyewitness to an event of this sort (see also Gal. 1:16 and 1 Cor. 9:1, though each of these texts uses different vocabulary).

In the following pages, I shall note varying assessments of this text on the part of contemporary theologians. Three points, however,

should be noted at this stage. First, the phrase "on the third day" in the third clause of the formula is applied to the resurrection itself, not to the discovery of the empty tomb or to the initial appearances. Recent authors have argued on the basis of biblical (see Hos. 6:1-2; Ps. 16:10) and intertestamental material that the phrase is not meant chronologically, but rather refers to a moment of decisive divine action.[110] (Modern references to rescue coming at the eleventh hour can serve as a remote analogy.) If this analysis is correct, the verse is an interpretation of the resurrection's theological significance, not a specification of its date.

Second, the formula emphasizes the sequence in which appearances took place and reflects a certain interest in the ecclesial status of their recipients. At the same time, in the judgment of many, the appearances are noted precisely as confirmation of the reality of the resurrection.

Third, the verb *ophthe*, "he was seen by" or "he appeared to," is of great significance. Paul does not use this precise form elsewhere. Its emphasis is on the active role of Christ, who lets himself be seen by chosen witnesses. In the Septuagint, the Greek translation of the Old Testament, *ophthe* is used frequently in narrating theophanies, where it serves as technical vocabulary for "appearing from heaven" (see, e.g., Gen. 12:7; 17:1; 18:1; Exod. 3:2; 4:1; 6:3). All uses of *ophthe* in the New Testament reflect similar contexts,[111] a fact that raises questions about interpreting the "seeing" literally.

Divergent assessments of this background are reflected in two distinct interpretations of

---

110. See especially Karl Lehmann, *Auferweckt am dritten Tag nach der Schrift* (Freiburg: Herder, 1968).

111. The term occurs eighteen times in the New Testament: Matt. 17:3; Mark 9:4; Luke 1:11; 22:43; Acts 7:2, 20, 26; 13:31; 16:9; 1 Cor. 15:5, 6, 7, 8; 1 Tim. 3:16; Rev. 11:19; 12:1, 3; 13:1. In each case, the reference is to an appearance from heaven. For an informative analysis of biblical terminology related to the resurrection, see the essays by Anton Vögtle and Rudolf Pesch in *Wie kam es zum Osterglauben?* (Düsseldorf: Patmos, 1975).

the fourth clause of the pre-Pauline formula. Most authors maintain that the text refers to a real seeing, though of a distinctive sort, that established faith in Jesus' resurrection and simultaneously established or confirmed the ecclesial position of the appearances' recipients.[112] Other theologians find that the ancient formula simply asserts the revelation of the resurrection and the ecclesial status of its witnesses, without providing information as to how such revelation occurred. To pursue this matter further, we shall have to consider recent treatments of the resurrection.

Modern Theological Discussion

Contemporary discussion of the resurrection entails both exegetical and systematic issues, and the positions of theologians on this subject are deeply entwined with their overall theological methods and convictions. While the resurrection has not been a traditional source of division along confessional lines, foundational differences among Catholics and Protestants on the nature of faith and on the relationship of divine grace to human activity often influence approaches to this topic. Despite overlapping concerns, it will be best to keep the presentations of Protestant and Catholic theologians distinct. Since intense modern debate about the resurrection developed first among Protestants and only later emerged in Catholic circles, the following survey will begin with a look at three major modern Protestant authors: Rudolf Bultmann, Willi Marxsen, and Wolfhart Pannenberg.

Rudolf Bultmann ⊛ Bultmann's thought on the resurrection, a standard reference point for later treatments, reflects his basic theological program of demythologization through existential interpretation. In Bultmann's judgment, the New Testament expresses its theological convictions in largely mythological form. While acceptable and even inevitable at the time the biblical texts were composed, mythological expressions pose unnecessary obstacles to modern believers. In addition, they entail the risk of a false objectification that subjects matters of faith to human control. Drawing on the early philosophy of Martin Heidegger, Bultmann advocates overcoming these problems by means of existential interpretation, a process that seeks to wrest from the ancient texts their underlying understanding of human existence as confronted by God and called to decision before God. The purpose of the texts is to awaken faith, not to provide objective historical information.

Applying these principles to the theology of the resurrection, Bultmann dismisses historical issues as irrelevant: "Christian faith . . . is not interested in the historical question." Far from being concerned with such data, Bultmann maintains that "faith in the resurrection is nothing other than faith in the cross as the salvation event" and that "to believe in the cross of Christ means to accept the cross as one's own and to allow oneself to be crucified with Christ." Contrary to all outward appearances, it is in the Word of the cross (see 1 Cor. 1:18-24) and nowhere else that Christ crucified and risen encounters us. To seek demonstration of the truth of this preaching or a historical basis for believing in it is an illegitimate effort to circumvent the demands of faith.[113]

---

112. The difficulty here lies in specifying what was seen; see William P. Loewe, "The Appearances of the Risen Lord: Faith, Fact, and Objectivity," *Horizons* 6 (1979): 177–92.

113. Rudolf Bultmann, "New Testament and Mythology: The Problem of Demythologizing the New Testament Proclamation," in *New Testament and Mythology and Other Basic Writings*, ed. Schubert M. Ogden (Philadelphia: Fortress

Bultmann's position recognizes that discussion of the resurrection cannot proceed in isolation, but requires reference to something else. Given his separation of Jesus' public life from his death, the resurrection could in principle be connected with either of these realities, but not both. But, as we have seen, Bultmann denies theological significance to the life of Jesus and conceives of theology as essentially a theology of the cross. In addition, his interest lies in the awakening of faith in the present moment, not in detecting significance inherent in past events. The result is a conception of the resurrection linked to the cross's paradoxical salvific character. The resurrection seems identified more with the rise of faith on the part of the disciples than with anything affecting Jesus personally.

Various interrelated elements of Bultmann's thought may well be challenged: the notion of faith as unsupported risk and consequent separation of faith from history; the denial of intrinsic significance to factual events; the option for existential interpretation and the resulting restriction of theological interest to the individual person and to the present time; the denial of theological significance to the historical Jesus; the false alternatives posed by separation of his death from his public life; the conception of the kerygma as immune from scrutiny. Nonetheless, Bultmann's insistence that the resurrection be subjected to critical interpretation has become an important reference point in subsequent discussion, even on the part of those who judge Bultmann's own position seriously flawed.[114]

Willi Marxsen ⊕ A stance similar in some respects to Bultmann's figures prominently in current discussion through the writings of Willi Marxsen, a German Lutheran exegete who shares Bultmann's notion of faith, interest in demythologization, and disjunction between Jesus' public life and crucifixion. Marxsen differs from Bultmann by insisting that nothing be permitted to detract from the Jesus of history. The result is a distinctive conception of the Easter faith and its origin: for Marxsen, "the question of the resurrection of Jesus is not that of an event which occurred after Good Friday, but that of the early Jesus."[115]

Arguing that the resurrection narratives, with their wealth of detail, are products of the early church, expressions of the Easter faith rather than reliable records of its origin, Marxsen identifies 1 Cor. 15:3-8 as the most significant historical testimony to the resurrection. Since even this ancient formulation is suffused with theological interpretation, historical investigation is unable to detail the events that lie behind the claims of the witnesses. From analysis of the biblical data, Marxsen concludes that occurrences after Jesus' death, above all a foundational experience on the part of Peter, enable the church to proclaim that Jesus lives, that Jesus' cause (*die Sache Jesu*, a characteristic phrase) goes on despite his death. Drawing on the nondualistic anthropology and apocalyptic vocabulary of

---

Press, 1984), 1–43; the citations are taken from pp. 40, 39, and 34. This much-debated essay was originally published in 1941.

114. For a detailed presentation of Bultmann's position and his exchange with Karl Barth on this subject, see Hans-Georg Geyer, "The Resurrection of Jesus Christ: A Survey of the Debate in Present Day Theology," in *The Significance of the Message of the Resurrection for Faith in Jesus Christ*, ed. C. F. D. Moule (London: SCM, 1968), 106–21.

115. Willi Marxsen, "The Resurrection of Jesus as a Historical and Theological Problem," in Moule, *The Significance of the Message*, 50; see, in addition to this entire essay (pp. 15–50), Marxsen's *The Resurrection of Jesus of Nazareth* (Philadelphia: Fortress Press, 1970).

contemporary Judaism, early Christians adopted resurrection language to express their faith. This vehicle of interpretation implied in turn that Jesus' grave was empty and thus led to legendary accounts of the women's discovery of the empty tomb. But resurrection terminology, inevitable under the cultural conditions of the New Testament, is neither intrinsic to Christian faith nor viable in the modern world. Nor is the anthropology of the biblical period the same as ours. Alternative confessions—that Jesus' cause goes on, that Jesus is the living one, that he still comes today—are more suitable for contemporary believers.

Many of the objections registered against Bultmann's treatment of the resurrection also apply to Marxsen's position. The vague account of the foundational experiences of Peter and the other disciples is a further weakness, and it is doubtful that all anthropologies are equally suitable for expressing Christian faith. Marxsen's interpretation of the resurrection is thus in many respects unsatisfactory. Nonetheless, his concern that events after the crucifixion not detract from the importance of Jesus is worth bearing in mind.

Wolfhart Pannenberg ◉ A conception of faith and theology diametrically opposed to those of Bultmann and Marxsen is operative in the work of Wolfhart Pannenberg, one of the chief critics of their thought on the resurrection. Pannenberg's treatment of the resurrection is part of an ambitious theological program, a context that accounts for many of his specific emphases and interests.

In Pannenberg's judgment, the central theological question posed by and since the Enlightenment is whether Christian faith is genuine faith or superstition:[116] whether, in other words, the Christian message is true. Theologians who dismiss this question as an act of unbelief fail to address the challenges posed by modernity. But the truth of the message can be judged only by reference to its content, for the authority of its sources is itself subject to dispute. Similarly, since Christians confess God as the all-determining reality, Creator of heaven and earth, no retreat from the realm of public history to the interior decision of the individual is legitimate. On the contrary, it is precisely in public history that revelation occurs, and the function of Christian preaching is to articulate the meaning inherent in the revelatory event when seen in its appropriate context. The validity of the Word is not exempt from critical scrutiny, and the point of reference for examining it is accessible to all.

Seen from this perspective, the resurrection of Jesus acquires central importance. First, the resurrection is decisive for Christology due to the inadequacy of the historical Jesus. Jesus' implicit claim to speak and act on behalf of God is not self-justifying, but requires divine legitimation. Such confirmation was not given during Jesus' lifetime, and Jesus' death, especially when its specific circumstances are taken into account, seems to constitute a final refutation of his claim to represent God.[117] The resurrection and public revelation of the resurrection are indispensable if Jesus is to be believed; without supporting his-

---

116. Wolfhart Pannenberg, "Insight and Faith," in *Basic Questions in Theology* (Philadelphia: Fortress Press, 1971), 2:41–42. It is consistent with this conviction that Pannenberg's *Systematische Theologie*, vol. 1 (Göttingen: Vandenhoeck & Ruprecht, 1988) begins with a chapter on the truth of Christian doctrine as the theme of systematic theology (pp. 11–72).

117. For Pannenberg, cross and resurrection constitute Jesus' double fate. *Jesus—God and Man*, 33, 210–11, 245–46. In both, Jesus has ceased to be active, and a response is given to his life. Yet the two are not on the same level of importance.

torical evidence, Christian faith would be indefensibly rash.

But the resurrection is also decisive from a second perspective. Any interpretation of world history must place events in context, for the context affects the interpretation. While the immediate context of past events can be determined to a greater or lesser extent, the overall outcome of history still lies ahead; we cannot position ourselves at the end of history and pass judgment on its outcome. Finding meaning in history as a whole thus seems impossible. Jesus' resurrection, however, is an anticipation of the end of history, an advance occurrence of what is expected one day for all. It thus provides an escape from this dilemma, a vantage point from which the whole of history can be assessed. Nothing else, not even Jesus' own life history, can do this. The resurrection is the key to interpreting both Jesus himself and human history as a whole.

The success of this theological program hinges on establishing the factuality of the resurrection as an event after Jesus' death. Strong historical warrant was needed for the first Christians to modify apocalyptic hope from envisioning general resurrection at the end of the world to confessing the resurrection of a single individual as already accomplished. Pannenberg's points of reference are the appearances and the empty grave. Appealing to 1 Cor. 15:3-8 as ancient material that includes eyewitness testimony, he argues that the appearance tradition is historically reliable. The emptiness of Jesus' grave is also historically demonstrable,

since otherwise the early Christian preaching of the resurrection in Jerusalem would have been exposed as false by reference to the presence of his body in the tomb. (In each case, Pannenberg classifies the detailed stories of the Gospels as later articulations of the theological meaning inherent in the resurrection, not as sources of further historical information.)

These historical facts require explanation, and the only plausible explanation is that Jesus is risen. While adopted from apocalyptic sources, resurrection language is the only vocabulary appropriate to the data; more general substitutes (e.g., of the sort proposed by Marxsen) fail to do justice to the historical facts. In Pannenberg's judgment, the core of apocalyptic hope for continued or renewed existence after death is a universal anthropological reality, not limited to the cultural conditions of the past. Far from rejecting this longing as evidence of non-Christian influence, he finds in it a reference point for Christianity's universal interests. Thus, the resurrection of Jesus, a historically demonstrable event, provides both the needed divine confirmation of the personal claims raised by Jesus' public life and a suitable vantage point from which to assess the meaning of history as a whole.[118]

Pannenberg's treatment of the resurrection, like other aspects of his work, is characterized by careful reasoning and thorough pursuit of foundational issues. The insistence on truth and the detailed examination of historical questions are particularly valuable. Nonetheless,

---

Pannenberg holds that the resurrection could be understood without the cross but that the cross could not be understood without the resurrection (p. 246).

118. Pannenberg, *Jesus—God and Man*, 53–114; idem, "The Revelation of God in Jesus of Nazareth," in *Theology as History*, ed. James M. Robinson and John B. Cobb (New York: Harper & Row, 1967), 101–33; idem, *Systematic Theology 2* (Grand Rapids: Eerdmans, 1994), 325–63. Pannenberg also attributes to the resurrection a type of retroactive effect, the possibility of which remains obscure; on this issue, see Brian O. McDermott, "Pannenberg's Resurrection Christology: A Critique," *Theological Studies* 35 (1974): 711–21.

questions remain. Does Pannenberg's conception of the need for subsequent legitimation of the historical Jesus require too much by way of extrinsic demonstration and unintentionally undercut Jesus' significance? Do references to Jesus' double fate (death and resurrection) imply a dichotomy between Jesus' public life (active) and his fate (passive)? Is the resurrection of Jesus historically demonstrable to an open-minded but neutral observer? Is apocalyptic expectation of general resurrection at the end of the world the most significant background of early Christian preaching that Jesus is risen? These issues are worth bearing in mind as we look at three major Catholic figures in the recent discussion of the resurrection.

As noted in the introduction to this chapter, Catholic theologians in the past few centuries typically relegated the resurrection to the domain of fundamental theology, where it was considered almost exclusively from an apologetic perspective; dogmatic Christologies of this period accorded the resurrection little attention.[119] As the biblical and liturgical movements awakened appreciation of the significance of the resurrection in the New Testament and renewed awareness of the paschal mystery's centrality in the life of the church, Catholic theologians of the 1950s and 1960s sought to enhance the position of the resurrection in dogmatic theology.[120] Extended treatment of the subject is now standard in Catholic textbooks on Christology.[121]

Such increased attention to the resurrection has been accompanied by the development of diverse theological positions on its nature and on the manner of its revelation. In addition, the salvific significance of the resurrection has been specified in different ways. The major systematic alternatives in recent Catholic thought are represented by Karl Rahner and Edward Schillebeeckx. In addition to considering these two authors, I shall also examine an innovative proposal advanced, with appeal to Rahner, by the exegete Rudolf Pesch.

Karl Rahner ◉ While attentive to the issues involved in exegetical discussion, Karl Rahner directed his thought on the resurrection primarily to systematic aspects of the question. Here as elsewhere, Rahner saw the content of Christian faith as a confirmation and fulfillment of human hope. His starting point in approaching the resurrection was therefore theological anthropology, more specifically his understanding of human freedom and death.

Rahner's theology of freedom focused on personal self-disposal before God, not on the choice of individual objects. Freedom is not only a power to select one thing over another but, on a deeper level, an ability to make something of oneself. Of its very nature, it seeks permanence, not reversibility, for constant change would be equivalent to indecision. For this reason, freedom must be limited temporally: the exercise of human freedom ends and culminates in death.

From this perspective, death is seen to contain both passive and active dimensions; it is at once the endured end of life, beyond one's control, and the completion of one's personal history of freedom. Human death is not extinction; rather, the freedom exercised over the course of a lifetime now bears eternal fruit in attaining a final state that includes all the constitu-

119. For a representative example, see Ludwig Ott, *Fundamentals of Catholic Dogma* (Cork, Ireland: Mercier, 1962). This work of 544 pages devotes pp. 192–95 to the resurrection and ascension.

120. The most influential work in this regard was F. X. Durrwell, *The Resurrection: A Biblical Study* (New York: Sheed & Ward, 1960).

121. See, e.g., Kasper, *Jesus the Christ*, 124–60; O'Collins, *Interpreting Jesus*, 108–32.

tive dimensions of human existence. While the way in which this occurs is beyond our ability to envision, the result is neither perpetuation of life in its current form nor substitution of a new mode of existence entirely unrelated to what has preceded it. Death leads rather to the permanent personal validity of an individual's life: "Death . . . is not the nullifying end of history, but the event in which history elevates itself, by God's own act, into the infinite freedom of God."[122]

Jesus' resurrection, while unique because of his uniqueness, incorporates the basic characteristics of resurrection in general. Divine causality and human causality are joined here, just as they are linked elsewhere. Jesus' death is the culmination of his free self-disposal before God, and his resurrection is the permanent personal outcome of his life. Far from being an extrinsically imposed sign of divine approval, it is the perfected and perfecting end of his specific death: "The resurrection of Christ is not *another* event *after* his suffering and after his death, but . . . the appearance of what took place in Christ's death: the performed and undergone handing over of the entire reality of the one corporal man to the mystery of the mercifully loving God through Christ's collected freedom, which disposes over his entire life and his entire existence."[123]

From these considerations on the unity of death and resurrection, Rahner concludes that the meaning of the resurrection is inseparable from the meaning of the crucifixion. The resurrection is the definitive stage of Jesus' salvific life; without it, nothing would be complete. But the resurrection is the only possible result of his salvific life and death, not a new event, separable from what precedes it. Therefore: "If the fate of Jesus has any soteriological significance at all, this significance can be situated neither in the death nor in the resurrection taken separately, but can only be illuminated now from the one and now from the other aspect of this single event."[124]

With regard to manifestation of the resurrection in events after Jesus' death, Rahner's position has varied. Generally accenting the appearances more than the empty grave, he emphasizes that the appearances involve a transposition of the risen Jesus into the range of the disciples' possible perception, and allow us to draw no conclusions about the specific characteristics of a risen body. In several writings, Rahner holds that such experiences were limited to the early church, so we are dependent on the first witnesses not only for the statement of fact but also for our knowledge of the possibility. Yet in some later texts, he tends to assimilate the appearances to the overall experience of grace and to argue that the indispensability of the apostolic message lies in its historical identification of Jesus.[125] While much of Rahner's later

---

122. Karl Rahner, "The Death of Jesus and the Closure of Revelation," in *Theological Investigations* (New York: Crossroad, 1984), 18:142 (corrected translation).

123. Karl Rahner, "Dogmatic Questions on Easter," in *Theological Investigations* (Baltimore: Helicon, 1966), 4:128 (corrected translation); see also idem, *Foundations of Christian Faith*, 266. The impact of Rahner's thought may be seen in the paraphrases of Kasper, *Jesus the Christ*, 150 (the similarity is far greater than the English translation suggests) and Küng, *On Being a Christian*, 359.

124. Rahner, *Foundations of Christian Faith*, 266. Kasper and Küng do not draw this conclusion, which seems to be entailed in the positions of Rahner that they do adopt.

125. For the first type, see Rahner, "Resurrection," in *Sacramentum Mundi*, 5:329–31; and idem, "The Position of Christology in the Church between Exegesis and Dogmatics," in *Theological Investigations* (New York: Seabury, 1974), 11:210–14. For the second, see idem, "Hope and Easter," in *Christian at the Crossroads* (New York: Seabury, 1975), 87–93;

writing sees the resurrection as a confirmation of Jesus' implicit claims, he remains unalterably opposed to understanding the resurrection as an extrinsically conferred sign of divine approval.

Rahner's conception of the resurrection as completion rather than correction is more akin to Johannine thought than to the Synoptic Gospels. While similar to Bultmann in associating the resurrection closely with the crucifixion, Rahner nonetheless insists that the resurrection affects Jesus personally and cannot be reduced to the first disciples' coming to faith. His position constitutes one pole of the contemporary Catholic theological spectrum.[126]

Edward Schillebeeckx ⊛ The next figure to be examine in our look at recent theologies of the resurrection is Edward Schillebeeckx, whose thought on the nature of the resurrection diverges sharply from Rahner's and forms the major contemporary Catholic alternative to Rahner's position. While a general overview of Schillebeeckx's Christology will be deferred until the next section of this chapter, some comments on his thoughts on death are needed to provide the background for his theology of the resurrection.

In contrast to Rahner, Schillebeeckx's theology of death pursues a phenomenological approach and identifies death as the extreme moment of human weakness and helplessness. In addition, he sees the crucifixion first and foremost as an act of cruelty and injustice. Given this background, the resurrection and death are not and cannot be seen as one event; the resur-rection is not death's "other," salvific aspect. To Schillebeeckx, the resurrection is more than the revelation of what happened in Jesus' death. It is a new and distinct event, a divine correct-ing victory over the negativity of suffering and death, a divine act that confers on Jesus' death new meaning. While the resurrection affects Je-sus personally and cannot be reduced to changes within his disciples, it remains metaempirical and metahistorical and must not be confused with a return to the conditions of Jesus' prior life. It is a confirmation that Jesus belongs to God, and thus of Jesus' person and message, yet it is not legitimation or confirmation in the nor-mal sense of those words: one statement of faith cannot legitimate another, and in any case, true legitimation of Christian faith remains a future, eschatological reality.

In addition to developing this interpreta-tion of the resurrection's nature, Schillebeeckx has also presented a distinctive conception of its revelation. In his judgment, discovery of Je-sus' empty grave is not a factor in the origin of faith in Jesus' resurrection.[127] Yet something is needed to account for the disciples' change of heart after the crucifixion. This "something" is tentatively identified as the disciples' grace-filled experiences of God's renewed offer of salva-tion in Jesus. Their essential component is not visual seeing, but the personal experience, pos-sible only through grace, of reorienting one's en-tire life on the basis of recognition of Jesus as the Christ. In keeping with this interpretation,

---

idem, "Jesus' Resurrection," in *Theological Investigations* (London: Darton, Longman & Todd, 1981), 17:16–23; and idem, *Foundations of Christian Faith*, 274–78.

126. For more thorough presentation of Rahner's thought, see John P. Galvin, "The Resurrection of Jesus in Contem-porary Catholic Systematics," *Heythrop Journal* 20 (1979): 125–30.

127. In *Jesus* (pp. 331–46), Schillebeeckx favors the view that the stories of finding the empty tomb derive from later liturgical celebrations at the place of Jesus' burial. He later grants that the tomb may have been found empty, but insists that this discovery did not in itself lead to faith. *Interim Report on the Books "Jesus" and "Christ"* (London: SCM, 1980), 86–88.

Schillebeeckx stresses similarities between the original disciples' coming to faith and the development of the faith of later Christians.

To specify matters further, Schillebeeckx undertakes a rather daring comparison of the tradition behind the appearance stories with the threefold account of Paul's experience on the road to Damascus in the Acts of the Apostles (Acts 9; 22; 26). The passages in Acts include a version that stresses conversion (Acts 9), an account that emphasizes mission (Acts 26), and a stage that incorporates both themes (Acts 22). Drawing on the work of Gerhard Lohfink, Schillebeeckx suggests that these three texts reflect different stages of a tradition in which the theme of conversion gradually yielded to that of mission. Noting the prominence of Peter in the resurrection tradition, and observing that the canonical stories of Jesus' appearances stress the theme of mission, Schillebeeckx tentatively suggests that the appearance narratives may be a later form of a tradition that originally concerned conversion experiences, but that has not been preserved in that earlier form. He therefore specifies the historical core of the appearance tradition as renewed experiences of forgiveness through Jesus, even after his death, which led to a reassembling of his followers at the initiative of Peter.[128]

Schillebeeckx's position has been misconstrued by some critics, as if he had reduced the resurrection itself, rather than the appearance tradition, to a conversion experience on the part of Jesus' disciples. Even apart from this misunderstanding, however, his historical reconstruction has been challenged as lacking textual foundation. Under the impact of such critique, Schillebeeckx has modified his position to some extent. While constant in insisting on the divine origin of faith in the resurrection and on the need for new experiences on the part of the disciples after Jesus' death, he no longer concentrates on the theme of conversion in his references to these experiences. Room is left for a possible visual component in the appearances, but explanations considered supranaturalistic remain excluded.[129]

Rudolf Pesch ◉ Drawing on Rahner's conception of the nature of the resurrection, Rudolf Pesch has proposed a novel exegetical interpretation of the background and origin of Christian faith in the risen Christ. Apart from its interest as a historical reconstruction, his hypothesis raises significant questions about the treatment of foundational christological issues.

As noted in earlier sections of this chapter, Pesch is optimistic in assessing the extent of critically assured historical knowledge of Jesus. Among other points, he is convinced of the disciples' pre-Easter faith in Jesus as prophetic Messiah, of Jesus' preparation of his disciples for his approaching death, and of Jesus' interpretation of his death, during the Last Supper, as salvific. It is against this background that he analyzes the New Testament texts concerning the resurrection.

Dissatisfied with the standard accounts of the origin of Easter faith, Pesch finds that the tradition concerning the discovery of the empty tomb is historically inconclusive, and that attempted explanations of the nature of the appearances often lack concrete information. In his judgment, the *ophthe* formula in 1 Cor. 15:5-8 expresses the ecclesial status of those listed as

---

128. See Schillebeeckx, *Jesus*, 329–97, 516–44.

129. In addition to Schillebeeckx, *Jesus*, 644–50 (a section added to the third Dutch edition), see his *Interim Report*, 74–93.

recipients of the appearances, but does not provide factual data about the origin of their status. Drawing on the work of Klaus Berger on Jewish belief in the resurrection or exaltation of individual figures (prophet; Son of man) while history continued its course, Pesch proposes that faith in the resurrection originated with the historical Jesus: given the events of Jesus' life and the way in which he died, the faith he elicited from his disciples was sufficient to survive his crucifixion and provide a basis for the (valid) conviction that God raised him from the dead. The resurrection of Jesus is an object of faith, not a basis of faith that can be established historically. Later inquiry into the grounds of Christian faith is therefore pointed to the historical Jesus, not to stories of events after his crucifixion.[130]

Pesch's hypothesis generated considerable controversy, and a number of serious criticisms were registered against his position. As far as exegetical issues are concerned, Pesch's account of the historical Jesus is disputed, as is his argument that the *ophthe* formula merely indicates the visionaries' ecclesial status. That conceptions of the resurrection or exaltation of individual figures were widespread in Jewish circles at the time of Jesus' death has also been questioned.

In christological terms, some critics find excessive Pesch's emphasis on the historical Jesus, and fear that a low Christology denying Christ's divinity will result. Significant christological issues are thus at stake in the discussion.[131]

CONCLUSION

As this survey of major recent interpretations of the resurrection shows, contemporary theologies of the resurrection vary widely in interest and content. Each conception is deeply embedded in its author's approach to Christology and theology as a whole, and can be fairly evaluated only with reference to these wider contexts. The following section of this chapter will examine the overall Christologies of Karl Rahner, Edward Schillebeeckx, and Raymund Schwager, in my judgment the most significant contemporary Roman Catholic christological projects. However, before taking up those matters, this section will conclude with some principles concerning the interpretation of the resurrection.

First, it is clear from the reflections described here that specifying the meaning of the resurrection is not an easy task. Given the unity of Jesus' person and message, I would argue that, as a minimum, the resurrection must be understood

---

130. See Rudolf Pesch, "Zur Entstehung des Glaudens an die Auferstehung Jesu," *Theologische Quartalschrift* 153 (1973): 201–28. For a summary of his position and the ensuing debate, see John P. Galvin, "Resurrection as *Theologia crucis Jesus*: The Foundational Christology of Rudolf Pesch," *Theological Studies* 38 (1977): 513–25.

131. For further reaction to Pesch's thought, see Francis Schüssler Fiorenza, *Foundational Theology: Jesus and the Church* (New York: Crossroad, 1984), 18–28; and Johannes Nützel, "Zum Schicksal des eschatologischen Propheten," *Biblische Zeitschrift* 20 (1976): 59–94. Pesch has subsequently altered his position; see "Zur Entstehung des Glaubens an die Auferstehung Jesu: Ein neuer Versuch," *Freiburger Zeitschrift für Theologie und Philosophie* 30 (1983): 73–98. He continues to find the empty-grave tradition unreliable and to hold that, in principle, sufficient grounds for belief in Jesus' resurrection were available by the time of his death. Now, however, he argues that, in fact, the disciples' breakthrough to faith in the risen Lord was mediated by ecstatic visions of Jesus as the exalted Son of man. The position maintained by Hansjürgen Verweyen is closer to Pesch's earlier views. On Pesch's current views and the reaction of other authors to his shift to a more traditional position, see John P. Galvin, "The Origin of Faith in the Resurrection of Jesus: Two Recent Perspectives," *Theological Studies* 49 (1988): 25–44. On Verweyen, see John P. Galvin, "The Role of the Resurrection in Christology: The Contribution of Hansjürgen Verweyen," in *Hoffnung, die Gruende nennt: Zu Hansjürgen Verweyens Projekt einer erstphilosophischen Glaubensverantwortung*, ed. Gerhard Larcher, Klaus Müller, and Thomas Pröpper (Regensburg: Pustet, 1996), 174–85.

to affect Jesus personally; it is not reducible to changes within and among his disciples. In addition, it is necessary to avoid conceiving Jesus' resurrection as a resuscitation that brings about a return to his previous conditions of life—as, for example, in the stories of the raising of Jairus's daughter (Matt. 9:18-26; Mark 5:21-43; Luke 8:40-56), the widow's son (Luke 7:11-17), and Lazarus (John 11:1-44). Paul's reflections (1 Cor. 15:35-57) on elements of continuity and transformation in the resurrection for which we hope may provide some useful guidelines for speaking of the resurrection of Jesus as well.

Second, the oft-neglected distinction between the resurrection and its revelation must be carefully preserved. Failure to do so results inevitably in confusion and misrepresentation of theological positions. The views of theologians on the historicity of the empty grave and of the appearances must be distinguished from their conclusions concerning the resurrection itself.

Third, while the initial position of Pesch may be exaggerated, examination of the grounds for faith in the resurrection should not be restricted to consideration of events after the crucifixion. The context established by Jesus' life and death is an indispensable factor in weighing the foundation of Christian faith that Jesus is risen.

Fourth, conceptions of the resurrection that undermine the significance of all that preceded it are open to telling objections on the grounds of escapism.[132] This consideration gives strong support to understanding the resurrection as confirmation rather than reversal.

Finally, the relationship of crucifixion and resurrection is the central point in any theology of the resurrection. Because of the influence of Bultmann's thought, a close association of death and resurrection is often identified with denial that the resurrection affects Jesus personally, yet in fact, the two issues are quite distinct. Analyses of this relationship are strongly influenced by varying theologies of death and corresponding theological interpretations of the crucifixion. While debate on this subject is likely to continue, a completely negative theology of the crucifixion seems in the long run incompatible with a positive theological assessment of a public life that led inexorably to its violent end.

Three Modern Christologies

The previous section of this chapter examined various items important in christological discussion. A plethora of issues emerged from a look at the contemporary literature, and it became clear that these themes are so tightly interwoven that none can be thoroughly weighed and adjudicated without reference to others. Against the background of what has been considered up to this point, this section of the chapter will outline in more systematic form the overall christological positions of three recent Catholic theologians: Karl Rahner, Edward Schillebeeckx, and Raymund Schwager. Their positions on several individual topics have already been noted; the goal now is to see the contours of their distinct interpretations of Jesus as the Christ.

Before considering the distinctive characteristics of these authors, it will be well to note some interests that are common to all three. While variations exist in the further specification of the issues and in the choice of means to

---

132. See Dietrich Bonhoeffer, *Letters and Papers from Prison*, rev. ed. (New York: Macmillan, 1967), 142, 176; Franz Schupp, *Vermittlung im Fragment: Franz Schupp als Lehrer der Theologie*, ed. Walter Raberger and Hanjo Sauer (Regensburg: Pustet, 2003), 118–59.

304

pursue them, the following four concerns are so widespread that they can be considered, in broad terms, characteristic elements of recent Catholic Christology.[133]

First, Rahner, Schillebeeckx, and Schwager share with many other theologians a desire to address in their Christologies questions of urgent contemporary significance. In major theologians, this interest implies attention to the serious underlying questions of modernity, not preoccupation with fleeting or superficial issues. Increasingly characteristic of Catholic thought since World War II, though always in danger of deteriorating into a frantic quest for relevance, a legitimate and properly pastoral concern for current problems prevents most modern Christology from pursuing a goal of timeless formulations.

Second, recent Christology reflects a widespread desire to receive the results and to address the problems posed by modern biblical research. Both Rahner and Schillebeeckx studied theology at a time when Catholic dogmatic theology was more attuned to speculative, philosophical issues and was much less interested in biblical matters than it is today. Yet each author, like Schwager and other colleagues from a younger generation, has sought in his own way to become aware of pertinent biblical questions and has made efforts to address them a substantial factor in his thought.[134]

Third, all three authors, again accompanied by many others,[135] wish to unify Christology and soteriology, and to link them with other branches of theology. This is not merely a pedagogical matter; it expresses an awareness that Christian faith is a unified whole whose various aspects cannot be grasped accurately when divorced from one another. In this connection, each accords a certain primacy to soteriology: our access to the person of Christ is mediated by his salvific deeds. Yet Rahner, Schillebeeckx, and Schwager also insist that Christ's work itself directs attention to his person.

Finally, each author combines acceptance of the classical Christology of the early councils with heightened recognition of its limitations. On the one hand, this twofold judgment implies a willingness to measure alternative christological formulations against the Chalcedonian dogma and to insist that proposed Christologies not fall short of that council's affirmations. On the other hand, it entails freedom to depart from the conciliar terminology and framework of questioning.

Karl Rahner

Karl Rahner's writings on Christology span a half century and pursue innumerable questions from a variety of perspectives. The closest approximation to a comprehensive summary of his Christology is found in *Foundations of Christian Faith*,[136] but even this presentation differs in intent and scope from an integrated christo-

---

133. In addition to Rahner, Schillebeeckx, and Schwager, these traits are reflected in the works of Walter Kasper, Hans Küng, Dermot Lane, Gerald O'Collins, and Roger Haight.

134. Biblical matters are treated in much greater detail and with much greater attention to specific exegetical works in Schillebeeckx and Schwager than they are in Rahner, but such differences should not obscure the extent to which all three authors are anxious to address, as systematic theologians, biblical questions they see as having direct impact on doctrinal issues in Christology.

135. Wolfhart Pannenberg is a notable and distinguished exception.

136. Rahner, *Foundations of Christian Faith*, 176–321.

logical synthesis. Without attempting to retrace the genesis of Rahner's thinking, the following pages will recapitulate the main elements of his Christology against the background of the chief concerns motivating his thought.

At the root of Rahner's Christology lie three theological concerns, each of which comes to bear in the elaboration of his christological conception: God's universal salvific will, Jesus' indispensable role in the mediation of salvation, and the completeness of Jesus' humanity. While none of these themes is new to the history of theology, each assumes in Rahner's thought a prominence that it has not always enjoyed in the past.

As is evidenced in his early writing on membership in the church,[137] Rahner has been preoccupied from the start of his theological career with the universality of God's salvific will. This theme received its classical biblical articulation in 1 Tim. 2:4 ("God wills that all men be saved and come to a knowledge of the truth") and has been reiterated in the Second Vatican Council's reference to the "universal design of God for the salvation of the human race" (*Ad gentes* 3). While pursuit of this issue is not limited to Christology, Rahner is anxious that christological formulations express the conviction that the divine offer of salvation extends to all, including those who lived before the time of Christ and others who, through no fault of their own, have never been exposed to the Christian message.

Juxtaposed to this foundational affirmation of the divine salvific will is an equally basic insistence on the indispensability of Jesus. The classical biblical texts on this score depict Jesus as saying, "I am the way, the truth and the life; no one comes to the Father except by me" (John 14:6), and proclaim that "there is salvation in no one else, for there is no other name under heaven given among men by which we must be saved" (Acts 4:12). The Second Vatican Council also speaks of Christ as the "sole mediator" (e.g., *Lumen gentium* 8) between God and the human race. While aware that such biblical and conciliar texts require careful interpretation, Rahner is convinced that the indispensability of Jesus is no less essential to Christianity than the universality of God's salvific will. The difficulty lies in reconciling the two principles, which at first sight seem to contradict each other.

In reference to the third of his root theological concerns, Rahner argues that widespread misunderstanding of classical christological doctrine causes major pastoral problems. In his judgment, the conciliar teaching is often misconceived in a crypto-monophysite manner. While verbally orthodox in their profession of faith, those infected by this tendency unconsciously abbreviate Jesus' human nature, especially his human intellect and human freedom. The result is a mythological notion of Jesus as part divine, part human. While, on a popular level, some accept this conception of Jesus, wrongly imagining it to be orthodox doctrine, others reject it, also mistaking it for the church's teaching but finding it incredible. Common to both positions, in Rahner's judgment, is a misunderstanding of what the church actually teaches.

To address these issues, Rahner developed a conception of Jesus as the definitive Savior, or the eschatological (final) Mediator of salvation. While the origins of his Christology lie in reflection on the church's teaching about Jesus, his

---

137. See, e.g., Rahner, "Membership of the Church according to the Encyclical of Pius XII 'Mystici Corporis Christi,'" in *Theological Investigations* (Baltimore: Helicon, 1963), 2:1–88. This article was originally published in 1947, four years after the encyclical was issued.

306

thought is best grasped against the background of his theological anthropology. Rahner understands the human being as spirit-in-world, finite openness toward the infinite mystery of God. For a human being, salvation consists fundamentally in participation in divine life—over and above all that human nature, of itself, might demand or achieve. It is a free gift of God, freely offered to all.

To constitute salvation for human beings, the operation of grace must address every facet of human existence. Thus, while an intensely personal appeal to the human freedom of each individual, grace also has a public, historical dimension. Here the figure of Christ is, in Rahner's judgment, essential. Located at the "fullness of time" (Gal. 4:4), the climax of the history of salvation, the incarnation is the definitive divine assumption of a portion of creation into the inner life of God. As such, the incarnation is salvific; it is not merely the establishment of a figure who will subsequently perform salvific deeds. (This aspect of Rahner's theology is a contemporary retrieval of themes common in Eastern patristic thought, which attracted Rahner's interest from the time of his own theological studies.) Rahner argues that the offer of grace intrinsically requires, at some point, such public, historical expression. Jesus not only makes known God's universal salvific will; his existence is a constitutive element of the divine offer of salvation, without which an essential component would be lacking.

Yet the incarnation is the assumption not only of a complete human nature, but of a human life history as well. This, too, is part of Jesus' being "like us in all things but sin."[138] It is only with his death, when the lifelong exercise of his individual human freedom is complete, that the definitive human acceptance of the offer of salvation takes place. As discussed earlier, this death leads of itself to resurrection, the permanent state of Jesus' existence before God. His multidimensional work as the definitive Savior is accomplished.

How does this conception enable Rahner to address the three concerns that underlie his Christology? First, his interpretation of the salvific significance of Jesus, and especially his interpretation of Jesus' death as the definitive public expression and acceptance of the divine gift of salvation, accent from the start God's universal salvific will and eschew any suggestion of a God somehow hostile to the world prior to Jesus' death. The Johannine insistence that the sending of the Son is an effect of God's love for the world (see John 3:16-17) receives full force. At the same time, the indispensable salvific role of Jesus is also safeguarded. Jesus is not a religious leader on the same level as other important figures in the religious history of the human race. He is *the* Savior, *the* Christ, not only unsurpassed but unsurpassable, since he has definitively mediated participation in God's inner life. Finally, Rahner's picture of Jesus, especially his stress on the presence and exercise of Jesus' human freedom, accents without abbreviation the integrity of Jesus' humanity. Thus, the concerns that motivate his christological reflection are adequately, if not exhaustively, addressed.

But does Rahner's notion of Jesus as the definitive Savior incorporate the early councils' teaching on Christ's divinity? The charge has been raised in some quarters that in fact (though not in intention) Rahner's Christology

---

138. DS 301; see Heb. 4:15.

falls short of the dogmas of Nicaea and Chalcedon.[139] While a full discussion of these issues is not possible here, the basic outline of Rahner's response may be noted. To Rahner, profession that Jesus is divine (in the nonmythological sense of the church's teaching) is not an addition to the confession that he is the Christ, but an explicitation of the latter statement's inherent meaning. Much as Anselm argued that only a divine figure can save by offering acceptable satisfaction for sin, Rahner argues that only a divine figure can save by definitively mediating participation in God's own life. In his judgment, at least, his understanding of Jesus as the definitive Savior includes the full content of Chalcedon's doctrine.[140]

Edward Schillebeeckx

In sharp contrast to Rahner's emphasis on salvation as perfection of the good, Edward Schillebeeckx finds the starting point and permanent context of his Christology in the universal human experience of evil. To Schillebeeckx, human history is an extended search for meaning and liberation in the midst of suffering. No purely theoretical account of evil is of value; what is needed is action to overcome what ought not be.

Yet action requires foundation and support: a source of inspiration and of hope, and a memory of past injustice and suffering. In these respects, narrative holds more promise than theory: "People do not *argue* against suffering, but tell a *story*. . . . Christianity does not give any explanation for suffering, but demonstrates a way of life."[141] The primary form of Christology, set from the start in a soteriological context, is to retell "the life-story of the man Jesus as a story of God."[142]

Aware that our access to Jesus is mediated through the church's response to his person and life, Schillebeeckx engages in detailed study of Jesus' preaching and conduct and evaluates them as an offer of definitive salvation from God. Since the general course of events offers no basis for this conviction on Jesus' part, Schillebeeckx posits a unifying source of Jesus' activity in his unique experience of God as unsurpassably close and as the committed opponent of all that is inhuman. (Alluding to Mark 14:36; Rom. 8:15; and Gal. 4:6, though not relying on these texts in isolation, Schillebeeckx designated this reality as Jesus' "abba-experience," a term that has become identified with his theology.) In both historical analysis and systematic reflection, Schillebeeckx favors the category of eschatological prophet, the long-awaited prophet-like-Moses with whom God speaks face-to-face (see Deut. 18:15-18), as a vehicle for articulating Jesus' status and significance. The eschatological prophet is not simply an apocalyptic preacher of a message about the approaching end of the world. Rather, the eschatological prophet is a unique figure, God's definitive salvific representative in human history.

---

139. For criticism of Rahner on this score, see Heinz-Jürgen Vogels, "Erreicht Karl Rahners Theologie den kirchlichen Glauben? Kritik der Christologie und Trinitätslehre Karl Rahners," *Wissenschaft und Weisheit* 52 (1989): 21–62. For a defense of the orthodoxy of Rahner's thought, see Joseph H. P. Wong, *Logos-Symbol in the Christology of Karl Rahner* (Rome: LAS, 1984); and idem, "Karl Rahner's Christology of Symbol and Three Models of Christology," *Heythrop Journal* 27 (1986): 1–25.

140. For brief articulations of Rahner's position, see his "Jesus Christ," in *Sacramentum Mundi*, 3:204–5; and *The Love of Jesus and the Love of Neighbor* (New York: Crossroad, 1983), 26–30.

141. Schillebeeckx, *Christ*, 698–99.

142. Schillebeeckx, *Jesus*, 80.

308   Since Jesus' person and message are inseparable, it is not surprising that the conflict engendered by popular rejection of his message culminated in his execution. Long aware of the possibility of a violent end, Jesus gradually became certain of death's approach. Retaining assurance of personal salvation and somehow integrating his approaching fate into his understanding of his mission, he left his death, as a kind of final prophetic sign, for his followers to interpret. In principle, his death is a triumph of evil, an assault on the offer of salvation that Jesus embodied, though the manner in which he confronted and endured death imbued the entire event with a certain salvific significance. (In a sense, Schillebeeckx argues, we are redeemed more despite the death of Jesus than because of it.) In any case, death was not the last word. Renewed experiences of grace and of forgiveness of sin through Jesus soon led to a reassembling of the disciples, scattered at the time of the crucifixion, at the initiative of Peter. Thus, the church experienced anew Jesus' salvific presence and recognized in faith that he had been raised from the dead.

Yet, for Schillebeeckx, the story does not end here. From the start, the narrative has concerned an encounter: "The starting point of the Christian movement was an indissoluble whole consisting on the one hand of the offer of salvation through Jesus and on the other of the Christian response in faith."[143] This structure is retained in later periods as well, from the New Testament to the present day.

While interpretive categories have varied widely, underlying the entire history is a common experience of definitive salvation from God in Jesus. Schillebeeckx is unwilling to flesh out this formula more fully with individual biblical categories, for he is convinced that "New Testament Christianity can only be a model indirectly, and not directly,"[144] for later believers. Instead, he distills from an analysis of the disparate New Testament material four structural principles, present throughout Christian history and normative for any Christian soteriology:

1. Salvation is offered in and through God's history with humanity.
2. Salvation has a christological nucleus, for the true countenance of God is shown in Jesus of Nazareth.
3. The history of Jesus is inseparable from our own history as his followers.
4. The conclusion of the story is eschatological, for it cannot be completed within the confines of world history.

Without these four ingredients (God, Jesus, church, and future), a story of salvation would cease to be Christian.[145]

Against this background, Schillebeeckx outlines a provisional sketch of soteriology. Axiomatic is the principle that God does not will human suffering. Salvation includes both earthly and eschatological dimensions. During the course of history, the divine promise of salvation is present in efficacious but fragmentary acts of reconciliation, anticipatory of future salvation.[146]

---

143. Schillebeeckx, *Christ*, 66.

144. Ibid., 561.

145. For the four structural principles, whose systematic importance is greater than the brevity of their presentation suggests, see Schillebeecks, *Christ*, 629–44; and idem, *Interim Report*, 37, 51–55, 122–24.

146. For a brief summary of Schillebeeckx's christological project, which in many respects remained incomplete, see "Jesus the Prophet," in *God among Us* (New York: Crossroad, 1983), 33–44.

Schillebeeckx's christological project has generated intense discussion. Critics have questioned especially the adequacy of his classification of Jesus as the eschatological prophet and of his reconstruction of the revelation of the resurrection. Further clarification of his views and explanation of their relationship to more traditional expressions of Christology may be found in his published correspondence with the Congregation for the Doctrine of the Faith.[147]

Raymund Schwager

In contrast to both Rahner and Schillebeeckx, Raymund Schwager, a Swiss Jesuit theologian and long-term professor of dogmatic theology at the University of Innsbruck, develops his Christology with particular attention to the problem of violence (including the relationship of violence to God) and to the coexistence of divergent soteriologies within the New Testament. To address these and other issues, Schwager opts for a dramatic structure, which enables him to locate different theological themes at different stages of a compressed but gradual revelatory exchange.

Foundational to Schwager's conception is his concern with violence as a universal human problem that religion seeks to address. Drawing on the analyses of René Girard (who later became a close friend),[148] Schwager identifies violence as a pervasive though often overlooked concern within the Bible. In the Old Testament,

reference to violence is widespread, and its relationship to God is envisioned in ways ranging from ascription of violent traits to God (e.g., Ezekiel 38–39) to divine identification with the victim who suffers on behalf of others (as in Isa. 52:13—53:12). Due to the contradictory nature of such texts, the question of the relationship of violence to God remains unresolved at this stage.[149]

A second issue, not immediately related to the first, is the presence within the New Testament of divergent and apparently incompatible conceptions of the mediation of salvation. While texts such as Mark 1:15 ("'The kingdom of God is at hand; repent and believe in the gospel'") seem to require no atoning activity on Jesus' part, other passages, such as Mark 10:45 ("'The Son of man came not to be served but to serve, and to give his life as a ransom for many'") and many Pauline texts (e.g., Rom. 5:1-11), attribute necessary mediation of salvation to Jesus' crucifixion. Addressing the tension between such diverse New Testament soteriologies becomes an important factor in Schwager's dramatic conception.

Schwager's dramatic soteriology is strongly influenced by the thought of Hans Urs von Balthasar,[150] but Schwager differs from von Balthasar in the weight he attributes to Jesus' public life and in his understanding of the way in which human sin is imposed on the innocent Jesus.[151] The result of this conception is an innovative presentation of the culmination of the

---

147. See Ted Schoof, ed., *The Schillebeeckx Case* (New York: Paulist, 1984).

148. Girard's chief work is *Violence and the Sacred* (Baltimore: Johns Hopkins University Press, 1979).

149. Raymund Schwager, *Must There Be Scapegoats? Violence and Redemption in the Bible* (San Francisco: Harper & Row, 1987). For a brief summary of Girard's thought and an analysis of Schwager's early work, see John P. Galvin, "Jesus as Scapegoat? Violence and the Sacred in the Theology of Raymund Schwager," *Thomist* 46 (1982): 173–94.

150. Von Balthasar, *Theo-Drama*.

151. Schwager studies von Balthasar's soteriology at length in *Der wunderbare Tausch*, 273–312; no other modern Catholic theology receives such treatment.

history of salvation as a drama in five acts.[152]

Act I begins with the initiation of the drama (against the dramatic background of the Old Testament relationship of God and Israel) when Jesus publicly proclaims the imminent arrival of God's salvific kingdom. While unconditional in the sense of not requiring any prior preparation on the part of his audience, his message does impose on those addressed a demand for repentance and conversion ("'repent and believe in the gospel'"; Mark 1:15b). Far from being complete in itself, the first act thus points ahead to the response to Jesus' word.

The second act comprises two elements: the negative collective response to Jesus and his message, and Jesus' intensification of the urgency of his preaching through emphatic exposure of the outcome that will [would] result from failure to heed his word. It is here that Schwager locates Jesus' threats of destruction (e.g., Mark 12:1-12) and even of eternal damnation (e.g., Matt. 25:31-46). Despite appearances to the contrary, such texts do not definitively link God with violence; they reveal instead the appalling consequences inherent in human misdeeds and thus constitute a renewed appeal for conversion.

In the central Act III, the dramatic dialogue advances to a new and decisive stage. Even Jesus' intensified proclamation of his message fails to elicit the desired response: in addition to Jesus' opponents, even Jesus' disciples fall short of expectations in many ways (e.g., Mark 8:14-21). Rejection of Jesus' message entails rejection of his person, upon whom human beings project and impose their own sin, and moves inexorably toward his condemnation and death. Threatened with the failure of his preaching, and recognizing that the fate of the kingdom now rests with him alone, Jesus in a new and distinct act takes on himself the sin of the world and offers himself to the Father in death on behalf of his adversaries (e.g., Mark 14:24), insofar as they too are victims of sin. The third act thus also points ahead, as it leaves open the Father's response to Jesus' self-gift.

It is only at this stage that the Father's decisive judgment occurs and is revealed. In Act IV, the Father raises the crucified Jesus from the dead and thus identifies himself with Jesus. Yet, instead of identifying himself with Jesus and against Jesus' opponents, as the parable of the vineyard (Mark 12:9) would lead one to expect, the Father identifies himself with Jesus precisely insofar as Jesus offers himself on behalf of his opponents. He thus reveals himself as even more gracious and forgiving than had hitherto been revealed.

But the drama of salvation is not yet quite complete. The final Act V concludes the story with the interior transformative mission of the Holy Spirit and the emergence of the church. Only then is the full opposition between God and violence fully disclosed.

Schwager's dramatic conception thus allows him to locate different New Testament soteriologies at different stages of the drama, to attribute greater significance than von Balthasar does to the events of Jesus' public life, and to analyze the relationship of God and violence from the perspective afforded by Jesus' life, death, and resurrection. While acknowledging the depth of Schwager's thought, some commentators have raised questions about his historical judgments and asked if his interpretation of the crucifixion

---

152. Schwager, *Jesus in the Drama of Salvation*. For a more popular and imaginative presentation, see idem, *Jesus of Nazareth: How He Understood His Life* (New York: Crossroad, 1998).

obscures necessary distinctions between perpetrators and victims of evil.[153] At the very least, however, Schwager's work provides considerable insight into easily neglected aspects of the theological significance of Jesus' life and death.

The differences among the christological conceptions of Rahner, Schillebeeckx, and Schwager, especially evident in their theological assessments of the crucifixion and resurrection, should not blur recognition of common themes in their analyses of the historical Jesus and other important christological issues. Nor should it be imagined that their works exhaust recent thought on Jesus; among other studies, Roger Haight's understanding of Jesus as symbol of God for Christians deserves special mention.[154] But Rahner, Schillebeeckx, and Schwager do stand as three prominent models of two traditional approaches to christological reasoning: reflection on Jesus as the perfection of God's good creation, and reflection on Jesus as the divine remedy for the problem of evil.

Conclusion

The bulk of this chapter has sought to identify central issues in the field of Christology and to examine Christian thought on its various facets from its origins to the present. After examining various strands of christological thinking contained in the canonical New Testament, I traced the development of the church's normative doctrine on the person of Christ and the articulation of the classical interpretations of his redemptive activity. Turning from the themes of the patristic and medieval periods to the critical historical questioning characteristic of modernity, I first surveyed the development and implications of research into the public life of Jesus, his crucifixion, and his resurrection, and then considered in outline form the christological conceptions of three recent theologians, Karl Rahner, Edward Schillebeeckx, and Raymund Schwager. In each of these areas, basic christological data have been presented, though none of the topics has been treated exhaustively. Now this compact reflection on Jesus Christ as the object and foundation of Christian faith will conclude with a few principles that may serve as reference points in developing and assessing Christologies.

First, despite the passage of time, the Christologies of the New Testament and the dogmatic definitions of the early councils retain their significance as norms against which later theological formulations must be measured. Contemporary Christologies need not, and presumably in many instances will not, make use of the terminologies and modes of inquiry of the biblical and patristic periods. But modern thought about Jesus can be assessed by reference to these standards, to determine if new formulations fall short of fundamental Christian affirmation.

Second, both Jesus' own preaching of the kingdom of God and the church's subsequent proclamation of the Christian message presuppose an intrinsic link between the person of Jesus

---

153. The most extensive assessment of Schwager's thought may be found in Jozef Niewiadomski and Wolfgang Palaver, eds., *Dramatiche Soteriologie: Ein Symposion* (Innsbruck: Tyrolia, 1992). This volume contains papers presented at a symposium at Innsbruck in September 1991 and Schwager's response to those presentations.

154. See Haight, *Jesus, Symbol of God*. Haight's Christology has been criticized by the Congregation for the Doctrine of the Faith in a Notification dated December 13, 2004. The chief point at issue is the universal salvific significance of Jesus, an issue rightly underscored in the same Congregation's Declaration *Dominus Jesus* (August 6, 2000).

and the content of the gospel. To sever that connection is to deprive Christology of its necessary foundation. In the past, this issue seemed easily resolved by appeal to Jesus' self-referential preaching in the Fourth Gospel, but in view of modern exegetical research, it now requires more nuanced examination. An important task of Christology is therefore to ascertain the relationship of Jesus' person and message and to elaborate its implications for understanding Jesus.

Third, as noted in this chapter, Christians have at various times related Jesus' salvific character to the incarnation, to his public life, to his death on the cross, or to his resurrection. Because each of these four reference points is intimately intertwined with the other three, it seems ultimately inconsistent to ascribe salvific value to one element of Jesus' existence in isolation from others. To speak, for example, of Jesus' public life as salvific without recognizing salvific value in his death (or vice versa) is to ignore the fact that Jesus' manner of life is what brought him to the cross. Christologies can therefore be tested by asking whether their theological interpretations of the various reference points are consistent with the interrelationships inherent in their subject matter.

This third principle suggests a final consideration. To attribute salvific significance to the incarnation, public life, crucifixion, and resurrection taken severally is to dissolve Christology into a series of disparate assertions without a unifying core. The usual way to prevent this from happening is to select one or another element as the integrative factor. There is inevitably an element of decision in this choice, though the decision ought not be arbitrary. Over the course of the history of Christian thought, each of the four reference points has at times been accorded pride of place: the incarnation in much patristic thought; the incarnation and the crucifixion in medieval reflection; Jesus' public life in modern liberal theology; the resurrection in many Christologies of recent vintage. That the public life of Jesus and the resurrection now receive such attention is in part a justified reaction against past neglect of these themes. Nonetheless, it may be doubted that they, alone or in tandem, are capable of sustaining the burden thus placed upon them. It is the crucifixion in which the public life of Jesus is epitomized and to which the resurrection is indissolubly linked. It is here that the focal point of Christology—and of a life lived in discipleship—is to be found.

For Further Reading

Grillmeier, Alois. *Christ in Christian Tradition*. 2 vols. 2nd ed. Atlanta: John Knox, 1975–87.

> Classic studies of christological thought in the patristic period.

Haight, Roger. *Jesus, Symbol of God*. Maryknoll, NY: Orbis, 1999.

> A provocative contemporary study, written from the perspective of a pluralistic theology of religions.

Johnson, Elizabeth A. *Consider Jesus: Waves of Renewal in Christology*. New York: Crossroad, 1990.

> An analysis of contemporary Christology by a leading American feminist theologian.

Kasper, Walter. *Jesus the Christ*. New York: Paulist, 1976.

> An informative textbook on Christology, written by a well-known contemporary theologian.

Küng, Hans. *On Being a Christian*. Garden City, NY: Doubleday, 1976.

> A presentation of the basics of Christian faith, intended for a wider audience, with particular focus on christological issues.

Matera, Frank. *New Testament Christology*. Louisville: Westminster John Knox, 1999.

> An informative account of the Christology of the New Testament, based primarily on narrative analysis of the texts.

Meier, John P. "Jesus." In *The New Jerome Biblical Commentary*. Edited by Raymond Brown et al., 1316–28. Englewood Cliffs, NJ: Prentice Hall, 1990.

> A compressed but informative exegetical account of the historical Jesus.

———. *A Marginal Jew: Rethinking the Historical Jesus*. 4 vols. New Haven: Yale University Press, 1991–2009.

> A balanced and encyclopedic presentation (not yet complete) of the historical Jesus.

Meyer, Ben F. *The Aims of Jesus*. London: SCM, 1979.

> An overview of research on the historical Jesus and a thoughtful study, influenced by the work of Bernard Lonergan, of Jesus' goals.

O'Collins, Gerald. *Christology: A Biblical, Historical, and Systematic Study of Jesus Christ*. Oxford: Oxford University Press, 1995.

> A textbook that informatively surveys the major issues of Christology.

Pannenberg, Wolfhart. *Systematic Theology*. 3 vols. Grand Rapids: Eerdmans, 1991–97.

> A comprehensive study that presents Pannenberg's Christology (in volume 2) in the context of his entire theology.

Rahner, Karl. *Foundations of Christian Faith*. New York: Seabury, 1978.

> A summary of many major aspects of Rahner's theology, with particular focus on Christology.

Ratzinger, Joseph. *Jesus of Nazareth: From the Baptism in the Jordan to the Transfiguration*. New York: Doubleday, 2007.

> The first volume of Pope Benedict XVI's theological reflection on the public life of Jesus.

Schillebeeckx, Edward. *Jesus: An Experiment in Christology*. New York: Seabury, 1979.

———. *Christ: The Experience of Jesus as Lord*. New York: Seabury, 1980.

> The first two parts of a contemporary christological synthesis by an eminent Flemish Dominican theologian.

314   Schnackenburg, Rudolf. *Jesus in the Gospels: A Biblical Christology*. Louisville: Westminster John Knox, 1995.

> *A thorough study of Gospel Christology by an eminent German exegete.*

Schwager, Raymund. *Jesus in the Drama of Salvation: Toward a Biblical Doctrine of Redemption*. New York: Crossroad, 1999.

> *An intriguing dramatic presentation of soteriology, with particular attention to the problem of the relationship of God to violence.*

von Balthasar, Hans Urs. *Theo-Drama: Theological Dramatic Theory*. 5 vols. San Francisco: Ignatius, 1988–98.

> *The central part of von Balthasar's "trilogy." Volume 4 contains the chief elements of von Balthasar's dramatic soteriology.*

Church 6

Church

Michael A. Fahey

The Contemporary Context of Ecclesiology

In presenting a summary account of present-day Roman Catholic teaching on the church, one is faced first with the problem of where to begin. A chronological approach would require beginning with the preaching of Jesus as recorded in the Gospel recollections of his public ministry. From there, one would follow historically the nascent church's growth during the apostolic era, concentrating on its interaction with civil society and political structures that century by century helped to shape the church. Such a chronological approach has its merits. However, the method preferred in this chapter, one also favored by a growing number of theologians reflecting on the reality of church (ecclesiologists), is to begin rather with the church's present-day context and attitudes. This approach takes stock first of Christians' convictions and feelings today about the church, at least among those members of the international Christian church who have expressed their views. Only after that description would one then retrace retrospectively selected questions about the origin and historical evolution of the church.

Beginning with a frank description of the present situation could create the impression that a writer is only critical, even disrespectful of sacred traditions, especially if one voices criticism of the church's faults. But critical remarks can surely also stem from an intense love of the church and can be motivated by a burning desire to see the church respond more effectively to its lofty vocation. In fact, critique of the church, especially when it is temperate and includes a keen awareness of one's own share in the church's faults, can be highly constructive. Critique is not the same as dissent, that activity so feared in some quarters of the church today and frequently judged to be only petulance or unwillingness to accept definitive or official church teachings. Critique may well be a prophetic invitation to the church's fuller self-realization under the power of grace.

This method of beginning a study of the church from a contemporary starting point is one used effectively by the French priest and theologian Jean Rigal. His book *L'Église: Obstacle et chemin vers Dieu* (*The Church as Obstacle and Path toward God*)[1] begins by discussing the church as it is judged by some in the modern world: as oppressive, dogmatic, pyramidal, lifeless, and remote from modern realities. Another example of this approach is found in a collaborative work published by several leading German Catholic scholars.[2] Their volume includes an overview of trenchant criticism of the church by the historian Victor Conzemius.[3] Another French theologian, Henri Denis, begins his study of the church with an examination of why there exists such "disaffection" toward the Catholic Church today.[4]

Critique has not always been welcomed. When Antonio Rosmini, the nineteenth-century prophet of renewed Catholicism, wrote his *Cinque piaghe della Chiesa* (*The Five Wounds of the Church*) in 1832 and published it in 1846 on the eve of the election of Pius IX, his reward was to have his work placed on the Index of Forbidden Books in 1849. (It was later removed from the Index before his death.) Yet today hardly

---

1. Jean Rigal, *L'Église: Obstacle et chemin vers Dieu* (Paris: Cerf, 1983).
2. *Traktat: Kirche*, vol. 3 of *Handbuch der Fundamentaltheologie*, ed. W. Kern et al. (Freiburg: Herder, 1986).
3. Ibid., 30–48.
4. Henri Denis, *Chrétiens sans église* (Paris: Desclée de Brouwer, 1979).

anyone would dispute the accuracy of his sober account of those five wounds that plagued nineteenth-century Catholicism: the division between people and clergy at public worship, insufficient education of clergy, disunity among bishops, nomination of bishops entrusted to the hands of civil government, and restrictions on the church's free use of its own temporal possessions. We know from the diary of John XXIII, the pope who convoked the council of renewal (*aggiornamento*), how impressed he was by the persuasiveness of Rosmini's critique.

The Catholic Church, together with other Christian communions, finds its self-understanding primarily from the gospel revelation expressed in the New Testament. For a Christian, this is the heart of divine revelation. Yet today's Catholics know they are also ineluctably marked by the aftermath of the Protestant Reformation and the Council of Trent (1545–63), convened to respond to the Reformers' challenge only after many delays. Further, today's Catholics' understanding of church and of its structure is still strongly affected by the decisions of the First Vatican Council (1869–70), long after the immediate problems that it addressed have become remote to present-day consciousness. Also, many modern Catholics read the New Testament and its comments about the church in the light of the Second Vatican Council (1962–65). The way that educated Christians reflect on the church nowadays is also affected by historical consciousness, awareness of the literary development of the New Testament writings, and insights born in the upheavals of the two world wars with the resultant dislocations of populations and massive persecutions.

In the creed, the church is mentioned in the enumeration of beliefs in the workings of the triune God, who sanctifies and consecrates this community of faith. Because the church is included in the Christian's act of faith, it necessarily possesses a dimension of mystery that can never be totally comprehended. Concentrating on the visible human aspects of the church does not mean denying the fact that it is a human-divine reality or that there is more to church than meets the eye. Still, some of what does meet the eye is disturbing and troubling.

Disillusionment and Disaffection

Those who keep abreast of the various media sources are well aware of an increased disillusionment and dissatisfaction among Catholics in regard to diocesan and even worldwide leadership. The most dramatic and stinging cause of this, especially in the United States, is the discovery of sexual abuse of minors by priests. Closely connected with this is the realization that, to a shocking degree, a number of bishops failed to take appropriate and prompt actions to prevent this, deciding simply to reassign offending clergy to another parish or parochial setting. The huge sums of money that certain dioceses or religious congregations have been or are being required to pay in court settlements have shaken the faith of numerous Catholics.[5]

---

5. For a comprehensive investigation of sexual crimes by Catholic clergy, see the report of the John Jay College of Criminal Justice, *The Nature and Scope of Sexual Abuse of Minors by Catholic Priests and Deacons in the United States 1950–2002* (Washington, DC: USCCB, 2004). Among the sizable literature analyzing this situation, one may consult Jean M. Bartunek, Mary Ann Hinsdale, and James F. Keenan, eds., *Church Ethics and Its Organizational Context: Learning from the Sex Abuse Scandal in the Catholic Church* (Lanham, MD: Rowman & Littlefield, 2006); Thomas G. Plante, ed., *Bless Me Father for I Have Sinned: Perspectives on Sexual Abuse Committed by Roman Catholic Priests* (Westport, CT: Praeger, 1999); and A. W. Richard Sipe, *Celibacy in Crisis: A Secret World Revisited* (New York: Brunner-Routledge, 2003).

At the same time, regular attendance at the Sunday liturgies of parishes has declined. The causes for this drop-off are not completely understood: absence of fear that "missing Mass" is a mortal sin, disenchantment with liturgical changes, dissatisfaction with the competence and concern of the ordained, and major competition from recreational and domestic priorities. The secular media report widely on any controversial statements or decisions of popes, bishops, clergy, or other faithful, and those accounts affect attitudes toward the church.

Some Catholics feel that certain papal actions are promoting a centralist style of governance in the church. There is a growing perception that the move toward regional autonomy in the local churches cautiously encouraged at the Second Vatican Council is gradually being replaced by a centralist policy of control, especially through the choice of bishops and diminishment of the theological status of national episcopal conferences. The so-called Cologne Declaration, a specific criticism by some European theologians about the procedures commonly used to choose bishops, particularly in Europe, is an example of this mood; similar reactions to problems that have developed in South America, especially in Brazil, can also be noted.[6] In earlier days, the Swiss theologian Hans Urs von Balthasar described this critical mood on the part of some Catholics as an "anti-Roman affect."[7]

In some parts of the world, Catholics have been disillusioned and shocked by charges of financial abuses by certain Roman Catholic priests, some of which have been verified as criminal in courts of law. This naturally has led to a distancing from Catholic leadership. It also raises questions about principles of accountability and concerns about the church's orthopraxis.

A Church Divided

Any reflections on the church in its present reality need to address that the obvious fact about the Christian church today is that it still remains divided along confessional lines. Not only are the churches of the East and the West existentially estranged and still living in mutual suspicion of one another after over a millennium, but the churches of the West have been tragically fragmented since the sixteenth century. Emphasizing this fact is not done in order to impute blame to any particular groups or to deny that the Reformation helped Christians reappropriate their vocation and live more evangelically. But the fact is that suspicions, anathemas, and de facto or psychological excommunications have separated the Catholic and Protestant worlds for centuries. It is true, especially since the famous 1910 meeting of the Edinburgh Missionary Conference, considered as the starting point for the modern ecumenical movement, that there have been major efforts to heal the separations among Christians that have been and remain a countersign to the preaching of the good news. First among Protestants, then between Orthodox and Protestants, and now between Catholics and other Christians, the modern ecumenical movement has struggled to overcome the ignorance and prejudices that the Christian churches have long harbored toward one another. Willingness to cooperate and mutually explore doctrinal and cultural differences

---

6. The Cologne Declaration appeared in the London *Tablet* 243 (February 4, 1989): 140–42; see a similar text from Brazilian theologians entitled "The Church in Rough Water," *Tablet* 243 (July 29, 1989): 882–83.
7. Hans Urs von Balthasar, *Der antirömische Affekt* (Freiburg: Herder, 1974).

among Christians was a hallmark of the twentieth century especially since the close of the Second Vatican Council.

But unfortunately, after high hopes, there is now much disillusionment and self-doubt among Christians, prompting one professional ecumenist to produce what he calls *A Survival Guide for Ecumenically Minded Christians*.[8] The Christian churches are far from overcoming their differences. More and more people are unhappy about the "non-reception" of ecumenical consensus statements by the leadership and rank-and-file members of the various churches. Christians find a growing hesitancy to progress ecumenically, especially by church leaders. For example, at official levels, there is considerable reluctance to recognize the sacraments of other churches or to permit Eucharistic sharing (intercommunion). It has been argued that the differences that exist today among the Christian churches are legitimate variations within acceptable theological, liturgical, or canonical diversity, but this view is not widely accepted by church authorities. The decision makers in the churches seem to be moving only very slowly toward full visible communion among the churches. Is it because these barriers will take centuries to dismantle? Or is there an unwillingness to budge if it would mean admitting that one's way is not the only way?

Whereas there is agreement among churches on the importance of confessing the one holy catholic and apostolic church, there are divergences regarding the divisions of church office into bishop, presbyter, deacon; the role of the bishop as the fullness of ordained ministry and successor to the apostles; the primatial function of the pope; the validity of allowing women access to ordained ministry; and theological explanations about sacraments, salvation, and certain moral imperatives. Still, on some issues, there is growing consensus. One effort that required some fifty years of research has led theologians within the divided churches to note basic agreement on the sacraments of initiation. *Baptism, Eucharist and Ministry*—a document produced by a broadly based Christian team of theologians, including Roman Catholics, under the direction of the Faith and Order Commission of the World Council of Churches—has been a notable achievement.[9] And more recently, also after extensive consultation and collaboration, a second major agreement has been reached by the Faith and Order Committee of the World Council of Churches (with Roman Catholic input), entitled *The Nature and Mission of the Church: A Stage on the Way to a Common Statement*.[10]

Despite the move toward ecumenical exchange, there is still the phenomenon that one specific confessional church will consider itself as "the" church of Christ. Denominationalism remains a fact of life. Among some sectarian groups, there is an unwillingness to share and interact in the preaching of the gospel. In other words, they are in principle antiecumenical.

New issues such as women's ordination as priests and even as bishops have placed a strain on interchurch dialogue and cooperation. The church of Christ at the visible level is, in fact, not one. This makes it particularly difficult for

---

8. Thomas Ryan, *A Survival Guide for Ecumenically Minded Christians* (Collegeville, MN: Liturgical, 1989).

9. *Baptism, Eucharist and Ministry*, Faith and Order Paper no. 111 (Geneva: World Council of Churches, 1982). For a collaborative Roman Catholic evaluation of this document, see Michael Fahey, ed., *Catholic Perspectives on Baptism, Eucharist and Ministry* (Lanham, MD: University Press of America, 1986).

10. World Council of Churches, *The Nature and Mission of the Church: A Stage on the Way to a Common Statement* (Geneva: WCC, 2005).

a theologian of a specific confession to write about the church in a way that is not sectarian or triumphalistic.

Ecclesiology after the Holocaust

One of the reasons why it is difficult for Christians to overcome disunity in the church is that, as a collectivity, they have not yet achieved reconciliation with the Jews. Among some Christians, a dramatic change has occurred in their perception of Judaism and of Christianity's relationship with the Jews. For them, a Christian theology of church is being articulated in the light of a slowly but certainly emerging understanding about the relationship of the church with Judaism.[11] A more positive assessment of Judaism has been developing, at least in some quarters, and new thinking has emerged about how Christians and Jews should overcome ancient antipathies. This reassessment follows upon the exposure of the Holocaust in all its horrors and the growing realization, at least among some Christians, that the Nazi extermination policy was indirectly aided by age-old Christian prejudices and pseudo-theological arguments about the collective guilt of the Jewish people for the death of Jesus, about an imagined cancellation of God's covenant with Israel, and about the Jews therefore having ceased to be "the people of God."

A closer critical look at Saint Paul's Letter to the Romans (especially chapters 9–11) and the covenantal theology found in the Hebrew Scriptures calls for a corrective in certain homiletic and devotional Christian discourse. The Second Vatican Council's declaration on non-Christian religions—despite its failure to condemn resoundingly every historical form of Christian anti-Semitism, which at times had been present even among certain leaders of the church—rejected in no uncertain terms the charge that Jews were guilty of "deicide" and urged Christians to appreciate better the bonds uniting the two interrelated religions.

Those Christians who have a keen awareness of Christian individual and collective guilt in breeding hateful attitudes toward the Jews and who also recognize their sins of omission especially during the Nazi era are obviously cautious about making grandiose statements about the vocation and role of the church, especially if formulated in exclusivistic terms. It is impossible for Christian ecclesiology to articulate accurately its self-understanding while disregarding the perduring vocation of Israel under God's plan of salvation. Christians need to see how their religion has been grafted onto the vine that remains Israel, whose covenant, initiated by God and made with Abraham and his descendants, has not been nullified. That Jesus was a Jew, that he and his disciples were nourished by the spiritual and religious teachings of first-century Judaism, and that Christianity has borrowed much of its Scriptures and spiritual traditions from the Jewish faith—these facts need continuous reaffirmation. Exclusivistic affirmations about salvation through the church alone must be rejected. Even provocative New Testament statements about the Jews and the Pharisees, which might be understandable against the background of first-century struggles, need to be contextualized before one can formulate a balanced ecclesiology.

11. Johannes B. Metz, "Christians and Jews after Auschwitz," in *The Emergent Church* (New York: Crossroad, 1981), 17–33; see also John T. Pawlikowski, *What Are They Saying about Christian-Jewish Relations?* (New York: Paulist, 1980).

The Experience of Being Marginalized

Another contextual factor that bears upon how one begins to reflect theologically upon the nature of church is the fact that growing numbers of people in the church, speaking primarily but not exclusively from a Roman Catholic perspective, have an acute sense of their own marginalization by those in charge of the church. They see themselves as, practically speaking, irrelevant in the way church leaders establish priorities or shape pastoral strategies.

In North America at least, but not exclusively here, the most visible persons distressed by this insensitivity to their aspirations and convictions are Christian women, especially in the Catholic Church.[12] Many women are now bluntly expressing how they see themselves subtly but effectively ignored or stereotyped by the ecclesiastical establishment. Certainly this is not true of all women, but the extent of this feeling cannot be ignored. One way for those in charge to try to protect themselves from having to deal with these voices is to categorize these women as "radical feminists" imbued with the questionable values of secularism or consumerist materialism.

That all in the church need to employ inclusive, nonsexist language is a growing and strong expectation, and not only among women. The basic hope is that neglected dimensions of Christian revelation about God, salvation, and grace will emerge more strongly. Catholic women want a greater voice in the way church teaching is formulated; in decision making about pastoral, liturgical, and educational concerns; in the organization of seminaries; in holding clergy accountable; and in the formation of advisory and regulatory committees and consultations in the Catholic Church.

At a 1987 international synod of Roman Catholic bishops on the topic "the role of the laity," Irish Cardinal Tomas O'Fiaich of Armagh, Ireland, noted that the hierarchy of the Catholic Church needs to set about "awakening the sleeping giant" that is the laity and noted that "feminism can no longer be considered middle-class madness or an American aberration."[13] Sexism is not a women's issue. It is also a concern for men.

More acute still is the perception that the powerless and oppressed are ignored by those in charge. This perception is growing among the poor and persecuted of the world and among those committed to preferential option for the oppressed. Whether this growing awareness be traced to the many forms of liberation theology that flourished in Latin America, Africa, the Caribbean, and among those in affluent nations who are discriminated against, or whether this awareness be traced to the experience of base Christian communities or to efforts at inculturation and contextualization of theology, the results are clear: Whoever neglects the insights of the poor, the oppressed, or the victimized does so at the peril of formulating an impoverished ecclesiology. Any ecclesiology insensitive to these matters cannot appropriately understand the special concerns of modern reflection on the church.

A significant number of persons perceive themselves as marginalized by both society and

---

12. See Joan Chittister, *Women, Ministry, and the Church* (New York: Paulist, 1983); Letty M. Russell, *Human Liberation in a Feminist Perspective* (Philadelphia: Westminster, 1974). For an insightful rereading of the New Testament from a feminist perspective, see Elisabeth Schüssler Fiorenza, *In Memory of Her* (New York: Crossroad, 1983).

13. *Origins* 17 (Oct. 28, 1987): 361–62.

church because they are the poor of the world. For them, much of what the Second Vatican Council and papal documents have articulated about the "modern world" rings hollow because it does not correspond to their own specific experience. Many of these economically disadvantaged people have a profound awareness of God and a Christian faith that perdures even amid injustice. Thus, theologians writing out of the experience of poverty and suffering in economically underdeveloped countries stress that doing theology must arise out of a prior commitment on behalf of those struggling for justice. They argue that many in affluent countries are unaware of how goods from poorer nations actually benefit the rich because of an unjust social order. Such theologians plead for a renewal in theological methodology that would include a critical analysis of the major structures of economic oppression. Beyond this, they feel that general descriptions of "the church today" often exclude their own experience. They expect therefore that more attention be given to their economic, political, social, cultural, and religious experiences. Their spokespersons reject an abstract conceptualization of God made outside their own historical struggle for liberation. Among these Christians and others too, there is an increased awareness about the earth as gift of creation, and about the need for ecological, creation-centered reverence. These concerns make new demands on ecclesiology today.

Similar unrest is found among those who suffer from racism even by churchgoers. The church in some regions and nations can be blamed for subtle (or not so subtle) discriminatory practices that affect, for instance, who is called to ordained ministry, who rises to higher office, and how finances are allocated for projects of particular groups.

Beyond Europe and North America

Because so much published material on the theology of church is written in North America and Europe, it is not surprising that people on other continents see European or North Atlantic Christians as exercising an unfair monopoly on how the church is administered. There is a growing feeling, especially among Christians in Africa and Latin America, and to an extent among Asian Christians, that such dominance gives a decidedly false perspective on the nature of the church. These Christians feel that they were evangelized by persons deeply marked by a post-Reformation theology that had less pertinence to their own setting.

One of the notable forums for expressing this frustration has been the Ecumenical Association of Third World Theologians (EATWOT), which was founded in Dar es Salaam, Tanzania, in 1976 and continues to publish a series of ecclesiological studies and consensus statements challenging to the West.[14] After five meetings held among themselves, these Third World theologians invited representatives of the First World to Geneva for the sessions in 1983. Problems were identified, such as the imposition

14. For the published proceedings of EATWOT 1 (Dar es Salaam, 1976), see Sergio Torres and Virginia Fabella, eds., *The Emergent Gospel: Theology from the Developing World* (Maryknoll, NY: Orbis, 1978). For EATWOT 2 (Accra, 1977), see Kofi Appiah-Kubi and Sergio Torres, eds., *African Theology en Route* (Maryknoll, NY: Orbis, 1979). For EATWOT 3 (Sri Lanka, 1979), see Virginia Fabella, ed., *Asia's Struggle for Full Humanity* (Maryknoll, NY: Orbis, 1980). For EATWOT 4 (São Paulo, 1980), see Sergio Torres and John Eagleson, eds., *The Challenge of Basic Christian Communities* (Maryknoll, NY: Orbis, 1981). For EATWOT 5 (New Delhi, 1981), see Virginia Fabella and Sergio Torres, eds., *Irruption of the Third World: Challenges to Theology* (Maryknoll, N Y: Orbis, 1983). For EATWOT 6 (Geneva, 1983), see Virginia

324 of Western anthropology upon people of developing nations, and of concepts of human nature based on individualism, competition, and struggle for power. Much of this was judged to be neocultural domination in the wake of colonial imperialism among the early missionaries.

Contextualization

Walbert Bühlmann, a Swiss priest who for many years served the church in sub-Saharan Africa, published in the late 1970s an important work regarding the "coming of the third church" (that is to say, the growing importance of churches in the Third World, especially in the Southern Hemisphere). According to Bühlmann's definitions, the first church is that part of the church "first born" in the Middle East; the second church is that of Europe and North America. In his book on "the third church," he predicted that by the first decade of the twenty-first century, Christianity would be distributed in the following way: the majority of the world's Christians would be a part of the third church. Among Roman Catholics, he predicted an even more dramatic geographical distribution with the majority of Catholics located in Africa, South America, Asia, and Oceania.[15] What he predicted has in fact proven to be accurate.

Another changing contextual situation is specific to North America. In the United States,

a large number of Catholics are now Spanish-speaking, having come from the various specific cultures often simply grouped together as "Hispanic." This growing population has already changed the way that ecclesiology is conceived in North America.

At the same time, since Vatican II, Catholicism has seen the emergence of a notable move toward what is called by several descriptions, one of which is "neoconservatism."[16] The term *neoconservatism* describes an international, religious mind-set found variously in different continents or churches. In general, Catholic neoconservatives might be described as believers who judge that doctrinal integrity and ecclesiastical structures are being threatened by some in the church who are lessening the solid base of authentic tradition because of misguided enthusiasm and selective emphases. Neoconservatives possess an acute but often a nonhistorical sense of tradition. Typically, they stress the value of established institutions and hold a wary, cautious outlook on theological plurality. The pastoral strategy of neoconservatives is to strive assiduously to protect the simple faithful from being misled by speculations of irresponsible theologians. In the Roman Catholic Church, neoconservatives exhibit concern about changes judged to be undesirable that followed the Second Vatican Council: wider participation of the laity in the liturgy, theological dissent,

---

Fabella and Sergio Torres, eds., *Doing Theology in a Divided World* (Maryknoll, NY: Orbis, 1985). For EATWOT in 1986 (Oaxtepec, Mexico), see K. C. Abraham et al., eds., *Third World Theologies: Commonalities and Divergences* (Maryknoll, NY: Orbis, 1900). For EATWOT in 1992 (Nairobi, Kenya), see K. C. Abraham and Bernadette Mbuy-Beya, eds., *Spirituality of the Third World: A Cry for Help* (Maryknoll, NY: Orbis, 1994). For the 2000 EATWOT Theological Commission (Johannesburg), see Ramathate T. H. Dolamo et al., eds., *Global Voices: For Gender Justice* (Cleveland: Pilgrim, 2003). For EATWOT Latin American Theological Commission, see Luis Carlos Susin et al., eds. *Pluralist Theology: The Emerging Paradigms* (London: SCM, 2007).

15. Walbert Bühlmann, *The Coming of the Third Church* (Maryknoll, NY: Orbis, 1977). See also his *Forward, Church!* (Slough, England: St. Paul, 1977).

16. See *Neoconservatism*, the entire issue of *Concilium* 144 (1981), especially the article on Joseph Ratzinger, 76–83.

assertiveness by national and regional conferences of bishops, and decline in vocations to the priesthood and to religious orders. They argue that the church—specifically, some of the hierarchy—has tolerated too much diversity and too much wandering from orthodox doctrine. Church life, they argue, has been neglecting spiritual concerns and exaggerating an overly particular inculturation of the gospel. Christian social teaching and praxis, they feel, have become in some parts of the world imbued with a kind of Marxist ideology through liberation theology. Furthermore, while official ecumenical dialogues may be desirable, neoconservatives feel that theological conclusions should not proceed too quickly and that all proposals emanating from bilateral conversations should be submitted to appropriate authorities for rigorous scrutiny.

In a book devoted to studying the reasons why the Brazilian liberation theologian Leonardo Boff was temporarily silenced by the Vatican Congregation for the Doctrine of the Faith, the American professor Harvey Cox, whose roots are in the Baptist church tradition, contrasted two kinds of pastoral strategy in the Roman Catholic Church: one typified in the approach of the Vatican's Congregation for the Doctrine of the Faith, the other found in persons such as Boff.[17] Cox argued that the then-prefect of the congregation, Cardinal Ratzinger, favored a "recentering" of the church intellectually and liturgically within its ancient homeland (Europe) and promoted a "restoration" of cultural Christendom in which theological formulations and their philosophical suppositions are clear and distinct. Boff, in contrast, was seen to favor "decentering," whereby the gospel takes root in a variety of disparate cultures and flourishes especially among the poor. Powerful forces at international bishops' synods and in the Vatican, argued Cox, favored opting for the model of recentering. Whether or not this distinction is totally correct, the fact is that some Catholics perceive a "restoration" strategy in a number of church leaders.

One question asked today is why neoconservative Roman Catholics are characteristically intense and driven in their efforts to protect the church. The intensity of their efforts is understandable in light of their conviction that the church is threatened even by insiders and that the consequences of failure to respond will be a severe decline in Catholic values and identity. This conviction reflects an often strict Catholic training and education they received earlier according to a teaching that stressed unchanging doctrines and customs.

New Methodology

In recent decades, ecclesiology has also been influenced by the introduction of the historical-critical method, especially as that method is used for interpreting Scripture, the historical documents of councils, and the development of doctrines. As the fields of theology and ecclesiology become more and more complex, it is not surprising to see that complete treatises on ecclesiology are rarely now composed by individual theologians. Among some of the leading Catholic theologians of the twentieth century (Bernard Lonergan, Karl Rahner, Hans Urs von Balthasar, even to a certain extent Yves Congar), no comprehensive ecclesiology was attempted. Instead, we were offered specific reflections on narrowly defined issues of ecclesiology, *quaestiones disputatae* (disputed questions). Attempts at

---

17. Harvey Cox, *The Silencing of Leonardo Boff* (Oak Park, IL: Meyer-Stone, 1988).

326 a comprehensive ecclesiology are typically becoming collaborative works.

An alert student of the church will need to practice wise discernment in assessing church situations. Merely because a theologian is under a cloud of suspicion at a particular juncture of time does not mean he or she has misread the signs of the times or distorted a specific truth relating to the church. If the experience of the Catholic Church in the past sixty or so years can today teach us a special lesson, it is the possibility that here and now there may be insights appropriate to the church that have been neglected in official church teachings. These forgotten truths may be disliked or considered suspect by persons in authority and may be kept alive in only small pockets of the church. Conceivably, these insights may one day be heralded even in official teaching as vital signs of the healthy life of the church. This paradox need not surprise those who see the church as a pilgrim people or a sojourning church.

The Origins and Early Development of the Church

Now that we have taken note of several of the church's present contexts, it is important that we look back briefly to the origin of the church in the life and ministry of Jesus Christ and the subsequent preaching and activities of the Christian communities that emerged in the following three or four centuries.

Jesus and the Church

Jesus' role in "founding" the church is a central conviction of Christian faith, although the event is not specifically cited in prayers such as the Nicene Creed. Catechetical materials used by Catholics traditionally stated that Jesus "instituted" the sacraments, and by extension, the term has come to be applied to the church itself. Jesus is described as having instituted or founded the church during his lifetime. Proof of Jesus' direct intention to found the church has been provided by appeal to the passage in Matthew's Gospel where Jesus confers the keys upon Peter and promises, "On this rock I will build my church" (Matt. 16:18). This New Testament proof-text was further buttressed by citing the words of Jesus' postresurrection appearance to Peter, during which the risen Christ, after the triple questioning of Peter ("Simon, son of John, do you love me?"), instructs him to feed and tend his sheep.

Modern exegesis has suggested that it may well be possible—indeed, is even likely—that the promise of Matt. 16:18 occurred after the resurrection and was retrojected by the Gospel writers into the earlier public ministry of Jesus. Historical-critical methodology applied to the genesis of the written form of the Gospel accounts argues that certain events presented in the Gospels as occurring before the resurrection may well have been shifted there in light of the writers' firm faith about the deepest identity of Jesus. This way of reading the New Testament has resulted in greater appreciation for the likelihood of the church's foundation in different stages. This perspective not only allows for growth in Jesus' own sense of his mission during his life on earth, but also stressed as crucial, for the founding of the church, the period after the resurrection, as well as the Pentecost experience beginning with the Holy Spirit descending upon the disciples gathered in the Upper Room, an event appropriately called the church's "birthday." From this perspective it is harder to prove that Jesus had a master plan or blueprint for structuring his church before his death.[18]

One disadvantage of describing Jesus' intention of founding the church during his preaching in Judea and Galilee is that, by placing so much stress on the public life of Jesus as the formative years of the church's foundation, one neglects the role of the Holy Spirit during Pentecost and the ensuing years of the apostolic age. Need all the formative factors in the emergence of the church be directly related to the lifetime of Jesus? The fact that certain church ministries were in a state of development during the apostolic period is incontestable. Also, it cannot be overlooked that the composition of the New Testament canon was in process over several generations, and the New Testament was only gradually collected into a whole. Both these events were "founding events" of the church under the inspiration of the Holy Spirit.

The care that Jesus took in training the Twelve and other disciples as teachers and evangelizers clearly reveals that Jesus intended his message to have a perduring value. It is even likely that he expected his closest followers to learn by heart summaries of his teachings and to memorize instructions such as the Lord's Prayer. The institution of the Last Supper, when Jesus instructs his disciples to "do this in memory of me," implies his wish that this ritual continue on in the midst of his community of disciples.

Whether Jesus in his humanity understood from the beginning of his public life that his mission was to extend beyond the Jewish people to include the Gentiles is not altogether clear from the Gospels. Some New Testament scholars conclude that initially Jesus' own understanding of his mission was linked with Israel, and that only gradually and toward the end of his life, under the influence of grace and through personal discernment, did he broaden its applicability to include the Gentiles. It is difficult, given the nature of the written Gospels, to know for certain the stages of Jesus' insights.

The central concept of Jesus' preaching in Aramaic is translated in the Gospels composed in the Greek language as *basileia tou theou* or *basileia ton ouranon*. Volumes have been written about this term, which had a Hebrew substratum and which has commonly been translated into English as "the kingdom of God" or "the kingdom of heaven." The German Catholic exegete Rudolph Schnackenburg stressed in his important monograph on *basileia* that a better translation would be God's "rule," rather than "kingdom," since the notion is not primarily a geographic but a theological one.[19] Recently, other English words have been proposed to translate *basileia*: "dominion," "reign," or even less royalist terms, such as "God's plan for the future" or "special presence."

Commentators on Jesus' use of the concept *basileia* stress the fact that it has a complex, dialectic meaning that describes, depending on the context, different stages of one and the same ongoing religious reality. In Jesus' preaching, God's *basileia* is neither already fully present at the time he is speaking (realized eschatology) nor wholly

---

18. See Daniel J. Harrington. *The Church according to the New Testament* (Franklin, WI: Sheed & Ward, 2001).

19. Rudolph Schnackenburg, *God's Rule and Kingdom* (New York: Herder, 1965). For a complementary view by a Protestant scholar, see Norman Perrin, *The Kingdom of God in the Teaching of Jesus* (Philadelphia: Westminster, 1963). Also useful here are two works by Daniel J. Harrington: *God's People in Christ: New Testament Perspectives on the Church and Judaism* (Philadelphia: Fortress Press, 1980); and *The Light of All Nations: Essays on the Church in New Testament Research* (Wilmington, DE: Glazier, 1982).

328 absent here and now, awaiting achievement in the near future (eschatologism). Rather, God's reign comprehends dimensions partially present and partially future (the "already here" as well as the "not yet"). Jesus prays in the Our Father in regard to God's reign: "[May] thy kingdom come [in a way that has not yet been realized]." But in other sayings, he states confidently that the reign is already present because of healings and deeds of wonder worked through his ministry: "If it is by the Spirit of God that I expel demons, then the reign of God has overtaken you" (Matt. 12:28; also Luke 11:20).

From a theological viewpoint, one can state that Jesus, by being manifested as Lord in the resurrection, becomes the personification of this kingdom at a decisive moment of its process. Christians believe that the reign of God has entered into a final and decisive stage with the incarnation of God in Christ. In no way does this denigrate or marginalize the covenant with Israel, but for Christians, it adds another dimension that builds upon the first covenant without dislodging it.

Another element to be stressed is that this reign or kingdom does not inaugurate for the very first time a special covenantal relationship between God and humanity. Earlier covenants established with Adam, Noah, Abraham, and Israel still remain in force. What the term *kingdom of God* implies in the preaching of Jesus is that, at that point in time, there began a special, intensified presence of God (which Christians would ultimately identify as the new covenant) that Christians denote as Jesus the Messiah, the incarnate Word of God.

The community that emerged from Jesus' preaching, life, death, and resurrection—namely, the church—cannot be identified purely and simply with God's reign, the *basileia*. The church is, rather, a privileged locus for the advancement of the rule of God still to be realized. Some modern Catholic writers describe the church as an instrument of God's reign. This formulation is potentially misleading if it suggests that God's reign comes about through our efforts, when clearly it occurs by God's gracious and free intervention. Between the church in the present and the kingdom in the future stands the decision of God that will be made in judgment (see the parable of the net cast into the sea [Matt. 13:47-50] and the parable of the weeds among the wheat [Matt. 13:24-30, 36-43]). The kingdom of God does not depend on our actions but is God's promised eschatological work.

In the first half of the twentieth century, it was not uncommon for Catholic preachers to speak from the pulpit as though the New Testament "kingdom of God" parables were actually descriptions of the Catholic Church. Even today, some churches speak as though their particular church were, in fact, identified with the kingdom, and they do so without any kind of nuance.

Liberation theologians in economically developing nations have stressed that this kingdom of God should not be etherealized into a "purely religious" concept that would imply that the building up of God's reign has nothing to do with the political and social order. This would be totally misleading, just as it would be to argue that God's offer of both freedom from slavery and inheritance of a promised land had no political or social implications for Israel.

Church in the New Testament

The New Testament term for church, *ekklēsia*, is a word that had appeared already in the Greek translation of the Old Testament (the Septuagint), where it is used about a hundred times to translate the Hebrew word *qahal*, Israel's assembly or congregation responding to God's call. In the Gospels, the word *church* (*ekklēsia*) is not placed on Jesus' lips except in two passages (Matt. 16:18; 18:17). As noted, these two passages are seen by some exegetes as constructions whereby the evangelist transposed their original setting in the postresurrection period of Christ to an earlier time frame. Luke does not use the word *ekklēsia* in his Gospel, but the term is frequent in Acts, where it designates first the community in Jerusalem (Acts 5:11), then mission communities (8:1; 14:23), and then both the local community (9:31) and the collective, dispersed church (8:3).

The Roman Catholic Church shares with other Christian churches the conviction that a theology of church rooted in the New Testament not only is formulated from the Gospels, especially the sayings of Jesus, but also is obviously based on a number of different canonical writings that emerged from various geographical and religio-cultural contexts. It is a temptation to emphasize one or another of these aspects to the neglect of others. This has sometimes been done by different church groups in the past and to a certain extent explains the variant models of church that lie at the base of modern confessional differences. In the New Testament, we have diverse aspects held together in creative tension; these tensions are not of themselves signs of fragmentation but of a dynamism whose inner spirit remains one. The whole New Testament is a product of a notable maturation process. Paul of Tarsus, arguably the first Christian theologian, played a key role in the formulation of the ecclesiology we associate with the New Testament. His views of church are expressed in his major letters, even though formulating a theoretical account of ecclesiology was not one of his primary pastoral concerns.

It has often been stated as axiomatic in theological summaries of Paul's doctrine of the church that he was at first exclusively concerned with particular churches in specific locations and only later (as in Eph. 5:25; Col. 1:18) did he or his closest associates focus on the transregional church dispersed throughout the Mediterranean basin. In an address delivered a number of years ago to the Catholic Theological Society of America, the Catholic exegete Raymond Brown reviewed the data underlying this common assumption and argued the need for much greater nuancing than is usually offered by the conventional wisdom on this matter.[20] It is true, he noted, that Paul in his letters speaks of "the church of the Thessalonians" (1 Thess. 1:1), "the churches of Galatia" (Gal. 1:1), "the church of God which is in Corinth" (1 Cor. 1:1; 2 Cor. 1:1), and "the churches of God which are in Judea" (1 Thess. 2:14). But, Brown argued, there are passages that reveal that Paul also had a wider conception of church. For example, when Paul stated in 1 Cor. 12:28, "God has appointed in the church first apostles, second prophets," it is clear that he was not thinking only of the local church of Corinth. Sometimes, too, Paul moved quickly from the singular to the plural. In Gal. 1:13, he spoke of having persecuted "the church of God," but in Gal. 1:22, he spoke of not being known by sight "to the churches of Judea which are in Christ." In 1 Cor. 14:34, Paul stated that "women should keep silence in the churches" but then continued in the next verse to say that "it is shameful for a woman to speak in church." In short, there is in Pauline usage a blend of plural (churches)

20. Reprinted as Raymond Brown, "The New Testament Background for the Emerging Doctrine of 'Local Church,'" in *Biblical Exegesis and Church Doctrine* (New York: Paulist, 1985), 114–34.

and singular (church), the many forming the one. The same is also true in other works of the New Testament. The reference in Matt. 16:18 to "my church" covers more than a local church, whereas in Matt. 18:17, the word *church* points specifically to a local community.

Brown found in Paul's writings the same ambiguity that we find today in using the terms *local* or *particular* relative to church. When Paul speaks of the churches of Galatia or of Asia, he may be referring to a church associated within the specific geographical confines of a political area. But he may also have been thinking of even smaller local churches—namely, "house churches"—of which there may have been several, especially in larger cities.[21] In a locale such as Antioch or Ephesus about the year 90 CE, there could conceivably have existed, as Brown noted, a variety of house churches resulting from different Christian missions—one house church of Christian Jews who still adhered to the Mosaic Law and for whom Jesus was the promised Messiah; one house church of Jewish and Gentile Christians stemming from the mission associated with the Jerusalem apostles and honoring the Twelve as founders; another house church from the Pauline mission, consisting mostly of Gentiles who saw themselves free of the Jewish Law; and even a house church of Johannine inspiration, which did not use the title "apostle" but regarded all as disciples and regarded Jesus as made present through the Paraclete. It is not clear if, in the beginning, any crossing over of believers from one house church to another occurred; in some cases, a transfer from one to another might have been difficult, at least initially.

Apparently after a period of some hesitation about which word to use to identify this new community reality, *ekklēsia* became the preferred term for the community that followed Christ. Two other terms used in the formative period could conceivably have been retained to describe the Christian community but in fact were not: "the Way" (*hodos*, from the Hebrew *derek*), as used in Acts 24:14 to describe the church; or "the communion" (*koinonia*), as used for instance in Acts 2:42.

Specific New Testament Churches

In New Testament scholarship, there has been special interest in trying to understand the diverse churches or Christian communities that existed shortly after the close of the so-called apostolic age. Raymond Brown identified six categories: (1) three forms of post-Pauline communities with specific characteristics (reflected successively in the Pastoral Letters, in Ephesians and Colossians, and in Luke/Acts); (2) two kinds of Johannine communities; (3) a community related to 1 Peter; (4) the Matthean community; (5) a community related to the Epistle of James; and (6) other communities associated with Mark, Hebrews, and Revelation, as well as perhaps with the *Didache* and *1 Clement*. Knowledge of the diversity of the reality called church in its early stages is especially relevant in ongoing ecumenical dialogues about the importance of total conformity to one modern-day church's structures as over against others.

Another focus that has been influential in the study of local churches has been to identify the large Christian centers associated with cities such as Rome, Ephesus, Jerusalem, and Antioch. A spate of books and ongoing seminars

---

21. For further study of the house church, see Carolyn Osiek et al., *A Woman's Place: House Churches in Earliest Christianity* (Minneapolis: Fortress Press, 2006).

was the result of this interest.[22] Also, there was a growing appreciation of the complex reality represented by the term *Jewish/Gentile Christianity* (in that form of Christianity wherein Gentiles shared the various theological emphases of the Jewish Christians who converted them), and much depended on whether the Jewish Christians' original ties had been with Hebrew Judaism or Greek-speaking Judaism. All these complexities of the original reality should make a modern church wary of identifying purely and simply its own polity with the ineluctable "will of God." The first-century church was a reality much more complex and diverse than frequently realized.

The point of all this is to suggest that the claims that members of individual churches make about being the only legitimate church can be exaggerated. In the situation of the dividedness of the church, one would have to ask whether it is reasonable for one church to require other churches to abandon distinctive characteristics of self-identity before they can enter into full visible communion with it. This is particularly pertinent in regard to churches whose self-identity was shaped during the first millennium not in the Christian West, but in the East. If Eastern churches are to be invited today to enter into full visible unity with the Roman church, is it appropriate to require a level of

sameness with Rome that never existed even in the first millennium?

Another special academic interest today is the social milieus of early Christianity. This is reflected, for instance, in the work of the American John Gager, who has explored early Christianity in comparison to its religious competitors of the time, such as Mithraism, Judaism, philosophical schools, and Hellenistic religions.[23] Also, greater attention is being paid to the religious milieus of classical Mediterranean spiritualities in late antiquity, especially Egyptian and Greco-Roman spiritualities.[24] This interest in the religious environment of the Mediterranean world at the time of the first preaching of Christians helps us to understand Christianity's particular appeal.

Pre-Nicene Christianity

The study of the growth of the early church cannot remain restricted to the New Testament alone. One way to measure the degree of development of church in the first centuries is to follow its expansion over several centuries. From the time of the death of Jesus (c. 30 CE) to 337 CE (the end of the reign of Constantine, the first Roman emperor to become a Christian) is an era of some nine generations, taking a generation to be thirty-three years.[25] During these

---

22. For a cross section of studies on this, see Margaret M. Mitchell and Frances M. Young, eds., *Origins to Constantine*, The Cambridge History of Christianity 1 (Cambridge: Cambridge University Press, 2006), esp. 295–412. See also Raymond Brown and John P. Meier, *Antioch and Rome: New Testament Cradles of Catholic Christianity* (New York: Paulist, 1983); Raymond Brown, *The Churches of the Apostles Left Behind* (New York: Paulist, 1984).

23. See John G. Gager, *Kingdom and Community: The Social World of Early Christianity* (Englewood Cliffs, NJ: Prentice Hall, 1975). See also W. V. Harris, ed., *The Spread of Christianity in the First Four Centuries* (Leiden: Brill, 2005); Wayne A. Meeks, *The First Urban Christians* (New Haven: Yale University Press, 1983); and idem, *The Moral World of the First Christians* (Philadelphia: Westminster, 1986).

24. See A. H. Armstrong, ed., *Classical Mediterranean Spirituality: Egyptian, Greek, Roman*, World Spirituality 15 (New York: Crossroad, 1986).

25. See Michael Fahey, "*Ecclesiae sorores ac fratres*: Sibling Communion in the Pre-Nicene Era," *Catholic Theological Society of America, Proceedings* 36 (1981): 15–38, which provides references to the primary sources.

332 nine generations, the external shape of Christianity solidified and underwent several developments that remain influential even to this day. During these three centuries, Christianity suffered a number of localized, violent persecutions resulting in the death of many Christians. Toward the end of this age of the martyrs, there occurred what is called the Constantinian turning point, brought on in part by the emperor's decision eventually to allow Christianity to become a licit religion in the empire. This tolerance eventually led to notable social changes in the life of the church, especially in the way in which the church hierarchy and the state interacted. Eventually, with Constantine's conversion to Christianity and his enrollment as a catechumen, the first of what came to be called ecumenical councils was held. But even in the second and third centuries, church officials were interacting with governmental agencies, and Christianity both in the West and the East assumed certain characteristics adopted from the secular Roman Empire. What happened during the period of nine generations regarding the liturgy, sacramental practices, and growth in monepiscopacy (the practice of having only one *episkopos* or bishop/overseer for each particular church instead of governance by a council of elders) sheds light on the developing shape of church.

Few individuals have the broad knowledge needed to understand fully the shifting nature of local churches in the second and third centuries. One needs humility and equilibrium to recognize that much of what was written by Catholics and non-Catholics alike about this period in the past was one-sided and apologetical/confessional. Following the Second Vatican Council, theologians came to recognize that the distinction between what had been considered in the church an aspect of the *ius divinum* (a feature traceable to God's specific instructions expressed by Christ or by the Holy Spirit to the apostles in the subapostolic period) and what in fact was *ius humanum* (an authoritative human or ecclesiastical decision about an aspect of church) may have unintentionally become blurred. What is needed, therefore, is careful study to determine what exists in the church because of a specific, divinely formulated "will" expressed formally through revelation and what is the result of human or ecclesial "will," that is, an element having its origin in an explicit or implicit decision of the church community.

To understand the interaction of one city church with another (for, in fact, Christianity was at first largely based in cities), it is helpful to refer to certain historical practices. Did these separate, geographically dispersed churches perceive themselves as interrelated into a reality that encompassed the entire Mediterranean? To what extent did the churches prior to the Council of Nicaea (325 CE) see themselves as a unified reality? And what means did they use to express their interest in being part of a worldwide church?

The need to identify various strands of Christianity as incompatible with orthodox Christianity—strands such as Gnosticism, Montanism, and Marcionism—led the churches in the second and third centuries to intensify efforts at keeping in touch with one another. Still, each local church was seen as possessing all that was necessary for its functioning as a church. Once it had been evangelized and equipped with supervisors and presiders, once the community had been initiated into the Christian Scriptures and had been taught about the mysteries of baptism and Eucharist, such a church associated with a city or with part of a city assumed its own identity. What needs to be explained about the early church is not how a local, city-based church came to see itself as autonomous, but rather how a local church came to choose various modalities for wider fellowship. For mainline Christian churches, being autonomous never meant sterile isolation.

Communion in Pre-Nicene Christianity

The German scholar Walter Bauer, as early as 1934, stressed the importance of focusing on a wide spectrum of local or regional churches—including the area around Edessa, Alexandria, Antioch, western Asia Minor, as well as Rome—for understanding how the churches of the East and West developed. Other historians of the early church, such as Ekkart Sauser, have tried to reconstruct what church life must have been like in the East in the Christian communities at Jerusalem, Antioch, Alexandria, Constantinople, Seleucia, and Ctesiphon, and in the West at Lyons, Arles, Carthage, Trier, Barcelona, Ravenna, Milan, and Rome.[26]

It is informative to see how Christian communities after the close of the New Testament period developed in pre-Nicene Christianity and how they promoted ongoing sharing. Although it is not possible to reconstruct the entire period, we do have some useful information about at least six practices used by local churches to foster a sense of solidarity and communion among the disparate communities: (1) praying for others at Eucharistic celebrations and sharing the Eucharist; (2) installing new bishops by inviting bishops from neighboring churches to come together in order to ordain them; (3) convoking regional synods or councils; (4) exchanging and circulating letters; (5) accepting attempts at coordination of the Western churches by the bishop of Rome; and (6) submitting to direct interventions by the emperor in the administrative life of the church.

PRAYING FOR OTHERS AND SHARING AT EUCHARISTIC CELEBRATIONS

Not surprisingly, some of the most ardent descriptions of the sense of solidarity among the churches occur in liturgical prayers. By the third generation, we have a famous passage from the *Didache* that may be an even earlier prayer: "As this broken bread was scattered upon the mountains, but was brought together and became one, so let thy Church be gathered together from the ends of the earth, into thy kingdom, for thine is the glory and the power through Jesus Christ for ever" (9:4). In the same document, we read a similar prayer: "Remember, Lord, thy Church, to deliver it from all evil and to make it perfect in thy love, and gather it together in its holiness from the four winds to thy kingdom which thou hast prepared for it" (10:5). These are clear signs that the local church was conscious of sibling counterparts in other parts of the world. Justin's *First Apology* also records a similar perspective in the context of the Eucharistic liturgy: "And on that day which is called after the sun, all who are in the towns and in the country gather together for a communal celebration. And then the memoirs of the Apostles or the writings of the Prophets are read, as long as time permits. . . . Then prayers in common are said . . . for ourselves, for the newly baptized and *for all others wherever they may be.*"[27]

Within the celebration of the Eucharist and to a lesser extent perhaps in baptism, there was a

---

26. Ekkart Sauser, *Woher kommt Kirche? Ortskirchen der Frühzeit und Kirchenbewusstsein heute* (Frankfurt: Knecht, 1978).

27. Justin, *1 Apology* 67; emphasis added.

powerful dynamism at work leading Christians to perceive themselves as belonging to a people gathered for the purpose of praising and adoring God. There was a sort of supratemporal awareness of community, already adumbrated discreetly in the New Testament, but growing stronger—namely, that those who participated locally in a Eucharistic celebration were involved in close intersubjective communion with the faithful who by death had "gone before" the living Christians.

Specific Eucharistic practices expressed this awareness of and love for sibling churches. To be in communion with another church or specifically with its bishop/overseer, Christians sent consecrated Eucharistic bread of communion to other churches. Eusebius records this practice in citing a letter from Irenaeus to Victor, the bishop of Rome, concerning an Easter controversy. Irenaeus commented that Roman bishops in earlier times did not allow disagreements about the date for celebrating Easter to interfere with the practice of sending Eucharistic bread to other churches as a sign of solidarity.

Another custom related to the Eucharist was the practice of sending a fragment of consecrated Eucharistic bread to neighboring churches. The custom seems to be of Roman origin, but it was adopted by bishops in other cities. On feast days, as a sign of union, the bishop would send a piece of the communion bread just consecrated to priests or to bishops in nearby outlying areas; upon arrival, the bread would be mixed into the chalice of the receiving church as a sign of oneness. This practice continued until the ninth century and has even left some traces to this day in the Roman liturgy, when the priest, before distribution of communion, breaks off a piece of the host and commingles it with the consecrated wine in the chalice.

Inviting Bishops from Neighboring Churches to Ordain New Bishops

It is difficult to date exactly when the practice began of appointing only one bishop (*monos episkopos*) for each Mediterranean city church. But certainly by the fourth generation of Christianity, any variant practice that might have existed (such as administering a church by a kind of Sanhedrin or council, as seems to have been the original practice in the church of Rome) was replaced by the monepiscopal model. What developed then in the second century was a monarchical concentration of authority for the bishop. Along with that went a certain sacralization of the office of bishop. As we see in a letter of Saint Cyprian of Carthage,[28] the lay community within a church was expected to provide a *suffragium*, a voice, along with priests and bishops in the choice of a local bishop.

The actual sacramental initiation into the bishop's office was done by laying on of hands by bishops from neighboring churches. Hippolytus of Rome, in his *Apostolic Tradition*, mentions the requirement of having other bishops present at the bishop's ordination. Shortly before the Council of Nicaea, at a local Council of Arles (314 CE), it was specified that there should be seven bishops on hand, but "if not seven, one should not dare to ordain with fewer than three bishops." This promoted an acute sense of the fact that a local church, though autonomous, needed to be in communion with at least neighboring churches.

But by now, there was at work more than

---

28. Cyprian, *Epistulae* 67.3. See Geoffrey Dunn, *Cyprian and the Bishops of Rome* (Strathfield, NSW, Australia: St. Paul's, 2007).

simply calling upon neighboring bishops to consecrate episcopal appointees. A network was taking shape that tended to establish an order of importance among the churches: it designated older churches and younger churches. Although it would be premature to speak of patriarchates before 451 CE, still some churches had greater supervisory roles to perform than did others. Particular prestige came to be associated with certain local or regional churches for a variety of reasons: the real or imagined evangelization of a church by one of the original twelve apostles, cultural prominence, political power, effective leadership, and so on. In this development, it seems clear that the civil system in use among the Romans partially influenced the way bishops assumed functions.

CONVOKING REGIONAL SYNODS
OR COUNCILS

A third institution in the pre-Nicene church that fostered exchange and coordination among churches was the increased convocation of synods or councils. Councils or synods (the Greek language employs one and the same word for these events: *synodos*) are first mentioned in the second half of the second century, when the Christians of Asia conducted a series of open-ended meetings to deal with the problems of Montanism. Synods also multiplied as regional churches tried to iron out difficulties associated with the choice of the date for Easter. These synods were not made up exclusively of *episkopoi*. We know, for example, from a synod held in 256 at Carthage concerning a baptismal controversy that "a great many bishops met together in Car-

thage together with the presbyters and deacons and a considerable part of the people [*plebis*]."[29]

Furthermore, the synods exercised only the binding force that individual bishops wished to attach to them. Cyprian makes this clear in a letter in which he summarizes the work of a provincial synod: "No one of us sets himself up as a bishop of bishops, no one of us compels by tyrannical terror any colleague to the necessity of obedience, since every bishop, according to his own right of liberty and power, has his own right to judgment, and can no more be judged by another than he himself can judge another."[30] Most importantly, these provincial synods, especially those in the seventh, eighth, and ninth generations of Christianity, created the conditions for what eventually came to be known as an ecumenical council.

EXCHANGING AND
CIRCULATING LETTERS

Another factor that was powerful in establishing contact among the sibling churches was the practice of exchanging letters. Since the time of Saint Paul, Christians had been familiar with this practice. Among Christians, letters often contained the views of groups and not merely one individual. Letters could be hortatory and informational. They were hardly all pious or inspirational. They could include angry outbursts, threats, and sarcastic, caustic remarks. What is interesting is not merely the fact that they were written in such abundance, but that they were so carefully guarded, copied, and translated when necessary, even filed away for future reference.

---

29. Cyprian, *Sententiae Episcoporum*, in *Opera Cypriani* (Hartel 3:435.7).

30. Ibid., 436.3ff. On the role of episcopal synods during the early centuries, see Brian E. Daley, "Structures of Charity: Bishops' Gatherings and the See of Rome in the Early Church," in *Episcopal Conferences: Historical, Canonical, and Theological Studies*, ed. Thomas Reese (Washington, DC: Georgetown University Press, 1989).

336

Among the principal forms of letters were the so-called *litterae pacis*, letters conveying absolution for sinners, especially for those who had lapsed at times of persecution; there were *litterae pacis ecclesiasticae*, containing a bishop's permission granted to one of the faithful to visit some high dignitary; *litterae festales*, containing information about liturgical calendars and celebrations; *litterae circulares*, encyclicals intended for wide audiences; and the so-called *contessaratio hospitalitatis*, a sort of passport or credit card permitting a visiting Christian to have access to distant Christian communities, a kind of letter of good conduct entitling the bearer to free room and board in a distant church community, at least for a short period of time.

Accepting Attempts at Coordination by the Bishop of Rome

Another factor that further contributed to contact among churches in the pre-Nicene church, especially in the Western part of the Mediterranean, was the gradual coordination of certain functions by the church of Rome. Rome came to be seen as enjoying a sort of *potentia principalis*, a hegemony of influence over other churches, especially but not exclusively the Western churches. As a local church, it was seen to preside in love over other churches. Before the Council of Nicaea, there was no juridical formulation about Rome's role, much less talk of jurisdictional primacy or of a kind of universal ministry of its bishop. Still, certain factors contributed to increased communion under the initiative of Rome. The church of Rome intervened to reestablish order in the trouble spot of Corinth (see *1 Clement*); it exercised a broad pastoral care for those troubled about penitential practices (see the *Shepherd of Hermas*); a Roman bishop undertook initiatives in regard to certain Eastern churches to settle disputes about the date

of Easter; Rome had available a list of episcopal succession and eventually drew ecclesiastical conclusions from that list; a member of the Roman church formulated in the *Apostolic Tradition* appropriate liturgical practices; and Rome undertook special acts of charity, notably financial support for other churches.

Submitting to Direct Interventions by the Emperor in Church Administration

A final element to consider in this survey of factors that fostered communion in the pre-Nicene churches concerns the policies of Emperor Constantine, who reigned from 306 to 337. Although often guided by more than simply religious motives, still Constantine's policies had enormous repercussions for the future shape of the church. In his later years, the emperor was haunted by a vision of coordinated and cooperating local churches. He tried to achieve his goal through his influence and initiatives, and he tried—in fact, unsuccessfully—to deal with the Donatists and Arians. He ordered synods to be held in Rome (in 313) and at Arles (in 314) in search of harmony. For Eusebius, the church historian and writer of lavish encomiums, Emperor Constantine was a "bishop for the outside"; his influence was felt by his sponsorship; his favors toward Christian churches made him a popular benefactor; and toward the end of his reign, he restored confiscated buildings and made available finances for church buildings, clergy being exempt from certain political duties and from paying taxes. Although it is premature to speak of Caesaro-papism, what Constantine initiated was the prototype to that special mixture of church and state that dominated so much of church history in East and West.

The growth of cooperation among churches in the period prior to the Council of Nicaea was due to many different factors. Some factors were principally religious, such as the celebration of the Eucharist and the sacramental installation of new bishops by neighboring bishops. Some were organizational and social, such as the convocation of synods or letter writing. Others concentrated coordination within one person or one institution, be it the episcopal see of Rome or the imperial court of New Rome. These were outgrowths of the New Testament and, although new solutions, were considered legitimate developments. Of course, even within the New Testament, there are references to attempts to address the need for the church to adjust to world history.

Based on this quick overview of developments from the New Testament and subapostolic period up to the churches of the second and third centuries, two key questions can be raised: Have not today's churches, especially when deciding what is needed for restoring full visible communion, absolutized specific, contingent developments in historic church orders or in conciliar decisions? And have they not thereby created unnecessary barriers to the restoration of full visible unity among the churches?

The Nature of Church in Modern Roman Catholic Teaching

From Hierarchical to Communitarian Models

The basic source for the Catholic Christian's understanding of the church remains the preaching of Jesus in the New Testament. Still, the community of faith has to continue to articulate its theological understanding of the church

under the inspiration of the Holy Spirit and by collective discernment of the signs of the times. In the present section, recognizing that we are leaping over centuries of intervening experiences of church, our focus is on how contemporary Catholic understanding of church has been formulated, especially in the Second Vatican Council, held between 1962 and 1965. In what follows, the emphasis is on modern Catholicism's teaching about the responsibilities of the various groups in the church. The council did not fall out of heaven, but produced a summing up of much of what had recently gone before in theological and pastoral reflections and experimentations by those in leadership roles. If the Second Vatican Council was creative in amassing and giving public approbation to collective wisdom gathered from the Catholic and wider Christian community, it was not creative in the sense of producing something out of nothing.

The council affirmed aspects of church life that risked being neglected or forgotten; it even accepted some attitudes and teachings that earlier had been frowned upon by those in authority. At the Second Vatican Council, the Catholic Church reaffirmed and encouraged themes that had been alive and healthy but that sometimes had not been emphasized in Vatican directives or even papal encyclicals.

To give a short account of the Catholic Church's self-understanding today, one can draw themes from the Second Vatican Council that weave together various currents of ecclesiology that had been under development in the years preceding the council. The principal text is the Dogmatic Constitution on the Church (*Lumen gentium*; hereafter cited as LG). But to treat *Lumen gentium* in complete isolation from other council texts that touch on other aspects of church life would be to produce a lopsided description. *Lumen gentium* was intended to describe the church's life *ad intra*—that is to say, its nature, its relationship to revelation, its inner structures, ministries, and mission. But a second far-reaching constitution, the Pastoral Constitution on the Church in the Modern World (*Gaudium et spes*; hereafter cited as GS), has much to say about the church *ad extra*, in relationship to society. To provide a fuller account of church, one would have to analyze other conciliar documents that treat specific concerns such as the vocation of all the baptized, the responsibilities of bishops and presbyters, the ecumenical relationship of the Catholic Church with other Christian churches, and the imperative of religious freedom. It would be a formidable task to provide a comprehensive synthesis of all the texts of the Second Vatican Council that touch upon the church's vocation.

Even when the church, the community of those called to believe in the triune God, remains faithful to its central beliefs, it must from generation to generation examine its relationships to cultural, historical, and political forces. Its institutional structures are attempts to express part of its inner reality. In the long run, changes and shifts may not always be for the better. The church is the community that keeps alive the memory of Jesus, but it is also the community that, because of weakness and sin, is capable of forgetting some dimensions of the message of Christ. Hence, it is quite appropriate to refer to the church as a community ever in need of reformation, a pilgrim church. "The Church, clasping sinners to her bosom, at once holy and always in need of purification, follows constantly the path of penance and renewal" (LG 8).

Theologians attempt to articulate scriptural revelation in terms that facilitate modern believers' understanding. Confessional differences emerge notably in this area. There has not always been a strong sense of the need for ecclesiology. In the West, treatises specifically on church were not written until the twelfth century, and for the most part, they emphasized jurisdiction or the relationship of the papacy to governmental leaders.

One long-standing theological model for explaining the essence of the church saw it as a visible or perfect society. The model enjoyed widespread support from the time of the Counter-Reformation to the first half of the twentieth century. This description of the "perfect" character of the church was an apologetical attempt to assert the church's independence from the state. Such a model was weak, since it neglected the role of the Holy Spirit, the pneumatological dimension. The Swiss theologian Bühlmann cites as a typical textbook description of ecclesiology the once widely used work of Adolphe Tanquerey, which comprises sixty-four pages showing that Christ founded the church as (1) an infallible authority, (2) a perfect society, (3) a hierarchical society, and (4) a monarchic society.[31] The sources of analogy here were drawn not from biblical sources but from civil society. Such a juridical approach was notably strong in post-Reformation Catholic theology. However, it neglected the mystical, invisible traits of church life that had been highlighted by medieval believers, including certain Reformers.

Such an approach to ecclesiology was sometimes found even in certain papal documents. An example is a remark of Pius X in his letter *Vehementer nos* to the bishops of France (February 11, 1906). Here the pope described

---

31. Bühlmann, *Forward, Church,* 19.

the church as "an unequal society" composed of two categories of persons, "the pastors and the flock"; this flock or multitude "has no other duty but to allow itself to be led and to follow its pastors as a docile flock." A widely used distinction at that time was the differentiation between the *ecclesia docens* (the teaching church, understood as the hierarchy) and the *ecclesia discens* (the learning church, those to whom the popes' and bishops' instructions were addressed). The gradual move from that model of ecclesiology to others favored at the Second Vatican Council came about especially in the twentieth century through a variety of causes and influences. One of these was the articulation of a more "spiritual" ecclesiology under the ongoing influence of the nineteenth-century German theologian Johann Adam Möhler (1796–1838), whose *Die Einheit in der Kirche oder das Prinzip des Katholizismus* (*Unity in the Church or the Principle of Catholicism*), originally published in 1825, did much to promote this shift. Other voices emerged in the middle of the twentieth century. One was Yves Congar (1904–95). His work on ecumenism—especially his pioneering *Chrétiens désunis* (*Divided Christendom*) (1937); his sketch on the mystery of the church, *Esquisses du mystère de l'Église* (*The Mystery of the Church*) (1941); and his work on the laity, *Jalons pour une théologie du laïcat* (*Lay People in the Church*) (1953)—were all influential. At the same time, there was a revival in Catholicism of scriptural, patristic, and liturgical studies that led to a closer look at the church of the first several centuries. Important here for ecclesiology was Lucien Cerfaux's publication *La théologie de l'Église suivant Saint Paul* (*The Church in the Theology of Saint Paul*) (1942).

The Second Vatican Council's Description of Church

In language strongly marked by biblical sources, the Second Vatican Council stated in the opening of its main document on the church that, just as in the Old Testament the revelation of God's reign is made known through symbols, so too in the New Testament, the church "is now made known to us in various images" (LG 6). These biblical images are drawn from rural life and include sheep raising, farming, building, family life, and marriage. By the use of scriptural images, the church is likened to a sheepfold whose one and necessary door is Christ (John 10:1-10), a cultivated field, the tillage of God, the building of God, the "Jerusalem which is above," "our Mother," or the spouse of the spotless Lamb.

Instead of beginning with a description of the church as a perfect society, the first chapter of the Dogmatic Constitution on the Church asserts that the inner life of the triune God is reflected in the church itself. Borrowing a phrase from Saint Cyprian of Carthage (d. 258), the council states, "Hence the universal church is seen to be 'a people brought into unity from the unity of the Father, the Son and the Holy Spirit'" (LG 4). This trinitarian dimension stresses the free and mysterious character of God's intervention in the world that was an "utterly gratuitous and mysterious design of his wisdom and goodness" (LG 2). Because of this emphasis on its trinitarian structure, Catholics have even described the church as "icon of the Trinity." The church is structured in its communion according to the image and likeness of trinitarian communion. The church comes from the Trinity, returns toward the Trinity, and is structured according to its image.[32]

---

32. See the work of the Italian Catholic Bruno Forte, *The Church: Icon of the Trinity* (Boston: St. Paul, 1991).

Another basic image adopted by the Second Vatican Council to describe the nature of the church is that of communion (*koinonia*). This notion was inspired by the theological and historical research of several theologians, among whom could be listed Ludwig von Hertling and Jerome Hamer.[33] The communion or koinonial model for understanding the reality of church overcomes much of the inconveniences of juridical or apologetic notions associated with Catholicism's ecclesiology since the Protestant Reformation.[34] The writings of Yves Congar had a major impact on the use of the communion model.

The term *communion* is an apt category that has roots in human consciousness. *Communion* (or its equivalents, *fellowship* or *participation* or *sharing*) was not originally a specifically religious term, but touched on the intersubjective sharing that we experience with other human beings through love, family, marriage, nation, or cultural heritage. Communion can also extend beyond human beings to communion with living animals or with the cosmos. Religious usage suggests that there can exist a sharing or communion with the transcendent God. In the Hebrew Scriptures, God is described as a loving parent, considerate friend, and powerful ruler, but the stress is frequently on the distance between God and the human person. Even the biblical notion of covenant stresses the distance between master and servant. In the New Testament, the notion of communion stands in continuity with the basic understanding of human sharing, and of close exchanges between God and the human. What is different is the newness of God's taking on human life in Jesus Christ. For Saint Paul, communion became a way of describing the most intimate union of human beings with God as well as with other human beings made possible through the coming of Jesus Christ.

Saint Paul uses the term *koinonia* to express, along with other images, the mystery of God's love made visible in Jesus Christ. To express the presence of Christ through the Holy Spirit in the believer, Paul speaks of *koinonia tou hagiou pneumatos* (communion brought about by the Holy Spirit; 2 Cor. 13:13). Paul's use of the notion of communion may be compared to his image of the body of Christ or to his formulas about living "in Christ" or "with Christ," and it may be compared to Saint John's imagery of the vine and the branches, or even John's formulas of reciprocity about the Christian's being or remaining in Christ. The New Testament concept, especially in the writings of Paul, is closely allied to the concept found in Eastern Christianity today about our gradual divinization in Christ.

In Saint Paul's writings, the term *communion* reflects a double relationship—one that enriches the individual, and the other that forms ecclesial unity. The Holy Spirit's presence affects first an individual, but this presence is not meant to be an individual possession enjoyed in isolation. Communion is a gift intended to foster unity within the body of Christ, the church. In Paul, the term *communion* indicates that Christians partake in Christ by receiving his Spirit and that they also enter a fellowship with one another all the while possessing different

---

33. Ludwig von Hertling, *Communio: Church and Papacy in Early Christianity*, trans. J. Wicks (Chicago: Loyola University Press, 1972); Jerome Hamer, *The Church Is a Communion* (New York: Sheed & Ward, 1964). For a more recent study, see Dennis M. Doyle, *Communion Ecclesiology* (Maryknoll, NY: Orbis, 2000).

34. See James Provost, ed., *The Church as Communion* (Washington, D.C.: Catholic University Press, 1978).

gifts. Sharing one's earthly possessions through financial support, sometimes also called by Paul *koinonia* (2 Cor. 9:13; Rom. 15:26; Heb. 13:16), is one outward expression of participating in the gift of the Holy Spirit.

More broadly, the term *communion* points to a theological assertion about God's loving-kindness shared especially by those who have been called to faith in Christ. In this sense, *communion* does not refer to God's salvific will for all humankind, nor does it refer to the different graces bestowed on persons sanctified by other living faiths or religions distinct from Christianity. In the New Testament, *communion* stresses first and foremost not so much the "horizontal" sharing among Christians but the Christian's "vertical" sharing with God. The term describes the relationship between God and the believer, and especially the ongoing activity of the Holy Spirit who vivifies the person in the church.

In a previous section, we listed some of the ways that the Christian community expressed ecclesial communion or *koinonia* in the period between the New Testament and the Constantinian era. The basic Pauline term and its equivalency in the Johannine literature were retained and expanded. This is especially true in the writings of Irenaeus of Lyons, who uses the term *koinonia* over eighty times to describe our access to salvation. In his opposition to the false divisions and separation that he saw as introduced into Christianity by Gnosticism, Irenaeus appealed to *koinonia* to describe the communion among humans who share in the Spirit's life. Irenaeus's pneumatological emphasis was rather short-lived, however, since the church of the West came more and more to focus attention on the institutional aspects of communion rather than on its source in God. The term *communion* after

Irenaeus was seen, to be sure, as indicating a living relationship between believers and God, but much more stress was placed on the relationship of mutual acceptance between various local churches. This relationship was externalized by various regulations regarding baptism, penitential reconciliation, and Eucharistic hospitality. In itself, such a shift was quite legitimate and not undesirable. The only disadvantage was that in the expansion of the concept, some of its original multiplicity latent in the biblical texts was overlooked.

To the extent that the bishops in the early church assumed more and more responsibility for unifying the church, the regulatory aspects of communion became more marked. In his classic study of communion in the early church, the Roman Catholic scholar Ludwig von Hertling described how this word ultimately came to refer to "the bond that united the bishops and the faithful, the bishops among themselves, and the faithful among themselves, a bond that was both effected and at the same time made manifest by eucharistic communion."[35]

The term *koinonia* or *communion* occurs in a citation from Paul used today as a greeting at the beginning of the Roman Eucharistic liturgy: "The grace of God our Father, the love of Christ, and the communion [fellowship] of the Holy Spirit . . ." It also occurs in the Nicene Creed, the reference being to the *communio sanctorum*. This term can be understood in three ways, all of which are legitimate: the communion of the Holy Spirit that brings us into communion with other believers; the communion of holy things or realities (taking the antecedent of *sanctorum* to be the Latin neuter plural *sancta*), especially baptism and the Eucharist; and the communion of the saints (taking the antecedent of *sanctorum*

---

35. Hertling, *Communio*, 16.

342 to be the Latin masculine plural *sancti*), or sharing in the fellowship of other believers both living and dead.

Communion in the New Testament refers therefore primarily to the vertical relationship between believer (as member in a community) and redeeming God. Modern theological usage more commonly employs the term to describe the horizontal or ecclesiological implications of the church's charismatic structure, shared responsibility, and collective accountability. Other terms, such as *grace*, *divinization*, and *sanctification*, came to replace *communion* in its first sense. Communion has become a highly flexible concept, admitting a variety of degrees and modalities that are valuable in an age of pluralism or ecumenism. The concept now refers to communion among churches with identical doctrine and practice (united churches), or to communion among divided churches that lack full organic unity but are nonetheless one through baptism and belief in the divinity of Christ.

God's People in Christ

Chapter 2 of the Second Vatican Council's text on the inner life of the church describes the church as the "new people of God" (LG 9) or the "new Israel."[36] This echoes what is said in the New Testament, especially in Rom. 9:25-26; 2 Cor. 6:14; Titus 2:14; and 1 Peter 2:10: "[You] are now the people of God." Christians should be cautious, however, in how they use the title, since it might suggest that the Jewish people have ceased to be the people of God, a view contrary to the New Testament statements (see Heb. 11:25; Matt. 1:21; Luke 1:68; Rom. 11:1-2). The correct teaching of the church about Israel's continuing vocation has not always been

translated into the church's practice. The church regards itself as the "new people of God" but in a way that does not annul the first covenant given to Israel (Luke 1:72; Acts 3:25; Gal. 3:17). The Jews remain God's people (Rom. 9:6); God has not cast off Israel (Rom. 11:1). The vocation of the Jewish people of God is continuous, irrevocable, indestructible; the Jews are and remain God's chosen and beloved people. The new situation of the church does not destroy the old (Rom. 9:3). The Jews remain the people God addressed first. The Second Vatican Council's Declaration on Non-Christian Religions, *Nostra aetate* (NA), states, "Although the Church is the new people of God, the Jews should not be presented as repudiated or cursed by God, as if such views followed from the Holy Scriptures" (NA 4).

In claiming the title God's new people in Christ, the church also affirms that it is a pilgrim people, constantly in need of forward movement toward holiness. Such is the concern of chapter 7 of *Lumen gentium*, which is entitled "The Eschatological Nature of the Pilgrim Church and Its Union with the Church in Heaven" (LG 48–51).

Church as Sacrament

Another component of modern Catholic teaching reflected in the Second Vatican Council is the notion that the church itself is a sacrament. The opening section of *Lumen gentium* states, "The Church in Christ, is in the nature of sacrament—a sign and instrument, that is, of communion with God and of unity among all human beings" (LG 1). Whereas late medieval Western theology came to restrict the word *sacrament* to refer to only seven sacraments, the

---

36. William Henn, *Church: The People of God* (New York: Burns & Oates, 2004).

Second Vatican Council, partly influenced by Catholic theologians from the 1950s, referred to the church in Christ as a kind of sacrament (*veluti sacramentum*).

As Israel and Jesus himself had been visible expressions and signs of God's loving-kindness, so now, it was reasoned, the church itself is a sacrament or "mystery." This notion was adumbrated in the nineteenth century in the writings of Möhler and Scheeben and was further developed in the twentieth century by Karl Rahner and Otto Semmelroth, who portrayed the church as the first of all the sacraments, a kind of primordial sacrament (*Ursakrament*). The church was described as a sacramental sign, effect, and gift of God. At the heart of the sacramental insight is the conviction that God can and does use the physical, tangible, and historical aspects of human life as "bearers" of divine love. Some have called this use of the material to convey the spiritual as a kind of incarnational principle. The Dominican theologian Edward Schillebeeckx also expanded the traditional use of the terminology by describing Christ himself as the "sacrament of humanity's encounter with God."

Describing the church as a sacrament does not minimize the centrality of "word of God" in biblical revelation. A popular caricature that describes Catholicism as a Christianity of sacrament and Protestantism as a Christianity of word is completely misleading. Sacraments are in fact gospel words enhanced in such a way that the words are intensified by ritual gesture. As Saint Augustine remarked in his commentary on John's Gospel, a word is united to a sensible element and becomes a sacrament, or a visible word (*tamquam visibile verbum*).[37]

Later in chapter 9 of this volume there is discussion about the relationship between the church and the sacraments. Suffice it to say here that the church, when celebrating any sacrament, but especially at the memorial of the Lord's Supper, the Eucharist, attains an intensity of its very being and self-identity. The sacraments of initiation afford a person entry into the community of faith. Marriage and ordination are two sacraments of vocation to life in the church and in society. Through the celebration of the sacraments and through the expression of the community's faith, the church realizes one of its special functions, which is to keep alive the memory of Jesus by worshipping the triune God and giving expression to its hope for the final coming of God's reign.

The Local Church as Church of Christ

One central affirmation of the ecclesiology at the Second Vatican Council is this: "This church of Christ is really present [*vere adest*] in all legitimate local congregations of the faithful which, united with their bishops, in the New Testament are also called churches" (LG 26). This emphasis on the local church in Roman Catholic thought is close to Eastern Orthodox thought, where this form of ecclesiology goes by the name of Eucharistic ecclesiology. In this view, local churches are seen not as portions or parts of the church, but as the ecclesial body of Christ present in fullness in each local Eucharistic community, realized in a particular place and time. These local churches are the church of Christ called upon to live in communion with other churches lest they run the risk of becoming sects.

There is some potential ambiguity in the term *local* church, since it might refer to the

---

37. Augustine, *Tracatus in Evangelio Joannis* 80.3 (*Patrologia latina*, ed. Migne [hereafter PL], 35, 1840).

344 Catholic community within a specific nation (such as the American church), or to a diocesan church under a presiding bishop (such as the diocese of Bridgeport), or even to a parish or specific Eucharistic worshiping community (such as St. Rita Church in such and such a township). For that reason, some writers prefer to use the word *particular* instead of *local*.

Church as Charismatic Community

Another way the church is described in the perspective of the Second Vatican Council is as a community of charisms. In the Catholic community, as in the Christian community in general, except possibly for Pentecostal Christians, there had been a neglect of the term *charism*. It was as though charisms were once important in the early church, but eventually the age of charisms ceased to exist. In a famous speech at the Second Vatican Council, Cardinal Leo Suenens of Malines-Brussels urged the restoration of the belief in charisms. A charism is a gift or ability bestowed on an individual within the Christian community that enables that person to fulfill a specific service, either over a long period of time or in a relatively short period of time.

Thus, in the council's Decree on the Apostolate of the Laity, it is noted, "From the reception of these charisms, even the most ordinary ones, there arises for each of the faithful the right and duty of exercising them in the church and in the world for the good of human beings and the development of the church, of exercising them in the freedom of the Holy Spirit who 'breathes where he wills,' and at the same time in communion with his brothers/sisters in Christ and with his bishops especially" (*Apostolicam actuositatem* 3). Earlier in the constitution on the church, it was noted, "Whether these charisms be very remarkable or more simple and widely diffused, they are to be received with thanksgiving and consolation since they are fitting and useful for the needs of the church" (LG 12). Also, in speaking of the role of priests or presbyters, another Vatican II text states, "While testing the spirits to see if they be of God, they [presbyters] must discover with faith, recognize with joy, and foster with diligence the many and varied charismatic gifts of the laity whether these be of a humble or more exalted kind" (*Presbyterorum ordinis* 9). The same admonition is given to bishops: "For they [bishops] know that they themselves were not established by Christ to undertake alone the whole salvific mission of the church to the world, but that it is their exalted office so to be shepherds of the faithful and also to recognize the latter's contributions and charisms that everyone in his or her own way will, with one mind, cooperate in the common task" (LG 30).

Fearing that a vast affirmation of charisms might threaten proper order and authority in the church, the drafters of the Vatican II document on the church inserted a distinction (which is not biblical but has historical relevance) between two kinds of charisms: The Holy Spirit "bestows upon the church varied hierarchic and charismatic gifts and in this way directs the church and adorns it with his fruits" (LG 4). And in a similar vein: "Among these gifts stands out the grace of the apostles to whose authority the Spirit himself subjects even those who are endowed with charisms" (LG 7).

The Greek word *charisma* or the plural *charismata* is used seventeen times in the New Testament, all (except 1 Peter 4:10) in the Pauline corpus: Rom. 1:1; 5:15 (twice); 6:23; 11:29; 12:6; 1 Cor. 1:7; 7:7; 12:4; 12:9; 12:28; 12:30; 12:31; 2 Cor. 1:11; 1 Tim. 4:14; 2 Tim. 1:6. For Paul, the term is not always a *terminus technicus*, since for him it is a concept in development. In Rom. 5:15, it is a variant for the notion of salvation in Christ; in Rom. 11:29, it refers to Israel's privilege in the sealing of the covenant or the conferral of the Law, etc. But the classical text is 1 Cor. 12:4: "Now there are varieties of charisms [*charismatōn*], but the same Spirit; and there are varieties of service [*diakoniōn*], but the same Lord; and there are varieties of working [*energematōn*], but it is the same God who inspires them all in every one."

Besides the use of the word *charism(s)* St. Paul, in various places, enumerates a list of some eighteen different charisms, a few of which are difficult to differentiate: apostles, prophets, evangelists, teachers, admonitors, almsgivers, administrators, mercy workers, those who utter wise statements, those gifted with special faith, healers, miracle workers, discerners of spirits, those with the gift of tongues, interpreters of tongues, and those providing help, counseling, and service.[38]

Collegiality and Conciliarity/Sobornicity of the Church

One characteristic emphasis of the ecclesiology of the Second Vatican Council was its stress that pastoral responsibility for the worldwide church rests not only with the pope but also with all the bishops, especially those who are responsible for a diocese. A new word was introduced into Catholic usage, namely *collegiality*, which refers to the teaching that a bishop,

by reason of his episcopal ordination and not simply by reason of his appointment by the pope, also bears responsibility for the church universal. The term collegiality is much more specific than the general term *shared responsibility*, which applies to all the baptized and designates that by reason of baptism and charismatic gifts from the Holy Spirit, each believer must somehow be involved in promoting the teaching and embodiment of the Christian faith. Those who planned the Second Vatican Council and partook in its deliberations recognized that emphasis on the role of the pope since the First Vatican Council had somewhat clouded the reality of "collegiality," or the ministry of the world's bishops acting as a "college" either at a general synod or by worldwide involvement from within their home dioceses.

One of the ways that bishops' cooperative teachings about reading the signs of the times has been expressed since the Second Vatican Council has been through the meetings and publications of the various national episcopal conferences. Occasionally, these episcopal conferences sometimes reach prudential judgments that might differ from the priorities in the central offices of the papal administration, namely, the various congregations or councils of the Vatican curia. This tension between the bishops and the curial offices existed from time to time prior to the Second Vatican Council; some of the more dramatic interventions by bishops at the council pointed to these conflicts. The Congregation for the Doctrine of the Faith, the chief papal office for supervising the content and

---

38. The classic study on charisms in Paul and in Vatican II is that of Heinz Schürmann, "Les charismes spirituels," in *L'Église de Vatican II*, Unam Sanctam 51b, ed. G. Barauna (Paris: Cerf, 1967), 2:541–73. The scriptural texts that include partial lists of charisms are 1 Thess. 5:12; 5:19-22; 1 Cor. 14:1-5; 14:6; 14:26; 14:27-33; 1 Cor. 13:18-22; 1 Cor. 12:8-10; 12:28-30; 1 Cor. 13:1-3; Rom. 12:6-8; Eph. 4:11. These are largely charisms related to preaching, leadership functions, and charitable deeds.

manner of articulating official doctrinal teaching, has recently suggested that whereas these episcopal conferences have pastoral usefulness, they are not, strictly speaking, official teaching organs of the church. Not all have felt comfortable with this conclusion. In the meantime, bishops and theologians alike are carefully studying historical precedents for the modern episcopal conference and are showing how they do in fact represent a valuable source of authentic teaching for the church. On the occasion of a working draft on the status of episcopal conferences produced by a Vatican congregation, a number of Catholic bishops and theologians explored the function and necessity of these national conferences of bishops.[39]

The Eastern churches, especially the Eastern Orthodox, continue to stress another profound conviction—namely, that what is crucial to the life of the church is not only collegiality as a complement to papal ministry, but also "conciliarity" or "sobornicity." According to this view, the church is supposed to function as a harmonious symphony of believers who have been gathered in Christ and upon whom the Holy Spirit rests. Conciliarity seeks to fashion ecclesiastical life in a way that will express the church's nature and distinctiveness. Eastern theologians state that the church expresses communion in Christ through its synodal character.

One Holy Catholic and Apostolic Church

The Niceno-Constantinopolitan Creed—which was formulated in the fourth century at an ecumenical council and has been used since at baptism and other liturgical occasions as an expression of orthodox faith—affirms resoundingly that the Christian community sees itself as "one, holy, catholic, and apostolic" church. The original meaning of these attributes has not always remained clear, nor has the purpose of these dimensions been fully understood.[40] What is clear is that none of the four attributes was originally intended to be used polemically or apologetically to demonstrate the superiority of one church over another or to imply that one church possessed more unity, sanctity, catholicity, or apostolicity.

Just as in other parts of the Christian creed, the assertion of the church as one, holy, catholic, and apostolic is meant to be understood eschatologically. By that is meant that these characteristics are associated with the church to describe not purely what is now visibly evident to the beholder; rather, they are part of a prayer of longing and hope that the church may in fact become what it is called to be by reason of its lofty vocation. The attributes are meant to be both affirmations of fact and invitations to hope.

Oneness, holiness, catholicity, and apostolicity are possessed by the church because of the gracious gift of the Holy Spirit that effects these graces through God's mysterious design. But the gifts are clouded and distorted by the presence of sin and willfulness in the members of the church individually and collectively. Hence, just as in the Lord's Prayer we pray, "Thy kingdom come," so too in the community of faith do we need to pray, "May thy church become one, holy, catholic, and apostolic." Roman Catholics,

---

39. See the volume published under the auspices of the Woodstock Theological Center in Washington: Reese, ed., *Episcopal Conferences*.

40. Tamara Grdzelidze, ed., *One, Holy, Catholic and Apostolic: Ecumenical Reflections on the Church* (Geneva: World Council of Churches, 2005).

especially since the promulgation of the Decree on Ecumenism, have an acute awareness that their church, despite the presence of the Holy Spirit dwelling within, is not yet in fact visibly one, holy, catholic, and apostolic. The church is one because of the indwelling of the one Holy Spirit in all the baptized; it is holy because it is set apart by God's graciousness for the reception of a mysterious love of predilection; it is catholic in the original sense of the word, meaning that it is whole and entire, possessing all that is needed to make it integral; and it is apostolic because it remains in continuity in essentials with the original witnessing of the first-century apostles (and not simply the Twelve, but the entire apostolic community of believers in the first generation). Catholics are often inclined to apply these descriptive characteristics to the worldwide, universal church, yet they are beginning to learn that these characteristics are meant to apply just as truly to the local church.

Responsibilities within the Church

What follows in the next segment investigating the nature and mission of the church is a brief description of various "offices" or personal areas of responsibility characteristic of different members of the church. These will include the largest group, namely the faithful or laypersons, as well as a smaller group of women and men who are members of institutes of consecrated life, vowed individuals such as religious sisters and brothers. Next there is reflection on the roles of the ordained: deacons, priests, and bishops. Among the various pastoral duties of the ordained are the teaching and administrative tasks of the hierarchy with special attention to the ministry of the popes.

The Faithful

One fruitful way to better understand the nature of the church is to reflect on the various responsibilities bestowed upon its members. All members of the church are entrusted by God with specific responsibilities; these may differ, but they are complementary. The faithful, those who have responded to the call of God to accept faith in revelation, are expected to participate in the community's worship of God by joining with Christ in his heavenly liturgy of adoration and praise. By an active liturgical life turned toward God, they come to learn that faith consists not in a recitation of formulas but in a life imbued with Christian values.

The initial chapter of Vatican II's Dogmatic Constitution on the Church (*Lumen gentium*) relates the church to the inner life of the triune God. In the discussion of the structure of the constitution, there was some difference of opinion at the council as to what should be the following second chapter. Some participants argued for a section on the hierarchy. Despite their arguments for that option, the council next described the church as a whole ("God's People in Christ"), rather than immediately addressing the role of the hierarchy. This decision has widely influenced the Catholic Church's self-understanding and even affected the structure of the revised Code of Canon Law. The primary focus is on what all persons in the church share. Only later, in chapter 4, does *Lumen gentium* return to a discussion of the specific responsibilities of the *laity*, a term designating "all the faithful except those in holy orders and those who belong to a religious state approved by the church" (LG 31). The emphasis is not on the role of Christians taken as individuals but rather as members of the body of Christ. The faithful are said to find their dignity rooted in the gift of baptism through which as laypersons they share

348 in the priestly and prophetic office of Christ. The faithful, as has been seen, possess numerous charismatic gifts emanating from the Holy Spirit; these are bestowed upon all believers for the building up of the church.

Lumen gentium gives expression to the conviction that the entire body of the faithful possesses a *sensus fidei*, a supernatural instinct bestowed upon Christians that enables them to recognize what is authentic or inauthentic in church teaching, as well as what is central or what peripheral (LG 12). The entire body of the faithful, so states the constitution, cannot err in central matters of belief, which is another way of describing the basic "infallibility" of the church—namely, the conviction that the Holy Spirit maintains the church in truth by keeping alive the memory of the identity and significance of Jesus Christ. This religious "sixth sense" has special pertinence in connection with how teachings proposed by pastors or teachers find their "reception" in the church.

Modern ecumenical theology, through an extensive number of theological dialogues that attempt to go beyond ancient polemics, stresses that a believer can best understand the function of ordained ministry in the church by first gaining an insight into the ministry of Jesus and its continuation in the ministry of all the baptized.[41] One way of speaking that stressed the universal priesthood of all believers—a way of speaking considered rather suspect in post-Reformation Catholicism because it sounded too Lutheran, too Protestant—is affirmed by the council when it notes that the faithful "by virtue of their royal priesthood, participate in the offering of the Eucharist" (LG 10). In a period when the Roman Catholic Church in many countries is experiencing a notable decline in the number of persons presenting themselves for ordination, it is important that laypersons not be seen as a poor "substitute" for ordained presbyters. In fact, the faithful are included in participating in the mission of the church: "Each disciple of Christ has the obligation of spreading the faith to the best of his or her ability" (LG 17).

Another task that is applied today to the role of the faithful is coresponsibility or shared decision making. This may ring hollow in some parts of the church where the faithful, if called upon to speak, are rarely heard, or where members of the lay faithful are not consulted in crucial decisions, such as the naming of a local bishop.

Institutes of Consecrated Life

Another group of persons in the church given special attention in *Lumen gentium* (chapter 6) constitutes women and men traditionally identified as "religious" or members of religious congregations or orders. According to a new terminology, these persons are perhaps better referred to as members of "congregations of consecrated life." The responsibilities of these persons are described both in *Lumen gentium* and in the Decree on the Appropriate Renewal of Religious life (*Perfectae caritatis*). Central to their identity as religious are their public vows or pledges of the evangelical counsels: poverty, chastity, and obedience, promised within the context of a life in community. *Lumen gentium* describes the powerful sign-value emanating from those persons who wish to mirror Christ

---

41. From 1982 to 2005, Paulist Press published seven volumes of the series Ecumenical Documents, which contains many of these consensus statements. A shorter collection is *Modern Ecumenical Documents on the Ministry* (London: SPCK, 1975).

in the world (LG 40). Their lifestyle is meant to be a sign of fidelity and dedication to the fulfillment of the spiritual and material needs of the wider human family.

The idea of consecration does not imply separation from the church's mission, a subject I will treat in the next section. Women members of these communities have had a significant role in the education and evangelization of generations of young Christians. The decline in numbers among these religious communities has dramatically affected Catholic education. Also included in this category are communities of brothers. Groups of these men and women see themselves gifted by the Holy Spirit with similar kinds of charisms and for that reason choose to live together in community for the development and nurturing of these charisms conferred upon them for the life of the church.

The Ordained

A third group of persons in the church, the ordained, are assigned distinctive sacramental and liturgical responsibilities. Persons are ordained to become bishops, priests, or deacons. Ordination is understood as one sacrament that is conferred according to different degrees or different responsibilities.

The Latin texts of the Vatican II documents usually avoid the term *priest* (*sacerdos*), mainly because the New Testament shuns the Greek equivalent word to describe that specific group of ministers in the church. Rather, the texts of Vatican II use the term *presbyteros* (its English equivalent is not always retained in translations) to refer to those who have been ordained. Many Catholics may be puzzled by the introduction of this new term, "presbyters," which sounds rather "Presbyterian." There does, however, seem to be a gradual preference for the term *ordained*

rather than the word *priest*. To prevent anyone from drawing too sharp a distinction between ordained and nonordained, the Second Vatican Council specifically stated that "the common priesthood of the faithful and the ministerial or hierarchical priesthood, though they differ in essence and not only in degree, are nonetheless ordered one to another" (LG 10).

The more that the Second Vatican Council's documents describe the responsibilities of the bishop, presbyter, or deacon, the more the texts draw not only on Scripture but also on later categories. According to the document on the church, there are two forms of ministry (that of the ordained and the nonordained): "The ministerial priest, by the sacred power he possesses, forms and governs the priestly people; he effects the eucharistic sacrifice in the person of Christ, and he offers it to God in the name of all the people" (LG 10).

Later in the section on bishops, the task of presbyters is again touched upon. There they are described as "vigilant collaborators with the episcopate, called to assist and serve it, called to serve God's people, and constituted with their bishop one presbyteral college dedicated it is true to a variety of duties. . . . In each local congregation of the faithful, presbyters, in a way, represent the bishop with whom they are associated in all trust and generosity; in part they take upon themselves his duties and solicitude and fulfill them in their daily labor" (LG 28). If descriptions of the tasks of the ordained presbyter seem rather sparse in *Lumen gentium*, it is in part because two other decrees of the Second Vatican Council treat the role of presbyters: the Decree on the Ministry and Life of Presbyters (*Presbyterorum ordinis*) and the Decree on the Training of Presbyters (*Optatam totius*). Still, it is true that the Vatican II texts are more attentive to the bishop's role than to the presbyter's role.

A distinctive contribution of the council was to restore the diaconate as a permanent office in the church, and not simply as a stepping stone to the presbyterate. Married men would also be ordained to this particular ministry, now commonly called the "permanent diaconate," which would include preaching, administering various sacraments, and assisting presbyters and bishops in their apostolates. The Constitution on the Church (no. 29) spells out in some detail the valuable ministries that the permanent deacons fulfill in the life of the community.

Pastoral Office

Another distinct group closely connected with the presbyterium is that of the bishops, who are seen as continuing the work of the *episkopoi* in the New Testament. One of the most remarkable consensus statements related to this form of ministry produced in recent decades is a document on the role of the church's concept of *episkopē* ("oversight"); the document was produced by a French-speaking joint Roman Catholic and Reformed Christian commission known as the Group of Les Dombes (a village near the historic monasteries of Cluny and Taizé). Published in 1976, this document, entitled *Le ministère épiscopale* (*Episcopal Ministry*), makes an excellent companion piece to what the Second Vatican Council said about the tasks of the episcopal office.[42]

At the Second Vatican Council, the role of bishop was described in two documents: *Lumen gentium* and *Christus Dominus* (the Decree on the Bishops' Pastoral Office in the Church). These documents include sections on apostolic succession, the sacramentality of the order of bishop, the relation of the college of bishops to

its head (the pope), episcopal authority in the diocese, and finally, the governance and teaching authority of the local bishop.

Because of the heavy stress placed on the role of the pope in the previous council, (the First Vatican Council), it was important that the Second Vatican Council expatiate on the complementary functions of the bishop and show that the service he undertakes for the community is based not on delegation by the pope but on his sacramental ordination or consecration as a bishop. Thus, the document on the church explicitly states, "The fullness of the sacrament of orders is conferred by episcopal consecration.... Episcopal consecration confers, together with the office of sanctifying, the duty also of teaching and pastoring, which, however, of their very nature can be exercised only in hierarchical communion with the head and members of the [episcopal] college" (LG 21).

Historical studies suggest that those who came to be called *episkopoi* were persons who held responsibilities resulting from a blending of two originally separate functions: each was a successor of the apostles (thus having apostolic oversight) and the president of a presbyterium (the single local leader of the community). In appealing to apostolic succession, one should not lose sight of the fact that some characteristics possessed by the original apostles were of their very nature unrepeatable and noncommunicable. In the early church, a multitude of forms for exercising apostolic responsibilities existed side by side. From these varied and sometimes conflicting sources, the office of bishop eventually took shape. Even the notion of apostolic succession had a variety of meanings.

The Second Vatican Council stressed that the triple role of the bishop (teaching, sancti-

---

42. An English translation is given in the journal *One in Christ* 14 (1978): 267–88.

fying, and shepherding) derives directly from sacramental ordination and not from canonical appointment by the pope. The local bishop possesses the authority to govern in such a way that his canonical power is "ordinary, proper and immediate" (*Christus Dominus*, 8) In the administration of his diocese, the bishop retains a certain autonomy from national episcopal conferences, from the Vatican congregations, and even from the pope himself.

By reason of sacramental consecration into the episcopal college, bishops share in "collegiality," a responsibility for fostering communion among churches throughout the world. Hence, the ministry of a bishop, although focused primarily on a local diocese, is not restricted exclusively to his own particular church. The role of bishops in the Catholic Church is much more important than in many other churches. In a real sense, they are seen as in continuity with the role of the apostles in the earliest Christian communities.

The three major functions of the bishop according to Catholic teaching are teaching, sanctifying, and being a pastor.[43] Catholic teaching also stresses that it is crucial for the maintenance of visible unity at the universal level that there be an exercise of *episkopē* on a worldwide basis. How this form of more comprehensive pastoral care or *episkopē* has been and is now realized concretely in ecclesial life must be kept in proper balance between conciliarity and primacy. Could such a service of unity among churches be acceptable within the wider communion of churches beyond Roman Catholicism? What would Catholics and non-Catholics alike wish as the proper maintenance of a primacy that serves unity and diversity among the *koinonia* of churches?

Some of the language of the Second Vatican Council shows signs of haste and compromise in the way it treats historical texts and movements relating to the ordained ministry. In its desire to show that there is a continuity between New Testament apostles (perhaps without paying sufficient attention to the fact that, even in the New Testament, the word *apostle* is used with different shades of meaning) and modern-day bishops, the Second Vatican Council states, as though there are no historical problems in this succinct formulation, that "the apostles were careful to appoint successors in this hierarchically constituted society" (LG 20).

Magisterium

One perspective on church life that has received close attention in the Roman Catholic Church during the past two centuries is that associated with the term *magisterium*. This is a loanword from Latin that originally designated functions or activities engaged in by a *magister* or teacher, but which nowadays, especially in documents emanating from the pope or Vatican congregations, refers principally not to the function but to specific functionaries, namely, that group of persons entrusted with the task of overseeing and articulating official church teaching. It is curious that a notion that has grown to assume such central importance in an episcopally structured church such as the Roman Catholic Church apparently does not have a recognizable equivalent even in the other episcopal communities such as the Orthodox, Anglican, or Lutheran churches. Still, upon closer investigation, it is clear that other churches understand this function in terms of "teaching authority."

---

43. James K. Mallett, ed., *The Ministry of Governance*, With Oars and Sails 1 (Washington, DC: Canon Law Society of America, 1986).

352

One would be hard pressed to find any other term in Catholicism that has no obvious counterpart in the Byzantine or Reformed traditions. Hardly any other term at the heart of modern Catholic teaching has been able to maintain its modern usage without being contextualized by reference to its historically original connotation. In the past sixty or so years, most Catholics have shown themselves willing to understand the word *magisterium* as referring to a particular person or group of persons in the church entrusted with the task of providing ecclesiastical teaching that is *magisterium authenticum,* to use the language of the nineteenth and twentieth centuries, including that of the Second Vatican Council. In this case, the Latin adjective *authenticum* is often translated (incorrectly) as "authentic" teaching (as opposed to inauthentic?), rather than correctly translated as "authoritative" (in the sense of bearing the force of a teaching from a duly constituted source).

Crucial to restricting the word *magisterium* to that identifiable group of ecclesiastics entrusted with the task of authoritative teaching is the distinction—again rather recent in the church's history—between the *ecclesia docens* (the teaching church, that is, the bishops) and the *ecclesia discerns* (the learning church, referring to the rest of the church, especially the laity). Several theologians have recently attempted to show that the distinction between these two parts of the church is not as simple as it seems.[44] But most official modern Catholic documents accept without objection the use of *magisterium* to refer to the pastoral authoritative teaching of the hierarchy, as opposed to other forms of teach-

ing, such as that proposed by the theologians, prophets, mystics, or the ordinary faithful. The inconvenience in this usage, now conventional, is that it could trivialize the complexity of how church teaching is formulated, especially in regard to how the present-day church reads the signs of the times.

The medieval usage of *magisterium* was more nuanced and allowed for serious weight to be given to the teachings of competent church historians, canonists, or theologians who spoke out of their knowledge of the tradition. The insight behind this distinction between the ministry of bishops and of other teachers in the church, such as theologians, an insight that is blurred by present terminological usage, is that ordained bishops and responsible theologians have distinctive, though complementary, functions in the church. Where they may differ often pertains to prudential judgments about the wisdom of proposing teaching that may be seen as provocative, innovative, or lacking in rigor.

Naturally, in the context of this brief exposition of magisterium, one of the key concepts of papal and episcopal teaching today, it is not possible to give a totally adequate account of the sources and scope of ecclesiastical "magisterium." One can, however, urge that the notion be carefully contextualized historically and explained in a way that fully accounts for the demands of collegiality, reception of teaching by the faithful, the vocation of learning in the life of the church, and the importance of listening, especially to those through whom the Holy Spirit may be speaking to the church in our time. St. Cyprian of Carthage in the third century wrote

---

44. See, for instance, Ladislas Orsy, *The Church Learning and Teaching* (Wilmington, DE: Glazier, 1987), as well as the volume by Francis A. Sullivan, *Magisterium: Teaching Authority in the Catholic Church* (New York: Paulist, 1983). See also Michael Fahey, "Magisterium," in *The Routledge Companion to the Christian Church*, ed. Gerard Mannion and Lewis Mudge (New York: Routledge, 2008) 524–35.

to a fellow bishop, "It is thus a bishop's duty not only to teach; he must also learn. For he becomes a better teacher if he makes daily progress and advancement in learning what is better."[45]

Papal Primacy

The Catholic Church has strongly expressed the conviction that there must be a form of primatial authority exercised in the church. The function of papal primacy may have changed notably since the invention of new methods of communications (radio, television, Internet, etc.). The pope's function is explained as being in continuity with the role of Peter among the rest of the Twelve in the New Testament. Peter's role was as a missionary, as one who first received the promise of the keys (Matt. 16:18).

To understand the central importance that the primacy of the pope holds in the Catholic Church, it is important to look back at the nineteenth-century general council, the First Vatican Council (1869–70). Because it is more remote from our times and its preoccupations are less obvious to us today, some historical background is necessary. The Second Vatican Council, which was more interested in focusing its energies on the role of bishops, decided not to reformulate earlier descriptions of papal primacy and infallibility. One can be a loyal Catholic theologian and still regret that the Second Vatican Council did not sufficiently nuance what the First Vatican Council had stated about the papacy.

Canon Roger Aubert, whose special area of competence is the First Vatican Council, has clearly established through his research that those bishops at the First Vatican Council who hoped for the most extensive statement of papal infallibility (the maximalist position) were roundly rejected.[46] However, some of the popular commentaries later published in England and in other parts of the English-speaking world subsequently exaggerated what the First Vatican Council had stated about papal infallibility. These exaggerations were in part based on a famous two-hundred-page pastoral letter on papal infallibility circulated by the English cardinal Henry Edward Manning. His letter, published shortly after the council and written from an unabashedly maximalistic perspective, was interpreted as a commentary on the conciliar doctrine. It exercised an enormous impact on teaching in seminaries in England and other seminaries where English was spoken, which may help to explain why there were different emphases about papal infallibility among bishops from the English-speaking world and from other countries (such as Germany and France) at the beginning of the Second Vatican Council. Some of the subsequent theological explanations of what the First Vatican Council was purported to have stated may have been at the root of a maximalizing tendency that predicates infallible status to a wide spectrum of papal utterances. The more moderate positions of John Henry Cardinal Newman were not generally as well known as those of Cardinal Manning.

One astute explanation of what the First Vatican Council had said came from some twenty-three German bishops who had attended the council and who in December 1874 responded in a newspaper article to a dispatch from Germany's Chancellor Otto Bismarck. This dispatch argued that the council had effectively nullified the power of the bishops. These German bishops reasoned that in the mind of the

---

45. Cyprian of Carthage, *Epistula* 74, no. 10 (Hartel, *Corpus Scriptorum Ecclesiasticorum Latinorum*, III, par. 2, p. 807).
46. See Roger Aubert, *Vatican I* (Paris: Orante, 1964).

354 council, the pope clearly did not have unlimited powers, but that he remained subject to divine law and to Christ's intentions for his church. Nor are the bishops simply instruments of the pope, bereft of personal responsibility. The notion that the pope is an absolute monarch, they argued, is a wholly false interpretation of the dogma of infallibility. On March 4, 1875, in an apostolic letter to the German episcopate, Pope Pius IX praised the interpretation of the German bishops and wrote, "Your declaration is an expression of that true Catholic doctrine which is at once the teaching of the Vatican Council and of the Holy See."[47]

What did the First Vatican Council say? The circumstances under which that council began were not the most auspicious, when on December 8, 1869, 660 prelates assembled in Rome. There was reason to think that the council might be brought to a halt if the military forces seeking Italian unification (the *Risorgimento*) were to overrun the remaining papal territory. Such fears of invasion proved founded, and less than a year after the opening ceremony, on September 20, 1870, Rome was occupied by troops who laid claim to the city as the capital of the new Italy.

The accomplishments of the First Vatican Council were very limited and restricted because of the constraints of time. Two lengthy drafts on "The Church," the first prepared by the Roman theologians Giovanni Perrone and Giuseppe Cardoni, and the second developed by Joseph Kleutgen, were never discussed in any detail, much less ratified, because of the rush of time at the council. In regard to ecclesiology, all that was promulgated was the Dogmatic Constitution *Pastor aeternus* (*Eternal Shepherd*; voted

upon July 18, 1870), which describes basically only the function of the papacy in the church. Still, its preamble sets the doctrine regarding the institution, perpetuity, and nature of Petrine primacy in the context of preserving the unity of the bishops "in order that the episcopate itself might be one and undivided, and in order that the entire multitude of believers might be maintained in unity of faith and of communion by means of the close union of the bishops one with anther" (Denzinger-Schönmetzer, *Enchiridion Symbolorum* [hereafter DS], 3051). The necessity for expounding the doctrine of papal primacy is attributed to contemporary threats to the security of the Catholic Church: "With daily increasing hatred the forces of hell are rising on all sides against this divinely established foundation to overthrow the church, if possible" (see DS 3052). The text of the First Vatican Council did, in fact, try to situate the Petrine function in the context of serving the unity of faith and charity. According to the text, the twofold unity of faith and of communion ("charity" earlier in the text) was said to be maintained by the bishops as a whole. Far from being a "juridical" perspective, the primacy of the pope was located in the context of an episcopate that serves the unity of faith and of charity/communion.

After the introductory section to *Pastor aeternus*, there follow four chapters, each devoted to a central theme: (1) the institution of the apostolic primacy in Peter; (2) the perpetuity of the primacy of Peter in the Roman pontiff; (3) the power and nature of the primacy of the Roman pontiff; and (4) the infallible teaching power of the Roman pontiff. In this present exposition, I focus principally on the last two chapters.

---

47. For an English translation of the text of the German bishops, see F. Donald Logan, "The 1875 Statement of the German Bishops on Episcopal Powers," *Jurist* 21 (1961): 285–95.

The declaration's appeal to the scriptural texts (Matthew 16 and John 21)—its claim in chapter 1 that in the New Testament Peter had a leading role among the apostles—would not be challenged by the consensus of biblical scholars today.[48] What non-Catholics object to in chapter 1 of *Pastor aeternus* is the claim that this "primacy" is one not only of "honor" but also of "jurisdiction."

Chapter 2 states that "what was instituted in blessed Peter for the constant protection and unceasing good of the church must, by the will of the same Founder, remain continually in the church" (DS 3056). The objections of other churches, such as the Orthodox Church, to this teaching about the papacy, if I understand correctly, have been not that in some sense the bishop of Rome inherited Petrine functions, but rather that too many other kinds of functions have been bestowed on him.

Chapter 3 contains five lengthy paragraphs and concludes with a canon or anathema. To begin with that concluding canon is helpful, since it succinctly summarizes the entire chapter. The canon anathematizes those who deny that the pope enjoys "full and supreme power of jurisdiction over the whole church not only in matters pertaining to faith and morals, but also in matters pertaining to the discipline and government of the church throughout the entire world" (DS 3064). It anathematizes those who deny that he possesses "the full plenitude of this supreme power" or that this power is "ordinary and immediate over all churches and over each individual church, over all shepherds and all the faithful." The terminology used here requires some clarification. "Power" in this context (*potestas* or

exousia) refers to the holder's rightful freedom to act, the authority that he has been granted, and not to his having the power to impose his will on others by force or by intimidation. But *potestas* in the sense of "right" easily becomes confused with *potestas* in the sense of "might." The phrase *potestas jurisdictionis seu regiminis* (the power of jurisdiction or governance) had become standard since the early Middle Ages to describe the governing aspect of pastoral care in the church. Unfortunately, the gospel figure of the shepherd came to be focused on jurisdiction.

To say that papal jurisdiction is "ordinary" does not mean it is likely to be used ordinarily, habitually, on a day-to-day basis. On the contrary, it requires extraordinary circumstances for this "ordinary" authority to come into play. It means simply that the authority belongs to the holder, in this case the pope, *ex officio*, that is, as part of his papal office and is not delegated to him (for example, by a general council) or conceded to him (for instance, on the initiative of some bishop or local church). To say that his jurisdiction is "immediate" is to say that the pope is not obliged to work through intermediary authorities; access to him is direct, and his intervention need not be channeled through the local bishop or the local civil powers. These somewhat abstract "rights" begin to make better sense when one reads the rest of the chapter and reconstructs the kinds of situations being envisaged.

The burden of the first paragraph of chapter 3 is that "full power was given to him [the pope] in blessed Peter, by Jesus Christ, to rule, feed and govern the universal church" (see DS 3059). This means the pope is given a universal pastoral care,

---

48. See William R. Farmer and Roch Kereszty, *Peter and Paul in the Church of Rome: The Ecumenical Potential of a Forgotten Perspective* (New York: Paulist, 1990). See also Raymond Brown, Karl P. Donfried, et al., eds., *Peter in the New Testament* (New York: Paulist, 1974).

356 an ecumenical shepherding function, that remains, so far, remarkably vague and undefined, for all the document's grandiloquence.

The second paragraph of chapter 3 continues by stating that the power of jurisdiction is ordinary, immediate, and "truly episcopal." The addition of "truly episcopal" has led some persons to think that the only *truly* episcopal authority is that of the pope, and that consequently bishops are merely his delegates. This was in no way the intention of the formulation, as is clear from the acta of the First Vatican Council. "Truly episcopal" was included because some "Gallicans" were suspected of calling the pope's ordinary authority "primatial," as opposed to "truly episcopal," thereby wishing to limit it to emergencies and very rare circumstances. The First Vatican Council saw the pope as a symbolic center even when nothing was going wrong.

The third paragraph of chapter 3 of *Pastor aeternus* continues on a theme touched on in the preface to the constitution, stating that "this power of the supreme pontiff is far from obstructing the ordinary and immediate power of episcopal jurisdiction by which individual bishops, placed by the Holy Spirit and successors of the apostles, feed and rule as true shepherds the individual flocks assigned to them" (DS 3061).

The fourth paragraph (DS 3062) rejects the opinions of "those who hold that communication between the pope and the bishops and their flocks can lawfully be impeded; or who make this communication subject to the will of the secular power, so as to maintain that whatever is done by the Apostolic See, or by its authority, for the government of the church, cannot have force or value unless it be confirmed by the assent of the secular power." Behind this text, of course, was the memory of Pius VI's and Pius VII's humiliation by Emperor Napoleon Bonaparte.

The fifth and final paragraph in the third chapter on papal jurisdiction (DS 3063) states that, for the faithful, the pope is the court of last appeal. While not laying down the limits within which papal jurisdiction may function in any detail, the instances referred to clearly indicate that its purpose is to maintain the rights and liberties of the local church and its bishop while also enabling any who feel badly treated by the local leadership to appeal to a higher judgment.

The fourth and final chapter of *Pastor aeternus* states that "that infallibility with which the divine Redeemer willed His church to be endowed in defining a doctrine concerning faith or morals" may, in certain circumstances, enable the bishop of Rome, in his capacity as successor of Saint Peter, to define a doctrine to be held by the universal church. What the church has as a permanent endowment, the successor of Saint Peter may on occasion have available to him, enabling him to so act.

The three councils that the text cites—Constantinople IV (869–870), Lyons II (1274), and Florence (1438–39)—are not received as ecumenical councils by other churches. It is well to note that in 1974, for the anniversary celebration of the Council of Lyons II, Pope Paul VI took special pains to refer to that council as "the sixth of the general synods of the West." Whether that initiative opens the way for Catholics to regard Trent and the First Vatican Council as "general synods of the West," rather than ecumenical councils in the full sense of the term, and what effect that would have on the status of their decrees, is another matter. Despite what is commonly supposed in popular Roman Catholic listings of ecumenical councils, there is no definitive official list, and the numbering system dates back only to Saint Robert Bellarmine (1542–1621).

The functioning of the pastoral office of the

pope is described in some detail: "The bishops of the entire world, sometimes individually, sometimes assembled in synods, have followed the long-standing custom of the churches and the form of the ancient rule by referring to this Apostolic See dangerous situations, particularly those that have risen in matters of faith" (*Pastor aeternus*, ch. 4). The context of action by the pope is thus always envisaged in terms of his being approached by other bishops who find themselves unable to deal with some dissension or heresy. The text concludes with the following assertion:

> When the Roman Pontiff speaks *ex cathedra*, that is, when in the discharge of his office as shepherd and teacher of all Christians, and by virtue of his supreme apostolic authority, he defines that a doctrine concerning faith and morals must be held by the whole church, he possesses through the divine assistance promised to him in blessed Peter that infallibility with which the divine Redeemer willed His church to be endowed in defining a doctrine concerning faith or morals; and therefore such definitions of the Roman Pontiff are irreformable of themselves, not from the consent of the church [*ex sese non autem ex consensu Ecclesiae irreformabiles*].

It is well to clear up misunderstanding about the meaning of this last phrase. Readers cannot be blamed if they assume that these words mean that papal judgments may be issued independently of other bishops and of the church, and that such judgments are never open to revision in any sense. Several historical studies based on the acta of the First Vatican Council appeared in the years immediately preceding the Second Vatican Council so that the 1962–65 council could officially clarify the misleading terminology with this statement in *Lumen gentium*:

His definitions are rightly said to be irreformable by their very nature and not by reason of the assent of the Church, inasmuch as they were made with the assistance of the Holy Spirit promised to him in the person of blessed Peter himself; and as a consequence they are in no way in need of the approval of others, and do not admit of appeal to any other tribunal. For in such a case the Roman Pontiff does not utter a pronouncement as a private person, but rather does he expound and defend the teaching of the Catholic faith as the supreme teacher of the universal Church, in whom the Church's charism of infallibility is present in a singular way. (LG 25)

In stating that such decisions are "irreformable," the First Vatican Council did not mean that they could never be improved, clarified, expanded, developed, or placed in a new perspective so that in a sense they might be called "revised." The intention was to state that episcopal or conciliar validation or confirmation was superfluous. The specific terminology regarding the consent of the church was a direct reference to the Fourth Gallican Article of 1682, which stated that the pope's judgment in doctrinal controversies is irreformable only when covered by the subsequent consent of the church (*nec tamen irreformabile esse judicium nisi ecclesiae consensus acceserit*). Some readers of the documents of the First Vatican Council mistakenly translate the term *consensus* as though it means prior consultation, as though the pope can reach conclusions without prior consultation of the church. In fact, prior consultation is presupposed. What is excluded by the term *consensus* is rather the idea of subsequent approval. It is because a papal infallible judgment articulates the *consensus Ecclesiae* in the real and deep sense that it requires no *consensus ecclesiae* in the merely juridical or formal sense.

Many questions remain. To admit that the pope on occasion might be called upon to make such a prophetic judgment is not to specify the circumstances in which it might happen. Nor is it to say that an ecumenical council might not equally well make such a judgment. (In fact, historically, the councils have de facto been the means of dogmatic clarifications needed to settle trinitarian and christological controversies.)

It is true that the Second Vatican Council repeated much of the language and statements of the First Vatican Council and that there seems to be little further nuancing on an issue that has vexed other Christian churches since 1870. But in the way that the Second Vatican Council balanced the papal prerogatives with a fuller statement of the responsibilities of the episcopacy, and in the way that it describes the *sensus fidelium* (the believers' sense) found in the people of God, there is some movement toward refining the earlier teaching.

Alois Grillmeier, a German theologian later made a cardinal, commented on the key passage in paragraph 25 of *Lumen gentium* by noting, "In the mind of the faithful, as in that of the magisterium, the gift of infallibility had been too one-sidedly concentrated on the office, and even on a papal primacy which was considered in isolation from the episcopate as a whole. This could only lead to passivity and indifference with regard to responsibility for the word of God."[49]

Stating that the consensus of the entire people of God is infallible does not solve the complex questions that follow from that. How, in fact, is the truth, implicitly present in the mind or tradition of the faithful, discovered? Is it enough that the laity throughout the world takes for granted that a particular doctrine is true without having seriously examined it? Fifty years ago, for instance, the vast majority of Catholics believed that unbaptized infants were destined for limbo. Few hold this doctrine today. Is it that, placed in a new perspective, the truth that this doctrine expressed can now be better said by denying it? If that is the case, our faith in the undeceivable and undeceiving *sensus fidelium* in the people of God must allow for changes of direction.

The primary perspective within which the apostolic primacy in Saint Peter was envisaged and presented at the First Vatican Council is that of the papacy's being "the abiding principle of this twofold unity [of faith and communion] and its visible foundation." This description is repeated again in *Lumen gentium* 23. But this primacy of the papacy leaves room for a principle of unity that is other than "perpetual" (such as the Eucharist, which is frequently repeated but is not a continuous celebration), and it leaves room for an invisible foundation of this unity, namely, the presence of the Holy Spirit at work in the church. The papacy is not the only, or even the most important and fundamental, principle of unity of faith and communion.

The real stumbling block to the reunification of the Roman Catholic and other churches lies less in the actual verbal formulation of the Roman doctrines in the last two general councils and more in the real or de facto exercise of the papal functions, marked as they are at times by a notable Romanizing tendency, by a sometimes rigid selection process for the appointment of bishops, and by an isolation from the convictions of its own believers and from the insights of non-Catholic Christian saints and scholars. The distinguished theologian and church historian who taught for many years at the Pontifical Oriental Institute in Rome, Wilhelm de Vries, was convinced that it was regrettable that the

---

49. See Herbert Vorgrimler, ed., *Commentary on the Documents of Vatican II* (New York: Herder, 1967), 1:164–65.

Second Vatican Council lacked the resoluteness to reformulate in a more satisfactory way the obscure expressions of the First Vatican Council on this topic. For instance, the First Vatican Council did not indicate the limits of papal primacy. Clearly, however, the *plenitudo potestatis* (fullness of power) has its limits in the will of Christ's institution of the church. The fact that the Second Vatican Council did not give non-Catholic observers voice to raise questions from the council floor meant that clarification did not come from the conciliar texts, but only later from official bilateral consensus statements.

Evangelization and Other Church Tasks

One frequently asked question about the church is, What exactly are its tasks? Some obvious answers include keeping alive the memory of Jesus and his teachings, preaching the gospel within the Christian community, organizing and celebrating public worship, and teaching the faithful how to praise God in prayer. But there are also other tasks that relate to the church's mission to the world. The church is called upon, in the words of the Second Vatican Council, to read the "signs of the times" (GS 4) in order to understand its role in the world. Although the Pastoral Constitution on the Church in the Modern World spoke of humanity's "joys and sorrows," some have felt that the perspective of the text was too optimistic, too mesmerized by the progress of technology, and not sufficiently imbued with a solid "theology of the cross." At any rate, in the 1985 international synod of bishops that assessed the Second Vatican Council's impact during the twenty years since its close, it was suggested that the signs of the times had become bleaker, with an increase in hunger, oppression, injustice, war, sufferings, terrorism, and other forms of violence. It was noted that a new challenge for the church was to show how humanity's history of suffering and salvation history are intertwined and can be understood only in light of the paschal mystery. Another issue touched upon in the 1985 international synod of bishops was inculturation. The church, because of its present understanding of diversity and unity and in order to communicate its message more appropriately, needs to commit itself to draw from every culture all that possesses positive values for the communication of God's revelation in Christ. Inculturation tries to facilitate an intimate enrichment of authentic cultural values through their integration into Christianity. This requires a process of discernment that demands prayerful reflection and contemplation to communicate the gospel.

The Church's Mission

No account of the nature of the church is complete without an understanding of its mission.[50] What is the function of the church toward the large segment of humanity untouched by Christian revelation? What is it that Christians are asked to do for those persons? The concept of mission, however, is fraught with possible misunderstandings, not the least of which is a potential confusion between mission and proselytism.

The original Christian concept of mission reflected in the New Testament employed a

---

50. See Faith and Order Commission, World Council of Churches, *The Nature and Mission of the Church* (Geneva: World Council of Churches, 2005). See also Francis Schüssler Fiorenza, *Foundational Theology: Jesus and the Church* (New York: Crossroad, 1984), esp. chs. 7–8.

360

specific metaphor, which was inspired largely by John's Gospel, to express how God's love had reached out toward the created universe, especially the universe of humankind.[51] In the Fourth Gospel, Jesus refers with reverence to "the Father who sent me." Jesus speaks too about a second, interconnected mission or sending of the Paraclete, whose role would be to continue and perfect the work begun by him. The term *mission* described in pictorial language God's redemptive concern for the human community. The preexisting Word of God was perceived as having been sent to put on humanity, to "dwell among us," and to fulfill a salvific mission that would eventually be complemented by the Holy Spirit.

In medieval theology, these divine "missions" were expressions of the inter-trinitarian processions' outreach toward humanity. Missionary theology is first and foremost theology about the work of the three persons of the triune God as they communicate grace toward human beings. Nowadays, the church applies the word *mission* to what the community is called upon by God to undertake. It is important to remember that the church participates in a mission, rather than performs a mission. Mission is better understood by its origin than by its objective.

It was quite late in the history of the church, after the medieval synthesis of Thomas Aquinas, that theologians began to speak specifically about the "mission of the church." At first, influenced by the Western canonists, there was a gradual introduction of the idea of a *missio canonica* to describe the church's authoritative commissioning of clerics to preach the gospel. Even in the manualist Catholic theologians of the nineteenth and early twentieth centuries,

one rarely finds mention of the "mission" of the church. The only indirect reference is mention of the church's end (*finis*) or purpose. This perspective is reflected in the language of the First Vatican Council's decree *Pastor aeternus* (1870) that describes the church's finality as acting "so that Christ might render lasting the saving work of redemption" (DS 3050).

However, it is true that John's Gospel twice cites sayings of Jesus to members of the nascent church about "sending." At the Last Supper, Jesus is said to "send" the disciples gathered for the paschal meal in the Upper Room: "As you [Father] have sent me into the world, so I have sent them into the world" (John 17:18). Later, in a postresurrection appearance, Jesus says, "As the Father has sent me, so I send you" (John 20:21). In popular piety, these sayings from John are connected with the various "go" commands of Jesus ("Go into the whole world . . .") as found in Mark 16:15 and Matt. 28:19. Can these sayings, originally addressed to the Eleven, be extended to each and every member of the church so that mission is part of every Christian's mandate? The answer is doubtlessly yes, but it is important to distinguish between the mission of the triune God, the all-embracing power of salvation at work wherever the reign of God is in effect, and the mission of the church, obviously a modest participation within that broader process.

In recent times, Catholic theologians, including even the drafters of texts at the Second Vatican Council, have been hesitant about using the word *mission* to explain the church's activities in the world. One reads rather about the church's task, role, concern, function, presence, need to witness, challenge, mediation, and responsibility, concepts that are related to the

---

51. Michael A. Fahey, "The Mission of the Church: To Divinize or to Humanize?" *Catholic Theological Society of America, Proceedings* 31 (1976): 51–69.

general notion of the church's mission. The participants at the Second Vatican Council, as we have seen, chose to describe the church from a double perspective: the church's internal life (*ad intra*) and its external life (*ad extra*). At the council, rather than appealing to the church's *missio*, they spoke of its *munus* instead: *de munere ecclesiae in mundo hujus temporis* (concerning the task of the church in today's world). This Latin term *munus* is usually translated into English as "task" (perhaps the plural form, "tasks," would have been better) and sometimes as "role(s)," reflecting the various responsibilities the church is called upon to shoulder. The decision at the Second Vatican Council to use the word *task(s)* rather than *mission* had the advantage of removing an exaggerated parallel between the trinitarian missions and ecclesial mission. Also the church's "tasks" are much more comprehensive than the specific responsibility exercised by those formally involved in preaching the gospel to believers or to potential believers.

Evangelization

Among its own family, the Christian community celebrates a common vision of God through its preaching and sacramental worship. This vision can grow dim or seem unimportant to individuals or can even conceivably become distorted by lack of proper instruction. Hence, even within the church, the Christian vision needs to be rekindled, refined, and made more attractive, more central to the life of individual Christians or regional or national churches. The church needs to give more thought to how it can keep the gospel message ever fresh and attractive, especially when the level of preaching by the ordained is poor, and when the quality and quantity of instructional and devotional literature are problematic. Neglect of "distant" Catholics by the institutional structures of the church should be a major concern today. The more distant from church those people become who by family ties or national origins once identified themselves as Catholic Christians, the more that what is preached to them parallels the message to the non-evangelized. Reaching out to the distant members is often referred to as the new evangelization.

Besides the church's preaching to its own inner family members, the church is called upon to share its vision with the wider human family. This outreach is the task of evangelization exercised according to different styles and approaches. This evangelization needs to be undertaken within the context of a hierarchy of truths that reaffirms God's universal salvific will and the possibility that for many (even the majority?), a religious or even a humanistic tradition that is not Christian will be a source of holiness. Hence, evangelization undertaken out of love for the sacredness of Christianity, a sense of commissioning by God, and the desire to share a precious value in one's life must be done in a way that is respectful of the value of other religions and the human person's freedom of conscience.[52]

Even after explicit evangelization has been practiced (and clearly this will not always be successful) or even before evangelization is begun (postponed temporarily, for instance, until one feels better equipped to understand the potential recipients' value systems and cultural setting), Christians are expected to perform other tasks besides "preaching the gospel" in the strict sense of the phrase. Formulated in other words,

---

52. Pope Paul VI, *On Evangelization in the Modern World: Post Synodal Apostolic Exhortation, December 8, 1975* (Washington, DC: United States Catholic Conference, 1976).

362 the question is this: Apart from direct evangelization (sharing the gospel), what is the Christian community expected to "do" in the world? Christians should be careful not to have an exaggerated sense of their own importance. They should not be so self-congratulatory that they fail to recognize that others who are neither Christian nor religious may well possess many acute insights and sensitive moral commitments for improving the human condition that even some Christian leaders lack. This is said on the level of theoretical possibility, not stating that this is always or even frequently the case.

In their relationship to the "world" (taken here as meaning specifically the non-Christ-confessing community), Christian communities are expected to exercise three functions, which can be described as integrational, prophetic, and eschatological.

INTEGRATIONAL FUNCTION

Christian communities have the ability to exercise an "integrational" role vis-à-vis those who do not share their religious creed by illustrating the basic unity of the order of creation and the order of redemption. This means that becoming more fully human and becoming more fully sanctified have a common finality, since the gospel fulfills the most profound needs of humankind. Christians can be conscious collaborators with God in the functions of creating, redeeming, and glorifying the world through Christ. What the Christian "knows" is that humanity has been raised to a new level of dignity through God's personal communication with the world through Christ. Because of language barriers, geographical isolation, cultural prejudices, human frailty, and so on, none of this may be recognized by those to whom this is proclaimed. Classical theology stated that the gift of faith is unmerited and that, in the inscrutable design of God, not all receive the gift of faith during their lifetime (though they may still be slated to enter eventually into glory with God). Every individual sin, especially those sins that directly abuse others, and every corporate sin or scandal associated with the community called church, makes the possibility of responding to Christian revelation more difficult.

PROPHETIC FUNCTION

Christian communities have the ability to exercise a prophetic role in the world. The communities inspired by faith in Christ are called upon to express disdain for every form of evil, injustice, and abuse of power. Obviously, this does not imply that Christians have special insights into the concrete proposals that will correct social evils for sure. Christians' specific suggestions will be only as good as the expertise and competence of individuals skilled in politics, economics, or psychology.

The word *prophetic* is not meant to suggest purely denunciatory discourse. Ecclesial communities can also mobilize energy behind positive, beneficial initiatives, even those initiated in non-Christian communities. By acting as a leaven in the world, in family, professional, social, cultural, and political life, the Christian communities can mobilize forces that are creative; this is one step beyond pure denunciation of injustices and abuse.

ESCHATOLOGICAL FUNCTION

Since redemption remains an ongoing, unfinished process dependent both on God's grace and on human response in freedom, a response often weakened by sinfulness, the full appropriation of salvation is incomplete, even in the church. Christian communities are expected to reflect the truth that our true home is in God, that we are called to a "beatific vision." As explained by theologians such as Jürgen Moltmann in his *Theology of Hope*, Christianity's function is carried out not within the horizon of expectation provided by the role that society concedes to the church, but within its own particular horizon of eschatological expectation of the coming reign of God, of future righteousness, and of future peace and freedom.[53]

This eschatological perspective (meaning a perspective that is not yet fully realized) emphasizes that the social aims of Christian communities are not merely progress, movement toward affluence, and elimination of struggle. Christianity, because of its understanding of the transitional character of this world, stresses the radical ambiguity of human activity. The centrality of the cross and the paradox of life emerging from death that mark the Christian vision of life as well as its paschal dimension prevent the new humanity in Christ from subjecting the gospel to political reductionism.

The Pastoral Constitution on the Church in the Modern World (*Gaudium et spes*) touches on a number of aspects of the church's responsibilities to the world never before treated in conciliar texts. The document recognizes that the church has "a feeling of deep solidarity with the human race and its history" and that "the joy and hope, the grief and anguish of persons of our time, especially of those who are poor or afflicted in any way, are the joy and hope, the grief and anguish of the followers of Christ as well" (GS 1). The church offers its services to cooperate unreservedly with the rest of humankind in fostering a sense of family ties within humanity.

This pastoral constitution analyzes the present situation of humanity, its successes and its failures. It first treats the theoretical framework. Part 1, entitled "The Church and the Human Vocation" (nos. 11–45), treats specifically these themes: the dignity of the human person (12–22); the human community (23–32); human activity in the universe (33–39); and the role of the church in the modern world (40–45). Part 2, "Some Problems of Special Urgency" (46–93), treats marriage and family, culture, economic and social life, politics, and peace.

A study of the pastoral constitution's numbers 40–45, which treat the church's role in the modern world, may help elucidate Catholic teaching on the tasks of the church. At first, the perspective is simply that of *Lumen gentium*— namely, that the church is a visible organization and a spiritual community. But the document continues by saying that the church can contribute greatly to humanizing humankind and its history through each of the church's members and its community as a whole.

In a display of humility, the participants of the Second Vatican Council, in regard to the aim of humanizing the world, admit that the Catholic Church "values what other Christian churches and ecclesial communities have contributed and are contributing cooperatively to the realization of this aim" (GS 40). The council even states that the Catholic community is convinced that it can receive considerable help from the world in preparing the ground for the gospel, both from individuals and from society as a whole by means of the talents and activity found in the world.

These sections of *Gaudium et spes* have not received as close attention as some other texts. There is stress on the need for exchange, on the church's need to listen to the experts in the world. "It is the task of the whole people of God,

---

53. Jürgen Moltmann, *Theology of Hope: On the Ground and the Implications of a Christian Eschatology*, trans. J. W. Leitch (New York: Harper & Row, 1967).

364 particularly of its bishops and theologians, to listen to and distinguish the many voices of our times and to interpret them in the light of the divine Word" (GS 44). It even adds, echoing an idea of Justin Martyr, that "the church itself also recognizes that it has benefited and is still benefiting from the opposition of its enemies and persecutors" (GS 44).

Much of what is said in this document on the church in the modern world is traceable to the efforts of some European theologians, especially the Belgian Catholic theologian Gustave Thils (1909–2000), who in the 1940s and 1950s developed what Thils called a "theology of earthly realities."[54] The biblical teaching of this interrelatedness of church and world was given a strong christological basis. Cooperating with the modern world is helping to complete the journey that has as its goal "to unite all things in him [Christ], things in heaven and things on earth" (Eph. 1:10).

It is arguable that some church leaders do not in fact follow these remarks about the need to learn from the world, especially when they prematurely condemn certain political or medical procedures they may not completely understand. One example of broad consultation among a specific hierarchy that respected the need for this listening was the preparatory work of the U.S. Catholic Conference of Bishops in formulating two pastoral letters (*Challenge of Peace*, 1983; *Economic Justice for All*, 1986). Not only was a broad spectrum of informed opinions consulted, but the texts were formulated first in drafts with requests for reactions by experts before their final formulation. By consulting persons with special competence, even outside of the ecclesial community, the bishops communicated an important fact: the task of humanizing

the world can in no way be the exclusive work of the hierarchical church that fails to listen to the experience and insights of others.

Since the Second Vatican Council, the Catholic Church has become more acutely aware of its responsibilities in the service of the poor, the oppressed, and the marginalized. In this "preferential option" for the poor (which is not intended to be exclusive), special attention is given to Jesus' sayings in the Gospels about how the poor are blessed (Matt. 5:3; Luke 6:20). The Catholic Church also stresses that, besides material poverty, lack of spiritual goods may well be considered a form of poverty. Hence, the church is committed to denounce prophetically poverty and oppression and to promote the inalienable rights of the human person.

The Church's Call to Holiness

Another dimension of modern Catholic teaching about the church is treated in two sections of *Lumen gentium*. One section, in chapter 5, explores "The Call of the Whole Church to Holiness"; a second complementary section treats "The Eschatological Nature of the Pilgrim Church and Its Union with the Heavenly Church." These perspectives may also be considered part of the mission of the church, a call to sanctity of life. Regarding the first section, on the call to holiness, Catholics have left themselves open to criticism in the past in the way that they seem to exult in "good works" without acknowledging the fact that even our remote desire to practice a virtuous act is itself the result of divine grace. Concerning union with what the second section calls the "heavenly church," Catholics have a distinctive way of re-

---

54. Gustave Thils, *Théologie des réalités terrestres*, 2 vols. (Paris: De Brouwer, 1946–49).

lating to the saints in glory that they share with the Eastern Orthodox and Anglicans. Some of the prayers of petition that Catholics formulate to the saints, especially to Mary the mother of Jesus, seem to other Christians somewhat odd because they appear to circumvent direct invocation of Christ the Savior.

Unanswered Ecclesiological Questions for Future Resolution

A venerable practice of Western theology since the Middle Ages has been holding open debates on various *quaestiones disputatae* (disputed questions). These are not matters of definitive dogma, but are doctrinal issues where there is not complete unanimity, but issues that bear on important aspects of the church's corporate self-identity and are of more than mere academic interest.

In this section, I address four issues of this type. They are obviously not the only serious questions that could profit from further discussion, but they are ones I wish to address here. The topics are: (1) the binding force of the general councils held in the West in the second millennium, from the ninth council, Lateran I (1123) to the twenty-first, Vatican II (1962–65), with special attention given to the Council of Trent (1545–63) and Vatican I (1869–70), which have had such an impact on Roman Catholic life even to these days; (2) Eucharistic sharing or hospitality (intercommunion) between believers in the Roman Catholic Church and in other Christian churches not now in full visible communion; (3) recognition of the ordinations

of persons commissioned within other Christian churches, especially women ordained to the presbyterate or to the episcopate; and (4) new ways of exercising papal primacy in the context of the worldwide network of churches.

Ecumenical or General Councils

In the second millennium, the church of the West and then—after the Reformation—the Roman Catholic Church held a series of councils that have given a particular stamp to life among large segments of the Christian community. Some Roman Catholics are now beginning to note that, in fact, there is no definitive list numbering the councils that has been imposed with dogmatic authority. True, Rome designates certain councils held in the West (e.g., Trent, Vatican I, Vatican II) with a specific enumeration and with the specification "ecumenical." But this attribution is not a dogmatic pronouncement and reflects simply a common enumeration of the ecumenical councils traceable to the relatively late work of Robert Bellarmine in his *De Controversiis* (1586).

In recent times, under the leadership of Pope Paul VI, an important initiative of the See of Rome took place that unfortunately has gone largely unnoticed. Paul VI expressed the conviction that in fact there are two sorts of councils in the patrimony of the West: the early ecumenical councils of the undivided church and then the later general synods of the West. In an important letter dated October 5, 1974, and addressed to Cardinal Willebrands on the occasion of the seventh centenary of Lyons II (1274), the pope wrote, "This Council of Lyons counted as the sixth of the general synods held in the West."[55] This terminology of "general synods" suggests

---

55. French text in *Documentation Catholique* 72 (1975): 63–67. See also Yves Congar, "Church Structures and

that Catholic teaching is willing to accept the notion of varying levels of councils, what Yves Congar has called a hierarchy or relative order of importance among councils and synods (*hierarchia conciliorum*). If this distinction were to be widely accepted, then the anathemas pronounced against those who did not accept the canons of these general synods would seem to be softened or eliminated. This would have considerable import in the event of other churches reestablishing full visible communion with the See of Rome.

The ecclesiological questions raised in this connection are extremely interesting. Does this not imply then that the Church of Rome would at least in principle be willing to accept the notion of full communion with certain churches, especially the Orthodox churches, who would not be required to assent to the dogmatic status of certain teachings adopted by Rome at general synods? This would give much wider scope to the possibilities of other churches being associated in communion with Rome. It would not in any way imply that members of the Roman Catholic Church could ignore or neglect these teachings, but they would be seen as attempts by their own church to explain a profound truth of revelation, which might be understood by other Christians in a different way, and even with different terminology.

Shared Eucharistic Hospitality

Another matter of some disputation even among Catholic theologians and church leaders today is the appropriateness of divided Christians celebrating together and sharing in the Eucharist, occasionally or regularly, and that not on the basis of a spontaneous personal decision but rather on the basis of expectation of eventual official approval.[56] Many theologians prefer to speak of "Eucharistic sharing" or "Eucharistic hospitality," rather than using the term *intercommunion*, a word that is ambiguous if one thinks of the *koinonia* or *communio* that already exists among different Christians on the basis of their baptism in the same Holy Spirit.

In its decree on ecumenism, the Second Vatican Council wrote of "the wonderful sacrament of the eucharist by which the unity of the church is both signified and brought about" (*Unitatis redintegratio* 2). The official position of the Catholic Church on Eucharistic sharing, a position expressed at the council and in subsequent guidelines, is that this sharing should normally take place only when it signifies an already existing unity. Shared Eucharist, the Catholic Church argues, should not take place indiscriminately as a means of achieving unity. The precondition would be doctrinal unity and not only that unity in Christ already present through baptism. But these guidelines do not seem to be permanently fixed. In fact, the official bilateral and multilateral ecumenical dialogues that have taken place since the council have made it clear through their consensus statements that, in very many cases, what divides churches on Eucharistic or sacramental teaching is not related to the core of belief—that is, to the dogmatic heart of faith—but centers rather on theological elaborations of that faith, elaborations that may properly allow for different emphases.

Councils in the Relations of East and West," *One in Christ* 11 (1975): 224–65; Francis Dvornik, "Which Councils Are Ecumenical?" *Journal of Ecumenical Studies* 3 (1966): 314–28.

56. See "Eucharistic Sharing (Intercommunion)," in *New Catholic Encyclopedia*, vol. 17, *Supplement: Change in the Church* (Washington, DC: Publishers Guild, 1979), 215–17, with full bibliography.

What would be the implications of such a shift in discipline within the Roman Catholic Church? One closely related issue, of course, would be the need to recognize unequivocally the genuine character of ordinations in churches that apparently do not understand apostolic succession in the same way as do Catholics and that practice ordinations without the presiding function of a bishop.

Recognition of Ordinations

For the sake of its future self-understanding, the Catholic Church needs to turn its attention to the recognition of ordained ministries in Anglican and Protestant churches along the lines of its already stated recognition of orders in the Eastern Orthodox and Ancient Oriental churches. For purposes of discussion, I will limit discussion for the moment to the Anglican Communion. As is widely known, the Anglican Communion has in principle always recognized the validity of orders received by Roman Catholic priests or presbyters. For complex historical and theological reasons, the Church of Rome has not recognized orders in the Anglican Communion as "validly conferred." In part, this was due to the way that Rome perceived the Church of England's understanding of the sacrificial nature of the Mass and the finality associated with ordination rites in the sixteenth century. In 1896, after a long study by a papal committee on this question, Pope Leo XIII (who disagreed with the conclusions of the majority of the committee he had appointed to study this matter) published a bull, *Apostolicae curae*, on Anglican orders which concluded that, in fact, Anglican orders were "absolutely null and thoroughly void."

Based on the intense ecumenical investigations of the Anglican/Roman Catholic International Commission, culminating in the publication of its *Final Report*, it seems possible to assert that, in fact, the differences regarding both Eucharist and ordination are not dogmatically divisive issues. Rather, it seems, if we are to accept the agreed statements, that these differences are based on theologically diverse but complementary insights that are not necessarily exclusive.[57] Were the authorities in the Roman church to become convinced of this, it would conceivably be possible to change that church's previous assessment of this matter.

How this would apply to other Christian churches—both those that have formally retained the episcopal structures of church polity that Catholics find so imperative and those "free churches" that express the need for *episkopē* in other ways besides the office of "bishops"—remains a major issue that will require much further study and discernment.

The matter becomes all the more complicated today by the fact that some of those ordained as priests and bishops in churches of the Anglican Communion are women. The Roman Catholic Church (like the Orthodox Church) does not recognize the possibility of a woman being ordained, and has expressed this view in a document issued by the Congregation for the Doctrine of Faith, *Inter insigniores* (Declaration on the Question of the Admission of Women to the Ministerial Priesthood), published on January 27, 1977. While the declaration intends to be authoritative and argues in favor of maintaining the present position, theological discussion of the question continues at least in some sectors of the Roman Catholic community. The present official teaching—especially reasons given

---

57. Anglican-Roman Catholic International Commission, *The Final Report* (London: SPCK, 1982).

368   about the impossibility of a woman being an appropriate *repraesentatio Christi* (representation of Christ)—has not found full "reception" among Catholic theologians.

Papal Ministry

Another controverted question that will need to be discussed both within the Catholic community and among other Christian churches is whether it would be possible to reformulate the ministerial role of the bishop of Rome, the pope, in such a way that what Catholics see to be his primatial service of unity may become acceptable to other Christians outside the boundaries of the Roman Catholic Church. This is an issue about which there are many different perspectives stemming from the specific polity of a historical church or the distinctive theological emphases of a Christian community. The issue has received added centrality because in his encyclical *Ut unum sint* (1995), Pope John Paul II invited non-Catholic "church leaders and their theologians to engage with me in a patient and fraternal dialogue on this subject [of papal primacy], a dialogue in which, leaving useless controversies behind, we could listen to one another, keeping before us only the will of Christ for his church" (no. 96). Because of the diversity of perspectives, resolution of how papal ministry could be extended to other churches also will be achieved only slowly and step by step. The hope is that, through this exchange, not only will one segment of the church be enriched, but the entire body of Christians would come to understand more profoundly the mystery of the church.

For Further Reading

New Testament Studies

Collins, Raymond F. *The Many Faces of the Church: A Study in New Testament Ecclesiology.* New York: Crossroad, 2003.

   The writings of the earliest Christians reflect a variety of distinct and complementary emphases on church life.

Congar, Yves. *The Mystery of the Church.* Baltimore: Helicon, 1960.

   A characteristically insightful work on the biblical origins of the church by one of the major twentieth-century Catholic ecclesiologists.

Cwiekowski, Frederick J. *The Beginnings of the Church.* New York: Paulist, 1988.

   A study that traces how modern scholars understand the first three generations of the church.

Dunn, James D. G. *Unity and Diversity in the New Testament: An Inquiry into the Character of Earliest Christianity.* Philadelphia: Westminster, 1977.

   Written by a Protestant, this work provides a solid account of complementary biblical theologies of the church.

Harrington, Daniel J. *The Church According to the New Testament*. Franklin, WI: Sheed & Ward, 2001.

> The American Jesuit, long-time editor of **New Testament Abstracts**, *provides a useful summary of how the church is described in the canon of Christian Scriptures.*

Meeks, Wayne A. *The First Urban Christians*. New Haven: Yale University Press, 1983.

———. *The Moral World of the First Christians*. Philadelphia: Westminster, 1986.

> *Taken together, these two volumes enrich our understanding of the cultural and social context of various local Christian communities in New Testament times.*

Minear, Paul S. *Images of the Church in the New Testament*. Philadelphia: Westminster, 1960.

> *An extensive study of the metaphors and similes used by the New Testament writers to describe the church.*

Theissen, Gerd. *The Social Setting of Pauline Christianity*. Philadelphia: Fortress Press, 1982.

> *A major analysis of the sociological context of the communities associated with Saint Paul's churches.*

General Studies

Collins, Paul M., et al. *Christian Community Now*. Ecclesiological Investigations 2. London and New York: T&T Clark, 2008.

> *Part of a new international series, this volume engages four theologians (two Methodists, one Anglican, and one Roman Catholic) to discuss urgent priorities.*

Doyle, Dennis M. *The Church Emerging from Vatican II: A Popular Approach to Contemporary Catholicism*. Mystic, CT: Twenty-Third, 1992.

———. *Communion Ecclesiology: Vision and Versions*. Maryknoll, NY: Orbis, 2000.

> *The author's extensive teaching at the University of Dayton is neatly reflected in the clarity and accessibility of these modern presentations.*

Dulles, Avery. *Models of the Church*, rev. ed., Garden City, NY: Image, 1987.

> *A highly influential study of Catholic ecclesiological paradigms.*

Forte, Bruno. *The Church: Icon of the Trinity*. Boston: St. Paul, 1991.

> *This Italian Catholic ecclesiologist is well versed in Eucharistic ecclesiology and the pneumatology of the Eastern churches.*

Gaillardetz, Richard R. *Ecclesiology for a Global Church: A People Called and Sent*. Maryknoll, NY: Orbis, 2008.

> *The church is defined as called to community, mission, communion, ministry, and discipleship, and is sustained by memory.*

Haight, Roger. *Christian Community in History: Ecclesial Existence*. New York: Continuum, 2008.

> *This third volume in a comprehensive analysis of transconfessional ecclesiology draws heavily upon recent ecumenical consensus statements to illustrate the major agreements amid diversity in Christianity.*

Henn, William. *Church: The People of God*. New York: Burns & Oates, 2004.

> *This American Capuchin Franciscan friar, professor at Rome's Gregorian University, presents an accessible description of the church for a wide audience.*

Jay, Eric. *The Church: Its Changing Image through Twenty Centuries*. Atlanta: John Knox, 1980.

> *Ecumenically sensitive, the book gives a comprehensive overview of the history of ecclesiology.*

370   Kärkkäinen, Veli-Matti. *An Introduction to Ecclesiology: Ecumenical, Historical and Global Perspectives.* Downers Grove, IL: InterVarsity, 2002.

> The Finnish Lutheran author, who teaches at Fuller Theological Seminary, presents seven different confessional approaches to the nature of church, the views of seven leading contemporary ecclesiologists, and seven contextual ecclesiologies.

Lakeland, Paul. *Church: Living Communion.* Collegeville, MN: Liturgical, 2009.

> Besides offering a fresh analysis of the marks of the church, the book elaborates on ten challenges facing it today. The author then provides what is described as an "inductive" ecclesiology.

Lauret, B., and F. Refoulé, eds. *Initiation à la pratique de la théologie.* Vol. 3. Paris: Cerf, 1983.

> Part of a five-volume study on systematic theology, this volume develops the treatise on ecclesiology. It contains a matchless treatment on the theology of "local church" by Hervé Legrand, O.P., one of Yves Congar's protégés.

Lennan, Richard. *Risking the Church: The Challenges of Catholic Truth.* New York: Oxford University Press, 2004.

> The Australian theologian, an expert on the thought of Karl Rahner, describes the church's vocation to embody Christian beliefs in personal and communitarian discipleship.

Mannion, Gerard. *Ecclesiology and Postmodernity: Questions for the Church in Our Time.* Collegeville, MN: Liturgical, 2007.

> The author encourages church leaders to acquire new ways of reading the signs of the times in changing cultural settings and urges ecclesiology to link closely to ethical concerns.

McBrien, Richard P. *The Church: The Evolution of Catholicism.* New York: HarperCollins, 2008.

> The author's long involvement in teaching and lecturing shine through in this masterful yet accessible account of the developing theology of church. Solidly documented, the volume is an ideal text for colleges and study groups.

Phan, Peter C., ed. *The Gift of the Church: A Textbook on Ecclesiology in Honor of Patrick Granfield.* Collegeville, MN: Liturgical, 2000.

> The contributors to this Festschrift attempt to provide a comprehensive account of the nature and history of ecclesiology.

Prusak, Bernard P. *The Church Unfinished: Ecclesiology through the Centuries.* New York: Paulist, 2004.

> In seven chapters, the Villanova professor traces the church's self-understanding from the first century to modern times.

Skira, Jaroslav, and Michael Attridge, eds. *In God's Hands: Essays on the Church and Ecumenism in Honour of Michael A. Fahey, S.J.* Leuven: Peeters, 2006.

> To mark the honoree's seventieth birthday, the contributors account for the growth and progress in ecumenical ecclesiologies.

Sullivan, Francis. *The Church We Believe In: One, Holy, Catholic and Apostolic.* New York: Paulist, 1988.

> The work of an American Catholic ecclesiologist whose writings are steeped in tradition but attentive to contemporary issues.

Vondey, Wolfgang. *People of Bread: Rediscovering Ecclesiology.* New York: Paulist, 2008.

> Drawing upon his Pentecostal church affiliation, yet steeped also in modern Roman Catholic theology, the author, professor at Regent University, unfolds the nature and mission of the church through multiple layers of Christian imagination.

Studies on Vatican II and Its Impact

Alberigo, Giuseppe, ed. *Les Églises après Vatican II*. Paris: Beauchesne, 1981.

> *Unfortunately, this work has never been translated into English. It contains the talks of a number of major modern ecclesiologists given at an international colloquium in Bologna, Italy, in the late 1970s on central aspects of the doctrine of church.*

Alberigo, Giuseppe and Joseph A. Komanchak, eds. *History of Vatican II*. Maryknoll, NY: Orbis, 1995–2006. Vol. 1, *Announcing and Preparing Vatican Council II* (1995); vol. 2, *The Formation of the Council's Identity: First Period and Intersession October 1962–September 1963* (1997); vol. 3, *Mature Council, Second Period and Intersession September 1963–September 1964* (2000); vol. 4, *Church as Communion: Third Period and Intersession September 1964–September 1965* (2003); vol. 5, *The Council and the Transition: The Fourth Period and the End of the Council, September 1965–December 1965* (2006).

> *This international achievement painstakingly traces the month-by-month work of the council's genesis as reflected especially in its official acta.*

O'Malley, John W. *What Happened at Vatican II*. Cambridge, MA: Harvard University Press, 2008.

> *A thoughtful retrospective that compares the church before and after the council, with special attention devoted to the rhetoric and tone of its pronouncements. The impact of specific conciliar participants is further highlighted.*

Reese, Thomas J., ed. *Episcopal Conferences: Historical, Canonical, and Theological Studies*. Washington, DC: Georgetown University Press, 1989.

> *One of the first North American Catholic studies on the many-faceted aspects of bishops' collegiality, especially as expressed in their national conferences.*

Schultenover, David, ed. *Vatican II: Did Anything Happen?* New York: Continuum, 2007.

> *Four Catholic historical theologians (J. W. O'Malley, J. A. Komonchak, S. Schloesser, and N. J. Ormerod) look back after forty years to assess the changes initiated by Vatican II.*

Studies on Magisterium

Fahey, Michael. "Magisterium." In *The Routledge Companion to the Christian Church*. Edited by Gerard Mannion and Lewis Mudge, 524–35. New York: Routledge, 2008.

> *Addressed to an ecumenical readership, this overview articulates the concept of teaching authority as embodied variously in the principal churches.*

Gaillardetz, Richard R. *Teaching with Authority: A Theology of the Magisterium in the Church*. Collegeville, MN: Liturgical, 1997.

———. *By What Authority? A Primer on Scripture, the Magisterium, and the Sense of the Faithful*. Collegeville, MN: Liturgical, 2003.

> *By his numerous publications in this area, the author has become a leading spokesperson for how Catholics understand the concept of magisterium.*

Groupe des Dombes. *"One Teacher": Doctrinal Authority in the Church*. Translated by Catherine Clifford. Grand Rapids: Eerdmans, 2010.

> *The renowned French ecumenical association provided in 2006 a crystal-clear study of how authoritative teaching functions in the church.*

Mannion, Gerard, et al., eds. *Readings in Church Authority: Gifts and Challenges for Contemporary Catholicism*. Burlington, VT: Ashgate, 2003.

> *This hefty reference work (572 pages) contains key excerpts from ecclesiastical documents and writings of theologians clustered around eight subsections. Bibliographies and discussion questions are included.*

372

O'Donovan, Leo, ed. *Cooperation between Theologians and the Ecclesiastical Magisterium.* Washington, DC: Canon Law Society of America and Catholic Theological Society of America, 1982.

> Two of the leading Catholic professional societies in America collaborated to prepare these background papers and recommendations aimed at resolving tensions between bishops and theologians on doctrinal issues.

Sesboüé, Bernard. *Le magistère à l'épreuve: Autorité, vérité et liberté dans l'Église.* Paris: Desclée de Brouwer, 2001.

> The French Jesuit, long associated with the Groupe des Dombes, provides a personal synthesis of the complex topic.

Sullivan, Francis A. *Creative Fidelity: Weighing and Interpreting Documents of the Magisterium.* New York: Paulist, 1996.

———. *Magisterium: Teaching Authority in the Catholic Church.* New York: Paulist, 1983.

> Two well-informed and balanced systematic treatments of how ecclesiastical magisterium is currently understood in the Catholic tradition.

Studies on the Papacy

Buckley, Michael J. *Papal Primacy and the Episcopate: Towards a Relational Understanding.* New York: Crossroad, 1998.

> A modern exposition of the ideal interaction of pope and bishops based on the doctrine of collegiality articulated by Vatican II.

Farmer, William R., and Roch Kereszty. *Peter and Paul in the Church of Rome: The Ecumenical Potential of a Forgotten Perspective.* New York: Paulist, 1990.

> By sketching possible distinctive roles of the two apostles in the early Roman church, the authors wish to provide expanded understanding of Petrine ministry today.

Granfield, Patrick. *The Papacy in Transition.* New York: Doubleday, 1980.

———. *The Limits of the Papacy.* New York: Crossroad, 1987.

> These twin volumes on the papal ministry are historically informed and ecumenically sensitive.

Pottmeyer, Hermann Josef. *Towards a Papacy in Communion: Perspectives from Vatican Councils I and II.* New York: Crossroad, 1998.

> The German Catholic professor provides one of the rare comparative studies of the ecclesiologies of the two Vatican Councils.

Quinn, John R. *The Reform of the Papacy: The Costly Call to Christian Unity.* New York: Crossroad, 1999.

> Archbishop emeritus of San Francisco undertook this research to respond to Pope John Paul II's request in Ut unum sint (That All May Be One) to help clarify the role of papal ministry.

Tillard, Jean Marie. *The Bishop of Rome.* Wilmington, DE: Glazier, 1983.

> This Catholic ecclesiologist was active in dialoguing with Orthodox and Anglican Christians. His volume contains historical background and helpful proposals for a renewal of papal ministry.

Ecumenical Consensus Statements

Bilateral Working Group of the German National Bishops' Conference and the Church Leadership of the United Evangelical Lutheran Church of Germany. *Communio Sanctorum: The Church as the Communion of Saints.* Collegeville, MN: Liturgical, 2004.

> Lutheran and Catholic church leaders in Germany labored long to articulate a comprehensive agreed statement on the nature of the Christian community.

The Church of the Triune God: The Cyprus Agreed Statement of the International Commission for Anglican-Orthodox Theological Dialogue. London: Anglican Communion Office, 2006.

> *During fifteen years of dialogue, some sixty hierarchs and theologians produced this extensive forward-looking consensus on the mission of the church.*

Faith and Order Committee, World Council of Churches. *The Nature and Mission of the Church: A Stage on the Way to a Common Statement.* Geneva: World Council of Churches, 2005.

> *The product of intense consultation and collaboration, this position paper ranks with the Lima Report as one of the major ecumenical statements of the past several decades.*

Lee, Randall, and Jeffrey Gros, eds. *The Church as Koinonia of Salvation: Its Structures and Ministries.* Washington: United States Conference of Catholic Bishops, 2004.

> *This North American consensus statement on the church was prepared by the Bishops' Committee for Ecumenical and Interreligious Affairs at the United States Conference of Catholic Bishops together with the Department of Ecumenical Affairs of the Evangelical Lutheran Church in America.*

Sin and Grace 7

Sin and Grace

Roger Haight

The doctrines of sin and grace define an anthropology, a Christian conception of human existence. Whenever revelation of God occurs, human existence appears in a new light, for God's disclosure always also reveals the human as standing before God. The doctrines of sin and grace, then, unfold the core of Christian self-understanding. They deal with the mystery of human existence in relation to the God revealed in Jesus Christ.

Introduction: Scope and Method

A concise account of these doctrines can be put forward only under severe limitations, and these should be stated at the very outset. First, what follows will be a constructive systematic theology of sin and grace; it is not historical. A thorough appreciation of the language of sin and grace demands a survey of the history of these doctrines because of the many developments and changes in understanding that have occurred in different periods. Knowledge of this history is presupposed and only schematically represented. At the same time, this systematic interpretation of the doctrines will draw on classical sources from the history of theology and doctrine.

Second, this systematic theology of sin and grace enters into dialogue with the tradition of the Reformation. The analysis will always seek to preserve the theological insights and values of that tradition even while they are drawn into the overall framework of a Roman Catholic imagination.

Third, the perspective governing this theology of sin and grace may be called liberationist, since some form of a theology of liberation alone

can respond to the problems we face. But at the same time, this synthesis will be attentive to the concerns of other theologies, and the classical issues underlying the doctrines of sin and grace will be integrated into the development.

Fourth, a short treatise on the theology of sin and grace that also seeks in some measure to be adequate to the many issues involved in these doctrines cannot fail to appear schematic. Arguments must be curtailed, full explanations foreshortened. For example, we must presuppose the historical and exegetical study of biblical sources, the historical conditions that led Augustine to his understanding of sin and grace, and the intentions behind the Roman Catholic formations of these doctrines at the Council of Trent. The goal of this account is to portray the theological logic underlying these doctrines in a way that makes them credible today.

Finally, this theological analysis of the doctrines of sin and grace does not pretend to be *the* Roman Catholic account. Roman Catholicism shares in the pluralism that currently characterizes all Christian theology. These doctrines, then, are Roman Catholic, but as in the case of all constructive theology, what follows can only be considered a particular account of them.

Context

This theological account of the doctrines of sin and grace adopts a perspective that responds to the question of the life of the Christian in history. It envisages a spirituality of committed freedom and participation in the everyday life of society and history. In the terms of Juan Luis Segundo, this theology of grace turns away from a spirituality of life in this world as a "test" for another life, and promotes a spirituality of Christian commitment to the "project" of

378 history moving toward resurrection.[1] While this focus has perennial relevance and viability, the conditions of its applicability shift across times and cultures. It continually has to be inserted into new larger frameworks of accountability because of the movement of history and new theological concerns. This section provides a description of emerging theological topics and perspectives that form the apperceptive background for understanding the theology of grace today.

Several new developments in theology have a bearing on the theology of sin and grace. This selection of five topics is not intended to be exclusive; it does not exhaust the field. In fact, the titles that have been chosen to represent developments in the theology of grace are so broad that in some measure they conceal large differences in the initiatives associated with each other. The categories do not typify but only name areas that differ from yet overlap with each other.

Methodological Concerns

The expandable compartment of "methodological concerns" contains several considerably different initiatives.[2] Catholic theology after Vatican II shifted abruptly from an objective style of Neo-Scholastic reasoning to an analysis of the human subject's encounter with God's revealing word. Just what was entailed in that transition—in the programs of Karl Rahner and Bernard Lonergan, for example—is still being refined. This examination of the very grounds of Christian theology provides a context of depth to the theological appreciation of the meaning of doctrinal formulas. Donald Gelpi has also contributed an inculturated Americanist approach to this task by his appropriation of principles from the pragmatist tradition: just what does "experience" refer to and mean in the theological appeal to it? We need new ways of conceptualizing the spheres of nature and grace that transcend the meanings defined by Thomist and other Scholastic theologies.

Another methodological concern takes up the sources of theological symbols in the tradition. A new, synthetic, and post-Scholastic interpretation of theological topics recognizes the degree to which the theology of grace is really the theology of the Holy Spirit. The theology of the Spirit has frequently been confined to a consideration of the doctrine of the Trinity. But the return to scripture has opened up the practical economic theology of the Spirit, that is, the Spirit effecting salvation in the community and across history. Pneumatology helps support a new experiential viewpoint on the theology of grace and an expansion of the field in which the Spirit is operative.

Feminist Theology

As development of the content of the theology of grace will show, this doctrine hides within the symbol "grace" the absolutely fundamental character of the relationship between God and human beings. So primal and elemental is this relationship that an essential flaw in its formulation weakens and distorts the whole vision

---

1. Juan Luis Segundo, *Signs of the Times: Theological Reflections*, ed. A. T. Hennelly (Maryknoll, NY: Orbis, 1993), 149–75.

2. David Coffey, "The Whole Rahner on the Supernatural Existential," *Theological Studies* 65 (2004): 95–118; Ralph Del Colle, "The Holy Spirit: Presence, Power, Person," *Theological Studies* 62 (2001): 322–40; Donald L. Gelpi, *The Gracing of Human Experience: Rethinking the Relationship of Nature and Grace* (Collegeville, MN: Liturgical, 2001); Christiaan Jacobs-Vandegeer, "Sanctifying Grace in a 'Methodological Theology,'" *Theological Studies* 68 (2007): 52–76.

of Christian self-understanding. This has been demonstrated by feminist theologies of grace.[3] Discovery of an androcentric defect has released a tide of reexamination and revision of fundamental images of God, the human, and the mutual relationship of gratuity between them that have influenced all of theology.

The dynamics of this reinterpretation can be described in terms of three dimensions of a negative experience of contrast: (1) something is experienced as fundamentally wrong; (2) this simultaneously reveals a better way, the way things should be; and (3) this in turn provokes action to repair the situation.[4] Traditional theological conceptions of sin and grace did not express but actually demeaned women's experience. Recognition released positive revisions, and the result is feminist reinterpretation of the whole range of Christian doctrine. All the topics within the traditional theology of grace have been revitalized by voices that were previously not heard. The work of Michelle Gonzalez demonstrates the extensive and substantial resources feminist theologians have brought to the theology of grace.

Non-Western Inculturated Theology

Culture in large measure defines and is defined by language. Culture is a second-level identity marker; it defines a person's second nature. All theology bears with it some culture, and it will communicate well with the people of any culture only when it is written in the terms of their culture.[5] The relevance of these axioms intensifies when the subject matter is anthropology, where each culture carries a fundamental conception of the human.

Since Vatican II, Asian and African cultures have become self-conscious and intentional about bringing the Christian message home to the thousands of subcultures of these continents. How is grace experienced amid the bonds of kinship and the reverence of ancestors in Africa? How do whole peoples who are poor and live close to nature in Asia encounter the Spirit released in Jesus' name? How is salvation appropriated in a grace-filled life in these cultures? The dialogues between faith and culture in Asia and Africa, the correlation between the Christian language of the West and these complex cultures, provide opportunities for the discovery of new meaning in the doctrines. Since Roman Catholicism spans these cultures and the lines of communication among theologians is open, global inculturation of theology will begin to affect all members of the church as theology is shared cross-culturally. Western theologians can expect to learn new ways of appreciating God's grace.

3. Kari Elisabeth Børresen, ed., *The Image of God: Gender Models in Judeo-Christian Tradition* (Minneapolis: Fortress Press, 1995); Ivone Gebara, *Out of the Depths: Women's Experience of Evil and Salvation* (Minneapolis: Fortress Press, 2002); Michelle A. Gonzalez, *Created in God's Image: An Introduction to Feminist Theological Anthropology* (Maryknoll, NY: Orbis, 2007); Donna Teevan, "Challenges to the Role of Theological Anthropology in Feminist Theologies," *Theological Studies* 64 (2003): 582–97; Tatha Wiley, *Original Sin: Origins, Developments, Contemporary Meaning* (New York: Paulist, 2002).

4. Edward Schillebeeckx, *Church: The Human Story of God* (New York: Crossroad, 1990), 5–6.

5. Augustine C. Musopole, *Being Human in Africa: Toward an African Christian Anthropology* (New York: Lang, 1994); Andrew Sung Park, *The Wounded Heart of God: The Asian Concept of Han and the Christian Doctrine of Sin* (Minneapolis: Fortress Press, 2001).

Interreligious Dialogical and Comparative Theology

A positive appreciation of other religions has revolutionized fundamental attitudes of vast numbers of Christians in the Western world. Historical consciousness has affected so many people that those who used to be regarded as hostile competitors in belief are now reckoned as friends who are valued for the religious truths they bear. These convictions mark a new age of Catholic theology that values interreligious dialogue and comparative theology.[6]

One of the doctrinal and theological convictions that has both nurtured and accompanied these developments lies in a conviction that God's saving grace reaches out to all human beings, so this grace must become manifest in and through the world's religions. This new, spontaneous, and prior conviction drives the many theological attempts to understand how this saving grace of God works and how it relates to the historical event of Jesus Christ. These questions are far from being settled in the Catholic Church, and they give the theology of grace a particular pointed relevance to our general self-understanding.

Theology in Dialogue with Science and Ecology

Every educated Catholic today lives in an evolutionary universe and planet.[7] Only sectarian Christians are able to seal off and compartmentalize their fundamentalist faith and isolate it from the ordinary knowledge mediated by general education. Everyone else knows that the story of Adam and Eve is a mythic expression of faith in God as the ultimate Creator of heaven and earth in whatever way this creation is unfolding. But while this seems somewhat obvious, this common appreciation of faith contains many tensions that have not been satisfactorily addressed.

A couple of examples of outstanding problems will show that theology stands before an open challenge in this area as well as the others. One example accompanies the recognition of the symbolic character of the story of Adam and Eve. This does not affect an appreciation of a prevailing human culture of sin, but it does undermine the notion of a "fall" in relation to which incarnation and the cross are understood as a response. Adjusting redemption theory to the new scientific story of the rise of the human will have an impact on how the economy of grace should be construed. Another example of the impact of science on theological understanding accompanies a new understanding of creation itself as an ongoing evolutionary process. This story encourages a Christian interpretation of the Spirit and Wisdom of God as the inner constituent divine power of evolutionary creation. But this posits the Spirit of

---

6. Francis X. Clooney, "Learning to See: Comparative Practice and the Widening of Theological Vision," *Proceedings of the Catholic Theological Society of America* 58 (2003): 1–15; Rita M. Gross and Rosemary R. Ruether, *Religious Feminism and the Future of the Planet: A Christian-Buddhist Conversation* (New York: Continuum, 2001); Keith Ward, *Religion and Creation* (New York: Oxford University Press, 1996).

7. Daryl P. Domning, *Original Selfishness: Original Sin and Evil in the Light of Evolution* (Burlington, VT: Ashgate, 2006); Geiko Mueller-Fahrenholz, *God's Spirit: Transforming a World in Crisis* (New York: Continuum, 1995); Karl Schmitz-Moorman with James F. Salmon, *Theology of Creation in an Evolutionary World* (Cleveland: Pilgrim, 1997); Raymund Schwager, *Banished from Eden: Original Sin and Evolutionary Theory in the Drama of Salvation* (Herefordshire, UK: Gracewing, 2006).

God, which is often considered as synonymous with grace itself, as prior to Jesus Christ in the economy of salvation. In other words, the whole creative evolutionary process finds its source and ground in the power of the Spirit and thus grace. When this "picture" then begins to function as a primary imaginative framework of understanding the economy of salvation, it produces a decidedly different worldview than what was previously in place. A cosmocentric way of thinking suggests an ordering of the Trinity as Father, Spirit, and Son; the Son is the revealer of what has been going on from the beginning. These examples suggest that the dialogue with science is drawing the theology of grace into a new place.

Method

A systematic understanding of any doctrine consists of a methodical unfolding of its meaning and an attempt to display its truth. The doctrines of sin and grace make up part of the tradition of the self-understanding of the Christian community from its beginning. These teachings lie embedded in the founding Scriptures and the history of the church's confessional witness. Thus, these categories may be considered as simply given; the notions of sin and grace are intrinsic parts of Christian language and belief. But what do they mean? Do they indeed correspond to and accurately describe human existence as it is experienced today by Christians and others?

These questions, which arise automatically in any reflective consideration of any doctrine, define the overall method employed here. The general logic of that method may be stated concisely in the following way: Given these doctrines of the church as they appear in its foundational sources and classical symbols, an effort will be made, first, to make sense out of the doctrines and, second, to show how they illumine the actual situation of human existence. The truth of these doctrines then will appear in the measure in which they actually disclose our human existence in a mediated but self-evident way.

This general logic can be specified in the following two steps: First, the analysis begins with a preliminary anthropology. This description of human existence as it is experienced today serves as an a priori of the investigation of sin and grace. On the one hand, this can represent only a particular interpretation of our common situation. On the other hand, this description is not closed, but meant to open up the mystery that human existence is to questions that demand some kind of response.

Second, the questions arising out of common human experience today will be addressed to the traditional symbols of sin and grace. In this procedure, then, the doctrines of sin and grace will be interpreted in such a way that they will shed light on the human existence that embodies these questions. The doctrines of sin and grace will appear intelligible in the measure in which the questions to which they respond genuinely represent our situation, the doctrines themselves appear coherent, and they open up human freedom to meaningful action in the world. The interpretation will be faithful to tradition and authentic by being open to the symbols of the past, allowing them to shape our understanding.

From beginning to end, the method employed here is dialogical and interpretative. The point is not to represent the historical understanding of the doctrines of sin and grace at any point in the past of the church, although this is where one must begin. It is rather to draw that meaning forward into our own context to shed light on human existence today.

Division

The method involved in this systematic account of the doctrines of sin and grace yields the following division of the material: The first part will contain a preliminary anthropology showing that human existence must be considered from both an individual and a social perspective. These two levels of human existence account for a twofold perspective on sin and grace. The second and third parts will then deal with sin individually and socially. The fourth and fifth parts will treat the symbol of grace from the same two perspectives. The final part of this chapter will discuss the relevance of these doctrines for spirituality. No doctrine has a greater bearing on Christian life than the doctrine of grace in response to sin, death, and ultimate human destiny.

A Preliminary Anthropology

The following characterization of human existence will be no more than preliminary. It seeks to describe the essence of the way the human phenomenon appears in common experience. What are the profound junctures at which human existence today becomes a question to itself?

Human existence may be characterized as freedom. In such a definition, however, the term *freedom* should be understood both substantively and analogously. Ordinarily, the word *freedom* points to a quality of human existence. In this case, however, the term indicates what human existence is in distinction from the existence of other creatures. Human existence is freedom. The definition of human existence as freedom enables one to transcend the alternatives of substance and process philosophy, for existential freedom always is the act of becoming. But the

term is analogous as well, for the freedom that constitutes the human manifests itself on a large variety of levels.

On the most fundamental level, freedom may be understood as synonymous with the human spirit; the human spirit is freedom, a freedom that always in some measure transcends the determinations of matter. The elemental freedom that constitutes the human appears everywhere in human action: in self-consciousness itself, in thinking, in synthetic understanding, in weighing options, in deciding, in acting this way as opposed to that. The human spirit is spirit by being freedom: the freedom of the spirit to transcend physical necessity by bending back on itself in reflection, to stand outside itself by a consciousness of its own consciousness, and to choose against an impulse to do otherwise. Thus, freedom reveals itself in the individual psychologically as the self, and corporately it manifests itself in the culture with which human beings inform nature. If the category of freedom is neither exaggerated nor minimized, but allowed to refer to the inner core of the spiritual existence that constitutes humanity, then human existence may be defined as freedom.

Human freedom is constituted at a variety of distinct but inseparable levels that one might call dimensions of human being. For example, human freedom bears an essential relationship to the external world. It is intrinsically related to matter, to the physical world of nature and the environment; human existence is in continuity with other forms of life. One cannot understand human freedom simply as standing over against the worlds studied by the sciences; freedom unfolds within them. An understanding of human existence, even theologically, should include analogous correlations with the world and other forms of life. Another dimension is temporal-historical: human freedom at any given time is intrinsically related to and constituted by a solidarity with and responsibility to the past and the future. These dimensions will not receive the explicit attention they deserve, but remain implicit in the analysis that follows.

Two dimensions bear a special importance for understanding human existence today: the individual and social dimensions of freedom. The individual dimension of human freedom appears readily enough to immediate self-consciousness. Existentialism has thoroughly analyzed the presence to and responsibility for oneself that constitute the individual's freedom. In the West, the inviolability of personal autonomy hardly needs an apology; in North American culture, various forms of individualism are accepted implicitly as dogma. By contrast, the social constitution of human freedom is not self-evident and needs to be demonstrated to ordinary consciousness.

That human beings are not totally autonomous subjects can be shown from many points of view. Human freedom begins at birth, when human beings are in a state of total dependence on their environment, and freedom matures over a long period of time in which individuals gain their personal identity within the second womb of society. Society provides each person's language, which largely mediates the very power to think; culture provides a set of values that largely determine the concrete things that people hold dear. Psychologically, one's objective image of the self is derived from interaction with other selves. Fundamental moral dispositions and the conscience by which people judge and are judged are partly fashioned within us by those outside us.[8] The social environment that is internalized in the becoming of each individual cannot be considered a function of any single person's freedom. Objective patterns of interdependence are prior to any individual freedom and mold it in some measure. On the social level, then, human existence or freedom cannot be considered a collection of individual freedoms. Corporate and social existence enjoys a certain autonomy relative to each individual, and all individual freedoms are drawn up into this shaping solidarity.

These two dimensions of human existence unfold in a reciprocal, dynamic, and tensive relationship. On the one hand, each individual enjoys an inner autonomy that appears in self-consciousness as personal responsibility. But on the other hand, the self is always inescapably a responding self.[9] Individual freedom is always fashioned by interaction with the material world and the social world of behaviors and meanings that shape the self. The self is a social self. Viewed from the other direction, human freedom is a corporate and solidaristic phenomenon; individuals come into being and are sustained only within the relationships that help to define the very self of each one. After one has granted the dimension of the personal-individual constitution of human freedom and responsibility, one must also emphasize the social constitution and responsibility of human freedom.

On both levels, the modern experience of freedom indicates a power of creativity. The meaning and exercise of freedom extend well beyond a capacity to consider options and choose among several objects. Freedom makes

8. H. Richard Niebuhr, *The Responsible Self: An Essay in Christian Moral Philosophy* (New York: Harper & Row, 1963), 69–79.

9. The notion of the human person as a responding self, taken from H. Richard Niebuhr, implies that the self is intrinsically and essentially social.

new reality come into being; it creates, not in the theological sense "out of nothing," but out of the subjectivity of freedom itself and the raw material of the environment. Freedom fashions genuine novelty, what did not exist before. Thus, both personally and in the solidarity of corporate existence, human freedom continually refashions the world and in so doing re-creates itself. This modern insight of the awesome power and creativity of human freedom gives a new dimension to the patristic image of human existence as the image of God.

The shadow side of the capacity of human freedom for creativity consists in its power to destroy. Exhilaration at freedom's potential creativity cannot evade a sober analysis of what it has actually wrought. On the individual level of personal history, a lifetime of striving often ends in failure or in success at the expense of others. It seems a law of life. On the social level, enormous advances in science and technology have been turned into more effective instruments of human oppression and death. The statistical or quantitative increase of the human population of our planet is more than matched by an increase of human suffering. The sheer amount of poverty, hunger, lack of medicine, and early death of so many demonstrates that the actuality of human freedom cannot be conceived as simple creativity. The dark side of human freedom, its capacity for perversity, its aggressive self-seeking, its passive lack of concerned reaction, does not allow an easy optimistic anthropology. If this appears too strong a judgment, it is only because each person is all too able to make an accommodation, to define a small world for the self that is tolerably acceptable, to ignore the twentieth century as largely a century of death by human causes.

This hasty phenomenology of human existence as a praxis of freedom across time yields a fundamental experience of contrast that must structure all understanding of the human. On the one hand, human freedom appears to be a transcendent and creative power that constructs new reality and meaning in history. On the other hand, that very creativity appears fatally flawed. What ought to be is not; what should be is negated at every turn. The two experiences reinforce and augment each other; evil appears more pervasive against the background of the ideals that human freedom projects, the dreams dreamed and the values hoped for. And against the background of the chaos of human history, every little breakthrough of self-transcending love fuels new efforts of creative energy in hope.

Many questions arise out of this experience of duality and contrast. Two are especially crucial in our time for a Christian understanding of the nature of human existence. Both of them arise out of the context of the relation of human freedom to God, which has been explored in other doctrines, especially creation and Christology.

The doctrine of creation reveals that human existence has been constituted by God, who sustains it in its semiautonomous freedom. By "semiautonomous," I mean the autonomous creativity enjoyed by human beings within the larger context of being absolutely dependent on God for existence itself. Beyond this, Jesus Christ is the disclosure of God's salvation, God's initial and final benevolence in regard to human beings. In this context, the experience of the radical duality in human existence generates a first line of questioning relative to the status of human freedom before God. The first set of questions includes these: Given the experience of semiautonomous human freedom and its dual propensity for creativity and self-destruction, how does human existence stand now before God and relate to God? How does

God relate to it? Concretely, what is the character of the ongoing, saving dialogue between God and human existence across time? Within the context of the doctrine of creation and God's salvation revealed in Jesus, these questions concern the way God's salvation is played out concretely in actual historical existence.

A second line of questioning is equally important for any final understanding of human existence. One must suppose that in creating human existence as freedom, God had a purpose for that freedom. The question of the destiny and purpose of human freedom is inescapable; it necessarily arises, and one cannot avoid answering it at least implicitly by the logic of one's intentional action. Moreover, it is crucial in our time to recognize the two distinct aspects of the question—the one regarding freedom's ultimate destiny, the other concerning the purpose of human freedom within this world and history. For while the question of final destiny has long been given attention in the history of theology, the question of the purpose of human freedom in this world takes on an entirely new aspect in a historically conscious age. What is the inner reason for each person's creative freedom in the world? What are the intention and will of the Creator who bestows meaning and purpose on the collective exercise of human freedom *in this world?* This question is new today because it arises out of the new experience of the creativity of human freedom within the context of historical consciousness. Yet it is this purposiveness that is most threatened today. The diversity of responses to this issue, both theoretical and lived, amounts to a confusing chaos. And the massive human suffering witnessed in the world today throws into doubt the very meaningfulness of the history of this world. What is the Christian conception of the purpose of human freedom in history?

The two sets of questions proposed here find their Christian answer in the doctrines of sin and grace. These questions also help to illumine these doctrines by providing a way of interpreting their meaning relative to secular existence in the world and history. In addition, this preliminary anthropology provides a way of structuring an approach to the doctrines of sin and grace. On the one hand, because of the two distinct but inseparable dimensions of human freedom, sin and grace must each be explored on both the individual and social levels, for sin and grace qualify the whole history of human freedom. Individually and socially, both symbols disclose real transcendental dimensions of human existence as such and the concrete historical working out of these dimensions. On the other hand, the realities of sin and grace must be understood within the context of the purpose of human existence in this world and its final destiny. The following account, then, will deal with sin and then grace, first on the personal and then on the social level of our corporate existence, and always within the context of the questions of God's interaction with human existence in history and the purpose of human freedom.

Sin as a Dimension of Individual Existence

The subject of this discussion is the sinful condition of human existence as distinct from sinful acts. Unless explicitly stated to the contrary, the word *sin* refers to what has traditionally been called original sin. The term *original sin* has had simultaneously two interrelated referents: the originating sin at the dawn of human existence, often called the fall, and the damaging effects of that sin, resulting in a sinful condition of the

386 whole race. These two aspects will be merged together in this account.

The recognition of this sinful condition is a matter of faith. The doctrine of sin depends on some form of revelation. Despite the obvious moral evil massively displayed in human history, only a revelation of some other possibility can unveil the fact that this is not what human existence could or should be. The more obvious perception would depict human existence in continuity with the animal realm, where survival through competition, power, and violence is natural. Sin and grace then are simultaneously revealed, and each is perceptible only in the light of the other. An experience of grace thus enters into the account of sin, and sin will be the horizon for describing the experience of grace.[10] From the outset, one should understand that the doctrine of sin can be understood only in the context of an experience of standing before God.

It follows that, on its deepest level, the doctrine of sin is a doctrine of human freedom. In the end, it says the moral evil in the world is not due to either God or nature but emerges out of human freedom. Paradoxically, the bondage that the doctrine of sin points to is a bondage of spiritual freedom to itself.

The term *sin*, representing what has been called original sin, is used analogously. What is being described is not personal sin but a "condition" of freedom prior to its actual exercise. If one is to retain a doctrine of sin, one must link it to freedom itself. Sin, to really be sin yet not personal sin, must be a quality, structure, and dynamic process of freedom itself.

Before we turn to the sources for the doctrine of sin, a consideration of the state of the question in Catholic theology is in order.

Recent Catholic Theology of Sin

Current Roman Catholic theology of original sin is undergoing a radical transition and is marked by considerable pluralism. The reason for the many different theologies of sin is not difficult to pinpoint. The latest, most official teaching of the Catholic Church stems from the Council of Trent and is a reexpression of the doctrine formulated in the time of Augustine, largely through the influence of Augustine himself. But that early fifth-century expression of doctrine clashes with current conceptions of the world: our knowledge of the age of the planet; our sense of the evolution of the species; our growing knowledge of our continuity with other forms of life; our psychological views of the destructiveness of guilt; our attempts to formulate a more positive view of matter, the human body, sexuality, and emotion; the inadmissibility of guilt without responsibility. Truly, the doctrine of original sin in its received form does not appear credible.

The theological reinterpretation of the doctrine of sin progressed mainly on three fronts since Vatican II. The first has run parallel with the renewal of biblical studies. The historical-critical method allowed exegetes to understand Scripture in its own terms. It enabled theologians to get behind the doctrinal framework and see the degree to which later doctrine exceeds the scriptural witness. Indeed, in many respects,

---

10. Because of this mutuality of sin and grace, the account of sin that follows will be incomplete in itself and must be understood in relation to the theology of grace.

the Scriptures provide little support for some details of the developed doctrine.[11]

Second, patristic scholarship and the study of Augustine provide insight into why and how Augustine came to his formulation of the doctrine of sin. In effect, this critical, historical work relativizes Augustine's theology and the particular formulation of the doctrine that resulted from it. By displaying Augustine's teaching as a function of his time and experience, this historical work opened up further the possibility of reinterpreting the doctrine of Trent that is so dependent upon it.[12]

Third, current systematic theology displays a host of different constructive reinterpretations of the doctrine that attempt to make it intelligible.[13] In one form or another, these constructive, speculative theologies proceed by a method of correlation. Such a method brings the received doctrine into dialogue with current theological conceptions of human existence that are themselves informed by scientific and philosophical thought. The following examples represent some advances made after Vatican II that led to the current context described earlier.

In the theology of Piet Schoonenberg, the distinctiveness of original sin is correlated with the sin of the world. The concept of the sin of the world is drawn from Scripture and points to the accumulation of sin in history, which in turn constitutes the situation into which everyone is born. The notion of "situation" is key here: "Situation may be defined as 'the totality of the circumstances in which somebody or something stands at a certain moment, the totality of circumstances prevailing in a certain domain.'"[14] Thus, the situation of sin is prior to the exercising of freedom of each one and intrinsically enters into human freedom to determine the direction of the commitment and decisions of all individuals. Schoonenberg believes that all the assertions of Trent can be preserved by reinterpreting them within the framework of the sin of the world.[15]

A considerable amount of reflection has been devoted to the doctrine of sin within the context of an evolutionary view of the emergence of human freedom. Paradise is not a state at the beginning of the human race, but a utopian symbol of the goal of human existence. Moreover, an evolutionary framework postulates elements of analogous continuity between human existence and the physical and organic world out of which it arose. Thus, for example, Juan Luis Segundo sees analogies in human existence of a tension between two fundamental evolutionary forces, entropy and negentropy. In human freedom, these are represented by the pull of spontaneous, routine, mechanistic, and unfree behavior over against the liberating, creative energy of

11. For example, A. M. Dubarle, *The Biblical Doctrine of Original Sin* (London: Geoffrey Chapman, 1964); Herbert Haag, *Is Original Sin in Scripture?* (New York: Sheed & Ward, 1969); Kevin Condon, "The Biblical Doctrine of Original Sin," *Irish Theological Quarterly* 34 (1967): 20–36.

12. See Henri Rondet, *Original Sin: The Patristic and Theological Background* (Shannon, Ireland: Ecclesia, 1972).

13. Several works survey the developments in the systematic theology of original sin: James L. Connor, "Original Sin: Contemporary Approaches," *Theological Studies* 29 (1968): 215–40; George Vandervelde, *Original Sin: Two Major Trends in Contemporary Roman Catholic Reinterpretation* (Washington, DC: University Press of America, 1981); Brian McDermott, "The Theology of Original Sin: Recent Developments," *Theological Studies* 38 (1977): 478–512; Peter Gill, *Original Sin* (London: Faber & Faber, 2002).

14. Piet Schoonenberg, *Man and Sin: A Theological View* (Notre Dame, IN: University of Notre Dame Press, 1965), 104–5.

15. Ibid., 177–91.

grace that urges loving and humanizing acts of freedom. Sin, then, is part of a permanent structure of human existence always in tension with grace.[16] It is not that God the Creator willed sin; sin is still a function of freedom, but there is a deep tensive structure in human existence that leads to sin and is analogous in all of reality. The price of a really creative human freedom is a situation in which actual sinning remains an ongoing fact.

Some theologians deny the existence of original sin as a distinct reality in itself, that is, as distinguishable from personal sin. What the doctrine really signifies is the profound entrapment of human freedom in a tendency to sin. And this is manifested, as it were, in the "fact" that all human beings sin. The point of the doctrine of original sin is simply that all are sinners and depend absolutely on God's power of grace for the salvific exercise of freedom.[17]

Many of the insights of the recent theology of sin are drawn together in the reinterpretation of Stephen J. Duffy.[18] The distinctiveness of his essay lies in the method underlying it. Duffy is less interested in a systematic accounting for all the elements of the received doctrine, and more interested in examining what it reveals about ourselves. His method is hermeneutical. He reviews the Adamic myth, Paul, and Augustine with a view to uncovering the dark side of human existence that they open up to our self-awareness. He then weaves together insights from a variety of contemporary authors to explore several dimensions of the sin that works its way in us. In short, the analysis is descriptive of an anthropology of sin.

The treatment of sin and grace that follows employs a similar hermeneutical method. The focus of attention is human life; the goal is to illumine human existence under the light of the traditional doctrinal symbols of sin and grace. In this way, the doctrines themselves are reinterpreted. The result will be an analytic, descriptive account of the meaning of these doctrines for Christian life and spirituality. This analytic description of sin unfolds on two levels, the individual and social. These correspond to a need for both transcendental and historical methods of analysis. Neither is complete in itself; the complexity of sin demands that both of these dimensions always be understood together. I begin with the sources of the doctrine.

The Symbolic Sources of the Doctrine

An account of the doctrine of sin should begin with the data of Christian witness to the experience of it, with the sources of the doctrine and its traditional symbols. The term *symbol* refers to any concept, word, event, thing, person, or literary expression that mediates an experience of transcendent reality. As a modern equivalent of the analogy of faith, the religious symbol shares in the reality it mediates to consciousness. But a religious symbol does not represent or correspond to the transcendent mystery it points to in the same direct manner that concepts represent the objects of our knowledge of this world. Symbols should not be understood as a weak mode of understanding doctrinal expressions of faith, but as vehicles that expand the hori-

---

16. See Juan Luis Segundo, *Evolution and Guilt* (Maryknoll, NY: Orbis, 1974); idem, *An Evolutionary Approach to Jesus of Nazareth* (Maryknoll, NY: Orbis, 1988). See also McDermott, "The Theology of Original Sin," 496–502.

17. See Alfred Vanneste, *The Dogma of Original Sin* (Brussels: Vander, 1971). See also McDermott, "The Theology of Original Sin," 493–96.

18. Stephen J. Duffy, "Our Hearts of Darkness: Original Sin Revisited," *Theological Studies* 49 (1988): 597–622.

zon of human perception toward an encounter with reality not available to ordinary conceptual knowledge. The original symbols that are the source of a doctrine and provide the first expression of it are fundamental to its interpretation.

One of the principal sources of the doctrine of sin is the classical biblical story of a first pair of human beings, originally at peace with God and completely integrated within themselves, with each other, and within their environment. Through outside temptation, they rebelled and disobeyed God, in the wake of which came a history of sin (Genesis 3ff.). This story is a narrative and mythic symbol. It deals with human existence by depicting it in a primeval or mythic time, after creation but, as it were, prior to actual history.[19] It thus preserves deep experiences about the nature of human existence, a subject to which I shall return in dealing with how it should be interpreted. But the single most important conclusion of Catholic biblical studies relative to original sin consists in breaking down the misinterpretations of the story of Adam and Eve and their "fall" as a descriptive historical account, and breaking it open as an interpretation of ourselves.

A pastoral note may be helpful in the use of the category of myth. There is no common definition of myth, because myths can be studied and analyzed from many different points of view. A myth may be understood as a traditional story that represents the deep truths about the world, nature, and human existence. The story

of Adam and Eve is also etiological; it represents the "origins" of sin as if it were an "explanation" of the present situation of sin in the world. Transcendent mystery is depicted in anthropomorphic forms. But the term *myth* will be received differently by different audiences. For example, young people may have grown up believing that the story of Adam and Eve is a literal historical account of the origins of the human race. Particular attention, therefore, is needed to explain and mediate an understanding of this biblical symbol.[20]

The second major biblical source of the doctrine of sin is found in Paul. In his Letter to the Romans, Paul personifies sin as a power or force in world history and in the human person that keeps human freedom in bondage. The self is divided: "For I do not do the good I want, but the evil I do not want is what I do. Now if I do what I do not want, it is no longer I that do it, but sin which dwells within me" (Rom. 7:19-20). The power of sin, a universal force in the world, resides in each one of us.

In Rom. 5:12-21, Paul gives an extended contrast between Christ and Adam. Adam is taken as a real person, the progenitor of the race. The point of the comparison is to show that, whereas the powers of sin and death originated with Adam, the righteousness and eternal life caused through Christ abound even more. In the course of this comparison, however, Paul indicates that the sin of Adam is the cause of the universal condition of sinfulness and of spiritual

---

19. "The narrative explains human existence in its essential elements as something which came about in primeval time, and indeed the created state in contrast to the state of humanity limited by death, suffering and sin. It is a misunderstanding of the narrative as a whole to explain it as a succession of historical or quasi-historical incidents." Claus Westermann, *Genesis 1–11: A Commentary* (London: SPCK, 1984), 276. Westermann provides a full commentary summing up current exegetical opinion on the narrative of Genesis 2–3.

20. See John L. McKenzie, "Aspects of Old Testament Thought," in *The New Jerome Biblical Commentary*, ed. R. E. Brown, J. A. Fitzmyer, and R. E. Murphy (Englewood Cliffs, NJ: Prentice Hall, 1990), 1288b–90a. On religious symbols and how they communicate, see Roger Haight, *Dynamics of Theology* (Maryknoll, NY: Orbis, 2001), chs. 7–8.

and bodily death. Since the narrative in Genesis is etiological, that is, a projected explanation of the present condition of humankind, Adam is depicted as affecting that situation, which is then compounded by a history of actual personal sinning. Paul, however, does not explain this causality by inheritance. Although the later doctrine of an original sin in which all participated by inheritance was read back into this passage of Paul, it is agreed today that it cannot be found there. The intention of Paul is to assert that all are sinners and share in a situation that is universal from the beginning. But rather than providing a developed doctrine of original sin, the emphasis of the entire passage is on Christ as Savior.[21]

More than any other single source, Augustine is responsible for developing the doctrine of sin as it is known in the Western tradition. Augustine's basic position on sin and grace was in place before he encountered the doctrine of Pelagius and his followers in 411. The Pelagians had a more optimistic view of human nature and of the power of human freedom than Augustine, and thus a very different notion of grace. For example, part of God's grace is God's commands, and if God commands, it must be presupposed that human freedom can obey. For Augustine, all possibility of salvation originated not with human freedom but with God's grace; even the impulse toward God was impelled by the love of God that "has been poured into our hearts through the Holy Spirit which has been given to us" (Rom. 5:5). The completely prevenient or initiating quality of grace, passively received

without any merit, is supremely illustrated in Augustine's doctrine of original sin.[22]

It is often pointed out that Augustine's Latin text of Scripture led him to interpret Rom. 5:12 as saying that all humankind sinned in Adam. All human beings were sinners in the progenitor's sin insofar as all emerged from him as sinners, propagated sinful along the line by inherited sinful flesh. But far more deeply than exegesis ran Augustine's fundamental conviction, the central point to which he always returns: if all are not sinners, then Christ is not the Savior of all. But this conviction was indeed radical; it knew no exceptions; it applied even to infants. The practice of infant baptism was already in place, a baptism that was for the remission of sins. And other Latin theologians had already linked infant baptism to an objective sinful condition. For Augustine, then, the conviction of the absolute necessity of God's salvific grace through Christ was confirmed by infant baptism, which entailed an inherited sin. Thus, the doctrine of original sin appears as the dramatic counterpoint of Augustine's theology of grace.

The Pelagians were the occasion for Augustine's doctrine of original sin becoming the doctrine of the church. At the Synod of Carthage held in 418 to take up the teachings of the Pelagians, the doctrine of an original sin inherited from Adam was affirmed (Denzinger-Schönmetzer, *Enchiridion Symbolorum* [hereafter DS], 222–30). But the issues of human nature, freedom, grace, and original sin lingered on and had to be taken up again a century later. In 529, at

---

21. See Joseph A. Fitzmyer, "The Letter to the Romans," in *The New Jerome Biblical Commentary*, 844b–47a, for a concise but thorough commentary on this passage. See also Fitzmyer, "Pauline Theology," in ibid., 1402a–3a. For a survey of the notion of sin in the Bible as a whole, see Stanislas Lyonnet, *Sin, Redemption, and Sacrifice: A Biblical and Patristic Study* (Rome: Biblical Institute Press, 1970), 1–57.

22. Jaroslav Pelikan, *The Christian Tradition*, vol. 1, *The Emergence of the Catholic Tradition (100–600)* (Chicago: University of Chicago Press, 1971), 302.

the Synod of Orange, the essential Augustinian theology was reaffirmed (DS 370–97). These canons and decrees from Carthage and Orange became the substance of the church's doctrine, and their content was reaffirmed at Trent.

In the Roman Catholic tradition, the Council of Trent contains the fullest doctrinal teaching on original sin. This teaching is put forward in the council's Decree on Original Sin of 1546 (DS 1510–16). But it is not substantially new doctrine; for the most part, it repeats the teachings of Carthage and Orange, which stem from Augustine's interpretation of the doctrine. The major assertions of the Council of Trent, which are a reprise of fifth-century doctrine, are the following: Adam (and Eve), the first parents, sinned and thus lost the original holiness and justice in which they were created, and incurred God's wrath and the punishment of death. The consequences of this one sin were subsequently transmitted to all human beings by propagation, not by imitation; all human beings are born into a state of sin and guilt, a state of spiritual death, which the salvation of Christ alone, mediated by baptism, can remit. In reaction to Luther, the council also taught that although concupiscence, which stems from sin, remains after baptism, it is not properly sin in itself.[23]

This history of the doctrine of sin is not smooth or continuous; it contains a sharp break. That break begins to show itself in late Jewish literature, where Adam is presented as a real human being. This understanding continues through Paul to its climax with the doctrine of original sin in Augustine.[24] But the break goes much deeper than this interpretation. What has occurred by the time of Augustine is a passage from a symbolic understanding of the story of Adam and Eve to a false claim of theoretical or rational knowledge.[25] In other words, the primal symbols of faith stimulated theological reflection and the desire to understand in more conceptual ways, and based on that, the faith experience contained in the foundational symbols was changed into beliefs conceived as knowledge. This was hardened into doctrines that seem to convey religious truth in historical terms or propositions that seem to describe reality directly, if not literally and univocally. The result is that the doctrine of Trent seems at several points to be contradicted either by the descriptions of human origins by science or by current religious sensibility. For example, what does it mean to say that a newly born baby is sinful and guilty?

This split between the traditional doctrine and current understanding of reality has resulted in the large number of essays and books that reinterpret the Tridentine doctrine of sin. A study of these reinterpretations and of reinterpretations of Augustine can be depicted in a typology of models for understanding the doctrine of original sin.[26] The different models exemplify attempts to preserve the inner truth

---

23. Council of Trent, Decree on Original Sin (1546), in *The Christian Faith in the Doctrinal Documents of the Catholic Church*, ed. J. Neuner and J. Dupuis (Westminster, MD: Christian Classics, 1975), 129–32.

24. See Westermann, *Genesis 1–11*, 275–77. See also Fitzmyer, "Pauline Theology," 1402a–b.

25. See Paul Ricoeur, "'Original Sin': A Study in Meaning," in *The Conflict of Interpretations: Essays in Hermeneutics*, ed. Don Ihde (Evanston, IL: Northwestern University Press, 1974), 269–86. For the same point, made in terms of the philosophy of language, see Gabriel Daly, "Theological Models in the Doctrine of Original Sin," *Heythrop Journal* 3 (1972): 121–24.

26. Daly, "Theological Models," 121–42, sees the main problem of the doctrine of original sin stemming from a literal use of language. He considers reinterpretations of the doctrine in terms of other models than the "genetic model" of Augustine.

of the doctrine, while at the same time transcending but not bypassing the formulas of the Council of Trent, and to reconcile them with contemporary conceptions of the origins of human existence.

Another way of interpreting the doctrine of original sin would be explicitly to employ a hermeneutical method of correlation, a method that in some respects is implicitly operative in all recent theology of original sin. A brief outline of what this entails will explain how the sources of the doctrine come to bear on our understanding of sin today. Such a method involves going back to the primal symbols through which the doctrine was first mediated in the Jewish and Christian traditions. The historical-critical approach to Scripture has uncovered the symbolic quality of the Genesis account of Adam and Eve. The first premise in such a method requires that the symbolic nature of this account be respected.

This premise raises an issue that is crucial for the theological interpretation of the doctrine of original sin. The language of Augustine, the early councils, and especially the Council of Trent does not appear to be symbolic language and may not have been considered such by its authors, at least not in those terms. Rather, it is clear that their assertions unfolded within a historical framework. In other words, the language presupposes Adam and Eve as historical persons; this is the context of the thought. But doctrinal language generally, insofar as it deals with God and the mystery of human existence before God, entails the language of faith, which is always symbolic. This is even more clearly the case insofar as the language of Trent actually reflects the imaginative symbolic framework of an etiological story or narrative. Thus, the Tridentine doctrine of original sin is really symbolic; it shares in the same character of the story of Genesis upon which it depends. Thus, it is to be understood and interpreted in the same way as one would interpret the myth of Adam and Eve. And, inversely, by unfolding the symbolic significance of the narrative of the fall, one is at the same time reaching the deepest intentionality of the doctrinal tradition as well.

An intentional analysis of the primal myth of the sin of Adam and Eve will reveal the deep themes concerning human existence that are embedded in it.[27] Beneath the story lies the experience of sin and guilt; this penitential experience forms the context in which the story was composed, and the experience it expresses and interprets. By analyzing the structure and dynamics of the story, one can uncover that experience, not in merely psychological terms, but precisely in the terms of the symbols themselves. For example, the story indicates that human existence is fallen, not from a past state, but from its essential potentiality and what it is designed by God to be. Human existence is not what it should be when viewed in the light of God's single creative and salvational intention. Worse, this condition includes a certain propensity to sin. This experience is universalized; sin is a universal condition affecting all human beings, both as individuals and as groups. The external-

---

27. "On the one hand, it must be said that the concept [of original sin] refers back to the myth, and the myth refers back to the penitential experience of ancient Israel and the Church. Intentional analysis goes from pseudo-rationality to pseudo-history, and from pseudo-history to ecclesiastical *lived experience*. But the path that must be taken [in interpretation] is the opposite one: myth is not only pseudo-history, it is a revealing. As such, it unearths a dimension of experience which otherwise would have remained without expression and which would have aborted precisely as lived experience." Ricoeur, "'Original Sin,'" 285. For a more general discussion of the method employed here, see Haight, *Dynamics of Theology*, chs. 9–10.

ization of temptation reflects the universal tendency of human beings to find excuses, and the deceit of the serpent thematizes the illusion of unlimited human freedom and autonomy. The condition of sin is "objective" in the sense of being prior to the exercise of our human freedom, prior to conscious responsibility; human beings do not simply participate in sin, they discover it as a power that is there already. And this situation is not from God, for God's creation, complete before the symbolic first sin, is good; sin thus emerges out of freedom itself.[28]

But the interpretation of the doctrine of sin does not end with a consideration of the sources. These themes must be brought forward and made to interpret human existence today. In other words, we must apply this symbolic doctrine and use it to understand ourselves. The doctrine must be expressed in more reflective and universal, but still symbolic and theological, language. The story of Adam and Eve is the story of human existence itself. It points to a drama that transpires in every person, in society, and in the interaction between the individual and the social dimension of the human. The story accurately portrays point by point the concupiscence, temptation, and sin of all human beings personally and collectively. Its narrative represents a pattern of behavior that is reenacted in every age.[29]

It is important to grasp the reasons that underlie this doctrine of sin. What is the need for such a doctrine, and why have Christians always insisted on it? Besides the fact that the doctrine of sin truthfully portrays human existence, the necessity of the doctrine can be recognized in the fundamental questions to which it responds. The question underlying the Adamic story is basic in the light of the doctrine of creation: What is the source of moral evil in the world? The doctrine is central for understanding God and human existence in the context of God's creation. The biblical doctrine is that what God creates is good. The doctrine of sin maintains that its origin is not God; the source of sin is human existence itself.

In the Christian tradition, another reason for the doctrine was added to the rationale found in the Jewish writings. The doctrine of sin underscores the universal need for God's salvation revealed in Jesus Christ—thus, Paul's contrast between Adam and Christ. The doctrine of sin may be seen as a negative way of asserting the universal relevance of the event of salvation in Jesus Christ. The final argument of Augustine against Pelagius is always that, if human beings do not need grace, then Christ came in vain.

While both of these traditional logics remain valid today, there is a new exigency for the doctrine of sin that is more pointedly anthropological. The doctrine accurately portrays human existence as it is—that is, as both sinful and free. The present context for understanding this doctrine, however, is quite different from that of Augustine and Trent in two ways. First, unlike Augustine, Christians today do not live in a world marked by an elitist striving for Pelagian self-perfection; rather, our world is marked by a complacent acceptance of the world as it is and an acceptance of sin as if it were not sin but merely "the way things are."[30] Sin then must be highlighted as a misuse of human freedom, and grace

---

28. See Paul Ricoeur, *The Symbolism of Evil* (Boston: Beacon, 1969), 232–60; idem, "'Original Sin.'"

29. Langdon Gilkey, *Message and Existence: An Introduction to Christian Theology* (New York: Seabury, 1979), 135–39.

30. Gabriel Daly, "Original Sin," in *The New Dictionary of Theology*, ed. Joseph A. Komonchak, Mary Collins, and Dermot A. Lane (Wilmington, DE: Glazier, 1987), 730.

394   as the power to resist it. Second, and theologically, grace and sin cannot be reified; they should be understood, not in objective and quasi-physical categories, but in the personal, dialogical terms of God's self-communication as Spirit to enable the potential of human freedom and the sinful resistance of freedom to that grace. In this context, sin will appear as an inhibiting structure within the emergence of freedom itself.

In sum, given the traditional testimony to the experience of the sinfulness of humankind, the task of theology is to provide a descriptive analysis of human existence that both makes sense of the doctrine and at the same time allows it to shed light on actual existence, on the understanding of individual and collective history. I turn now to that descriptive analysis.

Concupiscence and Temptation

Concupiscence has traditionally been understood as an effect of sin, a concomitant of the condition of sinfulness. I begin the analysis of sin with concupiscence because it is most prominent in human experience.[31]

The freedom that is human existence is not unmixed; there is no pure freedom. Human existence is limited, qualified, and determined by physical nature—the physiological, biological, psychological, temperamental, and emotional structures that help constitute the one single and whole person. Each individual person is both free and unfree, free and determined.

As a result, human life unfolds within a fundamental tension of forces that have a bearing on the actual being of each one. For on the one hand, freedom is oriented to posit or dispose the self completely, fully, and without reserve in being before God. But on the other hand, because of the resistance to freedom that stems from the spontaneous and determining desires or impulses of nature, it is impossible to commit the self completely and fully. On a first and fundamental level, then, concupiscence refers to the sheer resistance of the whole of an individual to the freedom of self-actualizations for good or for evil. Concupiscence in this sense is not an evil; it is simply the finite condition and actual situation of human existence.[32]

Because the intrinsic finality of human freedom is toward a self-disposition in basic trust, faith, and love relative to God and according to God's will, the tension between freedom and unfreedom or determination becomes temptation. On the one hand, the infinite reach of freedom tends toward absolute existence, which can be guaranteed only by God, but on the other hand, the finite, limited, and determined aspects of human nature make it subject to the laws of diminishment and ultimate death. This tension creates a fundamental existential anxiety in and of human being itself, which may or may not come to psychological awareness, but which is always operative within human freedom.[33] This anxiety is ambiguous, both positive and negative at the same time. On the one hand, anxiety is the

---

31. This analysis of the dynamics of concupiscence and the "prior sin" is dependent on Karl Rahner, "The Theological Concept of *Concupiscentia*," in *Theological Investigations* (Baltimore: Helicon, 1964), 1:347–82; and Reinhold Niebuhr, *The Nature and Destiny of Man* (New York: Scribner, 1964), 1:179–86.

32. Surely concupiscence may be *experienced* as negative with respect to the revealed final destiny of human existence as union with God. See Rahner, "The Theological Concept of *Concupiscentia*," 375–76. But in itself, concupiscence is simply the entailment of the finite structure of existence as freedom in tension with nature.

33. This anxiety is a transcendental or universal structure of human existence. But it unfolds concretely and historically in a different way in each person. For example, anxiety about one's being will undoubtedly manifest itself in a

condition for the possibility of human creativity and achievement; on the other hand, it is a temptation to posit the self in being now against the threat of nonbeing or being-unto-death by proclaiming the self a fully autonomous center of being. This anxiety about being is so deep that motivational analysis cannot sort out the ambiguity in the exercise of human freedom. Because freedom cannot fully commit or determine the self in being, because it always suffers the threat of nonbeing, it is always tempted and in some measure seeks to secure itself in being on its own terms.

This initial approach to sin in descriptive analytic terms corresponds to Paul's dramatic and classic description of the divided self already cited. That description continues as follows: "For I delight in the law of God, in my inmost self, but I see in my members another law at war with the law of my mind and making me captive to the law of sin which dwells in my members. Wretched man that I am!" (Rom. 7:22-24).

Sin

Adam, it was said, is the symbol for every person and for the collectivity. The story of Adam and Eve is also the symbol for the emergence of freedom in history. To understand the significance of these symbols, therefore, one must understand the sinful condition of human existence as a process, a historical drama in each person and, as we shall see, in society; that drama characterizes human existence in its very unfolding as freedom. On the level of the individual, the imagination should be focused equally on the emergence of freedom from infant potentiality to its flowering in responsibility and on the exercise of freedom in every moment of conscious adult life. The dynamics of sin can be understood through the elements that are involved in it.

The point of departure for the emergence of sin is the coming into existence of human freedom that lacks an appropriation of God's self-communication in grace.[34] But grace should not be understood primarily in objective terms, because foundationally, grace is the personal self-presence of God to human beings in love. Therefore, the objective condition of not being able to respond to God's grace because of a lack of responsibility should not be considered as sin in any sense. One obviously cannot respond to grace at the beginning of human life. Freedom begins as a potentiality that is meant to grow into responsibility and actual response to God's grace.

This condition of coming into existence without an appropriation of God's grace is made more complex by the dynamics of concupiscence and temptation. In the beginning, human freedom exists as a mere virtuality that must emerge within the determinisms of nature that also constitute each person. Indeed, the historical process of that emergence depends on those determinisms and can never overcome them.

Within this complex structure and not apart from it, the sinful condition of human existence appears within the emerging exercise of freedom itself. The permanent threat of

---

distinctive way among the poor who have no job, little to eat, and no access to medical service. See Gregory Baum, *Theology and Society* (New York: Paulist, 1987), 263.

34. This theological construct is an attempt to account for the universal operation of God's grace in all people. The terms "God's self-communication," the "Spirit of God," and "grace" are used synonymously. It should be noted that appropriation of God's presence and initiative does not necessarily entail explicit awareness of the provenance of this empowerment.

nonbeing involved in the condition of finitude and the contingency of being, the resistance of nature to the full disposition of the self before God, and the positive temptation to posit the self in being autonomously—these qualify every human act. Every human exercise of freedom is in danger of becoming an autonomous assertion of the self and, in that measure, a failure of total trust, complete faith, and absolute self-disposition before God, who alone can secure human existence in being. This is not to be construed as formal, conscious, and intentional sin; it is an existential condition that is actualized in an emergent exercise of freedom.

Sin is both a structure prior to the exercise of freedom and one that is actualized by freedom itself. The inherent lack of openness, faith, and love—the measure of failure in fully appropriating God's grace or even rejecting it—retains the status of "prior sin," the prior reason for this or that sinful action. Paradoxically, this emergent condition is prior to the concrete exercise of freedom (not chronologically, but as the deep structure out of which freedom operates) yet becomes actualized only with the exercise of freedom itself. Paradoxical, too, is the fact that the actualization of this structure, resulting in actual sins, is both inevitable and free. Sin cannot be considered necessary or caused by God's creation because, emerging with the exercise of freedom, especially within the context of God's ever-present offer of grace, human beings could act in a totally self-transcending trust in God as the security of their being.[35] They don't, however, and personal sinning is a universal phenomenon.[36]

But there is more to it than a lack of an adequate response to God as Spirit. Out of the structure of temptation and prior to particular personal sins, one finds a certain propensity to sin, an aversion to God and God's will for human self-transcendence, an active resistance to God. As Piet Smulders expressed it, "In the heart of human beings lies a kind of will not to love God; anterior to personal choice, it encompasses and fetters that choice."[37] This is what Augustine called the curvature of the self in upon the self, resulting in a kind of tendency away from God in the direction of self, and drawing all things into the self as means to end.[38]

In sum, sin on the individual level may be described as a structure and a process of human freedom that begins with a lack of an appropriation of God's grace but then qualifies every moment of a human being's existence in this world. This structure leads through concupiscence and temptation to the prior sin—that is, some measure of a lack of openness and surrender in self-actualization before God and according to

---

35. Reinhold Niebuhr, *The Nature and Destiny of Man*, 1:183.

36. This is not an empirical judgment, of course. It stems from the correspondence of the scriptural and doctrinal witness with the inner experience of repentance and remorse of the sinner. See Reinhold Niebuhr, *The Nature and Destiny of Man*, 1:255–60. Sin can be recognized only by the sinner. But the transcendental analysis of this experience reveals a structure in which all participate. Inevitability, then, is not necessity, because sin is a function of freedom. The notion of inevitability remains paradoxical and cannot be fully understood. It points to a *historical* rather than a metaphysically necessary condition of estrangement, and this will be developed further on the social level of human existence.

37. Piet Smulders, *The Design of Teilhard de Chardin: An Essay in Theological Reflection* (Westminster, MD: Newman, 1967), 176.

38. From this analysis, it is clear that baptism, as the Christian community's mediating sacrament of grace and faith in the name of Jesus, bears a direct relationship to the condition of the lack of grace and the lack of faith in the emergent freedom even of a child. He or she is initiated into the explicit community of grace and faith. This will become clearer in the discussion of the social dimensions of sin and grace.

God's will—and, more aggressively, to a propensity against the designs of God and for the self. Sin emerges as a fallen condition only when it is actualized through human freedom. But at the same time, it is not identical with any personal sin; it is a structured dynamic process of a lack of basic trust, faith, and love that is prior to and underlies every personal sin.[39]

This description of the sinful condition of human existence does not remove the ultimate mystery involved here. One cannot fully distinguish the propensity to evil that this sin generates from the structure of human existence itself, which comes from the hands of God.[40] Some reflections, however, are helpful in considering this mystery. In fact, God has chosen to create human existence through an evolutionary process, and now human history lies open to the future as a function of human freedom. The God who creates human freedom respects the creative autonomy that God established. So serious is this freedom that it contains the possibility of a rejection of God's own address in love together with the responsibility and power for true creativity within God's love.[41]

Finally, one must consider the nature of the personal sins that arise out of this emergent structure of sin. Sin itself can exist only in human freedom, in the spiritual dimension of human existence. But the roots of sin reach back into the polar tension between spirit and nature that structures human freedom. Thus, personal sins may be characterized according to the predominance of the one or the other pole in the dynamic structure of existence.[42] Such a description, however, remains abstract and simply points to two extreme possibilities on a continuous spectrum. On the one hand, the freedom and autonomy of the human spirit spawn aggressive and domineering acts of egocentrism and pride. All the power, creativity, generativity, and potential for achievement by human freedom become autonomous self-assertion over against what is other: other persons, society, the world, and even God. These are the active sins of aggression. But on the other hand, the intrinsic link of the human spirit to the determinisms of nature also spawns what may be called sins of passivity or omission. Still rooted in the dynamism of spirit, here freedom negates itself, refuses to act, and tries to escape the responsibility and potentiality intrinsic to freedom itself. Often, active sins are regarded as the more typical and destructive. But since the structure of anxiety is also the basis for creativity, when the sins of passivity or omission are viewed against the horizon of God's grace, and on the assumption that God has assigned a purpose for human freedom within this world, they appear as an abdication of responsibility that is equally serious

---

39. It is crucial to see that sin is both a structure and a dynamic process. If sin were not a process culminating in inherent attitudes prior to any actual sin, it could not itself be called "sin." The tradition supplies many defining names for this prior sin: pride, unfaith, idolatry, disobedience, rebellion, egocentrism, and so on. All of them bring out particular aspects of sin. Perhaps the most central is an egocentric autonomy that can manifest itself actively or passively, as aggressiveness or escape from freedom and responsibility.

40. In other words, the problem, not of sin but of the propensity to sin that seems to emerge out of the very structure of human existence, is similar to the problem of evil and suffering generally in the world; it is insoluble and transcendentally mysterious.

41. If one conceives of history as involving a genuine dialogue between God and human beings in such a way that human beings are real dialogue partners in freedom, then the possibility and even the temptation to reject God's free initiative can be coherently encompassed in this worldview.

42. Reinhold Niebuhr, *The Nature and Destiny of Man*, 1:186–203, 228–40.

398 and ravaging.[43] This will become more apparent within the context of the social dimension of sin.

The Social Dimension of Sin

Any reduction of sin to its personal dimension and dynamics trivializes its power in the world. The history of the theology of sin has not been wrong in conceiving sin a kingdom of evil or personifying it as a cosmic agent that holds human existence in bondage. An adequate analysis of sin cannot remain on the level of the personal dynamics of each individual and at the same time do justice to the awesome hold that sin has on human existence. The analysis of the social dimension of sin is thus not simply "added on" to the previous understanding as some complementary reflection. Rather, sin *is* social as well as individual, and what follows could well be the point of departure for understanding sin in itself.

The idea of the social is used loosely to designate any and every form of routinized behavior of groups. It refers to constant relationships and patterns of actions that human beings have with one another and with the world. Thus, society or the social denotes any form of institutionalized behavior or the systems that govern and are implicit in such behavior. A society or institution is not an entity with an autonomous existence, however, for societies do not exist apart from the subjects that make them up. Yet the routinized or formalized patterns of behavior can be spoken of in objective terms, as the social sciences suggest.

Few people would deny the existence of moral evil in human history. If one steps back and views history generally, it can be seen as a process of sin, guilt, and consequent suffering from which no one is exempt. Viewed especially from the point of view of the victims, it would not be too strong to say that human history consists of human beings preying on others. Momentary peace, harmony, and community, usually experienced within definable groups, are the wonderful exceptions that prove the rule. But one cannot rest with this abstract and impressionistic statement. Because human existence is essentially social, human egocentrism, competitiveness, hostility, aggression, and lack of concern are always mediated through concrete organized structures of behavior and institutions.[44] The issue, then, is to show how and in what measure social evil in history not only is objective evil, but is really sin as distinguished from evil—that is, a function of responsible human freedom. How is this sin constitutive of the human freedom of every person prior to the actual exercise of his or her freedom? How is social sin not personal sin or actual sinning but an existential propensity toward it?

---

43. See Juan Luis Segundo, *The Humanist Christology of Paul* (Maryknoll, NY: Orbis, 1986), 177. The theme of passivity, omission, and failure to assume the responsibility of love underlies all of Segundo's work on sin and grace. The analysis here also takes into account feminist critiques of an overly masculine depiction of sin in the tradition. It would be wrong, however, to correlate the two poles of sin with gender. Historical consciousness excludes "essentialization" or "stereotypization" of either male or female structures of behavior. See Gonzalez, *Created in God's Image*, 103–7.

44. This description of social sin consists in a historical and social analysis. Very often, what is called "the sin of the world" in current theologies of sin is the product of a transcendental imagination that is abstract and general. By translating this abstract notion into the concrete and historical analyses of social sin from liberation and political theologies, one arrives at a more historical and realistic view of sin. See Patrick Kerans, *Sinful Social Structures* (New York: Paulist, 1974). Because of restrictions on space, what is lacking in the account of social sin here is an adequate historical phenomenology of sin.

The Objectivity of Sin and the Social Constitution of Human Existence

From one point of view, social institutions and structures seem to be objective. They are in some degree invariant relationships or patterns of behavior. Language is governed by grammar and standard usage, society by law, culture by sets of values and ideals established in tradition, and corporations by constitutions, bylaws, and customs. This objectivity is precisely what allows social "entities" to be studied in a disciplined manner. This objectivity appears most clearly in relation to each individual, for society and its institutions exist prior to the freedom of any single person. Human beings are born into society, and they voluntarily join a whole host of established institutions.

Social arrangements are meant to enhance human freedom. The organization and regularization of patterned behavior should and to some extent always do release freedom through memory, habit, and instinctive routine to grapple with new issues. But institutions also limit and determine behavior. Moreover, they invariably involve oppressive elements. All institutions that enhance the freedom of some always exclude or repress in some measure the freedom of others. The larger groups and organizations become, the less they possess an inner self-identity or autonomously conscious and reflective center, the more they become the projected and glorified self of the individual members, and the more corporate self-transcendence is impeded.[45] The identity of every group is defined by its boundaries over against other groups. Generally speaking (for one must speak generally about social institutions), individuals do not transcend the limits of the institutions that govern their lives; rather, social structures set them over against those in other groups. One is inclined to be loyal to one's family, tribe, cast, corporation, professional guild, economic class, regional society, race, nation, and sex—right or wrong.

The objective structures that define social institutions are internalized by those born into them or joined to them. Thus, either by the necessity of birth or by choice through voluntary association, the ideas, values, and patterned relationships between people help constitute each individual in the group. The most dramatic example of this is the already-cited phenomenon of language, where one's very power to think, and hence judge, evaluate, and decide, is in some measure determined by the learned system of speech with all the social and cultural biases and prejudices it carries. This objective determination of human beings does not remain an external influence; it is certainly more than a question of imitation and learning by example. The influence of the multiple levels of society enters into the personhood of each individual as a "second nature." Thus, every individual *is* social or socially constituted in being. This accounts for the infectious quality of the sin of the world and its contagion.[46] All human beings are in some way tainted by the negativities of the social institutions they inherit or join.

In terms of the previous analysis of sin on the individual level, one must speak of social concupiscence and temptation. The social determinants of every human being, generally speaking, cannot be controlled. From one point

---

45. Reinhold Niebuhr, *Moral Man and Immoral Society* (New York: Scriber, 1960), xii, xxiv, 35, 73–75, 83–93.
46. Schoonenberg, *Man and Sin*, 98–123; idem, "The Sin of the World," in *Sacramentum Mundi* (New York: Herder & Herder, 1969), 5:90–91.

400

of view, they are internalized as part of the self; from another point of view, one acts within them. Thus their positivities and negativities channel human freedom and determine human behavior. The positive and negative impulses of this second nature of each person, this social concupiscence, become temptation. The aggressive aspects of institutions enhance the power of the group, and hence individual autonomy, power, and dominance, over other people in other groups. They also tempt negatively, because it is very difficult for individuals to transcend the institutions that nurture them and assume a responsibility against their evil effects. Thus, social structures are also temptations to escape from freedom by sins of omission. In sum, the social determinisms of the institutions that make up the second nature of human existence amount to a concupiscence and temptation that can be stronger than the impulses of one's individual nature.

The Subjectivity of Society and the Phenomenon of Social Guilt

While from one point of view, society and its institutions appear to be objective, from another, they must be considered subjective. This is easily demonstrated by their changeability and pluralism. Social institutions gradually change over time and become quite different from what they were. And at any given time, the differences in the way even the most fundamental structures of human living unfold in various cultures show their relativity. No institutions, not even those governing sexual behavior, eating, or communicating, are sheerly the product of nature; every human institution is cultural, a product of human freedom and creativity.

Social institutions, then, are grounded in human freedom. Born out of creative human response to the world and others, they are carried along by a human freedom that continually internalizes these patterns of meaning and behavior. From this point of view, then, one passes from the sphere of objective evil to that of sin. The destructive aspects of social institutions are more than objective evils that are contrary to the will of God; they are also sin because they are produced and sustained by human freedom. This sin, however, is not personal sin, nor is it necessarily formal sin in the sense of being deliberate; it is precisely social sin. As distinct from personal sin or actual sinning, this social sin is an integral part of what has traditionally been called original sin.

The sinful aspect of social involvement can be drawn out by a consideration of the phenomenon of social guilt—not guilt for society of the past of which one was not a part, but responsibility for the present and future sin of society. This is a very delicate issue, because people rarely admit to guilt even in their individual lives, and this guilt is so difficult to measure that it tends to escape evaluation. Thus, one should be clear at the outset about two qualifications. First and foremost, social guilt is not individual guilt, but precisely an analogous reality that is social. The sameness and difference that constitute this analogy are crucial. We do not control society in the same way we control ourselves. Yet at the same time, we participate in society and contribute to its functioning. As prior to individual guilt, social guilt is part of the complex of prior sin. Second, it is impossible to quantify this social guilt, because it exists on so many different levels and in so many different degrees. Within the framework of these qualifications, however, social guilt remains inescapable.

This becomes clear from the fact that no one can escape participation in social structures and institutions that inevitably harm some people.

By their action within these institutions, prior to the immediate object of any particular action, all participants in some measure help perpetuate the social institutions in which they live. Individuals and groups can react against various aspects of social sin; human freedom can transcend society at any given point and become countercultural. But no one can escape all the aspects of one's social existence and participation. Even an attempt to escape from society and its structures can be an escape from the social responsibility that should be enlisted to change them.

But variables in responsibility and guilt can be located along the axes of knowledge and power. Some elements of society are more responsible than others for society itself and for all institutions. People are not explicitly responsible for what is unknown or beyond the sphere or capacity of their freedom, but some measure of knowledge and power is inherent in freedom itself, so that social guilt may vary from the merely virtual to the conscious and explicit. Often social situations appear as genuine entrapments; they entail dilemmas from which no course of action emerges that will not cause damage to whole groups of people. At this point, one begins to experience the all-encompassing power of sin and one's own and society's inability to escape it.

In the end, however, apart from these distinctions, the final demonstration of social sin and guilt is experiential, and it stems from the ontology of human solidarity. All are part of the concrete human condition. One cannot regard a social tragedy with indifference by saying, "It does not concern me." The strongest testimony to social sin and guilt is conscience, which is at the same time a consciousness of solidarity with others and implicitly a standing before God, the loving Creator and friend of all.

The Prior Situation of Sin and the Purpose of Human Freedom

The Christian doctrine of sin is intrinsically paradoxical, for it teaches that a universal condition of a propensity to sin, prior to the exercise of freedom, is part of freedom itself and affects every exercise of freedom. It states that human existence is fallen in such a way that sin, which is a function of freedom, is omnipresent. A gentler way of expressing this would characterize every exercise of freedom as ambiguous. But this fails to express the power, contagion, and aggressive force behind moral evil in history and in the individual self.

The power of sin in the world is simply inescapable. Sin is the condition prior to the exercise of personal freedom, constituted by the native structure of each individual and by a socially inherited second nature. It is sin inasmuch as these structures are appropriated and ratified through a lack of basic trust, faith, and love. This entails in some measure an assertion of the self or an escape from freedom over against others and implicitly God, who alone can guarantee security in being. On the one hand, sin is simple: it is the emergence within human freedom of false autonomy and egocentrism over against other human beings and God. On the other hand, it is complex, for it is fed by multiple factors, transcendentally on the individual level and historically on the social level. Sin is an aggressive power within each person's freedom that cumulatively projects itself out into history, or a recessive negation of freedom that fails to be responsible for the self and the world in response to grace. It is also a concrete historical sphere, region, or environment that enters into and influences each person's freedom. Both of these dimensions are necessary factors in its description. Social sin cannot be explained without the

402 individual dimension; the sheer power of sin and its hold on the race cannot be explained without the social dimension. This sin is both outside individual human freedom and within it, "objective" and subjective at the same time. It inescapably qualifies all human behavior, every exercise of freedom.

The inescapability of sin provides a first negative answer to the questions arising out of a preliminary anthropology. First, what is the status of human existence before God? In straightforward language, human existence is sinful. No human being can measure the self against its transcendent ideals and say, "I am what I should be," any more than any Christian can stand before God and confess personal holiness. No society or collectivity, no institution or group, can claim to measure up to what it should or could be. Thus, insofar as human existence is freedom, it is also both "objectively" and freely sinful.

The second question concerns the purpose of human freedom. The issue of its final destiny will be resolved in a consideration of grace as the kingdom of God. But relative to the purpose of human freedom within this world, the inescapability of sin provides a preliminary negative answer. There is no escape from sin in this world. One should not interpret the transcendence of human freedom as an escapist drive to live above the sphere of limits, determinants, concupiscence, and temptation. Rather, within this world, the purpose of freedom is the struggle against sin. Though sin is inescapable, it can be resisted and its power and effects minimized within the self and in history. A more positive indication that this is the intrinsic God-given purpose of human freedom lies in the doctrine of grace.

Grace on the Individual Level of Human Existence

Speaking generally, the notion of God's grace refers to God's goodness, graciousness, and benevolence toward human beings. Grace is God's love for human existence. But this grace is always understood against the background of a human dilemma. In relation to human sinfulness, God's grace appears as mercy and forgiveness. Against the background of human finitude and death, God's love appears as a power unto ultimate salvation in eternal life.[47] The history of the theology of grace yields no single systematic understanding of the term. Moreover, the same history deals with a whole host of different questions, not all of which can be subsumed into this account.

The theology of grace that follows rests on the following premises: First, it aims at a systematic theology by drawing the diverse notions of grace into a single consistent language. Second, grace is understood against the background of both sin and the finitude of human existence leading to death. Third, in defining God's salvation from sin and death, the theology of grace provides the Christian response to the fundamental questions that run parallel to those underlying the theology of sin. They concern the way God relates to human beings in their sinful existence leading to death, the consequent standing of human beings before the God who

---

47. In Protestant theology, grace tends to be understood against the background of the horizon of sin; Catholic theology tends to define grace in response to the finitude of human nature and death, although it does not neglect the problem of sin. There seems to be no compelling reason to consider these two frameworks in exclusion of one another; they can be combined.

approaches them in grace, the character of the ongoing dialogue between God and human existence, and the very purpose of human freedom in history.

The fundamental character of these questions that underlie the whole history of the theology of grace should not be underestimated. So basic are these issues that the theological anthropology developed in response to them casts its interpretation on the understanding of Christianity as a whole.[48] The theology of grace interprets the concrete appropriated meaning of God's salvation revealed in Jesus Christ.

Before examining the sources and analysis of this doctrine, however, I turn to a review of the state of the question in Catholic theology today.

Catholic Theology of Grace Today

The theology of grace contained in Catholic manuals before the Second Vatican Council consisted in a highly technical treatise divided into the specific topics of actual and sanctifying grace. It employed a variety of distinctions of various aspects of what was called grace, these distinctions having developed over the centuries in response to different problematic issues.[49] The treatise bore little relation to everyday Christian experience. Even the precise subject matter—what was being studied and its significance relative to the substance of Christian faith—was not self-evident.

The doctrine of grace as an explicitly distinct topic or area of reflection was most decisively determined for Western theology by Augustine. For him, the notion of God's grace, as God's agency of human salvation, contained a central datum for the whole Christian vision. In his fight with Pelagianism, Augustine insisted that God alone saves through the grace mediated by Christ. By firmly positing the absolute priority and gratuity of grace over against sin and human impotency for our own salvation, Augustine laid the groundwork for a fundamental Christian conception of human existence. But his theology also opened up many areas of mystery that pervade the ongoing relationship between God and human life, such as a precise understanding of what "grace" is, the relationship between grace and human freedom, and the balance between God's providence and the unfolding of human history.

In the twentieth century, no Catholic theologian has done more than Karl Rahner to restore the theology of grace to its position close to the center of Christian thought. The renewal of the theology of grace began on a foundational level with modernism, and a number of modernist theologians anticipated some of Rahner's conclusions. Other theologians contributed to the questioning of the theology of the manuals by historical studies of Aquinas and the medieval tradition.[50] But it was Rahner who most effectively transformed the theology of grace in Catholic theology. His theology, or at least

---

48. It is not surprising, therefore, that the fundamental theological issue underlying the Reformation concerned grace. The differences between Catholic and Protestant understandings of grace lead to basic differences in anthropology and spirituality that color their whole interpretation of Christianity and that are still operative. Today, however, they are not generally considered church-dividing.

49. Quentin Quesnell, "Grace," in Komonchak et al., *The New Dictionary of Theology*, 437, 442–44.

50. For example, Henri Bouillard, *Conversion et grace chez S. Thomas d'Aquin* (Paris: Aubier, Éditions Montaigne, 1944); Bernard Lonergan, *Grace and Freedom: Operative Grace in the Thought of St. Thomas Aquinas*, ed. Patout Burns (New York: Herder & Herder, 1970); Henri de Lubac, *Surnaturel: Études historiques* (Paris: Aubier, 1946).

404 many of the conclusions of this thought, are almost presupposed in the theology of grace today. Some of the force of Rahner's theology of grace, especially when viewed in contrast to the Neo-Scholasticism to which he was reacting, will help define the state of the question today. One can see four reversals at work in his reinterpretation of grace:[51]

1. Since the time of Aquinas, the term *grace* designated primarily, although not exclusively, "created grace," a habit or quality of the human soul infused by God. Concomitantly with this sanctifying grace, God, who is "uncreated grace," was present to and dwelt in the human person. Rahner simply reversed this relationship between created and uncreated grace. Grace is first and foremost God's self-communication and presence to human existence. This simple shift completely reorients one's thinking about grace and opens up the possibility of interpersonal categories to analyze it.

2. In response to the implied extrinsicism of Neo-Scholastic theology, Rahner defined the offer of grace as constitutive of the actual condition of human existence. The supernaturality of grace does not mean it comes to a purely self-enclosed human nature as an alien, arbitrary, and merely additional factor of the human condition. Rather, God's presence as an offer of salvation is part of the historical condition of a human existence, whose salvation God wills from the beginning.

3. Against the implication that grace is scarce, then, or that there is no salvific grace outside the Christian sphere, Rahner argued theologically to the universality of grace on the basis of the universality of God's saving will. The implication of this position is dramatic: it means that the whole sphere of human life, even in its most secular aspects, is potentially "graced." The position breaks down barriers separating the church and the world and unveils to Christian vision a kingdom of grace beyond the church.

4. Against the widespread Neo-Scholastic position that grace cannot be experienced, because it is supernatural, Rahner proposed that people do experience grace. This is a qualified view, however, since grace is still not known directly or distinctly as grace but in and through experiences of genuine self-transcendence. At the same time, however, this conclusion opens the theology of grace to phenomenological and narrative methods of analyzing grace in and through experience.

With these theological moves, Rahner returned the theology of grace to a consideration of the very nature of salvation and how it is experienced in human existence. In some ways, Rahner's theology of grace was transitional: he broke open the narrow objectivist treatise on grace and reconceived it in foundational anthropological terms. Yet to a large extent, the current Catholic theology of grace, even when it moves beyond Rahner, is dependent on him.

The movement beyond Rahner has occurred in several areas. One clear instance of this development lies in the explicit context of ecumenical theology. In an early work, Hans Küng succeeded in bringing much closer together the teaching of the Council of Trent on justification and the widely respected Neo-Reformation theology of

---

51. See Karl Rahner, "Some Implications of the Scholastic Concept of Uncreated Grace," in *Theological Investigations*, 1:319–46; idem, "Concerning the Relationship between Nature and Grace," in ibid., 297–317; idem, "Nature and Grace," *Theological Investigations* (Baltimore: Helicon, 1966), 4:165–88; idem, *Foundations of Christian Faith: An Introduction to the Idea of Christianity* (New York: Seabury, 1978).

Karl Barth.[52] Today the Lutheran and Roman Catholic Churches no longer regard their teachings on the theology of grace as incompatible.[53]

The significance of the theology of grace has also been expanded by liberation theology. Building implicitly on conclusions shared by Karl Rahner, liberation theology stresses grace as a liberating force in public, social life. It offers a conception of the Christian life of discipleship as participation with Christ in the mediation of grace to society and the building up of social grace.[54]

The concept and theology of grace have also been deepened by a return to biblical sources. Reaching back especially into the New Testament for the foundations of a theology of grace, which of course are prior to Augustine's formulation of the issues, Edward Schillebeeckx has opened up the rich pluralism of the symbolism of grace. By merging the theological notion of grace with the very experience of salvation that is expressed in so many different ways by early church communities, Schillebeeckx has again demonstrated the centrality of this concept.[55]

Finally, the initiatives after Vatican II have led to the present situation in which the exigencies of gender equality, inculturation outside the West, dialogue with other religions, and the new worldview opened up by the sciences have provided a new context for the theology of grace. That context requires a method that draws the tradition into the present and is open to new appropriations of how God's grace is operative in our world.

In the interpretation of the theology of grace presented here, the framework of Rahner's theology is foundational. In the light of a preliminary anthropology that raises questions and provides a hermeneutical standpoint, this initial concept of grace will be developed along the lines of liberation theology, in dialogue with the landmarks of the history of the theology of grace, and attentive to the demands of the future.

The Sources
for a Theology of Grace

The Jewish-Christian Scriptures as a whole are depictions of God's grace. God is gracious, and God's grace is God's salvation, and human salvation from God in all its aspects is grace. This substance of the Scriptures, this grace, is approached from every imaginable viewpoint throughout the whole of the Bible. An integral approach to grace in the Scriptures can never be reduced to a word study of the Greek and Hebrew terms associated with "grace" or to any particular concept. Most fundamentally, the

---

52. Hans Küng, *Justification: The Doctrine of Karl Barth and a Catholic Reflection* (New York: Thomas Nelson & Sons, 1964).

53. Lutheran World Federation and the Catholic Church, *Joint Declaration on the Doctrine of Justification (October 31, 1999)* (Grand Rapids: Eerdmans, 2000).

54. See especially the work of Juan Luis Segundo as represented in *Grace and the Human Condition* (Maryknoll, NY: Orbis, 1973); and *The Humanist Christology of Paul*; see also Leonardo Boff, *Liberating Grace* (Maryknoll, NY: Orbis, 1979). The liberation theology of grace has had an influence on the theology of the church's center. For example, it is clear that the Congregation for the Doctrine of the Faith's *Instruction on Christian Freedom and Liberation* (Vatican City, 1986) deals with human freedom as merely one aspect of human life, much as, for example, one might address the themes of work or sexuality. But if freedom is considered as the central constitutive factor that distinguishes human existence, thereby encapsulating an integral anthropology, the significance of this instruction is enhanced far beyond the intentions of its authors.

55. See Edward Schillebeeckx, *Christ: The Experience of Jesus as Lord* (New York: Seabury, 1980).

term *grace* applies to God as God acts for human salvation. And Scripture is a record of the Jewish and Christian experiences of God's grace in myriad different ways. The Scriptures contain innumerable images and symbols characterizing the way God deals graciously with the world and human existence.

But a systematic account of grace must contain a center of gravity, a symbolic and conceptual focus. This account of grace fixes on the notion of God as love and the outpouring of this love on humankind. In the Jewish tradition, God is depicted as the God of steadfast and faithful love. In the New Testament, in John, God *is* love. Jesus is the manifestation of that love of God; Jesus is grace. The risen Christ is grace. Grace is God as Spirit poured out anew through Jesus and dwelling in human hearts (Rom. 5:5). Often the risen Christ and God as Spirit are scarcely distinct.[56]

The effect of grace is salvation, and what that salvation consists of is depicted in many different ways. The Christian undergoes a spiritual rebirth, becomes a child of God, or is adopted by God. The Christian receives the gift of the Spirit and experiences God as Spirit in his or her life. One is formed in the image of Christ and is impelled to follow Jesus. All of this unfolds within a tension between an "already now" and the "ultimate future." Grace now leads to fulfillment and eternal life.[57]

In the Scriptures, there is no single symbolic conception of grace or the salvation it brings. Rather, there is a pluralism of different and, on the level of symbolic representation, irreducible images. Yet, as Schillebeeckx notes, "A fundamentally identical experience underlies the various interpretations to be found throughout the New Testament: all its writings bear witness to the experience of salvation in Jesus from God."[58] This experience is captured by the symbol of God as Spirit being poured out anew in the world through the mediation of Jesus. This symbol will become the central focus for this account of grace.

Among the most prominent and consistent images in both the Jewish writings and the New Testament is the Spirit of God. For Israel, the Spirit of God is God—like the wind, the unseen but sensible presence, power, and force of God at work in the world. God's Spirit is spontaneous; it comes and goes. Never static, never possessed, uncontrolled, God's Spirit effects what it will in the world but remains transcendent. God's Spirit gives life to human beings; its absence is death. God's Spirit inspires; it moves great figures "to deeds above their known capacity and habits of behavior—deeds of delivering Israel from its enemies."[59]

In the New Testament, the Spirit of God is the same God as Spirit from the Jewish tradition specified now through Jesus, who is seen as

---

56. Ibid., 463–68.

57. Ibid., 468–77. Schillebeeckx goes on to describe the many different ways in which the New Testament literature characterizes the salvation or liberation that is effected by the grace mediated by Christ. How are we saved? What are we saved from? What are we saved for? Salvation is from death; it is freedom and redemption from slavery to sin; it is reconciliation with God; it is peace with God through satisfaction. Redemption is an expiation through a sin offering; it is forgiveness of sins; it is justification and sanctification. Salvation is accomplished through Jesus' intercession. Human beings are freed for love in the community, for renewal of the world, from the demonic powers, and for life in its fullness. Ibid., 477–514.

58. Ibid., 463.

59. John L. McKenzie, "Aspects of Old Testament Thought," in *Jerome Biblical Commentary*, ed. Raymond E. Brown, Joseph A. Fitzmyer, and Roland E. Murphy (Englewood Cliffs, NJ: Prentice Hall, 1968), 742.

Messiah; hence the Spirit is poured out on human beings in a new way. In Paul, for example, the Spirit represents "the indwelling of God in Christian experience."[60] The Spirit of God within is the source of basic trust, faith, and love. The Spirit within inspires and frees one from external law. It frees from sin, from immoral conduct; it assists in prayer; it enlightens the mind to make one aware of one's relation to God. In his Letter to the Romans, Paul follows up his classic account of the divided self, torn apart by concupiscence, temptation, and sin, with a description of how God's Spirit within the human spirit overcome, this sin and death. In a systematic summary of the work of the Spirit, John Calvin argues that God's Spirit is the internal working of God that accounts for the appropriation into human life of God as God is revealed in Christ.[61]

A Definition of Grace

Can the diffuse idea of God's love for humankind manifested as Spirit be formulated in more specific theological language? The following definition of grace consists of an attempt to be faithful to the scriptural symbol of God as Spirit at the same time that it adopts the theological framework of Karl Rahner.[62] The method underlying this move is similar to the one used in the understanding of sin. Although Karl Rahner is not ordinarily considered a biblical or evangelical theologian, his conception of grace can be understood in terms of a critical hermeneutical method of correlation. Beneath the multiple biblical symbols for salvation lies the experience of God as Spirit in the community. That experience is also had today, so the experience expressed in the biblical symbols can be drawn forward and restated in more reflective, intellectual symbols and a generalized theological concept of grace.

In Rahner's theology, grace may be considered the sum and substance of the whole Christian message. Grace is salvation. If one were to ask what salvation ultimately consists of, the New Testament as a whole would yield the answer that salvation is participation in God's own life. Human existence is called in the end to personal communion with God, but in such a way that, even now in this world, God communicates God's self to human beings. Grace then is God's personal communication of God's own self to human beings.[63]

This first definition of grace can be seen as theologically synonymous with the scriptural symbol of God as Spirit. In other words, the two symbols refer or point to materially the same thing. Thus, the presence of God's Spirit can be interpreted theologically to mean God's

---

60. Joseph A. Fitzmyer, "Pauline Theology," in Brown et al, *Jerome Biblical Commentary*, 814. For the consistency with which the Spirit of God recurs as the symbol of grace and salvation in the New Testament, see also Schillebeeckx's survey in *Christ*, 463–514.

61. John Calvin, *Institutes of the Christian Religion*, ed. John T. McNeill (Philadelphia: Westminster, 1960), 3.1.537–42.

62. This systematic move to identify grace and God's Spirit entails both a loss and a gain. On the one hand, it does not reproduce the richly differentiated accounts of grace in Scripture or of such tradition-defining theological figures as Augustine, Aquinas, Luther, and Calvin. On the other hand, the very diffuseness of the concept of grace in the tradition often undermines an appreciation of the precise meaning of the doctrine and its place in systematic theology. What is needed today is a retrieval of developed doctrines in their most fundamental forms. This will be successful insofar as it does not distort but releases the same Christian experience of grace that is expressed in the differentiated language of the tradition.

63. Rahner, *Foundations of Christian Faith*, 116–26.

408

self-communication to human beings, or God's personal presence to and influence on human subjects. Inversely, this self-communication of God to human beings can be referred to and in turn be interpreted in relation to the meaning and function of God's Spirit in Scripture. Grace, then, quite simply refers to God. But God is understood here as God at work outside of God's self, so to speak, and immanently present within human subjects as an offer of personal encounter. By extension, grace includes the influence that God's Spirit has upon human beings and the effects it has when accepted. Grace is God's Spirit, which is God's personal communication of God's own self in love. This is what is revealed in and through Jesus of Nazareth; this is the message of salvation in the New Testament.[64]

Intrinsic to this concept of grace is the total and absolute gratuity in every respect that makes grace grace, and that is uncompromised in the whole history of the theology of grace. The very logic of a personal communication of God's own self indicates that this self-giving or opening up to human beings in personal love is totally free; it emerges out of God's inner freedom and cannot be other than gratuitous, unowed, unmerited, prior to any value or claim that might be construed as human deserving. No love that is authentic love, that is self-transcending giving over of the self to another, can be claimed or forced, and this applies absolutely to God. Thus, even before the unworthiness caused by sin, God's impulse to communicate with human existence is absolutely gratuitous with the full literal force of absoluteness. All

merit in any strict sense of the term is totally ruled out because, quite simply, to admit this in any degree distorts the very notion of grace and salvation. In the simple formula of Augustine, grace would not be grace.

This conception of grace should be projected into the broadest possible cosmological framework. What is revealed in the event of Jesus and mediated to us through the New Testament is the very nature of God and not an arbitrary decision on God's part. This means that, although completely gratuitous, grace describes God's nature. This is the way God relates to human existence absolutely and universally. Grace describes the universal attitude and relation of God to all human beings always. In this supralapsarian framework (that is, a view that regards things prior to any notion of a fall), God's gracious and salvific intent precedes creation. God creates human beings because God intends an interpersonal dialogue with creatures who can respond. This dialogue is genuine. God engages a human freedom that is so other than God and so free that, through sin, it can refuse God's offer of grace. But grace is intrinsic to the very purpose of creation; grace is not "added on" as an "afterthought" to "repair" a human history run afoul. God's saving self-communication is absolutely gratuitous yet an intrinsic and "objective" sphere or context of human existence itself. It is the milieu into which every human being is born.[65]

The universal dialogue of God's Spirit with human beings is not merely a theoretical construct but concrete and historical. Because

---

64. The phrases "the Spirit of God," "God's Spirit," and "God as Spirit" are used in a theocentric framework that envisages God as Spirit at work in all of history. In the Christian community, the Spirit of God is revealed and identified by Jesus. In terms of trinitarian theology, the stress is put on the doctrine that the Spirit is not less than or other than God.

65. Karl Rahner, "The Order of Redemption within the Order of Creation," in *The Christian Commitment* (New York: Sheed & Ward, 1963), 38–74. The existential but not individualistic interpretation of the fall, of course, rules out a chronological interpretation of the meaning of supralapsarian. But the point is still valid—namely, that salvation through grace is

human freedom is tied to matter, the only way human beings and God can interrelate is through the world and history, in concrete moments through the actual conditions and circumstances of each human life. It follows that for every human being, the place, the medium, and the point of historical contact with God's love consist in those things that make up the ordinary conditions of everyday living. The ordinary place of encountering God's grace is the historical world. Granted, God's presence as Spirit and offer of love is within each one always. In the light of revelation, one cannot imagine God's presence to human beings by creative power except as including God's gracious personal love. But God's love is meant to be appropriated by a personal response mediated through the concrete situation of each person. Thus, on the one hand, concrete history unfolds within a sphere or region of God's salvific love, present to each one in such a way that all human beings, from the beginning of their existence, live in the condition of God being personally present to them in an offer of love. But on the other hand, God's Spirit calls for response. Thus, the concrete events of history become the media of the actual dialogue between human beings and God present and at work through them.[66]

This vision corresponds to the biblical symbolism that from the beginning, God's Spirit hovers over all creation, giving it form and life and offering it salvation (Gen. 1:1-2). It remains now to unfold the theological testimony regarding the effects of this grace and how it supports human existence over against sin and death.

The Effects of Grace

The effects of God's Spirit within human existence testified to by Scripture are too many to list. But the history of the theology of grace dwells on certain dominant effects, and each one of these, from different points of view, could be considered central to the Christian life. The following four effects of grace—liberation from sin, liberation to love, active cooperation of God with human freedom, and participation in God's life—are presented in terms of the thought of theologians who focused on each of these aspects and offered important analytic descriptions of them.

LIBERATION FROM SIN

Viewed in Luther's terms, God's grace, by accepting the sinner as sinner through forgiving and re-creating grace, is justifying. The first effect of grace in human existence is liberation from sin.[67]

Luther conceives of grace and salvation not in terms of God's Spirit, although the Spirit

---

conceived as the purpose of God's creation, that there can be no separation between the spheres of creation and redemption, or nature and grace, and that human freedom emerges from the beginning, in each instance, into a region of the offer of God's personal love to which it is invited to respond. Despite the primacy of salvation to creation, one may but does not have to maintain with Rahner the Augustinian tradition of double gratuity (that is, the gratuity of salvation over and above creation) in order to protect the gratuity of grace and the semiautonomous character of human freedom. The controlling metaphor is history as God dialoguing out of freedom with genuine human freedom. But this does not require a distinction within the love of the one God for creation.

66. Rahner, *Foundations of Christian Faith*, 138–52.

67. A historical developmental account of the effects of grace is broken here in the interest of a systematic concern. The prevenient character of grace is also stressed by Augustine, who is the first theologian in the Western tradition who focused attention on the term *grace*. Luther is even more anti-Pelagian than Augustine, if such is possible. And God's initiating grace and salvation have to be the logical points of departure in considering the effects of grace. A classic statement of

410 has a role in leading one to faith, but in terms of God's Word, who is ultimately Jesus Christ. Following Paul, he sees all human beings as fallen and inextricably caught in the web of sin. No amount of external works can release the inner bondage of sin and guilt one must experience when standing before the holiness of God. The only escape from sin can come from another, outside the self, who is the realization of God's promise of acceptance and forgiveness. Christ, by taking sin upon himself, and by a cosmic victory over the personified power of sin itself, is himself the grace of God, God's promise of forgiveness, acceptance, and re-creating love of human beings. This grace is mediated by faith, a personal clinging to God in Christ, in such a way that human existence is transformed by a mystical union in which the person of faith takes on and is re-created by the qualities of Christ, with whom one is united, even as Christ absorbs human sinfulness and guilt.

Through a shift in language, it is possible to retain significant features of Luther's account within a vision that conceives salvation in terms of God as Spirit. Such a move is encouraged by the already-arrived-at conclusion that the dynamics of grace operate universally and thus outside a historical or explicit encounter with Jesus. The main point to be expanded concerns the way grace liberates from sin.

One of the major contributions of Luther consists of his return to scriptural language and his presentation of the dynamics of grace in the personalist categories of faith. Faith is not mere belief or assent to objective truth, but a total surrender of self, a clinging, that in this sense includes hope and love of God. Thus, the release from sin must be understood as occurring within the context of an interpersonal relationship between God and each human being. But this personal offer of God's forgiving love is precisely given universally by God as Spirit. Human existence itself "objectively" unfolds within the context of God's loving and forgiving presence, which reaches human consciousness implicitly in every human decision as a call to faith and as an opportunity for self-transcending hope and love.[68]

The release from sin that Luther describes is forgiveness; it is not a negation of past sinfulness, which is impossible, or an escape from fallenness.[69] Human existence is constituted in a condition of concupiscence and temptation to which it freely yet invariably succumbs. The liberating effect of grace lies precisely in God's acceptance of human beings as they are. Grace means that God is the lover of every single human being, infinitely and as if there were no other, with a love that makes each person infinitely valuable despite sin.

This liberation from sin is thus profoundly ontological, and when it reaches into consciousness in any form, but particularly in its explicit mediation through Jesus, its psychological pow-

Luther's view of the working of grace in contrast to works is "The Freedom of the Christian," in *Luther's Works*, vol. 31, *Career of the Reformer*, ed. Harold J. Grimm (Philadelphia: Muhlenberg, 1957), 1:327–77. See also *Luther's Works*, vol. 26, *Lectures on Galatians, 1535*, ed. Jaroslav Pelikan (St. Louis: Concordia, 1963). For a summary of Luther's concept of grace as justification, see Paul Althaus, *The Theology of Martin Luther* (Philadelphia: Fortress Press, 1966), 201–73.

68. Rahner, *Foundations of Christian Faith*, 129–33.

69. In the objective ontological categories of Aquinas, it was possible to say, after the pattern of an ontological change in substance, that one is either in grace or not. A person either does or does not possess sanctifying grace. See Roger Haight, *The Experience and Language of Grace* (New York: Paulist, 1979), 71–72. When the framework for understanding grace is interpersonal communication and response, one can think of degrees of intensity of communication and union with God. One can also speak of a person as simultaneously a sinner and justified.

er can be total. Human existence, sinful though it be, is freed, released, liberated from the burden of sin, especially of the impossible, frustrating, and crushing illusion of trying to prove one's worth before God. Forgiving mercy is the very name of God. It is hard to imagine other effects of grace becoming operative without this prior and primary liberation. The sacraments of baptism and penance are symbolic mediations of this specific aspect of God's forgiving and universally available self-presence as Spirit.

Before moving to the second effect of grace, we must consider briefly the Roman Catholic response to Luther's view of salvation as justification by grace through faith. Without attempting to determine the precise thought of the individual Reformers, the Council of Trent (1545–63) sought to articulate Catholic teaching on the disputed issues. Its Decree on Justification, adopted in 1547 after seven months of discussion, is the Catholic Church's most complete official statement on the doctrine of grace. Trent did not seek to provide an exhaustive account of the topics it addressed; in addition, aware of diversity among Catholic theologians on such topics as justification, it refrained from passing judgment on matters controverted within Catholicism. Only the chief points of its teaching relevant to Luther's theology of grace will be summarized here.

Trent identifies faith as the "beginning of human salvation, the basis and root of all justification, without which it is impossible to please God" (DS 1532; see Heb. 11:6). It teaches that grace effects an internal transformation of the sinner, so that we are not merely considered just but become just (DS 1529). Faith, hope, and love are conferred with justification (DS 1530), but if separated from hope and love, faith "neither unites perfectly with Christ nor makes one a living member of his body" (DS 1531). In keeping with this distinction, Trent holds that

the grace of justification is lost by every mortal sin, even if faith is not lost (DS 1544, 1577). Finally, the council presents a dialectical description of the life of Christians. Aware of Christ's promise that one who gives even a cup of cold water to one of his little ones will not lack a reward (Matt. 10:42), Christians are nonetheless to confide and glory only in the Lord, not in themselves. Since we all offend in many ways (see James 3:2), we should keep before our eyes God's severity and justice as well as mercy and goodness. Even if conscious of no fault, we should be unwilling to judge ourselves, for each human life will ultimately be subjected, not to any human judgment, but to the judgment of God (DS 1548–49).

The reasons for the differences between Lutheran and Roman Catholic theologies of grace, most evident in the varying usages of the central term *faith*, lie below the surface within fundamentally different paradigms of interpretation. The theological tradition from Augustine to Aquinas sees grace working in and transforming human freedom. In Luther, human freedom is minimized to leave complete room for the total priority and gratuity of God's gracious forgiveness. Grace is identified as Christ and God's Word, and faith's passivity means that human justification is always the justice of another, Christ, with whom the Christian is united. In contrast to this, a constant underlying theme in Trent's Decree on Justification, while granting the priority and gratuity of grace, deals with human responsibility and freedom. The differences of conception that this underlying concern produces are reflected in the decree, especially in its canons.

Many of these differences between the Lutheran and Catholic languages of grace still persist today. Yet they are not church-dividing, since so much of what is essential to the doctrine of

412 grace is held in common. In other words, while these two languages of grace cannot quite be reconciled, they fall within the range of legitimate theological pluralism.[70] It will be clear from the emphasis on human freedom and responsibility in what follows that the account of grace given here represents the language of grace behind the doctrine of Trent, even though it incorporates the basic themes of Luther's theology.

Liberation to Love

Viewed in terms of Augustine, God's prior grace liberates human existence from the bondage of egoism and opens up freedom by an impulse to love, pushing or drawing freedom toward self-transcending values and, through faith, toward God.[71]

In Augustine, one finds an understanding of grace predominantly, but not exclusively, in terms of God's Spirit. We have already seen Augustine's instinctive and total reaction against any Pelagian hint of self-reliance for salvation. Like Luther, Augustine views grace against the background of sinful human nature, but not outside a teleological context that implies a life of sanctification leading to salvation as victory over death. Augustine understood human existence in a Neo-Platonic framework as having come forth from God by creation and tending to return to God as creation's final resting place. In terms of spatial imagery, human existence is meant to rise through finite truths and goods to the supreme Truth and Goodness of absolute Being. But human existence is fallen. Augustine was overwhelmed by the dynamics of concupiscence, temptation, and sin, which have already been analyzed. Human existence for Augustine is freedom, and this freedom is clearly manifested in the power of free choice. But on another level, this freedom is held in bondage. The captivity of concupiscence, the sheer weight of materiality and the bonds of sensuality, complicated by the entanglement of ingrained habit and custom, is one thing. But the real mystery lies in the way human spirit or freedom, which is precisely other than matter, is a prisoner to itself. Human freedom, which can command the body to act, cannot command or will itself out of itself in self-transcending love.[72] Without the prior impulse that must implant even the desire for self-transcending values or objects, human freedom is incapable of the love that constitutes real freedom—namely, actuating the self beyond the self. In this framework, then, grace is God's Spirit expanding freedom, opening it up, in a desire and impulse of love.

Augustine's position on grace—that no authentic love exists in the world apart from the impulse of God's Spirit—may seem difficult to accept from an objective and detached point of view. Appreciation of it requires two things. First of all, one must ask the right question. Today people agonize over the question of why there is evil in the world. But Augustine also asked *how*, in such a damaged and sinful world, one could account for goodness and love: "From what source is there in people the love of God and of one's neighbor?"[73] Second, Augustine's

---

70. See George Anderson, T. Austin Murphy, and Joseph A. Burgess, eds., *Justification by Faith: Lutherans and Catholics in Dialogue VII* (Minneapolis: Augsburg, 1985), especially the "Common Statement" at 13–74.

71. Several of Augustine's treatises against Pelagius and on grace can be found in *Basic Writings of Saint Augustine*, vol. 1, ed. Whitney J. Oates (New York: Random House, 1948).

72. Augustine, *Confessions* 8.9, in *Basic Writings*, 1:122.

73. Augustine, "On Grace and Free Will" ch. 33, in *Basic Writings*, 1:763.

response to the question can be understood as correct only from within the context of religious experience itself. Referring to a foundational experience, Augustine responded to his own question by another question he appropriated from Paul: "What have you that you did not receive?" (1 Cor. 4:7, RSV).[74] Augustine realized that, in the religious context of standing before God, Jesus' parable of the Pharisee and the publican provides the only answer possible.

God as Spirit, then, expands the horizon of freedom and opens up human creativity to values beyond the self, implicitly in the direction of God and divine values. At this point, one can see a mutual complementarity in the understanding of the effects of grace in the systems of Augustine and Rahner. On the one hand, in the light of Rahner's and the Second Vatican Council's theology, one should reverse the Augustinian presupposition that grace, because it is absolutely gratuitous, is also rare in human history. If love abounds in the world, it is because all human existence unfolds within the context of God's love, which impels human freedom toward self-transcendence. On the other hand, Rahner's whole system is strictly Augustinian, for it presupposes that any acts of self-transcendence must also be an effect of God's grace.

COOPERATIVE GRACE

Augustine distinguished and defined cooperative grace in relation to operative grace in the following way: "God operates, therefore, without us, in order that we may will [love]; but when we will [love], and so will [love] that we may act, God co-operates with us."[75] Augustine

saw this distinction as a way of protecting free choice while still affirming the role of grace. But while the distinction is sound, Augustine's cosmic doctrine of double predestination finally undermines his conception of personal freedom. Otherwise, God does not have a free dialogue partner in history.

In the twelfth century, Bernard of Clairvaux also took up the concept of cooperative grace as a way of dealing with the problem of the determinism of grace versus freedom. But in Bernard, free choice under the influence of grace appears as little more than consent, an "allowing" or "going along with." Freedom is a weak concept suggesting at best pliability, a mere choice that allows the self to be moved.[76] Like Augustine, Bernard cannot have been expected to accommodate the modern experience of freedom. Human beings today experience freedom as much more than mere choice or consent. Human freedom is commitment to values that results in creativity or destruction. In either case, human freedom is a power to produce what is new. The question, then, is whether Bernard's reflection on cooperative grace can sustain both the absolute primacy of grace in all salutary actions of human freedom and the modern experience of freedom's initiating creativity.

Three reflections help to soften the paradox involved in cooperative grace, although the relationship between grace and human freedom remains mysterious. The first is the principle of Aquinas that God always acts upon creatures according to their nature, and since freedom is of the nature of human existence, God acts

---

74. Augustine, "On the Spirit and the Letter" ch. 57, in *Basic Writings*, 1:509.

75. Augustine, "On Grace and Free Will" ch. 33, in *Basic Writings*, 1:761.

76. Bernard of Clairvaux, *On Grace and Free Choice*, in *Treatises III: On Grace and Free Choice* (Kalamazoo, MI: Cistercian, 1977), nos. 46–47, pp. 105–6.

414 within and not against that freedom.[77] Thus, one cannot conceive of human freedom as a merely passive instrumental cause of the activity and effects stemming from God's presence within a human subject, because the instrument in this case is the free power and self-initiating energy of human freedom. The personalist context for understanding the dynamics of grace completely transcends images of mechanical force, power, or coercion.

Second, insofar as grace is genuinely cooperative, the initiatives of grace and human freedom should not be seen in competitive terms. Very often, this tacit presupposition underlies the dichotomous alternative that concessions to either God or human freedom somehow undermine the real initiative of the other. Granted that the sinful aspect of human action is precisely in competition with God, that which is sustained by grace need not be. As Luther said, works performed out of faith give glory to God.[78]

Third, the power of grace and of human freedom should never be conceived as operating on the same level. God is God; human beings are creatures operating on the level of finite history. A distinction of levels allows one to grant the power and efficacy of freedom on the overt level of conscious action in the world, while at the same time allowing one to insist on the presence of God's influence within the ontic depths of the sheer existence and animation of this particular exercise of freedom.

With these qualifications, the formula of Bernard takes on new meaning:

> [Grace] so co-operates with free choice, however, that only in the first case [thinking] does it go a

step ahead of it; in the others [willing and doing], it accompanies it. Indeed, the whole aim in taking the step ahead is that from then on it may co-operate with it. What was begun by grace alone, is completed by grace and free choice together, in such a way that they contribute to each new achievement not singly but jointly; not by turns, but simultaneously. It is not as if grace did one half the work and free choice the other; but each does the whole work, according to its own peculiar contribution. Grace does the whole work, and so does free choice—with this one qualification: that whereas the whole is done *in* free choice, so the whole is done *of* grace.[79]

The remnant of Bernard's weak concept of freedom is contained in the italicized prepositions. It would be more accurate to say the whole work is done *by* freedom and *by* grace. For this is the paradox: the whole of the salutary exercise of human freedom is both a work of God's grace and one of human freedom. On one level, God sustains human freedom in being by creation, while God's presence and influence of love inform its self-transcending character. On another level, what is done in this world on the level of history is manifestly the creation of human freedom. Thus, the whole of salvific action is performed by human freedom wholly sustained by grace. This view of cooperative grace is radically anti-Pelagian and respects the absolute gratuity of salvation in every respect. Yet it supports the semiautonomous character of human freedom.

PARTICIPATION IN GOD'S LIFE

A fourth effect of God's personal self-communication as Spirit is a bestowal on human exis-

---

77. Thomas Aquinas, *Summa theologiae* I–II, q. 113, a. 3, in *The Gospel of Grace*, ed. Cornelius Ernst (Oxford: Blackfriars, 1972), 30:170–71.

78. Luther, "The Freedom of the Christian," 353.

79. Bernard of Clairvaux *On Grace and Free Choice*, 47, p. 106.

tence of a participation in God's own personal life, already in this world but destined toward completion in eternal life. Another way of expressing this bestowal anthropologically would be in terms of the transformation of human existence that this participation entails.

This sanctifying and divinizing effect of grace is more typical of Greek than Latin theology, but it has been a standard feature in Catholic thought on grace since the medieval synthesis. In Aquinas, the primary referent of the term *grace* is a new and infused supernatural quality of the human soul. This habitual grace raises up human nature to a new supernatural level of participating in the divine life of God. In Rahner's system, however, infused created grace becomes the effect of God's personal self-communication to the human person. Since Catholic theology frequently and mistakenly has denied that Luther too affirmed this effect of grace, it might be fitting to describe it in his personalist terms, which are coherent with those of Rahner, while at the same time shifting Luther's Christ-mysticism into a framework of Spirit-mysticism.

Luther gives two metaphors that illustrate the transformation through participation in divine life that is effected by grace. One metaphor says, "Just as the heated iron glows like fire because of the union of fire with it, so the Word imparts its qualities to the soul."[80] This metaphor displays in physical terms the total transformation of the human person through a "transfer of qualities" effected by union. In other words, the human person, with God's life within, takes on divine qualities—it is sanctified, but in and through the presence of God's life. More

dramatically, because Luther relies on a more interpersonal account of the dynamics of love, he describes the same process in terms of a divine bridegroom marrying a "poor, wretched harlot."[81] The dynamics of the transformation occur in this instance through creative or re-creative love. The sheer personal love and personal self-communication of the divine lover raises up and reconstitutes the beloved on a new level of being. This is not simply a communication that makes the beloved feel better. Rather, in the case of God's real self-communication in the love that is God's Spirit, human existence is reconstituted as God's own.

These, then, are the four principal effects of grace, and they respond directly to the existential structure of sin and the personal sins it spawns. Grace is God's Spirit, which is itself God's personal self-communication offered to every human being. But God being present to a human being is also a force and a new power within human freedom. This is not to be conceived mechanically as a physical or determining causal agent. The whole logic of grace must be conceived in terms of a dialogue between two freedoms. Within human subjectivity, the personal presence, love, concern, and influence of a personal God are immanently at work. In the unfolding of freedom from mere potentiality into responsibility, one should not expect responses completely lacking in openness and basic trust, or every measure of faith and love. Where sin abounds, grace abounds even more. Whatever the measure of hope, faith, and love, it is a product of the impulse of, and drawing out by, God's own loving presence.[82] The tension

---

80. Luther, "The Freedom of the Christian," 349.

81. Ibid., 351–52.

82. As in the case of sin, the final "proof" of the role of God's grace in self-transcending human action is experiential. It cannot be demonstrated objectively, but only "recognized" after the fact as due to a power within one. Thus Paul exclaimed, "I live, yet not I, but Christ lives in me" (Gal. 2:20).

416 between sin and grace cannot always be measured in the absolute terms of No or Yes; it is not always a question of either sin or grace. For sin and grace and their appropriation involve subjectivity, the personal responses of freedom in existential dialogue. It is hard to imagine either an absolute No or Yes to God in a finite condition filled with ignorance and concupiscence that impede an absolute self-disposition of self, even though one cannot rule out these potentialities of freedom for acceptance and refusal.

This account of grace on the level of the individual person synthesizes ecumenical resources into a Catholic statement. A rather different perspective is opened up by the bilateral dialogue between Lutherans and Catholics. That dialogue recorded a milestone in 1999, and a description of that stage of its progress provides another helpful look at the effects of grace in a person's life.

Joint Declaration on Justification

On October 31, 1999, in Augsburg, Germany, representatives of the Roman Catholic Church and the Lutheran World Federation confirmed the "Joint Declaration on the Doctrine of Justification."[83] Since this doctrine was and has remained a major factor in the division between Lutherans and Roman Catholics since the sixteenth century, and since other Christian churches have endorsed this document, and since its significance contains lessons relevant to other doctrines as well, it deserves some attention here. A brief consideration of the declaration's goal, logic, content, deep structure, and significance will communicate much in a short space.

Goal

The two parties that authored this document state its goal in a straightforward way: "to articulate a common understanding of our justification by God's grace through faith in Christ" (5). In the face of division, ecumenical discussions since Vatican II have achieved a "high degree of agreement," and this document seizes an opportune moment to appropriate the results of many initiatives.

Logic

The logic of the declaration appears on two levels. The rationale of the presentation concedes that the history and development of these two communions and new insights into scripture have generated a new understanding of the doctrine that allows a consensus on its fundamental meaning. But this consensus welcomes different languages, theological elaborations, and emphases that leave the two traditions intact. Moreover, as distinct as these differences remain, they are not such that they warrant division among the churches involved but represent a legitimate pluralism, where pluralism means differences within a larger, more profound unity of consensus (7, 13–14, 40).[84]

This logic governs the way the declaration lays out its presentation. It begins with a preamble that sets the context of the document (1–7). It then turns to the rich biblical tradition that enshrines this doctrine (8–12). After defining the ecumenical problem (13), it lays out its

---

83. Lutheran World Federation and the Roman Catholic Church, *Joint Declaration on the Doctrine of Justification* (Grand Rapids: Eerdmans, 2000). Citations in the text represent paragraph numbers.

84. This means that all the problems regarding this doctrine have not been resolved. While both sides stand by the declaration, some serious differences remain.

nuanced consensus in two major constructive parts. The first defines as clearly and concisely as possible what is shared by Catholics and Lutherans about the core doctrine of the priority of grace and forgiveness of sin through the grace of Christ. The second takes up the many sub-doctrines or theological conceptions that surround the doctrine or are entailed in it. The declaration concludes by assigning the mutual condemnations of the sixteenth century the value of warnings against certain extremes.

CONTENT

The declaration sums up the content of this doctrine, which strongly upholds the absolute priority of God's grace for human salvation, in this full statement: "All people are called by God to salvation in Christ. Through Christ alone are we justified, when we receive this salvation in faith. Faith is itself God's gift through the Holy Spirit who works through Word and sacrament in the community of believers and who, at the same time, leads believers into that renewal of life which God will bring to completion in eternal life" (16). This core consensus, however, conceals a host of distinct theological loci that have been contested. The declaration deals with seven of these.

On human powerlessness relative to justification due to sin, both sides affirm an absolute dependence on God's grace for salvation. Catholics speak of cooperation with grace but do not deny the priority of grace. Lutherans speak of sin disabling cooperation because of the priority of grace and do not deny that one can reject God's grace (19–21).

On justification as forgiveness of sin and its making a person righteous, both sides agree "that God forgives sin by grace and . . . frees human beings from sin's enslaving power and imparts the gift of new life in Christ." However, Lutherans emphasize that one's union with God is constituted in and through Christ, while Catholics emphasize the internal renewal of a person from whom acts of love are now possible (22–24).

On justification by grace through faith, both sides admit this formula as descriptive of the process of justification. Lutheran language stresses the idea of faith "alone" without any intention of separating it from the acts of love that follow from it, whereas Catholic language tends to emphasize the reconstitution of a person that precisely allows acts of faith, hope, and love (25–27).

On the justified person as sinner, the parties confess together that a person is truly and really justified in Christ, even though the person is continually exposed to concupiscence and is in need of constant forgiveness. Still, the Lutheran notices that the self on its own still struggles with proclivities to sin despite being justified, and the Catholic, while not denying these inclinations are dimensions of the self not aligned with God, does not normally call this "sin" in a formal sense (28–30).

On the classic contrast between law and gospel, all confess that one is justified by faith "apart from works prescribed by the law" (Rom. 3:28) and that the commandments are valid indications of God's will. Lutherans stress the way a person stands accused by the law and thus is urged to faith, while Catholics stress the good actions that flow from faith (31–33).

On the question of certainty of salvation, Lutherans and Catholics together insist that despite human weakness, one can have absolute confidence in God's promise of grace in Christ. Within this tension, Luther looked only at Christ with the eyes of faith and was certain of salvation, while Catholics noted human weakness, not Christ, as a source of uncertainty (34–36).

418

On the question of the good works of the justified, both parties admit the goodness of the works that flow from justification and the obligation to pursue them. When Catholics speak of merit, they are focusing on human responsibility but not contesting that the good works themselves are gifts of grace. Lutherans, too, recognize growth in sanctification but underline that good works flow from justification and see eternal life as unmerited reward (37–39).

In sum, these concrete syntheses show how this declaration was forged in an irenic spirit of understanding the language and viewpoint of the other and recognizing its positive yield.

DEEP STRUCTURE

Before pointing out the wider significance of the declaration, it will be helpful to notice more attentively the deep structure of the common understanding that underlies it. Neither party wants to deny the validity of the mutual condemnations of the sixteenth century: they had merit, they were serious, and they "remain for us 'salutary warnings' to which we must attend in our teaching and practice" (42). What has changed, then, are the two church communions and present-day self-understanding, so that the condemnations of both, thought "not simply pointless," no longer apply (41).

WIDER SIGNIFICANCE

This deeper logic opens up the theological imagination to the wide significance of this declaration. The condemnations of the past were not untrue, but they were contextually bound, so that, when reality changed, their concrete reference and applicability disappeared. This is so because churches grow and change. Each church recognizes newness in the other. More importantly, this growth also allows the creative impulses of an analogical imagination and a dia-

lectical imagination to guide Christian response to the other church. An analogical imagination recognizes similarity within difference; it penetrates below surface unlikeness to discover resemblances and commonalities within. This is represented in the consensus statements. A dialectical imagination too lives in tension, but is dialectical precisely in holding together forces that pull in different directions. This is seen in the distinctive perspectives and languages. When such a tension is embraced and internalized, in a community, for example, and especially when it is coupled with an analogical imagination, it can be a positive, dynamic, and generative force promoting Christian life. We need pluralism in theology, and the joint declaration illustrates this.

The Social Dimension of Grace

If in dealing with sin, one cannot ignore its social dimension, it follows that there must also be a social dimension to grace. As in the case of sin, to reduce the intentionality and power of God's Spirit of love in the world to its manifestations in the behavior of individuals would trivialize its significance. Appreciating the significance of social grace, however, requires an appreciation of historical consciousness and the shift that has occurred in regard to the context for thinking about grace. This may be introduced by a consideration of the groundwork of the theology of grace of Thomas Aquinas and the need to reappropriate it in a new historical and eschatological framework.

From Teleology to Eschatology

The theology of grace of Aquinas is often characterized as static and mechanical. In fact, however, it is not, and this can be shown by looking at its foundations. Two fundamental conceptions work together to supply the groundwork that supports a dynamic conception of the working of grace.

The first is teleology. The whole of Aquinas's theology of grace is governed by teleology, which means a logic or rationale that determines the intelligibility of being or a being by its *telos*, or purpose and goal. All beings exist for a purpose or goal to which they are oriented. Since there is a correspondence of proportionality between the kind of being any being possesses and its purpose, one can understand a particular form of being in relation to its goal, and inversely, one can discern its goal by the kind of being it is.

The second concept is that of nature. In one respect, the nature of a being is that which makes it the kind of being it is. From this logical point of view, nature denotes the essence of what a being is. But in Aquinas, nature also determines how a being acts, for nature is a principle of operation and action. As the principle of activity, informed by its proper powers and faculties, a nature governs the kind of actions performed by a being, and as the source of action, it generates behavior typical of its kind of being. In a teleological framework, natures correspond to their goal or final end and purpose, and thus elicit actions that tend toward this goal.

In the confluence of these two conceptions, one can see the fundamental rationale of Aquinas's theology of grace. For revelation discloses that human existence is called to a supernatural goal of personal union with God, one that exceeds the power and the activity of human nature in itself. Grace, as a supernatural quality of the human soul, in effect creates a new

and supernatural nature with concomitant new powers of faith, hope, and love that enable a raised human nature to become the source of a supernatural kind of activity corresponding to a supernatural goal.[85] In all of this, it is important that one see the dynamic action-oriented logic of this conception, for it has become one of the hallmarks of a Catholic theology of grace. Human existence reaches its final goal of divine salvation through action—action played out in the world but at the same time filled with a supernatural or divine potency and power that overcome the "natural" limits of its finitude.

From today's perspective, the weakness in this teleological conception can be appreciated on the basis of certain aspects of historical consciousness. Historical consciousness refers to the contemporary sense of being in history, the awareness that human beings have emerged out of a long and distant past and are moving toward an unknown future in this world. It also involves an expanded horizon of consciousness, a product of modernity, by which people are aware of the multiple histories of other peoples and their own interrelatedness with them and interdependence upon them. History implies change and the relatedness to time and place or contextuality of all human values and ideas.

But two characteristics in particular of current historical consciousness have a direct bearing on Thomistic teleology. The first is the realization that the social and cultural structures of history were not given with nature, but were created out of and by human freedom. In other words, the journey of human existence to its end does not lead through naturally given and unchanging structures but through structures and forms that are themselves changing because they are the creations of human beings

---

85. Thomas Aquinas, *Summa theologiae* I–II, q. 109, a. 2; q. 110, a. 1–4, in *The Gospel of Grace*, 30:72–77, 108–23.

420

themselves. Classical culture and the teleology of Aquinas cannot do justice to this current appreciation of things.

Second, this new awareness brings with it a new concern that focuses attention on the meaningfulness and direction of human creativity *within history*. It is not enough to so focus on the end or goal of human existence that actual historical conditions are seen as the mere means to attain it. There must be some intrinsic meaning to historical existence itself, to the corporate project of human creativity. Some intrinsic continuity should connect the activity on the grand social level and its final goal. Although this is not necessarily the case, in fact the teleological conception tended to focus on the end so much that it minimized the intrinsic value of the means themselves. And although human nature is by definition a generic concept, it often operates individualistically; each human being was called upon through grace to behave in such a way as to save his or her own soul.

Given our historical consciousness and concern for the meaning of human history, the theology of grace should reappropriate Aquinas's Aristotelian metaphysical perspective of teleology into a biblical eschatological framework. This is, in fact, what has occurred in Catholic theology of grace. In systematic terms, however, it is not so much a negation of the Thomistic theology of grace as a reinterpretation and retrieval.

Eschatology refers to a theory or understanding of the eschaton, or end-time. It deals not only with end in the sense of *finis* or end point, but also with the goal of human existence. Thus, it is structurally analogous to teleology. But biblical eschatology was not fashioned within the framework of analytically defined principles of being. Rather, it was constructed as a theory of history and sought to define the corporate direction in which the people of God were

heading. Eschatology has a social character. It also is metaphysical and deals with being, but that which determines the end-time is God, the source of all being and the ruler of history. The eschaton will be determined by God's will and power. But this end-time is not totally discontinuous with the history of Israel or the world. History is leading there, and "signs of the times" indicate that God's final establishment of what is to be in the end is not totally disconnected from God's rule within history.

Implicitly and sometimes explicitly, the Roman Catholic theology of grace is being reinterpreted within an eschatological framework. This does not mean retreating from a medieval mode of thought to an even more culturally distant one. For the biblical eschatological perspective, too, is being refashioned by current post-Enlightenment conceptions and concerns. As a reinterpretation of Aquinas, this means that while changing his thought, one seeks at the same time to be faithful to elements that are fundamental to it. In this case, one should continue to regard human existence dynamically as a principle of action in the world and heading for its goal. But within the framework of eschatology, three things are added as explicit foci of attention. First, the *telos* of human existence is not translated into the individual or private concern of each one for his or her own destiny. Rather, the question of the direction of human history is raised for human existence socially, not merely as a particular social group or nation, but as a race. Second, the question of both the goal and the end (*finis*) of history is merged with the question of the purposiveness of human creative action within history itself here and now. Third, within this new context, the question of the purpose of human freedom takes on a new meaning when compared with the theology of Aquinas. Over and above the metaphysical meaning that is realized in each person, the purpose of human freedom also takes on meaning in sociohistorical terms. Eschatology opens up the question of the use of human freedom corporately in history. In short, the question of grace also concerns human society here and now and into the future. This leads to the question of social grace.

Grace within the Social Sphere

One cannot avoid speaking about social grace today for two reasons. The first is negative: there has never before been such an awareness of social evil, which is not simply objective evil but sin. The great sin that bears down on individuals and corporately on human existence as a whole is social. If grace is understood only and exclusively on the individual level, then it leaves this world in its sociohistorical forms to sin. Second and positively, since human existence is social, one must ask the question of the relationship of grace to social existence. What is the impact of grace on society? If, by analogy with personal sin, one can speak of social sin, there must also be a correlatively analogous reality of social grace. The question then concerns the way one should define, explain, and talk about this grace.

The idea of social grace, like the recognition of grace generally, can be conceived only against the background of sin and death. On the individual level, sin and grace are revealed together. Sin appears as sin against the background of grace as that which should not be, and grace appears against the background of sin as God's movement within human existence that overcomes a "natural" but free propensity to sin. The same is true on the macro or social level of sin. However one explains the phenomenon of social sin, the contrary to it will appear as social grace. One may define social grace, then, as the institutionalization and objectification of the dynamics of grace originating in personal-individual freedom.

There are many examples of social grace; one should not imagine that social grace is rare. Any group, institution, organization, or society may be considered social grace insofar as it is concerned with human life and enhances the common good. From a Christian point of view, the tendency is to describe the church as the prime example of social grace. Objectively, it is an institution that serves as the sacrament of God's grace after the pattern of the revelation of God in Jesus. But other institutions may also serve the same function anonymously in the social sphere.

Given the parallelism just mentioned, the analysis of what social grace is will follow the pattern found in the analytic description of social sin. On the one hand, social grace accounts for just and life-giving institutions because it is within human beings, and human institutions are subjective. On the other hand, social grace is embedded in objective social institutions in the sense that they objectively mediate God's grace when they impel self-transcending concern for others.

Human beings create social institutions; they are not given with nature. When one finds just institutions, organizations that are dedicated to the nurture and care of human life not only of their members but also of those whom the institutions affect, it may be assumed that they derive from the wills of people who are concerned about others. Institutions dedicated to the enhancement of the common good stem from self-transcending freedom that is actively concerned with equality and the protection of life. This is the subjective side of social grace.

But institutions are also objective relative to the freedom of any individual; they are prior to and become the internalized context for

422 the exercise of any particular person's freedom. They appear in every sphere and phase of life, helping to form that second nature that in turn shapes ideas, values, and concrete modes of behavior. When the influence of these structures urges self-transcendence in the service of other human beings, the institutions in question may be considered objective channels of God's grace.

Finally, it is important to realize exactly what one is talking about in the discussion of social institutions. There is no such thing as an institution that is purely sinful or a pure social grace. Of course, some social movements may spring to mind that appear to be the very archetype of a social sin or grace. But generally, both of these antithetical concepts—social sin and social grace—are heuristic. They are questioning categories that shed a particular light on certain aspects of social constructions and allow one to perceive them in a certain way. These categories raise questions and provide a perspective and a tool for regarding social institutions in a theological way. They enable a critical theological examination of the just and unjust aspects of every social institution.

Social Grace and the Purpose of Human Freedom

We come now to the question of the purpose of human freedom that was raised in the preliminary anthropology, then negatively relative to sin, and again in the discussion of eschatology. Since God has created human existence as freedom with the potentially creative and destructive power that we experience today, what is the intrinsic raison d'être written by God into that freedom? The question is directed first of all to the immediate purpose of freedom, to its exercise in this world. Another way of asking this question would be in terms of the direction in which the effects of grace lead.[86]

The analysis of social grace leads to the conclusion that the purpose of human freedom in this world under the influence of grace is the creation of graced social structures. This position can be made persuasive from two points of view—the one from the present looking forward into the future, the other from the perspective of eschatology itself.

The purpose of human freedom in this world can be understood as the direction in which the effects of grace lead. The forgiveness of sin and opening up of freedom in self-transcending love, cooperative grace and the participation in God's life that gives human freedom a capacity for creativity that it does not have on its own—all these lead to the classical Christian virtue of love of neighbor. But in the light of a new appreciation of the social constitution of human existence, and of interdependence and solidarity in social existence, love of neighbor cannot be reduced to interpersonal relationships; it must also be understood in social terms. Participation in the formation of emancipatory social structures is a necessary form of love of neighbor.

Our actual situation today is one in which the massive amount of social suffering calls the very meaningfulness of our corporate history

---

86. From one point of view, this is not a new question in theology, for the pre-Enlightenment churches did have a body of social teachings. But when one considers practical spirituality and theological conceptions of the Christian life, the tendency was to so focus on final salvation that the issue of the use of freedom in this world did not receive the attention that the present cultural context demands. There are, of course, exceptions to this in some of the Anabaptist movements. And John Calvin, with his doctrine of sanctification and his theology of the Christian life in this world, including the principle of stewardship, stands out in this regard. See *Institutes of the Christian Religion*, 3.10.719–25.

into question. But the meaningfulness that human beings long for is not simply there in history as an objective given to be discovered. It is a possibility that must be created by human freedom through the power of grace. In other words, God's grace calls upon and impels human beings to establish the meaningfulness of history in the open future.

More specifically, the movement of grace in human freedom has a double direction. The first is to resist social evil and sin. Negatively, the purpose of human existence as freedom in this world is not to escape social sin, but to resist it. Within history, the dynamism of God's Spirit moves human freedom against sin; militancy in the Christian life counteracts sin by fighting against it. Positively, the movement of grace is toward the construction of social institutions of grace in every sphere of human life. No area of institutionally structured human life is alien to the influence of graced freedom patterned on the life of Jesus.

The Eschatology of Grace

The second perspective that yields a conclusion about the purpose of human freedom comes from eschatology. One cannot avoid the eschatological question of the end of history. In response to this issue of the goal of history, the Christian has only the one answer contained in the symbol "the kingdom of God." No other symbol was more important for the teaching of Jesus than the kingdom of God; it formed a center of gravity for the whole of his message and for the activity of his ministry.

It is, of course, difficult to determine exactly what Jesus meant by the kingdom of God. Not only is it a religious symbol about something transcendent and eschatological, but also Jesus' teaching about it in parables and figures of speech does not yield a precise conceptual formula. But even if one could determine exactly what Jesus meant by the kingdom of God, its meaning would still have to be interpreted anew to be intelligible to twenty-first-century culture. From this perspective, the symbol means with surety at least this: The kingdom of God is God's rule, an order of reality according to God's will, "on earth as it is in heaven" (Matt. 6:10).[87] The kingdom of God implies an order of justice, of peace and harmony among people (for the kingdom of God is made up of people), who all give glory to God by being in accord with God's will in the final order of things.

The kingdom of God is an eschatological symbol. But it has a bearing on human history. On the one hand, the New Testament testifies to the breaking in of God's kingdom in a new way with Jesus, and on the other hand, it would make little sense to exempt history from the intention of the will of its Creator. The kingdom of God, then, as God's will, God's values, God's intention for historical existence, also applies to history "on earth." As in teleology, so too in eschatology: the end of history illumines what history should be like at any given time. The view that the purpose of human freedom is found in its dedication to social grace is not imposed upon the idea of the kingdom of God but is a faithful interpretation of its intrinsic meaning today.

The continuity between history and the end-time under the symbol of the kingdom of God reaches further. The eschatological question is the question of the ultimate meaningfulness of human existence as freedom in history.

---

87. E. P. Sanders concludes that "we know perfectly well what [Jesus] meant in general terms [by the kingdom of God]: the ruling power of God." *Jesus and Judaism* (Philadelphia: Fortress Press, 1985), 127.

424

From this perspective, it follows that for human life to be ultimately meaningful, it must actually contribute to that eschatological reality that Jesus called the kingdom of God.

Several considerations lead to this conclusion. The first is the reasonable inference that if the exercise of human freedom does not have a bearing on and enter into the construction of final reality, it is then finally and ultimately meaningless. In other words, the only way that one can affirm the meaningfulness of the creativity of human freedom in history is to affirm that it contributes to the ultimate and final condition of reality itself.[88] Second, it is also reasonable to think that this accords with the intention of God, who created in God's image the creative and world-fashioning freedom of human existence. It would seem to frustrate the creative intention of God if the positive achievement of human freedom were in the end worthless, made no difference, and counted for nothing. Third, Catholic theology of grace has always maintained a continuity between the operation of grace in this world and final union with God.[89] It is not unreasonable to extend this continuity to cooperative grace. This means that what is accomplished by human freedom in grace, the works and achievements of human freedom done in love, is constitutive of the ultimate reality of the end-time.[90] Finally, in current interpretations of the theological significance of the

resurrection of Jesus, many theologians see the resurrection as God's ratification and validation of Jesus and his message. Extending this view, faith in the resurrection of the life and actions of Jesus becomes a witness to and hope in this eschatology. He is the "first-born among many" (Rom. 8:29), the one whose whole life and praxis of love have been raised up and preserved in a salvation paradigmatic for all.

In sum, the theology of grace, in tension with the theology of sin, proposes an anthropology of creative human freedom and action. As stated in an earlier section, in this view of God's grace, the intention of God for salvation was prior to that of creation itself, so that prior to all sin, God's offer of personal love and self-communication provides the actual context of all human existence or freedom. God's Spirit is the symbol expressing this constant personal presence to and dialogue with human freedom. The effects of this grace are the accepting and forgiving of sinful human existence and the opening up of human freedom in self-transcending love. But this means that, when viewed from a new historically conscious perspective, new creation appears to be the intention prior to grace, and grace is *for* new creation.[91] In other words, the purpose of grace and human freedom together is the struggle against sin and the fashioning of ever-new history in love. What is done in freedom informed and sustained by grace will be

---

88. As Segundo puts it, "The values to which Jesus of Nazareth bore concrete testimony in his message and life can be realized only if the 'I' of each person has the power to accomplish a project that is both personal and definitive." *The Humanist Christology of Paul*, 133.

89. Rahner, "Some Implications of the Scholastic Concept of Uncreated Grace," 319–46.

90. Segundo, *The Humanist Christology of Paul*, 123–25, 157. Segundo also adds that God in the end-time will not make up what is not accomplished by human freedom in love. It should be noted that, although Segundo works within a framework of evolution, this does not imply a theory of moral progress or the view that love accumulates in history. On the level of empirical history, the effects of sin are more manifest than the effects of grace. Segundo is thus not subject to the critique leveled against nineteenth-century liberal theology insofar as it professed a progressive view of history.

91. Frances Stefano, *The Absolute Value of Human Action in the Theology of Juan Luis Segundo* (Lanham, MD: University Press of America, 1992), 335.

transformed into the permanent, definitive, and ultimate reality of the kingdom of God.[92]

Sin, Grace, and Spirituality

The point of theology is to open up an understanding of God, the world, history, and human existence in such a way that it provides a vision for human living. Just as all knowledge is for human life and action, so, too, the value of theology lies in the way of life it opens up to Christian imagination and freedom. No area has more direct bearing on Christian life than Christian anthropology. Insofar as the doctrines of sin and grace are anthropological, they contain the fundamental principles of Christian spirituality.

The Meaning of Spirituality

The term *spirituality* refers to the way human beings, individuals and groups, lead their lives considered from the point of view of union with God. Spirituality in this sense can be considered on a few different levels. On the existential level, spirituality is constituted by the actual way any given person leads his or her life. The point here reaches deeper than the superficial notion of lifestyle. Spirituality refers to the way people *lead* their lives; it includes the deepest purpose toward which a life is directed and the values and goals that underlie motivation. Spirituality is thus a general anthropological category; all persons have some form of spirituality insofar as they consciously direct their lives. Christian spirituality refers to the way Christians actually live. But on an abstract, reflective, and cognitive level, spirituality refers to the theory of how human life should be led. Here the meaning of spirituality approaches the meaning of theology insofar as theology has bearing on Christian life.[93]

The point of this concrete, existential, and historical definition of spirituality lies in the problems it seeks to overcome. First of all, as a common anthropological category, spirituality places the Christian way of life in dialogue with other human conceptions of life. Second, the definition is inclusive of all the dimensions of Christian life. By not identifying one aspect of Christian life, such as prayer or sacramental worship, with the whole of Christian spirituality, it does not evacuate the full range of human behavior of spiritual value. Thus, third, the definition is integrative. It seeks to bind together the many dichotomies—between the spiritual and material, sacred and profane, eternal and temporal, supernatural and natural—that have marked Christian life. In sum, this conception sees all aspects of human life as sacred because, suffused with the offer of God's Spirit, all human action can mediate response to God's grace.

Although the object of spirituality is actual human living, its formal and defining perspective lies in the question of life's conformity with the ultimate reason of things. What is the ultimate truth of human existence? Thus, the question of union with God is the fundamental issue or formality that defines the subject matter of spirituality. How is human life united with God? Or what is it in Christian life that unites people to God?

The subject matter of spirituality may be thought of in terms of action, where action is

---

92. Segundo, *The Humanist Christology of Paul*, 157. For Segundo, what is not done in love will not survive.

93. One may also refer to different schools of spirituality surrounding specific historical conceptions of the Christian life. Spirituality may also refer to a discipline that studies the literature of various aspects and forms of the Christian life.

426 understood in a comprehensive way to include the whole of human existence.[94] Although logically distinct, the notions of human freedom and action are intimately related. Human existence is freedom, but it is always freedom in action. The point of using the term *action* is to highlight the dynamic nature of human existence. Thus, spirituality most generally may be looked upon simply as the logic of human action.

By helping to define a Christian anthropology, the doctrines of sin and grace relate directly to Christian spirituality. The theology of sin and grace functions as second-level or reflective spirituality. By responding to the questions of how human existence stands before God; how God relates to human beings; how human existence should respond to God, other human beings, and history; and the purpose of human freedom in this world, this theology provides the fundamental theological framework for understanding how concrete Christian life should unfold.

God's Purpose for Human Freedom and Action

From the theology of sin and grace, it appears that the purpose of freedom and action in this world is, on the one hand, to resist sin; on the other hand, it is to love and serve the neighbor both on the individual level of personal relationships and socially through the mediation of social structures. This flows from the recognition of sin and the nature and effects of grace.

On the most fundamental level, the doctrines of sin and grace refer to the structural condition of human existence. The prior sin,

the fallen condition of human existence, describes the existential situation of human freedom as such. This sin cannot be escaped; sin lies within human freedom as a dynamic structure and process, and human freedom exists in it as in an "objective" sphere. So, too, God's permanent, universal, yet gratuitous offer of personal self-communication constitutes another sphere or region for the unfolding of human action, on both the individual and social levels. This divine milieu of God as Spirit or grace tends in the opposite direction of sin; it is God's energy for the freeing of freedom from the imprisonment of sin and its effects, both individually and socially.

The dynamic nature of human existence as freedom in action, combined with the permanent situation of sin and grace, implies that the purpose of human freedom in this world is to resist sin. Only the end of human life will provide a resting place from this struggle. But this implies that the fundamental logic of human freedom and action lies not in escape from this world, not in a religious society separated from this world, and not in a mere passing of time waiting for the end. Human life is not merely a "test" or a "prelude" to the real life of eternity.[95] Rather, the fundamental theme of Christian spirituality is responsibility, the assumption of the God-given purpose and intentionality of human freedom to establish the works of love in the world in contrast to the effects of sin and final death.

This dynamic and activist understanding of Christian anthropology and spirituality should not obscure the tensions out of which it unfolds. Sin and grace are in constant tension, and there

---

94. This broad concept of human action, which makes it synonymous with existential human existence itself, is drawn from Maurice Blondel, *Action (1893): Essay on a Critique of Life and a Science of Practice* (Notre Dame, IN: University of Notre Dame Press, 1984).

95. Juan Luis Segundo, *The Christ of the Ignatian Exercises* (Maryknoll, NY: Orbis, 1987), 41–124, passim.

is always both a passive and an active dimension to human life understood in Christian terms. Human beings are in bondage, captive to, and imprisoned by sin, even as God's Spirit is a power, force, and energy within human existence drawing human existence out in a freedom that transcends these bonds. One can understand the active, responsible, self-transcending exercise of freedom in love only against the background of our release from the anxiety for our own being through basic trust and faith in God.

What is important for the dynamics of sin and grace in today's world is the recognition of their social dimension. At no time in history has historical consciousness made human beings more aware of the significance and power of this dimension of life. The movement of grace is not merely a power to resist sin in one's individual life. In fact, the strongest bonds of sin in individual lives are mediated by social concupiscence, temptation, and sin. Thus, inversely, the dynamic teleology of grace, reinterpreted in an eschatological framework, leads human freedom in a sociohistorical direction to the exercise of responsibility in resisting social sin. The overriding purpose of human freedom in this world, and the direction in which God's grace impels it, is toward the construction of social grace in history. Sin will be resisted in one's individual life in the very dedication to that immediate goal.

Union with God

What makes human action spirituality is the way it binds human existence to God and God's grace. What makes Christian anthropology a study of spirituality is the way it explains how union with God is effected in this world through the exercise of human freedom. Is it by faith? Works? Worship? Retired contemplation?

An anthropology of sin and grace that is set within the context of human freedom implies that the only way one can be united with God is through responsive human action. But since action is such a general category, does this formula not raise the question of which particular actions forge this union with God? Such an approach to the problem cannot avoid reintroducing dichotomies into the Christian life.

One is finally united with God by the whole of one's life and action and not by any single kind of action. All of one's actions in every sphere, and the whole history of one's actions up to the present, constitute and carry one's fundamental option. The sum total of one's action defines the form of one's basic trust, faith, and love. All individual actions—including those commonly associated with the domain of spirituality, such as sacramental and liturgical worship, retreat, and prayer—are concrete and more or less conscious mediations of God's grace that merely feed into the generalized action where union with God or rejection of God is finally effected. All human actions performed out of self-transcending love mediate union with God.

The ability of action to actualize union with God can be understood on three levels. First, by defining a person's fundamental option, action effects a union of wills. One is united with God by doing God's will. Such a union with God is possible without being aware of it.

Second, on a conscious level of awareness of God, action mediates a possessive knowledge.[96] Through action, one does not merely know *about* God and God's will in a kind of objective

---

96. Blondel, *Action*, 434.

428 knowledge in which subject and object are separated. Through action, God is appropriated by the connatural knowledge that can be mediated only by doing God's will. Human action—a taking up and acting on the basis of that which is known theoretically—makes the doctrine of grace a principle of one's behavior. In this qualitatively different kind of knowledge mediated by action, the distance and separation between the object of faith and the believer are overcome. One possesses because one is possessed by the Spirit of God.

Third, through action one is ontically united with God through the response to grace that becomes cooperative grace. This is participation in God's life, though not in a static way that overlooks the dynamic quality of human existence as a principle of action. Rather, this participation in God's life implies new capacity, energy, empowerment, and coactions within the power of God's Spirit.

The crucial point in the spirituality of sin and grace, however, turns on the recognition that action for social grace and justice in this world is of itself genuine spiritual activity that unites one to God. This is not an addition to or the consequence of Christian spirituality that is somehow defined as complete in other terms. Action in the world and history that resists social sin and is engaged in the construction of social grace out of love *is* Christian spirituality. Of itself, by the power of grace, it unites one to God.

Resurrection Hope

Finally, intrinsic to Christian spirituality, as the depth dimension that sustains the whole of it, is Christian hope. This is openness to the future that trusts in God's power of creation and gratuitous love despite the destructiveness of time that leads to death. The life of Jesus and faith in his resurrection enter intrinsically into and constitute this hope. But this hope is not a mere wish and desire for survival. In Christian anthropology, this hope bends back and gives meaning to history itself and to the exercise of human freedom in creative action. Christian hope, then, is a fundamental trust that human freedom and action count, and that both individual freedom and history are meaningful because, in the end, what is done in love supported by God's grace will constitute the kingdom of God.

Conclusion

This short treatise on Catholic theology of grace or the practical doctrine of the Spirit and the Christian anthropology contained in it has to be situated in the larger theological picture suggested in the opening pages on context. That section drew together some of the major work being done in Catholic theology generally and, more specifically, in the theology of grace. From those sources, it extrapolated elements of a new Catholic vision that is emerging. This expansive framework for understanding reality is evolutionary in its conception of creation; it interprets God's presence and power in Wisdom and Spirit as the ground of this creativity. God as Spirit is revealed by Jesus also to be gratuitous love. As such, God establishes in being and accepts creation as it is; God empowers creation, urges self-transcendence in human freedom, and forgives human sinners. The loving, creative energy of God is universal and thus appears in different forms among the religions. As Jesus embodied, preached, and acted out God's Spirit of wisdom and love and thus revealed it in history, so, too, does the power of God's Spirit become actualized in human beings doing God's will, "on earth as it is in heaven," so that one can on occasion and in fragments find signs of hope in God's kingdom. Grace thus works both individually in persons and publicly in social endeavors, in human subjectivity but also as the creative energy of the universe. Here is a vision of what God is doing that encompasses individuals in their freedom and their concrete situations and reaches out to include the whole of human history and the universe.

For Further Reading

Augustine, *Basic Writings of Saint Augustine*. Edited by Whitney J. Oates. New York: Random House, 1948.

> *Contains several of Augustine's anti-Pelagian writings that formulated the fundamental categories of the theology of grace for the Western tradition.*

Clooney, Francis X. "Learning to See: Comparative Practice and the Widening of Theological Vision." *Proceedings of the Catholic Theological Society of America* 58 (2003): 1–15.

> *An essay that opens up a perspective for theological reflection on the theology of grace based theologically on the premise set by Vatican II that the Spirit of God is at work in the world and the religions reflect its saving truth and power.*

Duffy, Stephen J. "Our Hearts of Darkness: Original Sin Revisited." *Theological Studies* 49 (1988): 597–622.

> *A well-written interpretation of the doctrine that takes account of its genesis and combines several levels of understanding from other contemporary authors.*

Gonzalez, Michelle A. *Created in God's Image: An Introduction to Feminist Theological Anthropology.* Maryknoll, NY: Orbis, 2007.

> *An analytical interpretation of the theology of grace written from a feminist perspective that is readily accessible and demonstrative of the insight generated by feminist theologians.*

Haight, Roger. *The Experience and Language of Grace.* New York: Paulist, 1979.

> *An accessible historical treatment of the theology of grace in terms of important theological landmarks followed by a constructive liberationist interpretation.*

Rahner, Karl. *Foundations of Christian Faith: An Introduction to the Idea of Christianity.* New York: Seabury, 1978.

> *Contains the basic elements of Rahner's theology of grace, which has been the main influence on the Roman Catholic systematic interpretation in the post–Vatican II period.*

430   Ricoeur, Paul. *The Symbolism of Evil.* Boston: Beacon, 1969.

> *An authoritative investigation and analysis of various levels of the symbolism of evil. It may serve as a background for the more direct and methodological study of the doctrine in Ricoeur's "'Original Sin': A Study in Meaning," in* The Conflict of Interpretations: Essays in Hermeneutics, *ed. Don Ihde (Evanston, IL: Northwestern University Press, 1974).*

Schillebeeckx, Edward. *Christ: The Experience of Jesus as Lord.* New York: Seabury, 1980.

> *Contains a masterful synopsis of the theme of grace in the New Testament terms of salvation.*

Schoonenberg, Piet. *Man and Sin: A Theological View.* Notre Dame, IN: University of Notre Dame Press, 1965.

> *An early Catholic effort at interpreting the doctrine of original sin in historical and social terms; important for its independent grounding of liberationist understandings of sin and grace.*

Segundo, Juan Luis. "Ignatius Loyola: Trial or Project?" In *Signs of the Times: Theological Reflections*, edited by Alfred T. Hennelly, 149–75. Maryknoll, NY: Orbis, 1993.

> *This essay defines a perspective on the theology of grace that orients understanding toward a spirituality of engagement in history and society.*

Thomas Aquinas. *Summa theologiae.* Vol. 30, *The Gospel of Grace.* Edited by Cornelius Ernst. Oxford: Blackfriars, 1972.

> *The classic statement of the medieval interpretation of the theology of grace in Aristotelian categories that remained authoritative for the Roman Catholic Church up to the Second Vatican Council.*

Wiley, Tatha. *Original Sin: Origins, Developments, Contemporary Meaning.* New York: Paulist, 2002.

> *A clear yet subtle interpretation and retrieval of the doctrine of original sin that attends to the problems connected with this doctrine and is faithful to the tradition, ecumenically sensitive, and accessible to the general reader.*

Communion of Saints and Mary

Elizabeth A. Johnson

Down through the centuries, as the Holy Spirit of God graces person after person in land after land, they form together a grand company of human beings, sinful yet redeemed. The Christian doctrine of the communion of saints, based on Scripture and expressed in creed and liturgy, articulates this holy community in its many dimensions. It posits a bond of companionship among living persons themselves who, though widely separated geographically, form one church community around the globe. Since death cannot separate people from the love of Christ, it also stretches backward and forward in time to connect the church today with faithful dead of all ages. Insofar as the range of those who are graced by the Spirit is as broad as the human race itself, it likewise affirms a link between all who live by the light of their conscience, whether baptized with water or not.

The original Latin term *communio sanctorum* (communion of holy ones) is grammatically ambiguous, referring in one instance to a communion of holy people but in another instance to a communion of holy things. Thus, this symbol also traditionally signifies sharing in the bread and wine of the Eucharist. Given the ecological interrelationships of the community of life, it points in its widest reach to the sacramental fellowship of all creation formed by the power of the indwelling Spirit. From every angle, this doctrinal symbol crosses boundaries, bespeaking a communal participation in the gracious holiness of God brought about by the play of Spirit-Sophia from generation to generation and across the wide world.

Throughout the centuries, Christians have honored Mary of Nazareth, the mother of Jesus, the Mother of God (in Greek, *Theotokos*, the God-bearer, the one heavy/pregnant with God). Since she was abundantly graced by the Spirit, walked faithfully with her God during her life,

and now lives embraced by the glory of God, she also belongs in this company. Her location there provides a sound entryway to theological reflection on her significance.

The Living Tradition

This is clearly one area where the priority of praxis has held sway, with doctrine being led by piety and practice. A thumbnail sketch of the colorful history of the communion of saints, including Mary, will shed light on its basic meaning and provide significant elements for theological interpretation in our day.

Scripture

The idea of being a holy community is deeply rooted in Jewish tradition. This holiness is not primarily an ethical matter—that is, being holy as being innocent of sin or morally perfect. Neither is it something that individuals merit by their own worthiness. Rather, it is a gift freely bestowed by God in view of the inscrutable divine choice to forge a covenant relationship with this small, powerless, enslaved people. The community is consecrated by the God of Israel's own choice: "For I am the Lord who brought you up from the land of Egypt, to be your God; you shall be holy, for I am holy" (Lev. 11:45). This communal dedication is the innermost secret of the people's identity, and it flows into their responsibility to bear witness to the world.

Early Christians drew upon this biblical tradition to articulate their own sense of identity. Inspired by the waters of baptism and the shared Eucharistic meal, they understood that they participated in the very life of God through the life, death, and resurrection of Jesus Christ. As a result, they referred to each other in the church

434 as "saints" or "holy ones" (*hagioi* in Greek).[1] Over sixty times in the New Testament, this term points to the whole community, as Paul's letters attest: "To all God's beloved in Rome, who are called to be saints" (Rom. 1:7); "To all the saints in Christ Jesus who are in Philippi" (Phil. 1:1); "To the church of God that is in Corinth, to all of you who are sanctified in Christ Jesus, called to be saints" (1 Cor. 1:2); "All the saints greet you" (2 Cor. 13:13). All together and without discrimination, Christians are a community of holy people consecrated by the power of the Spirit. While sinners, they are yet redeemed in Christ, and their lives must reflect this in their faith-filled ethical behavior.

In time, the term *saints* expanded beyond the living to include those who had died and are now with Christ in glory. Between these saints and the saints on earth exists a strong communion, a mutual sense of appreciation and support. The letter to the Hebrews presents a memorable metaphor for this relationship. After a long roll call of Jewish ancestors, each of whom responded with faith to the challenging call of God in their lives, the text proclaims, "Therefore, since we are surrounded by so great a cloud of witnesses, let us also lay aside every weight and the sin that clings so closely, and let us run with perseverance the race that is set before us, looking to Jesus the pioneer and perfecter of our faith" (Heb. 12:1-2). The image in play here is that of a stadium packed with a throng of people in the stands, all of whom had once run the race and are now cheering for those on the field. Here the faithful dead are not proposed simply as exemplars to be imitated, let alone the objects

of a cult, but as a multitude of faithful people whose own struggles galvanize the energies of those presently running the course. Their witness, now configured paradigmatically in Jesus Christ, awakens hope that those running today might also win.

The story of Mary of Nazareth appears in the New Testament in thirteen discrete scenes concerning the conception, birth, growing up, ministry, and death of her firstborn, Jesus. After the resurrection, she appears explicitly in the early Christian community, being named among the 120 persons gathered in the upper room in Jerusalem awaiting the coming of the Spirit (Acts 1:14-15). A Jewish woman who sings prophetically of God's justice to the poor, she is depicted in different ways from Gospel to Gospel. The New Testament, while including Mary and other significant persons whose lives interweave with the story of Jesus Christ, presents no evidence for pious practices that later became characteristic of their veneration.[2]

Age of Martyrs

As Christianity spread, Roman persecution created conditions for some disciples to give the ultimate witness to Christ, their very lives. Condemned, tortured, bloodied, and executed, martyrs were perceived by others in the church as entering in a graphic way into the dying of Jesus, and so into his rising. They were icons of Jesus Christ, awesome signs of the victory of his power in the face of the evil of this world. Christians loved these martyrs and found ways to express their esteem. Their graves became

---

1. "Ágios," in *Theological Dictionary of the New Testament*, ed. Gerhard Kittel (Grand Rapids: Eerdmans, 1964), 1:88–115.

2. For critical discussion of all biblical Marian texts, see Raymond Brown et al., eds., *Mary in the New Testament* (Philadelphia: Fortress Press, 1978).

places of pilgrimage and prayer. On the yearly anniversary of their death—which, unlike in pagan custom, was considered the day of their true birth—nightlong vigil was kept at their graves, culminating at dawn in a Eucharist and common meal. Their memory continued to be cherished even through subsequent generations.

An early interpretation of the meaning of the martyrs was given in the second century by members of the church at Smyrna. Responding to the trumped-up charge that they were abandoning Christ in order to worship their martyred, beloved bishop Polycarp, they wrote, "Little did they know that we could never abandon Christ, who suffered for the redemption of those who are saved in the whole world, the innocent one dying on behalf of sinners. Nor could we worship anyone else. For him we worship as the Son of God. But the martyrs we love as disciples and imitators of the Lord, and rightly so because of their matchless affection for their own king and teacher. May we too become their comrades and fellow disciples."[3]

Veneration of the martyrs was pervaded by this lively sense of comradeship between the still-struggling living and the victorious dead, joined in the Spirit of Christ. This comes to particularly clear expression in Augustine's preaching on the feasts of the martyrs, which provides a vocabulary of relationship. If you think you can't do what they did, he encouraged

his congregation, just remember that they lived by the grace of God, and "the fountain is still flowing, it hasn't dried up."[4] Indeed, we have it easier, thanks to their efforts: "How can the way be rough when it has been smoothed by the feet of so many walking ahead of us?"[5] People who believed before us had no idea that one day there would be a community in this place, a church of the future praising God: "they weren't yet able to see it; yet they were already constructing it out of their own lives."[6] Like fragrance that perfumes a room, their lives leave us "lessons of encouragement,"[7] giving us strength and joy. Their adventure of faith opened a way for us, and now we go ahead of others in an ongoing river of companions seeking God. The feast of the young mother-martyrs Perpetua and Felicity, now dwelling in "perpetual felicity," occasioned deep insight into this mutual interrelation: "Let it not seem a small thing to us that we are members of the same body as these. . . . We marvel at them, they have compassion on us. We rejoice for them, they pray for us. . . . Yet do we all serve one Lord, follow the same teacher, accompany the same leader. We are all joined to the one head, journey to the same Jerusalem, follow after the same love, embrace the same unity."[8] In this era, the communion of saints was practiced as a disciplined way of remembering across the generations that empowered Christian life.

---

3. "The Martyrdom of Polycarp" par. 17, in *The Acts of the Christian Martyrs*, ed. Herbert Musurillo (Oxford: Oxford University Press, 1972) 16–17.

4. Augustine, Sermon 315.8, in *Sermons*, trans. and notes by Edmund Hill (Hyde Park, NY: New City, 1990–95), 9:133.

5. Augustine, *Sermon* 306.10, in ibid., 9:24.

6. Augustine, *Sermon* 306c.1, in ibid., 9:36–37.

7. Augustine, *Sermon* 273.2, in ibid., 8:17.

8. *Sermon* 280.6, in *The Passion of Perpetua and Felicity, with the Sermons of St. Augustine upon these Saints*, trans. W. H. Shewring (London: Sheed & Ward, 1931), 49–51.

Once the age of Roman persecution ceased, other types of holy women and men joined the ranks of martyrs who were venerated in the church. The Christian cloud of witnesses grew to include confessors who had been tortured for the faith but not killed; ascetics, especially those who lived a life of celibacy; wise teachers and prudent church leaders; and those who cared for the poor.

During these early centuries, Mary of Nazareth was also honored because of her fidelity to the divine call to bear and mother Jesus Christ. Theologians such as Justin and Irenaeus extended the biblical Adam-Christ parallel to include Eve-Mary, seeing that Mary's obedience to God's call overturned the disobedience of Eve. The axiom "death through Eve, life through Mary" captured the importance of her life as mother of the Redeemer. In a direct outcome of the controversy over the unity of natures in Christ, the Council of Ephesus in 431 legitimated the title *Theotokos* for Mary, reasoning that if Jesus Christ is in truth the Word incarnate, then she who bore him can be called the Mother of God (DS 251).[9] During these centuries, belief in Mary's physical virginity developed to include not only the scripturally attested virginal conception of Jesus but also her virginity during his birth and forever after (virginity *ante partum, in partu, post partum*), a belief given official status by an anathema of the Lateran Council of 649 (DS 503).

Late Antiquity: From Companionship to Patronage

The companionship model of relationship between the saints in heaven and on earth, typical of the New Testament and the age of the martyrs, receded under the impact of new circumstances. Studies have shown how significant the political, social, economic, and religious world of late antiquity was for shaping a new form of relationship to the saints in heaven.[10] Modeled on the Roman system of civic patronage, a spiritual patronage system emerged whereby the saints became heavenly patrons of individuals or communities. Prayers for their intercession before the throne of God or even their direct aid became common. Building churches over or near their graves, moving their bodies into more distinguished settings, and distributing pieces of their bodies or belongings as relics served to broaden access to their influence. Given that the saints were such strong conduits of divine favor, their presence evoked prayer for healings and other miracles; when these prayers were granted, saints were seen as a locus of the breakthrough of divine power.

In the case of Mary, patronage, presence, and power coalesced in a uniquely effective way as popular piety transferred elements from the Mediterranean cult of the Great Mother to the Jewish mother of Jesus.[11] Titles such as Queen of Heaven, imagery of the blue cloak and crown of

---

9. References to official church teaching are taken from J. Neuner and J. Dupuis, eds., *The Christian Faith in the Doctrinal Documents of the Catholic Church* (New York: Alba House, 1981). The notation DS followed by an Arabic numeral indicates the 1962 Denzinger-Schönmetzer collection of doctrinal documents (entitled Enchiridion Symbolorum) as translated in Neuner-Dupuis.

10. For studies using the approach of social history, see Peter Brown, *The Cult of the Saints: Its Rise and Function in Latin Christianity* (London: SCM, 1981); and Stephen Wilson, ed., *Saints and Their Cults: Studies in Religious Sociology, Folklore and History* (Cambridge: Cambridge University Press, 1983), with annotated bibliography, 309–417.

11. Jean Daniélou, "Le culte marial et le paganisme," in *Maria: Études sur la Sainte Vierge*, ed. Hubert du Manoir (Paris: Beauchesne, 1949), 159–81; R. E. Witt, *Isis in the Greco-Roman World* (Ithaca: Cornell University Press, 1971), 269–81.

stars, and roles of maternal protection and care migrated from the goddess to Mary, being "baptized" into a Christian framework. Figurines of the Egyptian goddess Isis presenting her little son Horus to the world became the model for Mary, Seat of Wisdom, presenting Christ to the world. As a missionary strategy this transfer was successful, making Christianity attractive to peoples who had long venerated female representations of the divine. Theologically, the success of this adaptation was less certain, as the figure of Mary in piety assumed the function of being the maternal face of God.

By the end of the early Christian centuries in both East and West, it was clear that while the communion of saints included all the redeemed in Christ, particular saints, besides being comrades in the following of Jesus, were also powerful patrons and intercessors. In the context of this growing popular cult of the saints, increasingly expressed in the use of icons, and in the context of strong criticism of these practices, the last ecumenical council to occur before the split between East and West made clear the distinction between honoring God and honoring the saints. In 787, the Second Council of Nicaea noted that God alone is to be worshipped and adored (*latria*), while the saints should be given simple respect and veneration (*dulia*) (DS 601).

Second Millennium

In medieval times, all of the previously described characteristics of devotion to the saints and Mary blossomed with a profusion that is impossible to codify. On the one hand, the church in its public liturgy soberly honored the memory of those whose lives had given splendid and striking witness to Christ, praising God in their company and holding up their example. On the other hand, popular piety petitioned uncounted thousands of local saints, some of them legendary. Credulity and superstition abounded, as evidenced by zeal for collecting relics, reports of frivolous miracles, superheated hagiography, and the divorce of piety from ethics. Mary, Mother of Jesus, Mother of God, assumed a magnified role in piety as beautiful virgin, merciful mother, and powerful queen of heaven and earth who could command even her Son.[12] Conviction grew that she ruled the kingdom of mercy in face of the severe justice of Christ. All of this occurred at a time when the Latin liturgy and scholastic theology became ever more remote from ordinary people's experience, where daily life was hard and dangerous. There was a felt need for human mediators who were closer to ordinary people and unworthy sinners than was the magnificent Savior and just Judge, Jesus Christ.

For the first thousand years of the church's history, precisely who among deceased believers were to be honored in a special way had been decided more or less spontaneously by the people and their bishops in different locales. In the tenth century, bishops in council at the Lateran involved the pope officially in this decision for the first time. Papal participation grew to the point where, by the thirteenth century, naming new saints (canonizing them, or inscribing them on the list or canon of officially recognized holy people) was restricted to the papacy alone.[13]

12. See Jaroslav Pelikan, *The Growth of Medieval Theology* (Chicago: University of Chicago Press, 1978), 158–84; and Heiko Oberman, *The Harvest of Medieval Theology* (Cambridge: Harvard University Press, 1963), 281–322.

13. For the history, see Michael Perham, *The Communion of Saints* (London: SPCK, 1980). Kenneth Woodward, *Making Saints* (New York: Simon & Schuster, 1997), presents current practice.

438

In spite of the efforts of some bishops and theologians to curb abuses, these did continue, becoming part of the late medieval distortion of the gospel criticized by the Reformers in the sixteenth century. The theological leaders of the Reformation did not turn against the saints or Mary in themselves. Luther, for example, wrote movingly of the community of saints and penned a commentary on the Magnificat, which described Mary as a woman of faith and "the foremost example of the grace of God."[14] The historic *Apology of the Augsburg Confession* makes clear that, for Lutherans, there remains a proper veneration of the saints expressed in three ways: thanking God for them, letting faith be strengthened by them, and imitating their example where appropriate. But what the Reformers forbid is invocation, or calling upon the saints for their prayers and favors. Not only is there no scriptural warrant for this practice, but it dangerously detracts from Christ as the sole mediator between the human race and God. In response, the Council of Trent, while giving regulatory authority over the cult of the saints to bishops in order to correct abuses, declared that it is "good and useful" to thank God for the saints and to ask them for their prayers, thus maintaining the legitimacy of invocation.[15]

Succeeding centuries saw these two divergent paths intensify as the Reformation tradition developed a case of amnesia about the saints and Mary, while Catholic piety and doctrine concentrated more fixedly upon them. Protestants tended to fulfill Luther's prophecy that when the saints were no longer thought to give people benefits, they would be left to rest unmolested in their graves.[16] Catholics meanwhile, with egregious abuses held in check, continued to venerate the saints through old and new practices. Polemics abounded. By the nineteenth century, a resurgence of interest in Mary led to a new exercise of papal teaching authority. In 1854, Pius IX defined the dogma of the immaculate conception, which declared that from the first instant of her conception, by the grace of God and the merits of Jesus Christ, Mary was preserved free from original sin (DS 2803). Almost a century later, in 1950, Pius XII defined the dogma of the assumption, which declared that after her life on earth, Mary was assumed body and soul into the glory of heaven (DS 3903). Piety and theology kept pace with these official developments. New "true" devotions were practiced, apparitions of Mary multiplied, and new places of pilgrimage such as Lourdes and Fatima attracted millions, while some theologians developed a theology of Mary as mediatrix of grace and even co-redemptrix.

Such was the situation on the eve of the Second Vatican Council (1962–65): centuries of silence and high suspicion of the veneration of the saints in the churches of the Reformation, and overly luxuriant growth of devotion in the Catholic Church. Fueled by the biblical, patristic, and liturgical renewals already under way, as well as by genuine ecumenical concern, Vatican II produced the first extended teaching on the saints and Mary ever given by a church council. By deciding to locate this teaching in the Constitution on the Church and to apply its insight in the practical norms of the Constitution on the Liturgy, the council set a promising

---

14. Martin Luther, "Commentary on the Magnificat," in Luther's Works, ed. Jaroslav Pelikan (St. Louis: Concordia, 1953), 21:295–355.

15. DS 1821–23.

16. Luther, Smalkald Articles, part 2:2, 28, in *The Book of Concord* (Philadelphia: Fortress Press, 1959), 297.

direction for subsequent Catholic theology and practice.

Turning Point: Second Vatican Council

Early in the council, the teaching on Mary was presented in a stand-alone document that reiterated the Neo-Scholastic theology of her unique privileges. This document had the support of over five hundred bishops who wished to have the council declare a new dogma, Mary as mediatrix of all graces, thereby adding a third jewel to her crown. Drawing on biblical and patristic sources and with an eye to the church's ecumenical relationships and mission in the modern world, other bishops proposed considering Mary in connection with the saints in heaven and on earth. After fierce dispute accompanied by weeping and bitter recriminations, the closest vote of the council (1,110–1,070) decided the issue. Teaching on Mary would be enfolded into teaching about the church, rather than issued as a separate document. To complete the picture, another stand-alone schema on the saints would also be incorporated.

Structure of Conciliar Document

The resulting document, the Dogmatic Constitution on the Church (*Lumen gentium*; hereafter cited as LG) passed to enormous enthusiasm, with over two thousand positive and only five negative votes. Its structural design provides a crucial hermeneutical clue for interpreting the

saints and Mary in contemporary theology.[17] **439** There are eight chapters in all, each exploring an aspect of the church. The first, entitled "The Mystery of the Church," opens with the proclamation that "Christ is the light of all nations" (LG 1). The radiance of this light shines on the church, which, by proclaiming the gospel to every creature, helps to shed on all people the light of Christ. This, then, is the foundational relationship that constitutes the very essence of the church: Christ the saving Redeemer and the church as the community of those who, graced by his Spirit, witness him to the world.

The next five chapters then consider aspects of the church as it exists on earth. These include the whole church as the pilgrim people of God (chapter 2); the various functions of episcopacy and clergy (chapter 3); the role of the laity (chapter 4); the call of the whole church to holiness (chapter 5); and the life of religious, who live this out in a special way (chapter 6). The document could have ended there, but the reality of the church is not exhausted in those who are alive at any given moment. Some of its members have already arrived in the promised future. They are still united with the pilgrim church, for the bonds that join believers to Christ in the Spirit are so strong that not even death can break them. One does not leave the church by dying. Therefore, the constitution goes on in its penultimate chapter (chapter 7) to turn its attention to the faithful dead, those "friends and fellow heirs of Jesus Christ" (LG 50) with whom the living form one community. This it does in tandem with reflection on the eschatological nature of the pilgrim church,

---

17. See Herbert Vorgrimler, ed., *Commentary on the Documents of Vatican II*, vol. 1 (New York: Herder & Herder, 1967), especially Gérard Philips, "Dogmatic Constitution on the Church: History of the Constitution," 105–37. See also Giuseppe Alberigo and Joseph Komanchak, eds., *History of Vatican II* (Maryknoll, NY: Orbis, 2000), 3:95–98, 366–72, 425–28.

440 to which these definitively redeemed persons give concrete expression. Within this assembly of those believers who are now forever with God, the final chapter (chapter 8) focuses on the Blessed Virgin Mary, faith-filled Mother of Jesus Christ and preeminent member of the church. Thus, it comes about that the precise location of the saints and Mary in this constitution reveals a theological order of relationship basic to the subject. The doctrinal content of these final two chapters draws out the significance of their placement.

Saints

Entitled "The Eschatological Nature of the Pilgrim Church and Her Union with the Heavenly Church," the teaching on the saints begins by considering the church's promised future when all people and the cosmos itself will be brought to *shalom* in Christ. Until the coming of that new heaven and new earth where justice dwells, the church on earth groans in travail on its way through history. But some of its members are already being gathered up in the great harvest. Between them and living disciples there is a genuine community. In an age of individualism, the constitution thought it important to clarify the foundation of this fellowship (*koinonia*). This lies in the truth that "in various ways and degrees we all partake in the same love for God and neighbor, and all sing the same hymn of glory to our God. For all who belong to Christ, having his Spirit, form one church and cleave together in him" (LG 49).

This is not a new belief. Historically, the church from its beginning centuries has understood that the apostles and martyrs as well as Mary and other holy people are united in Christ with those still alive, and has therefore venerated their memory in special ways (LG 50). In the lives of these people who shared our humanity yet were transformed into successful images of Christ, God vividly manifests to us the divine presence and the divine face. Through them, God speaks a word to us and gives us a sign of the kingdom to which we are powerfully drawn, surrounded as we are by such a great cloud of witnesses (LG 51). While not claiming detailed knowledge about the condition of the saints, the church believes they are definitively united with God. In this relationship, they contribute to the upbuilding of the church on earth through their "bright patterns of holiness" (LG 41) and their prayer offered in and with Christ. The right response of living disciples is to love these friends of Christ, to thank God for them, to imitate them in their following of Christ, to invoke their intercession (which means to ask them to pray for us), and to praise God in their company, especially during the Eucharistic liturgy. Each of these actions terminates through Christ in God, who is wonderful in the saints (2 Thess. 1:10).

Concerned that veneration of the saints has not always hewn to a rightly ordered pattern, the constitution calls for hard work to correct abuses that have crept in. To restore the veneration of the saints to ample praise of God in Christ, it exhorts, "Let the faithful be taught, therefore, that the authentic cult of the saints consists not so much in the multiplying of external acts, but rather in the intensity of our active love" (LG 51). Provided it is understood in the adequate light of faith, communion with those in heaven serves but to enrich our service of God through Christ in the Spirit. The council's Constitution on the Sacred Liturgy (*Sacrosanctum concilium*; hereafter cited as SC) translates these exhortations into concrete directives. Saints' festival days proclaim the victory of Christ's paschal mystery in their lives. Consequently, feasts of

Christ take precedence over those of the saints, the number of universal feasts of the saints is to be pruned, and private devotions should be harmonized with the liturgy, which far surpasses any of them (SC 102–11, 113). On balance, the council developed a theology of the saints centered in Christ, based on the vital community of all disciples in the one Spirit, and evocative of the hope of future *shalom*. In essence, "Just as Christian communion among wayfarers brings us closer to Christ, so our companionship with the saints joins us to Christ, from whom as from their fountain and head issue every grace and the life of God's people itself" (LG 50).

Mary

Within this context of the whole church together, living and dead, centered in Christ, the constitution's final chapter turns to one special saint, Mary. Entitled "The Role of the Blessed Virgin Mary, Mother of God, in the Mystery of Christ and the Church," the text begins by noting that it does not intend to present a complete mariological doctrine, but rather to highlight Mary's role in the mystery of Christ and the church. The key to interpretation is this dual relationship. If certain trends of the nineteenth- and twentieth-century Marian era had tended to imagine Mary in privileged and splendid isolation, the council makes clear that her religious significance resides in these relationships. She is the mother of the Son of God and at the same time redeemed by him, being a daughter of Adam and, as such, "one with all human beings in their need for salvation" (LG 53). In addition, she is that "preeminent" and singular member of the church who embodies the church's calling and hope. Christ and church, then, form the grid on which her theological meaning can be understood.

By means of a running commentary on biblical texts woven together in a harmonious, noncritical narrative, *Lumen gentium* tells the story of Mary's life in relation to the gospel events of the life of Jesus. Two themes emphasized throughout the story are her maternity by means of which the Redeemer entered the world, and her faith that led her to respond creatively to the call of God in different situations. The dynamism of her life is seen to lie in the way she advanced in her "pilgrimage of faith" (LG 58), all the way to the cross. This same dynamism led her into the midst of the community of the first disciples as they awaited the outpouring of the Spirit. Ultimately, it led her into the glory of Christ. The reality of her life, then, is intertwined with the great events of the coming of salvation.

MARY AND THE CHURCH

Recovering the patristic theme of Mary as a model (*typos*) of the church, this chapter offers a running reflection on the ways in which she shines forth to the whole community as an exemplar of integral faith, firm hope, and sincere charity. As the Constitution on the Sacred Liturgy phrased the same insight, in Mary the church "holds up and admires the most excellent fruit of the redemption, and joyfully contemplates, as in a faultless model, that which she herself wholly desires and hopes to be" (SC 103).

Since preconciliar development had given so much attention to the question of Mary as mediatrix of grace, the chapter pays special attention to this issue. Repeatedly it stresses that we have but one mediator, Christ Jesus, who gave himself as a ransom for all. Risen in the Spirit, he continues in this role. And then comes the key move: Christ's role as mediator does not operate in isolation but shows its power by drawing all believers into his prayer, so that they pray

442 for one another. This participatory dynamic does not overshadow Christ's sole mediation but rather shows its effectiveness. A nest of examples attempts to explain how this works. There is only one priest of the new covenant, Jesus Christ, but this priesthood is shared in different ways by all the baptized (the priesthood of all believers) and by ordained ministers. Again, God alone is good, but this goodness is shared in different ways with all creatures. In a similar way, only Jesus Christ is mediator, but this mediation gives rise to "a manifold cooperation which is but a sharing in this unique source" (LG 62). The mediation of the saints—and in this case, of Mary—in no way obscures the unique mediation of Christ, but reveals its strength as they participate in his prayer for the world.

Having thus illustrated the typical Catholic analogical imagination, which opts for a both/and rather than an either/or pattern, the chapter turns directly to Mary. In union with the prayer of Christ, she too prays for those who are beset with difficulties. Hence she can be called mediatrix. This title is not given dogmatic status as some had wished. Rather, in carefully chosen language, the text states that she "is invoked in the church" under the title of mediatrix (LG 62), thus placing the title in the context of prayer. Originally, the text had read she is invoked *by* the church, but this was changed to clarify the council's intent to describe a legitimate, optional pious practice rather than an official stance.

The chapter ends by giving attention to the special reverence with which the church should venerate Mary's memory. Differing essentially from the adoration due to God alone, this veneration has taken diverse forms in various cultures and should be encouraged. But theologians and preachers are earnestly exhorted to avoid the opposite excesses of either false exaggeration or narrow-mindedness. With ecumenical sensitivity, all members of the church are encouraged to remember that "true devotion consists neither in fruitless and passing emotion, nor in a certain vain credulity. Rather, it proceeds from true faith, by which we are led to know the excellence of the Mother of God, and are moved to a filial love toward our mother and to the imitation of her virtues" (LG 67). The chapter—and with it, the constitution as a whole—ends by circling around to the eschatological theme with which it began its treatment of the saints and Mary. In glory with Christ, Mary is an image of the church as it will be in the age to come. As such, she is a sure sign of hope and comfort for the pilgrim people of God.

The theology of the saints and Mary developed and taught by the Second Vatican Council finds its place integrally among major tenets of Christian faith. Rooted in Scripture and the patristic tradition, it is christological and eschatological in perspective, and ecumenical in tone. Walking in reverse through *Lumen gentium*, we see Mary in the midst of the community of saints in heaven, the saints as friends of God sharing community of life with the pilgrim people of God on earth, and the whole church itself reflecting the light of Christ as the moon does that of the sun. Such is the vision of the Second Vatican Council.

Paradigm Shift

The council's emphasis on the holiness of all the baptized spearheaded a basic shift in theology of the saints. In the centuries after Trent, although people approached saints in heaven with the correct intuition that all believers in Jesus Christ can be of help to one another, there was heavy stress on personal neediness. With a kind of naive realism, people pictured the saints as being closer to the human struggle than was the living God. With their sympathy to the human condition, these "friends in high places" could obtain help for sinners from the almighty God, though no clear theological explanation of this was ever given. The saints, including Mary, were thought to be mediators in the sense that they came *between* Jesus Christ and believers, obtaining favors even while being subordinated to him. It may be simplistic to sum up a complex history in a single model, but there is truth in the notion that from the sixteenth to the twentieth centuries, in the context of a strongly juridical experience of church, veneration of the saints took the predominant form of a patron-petitioner model.

The effect of conciliar teaching has been to shift the basic model to the more ancient one of companionship and solidarity. All are blessed and praying together in this community called church. As early Christian writers described it, saints in heaven are comrades and fellow disciples with pilgrims on earth, all following after the one love. To continue with the spatial metaphor, these saints are not situated *between* Jesus Christ and believers, but *alongside* their sisters and brothers, cheering them on. It is not distance from Jesus Christ or fear of his judgment or any other such motivation sometimes found in the patron-petitioner model that impels approach to the saints. Rather, the church on earth rejoices in this cloud of witnesses because we share with them a common humanity, a common faith, and a common life in the Spirit. This does not mean there is no difference between those on earth and in heaven, nor that petitionary prayer is unimportant. But it emphasizes that in the light of salvation by God in Jesus Christ, the relationship between all of the redeemed is fundamentally mutual and collegial.

The Postconciliar Era

In the years after the Council, new insights developed from many sources: theologies crafted in different cultural contexts, the teachings of popes, and the contributions of ecumenical dialogues.

Devotion in Global Perspective

The council's teaching affected the popular phenomenon of the saints and Mary in multifaceted ways. Perhaps most unexpected was the noticeable diminishment of private veneration of the saints and Mary among numerous people in industrial societies. This may well be a direct result of the biblical, christocentric, Eucharistic spirituality to which the council gave impetus. With access to God in Christ through Word and sacrament, there is no longer such felt need for approachable intercessors.

The phenomenon in all likelihood also arises from life in the modern secular world, where the imaginative link between heaven and earth has broken down. People experience that those who die have truly disappeared from this world; they are no longer accessible to the living in any direct fashion. Karl Rahner's analysis roots this situation most profoundly in the contemporary Western experience of God. God is eclipsed, hidden, silent, experienced as utterly remote and incomprehensible even if known as the holy mystery who is ineffably near. "Into this silent, unfathomable and ineffable mystery the dead disappear. They depart. They no longer make themselves felt. They cease any further to belong to the world of our experience."[18] If this is the Western experience even with loved ones

---

18. Karl Rahner, "Why and How Can We Venerate the Saints?" in *Theological Investigations* (New York: Herder & Herder, 1971), 8:7.

444 who have died, it is not surprising that saints of the past seem inaccessible and interest in them wanes.

In other cultural milieus, however, the situation is decidedly different. In Latin America, Eastern Europe, and the Mediterranean countries, veneration flourishes, sometimes related to national aspirations but more often as the expression of a national character that is warmhearted and affectionate. Among Latino/Latina communities in the United States, love of the saints and Mary in different configurations (Our Lady of Guadalupe from Mexico, Our Lady of Charity from Cuba, and many others) is an essential characteristic of popular religion. In Africa, drawing on that continent's tradition where the unseen presence of ancestors is foundational for the whole social fabric, the church is adapting the cult of ancestors into veneration of the saints, with several corrections: only God is powerful, so ancestors can do no harm, and Christ rather than family blood ties is the foundation for relation with the living dead.[19] The situation is, then, complex, with the experience of church members in different cultures reflecting basic mentalities of their time and place.

In addition to older locales that serve as centers of spiritual pilgrimage—Mexico City, Lourdes, Fatima—newer places such as Medjugorje in Bosnia/Herzegovina have claimed Marian appearances in the postconciliar decades. There is no definitive church teaching about what actually happens during an apparition. Theologians offer various explanations. In Rahner's view, such an occurrence is a manifestation of the charismatic element in the church, an unpredictable moment in which the Spirit of God seizes the imagination of a person to receive a message from heaven.[20] According to Schillebeeckx, such an event is a hermeneutic of the nearness of God to poor people who are outside the normal channels of official church power: the young, the uneducated, and rural women.[21] In all cases, the church considers such happenings to be a matter of private, not public, revelation. This means they are not essential to the faith. As with other devotional matters, church approval does not bind consciences to believe in the apparition or its historicity. Rather, ecclesial approval indicates that the practices and prayers associated with the apparition are in accord with the gospel, so participating in them will not lead one astray. The U.S. Catholic bishops explained this clearly in their pastoral letter on Mary:

> Even when a private revelation has spread to the entire world, as in the case of Our Lady of Lourdes, and has been recognized in the liturgical calendar, the Church does not make mandatory the acceptance either of the original story or of particular forms of piety springing from it. Within the Vatican Council we remind true lovers of Our Lady of the danger of superficial sentiment and vain credulity. Our faith does not seek new gospels, but leads us to know the excellence of the Mother of God and moves us to a filial love toward our Mother and to the imitation of her virtues.[22]

---

19. Edward Fasholé-Luke, "Ancestor Veneration and the Communion of Saints," in *New Testament Christianity for Africa and the World*, ed. Mark E. Glasswell and Edward W. Fasholé-Luke (London: SPCK, 1974), 209–21.

20. Karl Rahner, *Visions and Prophecies*, trans. E. Henkey and R. Strachan (New York: Herder & Herder, 1963).

21. Edward Schillebeeckx, *Mary, Mother of the Redemption* (London: Sheed & Ward, 1964), 131–75.

22. U.S. Catholic Bishops, "Behold Your Mother: Woman of Faith," *Catholic Mind* 72 (1974): 26–64, no. 100.

Papal Contributions

Since the Second Vatican Council, Paul VI and John Paul II have both contributed further insight into a Catholic understanding of Mary.

PAUL VI

Ten years after the council, distressed at the postconciliar falling off of Marian devotion in the west, Paul VI wrote the apostolic letter *Marialis Cultus*, seeking to encourage this devotion while placing it on a firm footing.[23] Acknowledging that some inherited practices of former eras show "the ravages of time" (MC 24), the pope encouraged people with their pastors to be creative in shaping new practices of devotion suitable to the temperament of this era. Toward this goal, he laid down five guidelines drawn from conciliar teaching: The honoring of Mary should be theological, set within the trinitarian structure of belief in the one God who creates, redeems, and makes holy the world. In addition it should be biblical, steeped in the great themes of salvation history; liturgical, shaped by the seasons and feasts of the year; ecumenical, sensitive to any expression that would give rise to misunderstanding, especially regarding the centrality of Christ; and anthropological, attuned to cultural realities of time and place, especially the emergence of women as equal to men in all fields of public endeavor (nos. 25–37). Taken together, these norms ensure that honoring Mary respects "her pre-eminent place in the communion of saints" (no. 28) while remaining coherent with the essential structure of Christian belief.

Concerned that a submissive, passive image of Mary inherited from previous generations could be repugnant to modern persons, the pope risked a new description. Mary was a strong and intelligent woman, he wrote, who consistently made courageous choices, giving active and responsible consent to the call of God. Her life was difficult, filled with the suffering of poverty, flight and exile, and grief. In this perspective, she is "truly our sister, who as a poor and humble woman fully shared our lot" (no. 56). In the midst of these troubles, however, far from being repellently pious, she did not hesitate to proclaim that God vindicates the oppressed. The church honors her memory not because of the social or cultural circumstances of her life but because of her own active discipleship: "She is held up as an example for the way in which, in her own particular life, she fully and responsibly accepted God's will (see Lk 2:38), because she heard the Word of God and acted on it, and because charity and a spirit of service were the driving force of her actions. She is worthy of imitation because she was the first and most perfect of Christ's disciples" (no. 35). Thus did Paul VI carry forward the council's theme of Mary in relation to Christ and the church.

JOHN PAUL II

During his long pontificate, John Paul II presented insights on Mary in a multitude of writings, speeches, and homilies. Carrying forth the teaching of the council, he noted how her maternal relationship to Christ and her relationship to the church as an inspiring and guiding member, are both rooted in her life of faith. The pope's discussion of her faith brings depth and poignancy to her humanity: her life was a "pilgrimage of faith" (quoting LG 58); she gave herself to God's word in the "dim light of faith"; like Abraham, she had to "hope against hope"; though the mother of Christ, she was in contact with the mystery of his truth only through a "veil," having

---

23. Paul VI, "*Marialis Cultus*" (Devotion to the Blessed Virgin Mary), *The Pope Speaks* 19 (1974–75): 49–87.

to be faithful even through the dark "night of faith."[24] In other words, even where it is most religiously crucial, she struggled through without extra advantages, lighting a path for disciples today to tread.

John Paul II's desire to promote the dignity of women, a movement that grew to global proportions in these decades, led him to turn to Mary as the exemplar of women's greatness. Thanks to her response to God's plan of salvation, she signifies "the fullness of the perfection of what is characteristic of woman, of what is feminine. Here we find ourselves, in a sense, at the culminating point, the archetype, of the personal dignity of women."[25] Blessed among women, Mary functions as a mirror into which women can gaze to discover the secret of how to live in accord with their own true advancement. There they will find that women's true vocation is motherhood, whether physical or spiritual. Like the maternal Mary, women need to emulate a "style" that makes no proud demands but maintains an attitude of humble service. Like her, women should develop virtues that will enable them to live their true vocation to the utmost; these include self-offering love, limitless fidelity, and tireless devotion to work. Functioning in a discreet and hidden way, they fulfill their vocation in union with Christ.

John Paul II insistently taught that women are fully human persons, created along with men in the image and likeness of God and endowed with equal human rights. He also advocated social justice for women, as when he urged "equal pay for equal work," equality of spouses with regard to human rights, and vigorous resistance to sexual violence.[26] His teaching brought about real advance in the church's anthropological doctrine. A difficulty arises, however, due to the unrelenting gender dualism of his thought. His anthropology of complementarity, which assigns personal characteristics to men and women on the basis of their reproductive functions, credits men with intelligence and decisiveness, and women with ability to love and care for the vulnerable. This translates into assigning leadership roles in the public realm to "man," whose essential nature is to act, while restricting "woman," who naturally receives, to private, nurturing roles.[27] The tension becomes apparent when the pope's words about Mary's "feminine" nature are laid beside his praise of Mary of the Magnificat, whose stance moves the church toward a preferential option for the poor.[28] Her assertive proclamation that God pulls down the mighty from their thrones and lifts up the lowly, and fills the hungry with good things but sends the rich away empty (Luke 1:52-53) embodies a greater resistance to oppression than her femininity, as he defines it, would allow. Beyond dispute, John Paul II was standing on firmer ground when with the council he emphasized Mary's faith-filled life, which inspires hope in the pilgrim church.

---

24. John Paul II, *"Redemptoris Mater"* (Mother of the Redeemer, an encyclical), *Origins* 16, no. 43 (April 9, 1987): nos. 14, 17.

25. John Paul II, *"Mulieris Dignitatem"* (On the Dignity and Vocation of Woman, an apostolic letter), *Origins* 18, no. 17 (October 6, 1988): no. 5.

26. John Paul II, "Letter to Women/Beijing Conference," *Origins* 25, no. 9 (July 27, 1995): paragraph 4.

27. Christine Gudorf, "Encountering the Other: The Modern Papacy on Women," in *Feminist Ethics and the Catholic Moral Tradition*, ed. Charles Curran, Margaret Farley, and Richard McCormick (New York: Paulist, 1996) 66–89.

28. John Paul II, *"Redemptoris Mater,"* nos. 12–19.

Ecumenical Dialogues

During these postconciliar decades, church-appointed ecumenical dialogues at the national and international levels met to study, pray, and argue over issues that have long divided the churches. In the area of Mary and the saints, particularly problematic areas included the practice of invocation, the role of Mary in God's plan of salvation, and the two papally defined Marian dogmas. Since the Reformation, a wide chasm on these issues had opened up between Catholics and Protestants. To find a way forward, the dialogues used the fruitful method of going back before the sixteenth-century split to examine what both sides held in common—namely, the biblical and patristic traditions, which can then form a basis for mutual understanding. Several major documents have issued forth that, while not constituting official church teaching, point toward major breakthroughs that would enable the churches to transcend the controversies. Chief among these are the U.S. Lutheran–Roman Catholic Dialogue study of Christ the unique mediator along with the saints and Mary, the study of Mary in the plan of God and the communion of saints by the Reformed–Catholic Dombes group in France, and the study of Mary as a sign of grace and hope in Christ by the Anglican–Roman Catholic International Commission.[29]

Each in its own way arrives at similar insights. On invocation, when set within the communion that is the being and gift of God in Christ, asking the saints to intercede for us expresses the solidarity of the church wherein all are meant to be of mutual support to one another. Analogous to what is done among living persons, the request directed toward a saint in heaven to pray for us is a precise expression of solidarity in Jesus Christ, through the ages and across various modes of human existence. On the Marian dogmas, understood within the biblical pattern of grace and hope, the two modern Marian dogmas can be seen to be consonant with the Scriptures and early Christian tradition. In terms of grace, the immaculate conception affirms that in view of Mary's vocation to be the Mother of God, Christ's redeeming work reached back to the depths of her being at her earliest beginnings—surely the starkest example of justification by grace alone without merit. In terms of hope, the assumption focuses on the action of God, who took her in the fullness of her person into divine glory. In this, she embodies the destiny of the church.

In the process of forging these insights, the ecumenical dialogue groups have pioneered for the churches deeper appreciation for their own and each other's traditions. They point to the possibility that ongoing differences in doctrinal articulation and devotional practice may in the future be seen as the work of the Spirit rather than automatically be church-dividing.

Diversity of Interpretations

The conciliar river has split into many streams. Catholic theology of the communion of saints and Mary now exhibits the pluralism characteristic of this era's theology as a whole. Some of the most influential insights have come from

---

29. George Anderson et al., eds., *The One Mediator, the Saints, and Mary,* Lutherans and Catholics in Dialogue 8 (Minneapolis: Augsburg Fortress, 1991); Alain Blancy, Maurice Jourjon, and the Dombes Group, *Mary: In the Plan of God and in the Communion of Saints* (New York: Paulist, 1999); and Anglican–Roman Catholic International Commission, *Mary: Grace and Hope in Christ* (New York: Continuum, 2006).

transcendental, political, and liberation theologies, the various strands of feminist theology, and Latino/Latina theology.

Transcendental Theology

Predating the council and influencing its teaching, transcendental theology utilizes the modern philosophical "turn to the subject" in an effort to speak a meaningful word to an increasingly secular age. It begins by investigating the human being's seemingly endless desire for knowing and loving, which leads to the interpretation of the human person as dynamic, unrestricted openness to the infinite. It then takes this anthropological analysis into theology and connects it with the teaching on grace, understood as God's own self-communication in the Spirit mediated through Jesus Christ, which fulfills this desire. Karl Rahner, pioneer of this method, presents the saints in heaven, especially those named by the community, as manifestations of the charismatic dimension of the church.[30] In this perspective, they have rich significance. They embody the grace of God in the concrete, showing that this gift actually arrives and can be victorious in the world, thus strengthening hope. In addition, since the grace of God does not work in a vacuum but in the midst of history, saints serve the community by taking risks to initiate new styles of holiness geared to the challenges of a particular age. Their success opens new paths of discipleship for others to tread with confidence. Ecclesially, the church's proclamation of their holiness is a function of its own identity as holy church, a signal that the saving power of God exists not only in sacraments or other institutional aspects, but also in surprising ways in people. As both redeemed sinners themselves and creative models of holiness for others, they are a vital part of the history of grace in the world.

In a particular way, Mary carries out this vocation of the saint. She is full of grace, and as a hearer of the word par excellence, she is a sign of redeemed humanity.[31] In God's favor to her and the pattern of her faith-filled life, the mystery of victorious grace is made uniquely manifest to people who are similarly called through grace to ultimate glory. In this transcendental approach, the meaning of the saints and Mary receives ultimate definition from the perspective of eschatology. This means that God's victorious grace has already won through in them, as pledge of a blessed future for all: "We hope because there are saints."[32]

Political Theology

Developed in Europe in response to the devastation of world war, political theology articulates the meaning of faith for the *polis*, the city or body of citizens, especially those whose lives are pervaded with suffering or destroyed by massive public violence. To rescue the identity of such vanquished nonpersons, theology turns to the passion, death, and resurrection of Jesus Christ. There it finds a pledge of future life for all the defeated and the dead. The categories of memory, narrative, and solidarity, drawn from the wellsprings of Scripture and liturgy, provide strong conceptual tools for interpretation. Remember-

---

30. Karl Rahner, "The Church of the Saints," in *Theological Investigations* (Baltimore: Helicon, 1967), 3:91–104.

31. Karl Rahner, *Mary, Mother of the Lord* (New York: Herder & Herder, 1963); see Max Thurian, *Mary, Mother of the Lord, Figure of the Church* (London: Faith, 1963).

32. Karl Rahner, "All Saints," in *Theological Investigations* (New York: Seabury, 1977), 8:24–29.

ing the dead, telling their stories of struggle and sometime victory, and walking in solidarity with their unfinished projects set up a vital community between the living and the dead in face of the power of evil. This narrative remembrance is not nostalgia that bathes the past in a rosy glow, but a telling that brings the past into the present, bearing the seed of future possibility. Such recall stirs up resistance against injustice, startling those who are apathetic or despondent into action and thus alerting tyrants that they do not have the last word. Little wonder that Johannes Baptist Metz described such practice as "dangerous."[33] The future opens up in a new way by the protest and hope carried in the act of remembering—that incalculable visitation from the past that energizes persons.

As used in political theology, these categories bring critical, productive power to theology of the saints and Mary. When the church venerates their memory, it lifts up many whom the world has scorned but God has loved, others who gave courageous witness of telling the truth in the service of justice, and still others who poured out loving compassion against the wishes of society. All lived discipleship amid the needs of their time according to their own brokenness and gifts. Based on vital solidarity, the narrative remembrance of these friends of the crucified and risen Jesus mediates the experience of saving grace in the midst of the disasters of history. Inevitably critical of the banality of evil, this theology orients believers to praxis—to action on behalf of the reign of God in the face of a godless world.

Liberation Theology

Latin American theologians, rediscovering the biblical idea of the living God as liberator of the oppressed, reclaim the saints as partners in the struggle for life. They criticize the present roster of canonized and liturgically celebrated saints, the majority of whom are white Europeans of upper- and middle-class standing and thus unrepresentative of the colonized, indigenous, mestizo and mulatto people who constitute the church of the poor. Responding to their own context, they search for new models of holiness among those who have struggled for justice. Leonardo Boff rereads the significance of Francis of Assisi, finding in his story powerful witness to God's love for the poor and the need to speak truth to power on their behalf.[34] Taking poignant note of the new generation of martyrs being created on his continent, Jon Sobrino lifts up their witness and its call to conscience as revelatory of the grace of God in the midst of conflict.[35]

In this perspective, Mary in particular steps forth as a herald of liberation. In reflection on the Gospels, the poor have rediscovered her solidarity with them as a village woman, a poor woman of the people, a member of a people oppressed by an occupying force, a refugee woman fleeing with her newborn child from the wrath of a murderous ruler, a bereaved mother of a victim of unjust execution by the state.[36] This solidarity carries political significance, for it is to *this* kind of woman that God has done great things. The poor of the land are the subjects of divine favor.

---

33. Johannes Baptist Metz, *Faith in History and Society* (New York: Seabury, 1980).

34. Leonardo Boff, *Saint Francis: A Model for Human Liberation* (New York: Crossroad, 1982).

35. Jon Sobrino, *Witnesses to the Kingdom: The Martyrs of El Salvador and the Crucified Peoples* (Maryknoll, NY: Orbis, 2003).

36. Ernesto Cardenal, *The Gospel in Solentiname*, 4 vols. (Maryknoll, NY: Orbis, 1976–82).

The liberation framework delivers new insight into the two modern Marian dogmas. Brazilian theologians Ivone Gebara and María Clara Bingemer write that while the immaculate conception and assumption carry the memories of other generations and do not bear immediate relevance on a continent marked by the suffering of millions, they can be made to work as allies in the struggle for life. For the *Immaculata* venerated on church altars is the poor Mary of Nazareth, insignificant in the social structure of her time. Similarly, the assumption exalts the woman who gave birth in a stable, lived a life of anonymity, and stood at the foot of the cross as the mother of the condemned. "The Assumption is the glorious culmination of the mystery of God's preference for what is poor, small, and unprotected in this world," they write; it sparks hope in the poor and those in solidarity with them "that they will share in the final victory of the incarnate God."[37] These Marian doctrines reveal the unrepentant ways of the living God whose favor shines on those whom the elite of the world see as insignificant or do not see at all.

Feminist/Womanist/ Mujerista Theology

The struggle for the full human dignity of women, which has reached global proportions, affects theology in the work of white (feminist), African American (Womanist), Hispanic (*Mujerista*), and Asian women who critically recover unnoticed dimensions of the communion of saints and Mary. A major criticism focuses on the official roster of saints, a large majority of whom are men, mostly celibate. Noticeably absent are happily married, sexually active women. Women who make the list are mostly virgins or martyrs, described with stereotypical feminine virtues. This official silence about the history of women's holiness and creative religious initiatives is no accident, but is a function of the patriarchal worldview that privileges male humanity as normative while leveling deep suspicion at female bodies.

In face of this prejudice, women's theology seeks to restore a lost heritage of women, their struggles and contributions. With a range of hermeneutical methods, Elisabeth Schüssler Fiorenza unlocks the New Testament to reveal the myriads of women who were active and influential in the ministry of Jesus and the founding of the church, shedding unique light on the leadership of Mary Magdalene, no repentant sinner at all.[38] Redescribing the early church's virgin martyrs, Maureen Tilley challenges traditional interpretations, which pose either rejection of sexuality or death as the only options for holy women's self-definition. Rather, these were self-actualized young women whose identity was so empowered by relationship to Christ that they could resist state-imposed patriarchal marriage.[39] Feminist liturgies of communal remembrance and litanies of the saints celebrate these and other rediscoveries, which provide impetus for mature adult personhood for women as well as men.[40]

---

37. Ivone Gebara and María Clara Bingemer, *Mary, Mother of God, Mother of the Poor* (Maryknoll, NY: Orbis, 1989), 120–21.

38. Elisabeth Schüssler Fiorenza, *In Memory of Her: A Feminist Theological Reconstruction of Christian Origins* (New York: Crossroad, 1983); and idem, *Wisdom Ways: Introducing Feminist Biblical Interpretation* (Maryknoll, NY: Orbis, 2001).

39. Maureen Tilley, "The Passion of Perpetua and Felicity," in *Searching the Scriptures*, ed. Elisabeth Schüssler Fiorenza (New York: Crossroad, 1994), 2:829–58.

40. Rosemary Radford Ruether, *Women-Church: Theology and Practice* (San Francisco: Harper & Row, 1985).

The struggle to broaden and redefine the company of saints to include women of all types is also transforming traditional pious images of Mary. The passive, obedient woman who stands ready to do whatever men in authority direct, the desexualized figure whose lack of experience is taken as a sign of holiness, the woman whose *sole* purpose in life is to bear a child (which is not to downplay the value of women's fertile ability to give life), the silent embodiment of the so-called feminine ideal of sweetness and nurture—none of these construals promotes women's flourishing in an age of expanding social roles and independent notions of the female self. None offers a firm ground for resisting male dominance with its all too often physically violent manifestations. By contrast, reading Mary of the Gospels through the lens of women's experience of struggle offers an empowering view of this woman through whom God became a child of earth, and a concomitantly liberating understanding of the holy God whom she praised.[41] This is a woman who took risks, asked questions, made her own decisions, pondered what God was doing in her life, knew how to say no, prophesied, tasted firsthand the bitterness of male-inflicted violence done to loved ones, and survived. Discerning the presence and creativity of the Spirit of God in her life, women connect with her in their own struggle against sexism in combination with racism, classism, heterosexism, and other demeaning injustice. "Mary's song is precious to women and other oppressed people," writes Jane Schaberg of the Magnificat, "for its vision of their concrete freedom from systemic injustice—from oppression by political rulers on their thrones."[42] In particular for poor women, explains María Pilar Aquino, "Mary is not a heavenly creature but shares their lives as a comrade and sister in struggle."[43] In solidarity with her sisters, she becomes a lodestone of hope for those who have been cheated of their lives.

Latino/Latina Theology

In the United States, strong relationship to the saints and Mary plays a major role in the piety of Hispanic communities. A growing body of theological literature explores this popular religion as a genuine locus for theology, reflecting as it does the *sensus fidelium* (sense of the faithful) of a suffering people. This theology posits that the community's intuition of faith and the practices that express it, such as home altars, graphic images, processions, and fiestas, are legitimate bearers of authentic gospel tradition. These symbols point to God's compassionate solidarity with the oppressed and vanquished, and they do so in a way reflective of the late medieval Iberian Catholicism meshed with Amerindian and African traditions that formed this religious culture.[44]

---

41. Sally Cuneen, *In Search of Mary: The Woman and the Symbol* (New York: Ballantine, 1996); Chung Hyun Kyung, *Struggle to Be the Sun Again: Introducing Asian Women's Theology* (Maryknoll, NY: Orbis, 1994), ch. 5.

42. Jane Schaberg, "Luke," in *Women's Bible Commentary*, ed. Carol Newsom and Sharon Ringe (Louisville: Westminster John Knox, 1998), 373.

43. María Pilar Aquino, *Our Cry for Life: Feminist Theology from Latin America* (Maryknoll, NY: Orbis, 1993), 176–77.

44. Orlando Espín, "Tradition and Popular Religion: An Understanding of the Sensus Fidelium," in *Frontiers of Hispanic Theology in the United States*, ed. Allan Figueroa Deck (Maryknoll, NY: Orbis, 1992), 62–87; and Ada María Isasi-Díaz, *En la Lucha/In the Struggle: Elaborating a Mujerista Theology* (Minneapolis: Fortress Press, 1993).

The numerous instantiations of Mary honored by communities of different Latin American and Caribbean origins defy neat systematization. Yet they are always and everywhere a symbol of God's faithful presence and concern in the midst of struggle. Virgilio Elizondo eloquently shows how Our Lady of Guadalupe, from the time of her first encounter with the indigenous Juan Diego, has represented an outpouring of divine compassion for a people colonized, robbed, raped, and defeated. He advances the thesis that the origin of devotion to Our Lady of Guadalupe involved resistance by conquered native people not only to the European invaders but also to the all-male God in whose name they conquered. In the process of this resistance, the poor and vanquished people became the recipients of a major disclosure in the development of the understanding of God: here "the male Father God of militaristic and patriarchal Christianity is united to the female Mother of God (Tonantzin), which allows the original heart and face of Christianity to shine forth: compassion, understanding, tenderness, and healing."[45] Others have analyzed Our Lady of Guadalupe as a brilliant popular pneumatology that puts people ultimately in touch with the Holy Spirit of God.[46]

The diversity of interpretation all points in one direction. As Miguel Díaz observes, "Whether understood as the female face of God (Rodriguez, Elizondo), a symbol of the Holy Spirit (Espín), the poetry of the trinitarian God (García), or the *mestizo* face of the divine (Goizueta), it is clear that U.S. Hispanic theologians understand Marian symbols as mediators of the life of grace, especially to and within the experi-ence of the poor and marginalized."[47] For Hispanic communities under pressure to assimilate, rites and symbols connected with Mary and the saints actually function as a protection and protest against the dominant U.S. culture, fueling their spiritual and cultural identity and their struggles for basic justice.

Elements of a Theological Synthesis

Enriched by biblical, patristic, conciliar, liturgical, spiritual, and practical developments of the previous decades, contemporary theology is able to lay down markers for solid understanding of the communion of saints and Mary. Without erasing the diversity of thought or devotional practices that perdure in different cultures, it identifies elements of a synthesis that will anchor this precious heritage securely within the wider framework of Christian belief.

Communion of Saints

The communion of saints is a most inclusive belief. It joins all living people who seek the face of God into a company of grace, connects them with the faithful dead of all ages, and links this community with the living matrix of the natural world, all embraced under the outstretched wings of the Spirit of God. From every angle, the communion of saints crosses boundaries, linking those whom the book of Wisdom calls "the friends of God and prophets" (Wis. 7:27) from generation to generation and across the wide world. A contemporary interpretation of

---

45. Virgilio Elizondo, *Guadalupe: Mother of the New Creation* (Maryknoll, NY: Orbis, 1998), 126.
46. Orlando Espín, *The Faith of the People* (Maryknoll, NY: Orbis, 1997), 6–10, 73–77.
47. Miguel Díaz, *On Being Human: U.S. Hispanic and Rahnerian Perspectives* (Maryknoll, NY: Orbis, 2001), 125.

its meaning brings at least five elements into play.[48]

THE LIVING COMMUNITY TODAY

First, as in the New Testament, the communion of saints comprises all living persons who respond to the Spirit's call of grace and, while sinful and imperfect, seek to live truthfully and lovingly with others. The point is that corporately, inclusively, without discrimination, the whole church around the world is a communion of saints. Too often, theology has squeezed this meaning dry, eliminating most of the baptized from sainthood in favor of a small group of elite officeholders or exceptional leaders. But this strategy woefully shortchanges the gift of God who, in gracious mercy through the life, death, and resurrection of Jesus Christ, calls, blesses, and sends forth all the living people who form the beloved community.

Drawing on biblical and early Christian insight, Vatican II underscored this truth in its luminous teaching on "The Call of the Whole Church to Holiness," positioned at the center of the Constitution on the Church (LG chapter 5). Through baptism, persons are justified in Christ and become sharers in divine nature: "In this way they are really made holy" (LG no. 40). This holiness, furthermore, is essentially the same for everyone. There is not one kind of indwelling of the Spirit for laypersons and another for those in religious life or ordained ministry. Rather, "in the various types and duties of life, one and the same holiness is cultivated by all who are moved by the Spirit of God" (LG no. 41). In other words, the church is not divided into saints and nonsaints. Vivified by grace, every woman, man, and child, in whatever diverse circumstances and of whatever race, class, ethnicity, sexual persuasion, or any other marker that at once identifies and divides human beings, participates in God's holy life. If this be the case, the holiness of ordinary persons in the midst of ordinary time needs to be ever more strongly emphasized if people are not to be robbed of their heritage and true identity.

CLOUD OF WITNESSES THROUGH TIME

It is a fundamental Christian hope that just as the death of Jesus had no ultimate power to separate him from God, so too communion with God extends beyond death for others. The power of the Spirit is so strong that death cannot break it: "Whether we live or whether we die, we are the Lord's" (Rom. 14:8). Hence the communion of saints is not restricted to persons who live and breathe at the present moment but also embraces those who have died. While this is utterly unimaginable, it fuels hope that the dead are not annihilated but are enfolded into the embrace of the living God, which to us is darkness but to them is the fulfillment of their lives in the sphere of the Spirit.

If we ask after these persons, seeking where they are to be found, the only possible answer, since they do not belong to the empirical world around us, is that they abide in God. In Karl Rahner's careful words, "We meet the living dead, even when they are those loved by us, in faith, hope, and love, that is, when we open our hearts to the silent calm of God's own self, in which they live; not by calling them back to where we are, but by descending into the silent eternity of our own hearts, and through faith in the risen Lord, creating in time the eternity

---

48. For full presentation of these themes, see Elizabeth A. Johnson, *Friends of God and Prophets: A Feminist Theological Reading of the Communion of Saints* (New York: Continuum, 1998).

454 which they have brought forth forever."[49] In other words, we meet them not by reducing their reality to our own earthbound, imaginative size but by going forth to where they dwell in the mystery of the living God as the beginning of the new heaven and the new earth.

The company of saints in heaven beggars description. While some few are remembered by name, millions upon anonymous millions of others are also included, celebrated on the feast of All Saints. In different times and places, their bright patterns of goodness traced in the sheer ordinariness of daily life shaped the religious world we inhabit today. Among these saints are also some whom we know personally. Their good lives, complete with fault and failure, have reached journey's end. To say of all these people that they form with us the company of the redeemed is to give grief a direction, affirming that in the dialogue between God and the human race, the last word is the gracious word of life. In instances where persons have wrought real and lasting damage by their actions, faith holds out the possibility that at their deepest core they did not concur in diabolical evil. The church's prayer is that God will be more merciful toward them than they have been to others. On their behalf, at least we may hope.

Paradigmatic Figures

Throughout history, particular persons emerge who focus the energies of the Spirit for a local community with its own needs and dreams. If and when the common spiritual sense of the community responds to these persons, recognizing their gifts, they become publicly significant for the life of the church. Theologically they have no essential spiritual advantage over the rest of the community who are saints in the

biblical sense. But the confluence of their own unique giftedness with the needs of a moment in history gives them a special function among their fellow pilgrims. Their names are remembered as a benediction, an act of resistance, a call to action, a spur to fidelity, a summons to encouragement.

Some among these saints are canonized and celebrated with a liturgical feast; some are not. But all paradigmatic figures have a significant role in the community. They are women and men who distill the central values of the living tradition, making them accessible in concrete form. The direct force of their example acts as a catalyst in the community, galvanizing recognition that, yes, this is what we are called to be. The uncanny integrity of their lives leavens the moral environment, luring others ever more deeply into life lived for God. They are like a Milky Way, a shining river of stars spiraling out from the center of the galaxy to light a path through the darkness back to that center, the divine mystery. The light of their memory encourages the creative witness of others; one fire kindles another. This is their irreplaceable role at the same time we recognize that the parameters of what it means to be holy can be given only by the whole communion of saints.

Practices of Memory and Hope

Inspired by the Spirit, relationships among the communion of saints have the effect of encouraging faithful discipleship. In the companionship model, with its lively sense of mutuality, those who are alive today understand their relationship with those who have gone before in dynamic terms: they walk with the community, accompany us, relate to us as fellow travelers on the road of discipleship. While prayers of

---

49. Karl Rahner, "The Life of the Dead," in *Theological Investigations* (New York: Seabury, 1974), 4:353–54.

petition are not absent, the key practice entails remembering them in the dangerous sense explored by Metz. One concrete example of how this "works" comes from El Salvador. In the villages and cities, people recite the traditional litany of the saints, adding the names of their own martyrs for the cause of justice. To each name, the people respond *Presente!* (Here). Oscar Romero: *Presente!* Ignacio Ellacuría: *Presente!* Celina Ramos: *Presente!* Young catechists, community workers, and religious leaders of the pueblos: *Presente!* This prayer summons the memory of these martyrs as a strong, enduring presence that commits the community to emulate their lives. The fire of each martyred life kindles a new spark, releasing the power of their witness into the next generation. Empowered by their memory, we become partners in hope.

The Community of Nature

On the face of it, the communion of saints seems to be thoroughly focused on the human community, living and dead. However, an intriguing duality in the original Latin term *communio sanctorum* enables this doctrine to include the natural world in a compelling manner. On the one hand, *sanctorum* is a form of the noun *sancti*, in which case the term means "holy persons." On the other hand, *sanctorum* is also a form of the noun *sancta*, in which instance the term refers to holy things. This latter reference was clearly intended when the phrase was first used in the Eastern churches, where *koinonia ton hagion* (fellowship of the holy) meant participation in sacred things—specifically, the Eucharistic bread and wine. Medieval theologians played with both meanings, the personal/subjective and the sacramental/objective, as have mystics and spiritual writers. In truth, there is no need to choose between the two, for they reinforce one another. The *communio sanctorum* is

a complex, multilayered reality made up of the Spirit-filled community sharing in each other's lives and in the sacraments, holy people and holy things inextricably linked.

In light of the contemporary moral imperative to treat the earth as a beloved creation with its own intrinsic rather than instrumental value, the elusive quality of the phrase's original meaning is a happy circumstance. Sacramental theology has always drawn on the connection between the natural world and the signs of bread, wine, water, oil, and sexual intercourse which, when taken into the narrative of Jesus' life, death, and resurrection, become avenues of God's healing grace. Now, in the time of the earth's agony, the *sancta* can be pushed to its widest meaning to include the gifts of air, water, land, and the myriad creatures that share the planet with human beings in interwoven ecosystems. The universe itself is the primordial sacrament, indwelt by the Spirit. The same divine creativity that lights the fire of the saint also fuels the vitality of the natural world. "Communion in the holy," then, embraces holy people and a holy world in interrelationship. Here this symbol reveals its prophetic edge as its cosmic dimension calls forth an ecological ethic of restraint of human greed and promotion of care for the earth.

Mary, Galilean Woman of Grace

Within this great cloud of witnesses stands Miriam of Nazareth, a woman of faith who heard the word of God and kept it, partnering God in the great work of redemption. In no way does this placement in the communion of saints diminish her unique historic vocation to be the mother of the Messiah or the specific grace that accompanies this vocation. It remains true, however, that a woman's maternal function does not exhaust her identity as a person before God.

456 While honoring her unique relation with Jesus, seeing Mary as "truly our sister" refocuses her significance for the church today in terms of her whole graced life lived before God.[50]

This theological synthesis proceeds in two steps. First, it discovers Mary as an actual historical woman who lived with faithful response to the Spirit. Second, it draws comfort and challenge from the living memory of her life as she walks with the community today. This then/now method springs from the insight that God's saving revelation takes place precisely in history, in specific times and places, rather than in the platonic realm of eternal ideas. Hence it entails a paradigm shift from a primarily doctrinal or devotional Marian imagination to an imagination colored by history—that is, to a picture of the historical Mary fed by the Gospels. This does not mean that doctrine and devotion have no part in interpretation, but their symbolizing needs to be tethered down by her concrete gospel reality at every point.

MEMORY:
THE WOMAN OF GALILEE

Envisioning Miriam of Nazareth as a real woman of history who walked faithfully with her God does not have to begin with a blank slate. By a happy providence, the quest for the historical Jesus, now two centuries old, provides a cornucopia of information about first-century Galilee that can spill over into rediscovery of Mary's actual life. The spade of archaeology, the measuring tools of social-scientific studies of the Roman Empire, and the quill of ancient authors all help to paint a picture of her world. Archaeologically, for example, the hard remains uncovered in Nazareth include olive presses, wine presses, and millstones for grinding grain, indicating the rural character of this village. What has not been found is just as significant. To date, nothing that indicates wealth has been uncovered in Nazareth: no paved roads or civic buildings, no inscriptions, no decorative frescoes or mosaics, no luxury items such as perfume bottles, not even any simple glass. Economic studies locate this village on the impoverished underside of a two-tiered monetary system of empire, in which the work of 90 percent of the population was taxed to expand the wealth of the elite few. Political studies make clear the violence of the Roman pattern of occupation, as when in 4 BCE, three legions put down a Jewish uprising; they crucified two thousand men around Jerusalem and, marching on Sepphoris, four miles from Nazareth, "burned the city and enslaved its inhabitants."[51] Religious studies uncover the lay style of Jewish synagogue practice, far from the Jerusalem temple with its priests and sacrifices. These studies combine now with cultural studies of Galilean marriage and family customs as they affect women to locate Mary squarely in her own time and place.

Granting Mary her own historical existence makes clear that her context was an economically poor, politically oppressed, Jewish peasant culture marked by exploitation and publicly violent events. Committing to a dangerous pregnancy, giving birth in a barn, fleeing to a foreign country as a refugee, asking questions, pondering meaning, doing the hard work of women in a farming village, anxious about her firstborn's ministry, losing him to execution by the state, living as a widowed elder in the post-Pentecost

---

50. For exploration of this approach, with historical details and close reading of Scripture, see Elizabeth Johnson, *Truly Our Sister: A Theology of Mary in the Communion of Saints* (New York: Continuum, 2003).

51. Josephus, *Antiquities*, 17.289.

community: in all these stressful biblical scenes, she lived out her fidelity to God's call on a low rung of the social ladder.

The relevance of this historical picture becomes clear when theology reflects that it is precisely to such a woman (such a nonperson) that God has done great things. Commenting on the Magnificat, Gustavo Gutiérrez observes how this prophetic song, sung by a lowly woman, "tells us about the preferential love of God for the marginalized and abused, and about the transformation of history that God's loving will implies."[52] At the same time, the power of her words consists in their ability to make us see that the quest of justice must be located within the dynamism of God's love, or it loses its meaning in Christian life. Take Mary's social location out of this analysis, and exegesis loses its sting.

HOPE:
HER DANGEROUS INSPIRATION

Memory links with hope when this method shows that the historical woman of the Gospels walks with the church today, accompanying believers as a comrade, a *compañera*. While the precise circumstances of her actual life can never be repeated, in company with her, we find strength to face up to our own encounters with the Spirit and go forward with the best of our faithful wits. The wedding feast at Cana (John 2:1-11) provides one illustration of how this relationship works. A typically poor family in Galilee hosts a wedding banquet. Amid the dancing and singing, the wine gives out. Miriam of Nazareth notices and decides to act. "They have no wine," she says to Jesus. Despite his hesitation, she gets results: six water jars filled with excellent wine. In this Johannine story, the wine,

more than one hundred gallons of it, signifies the abundant gift of salvation joyfully poured out by the presence of Christ. But Mary's words have a critical edge. People in poor nations hear her say, "They have no wine," and continue: nor any food, clean drinking water, housing, education, health care, employment, freedom, security from rape, human rights. Mary stands among the marginalized, herself a member of the group without wine, and speaks the hope of the needy. Her strong impulse to call for relief corresponds to God's own compassionate desire to spread bountiful life on earth. Just as her words propelled Jesus into action at Cana, her challenging plea addresses the conscience of the church, which is the body of Christ in the world today. Even though people in wealthy nations might prefer not to be disturbed, her voice reverberates through the centuries: "They have no wine . . . you have to act."

The hermeneutical method that interprets Mary as a genuine human woman who companions our lives today in the communion of saints contributes to a theology coherent with elements of biblical, classical, and conciliar church teaching, capable of promoting action on behalf of global justice and peace, particularly empowering to the flourishing of women, and productive of religious meaning for our time. Mary of Nazareth, Mother of God: *Presente!*

Conclusion

The religious symbols of creation, covenant, messianic promise, incarnation, sin, redemption in Christ, and eschatological hope have always carried a universal intent, relating the whole

---

52. Gustavo Gutiérrez, *The God of Life* (Maryknoll, NY: Orbis, 1991), 185.

world in a common origin, history, and destiny through the one Spirit. The communion of saints is another such symbol, developed in Christian vocabulary to express the reality of people's connection to one another in virtue of being graced by the mystery at the heart of the universe. It is a most inclusive symbol, for it interrelates not only diverse cultural, ethnic, and racial groups, and women with men, and the most socially marginalized with the powerful, all within a commu-

nity of grace, but also the living with the dead and the yet to be born, all seekers of the divine, in a circle around the Eucharistic table, the body of Christ, which encompasses the earth itself. Allowing this doctrine its full play in ecclesial life through remembrance and hope assures that when the church venerates the saints, including Mary, and reflects on their significance, it truly serves the power of the God of life.

For Further Reading

Saints

Anderson, George, et al., eds. *The One Mediator, the Saints, and Mary.* Lutherans and Catholics in Dialogue 8. Minneapolis: Augsburg Fortress, 1991.

> *The common statement of this ecumenical dialogue, supported by extensive background studies in Scripture, history, church teaching, and theology.*

Brown, Peter. *The Cult of the Saints: Its Rise and Function in Latin Christianity.* London: SCM, 1981.

> *Using methods of social history, this study links the emergence of the cult of the saints to cultural, political, and economic contexts of late antiquity. It is especially clear on patronage.*

Cunningham, Lawrence. *The Meaning of Saints.* San Francisco: Harper & Row, 1980.

> *A systematic presentation that focuses on the significance of saints as exemplars.*

Johnson, Elizabeth. *Friends of God and Prophets: A Feminist Theological Reading of the Communion of Saints.* New York: Continuum, 1998.

> *A historical and systematic exploration of the companionship model of the communion of saints and its ramifications for social justice, especially for women.*

Perham, Michael. *The Communion of Saints*. London: SPCK, 1980.

> *A study rich in patristic references and later developments in the Anglican tradition.*

Rahner, Karl. "The Church of the Saints." In *Theological Investigations*. Vol. 3. New York: Crossroad, 1972, 3:91–104.

———. "The Life of the Dead." In *Theological Investigations*. Vol. 4. New York: Crossroad, 1974, 4:347–54.

———. "Why and How Can We Venerate the Saints?" In *Theological Investigations*. Vol. 8. New York: Crossroad, 1983, 8:3–23.

> *Key essays that explore the significance of saints within a theology of grace.*

Sherry, Patrick. *Spirit, Saints, Immortality*. Albany: State University of New York Press, 1984.

> *A philosophical study of the meaning of spirit applied to the saints.*

Woodward, Kenneth. *Making Saints*. New York: Simon & Schuster, 1997.

> *A detailed study of the current process of canonization in the Roman Catholic Church.*

Mary

Anglican–Roman Catholic International Commission. *Mary: Grace and Hope in Christ*. New York: Continuum, 2006.

> *Fruits of ecumenical dialogue that break new ground for mutual understanding and develop the Marian tradition even for Catholic thought.*

Brown, Raymond, et al., eds. *Mary in the New Testament*. Philadelphia: Fortress Press; New York: Paulist, 1978.

> *A breakthrough ecumenical scripture study that uses historical-critical methods to deal with every New Testament verse concerning Mary.*

Elizondo, Virgilio, Allan Figueroa Deck, and Timothy Matovina, eds. *The Treasure of Guadalupe*. Lanham, MD: Rowman & Littlefield, 2006.

> *Studies of the significance of Guadalupe for Latino/ Latina peoples and all the Americas.*

Dombes Group. *Mary: In the Plan of God and in the Communion of Saints*. New York: Paulist, 1999.

> *A European ecumenical common statement.*

Gaventa, Beverly. *Blessed One: Protestant Perspectives on Mary*. Louisville: Westminster John Knox, 2002.

> *Essays retrieving the meaning of Mary and her faith for Protestant churches today.*

Gebara, Ivone, and Maria Clara Bingemer. *Mary: Mother of God, Mother of the Poor*. Maryknoll, NY: Orbis, 1989.

> *A liberation/feminist study of Marian doctrine and devotion in the Latin American context.*

Graef, Hilda. *Mary: A History of Doctrine and Devotion*. 2 vols. 1963. Reprint, Westminster, MD: Christian Classics, 1985.

> *A classic compendium of historical data through two millennia.*

John Paul II. "Redemptoris mater" (Mother of the Redeemer). Origins 16, no. 43 (April 9, 1987).

> *Encyclical on the Mother of the Redeemer.*

460   Johnson, Elizabeth. *Truly Our Sister: A Theology of Mary in the Communion of Saints.* New York: Continuum, 2003.

> *A theology of Mary drawing on women's experience, with attention to the Galilean context of her life as the framework for a liberating understanding of the Gospels.*

Küng, Hans, and Jürgen Moltmann, eds. *Mary in the Churches.* Concilium 168. New York: Seabury, 1983.

> *Succinct studies of biblical, ecumenical, and theological new directions.*

Paul VI, *"Marialis Cultus"* (Devotion to the Blessed Virgin Mary), *The Pope Speaks* 19 (1974–75): 49–87.

> *Papal letter that remains a classic regarding Marian devotion.*

Rahner, Karl. *Mary, Mother of the Lord.* New York: Herder & Herder, 1963.

> *A series of meditations in the manner of transcendental theology, which links Mary to the mystery of grace in communion with all human beings.*

Tavard, George. *The Thousand Faces of the Virgin Mary.* Collegeville, MN: Liturgical, 1996.

> *Ecumenical exploration of Mary's meaning through the ages, including her significance in Judaism, Islam, and other world religions.*

Sacraments 9.1

Sacraments in General

David N. Power

Inspired by the Constitution on the Liturgy of the Second Vatican Council,* the *Catechism of the Catholic Church* places the discussion of what are traditionally named the seven sacraments in the Roman Catholic Church in the larger setting of liturgy.[1] The church is a worshipping community, and it is as a worshipping community that in receiving God's grace it expresses its own identity as the church of Christ. The sacraments are key moments in the organic whole of common ecclesial worship. They cannot be properly considered apart from their celebration within the total liturgy, and in early times, they were given an appropriate place on the liturgical calendar, with implications for how they were understood. Eucharist was celebrated primarily in the gathering of the community on Sunday, initiation at Easter or Epiphany or Pentecost, penance and reconciliation in Lent in preparation for the Pasch, ordination on Sunday or on Ember Days. The anointing of the sick was related to the mystery of the Pasch by the blessing of the oil in Holy Week and by its celebration within the Eucharist whenever possible. The rites of marriage emerged over time from an initial blessing of the couple within the Eucharistic assembly. Within this liturgical setting, sacraments are celebrations of an ecclesial communion in the Spirit and have a ritual that combines word, prayer, and ritual action.[2]

---

* Acknowledging the contribution of the late Regis Duffy in the 1991 edition of this volume, this essay develops the topic further, with inclusion of more historical material and with attention to contemporary influences not noted before (e.g., that of Hans Urs von Balthasar and that of feminist theology, as well as material from the past twenty years).

1. *Catechism of the Catholic Church* (Vatican City: Libreria Editrice Vaticana, 1994), part 2, The Celebration of the Christian Mystery (hereafter cited as CCC).

2. Sacramental celebration is about making the invisible visible and about realizing the presence in this world of the eternal communion of Father, Word and Spirit. It is likewise the ecclesial enactment of the Paschal Mystery of Christ prefigured in the Paschal Feast, realized in the flesh of Christ, and celebrated in the liturgy. The use of capitals for certain terms in this and the following chapters is prompted by the desire to show the continuity within earthly enactment, and

Sacramental theology is now developed not only by considering the development of doctrines and theological writings and systems, but also by attending to the modes of their celebration. On this account, attention is given to the maxim *Lex orandi lex credendi*, sometimes translated as "The law of praying establishes the law of believing."[3] Without the addition of a verb in the translation, the phrase indicates quite simply that worship is the most basic evidence of what is believed, and that it is first and foremost through acts of worship that the church enacts its beliefs. This does not mean forms of worship are to be uncritically received, nor that doctrine always follows from worship; in fact, worship itself changes under the influence of how doctrines are formulated. The maxim may serve simply to denote the interaction between doctrine and celebration, rather than the primacy of one over the other. This is sometimes explained by saying worship is a first-order articulation of faith and doctrine, and theology is a second-order and more theoretical reflection, so the two orders of expression interact throughout the history of the church.

General sacramental theory, even when it is taught as an introduction to the study of sacraments, is an attempt to find a synthetic and methodological way to present the place of sacraments in the life of the church, as this is known from studies on particular rituals and celebrations. At the origin of such reflection are the sacraments of baptism and the Eucharist, to which the others are related. Since medieval times, writers in the West looked for a definition that could be applied analogously to all sacraments that belong to the essence of the church's memorial of the Christ event or that mediate the grace of communion with and in Christ. However, definitions alone give little understanding and belong properly in the context of reflection on the organic system of interconnected rites that have the Eucharist as their center. As the *Catechism of the Catholic Church* sums it up, "The sacraments form an organic whole in which each particular sacrament has its own vital place. In this organic whole, the Eucharistic sacrament occupies a unique place as the 'Sacrament of sacraments.'"[4]

This introductory section begins with a word about how sacraments originated within the life of a historical organic ecclesial community, so that we may see what is meant by saying they are instituted by Christ. This introduction is followed by an overview of the development of sacramental doctrine and theology, beginning with early centuries. Since the major concern of this compendium of systematic theology is to offer Roman Catholic perspectives, the section then turns to the influence of Saint Augustine, to Scholastic theology, and to the positions taken at the time of the Reformation by the Council of Trent. The section ends with a look at the contemporary renewal of Catholic sacramental theology, beginning in the nineteenth century and receiving a particular impetus through the work of the Second Vatican Council.

---

the continuity of the earthly with the Divine. For example, to be faithful to the continuity between the eternal utterance of Divine Word, the Word made known in human words, and the mystery of the Word made flesh, *Word* is capitalized. Other terms for which capitals are similarly used are *Paschal Mystery, Pasch, Risen Christ/Lord*, and *Cross*.

3. *Indiculus Caelestinus*, cap. 8 (Denzinger-Schönmetzer, *Enchiridion Symbolorum* [hereafter cited as DS], 246). For a discussion of this axiom, see Paul De Clerck, "'Lex orandi, lex credendi': Sens original et avatars historiques d'un adage equivoque," *Questions liturgiques* 59 (1978): 193–212.

4. CCC 1211.

Origin of Sacraments

Catholics in the Roman Catholic tradition were long accustomed to the definition of a sacrament as a sacred sign instituted by Christ to give grace. In the light of particular historical circumstances of doctrinal dissension, this was given an important place in doctrine by the Council of Trent and the catechism of that council. Taken in the abstract, it often led to the exaggerated quest to find the origins of each sacrament in the New Testament, and indeed even in specific words and actions of Jesus.

Supposing some knowledge of the liturgical history of particular sacraments, general theory begins appropriately with a word about the origins or institution of the sevenfold sacramental system of Roman Catholic tradition. This belongs within an organic system of worship that continues to develop over centuries and that is affected by the position of communities within the political, social, and cultural circumstances of different places and times. So that we can properly allow for the place of sacramental celebration in the ongoing life of the church, we must place queries about its origins and history against the background of an ecclesiology that sees the church as a living organism, influenced by conditions of time, place, and culture.

Appeal to specific scriptural texts may be made not as a quest for a moment of institution but as the attempt to relate sacraments as they developed to the gospel and the apostolic beginning of the church. According to our present knowledge of the history of the church's liturgy, the Lord's Supper and baptism are the only rites numbered as sacraments that have specific origins in New Testament times. Even with regard to these two, one cannot say that they were clearly set in place by Christ himself; rather, they need to be related to the importance and the form they took in the life of the apostolic community.

Leaving development to later chapters, a few things may here be noted about the appearance of other sacramental rituals over a period of time. Ordination rites pertained to governance of local churches and were celebrated within the Eucharistic community. Other ceremonies, such as those for penance, the care of the sick, and marriage, appeared over the course of time to express modes of belonging to the body of Christ that pertained to its fidelity to its apostolic origins and to the mystery of Christ. The theological task is to explain why, taking their diversity over time into account, they may be attributed to the guiding action of the Holy Spirit and became integral to the life of the church as Christ's body. Though there is certainly continuity, we must make reference to changes in the church's position in society and to peoples' cultures if we are to understand, for example, how rites of penance and reconciliation, rites of infant baptism, or rites of marriage took the forms known to us from the history of liturgy.

Looking for scriptural warrants, then, does not mean finding texts that indicate their institution by Christ in a narrow or legal sense. What these offer, rather, is an understanding of worship in spirit and in truth to which the Scriptures give testimony and to which sacramental rites belong. The meaning of sacraments is pertinent to the meaning of the church itself, as it is the living body of Christ and a community that lives from the Word of God offered in the Scriptures—one that remains truly his, though earthly conditions change over time and space. Giving such an ecclesial and historic setting to the discussion of sacraments and to offer a better theological meaning to the tradition about institution, Karl Rahner described the church as "the abiding presence of that primal sacramental word of definitive grace,"[5] which is given in Christ. It is the truly fundamental sacrament in that it is a community of faith and charity that lives as the visible expression of divine self-communication through Word and Spirit. This allowed Rahner to present the sacramental organism developing through history as an expression of the living grace of Christ and Spirit in the church according to time and place, or indeed as the visible presence of Christ and of his salvation in the world. Looking in this way at the relation of sacraments to Christ and church, we are in a better position to speak of their origins than when the matter is settled in a strictly institutional manner.

Faithful to the reality of Christian worship as one offered in spirit and in truth, theology and practice should not lose sight of the original and domestic simplicity of sacramental practice. Much ritual has been added to the celebration, different from age to age and from place to place, but this should not betray the sacraments' innate simplicity. When the need for revision and renewal imposes itself, this has to be achieved by way of a restoration of the original simplicity that marked the worship of a community that listened to the word of God and confessed the presence of the Lord through the power of the Spirit in the awesomely simple realities of bread, wine, water, and oil.

As the sacramental organism took shape, particular sacraments were related to specific Gospel texts, words and actions of Jesus in the course of his earthly dwelling, whether before or after his death and resurrection, and this pertains to their understanding as sacraments of Christ. On how this was done, we may learn something from the method pursued by the fathers of the church, even though we need to show some reserve about their typological uses of texts and stories. Referring the celebration of the mysteries to scriptural texts, they had in view the full reality of the salvation given in Christ and illustrated the meaning of sacraments through a mystagogical interpretation of the rites that was based on texts of both Old and New Testament. Sometimes they referred to particular words and actions of Jesus, but in a quite comprehensive way, as when they attributed the origins of water baptism to his own baptism, to the marriage feast at Cana, to his walking on the waters, to the water flowing from his side on the Cross, or of course to the Great Commission at the end of Matthew's Gospel. In this way, they expressed the belief that particular sacraments have their origin in his deeds and words, but most of all that they offer a participation in his mysteries. Only for the Lord's Supper or Eucharist is a specific time consistently allotted to the origins of the sacrament—namely, the Last Supper of Jesus with his disciples. Even then, discourse on its meaning required reference to other texts, such as the supper at Emmaus, the feeding of the crowds in the desert, the marriage feast of Cana, and of course, the paschal meal and the manna of the Old Testament dispensation. Taking several texts into play, preachers and writers expressed the belief that the church's sacramental action goes back to Christ himself and to the initial apostolic tradition.[6]

---

5. Karl Rahner, *The Church and the Sacraments* (New York: Herder & Herder, 1963), 18.
6. Karl Rahner, "Reflection on the Concept of *ius divinum* in Catholic Thought," in *Theological Investigations* (Baltimore: Helicon, 1966), 5:219–43.

466

Scholasticism

A more legal concern about how sacraments were instituted is found in early Scholasticism at the beginning of the second millennium, but this was in face of other theological issues. The attribution of the origins of matter and form to the will of Christ, as found in specific texts, fitted with a linear sense of institutional development, but the key question was the attribution of sacramental power and grace to Christ. According to what was a common way of thinking at the time, a rite could not be said to represent the action of Christ unless its ritual code had been determined by him when he was present among his disciples in the flesh. More important, however, was the belief that his forgiving and sanctifying power worked through the celebration of the rites.

It has been suggested that several things were at work in the ways in which the question of institution was formulated during the early medieval period.[7] First, the justification for calling rites other than baptism and the Eucharist sacraments came from criteria taken from these two—namely, origin in Christ and the offer of some grace necessary to salvation and to participation in the life of the church. Second, inasmuch as the church was thought to be an institution coming from God, Christ had to be the legislator who put the instruments of grace in place. According to Wendelin Knoch, a third factor in establishing the divine origin of the sevenfold system of sacraments was related to the church's quest as an institution of divine right to be free of the control of secular authorities. It needed to be seen as a body with its own inner coherence and gifted with autonomy above any earthly authority. Granted, therefore, that from Scholastic theology, Catholicism inherited a belief that Christ instituted sacraments at some historical moment by fixing their specific rites, the underlying concerns were the sanctifying power of Christ active in the church, the origin of sacramental life in the mystery of Christ, the maintenance of an organic system of ritual celebration that accommodates growth in the grace of Christ and of the church, and the preservation of the life of the church as an institution in its own right.

Council of Trent

The Council of Trent found this appeal to specific institution of each sacrament by Christ useful in the context of Reformation controversies.[8] Trent was not simply trying to resolve historical questions about the moment of institution of each sacrament but, in face of the critique of the Reformers, wanted to connect the church's seven sacraments with Christ and with the beginnings of his church. Its purpose was to assert the action of Christ's saving power in each and all of these rites, as celebrated in the Roman Catholic tradition.

Referring specifically to what the Council of Trent said on institution by Christ,[9] the *Catechism of the Catholic Church* composed after Vatican II adopts a contemporary perspective that is also more patristic. It places the roots of sacramental rituals in the words and actions of Jesus that express the mystery of incarnation, death, and resurrection but forgoes the desire to

---

7. Wendelin Knoch, *Die Einsetzung der Sakramente durch Christus: Eine Untersuchung der Frühscholastick von Anselm von Laon bis zu Wilhelm von Auxerre* (Münster: Aschendorff, 1983), 411–14.

8. Council of Trent, *Decretum de Sacramentis*, canon 1 (DS 1601).

9. DS 1600–1601.

assert any given moment of specific institution: "Jesus' words and actions during his hidden life and public ministry were already salvific, for they anticipated the power of his Paschal Mystery. . . . The mysteries of Christ's life are the foundations of what he would henceforth dispense in the sacraments."[10]

Quoting from Leo the Great, the catechism adds, "What was visible in our Saviour has passed over into his mysteries (*in sacramenta transivit*)."[11] With this origin in mind, it defines sacrament in the specific sense applicable to the sevenfold as follows: "Sacraments are powers that come forth from the Body of Christ, which is ever living and life-giving. They are actions of the Holy Spirit at work in his Body, the church." This makes a connection between the visible manifestation of Christ's mysteries on earth and the action of the Holy Spirit in the visible signs of the life of the church. It relates sacraments and their history to the life of an organic body. Institutional developments occur within this life and are monitored by ecclesiastic authority, but they do not provide exclusively for the meaning and fecundity of sacramental celebration, and they have to be seen within a larger historical perspective that takes into account time, place, social reality, and culture. One cannot trace a linear and homogeneous development of sacraments, so one has to ask whether at any given moment of the life of the church, locally and universally, the place that they take in the life of believers may be accommodated to how their communion in Christ affects their lives, offering salvation in fidelity to the gospel and apostolic tradition as this is lived out in current realities.

Sacramental Theology in the Patristic Era

With the foregoing words on the origin of sacraments in place, it is possible to offer a survey of the history of sacramental theology, or of how reflection on their place and meaning in the life of Christian communities kept pace with liturgical development and celebration.[12]

Early historical reflection on the sacraments is usually connected with the Greek word *mystérion* and the Latin word *sacramentum*. Both words place the sacraments in the larger setting of the mysteries of Christ's flesh as visible manifestation of God's design for salvation. In the first three centuries of Christian writings, *mystérion* was given a more general use from which its application to baptism and Eucharist follows. Employment of the term by Christian writers originates in the use made of it in the New Testament to designate the immanent appearance before the whole world of the reign of God, the revelation in Christ of the divine design for salvation, which had been hidden from eternity (cf. Rom. 16:25-26; Ephesians 1). Influenced by intertestamental literature and not only by the Hebrew and Sapiential scriptures, this term means the eternal wisdom of God now revealed

---

10. CCC 1114–16.

11. In the English translation, *sacramenta* is translated as "mysteries" to be faithful to the sense of the word in Leo— namely, making visible Christ's mysteries as they are celebrated in a number of different ritual actions and practices. This includes what we call the seven sacraments but is not confined to them. The quotation from Leo is from *Sermo* 74, 2 (PL 54, 398).

12. For an overview, see Carlo Rocchetta, *Sacramentaria fondamentale: Dal "Mysterion" al "Sacramentum"* (Bologna: Edizioni Dehoniane, 1990), 95–284.

468

in his plan of salvation. It brings to the fore that what has been unknown and invisible but has existed in the mind of God from all eternity has been revealed and made visible in Christ. The signs or events that have anything to do with this revelation belong to the mystery or can be spoken of as mysteries.

Application to liturgical rites is made against this background. One example worth citing is that of Irenaeus of Lyons, who uses the term to speak of baptism and the Eucharist because they offer a remembrance of and a participation in the mystery of the Word made flesh and an offer of human salvation.[13] Irenaeus strongly contrasts this with the sense of mystery in Gnostic wisdom and practice, which is reserved for the elite and kept secret from the general populace. When Origen uses the word *mystérion* in writing of the Word made flesh, of the Scriptures, or of worship, it is to underline that what is hidden in God is thus made visible, or that the divine reality is both revealed and hidden in its manifestation.[14] An expression that is now often seen as important comes to the fore in Melito of Sardis's homily on the Pasch, that is, the mystery of the Pasch, or Paschal Mystery.[15] Salvation is offered to humanity through the death of Christ, in whom all the figures of Old Testament history find their fulfillment.[16] The understanding of sacraments is properly found within the celebration of the annual Paschal feast, with its reading of the Scriptures and its celebration of baptism and the Eucharist.

The use of *mystérion* to designate the Eucharist, baptism, and attendant rites became common from the fourth century onward, especially in connection with commentary on the rites of initiation into the church at the Paschal Vigil.[17] There is not the danger of confusion with pagan mysteries, as there may have been earlier, and the use of the term and the context of participation in the mystery of Christ as Mediator and God's revelation is clear. The mystagogy of sacrament takes the death and resurrection of Christ as the key manifestation and realization of salvation, or of the "now" in time of God's kingdom, its eschatological advent. Connected with this idea of "Christian mysteries," there is the image of the *oikonomía*, or economy of salvation, and this too enters into much explanation of the symbolism of liturgical rites.[18] While the influence of Neo-Platonic philosophy on Christian language and understanding is continually undergoing study, it is clear that for early fathers of the church, the visible is related to the invisible in that it makes the invisible known, and the visible is light because it participates in the eternal light of God. Only in the sixth century, with the writings of the Pseudo-Dionysius, is a clearly Neo-Platonic and apophatic foundation given to this type of discourse to underline the enduring hidden character of what is made visible in sacraments

---

13. *Adversus haereses* IV, 18, 5.

14. See Hans Urs von Balthasar, "Le mysterion d'Origène," *Recherches de science religieuse* 26 (1936): 513–62.

15. Melito of Sardis, *On Pascha and Fragments*, ed. Stuart George Hall (Oxford: Clarendon, 1979).

16. It might be noted that for Melito, Pasch meant the suffering of Christ, whereas later it came to mean passage or transition through death to life.

17. English translation of texts and commentary in E. J. Yarnold, *The Awe Inspiring Rite of Initiation* (Collegeville, MN: Liturgical, 1994). For a study of these texts, see Enrico Mazza, *Mystagogy: A Theology of Liturgy in the Patristic Age* (Collegeville, MN: Liturgical, 1992).

18. There is reference to this use of mystery or Paschal Mystery in the Constitution on the Liturgy of the Second Vatican Council, *Sacrosanctum concilium* 2, 5.

and encouraging a contemplative participation in the divine mysteries of ecclesial celebration.[19]

Latin writers translated the Greek word as *sacramentum*, and use of the term underwent its own evolution.[20] Its use in ritual context is in line with Greek usage, but Tertullian gave it a specific meaning that had much influence later on Latin theology. In commenting on the rites of baptism, Tertullian not only used the word in the same general way as Greek writers used *mystérion*, but he also adopted a secular use, which understood *sacramentum* to mean a military oath by which one committed oneself to service on the basis of a promise and an agreement given by the emperor or his representative. Adopted for theological purposes, the word underlined the covenantal character of initiation ritual and helped to convey the ethical imperatives of entering the church through the rites of baptism and Eucharist. This is said to have some affinity not only with military inscription but also with pagan mysteries whereby the initiate is consecrated to pursuit of the knowledge of the hidden mysteries behind what is visible. Tertullian is thus an example of how secular vocabulary can be adopted to Christian meaning with the change effected by being set in a new context.

For Cyprian of Carthage, whose work is in many respects associated with the thought of Tertullian, the comparison with the military oath accentuated the participants' commitment to ecclesial communion, particularly when the bishop had to deal with defections. This is behind Cyprian's initial demand for the rebaptism of those who lapsed under persecution through a public denial of faith, either by word or action. Ecclesial communion is established through the bishop recognized by all, who prays over them in the communion of the Spirit.[21] Since Christ committed these sacraments to the Catholic Church, to which his followers are to remain faithful, there can be no sacraments outside this communion. The role of the bishop in the community, which was quite extensive in the mind and practice of Cyprian, is heightened through his presidency of the Eucharist. When the bishop says the prayer of thanksgiving over the gifts in the place of Christ (*vice Christi*), Christ himself is present and active in the life of the church. The ideal celebration is to celebrate as Christ celebrated, following the same ritual performance, meaning the way Cyprian found in the Scriptures, even down to such a minute detail as the pouring of water into the cup of wine.[22]

In summary, from these early centuries, we see the necessary context in which to pursue a theology of sacraments. First, the sacraments are about participation in the mystery of Christ and the salvation this offers, with a special appeal to the imagery of the Pasch. Second, they are about the mystery of the church and its members' belonging to it. Third, they are an eschatological manifestation of God's intention to save humanity in Christ. This fits with the imagery of Christ's Paschal sacrifice, which is the key eschatological moment of the revelation of the mystery and the entry into the human story of the kingdom of God. Fourth, understanding of the mystery is enhanced through commentary on the symbolic meaning of rites and words.

19. For his ideas on worship, see Dionysius the Areopagite, *The Ecclesiastical Hierarchy*, trans. and annotated by Thomas L. Campbell (Washington, DC: University of America Press, 1981).

20. For an overview of Latin literature, see J. de Ghellinck, *Pour l'histoire du mot sacramentum* (Louvain: Spicilegium Sacrum Lovaniense, 1924/1947).

21. Cyprian, *Epistola*, Corpus Scriptorum Ecclesiasticum Latinorum 74, 5.

22. *Epistola* 63, Corpus Scriptorum Ecclesiasticum Latinorum 3, 2.701–17.

Fifth, the ineffably invisible is made visible without abolishing the difference between the two orders. In the effort to go back to sources advocated by the Second Vatican Council and its subsequent liturgical reforms, contemporary theology has gleaned from this early history in explaining the place that sacraments have in the life of the church and presents their relation to Christ not simply in terms of his power but also in terms of how they symbolize his mystery.

Augustine

In the Latin West, Augustine stands behind all later developments.[23] Even when writers are not fully true to the meaning of what he said, he remains a constant point of reference, and his words are often cited, in or out of their original context.

In the vocabulary he used, Augustine followed the identification between sacrament and mystery, while accentuating the sacramental economy of the Pasch. All he says of the mysteries or sacraments through which this is celebrated supposes a community assembly, a gathering in word, action and prayer, presided over for each church by its bishop. This is an ecclesial communion in which the Spirit is the bond of life and Christ is present and active in giving salvation to those who approach in faith. The invocation of the Trinity, confession of the name of Christ, and visible ecclesial communion in the Spirit are essential to the mysteries and to their working within the life of Christians. His explanation of signs and words is rooted in the Bible, and to show the meaning of things and actions, Augustine pursues the relation between the word proclaimed, the word prayed, and the

things used or actions performed. What is visible to the eye is thus a visible word, according to the oft-quoted description of this interplay: *Verbum accedit ad elementum et fit sacramentum*, which could be translated, "The word is connected with the element and from this is made a sacrament."[24] His teaching on the mysteries or sacraments conveys an eschatological expectation, for all belongs within the mystery of the kingdom of God as it is now active in the church on earth and fully realized only in the communion of the saints in heaven.

In keeping with Augustine's doctrine on the church as the body of Christ, it was in controversy with the Donatist church that he refined his thinking in ways that were to exercise a great influence in later centuries. Unwilling to reject a sacrament celebrated according to the rites of the church—that is, initiation through water baptism, anointing with the Spirit, and Eucharistic communion, where the Trinity is properly invoked—he could not totally reject the sacraments of schismatics who refused to live within the visible communion of the Catholic Church. At the same time, because these rites were placed outside the communion of the true church, he could not allow that they have their sanctifying power. While truly given and received, the sacrament of baptism could not give life until the recipient joined the communion of those united in the Holy Spirit. Hence, it was necessary to make a distinction between a sacrament, the obligation to live and act in the church, which went with this external and public action, and the grace of Christ or a living communion in the Spirit, which the sacrament offers. This meant distinguishing between the sacrament and the

---

23. Augustine's best-known work on sacraments is *On Baptism against the Donatists*, NPNF I/4, 407–514. On his use of terms throughout his works, see C. Couterier, *Sacramentum et mysterium dans l'oeuvre de St. Augustin, Etudes Augustiniènnes*, ed. H. Rondet (Paris: Aubier, 1953), 163–332.

24. Augustine, *In Ioannem* 80, 3.

res sacramenti (the fruit; the thing signified), as well as distinguishing a belonging to Christ and to the church that followed on a correct celebration from the true belonging in the Spirit that could come only within the visible communion of the Catholic Church. To illustrate this point, he used the metaphor of character or mark, comparing what is done in baptism with the bodily branding of the emperor's soldiers, or even of cattle. Inasmuch as it may be seen to make a visible mark, the celebration of baptism indicates that the recipient belongs by right to Christ and his church.[25] To move from a schismatic group to enter the true church was to enter that communion in which this mark or claim would come to be in truth that which it signified in sign. In any celebration within true ecclesial communion, these three things are realized together: the ritual sign posited in faith, the belonging to Christ and church for which the image is the mark imprinted, and the communion in the Spirit and sanctifying grace of Christ, which is not only signified but truly given.

Though first employed in writing of baptism, when they were applied to resolve problems about unworthy ministration by men ordained according to the accustomed rites, Augustine taught that these rites belong to Christ and not to the minister. Whoever is the minister, it is Christ who acts, according to the celebrated quotation "Sive Petrus baptizat vel Judas baptizat, Christus baptizat" (Whether Peter baptizes or Judas baptizes, it is Christ who baptizes).

To appreciate the meaning of the sacrament for people of that period, along with Augustine,

it is worth recalling some elements from the sermons of Leo the Great.[26] While he centers all worship on the Eucharist, his use of the term *sacrament* includes not only liturgical rituals but also things that belong to the daily life of Christians, such as prayer, fasting, other acts of penance, and whatever expresses devotion to God and to Christ. In the celebration of the liturgy, all these sacramental things are taken into the fullness of the sacramental significance of the commemoration of the sacrifice of Christ, where what was done once and for all in the sacrifice of his death is now present by visible sign and by grace in the life of the church. To elaborate on the meaning and reality of ritual celebration in the church, Leo appealed to the teaching of 1 Peter 2:1-11 on the priesthood of those who form a people comparable to the people of the former testament of Sinai. They gather in church as one priesthood to celebrate the sacraments, presided over by their high priest ,the bishop, who is their leader, their teacher, and their pastor, and whose power and authority for the good of the whole come from Christ and is exercised in the Spirit.[27]

Sacrament in an Era of Change in Cultural Settings

In a later period, the cultural setting in Spain and in the Carolingian Empire brought about a kind of wedding between social order and

---

25. Unfortunately, in later theology, this metaphor of character was reified, and the relation to the invocation of the Trinity and membership of Christ's body obscured. Even today, Augustine's thought can be grossly misrepresented as a theory of sacramental minimalism and a mechanical *ex opera operato* efficacy. See, for example, Maxwell E. Johnson, *The Rites of Christian Initiation: Their Evolution and Interpretation* (Collegeville, MN: Liturgical, 1999), 151–58.

26. M. B. de Soos, *Le mystère liturgique d'après S. Léon le Grand* (Münster: Aschendorf, 1958).

27. Leo the Great, *Sermon 4* (PL 54:143–48).

472 ecclesiastical order, which had an impact on the forms and moments of celebration. It also brought about changes in doctrinal understanding, with a new conception of the ordained priesthood that accentuated the minister's power to offer sacrifice and referred less to the mystery of the body and the one priesthood of all. The practical changes affecting infant baptism, confirmation, penance, anointing of the sick, and ordination went along with changes in the theology of these sacraments as they relate to the church and to Christ. This has to be seen in treating of specific sacraments, but any general theory of sacrament has to keep in mind the relation of ecclesial order to public order as a necessary element in the understanding of ritual and sacrament as practiced in these realms.

Given the social respect for cultures of antiquity, which was general, there were attempts to elaborate on doctrines in a more systematic, or scientific, fashion. Isidore of Seville did this chiefly through the use of etymologies, as this had become known in other disciplines. He thus gave a generic definition of sacrament, applicable to all key rites of the church's liturgy: "Sacramentum est in aliqua celebratione, cum res gesta ita fit ut aliquid significare intelligatur, quod sancte accipiendum est" (A sacrament is found in a celebration when the thing is done in such a way as to signify something that is to be received as holy).[28] This definition places the signifying action in the context of celebration, highlights its nature as sign, and takes this to signify what is holy. Elaborating on the role of sign, Isidore stressed that what is made visible is perceived only as through a veil. Following

Isidore, writers in the pre-Scholastic period wrote at length of the veiled action of divine power. The purpose of the sacramental sign is as much to conceal as it is to make known, and then, of course, the signified can be known only by faith. Rather than being things and actions that are suffused with light and give knowledge of the mysteries celebrated, signs could easily be seen as things whose presence would tell the faithful that God is at work but in a way whose meaning is hidden rather than illuminated through the sign itself.

Scholastic Theology

At the turn of the millennium, Berengar and Abelard had an impact on the discussion of sacrament because of the dialectic they posited between sign and signified, showing the need for a more systematic treatment of this relationship.[29] This anticipates the developments found in Scholastic theology. These, too, were affected by cultural changes, pertaining especially to the promotion of knowledge. Doing theology moved from monastery and ecclesiastic schools to the university, where it was taught alongside other branches of learning, such as logic, law, medicine, and philosophy. Scholastic theology sought a form of teaching that would fit a cultural description of *scientia*, the acquisition and presentation of knowledge. Hence, writers followed new methods of investigation and exposition and looked for a definition of sacrament that would fit the demands for formulas that could sum up the core of what was known about something. Each sacrament would retain its own

---

28. Isidore of Seville, *Etymologiae* 6.19, 39–42.

29. Rocchetta, *Sacramentaria fondamentale*, 285–325. See also Josef Finkenzeller, *Die Lehre von den Sakramenten im allgemeinen: Von der Schrift bis zur Scholastik* (Freiburg: Herder, 1980).

specificity but would have to fall within the general definition.[30]

Two definitions that became standard points of reference in this quest were that found in the eleventh-century *Summa sententiarum*, whose authorship is disputed, and that of Peter Lombard. The first distinguished the mystery signified from the sacrament that signified it: "Sacramentum est visibilis forma invisibilis gratiae in eo collatae, quam scilicet confert ipsum sacramentum" (A sacrament is a visible form of the invisible grace contained in it, that is which the sacrament itself confers). This definition highlighted the idea of the grace signified as something veiled but opened to perception through the sacramental sign, as it also spoke of the efficacy of a sacrament. Peter Lombard in turn circulated this definition: "Sacramentum proprie dicitur quod ita signum est gratiae Dei et invisibilis gratiae visibilis forma, ut ipsius imaginem gerat et causa existat" (A sacrament is properly so called when it is a sign of God's grace, the visible form of invisible grace, in such a way that it is its image and its cause).[31] This definition put the focus on the grace received through the sacrament and on the way in which the sign may signify it by bearing some perceptible relation to it, as it also speaks of the efficacy of the sacrament. Lombard wished to distinguish what is properly called a sacrament from other signs that may point to grace but do not confer it. In particular, he and others at the time wished to make a clear distinction between sacraments or rites of the Old Law and those of the New. While these definitions brought to the fore the question of how a sign may be the image and vessel of divine grace, this was thought of conceptually, and there was little attention to the mystery of God's design to send the Son and the Spirit for human salvation, which was prominent in the patristic era. In other words, the definitions point to grace as something given and much less to the mystery of the Pasch through which humanity is redeemed and in which sacramental celebration participates.

With such definitions in mind, later writers sought to investigate logically other elements belonging to an understanding of sacrament. They wanted to relate them to Christ himself by attributing their institution to him in a formal sense, even scrutinizing the Gospels for the moment at which it could be said each sacrament was determined by fixing its meaning and its matter and form. They found the necessity or what was called the suitability of sacraments as the means whereby God chose to communicate saving grace in their accommodation to human nature and its way of perceiving, as well as to the weakness of its fallen condition. On this score, distinctions were made between sacraments as remedies for sin and sacraments as conferring the elevating grace of participation in the grace of the Head.

In a special way, Scholastic theology took up the issue of how sacraments could signify both the grace of Christ and church membership, and how some sacraments could at times in truth signify but not communicate grace because of a defect or block on the part of the recipient. These discussions gave rise to the distinctions in sacrament of the sign, the grace, and an intermediary factor. The terminology adopted

---

30. Several definitions from this period may be found in D. Van Den Eynde, *La définition des sacrements pendant la première période de la théologie scolastique, 1050–1240* (Rome: Antonianum, 1950).

31. Peter Lombard, *Liber sententiarum* 4.1.4.

was that of *signum tantum, res et sacramentum,* and *res sacramenti* (the sign only, the thing and the sacrament, the thing of the sacrament). The visible sacrament was the sign performed, inclusive of necessary word and ritual action. The *res* was the grace signified but which to be given required a disposition on the part of the recipient. The *res et sacramentum* signified the place of the recipient in the church, this itself signifying the offer of grace but not guaranteeing it. It was always given in the administration of the sacrament, even when grace was blocked. The most important elaboration of this way of seeing a sacrament was found in the explanation of the sacramental character given in baptism, confirmation, and order, but there were also attempts to apply the distinction to other sacraments. For example, the marriage rite was said to signify the bond of marriage and, through it, the grace of marriage. In penance, the contrition expressed in confession was seen to be the *res et sacramentum* linking the act of the penitent to what was signified in absolution, namely, the grace of remission of sin. In the Eucharist, the grace or *res* is communion with Christ, the sacrament the commemorative words and elements, and the *res et sacramentum* the body of Christ into which the elements are transformed.

The most thorny question had to do with the efficacy of sacraments, the role of the properly designated minister in assuring this efficacy, and the connection between sign and efficacy. The first thing settled was that the sacraments work *ex opere operato,* that is to say, they confer the grace they signify not by reason of the merits or faith of the minister or of the recipient but by reason of the merits and the grace of Christ working in them. This could be expressed as

the *opus operatum Christi,* or the work done by Christ. The faith of the recipient is indeed a necessary disposition to receive grace but in no way its cause. From this there followed an involved discussion as to how the sacraments confer grace and how much the analogy of instrumental cause could be employed to explain them.

While the discussion was over a period of time quite intricate, here we can simply summarize the positions taken by Bonaventure, Thomas Aquinas, and later Duns Scotus. In considering the sacraments, Bonaventure looked to them first as remedies for sin, enlightening the mind, releasing it from darkness, and strengthening the will against the passions by the discipline of ritual.[32] Beyond that, God gives his grace to those who approach these signs in faith, but their efficacy in this regard can be spoken of only as quasi causality. Relating the signs more fully to the grace that is given, Thomas Aquinas could say that sacraments effect the grace they signify. He opted for an analogous application of the Aristotelian idea of instrumental efficient cause and linked it closely with the Platonic notion of a participation in the form or exemplar of the one who causes, Christ.[33] Duns Scotus distanced himself even more than Bonaventure from the category of causality, relying on how he understood the covenantal nature of sacraments and the promises God attaches to them, making them more the occasions on which God grants grace to those who receive them with faith in the promises given in the redemptive death of Christ.

In none of these authors should it be thought that sacramental signification, however related to causality, was reduced to an analysis of the essential matter and form, for they were

---

32. Bonaventure, *In IV Sententiarum,* d.1, qq. 1–4.
33. Thomas Aquinas, *Summa theologiae* III, q. 64.

quite wide-ranging in their investigation of sign and signified. Sacramental meaning for them embraced first and foremost the role of Christ as mediator and priest. It included a conception of grace as participation in this reality and as entailing the gift of the indwelling Spirit. It reached out to include creation and the reality of the church as body of Christ, royal priesthood, and communion in the Spirit.

Thomas Aquinas

Following up on what has been said about Thomas's appeal to the analogy of instrumental causality, several things worked out in his systematic synthesis of sacramental teaching are worth recalling, since they still have importance for contemporary theology. He placed his explanation of sacraments in the *Summa theologiae* directly after his treatise on the mysteries of the Word Incarnate. This was because what the sacraments give is a share in the grace of the Head, in that *gratia capitis*, which Christ enjoyed in his humanity as the person of the Word who took on flesh and became the redeemer of the human race, remaining active in the church with which, through grace, he is as one person (*quasi una persona*).[34] Then, referring to the theology of the sacramental character inherited from the Augustinian tradition, he placed all sacramental action within the mystery of the one priesthood and worship of Christ and his church. Using the Aristotelian distinction between the active and passive powers of the soul, he attributed an active power to the ordained minister in the exercise of this priesthood and a passive power to all the baptized, which allowed them as members of the church and participants in Christ's priesthood to receive the sacraments and to offer worship.[35]

To explain the place of the ordained minister in relation to Christ, he used the expression *in persona Christi* (in the person of Christ) to describe the power of his sacramental action as a minister of the church and so of Christ. As already said, because of his use of the analogy of efficient causality, he was able to link the efficacy of the sacraments closely to their functioning as signs. Lastly, the central place of the Eucharist in the sacramental system is carefully preserved: it is that to which all other sacraments have a relationship by positing a desire for it in the soul, and it is the nourishment that unites the person who receives it directly with Christ. Because of this communion with Christ through his self-gift, it is also the ultimate sign of the unity and communion of the church of Christ.

Thomas elaborated on the other sacraments by positing an analogy with the process of growth in human life, thus offering an organic view of the sacramental system. Baptism gives new birth, confirmation the strengthening of this life for taking an adult responsibility in the community, penance and extreme unction serve as remedies for what impedes life, while marriage and order enable persons to assume responsibilities for the service of the whole. What many have found wanting in this synthesis is an account of the role of the Holy Spirit—a want that might in some respects be remedied by appeal to the articles in the *Summa* where he speaks of the Spirit who, as God's love, is the uncreated grace given to the members of Christ. It is also often said that Aquinas lacked an ecclesiology

---

34. Thomas Aquinas, *Summa theologiae* III, q. 8, art. 2, c.

35. Unfortunately, this terminology was often used later to support a passive participation in worship for the laity and a marked distance between the action of the priest and that of the faithful, though that was not the intention of Aquinas.

476 that could serve as a foundation for sacramental theology. One could, however, say that his sacramental theology was his ecclesiology, since it embodied an image of the church as a worshipping community and as a communion in the one priesthood and sacrifice of Jesus Christ, the mediator between God and humankind.

Meeting the Challenge of the Reformers

The inadequacies of the ways in which this Scholastic synthesis was transmitted in the centuries preceding the Reformation, and the inadequacies of sacramental celebration, with its marked distinction between priest and people, are the necessary background to an assessment of the challenge of the Reformers to sacramental action. While the teaching of the Council of Trent on sacraments draws much from the prevailing Scholastic synthesis, the particular points it teaches need to be seen in terms of its opposition to the teaching of the Reformers, primarily Luther, Calvin, and Zwingli.

The larger question of justification by faith framed the controversies about sacraments raised by Martin Luther and the other Reformers. To Luther and to others, the doctrine of *ex opere operato* efficacy, as put into practice by reception of sacraments without proclamation of the Word, suggested a mechanical justification where primacy was given to priestly mediation and little attention to faith. Sacramental practice, the Reformers argued, implicitly denied the gratuitous and initiating character of God's action in the work of salvation and the need for faith to receive the saving grace of God. One of the primary ways offered by the Reformers by

which to restore active participation of the faithful was to retrieve the patristic doctrine of the priesthood of all the baptized, or of believers. This was the foundation for their right to hear the Word, for the right to receive the sacrament of the Supper in both kinds, and for their communion with Christ in his sacrifice, when they cast themselves upon him in faith in the promises of the Cross and in obedience to God. Since Scholastic theology was couched mostly in philosophical terms, whose use seemed dubious to the Reformers, they preferred to speak in biblical categories and to give primacy to the Word of God, to the promises of the new covenant, and to faith.

Like the other writers of the Reform movement, Luther and Calvin would speak of only baptism and the Lord's Supper as sacraments in the proper sense, since only these have a New Testament guarantee of their institution by Christ and so of his promises. When Luther gave a definition of what constitutes a sacrament, he took his inspiration from Augustine's assertion that a sacrament is given when the Word comes to the element, adding that this makes it a holy sign of God's promise. As a visible word, a sacrament is an expression of the Word of God and derives its power from that fact and is to be received with faith in its promises.[36] It is not a sacrament because it is performed but because what it promises is believed. The Reformers insisted that the Word of God must specifically connect a sign with God's promise, and only baptism and the Eucharist meet this criterion. While Luther retained some use of confession, marriage ritual, and ordination to ministry, these were not to be considered sacraments. Their contribution, however, was to be related

---

36. Martin Luther, "The Holy and Blessed Sacrament of Baptism," *Luther's Works*, vol. 35, *Word and Sacrament I*, ed. Jaroslav Pelikan and Helmut T. Lehman (Philadelphia: Fortress Press, 1960), 29–43.

to the power to arouse faith and to give some important external mark of Christian profession. They could not be allowed in any way to derogate from the role of faith and from the primacy of baptism and the Lord's Supper.

In defining sacrament, John Calvin wished to avoid what he regarded as the major error in the Scholastic theologians' definitions: that sacraments confer justification even without faith as long as no obstacle is present.[37] In contrast, he said that Jesus Christ is the unique mediator and that it is by faith in him that sinners are justified. Calvin had a particularly rich covenantal and epicletic dimension to his sacramental teaching; according to that teaching, sacrament confirms the Word of God, and the Spirit enlightens the faithful to the meaning of both Word and sacrament. The Spirit vivifies faith, and in the Lord's Supper, it is through the Spirit that the communicant receives Christ in truth or is in communion with him through faith.

Thus, Calvin argued, three blessings that come from God are connected: God's Word teaches us, the sacraments confirm that Word, and the Holy Spirit enables us to welcome this enacted Word. What Calvin retained from Scholastic theologians was the teaching that sacraments are a concession to human weakness, and they have a pedagogical role in freeing the mind from darkness and in this way aid faith. Thus, Calvin defined a sacrament as an "external symbol by which the Lord seals on our consciences his promises of good will toward us, in order to sustain the weakness of our faith."

Of late, there has been some spirited defense of the late medieval cultic system and of how a whole gamut of devotions, holy places, ritual acts, and sacramental moments gave people access to the holy and transformed their lives.[38] This may be true, but one cannot set aside the essential Protestant critique of a religious practice that was quite distant from its New Testament roots, exaggerated the role of the ordained and failed to give the Word of God to the people, and with that failed to nourish an evangelical faith in Jesus Christ as Savior.

COUNCIL OF TRENT

An assessment of the response of the Council of Trent on sacraments[39] must take into account not only the canons but also the chapters preceding them. The decrees on the sacraments were placed after the decree on justification, and this made it clear that grace is totally gratuitous and is given only to those who approach Christ with faith. Since the sessions on sacraments followed a procedure that was principally restricted to a response to Reformers, there was no attempt to construct a systematic teaching on sacraments, nor to resolve points disputed among Catholic theologians.

Throughout the discussion of individual sacraments, the importance of faith as a necessary condition for sacramental participation was made clear. The summary canons on sacrament (DS 1601–13) reasserted the unique character of the Christian sacraments and their efficacious and objective nature, which is summarized in the term *ex opere operato*. For Trent, this emphasized the work of God and Christ, which the council members believed to be jeopardized by the Protestant teaching on justification by faith

---

37. John Calvin, *Institutes of the Christian Religion* (Grand Rapids: Eerdmans, 1975), 4.14–26.

38. Most notably Eamon Duffy, *The Stripping of the Altars: Traditional Religion in England, 1400–1580*, 2nd ed. (New Haven, CT: Yale University Press, 2005); Edward Muir, *Ritual in Early Modern Europe: New Approaches to European History*, 2nd ed. (Cambridge: Cambridge University Press, 2005).

39. A. Duval, *Des sacrements au Concile de Trente* (Paris: Editions du Cerf, 1985).

478 alone. In answer to the thesis that only baptism and the Lord's Supper could properly be called sacraments, the council affirmed the sevenfold system without showing how these sacraments interrelate. To uphold the role of the minister designated by the church, the council taught the need for him to act at least with the minimal intention of doing what the church does, or intends to do, in conferring sacraments. In answer to the position of the Reformers attacking the role of a consecrated priesthood, it affirmed the conferral of a permanent sacramental character in baptism, order, and confirmation. Beyond that, the council abstained from any explanation of what the character is or how it functions (DS 1601–13). Though some common ground between Catholics and Reformers might be suggested in these teachings, the polemic at the time was so great that this was not pursued.[40]

Renewal of Sacramental Theology

Nineteenth-Century Orientations

The renewal of sacramental theology has its roots in German writers of the nineteenth century, especially the Tübingen School and Matthias Scheeben.[41]

In the nineteenth-century efforts to renew sacramental theology, the relation to the cultural context in the work of these theologians means they attempted an answer to the rationalism of the Enlightenment and to the concerns with experience shown in Pietism, without being simply adversarial. In the search for a scientific understanding of doctrine, including that about sacraments, the Tübingen School affirmed that dogmas need to be interpreted in relation to the whole of Christian teaching, to the Gospel of Jesus Christ, and to the life of Christians. In this, the writings of these theologians display a growing awareness of the need for a hermeneutics of revelation, or for criteria of interpretation, something that must also apply to sacramental doctrine and practice.

Since these writers' positions are an important background to twentieth-century theology, a summary of their ideas is appropriate. Johann Sebastian Drey described revelation as a divine activity in continuity with God's creative activity. The church is the embodiment of revelation, an organism enlivened by the Spirit, and the setting for individual sanctification. It is a social reality in which people of diverse cultures are related as one.[42]

Johann Möhler, in what he says specifically of sacraments in his *Symbolism*,[43] where he compares Catholic and Protestant confessions,

---

40. The seeds of a revival of the proclamation of God's Word are here, as of a better explanation of the relations among sacrament, justification, and faith, but the liturgical revision that followed the council did not promote the use of the vernacular nor of a more active role of the faithful, with long-standing results.

41. For the nineteenth-century contribution to renewal of ecclesiology and sacrament theology, see Yves Congar, *Un people messianique: L'Eglise sacrement du salut* (Paris: Editions Cerf, 1975), 57–90.

42. See Wayne L. Fehr, *The Birth of the Catholic Tübingen School: The Dogmatics of Johann Sebastian Drey* (Chico, CA: Scholars, 1981).

43. *Symbolism: Exposition of the Doctrinal Differences between Catholics and Protestants as Evidenced by Their Symbolic Writings*, trans. James Burton Robertson, intro. by Michael J. Himes (New York: Crossroad, 1997). In the title of his book, the word *Symbolism* refers to Symbolic Books—that is, to the books of confessions taken as normative by different churches.

repeats what was standard, relying on the catechism of the Council of Trent. However, this work and his book *The Unity of the Church* offer principles that have since served the renewal of Catholic sacramental theology. Möhler describes revelation not first of all as truths revealed, but as God's active work through chosen intermediaries for the salvation of the world. He sees the church as the continuation of revelation in that it is the body in which Word and Spirit are at work, furthering salvation. His major emphasis in describing the church itself is not as a society or as a hierarchy, but as a living communion in faith and love. It is "a collective, organic self, with various ministries and charisms," and "its concrete, symbolic realizations of the Holy Spirit were its sacraments." He relates the sacraments to human experience, thus including the subjective element of understanding and action fostered by the philosophies of the nineteenth century. The relation to Christ, whose atoning and redeeming acts the sacraments constantly repeat, and the relation to human experience are thus both necessary to a theology of sacrament,[44] which he defines as "an outward act to be performed by men according to the commission of Christ, and which partly denotes, partly conveys an inward and divine grace."[45] The sacraments embody an eschatological perspective on the kingdom of God that is akin to what is found in the New Testament.[46]

Twentieth-Century Trends

Contemporary sacramental theology, before and after the Second Vatican Council, picked up on these points and was developed against the background of the role played in the life of the church by the liturgical movement as well as a renewed interest in studying early patristic and liturgical sources.[47] Intrinsic to the movement, especially as fostered by such persons as Lambert Beauduin and Virgil Michel, was a concern with social realities and the understanding that liturgy nourishes the role of the laity in the public sphere, since it is as members of Christ's body and Christ's priesthood that laypersons live out their lives.[48]

Common Principles ⊛ With the revival of interest in patristic sources and benefiting from nineteenth-century theology, as well as from dialogue with other churches and confessions, East and West, writers on sacramental theology have woven several principles into their work, so that even within a diversity of further explanation, these are taken as foundational:

First, the sacramental rituals or actions are related to the sacrament of God in Christ and in

---

44. Ibid., 236, 258.

45. Ibid., 305.

46. Not of this school, Matthias Scheeben is of interest to contemporary work especially through his retrieval of the patristic sense of *mysterion*, described above. With this, he was able to relate sacraments to the work of Christ and the Spirit, to the communion of the church, and to the origins of salvation in the communion of the Divine Trinity. See *The Mysteries of Christianity*, trans. Cyril Vollert (St. Louis: Herder, 1961).

47. For an overview up to 1994, see Regis Duffy, Kevin Irwin, and David Power, "Sacramental Theology: A Review of Literature," *Theological Studies* 55 (1994): 657–705; up to 1999, David N. Power, *Sacrament: The Language of God's Giving* (New York: Crossroad, 1999), 274–310. On the theology of Rahner, Schillebeeckx, von Balthasar, Chauvet, and Ross reviewed here, see the works cited in For Further Reading.

48. The major positions of this movement were made an integral part of the sacramental life of the church by the Second Vatican Council in its different documents and are now part of the teaching on liturgy and sacraments of the *Catechism of the Catholic Church*.

480 his mysteries. The church itself is the sacrament of Christ in the world, sign of the unity and reconciliation of the whole community of peoples. In this setting, sacraments are explained as a participation in the Paschal Mystery of Christ, however that may be understood. As memorials of this event, they are seen to have an intrinsic eschatological orientation, holding the present of Christian communion in tension between past and future.

Second is the principle that Word and Rite belong together in constituting a sacrament. This requires studying the relation between Word proclaimed, prayers of blessing, and ritual action, rather than isolating a consideration of matter and form from the celebration as a whole.

Third, in conjunction with the introduction of the epiclesis into the Eucharistic prayer and other prayers of sacramental blessing inspired by Eastern models, greater consideration is given to the work of the Spirit in sacramental action, along with that of Christ, Word incarnate. As a result, sacramental life may be related to the mystery of the divine communion of Father, Son, and Spirit.

Fourth, the explanation of the sevenfold division of sacraments is explained as an organic system of living worship through which the communion of the church is built and nurtured, all sacraments being related to the mystery of Eucharistic sacrifice and communion.

Fifth, the nature of Christian sacrament is symbolic action and symbolic communication whose fundamental signs and actions are those drawn from the domestic setting of the church, not from temple worship. This point could be summed up by saying that the Christian sacraments, as opposed to more elaborate rituals, are bread, wine, oil, and water, and that the place for worship is a place of household community gathering. This is integral to all efforts to explain the meaning of symbolic action and symbolic exchange.

Sixth, legal concerns about institution are replaced by an appreciation of the growth of sacramental life in a living organism of faith and charity.

Seventh, while mystagogy, or explanation of liturgy through a commentary on rites and texts, is more properly the work of catechesis, an interest in this method is integral to doctrinal and theological developments.

On the basis of these principles or theological perceptions, it is possible to elaborate on a number of currents of thought, associating them with particular authors.

Word Event: Protestant Influences on Catholic Theology[49]

Certain Protestant theologians—specifically, Gerhard Ebeling and Peter Brunner—have been significant partners in the development of Catholic sacramental theology. Lauding the approach of Karl Rahner and Otto Semmelroth in integrating the Word into the theology of sacrament as symbol, Ebeling suggested that Protestant theology could contribute a perspective that describes the sacrament as a Word event, itself relating to the Gospel as a Word event, or the event of God's Word coming into the world and into human history. The specificity of a sacramental event is found in the basic situation in which the Word event occurs. As a Word event, it keeps open the question of the nature of that responsive faith which is the proper approach to sacramental action.

---

49. This point was presented in the first edition of this book by Regis A. Duffy, "Sacraments in General," 203–4.

Peter Brunner, in dialogue with both Roman Catholic and Orthodox theology, linked Word, Spirit, and sacrament. The Word is addressed to the church and invites the trust of faith, but there can be no full response without an invocation by the church of Word and Spirit, in memorial of the death of Christ. For Brunner, the action of the Spirit is the ground for the eschatological character of sacramental worship, since Pentecost brought the outpouring of the eschatological and prophetic Spirit, which anticipates the advent of the fullness of God's kingdom.[50]

While others could be cited, these two important Protestant theologians who wrote in the early days of Catholic-Protestant dialogue have been mentioned to highlight the relation between Word and sacrament, which has become important to Roman Catholic sacramental theology and ecumenical exchange.

Symbolic Causality

Much theology in the twentieth century was marked by what was called the turn to the subject—that is to say, an effort to understand faith and revelation from the side of the human person, which must include attention to human experience and human consciousness. This effort has produced gains for sacramental theology, especially in the area of what is called either symbolic causality or symbolic exchange. Drawing on insights from contemporary philosophers and from anthropological studies, writers enlarged on the understanding of sign so that it could be better appreciated as an act of self-communication, both divine and human, and an encounter in grace within a living body. Thus, the development of the Thomistic analogy with causality along the lines of symbolic causality by Karl Rahner and Edward Schillebeeckx enriched it in a contemporary vein.

KARL RAHNER

Karl Rahner wanted to present a sacramental theology in continuity with that of Thomas Aquinas while enlarging upon it by pursuing the insight that the nature of sacraments as signs is at the heart of sacramental theology, thus avoiding an exaggerated sense of the causal production of an entity of grace.[51] Rahner found the embryo of a richer explanation of sacramental grace in Thomas's theorem that when grace is given outside the conferring of sacraments (as he deemed it to happen quite often), it includes a desire for sacraments, and in a special way for the Eucharist, even if this is only implicit. For Rahner, this showed that Thomas did not tie grace to its "production" in sacraments, and on this basis, he probed the relation between the grace that is already offered in human life and sacramental celebration. He located this in the necessity for a symbolic action that is native to human expression in order to integrate the gift of grace as knowledge, love, and communion into human life. Grace is present in the world by reason of God's self-communication in the very act of creation, when human beings were already called to that fullness of divine communion that theology has called supernatural because it is totally gratuitous and beyond humanity's natural capacities. It is, however, made concrete and is perfected in Jesus Christ as the embodied presence of God in the world, and sacraments are

---

50. Paul Brunner, *Worship in the Name of Jesus* (St. Louis: Concordia, 1968).

51. See especially Karl Rahner, *Theological Investigations*, vol. 4 (Baltimore: Helicon, 1966) and vol. 14 (New York: Seabury, 1976).

482 an expression of this in the existence of diverse communities and persons.

The understanding of the sacramental divine self-communication in its triune oneness through the sending of Word and Spirit is linked by Karl Rahner to the understanding of what constitutes revelation. Revelation is both an action within God and a historical act, or an act within history, reaching from particular history and event to embrace all history. It is the act of God that restores the divine presence in creation and the presence in love to humans, subverted by sin. As both event and speech, it makes known the divine salvific love. It reaches its acme in Jesus Christ, who is the Word of God incarnate, the ultimate presence of God in love in and to the world, of whom the Word of the gospel and of the church speaks. Because of its relation to history, Rahner spoke of the revelation of God in the Pasch of Christ as an event—an event that occurred at a particular time and place but is for all time and all place.

As living sacrament of this revelation, the church gives expression to this divine gift through its sacramental worship. The sacramental event is therefore a coming forth of God's grace into symbolic expression, so that reality may be seen and personally lived in the explicit faith of divine gift and presence. It is the power of the sacraments, and particularly of the Eucharist, to relate this pervading divine presence to the sacrifice of Christ in its eschatological significance for humanity and for cosmic reality. Sacramental celebration is the core expression of the nature of the church as a community and expresses its worship of God as a communion in the grace of the Paschal Mystery as well as its mission to be the bearer of the offer of God's grace to its members.

This can be further grasped through an understanding of symbolic action as self-presence and self-communication, embodying not only immediate knowledge and communion but the horizon of knowledge, not just of being but of the desire for being, not just of immediate love but of love without bounds. Jesus Christ in his Pasch is present in sacrament to a community in place and time, as total self-presence and total communication. The symbol that is given as sign of God's presence and love is the means whereby the human person and the human community can become self-present, both as being loved by God and as being in love with God.

Through symbol, and in the anamnesis of the passion, the Word comes with the gift of the Spirit to human persons in their oneness with the universe and in the surrender of all reality to the Father in sacrifice. The sacramental economy brings human and earthly realities beyond their suffering into a communion of joy and hope with Christ. In the Eucharist, the presence of grace in the world, the proclamation of this grace in the Word, the Word's climax in the gift of the body and blood, and the symbolic self-expression of the church in blessing and in meal come together as one. All other sacraments introduce or prepare persons for this Eucharistic encounter, and Rahner pursued this thought in theological essays on particular sacraments, as will be discussed in the following chapters.

EDWARD SCHILLEBEECKX

As suggested by the English title of Edward Schillebeeckx's book *Christ the Sacrament of Encounter with God*,[52] personal encounter is a key expression for his sacramental theology. Schillebeeckx believed that the accent on sign in the sacramental theology of Thomas Aquinas

---

52. Edward Schillebeeckx, *Christ, the Sacrament of Encounter with God* (New York: Sheed & Ward, 1963).

could be developed by appeal to categories and theorems used in modern personalist philosophies. Hence he wrote of symbolic causality as an encounter and exchange in shared meaning, the meaning given to the world through the redemptive work of Jesus Christ and expressed in ecclesial community through the symbolic language of sacramental celebration. To speak of sacraments as the action of the whole community, he had recourse to the theology of common priesthood and explained the character given in baptism, confirmation, and order as a relationship to and within the church whereby persons are empowered to perform certain acts and assume certain responsibilities. Here he benefited from the position of Thomas Aquinas, which explained the sacramental character as the empowerment to share in the priesthood of Christ and church, but Schillebeeckx gave greater emphasis to what this means for the role of the Christian in the world.

While in his early work on sacrament, he spoke of symbolic causality, to a number of readers, it was not clear how fully Schillebeeckx related symbol and cause, or how encounter in a shared meaning and ontological reality were related. It was in his small work *The Eucharist* that his simultaneous connection and differentiation between the symbolic and the ontological became clear.[53] In addressing what was then a current dispute over the respective merits of the words *transignification* and *transubstantiation*, he pointed to the benefits of the first in putting shared meaning and exchange to the fore and of the latter for expressing the density of what is given. Only an appeal to ontology can indicate that the meaning expressed and communicated

within the church is not identical with the full reality of the Christ who is given and present, and that shared meaning does not exhaust the mystery celebrated. Though it is indeed an act of Christ's gift, and a focus on sign and exchange is an important way of grasping it, it is beyond the threshold of what is expressed in sign. The contemporary insight into meaning and sign does not fully render the transcendent nature of that which is signified nor the horizon within which meaning is shared.[54] While we can affirm the presence of Christ in sacraments, particularly in the Eucharist, and find a meaning to that presence in the remembrance of event and in symbol, we have no adequate idea of what the reality is in itself. The modem emphasis on sign and symbol and encounter does not of itself sufficiently account for the transcendent aspect of the reality present and given in sacrament.

In early works, to express the relation to the eternal divine mystery whereby salvation of the human race belongs within the mystery of God in the communion of Father, Son, and Spirit, Schillebeeckx attributed a quality to the passion and resurrection of Christ and to their sacramental memorial that seemed to place them above history, even if taking place in history. This transhistorical quality appeared to be a condition both for the origin of the mystery in God and for the Pasch's symbolic continuation in the liturgy of the church. This explanation risked placing both mystery and the life of grace on a plane quite distinct from the flow of human events in its temporal setting. In Schillebeeckx's subsequent work on soteriology and ecclesiology, the historical reality of Christ's passion and the historical realization of grace have moved to

---

53. Edward Schillebeeckx, *The Eucharist* (1968; repr. London: Burns & Oates, 2005).

54. This was in keeping with Schillebeeckx's basic understanding of analogy. See Edward Schillebeeckx, *Revelation and Theology* (New York: Herder & Herder, 1967), 1:84–95.

the fore. Concentrating on the Abba experience of Jesus and the church's experience of the Spirit, Schillebeeckx points in the midst of human history to a filial and even mystical relationship to God in communion with the solidarity of Jesus with human suffering in his surrender to God in death. To this both liturgy and the testimony given in following the ethics of the gospel give expression. As the death of Jesus needs to be located in its social and religious context, so the memory of that death needs to be expressed in symbols and forms of prayer that are pertinent to the total historical situation of those who live in the faith of Christ, especially as this touches human suffering. The authenticity of liturgical memorial is, as it were, born from its immediacy to current historical reality and is verified in the ethical and liberating action of the community that keeps memory. The hope that is celebrated in liturgy must have its proper political dimensions—that is, a this-worldly and not simply an otherworldly quality.[55]

To Schillebeeckx's concern with the transcendent and the particular, we may relate the question posed by Ghislain Lafont when he asks whether a key element in the theory of sacramental causality does not need to be retained, that is, the way in which God's action affects our very being.[56] When Thomas Aquinas spoke of God as primary efficient cause, this was because only God touches humans in the foundation of their being and transforms them therefore in their action and suffering. To link suffering to God's action, Lafont argues for the importance

of attending to particular being in theories of causality. Sacraments do not simply conform the recipient to the form of Christ in a general way, but they do so for each one within the conditions of individual existence. In the face of God's healing and sanctifying action, persons are in their being open to this action and can be formed by it. What is given them is to participate in their own particular lives in the divine being of the communion of the Three in One.

GLOBAL LIBERATION PERSPECTIVES

In his concern for the redemption of historical reality, Schillebeeckx joins that of Latin American liberation theology, which when it treats of sacraments, accentuates the liberative force of the memorial of Christ's Pasch. Liberation theology explains the relation of sacrament to time when it speaks of the memorial of past event as a liberating event that is operative also in the present. In this, it gives great importance to the nature of Pasch as liberation, a liberation from captivity offered to the Israelites and offered to all in the Pasch of Christ. Some writers in this school highlighted the festal nature of memorial, thinking that festivity is symbolic of freedom from all that holds people captive in their current existence.[57] Sacramental anamnesis is a challenge to any earthly exercise of power, which puts it to judgment, and which for the suffering of the world, particularly in the social sphere, offers a hope for the future.[58]

The question of sacrament as a liberative and festal event figures likewise in African[59] and

---

55. See the homily given as epilogue to *Christ: The Experience of Jesus as Lord* (New York: Crossroad, 1980), 840–46.

56. Ghislain Lafont, *God, Time, and Being* (Petersham, MA: St Bede's, 1991), 257–324.

57. Francis Taborda, *Sacramento, praxis e festa* (Sao Paulo: CESEP, 1987).

58. The work of Johannes Baptist Metz built on the ideas of Latin American theology with his idea of the Cross as a dangerous memory.

59. For example, Elochukwu E. Uzukwu, *Worship as Body Language: Introduction to Christian Worship; An African Perspective* (Collegeville, MN: Liturgical, 1997).

Asian[60] theologians, not primarily as liberative from oppressive social structures but more as that which offers freedom from cultural oppression. The remembrance of Christ in his solidarity with victims celebrated in sacrament offers a cultural freedom that allows people to retrieve their own cultural heritage and give expression to their faith in the gospel through their own cultural forms of speech, act, and festivity. Only then is it a memorial that truly saves time, offering the oppressed the freedom offered them by God in the time of their present existence as it stands between past and future.

The Ecclesial Subject: Feminist Theology

Having drawn attention to the "we" of sacramental prayer and action, we must give special attention to the feminist contribution in retrieving the ecclesial subject of sacrament. The church has to overcome in its sacramental life the distinction, even division, of the community into its clerical and lay components. An important part of this retrieval of the ecclesial subject is to overcome male-female polarization and to include women as participating members in action, ministry, language, and symbolic expression. In the past, not only have women been excluded or marginalized in ritual celebration, but symbolic and linguistic expression has favored male dominance.

The current feminist contribution is no more homogeneous than that of other currents of thought, but various feminist writers address some key issues in different ways in the interest of redressing the gender imbalance of ecclesial life and thought. This implies a critique of patriarchal paradigms in language, rite, and institution; a theological reconstruction of liturgical history; and inventive modes of symbolic expression that are related to biblical and ecclesiastical tradition and to experience. Susan Ross has summed up the central concerns in saying that feminist sacramental theology addresses the human in the mystery of the incarnation and its remembrance, the place of gender in the way that symbols work in the community, and the connection between sacramental praxis and social justice.[61]

The work of Mary Collins represents one current of the feminist contribution to sacramental theology.[62] She has outlined five principles that attend to the close relation between interpretation of the sacramental tradition and its actual celebration. The foundational principle is "the ritualizing of relationships that emancipate and empower women." A second principle is that there are no elites in the liturgical assembly but that action and responsibility are community centered. This leads to the third principle: the call to overcome patriarchal domination so as to restore truly redemptive relationships that eliminate prejudices and the structures of exclusion or privilege. The fourth principle says the interpretation of the tradition from the perspective of an inclusive community means there is a need to develop a fresh repertory of symbolic speech and action. A fifth principle is that actual celebration and the way

---

60. For example, Felix Wilfred, *Beyond Settled Foundations: The Journey of Indian Theology* (Madras: Department of Christian Studies, University of Madras, 1993).

61. Susan A. Ross, "God's Embodiment and Women: Sacraments," in *Freeing Theology: The Essentials of Theology in Feminist Perspective*, ed. Catherine Mowray Lacugna (San Francisco: HarperSanFrancisco, 1993), 185–209.

62. Mary Collins, "Principles of Feminist Liturgy," in *Women at Worship: Interpretations of North American Diversity*, ed. Marjorie Procter-Smith and Janet R. Walton (Louisville: Westminster John Knox, 1993), 9–26.

in which it is done are as important as producing new liturgical texts, which means that studies of ritualization have to be incorporated into sacramental theology, which is a practical as much as a systematic science.

Another current in feminist theology owes its insights to French feminism, particularly that of the philosopher Julia Kristeva.[63] A critique of ecclesial language that resonates with writers dubbed postmodern is that language usage is often too focused on transmitting concepts or doctrines, with the result that it mishandles the symbolic order and the imaginary. Theological writers assume Kristeva's critique of Christianity when she says that the church in the course of its history has too often subjected women in its ritual and spirituality, or not made it possible for women to give expression to their own nature, interests, and feelings as women within the mainstream of church life and action. Making her own distinctive use of terms and with a look at cultural traditions, Kristeva has distinguished between the semiotic and the symbolic. The symbolic designates the public order or public symbolism grounding that order. This public symbolism is much concerned with social relations and social power and hence gives primacy to the conceptual and to structures within the assembly's expression. The negative factor in this is that it leads to an undermining of the kind of expression that Kristeva calls the semiotic and in which resides the seeds of creativity. This is corporeal in its roots and imaginatively associative, and it gives freedom to the pursuit of drives innate to the growth of persons or communities in process. In this kind of expression, women find themselves most at home and are able to contribute creatively to the common order.

A key religious and sacramental expression that illustrates the importance of attending to this distinction of modes of expression is sacrifice, to which Kristeva gives considerable attention. Very often, sacrifice has been understood as something that only a male or a consecrated priest can do in order to honor God, thus belying the traditional truth that Christianity has interpreted sacrifice as the spiritual sacrifice of interior disposition and as the public praise in which all engage. Sacrifice has often been seen as an act of suppression to make satisfaction for sin, and so as the renunciation of personal desire and creativity, whereas more traditionally, sacrifice speaks of a divine initiative of love in giving life to the people as a people. Christ's own sacrifice is a fully human and personal act in which he gives himself in full freedom and self-expression as an act of love and as a testimony to love and the justice that overcomes discrimination and division. With this one example in mind, it is important that feminist studies of sacrament, language, and ritual serve a more powerful and inclusive retrieval of biblical and liturgical symbols that is appropriate to the life of a church that acts as an inclusive community of subjects in the reception and appropriation of divine gift, in the sacrifice of praise, and in the ritual acts that express communion in the mystery of Christ and the life of the Spirit. Taking agapic love as that which is most essentially descriptive of God in the Judeo-Christian tradition, theologians may follow Kristeva when she writes of how the figures of the Mother who nourishes and the Father who sets down norms of behavior merge in the liturgical language and action through which God appears in sacramental celebration. In response to this, women and

---

63. On this influence, see Cleo McNelly Kearns, "Kristeva and Feminist Theology," *Transfigurations: Theology and the French Feminists*, ed. C. W. Maggie Kim (Minneapolis: Fortress Press, 1993), 49–80.

others who have been traditionally marginalized can find a voice that brings the semiotic and the symbolic together in the public ordering of Christian communion.

Theological Aesthetics

While Rahner and Schillebeeckx modified the language of efficient causality by speaking of symbolic causality and symbolic exchange, other writers moved even further away from ideas of causality in what they say of sacraments. It is to these that we now turn.

One of the important currents of contemporary theology can be called theological aesthetics. It is associated with such writers as Louis Bouyer and Henri de Lubac, but most of all with Hans Urs von Balthasar.

HANS URS VON BALTHASAR

The contribution of Hans Urs von Balthasar to sacramental theology lies in the way he sees sacrament as participation in the form of God's glory in the world, which is Jesus Christ, Son of God, in the mystery of his death, resurrection, and future coming, highlighting what is revealed on the Cross. This is to consider sacraments within a theological aesthetic and as something that flows from this a theological dramatics.[64] Like Rahner, von Balthasar works from the assumption that the economic Trinity, or the economy of God's salvific action in the world, reveals the immanent Trinity and that the mystery of redemption is the mystery of God's triune self-communication to humankind. But he does not look for an anthropological grounding in a connatural openness to being and language. The starting point has to be revelation itself, and the analogy of being holds inasmuch as it is thought from the vantage point of divine communication. Von Balthasar's theological aesthetics is the contemplation of divine beauty and glory as given to the world through the form of Jesus Christ in his self-emptying on the Cross and the abasement of his descent into hell. This theological beauty is the ground of all worldly beauty, for it is the self-communication and revelation of God's trinitarian communion. Von Balthasar complements his theo-aesthetics with his Theodramatik (theo-dramatic), where sacramental life also has its place, since in asking assent to the sacrifice of Christ and the reception of the form of Christ, the members of the church are invited to partake in the drama of the struggle between divine freedom and the claims to human freedom that will finish only at the Parousia.[65]

The divine mystery of eternal communion itself is manifested in revelation and in sacrament. The Father's self-emptying into Jesus at the time of the incarnation reflects analogously the Father's self-emptying into the Son from all eternity. This self-emptying means the Father's total gift of self to the Son. The Son's return of self to the Father also takes place from all eternity in the Holy Spirit, the Spirit of both Father and Son. The role of the Spirit in the mystery of divine gift through Christ belongs to the divine mystery and to the economy of salvation. In his resurrection, the Holy Spirit so fully penetrates Jesus' flesh that, in the church which is his body, Jesus is both the sender of the Spirit

---

64. Hans Urs von Balthasar, *The Glory of the Lord: A Theological Aesthetics*, vol. 1, *Seeing the Form* (San Francisco: Ignatius, 1989). The German original is dated 1961. For an overview, see M. Miller, "The Sacramental Theology of Hans Urs von Balthasar," *Worship* 64 (1990): 48–66.

65. Hans Urs von Balthasar, *Theodramatik*, vol. 2, *Die Personen in Christus* (Einsiedeln: Johannes, 1978), 311–30, 388–410.

488

and the self-gift offered in his transformed body and blood.

Von Balthasar fits baptism into this view of salvation by calling it a "letting-oneself-be-given the form of the death and resurrection of Christ for the life of the world as one's own affirmed form of existence" and at the same time being given the existential form of love and membership in the church, body of the Lord, which finds the form received from Christ in Eucharistic communion. The Eucharist into which baptism is entry is the form (*Gestalt*) of divine self-communication through Word and Spirit, as it is also the manifestation, at the heart of the church, of divine beauty. Participation in the mystery of divine self-communication and divine self-emptying out of love in the missions of the Word incarnate and the Spirit has to be contemplative and receptive to divine gift, which is exemplified by Mary at the incarnation and at the Cross. Not only baptism but other sacraments too are to be seen in their relation to the communion and contemplation of the Eucharist.

Symbolic Gift and Exchange

Some authors are even more reserved about the analogy of causality than Rahner and Schillebeeckx, even when inspired by Rahner or von Balthasar. In considering the manifestation of the divine, they are influenced by a double hermeneutical critique in modern thought. One current finds that the use of ontology often seems to contain God within the being of intercosmic agents. Another finds that communities are insensitive to the manipulative role of language when it is rigidly determined in its public use, to the detriment of its creative power. These authors, in writing of sacraments, therefore prefer the symbolism of gift to the analogy of causality.

Louis-Marie Chauvet

One of these writers is Louis-Marie Chauvet, in whose theology there is a distinctly Rahnerian accent placed on symbolic expression and symbolic exchange, as well as on the ecclesial context for discussing sacrament.[66] Chauvet's major work, *Symbole et sacrement*, is divided into four parts: (1) from metaphysics to the symbolic; (2) the sacraments viewed from within the symbolic web of ecclesial faith; (3) symbolization of Christian identity; and (4) sacramentary and trinitarian Christology. The first and foundational part sets the method for the rest of the book. Following a Heideggerian critique of Western metaphysics, he suggests that the language of sacrament is often instrumentalized when interpreted in causal terms. The relation of mutual and reciprocal gift between lovers is a much better analogy for grace and sacrament than is that of the making or producing of things through instrumental causes.

Avoiding manipulation of divine grace requires a better appreciation of the place of language in human exchange. Human communities must learn to see themselves as addressed and possessed through the language they inherit, rather than as the users of language systems to meet their programmatic purposes. In his section on the ecclesial symbolic web, Chauvet attends especially to the use of Scripture within liturgy, to symbolic rites that have roots in tradition, and then to the ethics that develop within

---

66. His major work is, under its English title, *Symbol and Sacrament* (Collegeville, MN: Liturgical, 1995). An abridgment of this work is given in *The Sacraments: The Word of God at the Mercy of the Body* (Collegeville, MN: Liturgical, 2001).

this context. The Bible has a primary and dominant role, since the church lives from the Word of God and from its interpretation, the chief site of which is liturgy.

As an act of performative language, sacramental expression is not, however, a matter of rote or mere repetition. To explain how the church may use the language of tradition, sacramental theology must incorporate a theology of the Spirit. By relating word to a selection of readings and to blessing prayer, Chauvet captures the presence and action of the Spirit as the way in which the Christian community is related to the Risen Christ and affirms his presence in a creative way. Through the gift of the Spirit, the church finds Christ in the hearing of the Word; through the Spirit, it invokes the Father in praise and thanksgiving; and through the Spirit, the gifts of the people are transformed and partaken in a communion of faith, hope, and love.

The symbolic presence of Christ in his church through word, ministry, prayer, and rite is properly grasped only when account is taken of the Spirit's role within the community. For Chauvet, this is the case because the symbolic as such conveys an absence as well as a presence, or indeed a presence that implies an absence. What is absent (the transformed body of the Risen Christ) comes into presence, and the distance implied in this can be kept only through symbolic expression. The Spirit active in ecclesial expression bridges the gap while keeping alive the sense of otherness in the exchange. Through openness to the gift of symbolic exchange, believers become one with the "other" in the communion of the Spirit, the body in time and place of the risen Lord. The language of faith required

to open the heart and mind to what is given or offered exacts openness to the other, to the invisible, to what is hidden as well as to what is revealed, and to what is in the future adumbrated in what is remembered. The nonreducibility of the sacramental to the localized, where it has to appear to make the mystery present, to the representative image it necessarily employs, or to the conceptual comprehension suggested by catechesis and doctrine is vital to the reality of what is given by the grace of Christ. This is, in effect, a contemporary exploration of what early Christian writers explored in addressing the relation between the invisible and the visible in sacraments, or of what Thomistic theology affirmed when saying that Christ is present *through* the sign so that the symbol or sign is not simply an indication of what is present but a unique mode of presence or of becoming present that is unique.[67]

In his discussion of sacrament, Chauvet draws on studies from the human sciences on rite and "institution." This latter word is given a human and dynamic meaning, rather than a juridical one. There is a developed and sanctioned tradition of sacramental practice, which cannot be treated in an arbitrary way. There are, however, semantic or constructive elements in the code that allow for creativity of expression. Hence, its use may be subjected to critique and renewal to allow for the diversified expression that is needed in different situations.

In the fourth part of this book, Chauvet gives his christological and trinitarian perspective on sacrament as gift. The starting point, in keeping with language's priority, is the *lex orandi*, which gives primacy to the proclamation of the Pasch. According to this proclamation, God

---

67. For a discussion of Chauvet's position that grapples with questions raised by postmodern approaches to language, see Nathan Mitchell, *Meeting Mystery* (Maryknoll, NY: Orbis, 2006), esp. 63–69.

gives his love to humanity in the self-effacement of the divinity on the Cross of Christ. Through the power of the Spirit and in the memorial of the Cross, God continues to reveal God's self as the other in human bodiliness, where he continues to efface himself. As sacramental celebration unfolds, it shows the presence of this self-giving and self-effacing God in the body of the church, which lives for others, and in the bodies of the suffering and despised of the earth, whom the church serves in Christ's name and Spirit. In the symbolic web of sacrament, the divine presence as other is manifest in the invitation to Cross over into a new way of seeing and acting, as also in sacrament, the church is configured to the Christ of the Pasch.

Jean-Luc Marion

Another writer who wishes to think of sacraments in terms of gift rather than of being and causality is Jean-Luc Marion.[68] Primarily a philosopher best known for his work on Descartes, he is influenced in this field by the thought of von Balthasar. Unlike Chauvet, Marion is not interested in a retrieval of the subject through an appeal to anthropological philosophies, since we should not think of sacrament in terms of some kind of collective ecclesial consciousness. What the phenomenology of Husserl says of appearances and perception is more important than Heidegger to theology. Things give themselves to be perceived, and attention should be paid to how they present themselves. The sense of revelation and sacrament that works by this phenomenology of sign and language allows us to appreciate the divine initiative better than the kind of discussion that looks for the roots of symbolic expression in human consciousness.

God's advent in self-giving as agapic love is revealed to us in the beauty and drama of Christ's self-giving, culminating in his death on the Cross. What appears in Christ's self-emptying is the earthly drama of his eternal relation to the Father. In sacrament, the faithful are drawn into communion with a loving God through their reception of the gift, their confession of faith, praise, and thanksgiving.

Three important words in the philosophy of Marion offer the meaning of Christian revelation and in particular of sacrament. These words are *idol*, *icon*, and *gift/giving* (donation). It is impossible to receive divine gift without knowing from practice the difference between taking something as an idol and respecting it as icon. The making of artifacts into idols comes from the fact that the gaze of the beholder stops at an expression of the divine, instead of trying to see beyond it. The idol retains for itself the admiration of the beholder instead of deflecting attention to the origin. The icon, on the contrary, presents itself as the face that endows the visible with the inexhaustible invisibility of God. It does not offer itself to human conceptualization but invites the one who sees it to bypass it, to venerate what is revealed through it and toward which it invites the gaze and desire.

The icon par excellence is the Word incarnate, in whom the gift of divine agape is given to us. It is given, however, not to be spoken of, to be conceptualized, but to be received and worshipped. Response is found in gratitude and jubilation, not in some kind of self-conscious appropriation. This icon is simply to be praised for what it is, as manifested in the Cross of the Word incarnate, divine agape. To know God is to let oneself be known by God, to cease to ap-

---

68. Jean-Luc Marion, *God without Being*, trans. Thomas Carlson (Chicago: University of Chicago Press, 1991). For other references, see Duffy et al., "Sacramental Theology," 688–93.

propriate the gift or the giving, and to receive it purely as gift. Within the ecclesial body gathered in sacramental celebration—and particularly in Eucharist, to which all others relate by their nature—what is made present are the gift of divine love within human time, the mystical reality of the Word's kenotic commitment to the Father and to humanity, and the anticipation of eschatological glory, of which this kenosis is the promise and guarantee.

Presence in Time through Gift

Since all sacramental action is engaged in memorial of Christ's Pasch and in the power of the Spirit, it is of particular interest to ask how it relates the community that celebrates to time. The three writers who will be quoted here on this point are Marion, Ghislain Lafont, and David Power.

On the basis of his explanation of the advent of the Word and of sacrament as icon and gift, Marion expands on God's eschatological presence in time through sacramental gift. As he puts it, "The memorial, because a real and past event, renders this day tenable,"[69] and inasmuch as it looks to the future, it defines the manner of human existence in the present. In the theology (such as that of Rahner) that considers symbolic action from the perspective of self-consciousness, Marion believes that because of this apparent self-sufficiency people are tied too irrevocably to the present, to what they can do in the present. If sacrament is considered as gift, it is the gift of Christ that was given in the event remembered, which offers the present its possibility of genuine

existence. The church is invited to live from gift, in openness to ever receiving the gift, and not from what its members do themselves by reason of their self-expression as beings in the here and now. The conception of time is not linear but of time lived in memorial of an event ever renewed, and in anticipation of the time of God's gift that is promised in this memorial.

Though he appeals to ontology, Ghislain Lafont also speaks of the relation of memorial to time in terms of gift, and indeed to the possibility of making time new.[70] The phrase he uses is "salvation of time," for the gift offered releases from all that is suffocating in our modern world, which ties human life to the achievements of reason and of reason alone. In considering sacrament as memorial, we have to give full importance to the principle of narrativity in order to grasp the manner of God's action and presence in time. In the repetition of the founding narrative of death and resurrection, the gift of a time unbound from sin is offered to those who live by faith in Jesus Christ. Through the sacramental action in the things of the earth, this memorial and this gift are related to the time of the present and offer it hope in the future opened up by the gift given in Christ. God's love for the particular and of each particular being is expressed through sacramental signs joined to narrative and gives a participation in the eternal of the divine being of trinitarian communion, which transforms how the present is lived.

David Power's writing on sacrament may be seen in relation to these presentations of the eschatological nature of the memorial of Christ and of his presence through this memorial.[71] As

---

69. Marion, *God without Being*, 173.

70. Lafont, *God, Time, and Being*, 325–44.

71. See David N. Power, "Sacrament: Event Eventing," in *A Promise of Presence*, ed. Michael Downey and Richard Fragomeni (Washington, DC: Pastoral, 1992), 271–99.

Power notes, the memorial character of sacramental celebration has been much discussed in the interests of achieving ecumenical understanding around the nature of what is done and how it is related to the Cross or to the Pasch of Christ. With this is allied the notion or symbol of representation. Sometimes it is said that sacrament, and especially the Eucharist, re-presents the Pasch (makes it present anew). This succeeds in removing any idea that sacramental action may add to what was achieved on the Cross. However, it fails in the attempt to address the relation of the Pasch and of its memorial to time, or to take account of the fullness or excess of the gift and of the fact that all representation of a past event is interpretation of the now in virtue of the past.

Sacrament as the action and presence of Christ in the church through the Spirit is the memorial of the one who has been raised up and ascended and who is yet to come but who is now present not in the being of earthly life but in the special form of sacramental presence. This is a "present" of one who is absent in his own proper form but truly present through Word, sign, the testimony of believers, and the inner testimony of the gift of the Spirit. This present is granted through the gift of the Spirit and offers a capacity for being and acting that is drawn forth from the memorial of what has been done and from the hope that is an anticipation of what is yet to be given by the grace of God. Memorial narrative in the language in which it is couched relates the Pasch of Christ to that particular community, which is represented in the symbolic action of sacrament: together they are an interpretation of the original event, which makes room for the fact that, grounded in the Scriptures, the Christ event is repeated anew in other cultural forms and related to the history of diverse peoples. Unlike Lafont, who emphasizes repetition in narrative, Power highlights the interpretative and hence culturally determined nature of memorial representation, leaving room for the creativity empowered by the gift of the Spirit. Though the rendering present of the Pasch grants the "today" of sacramental action, this is not a present grasped through the image or notion of linear time. It is the "today" of the action of Word and Spirit, or of God's gracious advent according to its own norms and patterns, rather than according to those of human fabrication and action. It signifies an ever new and gracious presence, an ever fresh gift, of Christ through the sacramental form in which memorial is embedded. Sacrament's necessary inclusion of narrative and its promise of a future are completed by a prayer and a symbolic action that is the work of the Spirit in the particular community assembled.

To speak of this relation to time, David Power has chosen to speak of "event-eventing." He suggests that sacrament is best understood in its relation to the Christ event if it itself is seen as an event of God's gracious action. Through a narrative that is given tangible expression in the sacramental signs and actions of a living faith-communion, Christ events again in the community as the "today" that is always newly given by God. This is a today lived in expectation, in the constant openness to the advent of God's grace and gift in the church's journey through human history, and in the ultimate hope of the consummation of God's kingdom, in God's own way and in God's own time.

Sacramental Language as a Word from God (Theology)

The theological and liturgical importance of language deserves to be pursued further. When it is said that the *lex orandi* is first-order language, this does not mean it expresses the mystery less effectively than doctrinal teaching or systematic reflection. Indeed, it says more and, in giving rise to thought, asks for a deeper immersion in the mystery of the triune God, who reveals and bestows the gift of the divine self in the celebration of the sacraments.[72] While the law of prayer is sometimes said to ground the *lex credendi*, the complex interplay between the two across time affects what is spoken and done in worship. To the two phrases *lex orandi* and *lex credendi*, writers now sometimes add *lex agendi* (law of action) by way of saying that the authenticity of worship needs verification in the ethical behavior of those who congregate for worship.[73]

Liturgical prayer engages the community as a body, as the "we" of the ecclesial communion that hears the Father and addresses the Father in the power of the Spirit. The language of prayer draws the hearer/speaker into the communion the Father gives through the sending of the Son/Word and the Spirit. There is polyphony to this language—verbal, corporal and visual—and a comprehensive attention to this reveals the mystery expressed and enveloping. While the different kinds of expression deserve attention, the blessing prayer serves as a hermeneutical key to the sapiential understanding of the divine gift.

Each sacrament at its core has a prayer of blessing, related to persons and the things they share. Each too is replete with scriptural references, central to which is the notion that sacrament is performed in obedience to Christ and in obedience to the revelation given in the mysteries of his flesh. While the memorial command and appeal to a memorial narrative are explicit in the Eucharist, these are present in some form

in other blessings. Two examples suffice here. The blessing of baptismal water has the scriptural warrants such as Christ's own baptism, his walking on the water, and the water flowing from his side on the Cross. The blessing of the oil of the sick appeals to Jesus' own healing ministry and his command to lay hands on the sick, as it also appeals to the biblical anointing of priest, prophet, and king.

Founded on the narrative of the mystery, these scriptural warrants guarantee that the sacramental action is done in memory of Christ, and the invocation of the Spirit guarantees the fidelity and inspiration of the congregation. Thus, blessing prayers draw the congregation in several ways into communion in the triune mystery of God. This type of prayer relates God's action through Word and Spirit to creation, to covenant, and to redemption from sin and death. It touches the congregation here and now and in its own cultural and social setting, because it is invoked over the things, persons, and events that bring them together. It is creedal, because it embodies a tradition that has its origins in the epiphany of the Paschal and Pentecostal events, and it is out of this tradition that the church has the power to live as God's people, always in expectation of the kingdom. It is prophetic because it is eschatological and in virtue of the presence of the living God awakens the congregation to this presence and to its promise of what is to come by God's grace. It is ethical because it supposes the ground of testimony in the Spirit that the people give in their lives as disciples. It is Eucharistic (a prayer of thanksgiving) in every sacramental action because the Eucharistic table is the center of communal life and because each

---

72. See Power, *Sacrament*, 76–80, 165–77. While Power and Irwin's ideas are comparable to Chauvet's reflections on the symbolic and symbolic exchange and draw on his insights, both give more attention to specific examination of the components of sacramental language and to a hermeneutics of texts and doctrines than does Chauvet.

73. Kevin W. Irwin, *Context and Text: Method in Liturgical Theology* (Collegeville, MN: Liturgical, 1994), 52–74.

494 prayer acknowledges the grace that comes from the Father in the bestowal of Word and Spirit. Finally, it is doxological in the wonder expressed before the mystery of God's triune and eternal holiness, open to the silence in which God is present beyond words.

Sacraments and Creation

In considering the place of the body in theology, it has been brought to the fore that it is through the body and symbolic exchange that Christians interact in liturgical celebration, and through the body, each person is related to the body of the church and to the social body. However, the earthly body that is touched by the use of bread, wine, oil, and water needs more consideration. Though the material elements used in sacramental celebration are things of earth (or as is said liturgically, fruits of the earth), the way in which humans are connected to earth, cosmos, and environment through this produce has been much neglected in Roman Catholic sacramental theology over the centuries. In face of the world's current ecological risk, this connection has come back into consideration in some publications.[74]

In writing of the eschatological orientation of the Eucharist (*Ecclesia de Eucharistia* 20), John Paul II reaffirmed the tradition that it puts those who celebrate into communion with the heavenly liturgy and arouses the hope of eternal life in the communion of the triune God and all the blessed. He added, however, that it also signals

the Christian commitment to this earth and to the world in the pursuit of justice and peace. Pope Benedict has taken up this theme in his apostolic exhortation *Sacramentum Caritatis* and expanded it to include concern for the environment and respect for the wonders and realities of creation. What is located primarily in the Eucharist, center of the sacramental dispensation, is found also in other sacramental celebrations.

In the Judeo-Christian tradition, the link with nature through material things and bodily action was a key point of the covenant between God and the human race, and in a particular way between the God of Sinai and the people of Israel.[75] Issues of respect for the earth and the just deployment of its resources are inherent to the practice of worship and the keeping of the Law and the celebration of Jubilee and Sabbath. The oneness of the mystery of creation and the mystery of redemption in Christ are a remarkable feature of Orthodox sacramental and liturgical practice and theology. The Orthodox vision of the universe can even be called a "sacramental cosmology," and sacramental remembrance and vision see Christ's death and resurrection as a divine embrace of the whole of creation, where the Spirit is continually at work.[76] Roman Catholic liturgy can regain a sense of humanity's general and local placement in earthly and cosmic mysteries through the way in which the material elements of sacramental action reveal the place of humanity within the totality of creation.

In use of things that touch the body and communicate in this way to the person, com-

---

74. Dionisio Borobio Garcia, *De la sacramentalidad creatural-cósmica a los sacramentos de la Iglesia* (Salamanca: Editorial Secretariado Trinitario, 2009); Linda Gibler, *From the Beginning to Baptism: Scientific and Sacred Stories of Water, Oil, and Fire* (Collegeville, MN: Liturgical, 2010).

75. Robert Murray, *The Cosmic Covenant: Biblical Themes of Justice, Peace and the Integrity of Creation* (London: Sheed & Ward, 1992).

76. Elizabeth Theokritoff, *Living in God's Creation: Orthodox Perspectives on Ecology* (Crestwood, NY: St Vladimir's Seminary Press, 2009), 181–210.

munities enter into the fullness of the mystery of creation, the mystery of God revealed in creation, and the mystery of the transformation of all creation through Christ. The generous and respectful use of the things of earth makes worshippers mindful of people's dependence on the earth and of their participation in the mystery of creation, even as they rejoice in the mystery of divine restoration through Christ and the Spirit. In the current human situation, we know that exploitation of earth's resources and of human labor go together and that redemption from sin promises release for those who live in community in communion with Christ and his Spirit from all the powers that hold humanity in thrall to sin, so that those who live by faith may be witnesses in the world to the full liberation from sin and death. While this sacramental hope is for eternal life, it engages those who profess it in witnessing and working here and now for a human community that lives by peace, justice, and communion with nature. Belief in the lordship of Jesus Christ over the church and over creation confessed in the hymn of Col. 1:15-20 can in the present day take on a fresh sacramental vibrancy.

Conclusion

The intention in this survey of Roman Catholic perspectives on sacramental theology has been to place present concerns in historical perspective. Advocating a more refined vision of the origin of sacraments, attention was first given to what is being retrieved from the patristic age. Next, a brief discussion of Saint Augustine aimed to give a better appreciation of the nature of his influence on all subsequent thought about sacraments. Following this was an effort to put the issues and theorems of Scholastic theology in focus, learning also from them how theology belongs to the interaction between it and cultural and social realities. To describe what Catholic theology inherits from the Council of Trent, the next section placed its teachings in the context of the challenge of the Protestant Reformation. The survey of contemporary renewal that followed showed its roots in nineteenth-century approaches and highlighted the work of several significant authors who represent the key current trends in sacramental theology. The nature of sacraments as ecclesial reality is to the fore, as well as the relation of their salvific intent to the mystery of the Trinity. An important element in this is the attention to symbolic exchange, as it is variously examined in different schools of theology. This attention to symbolic exchange retains the Scholastic tradition of sacramental efficacy but transforms it in a way that respects the nature of the sacramental action as an action of the whole body, Christ and all his members. At the same time, it was noted how some writers prefer the paradigm of gift to render an appreciation of what is offered to the church in sacrament. References to diverse writers then showed how a good grasp of sacrament as memorial action is essential to understanding the living sacramental organism of Christian worship, as is a due expansion of the constitution of the ecclesial subject that celebrates and receives the gift of God.

This survey of general principles or approaches lays the groundwork for considering the individual sacraments by attending to history and cultural realities and by retrieving the notion of mystery that relates sacraments to the life of the church as a living sacrament, to the work of Christ and the Spirit, and ultimately to the mystery of trinitarian communion.

For Further Reading

Chauvet, Louis-Marie. *Symbol and Sacrament: A Sacramental Reinterpretation of Christian Existence.* Collegeville, MN: Liturgical, 1995.

> A presentation of sacraments as sacraments of the church, using the paradigm of gift rather than causality. This work is attentive to issues of language, as well as to relation between Word, Spirit, and sacramental action.

———. *The Sacraments: Word of God at the Mercy of the Body.* Collegeville, MN: Liturgical, 1995.

> An abridgement of the previous work, more accessible to the general reader.

Duffy, Regis. *Real Presence: Worship, Sacraments, and Commitment.* San Francisco: Harper & Row, 1982.

> An interdisciplinary approach that focuses on the relation between commitment and sacramental action.

Duffy, Regis, Kevin W. Irwin, and David N. Power. "Sacramental Theology: A Review of Literature." *Theological Studies* 55 (1994): 657–705.

> A review of Catholic sacramental theology after the Second Vatican Council.

Fink, Peter E., ed. *The New Dictionary of Sacramental Worship.* Collegeville, MN: Liturgical, 1990.

> An important collection of articles on the theology and liturgy of the church's worship.

Kilmartin, Edward. *Christian Liturgy.* Vol. 1, *Theology.* Kansas City: Sheed & Ward, 1988.

> A restatement of sacramental theory from a liturgical viewpoint.

Mitchell, Nathan. *Meeting Mystery.* Maryknoll, NY: Orbis, 2006.

> An exploration of ritual and sacramental expression in conversation with postmodern philosophies and language studies.

Power, David N. *Sacrament: The Language of God's Giving.* New York: Crossroad, 1999.

> A hermeneutical approach to sacramental tradition and sacramental doctrines, relating these to the contemporary situation of liturgical pluralism.

Rahner, Karl. *The Church and the Sacraments.* New York: Herder & Herder, 1963.

> A landmark work that reestablished the ecclesial dimensions of sacrament.

———. *Theological Investigations.* Vol. 4. Baltimore: Helicon, 1966.

———. *Theological Investigations.* Vol. 14. New York: Seabury, 1976.

> Presentations of the key thoughts of Rahner's theology as related to sacraments.

Rocchetta. Carlo. *Sacramentaria fondamentale.* Bologna: Edizioni Dehoniane, 1990.

> A useful overview of the history of sacramental theology.

Ross, Susan A. *Extravagant Affections: A Feminist Sacramental Theology.* New York: Continuum, 2001.

> A feminist sacramental theology, placing it within a creative overview of current feminist theology. This work is very attentive to sacramental practice.

Schillebeeckx, Edward. *Christ, the Sacrament of Encounter with God.* New York: Sheed & Ward, 1963.

> A benchmark in sacramental theology, employing a personalist approach.

von Balthasar, Hans Urs. *The Glory of the Lord: A Theological Aesthetics.* Vol. 1, *Seeing the Form.* San Francisco: Ignatius, 1982.

> Pages 556–82 provide a synthetic presentation of von Balthasar's sacramental theology.

Sacraments 9.2

Baptism and Confirmation

David N. Power

Post–Vatican II Renewal of the Orders of Baptism and Confirmation

Present practices in the church are in a state of flux and show considerable diversity in the pastoral approach to the sacraments of baptism and confirmation and to the relationship between the two. To account for this, theology has to remain attentive to the nature of sacraments as sacraments of the church, living as a community of faith within the social and cultural settings of different times and places.

In the present time, adult initiation has taken hold in the life of the church in many countries, but the practice of baptizing infants is still common, with the celebration of confirmation and Eucharist at another stage of their lives. The renewal of the adult initiation process has certainly brought home its ecclesial significance, its nature as a process of conversion and growth in faith, and the way in which baptism, confirmation through the Spirit, and Eucharistic participation belong together. However, this does not suggest that what happens in the case of those baptized as young children is devoid of meaning. Theology, therefore, if it is to guide pastoral practice, has to address both adult and infant initiation.

Today the theology of baptism also has importance for the future of ecumenical exchange. It is a basic tenet of the Roman Catholic Church that any valid baptism introduces a person into membership in the people of God and that ecumenical relations are to be built on what a common baptism signifies about a common participation in the life of Christ and of the church.[1] Since other churches have also revised their liturgical books in the light of tradition, Catholic scholars keep their eye on these developments, knowing that it is together that the churches come to a better understanding of the meaning of baptism and of the ecclesiological implications of mutual recognition of how this ritual unfolds in different traditions.

Therefore, rather than an appeal to a common definition that fits all situations, what is needed is a hermeneutical practice of thinking, a way of relating to a baptismal tradition and to scriptural sources that allows the meaning of the ritual specific to each situation to be understood and appropriated. The teaching of magisterial doctrine is a necessary guide to the search for meaning, but of itself it does not determine the process of research, nor is it ever fully adequate to the sacraments' meaning.

Two quotations from contemporary documents of the Catholic Church may set the stage for a consideration of the sacraments of initiation as they belong together, even when they are celebrated separately. The Order for the Initiation of Adults states, "The order includes not only the celebration of the sacraments of baptism, confirmation and the Eucharist, but also all the rites of the catechumenate. Approved by the ancient practice of the church and adapted to contemporary missionary work throughout the world, this catechumenate was so widely requested that the Second Vatican Council de-

---

1. Baptism represents "a sacramental bond of unity linking all who have been reborn by it." Second Vatican Council, Decree *Unitatis redintegration* 22. As a point of departure in ecumenical exchange, it is "oriented toward a complete profession of faith, a complete incorporation into the system of salvation such as Christ himself willed it to be and finally toward a complete participation in eucharistic communion."

creed its restoration, revision and accommodation to local traditions."[2] This initiatory model presents the process as ecclesial, that is, as something that belongs to the life of the church and can be justly celebrated only within and with the church community. It also supposes that the process is a journey that assures maturation in faith and conversion, so that the celebration of the sacramental rites at the end of the preparation envisaged allows them to be wittingly called sacraments of faith. Furthermore, there is a clear relation to the Paschal Mystery of Christ, the preferred time for admission to full ecclesial communion through the threefold sacrament being the Paschal Vigil.

However, another order has these words for the baptism of children: "From the earliest times, the church . . . has baptized children as well as adults. . . . To fulfill the true meaning of the sacrament, children must later be formed in the faith in which they have been baptized. The foundation for this formation will be the sacrament itself, which they have already received."[3] Here, too, the sacrament is seen to be an ecclesial sacrament, one to be celebrated by the community and in the faith of the church. It is also a sacrament of faith, in which church and parents profess their belief in the saving power of Christ and its gift to the child. The transmission of this faith and grace to the child are only incipient, however. The child has yet to mature in the life of faith within the church and with its guidance. At what age it is appropriate to admit to confirmation in the Spirit and to Eucharistic participation has to be considered in the light of the reality of the church itself and of the child's own growth in the Christian life.

While much current theology therefore takes adult initiation as the paradigm, or even as normative in the sense that the meaning of baptism and baptismal practice is to be sought here first and foremost, it cannot be forgotten that the baptism of children expresses, when rightly celebrated, the basic fundamental meaning of baptism. How it may be fitting to relate the sacraments of baptism, confirmation, penance, and Eucharistic communion in developing a life of faith and of participation in the church community is a matter of greater dispute.

How the Sacraments Are Named

In considering the history of these sacraments now called baptism and confirmation, or bunched together with the Eucharist as sacraments of initiation, the terminology itself needs examination. The term *initiation* has become popular in recent Western theology to a great extent because of comparisons with anthropological discoveries of patterns of initiation among different peoples. In Catholic theology today, the term *initiation* seems firmly in place, mostly because it was adopted by the Second Vatican Council and the renewed liturgies for adults going through the catechumenate and receiving the sacraments at Easter. Despite that, not all are happy with the term, since it seems to press the parallel with cultural initiation rites too far. The word at best can be used only analogously.

In Christian history, it has a less established place for the introduction into the mysteries, and the entire process could simply be referred to as *baptism*. If any one word prevailed in speaking of the sacraments in early times, it was precisely

---

2. *Ordo Initiationis Christianae Adultorum* (Vatican City: Vatican Polyglot Press, 1972), 2.

3. *Ordo Baptismi Parvulorum* (Vatican City: Vatican Polyglot Press, 1969), 2, 3.

500 *mysteries*, since what they offer is a participation in the mysteries of Christ. Where there was any early use of the word *initiation* among Christians, this seems to have developed from comparisons with the process of initiation into pagan religions or mysteries, highlighting the superior and spiritual character of the process of entry into the mysteries of Christ as compared with others.[4] For example, Justin Martyr in his *First Apology* (61) referred to the process of Christian initiation when compared with other cults, but in writing his apology, he spoke of baptism as the "enlightenment" that comes with the knowledge of the revelation of Father, Son, and Spirit in whose name they are baptized.[5] Tertullian of Carthage (155–220) accepted the term *initiations* in reference to both Christian and pagan rites. Against the same cultic background, Origen of Alexandria (c. 183–253) explicitly referred to those "initiated into the mysteries of Jesus," and later John Chrysostom (c. 344–407), for example, frequently used the language of initiation. In the West, it appears that Cyprian of Carthage (155–220) made use of the word, though he is more likely simply to speak of baptism and to describe its rites. Even these recorded usages of the term *initiation*, then, show that it was more common to speak of the ways in which candidates were "introduced into the mysteries" revealed in Jesus Christ through the sacraments of baptism and Eucharist and the preparation leading up to them. Hence, despite what has become the common usage today, we need to be careful about calling the process of preparation and sacramental celebration *initiation* and focus more on the participation in the mysteries into which the elect are introduced.

Scriptural Foundations

It is from within the complex ecclesial life of our age that theology returns to its scriptural foundations to find the meaning of life in Christ that is transmitted in different ways and at different times.[6] Retrieving this scriptural foundation has perhaps been the most important theological move today in understanding these sacraments of incorporation into the church.

Synoptics

The relation to Christ is made clear in the narrative of his commandment to the apostles before his ascent into heaven (Matt. 28:19-20; Mark 16:15-16). While these are to be read as foundational narratives, they do not point chronologically to a given moment of institution. Their intent is rather that they connect the baptismal practice of the church with the proclamation of forgiveness through the death of Christ, with the need to spread the gospel to incite faith in him, and with the presence of the Risen Christ in his church through Word and sacrament.[7]

---

4. The information on this usage is taken from Pierre-M. Gy, "La notion chrétienne d'initiation," *La Maison-Dieu* 132 (1977): 33–54.

5. Justin, *First Apology* 61.

6. For a good overview, with references to literature, see Bryan D. Spinks, *Early and Medieval Rituals and Theologies of Baptism: From the New Testament to the Council of Trent* (Burlington, VT: Ashgate, 2006), 3–13; P. Tena-D.Borobio, "Sacramentos de iniciacion cristiana," in *La celebracion en la iglesia*, vol. 2, *Sacramentos*, ed. Dionisio Borobio (Salamanca: Ediciones Sigueme, 1994), 97–125.

7. It is even discussed whether these words may actually be attributed to Jesus himself or whether they come from the primitive church.

Mark adds that the preaching will be accompanied by certain signs giving testimony to the power of Jesus and having to do with the casting out of demons, with protection against diverse manners of evil and with the healing of the sick. These, in fact, point to the testimony of life in the community of disciples that accompanies the gospel proclamation and the invitation to discipleship.

While much has been written about it, there is no firm opinion on the origin of the baptismal rite as a rite of admission and welcome into the community of faith. What is known is that in New Testament times, the hearing of the gospel, the conversion of life in a turn to Christ, confession of faith in him, and water baptism were the mode of entry into the Christian community. The manner of baptism could probably be diverse, but it does seem that some kind of immersion was the most accustomed practice and one that was seen as most effectively imaging rebirth in Christ and the cleansing from sin. More, in fact, is known about the teaching on baptism and the work of the Spirit in bringing persons to the life of discipleship than about baptism's ritual origins.

The relation of Christian baptism to the baptism of Jesus himself, though assumed in much of patristic teaching, is a matter of dispute among scriptural scholars. Some think the link is intended by New Testament writers, while others argue against this. That the baptism of Jesus may serve as a paradigm is one matter, but that it may in any sense be seen as the origin of the sacramental practice is less evident.[8]

Pauline Teaching

Paul's summary words on baptism in Rom. 6:3-8 are understandable in the larger context of the teaching on justification constituted by chapters 5–8. The text itself expresses the immersion of those justified in the death of Christ, on which follows a share in the life of the Risen Lord. The sinner has been crucified with Christ, has died with him, and has been buried with him. Now he or she can be confident of being raised up with him. This teaching has been prepared in chapter 5 in what Paul says of justification by the superabundance of the grace of Christ and most of all through the image of Christ as the new Adam. As in one man, all are doomed to death, so through the death of one, all have been given new life. The contrast between the disobedience of the one and the obedience of the other is important to see what it meant for Christ to die, but it also portrays the "law of obedience in Christ" by which the justified live. This is then the background to the sense of baptism as a baptism into the death of Christ in Rom. 6:3-5. After the text on baptism, Paul discourses in chapter 7 on the combat between sin and good, between life and death, and between the law of the members and the law of the Spirit that goes on in the sinful person. This is what the person has been released from through the death of Christ to enjoy that life in the Spirit of which the letter treats in chapter 8.

That baptism pertains to life in the body of Christ is clear from the context, as is its relation to human solidarity in sin. On the one hand, the person is caught up in the sin of Adam, the sin of

---

8. Positions on the meaning of Jesus' baptism in the four Gospel accounts, as well as on its relation to ecclesial practice, are well laid out in Kilian McDonnell, *The Baptism of Jesus in the Jordan: The Trinitarian and Cosmic Order of Salvation* (Collegeville, MN: Liturgical, 1996), 1–28, 171–87. The relation of developing ritual and explanation to the life of the church in Christ explained in chapter 9.1 make it easier to see why different moments in Christ's mystery could be seen as the point of origin or "institution."

502 disobedience to God's law that affects humanity and each of its members, subjecting all to evil and death. But Christ, by becoming the new Adam, has associated himself in solidarity with humankind, sinners though we are. By the obedience of his death, sinners are justified, and not only sinners, but humanity itself through Christ's solidarity with it, is released from sin and death. One with Christ in his body, the baptized are freed from the law of sin and are given to share in the life of the Spirit, which drives out sin and fear and makes of them children of God in the Son.

Johannine Teaching

The most quoted text on baptism in John is from the meeting of Nicodemus with Jesus recounted in John 3.[9] This text is about entry into the kingdom of God, which comes from above. After the preaching and baptism of John and the announcement of the kingdom, Jesus here tells of the kingdom of which he is speaking. It is from above, and God is the one who gives the grace of this reign. It is from the Spirit, which blows where it will, by a gratuitous act and not by human design. With this pronouncement of the gift of the Spirit to bring about the kingdom, the Johannine narrative links baptism by water. It is possible that in some earlier version of this story, there was no mention of the water rite, but that it has been added as an ecclesial text to make the connection between the gift of the Spirit and the rite whereby believers are incorporated into the community of disciples. What comes to light later in the chapter, where Nicodemus seems to have been forgotten, is that acceding to baptism expresses faith in the life-giving and even glorious death of Christ on the Cross, from whose side the Spirit flows (John 7:37-39). While John uses the image of rebirth, it has to do with a conversion to faith in the Cross of Christ as light and salvation and with the work of the Spirit in bringing people to this faith.

Acts of the Apostles

The Acts of the Apostles provide ample evidence of the action of the Spirit in bringing forgiveness and new life in Christ, complementing what is said in both Paul and John and setting the teaching pertinent to baptism in narratives of early Christian life. The book presents the happenings of the day of Pentecost as the beginning of the apostolic mission and as a model for what it is to have faith in Christ and to belong to the company of his disciples. The hearers of the preaching of the Twelve on that day are invited to repent their sins, to believe in the power of the crucified Lord, who has been raised up from the dead, and to receive the Spirit promised by the prophets for the day of the advent of God's kingdom and now poured out on believers (Acts 2:37-38).

While the need for water baptism is clear, Acts never specifies a given rite by which the Spirit is given, but the book does in several scenes show that the gift of the Spirit is associated with entrance into the community. The point of the story about the Samaritans in Acts 8 is not to reveal another sacrament, but to relate the gift of the Spirit to the apostolic mission of the apostles and to their witness to Christ. In the story of Cornelius and his household (Acts 10:34-48), those who receive the word of Peter are filled with the Spirit and its gifts even before they are baptized. In another narrative, the plight of some who have been baptized but have never even heard of the Spirit (Acts 1:1-7) seems to lie in the incompleteness of their faith in Jesus

---

9. See Francis J. Moloney, *The Gospel of John*, Sacra Pagina 4 (Collegeville, MN: Liturgical, 1998), 88–102.

Christ, to whose death they look for forgiveness but without knowing too much about the new life that this assures. The preaching of the gospel needed to be completed by the apostle Paul before they could be awakened fully to its meaning and receive the Spirit.

Other Texts

Other ways in which baptism is seen throughout the New Testament may be summarized as follows, without claiming that there is but one New Testament interpretation, since authors vary somewhat on what it means to hear the Word, be converted, profess faith in Christ, and be aggregated to the community of disciples. To the images of immersion in the death of Christ and of rebirth in the Spirit may be joined that of being clothed with the righteousness of Christ (Gal. 3:27; Col. 3:9-10) and of putting on a new garment or a new nature. Given the baptism of Jesus himself and the promise of the Spirit, it is not surprising to find the images of anointing and enlightenment (1 Peter 2:9; Heb. 6:4). The gift of the Spirit is signaled by the imagery of pouring and blowing like a wind, but it is also called a sealing (2 Cor. 1:21-22; 1 John 2:20-27). All of these images recur in one way or another in diverse liturgical traditions, so that it is in sacramental celebration itself that the scriptural matrix is received into the life of the church.

Evolution of the Sacraments and Their Theology

Any survey of the history of initiation has to include both practice and theology, since they are so closely intertwined and since practice as mentioned in the chapter on the general introduction to sacraments in this book provides the *lex orandi* (law of prayer). After a general survey of the patristic era, special attention is given to developments in the West from the time of Saint Augustine onward. This concludes with a look at Scholastic theology.

Patristic Period

It is in the second century that we find the first evidence of a systematic and prolonged preparation for the sacraments and the use of the terms *catechumens* and *catechumenate*.[10] With the *Didache*, Justin, and Irenaeus, we already get some sense of an extended preparation, which included catechesis, moral instruction, and introduction to the Christian practices of prayer and fasting. More is learned of practice in the third century from Tertullian and the *Apostolic Tradition*. The cultural and moral milieu in which those seeking baptism lived seemed to demand this preparation, since they had to separate themselves from all that was incompatible with being a follower of Christ. We are also given some description of the ceremonies that took place on the Paschal night and that express the meaning given to sacramental initiation into the mysteries. These include the blessing of water, pure and flowing, the blessing of the oils of thanksgiving and of exorcism, the stripping of garments and the anointing of exorcism, interrogation on the creed to profess faith in the Trinity and its salvific action, immersion in the waters, and an anointing with the oil of thanksgiving, which included prayer for the descent of the Spirit.

In the pre-Nicene church, the appeal most often made to explain baptism was to the baptism

---

10. For a survey, see Spinks, *Early and Medieval Rituals and Theologies*, 14–67.

504

of Jesus himself in the Jordan. Good examples of this are the works of Tertullian and Ephrem of Syria. This certainly means that Jesus' baptism served as paradigm for the meaning attached to the rite, but beyond that, these writers appear to have seen Jesus' baptism as its moment of origin, even though they related it also to other mysteries of the Lord. As McDonnell puts it, for Tertullian and Ephrem, "the whole of Christ's incarnate life: the full range of mysteries, from conception through nativity, on through death and resurrection to the ascension, are all concentrated in the mystery of his baptism."[11]

Subsequently, the ritual and the explanations became more complex and admitted of differences between churches, especially with regard to anointings and the prayer for the Spirit. It is especially from the mystagogical catechesis of the fourth and fifth centuries that we can trace both the process and the theologies ascribed to these sacraments. At the conclusion of a detailed study of different rites, Bryan Spinks can conclude for the ceremonies practiced in the fourth and fifth centuries that while there was a basic pattern, there were differences, especially with regard to anointing and the gift of the Spirit.[12] In East Syria, the anointing was before baptismal immersion, whereas in West Syria, it came after the immersion but with anointings for exorcism beforehand, together with a renunciation of the devil. In Milan and in Rome, there was added a laying on of hands by the bishop, though its precise significance is unclear. In explanations of the meaning of the rite, cleansing from sin and the gift of the Spirit are always mentioned.

Otherwise, liturgies and commentaries most of the time highlighted the Pauline imagery of immersion into the death of Christ, but with attention to the rite of going down into the water and coming out again, the imagery of passage through death to life could be given prominence. This was aided by the appeal to the typology found in the story of the passage through the Red Sea by the people of Israel. Along with this went frequent reference to putting off the old Adam and putting on the new, being released from the slavery of sin, and renouncing Satan to be joined with Christ. Other writers, especially in East Syria,[13] seemed to prefer the symbolism of rebirth from the womb of the fount, with reference to John 3. This was connected with the idea that the baptism of the Christian had its prototype in the baptism of Christ in the Jordan, when he is revealed as God's Son and receives the anointing of the Spirit.

Whatever the ritual elaborations, the baptism that gave entry into the church or body of Christ was seen as the action of the Holy Spirit. Basil of Caesarea explains this succinctly in his treatise on the Holy Spirit, where he speaks solely of the rite of a triple immersion in water with an invocation of the three persons of the Trinity. To be baptized is to be born again of water and the Spirit, which means that "we die in the water, and we come to life again through the Spirit." Expanding on this life in the Spirit, he says, "Thanks to the Spirit we obtain the right to call God our Father, we become sharers in the grace of Christ, we are called children of light, and we share in everlasting glory."[14] He

---

11. McDonnell, *Baptism*, 190.

12. Spinks, *Early and Medieval Rituals and Theologies*, 38–67.

13. See English translations of pertinent texts in Thomas M. Finn, *Early Christian Baptism and the Catechumenate* (Collegeville, MN: Liturgical, 1992), 1:174–77.

14. Basil of Caesarea, *On the Holy Spirit*, English trans. (Crestwood, NY: St. Vladimir's Seminary Press, 1980), 15, 35–36.

also supports the idea of baptism as a commitment or pledge, saying that because baptism cleanses from sin, it is a pledge made to God in good conscience.

Western Practice and Theology

To find the practice and meaning of initiation in the Roman Catholic tradition, we have to consider developments in Western theology. The greatest influence in that regard has been that of Augustine, whose importance lies not only in his writings against the Donatists but in all that he wrote of the catechumenate and baptism of adults and in his promotion of the baptism of infants. It is to be assumed that, even in their case, he intended the use of the full rite of water, oil, and Eucharist.

As described in the general introduction to sacraments in this volume (chapter 9.1), Augustine is the parent of the doctrine and theology of the sacramental character. Of particular note here is that this involves an understanding of baptism within a theology of the church as the body of Christ. In the image that he uses of character, what is at stake is the belonging to Christ and the church, and what he says of baptismal grace shows that he means the life of communion in the Spirit, which can be known only in and through ecclesial communion.

Otherwise, the substance of Augustine's teaching on baptism is offered in the catechesis he gave the neophytes in the week after Easter. Dead to sin in Christ, they have new life in him as the chosen of the Father and members of his body, enjoying a communion beyond all differences, as expressed by Paul in Gal. 3:27. They have received forgiveness of sins, the pledge of the Spirit, and the hope of the resurrection.[15]

Though Augustine was a pastor who was much engaged in the catechumenate for adults and gave great importance to the reception of the sacraments at the Easter Vigil, he also gave the baptism of infants theological justification that prevailed in the Latin West. The baptism of infants was already well known at this time, but what he said of it gave good ground to the prevailing practice it later became.

Augustine's teaching on sin, and on original sin in particular, has been explained elsewhere in this compendium.[16] With regard to baptism, suffice it to note that his explanation fitted well with the solidarity and communion he believed inherent to sacrament. Though not guilty of any sin of their own, children stand in need of redemption, not because they would otherwise in death be condemned to suffering, but because they would not receive the grace of communion with Christ and could enjoy hereafter only a measure of natural happiness. One with humankind in the sin of the first Adam, needing grace to overcome this sin and its consequence, and in the communion of the church given them in baptism, they are given communion in Christ and in eternal glory.

Since baptism together with Eucharist is a sacrament of faith, Augustine had to explain how faith could be found in an infant or expressed by an infant in its celebration. Earlier in his ministry, his answer was to say that an infant is baptized in the faith of its parents, but since that seemed an unsatisfactory reply, he ended up by saying that infants are baptized in the faith of the church, an answer that fitted well with his idea of sacramental communion and solidarity.

---

15. Augustine, *Sermo 8 in Octava Paschae* (PL 46, 838–41).
16. Roger Haight, "Sin and Grace," ch. 7 in this volume.

506 It shows how children are incorporated into the living community of the church and may grow in faith in that ambience.

Separation of Rites

After the patristic period, in a cultural setting where the Christian faith became the normal pattern for all people and conversions to it were often a matter of people following their kings and leaders, Western practice was marked by the common administration of baptism to infants and by the separation of confirmation from baptism. These are two things that require what is best called a pastoral theology—that is, a reflection that can underpin the reasons for these practices, despite their novelty within the apostolic tradition, and uncover the meanings that were attached to them. Only then is it possible to know what may be properly done about them in the contemporary church.

The separation of confirmation, as well as of Eucharist, from baptism is a tearing asunder of the conjoined ritual of water baptism, anointing, laying on of hands, and Eucharistic communion. This is sometimes referred to as the dissolution of the original symbolic action of entry into the church or the disintegration of the rite of initiation. Today historians and theologians alike have difficulties in explaining why this took place and what precise meaning was attached to confirmation when separated from baptism, and even what ritual constituted this sacramental confirmation.[17] On the last issue, the question is whether it was anointing with chrism or the

laying on of hands by the bishop that was separated from baptism and thought to be the essential ritual action. In our time, Pope Paul VI has settled this matter by prescribing a laying on of hands with anointing as a joint act, but this does not resolve the historical question.[18]

The answers to the meaning of constituting a separate sacrament have to do with the role of the bishop in the church and with the need for a postbaptismal initiation when infants are sacramentally admitted to the church and come only later to a knowledge of the faith. With the growth of what we would call parochial communities and the common practice of infant baptism, it became impossible for the bishop of the territory to be present at all baptisms. From an ecclesial perspective, this meant he was not present to complete the rite, so that in some sense, the relation to the church was imperfect and needed to be brought to conclusion when the bishop made his pastoral visitation. This he would do by anointing or by laying on of hands, or both. To offer a theological meaning, this sealing was often explained as the gift of the sevenfold Spirit, giving maturity to the life of a Christian.

The association of first communion and confirmation with a process of personal growth or initiation is more post-Tridentine than medieval. It was after Trent that it became a common practice to defer confirmation to a later age, even to adolescence, so that preparation for it and the sacrament itself could be seen as moments in the growth of faith and grace fitted to the candidate's age. Since the practice of giving commu-

---

17. For a minute study of the ritual process whereby confirmation became a separate sacramental action, see Nathan D. Mitchell, "Confirmation in the Second Millennium: A Sacrament in Search of a Meaning," in *La Cresima: Atti del VII Congresso Internazionale di Liturgia*, ed. Ephrem Carr, Studia Anselmiana 144 (Rome: Pontificio Ateneo S. Anselmo, 2007), 133–75.

18. Paul VI, "Constitutio Apostolica de Sacramento Confirmationis," in *Ordo Confirmationis* (Vatican City: Vatican Polyglot Press, 1971), 14.

nion to infants had also ceased in the West, it was common to say that children could receive it when they reached the "age of reason." If they were given confirmation after instead of before Eucharist, the situation was complicated by introducing children to the sacrament of penance, so that the sequence of sacraments was baptism, first penance, first communion, and confirmation. Having these rites spread out over a period of years took on some importance in the combat against Protestantism; it was also considered to help counteract the influences of an increasingly secular culture and prolong the period of Catholic education.

A theologian has to say there is no warrant in early church practice for communion only at the age of reason, nor for a separate rite of confirmation for the giving of the Spirit. Hence, the issue is whether there is a pastoral theology that, in the light of sacramental tradition and historical change in the position of the church in culture and society, gives meaning and purpose to this sequence of rites.

Scholastic Theology

Scholastic writers from Hugh of Saint Victor to Bonaventure and Thomas Aquinas, in writing of baptism, pursued their general definition that sacraments are visible and efficacious signs of invisible grace.[19] In applying this, they included its various significations: washing or cleansing from sin, rebirth, and the immersion into the death and burial of Christ. Holding to the idea that baptism, like all sacraments, has to be a sacrament of faith, they adopted the Augustinian notion that infants are baptized in the faith of the church and cleansed and sanctified by the power of Christ's passion. As far as the

necessary rite is concerned, they were minimalists, placing matter and form in the use of water and the invocation of the Trinity that accompanies it. However, in teasing out the meaning of what is done, they made ample appeal to other parts of the ritual, such as the blessing of the water, exorcisms, anointing, and the clothing with a white garment. In other words, for the purposes of valid celebration, they were content with the minimum, but to arrive at the meaning of the sacrament through its signs, they looked to its fuller celebration. When it came to confirmation, they presented it as the sacrament of a mature faith with the obligation to profess this publicly, even though they did not require that it be given only to adolescents or adults. To describe it this way as a sacrament alongside baptism promoted the understanding that in becoming a member of Christ, a person received grace for forgiveness of sins and personal participation in his mysteries, and by confirmation took on active responsibility for living publicly as a Christian.

The Challenge of the Reformers and the Council of Trent

Unfortunately, in the course of the Middle Ages, the celebration of baptism was often done without much ceremony and outside its community setting, thus increasing the sense of an automatic effect and bringing attention most of all to the idea of a cleansing of the child from original sin. This is the factual background to the questions raised by the Reformers about Catholic practice and thought. The principal challenge, however,

---

19. For a collection of texts, see Spinks, *Early and Medieval Rituals and Theologies*, 140–51.

came from their teaching on justification as it was related to their teaching on baptism. Since justification requires faith and sacraments are the seal of the promises made by God's Word to those who believe, baptism must require faith and its apt expression. It was wrong to see in it an efficacy due to the positing of the rite through the ministry of the church. Though the Anabaptists rejected pedobaptism, most of the Reformers retained it, so they had to explain how it fit with their position on justification by faith.[20]

Both Luther and Calvin had to deal with the position taken by the Anabaptists supporting believer's baptism. As a biblical justification, Luther invoked Christ's blessing of children and the promise of the kingdom to little ones, but this left intact the need to offer some theology consistent with his position on justification.[21] For Luther, the authority of Augustine was enough to warrant the necessity of baptism, but over time, he formulated a hypothesis about infant faith. Given the personal nature of justification, it was not enough to say the child is baptized in the faith of the church. He thought that by God's saving power and gratuitous love, he assured in the child the faith that brings him or her into a believing church. With the idea that faith is a total openness to God's work and a trust strong enough to receive the promises, in the qualities of a child he could find the reality of a trusting and confident faith, which Luther called *fides fiducialis*.

Both Luther and Calvin gave ample mention to the role of the Spirit in baptism, and this sup-ported Luther's teaching about the faith granted a child. John Calvin, taking issue with the Anabaptists, added an appendix on infant baptism to the 1539 edition of his *Institutes of the Christian Religion*.[22] His position was that the work of the Spirit nurtures the beginnings of faith and repentance in infants, and that in receiving this sacrament, they partake of the covenant promise and are received as God's adoptive children when through the waters of baptism they are introduced into the family of Christ.

Because of the challenges to it, the Council of Trent offered its own justification of infant baptism and harmonized it with its teaching on original sin. The three Tridentine canons (DS 1625–27) dealing with the practice were intended to address the Anabaptist position on retaining solely "believer's baptism" and affirmed its legitimacy as warranted by tradition. Earlier in the decree on justification, the council had connected infant baptism with its teaching on original sin (DS 1514). In the canons on the sacraments, it asserted the legitimacy of early baptism and that baptized infants are to be counted among the faithful (DS 1625–27). On confirmation, the council had nothing more to say than that it is a sacrament instituted by Christ and that, through it, a special sacramental character is conferred.

What was generally lacking in the disputes about sacraments was an adequate consideration of their relation to the church as a communion in the faith of Christ. While Catholic teaching rested mostly on a doctrine of original

---

20. As noted in the general introduction to sacraments (chapter 9.1 in this volume), the Reformers also rejected the notion of the imprint of a sacramental character, primarily because of the teaching on consecration through the sacrament of order, but nonetheless, they did much to retrieve the patristic teaching on the priesthood of all the faithful founded on baptism.

21. For Luther's baptismal rite, see Bryan D. Spinks, *Reformation and Modern Rituals and Theologies of Baptism* (Burlington, VT: Ashgate, 2006), 9–14. On Calvin's relation to the Reformed traditions, see ibid., 40–44.

22. John Calvin, *Institutes of the Christian Religion*, 4.16:1–30.

sin and the need for redemption, the Reformers came closer to relating infant baptism to an understanding of the church as a covenantal community of faith. They also outlined a Christian anthropology that showed the openness to faith already present in the child as a human person, an openness to be nourished and engendered within a living dynamism of ecclesial life as the child matures in the power of the Spirit and as a member of the church.

Contemporary Theology

While many Roman Catholic writers today give most attention to adult baptism and treat this as normative for an understanding of the sacrament, the question of infant baptism remains a live pastoral and theological issue. While always to be seen as an act of Christ's justification and of introduction to ecclesial membership, one must ask how initiation may be properly celebrated for both adults and infants and with what signification particular to each case.

Some of the principles that have become common in Roman Catholic theology on the meaning of baptism and confirmation are outlined in the ceremonial books for their celebration, so these may be cited as a way of being in touch with a contemporary retrieval of Scripture and tradition that has been received into the liturgical practice of the church.[23] The ritual instructions also show how this is accommodated to pastoral settings.

On May 15, 1969, a general introduction to the sacrament of baptism was promulgated as prelude to the particular instructions on the baptism of small children.[24] This introduction offered several theological considerations: (1) In the sacraments of initiation, persons are freed from the power of darkness, die, are buried and rise in Christ, entering into the new covenant of the community of the redeemed. (2) They receive the Spirit of adoption as God's children. (3) Through the three sacraments, they join with the church in the memorial of the Lord's death and resurrection. (4) In baptism in particular, they are incorporated into Christ, made members of God's people, receive the forgiveness of sins, are made adoptive children of God, and become a new creation through water and the Spirit, built into a holy nation and a royal priesthood, and receive the indwelling of the Spirit. (5) In confirmation, they are signed and filled with the gift of the Spirit, conformed more perfectly to Christ, and empowered to bear witness and to work for the building up of the body of Christ. (6) In the Eucharist, they eat and drink of the body and blood of Christ and come to share in eternal life, are brought into the communion and unity of God's people, offer themselves with Christ and are offered by him, and join with the church in intercession for the whole human family.

On baptism in particular, the instruction gives four further theological principles and associates a practical rule with each one:

1. Baptism is the *sacrament of faith*, in which, enlightened by the Spirit, people respond to the Gospel of Christ. This requires a practical rule that points out the role of the word in the preparation

---

23. These principles are to be found in the teachings of the Second Vatican Council. While the document on the liturgy asked for a retrieval of the adult catechumenate and revision of the order of infant baptism, the teaching on the Paschal Mystery is found in *Lumen gentium* (LG) 7. LG 11 also speaks of incorporation into the priestly and liturgical community and calls all the baptized to witness to the world of their faith as one holy and apostolic people.

24. *Ordo Baptismi Parvulorum*, Introductio Generalis.

of catechumens and the preparation of parents and sponsors for the baptism of small children.

2. Baptism is the *sacrament of incorporation into the church* and requires the practical and traditional rule that it is never repeated.

3. Baptism is *the sacrament of the cleansing water of rebirth*, by which persons are made God's children and signed in the name of the Trinity. Therefore, in practice, the threefold profession of faith and invocation of the name of Father, Son, and Spirit are necessary to the sacrament.

4. Baptism recalls and effects participation in the *Paschal Mystery* through which persons pass from death to life. Hence, it is appropriately celebrated at the Easter Vigil or on a Sunday.[25]

Infant Baptism

The propriety of infant baptism was much discussed among Protestant writers before Vatican II, and this is worth recording here because it had some impact on Catholic theology. A defender of the opinion that baptism was known and practiced since New Testament times was the German scriptural scholar Joachim Jeremias. The strongest opponent of infant baptism was Karl Barth, on the basis of the view that baptism is union with Christ and partnership in the covenant offered to the church in him. He rejected on the one hand what he saw the Zwinglian subjectivism of sacraments as aids to faith and on the other hand the Roman Catholic position that, even in the case of children, sacraments work *ex opere operato*, that is through an efficacy built into the rite itself in virtue of Christ's power. In Word and sacrament, neither being complete without the other, Jesus Christ freely offers salvation, and response to this requires a response of faith, which is a cognitive act. Without this, baptism is without meaning, and the continued practice of baptizing infants is a wound on the body of Christ. What the church must do is uphold believers' baptism and celebrate it within a gathered community that freely hears and welcomes the gift of Christ.[26]

Within the Protestant tradition, Barth's position was rejected by his colleague at the University of Basel, Oscar Cullmann. For Cullmann, Rom. 6:1-11 means that Christ's justifying death and resurrection form one salvific event that is received as forgiveness of sins and the gift of the Spirit by all Christians, of whatever age. He adds that the passive form of the verb used in such texts as 1 Cor. 1:13, "you were baptized," shows that the effects of baptism are independent of the decision of faith and that thus, infant baptism is justified.

Among Catholic scriptural scholars, Barth's arguments were taken apart by Heinrich Schlier.[27] He, too, started with Rom. 6:1-11, arguing that as an instrument of salvation, baptism works *ex opera operato* and so is not dependent

---

25. To these considerations, it may be added how even before the Second Vatican Council, research into the theological tradition about the sacramental character helped to underline the fact that baptism in its complete form gives a participation in the royal priesthood of Christ and of the church. See, for example, Edward Schillebeeckx, *Christ the Sacrament of the Encounter with God* (Kansas City: Sheed Andrews & McMeel, 1963), 153–73.

26. For an extended discussion of Karl and Markus Barth's positions, see Dale Moody, *Baptism: Foundation for Christian Unity* (Philadelphia: Westminster, 1967), 57–71.

27. Heinrich Schlier, *Die Zeit der Kirche* (Freiburg: Herder, 1955), 107–29.

on the faith of the recipient. Though the response of faith is required of adults as a necessary condition, in the case of infants God's action through the instrumentality of Christ and the church grants the grace of salvation. The child is indeed empowered to live a life of faith, but faith is not required for his or her salvation at the moment of baptism. In other words, on the basis of scriptural exegesis, Schlier argued the accepted Catholic position against the arguments of Karl Barth and others.

While it does not have to do solely with infant baptism, it is worth recording that the Second Vatican Council in the decree *Unitatis redintegratio* paid particular attention to the common baptism whereby all recipients became members of God's people and of the body of Christ, at whatever age they are baptized. Hence, the Catholic Church will never repeat baptism given in other confessions when welcoming them into the communion of the Catholic Church. In later discussions among theologians of all churches, some ecumenical consensus is marked by what is commonly called BEM or the 1982 Lima Document of the Faith and Order Commission of the World Council of churches.[28] The document outlines the scriptural warrants for baptism and spells out its personal, ecclesial, and eschatological dimensions. That done, it acknowledges that both believer's baptism and infant baptism are known practices since the early days of the church. In both cases, what is signified is the initiative of God in Christ in offering salvation. In both cases, the sacrament is to be celebrated within a believing community, but care should be taken not to embrace any instrumental understanding of the sacrament that would preclude the necessity of faith in the sinner.

To develop an understanding of infant baptism that accommodates a good catechesis, Catholic theologians have to speak to the theology of grace implied and to its ecclesiological merits. A recent document of the International Theological Commission on Limbo makes it clear that the need for baptism in order to liberate children from eternal punishment is not viable and is not commonly accepted by either theologians or faithful.[29] The consideration given to infant baptism, rather, has to do with ecclesial belonging and with the offer of the grace of Christ within his church. Oddly enough perhaps, given the impact of teaching on original sin, Augustine can be of help on this topic because of his ecclesial understanding of both grace and sacrament. Any sacrament is an event of grace that takes place in the communion of the church and that involves all in sundry ways, not being merely a matter of what happens to an individual person.

Pastoral directives attached to liturgical books insist that those who present children for baptism must do so in faith and as members of the church. They have to receive proper instruction and be prepared to bring their children up in the Catholic faith, for otherwise, one could not speak of the baptized infant being introduced into the community of the church. What is broached here is the relation between family and church community, something that appears differently in different cultures, though as a basis for all, there is the teaching on family as "domestic church." For Western cultures, this tends to focus on the nuclear family, but African and

---

28. *Baptism, Eucharist and Ministry,* Faith and Order Paper No. 111 (Geneva: WCC, 1982).

29. International Theological Commission, "The Hope of Salvation from Infants Who Die without Being Baptized," *Origins* 36 (April 26, 2007): 725–46.

512

Asian peoples bring to their understanding of a living church a larger notion of extended family. Hence, the practical context within which to approach the integration of infants into the ecclesial community differs from culture to culture according to diverse practical understandings of the nature of family. In any case, what the theology and practice of baptism expect is that the baptism of infants be an ecclesial celebration of faith and hope, of which the place of the child in the family is an integral part. In this celebration, looking to the future, the community considers the hold that evil and sin exercise on the life of the child, the protection against this offered by the work of Christ and Spirit mediated within the church, and the life of grace and communion that the sacrament promises the child and in which it can grow.

On the celebration of confirmation, all will connect this rite with the gift of the Spirit, given to persons within the community of the church. This is what is accentuated in the revised ritual. As far as making it a separate sacrament is concerned, opinions are quite divided.[30] Some, mostly because of what is known from early tradition and because of a sense of sacramental integrity, think water immersion, anointing, laying on of hands for the gift of the Spirit, and Eucharistic communion should all be part of the one ritual of initiation into Christ, into his Paschal Mystery, and into the communion of the church. This should be the case, they believe, whether the candidate is an adult or a child. When the sacrament for the gift of the Spirit is separated from baptism, then the action of the

Spirit in the process of initiation—and, indeed, within baptism itself—is clouded. Catholics are also attentive to ecumenical repercussions, affecting relations with Orthodoxy on the place of the Spirit in introduction to the mysteries of Christ and the church, and with Protestants in what looks to them like an unnecessary multiplication of sacraments.[31]

Though the magisterium on principle holds to the unity of confirmation with baptism, it allows for giving it at a mature age where there are sufficient pastoral reasons for this. The introduction to the revised rite suggests that giving confirmation and Eucharist around the age of seven is appropriate and in keeping with the tradition of the Latin church. But it allows for its administration at a later age, should episcopal conferences deem this fitting for pastoral reasons that have to do with promoting personal adherence to Christ and the church.[32] Given this, there are those who hold for a later and separate conferral of confirmation and relate it specifically to the maturation in faith required of one baptized in childhood or infancy, whatever the inherent problems concerning the place of the Spirit in the life of the Christian when confirmation is separated from baptism. Their task is then to show that appropriating the gift of the Spirit for communion with Christ, for personal salvation, and for service is suited to whatever age group is to be confirmed. If the candidates are old enough, this then appears as a kind of sending on mission appropriate to a member of the church passing to an age of personal responsibility, akin to the mission in the Spirit of Jesus

---

30. There is a good presentation of the state of the question in Gerard Austin, *The Rite of Confirmation: Anointing with the Spirit* (Collegeville, MN: Liturgical, 1985), 125–46. See also P. Tena-D. Borobio, in *La Celebracion en la Iglesia*, vol. 2, *Sacramentos*, ed. Dionisio Borobio (Salamanca: Ediciones Sigueme, 1994), 167–80.

31. Many Protestant churches in their liturgies of baptism allow for an anointing and an invocation of the Spirit but see no reason why this should be taken as a distinct and separable sacrament.

32. *Ordo Confirmationis*, editio typica, 1971, Praenotanda no. 11.

himself at his baptism in the Jordan. While this does not seem in keeping with ecclesial sacramental tradition, perhaps it is the best pastoral solution so long as the separation between the two sacraments is canonically maintained and the celebration of confirmation integrates a proper understanding of baptism.

Conclusion

The greatest impetus to the contemporary theology of the sacraments of baptism and initiation comes from the revival of the practice of adult initiation after Vatican II and the renewal of the orders for adult initiation, infant baptism, and confirmation. Much of the theology of the conciliar period is incorporated into these orders, but they also give rise to ongoing considerations. For adult initiation, there is a renewed accent, learned from reading the fathers of the church, on relating the sacraments to a process of conversion and on the perception of water baptism, anointing with the Spirit, and Eucharistic communion as one complex sacramental act. There is also a historical consciousness at work that allows us to see changes in sacramental practice in social and cultural contexts. The question of infant baptism has been given consideration that is not focused on the remission of original sin but relates the baptism of the child to ecclesial and social setting. There is much discussion about the time for confirmation in the case of those baptized as children, and one has to say that it is hitherto an unresolved issue, both pastorally and theologically. One might say in brief that the theology of these sacraments has evolved in the light of the historical and cultural consciousness evident from a study of practice.

For Further Reading

Austin, Gerard. *The Rite of Confirmation: Anointing with the Spirit.* New York: Pueblo, 1985.

> *A succinct treatment of current approaches to the sacrament.*

Duffy, Regis. *On Becoming Catholic: The Challenge of Christian Initiation.* San Francisco: Harper & Row, 1984.

> *The catechumenal process is taken as a paradigm for a theology of initiation.*

Dujarier, Michel. *A History of the Catechumenate: The First Six Centuries.* New York: Sadlier, 1978.

> *A brief but useful overview of key historical catechumenal developments.*

————. *The Rites of Christian Initiation: Historical and Pastoral Reflections.* New York: Sadlier, 1979.

> *A pastorally informed précis of the theology of initiation.*

514

Ferguson, Everett. *Baptism in the Early Church. History, Theology, and Liturgy in the First Five Centuries.* Grand Rapids, MI, and Cambridge, UK: Eerdmans, 2009.

> An extensive study of the evidence on baptism in the first five centuries of Christianity.

Johnson, Maxwell E. *The Rites of Christian Initiation: Their Evolution and Interpretation.* Collegeville, MN: Liturgical, 1999.

> An analysis of the history and meaning of the rites of initiation throughout history, East and West.

Kavanagh, Aidan. *The Shape of Baptism.* New York: Pueblo, 1978.

> An articulate and challenging approach to the sacrament, based on its history.

Osborne, Kenan. *The Christian Sacraments of Initiation.* New York: Paulist, 1987.

> A summary of how baptism, confirmation, and Eucharist together constitute the Christian initiation process.

Spinks, Bryan D. *Early and Medieval Rituals and Theologies of Baptism: From the New Testament to the Council of Trent.* Burlington, VT: Ashgate, 2006.

> A helpful survey of theology and liturgy and their relationship, with close attention to primary sources.

Turner, Paul. *Confirmation: The Baby in Solomon's Court.* New York/Mahwah, NJ: Paulist, 1993.

> A study of the chequered theology and practice of the sacrament of confirmation through history.

Whitaker, E. C., ed. *Documents of the Baptismal Liturgy.* Revised and expanded by Maxwell E. Johnson. Collegeville, MN: Liturgical, 2003.

> A collection of documents on the baptismal liturgy from the major liturgical families of the church, East and West. This is an important resource book for liturgists and theologians.

Sacraments 9.3

Eucharist

David N. Power

Anoteworthy feature in contemporary Eucharistic doctrine and theology, Roman Catholic, Orthodox, or Protestant, is the sensitivity to the relation between liturgy, devotional practice, and theological reflection. Whatever the age under consideration, this link has always been present, but today it is given acute attention and consideration. In its development, theological reflection refers implicitly or explicitly to practice. It is influenced by it, it reflects it, it guides it, it consolidates it, or at times it tries to correct and change it. Current theology heeds these connections in the past of both East and West, inclusive of what is known of the heritage of the Lord's Supper in post-Reformation churches, and draws ecumenical conclusions. This has served the recovery of the sacrament as an ecclesial action, the sacramental reality of the body of Christ, head and members.

This chapter will first present the gains for Eucharistic theology of scriptural, liturgical, and patristic studies, drawing on work that is done by a fruitful collaboration between scholars of all churches and confessions. It will then place medieval, Reformation, and Tridentine developments against this background. Next, it will offer a summary of recent Catholic magisterial teaching and conside what has emerged in ecumenical dialogue that is important to the faithful of the Catholic Church. Finally, it will show some of the highlights and orientations of current Roman Catholic theologies.

Scriptural Foundations of Eucharistic Theology

Christian theology has always given much attention to the New Testament accounts of the Last Supper, found in the Synoptic Gospels and in Paul's First Letter to the Corinthians.[1] This is still the case, but methods of scriptural interpretation have changed the focus. Because of the broad use of the historical-critical method, much effort for some years was put into a historical reconstruction of the final meal of Jesus with his disciples, into a recovery of Jesus' own intentions in celebrating the meal, and into a retrieval of his exact words (*ipsissima verba*). Simultaneously, biblicists tried to recover the rituals of the early church in New Testament times from these accounts and other texts.

These investigations have not been without their fruits, but it has become apparent that it is impossible to uncover raw data about what Jesus did or intended. This has prompted scholars to recognize that authentic tradition is as much perspective as it is fact and that it is best recovered by reading the scriptural texts as literature. What is to be passed on is as much the meaning of the Lord's Supper expressed in literary form as it is a distinct and easily distinguishable rite. To give this a theological basis, scriptural texts need to be related to the existence of the church as the body of Christ within which there is an

---

1. Important works available in English on the scriptural foundations of Eucharistic theology are Joachim Jeremias, *The Eucharistic Words of Jesus*, trans. Norman Perrin (Philadelphia: Fortress Press, 1978); Edward J. Kilmartin, *The Eucharist in the Primitive Church* (Englewood Cliffs, NJ: Prentice Hall, 1965); Eugene Laverdiere, *The Eucharist in the New Testament and the Early Church* (Collegeville, MN: Liturgical, 1996); Xavier Léon-Dufour, *Sharing the Eucharistic Bread: The Witness of the New Testament*, trans. Matthew O'Connell (New York: Paulist, 1987); Edward Schweizer, *The Lord's Supper according to the New Testament*, trans. James David (Philadelphia: Fortress Press, 1968).

organic growth of liturgical forms.[2] For example, it is helpful to place Paul's recall in 1 Corinthians 10–11 of what has been handed down from the apostles in the context of his discourse on the communion of the church and on practices among the Christians of the city. Their experience of communion (*koinonia*) is grounded in their sharing of the bread and wine of the Lord's Supper, a sharing that derives its full vigor from their whole action as a community in gathering on the Lord's Day, in handing on the faith, in prayer, in their charismatic service to the building up of the body, and in their service of the needy.

Two Traditions

Even though there is ample discourse elsewhere on the Lord's Supper in New Testament texts, scholarly attention is always drawn to the narratives of the Last Supper. These narratives of Jesus' final meal are read in the setting of what is known of common life in early communities. As pointed out by Xavier Léon-Dufour, the early church had two different traditions regarding this meal or Last Supper—a cultic tradition and a testamentary tradition.[3] The former presented the Last Supper as the charter story for the celebration of the Lord's Supper and existed in two forms, the Markan and the Antiochene (Paul and Luke). The second, found principally in John, chapters 13 to 17, presented it as a farewell meal at which Jesus asked to be remembered by his disciples for his service to them, exemplified in the washing of the feet, and gave them the commandment to love each other as he had loved them. The fulfillment of this command and the promises associated with it were the guarantee of the presence of Christ among the disciples in the *agape* they practiced among themselves in the power of the Spirit. While John's Gospel makes no mention of the meal ritual or its memorial command, the cultic and testamentary traditions are brought together in Luke's Gospel. After narrating the sharing of bread and cup, completed by the memorial command, Luke recounts a kind of farewell discourse in which Jesus exhorts his followers to act toward one another as servants, an exhortation that applies as much to the one presiding at table as to the one serving (Luke 22:24-27). The promise of Jesus to remain with the church is realized both in the sacramental memorial and in the fulfillment of the love command through acts of service, the one being incomplete without the other.

Supper Narratives

Concerning the meal form of the Eucharist, historical reconstruction offers some findings that at first appear to raise serious questions.[4] For one thing, it is quite likely that the meal of Jesus with the disciples was not a Paschal Seder, despite the Paschal references of the Synoptic accounts. Second, we learn from Saint Paul that at a relatively early date, the ritual of bread and wine had to be distinguished from the other rituals of the full meal that early Christians were wont to take together, much in the manner of the domestic codes of the Jewish people. However, rather than weakening the ritual of the Lord's Supper, these findings help to make it clearer. The Paschal interpretation does not depend on the actual order of the Last Supper but has to

---

2. On this principle, see David N. Power, "Sacraments in General," ch. 9.1 in this volume.

3. Léon-Dufour, *Sharing the Eucharistic Bread*, 82–101.

4. On the supper narratives, see ibid., 102–79.

518

do with how Jesus is to be remembered. The memorial connection with the Pasch is made clear in the Gospel accounts, and in practice it is attached specifically to the blessings and sharing of bread and wine, rather than to the full order of the meal, though a fuller community sharing remains an important setting. In other words, the action in bread and wine does not forfeit its relationship to meal sharing and other acts of communion by being set apart within the meal or even over time detached from a fuller meal setting. As a commemorative act that includes an eschatological perspective, the sacramental action conjures up more than its own immediate context and expresses the total life and meaning of the church as the body of Christ in this world.

The actions and words attributed to Jesus in blessing and sharing the bread and wine have to be interpreted according to the place given them in each narrative and not merely by a semantic analysis of the individual sentences. From both context and actual words, one notes the importance of the references to the Pasch, the Exodus covenant and blood, and the Suffering Servant of Yahweh. These are historical master images evoked in the narrative by means of which the prophetic and symbolic actions and words of Jesus are fitted into the dispensation of salvation. What is done at the Supper thus appears as the fulfillment of past figures and events and as the eschatological anticipation of the fullness of God's rule. Jesus himself is the one by whose death these figures are realized and the end-time inaugurated. These historical images clarify the meaning of the actual words "this is my body"

and "this is my blood" (in whatever redaction they occur). They signify the double self-gift of Jesus—the one whereby he gives himself to the Father for humankind, and the other whereby he gives himself to the disciples at the Supper table as a means of sharing in the firstfruits of his Pasch. Of themselves, the words do not offer a univocal, clear concept of either sacrifice or presence, since they belong to the genre of metaphor, but all later theories are elaborated by way of reference back to these symbolic images. It is one of theology's ongoing tasks to ask what theories and concepts may serve to mediate the truth and meaning of the Lord's Supper to other generations and cultures, but in doing this, it has to respect the richness of meaning found in the symbols and metaphors of the New Testament narratives.

Memorial

One of the greatest helps that biblical interpretation has given to contemporary doctrine and ecumenical reconciliation is to set the memorial command against the background of Hebrew memorial, made up of commands, stories, prayers, and rites.[5] This makes it easier to read the command of Jesus to keep memorial as a ritual or liturgical command that embraces the entire Eucharistic action, inclusive of proclamation, blessing, and ritual communion in what has been blessed. While Christian writers are wont, naturally enough, to compare the Last Supper and the Eucharist with the meaning and rites of the Paschal Seder, it is incorrect to

---

5. On memorial in biblical tradition, see Fritz Chenderlin, *"Do This as My Memorial": The Semantic and Conceptual Background and Value of Anamnesis in 1 Corinthians 11:24-25* (Rome: Biblical Institute Press, 1982); Brevard S. Childs, *Memory and Tradition in Israel* (London: SCM, 1962); Cesare Giraudo, *La struttura letteraria della preghiera eucaristica: Saggi sulla genesi letteraria di una forma* (Rome: Analecta Biblica 92, 1981). For a summary of findings on memorial, see David N. Power, *The Eucharistic Mystery: Revitalizing the Tradition* (New York: Crossroad, 1992), 42–51.

focus attention too stringently or exclusively on this comparison. All Old Testament, intertestamental, and Jewish liturgies, both public and domestic, have a memorial character. There is also a memorial character to proclamation and to prayer, with special attention given to the prayer of the Psalms and to the varied traditions of *berakah* and *todah*, to use two standard terms for referring to Jewish blessings.[6] While studies on Hebrew memorial have helped enrich understanding of the New Testament memorial command, they have shown that the tradition recognizes a certain pluriformity of form and meaning. From within this multiplicity, however, certain things seem clear enough.

First, as the Jewish people continue to look back to the foundational events of the Pasch and the Covenant, so do Christians look back to the foundational event of Jesus' death and resurrection. A foundational event is one in which God enters into human history in such a way as to bring salvation and to change history's course. It is a guarantee of continuing divine beneficence and opens out to the promise and hope of final salvation from sin and death. In the memorial ritual, not only do the people keep memory, but they also plead that God will remember them in light of what the original divine intervention not only accomplished but promised.[7] In sharing, as it were, in the foundational event through the keeping of memorial, the people share in what it has given and in what it promises for the future. To establish the historical connection of the present with past and future, the memorial service has to include story, proclamation, blessing (comprehensive of praise, thanksgiving, intercession, and at times lament), and ritual action, chief among which is table ritual. While in Hebrew ritual, the persuasion that Yahweh is present among the people when they keep memorial can be expressed in the evocation of the figure of the angel, in the New Testament Eucharistic ritual, it is guaranteed that the mediator, Jesus Christ, is himself present through the gift of the Spirit and in the symbolic action and elements.

While it does not speak of the Eucharist, the Letter to the Hebrews adds something to its understanding as sacrament of the church when it elaborates on the original persuasion that believers enjoy communion in the benefits of Christ's death by describing Christian life and prayer as a share in the heavenly liturgy that the eternal High Priest continues to offer to the Father.[8] Christians in the postapostolic period readily applied this in a particular way to the Eucharist, but rather than finding this in the memorial command itself, it is more correct to see it as one of the elaborations on its meaning that time made possible. There is much indeed in the rhetoric and theology of memorial, both past and present, that cannot be simply drawn from the scripture text but has to be seen within the organic growth of communities that develop its meaning in a way that is persuasive and helpful to other generations and cultures.

Other Texts

Besides the Last Supper narratives, many other scriptural texts foster a better appreciation of

---

6. For the Psalms, see Claus Westermann, *Praise and Lament in the Psalms*, trans. Keith R. Crim and Richard N. Soulen (Atlanta: John Knox, 1981).

7. See Jeremias, *The Eucharistic Words*, 237–55.

8. See James Swetnam, *Jesus and Isaac: A Study of the Epistle to the Hebrews in the Light of the Akedah* (Rome: Biblical Institute Press, 1981).

520 the Eucharist.[9] An examination of the meaning of the "breaking of the bread" in the book of Acts has yielded no entirely conclusive results, but it does serve to put the Eucharist in the context of a gathering in which Word, prayer, food, and possessions were shared. Paul's interpretation of the Lord's Supper within this kind of gathering brings out its relation to the motifs of communion (*koinonia*) and service (*diakonia*).[10] It also underlines its proclamatory and eschatological characteristics and the moral implications of participation in the ritual. While there is continued discussion about the meaning of the discourse found in John 6, it points to faith in the Word of God made flesh as the foundation for faith in the Eucharist.[11] Finally, the composition of the stories of the multiplication of loaves in such a way as to reflect the ritual of the Lord's Supper brings out the value of the latter as eschatological sign and redemptive promise. These various features of the New Testament evidence facilitate a praxis-oriented understanding of the Eucharist whereby it is seen in relation to the church's mission in the service of God's kingdom and to the church's aspirations to truth and justice for all peoples, in the memory and hope of Jesus Christ.

Conclusion

Current theological retrieval of the New Testament evidence on the Lord's Supper or Eucharist offers the following pertinent considerations. Reading the texts commands entry into a world of symbols, textual and figurative, whose appropriation situates the Eucharistic celebration in the context of the history that has its center in the Pasch of Christ and unfolds in the memory of that event. By a better appreciation of what constitutes ritual memorial, it serves the renewal of celebration and the possibility of placing this ritual at the center of the entire life of the church as body of Christ and as eschatological people, called to service, proclamation, and mission. Finally, it offers this historical and memorial setting as the context within which to reconsider the doctrines of sacrifice, presence, and priesthood as they emerged and were disputed in later centuries.

Early Christian Centuries

The early Christian centuries are important to Eucharistic theology not only for the writers who treat of the Eucharist in a variety of contexts but even more fundamentally for the way in which Eucharistic liturgy and prayer developed. Indeed, the various forms of the anaphora or Eucharistic prayer have become an important source of a theology that is liturgical rather than doctrinal, as have the commentaries of the Fathers on liturgical rites.

---

9. These are treated in Léon-Dufour, *Sharing the Eucharistic Bread*, and even more amply in Laverdiere, *The Eucharist in the New Testament*.

10. See Jerome Murphy-O'Connor, "Eucharist and Community in First Corinthians," *Worship* 50 (1976): 370–85 and 51 (1977): 56–69; Gerd Theissen, "Social Integration and Sacramental Activity: An Analysis of 1 Corinthians 11:17-34," in *The Social Setting of Pauline Christianity: Essays on Corinth*, trans. J. H. Schutz (Philadelphia: Fortress Press, 1982), 145–74.

11. Léon-Dufour, *Sharing the Eucharistic Bread*, 253–72.

Christian Writers

It is next to impossible to give an adequate account of early writings on the Eucharistic sacrament.[12] The literature is homiletic, catechetical, mystagogical, and epistolary rather than tractarian. For the most part, authors explain the Eucharist by appeal to the symbols and the figures of the Eucharist in the Old Testament, such as the sacrifice of Melchizedek, the Paschal lamb, and the manna. In some cases, as in the letters of Ignatius of Antioch, a reflection on the Eucharist and on the celebration of the Eucharist is the most basic form of early ecclesiology.[13] When mention of the Eucharist occurs in a more tractarian form of literature, it is in connection with the doctrine of the incarnation, for the Eucharist confirms the incarnation and the incarnation the Eucharist, as is said by Irenaeus of Lyons.[14]

Any attempt to coordinate what comes from studies on this literature would have to center on the Eucharist's place in the life of the church and on the meaning of memorial, sacrifice, and the gift that Christ makes of himself as nourishment. Gathering on the Lord's Day, the assembly of the faithful was marked by its diversity of ministries, its proclamation of the Word, its memorial thanksgiving, and its communion at the table of Christ's body and blood. As an act of assembly in the local church, it is the sacrament of the body of Christ, through which each community is one with all who profess the Christian faith. Many practical rulings derive from and maintain this conception. The ruling of the one assembly, under the presidency of the one bishop, at the one altar preserved both unity and orthodoxy.[15] Mitigations of the rule, as when communion was taken on weekdays or occasions other than Sunday that brought people together, were not intended to take from the importance of the rule of one assembly on the Lord's Day.[16]

In different churches, East and West, the reading of the Scriptures was ordered with the memorial of the Christ event in mind, even when they related to God's deeds for the people who lived by the covenant of Sinai. Though the images used in prayer could be quite diverse, the many forms of the Eucharistic anaphora manifest a fundamental unity of structure and image that brings the memory of Christ's redemption to voice within the larger memory of all God's creative and salvific deeds, and in obedience to the memorial command given at the Last Supper. Catechesis and homily show the same intent and purpose in their elaborate comment on scriptural and sacramental figures or signs, in their constant exhortation to the imitation of Christ's passion, and in their repeated promise of an eternal share in his glory. Within this parenetic context, martyrdom appears as the most awesome configuration to the death and

---

12. For collections of texts in English translation, see Daniel J. Sheerin, ed., *The Eucharist*, Message of the Fathers, no. 7 (Wilmington, DE: Michael Glazier, 1986); Adalbert Hamman, ed., *The Mass: Ancient Liturgies and Patristic Texts*, trans. Thomas Halton (Staten Island, NY: Alba, 1967).

13. See Raymond Johanny, "Ignatius of Antioch," in *The Eucharist of Early Christians*, ed. Willy Rordorf et al., trans. Matthew O'Connell (New York: Pueblo, 1978), 48–70.

14. Sheerin, *The Eucharist*, 86–98.

15. See Hervé-Marie Legrand, "The Presidency of the Eucharist according to the Ancient Tradition," *Worship* 53 (1979): 413–38. For the development of order, see the chapter in this volume on that subject.

16. For more on this, see Robert Taft, "The Frequency of the Eucharist throughout History," in *Can We Always Celebrate the Eucharist?* ed. Mary Collins and David Power, Concilium 152 (New York: Seabury, 1982), 13–24.

522 resurrection that the church celebrates in the Eucharist, a perception that led to the devotion to the tombs of the martyrs and the celebration of the Eucharist over these tombs.

Beyond these practical manifestations of keeping memory, it has to be admitted that Christian thought about memorial shows some ambiguity in its more philosophical moments.[17] This is not unimportant, given the current search for ecumenical convergence around the idea of keeping memory. In many cases, Hellenistic speculation had as much influence as Hebrew precedent. Elaborations on Old Testament types of the mysteries, on their antitypical fulfillment in Jesus Christ, on their imitation in the Eucharist, and on their consummation in glory often show Neo-Platonic conceptions of an ordered and participated reality. This is especially the case when Christ is evoked not only as Redeemer but as the Word of God in whom the whole ordered reality of creation and redemption is divinely conceived in eternity. There are times when writers comment upon the liturgy as a recollection of the earthly and past realities of the passion, death, and rising from the dead in the abiding hope of final beatitude, and times when they stand in awe before the ritual participation in the heavenly liturgy that the glorious High Priest continues to render to God in the company of angels and saints.

Perhaps it is in commentary on scriptural figures, such as the Paschal Lamb or the manna, or on sacramental signs, that one notes more clearly an evolution in thought about representation. The earliest writers (as the earliest prayers) saw representation primarily in historical and eschatological terms. The events remembered brought salvation and promise and could be recalled in that way. The past lived on in the church of the redeemed, and people looked forward to possessing the full reality of what was promised and guaranteed in the future kingdom. By the fourth century, the scriptural types and the sacramental signs appear to have been endowed with a greater reality and were taken to be representations and realizations in iconic form of the events they reflected. Hence, either the historic events of Christ's Pasch or the heavenly liturgy to which he ascended could be said to be enacted in the Eucharist, just as the Old Testament figures could be taken to be an anticipated, if veiled, representation of the truth of Christ and of the Christian sacrament.

Though the salvific deeds of Christ are remembered in a variety of images, the imagery of sacrifice is increasingly applied to this ecclesial memorial action and seems to have found support in the sacrificial understanding of Christian prayer and of the life of discipleship.[18] In the New Testament, this meant the use of cultic terms to speak of the Christian life, given that the redeemed people in their following of Christ constitute the true worship of the gospel order. In the polemic about religion with both Jews and Gentiles, the great prayer of thanksgiving that culminated in the table action of communion is said to be the only sacrifice that Christians need to and can offer. Such worship is, of course, offered in and with Christ, so when the imagery of priesthood and sacrifice was simul-

---

17. Literature in English is not abundant, but see F. N. C. Hicks, *The Fulness of Sacrifice*, 3rd ed. (London: SPCK, 1946); Odo Casel, *The Mystery of Christian Worship*, ed. B. Neunheuser, trans. I. T. Hale (Westminster, MD: Newman, 1962); Enrico Mazza, *Mystagogy: A Theology of Liturgy in the Patristic Age* (Collegeville, MN: Liturgical, 1989).

18. See Robert Daly, *Christian Sacrifice: The Judeo-Christian Background before Origen*, Studies in Christian Antiquity, no. 18 (Washington, DC: Catholic University of America Press, 1978), 498–508; Kenneth Stevenson, *Eucharist and Offering* (New York: Pueblo, 1986).

taneously used to speak of Christ's death and risen life, it was almost a matter of course to say that the sacrifice of the church is a sacramental participation in Christ's sacrifice, whether this latter was thought of as the sacrifice of his death or the priestly worship that the Risen Christ offers in heaven to the Father. The memorial of Christ's Pasch as his obedient sacrifice to the Father, the sacrifice of praise and of intercession offered by him in heaven, the sacrifice of a worthy life of grace, and the thanksgiving sacrifice of the church's prayer together constituted one reality that made of the Eucharist the sacrifice of the body of Christ, head and members.

The participation of Christians in the sacrifice of Christ and in his worship, as well as the hope of their participation in his glory, could not be conceived except in connection with the nourishment they received at the table of his body and blood. It is because the command of Christ to keep his memory is obeyed in the prayer of blessing over the bread and wine that these are transformed into his body and blood. It is often stressed that the elements, when blessed, are the flesh and blood of the risen Lord, now endowed with incorruptibility and immortality. Hence, for Christians, this is nourishment for freedom from sin and death, the firstfruits of eternal life in the glory of Christ. At times, the cosmic significance of the table is derived from the notion of firstfruits as it applies to the bread and wine and to the resurrection of the body of Christ as firstfruits of creation's redemption.[19]

Despite the variety of these early writings, their unsystematic style, and their often occa-sional character, the unity of the church's Eucharistic vision that unfolds is impressive. In the Eucharist, the entire Christian mystery is ever present, celebrated and realized anew in the church. There the people are gathered as the redeemed and eschatological people, in the orthodoxy of the one faith, and in the unity of the one ordered assembly. There Christ is present in the power of the Spirit, in the sacramental action, and in the elements of heavenly nourishment. There his Pasch is remembered, and the worship of the church is gathered into his worship of the Father, as a living sacrifice of praise. There the martyrs are revered and venerated as the ideal of full sacramental and eschatological participation in the death and resurrection of the Savior. There Christians are instructed in the one mystery of the Pasch, their life is renewed at the table, and they are fortified in their discipleship and in the expectation of a final and unending share in Christ's glory.

The Eucharistic Prayer

No account of early Christian perspectives on the Eucharist would be complete without some reference to the anaphora or Eucharistic prayer traditions.[20] These present one of the richest sources for a contemporary theology of this sacrament that grasps at once both its essential unity and its cultural pluriformity. Scholarly debates on the origin and form of the prayer are by no means settled. Some relation to Jewish blessing is acknowledged, but beyond this general agreement, opinions differ. There is clearly

---

19. Augustine *Sermons* 227, 272, in Hamman, *The Mass*, 204–8; Sheerin, *The Eucharist*, 93–102.

20. The most exhaustive study of the Eucharistic prayer is that of Louis Bouyer, *Eucharist: The Theology and Spirituality of the Eucharistic Prayer*, trans. C. U. Quinn (Notre Dame, IN: Notre Dame University Press, 1968). For a survey of recent studies on its genesis, see Thomas Talley, "The Literary Structure of the Eucharistic Prayer," *Worship* 58 (1984): 404–20. For a collection of texts in English translation, see R. C. D. Jasper and G. J. Cuming, *Prayers of the Eucharist: Early and Reformed*, 3rd ed. (New York: Pueblo, 1987).

524 much to be learned from comparing the Christian prayer with Jewish table prayer, especially with the *birkat-ha-mazon*, or prayer of blessing that concluded a meal. It is impossible, however, to restrict the comparison to this prayer as though the Christian anaphora grew out of it in orderly fashion. Some writers have looked at the influence of other prayers—for example, the eighteen benedictions of the synagogue service. In recent years, considerable attention has been given to a fuller blessing tradition as represented in the genre of prayer referred to as the *todah*, which includes all prayers, whatever the occasion, offered in remembrance of the saving deeds of God.[21] Finally, one has to make room for the innovations in the nature of blessing introduced by Christian communities, not only in content but also in form.

With all of these precautions, it is still possible to speak of a theology that is rooted in the form and content of the anaphora. As a memorial prayer over bread and wine to be shared, it is the central and community form for keeping memory of the mysteries of Christ, the core around which the very identity of the church is built. Thus, it is important to note that it is the prayer of the people, proclaimed by the one who presides, and that it is raised up in the power of the Spirit as both thanksgiving and intercession. Through the blessing and the participation in the gifts blessed in the midst of the assembly in the communion of the Spirit, Christ and Christ's Pasch are sacramentally present in the community. The recitation of the Last Supper or institution narrative containing the words of Jesus over the bread and cup may not have been included in the earliest prayers, but before long, it gained a permanent and necessary place in the prayer.[22] Its meaning, however, derives not simply from its repetition but also from its position in the prayer, along with the invocation of the Spirit.[23] In that context, it represents the apostolic faith of the church, its intention to fulfill the commandment of Christ in praise and sacrament, in the power of the Spirit that from Christ's glory poured forth on believers. It also represents the persuasion that this very obedience, as well as the promise contained in the command, gives the sacramental action its power to represent anew the Paschal Mystery and to nourish the faithful for eternal glory.

While churches are now accustomed to prayers that include *sanctus*, anamnesis, epiclesis, and offering, it is helpful to remember that these are but elaborations on a fundamental form that is thanksgiving and intercession rendered in commemoration of the Lord's Pasch and its victory over sin and death.[24] The very earliest prayers known to us indeed are more wont to perceive in Jesus, God's servant, the very wisdom of God,[25] or to recall the death, the descent into hell, and the resurrection in the im-

---

21. The study to which all refer is Cesare Giraudo, *La Struttura Letteraria della Preghiera Eucaristica: Saggio Sulla genesi letteraria di una forma; Toda veterotestamentaria, Beraka giudaica, Anafora cristiana* (Rome: Biblical Institute Press, 1981). For a unique study of early anaphoras, see Enrico Mazza, *The Origins of the Eucharistic Prayer* (Collegeville, MN: Liturgical, 1995).

22. This question was raised by Louis Ligier, "The Origins of the Eucharistic Prayer," *Studia Liturgica* 9 (1973): 161–85.

23. See Edward Yarnold, "The Function of Institution Narrative in Early Liturgies," in *Comparative Liturgy: Fifty Years after Anton Baumstark (1872–1948)* (Rome: Pontifical Oriental Institute, 2000), 997–1004.

24. See David N. Power, "A Prayer of Intersecting Parts: Elements of the Eucharistic Prayer," *Liturgical Ministry* 14 (Summer 2005): 120–31, with references to the literature on the topic.

25. See the text from the *Didache* in Jasper and Cuming, *Prayers of the Eucharist*, 23–24.

agery of a conflict between Christ and the evil powers that besiege humanity, especially sin and death.[26] Thus, in light of later and present disputes about the relation of the sacrament to the sacrifice of Christ's death, it is helpful to note that sacrifice was one of several images used to express the meaning of what the prayer recalled and, when used, served to accentuate the communion in life and worship between Christ and his members.

The Medieval Sacrament

While Scholastic theology in its greatest accomplishment is a wondrously systematic and synthetic explanation of the priestly liturgy celebrated in the cathedrals, monasteries, and chapels of the medieval West, it remains something of a puzzle how the move was made from the actively participated local assembly of early centuries to the priestly offering of the Middle Ages.[27]

Already in the great ecclesiastical writers of earlier centuries, such as John Chrysostom or Augustine, even in the midst of their perorations on the sacrament of the body, one notes the traces of disintegration. The people needed to be exhorted to frequent and regular communion and to a responsibility for the celebration. Some of the writers, like Chrysostom or Leo the Great, themselves fostered a hieratic view of liturgy and of its ordained ministers, but they never lost sight of the sacrament as the action of the one priestly people. The liturgies of Rome

and Constantinople endeavored to reach a peak of splendor as some earthly realization of the heavenly court in ways that influenced celebration across the whole of Christianity. It is the opinion of some that the failure to continue to adopt the people's language in the liturgies of the West, once the first transition from Greek to Latin had been made, was the greatest force in separating the liturgy from the people and the people from the liturgy so that it became a priestly and clerical enactment done for and on behalf of the people, rather than together with them.[28] Language is indeed both a means of communication and a barrier. When access to the action through language was not possible, the people continued to have access to the visible, and the devotion to the consecrated and reserved species became the primary Eucharistic reality for the populace at large, all the way from kings to peasants.

One could appeal also to other influences, such as the hoary sinfulness of a virtually uninitiated baptismal throng whose deeds cried out for penance and propitiation, and who were at least helped to feel that way by monks and clergy.[29] The priestly role of offering sacrifice for sins in the name and person of Christ took on greater importance in such a climate, and this replaced the great sacrifice of thanksgiving offered together with Christ by the assembled faithful with a focus on the words of the minister spoken in the name or person of Christ.[30]

Though Scholastic Eucharistic theology explained the Mass as the action of the one

---

26. See the texts of Hippolytus and Addai and Mari, in Jasper and Cuming, *Prayers of the Eucharist*, 35, 42–44.

27. On the medieval sacrament, see Power, *Eucharistic Theology*, 22–30; Mitchell, *Cult and Controversy*, 66–195.

28. Mitchell, *Cult and Controversy*, 118, 380–418.

29. See David N. Power, "Sacrament and Order of Penance and Reconciliation," ch. 9.4 in this volume.

30. There are several theories on the reasons for the multiplication of Masses. For one theory and an overview of the literature, see Angelus Häussling, "Motives for Frequency of Eucharist," in Collins and Power, *Can We Always Celebrate the Eucharist?* 25–30.

526 priesthood of Jesus Christ and his church, it is a theology in which ordained priesthood has primary place and which lessens the part of the baptized in the action—this, no doubt, in keeping with what was the actual experience of the ritual. At the center is the priest, who in the person of Christ and of the church consecrates, confers grace, and offers sacrifice, parallel with his priestly role of forgiving sins through sacramental absolution. Since devotion centers on the consecrated species, much time is given to explaining the real presence of Christ and the manner in which this comes about through the words of the priest, which are in fact the words of Christ himself, whose power the priest has received. Though allegorical fantasies were frequent, the grasp of symbolic reality was on the wane, and categories adopted from Greek thought were used to explain the difference between presence in truth and presence in figure.

With the controversy surrounding Berengar of Tours,[31] the axiom *aut in figura aut in veritate* (either in figure or in truth) had become popular and replaced the mode of thought that could see the *veritas* in the *figura* not as the result of some supplementary action, but precisely because it was a figure. Thus, the real presence came to be explained, with much refinement that often eluded the people and the preacher, as substantial presence, and the means of this becoming present was explained as substantial change, or transubstantiation.

The thought of Thomas Aquinas on the real presence deserves a more wholesome consideration and respect than it often gets nowadays, but it cannot be denied that it was developed in a context that paid but scant attention to the presence of Christ and his mysteries in the liturgical action itself or in the assembly of the faithful. Its great achievement in its time was that it prevented a reduction of presence to the purely figurative and allegorical, while at the same time it avoided the risk of fleshly realism expressed in many a story of bleeding hosts and visions of the Christ child. Once Thomas has removed all possibility of presence through locomotion, corruption, generation, or copresence of the body with the bread, one is indeed left with the act of faith that the Christ who suffered and was crucified and is now enjoying glory in heaven is present in this sacramental form to which nothing else in human ken can be compared. He is there for the sake of the faithful, requiring indeed to be worshipped but most of all to be eaten by them for the forgiveness of sins, for grace, and for glory; and the communion in the body and blood of Christ given to all makes of the Eucharist the sacrament of ecclesial unity.

Reformation Controversies and the Council of Trent

The Reformation controversies of the sixteenth century were about both practice and doctrine, as these are essentially interconnected.[32] As far as practice was concerned, the Reformers objected to the concentration on the priestly acts of consecration and sacrifice and to the replacement of communion by the veneration of the species. They wanted the Lord's Supper restored as a sacrament, accessible in both kinds to all the faithful, in recognition of their royal priesthood, and they would not brook the language

---

31. Mitchell, *Cult and Controversy*, 137–63, summarizes these controversies.
32. For a summary, see Alasdair I. C. Heron, *Table and Tradition: Toward an Ecumenical Understanding of the Eucharist* (Philadelphia: Westminster, 1983), 108–45.

of sacrifice when this was associated with pro-pitiation or turned into the action of the priest apart from the faithful. For them, the once and for all sacrifice was that of Christ and the Cross, and the purpose of the sacrament was to make its mercy and forgiveness available to the communicants. Hence, they expurgated the Mass of all language of sacrifice other than that of thanksgiving and self-offering.[33] This, however, was not strictly a retrieval of the early Christian understanding of sacrifice, since the Reformers saw this metaphorical sacrifice not as essential but as accessory to the Lord's Supper, whose only essence was the offer of the sacrament of the body and blood to the faithful and communion in the sacrament.

For defenders of the Catholic faith, this undid the whole Catholic system of devotion and worship and stood as a denial of the essential doctrines of substantial presence, transubstantiation, and propitiatory sacrifice offered by the priest for the living and the dead. It takes many volumes to discuss anew the exact doctrinal and theological positions of both Catholic apologists and Reformers. Whatever is said about these, it has to be said that the situation was one of impasse and led to the defensive definitions of the Council of Trent that were concerned with both faith and practice and that established the medieval Eucharist as the core Catholic practice for four more centuries, even though the postconciliar reforms did purge it of many of its more impious and superstitious abuses.[34]

In the Decree on the Sacrament of the Eucharist, the Council of Trent defined real presence and the change of the bread and wine into the body and blood of Christ that this presence demands (DS 1651–53). It was emphasized that this is a sacramental and unique form of presence that is different to physical presence. The term *transubstantiation* was not said to be a necessary part of the definition of how the change comes about. Instead, the council simply said that it was a most suitable way in which to express the change that takes place in the elements.[35] In the Decree on the Sacrifice of the Mass (DS 1738–59),[36] the council abjured any idea of mere metaphorical sacrifice and sternly defined the propitiatory character of the sacrifice as offered by the ordained priest. One can certainly find language in the conciliar teachings that shows a healthy sense of the sacramental and representational relation of the Mass to the Cross, as one can also find encouragement of more frequent communion by the faithful, though not under both kinds, which could have smacked too much of Protestant persuasion (DS 1747, 1760). There is, however, no getting away from the fact that Trent favored a priestly conception of Eucharistic doctrine and practice and did nothing to overcome the clericalization of liturgy that was so much a part of the medieval heritage.

The mistake of later centuries, encouraged by the catechism of the Council of Trent, was to take the Tridentine decrees as the authentic

---

33. For an English translation of the liturgies of the principal Reformers, see Bard Thompson, ed., *Liturgies of the Western Church* (New York: Collins World, 1975), 95–307. For an excellent study that looks to both practice and theory, see Lee Palmer Wandel, *The Eucharist in the Reformation: Incarnation and Liturgy* (New York: Cambridge University Press, 2006).

34. See Josef Jungmann, *The Mass of the Roman Rite* (New York: Benziger, 1951), 1:134–35.

35. See Edward Schillebeeckx, *The Eucharist* (London: Continuum, 2005), 23–75.

36. For a study of this decree, see David N. Power, *The Sacrifice We Offer: The Tridentine Dogma and Its Reinterpretation* (New York: Crossroad, 1987).

528

and full teaching of the Christian faith on the Eucharist, rather than as the historically determined, apologetic, and defensive documents that they actually were. Without setting themselves up as judges of history, Catholics today can face their own critical issues only through a better understanding of what took place in the sixteenth century and of the reasons why the Council of Trent chose to define certain articles of the mystery of the Eucharist as essential to the faith and practice of the time.

Contemporary Roman Catholic Doctrine and Theology

This section of the chapter first presents developments in recent Roman Catholic papal teaching and explains the influence on Catholic theology of ecumenical dialogue. It then surveys the writings of some currently influential Catholic theologians.

Roman Catholic Teaching

As regards the Eucharist, in the wake of the teaching of Vatican II, the major components of official Roman Catholic teaching in recent decades are to be found in several papal documents. These are *Mysterium fidei*, a 1965 encyclical letter of Pope Paul VI; the 1980 Holy Thursday letter *Dominicae cenae* of Pope John Paul II; the 2003 encyclical letter of John Paul II, *Ecclesia de Eucharistia*; and the apostolic ex-

hortation of Pope Benedict XVI in 2007, following an episcopal synod on the Eucharist, *Sacramentum Caritatis*. Taken in their sequence, these documents reflect theological insights at play during this period, development of liturgical action, and magisterial concerns to respect these but maintain continuity with tradition.

In his 1965 encyclical, *Mysterium fidei*,[37] Pope Paul VI was anxious both to open the door to contemporary explanations of Eucharistic presence and to retain the Tridentine teaching on real presence and transubstantiation. The practical difficulty in the popularization of the Tridentine teaching was that it concentrated attention almost exclusively on the consecrated and reserved species and did not place the Eucharistic presence of Christ in the context of celebration and Eucharistic action. As a result, it encouraged adoration and devotion but not communion and active participation in the ritual memorial. To offer a teaching that would encourage the latter, some theologians took their examples and analogies from a phenomenology of rite and symbol and addressed their teaching primarily to an engaged participation in word, prayer, and table communion within the gathering of the Christian community.[38] Thus, words such as *transignification* and *transfinalization* became popular in the 1950s and 1960s. Pope Paul allowed for the usefulness of such explanations but insisted that it was impossible to bypass the medieval and Tridentine teaching on substantial presence and transubstantiation. What he asked for in contemporary theology was an integration of the old and the new, not a replacement of one by the other. It may be noted that Edward

---

37. Paul VI, *Mysterium Fidei, Litterae Encyclicae de Doctrina et Cultu ss. Eucharistiae*, in *Acta Apostolicae Sedis* 57 (1965): 753–74. English translation in *The Pope Speaks* 10 (1965): 309–26.

38. For a survey of the literature of this period, see Joseph M. Powers, *Eucharistic Theology* (New York: Seabury, 1967), 111–79.

Schillebeeckx responded to this by affirming the importance of both transubstantiation and transignification but related the doctrine to a phenomenology of symbolic gift and exchange to give primacy to the presence of Christ in the gift that is given.[39]

Not far into his pontificate, Pope John Paul II developed a practice of addressing a letter for Holy Thursday of each year to the bishops and priests of the Roman Catholic Church. In the postconciliar context of the church in which all the faithful assumed a more active part in ministry, John Paul continued to emphasize the irreplaceable role of the ordained in forms of ministry, but especially in sacrament. In 1980, this letter treated the mystery and worship of the Eucharist.[40] While it repeated and developed the position of the Second Vatican Council on the ecclesial nature of the mystery and on the participation of all the faithful, it singled out the doctrine of the sacrifice of the Mass, particularly the Tridentine formulation of this doctrine, and the role of the priest in celebrating this sacrifice in the person of Christ.[41]

This has been supplemented by the encyclical letter of 2003, *Ecclesia de Eucharistia*, a document that belongs to the term of his papacy.[42] One of the major preoccupations of this letter is to restore practices of Eucharistic adoration, albeit in their necessary relation to liturgical action and sacramental communion. The pope believes that the abandonment of Eucharistic action reflects deeper misunderstandings about the nature of the Eucharist itself. He feared that

while a necessary recovery of the sacrament as banquet and meal had occurred, this risked setting aside the sacrament's nature as sacrifice and representation of the sacrificial death of Christ. At the same time, he thought it necessary to preserve a correct understanding of sacrifice and described the sacrifice of Christ, which is sacramentally represented in this way: "The Eucharist is a sacrifice in the strict sense, and not only in a general way, as if it were simply a matter of Christ's offering himself to the faithful as their spiritual food. The gift of his love and obedience to the point of giving his life is in the first place a gift to his Father. Certainly it is a gift given for our sake, and indeed that of all humanity, yet it is first and foremost a gift to the Father" (13). Fearing that some accentuate a community-centered approach, the pope reminds his readers that the primary dimension of the Eucharist is vertical or God-centered: the Eucharist makes present Christ's sacrifice in which he gives himself in love to the Father for our sake.

On the basis of this understanding of sacrificial memorial, in which the faithful are made one with their High Priest, he underlined the proper Catholic understanding of Christ's presence and the fact that the bread and wine are transubstantiated. In some places, the Real Presence is affirmed while transubstantiation is ignored or denied, leading the faithful to think that Jesus is merely present "in the bread and the wine." Other times, the uniqueness of Christ's presence in the Eucharist is subverted

---

39. Schillebeeckx, *The Eucharist*, 107–52.

40. John Paul II, *Dominicae Cenae, Epistula de ss. Eucharistiae Mysterio et Cultu*, in *Acta Apostolicae Sedis* 72 (1980): 113–48. English translation in *The Pope Speaks* 25 (1980): 139–64.

41. For a commentary on the letter, see Edward J. Kilmartin, *Church, Eucharist and Priesthood* (New York: Paulist, 1981).

42. John Paul II, *Ecclesia de Eucharistia* (Vatican City: Libreria Editrice Vaticana, 2003); English translation, *On the Eucharist in Its Relationship to the Church* (Boston: Pauline, 2003).

by emphasis on Christ's presence "in the community," as if this were equal to his presence in the Eucharist. To counter the existence of such tendencies, the pope emphasizes that the "Mass involves a most special presence that—in the words of Paul VI—'is called "real" not as a way of excluding all other types of presence as if they were "not real," but because it is a presence in the fullest sense: a substantial presence whereby Christ, the God-Man, is wholly and entirely present'" (15; cf. *Mysterium fidei*, 39).

He was also concerned to affirm the necessity of the ministerial priesthood for a true and full celebration, placing it within his understanding of the apostolicity of the church and of the apostolic succession. This also serves to place each Eucharistic celebration within the communion of the whole church, united under the ministry of the pope.

A noteworthy feature in this letter is the way in which the pope relates the eschatological tension inherent to the Eucharist to the Christian's sense of responsibility for the world (20). He sees that participation in the Eucharist with a full understanding of the meaning of Christ's death and of the operation of the Spirit within human history constitutes a task of contributing to the building of a more human world, "a world fully in harmony with God's plan." Thus, he allies the church's promotion of justice and reconciliation with its memorial of the Pasch, done in the power of the Spirit.

Pope Benedict XVI's apostolic exhortation "On the Eucharist as the Source and Summit of the church's Life and Mission" of March 13, 2007, is a post-synodal document, bringing to light the major concerns and orientations of the synod of bishops with regard to both theology and practice.[43] It begins with the Mystery of the Eucharist as expression of the divine mystery, where the pope reflects on the action of the Trinity in the Eucharist (7–8), on Jesus as the true sacrificial Lamb (9–11), on the Holy Spirit, whose action brings about the memorial of the church and unites all in a communion of love (12–13), and on the church as an apostolic communion united in Christ through the Spirit and awaiting eschatological fulfillment (14–15). The second section considers the Eucharist as a "Mystery to Be Celebrated," in which the doctrines of the church are placed within the context of the worship of the church, with an examination of "the connection between the *lex orandi* and the *lex credendi*, and stressing the primacy of the liturgical action" (34). To this the pope adds remarks on Eucharistic adoration and devotion (66–69) in order to encourage the practices he thinks have fallen into desuetude. The third and final section is on the Eucharist as a "Mystery to Be Lived." The Holy Father considers topics connected with celebration and devotion, such as spiritual worship, Sunday obligation, Eucharistic culture, and the social implications of the Eucharistic mystery (70–93).

In explaining the structure of the exhortation, Benedict writes:

> I wish here to endorse the wishes expressed by the Synod Fathers by encouraging the Christian people to deepen their understanding of the relationship between the eucharistic mystery, the liturgical action, and the new spiritual worship which derives from the eucharist as the sacrament of charity. Consequently, I wish to set the present exhortation alongside my first Encyclical Letter, *Deus Caritas Est*, in which I frequently

---

43. Benedict XVI, *Post-Synodal Apostolic Exhortation* Sacramentum Caritatis, official English trans. (Vatican City: Libreria Editrice Vaticana, 2007).

mentioned the sacrament of the eucharist and stressed its relationship to Christian love, both of God and of neighbor: "God incarnate draws us all to himself. We can thus understand how agape also became a term for the eucharist: there God's own agape comes to us bodily, in order to continue his work in us and through us." (5)

One noteworthy feature is that the pope emphasizes the Jewish context and dimensions of the institution of the Eucharist, beginning with the Exodus (10). He places Jesus within the context of that great event and the Passover celebration and then expounds on how Jesus transformed the Passover meal into something far greater, bringing "his own radical *novum* to the ancient Hebrew sacrificial meal. For us Christians, that meal no longer need be repeated. As the church fathers rightly say, *figura transit in veritatem*: the foreshadowing has given way to the truth itself. The ancient rite has been brought to fulfilment and definitively surpassed by the loving gift of the incarnate Son of God" (par. 11). Benedict also notes that a proper understanding of the ecclesial and apostolic character of the Eucharist through communion with the bishop of Rome is necessary to advances in ecumenical dialogue and interchange.

Ecumenical Dialogue and Convergence

One of the things evident in these papal documents is that while advances on Eucharistic doctrine and practice in the dialogue between churches of the East and West have been brought about, reaching full communion in the celebration of the mystery is difficult to attain.

Under the sponsorship of the Vatican Secretariat for Christian Unity, there have been innumerable ecumenical dialogues on the doctrine and practice of the Eucharist at both the international and national levels.[44] Those between the Eastern churches and the Roman Catholic Church have resulted in documents that relate the mystery of the Eucharist to the mystery of the Trinity, with singular attention to the doctrine and action of the Holy Spirit.[45] To this dialogue Catholic theology owes deeper insight into the joint action of Christ and the Spirit in the Eucharist and into the importance of giving proper place to the celebration of the Eucharist in the local church as an expression of its apostolic and eschatological fullness.

Those between the Roman Catholic Church and Reformation churches have sought a path beyond the sixteenth-century impasse on questions of presence, sacrifice, and ordained ministry.[46] In these dialogues, the principal appeal has been to a recovery of the notion and reality of memorial and of the sacramental relation of the Eucharist to the Cross, so that it has become a broadly acceptable practice to speak or write of the Mass, Lord's Supper, Liturgy, or Eucharist as the sacramental memorial of the Cross or the Pasch of Christ, or even of the sacrificial memorial or the memorial of the sacrifice. This is placed in more recent documents in the context of the mystery of the church as communion or *koinonia*, an insight that owes much to

---

44. See Hardins Meyer and Lukas Vischer, eds., *Growth in Agreement: Reports and Agreed Statements of Ecumenical Conversations on a World Level* (New York: Paulist; Geneva: World Council of Churches, 1984).

45. See Joint International Commission for Roman Catholic/Orthodox Theological Dialogue, "The Church, the Eucharist and the Trinity," *Origins* 12 (1982): 157–60.

46. Meyer and Vischer, eds., *Growth in Agreement*, has collected many of these agreed statements.

532

dialogues with Eastern churches and that hearkens back to the teaching of Paul in his letter to the Corinthians.

Whatever doctrinal convergence has developed, and whatever official reserve or popular opposition it still encounters, it has been greatly helped by a simultaneous convergence in the forms of celebration that has resulted from a historically unparalleled effort of liturgical renewal in the majority of churches, a renewal based on a broad knowledge of early, medieval, and Reformed rites and practice and at the same time attentive to the potential of contemporary cultural forms.[47]

Since the Second Vatican Council, the Roman Catholic Church recognizes the action of Christ and the Spirit in the celebration of the Lord's Supper in post-Reformation communities and churches, but it continues to affirm that "especially because of the lack of the Sacrament of Orders they have not preserved the genuine and total reality of the eucharistic mystery."[48] While these churches observe the forms of Eucharistic celebration and keep memorial of Christ's Pasch, Eucharistic theology has to ask what is meant by the lack of the sacrament of orders and what this takes from the total reality of the mystery. This cannot be couched in terms of a lack of the Eucharistic presence nor by speaking of the absence of the sacramental memorial of the Pasch. It seems rather to have to do with the fullness of ecclesial communion that

Rome postulates, a communion that requires the recognition of papal primacy. That which is thought missing therefore seems to be an expression of full ecclesial communion, rather than the genuine reality of Eucharistic memorial or presence, once a legitimate difference in the terms in which these are expressed is recognized.[49]

Roman Catholic Theologians

In looking at current Roman Catholic theology, what is first presented is a set of core principles about the Eucharist that are commonly accepted. After this, an account is given of the positions of some major writers.

CORE PRINCIPLES

In the pages that Hans Urs von Balthasar devotes to "The Eucharistic Cult" in the Glory of the Lord, he gives a summary of the principles that give the basis for any synthesis of Eucharistic theology.[50] Locating the birth of the mystery of the church in the loving surrender that Jesus makes of himself in death, von Balthasar sees in the supper meal the covenantal seal of his communion with the church. Together, Supper and Cross constitute Jesus' "hour." In the social act of the Supper, Jesus gives the form whereby he is to be remembered, and it is the event of this communion between Christ and church that is sacramentally represented in the Eucharist. Christ and church encounter one another anew,

---

47. For a collection of recent liturgical texts from different churches and countries, see Max Thurian and Geoffrey Wainwright, eds., *Baptism and Eucharist Ecumenical Convergence in Celebration* (Geneva: World Council of Churches; Grand Rapids: Eerdmans, 1983), 136–209.

48. John Paul II, *Ut Unum Sint*, 67, citing Vatican II, *Unitatis redintegratio* 22.

49. On this, see Karl Lehmann and Wolfhart Pannenberg, eds., *The Condemnations of the Reformation Era: Do They Still Divide?* (Minneapolis: Fortress Press, 1990), 84–117.

50. Hans Urs von Balthasar, *The Glory of the Lord: A Theological Aesthetics* (Edinburgh: T&T Clark; San Francisco: Ignatius, 1982), 1:571–75. Elsewhere, von Balthasar supports the idea that the celebrant represents Christ the bridegroom of the church. E.g., "The Mass, a Sacrifice of the Church?" *Explorations in Theology*, vol. 3, *Creator Spirit* (San Francisco: Ignatius, 1993), 185–244.

and the doctrine of transubstantiation is to be understood in terms of the sign and proof that Jesus gives of his love in the gifts offered. It is in the eating and drinking with thanksgiving, that the sacrifice of his death is remembered as the continuing central event of the presence of Christ in the midst of his disciples. In this sacramental sacrifice in the signs of bread and wine given and shared, Christ is the one High Priest, and the celebrant is "no more than the delegate of Christ and the community."[51] In respect for the awesome simplicity of this Eucharistic encounter, von Balthasar augurs a sober and not excessively rigid liturgical form, of which the manner of celebrating in the early church is the exemplar.

With this kind of emphasis on the oneness of meal and sacrifice and on the ecclesial aspect of the Eucharistic memorial, ongoing theological reflection has to meet the challenge and invitation of the liturgical, doctrinal, and ecumenical developments described above. On the one hand, it is possible to speak of a legitimate plurality in unity, both practical and doctrinal. On the other hand, it is impossible to overlook a certain conflict of interpretations. What is needed is a mode of theology that takes both these factors into account. Some dialectic between apparently opposing positions is possible, as with the East-West positions on the Eucharistic epiclesis and on the matter appropriate to Eucharistic celebration. It is also necessary to be attentive to the distortions that can creep into belief, theology, and practice as a result of bias,

naive realism, or power structures that have inevitable effects on ritual and devotion.[52] Here we can account for some very materialistic conceptions of real presence and equally for some undernourished reductions of Eucharistic presence to subjective piety. We can also account for a theology of priestly power that virtually excluded the faithful from an active role in celebration.

Beyond such critical awareness, it is well to place and retrieve all teaching and practice in historical and cultural perspective. Most important of all, it is necessary to recover the language of symbol, ritual, and *poesis* as key to celebration and as origin of all theological reflection. In other words, a theology of the Eucharist has to be a theology of Eucharistic celebration. With these principles in mind, we can see how current theology appropriates biblical origins, early church developments, medieval synthesis, and sixteenth-century polemic, as well as the insight into the language and forms of ritual celebration that is provided today by the human sciences, hermeneutics, and aesthetics.[53]

This is done in an ecumenical context, with a proper appreciation of the contribution of Reformation and Orthodox thought to the Western churches. It is also more historically and culturally conscious, attentive to past context and to the possibilities of Eucharistic celebration and understanding in African and Asian cultures.[54]

Eucharistic theology and practice are enriched by a better grasp of the nature of symbolic action and exchange, as this is fostered by

---

51. Von Balthasar, *The Glory of the Lord*, 574. However for a developed understanding of Balthasar's position on the role of the priest, see idem, "The Mass, a Sacrifice of the Church?" *Explorations in Theology: Spiritus Creator* (San Francisco: Ignatius, 1993), 185–245.

52. See Nathan Mitchell, *Cult and Controversy: The Worship of the Eucharist outside Mass* (New York: Pueblo, 1982), 66–195.

53. Nathan Mitchell, *Real Presence: The Work of Eucharist* (Chicago: LTP, 1998), 87–100.

54. This is not much developed here, but see the examples in Thurian and Wainwright, eds., *Baptism and Eucharist*, 186–209.

534 current philosophies[55] and cultural, anthropological, and ritual studies. Moreover, a renewed sense of the Eucharist's eschatological horizon allows for more attention to such matters as its relation to peoples' histories, its ecological significance, and its relation to the ongoing quest for justice and reconciliation. All of this is as much agenda as it is accomplished fact. Indeed, it is next to impossible to find a Roman Catholic systematic theology of the Eucharist that incorporates this agenda fully and represents a system that could be compared with the Scholastic or post-Tridentine system. Nonetheless, a schematic and ordered summary is attempted here, by way at least of a guideline to reflection and practice.

Sacrament of the Church, Body of Christ in the Spirit

The core perception of this proffered synthesis is that the Eucharist or Lord's Supper is the sacrament of the church as the living eschatological sign of God's salvific rule, proclaimed and promised in the death and resurrection of Jesus Christ. This perception is elaborated upon from a liturgical starting point as a reflection on the action by which the church comes to be in the representation of Christ's mysteries through Word, prayer, and ritual. All the components of the action have to be taken into account: the gathering in the Spirit, the recall of God's saving acts in the proclamation of the Word, the great commemorative prayer of thanksgiving and intercession, and the communion in Christ's body and blood.[56]

Cultural and anthropological studies remind us that a people finds its identity in story and rebuilds its hopes in times of crisis from the recall and retelling of this story. The Eucharist is liturgically built around the narrative of Christ's passion and death, to which it relates a host of other stories—those concerning Jesus himself, those taken from the Old Testament, and those about the nascent church. Narrative is complemented by other genres of texts, especially prophetic, sapiential, and parenetic, which makes it possible to integrate what is narrated into a community basis for vision and action. The liturgy of the Word is not simply preparatory to memorial but is integral to it.

Rather than using a proclamation/response schema to explain the traditional two parts of the Mass, it is better to use the image of flow. The great thanksgiving prayer flows from the narrative and serves to bring it in an action-orienting way into the life of the church. From one point of view, one can say that people respond to story, but when story is viewed as that which forges identity, one has to ask what the means are by which it becomes a constitutive part of their lives and of their vision. On the basis of the relation between Word and sacrament advocated by Karl Rahner and key to Protestant theology,[57] one can ask how in practice a community is guided by the hearing of the Word of God in ways related to the Eucharist but not confined to the moment of its celebration. Ideally, those who gather for the Eucharist are communities that come together at other times to listen to God's Word and to attend to the Spirit,

---

55. See what was said in Power, "Sacraments in General" (ch. 9.1) about the contributions of Karl Rahner, Edward Schillebeeckx, and Hans Urs von Balthasar to the understanding of the symbolic, the connection between Word and sacrament, and how this makes a connection with Protestant theology.

56. See Power, *The Eucharistic Mystery*, 291–327.

57. See Power, "Sacraments in General" (ch. 9.1).

discerning the power of their presence in their lives. They are communities on a local level that share life and action together, care for the poor, and in testimony to Christ engage as a people in the struggle for justice and reconciliation. All of this is gathered into the Eucharistic communion, and even such a matter as the style and frequency of communion on Sundays celebrated in the absence of ordained ministers has to be assessed on this basis.

In the flow from Word to prayer, the Eucharistic prayer is to be considered for what it tells of the relation of peoples to their own histories and cultures. The prayer, even in the past, has been couched in fresh idioms, even when it adopts scriptural story and imagery. Though studies on the Eucharistic prayer ought to have made people aware of cultural diversity, its cultural rooting is not sufficiently respected in contemporary liturgical developments. Perhaps this is because the theological necessity of this rooting is not appreciated. The anaphora is actually a reinterpretation of the scriptural story in cultural context and idiom and in prayerful form. It is what can be called an appropriation by a people of their Christian tradition, worked into the fabric of their dominant perceptions and attitudes, even as they recognize in praise and obedience the priority of God's gift and of God's revealing Word in shaping the church as Christ's body. That these attitudes are expressed in the form of thanksgiving and intercession reflects the ways in which people see God's power active in their lives and history. Possible developments in the genre itself need deeper consideration, attentive to the ways in which people today, in face of contemporary history, might express their sense of configuration to Christ and of a divinely saving power in the life of humankind.[58]

The table ritual is associated with story and prayer. True appreciation of this ritual as the communion in hope in Christ's body and blood requires reflection on what the ritual signifies of the community that gathers.[59] Before it symbolizes Christ's presence, before it is changed by the transforming prayer, the table signifies and represents the people. Even after the prayer, when it represents Christ and his self-gift, it continues to represent the people, now invited into the fullness of their being in Christ. The significance of bread and wine and of the common table in themselves is important to an understanding of the presence of Christ in these elements. They represent fundamental human needs and desires and humanity's innate relation to time and place and to the fate of the earth. They represent the work that is done to bring them to the table. They represent humanity's communion with the whole of creation and with its cycles of production and reproduction. In concrete fact, as bread and wine of the people who come together, it often represents their struggle for existence and the joy or hope of working and searching together for a worthy human life. The breaking of bread and sharing of a common cup are ritual actions brought into many a human situation to express both a necessary mutual dependency and a common hope that comes from

---

58. On this account, some thought has been given recently to an inclusion of lamentation in the memorial prayer, though one can hardly say this suggestion has received widespread and popular acclaim. See David N. Power, "The Eucharistic Prayer: Another Look," in *New Eucharistic Prayers: An Ecumenical Study*, ed. Frank C. Senn (New York: Paulist, 1987), 239–57.

59. See Philippe Rouillard, "From Human Meal to Christian Eucharist," *Worship* 52 (1978): 425–39 and 53 (1979): 40–56; Enrique Dussel, "The Bread of the Eucharistic Celebration as a Sign of Justice in the Community," in H. Schmidt and D. Power, *Politics and Liturgy*, Concilium 92 (1974), 56–65.

536 the eschatological vision of reality embedded in the memorial of Christ's death and resurrection as God's gracious initiative in giving life to the world. When the bread and wine are transformed into the body and blood of Christ, they lose none of this significance but carry it with them into the reality of communion in Christ. The thanksgiving and the intercession that the communion renders to the Father in the life of the Spirit and in the appropriation of Christ's memory come now to center on this table, where human lives and human hopes are transformed. The vision of faith, love, and hope already expressed in the prayer is made more concrete, as is the sense of Christ's continuing presence in the church and in human history. The reconciliation and the justice of God's rule are embodied in the symbols that represent Christ and with and in him a transformed humanity and a transformed creation. From such action, the church emerges in the concreteness of time and place as the sign of the promise, the eschatological sacrament of what has been accomplished and promised in the Pasch of Christ, the pattern of its agapic praxis suggested to it by the very sacrament it celebrates.[60]

If this is the vision of the Eucharist that comes from a study of Scripture and tradition, related to the concreteness of human culture and history, theology has to develop several of its tasks from this center. Eucharistic theology needs to be critical of what impedes such a celebration. Even while it acknowledges many of the fruits of medieval devotion and practice, it cannot but see the human elements that impeded a more authentic development. It must be seen that a theology of real presence that removes

contact with the sacrament from all the senses but the visual is a long way from the communion of the supper room and from the command that Christ gave to the disciples to keep his memory. Similarly, it needs to be recognized that an excess of the language of propitiation prevents a retrieval of the sacrifice of thanksgiving as the core expression of what minister and community pronounce over the table. Finally, a theological explanation of the elements of bread and wine that withholds their power to represent people, their history, their culture, and their aspirations is a long way from the truth of the incarnation.[61]

SACRAMENTAL MEMORIAL

The sense in which the Eucharistic celebration is a memorial of Christ's Pasch or represents that Pasch in the midst of the assembly has received much attention of late and has been helpful in arriving at a consensus of belief among divided churches. However, the exact meaning of memorial is explained in different ways. Some think the memorial action brings the past event into the present; others think it brings those who celebrate back to the event commemorated. Attention to the flow of the action—comprehensive of word, prayer, and rite as a comprehensive language expression—gives its own insight into how the Christ event is present in its relation to past and future, as in the gift of the Spirit, the church is enabled to give it form. To be vital to history, events are brought to language, and the nature of the expression used serves their insertion into the lives of peoples. Through the memory and the offer couched in the entire flow of memorial language, Christ is present to his people and makes them one with him as his body,

---

60. See Tissa Balasuriya, *The Eucharist and Human Liberation* (Maryknoll, NY: Orbis, 1979); David N. Power, "Eucharistic Justice," *Theological Studies* 67, no. 4 (2006): 856–79.

61. This gives rise to discussion about the nature of the Eucharistic elements in different cultural settings.

a living presence in historically and culturally determined human communities.[62]

In this context, Roman Catholic theology must incorporate that which is permanently valid in the doctrines of real presence, substantial change, sacrifice, and priesthood and must open up to fresh considerations. Substantial presence and substantial change are to be reduced to neither metaphysical nor to purely anthropological or phenomenological categories. They can be better appreciated for what they say of Christ's presence if the starting point is the resurrection and the Spirit that assures the presence of the risen Lord in the church. After the memorial thanksgiving over them, the bread and wine are indeed no mere material substances. They belong in the world of communion with the risen Lord and thus assume a new reality whereby he is present in the midst of his faithful. Since our theology can hardly account for the transformation of the humanity of Christ through the resurrection in the Spirit, there is still much to be learned from the ascetically developed theology of Thomas Aquinas, which insists that all distracting images be removed before any positive explanation is offered. Because we do believe that the humanity of Christ has been transformed in the Spirit through his death and resurrection as the firstfruits of all creation, we believe that he is present in the sacrament, but what accounting is there for the nature of this change, except in the imagery of faith and hope? Important to a just retrieval of the doctrine of substantial change are the belief in this transformation and the hope that it carries with it. For this very reason, all talk of the presence in the elements and of their change is put in the context of the promise and guarantee of the Spirit given to the believing community. The presence in the elements is related to the presence in the community itself, in the word and in the prayer, as has been indicated by the conciliar and postconciliar documents of the universal Vatican synod.[63]

As for the Tridentine definition that the Mass is a sacrifice in no purely metaphorical sense but is propitiatory for the living and the dead, many problems have already been overcome through certain results of ecumenical dialogue. First, there is the common recognition that the Eucharist can be spoken of as sacrifice only in sacramental relation to the sacrifice of the Cross, of which it is the representation. Historical studies have made it clear enough that this language was already used at Trent but in the circumstances of the time was not enough to overcome oppositions between Catholic and Protestant interests and beliefs.[64] Second, the primary offering of the Mass is the offering of Christ himself to the Father and as communion gift to the church. The offering of the church is a communion in Christ's self-offering and has no validity aside from its inclusion in that offering. There is no unanimous agreement among Catholics as to whether it is appropriate to say that the "church offers Christ" by way of expressing its will to be taken up into his offering and its confidence in Christ's acceptance by God for the sins of the world.[65] Beyond these clarifications of the dogma, headway has to be made through overcoming the apparent opposition between a sacrifice of thanksgiving and a sacrifice for sin. Much that has already been

---

62. Power, *Eucharistic Mystery*, 304–27.

63. See Peter Fink, "Perceiving the Presence of Christ," *Worship* 58 (1984): 17–28; Mitchell, *Real Presence*.

64. Power, *The Sacrifice We Offer*, 69–76, 96–116.

65. This is the explanation adopted by the Catholic party to the Lutheran–Roman Catholic dialogue. See Lutheran–Roman Catholic Dialogue, *The Eucharist* (Geneva: Lutheran World Federation, 1980), 20.

538 explained above serves in that direction, for the study of the Eucharistic prayer makes it clear that it is through the memorial prayer of thanksgiving and intercession that the Pasch of Christ is represented and becomes efficacious for the community gathered in his name and in the Spirit. It has also become clear that the prayer is a prayer over bread and wine and leads normally to the communion table. To speak of what is done through consecration of the elements without a necessary reference to the communion table is unacceptable.

There is ever a risk of a reified grasp of Eucharistic presence and transubstantiation that is so fixated on what is visible and on a place and a moment that it borders on idolatry.[66] That is why Schillebeeckx wrote of presence as symbolic reality and placed it in the order of symbolic exchange.[67] The body of the Risen Lord "appears" as a gift in the mode of bread and wine that now, blessed in the power of the Spirit, are the sacrament of that gift within the body of the church and become the true appearing of Christ's offer of himself. Recalling this insistence of Thomas Aquinas that the gift can be received only by an act of faith, Schillebeeckx affirms, "The event in which Christ really present in the Eucharist appears, or rather, offers himself as food and in which the believer receives him as food" invites an act of faith that projects a vision of the present reality of the church as Christ's body in the Spirit, which in remembering him sees in it the sacrament of the Cross by which time is transformed, and in hope finds in it anticipated glory.

In a short essay appended to a philosophical work, Jean-Luc Marion locates the doctrine of presence and transubstantiation in a phenomenology of gift.[68] The body of Christ can be received as gift only in memorial. As icon, it is a pledge of God's kenotic commitment in Christ on the Cross, a presence beyond the present to the ecclesial body in its time-limited existence, and a gift not to be taken simply as a "here and now" reality but as an eschatological and mystical expectation of glory.

Whatever pastoral discipline may at times find appropriate, communion in both kinds is the ordinary rather than an extraordinary way to participate in the sacrament and in its fruits, while at the same time communion at the table cannot be separated from participation in the memorial prayer. This helps to get beyond the seeming conflict between the Protestant position that forgiveness of sins is given to the believer through communion and the Catholic position that the Mass may be offered by the priest for the sins of the living and the dead. The intercessory power of Christ's priestly prayer, with which the church is in communion, and the gracious efficacy of the sacrament stand together rather than in opposition. However, the distinctive note of Catholic belief embodied in the dogma that there is an abiding and salutary communion in Christ between the living and all the dead (not only the saints) and that this is given expression in the prayer of the church in the Mass is worthy of retention. Practices of Mass offerings may well need to be revised, if they are not already under revision, so as to do away with a note of superstition and certain connotations of priestly power. This does not, however, mean forgetting the fundamental tenet of

---

66. Here it is proper to recall what was said in chapter 9.1 in this volume on the insights of Schillebeeckx, Chauvet, and Marion.

67. Specifically, see Edward Schillebeeckx, *The Eucharist* (London: Continuum, 2005), 122–51.

68. Jean-Luc Marion, *God without Being* (Chicago: University of Chicago Press, 1991), 161–82.

the communion between the living and the dead that lies behind the remembrance of the dead in the Mass.[69]

These few remarks must suffice to show how the importance of the doctrines on real presence and sacrifice stands out more fully and clearly when they are put in the context of a theology of the Eucharist as the sacrament of God's eschatological people that receives its life and mission from the living presence of Christ in its midst, through the power of the Spirit. As explained, this theology is explored through a reflection on the order of the Eucharist, which includes in one integral memorial rite the narrative of the Pasch, the thanksgiving prayer, and the communion table. This reflection provides the needed context for the Catholic dogmas and their reappropriation.[70]

That the Eucharist is the sacrament of church within a framework of presence in time that is eschatologically perceived invites reflection on its place in the life of communities engaged in issues of justice, reconciliation, promotion of global fellowship, and protection of the integrity of creation.[71] Since all such concerns are local before they are global, celebration needs to be placed in the human, historical, and cultural context of peoples. Within such context, the eschatological Eucharistic communion of Christ's followers compels attention to the life-giving forces of the Spirit that assume and transform human energies and human goals, as they enable communities living in the memorial of Christ's Pasch to find a place in the historic present that aspires to a future that, while being eternal, already penetrates lives with hope for the present and with the sense of responsibility for the present of which, as has been said, Pope John Paul II wrote in his letter on the Eucharist and the church.

Conclusion

In the introduction to this essay on current Roman Catholic theology of the Eucharist, the threefold context of liturgical renewal, ecumenical convergence, and doctrinal concern was noted. It was stated that much of theology's work at present is a retrieval of the whole of tradition in that context. There followed a presentation of current biblical studies on the Lord's Supper or Eucharist. After that, material was culled from early Christian centuries, with specific mention of the theological import of the anaphora or Eucharistic prayer. This led up to a consideration of the particularities of the medieval sacrament and its consolidation at the Council of Trent. The essay concludes with the outline of a contemporary perspective, rooted in the recovery of the Eucharist as sacrament of Christ's body and of its proper liturgical form. This provided the context in which persisting doctrinal concerns can be considered and reappropriated.

---

69. Power, *The Sacrifice We Offer*, 158–60.
70. As for the role of the priest, that is dealt with in David N. Power, "Order," ch. 9.6 in this volume.
71. Power, "Eucharistic Justice."

540 ## For Further Reading

Bieler, Andrea, and Luise Schotroff. *The Eucharist. Bodies, Bread and Resurrection.* Minneapolis: Fortress Press, 2007.

> This book relates Eucharistic celebration to history and its tragedies by exploring its nature as memorial and by reflecting on the sign of bread.

Bouyer, Louis. *Eucharist: The Theology and Spirituality of the Eucharistic Prayer.* Translated by Charles Underhill Quinn. Notre Dame, IN: University of Notre Dame Press, 1968.

> An important book for the history of the Eucharistic prayer and its study as theological source, though more recent studies complement Bouyer's findings.

Irwin, Kevin W. *Models of the Eucharist.* Mahwah, NJ: Paulist, 2005.

> A study of the Eucharist on the basis of the relation between the **lex orandi** and **lex credendi**, outlining various models that serve as the framework within which this is done.

Laverdiere, Eugene. *The Eucharist in the New Testament and the Early church.* Collegeville, MN: Liturgical, 1996.

> An account of the full teaching on the Eucharist in the books of the New Testament.

Léon-Dufour, Xavier. *Sharing the Eucharistic Bread: The Witness of the New Testament.* Translated by Matthew O'Connell. New York: Paulist, 1987.

> The best available study of the New Testament data by a Roman Catholic scholar. This work is comprehensive, up-to-date on exegetical studies, and satisfying theologically.

Mazza, Enrico. *The Eucharistic Prayers of the Roman Rite.* Translated by Matthew O'Connell. New York: Pueblo, 1986.

> A theological study of the current prayers of the Roman Sacramentary, done with due attention to theological and liturgical concerns by an author well known for his studies on the liturgy.

Mitchell, Nathan. *Cult and Controversy: The Worship of the Eucharist outside Mass.* New York: Pueblo, 1982.

> The first part studies the development of this cult and relates it to theological and spiritual interests as they emerged in the first millennium. The second part is a pastoral and theological commentary on present directives and practices in the Roman rite.

———. *Real Presence: The Work of the Eucharist.* Chicago: Liturgy Training, 1998.

> An up-to-date presentation of this mystery, taking into account biblical foundations, history, and the contribution of the human sciences and language studies.

Power, David N. *The Eucharistic Mystery: Revitalizing the Tradition.* New York: Crossroad, 1992.

> A comprehensive survey of Eucharistic liturgical and theological tradition, relating it to contemporary concerns and developments.

———. "Eucharist in Contemporary Catholic Tradition." *New Catholic Encyclopedia.* 2nd ed. Vol. 5, 415–30.

> An overview of trends as indicated in the title of the article.

Schillebeeckx, Edward. *The Eucharist*. London: Burns & Oates. Continuum Imprint, 2005.

> *An important study of the classical theology of transubstantiation and of the doctrine of the Council of Trent, in relation to the issues raised by* **Mysterium fidei**, *an encyclical letter of Pope Paul VI.*

Seasoltz, Kevin, ed. *Living Bread, Saving Cup: Readings on the Eucharist*. Rev. ed. New York: Pueblo, 1987.

> *A collection of essays that appeared originally in* **Worship** *and address many of the current exegetical, liturgical, and theological questions important to Eucharistic theology.*

Sacraments 9.4

Sacrament and Order of Penance and Reconciliation

David N. Power

Present Discipline and Practice

In presenting a theology of the Sacrament of Penance and Reconciliation, it is best to start with the present discipline and practice as the context in which questions about it are now formulated. In the Roman Catholic Church over the past few decades, the discipline of penance and the practice of sacramental confession and reconciliation have been in flux. While continuity with the past can always be asserted, it is the case that penance took on diverse forms in the course of history. Despite many studies, it is by no means easy to have a clear picture of the history of penance and of the evolution of the sacrament.

Present practice or its disarray results not only from a changing cultural perspective, but also from the fact that over time, a number of things that were originally distinct converged and are still intertwined, leading to a lack of clarity on the purpose of the sacrament. The daily practices and prayers of penance considered integral to the life of any Christian, the consultation of spiritual guides in private form, and the need for public acts to exclude from communion those who had breached the Christian code of conduct in a serious and public way and then to reconcile them after doing due penance were distinct for centuries but were then included, as it were, under one umbrella. This was in part due to the privatization of the reconciliation of serious sinners in an era and cultural setting when public penance was inoperable for various reasons. Any pastor occupied today in hearing sacramental confessions knows that he

is dealing with two quite different types of penitent, though using the same form for both. One action asked of him is the reconciliation of persons who confess serious sins, called mortal, and the other is to receive the confession of devotion of those who in principle do not need sacramental forgiveness.

In some respects, the revisions made after the Second Vatican Council in the order of penance, to follow its ritual designation in official books,[1] attended to this. They were meant to address a changing esteem of penance and confession, but more deeply they represented the desire to aid people in a process of genuine and even ongoing conversion to the Lord, with specific attention to ways of highlighting the communal and ecclesial characteristics of penance and reconciliation. Following up on the principles enunciated in chapter 9.1, "Sacraments in General," one could say that this meant relating penitential and sacramental practices to the nature of the church as a community. While the *ordo* (order) works with the Tridentine distinctions between contrition, confession, penance or satisfaction, and absolution,[2] it does so in such a way as to promote diversity, flexibility, and attention to individual needs within this familiar schema. It also endeavors to give the sacrament a more liturgical form, attentive to the structures of word, prayer, and rite that belong to any liturgical celebration, expecting this to be observed in even the most apparently private realizations of sacramental action.

To ensure a proper ecclesial setting to penance and reconciliation, the new order provides for three ways of celebrating the sacrament and also offers texts for use in communal celebrations of penance, with or without the celebration of

---

1. *Ordo Paenitentiae* (Vatican City: Vatican Polyglot Press, 1974).
2. Ibid., Praenotanda 6.

the sacrament. The first mode of the sacrament is that of individual confession to a priest with individual absolution, but more liturgically ordered than before. The second mode allows for the possibility for individual confession and absolution within a communal celebration of penance. The third mode allows for confession in the heart, followed by general absolution, within a communal celebration. The task of current theology is to provide a theological understanding of this revision in the light of the history of practice and doctrine, seeing how the church as a body over time integrates the abiding promise of divine forgiveness, the process of doing penance, and the reconciliation of sinners with God and with itself.

Scriptural Warrants

In the light of how the origin of sacraments is to be understood, we may return to scriptural warrants.[3] From these, it is seen what aspect of the gospel is being given symbolic and efficacious expression in penitential practice and how this may vary over time. The scriptural warrants cited for the offer of sacramental forgiveness within the life of the church as a body are most commonly: Matt. 16:18-19; Matt. 18:18; and John 21:22-23. These texts have to do, on the one hand, with the power given to the church to preach and assure the forgiveness of sins and, on the other, in the case of Matthew 18, with procedures for the excommunication of a certain type of sinner, in the hope of reconciliation.

In inscribing the memory of these warrants into ecclesial life, it is clear that the call to repentance and the assurance of forgiveness through God's mercy can be given in several ways. This is implemented first and foremost in baptism for the forgiveness of sins but includes preaching divine mercy, reconciliation of sinners with the communion of the church, and even devotional confession. The theological task is to relate this diversity and the single items in it to the reality of the church as the place within which, through Christ and Spirit, penance is asked, and forgiveness offered and guaranteed.

It is not easy to know accurately how serious sinners were dealt with in the early beginnings of the church. While some New Testament texts exhort to compassion, and fraternal correction was advised (Matt. 5:23-24; James 5:16), there were occasions when some form of excommunication and some form of binding and loosing seem to have been deemed necessary, as seen with Matthew 18 and confirmed elsewhere (e.g., 1 Cor. 5:3-5; 1 Tim. 1:19-20). The "binding and loosing" passages of Matthew 16 and 18 are about entry into the kingdom of God but also about the connections between being reconciled with the community and with God. Other texts (Heb. 6:4-6; Mark 3:29; Luke 12:10) are harder to interpret in practical terms and may simply have to do with constant obstinacy in the conduct of some of the baptized, who thus remained outside the fellowship and should be shunned.

Early History and Canonical Penance

Though clarity is lacking, we have some idea of how the church passed from penitential teaching and practices of the New Testament era to

---

3. These are briefly recalled in the *Catechism of the Catholic Church* 1443, 1444.

546 a practical discipline.[4] This has to do with attitudes that developed when the church moved from an age of high eschatological expectation to an era that looked to a longer future for the church on earth. This may be illustrated by comparing the *Pastor of Hermas* with Tertullian. *Hermas*, thinking in terms of the end of days or of the coming final judgment, allows for reconciliation before those days come.[5] The writer did not look ahead to a long duration because of his eschatological persuasions, but he did not wish to deny penance in the face of the forthcoming judgment to the baptized who had sinned grievously but sought repentance. Tertullian, in contrast, thinks in terms of a protracted period of time and of how the church may organize a discipline or an institution for its members that could provide for once-in-a-lifetime conversion, a conversion and an eventual forgiveness, which he called a second plank, comparing it with baptism. The conversion envisaged by Tertullian and by those who followed needed the passage of time, the activities of penance, and the guidance that would assure it was firmly grounded before the penitent's restoration to Eucharistic reconciliation.

If catechumenal preparation had been stringent enough and moral conversion assured before the forgiveness of sins in baptism, not many would so fall away that their expulsion would be necessary. However, cases did arise for different reasons, as we may see in the history of the early North African church and in the dispositions provided by Tertullian and

Cyprian. Tertullian speaks to catechumens of a "penitence which is undertaken but once and permanently preserved" and then reluctantly admits that God has permitted the door of forgiveness "closed and locked by the bar of Baptism, still to stand somewhat open."[6] This is no private matter, however; it is the concern of the whole community, as appears in what he says to sinners: "When you stretch forth your hands to the knees of your brethren, you are in touch with Christ.... When they shed tears for you, it is Christ who suffers."[7]

Novatians and Montanists in these early centuries objected to reconciliation of serious sinners and singled out three sins for which there could be no pardon: idolatry, murder, and adultery. Ecclesiastical writers or canons included these sins among those for which reconciliation was possible but for which long penance had to be undergone. They did not, however, confine public penance and reconciliation to these categories. According to Tertullian, becoming a penitent was required for this list of sins: idolatry, blasphemy, homicide, adultery, fornication, cheating, lying and false witness, and taking part in spectacles at the circus and in the stadium. After him, writers (among whom Augustine is prominent) give similar lists but with some internal variety. It has to be understood that the sins mentioned are acts known to others and seen as harmful to others and to the moral code of the ecclesial community. In that sense, it can be said that there was public penance for public faults. However, there are also

---

4. For an overview, see James Dallen, *The Reconciling Community: The Rite of Penance* (New York: Pueblo, 1986). A selection of texts in English translation is given in Paul F. Palmer, *Sacraments and Forgiveness* (Westminster, MD: Newman Press; London: Darton, Longman & Todd, 1959–61).

5. *Shepherd of Hermas*, Commandment 4,3. Cited in Palmer, *Sacraments and Forgiveness*, 12–15.

6. Tertullian *On Penitence* 6, 7, in *Treatises on Penance*, trans. William Le Saint (Westminster, MD: Newman, 1959), 23, 29.

7. Ibid., 10, in Palmer, *Sacraments and Forgiveness*, 33.

admonitions—for example, on the part of Leo the Great—that the sins of those who are in the order of penitents should not be publicized.[8] This may have had to do with people whose sins were known to some but whose reputation in the community at large Leo considered ought to be respected, or with persons who on their own initiative asked to be admitted to the order of penitents.

The ecclesial sense of penance and reconciliation is evident throughout the work and writings of Cyprian of Carthage.[9] He was concerned mainly with the possible reconciliation of apostates or lapsed. This affected his approach to baptism and his approach to public penance and reconciliation, so that from him, a sense of the theological meaning of the procedure emerges. His struggle over the issue of rebaptism and his postulates for public reconciliation go together and are rooted in his conception of the church as a communion in the Holy Spirit. Deprived of the Spirit, a sinner must receive it anew within the womb of the community. Doing penance over a period of time and reconciliation with the Eucharistic table were both necessary. To guide this process was an important part of the bishop's role, but the community too had to take a part in the penitential process, which must be done in the Spirit, for there is no peace or reconciliation with the church that does not communicate the Holy Spirit anew. Just as catechumens were helped by the liturgical prayer and support of the whole community, so too were penitents to be aided in this way.

In one of his sermons, Augustine mentions three kinds of penance for sin that had their place in the life of the church.[10] First there is the penance done by catechumens in preparation for baptism. Then there is the daily penance of every Christian through prayer, fasting, and good deeds, a way of constant amendment and conversion to a deeper following of Christ. In the third place is the severe penance, embraced with tears, done by those who have to be excluded from Eucharistic communion. Though he mentions other sins elsewhere, in this sermon he makes particular mention of those guilty of adultery, murder, and sacrilege. Persons impugned for such serious sin he likens to a corpse; they are as dead persons without the life of the Spirit. What is to be done with such sinners is dictated by the prescriptions of Matt. 18:18. They are to be bound to doing penance but loosed from their sin when penance is done, as Lazarus was loosed from the cloths that bound his body in the tomb.

Talking in particular against those who have separated themselves from the church, Augustine identifies the sin against the Holy Spirit. It is "the sin of impenitence against the gift of God and the grace of regeneration or reconciliation which takes place in the Church in the Holy Spirit."[11] This is in line with the thought of Cyprian already noted and also in line with Augustine's own thought about the church as a communion in the Holy Spirit. He affirms both that reconciliation is open to sinners, even schismatics, and that reconciliation is given through reception into the communion of the Spirit. Elsewhere, in addressing a correspondent about the persecution of the church in North Africa by the Vandals, he writes that

---

8. Leo the Great, *Epistola* 168 (PL 5, 1210).

9. For a collection of texts from Cyprian, see Paul Palmer, *Sacraments and Forgiveness*, 40–50.

10. Augustine, *Sermo* 352 (PL 39, 1549–60).

11. Augustine, *Sermo* 71, 12.23 (PL 38, 455).

548 bishops and priests should stay at their posts to minister baptism, give communion, admit to the discipline of penance, and reconcile those who are ready for this.[12]

Though much about the practice is known to us from the writings of bishops and others, if the penance done during the early centuries of the church is called canonical penance, this is because it was regulated by the canons of such councils as Elvira (306), Arles (314), Nicaea (325), Orange (441), Angers (453), and Orleans (511, 538) and by those laid down by bishops for their own churches. In the main, the procedure was simple. The sinner was to be enrolled in the order of penitents and refused Eucharistic communion. This was followed by a prescribed period, lasting years, in the order of penitents, when the person was engaged in prayer, fasting, and deeds of mercy and service. To quote one example, writing in the middle of the fourth century, Basil of Caesarea cites canons that are quite detailed about periods of penance exacted of sinners.[13] He demands twenty years of penance for intentional homicide, ten years for unintentional homicide, and fifteen for adultery. During the period of penance, the penitent would proceed through the grades or ranks of weepers, hearers, and kneelers before eventual reconciliation. Exorcisms could be pronounced over them during this time, as was done for catechumens on the way to baptism. When penitents were to be admitted anew to communion, there had to be a liturgy of public reconciliation over which the bishop presided and during which he laid hands on the petitioners.

Entering the order of penance thus meant taking on a discipline of long duration, which would require abstinence from sexual activity as well as other bodily penances and which prevented persons from taking on certain kinds of office or occupation. This penance and reconciliation was allowed only once in a lifetime, but its imposition allowed of one exception. A dying person was never to be refused viaticum if this person showed true repentance. A consequence of this, however, was that if such a person recovered, he or she then had to enter the order of penitents for a time prescribed by the bishop.

In all of this, there is an integrated notion of church initiation, and the need for continuing communal and personal conversion. For contemporary Christians, it is sometimes difficult to appreciate how much the early churches regarded the initiation commitments made by adult converts as definitive. This initial and gratuitous forgiveness of sins was often referred to by the Greek term *aphesis* (gratuitous forgiveness) to distinguish it from the postbaptismal need to continue in the way of conversion (*metanoia*). What came gradually to light was that the mercy of God is without limit so that those who violated their baptism and sinned against God and against the church could be forgiven. Such forgiveness does not come lightly but supposes a true moral conversion, a true change in one's way of life comparable to what was required of catechumens.

If the lists of sinners on whom penance was imposed varied from place to place and from one period of time to another, this is because the gravity of sins and the harm done by them was affected by the social and cultural context in which churches lived, as well as by reference to the Scriptures and to common codes of conduct that people valued. The bishop is the leading figure in pronouncing on sin and effecting

---

12. Augustine, *Epistola* 228.8 (PL 33.1016).
13. Basil of Caeserea *Ad Amphilochium* (PG 32, 728). See Palmer, *Sacraments and Forgiveness*, 74–76.

reconciliation, but the process from entering the order of penitents to reconciliation can benefit from other pastoral and spiritual guides, and the whole community is expected to participate in strengthening and comforting sinners. The part of the community is expressed in the public liturgies of enrollment in the order of penitents and reconciliation, as well as in regular community prayer for them and for catechumens.[14]

There are principles grounding early practices that the church wants to retrieve in today's revision of its penitential system. It does not want to copy the discipline as it was then known, but it believes that even as we are trusting in the abundant mercy of God, any renewal has to take account of the gravity of sins that seriously violate a Christian mode of behavior, that true conversion from sin takes time, and that penance and reconciliation are matters for the church community and not simply for individuals.

However, there are also lessons to be learned from the ultimate failure of this discipline. The circumstances and devotional life of the members of the church changed in such a way that canonical penance did not fit into their lives. Many were baptized as infants and hence without the rigorous preparation for baptism supposed by the catechumenate. If they were to learn to live a more Christian life or to be healed of their sins, this could not be done practically by entering the order of penitents, since this impeded living a regular existence. Some pastors even therefore encouraged young people to put off penance until later in life and to continue going to church, even if not receiving communion, or indeed to receive communion with remorse for their sins and the intention of doing penance when this became possible. Frequent communion was also on the decline, so refusal of admission to the communion table did not seem so strong a penalty. On the other hand, for some, becoming a penitent seemed a desirable way of life, even if they were not obliged to it, so that by the sixth century, most of those who entered the order did so by way of adopting a way of life somewhat akin to the monastic life. They might even enter monasteries, not as choir monks but as *conversi*, or those seeking to sanctify themselves by a life of penance and work within the monastic enclosure. A lesson to be learned from all of this is that if penitential discipline and the possibility of reconciliation are not adapted to life's conditions, it fades into the background for the majority of people.

Daily Sins

To complete the picture for early centuries as background to our own age, we have to know what was done about daily sin. While those baptized had been forgiven and cleansed, it was never thought that they were free of all sinfulness and transgression. Thus, from the beginning, Christians were encouraged to confess their sins to one another, some public avowal of sin in community gatherings was normal, and the Eucharist itself was said to be for the forgiveness of sins. Following the instructions of Jesus, every believer had to pray often, fast, and practice deeds of mercy such as almsgiving for the remission of their sins. At special times of the year, the whole community engaged as one in such acts of penance. Tertullian thought that fasting was the proper preparation for communion, not just out of respect, but because we are sinners. Origen lists seven ways for the Christian to obtain the forgiveness of sins: besides baptism for those entering the church and the remission of

---

14. For examples of liturgies, see Palmer, *Sacraments and Forgiveness*, 120–22.

550 sins through following the discipline imposed on penitents, for others there are the suffering of martyrdom, almsgiving, fraternal forgiveness, fraternal correction, and charity.[15]

Both Eastern and Western traditions knew the practice of spiritual guidance from early days. By the time of John Chrysostom, we find him advising members of the congregation to seek guides among the monks and, along with other things, to be ready to confess their sins to their guides. Of course, there were frequent admonitions by pastors to confess one's sins before God in prayer, and this can be done without an intermediary.[16] Indeed, confessing to God is what is ultimately sought through any process, but confession to a holy person or spiritual guide was thought a fitting help to assure that one recognized and acknowledged offense against God in the hope of divine forgiveness. Confession to God or to a spiritual guide may well have been a common way of dealing in those days with what today would be considered serious sins, needing to be confessed to a priest. In those times, they would not have warranted entry into the order of penitents, since they did not bring public disrepute.

Over against these various ways in which people sought to be forgiven their daily sins, the need to be pardoned makes sense of the common exhortation of pastors that people should trust in God's forgiveness. In the Easter homily that is still read today in the Byzantine liturgy, John Chrysostom invites all to the Easter banquet, even those who have not done Lenten penance but have come only at the eleventh hour. Similarly, Maximus of Turin at the Paschal Vigil advises that no one, conscious of sins, should "withdraw from our common celebration," for "sinner though he may be, he must not despair of pardon on this day which is so highly privileged."[17]

In the West, and especially in Celtic Christianity, the way to perfection was conceived in more ascetic terms. In monasteries, each monk had to have a guide, but the people too could have resort to monks for guidance and, in this context, for the confession of daily sins. In neither case, Eastern or Western, was it necessary for the guide to be a priest, and women who followed the rule of life could act as such as well as men. This practice of confessing daily sins within the context of spiritual guidance has to be considered today when ordinary Catholics are recommended more frequent confession as a way of advancing in the way of spiritual growth and communion with God.

Medieval Changes in Penitential Practice

In describing the development of penance in the West, writers tend to move from canonical penance to what they call "tariff" penance, which spread across Europe through the missionary work of Celtic monks, who were often priests.[18] Using the term *tariff* could be misleading, since imposing a set penance established by a code was not the main feature of what the monks did. In its main outline, the work of the monks offered the possibility of being admitted to penance and reconciliation more than once in the

---

15. Origen On *Leviticus, Homily* 2. Cited in Palmer, *Sacraments and Forgiveness*, 35–36.
16. E.g., John Chrysostom, *On Lazarus, Homily* 4,4 (PG 48, 1012). Cited in Palmer, *Sacraments and Forgiveness*, 85.
17. Maximus of Turin *Sermo* 53, 4 (CCL, 23, 216).
18. For an overview, see Dallen, *The Reconciling Community*, 104–11.

course of a lifetime, of confessing privately to a monk/priest, of doing penance under his guidance according to the penance he imposed, and then of receiving reconciliation through his action. The two most striking characteristics of this historical shift are the disappearance of the public order of penitents doing penance in the bosom of the church and the possibility of recourse to penance and reconciliation more than once before the end of one's life.

In the context of a changing cultural scene, this was an adaptation of a monastic rule that provided for confession to one of the monks and doing penance under his guidance. Within monasteries, this penance had to do with infringements of the rule and the monastic way of life. Rules, as rules are wont, could be quite detailed, so they listed penances to be served for specific faults, and this is why historians find it suitable to speak of tariffs for sins. When what are known as penitential books adapted this to service among laypersons on the European continent, the list of sins and tariffs were, of course, wide-ranging. It needs to be remembered, however, that the first adoption of this procedure still required a considerable period of penance before reconciliation and that it incorporated a system of spiritual guidance known quite widely and not only in the Celtic church. With a discerning guide, the application of the tariffs could be flexible. Attaching specific penances to specific sins was in any case not simply a Celtic invention but was an idea of which we have found an example in the canons of Basil, previously mentioned.

As the church passed from the first millennium of its existence into the second, we also notice a marked emphasis on the act of confession to God made through confession to another person, whether it was a seriously sinful person's confession with remorse or a devout individual's confession of lesser sins. This involves the kind of communion between confessor and penitent that is expressed, for example, by Lanfrance of Canterbury: "The Lord in his person declared that confession is a threefold sacrament: it is a figure of baptism, it is one conscience formed out of two, and it is the sacrament of God and the human person united in one judgment."[19] He goes on to explain that the conscience of the one who confesses is fused with the conscience of the confessor in judging sin and that this itself is a sign of the unity resembling that of Father and Son, which Jesus besought for his followers.

The value attributed to confession itself as an expression of contrition explains why absolution from sin came to be proclaimed by the priest before the penitent performed the acts of penance imposed, though these were still intended as a spiritual remedy, a follow-up on the diagnosis of the malady. In this way, a new sequence of acts was introduced into sacramental reconciliation: contrition of the heart, confession of sin, absolution from sin, and acts of penance that would be medicinal as well as calculated to make satisfaction to remedy harm done. First and foremost, the priest confessor was to exercise his role as *medicus* (doctor). In practice, the image of making satisfaction or paying a debt seemed at times to prevail. This gave rise to the commutations that allowed some prayers to substitute for fasting and to the habit of giving stipends to monasteries, in exchange for which the women and men of the monasteries would offer prayers to satisfy the debt of the one giving the stipend or of the dead for whom prayers and Mass were offered. Hence, the evolution of how sacramental penance was understood was tied

---

19. Lanfranc of Canterbury, *De celanda confessione* (PL 150, 626–27).

552 to the development of the notions of purgatory, prayers for the dead, and indulgences.

The accent put on the salutary nature of an act of contrite confession had another consequence: It meant that quasi-sacramental value was attributed to confessions made to laypersons. This could be done in the case of serious sin when a priest was not attainable. In the case of venial sin, confession to a layperson was always possible, since this did not require priestly absolution. Thomas Aquinas takes account of this practice when he says confession to a layperson with the desire for the sacrament can bring forgiveness of serious sin and that all confession of venial sins to fellow Christians is a kind of sacrament.[20]

The official transition to mandated annual confession that followed the sequence of confession, absolution, and penance was made at the Fourth Lateran Council in 1215 (DS 812), obliging the Christian faithful to confess their sins annually on the occasion of the Pasch. This edict was given at a time when the church feared the diffusion of dualistic heresies, and it was conceived as an instrument for eradicating this from among the faithful. Once established, however, it became the means of dealing with all manner of sins, and manuals were composed to guide confessors in exercising this ministry in a way appropriate to the various kinds of sins, great and small, that people might confess.

Scholastic Theology

Scholastic theology worked with the procedures adopted in the previous centuries and explained the sacrament as something administered within the internal forum, without public confession or penance of any sort. The relations between confession, contrition, and absolution were diversely explained. Commonly sincere contrition, made out of love for God above all things, could be seen as the moment when the sinner was indeed one anew with God. It could not, however, be seen as the cause of forgiveness, which was the sacramental absolution given by the priest in the exercise of the power of the keys. Some thought such perfect contrition needed to accompany confession and hence precede the absolution, which pronounced forgiveness in the name of Christ as the priest imposed the penance to be done. Others thought imperfect contrition for lesser motives was sufficient and that the power of the sacrament gave the grace of true contrition perfected in charity. To explain the imposition of penitential acts, images of medicine were combined with those of making satisfaction for harm done so as to receive remission of temporal punishment remaining due. The two features together combined to present the image of Christ, primary instrumental cause of the sacrament, as both Shepherd and Judge.

Thomas Aquinas applied the distinctions of matter and form: the acts of the penitent are the matter, and the act of the priest in pronouncing absolution is the form. This was a way of showing how the acts of the penitent and the act of the priest are one sacramental reality. Aquinas was one of those who believed that perfect contrition is needed for a person to receive the forgiveness pronounced in absolution, but he explained that the power of the sacrament can give this at the moment when priestly absolution is imparted, even when it may have been missing before. Thus it is that the sinner always receives forgiveness with a truly sincere contrition.[21]

---

20. Thomas Aquinas, *Summa theologiae, supplementum,* q. 8, art. 2.

Reformers and the Council of Trent

The sequence of contrition, confession, absolution, and satisfaction was the one presumed in the decree on the sacrament promulgated by the Council of Trent. It was a procedure whose doctrinal and disciplinary value was affirmed in face of the accusations of the Reformers. Though Martin Luther retained the practice of confessing sin in his Large and Small Catechisms, he would not call that practice sacrament, since he found no scriptural warrant for its institution by Christ. Likewise, he found that as practiced in his time, confession to a priest instilled fear of punishment in the hearts of sinners instead of trust in the promise of forgiveness made known in the Cross of Christ.

Some of Luther's propositions condemned by Leo X in 1520 show what he refused to accept in confessional practice: "By no means presume to confess venial sins, and for that matter not even all mortal sins, because it is impossible for you to recall all mortal sins. Accordingly, only manifest mortal sins were confessed in the primitive church. When we sincerely desire to confess everything, we desire in effect to leave nothing for God's mercy to forgive" (DS 1458–59). His account of what was done in the primitive church was of course correct, but the fathers at Trent did not accept his reasoning about what was to be confessed in his and their own day.

In response to such a challenge, the Council of Trent defined the institution of the sacrament of penance by Christ and described it doctrinally according to the fourfold division that had become customary (DS 1667–93). In explaining the works of satisfaction, while proposing the remedial purpose of such penances, it puts a forceful accent on making satisfaction, pursuing an analogy with a tribunal of judgment. Even when sins are forgiven, according to this analogy, reparation has to be made and temporal punishment remitted.

How rigidly this analogy is to be taken has been queried by a number of contemporary theologians, anxious to retrieve the early church vision of penance done with guidance as the way of conversion and the act of the bishop as reconciliation rather than judgment. The Tridentine decree itself tempers the analogy with a tribunal of judgment. What it highlights is the need to overcome the disorders that remain in a person even after sin has been forgiven and that have to be remedied. Furthermore, it stresses that acts of satisfaction can be made only in Christ, "in whom we make satisfaction by bringing forth fruits of repentance," and that it is from him that they have their efficacy, as it is through him that penances are offered to the Father (DS 1691).[22]

When the 1614 *Rituale Romanum* provided a revised rite for the sacrament in the light of the council, it proposed a confession of sins made in the light of a careful examination of conscience in order to enumerate them to the confessor in number and kind. Other liturgical elements were neglected. Subsequently, in light of the theory of *ex opere operato* efficacy, many Catholics had recourse to the sacrament to receive the grace of the sacrament and its help in guarding against future sin.

In more recent times, historians and theologians alike brought into light the communal understanding of penance of the early church,

---

21. For a complex explanation of how a sinner moves from servile fear to filial fear, see *Summa theologiae* III, q. 85, art. 5.
22. This is cited in the revised *Codex Iuris Canonici*, can. 1460.

as well as the process of conversion involved in seeking sacramental reconciliation.[23] This was one of the influences that led Vatican II in SC 72 to ask for a revision of the rite that would show the social and ecclesial nature of the sacrament as well as the true nature of its effects.

Contemporary Theology: Sin, Reconciliation, the Personal, and the Social

The new order of penance and the *Catechism of the Catholic Church* both explain the sacrament in terms of its parts, which are confession, contrition, absolution, and satisfaction, so this will probably continue to dominate in Catholic theology and catechesis. However, this is put in a setting that is christological and ecclesial, indicating how it belongs to the mystery of the forgiveness offered in Jesus Christ and to the mystery of the church as a community. What contemporary writers seek to do is to accentuate the christological and ecclesial aspects of the sacrament and to bring out the human aspect by relating the four acts belonging to the sacramental process to an inner process of conversion in the heart and life of the sinner.

Access to the sacrament is placed within a large construct of ecclesial life, which includes communal and personal acts of penance, the pursuit of forgiveness or of perfection, communal prayer, and a proper relation to the liturgical calendar. This accentuates the celebration of the sacrament as the symbolic action of exchange, in which the pardon of God is extended to a sinful humanity and in which the repentant sinner is incorporated into the Eucharistic communion of the church or strengthened in it. When penance and reconciliation are considered in this way, some elements of the tradition are put in better focus.

Contrition

In line with the thought of Thomas Aquinas, Karl Rahner explains why contrition is placed at the heart of the sacrament. Contrition is a profound sorrow for having offended God's love, together with the firm purpose of sinning no more. One cannot truly expect forgiveness without this. Rahner points out that this is the oldest and most classical element of the church's teaching and practice. As he puts it, the penitent "is not only the passive recipient of this grace but is the one who, together with the priest, actively celebrates the sacred *mysterium* itself, which is the sacramental cause of grace which he receives."[24] If, as Aquinas says, the sacrament can transform imperfect contrition into true love, Rahner sees this as the ecclesial dimension of penance. The very fact that sinners bring their perhaps imperfect dispositions and their request for forgiveness to the public forum of confession is a way of relating oneself to the sacramental reality of the church as Christ's mystery in which the imperfect acts of a penitent may be perfected so that the ecclesial act is the sign of the effective presence of God's forgiving grace.

---

23. For example, Bernard Poschmann, *Penance and the Anointing of the Sick* (New York: Herder & Herder, 1964). Poschmann's original study in German appeared in 1940.

24. Karl Rahner, "Forgotten Truths Concerning the Sacrament of Penance," in *Theological Investigations* (New York: Crossroad, 1982), 2:135–74.

Personal Confession

To these considerations on contrition one can add the thought of Hans Urs von Balthasar on personal confession. In this he finds a model for the understanding of all sacramental life inasmuch as it is an exemplary instance of the encounter in Christ between the sinner and the forgiving God. While it is personal, this is not to be understood as a purely individual act. Sin has social consequences and consequences for the church community, but confession of sin and the offer of divine forgiveness also have communal implications. As von Balthasar says, "In me the whole Church confesses my solidarity with the sins of many, with the sins of all—just as in me the whole Church also goes to communion."[25] Whatever about the historical developments of the sacramental form recorded in history, its ground is found in the very reality of Christ as Redeemer, the one in whom a human person bearing the weight of sin and the God who forgives encounter each other.[26] While confession to an ordained minister is the primary form of penitence, confession to fellow Christians when grave sin is not involved can help rehabilitate the purpose and significance of confession as a celebration of the forgiveness given in Christ and the church. In this teaching, von Balthasar is one with the teaching of medieval writers.

The Sin Confessed

A challenge in renewing sacramental practice is to give importance to the ways in which sin is estimated and sins are numbered. In proclaiming that through the death of one, the Second Adam, all have been justified, Paul proclaimed that in the first Adam, all are sinners or are held in sin (Rom. 5:12-19). The sin of one cannot be seen except in relation to the sin of all and to the solidarity in sin, which can be overcome only in the solidarity with Christ of a renewed humanity. This sense of a double solidarity is constant in the church's penitential practice.

We learned further from history, noting the differences in different epochs, that the church over time specified what is sinful or what required sacramental forgiveness in different ways. In the early church, though lists differed from place to place or from time to time, those sins deemed pardonable only by public penance were ones that transgressed what is most fundamental to the life of the church and its respect for persons and communities. Apostasy had a prominent place on lists, as did such matters as murder, adultery, and harming the property or the reputation of others. In the introduction of a type of Celtic penance to the European landmass, the concern was with a new population and a new kind of Christianity where careful preparation for baptism could not be taken for granted. The penitential books in listing sins had in mind the conversion, often slow and gradual, of the already baptized to an ethical code that was truly Christian. Since sinners were never to be left without the hope of forgiveness and since they need the continual aid of a discipline of penance, pardon could be offered more than once in a lifetime.

In this light, today also the church has to consider the reality of sin and its consequences within the personal, social, and cultural context

---

25. Hans Urs von Balthasar, "Personal Confession," in *The Von Balthasar Reader*, ed. Medard Kehl and Werner Löser (New York: Crossroad, 1985), 281.

26. *The Glory of the Lord*, vol. 1, *Seeing the Form* (San Francisco: Ignatius, 1982), 581.

556 of these times. It is never enough to calculate sin on the basis of a mechanical reading of the Ten Commandments. These were never precepts that considered the person in isolation from the community, but they portray sin as the violation of the worship due God and of the tranquility of order in the life of the whole people. Helped by considerations of the past, we have some indications of how sin is to be estimated today. In administering its discipline, pastors of the church have to consider which sins are grave sins that need to be recognized as offenses against God and against neighbor, or indeed against society. Clearly, the more obvious violations of human life constantly require penance and pardon. Beyond this, within the compass of social reality today, Christians must reckon with different sorts of exploitation of others, especially where the rights and needs of the poorer are harmed by the ambitions of the richer, or where the fabric of society and of the environment is injured in the pursuit of personal gratification.

Communal Celebrations

Communal celebrations place confession and forgiveness within a larger sacramental structure, which includes proclamation of the Word, a communal quest to understand and confess sin, and prayer of both penitence and praise, making the confession of sin also a confession of praise. In line with earlier points, one of the reasons for giving a due place to communal celebrations of penance and the prophetic word to which they can allow space is to guide people—priests and the faithful—in reaching a true evaluation of what is sinful conduct in relation to the life of the community and to the world around it. We might well wonder about the gospel values held by Christians or about the values of their witness to Christ, and what a church community may see as sinful. On various occasions, church leaders have ruminated on the sins particularly harmful to morality today. They have spoken of such matters as different forms of sexual abuse, abortion, harm done to the ecology, discrimination of different kinds, dishonesty in one's way of meeting terms of employment, whether as employer or employee, and property speculation hurtful to others and to the economic order.

Such rumination has to fit into particular human and social realities, as we might see, for example, in the preparation of synods for churches from different continents. The preparatory document for the Synod of Africa held in 2008 speaks of such matters as racial violence, sexual misconduct that is harmful to others (especially in the time of AIDS), sexual violence, the exploitation of peoples on the part of governments and government servants, and graft and corruption.[27] It also takes note of relapse into superstitious practices that are not consonant with Christian faith, seeking to alert the faithful to what a conversion to Christ truly means within their cultures. Such fresh looks at sin are an attempt to guide moral behavior in relation to the order of our times.

The elements of penance brought to the fore in community prayer are those that were all too easily missed in the exclusive practice of private confession. These are (a) a new conscientization to what is sinful and its harmfulness and of how the sin of each belongs within the solidarity of sin within which humankind and particular peoples are joined; (b) a better appreciation of the nature of confession of sin within a fuller li-

---

27. "Synod of Bishops: Second Special Assembly for Africa; The Church in Africa in Service to Reconciliation, Justice and Peace (*Lineamenta*)," *L'Osservatore Romano*, Weekly Edition in English, no. 29 (1953), July 19, 2006, 3–14.

turgical context, especially the proclamation of the word and its prophetic interpretation; (c) a use of symbolic language suited to the relation that exists between moral judgment and faith commitment and including confession of sin within a confession of praise.

Apart from what is done through the sacrament of penance, for the Christian community as a corporate body, there is the need to review the avenues along which it embodies constant repentance and reconciliation. Fasting, vigil, deeds of mercy, and pilgrimage belonged to the communal past and to some extent still have their place. When communal celebrations of penance are related to the liturgical calendar, to pilgrimage, or to what are otherwise public occasions, this is an apt way of placing sin within the context of being a community that follows the Lord together and of relating the sacramental act to the total discipline of doing penance together.

Something else to keep in mind in today's practice is the constant relation between the confession of sin and spiritual guidance. This is helpful to those who need deep conversion or a difficult overcoming of sinful habits. It is also helpful to those who do not strictly need sacramental absolution but take confession as a means of pursuing a more devout life and mapping their lives by fidelity to the gospel. Confessors have to attune their ministry to this need and desire. It is something that may help pastors and the faithful value confession to competent laypersons as this was valued in the past, since faithful members of the laity may be good spiritual guides for those who seek to be faithful to Christ but are ever conscious of their sinfulness and need for God's mercy.

Penitential practice and its sacramental moment cannot be properly renewed without considering the place to be given to compassion toward sinners, as well as appreciating the Eucharist itself as a communion in the ultimate sacrament of forgiveness. In this, the church is inspired by some of the Gospel stories about forgiveness, such as that of the two sons or the stray sheep (Luke 17). Given circumstances of time, the pressure of cultural attitudes, and subsequent moral perplexities, such as new questions regarding those who have procured abortions, those divorced and remarried, the life of married persons who have to accept periodic separation from spouse and family due to working conditions, and homosexual conduct, we cannot act as though there were ready-made answers to these situations. In these cases, spiritual guidance has to be offered with the possibility of pursuing life in a Christian way, whatever has happened in the past or whatever one's situation has become. To pretend that there is already a formal or official answer to this would be wrong, but as the church continues its way of prayerful inquiry, all these persons and others not mentioned have to be treated as members of the church to whom God's forgiveness is ever offered.

In talking of the renewal of the sacrament in line with tradition, a word is needed about the third mode of celebration allowed by the official *Order of Penance*. This is general confession with general absolution. The possibility is certainly offered with care and restrictions in mind and with attention to the ongoing importance of personal confession. However, it is a genuine sacramental action that involves the community and is meant to help individual sinners. It is not to be dismissed as something to be avoided, but the opportunities it offers have to be judged wisely and with pastoral discernment. It is not intended solely for serious sinners who need to make a personal avowal, but it is intended for all who would be helped by a sacramental expression of God's call to conversion and of the ecclesial assurance of pardon and peace for

558 sinners. To forbid it because some might use it to seek cheap grace seems unwarranted. Given the difficulties often experienced by people today in finding personal confession possible, a more generous use of this form may be indicated.

Conclusion

Offering a theology of sacramental penance and reconciliation has been somewhat difficult because of its involved history of changing practices and perspectives. The gospel warrants for the offer of forgiveness have to be appropriated in accord with the reality of the church as a communion in Christ and the Spirit. The sacrament has to be put into a wider context of penitential requirements and practices. Its own inner liturgical and spiritual structure has to be duly respected, and the different components seen in relation to one another as constituting a complex whole.

For Further Reading

Coffey, David M. *The Sacrament of Reconciliation.* Collegeville, MN: Liturgical, 2001.

> *A theology of the sacrament, relating it to a theology of sin and to current Catholic practice.*

Dallen, James. *The Reconciling Community: The Rite of Penance.* Collegeville, MN: Liturgical, 1992.

> *The history, theology, and practice of sacramental reconciliation, with special attention to the revised order.*

Palmer, Paul J., ed. *Sacraments and Forgiveness: History and Doctrinal Development of Penance, Extreme Unction and Indulgences.* Westminster, MD: Newman, 1959.

> *A still very useful collection of conciliar, patristic, and theological primary sources, in English translation.*

Poschmann, Bernhard. *Penance and the Anointing of the Sick.* New York: Herder & Herder, 1964.

> *A summary of the history of penance and reconciliation by one of the great historians of the sacrament.*

Rahner, Karl. *Theological Investigations.* Vols. 2, 3, 6, 15. New York: Crossroad, 1982.

———. *Theological Investigations.* Vol. 10. New York: Seabury, 1977.

> *Several articles on the sacrament of penance that relate it to Rahner's basic sacramental theology.*

Sacraments

Anointing of the Sick

David N. Power

Post–Vatican II Revisions of the Order

The most recent revision of the liturgy for the sacrament of the sick highlights the fact that it is an ecclesial sacrament and should be celebrated as an act of the church,[1] not reduced to a minimal anointing, as tended to be the case when it was used primarily as extreme unction. It belongs in a fuller ecclesial context of care for the sick and dying, and this is why the order asks for at least a minimal gathering of faithful around the sick person and for a celebration that includes a liturgy of the Word and a prayer of blessing or thanksgiving. While allowing for the blessing of the oil by the priest celebrating the sacrament, it prefers the use of the oil blessed by the bishop during Holy Week, along with the blessing of the oils of chrism and catechumenate (OUI 21). It is also recalled that the proper sacrament for the dying is Eucharistic communion, food for the journey or *viaticum* (OUI 26).

While the order took seriously the prescription of the council that anointing is more properly called the sacrament of the sick than the sacrament of those who are at the point of death,[2] it remains open to interpretation on the recipients and effects of the sacrament. It says that, through it the grace of the Holy Spirit is given to help the person toward salvation (*salus*), aiding the infirm in both mind and body against the temptations that go with sickness (OUI 6). It may even empower someone to fight against succumbing to illness in such a way that health (*sanitas*) may be restored should it be appropriate to spiritual welfare. While the order says that the sacrament is given to the elderly or the sick who are dangerously ill (*periculose aegrotant*), it allows for repeated anointings within the same illness. Notably, the order says that the elderly who are weak may receive this sacrament even if not expecting immediate death, and that it can be given before surgery that carries the risk of death.

Practice and usage have to determine over time how these injunctions are to be interpreted and what constitutes a reasonable judgment about whether an illness may be considered sufficiently serious to warrant anointing (OUI 8). Whatever broad uses may be made by the faithful of holy oil as of holy water, the sacrament as such is not to be reduced to a passing remedy or treated lightly, no more than it is to be taken as a sign of rapidly approaching death.

Scriptural Warrants

Given the gradual way in which the sacramental system developed in the life of the church, it is difficult to say when exactly the anointing of the sick could be said to have assumed the status of a community sacramental liturgy. Healing as a charismatic ministry had a place from the beginning, as did care of the dying. To lay hands on the sick was part of the commission given by Jesus to the Twelve when he sent them forth to preach the Gospel, for this exercise of charism was to serve as testimony to the resurrection (Mark 16:18). Care of the sick was enjoined on early disciples as a community responsibility (1 Cor. 12:19; James 5:14-16).

---

1. *Ordo Unctionis Infirmorum Eorumque Pastoralis Cura* (Vatican City: Vatican Polyglot Press, 1972), 5–7, 33; hereafter cited as OUI.

2. *Sacrosanctum concilium* (Vatican II's Constitution on the Sacred Liturgy), 73.

The most common scriptural warrant given for the sacrament of anointing, sanctioned by the sacramental definitions of the Council of Trent, is James 5:14-15. This, however, is to be seen in tandem with the care for the sick that Jesus commended to his disciples, as well with his own ministry of healing, which attested to his mission from the Father for the salvation of humankind. As far as practice is concerned, that the early church gave a generous interpretation to James 5:14-15 is clearly stated by Innocent I in a letter to Decentius of Gubbio in 416. Of this text, he says, "This must undoubtedly be understood as referring to the faithful who are sick and can be anointed with the holy oil of chrism which the bishop has prepared and which is to be used for anointing not only by priests but by all Christians in their own need or that of their families" (DS 216).

Historical Overview

In keeping with this position on the meaning of James 5, we know that in early centuries, alongside the practice of laying hands on the sick, there was a rather fluid use of blessed oil. While it was deemed appropriate for bishops to anoint the sick when on pastoral visitation of a community, the oil could otherwise be used by any Christian to anoint someone else or even oneself. Besides using the oil for anointing, the sick might also drink it or rub it into infected parts of the body. This was not restricted, it appears, to use in serious sickness, and furthermore, the previous quotation from Innocent indicates that the oil used could be chrism, rather than an oil specially blessed for the sick.

Sometimes, however, the blessing of oil for this specific purpose appears in early liturgical formulas. For example, the *Apostolic Tradition* says that after the blessing of the bread and wine for Eucharist, the bishop could make thanks over oil that the faithful brought, wishing to use it for their comfort in illness, whether by using it externally or drinking it.[3] The earliest Latin or Roman formula we have is found in the Gelasian[4] and Gregorian[5] Sacramentaries, and there it is also placed within the liturgy of the Eucharist. These prayers relate the oil for the sick to the biblical anointing of priests, kings, prophets, and martyrs. This comparison would, of course, make sense if the oil were comparable to the oil of chrism, but it also indicates that its use made it possible for the ill to give the testimony of their faith in an act of worship, a testimony to be compared with that of all the anointed of the Lord. The Latin formulas suggest that the healing power expected of the oil is that it may serve as a safeguard for body, mind, and spirit. This respects the fact that persons who are ill are affected in every way or in the fullness of their being as humans, and not only in their bodies.

Liturgical rituals also place the anointing with oil in a fuller context of care for the sick.[6] Composed mostly for use in monasteries, these rituals include orders for visiting the sick, communion to the sick, the assistance of the dying,

---

3. *The Treatise on the Apostolic Tradition of Hippolytus*, ed. and trans. Gregory Dix (1968; repr. London: Alban, 1992), 18–19.

4. *Liber Sacramentorum Romanae Aeclesiae Ordinis Anni Circuli*, ed. L. K. Mohlberg (Rome: Herder, 1960), 382.

5. *Le sacramentaire Grégorien: Ses principales formes d'après les plus anciens manuscrits*, ed. Jean Deshusses (Fribourg: Editions Universitaires, 1979), 334.

6. For an overview, see A. G. Martimort, "Prayer for the Sick and Sacramental Anointing," in *The Church at Prayer*, ed. A. G. Martimort (Collegeville, MN: Liturgical, 1992), 3:120–22.

562

and viaticum for the dying, as well as formulas for the anointing either in the course of sickness or when the person comes close to death. A possible return to good health is often envisaged in these prayers, but whether the sick person awaits recovery or is thought to be ready for death, a healing in body and spirit is expected of the anointing. A person, even in a last illness, cannot be given spiritual help as a person and a child of God without also enjoying some corporal alleviation.

The medieval association of anointing with death, or its use as extreme unction, is related to the effective demise of canonical penance, when many deferred reconciliation until their deathbed. Gradually restricted to the ministry of priests, anointing was associated with the offering of pardon for sin and took on its appearance as sacrament of the dying, even when viaticum was given, sometimes even putting viaticum before the anointing when the two were done in sequence. What was done was then prescribed as the canonical rule, namely, that unction of the sick should be reserved as unction for the dying.

Scholastic theology took this practice as norm and hence wrote of the anointing of sick as extreme unction, given to those preparing for death. In the words of Thomas Aquinas, the effect conforms to the signification: "As baptism is a kind of spiritual rebirth, and penance a kind of spiritual resurrection, so extreme unction is a kind of spiritual healing or medication."[7] It is not meant as an antidote to mortal sin but is meant to give the spiritual strength needed for living a life of grace or glory. It offers the grace to overcome the debilities that remain after sin,

though when penance is impossible and with contrition on the part of the recipient, it can remit sins themselves.

The sixteenth-century Reformers did not eliminate all use of anointing the sick as an ecclesiastical custom, but they denied that it could be taken as a sacrament. The Council of Trent therefore defined that anointing of the sick is to feature in the sevenfold list of sacraments instituted by Christ (DS 1705). While not departing greatly from practice and from Scholastic theology, it did define anointing as a sacrament of the sick, to be given "especially to those who are so dangerously ill that they seem near to death" (DS 1694). This sacrament confers the grace of the Spirit to remove sin and its remnants and to strengthen the recipient through trust in God in the face of suffering and temptations. The council even added—with some reference to earlier church practice, it would seem—that the sacrament could give physical healing if this is helpful to salvation (DS 1696). Whatever broadening of the use of the sacrament this might seem to allow, it had no practical consequences in the Roman Ritual of 1614 or thereafter.

Theological Reflections

The retrieval by historical studies of the whole liturgical tradition clearly broadened the use and meaning of this sacrament as a sacrament of the sick.[8] A starting point for theological reflection is to see anointing as a particular participation in the Paschal Mystery and a participation in the life of the Eucharistic communion of the church. As the late Regis Duffy observed in the

---

7. *Summa theologiae, supplementum* q. 30, art. 1, c.
8. For a survey, see John Kasza, *Understanding Sacramental Healing* (Chicago: Liturgical Training, 2005).

first edition of this collection,[9] the mystery of suffering is placed through anointing into the ambit of the Paschal Mystery into which the sick person was initiated in baptism: "The calling down of the Holy Spirit, with the forgiveness of sins proper to anointing, enriches our understanding and experience of the forgiveness first extended in the initiating sacraments and then in penance and reconciliation."[10] What is expressed is faith in God's justifying and healing action as it is afforded us through the Son and the Spirit, in the passage from death to life. This is captured in the sacramental form: "Through this holy anointing may the Lord in His love and mercy help you with the grace of the Holy Spirit. May the Lord who frees you from sin save you and raise you up" (OUI 25). The linking between the worship of the church and those who are sick was expressed in some medieval prayers by way of asking that the person "be restored to worship" and, of course, by the sending of Communion from the assembly to the sick of the locality.

While the anointing of the sick is now restricted to the ministry of the priests, if the authority of the church chose to allow some form of anointing by laypersons, this would have a warrant in early ecclesial tradition. All the faithful, moreover, are encouraged to assume their ministry of aiding the sick, bodily and spiritually. This means meditating on the Scriptures with them, praying with them, and indeed praying over them, even with a laying on of hands, just as parents bless their children in this way.

This ministry creates the fuller context of the church's care for the sick, within which anointing and finally viaticum are given.[11]

Beyond these points, theological reflection has pursued two avenues of thought. One focuses on how a person may be helped by the grace of the Spirit in face of all that assails one physically, mentally, and spiritually in face of grave sickness. The other looks to how the celebration may embody a Christian theology of suffering in configuration to Christ, comforted by him and giving witness to faith and the hope of the resurrection even in weakness.

The first line of thought is inspired by a complete understanding of the human person, mind and body, individually and socially, and what this says to a grasp of illness as a human and not merely a physical phenomenon. The French theologian Claude Ortemann points to the disruption of human life caused by serious illness.[12] The sick person, prevented from engaging in normal human activity, is cut off from family, friends, and social belonging. With this go the sense of alienation from one's own body, remembrance of one's failings and feelings of guilt, an acute awareness of finitude, and a sense that time is passing and fleeting. What the sacrament promises is a restoration of wholeness and belonging, of reconciliation with one's finite condition. This comes through solidarity with Christ, through finding a place in the community of the church as one of its members, both receiving from others and giving to others the testimony and wisdom of suffering, and recon-

---

9. Regis A. Duffy, "Anointing of the Sick," in *Systematic Theology: Roman Catholic Perspectives*, ed. Francis Schüssler Fiorenza and John P. Galvin, 1st ed. (Minneapolis: Fortress Press, 1991), 2:253–57.

10. Ibid., 255–56.

11. For practical use, see *Pastoral Care of the Sick: Rites of Anointing and Viaticum Approved for Use in the Dioceses of the United States of America* (Collegeville, MN: Liturgical, 1983).

12. Claude Ortemann, *Le sacrament des malades* (Lyons: Ed. Chalet, 1971).

564 ciliation with finitude through the hope of the resurrection. In the vulnerability of illness, the sacrament comforts with the grace of Christ and of the Holy Spirit, in the midst of the church. All this is expressed in the Letter of James as being "raised up." In light of this, full attention may be given to the place of the ill person as the subject and celebrant of the sacrament, rather than a passive recipient. The ecclesial meaning of the sacrament is enhanced when the sick can be brought to the gathering of the church community and it is celebrated within the Sunday Eucharistic assembly.

The second line of thought draws primarily on Paul, where he relates human suffering to the sufferings of Christ. In 2 Cor. 13:4, he points to Christ, who both weak and strong is a model for the Christian in the face of suffering. In the Letter to the Romans, Paul invites his readers to participate in suffering with Christ, so that they may be glorified with him (Rom. 8:16-19). In contrast to a purely philosophical or even stoical approach to the power of evil and suffering in human existence, the gospel message proclaims God's victorious purpose as seen in the very sufferings and death of Christ, holding out the hope of resurrection. Through the grace of Christ, suffering and death do not hold sway over the human person, however feeble one may be as a result of sickness or old age.

Conclusion

Within the limits of space allowed, this essay has surveyed the place of the anointing of the sick in the course of the history of the church's liturgy and has noted the current effort to retrieve the meaning it once had for all the seriously sick, rather than only for those who are in immediate danger of death. We have also seen the sense in which it is a sacrament of the church, belonging within the entire pastoral care of pastors and community for the sick and dying. In this common life, the sick person is not a passive subject of care but participates fully in the life and worship of the church. Finally, the summary of recent theology offers some perspectives on the significance and the grace of the sacrament as a participation in the Paschal Mystery of Christ.

For Further Reading

Borobio, Dionisio. "Uncion de Enfermos." In *La celebracion en la iglesia*. Vol. 2, *Sacramentos*. Edited by Dionisio Borobia, 653–743. Salamanca: Ediciones Sigueme, 1994.

> *A fine presentation of the history, liturgy, and theology of the sacrament, in the context of the pastoral care of the sick.*

Duffy, Regis. *A Roman Catholic Theology of Pastoral Care*. Philadelphia: Fortress Press, 1983.

> *The author stresses that the ultimate goal of ministry of the sick has conversion and communion with Christ in his Paschas as its ultimate goal.*

Empereur, James. *Prophetic Anointing: God's Call to the Sick, the Elderly, and the Dying*. Wilmington, DE: Michael Glazier, 1982.

> *Surveying the tradition, the author brings out the prophetic role of the sick themselves as members of the church who testify to the Pasch of Christ.*

Kasza, John. *Understanding Sacramental Healing (Anointing and Viaticum)*. Chicago: Liturgical Training, 2005.

> *The author relates the theology of the sacrament to current practice, to canon law, to anthropology, and to medical care. An ample bibliography is included.*

Martimort, A. G. "Prayer for the Sick and Sacramental Anointing." In *The Church at Prayer: An Introduction to the Liturgy*. 2nd ed. Edited by Aimé Georges Martimort, 117–37. Collegeville, MN: Liturgical, 1988.

> *A survey of the history of the sacramental liturgy, relating it to the context of all liturgies for the sick and dying.*

Sacraments 9.6

Order

David N. Power

The current context for the theology of the sacrament of order in the Roman Catholic Church is set by the teachings of the Second Vatican Council and by the developments in the ecclesial life that belong to its aftermath. These include a large participation of the faithful in the works of ministry and a dialogue and cooperation in the mission of Christ and the Spirit with other churches, East and West, overcoming long-standing divisions and hostilities.

After the council, the Roman Catholic Church came to a fresh awareness of the vitality of Christian community and of the part played by all the baptized in building up Christ's body through the charismatic gifts of the Spirit and in serving the kingdom of God in the world. To express both the relationship to Christ and the relationship to the church, the Decree on the Ministry and Life of the Ordained Presbyter spoke of the presbyter's (like the bishop's) action *in persona Christi Capitis* (in the person of Christ the Head), rather than simply *in persona Christi* (in the person of Christ), as had become common since the Middle Ages. While the latter term designated specifically the role of the priest in celebrating the Mass and the sacraments, the new term covered the entire ministry of the ordained with the community, working along with all other members called to service.

While continuity is always a consideration, it is not possible to understand the place given to the sacrament of order today without seeing the difference with how the priesthood had come to be conceived and exercised. Since the high Middle Ages, the sacrament of order had been defined primarily in terms of priesthood and the offering of the Eucharistic sacrifice. Ordination to the priesthood was practically identified with ordination to the presbyterate, so that it was even a common opinion that the episcopacy was not a sacrament but a jurisdiction of divine institution. In its Constitution on the Church, *Lumen gentium* (cited hereafter as LG), the Second Vatican Council declared the sacramental nature of the episcopacy. It also taught that ordination means ordination to the threefold ministry of Word, sacrament, and pastoral care, with some preference for the image of shepherd, thus going beyond the idea that it was connected only with the ministry of sacrament or liturgical priesthood (LG 21, 26). It also asked for the restoration of that much-neglected order, the diaconate, which for centuries had been nothing more than a step toward priesthood but could be seen again as a lifelong ministry (LG 29). Thus, the council formulated the teaching that the sacrament of order includes the tripartite ministry of bishop, presbyter, and deacon, and that ordination to each one of these is, in its own specific way, ordination to the ministry of Word, sacrament, and pastoral care. Subsequent to the council, local churches on different continents underwent considerable development in fostering the participation of all the baptized in the work of the church and concomitantly in giving shape and focus to its mission. In such a context, there was a necessary reconsideration, both theoretical and practical, of the sacrament of order in its threefold structure.

In today's global church, there is a communion of many diverse communities made up of different peoples, cultures, and liturgical traditions, so that without breaking communion, each local community is more conscious of its own specific characteristics. The sacrament of order is to be understood within this context. There is an avowed starting point in what the Second Vatican Council says about the nature of the church as God's priestly people and the sacrament of the unity of the human race (LG 9), but this has to be put alongside what is stated in LG 11 about the difference between the participation of the baptized in the priesthood of Christ and that of the ordained as one of essence and not only of degree. It has been suggested that preferring the word *essence* over *degree* was a way of laying aside the idea of a distinction in rank between ordained and laity that seemed inherent to the word *hierarchy*,[1] but even if this were the case, one would have to ask how an essential difference may be explained.

New Testament Origins

It is part of the traditional teaching of the Roman Catholic Church that the origins of its hierarchical ministry are to be found in the New Testament and more specifically in the dispositions of Jesus himself, but magisterial teaching has always been circumspect about where these origins are to be found.[2] When accused by the Reformers in the sixteenth century of having distorted the evangelical reality of the church and of its ministry, the Council of Trent responded that the episcopacy as known at that time was the proper realization of the ministry to which Christ had commissioned the apostles.[3] This was in substance repeated at the Second Vatican Council (LG 18), but both councils, with some awareness of what the sacrament of order owes to ongoing development, were reserved in tracing origins back to the New Testament. Neither

Trent nor Vatican II wished to say that the tripartite ministry of bishop, presbyter, and deacon in its exact form could be traced back to the New Testament, but they did wish to maintain a factual and legitimate continuity of the tripartite ministry with the origins of the church in the community of Jesus' followers—or, in other words, with the apostolic church.

With this in view, as has been said in the chapter in this volume on sacramental principles, the idea of the institution of ministry has to be considered with attention to historical realities and in terms of the organic life of the church as sacrament of Christ in the Spirit. While we can look for the apostolic roots of order in the teaching of the New Testament and even in the words of Christ, it is impossible to locate a moment or an act when the sacrament of order was founded. It is not possible to trace an exact linear history of ministry from its origins and its ordering in New Testament times. The task is rather to see what understanding of ministry that is expressed in the New Testament needs to be constantly kept alive in the church, granted that this will always be in a form shaped by history and proper to any given place and time, as the Holy Spirit guides the community in its life and mission.

Different kinds of ministry and authority existed in early communities and need to be taken into account in forging a theology. One

---

1. For example, Otto Hermann Pesch, *Das Zweite Vatikanische Konzil: Vorgeschichte-Verlauf-Ergebnisse-Nachgeschichte* (Würzburg: Echter, 1993), 180–82.

2. See Bernard Cooke, *Ministry to Word and Sacraments: History and Theology* (Philadelphia: Fortress Press, 1976), 33–57; Raymond Brown, *Priest and Bishop: Biblical Reflections* (New York: Paulist, 1970); Jean Delorme, ed., *Le ministère et les ministres selon le Nouveau Testament* (Paris: Le Seuil, 1974); Andre Lemaire, "Ministries in the New Testament: Recent Research," *Biblical Theology Bulletin* 3 (1973): 133–66; Edward Schillebeeckx, *The Church with a Human Face: A New and Expanded Theology of Ministry* (New York: Crossroad, 1985), 40–121; John H. Schulz, *Paul and the Anatomy of Apostolic Authority* (Cambridge: Cambridge University Press, 1975); Edward Schweizer, *Church Order in the New Testament* (London: SCM, 1961).

3. Council of Trent, Decree on the Sacrament of Order, in Denzinger and Schönmetzer, *Enchiridion Symbolorum* (hereafter DS), 1767–69, 1777.

570 certainly has to take note of the role that the original Twelve, particularly Peter, and the apostle Paul played in proclaiming the Word and in binding local churches together in submission to the apostolic witness and the grace of the Spirit. The image of the apostle was important to development and historical continuity. The word actually owes more to Paul than to the Twelve. Broadly speaking, it is meant to express a witness to the resurrection of the Crucified One (a commission received from the Risen Christ), the proclamation of this gospel, and a life of faithful witness that commands authority. The designation covers Paul and the holy women of John's Gospel as much as Peter and the Eleven, but it was later associated in a particular way with the Twelve in order to express the origins of the church in the discipleship of Jesus' companions, in the witness of his deeds and teaching and of his death and resurrection, and in the mission to proclaim this gospel continually. That is the rather particular meaning that the church in subsequent centuries gave to the image of the twelve apostles and of a church founded on the apostles, while always recognizing that the proclamation of the original apostolic witness was, in fact, more complex than the image might suggest. Likewise, while the foundation on the apostolic witness is vital to the church's life and mission, and while bishops are frequently called successors of the apostles, it has to be borne in mind that they did not replicate the original apostolic ministry but bear the charge to assure that what the apostles preached is passed on with fidelity.

A comprehensive understanding of the place of charismatic and ordered ministry in apostolic times requires taking account of the relations between ministry, church, and kingdom of God. The church as community of belief and discipleship is the historical manifestation of God's rule in the world as it reached its prophetic fulfillment in the death and resurrection of Jesus Christ and in the Spirit-filled community of his followers.[4] It always exists in relation to the kingdom and as a sign of that kingdom for all humankind. It exists not for and of itself, but in service to the kingdom of God. Its ministry is the ministry of an apostolic community. That is to say, it builds up the community in itself as a community of apostolic witness, and it must promote both the inner life of the discipleship and its ways of proclaiming the gospel. The word, power, and service of Jesus are the paradigm for all ministry. The twelve who ate and drank with Jesus, listened to his teaching, and witnessed to his death and resurrection are the fountainhead of the church's life and ministry. However, they cannot be said to represent its definitive institutional form.[5]

In the communities of the apostolic era, we need to distinguish between the ministries that we find active in them and the order that governed their lives. There are several lists of charisms and services in the churches of different localities, but none that is exhaustive. The general impression is that ministry is wide-ranging, that it comes from the power of the Spirit, and that only on some occasions is there a specific commissioning, the community having recognized the charism and call of certain persons. The New Testament vocabulary is more often that of charisms and service. Charism stands for a gift received from the Holy Spirit for the service (*diakonia*) of the church and of the gospel. The one criterion of authenticity is that the

---

4. Schillebeeckx, *The Church with a Human Face*, 13–39.
5. See Sean Freyne, *The Twelve: Disciples and Apostles* (London: Sheed & Ward, 1967).

ministry contribute to the common good of the life of faith and the witness of the truth abroad. In contemporary writing, there is some discussion about the exact meaning of *diakonia*. Some see the word as all-embracing, so that all those who have gifts contribute to the building up and work of the church.[6] Others think that the meaning is more restrictive and, in the wake of the original apostolic ministry, applies only to those who exercise pastoral leadership.[7]

Theologians in reading the New Testament are wont to classify charisms and ministries for the sake of comprehension. This can help, provided one recognizes the tentative and provisional nature of the classification. Thus, one can distinguish between ministries of Word, inner service, and worship, and within the ministries of Word, between the apostolic or kerygmatic, the prophetic, and the didactic. Of the ministries of worship, little is said, but one may distinguish between the use of the many different gifts that enliven worship and the presidency without, however, having any clear signals as to who presided or how this was done. At the center of worship was, of course, the Lord's Supper, with its reading of the Scriptures, its apostolic Word, its blessing prayer, and its table ritual in the body and blood of Christ. It is quite possible that presidency over this service and the proclamation of the blessing and memorial prayer (in essence, a Word ministry) were at least at times done by different people.[8]

This already touches on the ordering of the community and on the ordering of relations between local churches. One has to look at the way in which order is served within each community and at the way in which the communities are bound together as the one body of Christ. By and large, one can distinguish between the internal order of the church in Jerusalem, that of the Pauline churches, and that adumbrated in the later pastoral letters.[9] Each seems to have adopted a different model from cultural surroundings, and it is in the pastoral letters that concern for the transmission of faith and ministry looms larger.

Several scholars, including James Dunn,[10] have pointed to some diversity in the ways in which particular communities were ordered and have highlighted some influences on this coming from religious and cultural realities. In the words of Dunn, it is necessary to distinguish between sociological influences and theological principles. Both allow for differences, but the former do so more specifically. It is then possible to see how communities borrowed from the organization of the Jewish synagogue, the household meetings and codes of Gentile peoples, and forms of voluntary association within which persons pursued a common interest. With all of this, the great concern was to live together in such a way as to be faithful to Jesus Christ and to the witness of the apostles.

To have a complete picture, apart from the

---

6. Markus Barth, *Ephesians: Translation and Commentary on Chapters 4–6*, Anchor Bible Commentary (Garden City, NY: Doubleday, 1974).

7. John N. Collins, *Diakonia: Re-Interpreting the Ancient Sources* (New York: Oxford University Press, 1990).

8. On presidency of the Eucharist in the early church, see Hervé-Marie Legrand, "The Presidency of the Eucharist according to the Ancient Tradition," *Worship* 53 (1979): 413–38.

9. See the summary of studies in O'Meara, *A Theology of Ministry* (New York: Paulist, 1983), 76–94. See also Raymond Brown, "*Episkope* and *Episkopos*: The New Testament Evidence," *Theological Studies* 41 (1980): 322–38.

10. James D. G. Dunn, "Models of Christian Community in the New Testament," *Christ and the Spirit*, vol. 2, *Pneumatology* (Grand Rapid and Cambridge, UK: Eerdmans, 1998), 245–59.

572 development of the image of apostle and twelve apostles, the role of Peter and of Paul in ministering to several churches is a reminder that besides the inner ordering of communities, some broader ordering of their mutual relations was required. They needed to be bound together in their common fidelity to Jesus Christ and in a life of communion and of witness to the power of God's kingdom, manifest in the works of the Spirit. Though Peter and Paul are the chief figures in this regard, the Council of Jerusalem, the apostolic work of Barnabas and Silas, the leadership of Stephen and six others among the Hellenists, the discipline exercised by Timothy and Titus, and the itinerant mission of prophets all have a role to play. It is not, however, until the subapostolic period that any clear lines of a commonly accepted order begin to emerge.

Early Christian Centuries

Looking to early Christian centuries, one can distinguish between the development of church order and the development of an ordination service.[11] Ministry in the service of the church and of its mission is more wide-ranging than is covered under these headings, though unfortunately it is true that all ministries tended to be absorbed in the course of time into the ordained ministry.

Ignatius of Antioch is an early witness to the appearance of the tripartite order of bishop, presbyterium, and deacons in the churches of Asia Minor. In the same period, however, other churches appear to have been governed by a presbyterium or college of presbyters. For Ignatius, the truly important significance of the one church under the pastoral care of the one bishop was that the community was maintained in its unity and in its apostolic faith by gathering for the Eucharist under his presidency.[12] With the *Apostolic Tradition*, often attributed to Hippolytus, one could say that the image of the church had come into bold relief as one Eucharistic communion, under the presidency of the one bishop, assisted in government by the presbyterium and in multiple services by deacons. It is in the context of Eucharistic communion that ordination to the threefold ministry took place. By all accounts, the faithful had an active part in electing the bishop and some say in the choice of presbyters, though this probably varied. Though bishops from other churches presided at the ordination of a bishop, the service was a liturgy of the entire community, allowing it to be said that the local church ordained its bishop in the communion of all churches, as represented by the bishops who took part in the ceremony.

The multiple ministerial tasks of his ministry brought the figure of the bishop into high profile. He was the steward of the household of the Father who was to govern it after the example of God the Father. He was shepherd of the people, expected in his person to conform to the image of Christ the Good Shepherd. He

---

11. See Cooke, *Ministry to Word and Sacraments*, 75–112; H. von Campenhausen, *Ecclesiastical Authority and Spiritual Power in the Church of the First Three Centuries* (Stanford, CA: Stanford University Press, 1969); Schillebeeckx, *The Church with a Human Face*, 125–55. For documents, see Paul Bradshaw, *Ordination Rites of the Ancient Church East and West* (Collegeville, MN: Liturgical, 1990).

12. Early evidence on the heightened figure of the bishop is found in the writing of Cyprian of Carthage and in the church order called the *Didascalia*. For a helpful collection of essays on episcopal figures in early centuries, see Richard N. Longenecker, ed., *Community Formation in the Early Church and in the Church Today* (Peabody, MA: Hendrickson, 2002), 129–80.

was responsible for preaching the Word to the faithful and where Christianity was not yet established for evangelization. To him belonged the reconciliation of penitents. To him also belonged the presidency of the Eucharist in the local church, a function that earned him the title of High Priest, ministering to the royal priesthood of God's people. He was also responsible for finances, particularly with regard to the care of the poor, and in this he was assisted by the ministry of deacons. In the communion of churches in the one apostolic faith, he conferred in different ways with other bishops so that together they might build up the one catholic communion.

The central ritual action of the ordination service for bishop, presbyters, and deacons was the laying on of hands with a prayer of blessing, invoking the descent of the Holy Spirit.[13] The laying on of hands was, of course, a very common ritual action, used in many circumstances, but in appointment to ministry in the church, it was marked off as specific to these three orders. People appointed to such orders as those of widow, reader, or cantor did not receive the laying on of hands. As far as the purpose of this ordination rite is concerned, there are shades of meaning that distinguish an Eastern from a Latin perspective. In Greek-speaking churches, the service was called *Cheirotonia*, which meant primarily the invocation of the Spirit who blessed the candidate with those gifts of service that enabled him to perform a ministry. In Latin-speaking churches, the word *ordination* took precedence over the designation of the rite as the laying on of hands and emphasized the appointment to an order or office.[14] With the poorly developed pneumatology of the Latin West, the prayer of ordination often failed to include an invocation of the Spirit. This is important because it meant that in common understanding and theological reflection, the notion of an institutional transmission of office and power prevailed over that of a response of the Spirit to the prayer of the church and an enabling for ministry through its gifts.

With the passage of time, one of the factors that most strongly influenced the development of the theology of order was the change in the role of presbyters.[15] Their original office appears to have been to assist the bishop in governance and indeed to assure that this was done within each church in a collegiate way. In time, however, through varied kinds of development, they became pastors and sacramental ministers in smaller communities that remained under the supervision of the bishop. This meant that their ordination was to pastoral care, sacramental ministry, and at least some teaching. Indeed, it paralleled in miniature the ministry of the bishop, so that the question of the distinction between these two orders was blurred. Simultaneously, the ministry of bishops was less and less connected with Eucharistic communities and more and more devoted to ecclesial supervision and to communion between churches. One could say that this kind of ministry was devoted to keeping unity in the diocese, fidelity

---

13. See W. H. Frere, "Early Ordination Services," *Journal of Theological Studies* 16 (1915): 323–69; Pierre-Marie Gy, "Ancient Ordination Prayers," in *Ordination Rites*, ed. Wiebe Vos and Geoffrey Wainwright (Rotterdam: Liturgical Ecumenical Center Trust, 1980), 70–93.

14. See Gy, "Ancient Ordination Prayers."

15. Kenan Osborne, *Priesthood: A History of Ordained Ministry in the Roman Catholic Church* (Mahwah, NJ: Paulist, 1988).

574 to the apostolic tradition through teaching in communion with other bishops, and the catholic communion of all churches with each other. It was once an important and even powerful ministry involving much administration, but the order of deacon was gradually reduced to the performance of a ceremonial role in liturgical ministry.[16] For disciplinary reasons, much connected with the requirements of celibacy for presbyters and bishops, it even became nothing more than a stepping-stone to ordination to the presbyterate.

The distinction between those called clergy and the rest of the baptized comes to the fore in the work entitled *The Apostolic Tradition* and then takes on permanence in ecclesiastical vocabulary. This distinction needs close scrutiny, lest it be confused with the essence of ministry.[17] The place given to the ordained and their auxiliaries by this distinction does not pertain to the nature of the sacrament. It rather depicts what we would call a canonical distinction deemed useful to the life of communities, often giving those called clergy obligations of life that set them apart and a right to be provided sustenance by the communities they served. It took on sharper relief with the demand made by leadership for community life and for an exemplary lifestyle on the part of the ordained and other clergy that would adhere closely to the model of the church at Jerusalem, described in the book of Acts. This ideal of clerical life was fostered by writers such as Ambrose, Augustine, Basil,

and Gregory the Great in early centuries and in the medieval church, at a time when reform was needed, by the formation of orders of Canons Regular. Given this history, it is to be seen as a distinction that is today subject to further theological and disciplinary consideration.[18]

The Medieval Hierarchy and Priesthood

The influence of the thought of the writer called Dionysius the Areopagite, coupled with organizational developments, contributed much to a theology of order that accentuated hierarchy and priesthood.[19] Hierarchy, which etymologically means sacred power, represented a universal vision that portrayed creation as an ordered participation in supreme truth within which those possessing higher degrees of participation influence those below them. This universal law of creation operated also within the church and within its ministry, which the Pseudo-Dionysius represented as a spiritual hierarchy, whereby those more closely united to God are to care for those on the way of purification and ascent. The faithful were perceived as those who received the grace of God through the ministry of the ordained within an ordered community. The ordained themselves were ranked in the descending order of bishop, presbyter, and deacon, according to the degree of their participation in sacred power and their holiness of life.

---

16. John M. Barnett, *The Diaconate: A Full and Equal Order* (New York: Seabury, 1981), 1–131; Kenan Osborne, *Permanent Diaconate: Its History and Place in the Sacrament of Orders* (Mahwah, NJ: Paulist, 2007).

17. Alexandre Faivre, *Emergence of the Laity in the Early Church* (Mahwah, NJ: Paulist, 1990).

18. The 1982 Code of Canon Law restricts the use of the term *cleric* to those who have received the laying on of hands, whereas over time candidates for ordination and to those attached to the service of papal and episcopal households.

19. On the medieval hierarchy and priesthood, see Cooke, *Ministry*, 113–32; Schillebeeckx, *The Church*, 156–94. For Dionysius the Areopagite, see his *The Ecclesiastical Hierarchy*, trans. and annotated by Thomas L. Campbell (Washington, DC: University of America Press, 1981).

A variety of factual developments, including an increase of priests within monasteries and of clergy ordained exclusively to provide the landed with Mass and ritual, meant the presbyterate was increasingly seen as priesthood with the power to consecrate and offer the sacrifice of Christ's body and blood. This even became the definition of the sacrament of order, and the hierarchy or sacred power of the bishop was associated with his jurisdiction over the life of the diocese. In the ordered world of the high Middle Ages, represented by its Romanesque basilica or Gothic cathedral and by the divinely constituted offices of prince and bishop, spiritual jurisdiction, the offering of the sacrifice of the Mass, and priestly absolution of sins were powerful and important mediations of divine grace. Ordination rites, with the accent on anointing and instruments of office, reflected this world and this concept of mediation. Though the term had originally been used to underline that it was Christ who acted through the minister in the sacraments, the notion of the priest acting *in persona Christi* or representing Christ became the focal point of the theology of order.

Since the essence of priesthood was located in the celebration of the Eucharistic sacrifice, in Scholastic theology one of the matters disputed was whether the episcopacy, while clearly an order, could also be called a sacrament. With the focus on Eucharist, the contribution of Thomas Aquinas was to see in this public worship the exercise of the one priesthood of Jesus Christ on the part of all the baptized and in a distinctive way on the part of the ordained priest, who acted *in persona Christi* as well as *in persona ecclesiae*. In his discussions about the ordering of the church, Aquinas remained close to the spiritual view of hierarchy he had received from the Pseudo-Dionysius, even as some canonists and theologians entertained a more juridical concept of power in the church.

The order of things described above, the theology of ordained priesthood, and what this meant to the relation between priests and faithful appeared to the sixteenth-century Reformers as curtailing the freedom of divine mercy and grace and leaving little room to the faith of the baptized.[20] It seemed to absorb the community of faith into a powerful and power-controlled institution, with little respect for the ministry of Word and sacramental gift and for the exercise of the royal priesthood of all believers. Much of the criticism, both practical and theological, was on target, but the scene was obscured by polemics and reciprocal accusations. The very idea of hierarchy was spurned by the Reformers, and they professed but one divinely intended ministry of Word and sacrament, without internal distinction between bishop and presbyter. In response, the Council of Trent defined the power of the priest to consecrate and offer sacrifice, the institution of priesthood and hierarchy by Christ, and the divine origin of the episcopacy as it actually functioned in the church of the time, as well as the essential difference between the baptized and the ordained in their relation to Christ and to the church.[21] Much pastoral reform followed in the wake of the Council of Trent, but for centuries, there was little room for an integration of the just insights of the Reformers or for modification in the actual ordering of ministry.

20. See Cooke, *Ministry to Word and Sacraments*, 133–69.
21. Council of Trent, Decree on the Sacrament of Order (DS 1763–78).

Contemporary Roman Catholic Doctrine and Theology

In this section of the essay something will be said of recent magisterial teaching on the sacrament, ecumenical discussions, and the work of Roman Catholic theologians.

Magisterium

Present teaching on the sacrament of order belongs within a renewed ecclesiology and a renewed appreciation of baptism as a full induction into the life of the church. As is well known, the Second Vatican Council spoke of the church as the people of God and of its participation in the threefold office of Christ as prophet, priest, and king. It then spoke of the part that each and all of the baptized have in this threefold activity, through responsibility for the transmission of Christian faith, for the church's liturgical life, and for the apostolate in one or other of its many forms (LG ch. 4, *Decree on the Apostolate of the Laity*). In the aftermath of the council, the more active part that the baptized had already begun to take in ecclesial activities increased a hundredfold all over the world, so that people have come to dub this period as one of an explosion of ministries. Naturally, this has affected both the exercise and the conception of the ordained ministry.

There has been considerable debate over the use of the word *ministry*, as some would prefer to give it a restricted usage and employ it only for activities marked off by official designation, but in general, it is given much the same employment and meaning as the word *charism* or gift of service in the Pauline letters.[22] Consequently, it proves useful to note the distinction between ministry and order. This recognizes that some participation in ecclesial service or office is a normal part of all adult Christian life but that the order of the church, necessary to its existence, marks off the part of each and assigns specific sacramental and leadership roles to those who receive the sacramental laying on of hands.

Relationships are inherent to the meaning of order, and it is inadequate simply to list the offices and actions for which bishop, presbyter (or priest), and deacon are respectively ordained. In the course of his papacy, John Paul II devoted considerable attention to the place of the ordained in the community of the church. While on the one hand he advocated collaboration with the laity in all works of service, on the other hand he gave a distinctive physiognomy to the role of ordained pastors. He brought the two perspectives together in offering a relational model of church within which to place the role of the ordained.[23] This relationality is first to the Trinity and to the work of Christ and Spirit, for all Christian life and ministry has its origins in this divine communion. In this light, John Paul II spoke of the priest's relation to Christ, to the church, to the people, and to the bishop and fellow presbyters.

In the midst of discussions about the possible ordination of women, however, he was most emphatic that this could not be done, and he gave what he considered a definitive pronouncement in the apostolic letter *Ordinatio Sacerdotalis*. In that statement, he simply said that the church

---

22. See the discussion in Thomas O'Meara, *Theology of Ministry* (New York: Paulist, 1983), 134–75.

23. Most particularly John Paul II, "The Post-Synodal Apostolic Exhortation *Pastores Dabo Vobis*," *Origins* 21 (1992): 717–59.

has not the power to ordain women because of Christ's choice of males alone to take their place among the Twelve. In the apostolic exhortation on the laity, *Christifideles Laici*, however, he gave a symbolic meaning to this preference for the male by putting it in the context of the Eucharist, where the ordained minister represents Christ as bridegroom of the church.[24] Despite these pronouncements, debate has not been stilled, especially in the light of ecclesial experience and of questions put to the arguments, both scriptural and theological. Since these are subject to scrutiny and discussion, some are left to wonder whether a change in the dispensation may not indeed be possible within a divinely ordered dispensation.[25]

Ecumenical Conversation

It behooves theological reflection to explain the precise purpose and character of ordination, or of the sacrament of order. To do this, sacramental theologians and ecclesiologists look back to the origins and later developments of ministry in order to sort out issues pertinent to its future. As they do this, theologians in the Roman Catholic Church find themselves necessarily in dialogue with theologians of other churches who are faced with similar questions and are looking for a unified approach to order that will foster ecumenical reconciliation and unity.

Because of past dissensions, in its own way this ecumenical interaction draws attention to the relation between the common priesthood of the baptized and ministerial priesthood, as well as to the meaning of the tripartite division within the one pastoral ministry. Thus, Catholic theology is marked by the impact of official conversations and by collaboration among scholars.[26] From a vast literature on the topic, the following points are important to ongoing theological developments within ecumenical exchange.

Most basic is renewed consideration of the theological understanding of apostolic succession. By common agreement, the apostolicity of the sacrament of order, as well as its celebration, is to be seen in the fuller context of ecclesial apostolicity, whereby ecclesial communities live and practice their mission in continuity with the foundation of the body of Christ and of ecclesial communion on the witness of the apostles. With this in mind, Catholics and Orthodox find common interest in the importance of situating order within the Eucharistic celebration of local churches. While Catholics and Protestants are not in complete agreement on the necessity of linear succession in a process of laying on of hands, there is at least a common understanding of the value of this as a sign of apostolic continuity, of the presence of Christ in the church, and of the gift and action of the Holy Spirit in the call to ministry and in its exercise. Catholic

---

24. John Paul II, *Post-Synodal Apostolic Exhortation* Christifideles Laici (Vatican City: Libreria Editrice Vaticana, 1988). For arguments that offer theological justification of the papal decision, see Gerhard Ludwig Müller, *Priesthood and Diaconate: The Recipient of the Sacrament of Holy Orders from the Perspective of Creation Theology and Christology*, trans. Michael T. Miller (San Francisco: Ignatius, 2002).

25. For a fairly lengthy discussion, with reference to literature on the matter, see David N. Power, *Mission, Ministry, Order* (New York: Continuum, 2008), 298–314.

26. To date, the high points of discussions between many churches are the two documents of the Faith and Order Commission of the World Council of Churches, *Baptism, Eucharist and Ministry*, paper no. 111 (Geneva: World Council of Churches, 1982); and *The Nature and Mission of the Church*, paper no. 198 (Geneva: World Council of Churches, 2005). The Faith and Order Commission includes Roman Catholic representatives.

578

and Orthodox theology, however, gives a stronger sacramental weight to order and ordination, couched in the words of a statement of the joint theological commission of these churches, which speaks of the bishop (and, by extension, the presbyter) as "the icon of Christ the servant among his brethren."[27]

Questions of institution and canonical form are better understood by all when all ministry is seen to have its origin in charisms given by the Spirit. Particular institutional and canonical forms can then be seen as integral to the organic growth of ecclesial life within the communion of the Spirit. Rather than being opposed, charism and institution belong in a mutual relationship that serves ecclesial life and mission. In this perspective, an increasingly common reference for the theology of the ministry—and so for the sacrament of order in Catholic understanding—is ecclesial communion (*koinonia*). Viewed in its charismatic origin and in its sacramental and canonical elements, ministry is a participation in the communion of the Trinity and the sending of the Word and the Spirit from within this communion for the life of the church and the service of God's kingdom.

Of late, some ecumenical documents, after the first blush of agreement, appear to find some impasse on matters affecting the possibilities of communion between churches. As a result, they tend to list points of agreement and then juxta-pose positions not so far reconciled.[28] However, a fresh point of departure is located in a renewal of the sense of mission—indeed, of a common mission—and so of discernment of what this shows about ecclesial and ministerial realities. In other words, call to a common mission in today's world serves as a spur to cooperation and to fresh consideration of historical and theological principles.

Roman Catholic Theologians

As with much else, the major effort of Roman Catholic theologians engaged in the current theology of order and ministry[29] is to retrieve important aspects of the history of ministry and to relate them to present circumstances and diversity of cultures, and in this to find common ground with the confessions and theologies of other churches.[30]

Some theologians continue to emphasize the particular call of the priest and take the essential difference between laity and priest as the key element in a theology of order.[31] Though, as noted, the Second Vatican Council modified the traditional language of *in persona Christi* to *in persona Christi capitis*, these writers continue to underline the idea of the priest as representative of Christ in the community and particularly in the sacraments, pointing to the continued papal use of the term *in persona Christi*. Recognition

---

27. Joint International Commission, "The Sacrament of Order in the Sacramental Structure of the Church with Particular Reference to the Importance of Apostolic Succession," no. 33 in *The Quest for Unity: Orthodox and Catholics in Dialogue*, ed. John Borelli and John H. Erickson (Crestwood, NY: St. Vladimir's Seminary Press, 1996), 131–42.

28. Faith and Order Commission, *The Nature and Mission of the Church*.

29. Theology remains much indebted to Schillebeeckx and the early attempt at a comprehensive survey of Bernard Cooke. For recent work, see Osborne and Power.

30. See works by Cooke, O'Meara, Schillebeeckx. See also Bernard Cooke, "Fullness of Order: Theological Reflection," *Jurist* 41 (1981): 151–67; Jean Galot, *Theology of the Priesthood* (San Francisco: Ignatius, 1984); Edward Kilmartin, "Apostolic Office: Sacrament of Christ," *Theological Studies* 36 (1975): 243–64.

31. Thus, Galot, *Theology of the Priesthood*; Bonaventure Kloppenburg, *The Priest: Living Instrument and Minister of Christ the Eternal Priest* (Chicago: Franciscan Herald Press, 1974). More recently, Müller, *Priesthood and Diaconate*.

is given to the service of the laity, but it is subordinated to this principle or placed in another category, particularly that of apostolate in the world. The distinction between the responsibility of the ordained in the sacred sphere and that of the laity in the secular is then exploited and highly accentuated.

Other writers, however, look to the possibilities of creative originality within apostolic continuity. While respecting that which is particular to Catholic teaching, they are concerned with possible structural changes that situate the sacrament of order more firmly in the local community and in the exchange between local communities and see its evolution as inherent to the ongoing guidance of the church by the Holy Spirit. They look carefully at the difference between doctrinal principles and disciplinary practice, especially on issues such as the distinction between clergy and laity, the necessity in the Roman Catholic Church for clerical celibacy, and even the possible issue of ordaining women. They also ask how determining for ministry in general and for the ordained ministry in particular is the distinction originating in Vatican II between the sacred and the secular spheres of operation. If ministry and service are seen as expressions of the community, then it is not possible to push this distinction to great lengths.[32]

Seeing ministry and all forms of service as gifts of the Spirit and as ecclesial acts is more fundamental and comprehensive and puts order in its proper life context. This includes a wide variety of activities done for the spiritual good of the church and for its mission in society. On the one hand, exercise of the priesthood and mission of Christ is something in which all the baptized can participate and that requires both recognition of the diversity of gifts and discernment of the presence of the Spirit. On the other hand, lest this diversity bespeak an excess of individualism and split communities, a greater consciousness of ministries must be accompanied by a greater consciousness of the local church community as a Eucharistic communion. The church as a universal communion and in its particular existence in place and culture has a corporate mission. This mission is rooted in apostolic witness to the power of the Spirit of the risen Christ and is directed to the service of God's transforming and reconciling rule in the world. The needs of the faithful, spiritual and bodily, have to be taken care of while the community is built up as a body that in corporate witness and action can serve its apostolic mission. Ecclesial activities converge around the Eucharist, sacrament of Christ's body and communion table, and within all sacramental celebration as related to it as center. The community of discipleship is nurtured, bonded, and oriented to mutual service and apostolic mission through the gift of the Spirit that is bestowed in this celebration through Word and sacramental gift.

An understanding of the sacrament of order belongs in this context of reciprocal ministry, mission, and commonly celebrated Eucharist. The nature of order as relationship within the one body, proposed by Pope John Paul II, is to be well integrated into theologies of ministry and ecclesial activity. Like all other sacraments, order is a sacrament of the church that signifies something essential to its being and vitality, even while it engages specific individuals in a particular form of ministry and responsibility. It is not meant to bring about a monopoly of any

---

32. For discussions on what is implied by LG 31 in making this distinction, see Power, *Mission, Ministry, Order,* 318–22; Edward Schillebeeckx, *The Definition of the Christian Layman* (Chicago: Franciscan Herald, 1979).

ministry, sacrament, teaching, or pastoral care, either at the local or at the catholic level. It is rather an ordering of ministries within the one Eucharistic fellowship and in the communion of churches. The sacrament of order represents the need for unity and the need for the service of Word, sacrament, and pastoral care if each community is to be faithful to its apostolic origins and to its apostolic mission. With ordering goes a presidency, so that the ordained do indeed have some specific functions that are necessary to this ordering. Whereas for some centuries, the accent was on the functions to which the minister was appointed, today the good of ministry is better retrieved through attention to what the role of the ordained signifies for the church as people of God and sacrament of Christ, within particular Eucharistic communities and in the bond between them.

As alternative to a hierarchical theology, from early ecclesiastical history it is possible to retrieve a vision of the sacrament of order as organic reality, with its own interior diversity. This diversity represents different aspects and needs of ecclesial life. Present reflection needs to show how it is to be respected in shaping the future. Within individual churches, the role of the priest or presbyter carries much of the responsibility of the early episcopacy. The presbyter is the leading liturgical minister and the one who must attend to unity in the community and to the fidelity to the apostolic witness, as well as to the provision and encouragement of all those services that communities need. As matters now exist, the ministry of bishops is less tied to individual communities and is more directly in the service of the communion of

communities, both within a diocese and within the universal church. The risk is that a bishop loses touch with the reality of Eucharistic community and the episcopacy becomes an administration rather than a ministry. In this regard, much can be gained through a contemporary retrieval of collegiality in the diocesan church, a synodality that includes presbyters and faithful but that can be strongly fostered through the presbyterium and the pastoral council. One purpose of the presbyters in the early church was that, in key matters, the presidency of the bishop would be tempered by collegial responsibility. In the circumstances of the present time, it might be wise for bishops to take on a more directly pastoral role in the presidency of a local church or parish, and to attend collegially with the presbyters and people to the unity of the diocese and the fostering of multiple ministries and a synodal community that is inclusive of all the baptized.

It is within this model of organic and synodal communion that there are possibilities of interecclesial conversation on the ordination of women. While Roman Catholic authorities have ruled out this possibility, it is possible to have a better understanding of the reasons why other churches have decided to have women in the company of the ordained. This inclusion does not obscure gender differences but promotes the contribution of both women and men to ordained and representative leadership in the church.[33]

The restoration of a permanent diaconate is of vital importance to the organic ordering of the church's ministry and to what is represented by the sacrament of order.[34] There is much hesi-

---

33. For a longer discussion, see Power, *Mission, Ministry, Order*, 306–14. Herve Legrand, "*Traditio Perpetua Servata?* The Non-ordination of Women: Tradition or Simply Historical Fact?" *Worship* 65 (1991): 482–508.

34. Barnett, *The Diaconate*, 133–60.

tation and lack of clarity on this score in magisterial teaching, in theology, and in practice.[35] Some tendencies seem to emphasize the role of the deacon in liturgy and in preaching. The risk is that the deacon become either a liturgical ornament or a substitute for priests in times of scarcity. One does better to see that the liturgical ministry of the deacon is in necessary conjunction with that which is specific to deacons in the daily life of the church. In early centuries, the deacons were charged with the care of the poor and, in connection with this, with the administration of the community's patrimony and common funds. In the Eucharist, they received the gifts of the people and administered the bread and wine to the bishop at the Eucharistic table. This was an admirable and fitting sacramental expression of their broader responsibilities and service. A secular task, as it were, was integrated into the life of the church as a communion of charity through a sacramental action.

This points to considerable possibilities for the restoration of the diaconate that are very pertinent to the mission of today's communities. There is a great emphasis on the church's service of the poor and on the witness to justice and reconciliation that it needs to bear in society for the creation of a more just world. This is one side of the promotion of the involvement of all the baptized, but it can also contribute to the separation of people and clergy by how the laity's secular task is interpreted. The diaconate could serve,

in keeping with its origins, as the bridge. The apt choices for the diaconate are persons mature in Christian life and in a spirit of service. They do not need to give up their secular occupations but can guide the rest of the church in relating a Christian commitment to the poor to secular action. Their regular participation in the liturgy in receiving the gifts and in administering them outside the liturgy brings together the sacramental and the more specifically diaconal quality of ecclesial life. At the same time, their wider concern with Christian witness in the life of society expresses the link between it and worship.

These are some of the main lines of contemporary thoughts on ministry and order. They imply, of course, a host of questions that cannot be developed here more fully because of the necessary restrictions of allotted space within this compendium of essays. Such questions, as noted, include the relation between church and God's kingdom; the viability of the distinction between sacred and secular; the relation of each member of the ordained to the community served; the developing role of women in ministry and its proper recognition; a critical approach to the choice, image, formation, and spirituality of deacons, priests, and bishops; and of course, the mutual recognition of ministries between the churches. Each of these subjects could be developed in a separate work, but the present survey may offer a framework within which they can be creatively addressed.

---

35. In LG 29, the document seems to accentuate on the one hand the function of the deacon in liturgy and preaching, and on the other hand his function in works of charity and administration. What is important is to show how these belong together.

For Further Reading

Cooke, Bernard. *Ministry to Word and Sacraments: History and Theology*. Philadelphia: Fortress Press, 1976.

> A comprehensive study of the development of ministry and of the sacrament of order from New Testament times to the present, taking account of literature in several languages. Though much has been added to the literature since its publication, this is still a valuable text.

Galot, Jean. *Theology of the Priesthood*. San Francisco: Ignatius, 1984.

> A defense of the classical approach to ministerial priesthood done in the light of history and current magisterial teaching.

O'Meara, Thomas. *Theology of Ministry*. New York: Paulist, 1983.

> A survey, made in light of current issues, of the development of forms of ministry in cultural context. The author addresses present questions about priestly and lay ministry.

Osborne, Kenan B. *Orders and Ministry*. Maryknoll, NY: Orbis, 2006.

> A follow-up on the author's several works on order and priesthood. This historical and theological survey puts order and its developments in the setting of a global church.

———. *Priesthood: A History of the Ordained Ministry in the Roman Catholic Church*. New York: Paulist, 1988.

> An overview of the history of the sacrament of order, with specific reference to the presbyterate. After an initial presentation of New Testament and early church materials, it concentrates on priesthood in the Roman church. Its multiple references to historical texts make it a useful tool in course work.

Power, David N. *Mission, Ministry, Order: Reading the Tradition in the Present Context*. New York and London: Continuum, 2008.

> Based on the author's previous works dealing with ordained ministry and with the service of the laity, this volume offers an inclusive theology grounded in the understanding of the ecclesial community as essentially missionary and locates baptized and ordained in this common mission.

Schillebeeckx, Edward. *The Church with a Human Face: A New and Expanded Theology of Ministry*. Translated by John Bowden. New York: Crossroad, 1985.

> A revised and expanded version of an earlier work, adopting a critically hermeneutical approach to historical texts and developments. Important for addressing such current issues as the ministry of base Christian communities, lay preaching, and the ordination of women and married men.

Wood, Susan K. *Sacramental Orders*. Collegeville, MN: Liturgical, 2000.

> A historical, theological, and pastoral consideration of the sacrament of order that gives a key place to a study of ordination rites and texts.

Sacraments 9.7

Marriage

Francis Schüssler Fiorenza

Today marriage is a changing institution. The number of families with a single parent as head of the household continues to grow. Childbirth outside of marriage is an increasing trend. In the 1950s, four out of every hundred births took place outside of marriage; in the 1980s, it became one of six; and today, it is one out of three. A growing number of couples (almost 50 percent) decide to live together prior to marriage or without a civil or church wedding. In the 1970s, 60 percent of cohabitations ended up in marriage, but in the 1990s, only 33 percent. The rates of divorce have changed. After a steady increase in divorce rates, they have held steady in recent years and have even decreased for college-educated women. The more educated the husband and wife are and the later they marry, the greater the stability of the marriage.[1]

Changes in the labor market have increasingly contributed to a transformation in the structure of marriage relationships. The entry of women into the labor force means that the division of gender roles into breadwinner and home worker no longer applies, though women still take on an unequal share of household labor. The growth of feminism has led to an increased cultural sensitivity to violence within marriage (both the battering of wives and the sexual abuse of children). These cultural and economic changes challenge the traditional pa-

---

1. Betsey Stevenson and Justin Wolfers, "Marriage and Divorce: Changes and Their Driving Forces," *Journal of Economic Perspectives* 21 (2007): 27–52; Linda A. Jacobsen and Mark Mather, "U.S. Economic and Social Trends since 2000," *Population Bulletin* 65, no. 1 (February 2010): 1–16.

triarchal structure of marriage and lead many to argue for a more egalitarian understanding of marriage, though this ideal is still a long way off in practice.

What is taking place is a deinstitutionalization of marriage as traditionally understood and practiced. Deinstitutionalization refers to a change in the social norms that define a person's behavior and expectations for a social institution such as marriage. Consequently, marriage no longer entails the same norms and social expectations as it previously did.[2] Some see these changes as a challenge to the very institution of marriage and ask whether marriage or the family is obsolete.[3] They describe our society as "postmarital" and argue that the dominance of the single-parent family, the high rate of divorce, and the legal acknowledgment of survivorship and rights between unmarried persons are signs of the demise of marriage.[4] If this were to come to pass, people in the third millennium would obviously have no use for a theology of marriage as a sacrament and no sense for the religious significance of marriage. Others, however, do not envision such a gloomy future for marriage. Instead, they speculate about how current trends might predict what marriage might look like in

the remainder of the twenty-first century. They point out that trends—as with the recent decrease in divorce rates—are not necessarily one-directional.[5]

Within the Roman Catholic Church, Cardinal Joseph Ratzinger, now Pope Benedict XVI, reflecting on modern scriptural and historical studies, pointed to the inadequacy of traditional ideas of marriage as a sacrament. Commenting on these ideas, Ratzinger asserted, "If one remains with the classic catechism, whereby a sacrament is an external sign, instituted by Christ, that signifies and effects inner grace, then these phrases say little; indeed they are in every respect questionable: neither has Jesus instituted marriage nor given it a specific external sign."[6] Moreover, Ratzinger continued, if the sacrament of marriage is understood as mechanically providing a couple with a grace that both makes their relation similar to the Christ-church relation and enables them to fulfill their tasks in the face of the reality of marriage, then the traditional teaching can "no longer be understood as a convincing, meaningful understanding of the notion of the sacrament."[7] In such cases, "the representative of systematic theology must appear, in more than one respect, as a hopeless

---

2. Andrew J. Cherlin, "The Deinstitutionalization of American Marriage," *Journal of Marriage and Family* 66 (2004): 848–61. See his earlier book, *Marriage, Divorce, Remarriage*, rev. ed. (Cambridge, MA: Harvard University Press, 1992), as well as his recent collection, *The Marriage-Go-Round* (New York: Random House, 2009). For a characterization of the trend as disestablishment, see Nancy C. Cott, *Public Vows: A History of Marriage and the Nation* (Cambridge, MA: Harvard University Press, 2000).

3. Amitai Etzioni, "The Family: Is It Obsolete?" *Journal of Current Social Issues* 14 (Winter 1977): 4–10.

4. David B. Wilson, "Is Marriage Obsolete?" *Boston Globe*, August 6, 1989, sec. A. See more recently, W. Bradford Wilcox and Elizabeth Marquardt, *When Marriage Disappears: The Retreat from Marriage in Middle America* (Charlottesville, VA: The National Marriage Project, 2010).

5. Andrew J. Cherlin, "American Marriage in the Early Twenty-First Century," *The Future of Children* 15, no. 2 (2005): 33–55.

6. Joseph Ratzinger, "Zur Theologie der Ehe," *Theologische Quartalschrift* 149 (1969): 53–74, here 54. See also Ratzinger's expositions of sacraments in general in *Die sakramentale Begründung christlicher Existenz* (Friesing: Kyrios Verlag, 1973); and *Zum Begriff des Sakraments: Eichstätter Hochschulreden*, vol. 13 (Munich: Minerva, 1979).

7. Ratzinger, "Zur Theologie der Ehe," 54.

dilettante."[8] Although his challenge was written decades ago, it remains today.

Consequently, one needs to examine carefully and critically the Roman Catholic tradition about marriage as a sacrament. A study of this tradition should take into account not only historical evidence about the long and diverse development of the Christian understanding of marriage. It should also examine philosophical and social background theories that have been the underlying assumptions of this tradition. Moreover, it would need to explore our contemporary experience and social constructs as articulated within diverse religious and social groups.[9] This task can be approached here only in a very limited fashion. In this brief treatment, I shall first examine biblical teaching, then Roman Catholic theological and church traditions, and finally contemporary systematic expositions.

Biblical Teaching on Marriage

The canonical Hebrew and Christian Scriptures contain many chapters and verses touching on marriage and issues related to married life. Nevertheless, it would be highly inappropriate to look to the Bible for a theology of marriage, as if the Bible contained a "theology *of* marriage." Too often, the Bible is looked upon as a source book for various "theologies of," be they theologies of work, of nature, or of sex. The Bible does not offer such a comprehensive systematic or conceptual analysis of marriage. However, it would be equally inappropriate if we did not attend to some of the diverse views and images of marriage that are reflected in biblical texts, for they have decisively influenced Christian theology.

Hebrew Scriptures

The Genesis accounts of the creation of the first human couple have influenced the interpretation of marriage in the West as much as the horizon of subsequent experience has influenced the interpretation of these verses. Historical-critical scholarship has shown, moreover, that the first chapters of Genesis contain two distinct accounts of the creation of the first couple: the Priestly account in Genesis 1 and the Yahwist account in Genesis 2–3.

The central verses of the Priestly tradition on the creation of humanity are Gen. 1:26-28: "Then God said, 'Let us make man ['adam] in our image, after our likeness. . . .' So God created ['adam] in his own image, in the image of God he created him; male and female he created them. And God blessed them, and God said to them, 'Be fruitful and multiply.'" This text describes the creation of human persons in the image of God as a creation of "the human" as male and female. The creation of the first couple takes place simultaneously. The human as both male and female is what is created in the image of God and represents God. This text is rather limited: "It says nothing about the image which relates 'adam to God nor about God as the referent. . . . It is not concerned with sexual roles, the status or relationship of the sexes to one another or marriage. It describes the biological pair, not

---

8. Ibid., 53.

9. For a survey of the family and gender in such a historical context, see the collection of essays in Anne Carr and Mary Stewart van Leeuwen, eds., *Religion, Feminism, and the Family* (Louisville: Westminster John Knox, 1996).

a social partnership; male and female, not man and wife."[10]

The Yahwist account in chapters 2 and 3 of Genesis contains the story of Adam and Eve in the Garden of Eden. In this narrative account, Adam is created first, and Eve is created afterward, formed from Adam's side in order to be his helpmate (Gen. 2:18-25). These verses have puzzled scholars. Traditional rabbinic literature interpreted these verses to mean that God originally created an "androgynous person," and those who translated the passage into Greek expressed this meaning by writing "a male with female parts." A more recent interpretation, however, suggests that 'adam literally means "the earth creature." Consequently, the intent of the story is not so much to stress that God created a male being first as to emphasize that God created humankind.[11]

Throughout the history of Jewish and Christian literature, both biblical accounts have been diversely interpreted and the source of much philosophical and religious speculation.[12] Yet one must exercise a certain reserve in the appropriation and use of this material. The Genesis accounts do not contain an implicit theology of marriage that seeks to legislate for all time the meaning of male and female and their division into their proper roles. Rather, the Genesis accounts function as mythic accounts of the origin of the world and of its inhabitants.

The Scriptures contain many verses and images about marriage. These have been the source of much poetic inspiration and theological reflection. Images of marriage and marital love can be found in the prophetic traditions, the Song of Songs, the story of Tobit, the book of Proverbs, the Wisdom of the Son of Sirach, and Qoheleth. This literature is quite diverse in its conceptions and views. For example, the erotic imagery of the Song of Songs that so passionately exults in the beloved contrasts sharply with the skeptical advice of the Son of Sirach that there is no wickedness or wrath on the earth greater than that of a woman (25:13).

The diverse literary genres and the contrasting social attitudes in these texts alert us to what can still serve as a source of inspiration and what needs to be assessed within its limited historical context. The negative attitudes toward women are pervasive, from the prophetic use of the harlot imagery[13] to Sirach's attribution of the origin of sin to women (25:24). At the same time, the ideals of fidelity and love are present in these texts. The negative texts must be acknowledged for what they are. They reflect not God's views, but the views of God's people—a sinful and wandering people like other peoples. The negative texts should be compared with more positive texts, and they should not be elevated above their socially and historically conditioned status to an eternal divine teaching about the sacrament of marriage.

Early Christian Scriptures

The early Christian Scriptures, like the Hebrew Scriptures, contain a variety of statements about

10. Phyllis Bird, "'Male and Female He Created Them': Gen. 1:27b in the Context of the Priestly Account of Creation," *Harvard Theological Review* 74 (1981): 129–59, here 155. Bird's analysis counters Karl Barth's influential analysis of the *imago* passage; see Karl Barth, *Church Dogmatics* (Edinburgh: T&T Clark, 1958), 3/1:183–206.

11. Phyllis Trible, *God and the Rhetoric of Sexuality* (Philadelphia: Fortress Press, 1978).

12. See Elaine Pagels, *Adam, Eve, and the Serpent* (New York: Random House, 1988).

13. See the critical analysis by T. Deborah Setel, "Prophets and Pornography: Female Sexual Imagery," in *Feminist Interpretation of the Bible*, ed. Letty M. Russell (Philadelphia: Westminster, 1985), 86–95.

588 marriage in diverse contexts.[14] Quite often, certain of these statements (e.g., Jesus' statements about divorce, the adultery exception of Matthew, or the Pauline exception) are highlighted from a particular systematic perspective. These verses, however, should not be isolated, but should be understood and interpreted within the context of diverse biblical traditions.

RELATIVIZATION OF MARRIAGE FOR THE SAKE OF DISCIPLESHIP

The earliest texts in the New Testament that refer to marriage stem from the early Christian missionary movements. These texts indicate a disruption and disturbance of traditional family structures: "Jesus said, 'Truly, I say to you, there is no one who has left house or brothers or sisters or mother or father or children or lands, for my sake and for the gospel, who will not receive a hundredfold'" (Mark 10:29). Likewise: "Truly, I say to you, there is no man who has left house or wife or brothers or parents or children, for the sake of the kingdom of God, who will not receive manifold more in this time, and in the age to come, eternal life" (Luke 18:29).

The early Christian missionary movement, often referred to as the "Jesus movement," provides the context of these verses.[15] The earliest disciples of Jesus did not at first establish local communities. Instead, they became wandering charismatics—traveling apostles, prophets, and disciples who moved from place to place and who left everything behind. As wandering preachers, they were homeless, lacked possessions, and lacked a family. The disciples left these behind for the sake of their preaching and missionary activity. For the sake of preaching God's kingdom, they chose a life with neither family nor possessions.

ESCHATOLOGICAL VISION AND THE COMMAND AGAINST DIVORCE

Another tradition of texts about marriage concerns divorce and remarriage.[16] These texts are Mark 10:11-12; Matt. 5:31-32; 19:3-9; Luke 16:18; and 1 Cor. 7:10-11. These sayings against divorce belong to the oldest traditions in the New Testament. They are a part of the Jesus tradition. If any sayings can with some degree of historical certainty be attributed to the historical Jesus, then these statements would be among the prime candidates.[17]

Scholars offer diverse interpretations of these sayings. Some scripture scholars attempt to explain them away as allegorical. For example, Bruce Malina argues that when taken literally, the statements make "as little sense as 'you are the salt of the earth.'"[18] Such an interpretation patently waters down the verses and substitutes personal conjecture for historical interpretation.

---

14. Everett Ferguson, ed., *Christian Life: Ethics, Morality, and Discipline in the Early Church* (New York: Garland, 1993).

15. For a social analysis of the Jesus movement, see Gerd Theissen, *Sociology of Early Christianity* (Philadelphia: Fortress Press, 1978).

16. For general Roman Catholic exegetical treatments, see Rudolf Pesch, *Freie Treue: Die Christen und die Ehescheidung* (Freiburg: Herder, 1971); Rudolf Schnackenburg, "Die Ehen ach der Weisungen Jesus und dem Verständnis der Urkirche," in *Ehe und Ehescheidung*, ed. Franz Henrich and Volker Eid, Münchener Akademie Schriften 59 (Munich: Kösel, 1972), 11–34.

17. Paul Hoffmann, "Jesus' Saying about Divorce and Its Interpretation in the New Testament Tradition," in *The Future of Marriage as an Institution*, ed. Franz Böckle (New York: Herder & Herder, 1970), 51–60, orig. pub. *Concilium* 55 (entire issue).

18. Bruce Malina, *The New Testament World: Insights from Cultural Anthropology* (Atlanta: John Knox, 1981), 118–21.

Nothing in the text indicates metaphorical or allegorical language. In fact, a literal interpretation of the text conforms well to the historical situation within first-century Judaism.[19] During this period, Judaism permitted divorce but limited its conditions. Sectarian groups such as the Essenes, however, rejected divorce outright. They had a distinct eschatological perspective on which they based their rejection of divorce.

Instead of explaining away these verses, some scholars point to their context and trajectory, especially to the debate in Palestine between the Hillel school, with its more lenient interpretation allowing divorce for the husband, and the Schammai school, which permitted divorce only for the most extreme cases. This perspective suggests that Jesus sides with the stricter interpretation and goes beyond it. Some exegetes suggest that Jesus' interpretation offers a protection for women, as Matt. 5:28 implies.[20]

Other scholars suggest that these Matthean verses should not be interpreted as a debate between two schools, but as a part of Jesus' radical eschatological vision. These writers point out that in the Jesus traditions that predate the Gospels (these traditions being reflected in Mark 10:2-9 and 12:18-27), Jesus' eschatological vision critically challenges traditional patriarchal marriage. It interprets marriage structures not in relation to an order of creation, but in relation to an apocalyptic theology of the restoration of original creation. The eschatological being of men and women is not based on sexual difference, but on freedom from sexual differentiation.[21] Jesus' imperatives do not provide valid norms for the historically conditioned circumstances of this time, but show that God's coming kingdom has an eschatological character that transcends the limits of traditional moral interpretations.[22]

Some exegetes have observed that in view of its literary genre, argumentation, and textual quotations from the Greek version of Genesis, the controversial dialogue constituting the pericope Matt. 5:31-32 expresses not a Palestinian dispute, but a debate within a Jewish-Christian Hellenistic community.[23] Some argue, however, that this debate in the Hellenistic community presupposes as known a decision or statement going back to the historical Jesus.[24]

Since the "except for" clause (Matt. 5:31) has significantly influenced the systematic position concerning divorce, its interpretation has been controverted. Among contemporary Roman Catholic exegetes, two divergent interpretations have emerged about the meaning of *porneia* in the text. One suggests that *porneia* refers to illegitimate marriages between relatives that were impermissible for Jewish Christians and that pagan Christians were also to avoid (Acts 15:20, 29). According to this interpretation, the exception adds not so much an exception as a further

19. Joseph Fitzmyer, "The Matthean Divorce Texts and Some New Palestinian Evidence," *Theological Studies* 37 (1976): 197–226, repr. in *To Advance the Gospel* (New York: Crossroad, 1981), 79–111.

20. See Dieter Luhrmann, "Eheverständnis und Eheseelsorge im Neuen Testament," in *Ehe, Institution im Wandel*, ed. Günther Gassmann (Hamburg: Lutherische Verlagshaus, 1979), 67–81.

21. See Elisabeth Schüssler Fiorenza, *In Memory of Her* (New York: Crossroad, 1983), 140–45.

22. Kurt Niederwimmer, *Askese und Mysterium: Über Ehe, Ehescheidung und Eheverzicht in den Anfängen des christlichen Glaubens*, Forschungen zur Religion und Literatur des Alten und Neues Testament 113 (Göttingen: Vandenhoeck, 1975), 12–41.

23. See Pesch, *Freie Treue*, 10–60.

24. Rudolf Schnackenburg, *The Moral Teaching of the New Testament* (New York: Herder & Herder, 1965).

restriction. Divorce is not allowed except for marriages that are really impermissible.[25] The other solution points out that *porneia* can also mean "adultery." This interpretation suggests that divorce is allowed when the marriage is already broken.[26]

In 1 Corinthians 7 (one of the most difficult chapters to interpret), Paul touches on several themes of marriage. In the first instance, he affirms the early Christian missionary ideal of the excellence of ascetic celibacy. Such a priority of asceticism over marriage was significant in the early Christian movement, so much so that, as recent exegetical research has shown, many in early Christianity viewed baptism and marriage as incompatible.[27] Though Paul acknowledges a priority of the unmarried state and recommends that the unmarried remain such, he does display a realism that acknowledges marriage. Paul does not so much develop a theology of marriage as concede the possibility of marriage as a practical necessity. Despite the examples of married couples as missionary apostles in the early Christian movement, such as his coworkers Prisca and Aquila, Paul argues that commitment to the work of mission favors asceticism over Christian marriage.[28]

In charging that neither husband nor wife should divorce one another, Paul refers to a word from the Lord. Such reference to a word from Jesus is a rare instance in Paul's writings. Nevertheless, in spite of the authority of this word, Paul argues from experience for an exception. In the history of Christianity, Paul's action has led to a broadening of the exception, and it has raised the issue of the power and responsibility of the community.

Household Codes and Christian Marriage

The deutero-Pauline and Pastoral Epistles contain a third tradition, the household codes, which were given that name because they were meant to regulate the behavior of the household. In contrast to the early Christian affirmation of asceticism and to the Pauline commendation of the unmarried state, these epistles affirm the importance of marriage and of family. Indeed, the Pastoral Epistles stipulate that bishops must be successful in marital and family life before their election to office; they must be married only once and have raised a solid family: "Now a bishop must be above reproach, the husband of one wife. . . . He must manage his own household well, keeping his children submissive and respectful in every way; for if a man does not know how to manage his own household, how can he care for God's church?" (1 Tim. 3:3-5).

Ephesians 5:21-33 contains a much more explicitly theological analysis of marriage. These

---

25. Jean Bonsirven, *Le divorce dans le Nouveau Testament* (Paris: Desclée, 1948); Fitzmyer, "The Matthean Divorce Texts and Some New Palestinian Evidence," 79–111. See also David I. Brewer, *Divorce and Remarriage in the Bible* (Grand Rapids: Eerdmans, 2002).

26. Gerhard Schneider, "Jesu Wort über die Ehescheidung in der Überlieferung des Neuen Testaments," *Trierer theologische Zeitschrift* 80 (1971): 65–87. See also Hoffmann, "Jesus' Saying about Divorce and Its Interpretation in the New Testament Tradition," and Pesch, *Freier Treue*. In *The Moral Teaching*, Schnackenburg retracts his earlier advocacy of the first interpretation.

27. Niederwimmer, *Askese und Mysterium*, 42–124. Niederwimmer shows the ascetic, christological, and eschatological basis for such a priority in early Christianity. See Richard B. Hays, *The Moral Vision of the New Testament* (San Francisco: HarperSanFrancisco, 1996.), ch. 1, app., pp. 46–59.

28. See Schüssler Fiorenza, *In Memory of Her*, 160–204. See also Carolyn Osiek and David Balch, *Families in the New Testament World: Households and House Churches* (Louisville: Westminster John Knox, 1997).

verses have become the classic biblical reference for much theological reflection on marriage. The household codes in Ephesians deal not only with the relations between husbands and wives, but also with the proper relations in regard to children and slaves (6:1-9). The household codes provide three parallel orders of relation: husband and wife, parents and children, masters and slaves. The first member of each pair has the role of leadership and responsibility, whereas the second has the role of obedience. With regard to marriage, the husband as the head of the wife parallels Christ as the head of the church.

These household codes have been diversely interpreted. Some have viewed them as expressing a divinely ordered sphere of subordination.[29] Others underscore the element of Christ's love for the church with the concomitant demands of the husband's love for the wife. Recent scholarship on the New Testament has illumined the specific context and meaning of these texts. In the Greco-Roman world, the early Christians were considered disruptive of the sociocultural order. The earliest Christians were, in fact, called atheists because they did not participate in emperor worship. Moreover, insofar as Christian communities allowed a wife, child, or slave to convert and join the community without the permission of the male head of the household, they were looked upon as disruptive of the patriarchal family order of the time.

The early Christian communities, with their emphasis on equality of discipleship and their admittance of individual women or individual slaves to the community, seemed to bear out

this charge. Consequently, the household codes, which are in the later books of the Christian Scriptures, represent in part an apologetic attempt to show that Christianity was not opposed to the Roman sociocultural order. The texts, therefore, borrow from the Aristotelian philosophy current at that time, which was embodied in a set of codes that reinforced the patriarchal order. It is this apologetic context of the texts that should deter today's Christians from accepting the Roman social order of patriarchy in regard to wives, children, and slaves as a divinely ordained order.[30] Theological reflection and pastoral preaching, therefore, have to be alert to the socially conditioned background theories or assumptions in elaborating a theology of marriage for and in modern societies not based upon the Roman patriarchal order.

In assessing the theological appropriation of these verses from Ephesians, it is important to note that a specific translation has greatly influenced the understanding of these verses. Because the Greek word *mysterion* was translated in the Vulgate as *sacramentum*, Eph. 5:32 has often been used as the basis for justifying the Scholastic doctrine of marriage as a sacrament. Some medieval theologians (for example, Peter Lombard) were aware of this translation problem. Moreover, Luther's polemic against the Roman Catholic teaching on marriage as a sacrament included this charge of mistranslation. As Walter Kasper has observed, "Most scholars are agreed now that the later idea of sacrament should not be presupposed" when one reads this passage from Ephesians.[31] A theological justification of

---

29. Most recently, Hans Urs von Balthasar affirms, "There are 'hierarchical states' theologically substantiated in this primal sacrament." *Theo-Logic*, vol. 3, *The Spirit of Truth* (San Francisco: Ignatius; Einseideln: Johannes Verlag, 1987), 345n63.

30. Elisabeth Schüssler Fiorenza, *Bread Not Stone* (Boston: Beacon, 1984). For a more popularly written version, see her "Marriage and Discipleship," *The Bible Today* 102 (April 1979): 2027–33.

31. Walter Kasper, *Theology of Christian Marriage* (New York: Crossroad, 1983), 30.

marriage as a sacrament should not be based exclusively on this passage.

Not Really a Harmony

One cannot bring these diverse traditions into harmony with one another as theologians of previous generations did when they attempted to synthesize ideas from various early Christian Scriptures into unified systematic concepts within a biblical theology or a theology of the New Testament. There is not a biblical theology of marriage as a unified set of ideas and concepts. Instead, one has to view the richness and diversity of the various early Christian traditions.

The traditions I have highlighted are central to the early Christian Scriptures. These traditions have had an impact on Christian thought throughout the centuries and can serve to criticize a one-sided appropriation of any particular tradition. The eschatological horizon of the Jesus movement, with its emphasis on asceticism, subordinates marriage and family to radical discipleship. Its eschatological vision stands out in contrast to the deutero-Pauline praise of the standard of a respectable family. The commitment to Jesus in a radical discipleship of equals is other than the emphasis on the Roman patriarchal order in the household codes. Yet there is also the eschatological ideal of marriage in relation to the original human creation that represents a hope and a vision beyond the frailty in marriages. The insight that relations among humans are meant to mirror the divine-human relation provides a challenge for theological reflection that Christian theology has taken up in various ways throughout the centuries.

Marriage in the History of Roman Catholic Theology

The history of Christian theological views toward marriage displays diverse attitudes, and the development of the Roman Catholic understanding of marriage as a sacrament is a complex topic. This history shows a complex, developing relationship between civil law (going back to Roman law) and theological interpretations of marriage.[32] Rather than present a historical survey, I shall merely highlight a few salient points from the history of theology: (1) Augustine's understanding of the sacrament in marriage within the context of his influential treatment of the goods of marriage; (2) the development of medieval conceptions of marriage; (3) the affirmations of the Council of Trent; and (4) recent official teachings of the Roman Catholic church regarding marriage.

Augustine: The Sacrament in Marriage

Although many of the early Christian writers dealt with marriage, Augustine's views have most strongly influenced Western theology.[33]

---

32. For a detailed presentation of historical issues, see Philip Lyndon Reynolds, *Marriage in the Western Church: The Christianization of Marriage during the Patristic and Early Medieval Periods* (Leiden: Brill, 1994). For the medieval period, see David L. d'Avray, *Medieval Marriage: Symbolism and Society* (Oxford: Oxford University Press, 2005). For special emphasis on the Reformation traditions, see John Witte Jr., *From Sacrament to Contract: Marriage, Religion, and the Law* (Louisville: Westminster John Knox, 1997). See also Glenn W. Olsen, ed., *Christian Marriage: A Historical Study* (New York: Herder, 2001).

33. For a survey of the views on marriage in the ancient church, see Alfred Niebergall, *Ehe und Eheschließung in der Bibel und in der Geschichte der alten Kirche* (Marburg: Elwert, 1985), 101–253.

Augustine did not so much affirm marriage as one of the sacraments of the New Law; rather, he affirmed that there is in all marriages, and not just Christian marriages, a sacrament. Augustine used the term *sacrament* in both a broad and a narrow sense.[34] In a very general sense, sacrament refers to visible words, things, and actions that are signs of what is invisible and transcendent. In a narrower sense, sacrament refers specifically to the sacraments of the Catholic Church, among which baptism and Eucharist have a predominant role.

Augustine understands the sacrament in marriage in the broad rather than narrow sense, as is evident in his treatment of the goods of marriage—a specific teaching that has greatly influenced traditional Roman Catholic teaching about marriage. Though the words *goods* and to a lesser extent *blessings* or *benefits* are often used in the English translation of Augustine, the word *values* probably expresses more adequately Augustine's thought. In *The Good of Marriage*, Augustine taught that marriage has three values: fidelity, offspring, and sacrament.[35] Fidelity (*fides*) is the faithfulness in the mutual love that each spouse has for the other. Augustine interprets fidelity in relation to the sexual love and intercourse of the married couple. Yet he does so in a way that disallows the denigration of one partner or the other to a mere sexual object. In his view, even sexual relations open to procreation can be sinful if the partner is reduced to a mere object of libido. Fidelity relates to sexual love, but it entails more than a sexual commitment. Rather, it is a commitment of love and trust. Fidelity is the virtue that also supports the second value of marriage, offspring. This second value entails the acceptance of children in love, their nurturance in affection, and their upbringing in the Christian religion.

The third value of marriage is the sacrament of marriage. In chapter 18 of *The Good of Marriage*, Augustine explains that the sacrament is found in first marriages. It primarily refers to the union of the spouses as an indissoluble bond. For these marriages are a visible sign; that is, they signify the image of the one society of the blessed in eternity. A Christian marriage signifies visibly on earth the future unity of the people of God in eternity. The union of the spouses, their visible covenant with one another, is a tangible sign of the unity of all people in eternity.

These three values show that Augustine does not view marriage simply as a bond between two individuals. Instead, he understands marriage as a sign and sacrament. He describes its sacramentality within the framework of the distinction between the old and new covenant. The marriages of the Hebrew patriarchs symbolized the future church that consisted of many nations and peoples, and this was signified by their polygamous marriage (*sacramentum pluralium nuptiarum*). The marriage of a bishop, as a marriage with one wife, differs from the marriage of the patriarchs. The one church from many nations already exists as a reality, even though it is not yet perfect. Therefore, the marriage of a bishop constitutes a sign of the radical unity and peace of the eschatological city (*sacramentum nuptiarum*

---

34. Charles Couturier "'Sacramentum' et 'Mysterium' dans l'oeuvre de Saint Augustin," in *Études augustiniennes*, Théologie 28 (Paris: Aubier, 1953), 161–332.

35. Augustine, *The Good of Marriage*, in *Treatises on Marriage and Other Subjects*, Fathers of the Church 15 (New York: Fathers of the Church, 1955), 9–51. On marriage as a vocation, see Willemien Otten, "Augustine on Marriage, Monasticism, and the Community of the Church," *Theological Studies* 58 (1998): 385–405.

594   *singularum*).[36] This vision of marriage as a sacrament underscores that marriage is a sign of societal peace and unity. It is not simply that the fidelity of two spouses aids in the continued nurturing of children, but also that the visible union of the couple signifies the eschatological unity of all people and nations.

Too often, contemporary theologians tend to neglect these positive elements within Augustine's theology and mention only what they perceive as the negative elements—for instance, his view of marriage as a remedy for concupiscence and his negative assessment of sexuality.[37] Augustine also taught that marriage "does not seem to be good only because of the procreation of children, but also because of the natural companionship between the sexes."[38] Moreover, as Augustine matured as a Christian, his belief in the incarnation led him to move further away from his early Manichean attitudes to a more positive assessment of human corporeality.[39]

Medieval Theology: Marriage as a Sacrament

A considerable development took place from Augustine's view of the sacrament of marriage as a visible sign of a transcendent unity of the people of God to the view of marriage as one of the seven sacraments. The incorporation of marriage into the rank of sacraments occurred during the medieval period between the eleventh and twelfth centuries. The context for this development was cultural, doctrinal, canonical, and liturgical.[40] The doctrinal occasion was the spread of the Cathari or Albigenses, ascetics who viewed marriage as an evil. Their views prompted a theological response that affirmed the goodness of marriage and spurred the development of a theology of marriage as a sacrament. In fact, the first official explicit affirmations of marriage as a sacrament occur in statements condemning the Cathari. In 1184 the Council of Verona under Pope Lucius III anathematized the Cathari for their opinions about marriage. In 1208 Pope Innocent III required as a condition for return to Catholicism that the Waldenses subscribe to a profession of faith that accepted all the church's sacraments, including marriage. In 1274 the Second Council of Lyons proposed a similar requirement as a condition for reunion for the Byzantine emperor Michael Palaeologus.

THE DEVELOPMENT OF MARRIAGE AS A SACRAMENT

Liturgical celebrations also influenced the development of the notion of marriage as a sacrament.[41] The church's liturgical practice of the wedding ceremony appropriated Roman and Teutonic traditions. Germanic, Frankish, and Lombardic laws emphasized the handing over of

---

36. Augustine, *The Good of Marriage*, ch. 18: "Just as the many wives of the ancient fathers signified our future churches of all races subject to one man Christ, so our bishop, a man of one wife, signifies the unity of all nations subject to the one man Christ."

37. Augustine often argues against several fronts. It is in his writings against the Manicheans that his most positive evaluations of marriage are made.

38. Augustine, *The Good of Marriage*, ch. 3.

39. See Margaret Miles, *Augustine on the Body* (Missoula, MT: Scholars, 1979).

40. See the diverse studies reprinted in Carol Neel, ed. *Medieval Families: Perspectives on Marriage, Household, and Children* (Toronto: University of Toronto Press, 2004).

41. For a discussion of this development, see Edward Schillebeeckx, *Marriage: Secular Reality and Saving Mystery* (New York: Sheed & Ward, 1965), 302–43.

the bride, different from though not unlike the Roman custom of the handing over of the bride to the husband as the paterfamilias. As a result, people came to equate the blessing of marriage with the "handing over of the bride." A parallel was seen between the veiling and handing over of the bride and the veiling and handing over of the consecrated virgin, as a "bride of Christ," to the church. This analogy between the bride and the consecrated virgin was significant for the developing understanding of marriage as a sacrament. Whereas the virgin was consecrated directly to Christ, the bride was consecrated through the human relationship with her husband, the figure of Christ. The bride's visible relationship to the husband was a sign of her invisible relation to Christ. The text of Ephesians 5:21-32 influenced this development. Since the virgin was consecrated directly to Christ, this consecration was not viewed as a sacrament. Since the consecration to the husband was a visible sign of a more profound relation to Christ, marriage was a sacrament. Such a development and view went beyond Augustine's view of the mutual fidelity in marriage as a sign of the unity of the people of God.

The doctrine of marriage as a sacrament developed gradually within the medieval period. Moreover, theological speculation about marriage during the medieval period was quite diverse. Three distinct theories existed about what constituted the nature of marriage. Does the marriage bond derive primarily from the consent of the two partners, from the consummation through sexual intercourse, or from marriage's social function? The consent theory, also known as the French theory, was advocated by theologians in Paris. They argued that the essence of marriage was the free consent of the individual couple. A marriage continued to be a full marriage even when sexual intercourse played no role, as in the example of Mary and Joseph. Procreation belonged to the task (*officium*) of marriage, but not its constitution. The second view, known as the *copula* theory, was advocated by canonists, especially in Italy. They argued that marriage was constituted by sexual intercourse and believed marital consent to sexual intercourse was the essential element of the marital relation. A third view argued that marriage was an institution that provided the social and human foundation for the bringing up of children.

Between proponents of the first two views there was a significant debate concerning the relation between mutual consent and the community of marriage.[42] Both agreed that mutual consent formed the basis of marriage, but they made a distinction between the contracted marriage (based on consent) and the ratified marriage (sealed through sexual consummation). Theologians such as Peter Lombard argued that the marriage bond was established by the mutual consent. His position that simple exchange of consent established the marriage bond eventually led to the tendency to underscore consent of the couple and the consent of no other as essential to marriage.[43] The canonists argued that a marriage, though valid due to mutual consent, could be dissolved if it was not consummated. Even the growing stipulation that marriage should take place publicly and within a religious

---

42. For a description of the medieval controversies, see James A. Brundage, *Law, Sex, and Christian Society in Medieval Europe* (Chicago: University of Chicago Press, 1987).

43. Michael M. Sheehan, "Choice of a Marriage Partner in the Middle Ages: Development and Mode of Application of a Theory of Marriage," *Studies in Medieval and Renaissance History* 1 (1978): 1–33.

ceremony was seen both as the increasing emphasis on the sacred aspect of marriage and as a safeguarding of the rights of the couple. Lombard's successors developed this emphasis on consent to affirm that the husband and wife administer the sacrament to one another.

The influence of this debate, especially the Parisian emphasis on spousal consent, can be seen in Hugh of Saint Victor's theological treatment of marriage.[44] Hugh posited two sacraments of Christian marriage. The *sacramentum conjugi* consists of the love union between man and woman that signifies and images God's love for humans and the human love for God. The *sacramentum officii* is expressed in sexual intercourse that images the love of Christ and the church—a love in the flesh. The theological position that marriage requires consent led to an emphasis on love within marriage.[45] Richard of Saint Victor (d. 1173) gives a lyrical description of marital love in *Of the Four Degrees of Passionate Love*. His treatment gives a priority to human affection: "We know that among human affections conjugal love must take the first place, and therefore in wedded life that degree of love which generally dominates all other affections seems to be good. For the mutual affection of intimate love draws closer the bonds of peace between those who are pledged to each other, and make that indissoluble, life-long association pleasant and happy."[46]

The institution of the sacrament of marriage was viewed somewhat differently from that of the other sacraments. One could not simply affirm that Christ instituted the sacrament of marriage, since marriage existed before Christ—indeed, was present even in paradise. Therefore, Scholastic theologians refer to stages in the institution of this sacrament. Anselm of Laon argued that marriage, in contrast to other sacraments, was instituted before the fall. Christ did not institute it, but confirmed it at the marriage in Cana. Three stages of institution are outlined in Thomas Aquinas's *Summa theologiae*. (Since Thomas died before completing the *Summa*, Reynaldo of Piperno completed the treatise on the sacraments by drawing on Thomas's earlier commentary on Peter Lombard's *Sentences*, where Thomas had basically followed Albert the Great.) These three moments of the institution of marriage are the natural orientation before the fall, the healing institution of the Law of Moses after the fall, and finally, the institution of the New Law as a sign of union between Christ and the church.

Thomas Aquinas: Marriage as the Greatest Friendship

Although it has been often noted that Thomas was much more negative in his assessment of women than Augustine, due to the influence

---

44. See Hugh of Saint Victor *De beatae mariae virginis virginitate*, written between 1131 and 1141. His *De institutione sacramentorum* treats of marriage in book 2, 11: *De sacramento conjugi*. See Roy J. Defarrari, ed., *Hugh of St. Victor: On the Sacraments of the Christian Faith* (Cambridge: Medieval Academy of America, 1951). For a general treatment of diverse monastic views of marriage, see Jean Leclercq, *Monks on Marriage: A Twelfth-Century View* (New York: Seabury, 1982). For a broader historical survey, see Georges Duby, *Medieval Marriage: Two Models from Twelfth-Century France* (Baltimore: John Hopkins Press, 1978).

45. Although medieval marriages were first of all social and economic relationships, one should not underestimate the importance of affective criteria in the choice of partners. See David Herlihy, "The Making of the Medieval Family: Symmetry, Structure and Sentiment," *Journal of Family History* 8 (1983): 116–30.

46. Richard of Saint Victor, *Selected Writings on Contemplation* (New York: Harper & Brothers, n.d.), 215.

of Aristotle's biology,[47] he actually had a more positive view of human sexuality, as the debate about marriage in paradise showed. Some argued that in the Garden of Paradise before the fall, human procreation would have occurred without sexual intercourse. Against such a view Aquinas argued on the basis of the naturalness of human sexuality for procreation. What was absent was not human sexuality, but "excessive concupiscence."[48] Moreover, with a healthy realism, Thomas stressed the importance of friendship for marriage: "The greater that friendship, the more solid and long-lasting it be. Now, there seems to be the greatest friendship between husband and wife, for they are united not only in the act of fleshly union, which produces a certain gentle association even among beasts, but also in the partnership of the whole range of domestic activity."[49]

Bonaventure distinguished among three types of sacraments. The common sacraments of the old and new covenant are marriage and penance. They exist from the wisdom of nature and are merely confirmed by Christ.[50] Baptism, Eucharist, and ordination are partially prefigured in the Old Testament, but they flourish in the New Testament. Beyond these, there are sacraments distinctive to the New Testament: confirmation and the anointing of the sick. They were established in the church by the Holy Spirit.

The Council of Trent on Marriage

Prior to modern papal and conciliar teaching, two major councils were significant for the Roman Catholic Church's teaching on marriage: the "Union" Council of Florence (1439–45) and the Council of Trent (1545–63). Whereas Florence was concerned with Eastern traditions, Trent affirmed both the sacramentality and the indissolubility of marriage in the context of Martin Luther's criticism of Roman Catholic teaching and practice.[51] The notion that marriage is indissoluble is evident in canon 7 (November 11, 1563): "Whoever says that the Church errs when it has taught and still teaches that, according to the evangelical and apostolic doctrine, because of the adultery of one spouse, the bond of marriage cannot be dissolved and that both, even the innocent party, who has not given cause for adultery, cannot contract another marriage while the other spouse is still alive . . . may he be excluded."[52]

---

47. See Kari Elisabeth Borresen, *Subordination and Equivalence: The Nature and Role of Woman in Augustine and Thomas Aquinas*, rev. ed. (Washington, DC: University Press of America, 1981).

48. Thomas Aquinas, *Summa theologiae* I, q. 98. For a defense of Thomas's view of human sexuality, see Otto Hermann Pesch, *Thomas von Aquin: Grenze und Größe mittelalterlicher Theologie* (Mainz: Matthias-Grünewald, 1988), 254–56, and in regard to women, 20–227. See also Lisa Sowle Cahill, *Between the Sexes: Foundations for a Christian Ethics of Sexuality* (Philadelphia: Fortress Press, 1985), 105–22.

49. Thomas Aquinas, *Summa contra gentiles* 3.123.6 (trans. Vernon J. Bourke [New York: Image Books, 1956]).

50. Ratzinger, "Zur Theologie der Ehe," 59.

51. Martin Luther, "The Babylonian Captivity of the Church," in Theodore G. Tappert, ed., *Selected Writings of Martin Luther, 1517–1520*, vol. 1, ed. Theodore G. Tappert (Philadelphia: Fortress Press, 1967); for the section on marriage, see 444–58. See also idem, "A Sermon on the Estate of Marriage," in *Martin Luther's Basic Theological Writings*, ed. Timothy F. Lull (Minneapolis: Augsburg Fortress, 1989), 630–37, where Luther develops a complementary idea of marriage as an estate.

52. Denzinger-Schönmetzer, *Enchiridion Symbolorum* (hereafter DS), 1807. For literature on the Council of Trent, see Hubert Jedin, "Die Unauflöslichkeit der Ehen ach dem Konzil von Trient," in Klaus Reinhardt and Hubert Jedin,

598

The Council of Trent made two basic affirmations about marriage. The first states that marriage is a sacrament and within the provenance of the church. Marriage is not simply a matter of private, personal, or individual decision but concerns the community. Therefore, Trent required that Catholic marriages should take place in the presence of a priest. It thereby sought to curb the widespread practice of clandestine marriages. Second, Trent reaffirmed the church's teaching and practice (especially in the Western church) that prohibited divorce and remarriage for cases of adultery. The council maintained that this teaching and practice are "in accordance with" evangelical and apostolic doctrine. Scholars have maintained that the language used by the council pointed to obligatory teaching and practice, "not an ultimately obligatory dogma in the modern sense of the word."[53] It sought to underscore that the church's practice and teaching were in accordance with the New Testament. This affirmation was deliberately very nuanced. "In accordance with" is not the same as "identical with." In other words, "it is not simply the teaching of the Gospel."[54]

The decision of Trent, as Walter Kasper summarizes it, was limited: "The only intention was to come to a decision in the controversy that had been raging at the time between the Catholic Church and the Lutherans. Controversies within the Catholic Church itself were, however, left open. No previous decision of any kind was therefore made by the Council of Trent with regard to the pastoral problems of the twentieth century."[55]

Recent Official Roman Catholic Teaching

Within modern times, several statements on marriage provide the content of the Roman Catholic Church's official teaching on the subject.[56] In his encyclical on marriage (*Arcanum divinae sapientiae*, "secret of divine wisdom") published in 1880, Pope Leo XIII took issue with the trend toward seeing marriage as a purely secular event and as subject only to civil law. In contrast, he argued for the sacramentality of marriage and the marital contract as a sign that imaged the relation between Christ and the church. Fifty years later, in Pius XI's encyclical on marriage (*Casti connubii*, "chaste wedlock") took up many of the themes of Pope Leo's encyclical. He especially deplored the many abuses surrounding marriage. At the same time, he sought to further elaborate the religious meaning of marriage. In his view, "This mutual inward molding of husband and wife, this determined effort to perfect each other, can in a very real sense, as the Roman Catechism teaches us, be said to be the chief reason and purpose of marriage, provided marriage be looked at not in

---

Ehe-Sakrament in der Kirche des Herrn: Ehe in Geschichte und Gegenwart, vol. 2 (Berlin: Morus, 1971), 61–135; Piet Fransen, "Divorce on the Ground of Adultery—the Council of Trent (1563)," in Böckle, ed., *The Future of Marriage as an Institution*, 89–100; Peter J. Huizing, "La dissolution du mariage depuis le Concile de Trent," *Revue de droit canonique* 21 (1971): 127–45.

53. Kasper, *Theology of Christian Marriage*, 61.

54. See Karl Lehmann, *Gegenwart des Glaubens* (Mainz: Matthias-Grünewald, 1974), 274–308, here 285. Lehmann relies on the interpretations of Piet Fransen in Böckle, *The Future of Marriage as an Institution*, 89–100; and Joseph Ratzinger, "Zur Frage nach der Unauflöslichkeit der Ehe," in Henrich and Eid, *Ehe und Ehescheidung*, 35–56, esp. 49ff.

55. Kasper, *Theology of Christian Marriage*, 62.

56. See Benedictine Monks of Solesmes, eds., *Papal Teaching: Matrimony*, trans. Michael J. Byrnes (Boston: St. Paul's, 1963).

the restricted sense as instituted for the proper conception and education of the child, but more widely as the sharing of life as a whole and the mutual interchange and partnership thereof" (no. 24).[57] Pope Pius XII continued the basic teaching of his predecessor. In diverse talks to various groups, most notably his addresses to "Italian Catholic Obstetricians" and to "Italian Catholic Midwives," Pius XII sought to reaffirm the traditional papal teaching.[58] At the same time, he introduced some elements of the personalist philosophical approaches to marriage current at the time. These papal discourses provided the basic contours of Roman Catholic teaching prior to the Second Vatican Council.

The Second Vatican Council's Pastoral Constitution on the Church in the Modern World (*Gaudium et spes*; hereafter cited as GS) made a decisive attempt to reflect theologically on marriage in the modern world. The document is primarily concerned with the church in the modern world, so it is aware of the challenges that modern economic forces present to Christian life, including marriage. However, this constitution is also innovative in its treatment of marriage. It refers to marriage as an intimate community of love, a Christian vocation, a sacred bond and covenant, and a mutual gift of two persons.[59] The Christian family is described as a domestic church.[60] It is noticeable that the traditional language describing marriage as a contract is missing. Its main theological point

was to rethink the question of whether procreation constitutes the primary, natural, and end and purpose of marriage. Its formulation was very careful: though it speaks of children as the gift of marriage and of the orientation of marriage toward the procreation and nurture of children, it affirms that "while not making the other ends of marriage of less value, the true conduct of marital love and the entire meaning of family life that comes from it have this goal, that the spouses be willing to co-work courageously with the love of the Creator and Savior" (GS 50).[61]

Within Roman Catholic theology, contemporary reflections on many issues take as their starting point the documents of the Second Vatican Council. However, the situation differs in regard to marriage, especially the issue of human sexuality. On June 23, 1964, Pope Paul VI removed the issue of the control of human fertility from the agenda of the Second Vatican Council. He expanded the Pontifical Study Commission, which Pope John XXIII had established, and instructed it to report directly to himself. The commission recommended a change in traditional teaching. Pope Paul VI rejected their concrete recommendation. His encyclical *Humanae vitae* (1968) further developed the Roman Catholic understanding of marriage. In previous papal documents, the arguments against the limitation of birth were drawn from the end or purpose of marriage, namely, the procreation of children. Since the Second Vatican Council's

---

57. The English translation of the encyclical is in ibid., 219–21.

58. For a collection of Pius XII's discourses, see ibid., 301–506.

59. For a description of the debates within Vatican II and an attempt to use the notion of "covenant" to develop a theology of marriage, see Peter Jeffrey, *The Mystery of Christian Marriage* (Mahwah, NJ: Paulist, 2006).

60. See Michael A. Fahey, "The Christian Family as Domestic Church at Vatican II," in *The Family*, ed. Lisa Sowle Cahill and Dietmar Mieth (Maryknoll, NY: Orbis, 1994), 85–92.

61. For an exposition of the teaching of *Gaudium et spes* on marriage, see Joseph A. Selling, "A Closer Look at the Doctrine of *Gaudium et spes* on Marriage and the Family," *Bijdragen* 43 (1982): 30–48, and idem, "Twenty Significant Points in the Theology of Marriage and Family Present in the Teaching of *Gaudium et spes*," *Bijdragen* 43 (1982): 412–41.

statements broadened the understanding of the primary purpose of marriage, Pope Paul VI had to nuance the argumentation and gave it a more anthropological and personalist basis.

This argumentation has been echoed and further developed by Pope John Paul II's Apostolic Exhortation on the Family (*Consortium socialis*) and in his Wednesday general audience talks on the "Theology of the Body."[62] To develop his understanding of sex and marriage, John Paul II draws on phenomenology and personalist philosophy in order to explicate the importance of intersubjective bodily relations between the spouses. The human person is embodied as a sexual being with the task of integrating physical and spiritual acts. In the pope's view, this integration requires that loving sexual unions be procreative.[63] Although his general audience talks cannot be considered official teaching, three points deserve special mention:

1. The pope develops a theology of the body as the basis for an understanding of human sexuality and marriage. He argues against any kind of moral dualism between spirit and body. Lust is a matter of the spirit as well as the body, just as sin affects the spirit and the body. There is a spirituality of the body through which humans achieve a mature spontaneity with their hearts. Human senses and passions can point to the

true and the good. Nevertheless, he also suggests that as a result of original sin, the body is not subordinate to the spirit, and he emphasizes the need for self-control over sexual passion.

2. He seeks to interpret marriage in relation to the love of God for human beings. He gives a primacy to love (agape) as modeled on God's love as seen in God's creation and in the incarnation.

3. The pope affirms the equality of women and their basic rights, especially against violence and discrimination. He introduces into his understanding of male-female relations the idea of the complementarity between male and female that developed in nineteenth-century Romanticism and within the modern nuclear family. The woman's primary role is seen as mother. His understanding of gender appears to be based on biology and on a specific cultural construction of gender that differs from post–World War II societal changes in which women entered the workforce alongside men.

In recent decades, the issue of marriage has also been treated within the broader context of the nature and role of the family in modern society, as indicated by the documents of the bishops' synod and the International Theological Commission.[64] Pope Benedict XVI gave an address on the fortieth anniversary of the en-

---

62. John Paul II's Apostolic Exhortation on the Family is published with commentaries in Michael J. Wrenn, ed., *Pope John Paul II and Family* (Chicago: Franciscan Herald Press, 1983). For the "Theology of the Body," series, see vol. 3 of *Reflections on* Humanae vitae: *Conjugal Morality and Spirituality* (Boston: Daughters of St. Paul, 1983).

63. For a critical analysis and interpretation, see Lisa Sowle Cahill, "Community and Couple: Parameters of Marital Commitment in Catholic Tradition," in William P. Roberts, ed., *Commitment to Partnership: Explorations of the Theology of Marriage* (New York: Paulist Press, 1987), 81101; and Charles E. Curran, *The Moral Theology of Pope John Paul II* (Washington, DC: Georgetown University Press, 2005). For a different perspective that defends papal teaching, see Richard M. Hogan and John M. LeVoir, *Covenant of Love: Pope John Paul on Sexuality, Marriage, and Family in the Modern World* (Garden City, NY: Doubleday, 1985).

64. Jan Grootaers and Joseph Selling, eds., "The 1980 Synod of Bishops 'On the Role of the Family': An Exposition of the Event and an Analysis of Its Texts," *Ephemerides theologicae lovanieses* 64 (Louvain: University of Louvain Press, 1983); and International Theological Commission, "Propositions on the Doctrine of Christian Marriage," *Origins* (September 28, 1978): 235–39.

cyclical, elucidating its enduring significance.[65] More recently, the United States Conference of Roman Catholic Bishops issued a pastoral letter, *Marriage: Love and Life in the Divine Plan*, which summarizes Catholic teaching and offers an understanding of the family as the domestic church and as sign and an image of the communion among the persons of the Trinity.[66]

Marriage as a Sacrament in Modern Systematic Theology

Within contemporary theology, the sacrament of marriage has been the subject of many studies. Much of the writing on marriage within theological literature concerns moral, pastoral, and canonical issues. Nevertheless, several important directions for a clearer understanding of marriage have been elaborated within contemporary systematic theology. In this section, I shall briefly sketch some contemporary directions, then offer some of my own systematic reflections on the sacrament of marriage, and finally summarize some of the discussion surrounding two practical pastoral issues that result from the Catholic theological view of marriage.

Three Modern Directions

Approaches to a theology of marriage as a sacrament reflect the general theological emphases of their historical contexts. During the most recent decades, three distinct trends within Roman Catholic theology have affected these approaches to marriage: christocentrism, the salvation-historical view, and the anthropological-ecclesial view. Due to the influence of Karl Barth, a christocentric focus entered not only Protestant neo-orthodox theology, but also Roman Catholic theology. Roman Catholic "christocentrism," however, displays its own distinctive forms, with an emphasis on the sacramental notion of the body of Christ. Likewise, the salvation-historical approach, exemplified by Oscar Cullmann and influential in French theology, made an impact on Roman Catholic theology in the 1950s and 1960s and has affected the analysis of the sacrament of marriage. In addition, Karl Rahner's development of the anthropological-ecclesial foundation of marriage as a sacrament has deeply influenced Roman Catholic thought on the subject.

CHRISTOCENTRIC VIEW OF MARRIAGE

The christocentric focus that flourished within Roman Catholic theology in the 1950s has its roots in the nineteenth century. It was especially applied by Matthias Scheeben (1835–88) to marriage.[67] Within French Catholic theology, the notion of the body of Christ or the mystical body of Christ, as it was then understood, became the key metaphor used to interpret marriage as a sacrament.[68] Whereas the sacrament of baptism signals an incorporation of a person into the body of Christ, the sacrament of marriage entails a further incorporation within the

---

65. See my treatment, later in this chapter, of Benedict's address in relation to his earlier writings in the section on birth control.

66. Washington, DC: United States Conference of Catholic Bishops 2009.

67. Matthias Scheeben, *The Mysteries of Christianity* (St. Louis: B. Herder, 1961), ch. 21.

68. Gustav Martelet, "Mariage, amour et sacrement," *Nouvelle revue théologique* 85 (1953): 577–97; Henri Rondet, *Introduction à l'étude de la théologie du mariage* (Paris: Lethielleux, 1960).

602 body of Christ. As a result, the Christian couple participates in a distinctive and special vocation.

Salvation-Historical View of Marriage

Roman Catholic theology has always been aware that the understanding of marriage as a sacrament has changed and developed throughout the ages. Many theologians interpret these changes not just as changes in the theological understanding of marriage. Instead, they argue that the nature and meaning of marriage itself have changed within the history of salvation. Such a view is present within medieval theology, as exemplified by Bonaventure's understanding of marriage. Within recent decades, theologians have sought to relate marriage to salvation history in the same way they have related it to the evolving history of the world and to the history of religious experience.[69]

Edward Schillebeeckx has elaborated a theological interpretation of marriage as a sacrament with this basic thesis: "Marriage is a secular reality which has entered salvation."[70] The relation between secular reality and religious reality is not a static relation but has a history. Human thought changes and develops in the process of continually reflecting on historical experience. Marriage has significance as a reality of created life. However, the historical experience by God's people of God's covenant and the Christian experience of Jesus as paschal event also contribute to the understanding of the significance of marriage. Marriage is then no longer understood simply as a secular reality within

creation, but it is understood also as a promise in the light of the experience of God's covenantal promise. Created reality is both affirmed and relativized in the light of the eschatological hope. Love within marriage is understood not only in relation to natural attraction, but also in relation to the historical experience of Jesus' death and resurrection and the understanding of God and of love proclaimed by the gospel.

Anthropological-Ecclesial View of Marriage

Karl Rahner contributes to the understanding of marriage as a sacrament by bringing together several key ideas of his theology: God's universal will for salvation, the fundamental unity of creation and salvation, the idea of a real symbol, and his understanding of the church as the basic sacrament.[71] For Rahner, God's love and gracious self-bestowal constitute the innermost dynamism of the world and of the history of humankind. It is God's gracious love that empowers us to love God and to love each other. Consequently, genuine love as a theological virtue is an event both of God's love for us and of our love for God.

The radical and real symbol of the unity of God's love for us and the human response of love is in the incarnate Christ. The church as a basic sacrament is real sign and symbol of God's love for humanity and the human love of God. In this context, marriage "is the sign of *that* love which is designed in God's sight to be the event of grace and a love that is open to all."[72] Moreover, marriage is a sacrament that concretizes and actu-

---

69. Piet Schoonenberg, "Marriage in the Perspective of the History of Salvation," in *God's World in the Making* (Techny, IL: Divine Word, 1964), 106–34.

70. Schillebeeckx, *Marriage*, 384.

71. Karl Rahner, "Marriage as a Sacrament," in *Theological Investigations* (New York: Crossroad, 1973), 10:191–221. For his basic understanding of sacraments, see *The Church and the Sacraments* (New York: Herder & Herder, 1963).

72. Rahner, "Marriage as a Sacrament," 209.

alizes the church. As Rahner expresses it, "The love that unites married spouses contributes to the unity of the Church herself because it is one of the ways in which the unifying love of the Church is made actual. It is just as much formative of the Church as sustained by the Church."[73]

Toward a Theology of Marriage: A New Community

These three directions have greatly enriched our understanding of marriage as a sacrament. Nevertheless, recent advances in fundamental theology, Christology, and ecclesiology lead beyond these contributions. Recent shifts within fundamental theology regarding the foundation of the church and within ecclesiology concerning the nature of the church have suggested a new understanding of the church as a sacrament. It has thus become necessary to bring the conception of the sacramentality of marriage into accord with these changes. In addition, traditional theological expositions of marriage as a sacrament have, in some aspects, been based on patriarchal assumptions of marriage and family or have been shaped by outmoded social and anthropological assumptions about gender roles. It has become necessary to elaborate the meaning of the Roman Catholic vision and ideal of marriage in view of equalitarian assumptions about gender and marriage.

MARRIAGE AS SACRAMENT: THE COMMUNITY OF THE SPIRIT

Much of traditional theology focused on the text from Ephesians as the symbolic basis of the sacrament of marriage. Unfortunately, use of the image of the Christ-church relation as a model for the marital relation between husband and wife has certain shortcomings. In the image of the relation between Christ and the church, Christ is the one who rules, who saves, and who heals. The church is the one who is obedient and who needs healing and salvation. The application of such symbolism to the marriage relation between husband and wife places the husband in the role of ruler and savior and the wife in the role of sinner and subordinate.[74]

Even though the biblical verses emphasize that Christ's self-sacrificing love for the church should be paradigmatic for the husband's attitude and behavior, the symbolism still implies a superiority of the husband as the suffering redeemer in the marriage relation. Such imagery has as its background the prophetic tradition's description of the relation between God and Israel, with the images of a faithful God versus an unfaithful harlot. The image of the covenant relation between Christ and the church as the basic symbol of the marriage relation may stress God's fidelity but may also unintentionally associate the husband with a faithful God and the wife with a fickle harlot. It also makes the husband superior to the wife and places her, along with children and slaves, in a subordinate, obediential position.

In addition, the household codes' imagery and imperatives express the husband's superiority to the wife and have had negative consequences within the history and practice of marriage. We have become increasingly sensitive to the prevalence of the problem of physi-

---

73. Ibid., 212.

74. Whereas Rahner argues that the subordination of wife to husband depicted in Ephesians is time-conditioned in that it "belonged to *that period alone*" (ibid., 221), von Balthasar argues for its relevance (*Theo-Logic*, 3:343–45).

604

cal abuse of wives by husbands.[75] But within the Christian tradition, such abuse was explicitly condoned and recommended in legislation with appeal to the household codes. Under the doctrine of "moderate correction," a husband was enjoined to beat or physically chastise his wife "moderately," as distinct from "excessively," as a loving correction for the good of her soul. For example, Friar Cherubino of Ciena (c. 1450–81) advises husbands that if pleasant words do not work, "scold her sharply, bully, and terrify her. And if this still does not work . . . take up a stick and beat her soundly, for it is better to punish the body and correct the soul than to damage the soul and correct the body."[76] Customary law often sanctioned the husband's exercise of his authority in the form of corporal punishment of a wife.[77]

For these reasons, which serve as retroductive warrants, I would like to suggest a fundamental shift in the underlying imagery of the relation between husband and wife in their relationship to God, Christ, and the church. As a part of my argument, I would like to draw attention to an important shift in Roman Catholic systematic theology in the understanding of the church as a sacrament. Walter Kasper has argued for several good reasons that the church should be understood as the sacrament of the Spirit.[78] First, his proposal seeks to take into account the post-Easter emergence of the Christian community with its faith in the death and resurrection of Jesus. Kasper is following the Roman Catholic position elaborated by Eric Peterson, Heinrich Schlier, and Joseph Ratzinger concerning the origin and foundation of the church. In addition, the notion of the church as a sacrament of the Spirit takes into account the distinction between Christ and the church. If the church is viewed exclusively as the sacrament of Christ or as the continuation of the incarnate Christ, then the danger exists that the distinction between Christ and the church is neglected and the church is reduced to a "quasi-mythological hypostasis."[79] The metaphor of the church as the sacrament of the Spirit of Christ relates the church to Christ in a way that does not divinize the church. This metaphor allows one to understand the church as emerging in the post-Easter disciples. The church is the community of disciples that emerges under the impact of God's Spirit.

I suggest that an adequate theological understanding of the sacrament of marriage needs to take into account these developments in Roman Catholic theology concerning the foundation of the church and the sacramental nature of the church. If the church is understood primarily as the community of God's Spirit and as the sacrament of the Spirit, then marriage should be understood as a sign and symbol of the church precisely insofar as it is a sign of the community brought about by the Spirit of God and Christ. A marriage between two individuals is the be-

---

75. See Elisabeth Schüssler Fiorenza and Shawn Copeland, *Violence against Women* (Maryknoll, NY: Orbis, 1994).

76. Quoted in William J. Hawser, *Differences in Relative Resources: Familial Power and Abuse* (Palo Alto, CA: Mayfield, 1982), 8.

77. A customary law in thirteenth-century France stated, "It is licit for the man to beat his wife, without bringing about the death or disablement, when she refuses her husband anything." Quoted in Jean-Louis Flandrin, *Families in Former Time: Kinship, Household, and Sexuality* (New York: Cambridge University Press, 1979), 123. See also Edward Shorter, *A History of Women's Bodies* (New York: Basic, 1982).

78. Walter Kasper and Gerhard Sauter, *Kirche—Ort des Geistes* (Freiburg: Herder, 1976).

79. Walter Kasper, *Glaube und Geschichte* (Mainz: Matthias-Grünewald, 1970), 294.

ginning of a new community, a community of equal disciples and partners under the impact and power of the Spirit. The community of Christians arose after Jesus' death, in discipleship of Jesus, and in the proclamation of God's power in the face of death.[80]

To view marriage as both a symbol and an actual beginning of new community concurs with the insights of the recent salvation-historical approach, which argues for a specific meaning of marriage within the Christian dispensation. Christians who view marriage in the light of faith see the meaning of marriage in relation to their experience, their Christian belief in Jesus, and their act of Christian discipleship. For Christians, marriage has a specific Christian meaning. Marriage is not simply the new image of God's creative activity symbolized by the Adam and Eve narrative. Nor is marriage an image of the covenantal relation between God and Israel, as symbolized in the prophetic literature. Instead, marriage is the symbol of a new community of life, one that images the origin of post-Easter, early Christian communities and one that anticipates the Christian eschatological hope of community. By stressing that the sacramental and symbolic function of marriage relates primarily to the church as the emergent post-Easter community of disciples, rather than to the covenantal relation between Christ and the church, I seek to emphasize the fundamental equality of husband and wife in the role of forming a new community. Their equality in discipleship and in the formation of a new community of marriage and their hope for that community can symbolize the equality and hope of discipleship in the post-Easter Christian community.

SACRAMENTAL VISION AND ROMAN CATHOLIC IDENTITY

When Roman Catholic theology affirms that marriage is a sacrament, it is not simply making a statement about the number of sacraments. Much more fundamentally, it is bringing to expression the Roman Catholic vision of reality. We can distinguish two different cognitive and practical attitudes, in practice intermingled, in the way we relate to our world and society. One is instrumental or functional, the other symbolic or communicative. An instrumental attitude asks about how things function as instruments for some useful purpose. It asks: What utility or function does a particular institution have? A symbolic or communicative attitude is quite different. Its primary question focuses not on utility or function, but on meaning and value. What meaning does an action have? What ideal does an object symbolize? What do we want to communicate?

A similar distinction can be made with reference to C. S. Peirce's semiotic categories, which enable us to place signs on a continuum according to their representational and communicative aspects. Some signs or complexes of signs are used referentially to convey information; others are used to communicate in a way that evokes participation. An engineer's model of the Brooklyn Bridge is referential and iconic, whereas a painter's picture is presentational and sensory.[81]

---

80. For an interpretation of the post-Easter emergence of the church in relation to the life-praxis of Jesus and of the earliest Christian proclamation of God's power in relation to Jesus, see Francis Schüssler Fiorenza, *Foundational Theology: Jesus and the Church* (New York: Crossroad, 1984), 3–192.

81. See Stanley J. Tambiah, *Magic, Science and Religion and the Scope of Rationality* (New York: Cambridge University Press, 1990), 84–110.

606

For Roman Catholic theology, then, the affirmation that marriage is a sacrament is an affirmation that marriage is not only instrumental or functional, but is also symbolic and communicative. Marriage is not merely an instrument by which various societies perpetuate themselves, nor is it simply a useful social arrangement by which the human race propagates itself. Instead, marriage is also a symbol that communicates meaning—a meaning articulated in relation to a historical memory and a future hope. When Roman Catholic theology describes marriage as a sacrament, it is not so much giving a referential or iconic characterization of marriage as it is seeking a presentational vision that should evoke one's participation in marriage in a specifically meaningful way.

Louis-Marie Chauvet, a French sacramental theologian, has applied the distinction between sign and symbol to the sacraments in general.[82] Arguing that the traditional doctrine of the sacraments has been based on the classical binary notion of sign, he suggests the appropriateness of the notion of symbol. Classically, a sign refers to something else. For example, smoke is a sign of fire, and gray hair is a sign of advanced age. The sign leads us to a new knowledge of something else. A symbol, however, introduces us to the cultural order to which it belongs. The sign of the cross, a religious habit, and a Bible are symbols of Christian identity. They do not primarily present new information or lead to new knowledge, as smoke leads us to suspect a fire. Instead, they are visible ways in which we mediate our identity. The sign of the cross is more than a sign of something else; it is also a symbol of Christian identity.

It seems helpful in discussions about marriage to take up the distinction between sign and symbol and to ask how marriage is both a sign and a symbol. The liturgical celebration of the sacrament of marriage within the Christian community symbolizes the meaning that marriage has for Christians within the context of Christianity. Marriage takes place before a representative of the Christian community, the communities of two families and sets of friends come together, and the couple starts forming a new community. In many cases, and most appropriately, the celebration of marriage is linked with a Eucharistic celebration by which the Christian community assembles and actualizes itself.

In my opinion, some theological treatments of marriage make romantic love the central notion of their thematizations. Such treatments can have several weaknesses. First, they overlook that for many centuries and in many areas, the romantic love of the partners for each other was not the personal and social condition of marriage.[83] Second, they sometimes apply an abstract ideal of love as self-gift to marriage without attending to the specific characteristics of love in marriage. Third, such an approach of-

---

82. Louis-Marie Chauvet, *Symbol and Sacrament: A Sacramental Interpretation of Christian Existence* (Collegeville, MN: Liturgical, 1995). See also his earlier work, *Du symbolique au symbole: Essai sur les sacrements* (Paris: Éditions du Cerf, 1979). See also David Power's treatment on the understanding sacrament in chapter 9.1 of this volume.

83. Edward Shorter and Lawrence Stone argue that it was in the eighteenth century that a shift took place from marriages based on interest to those based on affection and romantic love. See Lawrence Stone, *Family, Sex and Marriage in England, 1500–1800* (New York: Harper, 1977); Edward Shorter, *The Making of the Modern Family* (New York: Basic, 1975). A nuanced correction of this view is offered by Herman R. Lantz, "Romantic Love in the Pre-Modern Period: A Sociological Commentary," *Journal of Social History* 15 (1982): 349–70. Lantz points to the existence of romantic love further back in Western history but sees its spread as a part of the process of modernization.

ten leads to an intensification of expectations about marriage and the endurance of passion and romance that heightens the possibility for disappointment.[84]

If the meaning of marriage is seen primarily in relation to community, rather than in relation to a romantic and individualistic ideal of love, then one is in a better position to understand the specific characteristics of both the marital community and the love that emerges in marriage, including the love of spouses for each other and the love of parents for their children and vice versa.

In a marriage, commitment is primarily to a community. Obviously, such a community has been differently understood. Traditionally, marriage was viewed primarily as the continuation of the community of a particular family, whereas since the eighteenth century, marriage has been viewed as the beginning of a new community. What is important, however, in the stress on community and not simply on partnership or love, is that marriage entails a combination of personal and impersonal relations. It is not simply that the outside world is the world of the impersonal, whereas the family is the realm of the personal. (Often, one-sidedly understood, the public, outside world has been designated as the realm of the male, and the private, personal world has been designated as the domain of the female and family.) In my view, the commitment in marriage to community implies that the impersonal as well as the personal, the objective as well as the subjective, become the object of discourse and of life's energy. One develops a relationship not simply as an intimate relation to a private other, but rather as a community of intersecting relationships and interests.[85]

Love within marriage is often associated and equated with sexual attraction. Yet marital love entails not only desire, but also generosity and an ability to relate on diverse levels. As an eros, marital love includes passion and attraction. It grows from an initial attraction, pleasure, and happiness with one another to a full sexual passion and desire for one another. This passion and desire expand not only into a deeper passion but also into solidarity and commitment. Each spouse learns to respect the other as other and to encourage the other in his or her personal autonomy and hopes. The friendship that may bring the two together as an individual couple has to grow and develop to include others, and has to broaden out to other tasks and other communities. The more this broadening takes place and the more multiple the relationships, the more solid the foundation for the marriage. In the love of spouses for one another, all these elements are intermingled: friendship and passion, desire and generosity, communality and individuality, personal and communal interests. One does not pass from one to the other as if a stage of eros leads to a stage of agape, as if desire leads to solidarity, or as if friendship leads to love. Instead, love, friendship, inclusion of others, and the intersection of diverse and common interests coexist, each strengthening the others.

Just as the love between two spouses involves an intermingling of love and sexual attraction that is both powerful and multifaceted,

---

84. Compare Ernest W. Burgess et al., *The Family: From Traditional to Companionship* (New York: Van Nostrand, 1971); Niklas Luhmann, *Love as Passion: The Codification of Intimacy* (London: Polity, 1986); George Levinger and Harold L. Raush, *Close Relationships: Perspectives on the Meaning of Intimacy* (Amherst: University of Massachusetts Press, 1977).

85. For some recent literature, see Mark Cook and Glenn Wilson, eds., *Love and Attraction: An International Conference* (Oxford: Clarendon, 1979); and Anthony Giddens, *The Transformation of Intimacy* (Stanford: Stanford University Press, 1992).

608 so too does there also emerge in marriage the ambiguity of the love of parents for children. It is a love that begins as love for children as one's very own offspring yet as such must give way and become transformed to give birth to a love and support that encourage freedom, independence, and autonomy, especially from the parents. The love of children for parents, to whom they owe their very existence, is at first a very dependent love and must eventually grow into a form of independence.

All of this suggests a dialectic of commitment and love in marriage that expresses a continued transformation parallel to the experience of the beginning of the Christian community. The Christian experience of Jesus' life-praxis solidarity, his suffering and death, is combined with an experience of new life after Easter and an experience of new life and hope. Yet this hope is based also on the previous experience and community with Jesus. The new community of the church understands itself at first also as part of the community of Israel. Similarly, the experience of a new community and love in marriage continually gives birth to a transformed love, desire, hope, friendship, and responsibility.

If we take marriage as a sign or symbol of the new community of Christians under the impact of the Spirit, then we can better understand ourselves as Christians in relation to historical remembrance and history. We can understand marriage not simply as a self-giving love, but as a sign or symbol of a community that understands itself in relation to time and history and that is committed to a faith that trusts in a reality of love, hope, and transcendence. This faith is not above history but is intermingled with disappointment, death, and weakness. For the Christian faith, reality is ultimately grounded in a gracious God, and this God is both manifest and present in Jesus. A couple's public promises of love and commitment within the context of a Christian assembly both signify and symbolize the Christian hope and faith. Their promises signify and symbolize a trust and hope in the face of the common experience of the fragility of marriage.

Meaning and Purpose of Marriage

Roman Catholic theological treatments of the meaning and purpose of marriage have discussed the question of procreation versus mutual fulfillment as the end of marriage and the question of individual gender roles within marriage. Whereas traditionally the procreation of children was considered the primary purpose of marriage, more recently a more personalistic view has gained favor. In my opinion, some reactions against traditional conceptions of the purpose of marriage have either caricatured the traditional position or have themselves offered an overly narrow understanding of the goal and purpose of marriage.

Contemporary treatments of marriage often announce an important shift between traditional and modern Catholic views on the goal and purpose of marriage. They often describe this shift as a shift from procreation to life partnership as the goal of marriage. They increasingly emphasize that the goal and purpose of marriage consist of this life partnership. They often present the Roman Catholic tradition as having asserted that the primary and exclusive end of marriage is the reproduction of children. It is important, however, not to caricature the tradition. Indeed, throughout the tradition, many theologians affirmed procreation as the purpose of marriage and often took Gen. 1:28 ("Be fertile and multiply") as a key code and biblical foundation for the meaning of marriage. Nevertheless, such affirmations were never exclusive.

The Roman Catechism (*Catechismus romanus*) of the Council of Trent (1566) affirms that "nature itself by an instinct implanted in both sexes impels them to such companionship, and this is further encouraged by the hope of mutual assistance" (II, 8:13). Pius XI in his encyclical "On Christian Marriage," (*Casti connubii*) distinguished between a narrow and broad sense of marriage. The former referred to the conception and education of the children, whereas the latter referred to "the mutual inward molding of husband and wife" and the "determined effort to perfect one another" as "chief reason and purpose" (no. 24).[86]

Many contemporary Catholic books on marriage view it primarily in the categories of interpersonal fulfillment, and the subject of marriage is seen as the individual couple. These writers argue against the traditional emphasis on procreation and children, and they stress the interpersonal love, intimate sexual encounter, and mutual fulfillment of the couple as the meaning and purpose of marriage. Marriage is essentially a profound I-Thou relation between two individuals.[87]

Although this literature contains much of value, it may also risk replicating the individualism of much modern culture.[88] It overlooks that the very emphasis on the nuclear family does not represent a long-standing tradition but is a creation of modernity.[89] The very experience and phenomenon of marriage go counter, in my opinion, to this view of the married pair as an isolated individual couple. Moreover, insofar as such theologies of marriage make interpersonal affection and love the central component of marriage, they not only mirror the individualism of modern culture, but also, contrary to their very intention, contribute to the breakdown of marriages. As one historian of divorce has noted, "The logical progress of this trend in modern Western society, where love is conceived as being the single most important consideration in the choice of spouse and in the relationship between husband and wife, is that the loss of sentiments of love on the part of one spouse toward the other (or mutually) is the more likely than ever to be perceived by them as indicative of the breakdown of their marriage."[90]

Rather, along with school and work, marriage socializes individuals beyond their intimate family into a new network of families and friends. Marriage is not just a life partnership, but the bringing together of families, groups of

---

86. See Benedictine Monks of Solesmes, eds., *Papal Teaching*; DS 2232.

87. Examples of the personalist direction are Dietrich von Hildebrand, *Marriage* (London: Longman, Green & Co., 1942); Herbert Doms, *The Meaning of Marriage* (London: Sheed and Ward, 1939). Mmore recently, Theodore Mackin, *The Marital Sacrament* (New York: Paulist, 1989). Mackin polemicizes against the traditional understanding of marriage as a contract at a time when feminist theory is pointing to the importance of contracts within marriage to underscore the mutual responsibilities and obligations in regard to the common tasks faced by a couple. See also Michael G. Lawler, *Secular Marriage, Christian Sacrament* (Mystic, CT: Twenty-Third Publications, 1985); Lenore J. Weitzman, *The Marriage Contract: Spouses, Lovers, and the Law* (New York: Free, 1981).

88. For a criticism of this individualism in relation to marriage, see Robert M. Bellah et al., *Habits of the Heart: Individualism and Commitment in American Life* (New York: Harper & Row, 1985), 85–112.

89. Stephanie Coontz, *Marriage, a History: How Love Conquered Marriage* (London: Penguin 2005). See her earlier historical analysis that debunks some myths about the history of marriage: *The Way We Never Were: American Families and the Nostalgia Trap*, rev. ed. (New York: Basic, 2000). See also her anthology, *American Families: A Multicultural Reader*, expanded ed. (New York: Routledge, 2008).

90. Roderick Phillips, *Putting Asunder: A History of Divorce in Western Society* (New York: Cambridge University Press, 1988), 359.

610

friends, and coworkers. Through children, parents often come into greater contact with other families and with the community. Along with offspring comes the heightened responsibility that individuals bear not just for the next generation, but also for society as a whole, and for the earth on which the next generations are to live. Marriage as an encounter with another leads to the acceptance of responsibility for others. To define marriage primarily in terms of an interpersonal relation of two without recognizing the social and communal responsibilities that marriage entails is to offer a reductionistic view of marriage. The communal and social meaning of marriage needs to be explicated, especially in the face of an individualistic overemphasis on personal fulfillment.

The inclusion of this social and communal dimension helps ensure an adequate understanding of the purpose of marriage. A theology of marriage must also steer the middle course between a romanticism of identity and a romanticism of difference. The romanticism of identity is present in writings that imagine some sort of mystical union takes place between two persons so that they become one. One popular Roman Catholic book on marriage divides the human person into three levels of being and action: the physical and biological (the animal level), the psychological (the level of human senses and emotions), and the spiritual (the religious level). The author concludes, "To become one biblical body, one whole person, a man and a woman must become one on all three levels."[91] The author does not critically reflect on the connection between his advocacy of the imagery of the couple becoming one body and the mythic

belief that at first an androgynous being was created and that marriage brings split sexes back into one body. Fortunately, the author concedes that a husband and wife need not agree about everything on all three levels. One should affirm instead that the goal of mutual perfection should encourage each partner not only to develop self-respect and individuality, but also to achieve autonomy and self-possession. Ideals such as partnership or common good are indeed fine ideals, yet they can become oppressive to individuals. One of the merits of feminist theology and theory has been to demonstrate that too often such ideals as partnership or the common good lead to a sacrifice of the woman's own personal development—a sacrifice often with negative consequence for the wife, as well as for the personal maturity of each spouse and the marriage itself.

The other romanticism is the glorification of sexual difference. This type of thinking became fully developed first in the Romantic period, when the differences between male and female were considered essential differences. The novelty of this development is often overlooked. It has been observed that two basic views of gender or the sexes have dominated the past two millennia of Western thought: the one-sex and the two-sex theories.[92] According to the one-sex theory, which dominated classical learning up until the modern Enlightenment, woman is an imperfect version of man. Her anatomy, physiology, and psychic makeup reflect this inferiority. The two-sex theory, which became dominant in nineteenth-century Romanticism, argues that the body determines gender differences and that woman is the opposite of man.

---

91. Lawler, *Secular Marriage*, 71.

92. Thomas Laqueur, *Making Sex: Body and Gender from the Greeks to Freud* (Cambridge, MA: Harvard University Press, 1990); Richard A. Posner, *Sex and Reason* (Cambridge, MA: Harvard University Press, 1992).

She has incommensurably different organs, functions, and feelings. If the one-sex theories were once accepted as reflecting the divine order of creation and were used to justify a subordinate position of women within marriage and the exclusion of women from ordination, today two-sex theories are often used in theological analyses of marriage and in the interpretation of the order of creation. Such views of male and female as complementary poles have been embraced in popular psychology and in a more nuanced fashion in Jungian psychoanalysis.

Within a theological analysis, one must acknowledge the degree to which gender roles are social and historical constructions. The inadequacies of the one-sex theory have been widely discussed, but it is important to point out that the two-sex theory also is historically limited and appears increasingly inadequate to deal with gender roles in marriage and in the church. Theoretically, the Romantic division of genders has been criticized by feminist theologians.[93] Socially, it is inadequate for understanding the roles of male and female in the marriage of a dual-career couple, where both spouses bear mutual responsibility and equal time for the diverse tasks of parenting. Moreover, associated with the Romantic division is not only the Romantic notion of love, but also the understanding of the family as a safe harbor from the rough seas of the world. With the prevalence of such idealistic images of marriage, family, love, and gender, it is no wonder that so many marriages shipwreck in the rough seas of life or against economic and societal reality.

Pastoral-Practical Issues

When the theoretical and cultural shifts described in the preceding section are combined with societal changes, several theological, pastoral, and practical issues emerge. The greater prevalence of the single-parent family, the importance of coparenting within a dual-parent family, and cohabitation prior to marriage or as a substitute for marriage have become significant pastoral problems. Also, the issues of birth control and of divorce and remarriage have intensified as pastoral and theological concerns in the decades since the Second Vatican Council.

Select Pastoral Issues

These three issues reflect demographic trends that are transforming modern Western society and therefore raise specific pastoral problems and concerns.

THE SINGLE-PARENT FAMILY

In the United States today, the single-parent family is increasingly prevalent (and dominant in some subcultures) as the significant child-rearing unit. A single-parent family often faces several challenges.[94] These include the increased financial hardship of a single wage earner, the pressures of time in dealing with parental issues, and the lack of mutual validation and authority in guiding the development of children. With these pressures, the local churches as communities need to expand their help to the single parent in a way that creates the multifaceted

---

93. I have been especially influenced by Elisabeth Schüssler Fiorenza's critique of Gertrude LeFort's advocacy of duality; see Elisabeth Schüssler, *Der Vergessene Partner* (Düsseldorf: Patmos, 1964). See, more recently, Rosemary Radford Ruether, *Christianity and the Making of Modern Family* (Boston: Beacon, 2001).

94. See, for example, John S. Weltner, "A Structural Approach to the Single-Parent Family," *Family Process* 21 (1982): 203–10; Sara S. McLanaham et al., "Network Structure, Social Support, and Psychological Well-Being in the Single-Parent Family," *Journal of Marriage and Family* 43 (1981): 601–12.

612 support that only a community can provide. The ancient proverb that it takes a village to bring up a child needs to be translated in the consciousness of churches and communities so that they understand the aid of the single-parent family as being integral to their religious mission.

COPARENTING

The structure of work in developed economies has changed in ways that require women as well as men to participate in the labor force outside the home, and this change has theoretical and practical implications for families. Theoretically, it underscores the inadequacy of the split between female and male in which the female has responsibility for the home within her role of nurturing and within her proper sphere (namely, the home) while the male has responsibility as the wage earner within the sphere of the public. Instead, it becomes obvious that both male and female are involved in coparenting. Both have responsibility for nurturing love within the family and for the children's growth and development. Statistics indicate that more and more young couples undertake these responsibilities and goals, though inequalities still exist. It becomes important that the rhetoric of the church not turn the nineteenth-century Romantic understanding of gender and the family into an eternal value that fails to do justice to the structures of modern society or to the increased awareness of women's abilities to engage fully in the public sphere and for males to engage fully in the sphere of the home.

COHABITATION

The prevalence of cohabitation prior to marriage in contemporary society has led to considerable discussion. Some have suggested that cohabitation should be looked upon as a modern version of the medieval notion of betrothal and therefore should be more accepted.[95] This suggestion overlooks that betrothal took place within a culture of more stable and contractual relationship both before and after marriage. Consequently, especially in the United States, cohabitation is often serial among different parties and often does not lead to marriage as betrothal did, especially in the United States.[96] Moreover, there is an increase in the divorce rate among those who cohabit prior to marriage. The level of education, however, is much more predictive of stability than cohabitation.[97]

The pastoral issue at stake is more properly the significance of marriage and the importance of understanding relationships not primarily or exclusively in personalist terms, but within societal and contractual terms. The significance and meaning of marriage needs to be articulated less in personalist terms and more in terms of the relation of the individual to the creation of a new community and in relation to the contribution of this community to others and to society.

Birth Control and the Purpose of Marriage

Two of the most controversial issues within contemporary Roman Catholic teaching on mar-

95. Michael Lawler, *Marriage and the Catholic Church: Disputed Questions* (Collegeville, MN: Liturgical, 2002), 162–92. For an Anglican position, see Adrian Thatcher, *Marriage after Modernity: Christian Marriage in Postmodern Times* (New York: New York University Press, 1999).

96. Anita Jose, Daniel O'Leary, and Anne Moyer, "Does Premarital Cohabitation Predict Subsequent Marital Stability and Marital Quality: A Meta-Analysis," *Journal of Marriage and Family* 72 (2010): 105–16.

97. See Andrew J. Cherlin, *The Marriage-Go-Round: The State of Marriage and the Family in America Today* (New York: Alfred A. Knopf, 2009). The charts on pp. 205–12 are instructive.

riage are birth control and divorce.[98] Papal teaching on the nature and purpose of marriage has consistently excluded "artificial means" of birth control. The Council of Trent unambiguously affirmed the indissolubility of sacramental marriage. These issues are usually treated within pastoral and moral theology. Since, however, these issues pertain to the nature and meaning of marriage, it is appropriate here to include a brief sketch of the state of the question within Roman Catholic theology concerning these issues today.

A sharply controversial topic in contemporary Roman Catholic teaching in regard to marriage is the ethical issue of birth control—an issue related to the meaning and purpose of marriage. Its full treatment can be adequately developed only within a theological discussion of moral and ethical norms. From a systematic theological point of view, a shift has occurred within recent official church teaching. The importance of responsible parenthood and the significance of mutual love as a primary purpose of marriage have received increasing affirmation within official church teachings. In turn, many Roman Catholic theologians and many married Roman Catholics infer from the shift that

responsible parenthood and mutual love would allow various methods of birth control. Many theologians concur with what Cardinal Ratzinger wrote some years ago: "It is clear that the orientation of marriage to 'the procreation of offspring' and the model of 'in accordance with nature' that is closely connected with that view can no longer in its traditional form be the standard for the ethics [of marriage]."[99] At the same time, Ratzinger notes that the ideals of partnership and mutual fulfillment do not suffice as ethical standards. He concludes his analysis of the ethics of marriage in the following way: "We stand firm: one certainly no longer has an easily managed norm that is established from physiology."[100] Instead, he argues, there is the responsibility before the totality of love, humanity, the future, the command of God, and the double mystery of death and hope. All of this means that there is "no unambiguity. These responsibilities can require the limitation of offspring, so that this limitation is what is ethically demanded and the opposite is immoral."[101]

Reflections similar to those of Ratzinger had led innumerable theologians to argue that the Catholic Church should change its traditional opposition to "artificial means of birth

---

98. Another important and controversial issue is that of same-sex marriage. Within Roman Catholic theology, the magisterium (pope and bishops) has consistently and explicitly rejected the possibility of understanding of such unions as sacramental. The American bishops have at the same time repeatedly rejected many forms of social discrimination against gays. In contrast, other Christian religious communities have seriously debated the issue, and in some, this debate has been divisive. Many have taken opposing positions not only in regard to same-sex marriage, but also concerning the ordaining of persons in such marriage to the clergy and to leadership roles within the churches. For two diverse positions by Roman Catholic theologians, see the essays by William E. May, "On the Impossibility of Same-Sex Marriage: A Review of Catholic Teaching," and Stephen J. Pope, "The Magisterium's Arguments against 'Same-Sex Marriage': An Ethical Analysis and Critique," in *Marriage: Readings in Moral Theology*, no. 15, ed. Charles E. Curran and Julie Hanlon Rubio (Mahwah, NJ: Paulist, 2009), 279–329. For a historical analysis, see the learned work of Mark Jordan, *The Invention of Sodomy in Christian Theology* (Chicago: University of Chicago Press, 1997); idem, *The Silence of Sodom: Homosexuality in Modern Catholicism* (Chicago: University of Chicago Press, 2000); and his more recent discussion of the controversy over same-sex union in contemporary Christianity, *Blessing Same-Sex Unions* (Chicago: University of Chicago Press, 2005).

99. Ratzinger, "Zur Theologie der Ehe," 70; my translation here and following.

100. Ibid., 71.

101. Ibid.

614

control."[102] At the same time, both Pope Paul VI and Pope John Paul II have consistently and unambiguously rejected that implication. Pope Paul VI withdrew the issue from discussion at Vatican II and appointed a commission to study it. After he did not accept the recommendation of the commission, he issued *Humanae vitae*. More than 450 North American Roman Catholic theologians protested against this encyclical. Several episcopal conferences responded by recommending that the faithful should indeed attend to papal teaching, but they also suggested that the faithful should form their own conscience; such suggestions seemed to intimate cautiously the possibility of dissenting decision. Many theologians, including Bernard Lonergan and Karl Rahner, elaborated the foundations for dissent, whereas many ethicists, such as Bernard Häring and Charles Curran, explicitly took dissenting views.[103] At present, a crisis exists in the Roman Catholic Church. There continues to be an enormous gap between the opinions of, on the one hand, the majority of professional theologians and the principled practice of a majority of Roman Catholic married laity within the modern industrialized West and, on the other, the unambiguous and legitimate official teaching of recent popes.[104] The recent pastoral letter of the United States Conference of Catholic Bishops

reaffirms the traditional ban on contraception and entreats young married couples to trust in divine providence.[105]

Despite this split and the controversy about the means of birth control, a fundamental unity of vision exists within the Roman Catholic Church about the meaning and purpose of marriage. Its vision of marriage as sacrament entails the responsibility of the individual couple not only for themselves, but also for the community and society at large. This social responsibility is an essential element of human love and sexuality. The married couple forms a new community that extends beyond the sphere of the individual family to encompass others in their community and society. This responsible love, as a sign and a promise, gives marriage a mission to be a sacrament of the presence and power of God's creative love on earth. Despite disagreements about birth control, this social goal and responsibility remains central to both sides of the debate.

On the occasion of the fortieth anniversary of the Encyclical *Humanae vitae*, Ratzinger as Pope Benedict XVI addressed an international conference at the Pontifical Lateran University. In his address, he conceded that the document had become a "sign of contradiction," provoked much discussion, and in his view was "too often misunderstood and misinterpreted." Pope Benedict XVI emphasized the importance of

---

102. For an invaluable historical survey, see John Noonan, *Contraception*, 2nd ed. (Cambridge, MA: Harvard University Press, 1988).

103. Karl Rahner, "On the Encyclical 'Humanae vitae,'" in *Theological Investigations* (New York: Crossroad, 1974), 11:263-87. See also his "Magisterium and Theology," in *Theological Investigations* (New York: Crossroad, 1983), 18:54–73. An important early article on the philosophical presuppositions of the debate was Bernard Lonergan's "Finality, Love, Marriage," in his *Collection* (New York: Herder and Herder, 1967), 16–53. See essays by diverse theologians in Charles E. Curran, ed., *Contraception: Authority and Dissent* (New York: Herder and Herder, 1969).

104. For a discussion of the reception of *Humanae vitae*, see Joseph Komonchak, "*Humanae vitae* and Its Reception: Ecclesiological Reflections," *Theological Studies* 39 (1978): 221–57.

105. *Marriage: Love and Life in the Divine Plan* (Washington, DC: United States Conference of Catholic Bishops, 2009).

"reflecting in an ever new and deeper way on the fundamental principles that concern marriage and procreation." He quoted the medieval theologian William of Saint-Thierry's *On the Nature and Dignity of Love* (21,8) as teaching what is profoundly valid for our time: "If reason instructs love and love illumines reason, they can do something great." In defining this "something great," he writes:

> It is the promotion of responsibility for life which brings to fruition the gift that each one makes of him or herself to the other. It is the fruit of a love that can think and choose in complete freedom without letting itself be conditioned unduly by the possible sacrifice requested. From this comes the miracle of life that parents experience in themselves, as they sense the extraordinary nature of what takes place in them and through them. No mechanical techniques can substitute the act of love that husband and wife exchange as a sign of a greater mystery which (as protagonists and sharers in creation) sees them playing the lead and sharing in creation.[106]

He concludes with an appeal for education in the meaning of life and the responsible exercise of sexuality in a way that honors a society based on the principles of freedom and democracy and expresses a dedication to the other.

Divorce and Remarriage

The other difficult question is divorce and remarriage. The indissolubility of marriage has remained the ideal of Roman Catholicism from its very beginning. Nevertheless, the fact remains that marriages do fail and remarried couples wish to participate actively as Roman Catholics in the church's sacramental life. Thus, a pastoral problem of some weight arises out of the tension between the ideal and the actual practice.[107] Despite all good intentions and all goodwill, marriages do break down.[108] Sometimes the breakdown results from a failure of commitment and trust. At other times, the breakdown results from a set of conditions and events beyond individual responsibility. In some situations, the two should quite clearly never have gotten married, and the eventual collapse of the marital relation was obvious. In some circumstances, a physical separation is best for the individuals concerned and for the children—though no cases exist where there is not hurt that affects all involved. Previously one considered the harm to children as a result of divorce; more recently, one traces

---

106. Benedict XVI, "Address of His Holiness Benedict XVI to Participants in the International Congress Organized by the Pontifical Lateran University on the 40th Anniversary of the Encyclical '*Humanae vitae*,'" Clementine Hall, May 10, 2008, http://www.vatican.va/holy_father/benedict_xvi/speeches/2008/may/documents/hf_ben-xvi_spe_20080510_ humanae-vitae_en.html. More recently, in response to a question about the use of condoms and the prevention of AIDS, Pope Benedict XVI has stated: "This can be a first step in the direction of moralization, a first assumption of responsibility, on the way toward recovering the awareness that not everything is allowed." Pope Benedict XVI and Peter Seewald, *Light of the World: The Pope, the Church, and the Signs of the Times* (San Francisco: Ignatius, 2010), 119.

107. See Margaret Farley, *Just Love: A Framework for Christian Sexual Ethics* (New York: Continuum, 2006), 245–312.

108. For the causes of the breakdown of marriages as well as of divorce (two distinct issues), there is much recent literature. For a survey of recent research, see Gay C. Kitson and Helen J. Raschke, "Divorce Research: What We Know; What We Need to Know," *Journal of Divorce* 4 (1981): 1–37; George Levinger and Oliver C. Moles, eds., *Divorce and Separation: Contexts, Causes and Consequences* (New York: Basic, 1979); Stan L. Albrecht et al., *Divorce and Remarriage: Problems, Adaptations and Adjustments* (Westport, CT: Greenwood, 1983); and Barbara Thornes and Jean Collard, *Who Divorces?* (London: Routledge & Kegan Paul, 1979).

616 the harm back to the conflicts and emotional struggles within the marriage itself.[109] Proclamation of the ideal of marriage as indissoluble remains an important reminder not only of one's commitments and what one hopes for, but also of the suffering and hurt one seeks to avoid.[110] It needs to consider not only the harm that arises from divorce but also the harm within disharmonious marriages themselves.

In the face of the conflict between the religious ideal and the concrete practice, two pastoral solutions seem to have emerged in practice. One approach is canonical insofar as it involves expanding the canonical acknowledgment of the annulment of marriages. This has resulted in a de facto increase in annulments. The new Code of Canon Law expands the traditional grounds for nullity to include lack of understanding, lack of partnership and conjugal love, psychological immaturity, psychopathic and schizophrenic personality, and several other reasons.[111] In addition, an increased leniency in granting annulments has sought to deal in a practical and pastoral way with the breakdown of marriages. Yet in practical terms, this solution de facto renders children into bastards by declaring that a marriage was from the start null and void. Such an approach appears, in my opinion, to go against the spirit, if not the letter, of what was defined at the Council of Trent and affirmed in traditional Roman Catholic teaching. It is with considerable justification that unofficial Vatican statements have criticized the widespread use of this practice.

Another approach within contemporary Roman Catholic theology deals with the problem as a pastoral, practical issue. This approach is pastoral insofar as it highlights overlooked practices in the tradition of the church concerning second marriages. Three theologians now occupying episcopal offices, Walter Kasper, Karl Lehmann, and Cardinal Joseph Ratzinger, have defended this pastoral solution, though in different degrees. This approach points to more lenient practices in the first millennium of Christianity.[112] Origen and Basil mention that in cases where persons had become divorced because of adultery and then remarried, church leaders had allowed them to participate in the Eucharist. Ambrosiaster and Augustine also made reference to this practice. In the beginning of the medieval period, several church

---

109. Betsey Stevenson and Justin Wolfers, "Marriage and Divorce: Changes and Their Driving Forces," *Journal of Economic Perspectives* 21, no. 2 (Spring 2007): 27–52; Cherlin, *Marriage, Divorce, Remarriage*; Frank F. Furstenberg and Andrew Cherlin, *Divided Families: What Happens to Children When Parents Part* (Cambridge, MA: Harvard University Press, 1991).

110. It should still be noted that despite the increase in the number of divorces in the West in the twentieth century, the majority of marriages do not end in divorce. Moreover, Robert H. Lauer and Jeanette C. Lauer have noted that in marriages lasting more than fifteen years, 83 percent of both partners consider themselves happily married. "Factors in Long-Term Marriages," *Journal of Family Issues* 7 (1986): 382–90.

111. As an example of such practical recommendations, see Joseph P. Zwack, *Annulment* (New York: Harper, 1983). For studies of marriage and the new code, see Ladislaus Orsy, *Marriage in Canon Law* (Wilmington, DE: Glazier, 1986); Michael Smith Foster, *Annulment: The Wedding That Was: How the Church Can Declare a Marriage Null* (New York: Paulist, 1998); and Robert H. Vasoli, *What God Hath Joined Together: The Annulment Crisis in American Catholicism* (New York: Oxford University Press, 1992). On the increase of annulments, see Pierre Hegy and Joseph Martos, eds., *Catholic Divorce: The Deception of Annulments* (New York: Continuum, 2000).

112. Henri Crouzel, *L'Église primitive face au divorce, du premier au cinquième siècle*, Théologie historique 13 (Paris: Beauchesne, 1971). For corrections and modifications of Couzel's arguments, see Peter Stockmeier, "Scheidung und Wiederverheiratung im Neuen Testament," *Theologische Quartalschrift* 151 (1971): 28–38.

synods and various penitential books permitted a second marriage even when the first partner was still alive. The Eastern churches tolerated the possibility of second marriage, whereas the Western church as a result of Gratian's Decree established a stricter practice.

Diverse proposals have emerged from the historical data. Whereas some advocate that the Roman Catholic Church should change its position and others advocate no change, the middle position takes a pastoral approach that affirms the Council of Trent's teaching on marriage yet suggests a change in pastoral practice.[113] Kasper writes, "The Church should act in accordance with God's way of acting and for this reason, it should be possible to admit divorced persons who have remarried to the sacraments on three conditions: 1) when they are sorry for their guilt and have made amends for it as well as they can; 2) when everything humanly possible has been done to achieve reconciliation with the first partner; and 3) when the second marriage has become a morally binding union that cannot be dissolved without causing fresh injustice."[114]

Kasper's solution seeks to be faithful to traditional teaching as well as to pastoral practice. Personally, I would modify his formulation of the first condition. Obviously, there should be sorrow over a failed marriage, and one should never consider oneself totally guiltless. Nevertheless, there are many situations where the failure of the first marriage results from situations and conditions for which an individual may not be primarily responsible. To admit this situation and to deal honestly with the issue of second marriages is not to reject what marriage is. To quote Karl Lehmann, "The toleration of a second marriage and the associated admission to the sacraments should in no way place in question the obligatory basic form of indissoluble marriage."[115]

One might even state that in the face of the fragility of marriage, the celebration of the sacrament of marriage gives visible manifestation to the unconditionality of love as present in the conditions of human existence. The Roman Catholic Church's affirmation of the indissolubility of marriage expresses the unconditionality of the commitment to a new community. It is the nature of solidarity, love, and commitment to be resolute, steadfast, and unreserved. To say that I am committed to you in solidarity on the condition that you stay healthy, wealthy, beautiful, and wise is absurd. Human commitment and solidarity have an unconditional, unreserved, transcending dimension. This dimension, which is symbolized in the sacrament of marriage, expresses the Christian faith in a transcendent hope and trust.

Such an ideal is often frightening, for we know too often of our own fragility and weaknesses. We know that marriages too often break down. We know that love and commitment are not certainties upon which we can rely. The mutual commitment in marriage is as much a hope as a faith or trust. It parallels in many ways our faith in God—an experience not of certainty, but of hope. It is this hope that the Catholic Church expresses through its teaching and through its celebration of marriage as a sacrament.

---

113. See Joseph Ratzinger, "Zur Frage nach der Unauflöslichkeit der Ehe," 35–56.
114. Kasper, *Theology of Christian Marriage*, 70.
115. Lehmann, *Gegenwart des Glaubens*, 292 (my translation).

For Further Reading

Barth, Karl. *The Doctrine of Creation*. Vol. 3, part 4 of *Church Dogmatics*. Edinburgh: T&T Clark, 1961, 116–323.

> An influential presentation by a major Protestant theologian. Barth develops the nature of marriage as a life partnership. See the reprint of part of this text in **On Marriage** (Philadelphia: Fortress, 1968).

Brundage, James A. *Law, Sex, and Christian Society in Medieval Europe*. Chicago: University of Chicago Press, 1987.

> Detailed historical research on neglected aspects of medieval law and practice.

Cahill, Lisa Sowle. *Between the Sexes: Foundations for a Christian Ethics of Sexuality*. Philadelphia: Fortress, 1985.

Written by a leading Roman Catholic ethicist, this work provides an exposition of marriage that takes into account recent developments in biblical studies, gender studies, and anthropology.

———. *Family: A Christian Social Perspective*. Minneapolis: Augsburg Fortress, 2000.

> Discusses the family as church through a survey of New Testament sources, Chrysostom, Luther, and the Puritans, within recent Roman Catholic social theology, and with reference to African American families.

Cott, Nancy C. *Public Vows: A History of Marriage and the Nation*. Cambridge: Harvard University Press, 2000.

> A study of the evolution of marriage through the history of the United States from the American Revolution until now that demonstrates the public and social character of marriage and its intertwinement with social and political issues.

Curran, Charles E., and Julie Hanlon Rubio. *Marriage: Readings in Moral Theology*. No. 15. Mahwah, NJ: Paulist, 2009.

> This comprehensive collection of essays deals with all aspects of marriage, theological as well as moral. The first section presents a historical survey of the meaning of marriage. The second section contains reflections on the theology and spirituality of marriage, and the final section deals with specific issues in contemporary Roman Catholic moral and theological reflection. The essays have been selected to display a broad diversity of views.

Farley, Margaret. *Just Love: A Framework for Christian Sexual Ethics*. New York: Continuum, 2006.

> A significant collection of essays from a leading moral theologian that takes into account interreligious as well as postcolonial perspectives. The final section deals with marriage.

Kasper, Walter. *Theology of Christian Marriage*. New York: Crossroad, 1983.

> A brief theology of marriage with special consideration of biblical and pastoral themes.

Lawler, Michael G. *Marriage and Sacrament: A Theology of Christian Marriage*. Collegeville, MN: Liturgical, 1993.

> A comprehensive treatment of marriage that surveys the biblical, historical, and theological understandings of marriage. It also focuses on divorce and remarriage as disputed questions. The book develops further the author's earlier publication, Secular Marriage, Christian Sacrament (Mystic, CT: Twenty-Third Publications, 1985).

Mackin, Theodore. *The Marital Sacrament.* New York: Paulist, 1989.

> This volume is a historical survey of the various religious interpretations of marriage from biblical to contemporary times. It contains excellent bibliographies, and it updates and complements the author's previous volumes on marriage, What Is Marriage? *(1982)* and Divorce and Remarriage *(1984).*

McCarthy, David Matzko. *Sex and the Home: A Theology of the Household.* 2nd ed. London: SCM, 2004.

> The author combines reflections from his own personal experience with classic, contemporary, and postmodern theology in a way that underscores the connection between the Christian household and the common good.

Phillips, Roderick. *Putting Asunder: A History of Divorce in Western Society.* New York: Cambridge University Press, 1988.

> A comprehensive historical and sociological survey of divorce in the West that covers religious beliefs, legal regulations, and social practice.

Rahner, Karl. "Marriage as a Sacrament." In *Theological Investigations,* 10:199–221. New York: Crossroad, 1973.

> Develops Rahner develops his fundamental notions of marriage as a sacrament with reference to his ecclesial understanding of the sacraments.

Roberts, William P., ed. *Commitment to Partnership: Explorations of the Theology of Marriage.* New York: Paulist, 1987.

> This collection of essays by diverse authors offers distinct contemporary perspectives (exegetical, ethical, theological, and pastoral) on the nature of marriage.

Rubio, Julie Hanlon. *A Christian Theology of Marriage and Family.* New York: Paulist, 2003.

> An excellent discussion of marriage and family with a specific emphasis on the dual vocation of Christian parents as mothers and fathers. It reflects on the nature of family and problems of parenting in a postmodern age.

Schillebeeckx, Edward. *Marriage: Secular Reality and Saving Mystery.* New York: Sheed & Ward, 1965.

> Two volumes have been printed together in the American edition. The first volume deals with the biblical writings, and the second with marriage in the history of theology. Although a promised third volume has not appeared, Schillebeeckx's systematic theology of the sacraments is applied here in a theology of marriage.

Scott, Kieran, and Michael Warren, eds. *Perspectives on Marriage: A Reader.* 3rd ed. New York: Oxford University Press, 2007.

> A diverse collection of essays dealing not only with theological and religious issues about marriage, but also with some practical issues: abuse of women in marriage, annulment, remarriage and the church, effects of divorce on children, and financial issues and marriage.

Eschatology 10

Eschatology

Jeannine Hill Fletcher

622

As the doctrine of the "last things" (Greek *eschata*), eschatology is the area of belief that speaks of the final destiny of humankind and the world, and articulates a vision of the ultimate aim toward which creation tends. It has traditionally been structured through the categories of the immortality of the soul, resurrection of the body, personal judgment, purgatory, the second coming of Christ, general judgment, heaven and hell, and the final consummation of the world, and it has often focused attention exclusively on what happens after this life. Yet eschatology is not simply about what happens after death, as if disconnected from the Christian understanding of life. Dwelling on what is to come in the ultimate future, eschatology is simultaneously an assessment of the here and now as it is illuminated by the life and person of Jesus Christ. As eschatological thought speaks of the final destiny of humankind and the future that is creation's telos, this future is in continuity with the present. So while we do not know with certainty what lies beyond our life in this world ("no eye has seen"; 1 Cor. 2:9), Christians nevertheless hope for a certain future based on the present experience of a life intertwined with the life of Christ. Thus, eschatology is not idle speculation but hope-filled expression of the whole of the faith.

Biblical Sources

Christian eschatology finds its rooting in the biblical vision of both the Hebrew Bible and New Testament. As such, it draws an orientation from the creation account, through Exodus and the Prophets anticipating the vindication of resurrection, and finally witnessing to the efficacy of the person of Jesus Christ. In these sources we see the key eschatological themes of resurrection, kingdom, and judgment.

Creation and the Human Condition of Sin and Death

Christian hope in the last things is rooted in an understanding of creation "in the beginning." Affirming with Genesis the goodness of creation (Gen. 1:9-31), Christian faith understands God as the source of the created world and therefore that the created world is destined for fulfillment by God and in God. Embedded in this good creation is the life and destiny of the human person.

Although destined for good, humanity fails to cooperate with the Creator, compromising the consummation of creation through selfishness and sin. Turning away from God's design, sin is, in a sense, de-creation as it "brings about a state of death and corruption 'phthora'—both physical and moral—which is really a decline from being toward nothingness."[1] In the Genesis account, the ultimate consequence for the human failure to participate in the vision of the Creator is not life but death, as God warns Adam and Eve: "For in the day you shall eat of [the forbidden tree], you shall die" (Gen. 2:17). At the broken promise of Adam and Eve, God articulates the consequence with the declaration, "You are dust, and to dust you shall return" (Gen. 3:19). Death as the result of human sin-

---

1. Richard Clifford and Khaled Anatolios, "Christian Salvation: Biblical and Theological Perspectives," *Theological Studies* 66 (2005): 739–69, at 757. This is the understanding of sin put forth by Athanasius, a fourth-century Christian theologian and bishop of Alexandria.

fulness is further indicated in the stories of the Noahide flood (Gen. 6:5-7) and the destruction of depraved generations (Genesis 19).

If Genesis affirms the goodness of creation, the human failure to participate in this goodness, and the serious consequence of this failure, the remainder of the biblical account offers an understanding of how humanity is to overcome this situation. The response offered in the pages of Scripture is the transformation of this condition through a hoped-for redemption.

Redemption in History and Beyond

In the Hebrew Scriptures, fulfillment out of this brokenness is pursued in the process of living righteously as God's people. The reintroduction of God's justice and righteousness are to be found in the present history, and thus the transformative hope of the ancient Jewish scriptures is firmly rooted in this world. From the saving actions of God in the exodus from Egypt to the calls of the prophets for change, the hoped-for end to the present human condition was the transformation of history: "The present cosmos, created as 'good' by Yhwh but temporarily marred by injustice, infirmity, war, and sin, and in general by evil will be reclaimed and redeemed by God."[2] While the focus of transformation is to be in this world, the ancient texts do offer a theological vision of a place beyond this world in the underworld known as Sheol, the place of the dead (see Gen. 37:35; Ps. 55:15; Isa. 38:18). But at best, the condition of the departed was seen as a "shadowy existence" with very little resemblance to or continuity with the condition of the living.[3] The description of Sheol as darkness, dust, and abandonment (Job 17:13; 17:16; Ps. 16:10) maintains a stark contrast between death and life and underscores the need for righteous transformation *in this life*.

The emphasis in the Hebrew Scriptures is on redemption out of the compromised human condition through righteous living and God's vindication in history. Yet ancient Jewish history admits the reality that the righteous are often *not* vindicated in this world. And so, according to scholars, when in the second century BCE the people experienced harsh persecutions and died undertaking resistance, there is evidence in Jewish sources of a new way of thinking beyond this world. For God's justice to be fulfilled, the Scriptures witness the emergence of hope in resurrection as vindication for the righteous dead. Thus, in the Maccabean period, a more detailed discussion of an afterlife emerges. As William La Due describes,

> The prophet Daniel (ca. 160 B.C.) alluded to the possibility of resurrection for those who died fighting the good fight against the Seleucid persecutors. "Many of those who sleep in the dust of the earth shall awake, some to everlasting life, and some to shame and everlasting contempt" (Dan. 12:2). This represents the first unambiguous reference to resurrection in the Old Testament. Second Maccabees takes up the theme again, affirming that those brave soldiers who had fallen in the battles against the

---

2. Bill T. Arnold, "Old Testament Eschatology and the Rise of Apocalypticism," in *The Oxford Handbook of Eschatology*, ed. Jerry L. Walls (Oxford: Oxford University Press, 2008), 24.

3. Zachary Hayes, *Visions of a Future: A Study of Christian Eschatology* (Collegeville, MN: Liturgical, 1990), 30–31. Hayes provides a succinct overview of the eschatology of the Hebrew Scriptures at pp. 15–42.

Seleucids can be aided by collecting funds and sending offerings to the temple in Jerusalem so that their sins can be blotted out.[4]

The ancient Jewish tradition includes both an intense focus on the future of this world in history *and* the hope for everlasting life beyond.

In the New Testament, the Christian outlook decidedly continues the sense that the human story does not end in death but continues beyond this world. Such a conviction is rooted in the death and resurrection of the Righteous One, Jesus Christ. Jesus' death is witness to his commitment to the will of God even in a world so clearly at odds with God's design. In the tradition of resurrection for the righteous, the confession of Christ's resurrection among the first Christians expresses "the conviction that Jesus lives in a new and transformed way in his own individual reality in the presence of the God whom he served so faithfully in his ministry."[5] Christian eschatological hope rests on and in resurrection. That is, the Christian vision of the final end rests in the hope for resurrection out of death rooted in Christ's resurrection. The early Christians experienced Christ resurrected and identified his resurrection as promise of their own. As Paul visions in his letter to the Corinthians:

> Now if Christ is proclaimed as raised from the dead, how can some of you say there is no resurrection of the dead? If there is no resurrection of the dead, then Christ has not been raised; and if Christ has not been raised, then our proclamation has been in vain and your faith has been

in vain. . . . But in fact Christ has been raised from the dead, the first fruits of those who have died. For since death came through a human being, the resurrection of the dead has also come through a human being; for as all die in Adam, so all will be made alive in Christ. (1 Cor. 15:3-4, 12-13, 20-23)

In the logic of Christian faith reflected in Paul's letter, not only was the resurrection of Jesus vindication for Jesus as the Righteous One, but his righteous death was vindication for others as well. Jesus' efficacious vindication for others was interpreted in two ways: as effective sacrifice for others' sinfulness and as pattern for future righteousness. With Christ's passion and death, death itself can now be seen as reunion and rebirth in God.[6] As Paul writes to the community in Rome, "If we have become united with him in a death like his, we will certainly be united with him in a resurrection like his" (Rom. 6:5). To those who follow Christ, there is offered not merely death as the end of material, physical existence, but "death in the Lord" that is the fullness of God's promise for creation.[7] With the inevitable persistence of death within human experience, resurrection focuses eschatological thought beyond this world, affirming that our material existence in time and history is not ultimate. Clearly resurrection is a key theme in Christian eschatological thinking.

Yet Christian eschatology cannot exclusively be focused on the "beyond," for the route to fullness of life in resurrection is in patterning oneself on the life of Christ. In the words of

---

4. William J. La Due, *The Trinity Guide to Eschatology* (New York: Continuum, 2004), 2.

5. Hayes, *Visions of a Future*, 55.

6. Ibid., 100.

7. International Theological Commission, "Some Current Questions in Eschatology," *Irish Theological Quarterly* 58 (1992): 228. The document was drafted and discussed in 1991 and published with the approval of Cardinal Joseph Ratzinger, then president of the commission.

Paul again, the earliest Christians were invited to "put on the Lord Jesus Christ" (Rom. 13:14). What it means to "put on Christ" can be understood in relation to Jesus' own ministry and his preaching of the kingdom. Against the human experience of an ambiguous world—at once grace-filled and humanly corrupted, hostile and beautiful—the Christian New Testament remembers the preaching of Jesus of Nazareth, which drew hearers toward the beauty and graciousness of creation through participation in it. If all of creation is God's handiwork, the fulfillment of that creation is found in the realization of the kingdom of God, the hallmark of Jesus' preaching throughout the Gospels. According to Zachary Hayes, "There can be no serious question about the fact that Jesus set about his mission by proclaiming the coming of the Kingdom of God (Mark 1:14-15; Matt. 4:17; Luke 4:14-30). If one were to speak of the eschatology of Jesus, surely the Kingdom-metaphor would have to stand at the center of it."[8] In the Gospels, Jesus' own eschatological vision might be captured in his preaching of a coming kingdom where the poor and the poor in spirit are found and where mercy, peace, and righteousness reign (Matt. 5:3-12; Luke 6:20-23). This kingdom is creation as God intended.

The kingdom breaks into human history in the life, ministry, and healing miracles of Jesus, making Jesus himself an "eschatological event" where the consummation of creation is found. Yet as evidence of human failings abound, it is clear that this kingdom is amid the brokenness of a world that has not yet reached its fullness. It is the call of the Christian, therefore, to carry on Jesus' very person toward the completion of this world in the coming of a new creation. The early Christians echoed the prophet Isaiah (65:17; 66:22) in actively anticipating the new heavens and a new earth where righteousness is at home (2 Peter 3:13; see also Rev. 21:1). The kingdom is a second key theme in Christian eschatology. In this way, Christianity's hoped-for redemption is constituted not only by resurrection beyond this world, but also continues the Jewish emphasis on the transformation of this world.

Particularity, Finality, and Judgment

Thus, the Christian promise of fullness through death in Christ (and resurrection) cannot be dissociated from the practice of a life in Christ and his kingdom. It is here that a third theme is found in New Testament eschatology: judgment. The eschatological connection of resurrection, kingdom, and judgment can be seen, for example, in Matthew's Gospel where the Son of Man separates the sheep from the goats for inheritance into the kingdom on the basis of their participation in the kingdom vision: "For I was hungry and you gave me food, I was thirsty and you gave me something to drink, I was a stranger and you welcomed me, I was naked and you gave me clothing, I was sick and you took care of me, I was in prison and you visited me" (Matt. 25:35-36). Just as creation envisions the distinctive fashioning of each individual life toward fulfillment and death affects lives in particularity, the singularity of the human person's time on earth (according to Christian tradition) makes one's life choices and actions important.[9] While judgment on human failings that compromise the kingdom vision are necessary, in the eschatological schema of Christian faith, so too

---

8. Hayes, *Visions of a Future*, 44.
9. International Theological Commission, "Some Current Questions in Eschatology," 234.

626 is trust in the promise of the biblical witness: that Christ's sacrifice justifies even the sinner. "Since all have sinned and fall short of the glory of God; they are now justified by his grace as a gift, through the redemption that is in Christ Jesus" (Rom. 3:23-24).

In the texts of the New Testament, there is the bold claim that the completion of creation as God intended is found in Jesus' own person. This is how the earliest Christians experienced the life and ministry of Jesus, and they responded with the faith statement recognizing Christ as "the resurrection and the life" (John 11:25). Historical-critical approaches to the Bible have unearthed the strong likelihood that Jesus himself anticipated the in-breaking of God's kingdom as an imminent reality. Thus, for Jesus and for the early Christians, there was the expectation of the consummation of the kingdom as an event in the not-too-distant future. Following Jesus' death, the early Christians anticipated his return (Parousia) as the marking of the new eschatological era: "Then we who are alive, who are left, will be caught up in the clouds together with them to meet the Lord in the air; and so we will be with the Lord forever" (1 Thess. 4:17). While the end was not imminent and history continued on, the tradition of anticipating Christ's return as judge inaugurating the eschaton resonates through the tradition.

Key Themes:
Kingdom, Resurrection, and Judgment

The biblical text bequeaths to the tradition a variety of eschatological themes. The most central theme is that life does not end in death but continues in the resurrection, guaranteed by the resurrection of Jesus Christ. The future fullness of the kingdom, while distinct from the present, does stand in continuity with this life; therefore, what is done in this life is of critical importance, hence judgment also is a central part of the Christian eschatological tradition.

With agreement that there is life to come and agreement that judgment can be anticipated in the eschatological future, the unresolved question in the New Testament is the scope of this future. On the one hand, there exists a wide horizon of Christian eschatological hope: that the God who creates all things will restore all things, that God desires the salvation of all (1 Tim. 2:4), and that Christian hope is for the eschatological time when "God will be all in all" (1 Cor. 15:28). On the other hand, strands of the tradition tend toward a much narrower scope, carrying on, for example, the biblical suggestions that there are few who find the "narrow gate" that leads to fulfillment (Matt. 7:14) and that some are destined to "suffer the punishment of eternal destruction, separated from the presence of the Lord" (2 Thess. 1:9).

In the history of Christian eschatological thought, these themes—kingdom, resurrection, and judgment—remain, as does the tension between a wide horizon or a narrow scope for ultimate fulfillment.

Historical Perspective

With the biblical themes as foundation for eschatological reflection, diverse historical contexts further informed the future visions that became part of the Christian tradition.

Historical Developments

In the early centuries of the church, the scope of Christian eschatology was, for some, as broad as could be imagined. In the views of several of the early defenders of the faith, all of creation is taken as the horizon of eschatological thinking. Irenaeus of Lyon (c. 202), for example, responds to Gnostic currents that stressed a spiritual, hidden truth accessible only to the privileged few by identifying salvation with the very fullness of creation as a whole, encompassing even material reality. Brian Daley describes Irenaeus's understanding of salvation as "not so much God's unexpected intervention in history . . . as it is the end-stage of the process of organic growth which has been creation's 'law' since its beginning."[10] While sin was evident since the fall, the eschatological process begun in Christ provided for the renewal of humanity in a recapitulation, or redoing of creation as all things are brought together in history through Christ, the center of time and space. Origen (d. 253/54) similarly underscores the creative initiative having its fullness in the salvific rendering of all creation unto God, seeing the shortcomings of this world brought back into harmony with God's intention in creation. For Origen, the possibility of this restoration (*apokatastasis*) for *all* was central to his understanding. Reconciling the hope for universal restoration with the evidence of human failings, the eschatology of Clement of Alexandria (d. before 215) allowed for the individual to be brought back into harmony with God through spiritual growth begun in this life and continued even after death in a progressive purification.

While some early Christian defenders argued for a wide soteriological horizon in their eschatologies—whereby the Christian outlook could encompass the restoration of all—others argued for a narrower eschatological scope. For example, in the context of discussing right practice within the Christian community, Cyprian, bishop of Carthage (d. 258), associated salvation with a unified church following the rules of its leaders: "Nor let them think that the way of life or of salvation is still open to them, if they have refused to obey the bishops and priests. . . . The proud and contumacious are slain with the sword of the Spirit, in that they are cast out of the Church. For they cannot live out of it, since the house of God is one, and there can be no salvation to any except in the Church."[11] His famous axiom, "Extra Ecclesiam Nulla Salus" (Outside the church, no salvation) becomes shorthand for the straight path of salvation available to those within the church.[12] As Cyprian continues, "Straight and narrow is the way through which we enter into life, but excellent and great is the reward when we enter into glory."[13] In the early centuries when Christians were a persecuted minority within the Roman Empire, the unfailing commitment to the church in the sacrifice of the martyrs saw their death associated with Christ's and guaranteed their immediate reward.[14] The narrow scope of salvation gave consolation to those who incurred suffering as a result of their faith.

---

10. Brian E. Daley, *The Hope of the Early Church: A Handbook of Patristic Eschatology* (Cambridge: Cambridge University Press, 1991), 29.

11. Cyprian, Bishop of Carthage, *Epistle* 61, in *The Ante-Nicene Fathers*, ed. Alexander Roberts and James Donaldson (Grand Rapids: Eerdmans, 1951), 5:358.

12. Cyprian used the idea of "salvation within the church" as a challenge to Christian communities who had broken from the authority of the local bishop. However, the phrase became consistently used to condemn those "outside the faith," whether these individuals were non-Catholics or non-Christians. For an overview of the life of this axiom in church history, see Francis Sullivan, *Salvation outside the Church? Tracing the History of the Catholic Response* (New York: Paulist, 1992).

13. Cyprian, *Epistle* 61, in *The Ante-Nicene Fathers*, 5:358.

14. Daley, *The Hope of the Early Church*, 42.

When Christianity gained social favor in the Constantinian Empire, two differing Christian eschatologies emerged. On the one hand, in the absence of persecutions, some Christian thinkers interpreted the state of favor as anticipating the state of salvation—for example when Eusebius saw in Constantine's rule "a new kind of 'realized eschatology,' a foretaste of the eternal Kingdom."[15] On the other hand, in the absence of martyrdom, an emphasis on asceticism as voluntary martyrdom offered another realized eschatology for those who stood apart from the world. This alternative is seen in the work of Athanasius.[16] In both of these readings, we see the tradition of recognizing the emergence of the eschatological within history.

Augustine's version of a realized eschatology drew out the eschatological within history through identification with the church. In Brian Daley's assessment, "Augustine undoubtedly laid the foundation for the widespread tendency of later Latin theology to identify the Kingdom of God, at least in its first stage of existence, with the institutional Catholic Church."[17] Augustine's eschatology hinged on division and separation as he elaborated the difference between the earthly city and the city of God. While the fullness of the city of God remains beyond this world, nevertheless, a present division anticipates an everlasting one. Those who reside in the city of God have eternal happiness to look forward to, and "they who do not belong to this city of God shall inherit eternal misery."[18] Augustine solidifies the theological tradition by sketching in great detail the distinct destinations that await the inhabitants of each city. Culling biblical references and elaborating on the tradition, Augustine dwells at length on the destination of hell (book 21 of the *City of God*), insisting on the eternal punishments that await the wicked, including bodily suffering. And of his predictions of heaven (book 22 of the *City of God*), the same attention to bodiliness accompanies Augustine's considerations of the types of bodies men, women, and children will have in their heavenly reward. It is hard to overlook the speculative nature of much of Augustine's descriptive account, yet given the influence of Augustine, the tradition is sealed with a sense of the divided destinations in our eschatological future.

Yet other influences infuse the tradition again with a more comprehensive vision of fulfillment. Take Aquinas in the Middle Ages, who reflects the visible tension between a wide eschatological horizon and the more concentrated locus of salvation through the church. His work draws explicitly on Augustine and his divided eschatology, yet the incorporation also of Aristotelian teleology sees all of creation destined for the good, which is God. For Aquinas, all of created reality comes from God and has its end in God: "God is the last end of man and of all other things."[19] God creates with the end of fulfillment in mind for all of created reality. Yet, while all things are destined for their intended end in God, nevertheless Aquinas also holds a special role for the church, as revelation (*Summa theologiae* I, q. 1, a. 1) and the church itself are necessary for salvation (*Summa theologiae* III, q. 73

---

15. Ibid., 77.

16. Ibid. See also John Thiel, "Time, Judgment and Competitive Spirituality: A Reading of the Development of the Doctrine of Purgatory," *Theological Studies* (December 2008): 741–85.

17. Daley, *The Hope of the Early Church*, 134.

18. Augustine, *City of God*, 19.

19. Thomas Aquinas, *Summa theologiae* II.1, q. 1, a. 8.

a. 3).[20] Further, according to Aquinas, the sacramental life of the church not only anticipates the eschatological as the sacraments are a "foretelling of future glory" (*Summa theologiae* III, q. 60, a. 3), but the sacraments also are necessary for salvation (*Summa theologiae* III, q. 61, a. 1). This would seem to suggest that some do not reach their intended ends, since clearly not all persons participate in the sacramental life of the church. Aquinas navigates this by accommodating those who are not explicitly part of the church, writing, "A man can obtain salvation without being actually baptized, on account of his desire for Baptism, which desire is the outcome of 'faith that worketh by charity,' whereby God, Whose power is not tied to visible sacraments, sanctifies man inwardly."[21]

While Aquinas stopped work on his *Summa* before arriving at a discrete discussion of the "last things," his emphasis on how things are created for a final end in God provides for a reading of his work as eschatological throughout. As Matthew Lamb describes, "The whole of theology is profoundly eschatological according to St. Thomas Aquinas' *Summa Theologiae*. . . . Aquinas' theological vision moves from the most sacred mystery of the Triune God to take in the cosmic sweep of the procession of all creation from God and the return of all to God. The end is in the beginning and the beginning in the end."[22] For Aquinas, eschatology is not merely a concern with the end-time, but the very

purpose of creation toward its telos infuses all created reality from beginning to end.

As Aquinas and the various strands of the tradition were transformed into the manuals of theology in the eighteenth century, the approach seems to have lost sight of the whole of theology as eschatological. Eschatology became focused merely on the "last things" beyond the world. In the manualist tradition, the "classic" formulation of eschatology comes to be structured around categories determined almost exclusively by what happens after this life. Not only did the manuals frame eschatology in terms of the "beyond," but they reflect a literalist approach to the theological vision of Scripture. In Peter Phan's assessment, "Biblical statements on the afterlife were for the most part taken as realistic *description*, an advance report as it were of what happens beyond death."[23] Eschatology becomes at this phase a mere appendix to theology, increasingly speculative and peripheral to the proclamation of the faith.

This marginalization of eschatology in Catholic theology came into conflict with the historical-critical "discovery" of Jesus' own preaching as thoroughly eschatological. With the publication of Johannes Weiss's *Jesus' Proclamation of the Kingdom of God* (1892) and Albert Schweitzer's *Quest of the Historical Jesus* (1906), scholarly approaches to Christianity began to see that for Jesus, eschatology was far from peripheral, as he seems to have preached an immanent

---

20. Thomas Aquinas, *Summa theologiae* III, q. 73, a. 3. "There is no entering into salvation outside the Church, just as in the time of the deluge there was none outside the Ark, which denotes the Church, according to 1 Peter 3:20-21. And it has been said above (Question 68, Article 2), that before receiving a sacrament, the reality of the sacrament can be had through the very desire of receiving the sacrament."

21. Thomas Aquinas, *Summa theologiae* III, q. 68, a. 2.

22. Matthew L. Lamb, "The Eschatology of St. Thomas Aquinas," in *Aquinas on Doctrine: A Critical Introduction*, ed. Thomas Weinandy, Daniel Keating, and John Yocum (London: T&T Clark, 2004), 225.

23. Peter C. Phan, "Roman Catholic Theology," in *The Oxford Handbook of Eschatology*, ed. Jerry L. Walls (Oxford: Oxford University Press, 2008), 216.

eschatology in the vision of God's kingdom on the verge of arrival. The focus at the beginning of the twentieth century then was to reconcile Christian doctrines on the end-time and Jesus' own preaching about the end of time. "As a result," writes Nicholas Healy, "the theme of eschatology has ceased to be a discreet treatise situated at the end of dogmatics but concerns the form and content of the whole of Christian revelation and theology."[24] As evidence of this twentieth-century shift, Healy reminds us of Karl Barth's assessment: "Christianity which is not wholly eschatology and nothing but eschatology has nothing to do with Christ."[25] In this vein, Jürgen Moltmann's *Theology of Hope* (1964) represents a flowering of the twentieth-century reemergence of eschatology.[26] With this text, Moltmann reframes eschatology once again to insist that Christian hope is not merely for an end-time beyond this world, but that faith in the resurrection of the Crucified One and faith in the God of promise in the Exodus renders Christian hope fundamentally grounded in the transformation of this world. In Moltmann's assessment, "From first to last . . . Christianity is eschatology, is hope."[27] And this hope is not merely in God, but in what God promises: "peace and righteousness on earth."[28]

The late-twentieth-century insistence on eschatology as central, rather than peripheral, to Christian faith is borne out in a sacramental approach to eschatology. That is to say, liturgically and sacramentally, the whole of the church's life is bound up with the ultimate end. As Christians throughout the centuries have together prayed, "Thy kingdom come," in the Lord's Prayer, the liturgical life propels Christians toward the final end of a fulfilled creation. In baptism, the initiate is accompanied by Christ on the journey to God and he or she enters into the life and paschal mystery of Christ, affirmed in confirmation. In Eucharist, Christians are reminded that the fulfillment of creation as God's kingdom requires sacrifice, as the sacrifice of Christ is remembered. In marriage and holy orders, Catholic Christians glimpse the social dimension of the commitment to christoform discipleship, in trust and work toward the kingdom. As a reminder of the hoped-for communion with God eschatologically *and* the undeniable judgment on our human failings, the recitation of the creed anticipates the return of Christ in the Parousia, when he will come to "judge the living and the dead." The sacrament of penance celebrates reconciliation and conversion as component parts of the eschatological vision in its dimension of justice and judgment. The sacramental practice of the anointing of the sick witnesses again the restoration of wholeness held as eschatological offer by God through Christ. And the anointing of the sick welcomes some finally into death in Christ, with hope rooted in the witness of the resurrection. Anticipating the end-time as an "eternal Sabbath," Augustine closes *City of God*

---

24. Nicholas Healy, *The Eschatology of Hans Urs von Balthasar: Being as Communion* (Oxford: Oxford University Press, 2005), 8.

25. Karl Barth, *Epistle to the Romans*, 6th ed., trans. Edwyn C. Hoskyns (Oxford: Oxford University Press, 1933), 314. Quoted in Healy, *The Eschatology of Hans Urs von Balthasar*, 8.

26. For an overview of how eschatology was recognized as central in twentieth-century theology, see Walter Kasper, "Individual Salvation and Eschatological Consummation," in *Faith and the Future: Studies in Christian Eschatology*, ed. John Galvin (New York: Paulist, 1994), 7–24.

27. Jürgen Moltmann, *Theology of Hope: On the Ground and the Implications of a Christian Eschatology* (London: SCM, 1967), 16.

28. Ibid., 119.

with the vision that "we shall be that Sabbath."[29] Understanding the sacraments and liturgy as eschatological events, Christians actively anticipate the redemption for which they hope.

While at times the tradition has lost sight of eschatology as central to the whole of the faith, strands of the tradition remind us that eschatology is not merely a speculative exercise to be relegated to the appendix of our theological thinking. Rather, eschatology itself—the final consummation of creation as God intended—is the very heart of the faith.

Continuing Themes

Witnessing the variegated tradition of Christian theological reflection, nevertheless certain themes are identifiable as repeatedly surfacing and might form a characteristic Roman Catholic eschatology discernible through time. These include continuity between this life and what is to come, the notion of bodily resurrection, and the outcome of judgment (in particular, purgatory and beatific vision).

CONTINUITY BETWEEN THIS LIFE AND WHAT IS TO COME

The systematic outlook believes in a good creation called forth by the God who promises its consummation in Christ and his kingdom. In light of the reality that this kingdom remains visibly unfulfilled in this life (even if evidenced and anticipated in part), Christian reflection on the last things consistently holds death as a critical point of understanding. In the tradition of magisterial teaching, the church consistently sees this nodal point as one that holds together

the reality of this life and the hoped-for future. In the view of the Congregation for the Doctrine of the Faith in the late twentieth century, while neither scripture nor theology provides sufficient data for a proper understanding of life after death, and what is to come remains in mystery, nevertheless, Catholic doctrine insists on the "fundamental continuity" between our present life in Christ and what is anticipated in the future.[30] With an eschatological focus on the kingdom, there is continuity in that, while our time in history is not ultimate, what happens in history matters eschatologically because what is anticipated beyond death is not dissociated from life.

RESURRECTION OF THE BODY

What is anticipated beyond death is the continuation of life in resurrection. Resurrection clearly has its roots in the Jewish tradition, as Christians identified Jesus as the Righteous One vindicated by God for the salvation of all. But as questions arose in the course of Christian history as to just what sort of reality resurrection entails, Christian resurrection has been affirmed as *bodily resurrection*. We might understand this first by extending the principle of continuity between this life and the future. The Catholic Christian systematic and sacramental outlook has fundamentally affirmed the goodness of creation and the material reality of the world. Against philosophies that would deny the goodness of the body in ultimately claiming that after death, the soul finally shakes free of its imprisonment in matter, the Eleventh Council of Toledo (675) insisted that the faithful shall rise "in this very body in which we live and are and

---

29. Augustine, *City of God*, 22.30.

30. Congregation for the Doctrine of the Faith, "Letter on Certain Questions Concerning Eschatology," *Acta Apostolicae Sedis* 71 (1979): 939–43.

move."[31] This was affirmed again at the Fourth Lateran Council (1215) right up through Vatican II and the most recent magisterial statements on resurrection. While the continuity of our earthly bodies in resurrection is affirmed, the tradition also insists on a radical difference in the transformed state. Tracing back to Paul's vision of bodily resurrection, Christians affirm also that the perishable body will be "raised in glory" (1 Cor. 15:43) as imperishable. In the words of Paul, "It is sown a physical body, it is raised a spiritual body" (1 Cor. 15:44).

How do we make sense of the continuity and the distinction between the bodies in which we move and the habitation of resurrection? The first step is to trace its formulation in relationship to the Christian witness of the New Testament. In the stories of the Gospels, Jesus appears after the resurrection in an embodied state, one so physical that his disciples are moved to embrace him (John 20:17), invited to touch his flesh and eat with him (Luke 24:36-43), and challenged to place their fingers in his wounds (John 20:24-29). The various appearances indicate that the very same body that was broken in crucifixion has been brought to new life in resurrection. Yet, in the gospel stories, the same disciples are slow to recognize Jesus: he is mistaken for a gardener (John 20:11-16) and walks the road to Emmaus with companions who do not know it is him (Luke 24:13-32).[32] The stories of the New Testament witness a resurrection of the body that both stands in continuity of identity with the earthly reality of Jesus and is quite different. Indeed, the resurrection "affirms a transcendent destiny for Jesus."[33] In the tradition, it is clear that resurrection is not mere resuscitation.

From this complex nexus of identity and difference, contemporary theologians suggest that we consider the continuity of embodiment as a statement that insists on resurrection of the *whole person*.[34] For example, with Karl Rahner, this affirmation rests on an understanding of the human person as both spirit and matter, integrated as one in the life of this world. At death, a holistic understanding is also required, as he articulates: "'Body' (*Fleisch*) means the whole man in his proper embodied reality. 'Resurrection' means, therefore, the termination and perfection of the *whole man* before God, which gives him 'eternal life.' Man is a many-sided being which in (and despite) its unity stretches as it were, through several very different dimensions—through matter and spirit, nature and person, action and passion, etc."[35] The fulfillment of the human person and its completion attends to all these various dimensions. Seeing the body as "intentionality-in-time," Anthony Godzieba suggests that we consider the continuity of embodiment as a statement that defends the continued reality of the self and its "unique ensemble of embodied experiences."[36]

---

31. Eleventh Council of Toledo (675), in *The Christian Faith in the Doctrinal Documents of the Catholic Church*, ed. Jacques Dupuis (New York: Alba, 2001), 1016.

32. John Thiel, "For What May We Hope? Thoughts on the Eschatological Imagination," *Theological Studies* 67 (2006): 530.

33. Hayes, *Visions of a Future*, 53.

34. For an overview of the perspectives of Karl Rahner, Joseph Ratzinger, and Edward Schillebeeckx on the resurrection of the body, see Bernard Prusak, "Bodily Resurrection in Catholic Perspectives," *Theological Studies* 61 (2000): 64–105.

35. Karl Rahner, "The Resurrection of the Body," in *Theological Investigations*, vol. 2, trans. Karl-H. Kruger (Baltimore: Helicon, 1963), 210–11.

36. Anthony Godzieba, "Bodies and Persons, Resurrected and Postmodern: Toward a Relational Eschatology," in

In continuity with our understanding of earthly embodiment, resurrection of the body ultimately affirms the goodness of creation and our material existence in its particularity, complexity, and relationality embedded as an integral part of all that is. This includes the idea that our embodied existence does not end at the limits of our skin, but extends out into relationship with God, others, and world: "We are all living in one and the same body—the world."[37] Bodily resurrection affirms this: "Eternal life does not isolate a person, but leads him out of isolation into true unity with his brothers and sisters and the whole of God's creation."[38]

Outcomes of Judgment: Purgatory and Beatific Vision

The continuity of embodiment in resurrection affirms the goodness, totality, and particularity of human lives, and is therefore connected with the second key teaching held throughout the tradition: that of judgment. The particular human person embodied in a particular material reality is the one who is judged "according to what each has done while in the body."[39] That the judgment of each individually is to take place upon death is affirmed by the tradition expressed by the Second Council of Lyons (1274), *Benedictus Deus* (1336), Council of Florence (1439), Council of Trent (1563), and *Catechism of the Catholic Church* (1992).

Depending on the assessment of the judgment, the Christian outlook has sketched a variety of destinies, particularly in the forms of heaven and hell. This outlook has its resonance with the New Testament stories of Jesus as judge and the various outcomes destined for those who participate in the kingdom vision of righteousness and those who reject it. In the Catholic tradition, hell stands as the place where those who cut themselves off from God in life are found after death, and heaven is enjoyed by those who in this life have participated in God's reign. The immediacy of heaven after death is framed as the face-to-face encounter with God identified by Pope Benedict XII as the "beatific vision."[40] In his 1336 Constitution *Benedictus Deus*, "On the Beatific Vision of God," Pope Benedict XII defined this state in which the blessed "see the divine essence with an intuitive vision and even face to face without the mediation of any creature by way of object of vision; rather the divine

Theology and Conversation: Towards a Relational Theology, ed. Jacques Haers and Peter de May (Leuven: Leuven University Press, 2003), 219, 224.

37. Karl Rahner, "The Body in the Order of Salvation," in *Theological Investigations*, vol. 17, trans. Margaret Kohl (London: Darton, Longman & Todd, 1981), 87–88.

38. Joseph Ratzinger, *Eschatology: Death and Eternal Life*, 2nd ed. (Washington, DC: Catholic University of America Press, 1988), 160.

39. Eleventh Council of Toledo (675), in *The Christian Faith in the Doctrinal Documents of the Catholic Church*, ed. Jacques Dupuis (New York: Alba, 2001), 1017.

40. The statement of Benedict XII indicates that the blessed enjoy the beatific vision immediately after death. However, according to the International Theological Commission, the tradition has affirmed a twofold eschatological phase constituted by the outcomes of individual judgment and the general judgment of Parousia. "In traditional Christian thought the eschatology of the soul is a state in which, during the course of history, brothers and sisters in Christ are successively united with him and in him. . . . Such a union reaches its culmination at the end of history when people will be led to their full, existential and therefore bodily reality, through the resurrection." International Theological Commission, "Some Current Questions in Eschatology," *Irish Theological Quarterly* 58 (1992): 222. The contemporary magisterium insists, therefore, on an "intermediate state" for the departed, while Rahner argues that this position is not dogma. See Rahner, "The Intermediate State," in *Theological Investigations*, 17:114.

essence immediately manifests itself to them, plainly, clearly, openly, and in this vision they enjoy the divine essence."[41] The beatific vision is held out as the ultimate consummation for the individual created by God and finally welcomed into union with God.

While the states of heaven and hell are evidenced in the New Testament and shared by Christians across the varied denominations, there exists within the Catholic outlook yet another alternative following individual judgment in death. Perhaps the most distinctive of Catholic doctrines in eschatology is the state of purgatory. First recognizably articulated by an ecumenical council in 1274 at the Second General Council of Lyons, the Catholic tradition has insisted on the opportunity for souls to be "cleansed after death by purgatorial and purifying penalties."[42] At the time of the Reformation, purgatory seemed to represent the corrupt practices in a church where intercessory prayer for the souls of the departed might be purchased at a price of value to church officials. Further, Martin Luther saw purgatory as contradicting a biblical understanding of the nature of grace as the guarantor of salvation. Nevertheless, at the Council of Trent (1563), the Catholic Church affirmed "that there is a purgatory, and that the souls detained there are helped by the acts of intercession of the faithful," albeit insisting that this teaching be applied in a way that is "con-ducive to an increase of piety."[43] In the words of Trent, "As for those things that belong to the realm of curiosity or superstition, or smack of dishonorable gain, they should forbid them as scandalous and injurious to the faithful."[44]

If the doctrine of purgatory is to abide by the fundamental rule of continuity between this life and the next, an understanding of the logic of purgatory is in order. The logic of purgatory relates back to some of the affirmations seen in resurrection, namely, that our "whole self" does not end in death and that the soul continues to be related to matter, that is, to the materiality of the world in time and history. In Rahner's words, there exists "a cosmic relation between the finite human spirit and matter, that is to say, the *one* matter of *the world*. This relation would then still remain and would be preserved even when the precise way in which, during its earthly life, the body is formed through this relation between matter and spirit ceased to exist."[45] While human beings are offered the lifelong invitation of communion with God, it is always simultaneously steeped in the sin of human failings. The church's teaching that personhood continues after death insists also that the relationships of communion with God and others aimed at in this life might find their fullness in a process that continues after death. As John Thiel interprets the teaching, "Salvation, becoming who [we] most are, to some degree entails becoming

---

41. Benedict XII, *Benedictus Deus* (1336), in Dupuis, *The Christian Faith in the Doctrinal Documents*, 1019.

42. Second General Council of Lyons (1274), in Dupuis, *The Christian Faith in the Doctrinal Documents*, 19. There are precedents that anticipate this thirteenth-century development, for example, in many of the eschatologies of the patristic era. For a discussion of the development of the doctrine of purgatory, see Jacques Le Goff, *The Birth of Purgatory*, trans. A. Goldhammer (Chicago: University of Chicago Press, 1984); Thiel, "Time, Judgment and Competitive Spirituality."

43. General Council of Trent Twenty-Fifth Session, "Decree on Purgatory" (1562), in Dupuis, *The Christian Faith in the Doctrinal Documents*, 1,021.

44. Ibid., 1022.

45. Rahner, "The Intermediate State," 17:119.

who [we] were not—persons broken by their sin and the sin of others."[46] Further, the affirmation of bodiliness in resurrection—"the holistic integrity of the saved self"[47]—means that our relationality continues and that the work of the blessed dead might include ongoing reconciliation and forgiveness. The doctrine of purgatory stands in continuity with the relationality of our earthly lives and the holistic vision of resurrection. As Joseph Ratzinger has articulated, "The network of human relationality belongs to human nature itself," and the love and guilt that are the fabric of human existence in this world continue in connections beyond death: "The guilt which goes on because of me is a part of me."[48] The tradition of purgatory offers purification as the opportunity to grow in perfection beyond the limitations of our earthly life.

The aforementioned destinations of heaven, purgatory, and hell are envisioned at death in light of individual judgment and in continuity with the individual's participation with God and communion with others in earthly life. But Christian eschatology includes a further stage in the form of a final, general judgment at the second coming of Christ (Parouisa). In the words of Jacques Dupuis, "At the end of time, the Second Coming of the Lord in glory will therefore usher in the definitive revelation of creation's total renewal in God: whatever God offered in promise to our forefathers and mysteriously extends to us in Christ, will manifest itself fully when all God's family will be one and the whole universe will attain maturity."[49] In Acts 3:21, the biblical account envisions the return of Jesus as the time of "universal restoration." This understanding of the consummation of creation is a holistic vision as Christians look toward the ultimate future when "God will be all in all" (1 Cor. 15:28).

Currents in Contemporary Eschatology

A common thread in contemporary Roman Catholic theology is eschatology as relationship with God. In addition, there is a strong desire to see this relationship extend to all created reality. The resurrection event, then, inaugurates the completion of creation as God intended as God acts as the "Creator who brings his creative action to its completion in the resurrection of the dead."[50]

Salvation of the Individual: Relationship with God through Christ

Viewing eschatology as expressed in the various strands of the tradition, the "last things" are intimately intertwined with everything that is. Two elements bear underscoring at this point: the rooting of a Christian eschatological vision in a radical hope in God and the link between anthropology and Christology. The Christian vision of the final end for human existence is essentially an anthropological vision, one that attempts to make sense of the nature of human existence by framing it in terms of its ultimate intended end. In this, the Christian places a deep trust in God as creator of all existence (including

---

46. Thiel, "For What May We Hope?" 540.

47. Ibid., 528.

48. Ratzinger, *Eschatology*, 184, 187.

49. Dupuis, *The Christian Faith in the Doctrinal Documents*, 1,013.

50. Hans Urs von Balthasar, Mysterium Paschale: *The Mystery of Easter*, trans. Aidan Nichols (Edinburgh: T&T Clark, 1990), 204.

636 human beings), that the one who called all things into existence does so for an ultimate purpose, not simply to see them pass away. The beauty and goodness of the created world (affirmed in Genesis and standing as the invitation of God's kingdom) attest to the careful creation of the one whom Christians call God. To recognize human contingency and dependence, and to hope ultimately in the Creator, rests as the foundation of Christian eschatology as hope. This hope is strengthened in faith through the experience of Christ crucified and risen. Christians place their hope in God because they have been expressly affected by the life, death, and continued presence of Jesus of Nazareth as the Christ. In the words of Peter Phan, "Eschatology is anthropology conjugated in the future tense on the basis of christology."[51] The ultimate future experience of all humanity is extrapolated from the singular experience of Jesus Christ, for Christians affirm, in the words of the poet and priest Gerard Manley Hopkins:

> I am all at once what Christ is, since he was what I am, and
> This Jack, joke, poor potsherd, patch, matchwood, immortal diamond,
> Is immortal diamond.[52]

Hopkins's poetry articulates the fundamental connection between incarnation and eschatology. In Christian belief, God's becoming human has inalterably wed God's own being with humanity's destiny. Just as theological anthropology asserts solidarity among humanity in our common human nature, in incarnation God joins that solidarity in Christ. The consummation of life in communion with God witnessed in the resurrection is promised therefore to all.

The framing of eschatology as the future tense of anthropology helps to identify a distinctiveness of contemporary eschatology in that its focus does not tend to be on speculative forecasts of a future beyond our reach. Rather, as Rahner has helpfully articulated, there is a distinction to be made between the "apocalyptic" and the "eschatological." Whereas the apocalyptic purports to offer a description of the endtime based on some preview of what is to come, the eschatological anticipates the future reality by writing forward what we know to be the case in the present.[53] What Christians know to be the case in the present is crystallized around the experience with Jesus Christ. Contemporary eschatology focuses on humanity's relationship with God through Christ, providing one key in which traditional themes are rendered. Here, eschatology continues to treat the last things, and the human experience of death remains a crucial touchstone. But death does not mark the beginning of the eschatological; rather, death is a nodal point when contemporary eschatology emphasizes *continuity* between this life and what is to come.

The Nodal Point of Death

Continuing the theme of continuity between this life and what is to come, contemporary es-

---

51. Peter C. Phan, "Eschatology: Contemporary Context and Disputed Questions," in *Church and Theology: Essays in Memory of Carl J. Peter*, ed. Peter Phan (Washington, DC: CUA Press, 1995), 241–75, at 252.

52. Gerard Manley Hopkins, "That Nature Is a Heraclitean Fire and of the Comfort of the Resurrection," in *Mortal Beauty, God's Grace: Major Poems and Spiritual Writings of Gerard Manley Hopkins*, ed. John F. Thornton and Susan B. Varenne (New York: Vintage/Random House, 2003), 52.

53. Karl Rahner, "The Hermeneutics of Eschatological Assertions," in *Theological Investigations*, vol. 4, trans. Kevin Smyth (Baltimore: Helicon, 1966), 337.

chatology asserts that eternal life in Christ begins in the experience of Christ in the ordinary of this life. For Joseph Ratzinger, eschatology is not about a "where" or a "when" of the last things, but about "relationship with Christ's person."[54] Just as the first Christians found authentic living through Christ and his kingdom, it is in relationship with Christ and his kingdom that persons today find their authentic humanity. In the fullness of the kingdom, Ratzinger writes, "It becomes clear that God's truth and justice are not just ideas or ideals but realities, the truth of authentic being."[55] Yet while we may experience a foretaste of this when truth and justice are found in this life, the fullness of creation is successively compromised by the failings of humanity in history, such that the kingdom of God that Christ promises requires the transformation of earthly existence: "Such a transformation can only take place through death. For this reason, the Kingdom of God, salvation in its fullness, cannot be deprived of its connection with dying."[56] Death remains a crucial moment in Christian eschatological thinking, underscoring humanity's inability to conform to creation's intended telos without the gratuitous intervention of God's salvific work.

While death remains an experiential reality and retains its connection with human sinfulness, Jesus' solidarity with humanity has transformed death itself. Highlighting the affirmation of the Christian creed, Ratzinger identifies this transformation taking place through Jesus' descent into Sheol: "At that moment, death ceases to be the God-forsaken land of darkness, a realm of unpitying distance from God. In Christ, God himself entered the realm of death, transforming the space of noncommunication into the place of his own presence."[57] Through Christ, God extends the solidarity of relationship even into the place of the dead. What death ushers in is not the end, therefore, but the fullness of relationship with God. The one who "dies into the righteousness of God does not die into nothingness, but enters upon authentic reality, life itself."[58]

For Christians, death is not the end of existence, but its center, linking the lifelong free decision for God and participation in the divine reality with its fullness of participation in God's communion. Hans Urs von Balthasar also draws out the theme of "continuity" of this life and the next through a Trinitarian lens. For von Balthasar, the world exists in the image of the Trinity, and created reality mirrors the divine life when it imitates God's own relationality and self-giving. The truest reflection of this in Christian perspective is, of course, Jesus Christ, who demonstrated with his life how relationality and kenotic self-giving are what it means to be human and what it means to be divine. Participating in trinitarian relationship of self-giving, creation is destined for this divine fullness: "The real 'last thing' is the triune life of God disclosed in Jesus Christ."[59] Through his life, death, and resurrection, Jesus has prepared a place for those who follow him (John 14:2); that place is in the trinitarian life.

---

54. Ratzinger, *Eschatology*, 8.

55. Ibid., 91.

56. Ibid., 62.

57. Ibid., 93.

58. Ibid., 91.

59. Hans Urs von Balthasar, *Theo-Drama: Theological Dramatic Theory*, vol. 5, *The Last Act*, trans. Graham Harrison (San Francisco: Ignatius, 1998), 57.

638

Whether focused on a relationship with Christ or the relationality of the Trinity, contemporary Roman Catholic eschatology invites Christians to a life that has continuity here and beyond. This life is not the end, Christian eschatology insists, and the critical moment of death brings us to a definitive relationship with God.

THE REAL POSSIBILITY OF HELL

Because the last things stand in continuity with creation as God intended and as humans are invited to experience it, von Balthasar reflects exhaustively on the possibility of universal restoration (apocatastasis), that is, that all persons may be saved. Such a hope is not only witnessed in Scripture (e.g., Acts 3:21; 1 Tim. 2:4), but also held in the foundational writings of many of the early church fathers, including Clement of Alexandria (d. before 215), Origen (d. c. 254), Gregory of Nyssa (d. 395), and Ambrose, bishop of Milan (d. 397).[60]

Yet while the self-giving communion of trinitarian relations strives toward a reciprocity that extends to all created beings, freedom requires that this invitation to communion can be rejected. Recognizing the juxtaposition of heaven and hell throughout the tradition, von Balthasar insists with the tradition that hell stands as a real possibility. And although Christians throughout the centuries may have been carried away in their imaginative fancies of the various eternal punishments for the wicked, von Balthasar insists that the scriptural images of hell have a different purpose: rather than forecasting a future destiny, the discourses on hell

serve to reflect humanity's present condition of turning from God. Created by sinners in the refusal of relationship with God, hell is the state of contradiction that consumes with a burning fire. The reality of sin that abounds in the world and in which each person participates reminds us that humans indeed apply their freedom away from the life-giving relationship of trinitarian self-giving. The purpose of hell discourse and hell visioning is not to condemn the world; instead, it ought to serve an orienting function that might be called a "spirituality of hell." That is to say, the pressing reality of hell as a real possibility leaves no time to look at how others are faring, but rather requires that Christians take account of their own participation in sin. Hell exists as a real possibility not for persons in general, but for *me*. This realization provokes the individual to ask, "How am I in authentic relationship with God?" Judgment, in the first place, is self-judgment, as the spirituality of hell encourages human persons to reflect on how their self-giving falls short of the trinitarian model. Here we see the traditional themes of judgment and hell recast as the individual takes stock of whether or not he or she truly is in authentic relationship with Christ.

A concomitant dimension of the spirituality of hell consists of von Balthasar's powerful reflection of Jesus' own standing alongside the sinner. Jesus' divine kenosis witnesses him stooping to the lowest position of humanity in its sinfulness, as he hangs on the cross a defeated criminal and experiences the descent into hell, realizing the agony of the world and its sins.[61] From the aban-

---

60. For a brief description of the various patristic outlooks, see William J. La Due, *The Trinity Guide to Eschatology* (New York: Continuum, 2004), 10–11. La Due also recognizes the subsequent statements against apocatastasis writing: "The doctrine of *apokatastasis panton* (the final salvation of all) was condemned by canon 9 of the provincial synod of Constantinople in 543" (11). See also, Dupuis, *The Christian Faith in the Doctrinal Documents*, 1,016.

61. Von Balthasar, Mysterium Paschale, 23, 52.

donment of the cross ("my God, why have you forsaken me?" Matt. 27:45) to the abasement of hell, Jesus experiences the dark night of the soul wherein God's seeming absence is witness to the hidden depths of God's abiding presence. Christ's being with the dead in the event of Holy Saturday witnesses the ultimate solidarity with sinful humanity, mirroring perfectly the divine self-giving of relationality and assuring sinful humanity of God's desire for reconciliation. Von Balthasar finds evidence in Scripture and the tradition that Christ stands in deep relationship with humanity, even in our failings.

TRANSCENDENTAL DESIRE FOR THE BEATIFIC VISION

Contemporary eschatology's emphasis on *relationship* between the individual and God through Christ underscores what Christ shares with humanity and therefore what humanity may hope to share with Christ. Rahner echoes this in his transcendental approach to eschatology where human experience at its best is christoform. For Rahner, the human person is structured with a fundamental orientation toward God in God's fullness, the Absolute Horizon and Infinite Mystery that surrounds and sustains creation and life itself. In so many human experiences that witness to a sustaining reality beyond themselves, the human person has the experience of eternity, an experience of God. When we make free choices, commit to irreversible decisions, or reach out from ourselves in love, for example, we experience a transcendence beyond our own finitude and into the infinite horizon of existence. God created humanity with this fundamental structure of transcendence toward eternity and ultimate fulfillment in a life united with God. Like Jesus, all persons are called into complete union with God—in their lives in the present and in the future fulfillment of those lives. Human life, therefore, bears a christoformity in the perfected form of its actualization. In fact, Jesus, by his life of perfect union with God makes this goal universally possible.

Eschatology articulates the consummation of growth already taking place in human experience. Heaven, salvation, and the beatific vision are terms that indicate the fullness toward which all human lives tend, and these "ends" stand in continuity with the definitive choices enacted throughout the very moments of one's entire lifetime. Each moment of each day is conceived as an offer of relationship with God, to which the human person responds daily with a fundamental yes or no. Each moment and each day afford opportunities for irreversible decisions that constitute the orientation either toward or away from God. Death, therefore, is simply a witness to the definitiveness of decisions humanity makes daily in the space and time of history. In Rahner's words, "Our death is a culmination of the unrepeatable *onceness* of our personal human existence."[62] Death is the event in which humans achieve their definitive destiny and eternity opens up as the consummation of time and history.

In recognizing the definitiveness of death as the completion/fulfillment of the individual's story, Rahner draws attention also to the fundamental desire that this story be ultimately meaningful. As human beings, we desire that the uniqueness of our story and the complexity of our distinctive decision making endure and not simply be erased at our passing into death. This desire reveals a transcendental hope in the resurrection—that is, a hope for an eternal validity to our historical existence that is part of

---

62. Rahner, *Spiritual Exercises*, trans. Kenneth Baker (New York: Herder & Herder, 1965), 90.

the universal human makeup.[63] Experiencing this transcendental desire for resurrection, humans search history, seeking confirmation that such eternal enduring of the individual's story is possible. The Christian experience and conviction that Jesus' life and ministry, his person and his cause have a permanent validity, affirmed by God in the event of the resurrection, provide confidence in resurrection as an object of faith. Finding confidence and confirmation in Jesus, the transcendental desire for resurrection actively seeks its fulfillment. But even if one does not know Jesus to find confirmation in his life, the structural universality of human christoformity extends salvation beyond the bounds of Christian confession and covers humanity exhaustively. In Rahner's words, "The relationship of God to man is basically the same for all men, because it rests on the Incarnation, death and resurrection of the one Word of God made flesh."[64] With heaven and the beatific vision as the structural goal of all human existence, and the uniting of God to all humanity in incarnation, Rahner hopes also in the possibility of apocatastasis.

Like other contemporary theologians, Rahner sees the goal of communion and relationship not only between the individual and God, but also among human beings. This communion brings us back to the solidarity among humanity, and humanity with God, witnessed in incarnation. As Ratzinger has written:

> Given, therefore, the real interdependence of all men and all creation, it turns out that the end of history is not for any man something extrinsic, something which has ceased to concern him. The doctrine of the body of Christ simply formulates with that final consistency that christology makes possible a truth which was quite predictable on the basis of anthropology alone. Every human being exists in himself and outside himself: everyone exists simultaneously in other people. What happens in one individual has an effect upon the whole of humanity, and what happens in humanity happens in the individual. "The Body of Christ" means that all human beings are one organism, the destiny of the whole the proper destiny of each.[65]

The solidarity of the human condition links, therefore, the fate of the individual with that of the collective. We are brought to another dimension of Christian eschatology, that of general salvation.

Corporate Salvation: Transformation toward a Time When God Will Be All in All

Having experienced the reality of Christ alive, Christians have reason to hope in the resurrection extending to all of creation. But this future hope is wrapped up with the spirituality of hell that recognizes both human failings and the need for active participation in the promised redemption as resurrection is entwined with mission. That is to say, the earliest witnesses to the resurrection of Christ both were consoled by the triumphing power of God *and* sent on mission to do likewise.[66] Mission propels Christians

---

63. Peter Phan, *Eternity in Time: A Study of Karl Rahner's Eschatology* (London: Associated University Press, 1988), 163.

64. Rahner, "Christianity and the Non-Christian Religions," in *Theological Investigations*, vol. 5, trans. Karl-H. Kruger (London: Darton, Longman & Todd; Baltimore: Helicon, 1966), 118.

65. Ratzinger, *Eschatology*, 190.

66. For a discussion of mission as part of the eschatological vision, see von Balthasar, *Mysterium Paschale*, 224, 251.

through the ages to continue Christ's work of self-giving love to the world. In the words of von Balthasar, "Christian hope, theological hope, goes beyond this world but does not pass it by: rather it takes the world with it on its way to God who has graciously prepared a dwelling in himself for us and for the world."[67] By self-giving and suffering in love for the well-being of the world, the Christian participates in this eschatological promise. Mission extends the eschatological scope beyond the individual to a corporate goal as "continuity" not only anticipates a particular future for individuals in Christ, but also allows this anticipated future to transform the present.

SALVATION AS LIBERATION:
THE HISTORICAL BEGINNING OF THE END

With the biblical witness offering a vision of God's promised fulfillment engaged as a process within history, the New Testament identifies Jesus Christ as the firstfruits of eschatological consummation breaking into history. This calls forth Christian mission encouraging the transformation toward a new earth, seeing a continuity between the promises of God fulfilled in history and the fullness of that fulfillment beyond history. With eschatology offering a foretaste of an ultimate future that is not yet here, there is, nevertheless, an anticipation of the fulfillment of God's promises already in the midst of the world. "The kingdom of God is among you," Christian scripture proclaims (Luke 17:21), and the practice of Christian mis-

sion and sacrament seeks to participate in the processes that make this promise a reality.

While the practice of Christian eschatology has frequently leaned toward the future vision of the "not yet" (emphasizing the "last things" of death and resurrection into eternal life), Catholic Christian sacramental and mission practices affirm the kingdom already at hand and the foretaste of consummation. This "already" insists that God is both the God of the absolute future and the God of history, actively engaged in the work of the world. The consummation of creation as God intended is already at work as God acts in history; Christians, too, are called to cocreate God's vision of fullness through the transformation of the world. In contemporary eschatology, the theme of continuity not only writes forward the future, but also calls Christians to transform the present on the basis of the telos for which they hope. In the writings of Vatican II, *Gaudium et spes* articulates the "deep solidarity" among humans in history and their common end in consummation.[68] The document goes on to envision the Christian response to this solidarity of humanity and its fullness: "Although we must be careful to distinguish earthly progress clearly from the increase of the kingdom of Christ, such progress is of vital concern to the kingdom of God, insofar as it can contribute to the better ordering of human society."[69] While the fullness of the kingdom promised in Christian scripture is ultimately a gift from God, nevertheless, contemporary strands

---

Liturgically, Christians are reminded of the connection between resurrection and mission, self-giving and hope in the words of the Eucharistic prayer, "Do this . . ." *Mysterium Paschale*, 95–100.

67. Von Balthasar, *Theo-Drama*, 176.

68. Vatican II's Pastoral Constitution on the Church in the Modern World (*Gaudium et spes*), no. 1. This translation taken from *Vatican Council II: The Basic Sixteen Documents*, ed. Austin Flannery (Northport, NY: Costello, 1996), 163; and *Gaudium et spes* no. 24, p. 189.

69. *Gaudium et spes* no. 39, in Flannery *Vatican Council II*, p. 205. Citing Pius XI's Encyclical "Quadragesimo Anno," *Acta Apostolicae Sedis* 23 (1931): 207.

642

of the tradition have affirmed the beginning of the eschatological end having roots in the transformation of history.

In contemporary eschatology, liberation theology is the approach that most strongly affirms this continuity of future salvation and present transformation. Taking seriously the vision outlined at Vatican II in light of the reality of poverty and oppression in Latin America, liberation theologians of the 1960s applied this understanding to the active transformation of social and political realities toward their fulfillment in Jesus' kingdom vision. Reminding Christians that the heritage of the Hebrew Scriptures sees God's actions in history as "political action" in Israel's release from slavery in the Exodus account, Gustavo Gutierrez insists that the religious event of God's salvation is not set apart from the historical, the social, and the political.[70] Consequently, "the struggle for a just world in which there is no oppression, servitude, or alienated work will signify the coming of the Kingdom."[71] Gutierrez concludes, "Salvation embraces all persons and the whole person; the liberating action of Christ—made human in this history and not in a history marginal to real human life—is at the heart of the historical current of humanity; the struggle for a just society is in its own right very much a part of salvation history."[72] Thus, for Gutierrez, eschatology as the fulfillment of God's promises in creation is bound up with the liberating processes recognizable in human history: eschatological promises are in continuity with the transformation of God's created world. As a historically tangible

process, the eschatological promises stand as the ends of political activity, calling Christians to understand mission as actively working on behalf of Christ's kingdom anticipated in the reality of justice in the world.

The individual and communal dimensions are intertwined here as Christians are called to commit to lives in a christocentric pattern (Rahner) that sees oneself poured out into the world (Moltmann) for the end of union with God (Balthasar) and others (Ratzinger). Communion with God means actively working toward cocreating God's fullness vision on earth. It means standing in willingness to confront the world in its godlessness even to the point of self-sacrifice. Here, liberation theologians remind us that Christian eschatology is not only rooted in Christ's resurrection but also intimately connected with the cross. In the words of Moltmann, "By accepting the cross, the suffering and the death of Christ, by taking upon it the trials and struggles of obedience in the body and surrendering itself to the pain of love, [faith] proclaims in the everyday world the future of the resurrection, of life and the righteousness of God."[73] In doing the will and work of God in the self-giving sacrifice for the wholeness of the world, Jesus Christ stands as pattern of human participation in the eschatological vision of completion that conforms to God's vision in life even in the face of death. In the words of Ratzinger, "Communion with God means a life stronger than death."[74]

Nowhere is this more powerful than in the witness of the martyrs, like the life and death

70. Gustavo Gutierrez, *A Theology of Liberation: History, Politics, and Salvation*, 15th anniv. ed., trans. Sister Caridad Inda and John Eagleson (Maryknoll, NY: Orbis, 1988), 86–91.

71. Ibid., 97.

72. Ibid.

73. Moltmann, *Theology of Hope*, 163.

74. Ratzinger, *Eschatology*, 91.

of Ignacio Ellacuria or Oscar Romero, who engaged the kingdom vision as both spiritual and political, being willing to stand with their very lives against the dehumanization of political oppression in Latin America. The willingness to stand with God for life in the face of death and all that dehumanizes is the christoform pattern that leads to resurrection. Here, the goal of eschatological fullness rests not merely in the transformation of individual lives (although this is a key component), but also in the transformation of the systems and structures of the anti-reign, which compromise human well-being. As Ellacuria writes, "The Reign of God is not possible as a community of human beings in perfect peace and total justice, without a radical change of the natural conditions that are present in human life, a change that is called the resurrection of the dead."[75] The conditions that are present in human life cannot be understood by speaking only of individual responses to the invitation to wholeness presented by the God of creation; rather, the reign of God is constituted also by the structures and systems that create a community of perfect peace and total justice.

That perfect peace and total justice might be a reality is affirmed because of the foretaste of resurrection in Jesus Christ. To recognize where this foretaste is found, we are retuned to the Jesus of history, recognizing that "the humanity God took on, in its littleness, reveals God."[76] For liberationist eschatology, the sal-

vific presence of God within history continues to be found among the weak and small, as the eschatological fulfillment heralded by the resurrection of Jesus Christ is announced by the crucified people of the world who hope, trust, and work for God's reign despite the crush of the anti-reign of sin and its systems that structure our world.[77] The crucified people who continue to live because they have "risen from the Death inflicted on [them]" stand as witness to the resurrection power in the risen Christ, their presence also a foretaste of the fullness of the eschaton.[78] Just as those who followed Jesus experienced the kingdom's healing in his presence, so too, the experience of God's reign amid the world's brokenness stands as experiential affirmation of the present reality of the eschatological process.[79]

Christians stand expectant that the promises of God will be fulfilled because they have experienced the foretaste of the new creation by the power of Jesus Christ. For the liberationist theologian, this new creation is glimpsed in the ongoing transformations that liberate persons to wholeness. In the vision of Letty Russell, God's gift of shalom to all creation is experienced in the table fellowship of persons even today: "The joyous meal offers a preview of the New Creation that God, in Jesus has promised to all . . . of the 'liberating eschaton' that stretches before all humanity. This glimpse of God's future is liberating . . . because here

---

75. Ignacio Ellacuria, "The Crucified People," in *Systematic Theology: Perspectives from Liberation Theology*, ed. Jon Sobrino and Ignacio Ellacuria (Maryknoll, NY: Orbis, 1996), 261.

76. Jon Sobrino, *Christ the Liberator: A View from the Victims*, trans. Paul Burns (Maryknoll, NY: Orbis, 2001), 294.

77. Ellacuria describes, "What is meant by the crucified people here is that collective body, which as the majority of humankind owes its situation of crucifixion to the way society is organized and maintained by a majority that exercises its dominion through a series of factors, which taken together and given their concrete impact within history, must be regarded as sin." Ellacuria, "The Crucified People," 266.

78. Ibid., 278.

79. For a discussion of the experiential presence of salvation in Jesus, see Elisabeth Schüssler Fiorenza, *In Memory of Her: A Feminist Theological Reconstruction of Christian Origins* (New York: Crossroad, 1992), 123.

644 people gather at a round table where no one is excluded, where power is shared, where multiple gifts are celebrated, and where those who have been historically marginalized are welcomed to the seats of honor."[80] For the liberation theologian, eschatology is the "anticipation of God's great reversal in a world of suffering and exile."[81] This anticipation is grounded in the experiential availability of such liberation in the present. The continuity between eschatological future and its impact on the present sees salvation as a process continually open to both present and future. In the words of Ivone Gebara:

> A process of salvation is a process of resurrection, of recovering life and hope and justice along life's path even when these experiences are frail and fleeting. Resurrection becomes something that can be lived and grasped within the confines of our existence. . . . This salvation is not a state one attains once for all. It is there like a glass of water that quenches thirst for the moment, but thirst comes again, sometimes stronger than before. It is there like a bit of land that one succeeds in acquiring after much anguish, but then the landowner takes over, and there follows drought or the lack of good conditions for cultivating the land. The moment of the hoped-for salvation comes, sometimes seen, sometimes unforeseen. No sooner it comes than it is gone: it escapes, flying away to prepare another and another. This fragile redemption is what we find in the everyday life of every person."[82]

In liberation eschatology, we see individual and collective salvation coming together. If the individual is called to christoformity in communion with God that is recognizable in a life of self-giving, solidarity, justice, peace, and righteousness, then the individual's salvation is bound up with the collective transformation of a world without righteousness into the world of God's reign that is the consummation of creation for all. In the words of Ratzinger, "True eschatology must be universal and aim at the salvation of all."[83]

Science and Nature: God's Action in Cosmic Consummation

The hope and promise of God witnessed in the Bible has been understood to include the transformation of the world eschatologically toward a new heaven and a new earth, understanding the new earth to be a transformation that has its roots in the present transformation of the world. For liberation theology, this transformation is actively engaged in the social and political lives and histories of persons throughout the world.

In the view of theologians in tune with the current discourses of the scientific community, the transformative hope of eschatological thinking encompasses not only all persons throughout the world, but the world itself. That is, the

---

80. Serene Jones and Margaret A. Farley, "Introduction," in *Liberating Eschatology: Essays in Honor of Letty M. Russell* (Louisville: Westminster John Knox, 1999), viii.

81. M. Shawn Copeland, "Journeying to the Household of God," in *Liberating Eschatology*, 38.

82. Ivone Gebara, *Out of the Depths: Women's Experience of Evil and Salvation*, trans. Ann Patrick Ware (Minneapolis: Fortress Press, 2002), 123.

83. Ratzinger, *Eschatology*, 65. While Ratzinger affirms the corporate dimension of salvation, he has been outspoken about what he perceives to be a danger in the liberationist emphasis on this-worldly renewal in its capacity to eclipse the gratuitous nature of eschatological consummation. See Congregation for the Doctrine of the Faith, "Instruction on Certain Aspects of 'Theology of Liberation,'" *Acta Apostolicae Sedis* 76 (1984): 876–909, http://www.vatican.va/roman_curia/congregations/cfaith/documents/rc_con_cfaith_doc_19840806_theology-liberation_en.html.

dynamic process evident to the scientific community shaped by evolutionary thinking opens a space for rereading the biblical texts with an ear to cosmic creation and cosmic consummation. As science increasingly reminds us of the human interaction and dependence on the whole of the created world, theologian John Haught recognizes "that we humans are indeed fully part of an evolving universe. And so, theology's preoccupation with our individual destinies can be separated only artificially from a deeper and wider concern about the cosmos as a whole and where it might end up."[84] Just as the natural world continually unfolds in newness that heralds a constant futurity to material existence, it stands as witness to the ultimate futurity of God and provides an experiential basis for our eschatological hope. The complexity and beauty of the created world similarly give witness to both hope and promise for a cosmic future. As Haught poetically reflects, "What has come into being already includes such an intensity of beauty that nature may be read as a great promise of more being and value up ahead."[85] Here, the goodness of creation and God's promises of consummation have experiential evidence in present human experience.

The cosmic eschatology outlined by Haught draws on strands of the systematic framework, just as we have seen in other eschatologies. Affirming that our knowledge of God is rooted in the witness of Jesus Christ, Haught envisions God as the one whose central attribute is self-giving love, and it is through this self-giving love that God creates. Both creation and incarnation indicate God's close association with the created world, indeed, God's self-emptying descent into this world. The world, while charged with an intimate connection with God, nevertheless is created with a fundamental freedom, exhibited both through human histories and through the cosmic evolutionary process. In this intimate connection with God, the created world is not primarily dead and static matter, but alive. The livingness of a dynamic universe is affirmed by the insights of science, as discoveries have identified the way the material world continues to come into being.[86] For Haught, this can be read as an "eschatological aliveness" that indicates a constant futurity of creation itself. Consonant with the biblical narrative of God as one who creates by way of promises and calls forth creation and history through participation in the promise making and promise keeping, the biblical God calls the whole universe into the future through promises. Haught sees the search for the kingdom of God and the building of the body of Christ as connected to the ongoing creation of the heavens and the earth, insisting that the cosmos itself is part of the creation and redemption envisioned in the Christian story:

Redemption must mean, then, that the whole story of the universe and life is embraced by divine providence. Not simply gathering our human stories into the trinitarian drama, the God revealed in Christ assimilates also the whole story of life on earth (and life elsewhere in the universe if it exists there). And since the entire physical history of the universe, as recent

---

84. John Haught, "Behind the Veil: Evolutionary Naturalism and the Question of Immortality," in *World without End: Christian Eschatology from a Process Perspective*, ed. Joseph Bracken (Grand Rapids: Eerdmans, 2005), 172.

85. John Haught, *Christianity and Science: Toward a Theology of Nature* (Maryknoll, NY: Orbis, 2007), 60.

86. Haught rests this vision threefold: (1) in the perspective of the vastness of cosmic history whereby humans have only recently emerged onto the scene; (2) in the evolutionary perspective of the created world developing ever-new forms; and (3) in the current scientific perspective of an expanding universe.

astrophysics had made clear, is tied into the existence of life everywhere, theology can no longer separate human hope for ultimate deliverance from the larger cosmic course of events. Because of the divine omnipresence, nothing in the universe story or in life's evolution can occur outside of God's own experience. If Jesus is truly the incarnation of God, then his experience of the cross is God's own suffering. And, by virtue of life's unbroken historical unity, Christian theology may be so bold as to assume also that the eons of evolutionary suffering in the universe are also God's own suffering. This would mean that the whole of nature in some way participates in the promise of resurrection as well.[87]

That the future includes resurrection is a statement of faith rooted in the experiential outlook of Christians in encounter with Jesus but also evidenced in the cosmic process itself. Evolutionary science indicates that the universe has a story that began long before humans entered the scene and that the story of the universe is yet unfinished. Cosmic events reflect both temporal perishing and constant creative transformation. Witnessing these events through the theological lens one sees a creative transformation borne by the Spirit of God. Haught writes, "In our theological understanding of this processive world there is abundant death and perpetual perishing, but there is also redemption, preservation and new creation."[88] By this, he indicates a compatibility between the Christian hope in resurrection and the evidence of science that identifies the transformation of material existence in a world in process. In a process outlook, the uniqueness of moments in their interconnectivity in the present, as well as to the past and future, can be understood to affirm that nothing particular is lost, but that resurrection faith can find reason for hope in the process of a world perpetually in motion, ever opening to future newness.[89]

The affirmation of God as creator of the *whole* of reality, along with the goodness of created reality and God's desire to bring it to consummation, has led Ratzinger to affirm that "no part of God's creation is too insignificant to be made perfect."[90] Increasingly, with insights from science, Christian theologians are willing to include all created reality, both human and nonhuman, in the vision of completion. Our eschatological future is no longer about which individuals get into heaven, but about our intimate interconnectivity with all that is and the responsibility that emerges as we are embedded in the network of a complex material and social reality and are carried along with it toward our common future.

Religious Pluralism: Many Ways of Salvation?

The embedding of humanity in the cosmos and the holistic vision of a total redemption provide a background for considering one of the pressing elements of contemporary Roman Catholic theology: the reality of other faiths. If Christian faith in the resurrection and eternal life lies with Jesus Christ ("I am the way, and the truth,

---

87. Haught, *Christianity and Science*, 92–93.

88. Ibid., 163.

89. This way of framing the interrelation of creation comes from "process thought." Haught and others have been influenced by the philosophical outlook of process philosopher Alfred North Whitehead, as well as the insights of the scientific community. Process theologians reflecting on eschatology include Marjorie Hewitt Suchocki, Joseph Braacken, John Cobb, and others.

90. Ratzinger, *Eschatology*, 175.

and the life. No one comes to the Father except through me"; John 14:6), the fate of persons who do not identify with Christianity could come seriously into doubt. With the broadening of our eschatological scope to include the cosmos as well as all that is in it, the question of whether and how persons of other faiths attain salvation remains a puzzling challenge to Christian eschatological thinking.

With the persistent axiom "Outside the church, no salvation" ringing through Christian history, we might think Christian faith has held that persons of other faiths are destined for the real possibility that is hell. Indeed, throughout the tradition, the eschatological future for non-Christians appeared dim, crystallized in such statements as this one at the Council of Florence (1442): "The holy Roman Church . . . firmly believes, professes and teaches that 'no one remaining outside the Catholic Church, not only pagans', but Jews, heretics or schismatics, can become partakers of eternal life; but they will go to the 'eternal fire prepared for the devil and his angels' (Mt 25:41)."[91] While this seems to be directed explicitly at condemning persons outside the faith, we can take heart in the magisterial affirmation that "the Church has never once declared the damnation of a single person as a concrete fact."[92]

Indeed, throughout the tradition, while "Outside the church, no salvation" was employed as a catchphrase to sum up the future for unbelievers, strands of Catholic theological thinking mitigated against the pessimistic outlook this entailed. One example is the patristic tradition of apocatastasis. Another can be seen in Thomas Aquinas's assertion that one can be saved through a "baptism by desire" in the absence of an actual baptism. This distinction develops into a tradition of recognizing persons as being part of the church through baptism *in re* (in reality) or *in voto* (in desire). The Council of Trent (1542) expresses this idea, stating that transition to the state of grace "cannot take place without the waters of rebirth *or the desire for them*."[93] Already there is some room for the salvation of those who are not quite Christian. By Vatican II, Catholic Christian eschatological hope explicitly embraced the future of all persons, Christian and non-Christian alike. With statements like "There are those who without any fault do not know anything about Christ or his church, yet who search for God with a sincere heart and, under the influence of grace, try to put into effect the will of God as known to them through the dictate of conscience: these too can obtain eternal salvation,"[94] the documents of Vatican II couple the vision of a universal offer of salvation with a broad scope for the workings of Christ: "Since Christ died for everyone, and since the ultimate calling of each of us comes from God and is therefore a universal one, we are obliged to hold that the Holy Spirit offers everyone the possibility of sharing in this paschal mystery in a manner known to God."[95] This form of eschatological hope for the

---

91. General Council of Florence, "Decree for the Copts," in Dupuis, *The Christian Faith in the Doctrinal Documents*, 309–10.

92. International Theological Commission, "Some Current Questions in Eschatology," 236–37.

93. "Decree on Justification," in *Decrees of the Ecumenical Councils*, ed. Norman P. Tanner (Washington, DC: Georgetown University Press, 1990), 2:672. Emphasis mine.

94. "Dogmatic Constitution on the Church," sec. 16, in Tanner, *Decrees of the Ecumenical Councils*, 861.

95. "Pastoral Constitution on the Church in the World of Today," sec. 22, in Tanner, *Decrees of the Ecumenical Councils*, 1,082.

non-Christian has been termed inclusivism, for the salvific workings of Jesus Christ *include* the future even of the non-Christian, even in ways unbeknownst to Christian and non-Christian alike.

The most extensive working out of an eschatological inclusivism comes in the writings of Karl Rahner, who identified persons of other faiths who participate in the salvific work of Jesus as "anonymous Christians."[96] Christians can hold on to the hope in God's universal will of salvation (articulated, for example in 1 Tim. 2:4, identifying God as Savior "who desires everyone to be saved"), as well as the affirmation that salvation comes through Jesus Christ, by recognizing a fundamental unity of humanity that underlies all of our religious differences. In God's creative activity, humans are endowed with an inclination toward the Ultimate Horizon, opening themselves up to the ever-greater, always-future of God's being in the universal activities of knowing, freedom, and love. When they do, they are participating in the creative activity of the one God and, in the process, saying yes to the God of all creation, just as Jesus Christ did to the fullest. The work done by Christ can be seen evidenced in the transcendence toward God taking place across the broad spectrum of humanity. For Rahner, the eschatological future for all humanity is the salvation made possible in Jesus Christ: "Anyone who does not close him [or her] self to God in an ultimate act of his [or her] life . . . this person finds salvation."[97] Participating in the foretaste of eschatological consummation in everyday transcendence, even the non-Christian is on the path to the Ultimate Future.

While recognizing that inclusivism moves in the direction of a positive assessment of the fate of people of diverse faiths, increasing contact with practitioners of other traditions and awareness of the distinctiveness of belief and practice have influenced the eschatological thinking of some Christian theologians to challenge Rahner's formulation. The specific ends Christian eschatology hopes in call forth particular practices patterned on Christ; the vision and practice of other faiths, these theologians insist, are simply different from the Christian ones. For these theologians, the future fate of humanity must take these differences into consideration. For some, differences must be overcome for salvation, while others envision a diversity of paths leading eschatologically to the fulfillment of all.

The particularity of the Christian eschatological vision through Jesus Christ leads some theologians to insist that the continuity between this life and the future cannot simply be broken by our theological hopefulness. That is, the path and practices one undertakes should determine the place where one arrives. This affirms both the distinctiveness of the christoform pattern of Christians and the diverse practices and forms of persons of other faiths. As Joseph DiNoia writes, "Conformity to Christ does not involve a finally anonymous uniformity. Rather, Christ's grace unlocks the potential for the realization of the unique personal identity of each disciple. The victory of Easter wins for Christ's disciples the resurrection of the body:

---

96. Karl Rahner, "Anonymous Christians," in *Theological Investigations*, vol. 6, trans. Karl-H. Kruger and Boniface Kruger (New York: Seabury, 1974), 390–98; idem, "The One Christ and the Universality of Salvation," in *Theological Investigations*, vol. 16, trans. David Morland (New York: Seabury, 1979), 199–226; idem, "Jesus Christ in the Non-Christian Religions," 17:39–52.

97. Karl Rahner, *Foundations of Christian Faith: An Introduction to the Idea of Christianity*, trans. William V. Dych (New York: Crossroad, 1978), 143.

the transfigured but perduring personal identities of an indefinite number of uniquely specific, 'named' persons. These persons dwell in the perfect union of *caritas* with each other and the Blessed Trinity, itself personally 'Named,' in the life to come."[98] Since the specific ultimate aim of Christian understanding is notably different from the ultimate aim identified by other religious traditions (Nirvana, surrender to Allah, or release from the cycle of death and rebirth), these various aims would call forth distinctive practices designed to achieve said aims. For DiNoia, the distinctiveness of practices that shape believers toward a particular aim requires that we recognize persons *will* be shaped differently toward these different aims. Not all practices are christoform, so the final state at which persons undertaking those practices arrive is not the same as what is envisioned as the ultimate end of christoform practice in trinitarian union.

While thinkers such as S. Mark Heim have envisioned this distinctiveness to develop into a diversity of ends for persons of various faiths (or "salvations," as Heim's work is entitled),[99] DiNoia wants to hold onto the universality and ultimacy of the Christian vision of consummation. He does so by employing the uniquely Catholic doctrine of purgatory. DiNoia writes, "The point of the doctrine is that a certain kind of life may render one unfit for the *immediate* enjoyment of fellowship with the Blessed Trinity, even though one is ultimately destined for it."[100] He continues, "The doctrine of purgatory permits Christian theology a wide measure of confidence about the salvation of non-Christians . . . without underestimating the distinctive aims they have pursued in life. . . . Presumably, for non-Christians purgatory would involve the realization of the continuities as well as the discontinuities between what they had practiced and believed and what is indeed the case about the true aim of life."[101] In wanting to affirm both the universality of salvation in the Christian eschatological vision and the ultimacy of the Christian vision in its particularity, DiNoia provides for a reading of the tradition that holds both together in light of the reality of religious diversity.

For other theologians, the universality of salvation held forth as promise in the Christian vision provides for a reading of the particular forms of religious practice as offering diverse ways to the ultimate future that Christians seek. Paul Knitter, for example, recognizes in the patterns of the world's religions the same desire for consummation of the world and its transformation. In working together for the liberation of the world, practitioners of every faith can participate in the kingdom vision "on earth," whose ultimate consummation remains bound with the mystery of God "in heaven." In Knitter's words, "Jesus as the Christ tells me not only that there is a universal Mystery that holds earth-humanity-Divinity together, but that this Mystery beckons us to struggle for a different kind of world and to do so with a particular concern for the victims and outcasts."[102] Since, for Knitter, religions in their many forms participate also

98. Joseph DiNoia, *The Diversity of Religions: A Christian Perspective* (Washington, DC: Catholic University of America Press, 1992), 60–61.

99. S. Mark Heim, *Salvations: Truth and Difference in Religion* (Maryknoll, NY: Orbis, 1995).

100. DiNoia, *The Diversity of Religions*, 105.

101. Ibid., 105–6.

102. Paul Knitter, *No Other Name? A Critical Survey of Christian Attitudes toward the World Religions* (Maryknoll, NY: Orbis, 1985), 168.

650

in the liberating transformation called forth by Jesus and enacted by those who would be his disciples, the ultimate eschatological transformation can be envisioned as encompassing other religions as paths to the eschatological future of God's kingdom.[103] In Knitter's words, "What Paul calls the Mystery of God's plan revealed so powerfully and savingly in Christ Jesus, can be revealed elsewhere and in sundry forms—without ever exhausting that Mystery."[104] Our eschatological future holds both promise and mystery that can be enhanced by an active engagement with the visions of other faiths.

While theological thinking continues to develop in the area of eschatology of religious pluralism, the mainstream Catholic position remains inclusivism that affirms a universal theological anthropology and a shared future destiny through the life, death, and resurrection of Jesus Christ.[105] At the same time, practitioners of interreligious dialogue often experience a sacramental restoration of wholeness and healing of interreligious relations that may foretaste the eschatological apocatastasis when the Creator of all in particularity brings creation to its completion. How this might happen out of our interreligious state remains mystery, for Christians continue to marvel at how inscrutable are God's ways (Rom. 11:33).

Conclusion

As seen from the various approaches to eschatology sketched out in this chapter, there is both continuity and innovation in eschatological thinking in the history of the Roman Catholic Christian tradition. Eschatology is, and remains, rooted in the biblical witness, and Catholic eschatology continues to be guided by magisterial articulations of the continuity between this world and our future in Christ. Like all theology, eschatology is infused and influenced by broader currents of thought and thus in each age is articulated in distinctive tones and with varying emphases and understandings. From Jewish, Greek, and Roman influences in the early church, to the vision of Augustine or Aquinas, and the philosophical and contemporary political currents, Christian eschatological thinking has been shaped by many sources.

Throughout the various movements in eschatology, important themes remain: our future hope is rooted in the life and mission of Jesus Christ, whose kingdom vision represents the consummation of creation as God intended it. This hope extends into the ultimate future beyond the confines of what we can know in this world, resting firmly on a resurrection faith. With experiential evidence, Christian eschatology envisions an ultimate future that stands in continuity with the relationality, transcendence, meaning, justice, and beauty of our life on earth. The continuity between Christian faith in the world today and the horizon of our ultimate future can be seen in the deep interrelation of eschatology with the many doctrines of Catholic Christian theology examined in this volume. Further, this intertwining of present and future is evidenced in the sacramental celebrations and

---

103. Ibid., 13.

104. Ibid., 157.

105. For a recent statement that reflects the inclusivist position, see Congregation for the Doctrine of the Faith, "*Dominus Iesus*: Declaration on the Unicity and Salvific Universality of Jesus Christ and the Church," *Acta Apostolicae Sedis* 92 (2000): 742–65, http://www.vatican.edu/roman_curia/congregations/cfaith/documents/rc_con_cfaith_doc_20000806_dominus-iesus_en.html.

liturgical life of the Catholic Christian community. Perhaps one might say that, in the end, the point of Christian eschatology (indeed, the point of Christian theology) is to live as if the consummation were a present reality, rooted in the experience in Christ that this eschatological future can be a present reality, and grounded in the hope that this eschatological future will become our final reality.

For Further Reading

Daley, Brian E. *The Hope of the Early Church: A Handbook of Patristic Eschatology*. Cambridge: Cambridge University Press, 1991.
> *A historical overview of the eschatologies that emerged in the first through seventh centuries of Christian thought.*

DiNoia, Joseph. *The Diversity of Religions: A Christian Perspective*. Washington, DC: Catholic University of America Press, 1992.
> *A theology of religious pluralism that focuses on the distinctive aims of the religious traditions. Outlines a response to other eschatologies of religious diversity and puts forth a Catholic Christian response, reintroducing the doctrine of purgatory in light of religious differences.*

Gebara, Ivone. *Out of the Depths: Women's Experience of Evil and Salvation*. Translated by Ann Patrick Ware. Minneapolis: Fortress Press, 2002.
> *A feminist perspective on liberationist eschatology that sees salvation as begun in the intraworldly events of the everyday.*

Gutierrez, Gustavo. *A Theology of Liberation: History, Politics, and Salvation*. 15th anniversary ed. Translated by Sister Caridad Inda and John Eagleson. Maryknoll, NY: Orbis, 1988.
> *A reading of salvation as intertwined with political transformation and liberation of oppressed peoples. The author argues with biblical resources for the active engagement of the eschatological in history.*

Haught, John. *Christianity and Science: Toward a Theology of Nature*. Maryknoll, NY: Orbis, 2007.
> *Outline of an eschatology that incorporates a critical engagement with science, including evolution, and includes the final ends of the cosmos.*

Hayes, Zachary. *Visions of a Future: A Study of Christian Eschatology*. Collegeville, MN: Liturgical, 1990.
> *A systematic treatise on eschatology as hope with foundational chapters on biblical outlooks.*

652 Knitter, Paul. *No Other Name? A Critical Survey of Christian Attitudes toward the World Religions.* Maryknoll, NY: Orbis, 1985.

> An investigation of the salvific fruitfulness of other religions as paths to a common end in the kingdom of God.

La Due, William J. *The Trinity Guide to Eschatology.* New York: Continuum, 2004.

> An accessible overview of eschatological thought from the biblical sources through various theological articulations, with an emphasis on diverse twentieth-century theologians.

Moltmann, Jürgen. *Theology of Hope: On the Ground and the Implications of a Christian Eschatology.* London: SCM, 1967.

> The crucial text of the twentieth century, marking the reemergence of eschatology as central to Christian theology. Moltmann articulates an understanding of eschatology as thoroughly informed by the social and political realities of this world in continuity with the fullness of God's kingdom promise.

Rahner, Karl. *Foundations of Christian Faith: An Introduction to the Idea of Christianity.* Translated by William V. Dych. New York: Seabury, 1978.

> The essential description of Rahner's theological anthropology, which envisions human becoming toward God as christoform and anticipates our eschatological aim as re-union with God. This work includes Rahner's theology of religious pluralism and explores the question of the salvation of non-Christians.

Ratzinger, Joseph. *Eschatology: Death and Eternal Life.* 2nd ed. Washington, DC: Catholic University of America Press, 1988.

> A systematic approach that incorporates biblical, historical, and magisterial perspectives on eschatology.

von Balthasar, Hans Urs. *Theo-Drama: Theological Dramatic Theory*, vol. 5, *The Last Act.* Translated by Graham Harrison. San Francisco: Ignatius, 1998.

> This volume completes von Balthasar's systematic theological anthropology with extended reflection on the ends of our human condition as illuminated by Christian faith in Jesus Christ.